APPLETON SERIES IN SUPERVISION AND TEACHING

Edited by A. S. Barr *and* William H. Burton

SUPERVISION

"It's all right in theory, but it won't do in practice," is another popular way of revelling in logical absurdity. The philosopher Schopenhauer said all that needs to be said about this sophism: "The assertion is based upon an impossibility: what is right in theory *must* work in practice; and if it does not, there is a mistake in the theory; something has been overlooked and not allowed for; and consequently, what is wrong in practice is wrong in theory too."

Max Black, *Critical Thinking:*
An Introduction to Logic and Scientific
Method (New York, Prentice-Hall, 1946),
p. 215.

SUPERVISION

A SOCIAL PROCESS

William H. Burton
HARVARD UNIVERSITY

Leo J. Brueckner
UNIVERSITY OF MINNESOTA

Dr. ARVIL S. BARR collaborated with the
authors by reading Chapters 11 and 15 on
the study and improvement of instruction,
an area in which he has specialized

Third Edition : New York
APPLETON-CENTURY-CROFTS, INC.

PREFACE

The question is whether the teacher shall make the undergraduates of 1954 skilled in discussing possible future changes and fully canvassing their advantages and disadvantages. Or shall he leave them to wander with bandaged eyes through "the inscrutable years which lie ahead," equipped with nothing to guide them except a strong love for the institutions among which they were born.

> "If the Salt Have Lost His Savour..."
> Charter Day address, University of Oregon, October 19, 1954, by ZECHARIAH CHAFEE, JR., Harvard University

The challenge in Professor Chafee's stirring address confronts all who teach, not merely those who stand before undergraduates. The entire range of agencies and processes of public enlightenment are being tested as never before in history. The "struggle for men's minds" is the most important and fateful characteristic of our times. The methods used, and the degree of success achieved in this intellectual Armageddon will inevitably affect the destiny of our society. The President of the United States has expressed the belief that the future of the free democratic world might well be decided in the public schools within the current quarter century.

First, fundamental changes are emerging in our Western society and civilization, in fact in all societies. Forces which have been gathering strength over the centuries now challenge current aims and values. The average citizen as well as the scholar is called upon to study and to discriminate between social trends of great magnitude. Education emerges ever more clearly as a basic social force that plays a major part in preparing each succeeding generation to live in and to manage a dynamic, emergent, precarious, revolutionary social order, our own especially. Education thus ultimately plays a part in the shaping of destiny.

Second, our older concepts of human nature and its limitations are giving way to newer knowledge which indicates the possibilities and growth of all individuals. Research in biology, medicine, anthropology, psychiatry, psychology, and in education itself open up new hopes and aspirations in the area of human growth and development. Creativity becomes more important than molding individuals to conformity. The new discoveries in the areas named challenge all who are engaged in any type of educational work to face courageously their implications. Scientific findings combine with philosophic contemplation and analysis of the nature of democracy to further sharpen the challenge and task of education. The administration and supervision of schools, the whole setting for learning, must be changed basically and radically.

Third, the current period is marked by a remarkable and possibly tragic discrepancy between technological and moral thinking. Technology has advanced beyond the dreams of early scientists, but our moral and ethical processes, particularly in dealing with each other, and fatefully on the international level, are still largely on a primitive level. The widespread immorality, or more properly unmorality, of our society, particularly in some of our economic and political leaders, is a genuine threat to our society. Fortunately, increasing numbers of our industrial and political leaders see the threat as clearly as do the scholars. The challenge to all leaders, those in education particularly, is for the revitalizing of our moral values and practices. Social invention and far-flung changes in education are demanded.

The authoritarian and coercive school must give way to a democratic institution that achieves its ends through co-operation and participation of all who are concerned with the growth and development of learners. Democratic administration and supervision are necessary to accompany the democratic processes that are characteristic of the modern schoolroom.

The authors, to the best of their ability, have tried to show how the principles of democracy, the findings of science, and the implications of trends within our dynamic social order may be utilized in a theory and practice of supervision. The basic concept of traditional supervision, imposition of training and guidance upon teachers, is replaced by the view that supervision is a co-operative enterprise in which all persons concerned with child growth and development work together to improve the setting for learning. The first edition of this volume, published in 1938, which succeeded the earlier volume by Barr and Burton, was well advanced along this line. The second edition published in 1947 elaborated the principles still further. The present edition contains the next logical step: a summary discussion of social process in general and a more detailed discussion of that process as carried on in small groups. The authors have worked earnestly to avoid inconsistencies or contradictions within their treatment of this extremely difficult discussion. Inconsistencies which may have escaped us will be, we believe, concerned with minor questions of technique and not with basic principles. Each author has contributed detailed criticisms and selected passages, some of them extensive, to chapters written by the other. Responsibility for chapters, however, was definitely placed. Chapters 1, 2, 3, 4, 5, 6, 7, 12, and 16 were written by Burton; chapters 8, 9, 10, 11, 13, 14, 15, 17, and 18 by Brueckner. A. S. Barr, who has been associated with these textbooks since 1928, assisted by reading and supplying expert advice on the two chapters dealing with the teacher. Professor Barr's interests have been for some time in the area of research into the evaluation of teacher effectiveness. His pioneer work in and contributions to the field of supervision are many and enduring, and are well known to all workers in education.

A feature in the preparation of this edition was the extensive and detailed consultation with practical field workers. Brueckner used most of his sabbatical leave in 1952-53 to make a leisurely swing around the country, coast to coast, north to south, consulting with literally dozens of superintendents, supervisors, and principals. Round-table discussions were widely utilized to note the types of problems, the practices, and the relation of our text to the field situation. Scores of documents covering every aspect of supervision were gathered and analyzed. Brueckner, further, drew heavily upon his long experience in varied field work as consultant and member of survey commissions. He is at this writing chairman of the state committee on the study and improvement of instruction set up by the Minnesota State Department of Education. Burton concentrated on the curriculum area, examining a wide range of city and state programs through both the available documents and personal contact. He has served as consultant on elementary curriculum to the Maine State Department of Education since 1943, and will serve the Oregon State Department in similar capacity from 1955. Similar experience is included on the city and individual school level, together with extensive field work, surveys, and the like.

The two authors met from time to time to analyze and prepare the material. This edition is heavily loaded, as were previous editions, with first-hand descriptions of actual practices, with extracts or paraphrases from documents prepared by school staff workers. Our sincere thanks goes to the scores of busy people who gave freely of time and energy, not to mention materials. The professional spirit displayed was a convincing demonstration of the eagerness of school workers generally to participate in the improvement of education.

Two features of previous editions need explanation here. The size of the volume has earned adverse criticism from several instructors and graduate students. Field workers, by contrast, value the detailed content which necessitates the size. We made a careful survey of desirable content and decided to cut down as much as possible but not to be unduly concerned with size. Field workers actually asked us not to sacrifice content. Most of them work far from college libraries and say they would be helpless in many instances except for the extensive compendium of information and reference in this and similar large volumes. Many instructors, furthermore, also voted against undue curtailment.

The second adverse criticism concerned the inclusion of concise summaries in the form of numbered points in outline form. The self-acknowledged sinner here is Burton, who uses this device to save many, many pages of print, and because students advanced enough to be studying this volume might be stimulated by these lists. Field workers were again less critical than instructors of these lists. The number of these summaries has been sharply reduced but the device seems valuable enough to retain in places.

Space has been saved also by including the bulk of the references in the body of the chapter and without repetition at the close.

The suggested activities have all been tried many, many times by a number of instructors. Several were, in fact, brought in from the field by advanced students who wished assistance with their immediate practical problems. The emphasis on the practical, however, has not been at the expense of theory. Basic theory is recognized as prerequisite to any reputable practice and is presented as thoroughly as we knew how.

W. H. B.
L. J. B.

CONTENTS

Part III

THE IMPROVEMENT OF THE EDUCATIONAL PROGRAM

Part IV

THE EVALUATION OF PROGRAMS OF SUPERVISION

Part **I**

◆·◆·◆·◆·◆

THE DEFINITION AND ORGANIZATION
OF MODERN SUPERVISION

Chapter 1

❖·❖·❖·❖·❖·❖·❖·❖

Supervision: A Social Process

A PRELIMINARY STATEMENT OF SUPERVISORY FUNCTION

THE CHIEF FUNCTION of modern supervision is the evaluation and improvement of the factors affecting learning. We hasten to add that this is not the chief function of *supervisors*. The seeming paradox will be explained as we develop the modern concept of supervision.

This major function, evaluating and improving the factors affecting learning, clearly necessitates certain subsidiary functions. First, we cannot evaluate except in terms of an accepted philosophy, an accepted and understood statement of aims. The co-operative formulation of these is a function of supervision. Common purposes, goals, and standards are thus established. Second, a process has to be developed for carrying on an educational program aimed at achieving the objectives. Third, a staff and organization, varying in size, complexity, and relationships, must be set up for implementing and improving the program. The policy, process, and organization should be of such nature as to protect and stimulate the individuality and creativity of the persons included. Human relations (as we shall see) are far more important than the mechanical efficiency of any process or organization.

Fourth, a policy and process for community relations must be devised, stressing co-operative participation [1] in policy-making and planning. Fifth, a theory and practice of evaluation must be developed consistent with the accepted aim and philosophy.

The school, supervision, and the social order. The relationships between these three will be developed at various points in this volume, chiefly in Chapters 2 and 7. Details aside for the moment, we must stress that the *aim and philosophy* of education and hence of supervision must reflect the aims and aspirations of the social order within which the school operates. The *process* must emerge from the same source. The development, use, and improvement of any of these three is a community-wide activity. Individuals, as well as all community agencies concerned with education and with any phase of social welfare, must participate in the operation of this major community undertaking, education. The democratic philosophy and process are the bases of guidance in this country.

Evaluation of the educational product is as much a community responsibility as are other phases of the educational program. But

---

[1] The concept and practice of co-operative procedure will appear throughout this volume. The writers believe that genuine social process demands the participation of both professionals and laymen. Ample material is available dealing with co-operation within the professional staff. We must extend co-operation to include the community. One of the first, if not the first, general volumes dealing with co-operation with and from laymen appeared as

this book was being prepared:
Citizen Co-operation for Better Public Schools, Fifty-third Yearbook, National Society for the Study of Education (Chicago, Univ. of Chicago Press, 1954).

The present writers believe that administrative and supervisory leaders should be quite familiar with this volume. A number of other brief treatments are also available.

measurement of pupil achievement is only one part of an appraisal process which evaluates any and all aspects of the teaching-learning situation. We must determine the degree to which co-operatively determined goals have been achieved. Details will be presented in later chapters.

The word *community* is used with both local and wider reference. The purposes and goals of our national and regional communities should be co-ordinated with those of local communities.

Arguments about supervision lead to clarification of function of supervisors. So far, so good. All the functions of supervision listed above seem clearly reasonable. Who can seriously object to the constant evaluation and improvement of the educational program, particularly a program based on and emerging from the community itself? To do so is to deny the basic reasons for the existence of schools. What fault can be found with establishing a common purpose, since without one neither individuals nor groups can progress? Surely we must have a personnel including a number of generalists and several kinds of specialists? No one could object to the stimulation of creativity within this personnel. And without evaluation, we cannot tell what we have accomplished.

Supervision, however, is a controversial aspect of education, with a long history of sound and fury. The bibliography of protest is lengthy, even though the tide has turned, as shown by an increase in the number of favorable comments. If we analyze the controversial literature, rather than merely continuing the argument, we can find significant guidance. Analysis leads directly to consideration of the crucial questions, "how" and "by whom." This leads in turn to the functions of *supervisors,* distinct from those of *supervision* as a *social process.*

The primary function of supervisors. Light is thrown upon the desirable functions of supervisors by (*a*) analysis of complaints about supervision, (*b*) analysis of commendatory statements, and (*c*) consideration

of the principles governing democratic human relations. All three contribute to a common conclusion.

Chief complaints deal with the imposition of a supervisor's personal views upon the teacher, or the imposition of a course of study unfitted to local conditions. We hear protests about disregard for the dignity, the feelings, and the considered conclusions of some of the persons within the group. But hold on, says a careful observer, *these complaints do not refer to supervision at all, but almost entirely to the mistakes of persons engaged in supervision.*

Most of the antagonists, and not a few of the defenders, make two simple but common blunders in logic. First, judgments are based upon specific illustrations of local practice, on "my experience," instead of upon fundamental purposes and principles and upon a comprehensive picture of practice elsewhere. Second, there is failure to distinguish between a striking but non-essential characteristic of something and its essence. The latter blunder is worse than usual in this case, since the striking characteristic is not merely nonessential, it is an illustration of actual malpractice. In short, most objectors are erroneously judging *supervision* by the specific acts of *malpractice of individual supervisors.*

Additional clarification comes from statements favorable to supervision. Studies show conclusively that supervisory practice, when well done, is not merely welcomed but is actively sought. Even more significant, these studies show that those reporting clearly discriminate between the *acts of individual supervisors* and the *essential purposes and practices of supervision.*

What is the significance of "well done"? Supervision is well done when it promotes the insights of all persons engaged in solving an educational problem; when it accepts leadership from any and all persons; when it recognizes and protects the unique individuality of every person in a given group. Supervision, well done, assumes that all persons are willing and recognize their obligation to work together on common problems, and that all are capable of creative contribution in one way or another. *Competent supervision does not merely aid persons to solve their problems; it provides the conditions under which all may participate as free agents in the solution of common problems.*

The primary function of supervisors of all types is leadership, plus the encouragement and recognition of leadership in any other person either on the professional staff or among the community participants.

The supervisor is not the only person capable of exercising leadership, but this is his primary function. The official *status* of the supervisor implies leadership under modern democratic theory, but leadership may *emerge* from any member of the group. We shall have more to say later (Chapters 4, 5, and 7) about status and emergent leadership and about the techniques of group process within which leadership appears and is used. The basic differences between (1) supervision as inspection, training, guidance and (2) supervision as leadership in the democratic, co-operative group attack on common problems, will be discussed in detail. Suffice it for the moment to say that supervision and supervisors should stimulate, encourage, give aid, and set up conditions wherein all may study and learn with security. Supervisors form but one of several groupings of persons, all of whom are participants in a self-regulating process. We shall see more clearly in the next four chapters just how purposes, processes, and organizations are developed by a group rather than by a few at the top of an administrative hierarchy. Supervision is a difficult but basic social process in which all persons affected by the process participate. This conception of supervision and of supervisors' functions differs widely from some concepts still held by many field workers, if we may judge by their practices. Supervision should not seek to regulate, direct, control, or impose the be-liefs and activities of one group of persons upon another group.

The historical development of supervision explains many difficulties and strengths in modern supervision. Supervision properly defined and practiced differs widely from supervision as often understood and practiced. It is just at this point that the educational worker who relies on "my experience" makes his greatest blunder, both in his own actions and in his interpretation of what he observes. What he often proudly calls the "practical" view as distinguished from the "theoretical" is neither practical nor theoretical but merely *uninformed*. The experience upon which the naïve practical man relies is always fragmentary, inadequate, and usually incorrectly interpreted. Experience, if it is to become a basis for conclusions, must be enlightened and illuminated by knowledge of basic principles and facts derived from philosophic reflection and from controlled research. *Critically analyzed experience* and the critical analysis of wide observation of practice are valid bases for conclusions. Historically, the philosophy controlling supervision has gone through a number of significant changes. The historical development of supervision is rarely known to the so-called practical field worker.

The concept of supervision as inspection is inherited from early beginnings. The General Court (legislature) of the Massachusetts Bay Colony directed in 1654 that the town selectmen should secure teachers of certain religious and moral qualities. Nothing was said about inspection or supervision. Other northeastern colonies had similar laws.

Inspection appeared in the early 1700's, specifically in Boston in 1709, when committees of citizens were appointed to visit and inspect the plant, the equipment, and pupil achievement. The latter is, of course, a form of inspection of the teacher. Specific mention of inspection of the teacher's methods did not appear for many years. Committees until about 1714 were made up largely of ministers, and learning was a qualification for membership. Selectmen increasingly served as inspectors, thus marking the beginnings of public responsibility for education. The early committees were largely concerned with the Latin grammar schools, but as time went on, inevitably they widened the scope of their activities to include all schools and the functions of criticizing and advising the teacher.

Schools increased in size, as towns grew, until several teachers were working in one building. One teacher was singled out and given certain administrative and managerial duties, thus becoming a *principal* teacher, later to become the building principal. Supervisory duties, even the meager one of inspection, were not delegated to principals until comparatively modern times. We are even yet struggling to make the principal an important supervisory officer. Another hundred years passed, and in the second quarter of the nineteenth century there appeared a new officer, the *superintendent of schools.* Boards of education often opposed this new office, since they were jealous of the administrative and supervisory functions still vested in the boards. The new officer was for a long time a minor administrative officer. Today in many places he is the leader of a school system, but there is still much difficulty because of imperfect demarcation between functions of lay boards and educational leaders. The leadership of superintendents in some regions, notably in New England and in some parts of the deep South, is practically zero because of failure to delegate important functions to the professional leader. Progress in vesting leadership in the trained superintendent has been made in all regions to some degree; notable progress has been made in several.

The special supervisor appeared in the period 1875-1900 as a result of the addition to the curriculum of such new subjects as art, music, manual training, and others. These officers were actually traveling teachers, since no one else knew how to teach the new ma-

terials. The effect of these new special supervisors on existing supervision was not seen at the time. The use of "traveling teachers" actually retarded the desirable development of both supervision and teacher education.

Many modern problems and shortcomings in supervision, it can be seen readily, arise from its early history.

Supervision as inspection combined with laissez-faire in modern times. The primitive conception still persists that teachers should be inspected and rated by someone. The accompanying assumptions are those of laissez-faire, for the ratings are rarely made the basis for any form of guidance or improvement. If teachers want to improve, they are free to do so. If not, and if no serious trouble arises—well, that is not a matter of great concern. In the event that trouble does arise, efforts are usually directed at getting rid of the teacher, not at guiding him toward improvement. This ancient and wholly reprehensible theory and practice persists far more widely than is thought. A considerable number of superintendents and supervisors even go so far as to defend it, saying that their teachers are left "free," are not to be "imposed upon" or "directed." Some even call this "democratic" supervision! The sweet-sounding terms are but euphemisms to disguise various reasons for inability to exercise leadership.

Supervision as coercion. The obvious need for improvement in teacher background and performance led other supervisors to the opposite of laissez-faire. A natural conception in pre-democratic thinking was that coercion would achieve the necessary changes in teachers and in teaching. Courses of study and classroom methods were prescribed. Performance was checked regularly to see that orders were obeyed. Extension courses, reading circles, various other forms of study were required both by local regulation and (sometimes) by law. The philosophy is obvious: Truth is vested in "those whom God hath called into authority over us." Responsibility and authority reside in the upper administrative levels. The best materials and methods are given to teachers who are merely employees to carry out the directions of those who see the ends and who plan the achievement of those ends. Worse than that, learning was conceived as an almost mechanical process. The teacher was compelled to use detailed techniques handed out ready made. Today we know that classroom techniques have to be a product of teacher ingenuity exercised on local conditions. The teacher was rarely introduced to the real aims of the supervisor. As we shall see, the process of modern democratic supervision is the direct opposite of coercion.

Supervision as training and guidance. An important gain was made when supervision was first comprehended as involving training and guidance. Upper administrative levels still knew best; extensive prescription of materials and methods was still present. The improvement of teachers was not confined to strictly technical matters, however; personal and cultural development was included. The gain came in the recognition, however slight, of *needs* as the foundation for improvement programs. Practices varied from benevolent despotism to the beginnings of adaptation to needs and local conditions. Teacher participation and freedom to experiment, as techniques of growth, were not yet recognized. Self-development was not yet even dreamed of. The utilization of teacher leadership was not even thought of at first, though all these possibilities began to come into discussion as time passed. It is true that even today the concepts of training and guidance dominate many supervisory programs.

This concept and practice was an improvement over earlier programs but had a serious flaw—one which has plagued supervision ever since. Training and guidance were focused on the teacher and were confined to the (supposed) improvement of this group and their techniques. The curriculum, the materials, the pupil, and, worst of all, the community were completely overlooked. The

modern participatory, co-operative programs which we shall emphasize aim to improve all aspects of the learning situation including the community, and all personnel including even lay participants.

Weaknesses of early forms of supervision should not be allowed to persist. Early workers did the best they could on the basis of knowledge then available, and for this all credit is due them. Some of the weaknesses could have been corrected earlier, but we all know how great are the difficulties in bringing about either major social change or change in smoothly working routines. In listing early shortcomings we do so not so much in criticism of early leaders as to set up guides for modern workers who possess wide knowledge which was unknown to their predecessors. *The persistence of earlier theory and practice of supervision until today is prima facie evidence that school leadership often is unaware of large bodies of available knowledge, or when aware of the knowledge, prefers instead a comfortable and comforting set of routines.* The needs of the learner are not allowed to disturb the peace enjoyed by vested interests.

The assumptions of principle and of practice for which there can be no excuse in the modern school include: (fallacies)

1. The assumption that a centrally devised theory of education, curriculum, or classroom practice (*a*) is better than any other that can be devised, and (*b*) can be imposed on the teaching staff. The implication is that there are best methods of doing anything; that these are known to the élite, and that they may be handed down from above.

This concept ignores everything we know of the precarious, uncertain, variable, and experimental nature of life, of the learning process, and of education.

2. The assumption that the teacher is the primary (or the only) factor to be dealt with in improving the setting for learning.

The curriculum, the quality and availability of materials, the dominant public opinion, the learners themselves, and many others are ignored. The failure of many teacher-improvement programs to bring about improvement in the growth and development of the learners should lead supervisors to see that other factors are involved.

3. The assumption that persons (in this case, teachers) are not fundamentally different from other factors affecting the learners.

Imposition, training, and guidance give no recognition to the processes through which persons change their values, beliefs, and attitudes, and thereby their behavior; make no provisions for bringing about these changes by reputable means; ignore the necessity for preserving security while making changes. The actual results in destruction of personality values, particularly initiative and originality, are either not recognized or blamed on the perversity of persons. Repressions, inhibitions, complexes, eventually frustration and revolt, are natural outcomes.

4. The assumption that the legal and status relationships between and among persons are sufficient and satisfactory.

The co-operative, participatory relationships now known to be most effective are unknown or overridden. The undemocratic relationship which must exist under coercion, regulation, imposition (even benevolent), and between groups when one group has power to control the other, is unknown or unrecognized. Fear and distrust enter, insincerity and dishonesty are inevitable. Productive interactive relationships are impossible.

Assumptions and practices based on current knowledge. Avoiding historic errors is one thing. Utilizing the advances in philosophy and science is another. A number of far-reaching influences, some of them well outside the technical field of education, have more and more affected education in all its functions. Education is indebted to new knowledge in the fields of social theory, cultural anthropology, biology and what may be called socio-biology, psychology, psychiatry, and medicine, to mention some major areas. The structure of society and the evolution of its institutions; the nature and development of human personality; and most important, the relation between the individual and the society within which he lives, are all necessary background for the modern educational worker. Detailed information is available and should have been included in the general education (though it probably was not) of all who work in education. The following paragraphs very briefly hint at some of the implications of the new knowledge.

Analysis of the transitional crisis in civilization and of the emergent social theory. The fundamental changes taking place in Western society and civilization have sharply challenged the average citizen in all walks of life. Questions of ultimate aims and values, of the relation of means to ends, are the business of the man in the street as well as of the philosopher. Sensitivity to aims and values is steadily increasing throughout society, with accompanying scrutiny of the means for achieving the values. Education is no exception. Educational workers deal with ultimate purposes and cannot complacently retain older ideas.

Social change is now seen as a basic principle of the universe and not the result of violence by the masses or theorizing by "crackpot" scholars. The process of social change can be studied and, within limits, managed. In any event, it can be understood and taken into account.

The democratic philosophy of life and of education establishes new emphases. Attention to ultimate aims and values and to the relation between means and ends is still further encouraged by current philosophic contemplation and analysis.

The democratic philosophy has, in addition, greatly affected our views concerning persons and relationships within a group. Extended treatment of the group process will be found in a later chapter, the brief reference here dealing only with those points which affect the definition of supervision and its functions.

Democracy is a social theory affecting all of life; it is not limited to political forms. The worth of the individual person is the first principle, together with the common good as the social aim. The individual has duties and obligations as well as rights and privileges. Democracy, supported by scientific findings, clearly recognizes that leadership and creativity appear on all levels and in all types of persons. Problem-solving by means of group attack is fundamental to progress within democracy. All of this makes the older relationships between leader and led wholly untenable, and the traditional processes of imposition and direction impossible. All persons ideally become co-workers and participants in the co-operative formulation, execution, and evaluation of everything from general aims and policies to the minutiae of everyday procedure.

Scientific studies in education, particularly of the growth and development of the learner, have given new insights. The application of scientific method to the solution of social problems is also one of the great advances of the present century. Its effect upon supervision as a part of education has been significant. Our understanding of, and sensitivity to, the vast complexity of the learning process has been greatly increased. The great range of factors affecting learning, many far outside the school setting, and the subtlety of many of them, has become much clearer. The total environment must be considered, which in turn greatly extends the scope of supervision. Knowledge of the growth and development of the learner, the organismic concept of the learner, and the concept of integration have had profound effect upon educational thinking. Supervision cannot proceed in defiance of these facts.

The implication of current knowledge for supervision. Avoidance of errors resulting from outmoded principles and practices must be supplemented by use of new principles and practices based on advances in knowledge. New and important assumptions and concepts include:

1. Education is recognized as a basic social force affecting the development of human personality and of a stable democratic social order. Education is not a mechanical process dealing with mechanics of learning through mechanical administration of details. Supervision thus becomes a basic part of a fundamental social process and cannot be effective if it relies on the unthinking imposition or enforcement of materials and methods.

2. A consensus must be developed within the group as to the ends and values of life, hence of education, before details of education, hence of supervision, can be developed. Provision for re-examination of goals and values as necessitated by changes in society must be included. A good deal of school work, as we all know, has gone on without any clear understanding of purposes, or has been based on purposes long outmoded.

3. Change is recognized as a principle of the universe, affecting all phases of life and of social organization. Changes in the educational program, often extensive, whether in administration, methods of financing, curriculum organization, methods of teacher, or any other factor, are recognized not merely as necessary but as highly desirable.

4. The process of social change is recognized and used. Changes in values, beliefs, attitudes, and behavior are best brought about by extending and improving the insights of the persons involved—staff, pupils, community members. Imposition, direction, even guidance, are supplanted by methods of identifying problems, group planning, group attack on problems, experimentation, and other related procedures.

5. Supervision is recognized as a social process; in our country the co-operative democratic process. Group planning, group attack on problems, experimentation, as above, are central. Co-operation among all agencies of society which deal with childhood and youth, with their protection and education, is inescapable. Supervision becomes co-extensive with, or at least intimately related to, the entire setting for learning.

6. The chief function of supervisors is leadership and the stimulation of leadership within the group. The supervisor must have skill in leadership, skill in managing human relations, skill in guiding group process, in addition to being an expert in his own field.

7. The improvement of the factors within the total learning situation is the over-all aim of supervision. Improvement is no longer directed solely at teachers. The focus is on the setting for learning and not on persons. Those who earlier directed programs of "improvement of teachers in service" were themselves in need of further study, experience, and improvement, but this was overlooked because of our undemocratic concepts. A co-operatively determined attack upon significant local educational problems is the best in-service education procedure known. The whole staff is stimulated to study and growth. *The improvement of teachers is not so much a supervisory function in which teachers participate as it is a teacher function in which supervisors co-operate.* Actually, the modern aim is improvement of the *staff* through co-operative procedures. The idea of growth is replacing that of improvement.

Supervision is increasingly derived from the setting for learning instead of imposed upon it. The influence of the principles and practices summarized above has led to supervision based on and derived from a given set of circumstances. Many supervisory programs today unfortunately are still planned and directed by those on the upper levels; many of these programs are valuable and helpful when accepted by the staff. Numerous research studies in industry [2] as well as in education,[3] however, have established beyond doubt that greatly improved effort results when programs are based upon the needs, purposes, and problems existing within the situation and are recognized by the workers therein. Extensive research also shows that co-operatively derived programs reveal great gains in morale and mental health of the staff, in addition to improved technical results.

Section 2

A DEFINITION AND PROGRAM FOR MODERN SUPERVISION

What, then, is supervision today? The previous section indicated that the functions of supervision are far more extensive than formerly because of wider application of the principles of democracy, the findings of research, and the changes within the social

[2] J. R. P. French, A. W. Kornhauser, and A. J. Marrow, "Conflict and Co-operation in Industry," *Journal of Social Issues* (February, 1946).

B. B. Gardner, "Employee Counseling in Private Industry," *Public Personnel Review,* No. 6 (1945).

J. David Houser, *What People Want from Business* (New York, McGraw, 1938). An older but very valuable study.

R. L. Hull and Arnold Kolstad, "Morale on the Job," in Goodwin Watson, ed., *Civilian Morale* (Boston, Houghton, 1942).

David Krech and Richard S. Crutchfield, *Theory and Problems of Social Psychology* (New York, McGraw, 1948). Ch. 14 on "Industrial Conflict" is excellent on needs of worker; tensions on the job; frustrations related to the job; channeling dissatisfactions; reduction of frustration and tension.

A. J. Marrow and J. R. P. French, "Changing Stereotypes in Industry," *Journal of Social Issues* (August, 1945), pp. 33-37.

Elton Mayo, *Human Problems in an Industrial Civilization* (New York, Macmillan, 1933). The original classic in this field.

F. J. Roethlisberger and others, *Management and the Worker* (Cambridge, Harvard Univ. Press, 1939). Account of the monumental research conducted at the Western Electric Company, Hawthorne Works, Chicago, begun in 1927. One of the basic references even yet. (An interpretive description of this study by Goodwin Watson will be found in *Progressive Education* (January, 1942), pp. 33-41.

Goodwin Watson, "Work Satisfaction," in George Hartmann and Theodore Newcomb, eds.,

Industrial Conflict (New York, Cordon, 1939).

[3] Kenneth D. Benne, *A Conception of Authority* (New York, Teachers College, Bureau of Publications, Columbia Univ., 1943).

Kenneth D. Benne and Bozidar Muntyan, *Human Relations in Curriculum Change* (New York, Dryden, 1951). Many sections. See also Circular Series A, No. 51, Illinois Secondary School Curriculum Program Bulletin No. 7, Springfield, Ill., Office of State Superintendent of Public Instruction, 1950.

Kenneth D. Benne, Leland P. Bradford, and Ronald Lippitt, *Group Dynamics and Social Action* (New York, Anti-Defamation League of B'nai B'rith, 1950).

William H. Burton, "The Teacher's Morale as an Important Factor in Teaching Success," *California Journal of Elementary Education* (May, 1938), pp. 218-226.

Clyde M. Campbell, ed., *Practical Applications of Democratic Administration* (New York, Harper, 1952). Contains a wealth of information.

Robert E. Cralle and William H. Burton, "An Examination of Factors Stimulating or Depressing Teacher Morale," *California Journal of Elementary Education* (August, 1938), pp. 7-14. An objective study.

Irving Knickerbocker, "Leadership—A Conception and Some Implications," *Journal of Social Issues* (Summer, 1948), pp. 23-40.

Kurt Lewin, *Resolving Social Conflicts* (New York, Harper, 1948).

Douglas McGregor, "The Staff Function of Human Relations," *Journal of Social Relations* (Summer, 1948), pp. 5-22.

climate surrounding education. Specifically, there may be noted the great changes in curriculum materials and organizations, the more functional organization of teaching programs, the greatly changed practices in pupil promotion, the introduction of heterogeneous grouping within unit teaching, with ability grouping confined to special subjects and more advanced students. Teachers are, in general, better trained and more professional, though literally tremendous progress still remains to be made. Secondary schools are receiving ever increasing numbers of students who are not fitted to the traditional secondary programs, many in fact who have not mastered the skills that one commonly associates with elementary schools. In place of complaints and rejection of these students, secondary schools need extensive supervisory assistance in adjusting programs to the new needs and in formulating new programs.

Changes in family life, in social relationships generally, renewed attention to delinquency, are all affecting education and hence supervision. The effects of competition wrongly applied in life, and the tensions of our times, particularly those of big city life, are producing mental health problems which the schools cannot avoid.

The rash of criticism directed at schools currently focuses attention on outmoded practices, on our efforts to improve, and, significantly, upon the serious failure of the schools to keep the public informed about the new curriculums and teaching practices.

The foregoing paragraphs list only a small number of factors from the scores that exist which explain the necessity for profound changes in education and in supervision; which will indicate the necessity for still further extensive changes.

All phases of supervision have been affected: definition, principles, administrative organization, the general and specific activities of supervisors. Each of these will be discussed in proper order in succeeding chapters. We are, for the moment, concerned with definition. The authors give below the revision of a definition first presented in 1938, and then revised in 1947, which even in its early forms reflected the contributions of new knowledge and the effects of social changes. The contribution of the present volume will be, it is hoped, a definition in keeping with current conditions, plus suggestions for better implementation of the definition.

A definition and a program in outline form. *Supervision is an expert technical service primarily aimed at studying and improving co-operatively all factors which affect child growth and development.* Everything in a school system is designed, of course, for the ultimate purpose of stimulating learning and growth. Supervision gives expert and specialized attention to these factors.

The basic characteristics of a comprehensive plan for the improvement of the educational program in any community may be outlined as follows:

1. The educational philosophy of the school, that is, the general and specific objectives to be achieved, must be co-operatively formulated as a first and fundamental necessity.

    a. The philosophy and goals are determined partly by the nature and purposes of the social order, and partly by the nature and purposes of each individual as a unique personality.

    b. Broad open-end goals, such as democratic socialization of the learner, help to unify and guide group action. Goals of this type must be supplemented with specific behavioral goals.

    c. Goals are not permanent, though general social goals change very slowly and over considerable periods of time.

2. Evaluation of the educational product should take place at various stages of development and in the light of the accepted objectives, for the purpose of determining the extent to which the objectives are being achieved. The objectives and the methods of evaluation themselves are likewise to be evaluated. (Despite reference to "stages of development," evaluation is actually continuous and is an

integral part of all learning and supervisory activities.)

The results of evaluation provide a basis for determining strengths and weaknesses of the educational program provided by the community so that steps can be taken to improve the program. Other needs and improvements will arise from study of new facts and insights developed by research, by philosophic analysis, or by social changes.

3. A quick review should be made of possible factors contributing to any unsatisfactory conditions revealed by the appraisal. The causes of unsatisfactory results may be found in:

  a. The curriculum.
  b. The instructional methods and the characteristics of the teaching personnel.
  c. The equipment and instructional materials, physical environmental conditions within and without the school.
  d. The general policy of the school on teaching, discipline, punishment, promotion, and others.
  e. The attitudes and expressed beliefs of the community.
  f. The learner, his physical, mental, social, emotional, and moral traits, experiential background, interests; physical and mental health, habits of study and work, and the like.

4. A tentative summary should be made to determine which of those general factors is *most likely* to be operative in the particular circumstances. This serves as a guide or search model for the systematic analysis in Point 5.

Points 3 and 4 indicate that general in-service study of the educational program by staff and all interested community members, including students, should be continuous. The search for specific factors and the development of remedial measures is thus ensured. It is not safe to jump to conclusions as to causes of weakness or to prescribe hastily without renewed acquaintance with the professional background easily available in standard references. Invited specialists are also of great assistance here. Preliminary (and really continuous) study by staff and community is doubly necessary when new departures, as distinguished from improvement of existing materials or processes, are under consideration.

5. A systematic analysis or search of the local situation should then be made to determine with some assurance the factors most likely to be actually contributory to the unfavorable growth of learners in the given situation. Here the staff is concerned with specific, rather than general or possible, factors.

  a. Self-study and evaluation by all staff members is essential, in addition to analysis of other influences in the setting for learning.
  b. The assistance of specialists in any subject area, in instruction, in group process, in any phase of educational psychology, may be invited at this point.
  c. The result should be a list of local needs, shortcomings, and problems to be dealt with.

6. An improvement program for *dealing with underlying conditions as well as immediate* factors should be developed.

  a. The needs, interests, capacities, contributions of all participants must be recognized.
  b. The contributions of experts or resource persons must be considered in terms of the actual existing conditions.

7. The effectiveness of this program should be appraised from time to time (actually continuously) to determine the desirable changes wrought in the educational product.

The appraisal should extend also to the changes in the factors themselves, such as the curriculum, methods of instruction, personalities, materials, environmental conditions as a result of the improvement program.

The detailed procedures of democratic co-operation by which supervisory programs can be carried on will be found in Chapters 4, 5, and 6.

The importance of self-supervision. The agelong tradition of imposed supervision, together with the desirable modern emphasis upon co-operative group endeavor, sometimes obscures one of the most important implications of modern educational philosophy, namely, the possibility of self-direction, self-guidance, self-supervision. The mature individual will not only serve as a leader in group enterprise, not only contribute to group discussion and decision, but he will often engage in purely individual effort. Experts do this when working independently on a frontier problem. A member of the rank and file does this when he studies his own needs, tries out new methods in his classroom, pursues a problem of his own through the available literature. Self-initiated attention to any problem often, perhaps usually, grows out of group activities, and can hardly avoid contributing to the group program.

Mature educational workers who have active, critical minds, a realization of the importance of education, and a dynamic view of the universe will engage in self-directed study as a matter of course. Many interested and willing teachers need only encouragement and assistance to spur them to work independently on their own problems. Many teachers not yet confident enough to participate extensively in group projects will be greatly aided in developing greater security by independent study. Individual growth and ability to participate in group action are both stimulated. Oddly enough, there is little material on self-supervision.

Contrasts between traditional and modern supervision. The definition given above clearly breaks with the earlier, narrower conception of supervision. Traditionally supervision was centered around the teacher and the classroom act, and was based largely on the thought that teachers, often being lamentably undertrained, need careful direction and training. Visiting the classroom, conferences, teachers' meetings were the bulk of supervision and, in many minds, were synonymous with supervision. Modern supervision, in contrast, is far more fundamental and diverse. Its characteristics may be summarized in outline form for brevity and clarity.

1. Modern supervision directs attention toward the fundamentals of education and orients learning and its improvement within the general aim of education.
2. The aim of supervision is the improvement of the total teaching-learning process, the total setting for learning, rather than the narrow and limited aim of improving teachers in service.
3. The focus is on the setting for learning, not on a person or group of persons. All persons are co-workers aiming at the improvement of a situation. One group is not superior to another, operating to "improve" the inferior group.
4. The teacher is removed from his embarrassing position as the focus of attention and the weak link in the educational process. He assumes his rightful position as a co-operating member of a group concerned with the improvement of learning.

The following outline, based on prominent catch words, notes in succinct fashion the salient differences between the two types of supervision.

CONTRASTS IN SUPERVISION

Traditional	Modern
1. Inspection.	1. Study and analysis.
2. Teacher-focused.	
3. Visitation and conference.	2. Focused on aim, material, method, teacher, pupil, and environment.
4. Random and haphazard, or a meager, formal plan.	3. Many diverse functions.
5. Imposed and authoritarian.	4. Definitely organized and planned.
6. One person usually.	5. Derived and co-operative.
	6. Many persons.

Put into sentence form, this means that, in the main, traditional supervision consisted largely of inspection of the teacher by means of visitation and conference, carried on in a random manner, with directions imposed on the teacher by authority and usually by one person. Modern supervision, by contrast, involves the systematic study and analysis of the entire teaching-learning situation, utilizing a carefully planned program that has been co-operatively derived from the situation and which is adapted to the needs of those involved in it. Special help is also given individual teachers who encounter problems that cannot be solved by ordinary group supervisory procedures.

The far-flung relationships and activities

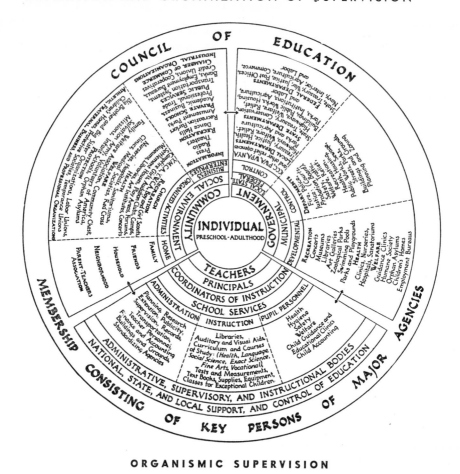

ORGANISMIC SUPERVISION

From L. J. Brueckner and R. H. Koenker, "Organismic Supervision," *Elementary School Journal* (February, 1940), pp. 435-441. Published by the University of Chicago Press.

of modern supervision will be developed throughout the volume. A preliminary view can be obtained through scrutiny of the chart above prepared by Brueckner and Koenker.

This chart was designed to call attention to the wide variety of agencies that impinge on the individual and affect his growth and development. These agencies include the school and a wide variety of public and private institutions and organizations, some of them identified in the chart. They ordinarily operate largely independently of each other. The chart indicates a plan for co-ordinating and integrating their functions through a council on education, represented by the outer ring. This council would consist of

representatives of all agencies, public and private, that are concerned with the educational program in its broadest sense. In many places this group is called the co-ordinating council. Such councils have often produced remarkable changes in community life. The chart represents the interaction of all of these forces as they impinge on the learner.

Principles underlying supervisory functions are vital. One and the same set of supervisory functions, based on different sets of principles, would produce greatly varying results because of differing aims, means, and attitudes. Supervisory functions, for instance, could be exercised autocratically or democratically, depending upon the social theory and process of the surrounding society. Extended treatment is given this problem in Chapter 4, but for the moment, we may re-emphasize two points presented previously in this chapter. The two desirable principles are those of science and democracy. Supervision must use objective evaluative and diagnostic techniques; an evolutionary, experimental attitude must permeate the whole activity. Democratic attitudes and the practices of participation and co-operation are equally fundamental. Respect for personality and courteous reception of contributions of varying worth to the common task must be dominant. Participation and creative individual contribution must be facilitated. Authority, when set up and used at all, will be derived from the setting for learning as determined and set up by the group. Authority will be the authority of the group over itself, exercised for the good of the group, delegated by the group to a person or persons and similarly withdrawn if not exercised effectively toward the achievement of commonly conceived purposes. The writers, as will be emphasized in the following chapter, deliberately reject the traditional concept of imposed authority and substitute therefor the concepts of responsibility and leadership, of derived authority.

It is sincerely hoped that the new definition, plus increasing emphasis upon democratic operation, will help to eliminate from our thinking the connotations of inspection, arbitrary rating, imposed improvement programs, and the superiority-inferiority relationship between groups of co-workers. The writers emphasize the possibilities in such terms as *educational consultant* (or *adviser*); *technical consultant* (or *adviser*), or *counselor,* or *instructional consultant* (or *co-ordinator*), or *resource person,* for use in place of *supervisor.* The term *co-ordinator* also seems to be gaining in use and perhaps the time is ripe for an even better term more in keeping with modern educational concepts.

Criticisms of supervision. Supervision has always had to meet criticisms from a propor-

tion of the teaching body. Analysis of these criticisms is revealing. Teacher criticisms, usually voiced orally or in articles written by individual teachers, vary from carefully worded, sincere discussions of poor supervision to wild, illogical, and incoherent denunciations of any and all supervision. The majority of casually expressed criticisms reflect narrow temperamental views. This is a matter for genuine regret, since real harm is done. The general attitude of thoughtless, antagonistic criticism is kept alive. Young teachers are given undesirable prejudices. Those persons who express unthinking, temperamental criticisms are unfavorably affecting their own opinions and attitudes. Rising levels of professional insight and spirit, plus increasingly co-operative practices in supervision, will tend to eliminate criticism on the level of "cloakroom gossip."

A number of valid and reliable studies of supervisory activities have been made, under controlled conditions, in which the sober judgments of many teachers concerning their value were recorded. These show conclusively that although teachers object, and rightly so, to formal, uninspired, and dogmatic supervision and to supervisors lacking personality and training, they are enthusiastically in favor of good supervision. Favorable judgments outnumbered the unfavorable on the ratio of approximately six to one. The evidence is easily available in both primary and secondary sources and is voluminous. It is not restated here because of easy availability and because advanced students may be expected to be familiar with such routine background materials.[4]

[4] The following samples of current articles are given as representative. A report may be made when groups need further information on this question. The articles are valuable also as a source of specific references to supervisory techniques.

The ten recently published texts in supervision, listed at the end of this chapter, each contain discussions of this topic. Use the index.

P. M. Bail, "Do Teachers Receive the Kind of Supervision They Desire?" *Journal of Educational Research* (May, 1947), pp. 713-716.

E. J. Goebel, "What Do Teachers Expect of

The chief criticisms derived from the serious judgments of fair-minded teachers and from more objective analyses may be summarized thus:

1. Supervision costs too much.
2. Supervision is undemocratic. It destroys the individuality of the teacher, represses his initiative, inhibits him emotionally, and otherwise interferes with his self-reliance and self-expression.
3. Supervision lacks basic principles that are objective, valid, and reliable; it lacks adequate criteria for self-evaluation.
4. Supervision lacks a staff of adequate training and personality.
5. Supervision lacks a planned program.

Brief comment only is needed. The first criticism, cost, cannot be discussed intelligently in general. This is a question of financial ability and policy in each local administration. There is overwhelming evidence of the value and results of supervision. Recent surveys show that with the sole exception of localities where political interference is severe, the more money spent the better the schools. Money spent on supervision will unquestionably secure desirable results. If money is simply not available, however, then any supervision costs too much.

Supervision is not inherently and automatically undemocratic. That it is undemocratic in given school systems is not a criticism of supervision but of local leadership. Democratic supervision can be observed in many places and it is on the increase.

The criticism that supervision lacks basic principles is incorrect. To be sure, there is some lack in the number and adequacy of the principles as they now exist, but the list is steadily expanding. Teaching, medicine, engineering, and other activities were all in the same situation in the beginning and they are still partly there. This criticism usually stems from a lack of information.

The lack of adequately trained staff with desirable personality traits cannot be a criticism of supervision but is again a criticism of local circumstances. A challenge exists for the development of better educational programs for supervisors.

Modern supervision in competent hands is planned and carefully organized. Ongoing programs of professional activities of the better types are constantly being derived cooperatively from the needs of particular conditions and democratically carried out with the participation of the whole staff.

Factual or logical arguments indicating that supervision is an unnecessary and detrimental addition to the educational structure do not exist. Justification of supervision must rest in the last analysis upon experimentally derived data, of which an abundance exists. (See Chapter 18.)

The need for supervision. Discussion has proceeded thus far upon the assumption that supervision is a necessary function or service within the educational organization. Opposition to and denials of the value of supervision do not today emanate from any influential source or from any person of standing in education. Isolated individuals who oppose supervision as such are usually honest, naïve individuals who do not know the facts; educators or laymen who do not recognize the technical or professional nature of education and of supervision. A few dishonest individuals oppose supervision for selfish reasons.

The state of affairs differs, of course, between the elementary school and the second-

Supervision?" *National Catholic Education Association Proceedings* (1952), pp. 421-425.

R. E. Gross, "Teachers Want Supervision!" *School Executive* (August, 1953), pp. 52-53.

G. C. Kyte, "This Is the Kind of Supervision That Teachers Welcome and Appreciate," *Nation's Schools* (July, 1951), pp. 33-34.

D. J. Lane, "What's Wrong With Teacher-Supervisor Relations?" *High Points* (February, 1953), pp. 29-53.

V. L. Replogle, "What Help Do Teachers Want?" *Educational Leadership* (April, 1950), p. 447.

Jane Sherrod, "Six Ways to Avoid a Supervisor," *ibid.* (November, 1952), pp. 132-133.

M. J. Whitehead, "Teachers Look at Supervision," *ibid.,* pp. 101-106.

Various professional periodicals devote an issue from time to time to supervision. Note, for instance, the November, 1952, issue of *Educational Leadership,* and other earlier numbers.

ary school. Reputable supervisory programs are found widely on the elementary level. The secondary school,[5] with its subject-matter emphasis and type of teacher preparation, has been very slow to develop this very effective and necessary supervisory service. Supervision on the functional service basis is a necessary, integral part of any general educational program and of any specific school system because:

1. Supervision as expert consultant service is an accepted principle in all difficult and complex human undertakings in any line of endeavor.

2. Education, particularly, is complex and intricate, and furthermore is carried on in minute divisions—classrooms—scattered throughout a community and over the nation. The great extension of educational opportunity, particularly on the secondary level, increases the demands for technical assistance.

Brief teacher tenure also complicates the situation. Supervision in the sense of leadership will contribute to unity (not uniformity) of purpose and co-ordination of effort.

3. The academic and professional training of all levels of professional workers, despite excellent progress, is still absurdly low. Supervision will contribute to the growth of all.

4. The teaching load, particularly in high school, is so diverse, so heavy, and so unrelated to teachers' previous preparation that technical assistance is necessary.

5. Education is developing so rapidly that educational workers in general cannot possibly keep abreast of current developments. Supervisory services will bring to all members of the staff analyses and discussions of research findings, new departures, creative suggestions.

6. Leadership and creative contributions may emerge anywhere, it is increasingly being realized. Supervisory leadership aids in discovering leadership and creative ability and in arranging opportunities for their emergence.

Section 3

THE DUTIES AND ACTIVITIES OF SUPERVISORS: A GENERAL STATEMENT

Early books on supervision usually included at this point an extensive listing of specific activities through which the definition of supervision became operative. Since then, however, a great change has taken place and is still taking place in what we regard as desirable activities for supervisors. The change is another illustration of the impact on education of democracy, of research findings, and of the great fund of new knowledge of human relations, personality, and mental health.

The major and minor duties of the supervisor are much more clearly discriminated. Certain newer duties are rated as more important than some previously prominent. General and specific activities have changed in number, type, and importance; some have been dropped. Trends within this area are, for the moment, more important than listings of activities. Detailed discussion of supervisory procedures in relation to major problems will be presented in succeeding

chapters. Meanwhile, an extremely abbreviated illustrative listing is included here to give some concreteness to the discussion.

Scrutiny of early discussions reveals a number of major duties for which illustrative specific activities are given.

1. Field work (usually inspection).
   Visit schools; answer calls.
2. Training activities.
   Individual and group conferences; demonstration teaching; arrange intervisitation; direct observation; provide social contacts; hold teachers meetings, study groups; and many others.
3. Preparing instructional materials.

[5] Two good books devoted specifically to supervision in the secondary school are available. General principles in all texts on supervision are also applicable to the secondary school.

Charles W. Boardman, Harl R. Douglass, and Rudyard K. Bent, *Democratic Supervision in Secondary Schools* (Boston, Houghton, 1953).

Thomas H. Briggs and Joseph Justman, *Improving Instruction Through Supervision*, rev. ed (New York, Macmillan, 1952; original, 1938).

Prepare course of study; prepare, list, and discuss instructional materials of many types; prepare oral or written materials on specialized problems of instruction, of testing, of improving specified aspects of instruction.

4. Making test surveys and other inquiries. Test widely for instructional results; make reports on observed conditions, requests; make and/or report research.
5. Giving special attention to new teachers.
6. Aiding in selecting and introducing texts, equipment, and any other materials.
7. Participating in selecting, assigning, and transferring teachers.

Other headings refer to professional activities, research, community relations, preparing publicity, and participating in professional organizations and programs.

Early studies emphasized details. A large number of objective studies appeared prior to 1930. Very few appeared during the decade 1930-1940, but there was renewal of interest after 1940. Significant differences appeared between studies prior to 1930 and after 1940.

The older studies surveyed all types of school systems from rural to large city; all types of supervisors, state, city, and country, general and special, department heads, principals, and superintendents. These studies *accepted supervision as it was and proceeded to count and list the supervisory activities performed.* Purposes for which the activities were undertaken were usually taken for granted. Sometimes they were overlooked or only hazily considered. The specific circumstances in which the activities occurred were often neglected. Appropriateness of the activity to the purpose was rarely considered. A few studies were made aimed at evaluating the worth of certain specific techniques.

Important trends, however, appeared early. Objective analyses, while very valuable, have definite limitations. First, supervisory practices are often traditional, commonplace, and mediocre but, since they seem to work in ordinary circumstances, are likely

to be faithfully recorded as "successful" practice, Second, valuable new departures, the beginnings of what may develop into a significant trend, are often overlooked, since they rank low in a frequency tabulation of current practice.

These objective studies need to be supplemented by the subjective analyses and new suggestions of competent, informed thinkers in the field. In any event, we must be on the alert for innovations and the development of new trends.

A distinct trend away from inspection and imposed improvement and toward assistance, guidance, and co-ordination was noted as early as 1925. By 1929, much less of the supervisors' total time than formerly was being given to indiscriminate visitation of the classroom. Large cities placed much less emphasis upon visiting the teacher at work and more upon research, study, and office conferences. Smaller cities continued the emphasis upon classroom visiting, with less attention to research and study.

The trend away from *confining* supervision to classroom visitation and individual conferences has continued steadily. Actual first-hand contact with the classroom will be important always, but this form of information gathering is not the most effective or economical method for getting the desired results. Visitation itself is changing, with scheduled visits greatly reduced in number in favor of the more effective visitation made on request. Many other functions now share the supervisor's time. Group conferences for study and attack on common local problems emerged early and have grown steadily in importance. Research, a function rarely included in the very early studies, now appears often.

Valuable guidance was found in studies of teacher judgment of the use and effectiveness of various supervisory procedures. One [6] of

[6] Ernest O. Melby, *A Critical Study of the Existing Organization and Administration of Supervision* (Bloomington, Ill., Public School Publishing Co., 1929).

the very early studies showed, for instance, that only 12 per cent of the teachers responding had experienced demonstration teaching as a supervisory technique but 64 per cent regarded that technique as of great value. Intervisitation was experienced by only 8 per cent but 64 per cent rated it as of great value.

Unannounced visits to the classroom had been experienced by 58 per cent of the teachers, but were regarded as very valuable by only 22 per cent. Reporting of lesson plans was required of 51 per cent but was regarded as valuable by but 32 per cent. *Required* professional reading and organized reading circles were rated very low (16 to 27 per cent) by teachers who at the same time rated very high (65 per cent in favor) the maintenance and *availability* of a professional library and magazine shelf. Again we note the early trend toward voluntary study of self-recognized problems. Other similar studies are available.

Teachers' evaluations of certain other activities need careful interpretation. One extensive study,[7] for instance, showed that teachers asked for very few items in "improvement in service" and rated low those that were available. Dozens of other items which they did ask for and valued highly are recognized as excellent improvement-in-service procedures, though not identified as such by the teachers. The teachers in this study asked overwhelmingly for "specific directions," "practical procedures to be followed." They demanded overwhelmingly that supervisors stop talking in "generalities" and "tell us specifically what to do!" These same teachers in another part of the investigation complained naïvely that a serious fault of supervision was that it "laid down procedures to be followed," demanded that "teachers do as supervisors say!" This contradiction is explained through reference to teacher-training and to the unwitting use of clichés and slogans. Many teachers complain automatically about "imposition" but at the same time demand to be told "what to do."

Better teacher-training and the increasing use of co-operative techniques will progressively eliminate this difficulty.

One of the most significant findings in the early study was that co-operative group study had been experienced by but 9 per cent but was voted as valuable by 45 per cent. Thirteen years later [8] this device, co-operative, participatory study, appeared at the very top of the list as the most valuable device.

Considerable latent leadership among teachers, a key belief in modern supervision, was clearly revealed in the very early studies. Teacher requests for certain types of supervisory assistance and teacher evaluations of services rendered clearly demonstrated good insight and a desire for improved settings for learning. Supervisory leadership also appeared in services offered to teachers but not requested by them, services which were later evaluated highly by teachers. It is evident that a number of important needs in any situation, not always sensed by those directly involved, will be recognized when revealed by good leaders, whether among teachers or supervisors.

Later and current studies reflect a new orientation and a better organization of major and minor supervisory activities. First, the mere listing of activities characteristic of the older studies has given way to critical listing. The purposes for which activities are performed are scrutinized, and hence appropriateness to given circumstances is established. Second, the static view reflected in statistical listing is giving way to notation of innovations and trends, though frequency listing is still important. Third, emphasis upon a multiplicity of detailed

[7] *Current Problems of Supervisors,* Third Yearbook, Department of Supervisors and Directors of Instruction (Washington, NEA, 1930).

[8] C. A. Weber, "Techniques of In-Service Education Applied in North Central Schools," *North Central Association Quarterly* (October, 1942), pp. 195-198.
C. A. Weber and S. L. Garfield, "Teachers' Reactions to Certain Aspects of In-Service Education," *Educational Administration and Supervision* (September, 1942), pp. 463-468.

techniques is being replaced by attention to larger categories, with specific procedures to be developed in the light of principles and given conditions.

An illustrative listing of these larger categories, selected from many current studies,[9] reveals a significant contrast with the listing from older studies given above.

1. Group attack upon self-defined problems and group study of self-selected topics or areas. This in turn means that group process with its participatory, co-operative procedures is supplanting the older techniques of imposition or direction. Group spirit and morale are created.

2. Leadership is increasingly exercised in place of authority, and opportunities for leadership to emerge within the group are fostered.

3. Recognition of the individual school as the unit of supervision and of the principal as the natural status leader is multiplying.

4. The use of consultants is increasing, with ever better definition of the function of a consultant.

5. Counseling with teachers, individually and in groups, is increasing, replacing the in part wasteful individual conferences, though these are valuable when appropriate. (This is also indicated in current studies.) Counseling may deal with personal problems and tensions as well as with professional matters.

6. Self-appraisal and self-direction are receiving more attention than for some time.

7. Open criticism by teachers directed at

certain older, stereotyped supervisory techniques is frequent, severe, and valid. (Teachers' meetings, for instance, are condemned severely, whereas group study of common problems by a staff or smaller group is highly commended.)

A recent statistical study [10] of the supervisory practice of elementary school principals, conducted by the National Department of Elementary School Principals in 1948, concludes with the recommendation:

Principals should seek to develop experimental and creative attitudes and procedures in the field of supervision. New ideas and processes, based upon research and study, are needed to lift supervision above dull and obvious methods.

Fifteen common supervisory practices were listed but only four were employed by three-quarters of the principals, and only nine by 50 per cent. Helping individual teachers was listed by 97 per cent of the principals, and while this is costly of time, it is a primary concern of principals. Dealing with individual pupils was reported by 84 per cent, which is again desirable but time consuming. The study shows the progress made since early days, and its recommendations for further improvement are sound.

A similar study [11] of the activities of gen-

[9] C. L. Amundson and L. W. Kindred, "What Is the Principal's Responsibility for Supervision?" *National Association of Secondary School Principals Bulletin* (April, 1954).

K. A. Cook and Harold Full, "Is the School Faculty Meeting Significant in Promoting Professional Growth?" *School Review* (November, 1948), pp. 519-524.

Educational Leadership, issue for November, 1952. Contains several articles, mostly of discussional type. Some of these report valuable factual information.

G. E. Flowers, "Relationships with Others Is the Key," *American School Board Journal* (June, 1952), pp. 25-27.

N. H. Glicksman, "Experienced Teacher under Supervision," *High Point* (January, 1949). (Commentary on this by another author in issue for April, 1949.)

Allen C. Harman, "Supervision in Selected Secondary Schools," doctoral dissertation (Philadelphia, Univ. of Pennsylvania Press, 1947). Good bibliography of these studies to 1947.

D. C. Keesler, "The Development of a Principal's Self-Appraisal Program," *American School Board Journal* (September, 1946), p. 78.

B. Miller, "The Superintendent as Educational Leader," *School Executive* (June, 1952), pp. 70-71.

D. A. Prescott, "Role of Supervisor in Reducing Tensions," *California Journal of Elementary Education* (November, 1951), pp. 87-91.

Fred F. Quinlan, "Faculty Meetings During School Hours," *American School Board Journal* (July, 1946), p. 46.

K. J. Rehage, "Analyzing the Administrative Job," *Elementary School Journal* (November, 1952), pp. 129-31; 125-29.

Review of Educational Research (October, 1949), Ch. 7.

[10] *The Elementary-School Principalship, Today and Tomorrow,* Twenty-seventh Yearbook, Department of Elementary School Principals (Washington, NEA, 1948), p. 109.

[11] *Leadership Through Supervision,* 1946 Yearbook, Association for Supervision and Curriculum Development (Washington, NEA, 1946), pp. 37-38.

eral and special supervisors, made in 1945 by the Association for Supervision and Curriculum Development, shows somewhat greater progress among the more general officers. More than 75 per cent of supervisors were using sixteen different processes, and 50 per cent were using as many as thirty different procedures. The important finding of this study was that integrated programs of supervision, co-operatively determined, were appearing with encouraging frequency. This means that detailed techniques are not as important as an over-all program which incorporates them.

Note in table below that many of the listed functions call for group planning, and that they in turn encompass many of the more detailed activities.

FUNCTIONS FREQUENTLY OR REGULARLY PERFORMED BY SUPERVISORS RESPONDING TO THE QUESTIONNAIRE

Per cent	Functions
100	Attending meetings of professional organizations.
97	Discussing educational philosophy or objectives with teachers.
96	Holding group conferences to discuss common problems.
96	Making classroom visits.
95	Holding individual conferences with teachers on problems they propose.
94	Discussing methods with teachers.
89	Working on committees in professional organizations.
88	Evaluating and selecting books for pupil use.
88	Leading teaching groups in formulation and development of a common philosophy of education.
86	Helping teachers organize and develop source or teaching units.
86	Giving suggestions or instructions on how to initiate or carry through an instructional unit.
85	Organizing and working with teacher groups in curriculum-revision programs.
82	Interpreting test data to teachers and helping them to use them for improvement in teaching.
81	Evaluating and selecting books for teachers' libraries.
79	Acting as consultant in local faculty group meetings.
78	Working with curriculum consultants in analysis or development of curriculum program.
73	Speaking to lay organizations.
72	Speaking to parent study-groups.
71	Holding office in professional organizations.
70	Interviewing parents or laymen regarding education matters.
69	Writing or developing curriculum materials.
67	Preparing descriptions of educational philosophy or objectives with teachers.
65	Preparing manuals or bulletins on teaching various subjects.
65	Setting up courses of study, scope, and sequence plans.
65	Developing pupil-accounting systems, such as cumulative record cards.
64	Interviewing prospective teachers, employees.
62	Setting up and administering program to evaluate school practices.
62	Directing testing programs.
54	Preparing source or teaching units for use of teachers.
53	Organizing and/or directing workshops for local teachers in the area.
47	Previewing films, still films, records, or recordings.
46	Instructing teachers in the use of audio-visual aids.
45	Preparing written reports of classroom visits for the superintendents.
44	Writing articles on education or the activities of the school for newspapers.
42	Administering standard tests.
39	Planning demonstration teaching.
39	Organizing audio-visual materials.
39	Working with a teacher to help her to demonstration teaching.
37	Organizing and/or directing work-type teacher meetings.
36	Distributing audio-visual materials.
30	Organizing and/or directing workshops for teachers on university campuses.
29	Writing for professional journals or magazines.
26	Correcting tests.
14	Writing or collaborating in writing of textbooks.

A recent general statement by Wiles[12] which defines the supervisor's major duties in terms of group process is a natural culmination of certain trends indicated in the preceding pages. Wiles lists the major skills in group process as (a) skill in leadership, (b) skill in human relations, (c) skill in group process, (d) skill in personnel, and (e) skill in evaluation. Helpful illustrations of each are included in the book. This is wholesome but it is not the whole story. Expertness in group process is not all of supervision. Specialists of various types are necessary and these must be expertly informed in their areas of specialty. Problems of relationship and co-operative function are not solved by group discussion alone, though such discussion is an important part of solving such problems.

The 1952 revision of Briggs and Justman,[13] *Improving Instruction Through Supervision,* contains in the first four chapters a practical and forward-looking analysis of trends in supervisory function but limits the discussion to techniques. Problems are not discussed.

Functions differ somewhat among various types of supervisors. Wiles's emphasis upon group process is stimulating, but it is necessary to go further. Problems and activities will of necessity differ within an entire supervisory staff. Emphasis currently, it is true, is upon co-operative performance of the same or similar functions, but staff differences in knowledge and function are still significant. Furthermore, group process,[14] it is now known, does not work equally well with all types of personnel or organization.

Generalists and specialists have somewhat different relationships to the groups with which they work. Superintendents and building principals will function better if they develop desirable permissive conditions, stimulate participation and emergent leadership, keep discussion and study moving along, summarize, head off digressions and impasses, give support to the project whatever it is.

The specialist called in must be informed and skilled in these things also, but his contribution is to a condition already existing. This calls for specialized knowledge and different skills: leading a specified discussion, persuading, meeting questions and disagreements. The general system-wide supervisors function in both capacities.

Specialists, moreover, are of many kinds. The first ones added in early days were to serve the subject-centered curriculum, as supervisors of reading, of arithmetic, of social studies, of testing. Later specialists were added to serve the needs of learners, as experts on diagnosis of learning difficulties, child psychology, guidance, research. Curriculum directors and co-ordinators represent still another group, usually standing between the two groups of specialists just mentioned.

A general supervisor assigned to new teachers has still different problems and activities from those of general supervisors, and from those of many specialists listed above. His procedures are also specialized and technical.

State supervisors and rural supervisors also have their functions and techniques, determined in part by the region over which they operate and by the legal and administrative relationships existing.

All types of specialists are necessary, though the services of the subject-area experts have changed through the years. The presence of both types of specialists within a school system poses important problems of function and relationships, as we shall see in Chapter 5.

Public relations and the supervisor. Field workers and students have asked insistently that we include a brief treatment of public relations. All types of supervisors should participate in whatever program of public relations exists in the given circumstances. A

[12] Kimball Wiles, *Supervision for Better Schools* (New York, Prentice-Hall, 1950).
[13] New York, Macmillan.
[14] See specific discussion of this, together with references to basic research, in Ch. 7.

large and growing literature on public relations is available, hence summary here is brief and confined to general principles.

The chief aim of a program of public relations is to develop mutual understanding and respect between the school and its community. A program adequate to achieve this aim is basically different from campaigns to "keep the public informed," different from "selling the schools to the public." These older practices are based on the assumption that the schools are one thing and the community another.

Understanding and respect between persons and groups may be built by co-operative action upon group problems, by common study of materials, by processes which produce information rather than disseminate information produced by others. Participation by the community in school affairs in all respects is advocated throughout this volume. Methods and illustrations are included in nearly every chapter. Public relations in the older sense are not necessary in communities where there is continuous lay-professional co-operation and interaction. Public relations today are achieved through this complete and continuous interaction.

Parents will come to understand the structure and operation of the school as they participate co-operatively in many of the regular ongoing activities of that school; they will come to understand the teachers as persons, with problems, pressures, aims, and abilities. Teachers will similarly come to understand the backgrounds on which parents base their questions, destructive or constructive suggestions; to understand the ambitions of the parents for their children, the problems and pressures within the community and within given homes. Parents will come in contact with the scientific or technological material now available in education which may materially change their opinions about school processes, children's abilities, and many other things. Teachers will come in contact with the level of educational thinking in the community, the factors determined by the socioeconomic status of neighborhood or total community, the resources, handicaps, and trends within the community.

A public relations program is a far-flung organization of systematically organized interaction between community and school. An adequate program goes far beyond the typical P.T.A. with a few formal committees on routine matters, beyond exhibits, room mothers' clubs, and the like.

The community will support a school with greater willingness and conviction when the program is well understood and approved. The school will develop a truly effective program when it knows the community resources, aims and ambitions, handicaps, and how these relate to the general aim of education.

Incompetent criticism [15] from the community rests usually on incorrect information, or on lack of information, concerning the aims, offerings, and processes of the school. (We are not considering here attacks based on dishonest motives, though they too are best repulsed through extensive, effective programs of public relations.) Incompetent criticism may also rest on lack of understanding between persons, on some emotional or temperamental friction between personalities.

Four general areas within which effective public relations can be developed are listed below, with some general suggestions as to projects and techniques. The detailed illustrations to go with these general areas would make a sizable pamphlet. School officers desiring specific illustrations of actual activities and organized programs can find unlimited materials in the periodical literature, in some of the bulletins on curriculum construction, and in various textbooks.

I. *A co-operative program for the continuous improvement of the schools* (see Chapters 14 through 17)

[15] *Forces Affecting American Education,* 1953 Yearbook, Association for Supervision and Curriculum Development (Washington, NEA, 1953).
William H. Burton, "Get the Facts," *Progressive Education* (January, 1952), pp. 82-90. Many similar articles available.

Parents and all community members should participate widely in all typical professional improvement activities within the school.

1. *Continuous, co-operative community surveys* of the schools.

2. *Participation in any typical improvement project:* organizing new curriculum structures (for instance the core, or "general" courses, or readiness programs in primary); reorganizing older courses, studying pupil and community needs, improving the marking system, the report card, guidance, getting children ready for entrance into the first grade, and so on.

The subsidiary techniques [16] available here include:

Curriculum Com-   Lecture-discussions
   mittees   by outside experts
Visits to other   Study Groups
   schools   Workshops
Systematic courses Committee work
Exhibits   Panel or Forum
                      Discussions

II. *A co-operative participation by school officers in community activities*
Co-operating in community enterprises. The teacher's talents will aid in making for successful outcomes, the respect and understanding by the community is increased.

(For instance, taking part in community dramatic or musical programs, assisting community chest, Red Cross, Boy Scouts, church work, and so on. Belonging to and participating actively in community organizations such as civic clubs, luncheon service clubs, women's clubs, patriotic societies. The teacher not only aids the community but is able to interpret the work of the teacher and the school to prominent citizens.)

Caution: This can very easily be overdone. Teachers can be overworked. Participation in community activities should include participation in the recreations, sports, hobbies, and all other forms of enjoyment such as symphonies, libraries, and so on.

A prominent need all over the country is joint effort between school and community for the desirable introduction of all new teachers into the community. There is a small amount of good periodical literature on this.

III. *A co-operative study of the community, its origin and development, its resources and handicaps, its advantages and depressed areas, its services, and so forth*

(Details are omitted here, since excellent outlines for making community surveys are easily available; lists of typical excursions and visits, etc. For an initial start on this literature see Chapters 13 and 17 in this volume, and part of Chapter 16; see also the numerous references in later chapters to the Yearbook on *Citizen Co-operation for Better Schools;* the numerous reference to volumes by Olsen on the community school.)

The foregoing activities will reach many parents but not all. Many community members who have no children in school may aid to make or break a school program. The understanding and respect of all citizens is necessary.

1. A systematically organized, long-range series of activities, probably under auspices of the P.T.A.

Lecture-discussions on what is going on in the school, plus new trends emerging in the country.

Lecture-presentation by school officers and outside speakers of specific items within the school of a more formal or routine nature.

Forum or panel discussions, parents and teachers putting on the program.

Lecture-discussions led by parents on their reactions, questions, beliefs about community needs, etc.

Exhibits to be visited.

Dramatizations or other presentations by children.

Smaller editions of these same activities, based on individual rooms instead of the whole school.

Small groups for study or discussion at school or in individual homes.

Mimeographed bulletins distributed regularly throughout the community.

Printed bulletins occasionally, particularly with pictures.

Continuous use of space in local newspaper for news items, explanations of professional activities and projects, if possible pictures of children's exhibits and activities.

When parents have gained an insight into the educational program through informational, observational, discussional, and study

---

[16] See Sec. 2 of Ch. 6, and all of Ch. 7 for detailed procedures.

activities, they have background and confidence for the kinds of participation outlined in I, II, and III above.

A BRIEF BIBLIOGRAPHY ON PUBLIC RELATIONS

The *periodical literature* is increasingly presenting excellent accounts of successful procedures from given school systems.

State departments of education, city and county systems publish bulletins, both reporting programs and giving general summaries of principles and procedures.

State and city associations of teachers publish similar summaries.

Annual reports of superintendents are increasingly developed for public relations purposes.

Collections of these materials should be built up locally, plus pamphlets, newspaper releases, scripts for radio programs, tape recordings, and motion pictures where these are available.

Departments of the National Education Association, particularly the *National School Public Relations Association,* publish much valuable material.

Building Confidence in the Schools, Association for Supervision and Curriculum Development, pamphlet (Washington, NEA, 1949).

Citizen Co-operation for Better Public Schools, Fifty-third Yearbook, Part I, National Society for the Study of Education (Chicago, Univ. of Chicago Press, 1954).

Citizens and Educational Policies, Educational Policies Commission (Washington, NEA, 1951).

Denver Public Schools, *Human Relations in Action: Pupils, Parents, and Teachers Work Together* (Denver, The Schools, 1952).

FINE, Benjamin, *Educational Publicity* (New York, Harper, 1943).

How Can We Organize for Better Schools: A Guidebook for Citizens Committees, National Citizens Commission for the Public Schools, 1953.

Metropolitan School Study Council, *Public Action for Powerful Schools.* Research Study No. 3 (New York, Teachers College, Bureau of Publications, Columbia Univ., 1949).

MOEHLMAN, Arthur B., *Social Interpretation* (New York, Appleton-Century-Crofts, 1938).

An earlier book by MOEHLMAN, *Public School Relations,* published by Rand McNally in 1927 is still valuable for many details. Considerable change of opinion and attitude has taken place, however, since that was published.

————, *School Administration,* rev. ed. (Boston, Houghton, 1951). An excellent chapter on public relations.

National Congress of Parents and Teachers, *Parent-Teacher Publicity Handbook,* 1949.

National School Public Relations Council, Washington, National Education Association:

> *It Starts in the Classroom,* 1951 (Study guide available)
> *88 Techniques in School Public Relations for Teachers and Administrators,* 1951.
> *The PR Guide—A Where to Look Handbook of Aids for Your School Public Relations Program,* 1951.

Public Relations for America's Schools, Twenty-eighth Yearbook, American Association of School Administrators (Washington, NEA, 1950).

Public Relations in Secondary Schools, National Association of Secondary School Principals (Washington, NEA, 1948).

REEDER, Ward G., *An Introduction to Public-School Relations* (New York, Macmillan, 1953). Excellent and extensive bibliographic listing of periodical references.

Science Research Associates, *Good Schools Don't Just Happen!* Chicago, Ill., 228 South Wabash Ave., undated.

STOREN, Helen F., *Laymen Help Plan the Curriculum,* Association for Supervision and Curriculum Development (Washington, NEA, 1946).

The Superintendent, the Board, and the Press, pamphlet (Washington, NEA, 1951).

TEAD, Ordway, *The Art of Administration* (New York, McGraw, 1951).

YEAGER, William A., *School-Community Relations,* rev. ed. (New York, Dryden, 1951).

YOUCH, Wilbur, *How Good Is Your School?* (New York, Harper, 1951).

A periodical presentation is of particular interest:

MORRISON, Wilma, "A Responsible Press and the Schools," *Pi Lambda Theta Journal* (Winter issue, 1952), pp. 75-80. An unusual and unique report of the development of school board-press relationships in Portland, Ore., over a long period of time.

CHAPTER SUPPLEMENT

REPORTS

1. Students with experience in the development of public relations programs, either of the older type or of the more modern co-operative type may report for class discussion. This presentation of experience reports has been found very effective.

2. Individuals or small committees may report on programs as reported in the periodical literature or in documents based on a given situation.

GENERAL QUESTIONS FOR QUICK INTRODUCTORY SUMMARY

1. List any new concepts or beliefs derived by you from the chapter, and which you readily accept. Clarified or amplified ideas may be included. (Differences in statement and in opinion usually lead to a clarifying class discussion.)

2. State any major ideas presented by the chapter which are not quite clear to you; ask for clarification.

3. List any ideas long held by you and regarded as sound but which now seem to be contradicted, or at least called into question, by the chapter.

4. List any concept or suggestion which you cannot accept at the moment, or about which you are in reasonable doubt. (This question is important in that it leads instructor and students to discover points of misunderstanding or misplaced emphasis.)

5. State three or four concepts or principles of a summary nature which seem to you to best present the guidance to be derived from the chapter. (This question may be repeated for sets of chapters or parts of the volume.)

6. List a number of prevalent practices in education which would have to be abandoned if the facts and principles in the chapter are accepted as valid and used by educational leaders, teachers, and laymen.

(The six questions have been found useful in getting before the class in the opening part of the period a quick summary of high points. They will not be repeated, but the authors present them to students periodically throughout the study of the volume.)

QUESTIONS CALLING FOR MORE EXTENDED ANALYSIS

1. Why is supervision necessary in business, industry, or in any human activity of any scope? In education? Are the problems the same in the three specific areas named? List specific likenesses and differences.

Describe very briefly illustrations of typical supervisory procedures found in the business world. Draw on your observation or reading.

2. Why emphasize leadership and democratic co-operative action in supervision? (Do not stop with one or two simple and obvious answers.) Has supervision always been democratic and on a co-operative basis?

3. How do you suppose the problems involved in the study and improvement of conditions affecting the improvement of learning and the development of the individual can be dealt with in small communities? In rural areas? (Only preliminary discussion is possible here. The question reappears for extended discussion after appropriate background has been acquired.)

4. Examine any ten consecutive pages in one of the ten recent books on supervision (or older references if desired). Select specific sentences which indicate adherence to the older theory of imposed education and of improvement through imposed supervision; or adherence to the newer functional education and to co-operative supervision.

5. Note the definition of supervision in the text examined. Make critical comparison with the definition on this volume; note agreement, disagreement, whether broader or narrower in scope.

6. One of the new volumes criticizes our definition, particularly the words *expert technical service,* as clearly "implying the issuance of orders to those who are being given the service. . . . The idea of supervisor as leader is completely absent from the definition."

Make a quick search of this chapter and list statements from the chapter which support this criticism or which contradict it.

7. Describe three or four areas in which advances made by educational science and philosophic analysis are such as to necessitate supervisory aid in co-operative interpretation and dissemination of the new materials. Be specific.

8. Add further points, if possible, to the

contrast between traditional and modern supervision on page 13.

9. Add any further arguments you may know which indicate the necessity for supervision, to supplement the list on page 17.

10. Examine critically the definition of supervision on pages 11-12.

a. Add any points you think should be included, giving your reasons. Be sure you have a new point and not something already clearly implied in the definition.

b. Present arguments against any point which you think should be excluded from the present definition.

INDIVIDUAL REPORTS

1. Present a brief oral report critically summarizing three or four recent studies of the supervisory duties of principals, or general supervisors, or certain special supervisors.

2. Summarize and interpret the significance for supervision of the facts presented in any recent investigations of the training levels of teachers in the United States. These will be found in periodicals, state bulletins, research monographs, and so forth.

3. Summarize three or four recent articles which report what teachers want of supervision or their attitudes toward it.

4. Select from the listing of articles in *The Education Index* three or four on supervision which promise to be objective and three or four which promise to be mere descriptions, or opinions, or casual comment. Critically compare the methods of presentation and the conclusions.

CLASS PROJECT NO. I
THE EVALUATION OF A MODERN TEXTBOOK IN SUPERVISION

Select one of the ten recent texts listed below. Write a brief, systematically organized, critical review of the selected text.

The reading may be done at any time, although the writing cannot be done until the last two or three weeks of the term. The course will then be far enough along to supply perspective and basis for a review.

Reviews may be organized in any way that suits the student. The following criteria, together with any others the student thinks of, should apply.

a. Adequacy. Does the book touch on and give assistance with all major areas in the field? With some but not all? Does it include any not included in the course?

b. Type of treatment. Is the presentation in the form of principles, or directives, or exhortations, or problems, or running discourse? Writing clear and direct or otherwise?

Are the principles well supported by illustrations, cases, incidents? By adequate philosophic and/or scientific references? Or are the statements simply offered for acceptance?

Are the principles and supporting material interwoven, where supporting material is given?

c. Organization. What is the scheme of organization? Is it sound in and for itself? Sound as a presentation of supervision as a field? Is anything included which is not within the field of supervision?

d. Teaching aids. Are there outlines, summaries, exercises, projects? If so, are they realistic? Adequate?

e. Validity. Is the treatment generally valid or not valid in the light of the democratic philosophy as generally understood in education in the United States; in the light of known scientific materials? Are there any specific items within the general over-all treatment which are valid or invalid on the grounds stated here?

f. Over-all commentary. Include within review, or separately at its end, a brief summary evaluation of the book as a basic text for the course.

TEN RECENT TEXTBOOKS IN SUPERVISION

Each student should select one of these volumes and use it consistently in connection with this text. The new books each have something to offer on one point or another. The materials should be used to supplement class discussion. This is good preparation for Project No. I.

An oral symposium at the close of the course may be held if time permits, with individuals or small committees reviewing the various books. The differences in approach and in coverage are quite striking.

ADAMS, H. P., and DICKEY, F. G., *Basic Principles of Supervision* (New York, American Book, 1953).

AYER, Fred C., *Fundamentals of Instructional Supervision* (New York, Harper, 1954).

BARTKY, John, *Supervision as Human Relations* (Boston, Heath, 1953).

BOARDMAN, Charles, DOUGLASS, Harl, and BENT, R. K., *Democratic Supervision in Secondary Schools* (Boston, Houghton, 1953).

BRIGGS, Thomas, and JUSTMAN, Joseph, *Improving Instruction Through Supervision,* rev. ed. (New York, Macmillan, 1952).

MCNERNEY, Chester T., *Educational Supervision* (New York, McGraw, 1951).

MELCHIOR, William T., *Instructional Supervision* (Boston, Heath, 1950).

REEDER, Edwin H., *Supervision in the Elementary School* (Boston, Houghton, 1953).

SPEARS, Harold, *Improving the Supervision of Instruction* (New York, Prentice-Hall, 1953).

WILES, Kimball, *Supervision for Better Schools* (New York, Prentice-Hall, 1950).

GENERAL REFERENCES

American Association of School Administrators, *Community Leadership; The Superintendent Works with Community Leaders* (Washington, NEA, 1950) (twenty-four page pamphlet).

Association for Supervision and Curriculum Development, *The Department Head and Instructional Improvement* (Washington, NEA, 1948) (fifty-page pamphlet).

————, *Leadership Through Supervision,* 1946 Yearbook (Washington, NEA, 1946).

(NOTE: The earlier name for the A.S.C.D. above was The Department of Supervisors and Directors of Instruction. Earlier yearbooks published by the department are, despite dates, of value still.

Supervision and the Creative Teacher, Fifth Yearbook, 1932. Valuable and stimulating early discussion of what is now the modern concept.

Effective Instructional Leadership, Sixth Yearbook, 1933. Another good discussion showing beginnings of substitution of leadership for authority.

Co-operation: Principles and Practices, Eleventh Yearbook, 1939. An excellent summary with much specific material.

Leadership at Work, Fifteenth Yearbook, 1943. One of most valuable references yet. Contains the new well-known fable of "Joe Brown" and how he learned the meaning of leadership. This story will be studied in connection with Chapters 4, 5, and 7.)

BENJAMIN, Harold, *Emergent Conceptions of the School Administrator's Task* (Stanford University, Calif., Stanford University Press, 1942).

CAMPBELL, Clyde M., ed., *Practical Applications of Democratic Administration* (New York, Harper, 1952).

Department of Education, State of Georgia, *School Leaders Manual* (Atlanta Ga., State Department of Education, 1947).

Department of Elementary School Principals, *The Elementary School Principalship—Today and Tomorrow,* Twenty-seventh Yearbook (Washington, NEA, 1948).

————, *The Public and the Elementary School,* Twenty-eighth Yearbook (Washington, NEA, 1949).

HALSEY, George, *Supervising People* (New York, Harper, 1946).

JACOBSON, Paul B., REAVIS, Wm. C., and LOGSDON, James D., *Duties of School Principals,* 2nd ed. (New York, Prentice-Hall, 1950).

LEWISOHN, S. A., *Human Leadership in Industry* (New York, Harper, 1945).

Bibliographies throughout the volume with a few notable exceptions will be brief and selective. Other similar volumes are available. We have followed the policy of including references freely within the body of the chapter, connecting them immediately with major topics. Current publications will have to be added by those using the book.

The Periodical Literature

The periodical literature is so extensive and appearing so continuously that a listing beyond the footnotes is a waste of time. Individual students or small committees may be asked to report with each chapter any recent articles of merit dealing with the content of the chapter.

General Sources Which Will be Useful Throughout the Course and to All Workers in the Field

The Review of Educational Research (published quarterly)

The Encyclopedia of Educational Research

The Education Index

Research Bulletins of the National Education Association

Yearbooks of the National Department of Elementary School Principals, Association for Supervision and Curriculum Development, American Association of School Administrators.

Chapter 2

◆·◆·◆·◆·◆·◆·◆·◆·◆·

The General Nature of Social Process and Social Change

A SPECIALIZED BOOK such as this cannot include a detailed exposition of social process and change. A compact summary of principles is necessary, however, first, because modern educational administration and supervision is a social process, and second, because the topic has been until the present omitted from the education of most school workers. A huge literature produced by sociologists is available. The readers should decide after finishing this chapter to what extent they need to consult this literature.[1]

Section 1

AN OUTLINE OVERVIEW OF SOCIAL PROCESS AND SOCIAL CHANGE

✗ **A brief definition.** Social process is that series of actions by which any social group of any size organizes the common life of the individuals in the group. Social process theoretically and generally aims at the progressive betterment of life for both individual and group. Practically and specifically, it very often interferes with improvement. The special benefits of small powerful groups may be preserved at the expense of greater good for the group as a whole.

The chief social processes through which any group carries on its life include government, education, protection, communication, production, distribution, consumption, conservation, religion. We will be concerned here with education as a social process.

All living organisms are motivated to satisfy their needs, wants, or interests. Any dissatisfaction, disequilibrium, or tension sets off efforts to bring satisfaction, equilibrium, relief from tension. The result is interaction between and among persons. The social process through which individuals satisfy their needs produces personality as we know it, produces the institutions and conventions of society.

Social process historically has shown four stages or levels which may be duplicated in any specific situation today. The stages are not necessarily mutually exclusive nor always consecutive, though they are often both. Characteristics might be a better term than level or stage. First, there is competitive effort, a struggle with other persons and groups, to secure what is wanted or needed. This may not in all instances be deliberate and conscious competition. Second, there is conflict or open struggle. This is the type with which we are most familiar in the past. This produces war, political strife, race antagonism and other cultural clashes, conflicts between capital and labor, cut-throat

[1] Excellent materials are available. A start may be made by examining pertinent topics in Emory S. Bogardus, *The Development of Social Thought* (New York, Longmans, 1942), which summarizes literature to date of publication. A selective bibliography is included which can be brought up to date very easily. Class reports may make the supplementation easier.

29

competition between business organizations. Conflict, however, stimulates study which often leads to the invention of new meanings and processes.

Conflict may continue to sustain itself. This type of conflict is disintegrative, perpetuating and aggravating the causes of conflict. Conflict may also be a starting point for activity leading to a new synthesis and integration. Conflict as an instrument for beating down minorities or dissenters, for perpetuating one's point of view, is a serious evil. Conflict which stimulates individuals and groups to seek sincerely for elimination or at least reduction of the causes of dissension is an instrument of learning and of progress. Realization of the stupidity of disintegrative conflict, and of the wisdom of resolving conflict through compromise, adjustment, or a new integration leads to another stage. Third, there is conscious adjustment by individuals and by groups to facts and conditions. Herein lies the crucial point in social process: changes in goals, values, motivations, attitudes. Adjustment can be greatly aided by education and by critical analysis of experience, and by any other agencies of enlightenment. The opposition of inert, uninformed, or selfish individuals may appear. Propaganda, pressure, or other efforts to prevent enlightenment may appear. But the inner changes manifest themselves eventually in changed habits, patterns of behavior, and in institutions. Leaders should emphasize the development and extension of insight, which is the basis for any changes made by individuals. Fourth, the new goals, values, and patterns are eventually assimilated and become habitual parts of individual and group life. They are said to have interpenetrated the values, attitudes, and sentiments of individuals.

Social process, and particularly social change, should become steadily more humane, eliminating or reducing disintegrative conflict, thus producing more rational, co-operative beings, that is, socialized persons, and hence more socially useful institutions.

We believe in the possibility of conscious direction of social process and social change, at least in some measure. This point will be discussed later in proper sequence. Meanwhile, we note the possibilities of education for the conscious acceleration of the humanizing process by modifying self-interest and aggrandizement toward service and the common good. Detrimental individualism can be turned toward co-operative group life, with ample opportunity for the development of creative individuals. Modern social theory is not opposed to individualism but only to antisocial distortions of the concept.

Modern times have forced us to realize the importance of human relations, of working and getting along together in groups. The prevalence of emotional instability, of more serious types of personality maladjustment, the problems arising within family life, within the political and economic institutions, are common knowledge. On the international scene, the obvious danger lies in the inability of national groups to get along. The mechanisms of co-operation, of communication, of interchange, and of common decision, so necessary to modern social process, do not exist on the international level on any large scale as yet.

Education is or should be a social process. That it is not in many places is a challenge, not a cause for discouragement. The social processes of education are the same as in the Great Society outside the school. Education must strive to become more successful in producing through social process more effective personalities and more effective human relationships, thus contributing to the improvement of social institutions. Education must introduce persons to the very processes of group life and to the creative process by which social institutions are produced and improved. In accomplishing this, education will inevitably point out the processes and factors may influence social process toward approved goals, or which turn it toward selfish, and limited ends.

Social change [2] is described and interpreted somewhat differently by anthropologists, sociologists, and psychologists. The professional educator should be familiar with the viewpoints of these other disciplines but should maintain the view of a generalist. The educational leader is interested in the dynamics of change as these operate in the world and in the school as a social system. One basic concept for the school is that social change is preceded by and is based on changes in people, in their values, concepts, and attitudes. This eventually brings change in institutions and ways of behaving.

Principles explaining social process and social change. Certain principles and facts can be derived from analysis of social process which explain that process and which supply guidance for directing that process whether in school, in the political world, in the economic order, or elsewhere.

PRINCIPLES OF SOCIAL PROCESS AND SOCIAL CHANGE

1. All the efforts of men are motivated, rightly or wrongly, by the usefulness to man of the proposed result.

2. The essence of social process is interaction between and among persons. The opinions, agreements, and decisions of the group are reached through study and discussion. This necessitates:

   a. Common agreement on values, attitudes, and meanings within the group or openly expressed desire to critically evaluate certain of these factors.

   b. Full and free opportunity for co-operative participation in all activities which affect the life of the group.

   c. Easy and effective communication without which interaction cannot take place.

   d. A process, channels, and controls through which interaction and communication are carried on, and through which common values, attitudes, and meanings may be disseminated and/or changed.

3. The essential result of the interactive social process is the development and extension of insight, which in turn brings changes in the values, beliefs, motives, patterns of behavior in persons and in the relations between persons.

4. The changes in social institutions and processes, while important, are incidental to the changes within persons. Cultural change can come only as persons come to see the value of, and to believe in, the proposed changes.

Changes by fiat or edict are usually not successful and do not result in lasting improvements.

Legislation may be very effective or quite useless as an instrument of social change, depending upon the circumstances. Legislation which has wide backing of an informed majority will compel the slow minority to make changes. Legislation in advance of wide public understanding is ineffective and sometimes produces new evils. One of the aims of public enlightenment is to develop backgrounds of valid fact and principle so that necessary changes can be brought about. Compulsory vaccination of school children, compulsory attendance, laws regulating the practice of medicine, and many others are cases in point.

5. The satisfaction of any set of needs or interests results in a stabilization which provides new needs or problems, hence more conflict, or co-operative study, or more social invention, and finally assimilation of newer values and processes, and so on.

Any group dealing with its own values and problems will profit from a comparative study of values in other groups, local or larger. This is particularly true of the study of the historical development of the group's own conception of value or progress.

We should realize that our own Western society has undergone in modern times the greatest and most violent changes. (Are the Oriental societies on the verge of revolutionary awakening?) The U. S. A. is now, because of historical circumstances, the trustee of progress in the West.

6. Change in society may be planned or unplanned. The social process and change go on constantly and continuously in either event. Modification of values, of meanings, of patterns of behavior, of institutions and conventions is incessant. Social inventions also appear.

---

[2] The discussion in a general volume must be abbreviated, hence the so-called cosmic or immanent causes of change are not included: change by natural cycle; by supernatural intervention; by mechanical or material evolution; or by other deterministic factor. The *laissez-faire* attitude toward social change is omitted. Readings are available if anyone wishes to explore these ideas.

It may seem trite and naïve to say that society is always either changing or not changing. Living civilizations are changing and must change in order to survive. The presence of crystallization, of a static view of life, or resistance to change as such are characteristics of a decaying civilization. The important question is: Shall social change go on without planning, in haphazard manner, or shall there be planning in so far as complex social processes are susceptible to planning? Planning, not planned change, is the essential. What then are some principles with which to explain and guide social change?

7. Change, at least so careful students of the problem hope, can be planned and managed to some extent, thus substituting orderly change based on insight for abrupt change through violent revolution.

Periods of rapid change have been, historically, marked by varying degrees of disorder, sometimes chaos. Historical traditions and historical experience are often disregarded, blacked out for a time. Certain so-called "practical" men and groups profess not to believe in "social planning," even though they engage in high-level planning in their own areas. In fact, "practical" men and aristocracies of any type are often the cause of the violent revolutions they so much fear. Opposing and delaying badly needed changes, refusing the orderly methods of change, inevitably precipitates revolutionary change.

The concept of controlling change, in part, in large-scale social organizations is so new that we have no great body of data available. So many factors are interrelated, so many variables enter, that cultural change can never be wholly controlled. Experiments are under way, particularly in political and politico-economic areas, with some appearing in the field of social problems. Experiments are hailed by some as the key to a better future; condemned by others as dangerous and subversive. The truth seems to be

that sufficient data are not yet available. Safety at the moment lies not in throttling experimentation but in ensuring systematic analysis of things as they are, planning in relation to existing conditions, and in full participation by all concerned. A beginning has been made by the present generation; the next generation will probably see the results. Meanwhile, we do know that casual, unplanned change, or change directed by narrow special interests, is as likely to be detrimental as beneficial. Failure to plan tentatively for change in an ever more complex society must become ever more risky. Uneven and random attack on maladjustments can only result in random and uneven benefits, and there is real possibility of damage.

Are there alternatives to conflict, to wasteful change, to violent revolution? It is hoped that there are, and certain guides may be noted:

8. Efforts at influencing social change must (*a*) be in accord with principles of human motivation and growth; (*b*) be preceded by and based on systematic study of the specific point under consideration and of the surrounding conditions; (*c*) include provision for experimental tryout in typical small areas and under typical conditions; (*d*) be in accord with prevailing legal controls.

9. The relationships of specialized experts, of the total group, and of minorities within either the experts or the group, to each other and to social process or change are delicate and not yet clearly understood. Nevertheless, the facts must be recognized and consciously analyzed with the object of developing desirable relationships.

Lynd [3] long ago pointed out, first, that knowledge possessed by trained experts is accruing much faster than this information can be assimilated into the thinking and behavior of the total group. Second, that we are accumulating maladjustments within our society more rapidly than we can deal with

[3] Robert Lynd, *Knowledge for What?* (Princeton, Princeton Univ. Press, 1939), pp. 108-109. Entire volume is extremely useful.

them. Education and other agencies of enlightenment, "reform" campaigns, and legislation are unable to make use of the new knowledge fast enough to reduce the rate of growth of maladjustment. An effort to speed up change, in so far as it can be done, would seem to be indicated. The expert has valuable guidance to offer but it must be offered in such way that groups accept it and are convinced.

Social invention comes very largely from an informed and trained minority, but no group has a monopoly on new ideas. First, we must remember that creativity may appear anywhere. Second, it is essential that the new ideas be accepted and permeate the thinking of the public. The public, in fact, are usually closer to certain aspects of life than specialists can be, and their group judgment on these matters may be better. The expert, on the other hand, is far better informed on historical developments and movements, is more facile in handling abstractions, likely to be less upset by change.

The thinking of trained experts who are socially oriented eventually becomes the thought and action of the public, but only if (a) the expert exercises conspicuous leadership toward the common good and in free dissemination of new materials, and (b) the expert is trusted by the public. Another way of saying this is that the experts will be important to the extent that they work for full participatory discussion and decision for all; the public will be important to the extent that they follow the moral urge to be informed and to make decisions based on fact and reason.

The fateful and pressing nature of social change. Why all this discussion of social change? As George Apley said: [4]

I wish there weren't quite so many new ideas. Where do they come from? Why is everyone trying to break away from what we all know is sane and good?

Politicians and industrial leaders who welcome change in their own fields resist almost with violence change in social thought. Many of them are, in Adlai Stevenson's phrase, "dragged kicking and screaming into the twentieth century." In education we see many superintendents, principals, department heads, teachers digging in their heels to resist any change or improvement in the school or the processes of education. Those concerned with elementary schools and many leading theorists are more hospitable to change than some secondary-school leaders and administrators. The latter are not being dragged into the twentieth century; they have not yet discovered it. They sleep warmly comfortable in the last half of the nineteenth century, some waking momentarily to cast nostalgic glances at the first half of that century. There are, needless to say, many brilliant exceptions to this indictment.

The speed of change is greater than in any past era; the dire necessity for change where maladjustment exists is one of the most fateful aspects of modern civilization. We have a clear choice: Make changes with reasonable speed to correct maladjustments and injustice and to improve our many desirable achievements, or have the evils corrected by violent upheaval with its attendant disorder and danger. In our special field of education we have seen again and again that a change long overdue often occurs hastily and without necessary preparation of either professional workers or lay public. A counterswing against new and clearly desirable improvements always follows. The height of intelligence in all human affairs is to study trends and scientific findings, to attempt to foresee changes which will be clearly validated, and to prepare for these changes. Blind opposition to necessary change, whether in national affairs or in the curriculum of the third grade, is the essence of stupidity and inevitably brings trouble.

Ample material on social change is available in the field of sociology and in some of

[4] J. P. Marquand, *The Late George Apley* (Boston, Little, 1937), p. 294.

the branches of anthropology. Far more is needed than can be summarized here. It is necessary, however, to give some convincing basis for the inevitability of social change, for the absolute necessity of taking change into account in our thinking. Our listing of causes of change cannot be exhaustive but it is given in the hope of quickly orienting students to such facts as we have.

First causes of social change in the modern world. Various methods of listing these appear in the literature. Another scheme may be devised by instructors and students who so desire. Prominent *first causes* in modern times include:

1. The rise of science and its attendant technology.
2. The rise of the democratic theory of life.
3. The rise of the masses.
4. The wide dissemination among all levels of society of information and insight, heretofore the possession of privileged groups.

Science and the resultant technology are prime causes of change in the modern world, but we should note that technology, broadly defined, began ages ago. The first manlike creature who used a stone or a stick as a weapon, who used a sharp stone as a tool, who built a shelter of materials, who used fire, was a forerunner of the men who developed the complex tools and weapons of today, who harnessed steam and electricity for power, who invented automatic machinery, who developed wireless communication, who split the atom. Technological advances from the most primitive to the most modern have always produced changes, superficial or profound.

The four causes of change listed are not the only ones, but these may be used as illustrations. They have brought about changes not only in the socio-cultural order within national groups but have profoundly changed the order of international relationships. Later we will examine the changes with special reference to education.

What are some of the secondary, or more immediate, disturbances of complacency or equilibrium, hence causes of change? Many students will disagree with some of the statements listed below, though probably the real issue is the degree of dissemination of information on the point among the population. Some changes are clearly operative on some levels of society, not on others. Again compartmentalization occurs, and certain contradictory or partly contradictory factors will be accepted by individuals and groups. There will be contradiction also between what some persons or groups accept verbally and their actions. Insight can be greatly extended by class discussion and the critical study of the process of change. How widely are these changes accepted? By what social classes or intellectual levels? What is the significance of some of the compartmentalizations which are observed? What are the probable causes of opposition to or denial of certain of these changes? A summary of the secondary, or more immediate, causes of social change follows:

1. *Changes in theory or philosophy of life*
   From the supernatural as sole and complete explanation, comfort, and control—to man's belief in himself and his powers of reason; from revelation as sole source—to reason; from regarding himself as a puppet of destiny—to believing that he can participate in "shaping his ends."
   From exclusive concern with spiritual matters—to a normal concern with material affairs also. (Note current, reversed trend toward discussion of moral and spiritual values.)
   From orientation of life toward life-after-death or to the past of human history—to effort to improve the present and to make a better future.
   From authoritarian views of life, men, and matters—to a democratic, co-operative view; from a static view—to a dynamic and experimental view.

2. *Changes in the economic and the socio-cultural orders*

A. *The changing world situation*

From independence and isolation among nations—to interdependence and propinquity.

From cultural isolation (or at least independence)—to aggresive battle between ideologies.

From wealth of natural resources—to increasing need for conservation (but with technological processes tending to compensate in some measure for past waste and approaching exhaustion).

From simple barter of natural products—to a system of international banking, credit, and exchange.

From simple communal government where all meet face to face to settle tribal affairs—to absolute rule by strong individuals, to feudalism, to limited monarchy, to democratic parliamentary government. (Current trends attempting to undermine democracy should be noted.)

From uncontrolled increase in population—to recognition of necessity for control. (This one causes considerable controversy, but it is significant that every reputable demographer and many in other areas agree that this is very probably the most dire and fateful problem in the modern world.)

From economic competition between business units—to economic competition between national units. (Students may wish to extend this list with references to intercultural tensions, conservation of human resources, ideological challenges, and others.)

B. *Changes in structure of society* (with special reference to the U. S. A.)

From a simple, independent, agrarian order—to a complex, interdependent, urban, industrial order.

From control by an élite who held power and authority—to increasing use of democratic process resulting in consensus of the group, or partial agreement operating through majority rule. (The rise of the common man has brought attendant shifts in money, power, prestige of certain life activities,

types of cultural attainments, and many others.)

C. *Changes in community organization and life* (with special reference to the U. S. A.)

(The illustrations here would cover a page or more and are easily available in education texts as well as in the sociological literature. A few quick illustrations should be given by students to identify the area. Students uninformed here should read immediately in any of several references.)

3. *Changes in our methods of dealing with the natural environment;* of providing food, clothing, shelter, recreation, expression of religious values; methods of maintaining health and curing disease; methods of dealing with our enemies.

From natural shelter—to hand made cover, to modern housing (See the volume *From Cave to Skyscraper*).

From skins of animals—to hand-woven garments, to mass produced clothing.

From natural foods—to planting seeds and scratching the ground with a stick, to scientific farming of thousands of acres with power machinery, to chemical fertilization.

From precarious subsistence dependent on natural foods—to the security resulting from curing and storing foods, thus achieving independence of drouth, flood, frost, or other natural hazards.

From the use of hands—to natural objects as tools, to the refinement of these objects, to the invention of tools, to the use of power, to the complex machines of mass production. (Note that the change from handcraft to mass production, with accompanying change in ownership of the tools of production, has brought profound social changes, e.g., in relations between employers and employees, relations between producer and consumer, and eventually in relations between both capital and labor and government.)

From sticks and stones (instead of tooth and claw) as weapons—to missiles, clubs, spears, bow and arrow, to catapult, to guns, to poison gas, to atomic bombs.

From magic and charms for treating ills—to torture, to potions from common roots and herbs, to bleeding, to surgery, vaccines, and wonder drugs, to chemical control of germ sources.

The superstitious savage, cowering in abject fear before an evil universe, has become chemist, physicist, and biologist, penetrating some of the inmost secrets of his universe; has become philosopher and contemplative thinker pondering upon ultimate purposes and values of life. Social changes over the centuries have produced the institutions which constitute civilization: the family, the community, the state, religion and the church, industry, systems of exchange, standards of living, methods of preserving health, habits of enjoyment and relaxation, the alphabet, language, number, music, and many others. The development of social institutions over the centuries has gone hand in hand with the development of modern man, with his values, purposes, social conscience, and ways of life.

The factors facilitating or resisting social change. A number of long-term factors may be listed first, to be followed by more immediate influences.

LONG-TERM FACTORS AFFECTING SOCIAL CHANGE

Factors Resisting Change	Factors Facilitating Change
Geographical isolation.	Diffusion of culture traits.
Severe or extreme climate.	Temperate climate.
Coercive universal language.	Permissive vernacular.
Conservative education.	Creative education.
Authoritarian leadership.	Democratic leadership.
Fundamentalist religion.	Social religion.
Dogma and scholasticism.	Science: invention and discovery.
Homogeneous cultural grouping.	Heterogeneous cultural grouping.
Familial and racial ties.	Cosmopolitan and universal experience.
Rural social forces.	Urban social forces.
Centripetal forces (dominance by older persons, vested interests, rules of order, and succession of officers).	Centrifugal forces (war, literature, radio, movies, travel).
Private property (when conceived as private advantage, special privilege, and exploitation).	Private property (when conceived as a public trust or regulated in the public interest; when accompanied by social responsibility).
Monopoly.	Division of labor.
Epicurean mode of life.	Saving and planning mode of life.

The listing of more immediate factors is illustrative.

1. *The more immediate factors initiating and facilitating social change*
   a. A current pervasive climate of opinion which is dynamic, hence susceptible to change and favorable to criticism and experimentation. An attitude of confidence toward future progress is present.
   b. New impetus toward religious values; effort to apply these to everyday life.
   c. New knowledge in the humanities, new knowledge in the social sciences, new social inventions.
   d. New knowledge and inventions in the technological fields.
   e. Recognition of maladjustments in our culture, evils, tensions, injustices, plus a genuine conviction on the part of leaders, or masses, or both that these conditions can be improved.
   f. The availability of an adequate process, of specific techniques; the availability of leadership within the process. (See Group Process later; also materials from the National Laboratory of Human Relations; from the Tavistock Institute.)
2. *The more immediate mechanisms for bringing about change*

a. The dissemination of new knowledge through all general agencies of public enlightenment: schools, churches, press, radio, television, public forums and discussions; the effort to influence the basis of desires.

b. The use of democratic group process (1*f* above and see later) both for disseminating information and for making decisions.

c. Conferences, commissions, workshops, and all other social planning groups and enlightenment processes.

d. Political methods such as pressure groups, legislation.

3. *The more immediate factors obstructing social change*

a. A current pervasive climate of opinion which is static, demanding retention of the status quo. An attitude of skepticism toward improvement, even despair of the possibility of improvement.

b. The concentration of power within any segment of a group.

c. The betrayal of the agencies of enlightenment, or betrayal by the agencies of enlightenment.

d. The lack of adequate, valid information.

e. The forceful prevention of free discussion and controversy.

Causes of change with special reference to education. All of the foregoing factors affect education, plus factors peculiar to the field. The following list refers specially to the United States, though much of it is applicable elsewhere.

1. *Changes in philosophy of education*

From belief that education is for an élite —to belief that education, if not actually a right for all, is essential to the safety of democracy.

From belief that education is ornamental, cultural in the abstract sense, exists for its own sake—to belief that education is useful in widest sense, in all senses and areas.

From belief that education is something partly or wholly removed from life, from current problems and tensions— to belief that education is inescapably concerned with controversial issues, and is itself a primary factor in social reconstruction.

From belief that the end is knowledge, is intellectual—to belief that the end is a thinking-doing-willing person, the development of the entire individual into an independent, informed, responsible individual; from adjustment—to the development of adaptability.

From belief that education can be carried on with little regard for the value system and the institutions of society —to belief that the institutions are dynamic elements and that the value system gives meaning to education.

2. *Changes in social temper toward education*

From limited period of compulsory education—to ever increasing length of schooling.

From limited, narrowly intellectual curriculum—to extensive, diversified offerings.

From inadequate plant and facilities— to increasingly adequate facilities for diversified education.

From acceptance of poorly educated and poorly trained teachers—to demand for higher and higher standards.

3. *Changes in knowledge of the nature of the learner, and of the teacher*

From belief that only the intellectual élite could learn; that common people could not, or at best learn only skills as hewers of wood and drawers of water—to knowledge that all can learn.

From belief that intelligence was correlated with social-class structure—to knowledge that intelligence appears anywhere (Leadership and creativity likewise). (A sequence of beliefs may be noted here; from belief that the learner is a tabula rasa to be written on—or a jug into which learning is poured—or clay to be modeled—to knowledge that learner is an active behaving organism with a personality [attitudes, motives, understandings, ambitions of his own which he brings to school]; and is an active participant in his own education.)

4. *Changes in knowledge of the nature of learning*

From belief that learning is a passive process of absorption—to knowledge that it is an active process of experiencing.

From belief that learning could be related to fixed, arbitrary standards—to knowledge that directional-process goals, developmental tasks, the adaptation of standards to the pattern and rhythm of the learner are necessary.

From belief that personality is inherited to knowledge that personality is a social product.

5. *Changes in goals and accompanying change in evaluative measures*
6. *Changes in curriculums and methods of instruction* (These in turn become causes of still other changes.)

Section 2

AN OUTLINE OF PRINCIPLES APPLICABLE TO CHANGE IN EDUCATION

This section will be confined to a minimum summary of principles with some indication of process. The actual operation of the methods of bringing about change will be illustrated by practically every chapter which follows.

The possibility of consciously directed change must be accepted. Fact and logic support the view that improvements in education (or in anything else) will be accomplished more efficiently if there is a systematic plan, consciously thought out in terms of needs and present conditions, to effect the desired change.

The alternatives, far too prominent in education, have been (*a*) change through tinkering with the present structure, (*b*) change by edict, and (*c*) change through indiscriminate borrowing and imitation of improvements worked out elsewhere. We have all seen the results of tinkering with administrative organization, the curriculum, the policy of promotion, and the like. The same is true for changes made by edict. Borrowing is not sensible, since conditions in the two places might be very different. Further, the new departures selected for borrowing may themselves have been developed by unsound methods.

These older methods of bringing about change lack a systematic plan based on actual conditions. There is no provision for the crucial factor: changes in the goals and motivations of the personnel. Participatory discussion and decision are missing. The new is often imposed on the whole system with no preliminary experimental tryout. No one knows whether the change will work or not. There is no provision for honest evaluation.

Desirable change rests upon the development and extension of insights. All human activity is controlled by, and all social institutions are based upon, a complex constellation of influences and the interaction between and among them. Chief of these influences are the goals and values of the individual, his motivations, attitudes, beliefs, and abilities. Change is basically change in these things. It is often said that we wish to bring about changes in the goals, motivations, and attitudes of individuals or groups. This is true, but the statement is often interpreted to mean that one group knows the truth and will operate to bring about changes in other persons. A better statement is that we wish to participate in the development and extension of insight, our own as well as that of others. Persons with better and better insights will make their own changes in goals, motivations, relationships, and processes. This approach is sound, both psychologically and democratically.

Change, it cannot be emphasized too strongly, is not the goal. Change for the sake of change is witless. Individuals and groups seek to solve their problems, to relieve tensions. They discover that certain conditions must be changed or the problem cannot be solved, nor the tension reduced. Change, that is, improvement, in the situation then should follow any careful consideration of problems and needs. The needs will be revealed in several ways, such as unrest and protest, by public inquiry, by discussion of the possible bearing of new discoveries or ideas. The need for change in education is made apparent not only in these ways, but also by deliberate appraisal programs, surveys, diagnosis, and the like. The processes for revealing educational needs are included in Parts II and III of this volume. Change should take place in education, not blindly, but because need for change is clearly indicated and understood.

Change must guarantee security, growth, and desirable results. One of the first, if not the first, and one of the best discussions of change was presented by Miel,[5] with special reference to changing the curriculum. Her views are equally applicable to all phases of educational change. Change or even proposed change is a natural threat to the security of all who are successful under current conditions. Doubt as to continued growth and success, doubt as to the results of the proposed changes are natural; these things cannot be shrugged off since they affect the very heart of human life and effort. The psychological factors involved in any approach to change or plan for change must be given full consideration. Planning in terms of material conditions alone is doomed to failure. The security of the personnel, their natural doubts about the desirability of any given change, and their fears concerning results should be given attention as the need for changing accepted procedures is shown, as the situation is studied and plans developed. The dissemination of information, the development of the actual mechanisms of change, and the methods for determining success and failure must be planned and carried out with the participation of the group. Understanding is thus more likely to result, with accompanying reduction of insecurity and doubt.

General preliminary procedures for initiating change. A summary, including the repetition of important points made earlier, should be valuable here. Changes occur whether we like it or not. We believe that beneficial control, or at least direction, can

be exercised. We should try to establish first, then:

1. The need for change, through evidence derived from the situation.
2. Acceptance of change as natural.
3. Facilitation of communication between and among all concerned.
4. Conviction among enough persons that we can affect social change for the better. (Better in the light of our known goals.)
5. Willingness to experiment on basis of known facts, and systematic planning in the light of actual conditions.
6. Willingness to accept experimental procedure for what it is—an experiment which cannot be guaranteed in advance. (This is a basis for security to replace the familiar, the known, the old. When we know that lack of desired results is not a failure of persons but a common result in experimental work, security is enhanced.)
7. Operation of group process: the pooling of wisdom, the participatory discussion of all factors by all persons, and co-operative judgment and decision.
8. Skill in leadership in group process and in human relations everywhere.

Wiles [6] regards the group process, skill in leadership, and in human relations as so important that he makes supervision equivalent to the operation of that process under skilled leadership. Ordinary observation indicates that school systems are affected fundamentally by this process and by leadership. Communities where the group process under leadership has been fully participatory accept change in education easily, because understanding accompanies the very study, development, and tryout of the change. Communities where changes are thought out and tried without participation by staff and lay public often suffer severe upheavals. Opposition is often violent because of complete misunderstanding of goals and means. Change thrust upon a staff and community is practically never successful. Many a desirable change has been killed because of failure

[5] Alice Miel, *Changing the Curriculum: A Social Process* (New York, Appleton-Century-Crofts, 1946).
[6] Kimball Wiles, *Supervision for Better Schools* (New York, Prentice-Hall, 1950).

to provide for the growth in human relations necessary for the success of any social endeavor.

A list of tentative principles for the guidance of change in education. Readers may wish to extend, curtail, or rearrange this list which is given by way of illustration. In any situation the following principles should be of aid:

1. Establish not only the necessity for change in some area, but also establish belief in the necessity for attempting change. The latter is often missing even though the first is clear.

2. Identify and openly list the shortcomings and weaknesses of the present setting for learning which must be recognized and acknowledged.

The loss of security, referred to earlier, usually is evidenced at this time. The listing of needs and shortcomings and its implications often challenge the basic motivations of many of the persons involved. Conflict is inevitable. The group through its own study should eventually see the greater security implied in the changes. Study and group attack give the immediate security of group process—we are all in this together.

3. Develop a strong desire to attack the weaknesses, to invent and try new procedures.

4. Make a systematic study of the amounts and kinds of opposition, whether due to inertia, insecurity, or skepticism.

5. Make a systematic study of the amounts and kinds of power in the community; of the surrounding conditions which favor study and change.

6. Watch for counter-forces and counter-motives within any new movement itself, for instance, the tendency to be satisfied with the group process itself, or with verbal results.

The very interest and enthusiasm of the process may be eminently satisfying, with outcomes and resultant action minimized or actually omitted. The issuance of printed materials with no realization of the necessity for or methods of translating the ideas into action is common in education.

7. Watch for experiments under way, for social inventions in the area under study, for creative suggestions of any sort that can be adapted and utilized.

8. Accept the pace of social change as slow, tedious, annoying, and subject to opposition because of inertia, distrust, and skepticism.

Many small changes must be accepted as evidence of progress. These may then be capitalized for further study and experimentation.

9. Make initial attack at those points where dissatisfaction seems strongest; where favoring influences seem strongest or may be developed with ease. Attack may be direct or indirect, depending upon circumstances. Attempt to create situations out of which the group initiates the attack itself.

10. Work earnestly for participation of all in the group process and endeavor to develop skilled leadership; work for a permissive atmosphere which encourages both participation and leadership by all. Use outside help when needed (experts—specialists—consultants).

11. Develop means of evaluation so that direction and amount of progress can be seen.

Factors facilitating change that are subject to some control. Certain factors are more readily manipulated than others. Borrowing again from Miel's [7] analysis of curriculum change, these are:

1. The motivations of the individuals and groups who alone can bring successful change.
2. The conditions under which groups work.
3. The extent of social invention.
4. The amount and quality of leadership present and developed.

Motivations. We need not labor the basic importance of motivation. Educational workers have long since accepted the facts. Industry has discovered the relation of motivation to individual and group results, and spends millions to motivate in accord with the psychology of the worker and to provide conditions wherein this type of motive will operate. Prose and poetry testify to universal recognition of the basic truths regarding human motivation. Long ago Fyodor Dostoevsky [8] said: "If it were desired to reduce a

[7] Alice Miel, *op. cit.,* p. 29 and Chs. 3, 4, 5.

[8] Fyodor Dostoevsky, *The House of the Dead* (any edition), Ch. 3, third paragraph.

man to nothing it would be necessary only to give his work a character of uselessness."

Motives range from the basic human drives to the simple purposes of the moment. Individuals work and will fight to protect *values* which they believe to be basic to their lives and to their society. They will work steadily and persist through difficulty to achieve *goals* which are sensible to them. They will work readily to improve conditions that produce *dissatisfaction.*

How does one heighten values so that life activity may move toward more desirable goals? The whole experience theory of learning is at our service here. Values, like all other learning outcomes, are produced through experience and through reflective contemplation of experience. The experimental attack on problems which are real for the individual or group supplies the conditions out of which values emerge, are stated, and translated into operational terms. The mere verbalizing of values so common in life activities is worse than useless. A value merely verbalized is unreal and does not motivate to action. It may actually prevent much needed action.

The pursuit of goals and the removal of tension due to dissatisfaction move ahead as a result of the problem-solving process pursued by the group.

This brief summary hints clearly at the cause of so much unsatisfactory endeavor, individual or group, in education. The values, the goals sought, are imposed by authority and are not necessarily those of the working group. The road to successful attack is clearly indicated.

Conditions for satisfactory group work. Expressed in a few sentences the conditions are: a *social climate* in which a *unified group* can identify and work *freely and co-operatively* on its *problems.* This implies that the group is *functional,* that is, set up to achieve real purposes and not as an organizational stereotype; that there is facile *communication* and ease of *interpersonal relationships.* The group should be unified through common aims and values and through good *leadership* but should actively preserve *flexibility* and give special attention to the contributions of *individuals* and *minorities. Heterogeneity* is fully as important as *homogeneity.* The latter aids in arriving at common purposes and methods and makes co-operation possible. The former stimulates closer definition of purposes, more critical use of means, and above all favors the invention of new means and solutions. The *size* of the group should be *small,* ordinarily twenty-five or less, with sub-groups arranged as needed. *Co-ordination* between groups must be provided. Further discussion of details is given in Chapter 7. An *organization* should be set up by the group to facilitate intragroup activity and intergroup co-ordination.

Social invention. This factor might seem to be the least susceptible to guidance. Creativity cannot be commanded or assigned, "called from the vasty deep" at will. Today, however, we know far more than formerly of the conditions out of which creativity or invention is likely to emerge.

The first and perhaps the most important stimulus to invention is the sincere belief that any of our processes or institutions can be improved. We have not discovered the last word; nothing is sacred within our democratic process and organization. Everything we do can be improved. A second stimulus is historical knowledge of social progress. Study of the conditions and of the emergence of new social mechanisms does help.

The self-conscious analysis of the whole range of democratic process and of the techniques of problem-solving—definition of problems, discussion of problem and related information, sources of data, the techniques of communication, and particularly of decision-making—may at any time strike fire with an individual or group. Improvements on present procedures or new techniques may appear.

The relation between facts and evidence, beliefs, and desires or feelings is not at all what most persons think it is. Desire is by far the more powerful determinant of our beliefs and decisions than are fact and reason. Desires, however, are subject to modification, though we know too little about how to effect this at present. The method of experience again seems the best route to improved thinking and to invention of new procedures.

New knowledge and fact do, however, stimulate invention as they create doubt about present beliefs and procedures, create awareness of one's ignorance. This awareness directly prepares the way for new ideas to appear, heretofore blocked by the certainty and insistent acceptance of our present "wisdom."

Comparison of one's values, beliefs, and processes with those of other groups stimulates analysis of one's own views. The very awareness of other ways of doing things is particularly stimulating to all except those with aggressively closed minds.

The study of the distribution of power and control [9] *within any group and within the school system is of value.* A summary of methods of studying power structures in a community, together with a concrete example, is given in Chapter 16. Suffice it to say here that we are developing better methods of utilizing the power of the co-operative group as contrasted with power vested in given positions or persons. The same study and invention is needed in the areas and sources of public information.

The use of experts (discussed earlier) may be an excellent source of new ideas, or questioning, and hence of new inventions.

Leadership. This factor, in contrast to invention, is subject to great growth and development. The principles and processes are summarized in Chapters 4, 5, and 7.

CHAPTER SUPPLEMENT

GENERAL INTRODUCTORY QUESTIONS

This is one of the most important chapters in the volume. Considerable discussion is necessary and will prove to be rewarding. At the same time, it has proved to be one of the most difficult chapters to interpret and to extend through class discussion.

The six questions listed for introductory discussion of the end of Chapter I have proved very valuable when used here.

1. Give illustrations from everyday life of the four characteristic stages in the development of a mature social process.

2. Describe as accurately as possible an actual case of disintegrative conflict; of integrative conflict. Describe characteristic verbal expressions and behaviors (attitudes as far as they can be inferred) of persons engaged in either type of conflict.

The illustrations may range all the way from family life to international affairs. Continue this discussion with similar specific cases from within the school.

3. Describe a life situation on any level in which you yourself underwent a change in values, concepts, or attitudes. Describe as best you can the influences and experiences which brought about the change.

4. Describe similarly a situation in which a community group, large or small, apparently experienced such changes. Community changes may involve a long period of time and may be difficult to report in a satisfactory manner.

5. Give specific illustrations of the proper and of the improper use of legislation to speed up social change. (Do not stop with the Prohibition Amendment as an unsuccessful effort).

6. Read any discussion of social planning available, preferably brief arguments in the general periodicals. Include some by economic and industrial leaders as well as by social scientists. Analyze as carefully as possible the reasons, particularly the implied or hidden reasons, which seem to underlie the views expressed.

7. Relate briefly any personal experience with the useful participation of specialists in a project; of unfruitful participation by specialists.

8. List a few illustrations for Point 2c on page 37.

9. Take any one of the broad general factors

---

[9] Methods of studying forces and influences within a community are presented briefly in Ch. 16. We preferred to analyze this not in general terms, but in relation to a problem, the improvement of the curriculum.

in the table on page 36 and show very briefly how the selected factor probably operates. Illustrate from history if you can.

10. Illustrate very briefly any one of the immediate factors facilitating or obstructing social change. Give cases.

(The details of the processes for facilitatiing change are developed in many of the remaining chapters. A return to this chapter at the end of the course for re-analysis and scrutiny of one's earlier views has proved of value.)

11. List a number of changes in our social-political-economic order which now seem accepted despite continuing opposition from some groups. Consider the past twenty-five years, the nineties, the past 100 years in selecting changes.

What part does education seem to have played in bringing some of the changes about? Cite cases wherein education could have been used to advantage?

12. What might be social changes which we can reasonably expect to be made and to which education might contribute?

13. What changes might take place in society which would exemplify the principle that we should have a flexibly organized society with mobility between groups?

14. Illustrate with specific cases wherein our social order is experimental; wherein it is not. List evidences of the democratic process at work, or the opposite.

15. Repeat the first ten questions, substituting educational illustrations and problems for the more general life illustrations.

SUGGESTED READINGS

BARNES, Harry E., *Social Institutions in an Era of World Upheaval* (New York, Prentice-Hall, 1942).

————, *Society in Transition* (New York, Prentice-Hall, 1946).

————, RUEDI, O. M., and FERGUSON, R. N., *The American Way of Life* (New York, Prentice-Hall, 1942).

BUNDY, McGeorge, *The Pattern of Responsibility* (Boston, Houghton, 1952).

CHILDS, John L., *Education and Morals* (New York, Appleton-Century-Crofts, 1950).

CONANT, James B., *Modern Science and the Modern Man* (New York, Columbia Univ. Press, 1952).

CUBER, J. F., and HARPER, R. A., *Problems of American Society: Values in Conflict* (New York, Holt, 1951).

DAVIS, Kingsley, BREDEMEIR, H. C., and LEVY, Marion J., *Modern American Society* (New York, Rinehart, 1949).

DOUD, Jerome, *Control in Human Societies* (New York, Appleton-Century, 1936).

DRUCKER, Peter F., *The New Society* (New York, Harper, 1949).

FRANK, L. K., *Society as the Patient* (New Brunswick, N. J., Rutgers Univ. Press, 1950).

HERSKOVITS, Melville, J., *Acculturation* (New York, Augustin, 1938).

MACIVER, Robert M., *Society: Its Structure and Change* (New York, Long and Smith, 1934).

————, "The Historical Pattern of Social Change," in *Authority and the Individual,* Harvard Tercentenary Publications (Cambridge, Harvard Univ. Press, 1937).

————, *The Web of Government* (New York, Macmillan, 1947).

MANNHEIM, KARL, *Man and Society in an Age of Reconstruction* (New York, Harcourt, 1940).

————, *Diagnosis of Our Time* (London, Kegan-Paul, Trench, Trubner, 1943).

OGBURN, William S., *Social Change with Respect to Culture and Original Nature* (New York, Viking Press, 1950).

————, *Social Change* (New York, Huebsch, 1922).

————, and NIMKOFF, Meyer F., *Sociology* (Boston, Houghton, 1946).

RUSSELL, Bertrand, *Impact of Science on Society* (New York, Columbia Univ. Press, 1951).

SOROKIN, Pitirim, *Social and Cultural Dynamics* (New York, American Book, 1937).

————, *Sociocultural Causality, Time* (Durham, N. C., Duke Univ. Press, 1943).

————, *The Crisis of Our Age* (New York, Dutton, 1941).

————, *Society, Culture and Personality* (New York, Harper, 1947).

STANLEY, William O., *Education and Social Integration* (New York, Teachers College, Bureau of Publications, Columbia Univ., 1953).

TODD, Arthur J., *Theories of Social Progress* (New York, Macmillan, 1924).

ZIMMERMAN, Carle C., *The Changing Community* (New York, Harper, 1938).

The list of references in this field could be extended interminably. The foregoing contains a few of the older references and brings the list quite closely up to date. Interested students and instructors can extend to any desired length.

The periodical literature contains a large number of articles currently on this topic and this literature should be searched briefly by the students and by field workers.

◆·◆·◆·◆·◆·◆·◆·◆

Chapter 3

The Aims of Education and Supervision

Section 1

HISTORICAL AND THEORETICAL CONSIDERATIONS

THE AIMS OF EDUCATION are taken for granted by large numbers of educational workers on all levels, particularly on the operational level. The determination and clear definition of aims, on some levels, receives less time and effort than it actually deserves. This may be a real tragedy. Attention to aims is vital in all societies at all times. Our society is in a period of crisis, and it is to some extent divided and fragmentized. Failure to determine the goals of education, failure to understand and give loyalty to the moral commitments of our society, may make a tragic contribution to further crisis and division.

Aims cannot be taken for granted. Aims should not be stated in vague, high-sounding terms. Aims cannot be spun out of thin air. Aims must be known and clearly stated and must be derived from the goals and life of our society. The life of society includes aspirations, hopes, and values, as well as the common workaday knowledges, skills, and abilities useful in that society.

Educational workers of all types and supervisory leaders in particular have a real and fateful challenge, have an opportunity to contribute immeasureably in formulating the aims of education. The nature of the challenge and of the opportunity will be apparent as the chapter develops. Meanwhile let us begin by examining the necessary background.

The ultimate sources of general educational aims. Sources range from the materials constituting the long Judaic-Graeco-Christian tradition to the activities and needs of local community groups.

The general sources of general aims usually include:

1. The Judaic-Graeco-Christian cultural heritage and tradition.
2. The organic and social nature and needs of mankind.
3. The historic development, present status, and trends within the institutions and conventions which constitute our social order.

The core of values derived from the cultural heritage. The Judaic-Christian stream of thought, together with other religious influences, has furnished us with our core of spiritual and moral values. The Greek thinkers gave us the beginnings of esthetic, intellectual, and political values and concepts. These more remote goals of our society are found in certain documents which are both source and guarantee of the aims. The Old and the New Testaments provide moral and spiritual guidance for Christians and Jews. Other great religious documents could be added to the list within and without the Judaic-Christian heritage. The writings of the Greeks, from which we have drawn so many of our esthetic, intellectual, and political values and aims, are too numerous to list. The same is true of the Roman documents on law and government. Our Western society has produced certain later documents, largely political in nature but clearly indicat-

44

ing other aims of life and hence of education. The Magna Carta, the American Declaration of Independence, the French Rights of Man, and the Constitution of the United States are but a few. American, British, French, and many other national documents can be listed.

2) *The organic and social needs of mankind.* The *organic* needs are usually listed briefly as food, clothing, shelter, sex, protection, rest, warmth, and other creature comforts. These arise from the biological nature of the living organism.

The *social* needs are for response and recognition from one's fellows, for purpose in life; for ability to participate in both the competitive and the co-operative aspects of group life, to exercise religious impulses, to play and refresh one's self. These major social needs imply a host of subsidiary needs which become our ways of earning a living, of adjusting to the physical and social environments. Social needs, whether basic or derived, may vary from society to society and between levels within a society. Social needs, even the derived ones, are as imperative as the basic organic needs under modern conditions of life. The connection between basic organic needs and the immediate, practical needs (and immediate aims of education) is often tenuous and uncertain. The connection is further complicated when we consider the individual as occupying a given social position, or as member of a society regardless of social prestige or the lack of it.

3) *The institutions, conventions, and trends within our society.* These are treated by some writers, not as source of ultimate aims, but as a source of derived aims based on the interaction of man's organic nature and the world around him. We may avoid this argument, and note only that an aim of education must be to introduce individuals to the particular structure of his society, to the historic development of that structure, and to the strengths, failures, and tensions within the structure. More important than

the structure are the methods that men have used to develop and change their institutions and conventions. No institution is immutable or eternal; all were invented and developed by men trying to order their lives together. Institutions should be altered constantly to better serve the needs of those who live with the social structure. The Western democracies should educate for orderly change within the democratic methods of discussion and consensus, of parliamentary procedure. Successful democratic process precludes the necessity for violent revolution as a method of change.

The sources of immediate and limited aims for specific educational experiences. The direct and specified aims for subjects, activities, school levels, for units, for lessons or series of lessons may be numbered in the thousands. They include the innumerable understandings, attitudes, appreciations, achieved abilities, and skills necessary for carrying on the affairs of life. Illustrations are to be found widely in curriculum documents and in texts on teaching and the curriculum. Illustrations will be found in brief in Section 2 of this chapter, and in Chapters 12 and 16. The relation of the remote, general aims to the more specific aims is also presented in the same places.

The formulation and statement of aims. Philosophic scholars who interpret our cultural heritage and attempt to predict from it supply material for educational aims, and these men often state aims. The students of society and its institutions, the sociologists, the cultural anthropologists, and the students of political life contribute here also. The biologist and bio-chemist, psychologists, medical research men, and all those who study the life and growth of living organisms, and of personality, give guidance on the organic and social needs of men.

Many community agencies, such as courts, or those concerned with welfare, or with recreation, supply much data useful in establishing human needs, hence objectives of education. Students of the professions and industry indicate still other immediate needs.

The methods by which aims are determined, whether by scholars or by local committees of the parent-teacher association, include reflection and contemplation (remote as that may sound), the analysis and clarification of historical backgrounds, and the application of objective research methods to social problems (social analysis, activity analysis, job analysis, consensus of experts, studies of the errors, shortcomings, and difficulties of adults, and others).

The efforts of scholars and of social agencies, working by various methods, produce lists of core values and beliefs within our society, lists of organic and social needs which must be satisfied, particularly needs peculiar to childhood and adolescence; lists of tensions and maladjustments, and of controversies within our common life.

The actual statement of an educational aim may be made by a great individual, by a committee, by a national or local organization. Occasionally a statement appears which is international in origin and implication. Statements at all levels until modern times have been made almost exclusively by scholars or professional groups. Today local groups participate in study and aid in formulating statements of aim. Study on the community level not only clarifies the historical and scholarly background for everyone but produces aims based on local aspirations and needs. Above all, local participation in study and statement of educational aims is excellent public relations, bringing professional and layman into understanding and agreement. Communities will support educational aims and programs which they have helped to build and which they therefore understand.

The aim of education is social, but with due regard for individuals making up the social group. The individual man, who has come into his own in modern times, lives in and through the culture into which he is born. The goal of education is therefore so-cial and cannot be otherwise. A society may use its educational system to subordinate the man to the culture, but that is the fault or the dishonesty of the leaders at the time. A society may, in the effort to develop man as the unit of society, unduly exalt the individual to its own detriment.

Current revival of interest in aims of learning. The world situation has focused attention sharply on schools and on education. The subordination of the school system to the aims of state is no new thing, but this relationship in Nazi Germany and in Communist Russia has startled many persons. The attempts to capture the schools of the United States by both subversive and loyal groups, by both open and undercover methods, have caused our citizens to study as never before not only the ultimate aims of education but also the immediate classroom goals of learning.

All education takes place within a culture containing its own values and processes. *Education serves the culture* by preserving it and providing some of the conditions for improving it. *Education serves the individual* by providing him with opportunity for the optimum development of his capacities. *Education serves both* when it develops moral beings with purposes and loyalties which are valuable both to the individual and to his society.

Serving the two ultimate ends is no easy task. Ulich writes: [1]

No country, so far, has been able to reconcile the two goals of modern education, that is, to supply on the one hand some degree of cultural unity within the nation and, on the other hand, the full development of individual talent. Nor has any country solved the dilemma which stems from the twofold obligation of education; namely, to serve specific interests such as preparation for a vocation and for loyal citizenship within an individual nation, and to represent at the same time the universal values of humanity as a whole. Much of our present futile

[1] From pp. 11-12 of the book *Conditions of Civilized Living* by Robert Ulich. Published by E. P. Dutton & Co., Inc.

discussion about the contrasts between practical and liberal education stems from lack of insight into these deeper issues of education.

But the deepest reason for our present feeling of dissatisfaction with public education lies in the present lack of a generally recognized hierarchy of values which tells us what to put first and what to put last, and what, if deeply understood, can go together; and as, at least in such complex fields as education, there can be no good structural planning without a clear philosophy behind it, we have not yet built up a type of school which could show to the nation that there can be unity in a variety of educational goals, learning in connection with real experience, and responsibility and harmony between practical and liberal education. So far we have nothing but bad compromises.

Educational objectives must take into account the value system and conventions of society, the beliefs, attitudes, skills necessary for living in that society. Loyalty to our social system plus freedom to evaluate critically and to suggest changes are basic objectives.

Educational objectives must also provide for the best possible development of the unique individuals making up society. The development of all desirable aspects of the capacity or potentiality possessed by each unique individual is a basic objective.

Society and the individual are inextricably interwoven. The security and improvement of a democratic society depends upon the loyalty and intelligence of the individual citizens. The security of the individual, and particularly the improvement of his life and opportunities, depends upon the maintenance of a truly democratic society. Society will move toward cultural disintegration to the degree that its members do not believe in and uphold a common value system, a common moral and intellectual orientation. The individual will suffer if society is torn by unresolved conflicts or resorts to totalitarian suppression of individual liberties.

Contrast of extreme positions clarifies relationship between social and individual sources of aims. Education until the beginning of modern times was dominated by the society in which the educational system developed. The objective was to produce an individual who would fit into the society as it existed. The capacities, desires, or interests of individuals could not be wholly overlooked, but they were not important in determining the aim or content of education. The aim was stated clearly as preparation for adult life as then lived. Discipline leading toward conformity was the method. The cultural heritage in static and adult-formulated organizations was the material taught.

The value of the society-centered aim was its emphasis upon cultural unity and upon orientation of the individual within that unity. The weaknesses were, first, neglect or defiance of one primary value of the Judaic-Graeco-Christian system, namely, the supreme moral worth of the individual. This value is incorporated into the democratic social view in the form of respect for the individual. Second, this view was based on ignorance and, in later times, on refusal to accept the findings of modern psychology concerning the nature of the individual, of his learning processes, and of individual differences.

The individual-centered (child-centered) view arose within this century. Its objective was the production of the best possible individual personalities. Aim and content of education were both derived from the experience, the needs, interests, and capacities of the individual. Individual success and social improvements via the efforts of well-educated individuals were both within the thought of the leaders of this view. Preparation for adult life would be cared for through progressive growth at all ages toward maturity. Freedom and permissiveness were prominent. The content was anything in the real life of the learner which would further his growth and development.

The value of the individual-centered aim was that it was based squarely upon valid facts about individuals and how they learn. Individual differences were recognized as basic. The moral principle that children are persons in their own right and entitled to status and treatment as such was basic to this position. The child-centered view, when it appeared, had the immediate value of balancing the serious overemphasis upon the society-centered view with its stress upon formal materials. A weakness of the individual-centered position was that the development of the individual was often defined in strictly selfish and private terms. A corollary weakness is that extreme individualism is inimical to the very social organization without which the individual cannot exist and realize himself.

Schools operating with society-centered aims are fairly common; those with child-centered aims very rare. Leading theorists have long stated aims and advocated practices which reconcile both the society-centered and child-centered views. The practical operator of the schools, however, has far too often held fast to an adult-society-centered aim. Untold numbers of secondary schools are obviously operating with an aim related to a distant and nebulous adult life, with a minimum of regard for the individual. Elementary schools have moved steadily toward recognizing both objectives.

The child-centered school, despite the widespread uproar over "progressive" education, over using the "whims and caprices" of immature children as sources of aims, is practically nonexistent in the form in which it is criticized.

Societal and individual aims are actually interrelated. The interrelationship, as indicated above, has always been recognized by leading thinkers and is now slowly permeating the thinking of the practical school worker. The felt needs, the purposes, the interests and problems of the learner are inescapable necessities in any learning situation, especially on the lower levels. Education begins but does not end there. Failure to go beyond "felt needs" would keep the aim and process of education on an immature level. The learner must eventually be concerned with the goals of his society.

The development of the unique capacities of the *individual* is a *socially determined* aim. The exaltation of the worth of the individual is a social decision. The definition of what constitutes the best development for an individual is determined by the aims and values of the society within which the individual will realize himself.

Recognition of both societal aims and of aims centering upon individual worth and development is no weak compromise. No logical inconsistency is involved. Socialization and individualization are both necessary aims of the educational process.

The interested student may read at this point:

SMITH, B. Othanel, STANLEY, W. O., and SHORES, J. H., *Fundamentals of Curriculum Development* (Yonkers, World Book, 1950). Ch. 7 contains an excellent extended discussion. Note other basic readings in bibliography. Read also Chs. 5 and 8.

THAYER, V. T., ZACHRY, Caroline B., and KOTINSKY, Ruth, *Reorganizing Secondary Education* (New York, Appleton-Century-Crofts, 1939). An earlier statement similar to that presented here.

Statements of aim as "preparation for life" need careful interpretation. Failure to ask two questions about this familiar statement of aim has over the years led to tragic errors. Broadly speaking, preparation for life is always and can be the only ultimate objective of education. But we may ask: "Whose life?" and "What does preparation mean—what is the desirable method?"

An unfortunate assumption still underlying much educational practice is that preparation is for adult life and is best achieved by imposition upon the child of adult-organized materials. The child's life is ignored as are the materials and processes useful in his life and learning. We know now that the child grows through achieving ever increasing levels of maturity, of insight, of skill. By progressing through a series of learning experiences geared to his level of maturity, he grows naturally into the adult level.[2] The meanings, behavior patterns, skills, values, the learner needs *now* are simply less mature forms of the ones he will use as an adult. The learner will eventually see for himself the necessity for setting up and achieving goals more remote than those of immediate living. He learns by direct experience with problems on his own level of the necessity of looking ahead for consequences of his aims and acts. He sees the social consequences within his own peer group of his aims and those of his social group. He learns the value and processes of working together, the importance of common values and beliefs, of being able to communicate with others and to rely upon them. Above all, he will realize the importance of aims beyond immediate circumstances, the value of working for deferred aims and values. Finally, he will recognize the values of the social aims of organized social groups, and the place of individual aims within the society. Given a chance to arrive at adult life through his own growth processes and experiences, he will not need to have vague and meaningless "aims" and meaningless processes of preparation thrust upon him.

Preparation for life is a growth process. It is neither imposition nor indoctrination. Two terms of recent origin embody the modern concept. Hopkins suggested the term *directional-process goal* to indicate that learners progress along lines of development from earliest contacts in the direction of ever widening grasp of values, meanings, or whatever is being learned. The term *develop-*

mental task, suggested by the University of Chicago Committee on Human Development, defines such a task as one which arises as a need at certain periods of life development.

The directional-process goal.[3] The ultimate objective of education is to develop those patterns of conduct, values, meanings, and attitudes necessary for effective living on the adult level within an evolving democratic society. The immediate objectives are less mature forms of the remote goals—the directional-process goals toward which the pupil grows by achieving increasing levels of maturity, insight, skill, and understanding. The learner, progressing through a series of directional-process goals, will eventually see for himself the necessity for achieving socially desirable goals. All teaching or learning situations bear upon the remote aims. The learners do not know this, and to tell them would merely confuse them or, as often happens in traditional schools, antagonize them. The teacher, as the better-informed and more mature adult, exercises leadership and guidance so that the less obvious needs are not neglected. Thus a balance between immediate purposes (felt needs) and remote purposes is achieved functionally.

Students may find it helpful to examine certain modern courses of study, for instance, the New York State Curriculum Guide for Mathematics; the San Francisco Teaching Guide in the same subject; the Cincinnati Tryout Course in Science, Kindergarten—Grade Eight. Each course shows the progressive development within the field. Math-

[2] For further elaboration of this general view see:

Roy O. Billett, *Fundamentals of Secondary School Teaching* (Boston, Houghton, 1940), pp. 169-170.

William H. Burton, *Introduction to Education* (New York, Appleton-Century, 1934), pp. 22-30. 33-36, 60-66.

———, *The Guidance of Learning Activities,* 2nd ed. (New York, Appleton-Century-Crofts, 1952), pp. 50-56.

John Dewey, *Experience and Education* (New York, Macmillan, 1938), pp. 44-52.

L. Thomas Hopkins, *Interaction* (Boston, Heath, 1941), pp. 344-347.

James L. Mursell, *Successful Teaching* (New York, McGraw, 1946), pp. 4-11.

———, *Developmental Teaching* (New York, McGraw, 1949), pp. 5-27.

[3] This term was originated by L. Thomas Hopkins and elaborated in his volume, *Interaction* (Boston, Heath, 1941). See also his *The Emerging Self* (New York, Harper, 1954). Another similar discussion which does not use this terminology is found in James L. Mursell, *Developmental Teaching,* pp. 17-21, 22-27, and Ch. 2.

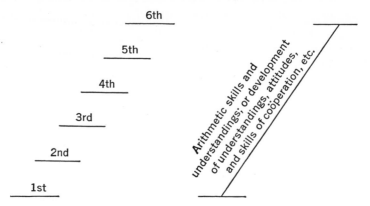

ematics progresses from the simplest experiences children have with number up to the formal arithmetic which can be handled at upper grade levels. The pupil progresses along the line of development as his capacity and maturity permit.

Modern curriculums and guides list flexible social objectives for various age groups, thus enabling teachers to select immediate objectives for units or assignments.

The nature of the directional-process (or directional-progress) goals may be clarified by comparison with traditional grade-level or grade-progress goals. The formal school divides subject matter into segments and arbitrarily assigns certain segments to successive grade levels. Children who do not achieve the grade level are failed, even though they may have made all the progress possible for them. The directional-process goal is represented not by grade steps but by a continuous line. The line represents any given subject area or area of personality growth. The child progresses along that line as his capacities and rate of learning permit. Many children who learn equally well, learn at quite different rates. The line represents a sequence through which learners grow as each individual's pattern permits. This type

of goal is obviously based on the way pupils learn. The grade-level system often interferes with learning.

The learner progresses from his earliest contacts with number experiences as a baby to such levels of mathematics as his capacity allows. The same is true with language expression, getting along with others, or any other given ability.

Developmental tasks as goals. The Committee on Human Development at the University of Chicago has contributed the concept of the "developmental task," [4] which is useful in considering the goals of education. This statement by the Committee aids in reconciling the "felt needs" of the learner with the more remote social ends:

The developmental task concept occupies middle ground between opposed theories of education: the theory of freedom—that the child will develop best if left as free as possible; and the theory of constraint—that the child must learn to become a worthy responsible adult through restraints imposed by society. A developmental task is midway between an individual need and a societal demand. It partakes of the nature of both.

A developmental task is a task which arises at or about a certain period in the life of the individual, successful achievement of which

[4] Robert J. Havighurst, *Developmental Tasks and Education* (Chicago, Univ. of Chicago Press, 1948), pp. 4, 5, 6. Used with permission of the author.

An excellent elaboration is found in *Fostering Mental Health in Our Schools*, 1950 Yearbook, Association for Supervision and Curriculum De-

velopment (Washington, NEA, 1950), Chs. 6 and 7.

A summary of the developmental tasks of early adolescence only will be found on pp. 190-196 in Arthur W. Blair and William H. Burton, *The Growth and Development of the Preadolescent* (New York, Appleton-Century-Crofts, 1951).

leads to his happiness and to success with later tasks, whereas failure leads to unhappiness in the individual, disapproval by society, and difficulty with later tasks. . . .

Living is learning, and growing is learning. One learns to walk, talk, and throw a ball; to read, bake a cake, and get along with age-mates of the opposite sex; to hold down a job, to raise children; to retire gracefully when too old to work effectively, and to get along without a husband or wife who has been at one's side for forty years. These are all learning tasks. To understand human development, one must understand learning. The human individual learns his way through life.

The original source lists the appearance and growth of the developmental tasks from early infancy to adulthood. The concept is closely similar to that of the directional-process goal mentioned earlier.

Indoctrination of the values and principles of democracy is as ineffective as imposition. One of the precepts of democracy itself is that we should not indoctrinate. We may say without flippancy that the only thing that might possibly be indoctrinated in a democracy is the postulate that we should not indoctrinate. Belief in and loyalty to democracy will be more secure if the learner achieves these things as a result of natural learning processes. If we set out to develop free moral beings within an organized society, we will inevitably introduce learners to, among other things, the nature of the world and of man. The history of mankind and the development of his institutions will be studied. The institutions of society come before the individual neither as things imposed upon him, nor as things which he may freely and without consequences accept or reject. They come into his thinking as impersonal aspects of the environment. The institutions are seen not as arbitrary forms, nor as outmoded traditions stifling to the individual, but as the means by which and within which men have organized their life together. The organization of a dynamic society actually provides opportunities for the individual to realize his freedom and growth.

The impersonal, historical study of man and his institutions will show the individual how the institutions and conventions were organized by men like himself trying to meet their needs. He will see how changing needs and conditions, new ideas and new ideals, bring change in institutions. A learner who has been prepared for life by growing into it will not hesitate to exercise his own initiative and judgment in modifying his institutions. The life of society and the good life for the individual depend upon the intelligent use and progressive improvement of institutions built up through centuries of experience. Improvement of the social order and of life for the individual lies in the progressive betterment of the institutions. Freedom for the individual within society is not anarchy, whim, or caprice; it is freedom to make decisions about the important issues in society.

We may repeat for emphasis that the aim is not the imposition or indoctrination of the cultural heritage. The aim is (1) growth, in a continuous, ever widening understanding of one's society, its cultural heritage and institutions; and (2) a continuous development toward an integrated personality, toward realization of individual capacities within one's social order, toward a conviction of personal worth.

Lest this sound like advanced or philosophic discourse, let it be said that the lines of growth suggested start in infancy and continue through all of life. The kindergarten and primary will have many activities which give the children their first, simple, and specific glimpses of institutions and processes which later may be studied directly and formally.

All goals of education must be adapted to the level of maturity of the learner at any given time. The acceptance of more remote social goals is itself partially a result of the advancing maturity and insight of the learner. All the traditional goals of education as conceived by laymen and by many teachers are actually achieved better under growth con-

cepts and processes [5] *than under the concepts and processes of imposition or indoctrination.*

Finally, we may point out that no one can know the explicit nature of the adult life that will be lived by the rising generation. Educators, or any other group, would be presumptuously impertinent if they laid down a design for the future and educated for it. Authoritarian societies have tried to do this in some measure. We can, however, also avoid the opposite error of educating toward an adult life which has passed or is passing. Scholars in the social sciences do not know the "shape of things to come," but they do know the shape of things that are dead and gone. The best we can do is to prepare all individuals to know that change is a law of the universe; lead individuals to examine and evaluate data, to become familiar with social movements and their history; to make judgments, to come to decisions, to solve problems as effectively as possible. We might abandon some (not all) of the procedures and materials inherited from the eighteenth and nineteenth centuries, some from the seventeenth, and endeavor to introduce future citizens to the twentieth century—at least as far as it has gone. Where this century goes during its second half might be in part determined by the range and effectiveness of popular education guided by known facts and democratic values.

Section 2

KINDS AND LEVELS OF EDUCATIONAL AIMS

The discussion of sources of aims did not contain a single illustrative statement of an aim, except in most general terms. What kinds and levels of aim are there? Who states them? In what form? What is the relation of aims to actual procedures in the classroom or to the operation of the school system as a whole?

Relation of ends to processes often overlooked. Problems in education cannot be solved safely without reference to the objectives of education. To begin on the firing line, effective learning by pupils will not take place except as the learning experiences are unified around a goal real to the learner. The use of classroom techniques without thought of the ends involved is pseudo-education of the worst type. The actual results of this are far-reaching and can be truly dangerous. The teacher whose aim for the pupils is "to cover the text" or "to follow the course of study" is far more common than we think. "Why are you teaching this lesson? What is the aim or purpose just here?" is too often answered by "It's the next lesson in the text (or course)." Sometimes it is answered with blank amazement as to why the question should be asked. Teachers should not feel hurt over these statements of plain fact. Teachers are no worse than their leaders; in fact, confusion on the teaching level often stems from unenlightened guidance on the teacher-education level.

Materials and methods of instruction cannot be chosen sensibly except by guidance from the objectives to be achieved through their use. Teachers' guides and curriculums must be organized within a framework of social and personal goals; otherwise a curriculum is a senseless collection of experiences and materials.

Administration, from simple routines to the determination of public policy, will be worth while only as it is directed toward a socially desirable goal. Exercise of the skills of supervisory leadership without thought of

---

[5] The statement refers to general education within which the standards, criteria, and outcomes can only be in terms of the growth of the individual. Standards of achievement within subject-matter areas, in degrees of skill, mastery of concepts, and the like are clearly justifiable within special education. For quick summary see:

William H. Burton, *Guidance of Learning Activities*, pp. 22-24, 622-623.

goals is mismanagement of the worst type. Administration and supervision can affect the whole structure of the school, but whether for good or for ill depends, among other things, upon the accepted goals.

Learning experiences can be educative or miseducative. Policies for promotion and progress of pupils can be dictated by immediate and nonbasic factors, by ignorance of the facts, or by the facts interpeted in the light of a fundamental aim. The setting for learning can be enlightened and improved by supervisory leadership, or it can be confused or even partially destroyed.

The appraisal of any and all aspects of the educational program would be impossible except when directed by stated objectives for the program. The relationship of objectives to appraisal is outlined in detail in Chapters 8 and 9.

An excellent illustration of subordination of means to ends is found in the procedure of Pittsfield, Mass., school and community leaders recently when constructing two new junior high school buildings. They employed consultants who participated in staff and community deliberations designed to set up objectives and a program for the populations to be served by the schools. Aims and programs were tentatively developed first and then architects were employed to plan buildings to meet these objectives and programs.

Confusion between levels of aim is common. Remote general aims and immediate limited aims are often not discriminated. Immediate pupil goals, "felt needs," are often accepted as a basis for organized instructional procedures to the neglect of long-time lines of growth. Or remote, adult-conceived goals may be accepted as sufficient, with no listing of learner's goals.

Teachers, supervisors, and curriculum committees may list as *lesson* aims vague abstractions such as wisdom, citizenship, good use of leisure, and the good old stand-by, "learning to think." At the other extreme, narrow immediate aims may be accepted with no further reference to the more *remote* aims. Learning the table of 4's, mastering the spelling list, reading ten books, are often the only aims given.

Confusion is increased if it is not recognized that any one curriculum area may warrant several different types of aim. For instance, the following may be listed as different levels of aims in the teaching of arithmetic:

Peculiar to the curriculum area
Skills in counting, ordering, grouping, uses of decimals, others.
Functional knowledge enabling one to choose the proper procedure to use in a given situation.
General abilities to compute, to find percentages, ratios, others.
Insight into the structure and use of the number system.

In the area of child development
An interest in mathematics, with liking for the subject and its operations. Desire to be mathematically precise and accurate in problems where numerical data are used.

In the area of societal outcomes
A possible generalization of the process of problem-solving.
Attitudes and skills useful in exercising leadership in the solution of group problems.
Attitudes and skills of democratic cooperation and of social sensitivity.
Creative abilities and skills in dealing with actual problems that arise in life outside the school.

A clear conception of scope of aims, levels of aim, of kinds of aims, and of defensible wording and organization of aims will be of inestimable assistance. Supervisory leadership can render vital service at this point.

Levels of aim [6] need clarification and definition. The hierarchy of aims may be organized usefully in several ways. Readers

[6] The writer is indebted for this conception of levels of objectives and for the analysis of levels to Dr. Merritt M. Thompson, School of Education, Univ. of Southern California. Unpublished material. A valuable summary of Dr. Thompson's view appears in his article, "The Levels of Objectives in Education," *Harvard Educational Review* (May, 1943), pp. 196-211.

may prefer another rather than the one offered here. Any logical organization will aid in preventing some of the errors noted above.

1. *The broad social purposes or objectives of society (in so far as society can be thought of as having objectives) and hence the remote general aims or purposes of education.* The aim of every society is to secure the good life for its members. This aim has been stated variously by different men for different societies and at different times: morality; character; preservation and transmission of the culture; citizenship; democracy; collectivism. Many printed courses of study have a page or a small chapter giving a statement of remote aims developed and worded by the local group. These remote, abstract categories are satisfactory for designating the all-inclusive end point, and for use among advanced scholars for whom such terms have meaning. As immediate classroom objectives, they are absurd.

2. *The more specific social purposes or objectives of education as formulated by social groups.* If we are to come to closer grips with educating members of society, we must know the more specific social needs and purposes to be fulfilled. Lists have been appearing since early times, and with increasing definiteness since about 1860. In 1859 Spencer stated that the definite objectives of education were to prepare individuals for (1) self-preservation, (2) securing the necessities of life, (3) rearing a family, (4) maintaining proper social and political relationships, and (5) enjoying leisure time.[7] In 1918 the United States Office of Education presented its now famous Seven Cardinal Principles: training for (1) health, (2) command of the fundamental processes, (3) worthy home membership, (4) vocational efficiency, (5) citizenship, (6) worthy use of leisure, and (7) satisfaction of religious needs. Various cultural-anthropological lists may be combined into a list of definite social objectives of education as follows:

1. Physical adequacy—health and vigor.
2. Satisfying home and family life.
3. Gainful employment—satisfying to the person and adequate for support.
4. Participation with others in community activities—social and political.
5. Participation with others in religious activities—satisfaction of desire for some relation with the universe at large.
6. Participation with others in desirable recreational activities.
7. Ability to communicate thought to others and to understand their expression.

Recently, lists of definite social objectives with a socioeconomic emphasis have been sharing attention with the cultural-anthropological statements. The major functions of social life become the categories. Those used in the Virginia Curriculum, which have been widely used and modified, are as follows:

1. Protection and conservation of life, property, and natural resources.
2. Production of goods and services and distribution of the returns of production.
3. Consumption of goods and services.
4. Communication and transportation of goods and people.
5. Recreation.
6. Expression of esthetic impulses.
7. Expression of religious impulses.
8. Education
9. Extension of freedom.
10. Integration of the individual.
11. Exploration.

The general organization of aims on this level was repeated in the statement of the Educational Policies Commission in 1938: [8]

1. *The Objectives of Self-Realization:* the inquiring mind, speech, writing, reading, number, sight and hearing, health, health habits, public health, recreation, intellectual interests, esthetic interests, character.

[7] Herbert Spencer, *Education* (New York, Appleton, 1874). U. S. Bureau of Education, Bulletin No. 35, 1918. A similar bulletin published in 1929 by the University of the State of New York, entitled "Cardinal Principles in Elementary Education," is of interest.

[8] *The Purposes of Education in American Democracy,* Educational Policies Commission (Washington, NEA, 1938). This volume is no longer available but the same statement substantially is found in a later publication, *Policies for Education in American Democracy.*

2. *The Objectives of Human Relationship:* respect for humanity, friendships, cooperation, courtesy, appreciation of the home, conservation of the home, homemaking, democracy of the home.

3. *The Objectives of Economic Efficiency:* occupational information, occupational choice, occupational efficiency, occupational adjustment, occupational appreciation, personal economics, consumer judgment, efficiency in buying, consumer protection.

4. *The Objectives of Civic Responsibility:* social justice, social activities, social understanding, critical judgment, tolerance, conservation, social applications of science, world citizenship, law observance, economic literacy, political citizenship, devotion to democracy.

This statement is, to say the least, certainly less scholarly than most of the earlier ones and is much less well organized.

This level of objective is usually summarized in printed courses in the form and wording satisfactory to the local group. Source volumes often contain discussions and diagrams showing the relation of objectives on this level to the materials and experiences for the learners. Objectives stated in the terms given above are out of place and detrimental in a teacher's unit.

3. *The teacher's purposes or objectives.* These are the typical results the teacher desires for his pupils. Objectives here are stated in the form of definite understandings, attitudes, values, behavior patterns, skills, and so forth. Those which the given unit may develop in the pupil should be stated in the teacher's unit. He may then plan materials and experiences to bring about pupil activity toward these goals.

Illustrations of understandings (on varying levels of generalization) might include the following taken at random from several courses and unit plans:

The development of a culture is an evolving process.

Newspapers play an important role in molding public opinion.

Newspapers carry propaganda very often as well as news.

The movements of the various bodies which compose the universe are determined by the action of certain forces, and as a result there is order.

Experimentation and invention are stimulated by competition and in turn modify the growth of industry.

Appreciations are easily stated:

An appreciation of good poetry (or of music, or of the ballet, etc.).

The appreciation of the contributions of various cultural groups within American life to our life.

The appreciation of the contributions of various nations, races, and individuals to the masterpieces of literature (or art, or scientific invention, etc. Appreciation of these things is distinctly different from understandings about the same things)

An appreciation of design, harmony in color, and of standards of taste (for instance, in making one's home beautiful and tasteful).

Attitudes (may often be of appreciation):

Attitude of tolerance and respect for other persons' opinions, together with maintenance of independence of standards and opinions during discussion.   .

Active tendency to participate in the civic responsibilities of a citizen.

Attitude of willingness to co-operate and to contribute to common tasks.

Abilities as commonly stated are easily recognized:

Ability to read (to write, to spell).

Ability to compute with speed and accuracy. (Goals of this type are increasingly stated as quantitative, behavioral terms).

These common but highly generalized abilities may be broken up into several dozen subsidiary abilities, each of which is a desired outcome of learning. Abilities, for instance:

To read with acceptable speed and comprehension.

To grasp at one glance an ever longer group of words.

To skim.

To find new materials in the solution of problems.

To read more rapidly silently than orally.

To evaluate what is read.

Before proceeding, it should be noted that many of the abilities listed above either can be classified as skills, or can be broken down into more specific skills, as we shall see presently. The fragmentary list does, however, indicate the complexity of outcomes in one supposedly simple subject. An even simpler subject—spelling—contains a diversity of outcomes undreamed of by the average citizen. Understandings, attitudes, abilities, and skills appear as follows:

Increasing sensitivity to one's own misspelling.
Awareness of society's attitude toward misspelling.
The attitude of desiring to spell correctly.
The development of systematic methods of studying spelling.
The attitude and habit of systematically attempting to determine causes for one's own misspelling.

Other general abilities often mentioned in courses and units are:

To co-operate with others in given undertakings.
To use newspaper and magazine reviews and criticisms in guiding one's selection of motion pictures to see or books to read or plays to attend.
To use logarithms and other mathematical formulas.
To conduct group discussion in orderly fashion.
To be able to check newspaper reports against standards, references, and sources of fact.

A skill is facility in performance of any given response; it is a relatively fixed, relatively automatic response to similar and recurring situations. Skills may be either mental or motor. The special abilities referred to above include within them scores and scores of skills. In the general ability to compute, for instance, there are found such minute skills as counting, using tables, adding odd and even numbers, adding two-place numbers, adding columns of more than four, five, or six numbers, measuring weighing, estimating. What we commonly call addition, subtraction, multiplication, and division have within them a number of specific skills, most of which have to be learned.

Reading involves such subsidiary skills as skill in recognizing new words, skill in pronunciation, skill in combining contextual clues in order to interpret unfamiliar words. Other related skills are the skills in using a table of contents, an index, topic headings, footnotes, bibliography. Library skills include the use of the card catalogue, the *Reader's Guide,* the dictionary, book reviews, and similar tools. Skills useful both in securing content from reading material and in organizing outlines are skills in selecting a topic sentence, a summary sentence, and key words. Skills in punctuation also are necessary here. The reading of a map in general is an ability, but there are certain specific skills within it, such as the reading of symbols for various elevations, types of vegetation, natural resources, cities, and rivers. In the field of mechanic arts, there are any number of subsidiary skills in using certain tools.

4. *The pupils' purposes or objectives.* These are always the immediate things the learner wishes to accomplish. Illustrations are scattered through following pages, hence a brief summary statement only is given here. The questions asked, the problems raised for discussion, and free discussions among children and youth reveal many of their real objectives.

What keeps airplanes from falling?
What kind of tree should we plant in the school yard?
Could we repair this radio in the school shop?
Could we make dresses in the sewing class for the school party?
Why do the baseball teams generally train in Florida and the Southwest?
What does the Driscoll School have that we haven't which got them in the Sunday paper?
Why is our town named ————?
Why is the bay entrance called the Golden Gate?
What are Forty-Niners?
How can we tell a good cold cure from a poor one?
Why did people come to live here in the first place?
Can we write a play and act it out?
Can I get a book on how to be popular?

Can I learn to get along with girls (boys) at parties?

Where can I find out about courtship, marriage, sex, rearing children?

Am I too young to "go out with a boy," to go to dances, to use lipstick?

When is "old enough" to be seriously interested in a boy (or girl)?

Hundreds are available in the many studies of children's problems and the dilemmas of youth.

Some of these are major purposes as stated, around which units or assignments can be organized. Others are fragments which hint at larger objectives that can be developed by the individual or by the group and the teacher.

Illustration of the levels. Let us examine specific classroom projects and note how the various levels of objective enter. The *broad social objective* of a fifth-grade reading lesson is literacy for the nation. Literacy of the population is a measure of a civilization and is necessary to the development of the best life therein. This objective is not an immediate concern of either teacher or pupil. To state it as a lesson objective would be ludicrous. A *definite social objective* of this lesson would be the development of reading skill in order to facilitate the continuous activities of communication. Social processes are immensely improved through easy communication of information. Again, this objective is not stated as a lesson aim. The *teacher's objectives* in the fifth-grade lesson might be to increase speed and comprehension, to improve vocabulary, to develop better taste in reading. The *pupils' objectives* may be to enjoy a good story, to find out something, or to see what happens next.

A lesson in general science, or one using scientific materials in core units, illustrates the levels in a field quite different from reading. The *broad social objective* would be an understanding of the technological civilization in which the learner lives, and certain skills in getting along in that world. For instance, we educate toward the substitution of scientific fact for lore, superstition, and neighborhood beliefs. We educate for the belief that certain discomforts, shortages, and physical ills are not necessary in modern scientific society. We educate for the use of the scientific method in place of the method of uncontrolled, biased, fragmentary personal experience. These do not appear as objectives for units or lessons. A *definite social objective* might be certain scientific understandings and abilities in choosing a vocation and succeeding in it; another, scientific interests as recreational pursuits. *Teachers' objectives* here would be some definite scientific understandings, laboratory skills, recreational interests, and attitudes toward the world of science, its methods and achievements. *Pupils' objectives* might be to find out what makes firecrackers explode, how to remove a stain, how to prepare the soil for growing flowers in the school garden, or how to make an electric buzzer.

Failure to distinguish between remote general objectives of education and the immediate objectives of units or assignments. Many teachers and some leaders, when stating objectives for teaching situations, indicate incredible confusion between certain *levels* of purpose or objective.

One group lists remote, general, often abstract, long-term objectives of education as immediate, quickly achievable objectives for limited learning situations covered by a unit or an assignment. In fact, these are often given as objectives for a single lesson. For instance, objectives for these limited units or assignments are often stated as the appreciation of beauty, the ability to think, good character, co-operation, understanding of democracy, citizenship. The use of this type of objective for single units or assignments is absurd for several reasons:

1. These objectives are achieved only through a continuing program over a period of time. They are properly the remote objectives to be achieved through many series of units in general education, through whole courses or groups of courses in specialized education.

2. These objectives give no help whatever in determining the immediate materials and procedures to be used for teaching processes.

3. These objectives are not dynamic. They do not stir to action.

Teachers and leaders enamored of this type of statement for objectives—who list "beauty," "culture," "ability to think," "democracy" as outcomes for limited learning situations—usually proceed in a vague, unorganized, pointless manner. They neither define nor specify. Materials and learning experiences are casual and random. Evidences of achievement cannot be produced, because the vagueness of the objective makes achievement difficult to measure. Demands for evidence bring the defense that "analysis kills the spirit." (The presence of the "spirit" seems to be accepted without evidence.) There is much lovely language about "higher things," but little attention to the workaday details necessary to achieve the valuable higher things which are hidden behind the flowery language. The euphemistic language, combined with the lack of forcefulness in the statements, actually lulls to inaction.

A natural error regarding methods of teaching and of learning results. This group tends to sneer at the necessary tasks of preparation, of gathering and organizing materials and experiences, of studying and knowing children; it tends also to sneer at the daily routines, at practice, at the necessity for evaluating and producing evidence of effect.

Another group reverses the error above and states as objectives, not merely for limited lessons but for education in general, a series of narrow, limited, bread-and-butter aims. These are the *ad hoc* aims of the limited utilitarian; the aims of those who interpret literally and narrowly the principle that learning must be based upon the felt needs of the learner. The ability to pass college-entrance board examinations is a prime example of the narrow, noneducational objective. This group very often teaches pupils to read, but not how to discriminate

news from propaganda; to read, but not to see the relation between a critically literate populace and the stability of the social order.

This group fails to see the fundamental, long-time objectives which, as such, may properly be stated in general, abstract terms. This group is likely to be mildly contemptuous toward "culture," "beauty," "appreciation of poetry." There is likely to be much hard-boiled language about the "practical," about "facts," with derogatory references to the "theoretical."

The natural error here regarding methods of teaching and learning is that much use is made of daily assignments, recitation of facts, drilling upon isolated skills, daily marking of performance. This group is impatient with the subtle developmental methods designed to develop understandings, to cause appreciations to emerge, to stimulate creative effort.

The exclusive use of this type of objective is detrimental because:

1. These objectives exclusively employed may very well prevent the teacher from seeing the fundamental, long-term objectives and thus prevent pupil progress toward them.

2. These objectives might be achieved without making any contribution toward the achievement by the pupil of desirable generalized controls of conduct and behavior patterns.

Failure to distinguish between teacher's objectives and pupils' objectives. In the traditional school, typical teacher objectives are memorization of facts by the pupil; achievement of designated skills in reading, arithmetic, language art, manual art; certain vocational skills; and many others. The teacher who is moving toward modern methods adds to these objectives others in the form of study habits, psychological traits, attitudes, and understandings which he hopes will develop in the learner. The modern teacher usually states his objectives in terms of understandings, attitudes and appreciations, general abilities, skills, and general behavior patterns which he hopes will develop in the learner. He may add fact and other subject-matter learnings if he wishes.

The pupils' objectives are, typically, things which they wish to do. They may wish to read a story to see what happens next, or for enjoyment of the exciting adventures narrated, or to secure definite information. They may wish to find out what keeps an airplane from falling or how a thermometer works. They may wish to make a model airplane or a thermometer that works. They may wish to know how newspapers are published; whether one can rely on news statements; whether advertisements are truthful or not.

The teacher's objectives and the pupil's objectives in any learning situation are not similar in form, but they are intimately related. The teacher's objectives are the desirable educational outcomes in the forms stated above which he hopes the pupil will achieve. The pupil's objectives are the immediate results which he sees and desires and which will result from his activity in solving the question in which he is interested. The teacher hopes so to guide the learning experience that desirable educational results (the teacher's objectives) will be achieved while the pupil is achieving his objectives. Failure to realize the difference and relation between teacher's and learner's objectives has caused not only much ineffective and useless teaching but has resulted in detrimental attitudes and practices, and much pupil antagonism toward education. In many schools the pupil does not know or care what the teacher's objectives are. Worse, the teacher too often does not know or care what the pupil's objectives are. Because of this, teachers often cover the ground, go through the motions, and think that they have achieved their objectives when, in fact, they have achieved no educative results. The pupil has realized neither objectives of his own, nor those of the teacher.

Section 3

SUPERVISION AND THE AIMS OF EDUCATION

A service of great value can be rendered by supervisory leadership through stimulation of the study of aims. Any activity which proceeds without identifiable aims is witless. This is particularly true of education, whether we are dealing with classroom teaching or general administration of the system.

Organized study of aims and their functions should result in

1. Clarification and better understanding on the part of all staff members of (*a*) the kinds of educational aims, (*b*) the relationships between levels of aims, and (*c*) the relation of aims of education to the life of the society within which the schools operate.
2. The ability and habit of critical evaluation of all statements of aim on any level.
3. Conscious use of aims as guides in all the processes of education.
4. Effective selection of means of appraising the outcomes.

Supervisory leadership and the remote social goals of education. School workers generally will probably never participate in the derivation and statement of remote goals, but they should be aware of those accepted by society. Goals on this level are presented by contemplative scholars, by students of society, individually or in groups. Despite differences of wording, the various statements of general aim have fallen into well-defined classifications. Student reports may be made here, if desired, on statements of aim which differ from those presented in this chapter. The writers are committed to statements of general aim which

a. Are derived from our society and our cultural tradition.
b. Are based on both social analysis and contemplation.
c. Uphold and enhance the democratic way of life.
d. Care for the basic organic and social needs of men.

Consistency and absence of contradiction within the statement of aims would be highly desirable. The diversity of society in the

United States, and the social crisis in the world, generally results, however, in normal differences of opinion on the beliefs and values which should be the core of our culture. Controversy over statements of general aim is therefore accepted as normal. We should strive for a consensus on statements of aim within given situations.

The important service of supervisory leadership in this connection can be stated as:

1. Provision of opportunity for critical study of existing statements of aim, and of their methods of derivation.
2. Provision for development of a statement of these general aims in form and words determined by the local staff.

The fact that school workers generally will not participate in the original derivation of social goals does not mean that existing statements of goal must be accepted as they stand. Statements of general aims differ considerably in adequacy, in clarity of statement, and in form of organization. Methods of study on which the statements are based may vary from a superficial survey of secondary sources to the critical methods of primary investigation. A program of critical study based on several existing presentations is an excellent procedure. The staff and community become not only more critical of what is presented in print, but gain a far more adequate understanding of the nature and use of general aims. Finally, such study leads directly to the next point: development by school leaders and laymen of a statement for local publication and use.

Excellent existing statements of general aim could be (and often are) accepted by school systems and printed in the general teacher guides or other curriculum documents. A better procedure is to produce one's own statement based on study of other lists of aims. One may say that nothing new can be produced this way. This is true, but the important thing is the greatly improved understanding of and adherence to a statement produced by the group. The very effort to word and organize the statement, plus the preceding study program, brings the insight and sense of possession which accompanies learning by experience.

Supervisory leadership and the more specific divisions of the general aims. The same general program holds here as for the remote general aims: critical study, followed by development of an acceptable statement.

Supervisory leadership and the teacher's objectives. The teacher's objectives, as stated earlier, are those patterns of behavior, understandings, attitudes, values, abilities, and skills which are necessary for successful membership in one's society and at the same time which promote individual development. The teacher's objectives, it should be re-emphasized, are determined both by the needs of our world, of our society, and of the individual. The increasing maturity of the learner, the beginnings of specialization with its introduction of special subjects, will introduce certain substantive outcomes derived from organized subject matter which become teacher objectives.

The general procedure for formulating teachers' aims probably should be (a) a study by the staff and laymen together of the core of beliefs and values held by our society, the contradictions and tensions within what is inevitably a changing society, and (b) a study of the nature and development of human beings. The first will have been accomplished during the study of remote social aims indicated in earlier pages. The second study is an excellent one for group work.

The study of the nature and development of human beings may be subdivided as follows:

a. The growth and development of human beings.
b. The nature of the learner and of his learning processes.
c. The characteristics of the various maturity levels.
d. The needs and problems of children and adolescents in an urban industrial society which largely excludes young people from important community activities.
e. The needs and problems of children and

youth in a society which presents contradictory values and actions, which presents a diversity of interest groupings.

f. The necessity for bringing individual and social goals into relationship with each other.

Each one of these is a major topic of study in itself. Each could be made the core of a program of supervisory activity or community group study lasting some time. Study of the concepts of the directional-process goals and of the developmental tasks as goals, together with related practices, will be another fruitful area for study.

The general intent of study here is to aid the teacher in seeing and formulating the objectives of instructional units or integrated assignments to accord with the general social aims, with the major aims of individual development, and with the immediate experience, interests, and needs of the learner. The general structure of these study programs with meetings, readings, and scrutiny of illustrations is outlined in Chapter 6.

Supervisors and teachers may become very conscious of aims, conscious of discrepancy between stated and actual aims, sensitive to the relationship between general and specific aims, as a result of co-operative surveys of instruction in a given curriculum area or for a particular level of growth. Self-analysis of the general results of surveys of this type can be very revealing yet without loss of security. Teachers, in fact, often request this type of survey. The Minneapolis program in work-reading, reported in Chapter 18, is an excellent example. Another is Whipple's survey of reading in Detroit reported in Section 4 of Chapter 11. Similar surveys may be undertaken by supervisors, teachers, and laymen. Accounts of such surveys found in the periodical literature are useful. (See Exercises Nos. 5 and 6.)

Supervisory leadership and the learner's aims. The learner's aims, as illustrated earlier, are usually to solve problems, to answer questions, or to satisfy interests of immediate concern.[9] These aims are usually stated in the pupil's own words. The learner will, as explained earlier, move toward interest in more remote social and less personal aims, toward deferred values, as he matures and as he gains insight into himself and life about him.

The pupil's needs, which are the bases for his aims and those of the teacher, may be presented from two points of view. Each view must be considered. First, there are summaries of pupil needs as seen and stated by adults. Second, the immediate felt needs of individuals or groups may be listed as they appear in pupils' questions; as they are derived from observed behavior, or as they may be stated directly by the learners themselves.

Needs of childhood and of adolescence as stated by adults. The literature on this topic is extensive and valuable. Needs fall into several categories.

Needs growing out of the facts of physical and motor development. The child is a growing, developing, maturing physical being. He is aging chronologically; growing in height and weight; developing in strength, motor skill, and co-ordination; and maturing physiologically. His needs are chiefly those of a good physical environment: protection against disease; good nutrition; opportunities to be active; adequate rest, sleep, and relaxation; proper clothes; and good physical management.

Needs growing out of the facts of mental growth. The child is growing mentally: in sustained attention, in intelligence, in the development of concepts and reasoning, and in the acquisition of mental skills and language. His needs are for activity and experience. The facts of mental growth appear to

[9] Teachers may sometimes ask how children actually set up aims or suggest problems, how participatory planning for aims and their development is carried on. Preservice training is at fault. The supervisor will need to give help similar to that available in special-methods courses and in general principles of teaching texts. A large volume of materials is available in standard texts, in logs or other accounts of actual teaching, and in the better type of plans for given units.

be better known than those of other types of growth.

Needs growing out of the facts of emotional growth. The child is growing emotionally: in becoming acquainted with the fundamental emotions of fear, anger, and affection; in adjusting to conflicts and in developing emotional control. There is a growing need for security, social approval, and success.

Needs growing out of the facts of social growth. The child is growing socially: developing sympathy, friendships, aggressive and submissive behavior, competitive activities, leadership, understanding of other people and skill in working with them, and moral values. The needs in these areas are for understanding and sympathetic assistance. There will be problems unique to early childhood later childhood, and adolescence.

Needs growing out of the growth of the child as a whole. The child is a developing whole. There is need for well-integrated, wholesome, pleasant, forceful, and well-adjusted personalities. The personality needs of children are many. The need for religious experiences is related to several of the categories.

A school staff may engage in detailed study of these lists in original references. The implications are highly important as aids in determining the teacher objectives described in preceding pages. The summary here could have been included logically with the preceding discussion of teacher's aims and may be studied in connection with the list of six areas given there if desired.

A general volume such as this one does not pretend to include detailed discussions of subsidiary subjects, especially when an extensive literature exists. Good references are:

BRECKENRIDGE, Marian E., and VINCENT, E. Lee, *Child Development,* 2nd ed. (Philadelphia, Saunders, 1949). Comprehensive discussion.

BRUBACHER, J. S., and others, *Public Schools and Spiritual Values,* Seventh Yearbook, John Dewey Society (New York, Harper, 1944).

CARMICHAEL, Leonard, ed., *Manual of Child Psychology* (New York, John Wiley, 1946). Comprehensive summary of major research in field of child development.

JERSILD, Arthur T., *Child Development and the Curriculum* (New York, Teachers College, Bureau of Publications, Columbia Univ., 1946).

MURPHY, Gardner, MURPHY, Lois B., and NEWCOMB, Theodore M., *Experimental Social Psychology,* rev. ed. (New York, Harper, 1937). The sociological development of the child in all aspects.

OLSON, Willard C., *Child Development* (Boston, Heath, 1949). One of the best summaries.

STRANG, Ruth, *An Introduction to Child Study,* rev. ed. (New York, Macmillan, 1938).

TYLER, Leona E., *The Psychology of Human Differences* (New York, Appleton-Century-Crofts, 1947). Very readable.

Child Growth and Development Emphasis in Teacher Education, American Association of Teachers Colleges (Oneonta, N. Y., State Teachers College, 1944). An excellent summary.

How Children Develop (Columbus, O., University of Ohio, 1946). An illustrated pamphlet, exceptionally valuable for beginning teachers and parents.

JENKINS, Gladys G., SHACTER, Helen, and BAUER, William T., *These Are Your Children* (Chicago, Scott, 1949). An unusually valuable reference.

PRESCOTT, D. A., *Emotion and the Educative Process* (Washington, American Council on Education, 1938).

FENTON, Norman, *Mental Hygiene in School Practice* (Stanford University, Calif., Stanford Univ. Press, 1943). Excellent.

BAKER, Emily V., *Children's Questions and Their Implications for Planning the Curriculum* (New York, Teachers College, Bureau of Publications, Columbia Univ., 1945).

Innumerable periodical references are available describing specific studies of value to all supervisors and teachers.

The discovery of the immediate needs of the learner. Education begins with the felt needs of the learner, though it must eventually progress to more remote societal and individual needs. The values, interests, and problems of children are not those of adults, but must not be ignored as they too often are. Many methods have been developed for studying learners at all educational levels.

Testing to determine skills, abilities, attitudes, etc.
Observation of behavior with anecdotal records thereof.
Participation in the activities and conversations of learners.
Collection of questions asked by children and youth.
Sociometric analysis of group structure and the interrelationships of individuals within the group.
Projective techniques (many available).
Questionnaires directly to the individuals.
Inventories, interviews.
Case studies.

All these are designed to reveal needs, interests, problems, which in turn aid in establishing good pupil aims. Details are given in Chapter 9.

1. *The various methods of investigating needs may be used simultaneously.* The Florida state course of study,[10] for instance, lists the following helpful suggestions to teachers who wish to discover and understand the needs of the individual pupils:

1. Ask the members of the class to answer questions somewhat similar to these: Why do you want to come to school? What do you want to learn this year? Have you seen something lately about which you have wondered but about which you could not find the answer? What do you like to do at school, at home? ...
2. Watch the children while they are playing or working during their free time. The books which the children use voluntarily, the objects which they make, the playthings which they choose, the groups which they join, and the free discussions—all give to the teacher an excellent idea of the things about which the children are concerned.
3. Talk casually to individuals and to small groups, letting them take the lead in the conversation. Occasionally, when questions are asked, the teacher may make mental notes without comment. As soon as possible these notes should be recorded for future reference.
4. Give the children an opportunity to tell the others about good times they have enjoyed,

about the interesting things they are doing or have done, and about the things they would like to do. ...
5. Ask the children to collect pictures which appeal to them or which they think would appeal to some member of the group. (These pictures may be brought to school and classified by the teacher for her own guidance. Other objects of interest may be used in a similar manner.)
6. Distribute to small groups of children catalogs from ... mail order houses and give the pupils directions for using the index. The teacher may watch to see what the children look for. ...
7. Talk to the parents to find out how the child spends his free time at home and what interests are his which his parents know about.

Curriculum guides and documents based upon the study of children and adolescents often contain similar aids for discovering interests and problems.

2. *Studies of interest in particular subjects.* Teachers often ask students what they expect to get from a subject area about to be studied. This is a valuable guide to setting up objectives in that subject area. Wendell Bragonier of Lincoln Junior High School, Des Moines, used questions asked out of interest by his students about the coming year's work in science. The following is a sample [11] of the things the students hoped to learn. Lists of interest questions in any subject area as noted elsewhere, must be supplemented by a listing of the requirements of that systematically organized area.

A. *Air and Air Pressure*
1. How dense is the air?
2. What causes the different densities of the air?
3. How is artificial air made?
4. What causes air pressure?
5. Why is air at an altitude lighter than air here?
6. What makes air pockets?
7. How is air transformed from hot to cold and back again?
8. How is liquid air made?

[10] *The Course of Study for Florida Elementary Schools, Grades 1-6* (Tallahassee, Fla., State Department of Education, 1933), p. 13.
[11] Quoted in H. H. Giles, *Teacher-Pupil Planning* (New York, Harper, 1941), pp. 263-266.

B. *Sound*
   1. How are sound waves picked up by radio?
   2. How are sound waves sent out for radio?
   3. What causes thunder?
   4. Difference between mucrote and speaking voice?
   5. How does the voicebox vibrate?
   6. How is a voice recorded on a victrola record?
   7. How does sound affect work?
   8. Why do different musical notes have a different number of vibrations?
   9. How can sound travel through wires?
   10. Why is air necessary in hearing musical sound?
   11. What is an echo?
   12. Why is it difficult for one speaking in the open air to be heard?
   13. When calling to someone at a considerable distance, is cupping the hands before the mouth any advantage? If so, why?
   14. How can deaf children listen to music by resting their hands and head upon the frame of a piano?
   15. How does opening the holes of a saxophone or clarinet affect the pitch?

Sets of questions similar to these are presented for a number of subjects such as weather and climate, water, machinery, electricity, and light.

3. *Studies of the problems of adolescents.* Currently much use is being made of the problems of learners in determining needs, and hence some of the aims of teaching. Pupils may be asked to list their problems in running discourse without controls, or may be asked to mark a set check-list of problems.

An early study by Mooney [12] used a check-list of short statements representing common problems of students. The student used the list by marking the problems which are of particular concern to him and by writing a summary in his own words. The college and high-school forms contain 330 items each, grouped into eleven categories: (1) Health and Physical Development; (2) Finances, Living Conditions, and Employment;

(3) Social and Recreational Activities; (4) Courtship, Sex, and Marriage; (5) Social-Psychological Relations; (6) Personal-Psychological Relations; (7) Morals and Religion; (8) Home and Family; (9) The Future: Vocational and Educational; (10) Adjustment to School Work; and (11) Curriculum and Teaching Procedures. The items are phrased as follows: "In too few school activities," "Shyness," "Having no close friends," "Lost—no sense of direction in my life," "Confused in my religious beliefs," "Moral code weakening," "Needing to decide on an occupation," "Family opposing my choice of vocation," "Not liking school," "Wanting more help from the teacher," "Slow in reading," and the like. The method provides an excellent means of discovering the felt needs of pupils. It is limited to the extent that the problems of the persons concerned are circumscribed by their insight and the scope of their experience.

Cary [13] investigated the problems recognized by a group of 620 students in the ninth, tenth, eleventh, and twelfth grades in Southwest High School, Minneapolis, and found:

Areas Checked Most Frequently	*Frequency*
Adjustment to school work	2471
Curriculum and teaching procedure . .	2309
Personal-psychological relations	1935

The ten most frequently reported personal problems in order of rank are:

   1. Wondering what I'll be like ten years from now.
   2. Wanting to earn some money of my own.
   3. Wondering if I'll be a success in life.
   4. Forgetting things.
   5. Not taking some things seriously enough.
   6. Learning how to spend money wisely.
   7. Having to ask parents for money.
   8. Learning how to save money.

[12] Ross L. Mooney, "Exploratory Research on Students' Problems," *Journal of Educational Research* (November, 1943), pp. 218-224.

[13] Miles E. Cary, "Looking at Teen Age Problems," *Journal of Home Economics* (December, 1948), pp. 575-576.

9. Can't forget some mistakes I've made.
10. Losing my temper.

Remmers and Shimberg [14] studied a sample of 2500 high-school freshmen, using the Science Research Associates Youth Inventory, and found the ten problems reported most frequently to be:

Problem	Per cent
1. My courses are too far removed from everyday life	77
2. I wish I could be more calm when I recite in class	63
3. For what work am I best suited?	58
4. How much ability do I actually have?	58
5. I want people to like me better	55
6. I get stage fright when I speak before a group	54
7. I want to gain (or lose) weight	54
8. I want to make new friends	52
9. I have difficulty keeping my mind on my studies	51
10. I wish I knew how to study better	51

Grant's [15] study of freshmen in Antelope Valley Joint Union High School, Lancaster, California, used a list of eighteen categories somewhat similar to those of Mooney, listed above. The ten problems listed most frequently differ in an interesting manner from those found by Remmers and Shimberg, though it is obvious that several items in Grant's list could be combined under some of those in Remmers and Shimberg's list.

Problem	Frequency
Concerned about getting good grades	120
Lack of transportation to attend sports and social activities	118
Wanting a job during vacations	115
Forgetting	114
Not having enough money	105
How to date	104

Making mistakes	103
Don't know how to dance	97
Live too far from friends	96
Knowing the correct thing to say in all social occasions	96

Lists of problems do differ with groups from different social or economic backgrounds, or geographic areas. Problems differ also by maturity levels. Preadolescents are concerned in considerable degree with personal needs, whereas older boys and girls are more concerned with social problems. Young children are concerned with fears and securities, with their expanding understanding of the physical and social worlds.

4. *Studies of the problems of children.* Similar analyses can be made of the interests and problems of very young children and of those in the elementary grades. Space prohibits an extended listing. The illustration which follows is from Raths and Metcalf, [16] who devised a list on which children could check their immediate problems.

The instrument contains 160 items indicative of eight groups of needs as follows: (1) a feeling of belonging, (2) a sense of achievement, (3) economic security, (4) freedom from fear, (5) love and affection, (6) freedom from guilt, (7) a share in making decisions, and (8) integration in attitudes, beliefs, and values. Some excerpts from the list are given below.

The following statements relate to the feeling of belonging:

1. I wish I did not have to play by myself so much.
9. I wish I liked more children.
17. I wish I felt as though I really belonged in my school group.
33. I wish there were more children my age to play with.

[14] W. H. Remmers and Benjamin Shimberg, *Examiner Manual for the SRA Youth Inventory* (Chicago, Science Research Associates, 1949), pp. 15-20.
[15] Bruce Grant, "Problems of Freshmen in the Antelope Valley Joint Union High School," unpublished study, 1951, pp. 1-12. Summaries are found in Grant's, "Survey of Research Studies on Problems of Adolescents," *California Journal of Secondary Education* (May, 1953), pp. 293-297. This is a good brief commentary on the best recent studies.
See also many modern volumes on adolescent psychology or on development of the adolescent.
[16] Louis Raths and Lawrence Metcalf, "An Instrument for Identifying Some Needs of Children," *Educational Research Bulletin* (October, 1945), pp. 169-177, 196.

129. I wish children in our neighborhood were friendlier to me.

The following statements relate to the desire for economic security:

11. I wish I could be sure that my father would always have a steady job.
27. I wish I could have money of my own to spend as I please.
43. I wish our family could afford to give each other better presents at Christmas and on birthdays.
107. I wish our family could afford to go to doctors and dentists whenever we needed them.
122. I wish our family had enough money so that we didn't have to worry so much about food, clothing, and rent.

The following statements relate to the feeling of guilt:

14. I wish I liked Negro children as much as I like white children.
22. I wish I had never lost my temper.
38. I wish I had never cheated.
46. I wish I had never looked down on people who are poor and uneducated.
62. I wish I had been more obedient.

Teachers need assistance and further study in order to interpret the investigations which have been made of children's problems. Teachers must discriminate and aid children to discriminate among several aims which may be chosen for definition and study by the learners. Pupils' interests and choices of activity are not all of the same importance; some may be miseducative. The teacher may undertake this task with courage when armed with information and valid procedures. Many good references are available of which the following are but a few:

BAKER, H. J., and TRAPHAGEN, Virginia, *The Diagnosis and Treatment of Behavior-Problem Children* (New York, Macmillan, 1935). An older references of value. Case studies. Detroit Behavior Scale in detail.

BELL, J. E., *Projective Techniques* (New York, Longmans, 1948).

BIBER, Barbara, MURPHY, Lois B., WOODCOCK, Louise P., and BLACK, Irma S., *Child Life in School: A Study of a Seven-Year-Old Group*

(New York, Dutton, 1942). Detailed analysis with much valuable material for all teachers.

BONNEY, Merle E., *Popular and Unpopular Children, A Sociometric Study,* Sociometry Monograph No. 9 (New York, Beacon House, 1947).

BURTON, William H., *The Guidance of Learning Activities,* 2nd ed. (New York, Appleton-Century-Crofts, 1952). Sec. 1 of Ch. 9 contains quick summary. Skim Chs. 7 and 8 also.

CUNNINGHAM, Ruth, and associates, *Understanding Group Behavior of Boys and Girls* (New York, Teachers College, Bureau of Publications, Columbia Univ., 1951). Chs. 4 and 9 of value to everyone.

DRISCOLL, Gertrude. *How to Study the Behavior of Children: Practical Suggestions for Teaching,* No. 2 (New York, Teachers College, Bureau of Publications, Columbia Univ., 1941). Very useful.

ENGLISH, Horace B., and RAIMY, Victor, *Studying the Individual School Child* (New York, Holt, 1941). An older reference containing excellent material.

Helping Teachers Understand Children (Washington, American Council on Education, 1946).

HYMES, James L., Jr., *A Pound of Prevention; How Teachers Can Meet the Needs of Young Children* (Caroline Zachry Institute, 17 East 96th St., New York 28, 1941). A very practical treatment.

JENNINGS, Helen Hall, *Sociometry in Group Relations, A Work Guide for Teachers* (Washington, American Council on Education, 1948). Step-by-step techniques for diagnosing relationships in school groups.

LEE, J. Murray, and LEE, Dorris M., *The Child and His Curriculum,* 2nd ed. (New York, Appleton-Century-Crofts, 1950). First five chapters.

SNYGG, Donald, and COMBS, Arthur W., *Individual Behavior* (New York, Harper, 1949).

TORGENSON, Theodore L., *Studying Children* (New York, Dryden Press, 1947).

WOOD, Ben D., and HAEFNER, Ralph, *Measuring and Guiding Individual Growth* (New York, Silver Burdett, 1948). Very readable presentation of individualized education based on study and cumulative records. Guidance of students toward their own unique goals.

See also among others:

ENGLISH, O. Spurgeon, and FINCH, Stuart M., *Emotional Problems of Growing Up* (Chicago, Science Research Associates, 1951). Covers both childhood and youth.

IMELDA, Sister Marie, "Attitudes and Appreciations of the Pre-school Child," *National Catholic Educational Association Proceedings* (1950), pp. 437-440.

KUDER, G. F., and PAULSON, Blanche B., *Exploring Children's Interests* (Chicago, Science Research Associates, 1951). A well-written summary and introduction to the field. Nontechnical language for teachers and laymen.

————, *Discovering Your Real Interests* (Chicago, Science Research Associates, 1949). This is addressed to high-school students but equally useful to teachers and parents.

REMMERS, H. H., and HACKETT, C. G., *Let's Listen to Youth* (Chicago, Science Research Associates, 1950). Written for adolescents and for parents but useful to teachers, counselors, and others.

STRATTON, D. C., "What Youth Want from Their World," *National Parent Teacher* (April, 1953), pp. 4-6.

WHIPPLE, Gertrude, "Appraisal of Interest Appeal of Illustrations," *Elementary School Journal* (January, 1953), pp. 262-269.

General criteria for aims. A number of standards may be set up by which to evaluate aims. Some of the standards refer to general aims and others to the more specific objectives.

1. Are the general aims derived from our society, with particular reference to:
   a. The positive core of values and beliefs commonly held by the citizen; the conflicts in our society over beliefs and values; the diversity concerning some values and beliefs?
   b. The tensions, maladjustments, and social problems within our society?
   c. The necessity for supporting the principles of an emerging and developing democracy?
2. Are the goals in keeping with the organic and social needs of mankind?
3. Are the goals in keeping with the needs and developing maturity of the learners?
4. Are the goals in keeping with the function of the school as presently accepted in our society; achievable by the school; achievable by the learner?
5. Are the statements from general to specific internally consistent; sequential in development?
6. Is the principle of relative values clearly demonstrated in the exclusion and inclusion of aims?
7. Are the goals stated clearly enough to be subject to evaluation, that is, so that degree of attainment may be determined?

CHAPTER SUPPLEMENT

QUESTIONS FOR GENERAL DISCUSSION

1. Which ideas that you may have had about the aim of education are clarified by this chapter? Which contradicted? Which of the contradicted ideas persist in your mind, and which are you willing now to give up?
2. State what seemed to you to be the three or four most striking principles developed in this chapter. What is the value of these principles to the classroom teacher? To the supervisor?
3. Ignorance of the remote aims of education is responsible for much error and bad practice of educational policy and in classroom procedure.
   a. Explain as well as you can at this stage why there is, among educational workers, widespread ignorance of the general aims and of the hierarchy of aims.
   b. Note during your classroom observations two or three specific errors on the part of the classroom teacher due to unawareness of aims. Also note illustrations of good understanding of aims and relationship between aims, of relationship of means to aims.
   c. Explain in general terms with illustrations the types of error in which educational workers other than teachers will fall because of unfamiliarity with the aims of education.

4. The form in which educational objectives on any level are stated varies widely and often contributes to confusion.
   a. Explain in some detail why these variations occur.
   b. Indicate in some detail how the unnecessary and confusing variations

(as distinguished from natural and legitimate variations) may be corrected and eliminated.

5. Observe a lesson, or two or three consecutive lessons, and try to formulate the objectives that the teacher had in mind. What is the evidence on which you base your conclusions? If the pupils have their own objectives, how were the objectives established in the course of the lesson? Evaluate these objectives, as you derive them from the classroom procedure, in terms of the discussion of needs in Section 3 of this chapter.

6. Ask a number of teachers for the objectives of lessons which you have just observed. Do not indicate surprise if none can be stated; accept without comment any formal or absurd aims; accept with commendation any competently expressed objectives. Bring the list of any comments in for class discussion.

7. Review a number of current articles on the aim of education. Be sure to include one or more articles which include attacks and criticisms by laymen.

8. Examine a number of course-of-study guides (or professional books on the curriculum).

   a. Note the broad, general aim of education, if it is stated, and evaluate it.
   b. If no general aim is stated, examine the statement of specific objectives and also the objectives by subjects or units to see if you can infer the general aim.

9. Examine the content of several kindergarten or primary courses of study.

   a. Note how the far-away general aim of education is being approached even with these young children.
   b. Contrast, if available, older courses or teachers' guides with fairly recent ones.

10. Examine the general curriculum handbook of the type put out by many cities and states, or that part of the course-of-study document which does present the general aim and the methods of deriving this aim. Critically evaluate:

   a. The soundness of the general, remote, societal aims stated.
   b. The soundness of methods used to determine these aims. (Often this is omitted.)
   c. The clarity of language and the form used.

11. Examine the annual reports of school superintendents, and evaluate critically any statements made about aims. Examine any booklets which may be available such as those published by individual schools, public or private, setting forth the aims of the program or any other interesting views on their type of education. Critically evaluate the statements dealing with aims of education.

Examine similarly bulletins which deal with promotion policies, with counseling and guidance, the development of public relations, or any other thing on which school officers may be expressing themselves. Report direct statements or indications showing that the staff is fully aware of an aim and of the responsibility of working for that aim; or show that they are not aware of that aim or are actually working for outmoded aims.

12. What are the probable reasons for the neglect of aims and objectives by a large number of teachers and other school workers?

13. Why are aims or objectives stated very badly, not merely in language and form, but in content?

14. How do you account for the persistence of aims which have long since lost any usefulness for present schools or for the society in which the schools exist.

15. Evaluate the following practices in terms of accepted general aims of education:

   a. Memorization and recitation of certain paragraphs in geography, history, or other textbooks.
   b. Study of Indian life by third-grade children.
   c. An experiment on the relation of light to plant growth.
   d. Competition between groups, such as for prizes in spelldowns, etc.
   e. Use of motion pictures or the radio in the literature class.
   f. Preparation and exhibition of a mural dealing with transportation.
   g. Discussion of the question, "When we pay for a loaf of bread, what do actually pay for?"
   h. Experience unit, "What should our community do to provide us with a safer water supply?"
   i. A sixth-grade class undertakes the preparation of a special issue of the school paper as a report of the work of the school to parents.
   j. Special classes for talented or for retarded children.

16. Report for class analysis (1) the statement of objectives set up in any local program of curricular development in which you may

have participated, or (2) the methods used to determine the objectives.

17. Report from personal experience the actual consequences in a given situation of failure to develop an understanding and responsibility for aims. Reports may range from major effects on the school system, the curriculum, the administrative policy, to the minutiae of everyday education.

18. Make a similar report focusing now on the use of imposition and indoctrination; of adult-centered procedures versus the growth-and-development concept of procedures. (This is not as simple as it sounds. A good deal of curriculum material, a goodly amount of material on procedure, while seemingly modern, actually is based on hidden assumptions of imposition, indoctrination, and adult view.)

   a. For instance, give illustrations of current curriculum content of school practice, of materials and outcomes which are of no use anywhere in life.

   b. Give illustrations of materials and outcomes that could be acquired which are clearly useful to all citizens constantly, but which are not commonly included in current school curriculums.

   Develop other similar illustrations, focusing always on hidden imposition and indoctrination.

19. Report from personal experience, if you can, how a supervisor actually aids a group of teachers who say they cannot see any relationship between statements of remote aim and their classroom responsibilities. If you have not had this experience, attempt to answer the question on a theoretical basis

INDIVIDUAL REPORTS

1. Examine the statement of educational aim in societies outside the United States. Make comparison as to the statement of aim and probable methods of deriving these aims.

2. Take a text in some specialized aspect of education, for instance, administration, or principles of teaching, or evaluation, and note the statement of aim of education, provided one is included. Many of these books now do include such aims.

   a. Do you consider the statement of purposes which you found adequate and acceptable? Is the statement which you examined similar to previously published statements, or different?

3. Report briefly on ways the life of the community, the available instruction that is supplied to the type of school tend to contribute to the achievement of the aim or detract therefrom. What changes as much as is asked of the situation to which you are familiar.

4. How adequately does the program of teacher education which you underwent, or the program for the training of superintendents of which you may know, consider the purposes of education.

CLASS PROJECT NO. II

The class as a committee of the whole, or through a representative committee, will develop (1) a statement of aim in some curriculum area or level of the school, or (2) a statement of general educational aims, which is acceptable to the group. Report to the group, if the committee of the whole is not used, on the organization and procedure followed which ordinarily would be typical of the procedure used by any group in the field.

SUGGESTED READINGS

The necessary references have been included in the body of the chapter. Certain other general volumes dealing with the philosophy of education or with the aim of education are easily available in any catalog and should be examined in connection with this chapter.

Chapter 4

◆·◆·◆·◆·◆·◆·◆·◆

The Principles Governing Democratic Supervision

Section 1

PRINCIPLES CONSTITUTE ONE OF THE BASIC CONTROLS OF ACTION

A FASHION HAS DEVELOPED among certain educational workers to say of principles generally, of philosophic principles, and particularly of the principles of democracy: "We do not really know what the principles of democracy are"; "After all, who is to say what the principles of democracy are?"; "No one agrees on the principles of democracy, so how can we know what they are?"; "The so-called principles are but popular phrases"; "The so-called principles of democracy are always changing, so why try to state them?"

The writers stand squarely in opposition to this "know nothing" cult. Education or any other human enterprise cannot be conducted intelligently without aims and ends, without basic guiding principles. There is actually large agreement among competent thinkers on the aim of education and on principles of democracy. To profess ignorance of the principles of democracy may be because one actually is ignorant. It may also be because of indifference, because of refusal to engage in the intellectual effort necessary to derive and understand principles. Worse, ignorance is professed in some cases as a cloak for refusal to accept the basic responsibility which is inescapable with educational workers, namely, to serve the values of one's society.

Lack of agreement among all groups in our society concerning the values and principles of democracy is a challenge to leaders and cannot possibly be a criticism of the principles. Diversity is a normal condition in a democratic society. If some use the great values and principles as "phrases" to which mere lip service is given, again the fault cannot lie within the principles. (Unless, in fact, the principles are unwarranted by our social tradition, or are outmoded, or are imposed by a special-interest group.)

The democratic way of life is dynamic. Goals and principles will change. Change is slow and takes place over a period of time. It should not take place capriciously as a result of some unfounded pronouncement. Progress comes from change based on new evidence, on social inventions to meet new conditions, on new insights resulting from reflective contemplation. Progress may be capricious, sudden, or erratic, but this is mere chance. Difficult as it is to operate within a dynamic and changing society, nevertheless no one who deals with education can escape responsibility for working toward aims according to democratic principles. Educational workers not dedicated to this view, or who "do not know" what the principles are should seek other lines of endeavor.

One of the chief responsibilities of education from primitive to modern times is the introduction of the individual to the values, conventions, and principles of his culture, not merely as knowledge but as guides to life. We must not only *know* the principles of democracy, we must *act* upon them. Today there is desperate necessity that citizens of a democracy not merely know the principles but that they stand up and be counted in favor of democracy. Democracy, however, cannot be imposed or indoctrinated; it must be achieved and believed. Individuals can be aided in discovering or in stating values and principles by free inquiry, by study which includes all the facts, which considers strength and weakness in any value or principle. One may be a partisan for any doctrine or principle which he has accepted after full and free inquiry; a principle which, furthermore, can withstand open critical analysis. One may be partisan to any such principle, further, in so far as he maintains an open mind toward new evidence, new conditions, and legitimate criticism. To change a principle into a dogma, to allow it to crystallize, to refuse to allow further critical analysis, is to violate one of the chief tenets of democracy. Brameld [1] has suggested the term *defensible partiality* for the attitude of loyalty to principles when one's conviction is based on free inquiry. Education and supervision must be guided by and exemplify the principles of democracy.

Principles are one of several factors controlling action. When asked what generally controls action or conduct, the average citizen will usually reply, one's philosophy or principles. After a moment's thought he will usually add that action is controlled also by one's purposes (objectives). Confused discussion is then likely to ensue about the nature of objectives and principles and the relation of one to the other. A cynical citizen at this point may interject that purposes and principles are all window-dressing; action is really controlled by expediency! Cynical though it may be, this comment should not be brushed aside, since it points to another, often overlooked, factor in the control of action; namely, the hopes and fears of the individual, the successes and frustrations, the

hidden pressures, the basic temperament—in short, the human nature or personality of the actor. A more objective citizen weighing both answers might say that because human nature is good as well as bad, the individual will often spurn expediency but still be forced to act contrary to principles or desirable objectives because of limiting factors within the situation which are beyond his control. The realities of a given situation, the economic status of the individual, the opportunities available for better status, health, and strength, prejudices and discriminations present, facilities available, and so forth, are often determiners of conduct.

Controls over action, then, include *objectives, principles, human nature,* and the *realities of a given situation.* None of these by itself is sufficient to explain or to control action. All are usually operable in a given situation. Separate chapters of this book are devoted to objectives and to study and improvement of the socio-physical environment. The effect of human nature is indicated in several chapters. Extended treatments can be found in volumes on human motive. The present chapter deals with principles as one guide to supervisory action. The volume as a whole tries to indicate the desirable integrations of the several behavior controls.

The distinction between principles and techniques. The bulk of writing and thinking about education generally, about supervision specifically, has been concerned until quite recently with analysis of techniques, procedures, mechanisms. Leaders have always supplied excellent materials on aim and philosophy, but the rank and file has been concerned chiefly with details and processes. The majority, the huge majority, in fact, of teachers and educational workers generally, are either unaware of or but hazily informed upon the general aims and principles of education, upon the relation of education to the

[1] Theodore Brameld, *Ends and Means in Education: A Midcentury Appraisal* (New York, Harper, 1952), pp. 87-88, 92-94.

social order, to the philosophy (principles) of their own society. Criticism of educational workers is not intended; this is but a simple statement of fact. The remedy lies within the province of teacher education, preservice and in-service (supervision), and is emerging. Before turning to an organized discussion of principles, let us define and contrast techniques with principles.

Techniques are ways of doing things: principles are one of the controls for the doing of things. A teacher who is aiding children to learn to multiply, or to develop better language skills, or to suspend judgment while all evidence is examined, proceeds in a given and particular way which can be observed and accurately described. These specific ways of doing things are called *techniques.* For example, a teacher may give without any preliminary explanation a set of formal drill exercises printed on cards or worksheets. Practice with these will, it is hoped, develop skill in addition or multiplication. Another teacher may use a quite different technique, namely, present a number of simple but real problems. Objective materials may be included. Formal drill techniques will then follow the development of meaning and insight derived from the real problems. A teacher might drill pupils on long lists of grammatical forms, or he might approach these forms and practice thereon through language usage in real situations. The drill technique would again follow achievement of meaning. There are, however, usually several ways, techniques, available for use in any situation. Which technique is likely to be the more efficient, and how do we choose? Several factors influence choice: the purpose at the moment; the type of learner; the equipment available; the general policy of the school. Each of these factors may be interpreted as a set of *principles*. A principle may be defined for our purposes here, and in simple language, as a fundamental or general truth which may guide thinking or overt action.

Techniques in all fields arise in and are developed by efforts of individuals to achieve purposes. The efforts of teachers or learners may consist of simple trial and error, or their efforts may be guided by principles when these are available. Principles may arise either from critically analyzed experience or from systematic, controlled research. The modern process or "experience" units are designed to give learners at all levels opportunity to discover generalizations and principles. Modern methods are designed to teach (that is, give opportunity to discover) the principles and techniques of good thinking and problem-solving.

Education, for historical reasons we need not repeat here, has in the past dealt largely with techniques. The normal schools and early teachers colleges were often accused of overstressing *methods,* that is, techniques for teaching arithmetic, language, or spelling. Scholars in other fields have tended to criticize teachers colleges as superficial. On the other hand, techniques are inescapably necessary. To get anything done one must have facile command of techniques, that is, he must be able to perform certain activities with skill and dispatch. The real criticism should have been not that techniques were stressed, but that they were often stressed without reference to desirable goals and general principles.

Certain drill techniques widely used in arithmetic, for instance, will unquestionably produce speed and accuracy in computation, but at the same time produce a deep dislike for arithmetic. Drilling directly upon the material in standard arithmetic tests will undoubtedly enable learners to pass tests well above the expected norm, but the learning fades soon. The technique "got results" which were obvious, but its use violated principles of learning, which would lead us to consider other results. The use with all pupils of a technique which has worked with some pupils is also a violation of principle. Sample principles of learning applicable to the cases noted in the preceding paragraph, and to other similar cases, would include:

Learning should be purposeful.

Wide differences exist within all groups of learners in readiness, interest, level of understanding, and in many other traits.

Practice is needed to refine and perfect skills but this practice is more effective when distributed.

Pupils do not all learn at the same rate or in the same way.

Certain leaders in teacher education, disturbed by the criticism about stress on methods, swung to the opposite extreme and aimed at giving teachers wide contact with basic disciplines and the principles derived from these disciplines as applicable to education. The theory is that persons of good intelligence trained in basic principles would then evolve and invent techniques adequate in given situations. Unfortunately, this has not worked out. It has sometimes produced individuals who can speak well and correctly about goals and principles but who do not know what to do to achieve these goals.

A balance is necessary both in preservice education and in the supervision of in-service growth. Techniques are necessary and important—in fact, nothing could take place in any field without *ways* of doing things. Principles —that is, general truths or concepts or accepted tenets—are also necessary. New techniques are constantly being devised which are better ways of carrying out principles and which, furthermore, must be chosen discriminatively to fit given circumstances. Principles are guides that help in selecting techniques. Studies in both industry and education show that workers equipped with the "theory of the thing" are more efficient than those equipped only with sets of techniques which they may not fully understand.

Principles, techniques, and supervision. As we have indicated in the preceding paragraphs, supervision often has been engrossed in techniques with less attention to principles. Supervision has consisted too often of handing out techniques. In fact, in most instances the teachers who often complain temperamentally of "direction" or "control" by supervisors actually demand and desire the prescription of specific methods. They decry general or "theoretical" assistance from supervisors. This is true even today, despite the improvement of teacher training and the increasing understanding of teacher initiative and participation. The so-called "practical" teacher is the worst offender, since his level of training and insight is that of the device and not that of intelligent, independent invention of techniques based upon principles.

The spirit of modern supervision stresses not merely teacher growth but teacher participation in the study and improvement of the total teaching-learning situation. This necessitates a progressive movement away from the prescription of specific devices and toward the constant stimulation of the teacher to the understanding of principles and their use in guiding behavior. The teacher of the future should be a free, ingenious individual evolving his own minor, everyday techniques by intelligent use of principles. Hence, supervision, though still suggesting techniques when necessary, will always strive to develop in all workers the basic understandings underlying the various aspects of the entire educational organization and process.

The older volumes on supervision include elaborate discussion of everyday techniques. Subsequent chapters in this volume will present many, many illustrative techniques and explanations of their application. The chief emphasis, however, will be upon the basic structure of principles of education. The rest of this chapter is devoted to a listing of the principles of democracy as applied to supervision. The major techniques of supervision will be described in Section 2 of Chapter 6

Section 2

THE PRINCIPLES OF DEMOCRATIC SUPERVISION

The democratic philosophy will supply principles for supervision in the United States. A democratic philosophy will be a statement of those values, aims, and policies deemed valuable in the furtherance of democracy. Certain individuals claim that there is little or no agreement on the meaning and principles of democracy. On the contrary, there is very great agreement among competent students. Because of this argument in the field and because of the vital importance of democracy in the present era, a number of principles important in themselves and of particular importance for education and supervision will be described briefly. Detailed discussions are available in great volume. Simple, everyday illustrations may be cited.

The principles of democracy have for centuries rested upon reasoning from desired values. Today evidence, both clinical and experimental, supporting these principles is available and is steadily increasing in volume. Democracy can be shown in actual situations [2] to be less productive of frustration and maladjustment, less productive of pointless conflict, than any form of authoritarian control.

Democracy is a way of life and not limited to political forms. The average citizen thinks of democracy in terms of political organizations and procedures and rarely in any other way. This causes much of the confusion in current thought. Democracy did develop in the political field for reasons which are significant. Democracy and its political forms emerged as a defense against the constant violation of the rights of the common man by those in positions of power; in opposition to the doctrines of a class society, the divine right of kings. Catch phrases grew up, "all men are equal," "one man is as good as another." Participation in one's own government, through direct voting or through elected representatives, is the essence of political democracy.

Democracy actually is much broader, applying to the economic and social orders as well. We are engaged at the moment in a struggle to achieve an industrial and economic democracy parallel to the political. The principles of democracy apply to all of life.

Democracy's guarantee of political rights is not a universal equalitarianism. Political democracy guarantees to men the right to participate in their government, the right to a hearing before the law, the right to trial by their own neighbors, the right of access to those things which will enable each to develop his own unique personality and to live a decent life. All men are equal in these and similar things.

The political idea that all men are equal has been carried over by superficial thinkers, demagogues, and by the naïve populace to apply to any and all fields. The originators of the political doctrines of equality never intended this; a few even warned against it in the very beginning. Serious difficulties immediately arise. First, the incontrovertible facts of biology come into sharp collision with any such foolishness. Men are *not* equal in natural endowment of brains, in physical strength, in health, or in any innate characteristic. Second, training, opportunity, and the general effects of different environments still further increase and exaggerate the natural and inescapable *inequalities* among men. Men are enormously unequal in knowledge, in insight, in appreciation, in honesty, in ambition, in resourcefulness, in motor skills, and in many thousands of other characteristics.

[2] Clyde M. Campbell, ed., *Practical Applications of Democratic Administration* (New York, Harper, 1952). See Ch. 4 for an excellent elaboration of this point. The footnotes and bibliography contain what is practically an exhaustive listing of supporting references.

Abilities, contributions, and rewards will differ mightily between individuals. Men are guaranteed equality as citizens before the law. Legislative enactment cannot make them equal in any other way. It is nonsense to say that they are equal except as political beings or to attempt to treat them as equal in the home, in the market place, or in the kindergarten.

Democracy emphasizes the worth of persons. The clash between the concept of equality borrowed from the political field and flatly contradictory facts in other fields produced a new concept of inestimable worth. The basic principles of several religions, where they are not obscured by formulas and rituals, contributed. The concept was not the *equality* of men but the *worth* of men. The individual soul is of supreme value to God; the individual man, of supreme value to a decent society. Men are not equal in ideas or abilities. Men cannot be considered equal—but they can be considered. Men are not equal in their contributions to the common life, but they are equal in that each may contribute. Men are not equal in the worth of their contributions, but are equal in their right to the respect of the other contributors. Each individual is to contribute to the group life and to be respected for that contribution, however simple and humble. The concept of the worth of individual human beings, of respect for personality, and of development in creative ability is a principle of supreme importance everywhere in life.

Democracy has obligations as well as rights; a democratic conscience must be developed. Political rights within a democracy are guaranteed legally. The obligations and responsibilities which balance these rights cannot be demanded or required by law. Obligations and responsibilities must be freely assumed by free citizens. The increasing democratic participation in economic and social affairs must be balanced by self-assumed obligation to contribute one's share in making this participation work.

The weakest link in the democratic chain lies just here. Rights are accepted as a matter of course, are enjoyed, are demanded. We have not seen nor been properly educated to assume the inescapable obligations which the rights entail. Figures presented in *Learning the Ways of Democracy* [3] are disturbing. Two thousand high-school students were asked to define *democracy* in their own words. Ninety per cent could present acceptable statements, but of these over two-thirds defined democracy *solely* in terms of rights and liberties, with no reference to any responsiblities or obligations. Acceptable statements were confined also to political democracy; fewer than 8 per cent referred to economic democracy. Three out of four of the 8 per cent who did try to define economic democracy did so again in terms of privilege and not of responsibility.

Evidence of civic irresponsibility of youth was also discovered in the New York Regents Inquiry and is presented by Spaulding as follows: [4]

Despite some success in acquainting boys and girls with their rights as citizens, neither the school nor any other social influence has developed in these boys and girls an active social conscience. High-school pupils on the point of leaving school, display on the contrary, a disturbing inclination to evade social responsibility, and young people who have left school undertake few activities which will contribute in any way to the public good.

Members of the Educational Policies Commission, in the course of their tours to gather material, made another interesting discovery. Each high-school principal was asked to arrange interviews with three groups of students: (1) leaders in school affairs, (2) outlaws or nonconformists, and (3) "forgotten men," those who caused no trouble, attracted

[3] *Learning the Ways of Democracy,* Educational Policies Commission (Washington, NEA, 1940), pp. 46-50.

[4] Francis T. Spaulding, *High School and Life,* New York Regents Inquiry into the Character and Cost of Public Education Studies (New York, McGraw, 1938).

The same facts are revealed by current publications.

no attention, since they participated neither constructively nor obstructively. The leaders, those who led activities, held student offices, got things done, were a relatively small group but were getting considerable training in some aspects of democratic leadership. The outlaws and nonconformists were regarded unfavorably by the school staff, but the interviews revealed that these individuals were just as bright and just as loyal to the school as were the leaders. They came from less favored economic classes, were less well dressed, had less suave manners. Many were maladjusted, either mildly or seriously. These individuals were given little chance to participate democratically. They had been "outlawed" but clearly were not bad boys. Despite the incorrect attitudes of many school staffs, this group does not constitute a serious threat to democracy.

Coming to the third group, those who do practically nothing, the principals said that they had none or very few such students. The facts are that this group constitutes roughly 50 per cent of the student body. This group is a genuine drag upon the democratic process and may become in adult life the group easily led into viciously undemocratic beliefs and practices. They constitute a great challenge, that of getting them into the ongoing participatory life of the school which is the training for democracy.

The general problem, despite some of its darker aspects, is recognized; and excellent work is going forward. The volume quoted,

Learning the Ways of Democracy, is an excellent compilation of specific illustrations. Hanna's volume *Youth Serves the Community* [5] contains a provocative account of many projects together with an extensive bibliography. The article "Youth Has a Part to Play" [6] is also of great importance. The increased emphasis upon interrelation between school and community is a case in point.[7] The effort to provide learners at all levels with direct contact with the community as (*a*) observers, (*b*) participators, or (*c*) contributors to community processes is a direct effort to secure better education in the ways of democracy.

This all means that the problem of developing a "democratic conscience," the recognition and assumption of responsibility, is under increasingly effective attack. Everyone must receive education designed to develop social leadership and creative citizenship if democracy is not to fall upon evil days.

Adults are the victims of their training and experience. Democracy will not work without the development of the democratic conscience: a firm belief in the principles of democracy, a sincere and persistent attitude of desiring to conduct oneself democratically, and an unshakable faith in the ability of human beings to achieve the difficult levels of democratic life. Democracy will be successful to the degree that individuals gladly assume responsibility and fulfil obligations.

The individual who accepts respect for his individuality is under obligation to develop

---

[5] Paul Hanna, *Youth Serves the Community* (New York, Appleton-Century, 1936).

[6] M. R. Mitchell and others, "Youth Has a Part to Play," *Progressive Education* (February, 1942), pp. 87-109. Also published as a separate pamphlet.

[7] Edward G. Olsen, *School and Community,* 2nd ed. (New York, Prentice-Hall, 1954).

———, *School and Community Programs* (New York, Prentice-Hall, 1949). A companion book to the previous listing.

———, *The Modern Community School* (New York, Appleton-Century-Crofts, for the ASCD, 1953). Excellent cases.

Claude L. Williams and Gertrude C. Curtin, "The Development of Citizenship through Co-operation with Community Agencies," *Elementary*

Schools: The Frontline of Democracy, Twenty-second Yearbook, Department of Elementary School Principals (Washington, NEA, 1943).

S. E. T., Lund, *The School Centered Community* (New York, Anti-Defamation League of B'nai B'rith, 1949).

W. A. Yeager, *School-Community Relations* (New York, Dryden, 1951).

Clyde M. Campbell, ed., *op. cit.,* particularly Ch. 2. Excellent statement and supporting bibliography.

Many others are available.

Citizen Co-operation for Better Public Schools, Fifty-third Yearbook, National Society for the Study of Education (Chicago, Univ. of Chicago Press, 1954).

a personality worthy of respect. A society which wishes to be democratic must afford opportunity for such development. One who accepts the right to contribute to group discussion is under obligation to have something worth contributing. Koopman, Miel, and Misner present a brief, apt illustration of the relation between right and obligation: [8]

Fundamental Rights	*Fundamental Obligations*
To originate ideas regarding any question or problem having to do with individual or group welfare.	To be competent to originate worthwhile ideas, those that should command the attention of serious-minded members of the group.
To pass judgment upon the ideas expressed by others, more especially those pertaining to group welfare.	To be competent to criticize constructively rather than merely destructively, to get down to fundamental principles.
To initiate reforms, to "start something" which is believed to be for the benefit of the larger group rather than of a limited few.	To think things entirely through; to anticipate fully the consequences of initiating and promoting any movement; and to be prepared to accept gracefully the consequences of his action.
To propose or to promote sincerely and intelligently activities which are initiated by others until these have been finally accepted or rejected by the group.	To work vigorously to get one's ideas accepted. To co-operate fully in carrying out the expressed will of the majority.

Democracy emphasizes for the group the common good as social aim. Co-ordinate with emphasis upon the worth of the individual goes emphasis upon the constant improvement of group life, of society and its institutions. A democratic society, be it a nation or a school system, is a way of life which has for its aim the continuous improvement of the life of the group; the continuous discovery of higher values, improved

institutions, the continuously emerging and improving "good life." Democracy is not a fixed set of values and institutions to be perpetuated through indoctrination; it is evolutionary and flexible.

Society in its historical development has evolved mechanisms and institutions through which it lives and evolves. Certain institutions are regulatory in their effect upon the individual. This is not curtailment of individuality or disregard for personality. This is necessary to protect and conserve for all persons the values which are recognized as best for that society in the long run. Side by side with the controlling and regulatory institutions, others have evolved which free the individual and stimulate his growth. The individual grows in the worthy aspects of personality; society grows in those values which make for the highest type of life for the individual and for the group. To the extent that institutions of the group are participatory and the individual sees that they are, the institutions will be upheld.

Democracy emphasizes a flexible, functional organization of the group with freedom for all to contribute. The two preceding points lead naturally to a third, namely, the organization and functioning of a democratic group. Democracy means for some that there shall be no groups, divisions, or "classes" in our society. Currently there is both a social-class and an economic-class organization in our society. Upward mobility, though it seems to be decreasing at the moment, has saved us from the dangers of an undemocratic society. The words *groups* or *classes* have unfortunate connotations. Undemocratic groupings in society are based on the arbitrary and meaningless criteria of birth, wealth, "social position." Undemocratic groupings are relatively fixed. One

[8] D. J. MacDonald, "Democracy in School Administration—Some Fundamental Principles," *American School Board Journal* (September, 1921), pp. 31-32. Quoted in G. Robert Koopman, Alice Miel, and Paul J. Misner, *Democracy in School Administration* (New York, Appleton-Century-Crofts, 1943), p. 141.

class or group is superior or inferior to another. The Marxian concept of "class" is likewise wholly unacceptable in our society. The school society has suffered for generations from undemocratic organization with arbitrary divisions which gave some groups power over other groups.

Divisions or groupings of some sort are necessary in any organization. Democratic groupings should be based on necessary functions within group life and contributions to the common activity. Common interests and abilities are important. Democratic classifications must be flexible, open to all, and with free passage from group to group. Democratic groupings will not be distinguished as upper and lower; superiority and inferiority do not enter. Any function necessary and valuable to group life is therefore worthy of respect; the groups performing various functions are equally worthy of respect. Democratic groups are unified and integrated in their efforts not through external authority but through adherence to a set of ideals and to activities which have been set up by that group itself. Any and all members are free to initiate problems for discussion, to make suggestions, to volunteer to lead, to carry out commonly determined plans.

Democratic authority is derived from the situation, not from power under the law. The problem of authority and its exercise has puzzled many students of democracy. One group uses the slogans "This is a free country," "I can do as I please," "No one can tell me what to do." These slogans imply complete freedom from any restraint. Another group asks how anything is to be accomplished unless someone in authority directs and commands. How are incoherence and anarchy to be avoided unless authority is vested in someone and firmly operated? This implies authority in the traditional and legal sense, external authority applied by one group to another which had no part in setting up the authority.

Democratic thinking holds that the alternatives are not those of no authority versus external authority exercised without the consent of the governed. *Democratic authority is derived from the given situation under study.* What does this mean? A problem of policy or of procedure, let us say, has arisen and is being studied by a group of educational workers. Free discussion brings out that certain things should and could be done; they are demanded and made possible by known facts, by availability of local personnel and services. *Authority resides in the situation,* in educational science and philosophy, and in local resources. *Recognized and accepted by the group, this authority permeates the group.* What does this mean? The group has determined what should be done and how to do it. Various individuals will volunteer their expert services or will answer a call to serve. The group knows what to do and who is to do it. The group has authority derived from its co-operative study of the needs and possibilities. Within the plans carefully organized by the group in open meeting, everyone exercises authority. The authority is that of the group over itself and guaranteed by their study of the given situation. In place of "obedience to authority," we now have the voluntary and conscientious execution of one's own part in the common plan. This mutual recognition of responsibility is one of the obligations of democracy previously mentioned.

Democracy substitutes leadership for authority; recognizes that anyone may exercise leadership. Will co-operative group determination of policies and procedures "destroy" the "authority" of the superintendent, of the principal, even of the school board? This is an important question. Legally, authority is vested in certain boards and executive officers. This condition is likely to continue, at least on the books, for some time to come.

Leadership in democratic process. Distinction must be made between "status" leadership and "shared" or "emergent" leadership. A status leader is one who occupies a position of leadership through appointment, election, ownership, or force. A superintendent of schools, a classroom teacher, a chief of police, a factory owner, a gang leader, are all status leaders. Until modern times, status leaders exercised their leadership in authoritarian manner. Under democratic conditions the status leader can perform important functions. He should endeavor (a) to set a permissive tone for all affairs under his jurisdiction. This in turn encourages (b) free discussion, contribution, difference of opinion, and (c) leadership on the part of others as is necessary during the discussion or construction. The status leader, in addition to being primarily concerned with the improvement of human relations as indicated, may also (d) serve as resource person for certain phases of the work, and finally (e) aid in co-ordinating the efforts of all in the group.

Status leadership which operates democratically substitutes leadership for authority. Free expression is encouraged. Any member may at a given moment exercise leadership through a suggestion or an argument. Suggestions influence the trend of discussion, objections are raised, compromises are suggested. Each of these is a case of "shared" or emergent leadership. The study by Lewin, Lippitt, and White showed clearly the great superiority of democratic or shared leadership over both the authoritarian and the laissez-faire types. These concepts of leadership are further discussed in Chapter 7.

The superintendent may, however, be regarded as a professional leader and not as an executive; as one who exercises leadership by providing conditions for full participation and co-operation for the entire staff, for leadership on the part of others, and not as one who determines policies and issues orders to be carried out by others.

A community through its school board must have a trained, capable professional officer who can be depended upon to see that the school system is operated effectively. Citizens, teachers, and other educational workers need to have one person to whom they can go for certain types of advice and help. A designated head is necessary also to take action in cases of emergency and immediate need. Democratic thinking holds, however, that all this can be provided without relying upon "authority" in this person but by relying upon his skilled professional leadership. Leadership which provides for free group formulation of policies and programs of action will achieve desirable ends far better than authority ever can. A group so led thoroughly understands the demands of the situation and the action to be taken.

The superintendent who exercises leadership will further the ends of education far more effectively than one who relies on authority. A democratic educational system will further the ends of a democratic society far better than an authoritarian system. School administration in early days borrowed much from industry and business, both principle and practice, even though the ends to be served were quite different. Today it is interesting to note that business and industry, which so prided themselves on efficiency of organization and administration resting upon external authority, are increasingly using the methods of democracy in management. The literature on this is significant and rapidly increasing.

When all are imbued with democratic ideals, the imposition of the will of one person upon another is not an issue. It is only sensible to recognize, however, that not all will rise to the opportunity to participate co-operatively. Persons who are lazy, who are secure in their positions, who are obstinate either because of honest ignorance or because of mental inability to keep up with the group, will remain inert or will actively oppose and sabotage co-operative programs. The un-co-operative individual, no matter what the cause, is a challenge to democratic principles and methods. Each is entitled to honest consideration, to diagnosis, to sympathetic guidance and assistance. Opportunities for growth should be extended here just as with co-operative persons. Democratic means are winning uncounted victories and bringing to participation, even to important creative contribution, many who were unco-operative. It would be silly sentimentalism, however, to deny the exercise of legalistic authority for the removal of these persons when all else has been fairly tried and has failed.

Authority then, with the exception just noted which should occur so rarely as to be almost negligible, should give way to *responsibility* for leadership. Chief responsibility rests upon the designated leader but this responsibility is shared by each and every member of the staff.

Democracy uses the method of group discussion, deliberation, and decision for solving problems. The principles and processes of group discussion will be presented in detail in Chapter 7. We merely state the principle here to accompany other basic principles.

Democracy utilizes experts. Democratic discussion in which all may participate has a place for the expert. This is especially true when dealing with genuinely technical phases of education. Common sense, so valuable and sound when dealing with the nontechnical, often repeated, everyday concerns of human activity, is practically always wrong when it opposes strictly technical conclusions. Experts in all aspects of educational procedure should participate by supplying data and tested conclusions; sometimes by aiding in further experimental or logical investigation.

The differences in the use of experts in democratic and nondemocratic situations are significant. The expert participating in democratic discussion is (1) just one member of the group on a footing with the others, (2) whose contribution, no matter how expert, is not imposed on the group by authority, nor uncritically accepted by the group. The expert, (3) accepts responsibility for making his contribution clear to nontechnically trained colleagues, of reducing it to practical implications for various members of the group, of cheerfully supplying the background of experimental analysis which supports the conclusions. The contributions of the expert are (4) subject to revision, not through uncontrolled argument, but through further experimental work or critical logical analysis. The discussion in Chapter 2 may be recalled here.

Democracy emphasizes experimentalism. Group decisions are made for the purpose of directing action. Experience with the tryout of group decisions will influence later and continuing deliberations. There will be continuous experimental interaction between decisions and tryouts. The democratic spirit and the scientific attitude are at one in their emphasis upon experimentalism.

Section 3

SUPERVISION RECEIVES GUIDANCE FROM THE DEMOCRATIC PHILOSOPHY AND FROM THE FINDINGS OF SCIENCE

Guidance for supervision from the democratic philosophy. Democracy has, first, made untenable the older relationships between the leader and the led. Imposition and direction as techniques have been discredited. Second, it is recognized that leadership and creativity appear upon all levels and among all types of persons. Third, co-operative techniques replace those of central determination and direction. Policies, plans, techniques, and the evaluation of these are group-determined. All types of persons are invited to contribute to the formulation of plans and decisions which affect them: pupils, parents, community leaders and organizations, teachers, general and specialized educational workers, administrators and so forth. All persons from superintendent to humblest cadet teacher are regarded as co-workers on a common task. Each has a contribution worthy of respect, even though differing greatly in weight or importance. Fourth, authority is derived from analysis of the needs and possibilities of a situation.

Democracy anywhere is participatory group life enjoyed by free individuals possessing maximum opportunities for participation. This sounds silly and utopian when we consider the long tradition of absolute authority in the management of school affairs, the flagrant misuse of authority by many leaders. Educational workers on some levels are still looked upon as hired hands. Boards and superintendents often speak of "my" school or "our" school system. Democracy will not be achieved without many years of arduous effort and courage in leadership; without extended education in the nature of democracy itself—but it can be done. The proof is that along with autocracy in school administration in many places, there exists in other places excellent illustration of thoroughly democratic participation by all in forming policies, in setting up supervisory programs, in organizing for curriculum construction, and in many other activities.

Guidance for supervision from the philosophic method. Supervision will increasingly consider the nature, the remote aims, the values of the great society within which education operates. The immediate community as a whole, its resources and facilities, its problems, its aspirations, its whole social climate, will be considered as the matrix of immediate educational problems and procedures. Outcomes will be evaluated in the light of good both to local society and to the larger one within which smaller communities exist. Philosophic supervision will increasingly see education as a whole correlative with life as a whole, affecting individuals who are living wholes. Subject matter, materials, the immediate teaching-learning processes will be evaluated not in and for themselves but only as they serve a remote policy agreed upon by the society involved.

Philosophic procedures and conclusions differ significantly from the procedures and conclusions of the untrained thinker in that they are likely to be more *closely allied with some conception of life as a whole,* that is, to be more inclusive of all conditioning factors, more sensitive to remote consequences.

Definite limitations and difficulties exist in the use of the philosophic method. First, it rests upon mastery of the canons of logic, a system very difficult for the average thinker to master. Second, it is naturally liable to the well-known pitfalls and fallacies which attend subjective processes. Third, it depends upon objectivity in language in contrast to objectivity through measurement as in the scientific method. Competent, honest thinkers will differ because of inherent difficulties in language usage. The current emphasis on semantics is in part due to the increasing necessity of clarifying language and meaning.

The common criticism that philosophic conclusions are provisional, tentative, and incomplete is not a legitimate attack upon the method. All conclusions when properly understood, whether scientific or philosophic, are tentative.

Guidance for supervision from science and its method. First, the scientific method focuses attention upon getting the facts, upon determining the situation as it exists, upon diagnosis. Supervision, in setting up objectives, in determining needs, in examining resources, in planning procedures, and in evaluating results will be influenced by the methods and attitudes of science. Second, supervisors are increasingly using scientific methods or practical adaptations of them, particularly experimentation, and scientific attitudes in attacking practical everyday problems. Third, the scientific movement in education has amassed a huge body of background material. Many, many facts are known about various aspects of the educational process. Administrators, supervisors, and teachers, no matter how gifted and ingenious, can never be fully competent if ignorant of the technology of educational science. Though by no means the whole of it, training for supervision must include sound background in technology. The supervisor must know and utilize through adaptation to his own unique situation such conclusions as we have. Gross blunders can be avoided by knowledge and use of scientific methods and materials. Uncontrolled subjective judgments, sentimental or even temperamental judgments and conclusions, give way to controlled subjective judgments, to objectively determined facts, to reasonable standards and principles. Scientific findings always may be attacked if one can point to flaws in the original investigation, to failure in controls, to errors in the analysis of data or in drawing conclusions. The suggestion of refinements in techniques or of new inquiries to be made is always desirable. The rejection of scientific conclusions on the basis of one's "experience," or because one's opinions are different, is childish.

Scientific procedures, data, and conclusions differ significantly from the procedures, data, and conclusions of untrained workers in six respects: greater *precision,* greater *objectivity* (or *verifiability*), closer *impartiality,* greater *sufficiency of basis,* greater *expertness,* and more *systematic organization.*

Definite limitations appear when scientific methods are applied to the social sciences, of which education is one. First, education is a dynamic, complex, social process, hence very difficult to control and measure. Second, the materials of any social science, notably education, are different from the materials of the physical sciences. The data in education are not as discrete, as exact, as reliable in performance as the data in the physical sciences. Third, the sharply analytic attack, essential to scientific investigation may actually interfere with or invalidate an inquiry in education. The strict control and even exclusion of certain factors in an experiment upon children's learning, so necessary in controlled scientific investigations, may actually destroy the value of the study. The very factors excluded may be vital influences within any normal learning situation. Certain errors not inherent in the method are sometimes introduced by given individuals. A too rigid insistence, first, upon purely "objective" data leads into the

error of rejecting the valuable subjective data which can be produced by trained and competent thinkers. Second, there is sometimes a tendency to overgeneralize, or third, to undergeneralize.

Dynamic methods of problem-solving are more important than insistence on rigid adherence to formal methods. The philosophic and the scientific methods are not mutually exclusive. A real situation blends them into problem-solving procedures. Supervision is not the operation of formulas, routines, rules of thumb. It is not the inflexible application of experimentally validated conclusions, valuable as these are. Education and supervision within it is an intellectual adventure requiring ingenuity and initiative in meeting the succession of problems which constitute the day's work. The best scientific and philosophic training in the world will not show us how to supervise—it will show us how to find out how to supervise.

Supervision is both scientific and democratic. A few individuals still speak, write, and supervise as if science and democracy were antagonistic, or at least not easily combined. The truth is that each is necessary in any integrated theory and practice. Each is a fundamental, necessary, and inescapable factor in any mature thinking about anything of importance. They are one in their emphasis on experimentation. The misunderstanding arises from superficial thinking, or through contact with definitely poor practice. The terms *scientific supervision* or *democracy in supervision* may each be used by different persons in different situations with greatly differing connotations. In one situation, either term may mean supervision that is fine and splendid; in another situation, the same term may refer to supervision that is unfortunate and detrimental.

Scientific or democratic supervision at their worst. In order to emphasize the positive, we will examine first the negative conceptions. At its worst, *scientific supervision* means overemphasis upon quick and narrowly objective results in fundamentals. It may force teachers to adhere closely to the "normal curve" in distributing marks. Detailed rating schemes may be used. Remedial programs of a mechanical and "subject-matter" type may be utilized. There is danger of to much reliance upon limited, fragmentary, and misleading although truly objective, data. There is often no scrutiny of what is called "objective." Carried to extremes, the uncritical, unimaginative, bungling use of scientific tools antagonizes and discourages first-rate teachers. It results in a most undesirable formalization of procedure, whether of teaching or of supervision. Science aided us in disposing of the highly undesirable "personal" authority of individuals in power. There is often substituted an equally undesirable, woodenly "impersonal," authority of science.

At its worst, *democracy in supervision* is a euphemism covering genuine inefficiency and weak leadership. Superficial exponents of *democracy in supervision* wander around the school system scattering sunshine wherever they go. They pat teachers on the back, sympathize with their grievances, indulge their whims, give little help, and insist on nothing. These procedures, when accompanied by strong leadership in helping teachers to self-analysis and improvement, may be powerful influences for good. Operated at random and for the sake of the moment only, they constitute spineless supervision which is very likely to result in easy popularity and a great deal of sentimentality. If teachers do not grow, if pupils do not learn, there is much talk about "placing responsibility on the teacher," "stimulating growth by noninterference," "encouraging teachers to do things their own way," the "sinfulness of imposition." Not only is nothing required in the way of standards or results, but nothing is even suggested. In this sense, the phrase *democracy in supervision* means either extreme laziness or muddle-headed stupidity.

An ignorant enthusiasm for the science of education and for scientific method seems to make some persons harsh, arrogant, and dogmatic. Similarly unbalanced emphasis on democracy and freedom seems to send some dancing among the daffodils when they should be attending to the spring plowing.

Scientific or democratic supervision at their best. At its best, *scientific supervision* means securing as complete and accurate a picture as possible of current school practices. Then all scientific knowledge about the learning process, materials and methods of learning, is utilized to improve conditions. The scientific supervisor is critical, analytic, discriminating, and objective in thinking. He must know and use the findings of scientific research, know and use the best standardized tests in their proper place, know the limitations of these tests. He must know the experimental and statistical data on individual differences, on adapting the schools to individuals. Scientific supervision means respect for such facts as we have and proper use of facts. It means knowing how to derive and check for validity new and current facts. It means replacement of muddled "atmospheric" analyses and suggestions by competent, objective, analytic methods.

At its best, *democracy in supervision* means enlisting the abilities of teachers, principals, and superintendents in the co-operative enterprise of improving teaching or other aspects of the teaching-learning situation. The democratic supervisor has and expresses confidence in fellow-workers; he evaluates teaching on the basis of the understandings, attitudes, and skills actually acquired by the pupils, regardless of whether these were secured through teaching procedures suggested by him or not. His classroom interviews with teachers are real conferences characterized by interchange of ideas and suggestions; his teachers' meetings are participatory with opportunity for teachers to present opinions, to differ, to demonstrate. The democratic supervisor encourages self-direction, self-criticism, and self-control among teachers. He realizes that growth requires not only opportunity but time.

Functioning combination of science and democracy is necessary. It is futile to say that these two are antagonistic or that they cannot be combined. They have already been and are always used together in any competent thinking. Enough has been said in the preceding paragraphs so that a brief summary will suffice here. Science contributes precision, "factness," law, and a method of determining facts. The philosophic method in general contributes sensitivity to aims, purposes, and values, and focuses attention upon implications. The democratic philosophy in particular places emphasis upon the social outcome, puts attention upon personality and individuality, gives us a rational basis for authority, and emphasizes participation and co-operation within democratic authority. Both science and democracy utilize the experimental attitude and attack. Democracy implies fair dealing with all persons concerned, and science means fair dealing with all pertinent facts.

Good supervision is creative. The foregoing discussions, particularly of democratic procedure, make clear that democratic life in any field will develop creativity. Democratic supervision which provides ample opportunity for participatory discussions and group formulation of policies and plans, which treats all contributions with respect no matter how small or simple, inevitably stimulates creative expression from many, perhaps from all, of the group. Current belief is that every normal individual is capable of creative expression in some degree. Growth and development of the total personnel, including community members, is definitely stimulated through creative expression. Supervision, in addition to providing opportunities for creative contribution, will deliberately seek latent talent, will deliberately manipulate the environment to provide settings for creative expression.

Creative participation grows somewhat slowly. Leadership must be persistently resourceful in providing opportunities and in utilizing contributions as they appear. The effect of creative supervision and administration will be reflected directly in creative teaching and learning. Creative leadership in the long run is vitally necessary to the success of democratic life.

The term *creative* is used here in its original root meaning which has dominated usage for centuries: the suggesting, devising, inventing, producing something new, unique, not-before-existent. The more recent usage which regards as creative any recall of known materials or discovery of already existing materials is definitely rejected. Recall and discovery of known materials are necessary and valuable in all problem-solving. Contributions of this type and the individuals making them should be recognized, but this is not to be confused with creativity.

Supervision is increasingly professional. Supervision is a part of the general teaching profession, which is itself not yet fully professional. Supervision, like teaching, is moving steadily toward professional status. A specialized body of knowledge is growing up, together with a body of techniques which cannot be acquired easily or out of hand by amateurs. Broad cultural training in addition to the professional is increasingly demanded. Constant study is required to keep abreast of developments. Obligations and responsibilities are self-recognized and beginning to be stated in codes of ethics. Initiative and responsibility are increasingly earned by professional supervisors. Self-evaluation and self-directed study and growth are increasingly evident.

Supervision, like teaching, cannot eliminate incompetents from the profession. Physicians and lawyers can be disbarred, but educators have not yet recognized this professional obligation. Tenure is still flaunted as a defense even when gross incompetence and deliberate dishonesty are clearly manifest. Eventually education as a profession must face this problem of self-evaluation and self-regulation, of professional regulation of standards. A few rare instances are known in which teaching groups have themselves urged incompetents to leave the local situation for the greater good of the greater number.

Good supervision is judged by its results, seeks to evaluate itself in the light of accepted purposes. This principle is largely self-explanatory in the light of foregoing pages. The techniques of supervisory evaluation, together with some sample investigations, are set forth in Chapter 18.

Supervision proceeds through an orderly, co-operatively planned series of activities. The principles and procedures for supervisory planning are elaborated in Chapter 6.

Section 4

A SUMMARY OUTLINE OF PRINCIPLES GOVERNING SUPERVISION

A summary statement has been found valuable for quick reference. Many details will be developed in later chapters, general principles only being listed here.

PRINCIPLES GOVERNING THE OPERATION OF SUPERVISION

1. Administration is *ordinarily* concerned with providing material facilities and with operation in general.

2. Supervision is *ordinarily* concerned with improving the setting for learning in particular.

3. Administration and supervision considered *functionally* cannot be separated or set off from each other. The two are co-ordinate, correlative, complementary, mutually shared functions in the operation of educational systems. The provision of any and all conditions favorable to learning is the common purpose of both. (See Chapter 5 for detailed sub-principles and procedures.)

4. Good supervision is based on philosophy and science.

    a. Supervision will be sensitive to ultimate aims and values, to policies, with special reference to their adequacy.

    b. Supervision will be sensitive to "factness" and to law, with special reference to their accuracy.

    c. Supervision will be sensitive to the emergent, evolutionary, nature of the universe and of democratic society in particular, hence should be permeated with the experimental attitude, and engage constantly in re-evaluation of aims and value, of policies, of materials and methods.

5. Good supervision is (in the United States) based upon the democratic philosophy.

    a. Supervision will respect personality and individual differences between personalities, will seek to provide opportunities for the best expression of each unique personality.

    b. Supervision will be based upon the assumption that educational workers are capable of growth. It will accept idiosyncrasies, reluctance to co-operate, and antagonism as human characteristics, just as it accepts reasonableness, co-operation, and energetic activity. The former are challenges; the latter, assets.

    c. Supervision will endeavor to develop in all a democratic conscience, that is, recognition that democracy includes important obligations as well as rights.

    d. Supervision will provide full opportunity for the co-operative formulation of policies and plans, will welcome and utilize free expression and contributions from all.

    e. Supervision will stimulate initiative, self-reliance, and individual responsibility on the part of all persons in the discharge of their duties.

    f. Supervision will substitute leadership for authority. Authority will be recognized as the authority of the situation and of the facts within the situation. Personal authority if necessary will be derived from group planning.

    g. Supervision will work toward co-operatively determined functional groupings of the staff, with flexible regrouping as necessary; will invite specialists when advisable.

6. Good supervision will employ scientific methods and attitudes in so far as those methods and attitudes are applicable to the dynamic social processes of education; will utilize and adapt to specific situations scientific findings

Level	Social Theory	Program of supervision	Methods of Supervision	Flexibility of Program	Staff Relationships: Teacher-Supervisors	Teacher Freedom in Choice of Materials and Methods	Respect for Personality	Source of Individual Growth	Methods of Individual Growth
I. PURPOSING.									
A. By individuals									
1. Leaders, experts at work on frontier problems.	Democracy; leader devotes himself to a problem for common good.	Self-supervision; eventual contribution to group program.	Continuous self-initiated attention to needs, new discoveries, etc., science guides.	Complete; individual ability, insight and energy control.	General supervisory climate stimulates individual; supervisor on consultancy basis.	Complete under guidance of science and philosophy.	Complete whenever interaction takes place.	Individuals own desire for greater professional understanding and skill Urge to creative work.	Continuous self-directed study, experimentation or creative endeavor.
2. Any individual at work studying and striving to improve his own work.	Democracy; individual reconstructs his contribution to welfare of the group.	(Same as above.)	Continuous self-survey to locate needs; science guides	(Same as above.)	(Same as above.)	(Same as above.)	(Same as above.)	(Same as above.)	(Same as above.)
B. By groups working on self-selected problems to improve their own effectiveness.	(Same as above substituting *group* for *individual* in all instances.)								
II. CO-OPERATION.	Democracy; co-operative voluntary group formulation of policy and program.	Co-operatively derived from situation and based on needs.	Continuous co-operative self-survey of needs; aid on service basis.	Complete; needs and problems control.	Mutual recognition of worth; consultancy relationship; stimulation to creative work.	Teacher has large freedom of choice in terms of children's needs and problems, with due regard to science and philosophy.	Complete between persons guided by common science and philosophy.	General stimulation of climate of co-operative endeavor. Individuals own desire to improve and to contribute. Opportunities given for creative work.	Continuous co-operative group study of needs of situation; of new materials in educational science and philosophy; through experimental and creative processes.

III. PARTICIPATION IN PREDETERMINED PLAN.									
A. Liberal policy.	Benevolent autocracy leaning toward democracy; voluntary participation in carrying out plan of superiors would be hoped for.	Predetermined plan is imposed but suggestions and modifications within it are given a hearing.	Participation of all is invited in carrying out plan from central office; some freedom for research and creative work but within plan.	Some provision for choice of activities.	Training-guidance relationship dominant; some leadership with individual problems; inspection minimized.	Teacher selects from approved course of study which allows for considerable variation.	Partial, degree differing with situations.	Opportunities, few or many, to contribute and to be recognized.	Voluntary participation (sometimes required) in study programs suggested and supplied by superiors; some choice, a little individual experimentation.
B. Conservative policy.	Paternalism; directed and controlled participation in plan of superiors.	Predetermined plan is imposed; minimum only of suggestion and modification received.	Teachers assigned to activities and study groups with no or very little consideration of individual needs or interests; a little freedom for research and creative work.	A little provision for choice of activities.	Inspection and training-guidance are both prominent. A little choice permitted in choice of practices.	Teacher selects from list of designated methods and materials.	Recognition of individuals whom those in authority know best; attractive submission to authority.	Individuals acceptance and willingness to develop approved practices.	Assigned participation in study programs suggested and supplied by superiors; little choice; very little or no individual experimentation.
IV. DOMINATION.	Autocracy; reactionary effort to maintain existing order without change; obedience to authority, not to philosophy and science.	Predetermined plan often without reference to needs; carried out as it stands.	Imposition of practices approved by supervisor; may be based on tradition, even on prejudice: no research.	None; visits and meetings scheduled; attendance at conferences required; no variations.	Inspection and checking of performance. Imposition of practices.	Teacher has no choice; follows procedures laid down in advance.	None; individual does as he is told; complete submission to external authority.	Obedience to orders; fear of losing position.	None actually—growth if it can be called such comes through careful study of the demands of superiors.

* This chart was developed by the author of this chapter from one originally constructed by Brueckner and which appeared in the first edition of this volume. The seventh column in the chart is not co-ordinate with the others. The topic treated is actually a sub-point under the heading for column six, and is inserted for illustrative purposes. A complicated chart form would have been necessary to indicate this.

concerning the learner, his learning processes, the nature and development of personality; will co-operate occasionally in pure research.

7. Good supervision, in situations where the precise controlled methods of science are not applicable, will employ processes of dynamic problem-solving in studying, improving, and evaluating its products and processes. Supervision either by scientific methods or through orderly thought processes will constantly derive and use data and conclusions which are more objective, more precise, more sufficient, more impartial, more expertly secured, and more systematically organized than are the data and conclusions of uncontrolled opinion.

8. Good supervision will be creative and not prescriptive.

    a. Supervision will determine procedures in the light of the needs of each supervisory teaching-learning situation.

    b. Supervision will provide opportunity for the exercise of originality and for the development of unique contributions, of creative self-expression; will seek latent talent.

    c. Supervision will deliberately shape and manipulate the environment.

9. Good supervision proceeds by means of an orderly, co-operatively planned and executed series of activities. (See Chapter 6 for detailed sub-principles and processes.)

10. Good supervision will be judged by the results it secures.

11. Good supervision is becoming professional. That is, it is increasingly seeking to evaluate its personnel, procedures, and results; it is moving toward standards and toward self-supervision.

PRINCIPLES GOVERNING THE PURPOSES OF SUPERVISION

1. The ultimate purpose of supervision is the promotion of pupil growth, and hence eventually the improvement of society.

2. A second general purpose of supervision is to supply leadership in securing continuity and constant readaptation in the educational program over a period of years; from level to level within the system; and from one area of learning experience and content to another.

3. The immediate purpose of supervision is co-operatively to develop favorable settings for teaching and learning.

    a. Supervision, through all means available, will seek improved methods of teaching and learning.

    b. Supervision will create a physical, social, and psychological climate or environment favorable to learning.

    c. Supervision will co-ordinate and integrate all educational efforts and materials; will supply continuity.

    d. Supervision will enlist the co-operation of all staff members in serving their own needs and those of the situation; will provide ample, natural opportunities for growth by all concerned in the correction and prevention of teaching difficulties, and for growth in the assumption of new responsibilities.

    e. Supervision will aid, inspire, lead, and develop that security which liberates the creative spirit.

Levels of supervisory principle and operation. The chapter has developed, it is hoped, acceptable principles of supervision. Wide variation in understanding, in acceptance, and in operation of these principles are observable in the field. The chart on pages 86-87 presents an outline of levels which may contribute to better understanding, and which should enable students and field workers to identify the levels upon which they now operate or are forced to operate. Scrutiny of the chart [9] and identification of ways to improve local procedures may aid in raising levels of practice.

[9] A brief, compact chart similar to ours will be of interest to students. See F. C. Ayer, *Fundamentals of Instructional Supervision* (New York, Harper, 1954), p. 116. This entire volume is devoted largely to presentation of principles and may be used in conjunction with the present chapter.

CHAPTER SUPPLEMENT

QUESTIONS FOR GENERAL INTRODUCTORY DISCUSSION

Recall here the six questions at the close of Chapter 1. These questions will prove useful with groups of young students, to those with a limited amount of experience, and for field workers who are just beginning to explore this area. The next set of questions can be used with groups of more experience.

1. State in everyday common-sense language why the nature of the basic principles underlying any activity is of such importance.

2. State in your own words why principles are superior to techniques as guides to practice. Use the materials in the book, but go beyond them if possible. (Demonstrate your understanding by translating into words unmistakably your own.) Specific illustrations from your experience are desirable here.

3. Why is the "prescription of specific practices" very often a form of quackery? Many school workers are always demanding "practical" courses. What is the error in their thinking here? Again illustrations as well as reasons are desirable.

EXERCISES AND REPORTS

1. Examine critically the summary of principles in Section 4 of this chapter.
   a. If there are any principles omitted which you think should be included mention them and present arguments. Be sure you actually have a separate and new point and not one already legitimately subsumed under one of the present headings.
   b. If there are any principles with which you cannot agree, or which for any reason you think should be left out, present your arguments.

2. State in your own words what is meant by the principle, "authority is derived from the situation."

Give illustrations from life showing that, in truth, authority is always actually derived from the situation, even though this is not clearly recognized. What factors have blinded us to this fact?

Attempt to show how the application of this principle would change any given procedures now used or observed by you. If you know a system in which this principle does operate, you may substitute here descriptions of the practices which exemplify the principle.

3. State in your own words what is meant by the principle, "leadership should be substituted for authority." Give illustrations from life.

Give the arguments in support of this change if you did not include them in answering the above question.

Attempt to show how application of this principle would change any given procedures now used or observed by you. You may substitute descriptions of practice if you wish, as in the preceding question.

4. Develop a statement of specific implications for supervision of the first principle of democracy, namely, respect for personality.

5. Develop a statement of specific implications to supervision of the democratic principle that obligations are involved as well as rights. A statement may be made here also relating the teacher to the parent, to the administration.

6. Illustrate from real life the wise use of experts in problem-solving. Show, if possible, the consequences of refusal to consult informed persons, a thing which is very common in public life. Duplicate this question for education.

7. Give specific illustrations from experience or observation of the rise of democratic administration or supervision. The instances may be major or minor.

8. Give specific illustrations, preferably from your own experience or observation of the detrimental type, of scientific supervision or of democracy in supervision.

9. Mention a few specific changes which would need to be made in common or typical supervisory practices if we followed any one or several of the principles as set forth in this chapter. (This, of course, has been done for certain of the principles as noted in previous questions. Elaborate here for principles we have not discussed so far.)

QUESTIONS BASED ON SPECIFIED READINGS

Read the fable of Joe Brown which is contained in Chapter 1 of the Fifteenth Yearbook of the Department of Supervisors and Directors of Instruction, 1943.

State three or four principles which you can derive from this story of Joe Brown. Make any additional comments that you wish.

Read de Huszar, *Practical Applications of Democracy,* the preface, Chapters 1, 2, and 10.

State in your own words what is the meaning of "Consent Democracy," "Talk Democracy," and "Do Democracy." Make any other comments you wish.

This entire volume is very small and can well be read by all students. It is an exceptionally valuable reference.

Read in Koopman, Miel, and Misner, *Democracy in School Administration,* Chapters 1 and 2. What can you derive from these chapters which might be of use to you as a supervisor?

WRITTEN EXERCISE

1. Prepare a brief, critical, and well-organized account of the supervisory principles which actually operate in a situation where you are now working (or have recently worked). Distinguish clearly, if necessary, between the principles set forth in bulletins and reports in your system and those which actually operate as judged by the overt procedures used. Include printed or mimeographed materials if available. Use the chart on pages 86-87, if it is of aid, but ignore it otherwise.

Indicate in the course of your account wherein the principles both announced and actual, if the two do not coincide, need to be changed. What do you propose to do to bring about changes if you are in the position to do so in the given situation?

SUGGESTED READINGS

CAMPBELL, Clyde M., ed., *Practical Applications of Democratic Administration* (New York, Harper, 1952).

Department of Supervisors and Directors of Instruction, the Fifth, Sixth, Eleventh and Fifteenth Yearbooks. Titles and years are given in the bibliography at the end of Ch. 1. The Fifteenth Yearbook, particularly Chs. 1 and 2, is of interest here. Ch. 1 contains the famous fable of Joe Brown.

————, Eighteenth Yearbook, *Leadership Through Supervision* (Washington, NEA, 1946).

DE HUSZAR, George B., *Practical Applications of Democracy* (New York, Harper, 1945). A direct and vigorous demand for less talk and more action in democracy. An unusually valuable reference.

KOOPMAN, G. Robert, MIEL, Alice, and MISNER, Paul J., *Democracy in School Administration* (New York, Appleton-Century-Crofts, 1943). The whole volume is very valuable, and Chs. 1, 2 and 3 are of special value here.

MILLER, Van, and SPAULDING, Willard B., *The Public Administration of American Schools* (Yonkers, World Book, 1952).

MOEHLMAN, Arthur B., *School Administration,* rev. ed. (Boston, Houghton, 1951). This is a monumental volume covering all phases of administration with an excellent historical philosophical background.

MORT, Paul, *Principles of School Administration* (New York, McGraw, 1946). This book on administration contains one of the best set of general principles that is now available. It may be read in conjunction with this chapter.

RORER, John A., *Principles of Democratic Supervision* (New York, Teachers College, Bureau of Publications, Columbia Univ., 1942). This is an exhaustive, critical analysis of all writings to the date given. It is one of the most valuable single references on the Principles of Supervision under Democracy.

Each of the ten recent books on supervision listed at the end of Chapter 1 may be consulted here on this particular topic; namely, Principles of Supervision.

Chapter 5

♦·♦·♦·♦·♦·♦·♦·♦

Administrative Organization for Supervision: A Social Structure

ADMINISTRATION is commonly interpreted as referring to managing, operating, or directing an organization of any type. Traditionally the function of administration is to "run things," to get things done. Administration has usually achieved its purposes by issuing orders or directives. An organization or machinery is set up with defined channels through which operation proceeds. These common conceptions were rarely challenged until recent times. Let us examine some of the widespread and uncritically accepted beliefs about administration.

First, let us ask, are other persons besides administrators involved in "getting things done," in managing operations? Yes, there are many other persons. Second, to whom are orders and directives issued; who receives these orders? Orders are directed to persons. Third, does it make any difference in the carrying out of directions if those receiving them understand both the instructions and the purposes involved? Yes, it makes a great deal of difference. Fourth, and even more important, does it make any difference if the persons agree or disagree with the directives or the purposes? The older view was that those receiving orders should not "question the authority of those whom God hath called into power over us." The moderns are likely to be a bit contumacious about this. Fifth, do the beliefs, particularly the feelings and emotions of persons, affect efficiency either in carrying out orders or in operating on their own? The early view was that such questions were ridiculous. We know now that these questions are fundamental.

Two factors in modern times have changed our beliefs. First, the rise of the democratic view of life, the better understanding of democratic values as applied to life. We need not repeat here the summary of the preceding chapters. Second, the truly great amount of information developed by research concerning the motives of men, the dynamics of human behavior, the factors making for frustration or for creativity. The basic concepts of administration today differ materially from those of yesteryear.

Administration is a social process. The chief responsibility of administration is co-ordination, that is, developing relationships among persons within a group which will enable that group to function at its best. The chief activity of administration is the exercise of leadership toward this aim. The important but subsidiary processes of administration, "getting things done," will be far better achieved when all persons have had a part in setting up goals and processes, in differentiating the authority necessary, in developing an organization and process within which these persons are to live and work together. Participation is the key.

Commitment by all to democratic values and processes is necessary, as set forth in earlier chapters. First, group process, or group attack on common problems, does not merely pool experience and resource, it frees creative processes as does no other method. Second, the most effective authority is that of the group over itself, derived from the situation, and exercised for the good of the group. Authority of any group over another without consent of the latter is now regarded as being ineffective. Third, administrative directives are progressively replaced by co-operatively determined policies and programs.

The preceding statements are based largely upon philosophic analysis and upon research done outside education, or within educational areas outside administration. Administration as an area is characterized by a tragic lack of research, even though research is cited by all as one function of administration. First, there is little or no fundamental theory of administration. Areas and problems susceptible to basic research are therefore not clearly seen. Many texts in administration actually deal with operation and often make no mention of any theory. The many studies of operation, frequency of activity, of conflict between administrative personnel ap-pearing in the literature, have no meaning in and by themselves. The writers, in quoting these freely in following sections, have interpreted them always in the light of basic principles of education and of democracy as set forth in preceding chapters. Second, the average administrator is an operator of school systems who seldom studies controlling general aims and philosophy. The "cult of the practical man" has made great strides with administrators in all lines, many of whom are unaware that the practical man is often a mere manipulator of routines, and quite often the source of literally stupendous blunders in human affairs. No one decries practicality, but practicality unenlightened by systematic theory [1] is genuinely dangerous in complex social organizations. Theory developed without regard to facts is also dangerous but very rarely gets into operation.

Section 1

AN ORGANIZATION IS NECESSARY TO PROVIDE CO-ORDINATION OF EFFORT

Multiple educational services within a system need co-ordination. The word *administration* ordinarily brings to mind the machinery of organization. Machinery is necessary but it is not the end; it must be kept subsidiary to the functions it serves. Flexible, adaptable, made-on-the-spot machinery is more valuable than static, predetermined procedure. Principles and objectives are more important than the machinery.

The basic cause of problems necessitating administrative machinery of some sort is that the school system of the United States offers an ever larger number of services to the children, to the staff, and to community members. The trend toward increased service seems destined to continue, despite some opposition in a few quarters. The emerging social theory of the times supports the trends. These highly specialized services influence the setting for learning. Even small school systems are making a considerable number

[1] We need not digress into the area of basic administrational theory and research as this rightfully belongs to texts and courses in advanced administration. Advanced students may wish to examine several illustrative statements. Others are available.

J. W. Getzels, "A Psycho-Sociological Framework for the Study of Educational Administration," *Harvard Educational Review* (Fall, 1952), pp. 235-246.

Luther Gulick and Lyndall Urwick, *Papers in the Science of Administration* (New York, Columbia Univ., 1935). An early discussion.

G. Robert Koopman, Alice Miel, and Paul Misner, *Democracy in School Administration* (New York, Appleton-Century-Crofts, 1943). Practically the first treatment in education.

Arthur B. Moehlman, *School Administration, Its Development, Principles, and Future in the United States,* new ed. (Boston, Houghton, 1951). An encyclopedic treatment with extensive discussion of theory.

Clyde M. Campbell, ed., *Practical Applications of Democratic Administration* (New York, Harper, 1952). A practical treatment but indirectly suggests many basic research opportunities. Excellent bibliography.

Paul Mort, *Principles of School Administration* (New York, McGraw, 1946). Compact discussion of theory.

of them available. Rural schools secure them through the county school office or the state department. The divisions or departments in a school system fall usually within two types, those dealing with services, and those dealing with subjects, broad fields, or other major divisions of the curriculum. A trend is noted toward organization into three major divisions with subdivisions.

Service departments usually include a department of statistics, a department of research (sometimes confined to tests and measurements), a department of personnel which selects, assigns, and sometimes evaluates the teaching personnel, a department of textbooks and supplies, a department of buildings and grounds, a curriculum department. Curriculum and supervision are often combined in a department of instruction. Departments of attendance often include services to children who must work, to delinquents, and to problem cases. Larger systems, and many smaller ones, include departments of health, of home agencies, of libraries, of corrective physical education for exceptional or defective children, for the blind, for the deaf, for sight saving, for home instruction of shut-ins. Clinics which deal with guidance, with diagnosis of learning difficulties, with behavior problems and emotional disturbances, are widely distributed. Many other specialized services are found here and there.

Curriculum and supervisory departments were originally organized in terms of separate subjects, particularly the so-called special subjects—art, music, physical education, industrial arts, home economics, and the like. Later, subject supervision was extended to the academic subjects—reading, arithmetic, language—and to any additions to the curriculum. A recent development has been to organize by broad fields rather than by subjects: social sciences, physical sciences, fine arts, and so forth. The most recent tendency has been to organize the curriculum in terms of still larger divisions such as personal needs, social functions, areas of learning ex-

perience. A large system may have as many as fifty different subjects or areas, but the tendency is clearly toward organization in fewer larger areas.

All this means that an ever larger number of persons have come to participate in supervision. Superintendents, deputy or assistant superintendents, several kinds of general supervisors, any number of special supervisors, all participate in supervision. In addition to the great increase in number and kind of typical supervisory officers, the elementary principal and the department head in secondary schools are recognized as having important supervisory duties. Co-operating with all these will be school physicians, nurses, psychologists, psychiatrists, and many different research workers and clinicians. The teachers themselves are now participants in supervision.

The already complex problem is further confused by nomenclature for school officers which differs from system to system. One study revealed that in approximately 150 different school systems, a given officer may be named by any of twenty-one different titles, though status and duties are approximately identical. That these different titles convey different concepts of status and function to different persons is even more important than that the titles vary.

School services need to be co-ordinated with outside service agencies. We will indicate at several points in this volume the necessity for close school-community interaction. Originally the school and community were close, but influences arose which separated them. Modern times are seeing deliberate action looking toward ever closer interrelation. Details will be found in later chapters on materials and the curriculum. Here we are concerned with co-ordination of services. The school must be ever more closely identified with the life of the community—political, social, and economic—and particularly with the ethical life of the community. This means that the school on the one hand will participate widely in community projects while on the other it will be utilizing constantly the material and personal resources of the community. A large number of vitally important services similar to those offered by the schools are available from many community agencies. In nearly every city of any size there are child-guidance clinics, diagnostic clinics, health departments, recreation opportunities; all these are operated by various agencies, by juvenile courts, by police departments, by private foundations, by the Y.M.C.A., the Y.W.C.A., the Boy Scouts, and similar organizations. Important educational services are offered by museums, libraries, art galleries, zoos, and public parks. Schools will find frequent opportunity for cooperation with hospitals, clinics, private nursery services, the humane society, the orphans' or children's homes, private and municipal employment services. Many departments of municipal government either offer certain educational services of their own, or willingly co-operate with the schools. Prominent here are departments of fire, police, health, safety, traffic, parks, and sometimes public works. Many corporations, industrial plants, and industry-wide organizations also make available valuable educational services.

The churches, the welfare organizations, the fraternal orders, the service clubs, the labor unions, the employers associations, and many other community organizations need to be co-ordinated with the schools for common ends. The neighborhood clubs, parent-teacher associations, or any type of highly localized community effort will be found important.

The depression-born services such as the NYA, CCC, WPA, and various relief agencies, the wartime OPA, all served excellent educational ends. Many state and federal departments have educational materials and services available similar to those of certain municipal departments.

A glance at the "organismic chart" in Chapter 1 and at the several charts appearing later in this chapter will give an overview of the far-flung services which must be co-ordinated for the good of the child and of society. Speaking generally, services should not be duplicated between in- and out-of-school agencies. No one of the various agencies should be in control. The co-ordinating community councils, which have been developing rapidly, have been eminently successful in solving many problems. All agencies including school and parent are represented. Pupils have been called in for discussion in many instances with excellent effect. The co-ordinating council will be described later in this chapter.

Lay participation in educational planning and administration is necessary and desirable. The principles of democracy and the dictates of practical planning necessitate ever wider lay participation in the management of educational affairs. Policy and plan are thus kept closer to the needs of the total community. Stagnation followed by violent upheaval, followed in turn by uncritical acceptance of "new" practices, or by reactionary return to outmoded practices, is more likely to be avoided.

Public participation has been largely confined to supplying funds and to determining policy through the representative school board. A modern development has been the publicity campaign designed to advise, inform, and carry the public along with professional developments. These programs are useful as immediate means and as a correction for a serious error. Widely hailed as they are, these "public relations" campaigns nevertheless indicate that there was failure to provide for public participation in the first place. We do not have to "sell" a policy or a program to a public which has been participating from the beginning in its development.

Lay contribution must eventually go much further to include actual participation in many areas. A program of improvement in curriculum and methods of teaching in particular can succeed only as public leaders, publicists, and all lay groups concerned with the welfare of childhood and youth are carried along as part of the new program.

Public leaders and lay groups can contribute most effectively in surveys [2] of local needs, in discussions of policies and general plans for meeting needs, in determining general financial support, in selecting the professional leader of the school system. The lay public plays a less important rôle in the strictly professional or technical problems. The school board or other public groups should not be asked to pass upon the implications of research, upon the efficacy of given methods of teaching, upon in-service training programs, and the like. The professional leader appointed by the board, with his staff, must be responsible to the community for technical decisions and for demonstrating that the technical decisions were based upon adequate bases, for demonstrating that a reputable program is being maintained. The public participates in technical matters, first, through participatory observation, and second, through legitimate demands for explanation and proof.

An important administrative problem arises. Co-ordination of this huge list of services and of persons must be achieved for the greater good of the teaching-learning situation. School systems must develop common understandings within the total staff and community. Written statements of procedures for recurring routine items may be necessary; channels and machinery for intercommunication and for the sharing of activities need to be set up. Two broad general lines of solution have appeared. *Traditional administrative procedure* is that in which the superintendent, with or without a central cabinet, devises a set of rules, arranges definite machinery, and presents it as the operating procedure to be followed by the staff. The usual scheme is that of line-and-staff relationship. Varying degrees of participation by the staff in setting up the rules and machinery are found, but generally the traditional solution is an authoritarian one imposed on the system and based on the

legalistic authority of those at the top. *A more modern procedure,* long discussed in theory and now appearing increasingly in actual practice, is the co-operative determination on-the-spot of policies, mechanisms, and procedures by all those actually concerned with the problem. The modern solution is based on the democratic concept of authority-derived-from-the-situation, rather than upon the legalistic conception. Leadership is substituted for personal authority. Details will be elaborated a few pages further on.

Ignoring the problem constitutes a serious blunder. The whole problem of co-ordination was sadly neglected during the days when school systems in the United States were expanding with such astonishing rapidity. Total neglect rarely appears nowadays; but disregard for inadequate, undemocratic, and inefficient solutions is still too widely present. Certain serious difficulties and evils appear if no organization is set up, or if a poor one, either traditional or modern, is accepted.

First, friction developing into clash and antagonism may and usually does result. Second, there is often great waste from duplication (not sharing) of activities, even if no friction appears. Third, many important services or activities may be wholly neglected, since no one knows who is to perform them. This may be true in circumstances where all have the co-operative attitude and are willing to work together. There is no procedure for co-operative sharing of activity.

As we shall see, the great majority of supervisory duties are performed with almost equal frequency in some cases by as many as three school officers. Investigations cited below, showed also that many supervisory functions deemed important by all concerned were not being performed by a majority of supervisory officers; that a number of duties

[2] Note illustrations of lay participation with discussion of actual operation in later chapters, particulary Chs. 17 and 18.

judged to be of minor importance were being widely performed. Common understandings and procedures are necessary whether imposed from above or co-operatively formulated.

Supervisory officers and principals will inevitably proceed at cross purposes in any situation where system is absent. We are all familiar with the autocratic principal who says, "No supervisor is going to come into my building and tell my teachers (or me) what to do." The supervisor in turn often says, "These old principals are merely glorified clerks (or they have crystallized on the job), and I never bother to tell them anything." A serious misconception is indicated concerning the whole nature of education, of co-operation, of sharing functions, not to mention the absence of common understanding. Groups of principals and supervisors committed to traditional concepts of operation in the classroom will quarrel with groups of principals and supervisors who are committed to modern procedures.

The problem may be solved with reasonable ease if attacked seriously. Writers on administrative theory and administrators in the field are now well agreed that solution of the problem is not unduly difficult. A very few still seem to believe that because we are dealing with a very complex system, with personalities, and with intricate human relationships, solution is either impossible, or at best, inadequate and unsatisfactory. There exist, on the contrary, quite definite principles of administration in general, and of human affairs in particular. The principles governing co-operation and shared activity are reasonably clear. They are known to sincere students of the problem and are widely used in human affairs. The problem is, most emphatically, not a muddle or hodgepodge. It does not have to be left to luck, to Providence, or to the pious hope that everyone will be suffused with sweetness and light, causing them to co-operate without argument and without adequate knowledge of how to co-operate.

Before taking up details of organization let us clear one point, namely, the relation between administration and supervision.

The relation between administration and supervision is one of co-ordination, and not of contrast or competition. Early texts devoted considerable space to the question: Can or should supervision be separated from administration? Modern knowledge has made this an academic question. The two can be separated arbitrarily only for the sake of analysis. A separation in function is impossible.

The history of the relationship is, however, of importance. Arbitrary separations in function still persist in school systems. The remains of formal procedures are to be found side by side with efforts to develop more democratic organizations. Administrative procedure and our thinking about organization are both cluttered up by these vestigial remains. The newer, more democratic schemes which are emerging are incomplete, and are often misunderstood. The brief summary to follow may aid in clarifying relationships.

The present legal basis of education probably accounts for part of the difficulty. Financing the system, securing an adequate staff for the business and instructional activities, accounting for costs, determining curriculums, securing books and materials, preparing the budget, establishing standards of progress, supplying testing services, maintaining buildings and grounds, providing a large number of special services—all these are duties commonly associated with administration.

Supervision has had a number of meanings, as indicated in Chapter 1. The earliest meaning in colonial days was actually administrative: oversight of the schools by legally appointed laymen. Very early, however, those appointed for administrative oversight began to comment upon the curriculum, the teaching methods, and the teacher. The two developed together but without any recognized theoretical basis. Superintendents and school boards, as time went on, sincerely interested in improving the effectiveness of education, embarked upon programs for the improvement of teachers. Later this was extended to curriculums, texts and other instructional materials, teaching methods, and eventually to all facets of the setting for learning.

The problems and relations of administration and supervision were complicated considerably when the curriculum began to be extended about 1870. The curriculum previously had consisted largely of reading, writing, and arithmetic. A number of new subjects appeared: manual training, home economics, music, drawing, physical education, history, and literature. This extension of the curriculum is still going on. The superintendent, the principal, and the regular teachers were ordinarily quite unprepared to give instruction in these new subjects. Specialists had to be employed to teach them. The new subjects thus came to be known as special subjects. The special teacher, going from building to building to give instruction to the children, became a traveling teacher working out from and more closely related to the central office than to the local school units.

Fundamental changes were made in the duties of these traveling specialists. First, systems grew in size so that one elementary building could use whole-time teachers of the special subjects, particularly music and art. The traveling specialists thus became local teachers responsible to the building principal. Second, as levels of teacher training improved, the so-called "regular" teachers first accepted guidance from the so-called "special" teachers and traveling teachers, eventually taking over instruction in the new subjects. Third, it was increasingly recognized that the new subjects were as much a part of desirable education as the older offerings. Integration would be better achieved if the distinction between "special" subjects and the "regular" curriculum were eliminated. All teachers were increasingly required to teach any subject important enough to appear in the school.

The new specialists had thus both administrative and supervisory duties. Supervisors from the central office, special teachers, principals, and others were increasingly engaged in administering and supervising the same things. Relationships between officers increased in complexity.

The foregoing remarks apply chiefly to the elementary school. Supervision with its complexities appeared much later in the secondary schools.

The central supervision of "special" subjects had meantime been extended to many of the academic subjects. Supervision by department heads in secondary schools was developing, even if feebly. This multiplied the number of persons involved and eventually led to still further changes in relationships between generalists and specialists. The sum total so far was to emphasize the meaning of supervision as the professional training and assisting of teachers and to further differentiate it from administration. All this development complicated the relationship between administration and supervision, since meanings and practice could not be easily aligned.

A fourth factor turned out to be of great importance: the place and function of the elementary and secondary principals changed fundamentally. Increasingly critical analyses of the duties of school officers indicated that the building principal was one of the most strategically placed individuals. The administrative duties commonly associated with the office came to be supplemented by important activities of leadership and professional supervision. This led to minimizing the work of the special supervisor in many places, to clash and friction in others, and as we shall see later, to eventual co-operative relationships.

A fifth factor, which emerged only recently, has played a major part in breaking down the arbitrary distinctions between administration and supervision. A large group of new staff members has been added to state and city school systems, not as in 1870 and thereafter to develop an increasing number of separate subjects, but to develop an over-all picture, to co-ordinate, to bring integration and order into a compartmentalized educational scheme. Curriculum directors, research specialists, diagnosticians, remedial workers, guidance officers, deal not with separate subjects or materials but with all aspects of the child's personality, the whole curriculum, the whole educational program. The old distinctions arbitrarily defined cannot survive within a modern functional program. Organization around the total ongoing learning process instead of around compartments in the course of study necessitates cooperative interaction by all concerned with learning.

The school officers charged with authority to operate the schools are line officers, with authority delegated down the line from the superintendent. Officers charged with supervisory or advisory duties (or functions) constitute the staff. The general theory of line-and-staff organization is discussed later in this section.

Administrative and supervisory duties overlap. Even without the historical background, mere inspection of the typical division between administrative and supervisory duties would indicate that the division can be only an arbitrary one for purposes of discussion. Intimate interrelationship and overlap are inherent and inevitable.

The provision of a building and equipment, for instance, is a typical administrative duty. The planning and construction of this building will not be intelligently done, however, unless supervisors and teachers participate. Competent teachers know intimately and at first hand the desirable space requirements necessary for little children, the types of equipment and materials best suited to various age levels. Specialists in reading, in testing, in health education, or what not, all have technical information of value. School buildings have in fact often been

planned and built by administrators and architects without reference to teachers and other specialists. The result too often is a plant and equipment not well suited, even detrimental, to education. The most typical administrative duty, providing housing, cannot be properly carried on without active interrelationship with supervisory officers. A typical supervisory duty, carrying on programs of study for improvement, cannot be carried on without knowledge of the policy, the financial ability, sometimes of the political alignment of the administration. Administration is legally empowered to establish a curriculum and provide texts. Supervisors and teachers, however, have much important information about the maturation of learners which will affect the curriculum and the texts. Supervisors and teachers should provide the best possible instructional program. This involves purchase of books, pictures, crayons, paint, paper, materials, tools, and so forth. Supervisory activity here cannot proceed without co-operation from the administration which has knowledge of money available. Illustrations could be multiplied indefinitely. Suffice it to say that mere inspection will show that duties overlap and interrelate of necessity. No hard and fast distinction can be made.

The fact of overlap and sharing of duties is further confirmed by the objective analyses of actual practice. The early research studies in the field include a number of excellent time and frequency studies of the activities of all types of administrative and supervisory officers: superintendents, general and special supervisors, elementary and special supervisors, department heads.

The lists of duties performed were attacked critically by several analysts in the effort to determine the duties which various officers *should* perform as distinguished from those they now performed. Here began the effort to eliminate unnecessary and wasteful overlap which results only in friction, confusion, and waste. Attention began to shift toward the determination of the necessary and valuable co-operative interrelationships which are effective in furthering the work of education. Current studies do not discuss mere overlap but attempt to determine the necessarily shared responsibilities.

Analyses of duties performed and by whom, with overlaps or omissions counted, are still necessary. New duties appear, a few are eliminated, concepts of relationship between officers change. Discussions today, however, introduce a new emphasis, namely, the effort not merely to count overlaps but to determine how shared responsibilities can be carried on for the good of the system. Articles increasingly stress "co-operative democratic administration (or supervision)." Traditional organizations are questioned; new methods of organizing are appearing everywhere. The trend is toward a co-operative formulation of working relationships on the spot, on the basis of the needs of the situation and the personnel available. This leads directly into the important administrative problem of organization. We are at the moment concerned with a few facts only: administration and supervision have certain typical duties; practice in these fields is characterized by large overlap in performance of duties; sharp distinctions need not be made; there is need for a co-operatively determined scheme for sharing responsibilities.

Guidance is derived from the analysis of administrative and supervisory practices. The following facts derived from the studies of supervisory activities are of value in clarifying thinking:

1. Practically all supervisory duties are performed at one time or another by administrative officers. Many administrative duties are performed from time to time by supervisory officers.

2. A number of duties are difficult to classify as one or the other despite restricted definitions of administration and supervision.

3. Certain duties stand out as practically impossible to classify strictly under one or the other: curriculum construction, securing texts and other instructional materials, selecting the teaching staff, furthering the growth and welfare of the staff, testing or evaluating outcomes, child accounting.

4. Great but not complete agreement exists among competent judges as to duties which are deemed of major and of minor importance.

5. Duties judged to be of major importance were in the main performed by a majority of administrative and supervisory officers.

6. A considerable number of duties judged to be of minor importance were being performed by a majority of school officers.

7. The fact that a duty is widely performed is not a safe basis for judging its importance.

8. Great differences exist between administrators not alone in their sharing of supervisory duties but in their control of supervisory officers and duties.

9. Great need is shown for devising principles and mechanisms to provide for co-operatively shared responsibilities and activities.

Rorer,[3] in his remarkable analysis of principles governing supervision, shows that the differentiation between supervision and administration may be found in the function of leadership. The administrator will specialize in leadership, in taking the initiative in movements for the improvement of teaching and learning. The movements initiated, however, may be in response to suggestions from any member of the supervisory or teaching staff. Leadership then is not exclusively an administrative function, but a large responsibility for it does lie with the administration. The principle that leadership instead of authority be characteristic of administration was voiced very early (*circa* 1930) by Courtis in various publications. It was strongly stressed in the first edition of this book and developed in some detail in the Eleventh Yearbook of the Department of Supervisors and Directors of Instruction.[4] Current (1955) discussions continue to extend and amplify the views first stated long ago.

[3] John A. Rorer, *Principles of Democratic Supervision* (New York, Teachers College, Bureau of Publications, Columbia Univ., 1942), pp. 30-32.

[4] *Co-operation: Principles, and Practices,* Eleventh Yearbook, Department of Supervisors and Directors of Instruction (Washington, NEA, 1939), pp. 48-50; 110-113.

Section 2

ORGANIZATION BASED UPON AUTHORITY

The writers wish to make clear that in presenting a detailed summary of authoritarian organizations, together with the arguments for such organization, they are not advocating such methods. The authoritarian structures are still the most widely used in the country and will continue for a long time. Honest presentation of them, with discussion of strengths and of methods for alleviating the weaknesses, will be valuable to many persons for a long time to come. The modern procedures presented in Section 3, based upon leadership instead of authority and formulated co-operatively by all concerned, are definitely superior: first, in their fidelity to democratic principles; and second, in that they can be fully as "efficient" as the older procedures.

The principles underlying authoritarian organization. Rorer [5] makes an important distinction between principles of external organization and those of internal organization. The former deal with the machinery and personnel of a school system; the latter with the functioning of the machinery. The two are sometimes confused. The generally accepted principles of external organization are essentially as follows:

1. Authority is centralized in the legally appointed person at the head.
   a. The superintendent of schools is, in the last analysis, responsible for the general instructional policy of the school system.
   b. The principal must be the executive-in-chief with supreme responsibility in his school and must be directly responsible to the superintendent.
2. Authority and responsibility may be delegated by the superintendent to inferior officers.
3. The lines and channels through which this delegated authority will flow must be sharply and unambiguously defined.
   a. Provision must be made that each individual or area in the organization may be reached expeditiously from any higher administrative level.
   b. Provision must be made for appeal from any individual or level to higher administrative levels.
   c. No individual should receive suggestions covering the same item from more than one person. (Teachers should get all assignments, notices, directions from the principal.)
4. Duties and activities must be assigned down through the line of authority.
5. The performance of duties assigned to any level must be checked by the next higher levels throughout the system.
6. Staff officers are instructional experts and consultants; they are differentiated thus from the line officers and also by having no authority or executive power.
   a. A principal or department head is both an administrative and a supervisory officer.
   b. The principal in his supervisory capacity may render his most effective service through direct assistance: visiting and conferring with individual teachers, helping with individual pupils, making immediate suggestions, helping with lesson plans, devices, units, discussing devices.
   c. The general or special supervisors from the central office may render their most effective service through indirect and more remote assistance: making or taking leadership in making courses of study, providing materials, creating standards, training principals or large groups of teachers. (Research studies based on functioning within traditional systems clearly support this *general* division.)
   d. The bulk of everyday classroom visiting may be taken over by the principal; the supervisor's visits may occur mostly upon request.

These principles are practically self-explanatory and will be familiar to advanced students and workers in the field; therefore, detailed discussion is omitted.

The principles of internal organization seem to be:

[5] Rorer, *op. cit.,* pp. 124-250.

1. Facility for co-operation and co-ordination must be provided.
   a. A common theory of education, a common technology, and a common aim and philosophy must be established.
   b. The work of the line officers and that of the staff officers must be co-ordinated by common planning under a deputy superintendent or some form of supervisory council.
   c. Below the level of general co-ordination there must be many interlocking committees, conference groups, and small subcommittees.
   d. Cases of conflict or disagreement between any officers or groups must be settled by the next higher administrative officer, ultimately by the superintendent.
2. There must be flexibility of operation.
   a. Adjustment of strictly logical lines and duties must be made when local circumstances demand it (type of community, size of system, traditions, previous policies, the training, experience, and personalities of the personnel already there, and so forth).
   b. Line officers will have to perform duties in some instances which are ordinarily assigned to staff officers.
   c. Staff officers will have to perform duties in some instances which are ordinarily assigned to line officers.

These principles counteract in some measure, but never wholly, the inherently undemocratic nature of authoritarian organization.

Types of traditional or authoritarian organization. Several different schemes for organizing supervision administratively are found in the United States. The first one cited below is not sound even under traditional authoritarian principles. Many variations are found of schemes which are acceptable in the light of traditional principles. The variation is sound and desirable, showing that even under the rigid principles of authority there is effort to experiment, to adjust to local conditions and personnel.

The extrinsic-dualistic organization. The term was coined long ago by Barr. Supervision is "extrinsic" to the supposedly basic educational organization, which results in a "dualistic" conception of administration and supervision. Each proceeds with little or no attention to the other. The reasons for this appeared in the first chapter. Supervision was supplementary, adventitious, extrinsic. Teachers were responsible to both administration and supervision. Mechanisms for co-operation were not even thought of. This type was at one time almost universal and still is the actual operating scheme in too many places, despite surface efforts to develop either a reputable authoritarian scheme or a modern democratic one. The illogical and incompetent nature of this scheme is apparent. There is no centralization of authority, no definition of lines, no mechanisms for co-operation, nor any modern method for co-operative formulation of procedures.

The line-and-staff organization, general theory. This type of organization is found in nearly pure form in the army and is probably more easily understood through reference to the army. Line officers are those in authority. They issue orders. Authority descends along regularly defined "lines" from the general to the brigadier-general, to the colonels, to the majors, to the captains, to the lieutenants, to the sergeants, to the corporals. One line officer may be approached only through "regular channels," that is, by proceeding up or down along the defined lines of authority. Staff officers are specialized experts who are masters of technical services. They have no authority and issue no orders though they may have the rank of colonel, major, captain, and so forth. They supply advice, information, technical assistance to line officers. Generals issue orders for battle, but they do not do so without careful consideration of the advice and information turned in by staff officers in charge of espionage, service of supply, munitions, repairs, weather information, and so forth.

The line-and-staff scheme is found elsewhere than in the army. It appears in the church, in department stores, in publishing houses, in manufacturing concerns, in charitable and nonprofit enterprises, in purely eleemosynary institutions, in fact, wherever the activities of butcher, baker, or candlestick-maker are extensive enough to necessitate organization. Line-and-staff can be found in the spontaneously and democratically organized gangs of boyhood; will often appear in an elementary classroom where pupils are organizing their own learning activities.

Objection is often made to line-and-staff because it is found in the army and in industry. This is not wholly sound argument; the real objection lies elsewhere. Line-and-staff organization is merely a mechanism to facilitate human co-operation in complex undertakings. The crucial question is whether it must be operated in military fashion or with the rigid inflexibility of an industrial organization. *The fact that it appears in simple situations spontaneously and can be formulated co-operatively shows that some democracy is possible and that authoritarian imposition can be avoided in some degree.* Large organizations can reduce but not eliminate the evils of rigidity by (1) placing an officer as co-ordinator for all line-and-staff activities, (2) keeping all lines of action free and loose instead of rigidly dictated, and (3) providing certain specific mechanisms (see later pages) for flexibility and co-operative interaction.

The line-and-staff organization applied to school systems. The application of line-and-staff to educational organization raises a second crucial question, that of ends. The army and manufacturing plants deal with products which not only can but should be precisely standardized in large part. Persons involved are definitely subordinate to the

desired ends and to the processes for securing the ends. Doing and doing correctly by formula is the desired thing. Education deals with the development of unique personalities and with the enhancement of an emergent, experimental civilization. The staff operating the educational system is, moreover, made up of persons who should find growth and satisfaction in their work. The products and the processes not only should not be standardized but can be standardized only with dire results. Organization in education must provide for doing as it does in business, but in addition, must provide for creative thinking and individual contribution.

Logic and some evidence [6] shows clearly that these desired ends are attained far more easily through the modern co-operative form of organization. In circumstances where the authoritarian form prevails something can be done, however, to alleviate, counteract, or correct the undemocratic characteristics. Principles of internal organization cited above supply the guidance.

The line officers in a school system include the superintendent, assistant or deputy superintendents, district or divisional superintendents, principals, vice principals, department head, and any specially appointed committee chairmen or other officer given authority from the head of the system. Authority is delegated down defined lines from the superintendent. The line officers systematically operate the school program.

Staff officers supply expert technical information and advice to the line officers. Staff officers are of two types, those in charge of service departments and those in charge of subject departments or other major divisions of the curriculum. The first includes statisti-

[6] Clyde M. Campbell, *op. cit.* Excellent analysis of theory with good bibliography referring to specific situations.

David Krech, and Richard S. Crutchfield, *Theory and Problems of Social Psychology* (New York, McGraw, 1948).

Hadley Cantril, *The Psychology of Social Movements* (New York, Wiley, 1941).

Paul Mort, *op cit.*

John H. Martin, "We Tried Some Freedom," in Kimball Wiles, *Supervision for Better Schools* (New York, Prentice-Hall, 1950), pp. 310-318.

Kimball Wiles, *loc. cit.* Good discussion of general theory with bibliography.

Association for Supervision and Curriculum Development: *Leadership Through Supervision*, 1946 Yearbook; *Group Planning in Education*, 1948 Yearbook (Washington, NEA, 1946 and 1948).

cians, psychiatrists, psychologists, librarians, test experts, guidance officers, personnel officers of various types. Service divisions ordinarily serve the entire system. The curriculum divisions may, however, take any one of three forms. Many variations are found in practice. Three common systems are:

1. Line-and-staff with vertical supervision of instruction.
2. Line-and-staff with horizontal or divisional supervision of instruction.
3. Co-ordinate line-and-staff which usually follows the horizontal or divisional plan.

In *vertical* organization, supervisors are advisers on instructional conditions in a given subject or curriculum area throughout all grades from primary to the end of secondary school. In *horizontal* organization, they work only in given school divisions such as primary, upper elementary, secondary. Vertical supervision is strong in securing unity, co-ordination, integration, and articulation of materials and methods within each field. It is weak in that it tends to keep subjects or areas separate and provides less well for correlation between subjects or areas, and sometimes fails to secure integration of subjects or areas required by the objectives of the school. Horizontal supervision is strong in securing unity and integration between subjects or areas within the limits of divisional levels. Its weakness lies in the possible failure

to articulate between levels. Choice between the systems depends upon the training and attitudes of the given staff and upon local traditions.

The co-ordinate plan, the third system mentioned above, is really a variation of the second, the added feature being an emphasis upon the co-ordinate nature of the activities of line and staff officers. This is an effort to avoid certain weaknesses of conventional line-and-staff organization.

The strength of conventional line-and-staff organization is that it does provide clear and unambiguous assignment of duties and encourages specialization. The weaknesses grow out of the strengths. Co-operation between line and staff may actually be seriously impaired by too careful differentiation and overspecialization. Partial correction lies as indicated earlier, in the formation of supervisory councils, interlocking committees, conference groups.

The co-ordinate system is itself an extended effort to overcome weaknesses of conventional line-and-staff organization. The defined differences between line and staff are softened by stating that the activities of line and staff officers are co-ordinate functions in any given educational program.

Staff officers in conventional line-and-staff serve all principals and teachers alike and from the central office. Co-ordination takes

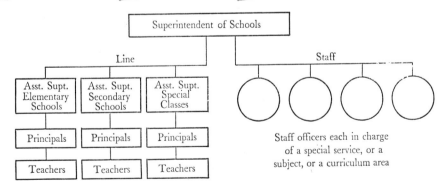

A SCHEMATIC REPRESENTATION OF LINE-AND-STAFF ORGANIZATION

From *The Superintendent Surveys Supervision,* Eighth Yearbook, Department of Superintendence (Washington, NEA, 1930), p. 55.

place through the primary administrative staff or council and for the system as a whole. Staff officers in the co-ordinate system serve given divisions, such as kindergarten, primary, intermediate, junior high, senior high, and so forth. Co-ordination takes place more directly through divisional and local officers. System-wide co-ordination is still necessary, of course.

In the co-ordinate system, the building principal engaged in unit supervision is held to be functioning at the same organic level as the special supervisor, a staff officer engaged in supervision or in a subject or area of learning experience. Each is assigned co-ordinate administrative responsibility: the principal over a group of teachers and pupils; the special supervisor over a group of assistants. Each is assumed to be equally interested in the improvement of the situation, hence will engage naturally in co-operative endeavor, each carrying out his specially allocated functions under direction of the divisional administrative staff.

The strength of the co-ordinate form is that it emphasizes and encourages co-operation and integration so far as these can be achieved under an authoritarian and defined system. The weakness is that it may reinstate some of the overlap we are trying to avoid and may minimize specialization. The correction of these weaknesses lies in more careful allocation of duties and in formation of interlocking committees.

The effort to overcome weaknesses in either system points surely toward the evolution of more democratic organizations to which we will turn in Section 3.

Variations in supervisory organization found in small cities. The larger cities usually have some form of line-and-staff organization in more or less accurate detail. Such systems have large staffs which permit greater specialization. Since the individual buildings are larger, the principalship is enhanced.

In the smaller cities there is less money, hence a smaller staff. Since the buildings are smaller, the principal is usually a part-time or full-time teacher. All of this places severe limitations on the smaller systems whose need of supervision, of curriculum reorganization, and so forth, is usually great. Furthermore, the superintendent, either because he is overworked or untrained, very often fails to recognize the importance of organization. He often does not take advantage of such facilities as he has.

The chief devices utilized in small systems are as follows:

1. One general supervisor is sometimes employed to give attention to the so-called regular or academic subjects. This is, of course, extremely helpful when a competent person is secured. The weakness of the plan is that this general supervisor must be a generalist as the superintendent and principal already are. Sometimes one or two special supervisors are employed to supplement the efforts of the general supervisor.

2. Instructional committees may be organized involving some or all of the entire staff. These committees may give attention to organizing courses or to selecting textbooks or to the interpretation of new movements or to devices for improving instruction.

3. One or more, usually two or three, special supervisors are employed. General supervision is done by the superintendent or by the principal or by specially designated supervising teachers. This is helpful when competent specialists are found. The weakness is that they may be merely special teachers.

The Eighth Yearbook of the Department of Superintendence cites the following advantages of the supervising teacher system.[7]

  a. In cities of a sufficient size, special supervision is thus made possible for all subjects, art, music, civics, arithmetic, reading, physical education, and the rest, at a minimum cost. The need for special supervision for all subjects has already been set forth.

  b. The plan assures a fund of practical ideas, plans, and materials for use in the school system. That is, such plans, procedures, and materials as are recommended are first tried out under

[7] *The Superintendent Supervises Supervision,* Eighth Yearbook, Department of Superintendence (Washington, NEA, 1930), p. 61.

actual classroom conditions. They represent workable ideas rather than theories.

c. The specialist is kept in close touch with actual classroom conditions. Critic teachers in teacher-training institutions, almost without exception, have found it necessary to teach one or two classes daily to retain a sympathetic understanding of the problems of actual teaching.

d. Such a plan avoids the embarrassment of an unattached group of specialists.

4. Building principals are given responsibility for special supervision. The principal of one building may be designated as a special supervisor of arithmetic in all buildings. His relationship to the other principals when in their buildings will be that of a special supervisor. Another principal will be responsible for language activities, another for the social studies, and so forth. This involves adjustment of load and clerical help.

5. A supervisor is employed by two or more small communities jointly. The supervisor's time is distributed among the schools evenly but with understanding that the schedule may be discarded on occasions as special problems arise. This is not widespread but has been found very satisfactory when the supervisor is truly interested in the problem. Other services may be shared similarly.

6. The extension and consultant services of colleges, universities, and state departments are being widely used. These services have increased in number and efficiency in recent years.

7. A local workshop and equipment are provided. This can be used by all interested teachers as need arises. The workshop can also be systematized with meetings during the year. Leadership may be local or secured from nearby colleges or from the state department.

8. Wider use is being made of special consultants for short periods to deal with a given problem; or of part-time consultants.

The great spread of curriculum programs currently gives many opportunities for introduction of supervisory services into smaller systems.

The special problem of county and rural supervision; the place of the state department of education. The principles developed in this volume, together with suggested practices, are applicable to all types of schools,

though details of procedure obviously must differ.

The day of the lone rural supervisor traveling slowly from school to school is passing. Many counties today have the money, the staff, and the leadership to provide programs similar to those in large cities. The work of the county office, for instance, in Los Angeles county, San Diego county, and San Bernardino county in Southern California is well known. Descriptions of similar work in other parts of the country are available in the literature. The consolidated central rural school and regional school makes possible better supervision.

An alert and professionally minded state department can be of inestimable aid to all rural, county, town, and city systems through advice on solution of problems, critical analysis of procedures and materials, supplying bulletin material, through consultant service and many other special services. Alexander's excellent analysis [8] of the work of the state department programs in Louisiana, Tennessee, and Virginia, though some years old, still supplies valuable information. He points out that state programs may be *directive, indirect,* or *co-operative* in their procedure, depending on local tradition, immediate conditions, and vision of the leadership at both state and local levels. The extensive work of the California state department in all areas, and that of the Maine state department in elementary education are both well known through their publications. Texas, Minnesota, and other states can be cited. Florida recently began to study the state department services. The best recent treatment will be found in Melchoir, *Instructional Supervision,* [9] Chapters 15 and 16. The first chapter contains detailed discusions of projects carried on jointly by state departments, colleges,

[8] William M. Alexander, *State Leadership in Improving Instruction,* Contributions to Education No. 820 (New York, Teachers College, Bureau of Publications, Columbia Univ., 1940).

[9] William Melchoir, *op cit.* (Boston, Heath, 1950).

John H. Jollief, *Evaluation as an Aspect of State*

or universities. The second chapter discusses the work of school-study or school-development councils in co-operation with universities. A list of these councils is given and material may be secured directly from them on a wide variety of topics and problems.

A major text on rural supervision has not appeared since that by Anderson and Simpson in 1932. Despite the copyright date, the general principles are still sound, though many of the detailed procedures suggested have been outmoded. Many detailed cases or projects will be found in Melchoir's book referred to above. Three bulletins may be noted here as representative of others available:

Instructional Leadership in Small Schools, a pamphlet, Association for Supervision and Curriculum Development (Washington, NEA, 1951).

Rural Leadership and Service; a Guide for Development of the District Superintendency (Albany, N. Y., State Department of Education, 1951).

The Rural Supervisor at Work, 1949 Yearbook, Department of Rural Education (Washington, NEA, 1949).

Another source of useful materials is the Division of Rural Service of the National Education Association. Similar materials are available from the Rural Division of the United States Office of Education. Other agencies with which the NEA division co-operates include the American Country Life Association; Rural Youth of the U.S.A.; the Alliance for the Guidance of Rural Youth. Bulletins on every phase of rural education and its leadership are available.

Associations of secondary schools and colleges. Great aid to whole regions may result if regional associations follow the example of the Southern Association, which has sponsored and aided the "Southwide Study" of school improvement. (This study will be discussed briefly in Chapters 8 and 15.)

Co-operative studies. Various state departments, universities, and associations formed for the purpose have stimulated co-operative studies of one or another aspect, as, for instance, the several studies which developed evaluative criteria. (See Chapters 8-12, 14-16.)

Section 3

ORGANIZATION BASED UPON DEMOCRATIC PRINCIPLES AND UPON RECOGNITION OF THE CHIEF AIM OF THE SCHOOL

The keynote for modern democratic organization is the maintenance of satisfactory human relations while co-ordinating the efforts of many persons engaged in a common task. This keynote is admirably stated in a fundamental monograph on administration

Supervision of Elementary Schools. Unpublished doctoral dissertation, Indiana Univ., 1944.

Muriel M. Kelly, *Trends in an Evolving Program of Supervision for Virginia.* Unpublished doctoral dissertation, George Peabody College for Teachers, 1945. Historical and evaluative.

Frank G. Dickey, *Developing Supervision in Kentucky.* Bulletin of the Bureau of School Service, College of Education, Univ. of Kentucky, Vol. XX, No. 3 (March, 1948). Evaluates local supervision under nine criteria.

John W. Litherland, *A Study of State Programs of Supervision of Schools and a Selection of the Practices and Procedures which Seem Pertinent to a State Program of Supervision in Nebraska.* Unpublished doctoral dissertation, Univ. of Nebraska, 1947.

Genora McFadden, *The Development of State-*

Authorized Supervision of Rural Elementary White Schools in Alabama. Unpublished doctoral dissertation, George Peabody College for Teachers, 1948. Largely historical.

See also:

Genevieve Bowen, *Living and Learning in a Rural School* (New York, Macmillan, 1944). A diary-type running account of teaching in a rural school. Valuable for teachers and supervisors.

Kate V. Wofford, *Teaching in Small Schools* (New York, Macmillan, 1946). Written for teachers, but is one of most valuable books available for rural supervisors. Modern up-to-date point of view throughout.

J. F. Butterworth and H. A. Damon, *The Modern Rural School* (New York, McGraw, 1952).

Lorene K. Fox, *The Rural Community and Its School* (New York, Kings Crown Press, 1948).

with special reference to government. Seven principles [10] are quoted below. Particular attention should be devoted to numbers 1, 2, 5, and 7.

1. Personnel administration becomes of extraordinary significance, not merely from the standpoint of finding qualified appointees for the various positions, but even more from the standpoint of assisting in the selection of individuals and in the maintenance of conditions which will serve to create a foundation of loyalty and enthusiasm.

The new drive for career government service and for in-service training derives its significance not so much from the fact that better persons will enter the service when the chance for promotion is held out to them, but from the fact that a career service is a growing and learning service, one that believes in the work and in the future of the enterprise.

2. Even where the structure of the organization is arranged to produce co-ordination by authority, and certainly in those realms in which the structure as such is wanting, the effort should be made to develop the driving ideas by co-operative effort and compromise so that there may be an understanding of the program, a sense of participation in its formulation, and enthusiasm in its realization.

3. Proper reporting on the results of the work of the departments and of the government as a whole to the public and to the controlling legislative body, and public appreciation of good service rendered by public employees is essential, not merely as a part of the process of democratic control, but also as a means to the development of service morale.

4. As a matter of public policy the government should encourage the development of professional associations among the employees of the government, in recognition of the fact that such associations can assist powerfully in the development of standards and ideals. In situations where it is natural, office and shop committees should be built up.

5. A developing organization must be continually engaged in research bearing upon the major technical and policy problems encountered, and upon the efficiency of the processes of work. In both types of research, but particularly in the latter, members of the staff at every level should be led to participate in the inquiries and in the development of solutions.

6. There is need for a national system of honor awards which may be conspicuously conferred upon men and women who render distinguished and faithful, though not necessarily highly advertised, public service.

7. The structure of any organization must reflect not only the logic of the work to be done, but also the special aptitudes of the particular human beings who are brought together in the organization to carry through a particular project. It is the men and not the organization chart that do the work.

The real importance of organization and machinery. An able article by Campbell calls attention to a curious neglect of the impact of organization in our national society. The framers of the Constitution and the Bill of Rights were determined to make the language express our freedom and privileges clearly and beyond all argument. We have not until immediately current times, however, been keenly or critically interested in a structure for administration of public institutions which would exemplify and exercise our freedoms. We do in fact, and particularly in education, often state and defend principles of democracy, and at the same time defend just as vigorously a structure which contradicts those principles. Pure democratic living is, as he points out, never attainable because man is not perfect. No structure will ensure democratic relationships but it can very significantly affect our attitudes and behavior one way or another. On the positive side Campbell [11] quotes from Huxley: [12]

Different kinds of social machinery predispose to different inner attitudes. The most admirable machinery is useless if the inner life is unchanged; but social machinery can affect the fulness and quality of life. Social machinery can be devised to make war more difficult, to promote health, to add interest to life. Let us not despise machinery in our zeal for fulness of life, any more than we should dream that

[10] Luther Gulick and Lyndall Urwick, *op. cit.* Principles found on pp. 37-38. Students may read with profit Ch. 1, "Division of Work" and Ch. 8, "The Process of Control."

[11] Clyde Campbell, "A Democratic Structure to Further Democratic Values," *Progressive Education* (November, 1952), pp. 25-29.

[12] Julian Huxley, *Man in the Modern World* (New York, New American Library, 1948), p. 144.

machinery can ever automatically grind out perfection of living.

Machinery we must have, but unless it is in line with democratic values and processes it will not improve the process it is designed to serve.

Increasing recognition of inescapable weakness in line-and-staff has increased dissatisfaction with it. A number of important weaknesses in the line-and-staff organization have been noted in educational writing for a long time. The efforts of field workers to improve the system or to evolve a better basic structure indicate that the practical workers are at one with the theorists in recognizing the difficulties. Several of these points are indicated in the very presentation of the system itself in immediately preceding pages; several were clearly indicated long ago in the first edition of this text. Writers of texts on administration have been for some time and with increasing vigor voicing fundamental criticisms. The principles of democratic supervision set forth in Chapter 4 contain still other inferential attacks upon line-and-staff organization.

We have already noted, first, that administrative and supervisory functions cannot actually be separated; second, evidence shows that the imposition of authority will not accomplish as much or as well as the exercise of leadership; third, truly democratic cooperation is likely to be more efficient in the long run than contact through strictly defined channels; and fourth, machinery and rules made on the spot, by those most intimately concerned and who will have to operate within the given situation, are superior to rules and machinery made by a central staff further removed from the learning situation which the machinery is to serve.

The fourth point calls attention to a serious difficulty. Machinery and procedures set up to facilitate human affairs are always in danger of becoming ends in themselves. The logical arrangement and smooth running "efficiency" of the system become more important than the ends served. This lapse

into formalism is greatly encouraged if the system was set up in the first place by persons remote from the scene of action. This type of formalism in school systems was doubtless enhanced by the concept of "efficiency" borrowed from the business world. The failure to stress the difference in desired outcomes between business and education, noted earlier, is unquestionably concerned here also. A product that can and should be standardized is produced better by machinery and processes that are also standardized. All educational machinery is ostensibly set up for the purpose of furthering the desired outcomes of education: the production of unique individual socialized personalities by securing growth and development within a social group of the individually different children; the ultimate improvement of society.

The machinery and its smooth operation may become the end if we are not careful; recognition of the true ends to be served may become purely verbal. The system comes to function for its own good, not that of the learner.

Line-and-staff may be inoperable in a truly modern system of education. Certain leaders are expressing the belief that it may actually be impossible to organize a good school system under traditional line-and-staff organization. Arguments are derived from an examination of (1) the type of educational theory and practice within which line-and-staff emerged, and (2) the implications of the new services added to school systems in comparatively recent times.

Line-and-staff organization was set up to organize a school system which accepted principles and practices concerning learning, the curriculum, the management of the classroom, the desired outcomes, and testing practices that are now largely passing out of the picture. Many of the new services added in recent years were designed not to serve the old subject-centered educational system but to serve the needs of the pupils. The new services indicate clearly that educational thinking is concerned increasingly not only with subject-matter outcomes, not with formal skill or fact learning, not with objective testing of limited results, not with uniformity in classroom procedure, but also with the life and learning of the individual pupils.

The problems just indicated have been presented in such clear and incisive language by Spears that a lengthy quotation is justified.[13]

The line-and-staff matrix came in when the curriculum was considered as something fixed, when it was looked upon as little more than a number of subjects and skills to be manipulated under well-regulated classroom conditions, when the theory of mental discipline still clung to its exalted pedestal, when psychologists were still flirting with the mind-body theory, when the out-of-class activities of youngsters were tolerated rather than encouraged, when efficiency in school operation took precedence over respect for personality, when the school was an institution operated apart from the rest of the community, and when supervision centered its attention upon teacher weakness rather than upon curriculum improvement. . . .

Even if [we] were to concede that the line-and-staff pattern of operation served in a fair way to unify instructional leadership a few years ago, it could not automatically be concluded that the pattern would fit today's situation. In recent years, general curriculum practitioners, guidance leaders, research workers, and similar directors have been added to the original headquarters staff of special subject supervisors. This new crop of workers represents the growing concern for the individual pupil, and has little in common with special subjects or special fields as such. As these newer instructional leaders were added, the administration again got out the old line-and-staff principle, dusted it off, and bent it here and there to fit the new situation. But fundamental differences between the new situation and the school situation existing at the time of the principle's origin have been ignored.

The recent deluge of new staff officers represents a unique situation. Whether the average school system actually appreciates it or not, behind this recent creation of the positions of curriculum director, research director, instructional co-ordinator, guidance director, and all their associates, rests a general dissatisfaction with the existing school program. The inception of these positions represents something much more revolutionary than did the inception of

special subject supervisors. Special subject supervisors were brought in to strengthen an existing order, not to change it. The task of changing the curriculum and moving the emphasis of the school program from subject to child is a Herculean endeavor that, if it is to be successful, is bound to call for a few revolutions that even a rigid statement of rights and duties cannot and should not offset. If it can be said that the creation of a curriculum department or the appointment of a curriculum director represents a definite dissatisfaction with the existing school program, it might be asked if it doesn't follow that it likewise represents dissatisfaction with instructional leadership that already exists in the system. It is quite likely that some of these appointments have behind them nothing more sincere than the desire to keep up with the Joneses, but in the main they indicate that philosophies of education are at stake, and the resulting situation calls for something more than a principle of staff organization to reconcile it. In fact, isn't friction in instructional leadership at times the first sign of possible advancement in instructional procedure? The school system that has done so much by law and precept to keep down instructional differences, may have been better off had it encouraged conflict, thus forcing antiquated purposes and practices into a death struggle with modern points of view. Actually, antiquated procedures are being sheltered by a line-and-staff principle that has vested their proponents with power. . . .

. . . As long as the activities of these new staff officers are limited to teacher discussions, committee meetings, the formulation of instructional objectives, and petty tinkering with existing courses, no conflict arises. But as soon as proposals are made that would transpose from mere conference-room talk to actual classroom practice such phrases as "pupil purposes," "the development of the whole child," and "learning to do by doing," a strain is placed upon instructional leadership that is apt to crack the unity that was verbally attested to in the conference room. . . .

. . . The reorganization of the school program demands not only unity of statement on the part of the leadership, but asks, above all, unity of purpose and effort.

[13] Harold Spears, "Can the Line-and-Staff Principle Unify Instructional Leadership?" *Educational Method* (April, 1941), pp. 343-349.

The article by Campbell in *Progressive Education* for November, 1952, quoted earlier, amplifies Spears's views on the level of principles.

Efforts to improve line-and-staff constitute one route to understanding of democratic organizations. Modern administrative organizations and processes have a sound theoretical basis of their own; they are not merely improvements of older mechanisms. They are basically different from the older procedures. Efforts to improve the old, however, if persisted in with sincerity, lead to study of aims and principles which in turn leads the student into the new. He does not go there under compulsion but through following his own needs and through study which he initiates.[14]

Spears,[15] in preparing for his report, queried the officers of forty school systems and found practically all to be operating under line-and-staff. Many of the officials, however, were making great effort to devise improvements within the line-and-staff organization which would secure greater unity of understanding and effort. The list constitutes an enlightening exhibit, and as Spears says, "many of these attempts go beyond the mere rededication to the line-and-staff principle."

1. Regular meetings of directors, supervisors, and principals to discuss policy.

2. Regular meetings of directors, supervisors, principals, and teachers to discuss policy.

3. The creation of a school policies council made up of representatives of line, staff, and teaching groups.

4. Changing the title of director of elementary education to *co-ordinator* of elementary education to promote unity of action among supervisors and principals.

5. Changing the title of supervisor to *consultant*.

6. The creation of a curriculum council, representing the supervisors, directors, and principals.

7. The creation of a council of teachers and administrators to establish instructional policy.

8. The retention of the usual line-and-staff relationship of supervisor and principal, with the centralization of instructional authority in one position in the central office.

9. The elimination of special-subject supervisors and the substitution of all supervision by area, both vertical and horizontal, that is, supervisors of primary, elementary, junior-high, and senior-high areas.

10. The careful manipulation of supervisors from the central office so that no two are in a building at the same time, thus enabling the principal and supervisor to visit together.

11. The careful designation in the central office of days of the week or month to be used for meetings of particular groups, thus avoiding conflicts and protecting time of teachers, directors, and administrators.

12. Curriculum building by subject areas, an area including representation from kindergarten through the senior high school.

13. Maintenance of the authority of building principal in all cases except those dealing with curriculum planning, in which instance the desires of the special supervisory officers take precedence.

14. For the purpose of guiding instructional leadership and practice, the development of a sound educational philosophy by the entire school family, administrators, teachers, and pupils—a philosophy which all will understand and attempt to practice.

Several of these points clearly indicate that strict line-and-staff is being deserted, whether consciously or not. We may now turn to principles and organizations which are radically different from the conventional systems.

The principles underlying democratic organization. The principles here stated are

[14] The present writer has found that one of the most effective methods of leading experienced teachers who are suspicious of "modern" or "progressive" education is to encourage them to improve their own present methods. Every assistance is given to improve methods which the teacher has used and approves. Honest effort to discover why certain methods are used and to discover the basis for the improvements leads an astonishing number of convinced traditionalists into acceptance and competent use of basically different methods.

Greater success attends this procedure than attends the effort to secure intellectual comprehension of the principles first, divorced from the teacher's practice. The method has been used in a number of workshops and in a curriculum reorganization problem in one of the most conservative New England states. Spears has shown the same thing in his exhibit concerning administrative organization.

[15] *Ibid.,* p. 348. Note list of readings on administrative structure, and the report suggested, at end of chapter.

simply the general principles of democratic supervision set forth in Chapter 4 and now applied directly to the specific problem of administrative organization. The exposition in Chapter 4 will be supplemented here briefly.

1. Authority resides in the situation, in its demands and needs, and in its resources.

2. Authority is derived by persons from the situation and is shared by all who participated in the study and planning for the situation and its solution.

3. Personal or legalistic authority is replaced by responsibility for educational leadership. Educational leadership is centered in the superintendent or any other person in a position ordinarily designated as that of leader, such as a principal or department head, and so forth.

4. Educational leadership and responsibility, however, are shared by all school officials from school boards to teachers. They are shared by pupils and by community members. Any person may suggest a problem, may exercise leadership in developing it, and may be asked to assume formal leadership by the group.

5. Leadership is exercised by securing the full participation of all concerned; not merely in carrying out a policy set up by the leader, but in the very formulation of that policy in the first place, in planning its execution, in carrying it out, and in evaluating it.

6. The new concepts of authority and responsibility are made operable through group-determined rules, mechanisms, and procedures. (A group setting up its own machinery will naturally distinguish between routine mechanics which are performed over and over again and the formulation and carrying out of important educational or instructional policies. The first can be standardized somewhat along the lines of traditional line-and-staff, but note that the entire attitude and point of view will be wholly different when these things are co-operatively formulated by the group and not imposed from above.)

7. Responsibilities and duties of all administrative and supervisory officers are shared with one another and with all other members who of necessity perform duties which interrelate and overlap.

8. The democratic formulation of plans will allow widely for assumption of responsibility for getting things done, for exercising initiative, and for self-evaluation. Any and all persons may assume responsibility, exercise initiative, and perform functions within a framework which has been previously set up by the group itself.

The foregoing eight principles govern external organization, that is, the provision of machinery and personnel. The following three are principles of internal organization, that is, governing the operation of the machinery. *3 prin here*

1. Supervision should be so organized that the fullest participation of all concerned, administrators, supervisors, principals, teachers, any other educational workers, pupils, parents, other community members, is secured in all aspects of carrying on educational programs. This means:

> *a.* All programs of activity will be organized around problems of direct concern to those participating and arising out of their own ongoing activity.
>
> *b.* Councils, committees, subcommittees, conference groups and individual effort will be organized as needed and to serve definite purposes. (See next principles for relation of this to continuity and flexibility.)
>
> *c.* Channels of communication will be free and easy in operation, open to access by all at any time. School officers will receive suggestions from anyone at any time, will be ready with assistance to anyone at any time; will be approachable and adaptable to individual differences in colleagues.

2. Supervisory organization must be flexible enough to adapt itself to the needs of each particular supervisory teaching-learning situation as it arises; must provide for continuity within this flexible adaptation and readaptation.

> a. Continuity will be provided through the co-operatively formulated minimum of rules, of standing and central committees which take care of routine administration and which can act in serious emergencies.
>
> b. The councils, committees, conference groups, and individual study noted in the previous principle as serving wide participation also serve flexibility, particularly as they are disbanded to be replaced by new ones for new problems, as they are reorganized and readapted, as membership changes.

c. Flexibility, like participation, depends upon the democratic conscience, the willing acceptance of obligations and responsibilities.

d. Flexibility, like participation, is aided through simplicity of machinery.

3. Supervisory organization must provide for co-ordination and integration of educational outcomes. Modern supervision will not confine itself to subject divisions; will not compartmentalize its service by grades. It will operate over large centers of interest and areas of experience, bridge gaps between school levels, and so forth.

The principles are, as stated earlier, applications of general principles which were expounded in Chapter 4. Discussion at this point will therefore be sharply curtailed and in summary form.

Regarding the delegation or the co-operative allocation of duties within an organization, Campbell [16] makes one of the most original and provocative suggestions to appear in years:

Creative workers should delegate routine duties to administrators rather than administrators delegating time consuming tasks to creative workers. Educational administrators should clear the way for teachers rather than teachers removing obstructions for administrators. In other words, the essential purpose of administration should be to strengthen and improve instruction. There is no other goal that is of such primary importance. Superintendents and principals who delegate onerous tasks to teachers are in false and untenable positions unless they can show that the assumptions of responsibilities by faculty members give, or will give, increased freedom to all members of the staff.

This is not interpreted as indicating lesser importance for administrators and their duties. It is more accurately an extremely sharp delineation of the important contributions which can be made by administrators in a modern organization.

Authority derived from the situation. We may recall from the earlier discussion that authority is derived from the situation. We derive and define it by asking: (1) What do the needs and demands of the situation authorize us to do? (2) What do the resources of the situation in material and in personnel authorize and permit us to do? (3) What do the known facts of educational science applicable to the situation and the accepted principles of philosophy within the group authorize us to do?

The replacement of centralized legalistic authority and its delegation along defined lines by democratic authority is well stated by Moehlman. [17]

Since the function of organization has been established as a means and not an end, the value of all agents, agencies, and organization forms and practices should be on the basis of their contributions to the achievement of educational objectives. All executive agents and agencies involved in the execution of the program are an entity or unit in terms of purpose. Any person involved in the carrying-out of any part of the educational plan is functionally a part of the executive activity. Every portion of the executive activity is relatively of equal importance to every other portion. Internal subdivision of the executive activity is merely specialization to promote efficiency.

The terminal validity of organization *per se,* the concept of each participating individual as a part of the organic total executive activity, the recognition of competency and conscience as essential to democratic operation and organization structure through which the exercise of civil liberties may be easily maintained are all indicated by these principles.

When public-school personnel is properly oriented in terms of function, the teacher becomes the most important agent in the executive activity, correlative with instruction as the supreme purpose for the organization and operation of the schools. The facilitating personnel essential is of relatively equal importance in the smooth operation of the teaching process. The degree to which these principles may be applied to operation depends upon the competency and conscience of the individuals involved. The practice of democratic procedures does not spring full-blown into life, but develops through laborious and often painful experimentation and slow growth. Neither can

[16] Clyde Campbell, "A Democratic Structure to Further Democratic Values," p. 28.

[17] Arthur B. Moehlman, *School Administration, Its Development, Principles, and Future in the United States* (Boston, Houghton, 1940), pp. 259-260.

it be legislated into the mechanics of organization, for, without competency and the spirit to work democratically, the best techniques are of little avail.

Responsibility for leadership replaces legalistic authority. Chief responsibility rests upon persons in positions from which leadership is expected. Not only is the responsibility shared with all other persons, however, but initiative in leading should be encouraged by the designated leader. Democratic functioning through leadership cannot succeed without genuine acceptance of democratic responsibility in obligation, without the possession of a democratic conscience. Growth of democratic operation is of necessity slow, but this is not cause for discouragement.

The legal authority and the legal responsibility for *adopting* and sustaining educational policies and programs rests with the local board of education where it should properly rest under our theory of local control. Certain legal duties and responsibilities are also vested in the superintendent. The *formulation* of policy, however, is a technical task and can be done only by the trained professional staff. Policies are then presented to the board for acceptance or rejection, not blindly but after consideration and questioning. The board performs a valuable service in asking for explanations, in suggesting changes for consideration. The board cannot formulate policies well but certainly does not have to endorse a staff-formulated policy without question and analysis. Thus the board participates in policy-making in an effective way. The staff works with the board in reformulating a policy if necessary. The co-operative interchange illustrates leadership in place of authority and in no way interferes with duly constituted legal responsibilities. Boards which usurp the policy-making function usually blunder disastrously, as witness the widespread incompetence of school policies in many New England and deep South communities where superintendents and professional staff are practically "hired hands" of the boards.

Shorter terms for, and rotation of, administrative officers might enhance leadership. A drastic change in the nature of tenure for administrative officers has appeared in theory but has not yet affected practice. Shorter terms with revolving tenure within a system or between systems is suggested. Revolutionary as the idea is, it is by no means absurd or impracticable. Good arguments exist in support. First, continued exercise of authority does clearly have detrimental effects upon the thinking and behavior of those possessing the authority. The outcome usually is arbitrary management. Authoritarian management may often be courteous and suave but nonetheless is arbitrary, *ex cathedra,* and unmindful of effects upon personalities under control. Harshness and dogmatism appear in some cases. Second, genuine errors are inevitable, honest though they may be, when persons in authority rely upon their own judgment instead of utilizing wide consultation among colleagues. A corollary under this point is that decisions are often selfish, deliberately disregarding the good of the group or the activity. Third, reversing the first, persons secure in their positions of authority often refuse to study local needs, to make decisions, to take a stand, to take incisive action. They actively avoid any discussion, any interest in progressive developments, any possible action which might endanger their tenure. Fourth, persons protected by tenure often coast along with no thought of study, growth, or leadership. They simply sit. This group is less active than that referred to in the preceding point. This is too obvious with numerous superintendents and principals to need discussion. (The evil is not confined to administrative officers; untold numbers of teachers on all levels are also affected. This is discussed elsewhere.)

Revolving tenure might affect many of these difficulties. The possibilities of shifting from one system to another neighboring one for given periods of time are provocative. The necessity and the freedom to exercise leadership, to achieve some observable results, might be more apparent. Rotation would, of course, not be automatic and all inclusive, able and trained personnel only being concerned. The stimulus to become eligible would be important. All members of a staff might expect to serve in rotation on the many committees dealing with curriculum, instruction, and other items.

Group administration might enhance leadership. Administration of a building by committees instead of by a principal was proposed many years ago for elementary schools and is in operation in some places. The legally appointed principal is a participating member of the committees, but it would not be impossible in the future to eliminate the permanent principal and to elect one from the group.

Staff participation in selection of leaders. The logical application of democratic principles does point toward a greater voice for teachers and the staff *in toto* in the selection of professional leaders. This could be done, as indicated in this and the preceding chapter, without impairing the necessary administrative responsibilities of the leader.

Tenure should become increasingly professional. The foregoing must not be construed as a plea for the abolition of tenure. Tenure, properly utilized, indirectly protects the community and secures efficient service by protecting the teacher from minority pressures, from interference by powerful individuals of local prominence, from arbitrary dismissal because of personal spite. Tenure, properly utilized, protects the teacher directly as indicated. Tenure as applied at present, however, often merely protects the educational worker in the possession of a job without reference to achievement or continued growth. Tenure actually produces in far too many cases individuals who defiantly flaunt

their tenure in the face of suggestions for improvement and growth. The remedy lies in the increasing professionalization of educational workers to the point of recognizing that the sole safe basis for tenure is not legal enactment but efficient service and continued growth in observable degree. Tenure within a professional group should be administered by the group in terms of recognized professional standards and not by legalistic process.

Democratic organization can be efficient. Another question constantly asked, especially by those responsible for large systems or divisions is: Can this loose, co-operatively organized, constantly reshaped machinery actually be efficient? [18] The evidence is not yet extensive, since democratic administration is still emerging slowly. The evidence is scattered widely in articles and bulletins, but it is available. Logical argument as distinguished from evidence is all on the side of democratic organization.

Democratic organization seems to be fully as efficient as the authoritarian in securing everyday routine functioning. Democratic organization seems far more efficient in securing the more important outcomes such as the personal growth of staff and pupils, maintaining mental health, eliminating fear and suspicion with their accompanying inhibitions and destruction of creativity, securing greater community participation in and respect for the educational system. The dynamic, variable, unpredictable aspects of any co-operative human activity are easily cared for by democratic administration but are often ignored by too rigid authoritarian procedure. Dynamic processes do not submit readily to cut-and-dried rules or mechanisms. Government and industry, from which we borrowed the authoritarian procedures, are discovering this and, particularly in industry,

---

[18] Excellent brief materials bearing upon the efficiency of democratic organization are scattered through *Democracy in School Administration*, by Koopman, Miel, and Misner. For an excellent detailed illustration see Arthur D. Hollingshead, *Guidance in Democratic Living* (Appleton-Century-Crofts, 1941).

See also many of the monographs and texts referred to in Ch. 4 of this volume.
Parallel arguments referring to classroom teaching with citation of six studies will be found in William H. Burton, *The Guidance of Learning Activities,* 2nd ed. (New York, Appleton-Century-Crofts, 1952), pp. 222-224.

are moving toward democratic organization.

Authoritarian administration is often not nearly as efficient as claimed because of indifference or antagonism within the structure. The actions of persons or committees to which authority has been delegated are often questioned. The limits of delegated authority are debated. Wrangling and waste motion often result within what is outwardly a logically organized mechanism.

Democratic co-operation operates within a framework. The problem of formal organization of machinery has been left out of the discussion up to this point so that the principles enunciated would receive all attention and emphasis. Democratic organization is not as some fear, amorphous, without recognizable and dependable structure. Democratic leadership operates within a framework. Without a framework, without mechanisms, without rules and controls, the results are inevitably incoherence and chaos. The contrast between authoritarian and democratic organization is not that of structure versus no structure. The contrast lies in the *origin* and *purpose* of the structures, in the *form, operation,* and *controls* within the structures. A brief resummary of points selected from the foregoing detailed presentation will throw the contrasts into sharp relief.

Origin and purpose. Authoritarian structure is set up by legally designated leaders and is in part itself determined by law. The real purpose of education may or may not be influential in the process of devising the machinery. The purpose may sometime become, whether recognized or not, the logicality of the system and its smooth operation. Duties may be and often are assigned functionally in authoritarian systems, but in an overwhelming number of school systems the duties are assigned in wholly arbitrary manner. In others, distribution is made in terms of the predetermined machinery instead of functional relationship. The distribution of duties in certain large cities could have been made equally well by drawing straws.

Democratic structure emerges through the co-operative effort of those who are to operate it. The purpose is to serve given teaching-learning situations. Duties are more likely to be assigned functionally. The improvement of learning is more likely to be the primary consideration; smooth operation secondary. Errors here are usually traceable to incorrect understandings of democracy.

Form. Distinction will be made, in setting up any forms, between the *simple, repetitive, routine* operations of a school system and the *dynamic, variable,* unpredictable, necessarily experimental aspects of the educational process which the system is to serve.

The informal organizations [19] which spring up within the formal in order to take care of the unpredictable variables, or for special *ad hoc* purposes, are now known to be a significant part of any organization.

Informal organizations are found within all formal organizations, the latter being essential to order and consistency, the former to vitality. These are mutually reactive phases of co-operation, and they are mutually dependent.

We have always known that informal, socially determined procedures will appear within the formal and officially established organization. Currently, however, this is being openly recognized and efforts are being made to take advantage of this inevitable and obviously effective social process. Cornell [20] says concerning this:

A number of studies and several action programs have emerged as a result of this development under the leadership of Paul R. Mort. See Paul R. Mort and Francis G. Cornell, *Adaptability of Public School Systems* (New York, Teachers College, Bureau of Publications, Columbia Univ., 1938); also by same authors, *American Schools in Transition* (New York, Teachers College, Bureau of Publications, Columbia Univ., 1941).

[19] Chester I. Barnard, *The Functions of the Executive* (Cambridge, Harvard Univ. Press, 1948), p. 286.

[20] Francis G. Cornell (with the assistance of Darrell J. Inabnit), "Administrative Organization as Social Structure," *Progressive Education* (November, 1952), p. 32.
The adaptability concept is concerned with the processes by which a school system adapts itself to its physical, social, and intellectual environment.

The key to the idea we wish to emphasize here is the term *vitality* in the quotation from Bernard above. For it is this unconventional grouping of people in uncharted and unexpected situations for which there are no formal rules, from which new structures, new institutionalized functions, develop. It is an interesting thing that this relates itself to the concept of adaptability in school administration, one of the few dynamic principles which has emerged in this field in the past quarter of a century.

The machinery for the more dynamic aspects can, under democracy, be made and remade as situations develop. Councils, committees, study groups will appear here as they did under the authoritarian scheme, but they will not be set up in advance of an actual situation, not set up by the central staff, and they will not remain fixed. Democratic mechanisms will be organized to suit the situations to be served and by the persons involved; mechanisms will come and go; membership will change. The flow will as often or more often originate in the committees of teachers, teachers and supervisors, teachers and pupils, or community members as it does in the central offices. All types of contact will be free and easy, instead of confined to sharply defined lines and channels.

With either authoritarian or democratic conditions, the machinery for everyday operation of a school system will appear *outwardly* to be very similar. *Inwardly,* however, the whole attitude and setting will be different because all persons concerned participated in the co-operative formulation of the scheme, all persons know it can be redesigned to meet new needs, all persons know that they individually may suggest modifications and participate in reshaping the structure.

Operation. The operation of typical traditional school organizations is of necessity mechanical and formal to lesser or greater degree; it may be, though not necessarily so, dictatorial and repressive. Democratic organization to be successful must operate with considerable flexibility, and with full recognition of the inescapable human factors involved whenever two or more persons work together. This leads us to controls.

Controls. Authoritarian controls seem to be easy and simple. Clearly stated rules, definition of areas of activity, lines of authority, control all actions. Rigidity differs with systems, workers being given considerable freedom in some, reduced to actual puppets in others.

Democratic organization provides for broad assumption of initiative in getting things done. What then keeps individuals from "going off in all directions at once"? What prevents confusion, incoherence, friction, clash? The first and simplest control is that of the co-operatively formulated general framework within which all are working. The second is the co-operatively determined policy and distribution of duties set up especially for any given project. The worker exercises initiative within a framework which he helped to set up, hence understands, and to which he gives loyalty. Initiative will be along the lines of bringing the individual's particular contribution to the aid of the common outlined plan and procedure. The third control is the recognition by any honest and sensible person that he loses the respect and confidence of his co-workers and actually destroys his own effectiveness if he ignores all controls. The fourth control is the most remote but perhaps the most powerful, the democratic conscience previously discussed. This is collective self-control. Individuals will need to possess firm and lasting belief in the democratic process and be determined to uphold it by working within its self-assumed obligations. If that sounds utopian and if we do not have faith that it will work, then we need not worry about the problem longer. Democracy is then merely an idle dream. The democratic process in school and in society will work only as it is based on convictions of democracy and upon willing assumption of its responsibilities.

Simple illustration of democratic procedure. A simple everyday situation and one which causes much trouble even under the carefully defined controls of the authoritarian system is the flow of assistance to an individual teacher or group of teachers. All suggestions and materials must reach the teacher, traditionally, through one source, the building principal. Under democratic supervision, advice and aid may flow from several sources to one person or group. Suggestions may come to a teacher (or pupil, or principal, or supervisor, or superintendent) from several fellow-teachers, from several supervisors or other consultants, from special service personnel. The suggestions may come in response to a request from a teacher who under democracy has the right to consult any co-worker, or the suggestions may be volunteered by co-workers who under democracy accept the obligation to offer help if the situation demands it. A problem in co-ordination is presented.

First, suggestions from various persons are not likely to be seriously contradictory and confusing when given by co-workers who set up in the first place the policy and plan under which they are giving and receiving advice. Second, the person receiving the advice, instead of giving way to complaint if advice does conflict, has under democracy not only the right but the obligation to weigh suggestions in the light of known facts; to accept or reject on the basis of logic and evidence. Third, the individual may discuss with the various advisers the possibility of attempting through round-robin conversations to sift and co-ordinate. Fourth, the teacher may ask the various specialists for a brief group conference for analysis of suggestions. The foregoing analysis holds for any officer in the system from superintendent to custodian, and for groups of persons.

Democratic organization should result from growth, not from an administrative order. The lengthy analysis of and plea for democratic organization does not mean that we are to throw overboard the traditional organizations we have. Democracy in school administration will result from long slow growth, as it has in all other human activities;

it will be evolved through long, patient, but constant effort by all members of the staff studying and working together.

Serious obstacles [21] stand in the way. First, and probably the most dangerous, is the long entrenched tradition of authoritarian administration. Second, and corollary to this, is inertia and unwillingness to change among those with vested interests in the old. Political patronage in some systems is a part of this point. Third, there is lack of knowledge of and experience with the democratic process. This is a challenge as well as an obstacle. Fourth, it is said that "human nature" is against change, against assumption of responsibility, against the constant alertness, the "eternal vigilance" which is the price of democratic freedom. Human nature has potentials of equal, if not greater, power for progress, for courageous assumption of responsibility, for persisting through disappointments toward ideal goals. Currently a fifth obstacle has emerged, namely, the interference of pressure groups whose interest is anything but the improvement of the schools. Organized for selfish, often even evil reasons, they constitute a serious threat to better school organization. Even those groups who are sincerely interested in school improvement become obstacles whenever they mistakenly assume that they speak for the community, and particularly when they become impatient and resort to the methods of pressure rather than of study and persuasion.

The chief point is that democratic organization is wholly possible of achievement by any group which desires it ardently enough and which will do something about it. Democratic organizations are beginning to appear in increasing numbers not merely in education but in industry as well. The cardinal sin

[21] Roberta Green, "The Obstacles to Democratic Administration as Seen by a Teacher," *Progressive Education* (November, 1952), pp. 35-37.
Russell Malan "Obstacles to Democratic Administration as Seen by an Administrator," *ibid.,* pp. 37-41.
Irvin R. Kuentzli, "What Group Does the Administrator Represent?" *ibid.,* pp. 46-50.

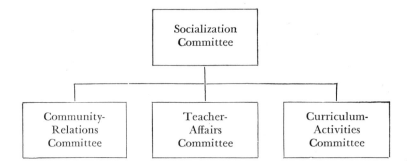

THE UNIT OF PARTICIPATION

From G. Robert Koopman, Alice Miel, and Paul J. Misner, *Democracy in School Administration* (New York, Appleton-Century-Crofts, Inc., 1943), p. 81.

is to sit around and discuss it without doing anything about it. Educational workers must not be discouraged by obstacles nor bamboozled by those opposed to democracy. They must study the principles and then endeavor to take action.[22]

Democratic organizations schematically represented. Democratic organization cannot be charted so easily as the traditional mechanisms. General outlines can be presented which, it is hoped, will stimulate groups to develop their schemes. Charts are static representations of dynamic processes. Councils, committees, and the like change; personnel is constantly changing within a democratic organization. Charts must be examined with those facts in mind.

Illustrations of the general theory of supervisory organization for a single school and for the system. Before taking up actual illustrations found in practice we may examine schematic outlines of the theory. One of the best discussions is found in Koopman, Miel, and Misner. The chart [23] on this page shows the set-up which they advocate for a single building and which is based upon the following assumptions.

1. Teachers as a professional group, charged with important social responsibilities, should continuously study their own professional problems if the school is to function as a dynamic social agency. The need for such study suggests the formation of a committee which is called here the "Teacher-Affairs Committee." The

essential functions of the Teacher-Affairs Committee are:

> *a.* Keeping faculty members informed concerning the activities of professional organizations to the end that the rights and responsibilities of all professional agents may be recognized and discharged effectively.
>
> *b.* Facilitating the personal and professional growth of all agents by making available the services of specialists and the results of significant studies, reports, and writings which will help each person to become an increasingly alert, informed, and useful member of the profession and of society.
>
> *c.* Promoting optimum security for teachers.
>
> *d.* Providing opportunities whereby professional agents may participate in recreational and social activities which will further normal human relationships.
>
> *e.* Representing the faculty in the translation of accepted policies into action.

2. A public school needs the application of intensive group thinking to the end that its activities may have unity of purpose. Opportunity for such group thinking is provided by a committee which is called here the "Cur-

[22] Alfred D. Simpson, "Critique of the Administrative Structure from the Standpoint of Democratic Concepts," *ibid.,* pp. 42-45.

For extended analysis see texts referred to earlier by Koopman, Miel, and Misner; Moehlman; Mort; Campbell.

Nolan C. Kearney, "Freedom-Responsibility," *Progressive Education* (November, 1952), pp. 51-52.

[23] Koopman, Miel, and Misner, *op. cit.,* Ch. 4.

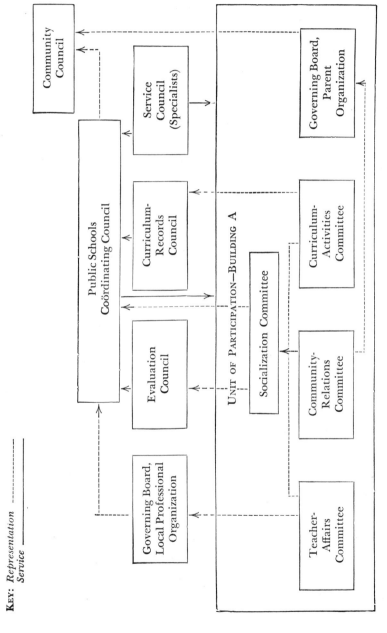

Key: *Representation* ----------
Service ——————

ALL-CITY ORGANIZATION

From G. Robert Koopman, Alice Miel, and Paul J. Misner, *Democracy in School Administration* (New York, Appleton-Century-Crofts, Inc., 1943), p. 86.

Community Council

Service Council (Specialists)

Governing Board, Parent Organization

Public Schools Coördinating Council

Curriculum-Records Council

UNIT OF PARTICIPATION—BUILDING A

Socialization Committee

Curriculum-Activities Committee

Evaluation Council

Community-Relations Committee

Governing Board, Local Professional Organization

Teacher-Affairs Committee

riculum-Activities Committee." The essential functions of this committee are:

 a. Adapting general curriculum policies for use in a given building.
 b. Organizing the learning experiences of students, including student participation in the administration of the school, and planning the use of specialists.
 c. Developing techniques of evaluating the curriculum experiences of students.
 d. Keeping curriculum records.

 e. Planning the instructional budget.
 f. Planning utilization of school plant.
 g. Planning replacements and additions to school plant.

3. Real experiences must be the basis of the educative process and, therefore, the total environment in which persons live must be recognized as the source of the most important learning experiences. This suggests the need for a committee that is called here the "Community-Relations Committee." The essential functions of the Community-Relations Committee are:

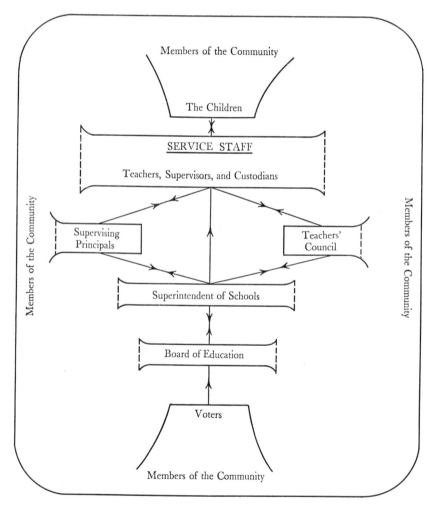

PROPOSED CHART OF THE ORGANIZATION OF A SCHOOL SYSTEM: NEW COMMUNITY-CENTERED SET-UP

Arrows indicate lines of policy formation and authority. Flares and broken lines indicate interplay between the school organization and the community. From Clarence A. Newell, "The Children Are at the Top in This Organizational Chart Based on Modern Educational Design," *The Nation's Schools* (June, 1943), pp. 24-25.

a. Facilitating the participation of all members of the community in planning, executing, and appraising educational policies and activities.

b. Planning interpretative programs and exhibits.

c. Making available objective data concerning community educational needs through the technique of the continuous community survey.

d. Co-operating with community groups in the continuous development of effective agencies and activities of adult education.

4. The activities of these basic committees must be co-ordinated if they are to be effective in promoting socialization. This requires the organization of a co-ordinating committee which is called here the "Socialization Committee." The essential functions of the Socialization Committee are:

a. Surveying and evaluating social life in order better to criticize the several

functions of the school in society.

b. Interpreting results of evaluation activities in terms of the unitary objective of education—democratic socialization.

c. Determining steps, emphases, and sequences—the strategy of school administration.

d. Reviewing, co-ordinating, and integrating activities of students, teachers, specialists, and community groups.

e. Maintaining balance among the activities of students, teachers, and community groups.

The chart on page 119 shows the general scheme for a city-wide organization. The assumptions given above for the building organization hold here. Other relationships are inferrable from the chart.

A very ingenious scheme proposed by Newell is seen in the chart on page 120. He

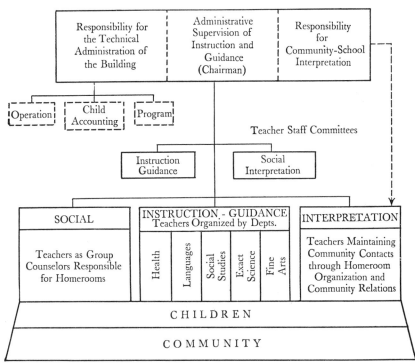

THE ADMINISTRATIVE COMMITTEE

ADMINISTRATIVE ORGANIZATION UNDER COMMITTEE PLAN OR MULTIPLE PRINCIPALSHIP

From Arthur B. Moehlman, *School Administration, Its Development, Principles, and Future in the United States* (Boston, Houghton Mifflin Company, 1940), p. 540.

wishes to emphasize that the school organization works not in a vacuum but within a community. The lines designating groups flare out toward the community and are set off from the community only by dotted lines indicating that no complete barrier should exist. Easy interplay should be indicated. The general principles set forth by Newell are similar to those in this chapter.

An excellent scheme for single building administration is given by Moehlman and is seen in the chart on page 121.

Illustrations of actual practice in small and large systems. The chart below shows a simple organization for the small system of Webster Groves, Missouri. The chart on page 123 shows the somewhat more complicated organization in Denver, Colorado.

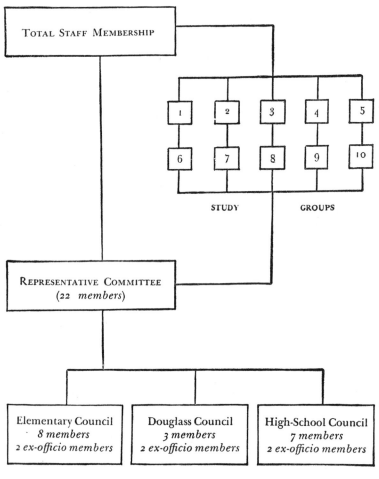

ORGANIZATION FOR PROBLEM-SOLVING, WEBSTER GROVES, MISSOURI

From G. Robert Koopman, Alice Miel, and Paul J. Misner, *Democracy in School Administration* (New York, Appleton-Century-Crofts, Inc., 1943), p. 95.

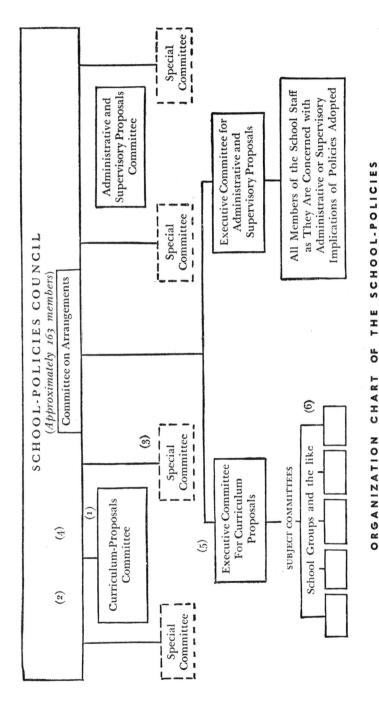

ORGANIZATION CHART OF THE SCHOOL-POLICIES COUNCIL OF DENVER PUBLIC SCHOOLS

The numbers indicate the order through which a curriculum proposal may pass from initial proposal to adoption and execution. An administrative or supervisory proposal would progress in the same manner through the committees indicated on the right-hand side of the chart. From G. Robert Koopman, Alice Miel, and Paul J. Misner, *Democracy in School Administration* (New York, Appleton-Century-Crofts, Inc., 1943), p. 98.

CHAPTER SUPPLEMENT

GENERAL QUESTIONS FOR INTRODUCTORY DISCUSSION

1. What are the characteristics of each of the following types of supervisory organization, their strength and weaknesses?

    a. Dualistic.

    b. Line and staff.

    c. Co-ordinate.

2. What is probably the most significant weakness of the line and staff system?

3. What is probably the one most significant influence which is bringing in the newer, more democratic organization? Other factors?

4. How can we avoid confusion, if not indeed chaos, within a non-authoritarian organization?

5. In what sense can organization be regarded as emergent rather than as fixed?

6. What is meant by organismic supervision?

7. What is the function of the community council, as discussed by Olsen? (See footnote 7, Ch. 4 for references.)

8. What should be the role of the State Department of Education in supervision?

9. How organize the staff of a fifteen-teacher elementary school for supervision? Tentative, brief analysis at this point.

10. Show that administration and supervision are mutually related and co-ordinated functions. Do not restate points from chapter. Go beyond this, using illustrations if available.

DISCUSSION QUESTIONS CALLING FOR MORE EXTENDED ANALYSIS

1. List several reasons of major importance showing why it is of the utmost importance that any given school system attack and make tentative solution for the problem presented in this chapter.

2. Examine critically the two outlines (authoritarian and co-operative) of principles given in this chapter.

    a. If there are any principles omitted in either scheme which you think should be included, mention them and present arguments.

    b. If there are any principles with which you cannot agree, present your arguments.

3. Cite from your own experience (either as teacher, supervisor, principal, superintendent) two concrete illustrations of difficulty arising from lack of good administrative organization within the school system. Describe the cases briefly, indicating how the application of principles in this chapter might have obviated the trouble.

4 Cite from your own experience any illustrations you may have encountered wherein organizations were operating effectively whether authoritarian or co-operative.

5. The chart on page 125, as the title indicates, represents an organization widely found in small and medium-size school systems. It has some merit and is susceptible to improvement.

Examine it carefully and be prepared to suggest important improvements or to justify the phases which you would retain.

(The writers have found that a large, wall-size reproduction of this chart (or other similar ones), hung where all can see it, is a great aid to class discussion. Instructors and field workers will find discussion here very rewarding but tending to become extended. The point of diminishing returns must be recognized.)

ORAL REPORT

A student can report with benefit to the class Chapter 12 in the Eleventh Yearbook of the Department of Supervisors and Directors of Instruction. (This material may be given as reading for the class instead.)

WRITTEN REPORTS

Superintendents, supervisors, principals, and others are urged to use their own situations in answering some of these exercises. Class members will recognize that frank discussions of local situations are confidential.

1. Describe in some detail with charts the administrative organization within your system with special reference to supervision.

    a. Include an analytic statement showing agreement or disagreement with principles.

    b. Include definite suggestions for improvement if the present organization is not satisfactory.

(Be specific in presenting the conditions within the situation; size of system, traditions, personnel, type of population, or other significant items.)

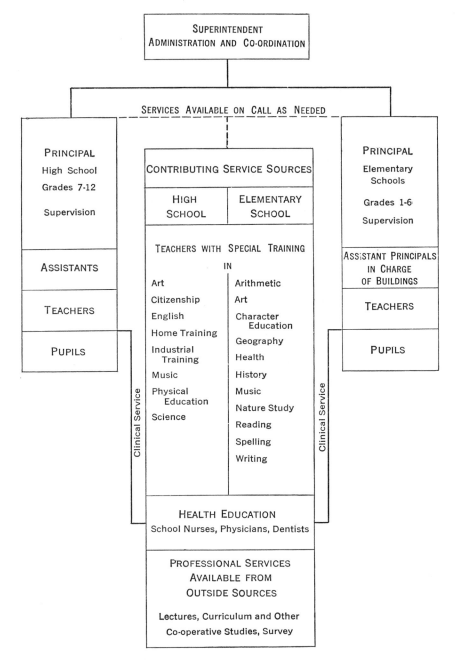

A COMMON TYPE OF ORGANIZATION

2. An individual, preferably a committee, should meet with the superintendent and central staff of any nearby co-operating school system or with several such systems and discuss the actual problems arising within the organization, methods of flexible adjustment, and so forth.

Superintendents and supervisors may be invited to meet with the class for similar discussion.

3. Individuals or a committee may examine the charts given in the concluding pages of this chapter with a view to improving on the

organization and relationships shown. Do the same for any recent charts appearing in current literature.

CLASS PROJECT NO. III
THE IMPLICATIONS OF DEMOCRATIC PRINCIPLES

Chapters 1, 3, and 4 have presented a new definition and aim for supervision. Chapter 5 has outlined a new view on administrative structure. All this has presented and explained the co-operative, democratic philosophy under which supervision should operate.

Make a list of important consequences which should flow from the extension in practice of the modern concept and democratic philosophy. The list should refer to basic and fundamental considerations and not to minor techniques or superficial aspects. Make at least seven or eight points, more if possible. (A total of nineteen has been compiled.)

This question is highly important because it first tests the student's understanding of the materials to this point, and second tests his ability to infer consequences and to foresee results.

(Students often make the mistake of including in their answers such statements as: "Supervision will be more co-operative," "more democratic," "more sympathetic," "teachers will participate," "there will result a more friendly spirit," and so forth. These answers are worthless, the points being themselves characteristics of democratic supervision. The real question is: granted all these and more, what results can one expect? The real answer includes effects upon any and all aspects of education, of the personnel, and the situation which should result from democratic operation of supervision.

Chapter 6

♦·♦··♦··♦··♦··♦··♦

The Co-operative Planning of Supervisory Programs

THE FOREGOING CHAPTERS have set forth in general terms what supervision is and why we must have it. Its major functions have been listed. The philosophy under which these functions should be exercised has been outlined. Various schemes for organizing personnel and allocating duties have been suggested. We come now to one of the most important problems in the whole field, namely, how the actual work of supervision should be planned and carried out.

We wish to emphasize at the very opening of the chapter that planning as presented here is continuous, emergent, and developmental, geared to actual situations. We do not mean formal planning wholly in advance, and slavishly followed. Constant re-planning is inherent in our conception.

Planning is a fundamental principle of supervision. One of the marks of intelligence and special ability is foresight and anticipatory planning. Careful planning for the future enables one individual or group, other things being equal, to accomplish things which unorganized individuals or groups not only cannot achieve but cannot understand.

Supervision particularly requires planning. It is an unusually complicated process. Many different factors must be considered. There is, first, a group of learners of various ages, chronological and mental, of varied purposes, interests, backgrounds, and degrees of intelligence. Second, there are many and different outcomes to be accomplished singly by the learner but simultaneously by those promoting learning. Third, there are subject matter, instructional material, and many learning activities of varying complexity and accessibility. The nationality of the pupils, their social and economic status, that of the school, and the types of buildings and rooms available will all complicate the matter. Furthermore, some of these factors change from term to term, from week to week, and even from day to day. Fourth, there is a group of educational workers who vary in age, background, and temperament as widely as do the pupils. These adults will differ greatly as to their philosophy of education and theory of learning, and as to their beliefs in the nature of subject matter. Fifth, important developments in the field of education are so rapid that it is a difficult task merely to keep the school system abreast of valuable new departures. Lastly, there is the necessity of securing unification or integration of educational effort through supervision. It may be repeated that supervision is highly complicated. Improvised, inspirational, opportunistic, random, desultory, and haphazard supervision inevitably results in chaos. The planning of this complex human activity necessitates the co-operative participation of all concerned.

An educational staff without a program has no point of departure and no destination. The value of supervision, furthermore, cannot be determined well, if at all, unless a plan is set up sufficiently definite so that the results of its operation can be measured. The staff must have clearly in mind the objectives which they wish to attain; they must know the methods by which these outcomes may be accomplished; they must know some of the obstacles which will likely appear; they must learn how to adjust the means and facilities available to the achievement of the desired end. A good deal of ineffectual supervision exists because groups have failed to make definite plans.

Several definite reasons may be advanced in support of planning. A planning program:

1. Secures a unification of effort by:
   a. Continuous scrutiny and restatement of the aims of education.
   b. Evaluation of extent to which outcomes are being achieved.
   c. Continuous reorganization and enrichment of the curriculum
   d. Functional administration for carrying on the program.
2. Secures an easier co-ordination of the work of all persons, teachers, supervisors, administrators, specialists.
3. Supplies professional stimulation to all staff members, keeps the system abreast of the times, improves levels of skill and of insight through:
   a. Opportunities to participate in co-operative formulation of policies and plans.
   b. Opportunities to exercise leadership.
   c. Opportunity to try out experimentally new departures agreed upon by the staff, or one's own creative contribution.
4. Insures for a specific situation that the staff has examined outcomes and procedures; has analyzed needs and resources; has selected certain needs or new departures for intensive study.
5. Insures an orderly sequence of professional activities directed toward the achievement of the objectives selected. Vague and general supervision, mere routine visitation and conference, un-co-ordinated meetings, are replaced by a dynamic, emerging series of diverse activities.
6. Gives the school board and lay public clearer understanding of the work being done by the schools.
7. Affords the necessary basis for evaluating the success of the educational program under direction by the local staff.
8. Gives security and confidence to the entire staff.

9. Furthers the crucial objective of the whole educational program, namely, the enhancement of learning through constantly improving the total setting for learning.

The necessity for planning of supervision is securing increasing recognition. A comprehensive survey of supervisory planning in 259 cities of all sizes, distributed over the country, was made in 1925 by students in the writer's seminar in supervision. Very few cities submitted plans. Some of the larger ones indicated that their work was well planned but was of such nature that it could not be reduced easily to a written statement. A large number submitted no plans at all, and several stated frankly that they did not know what was meant.

Many replies indicated that the so-called plan of supervision merely meant a routine schedule of visiting and conference, plus teachers' meetings, demonstration teaching, and the like. Very rarely was the work organized around central problems growing out of the needs of the schools. In those days supervision was still looked upon as visitation and conference. Supervisors were not adequately trained for the work, and even if they were, administrative and clerical duties very often prevented the exercise of constructive supervisory leadership. The authoritarian form of administrative organization was not always able to secure co-operation between defined fields and lines of contact. The very complexity of the circumstances, mentioned above, discouraged planning.

Great progress has been made since 1925. Summary compilations have not been made, but much evidence is available in magazine articles and in city, county, and state reports.

Long-term and short-term planning. Early statements concerning planning have recently been criticized as involving only short-term outlook; as being fragmentary and badly articulated, or not articulated at all. The criticisms are correct. We must distinguish between long-term and short-term plans.

Any school system, superintendent, or group of supervisors which is alert and progressive must set up and operate a long-term program and work on certain far-reaching major objectives. These objectives should involve fundamental aspects of education and will be both administrative and supervisory in nature. We are here concerned only with the more directly supervisory aspects of long-term planning.

The long-term supervisory objectives will be derived from some of the basic aims and purposes of education in general and from the more specific purposes of supervision.

The original edition of this text long ago pointed out that there are two general types of planning:

1. Co-operative planning of group attack upon long-term general objectives and problems (though sometimes also group planning of more limited attack on specific problems).
2. Planning assistance and encouragement to individual teachers in carrying on individual study and procedures on specific problems.

Spears,[1] in a good analysis, breaks this up into four different "fronts":

1. Co-ordinating the total instructional program.
2. Providing for the continuous in-service development of teachers and staff.
3. Providing proper and adequate instructional materials.
4. Helping teachers with their individual problems.

The four points are not, of course, separate operations. Spears then indicates that two approaches to the major objective are indicated. One is the continuous, long-term, general, or wholesale improvement of major aspects of the school program. The second is the concentration upon the limited objectives of an individual building, or small group, or a single teacher. He illustrates this view with the following listing:

1. Broad supervision.
   a. The development of science teaching guides for all elementary classrooms.
   b. Committee study and selection of social studies materials for city-wide use.
   c. A study of better adjustment of the school system's first-grade program to the maturity of the children.
   d. Helping to organize and to conduct a three-week workshop devoted to guidance and counseling in the county schools.
2. Concentrated supervision.
   a. Helping a beginning teacher who has had difficulty in classroom management.
   b. Arranging a schedule of visitation for two teachers of a junior high school who wish to inaugurate a combination citizenship-English core course.
   c. Providing additional reading material for a primary teacher who has been using a single set of readers.
   d. Working with the staff of a small rural high school which is to be evaluated later in the year by an accrediting committee.
   e. Working with a weak teacher who is serving the last year of a three-year probationary term.

The more concentrated type of supervision may range from trouble-shooting, through brief follow-up programs with a teacher or small group, to a fairly long series of activities. Spears points out that while this type of supervision lacks the broad sweep and glamour of the large programs in curriculum planning, it is nevertheless as essential as the broad type.

[1] Harold Spears, *Improving the Supervision of Instruction* (New York, Prentice-Hall, 1953), pp. 150-153.

Section 1

PRINCIPLES AND PROCESSES OF PLANNING

Principles governing planning. The nature of supervisory planning is made clearer and the objections or criticisms are further answered by scrutiny of its underlying principles.

Principle 1. *The supervisory program should be formulated co-operatively; should be an expression of the combined thinking of teachers, supervisors, administrators, pupils, and community members, concerning the needs of the situation.*

Supervisory programs indicate the direction of effort for all those involved with the instructional program. All concerned have their own typical contributions to make to the program and its operation. Teachers in particular will not be antagonistic or indifferent to supervision when they assist in setting up the objectives and in carrying out the program. The community likewise will support and defend a program in which laymen have participated. An organized program is always tentative; it will have to be redesigned freely as it progresses. A soundly derived program will be set up co-operatively; it will then guide the co-operative efforts of the staff in achieving it.

Principle 2. *The supervisory program should be derived from the setting for learning; be based on facts concerning the needs of the persons and the material setting.*

The principle here stated is really a corollary of the one preceding. Supervision, together with many other phases of education has suffered from the lack of careful reporting of facts, lack of critical scrutiny of facts, lack of unambiguous language in describing and evaluating facts. The derivation of reasonably complete and precise facts must precede and be continuous with the planning of supervisory programs. A good deal of so-called planning in both administration and supervision is really vague generalizing. It is often superficial and definitely inaccurate. Exhortatory and evangelical discussion, together with pious hope that desirable outcomes will somehow eventuate, is substituted for critically derived, evaluated, and carefully organized proposals for action.

The problem of finding a basis for a supervisory program is difficult; we are observing (1) an activity and not a situation, (2) a process which is constantly changing and not a routine repetition, (3) an activity and process of unusual complexity. Observers, furthermore, differ in their conclusions.

Principle 3. *The supervisory program should be flexible.*

The principles and general mechanisms for securing flexibility were presented in some detail in Chapters 4 and 5. These may be applied here. A planning program is constantly being readjusted, replanned, as the situation changes. General ideas may be repeated from the earlier chapter for the sake of emphasis:

a. Flexibility is enhanced when staff and community members have participated in the co-operative formulation of the plan. The group thus understands the aim and processes set up, understands the connections and ramifications. They are thus ready and able to make necessary changes and readjustments with a minimum of confusion.

b. Flexibility is enhanced by provision for free and easy contact of all persons with each other, by provision for easy meeting of groups for conference, by shifting membership on committees, and so forth.

c. The number of objectives may be kept small and plans for achieving them reasonably simple. This makes for flexibility in that fewer connections must be broken, fewer procedures upset as changes emerge.

d. The objectives, while definite, should not be prescriptive. Fixed goals, particularly of pupil achievement, make for rigidity and formality. Directional-progress goals facilitate flexibility.

Principle 4. *The supervisory program should include provision for its own testing or evaluation.*

An error easy to fall into is *post hoc ergo propter hoc,* that is, assuming that certain results are caused by certain preceding events. Very often the same results would have been achieved without the preceding events, or with another sequence of preliminaries. This naïve fallacy appears in many recent educational reports and research studies. Chapter 18 discusses this.

In educational reports, another weakness which in some instances skirts very close to unethical practice is to seize upon whatever results do appear, claim credit for them, and assert that these were the results which had been desired from the beginning.

It is necessary that supervisory programs state in advance, with such definiteness as precarious and emergent social plans permit, the evidence that legitimately may be expected to appear as proof of the efficacy of the plan. In simple situations it may be test scores or statistical statements. In others it may be the appearance of objectively observable and describable institutions, mechanisms, materials, and so forth. In still others it may be objectively describable changes in teacher or pupil activities or attitudes. In more complex situations it may be a subjective but organized evaluation of results in terms of predetermined criteria. In any event, the plan must include reference to tests, checks, criteria to be used in determining the degree of success attained. Needless to say, any evaluation of supervisory plans is to be made democratically, with all members of the staff free to participate.

There is now in existence a small but respectable body of evidence indicating the value and success of supervisory planning, or of supervisory devices singly. Experimental studies on this problem are summarized in Chapter 18.

The steps in planning for supervisory programs. The planning of any important enterprise goes through a number of steps,

mental and overt. The general outlines of this process are known. Specific application to supervision is made herewith.

1. *Evaluate the educational product at various stages of development, in the light of accepted objectives, by means of suitable instruments and procedures of appraisal. Achievement, behavior, and growth are to be included in the evaluation.* The methods of evaluating the products of learning are presented in detail in Chapter 9.

Fact-finding techniques are in general known to experienced supervisors and advanced students. The six chapters in Part II of this volume are devoted to these techniques and their uses. Facts will be sought concerning the pupil as a person, concerning outcomes and factors affecting outcomes, concerning the community attitudes, beliefs, and resources for education. The teaching staff, curriculum, and instructional materials must all be examined.

2. *List the shortcomings, problems, difficulties, or needs revealed by the appraisal. Study the situation to discover causes of the deficiencies.*

List at this point also any new departures which might be considered for introduction into the local situation.

The appraisal reveals needs. This, with analysis of causes of difficulties, leads to formulation of problems.

Needs and problems may range from the difficulty a teacher (or a few teachers) is having with classroom management, to system-wide curriculum reorganization. A fairly large number of problems may be revealed in some systems, a smaller number in other systems.

Possible new procedures must also be considered. Scientific experimentation is constantly producing new techniques in all phases of education. Philosophic analysis develops new aims and policies, with changed emphases on techniques. Empirical procedure in the field produces still other things worthy of attention and trial. Innovations may concern teaching procedures, organization of curriculum materials, administrative procedures, in-service training techniques, evaluational procedures, and so forth. The introduction, or at least the trial, of new procedures and policies is one of the most important characteristics of the dynamic field of education. Supervisory leadership should constantly be suggesting the trial in local situations of new ideas for the improvement of the educational product.

3. *Select through group discussion a list of problems, or needs, or new departures which seem most urgently to require attention. State these as objectives for the improvement program.* Certain items may be for long-term attack, others for short-term campaigns. Objectives may deal, as already indicated, with any and all legitimate needs which may be met through group attack. Statements of objectives, of course, should be definite and concrete, indicating clearly what the aim actually is. Typical errors in the statements of objectives are (1) failure to be definite, (2) confusion between the objective and the means, and (3) confusion between the objective and a statement of attitude or policy. The following specific illustrations, taken from actual plans, may be of assistance. The form of statement may be changed or abbreviated as desired.

Objectives which are broad in scope and sound are: [2]

To develop understanding of the theory and practice of unit organization of teaching materials.
To develop understanding of the theory and practice of creative activity.
To continue work on the construction or reorganization of the instructional guide in health (or social studies, or general science, or second-grade activities, and so forth).
To develop a more unified theory of supervision.
To introduce manuscript writing into the first grade and to improve cursive writing in the other grades.
To develop co-operatively an analysis sheet for use by teachers, principals, and supervisors in the study of instructional practice.

Objectives which are less broad in scope and sound are:

To establish a junior first grade to meet the needs of immature children who are not sufficiently developed to profit by typical first-grade work.
To improve the teaching of fundamental skills of arithmetic in fifth grade.
To improve the teaching of work-type reading in the seventh grade.
To assist teachers with the elimination of certain typical language errors found in given groups of pupils (sometimes in given groups of teachers).
To train teachers in the use of diagnostic tests in reading (or writing, arithmetic, and so forth) appropriate to the level involved.

Objectives which are vague or indefinite as stated, and which need accurate restatement are:

To diagnose the specific needs of different groups and to organize remedial instruction.
To improve instruction. (This is the whole long-time and continuous objective of all supervision.)
To improve teachers in service.
To reorganize the course of study.
To secure more worth-while use of textbooks.
To teach pupils to think.
To build character.
To assist unsatisfactory teachers.
To create good pupil attitude.
To give pupils an enriched environment and educational experience.

Objectives which are really not objectives at all but statements of policy, statements of means to be used, or statements of attitudes: [3]

To encourage teachers' contributions to the general improvement of instruction. (This has the additional fault of vagueness. While it could be a desirable objective in some situations where it is peculiarly necessary to get teachers to contribute at all, it

[2] Objectives listed here and designated as "sound" are drawn from situations representing different levels of development. "Sound" means sound for the given level of insight or development in local thinking.
[3] The first five items are by-products, not objectives. They may be objectives in the minds of the leader but are not objectives for the group. They will be achieved naturally through a good program based on legitimate objectives.

would ordinarily make a clumsy objective. It is more easily seen as a valuable by-product of a good co-operative program.)

To have a more helpful program of teacher conferences, group and individual. (While this could be an objective, it would be abstract and pointless. It is best used as a means.)

To establish a link between the supervisor and the teachers by common participation in activities whose purpose has been accepted by both.

To give teachers experience in the processes of democratic action; to secure (or encourage) teacher participation in the solution of supervisory problems.

Developing the mutuality of responsibility on the part of the staff and the community in regard to the individual educational growth of each child in the public schools.

To extend the use of demonstration lessons in supervision. (This could be an objective only by courtesy, as it is clearly a means.)

To encourage and stimulate the teachers. (This is vague and meaningless. It could be an objective but is more likely a statement of attitude.)

To keep records of visits.

To make use of bulletins and supervisory activities.

To give teachers credit for all contributions made (not an objective but a desirable attitude or policy).

Students often say they "cannot see why" certain of the vague, indefinite or incorrect objectives are not objectives. These students should be directed to attempt to develop an explicit plan to go with the objective in question. The weakness of improperly stated objectives will soon become apparent.

4. *Develop a program of activity under supervisory leadership designed to improve underlying conditions and to bring about improvement in the products of learning.* The problems once selected and defined, the next task becomes the co-operative organization of the actual activities of diagnosis and solution.

These will utilize any number of subsidiary techniques:

a. Conferences with individuals and small groups for the planning of any and all kinds of projects.

b. Series of local study groups, general or limited teachers meetings.

c. A local workshop with facilities and personnel available at stated times.

d. Extension courses, summer-school work, leave of absence for study or travel.

e. Co-operatively developed bulletins, usually with references and study guides.

f. Experimental work, either individual or group, for the development of new materials, new evaluational devices; for try-out of materials.

g. Committee and study groups to examine student interests, attitudes, problems, and needs.

h. Committee work on curriculum improvement or course-of-study writing.

i. Visiting teachers in local and outside schools according to plans devised by teachers and staff.

j. Visits and conferences by supervisory personnel, usually on call and for co-operatively determined purposes.

k. Co-operatively determined programs of directed observation and directed teaching.

l. Committees and study groups to examine new texts, to select texts and materials.

m. Exchange of teachers between schools and between systems.

Detailed discussion of these will be found in Section 2 of this chapter.

Special caution: necessity for specific statements regarding means. Many students in training and not a few supervisors fall into serious error when developing plans, that of vague generality in designating the means to be used. Groups which develop plans co-operatively are less likely to make this error, although many do. It is quite meaningless to say that a given objective will be achieved through "a series of meetings," "the use of bulletins," "organized demonstration teaching," "planning conferences," "study groups." The means must be related specifically and in detail to the definite objective. The topics for meetings must be specifically stated, the books to be studied named (often with page references given), periodical articles to be studied must be listed. The function of a workshop in a given program must be specified. Research projects must be clearly defined, with conditions, controls, and evaluations indicated. Bulletins must be organized around given topics. Methods of developing co-operative effort on any item must be outlined. Many of these items cannot, of course, be specified in advance in a dynamic program; however, forecasts can be made.

Emphasis upon specificity in describing one's procedures cannot be overemphasized; otherwise the plan is a pure verbalism. Many students prone to substitute words for meanings will, when pressed on this matter, take refuge in still further abstraction. One young superintendent, pressed hard in discussion to state exactly and specifically how he would get a certain thing done, or at least plan to get it done, said, "I would require my teachers to do original thinking!" Specificity is an absolute necessity and can be achieved within a flexible dynamic program.

There is no standard sequence of events in the attack upon any supervisory program. One may start with a series of meetings for presentation of evidence; another will use few or no meetings. Bulletins may be used extensively in one plan, conferences in another. Planning may come early or after certain crises have been allowed to arise. Many supervisory procedures will enter into any situation. The particular objective should ordinarily indicate the general line of procedure. The ingenuity and ability of the personnel will determine specific activities within the general framework.

Brief descriptions of specific supervisory programs. The written account of a plan or log of its development would be so extensive that lack of space prohibits such exhibits. Instructors should gather collections of plans and of logs from the field for use with students. Several good diary accounts are available in periodical literature. A few sharply abbreviated descriptions of the chief features of given plans are included here. Note that two of these programs started directly from the evaluation of the learning products; the other two less directly but

nonetheless from attention to the results being achieved by the learners.

CASE 1[4]

A PLAN FOR THE IMPROVEMENT OF LANGUAGE INSTRUCTION IN THE ELEMENTARY GRADES, SANTA ANA, CALIFORNIA

Observations and partial surveys indicated that the results being achieved by the pupils in oral and written language skills were not satisfactory. The entire staff participated in a detailed analysis of results and of conditions surrounding the achievements.

At the first meeting in September, attention was called briefly to the partial facts revealed the preceding spring. A more adequate survey was undertaken. There was placed in the hands of each teacher a bulletin entitled "Selected Readings in Elementary English." This contained classified references on various phases of language teaching. Teachers were asked to read briefly for orientation, selecting titles with specific reference to their own difficulties. They were also asked to summarize later their own difficulties and needs.

Based on teachers' suggestions and interviews, four meetings were arranged for October and November, each one discussing a problem raised by the staff. Staff members, teachers, and an outside expert served as chairmen.

As a result of discussions in the meetings, readings, and further observations, another bulletin was issued, entitled "Samples of Natural and Profitable Situations for Speaking." Teachers were asked to check these as natural and legitimate, or artificial and academic.

Simultaneously a summary of a lecture on language teaching by a state department specialist was handed out.

Based on their meetings, readings, and reactions to bulletins, the staff now worked out one or two record blanks and criteria for evaluation which they were to apply to the pupils' oral and written language.

This co-operative derivation of the objective and organization of means to achieve it unified staff thinking. From then on, meetings, demonstrations, and panel discussions attacked the various subpoints systematically.

Emphasis should be made here that these accounts are *general*. Bulletins, meetings,

[4] Taken from materials supplied by Superintendent F. A. Henderson and Miss Kueneman, elementary supervisor.

demonstrations, reading and study in all these programs are specific and definite. Problems are clearly stated, bulletins are specific, references to study materials are to definite materials dealing with stated problems. Demonstrations are preceded by preparation both of the lesson and of the group which is to observe. Observation outlines should be in the hands of the observers, and discussion should follow based directly upon the original needs which initiated the demonstration and upon the actual procedures in the lesson.

An account of a program to improve work reading in the Minneapolis elementary schools will be found in Chapter 18. The details are there made specific. The project is now some years old, but it is still an excellent example of a planned program for the improvement of instruction.

CASE 2 [5]

THE INTRODUCTION OF A GUIDANCE PROGRAM INTO THE CLIFTON, ARIZONA, HIGH SCHOOL

Interest in a guidance program arose from several sources. Parents asked questions about courses taken, the relation of these to future life work; pupils asked similar questions. A few criticisms and complaints indicated need for attention to guidance. The superintendent and teachers were interested through summer courses and casual reading in the emphasis being placed upon follow-up work done with graduates of high schools.

A survey of the school and of the community to secure facts bearing upon this emerging interest was the first step. The age-grade status, pupil load, drop-outs, and failures were all stated statistically. A study of those leaving school was made with reference to their success in other schools; to the kinds of jobs they take.

Second, the data from the survey were presented to the school staff and further comments emerged. The staff concluded that before the mechanics of a guidance program were set up it would be well to study the remote reasons and implications. (This is a superior reaction and very desirable.) The chairman of the Social Science Department was therefore invited, third, to lead a lecture-discussion on "Social Conditions and Their Implications for Guidance." The chairman prepared a ten-point dis-

cussion outline plus a few readings on the questions in the outline. The group was thus prepared well in advance to understand the more subtle and remote considerations.

The fourth step was to analyze local school conditions in the light of the background now developed together with possible local objectives. The high-school principal prepared a two-page study guide with readings as preparation for the discussion of local conditions and objectives. Out of this conference grew plans for several more detailed discussions of specific aspects of an actual guidance program. The fifth step was a meeting on "The Informative Phase of a Guidance Program," prepared and led by a classroom teacher who was interested in this and volunteered.

[The various other characteristics and processes of a program were taken up thus.]

The program then shifted to presenting this program to the community which was done through discussion of local needs, background material now in possession of the teachers. Panel discussions which included community leaders were used together with other typical methods of dissemination.

Presentation and explanation to the student body accompanied this. Student participation was prominent. Students organized and carried out a "Go to High School" campaign which involved extensive study. An occupational survey of students' interests was compiled.

The program led into a major and vital continuing objective, namely, the basic reorganization of the total curriculum offerings.

CASE 3 [6]

THE DEVELOPMENT AND INSTALLATION OF A SPECIAL CURRICULUM FOR THE NONACADEMIC PUPIL IN A SELECTED ELEMENTARY SCHOOL, FRESNO, CALIFORNIA

This was a proposed plan which might or might not be placed in operation. Need for the program was based on several considerations. Children came from very poor socioeconomic groups. Thirty-five nationalities were represented. The curriculum and teaching procedures had been for years unduly conservative, obviously unfitted to the children. Truancy and indifference were marked, disciplinary situations

[5] This account prepared from materials supplied by H. A. Liem, Superintendent of Schools at the time of the project.

[6] Account based on material supplied by Kenneth R. Brown, classroom teacher.

numerous. A few hit-or-miss adjustments had been attempted.

An analysis was proposed to cover percentage of failure, percentage of retardation, amount of A.D.A. lost, intelligence levels, numbers and types of disciplinary situations, case studies of selected students needing assistance. Data were to be summarized and presented to the faculty in charts and graphs with descriptive statements. A list of five penetrating questions was distributed well in advance of the meeting. Proportion of failures deemed inevitable? Located in given strata or areas of the school? Causes of these and other maladjustments? Might the curriculum be at fault? Would we be willing to study the relation between the type of learner and the curriculum?

The leader hoped to have a study of the objective of the school emerge together with a question as to the individual teacher's part. Excellent references on the problems of youth, together with others on adjustment programs being developed in other places, were provided.

Through a series of meetings on problems selected by the group out of preceding discussions and organized around a set of study questions developed in advance of the meeting, it was hoped that a number of basic problems would be considered that would lead to a comprehensive and co-operative attack upon curriculum and teaching technique. Problems which might emerge were: causes of failure; maturity levels and learning; relation of materials and methods to individual needs and interests; pupil participation in planning; "progressive" methods of teaching; type of discipline; classroom control with diverse activities; and others.

CASE 4[7]

A SUPERVISORY PROGRAM TO REDUCE INTER-
GROUP TENSION IN AN AMERICAN JUNIOR
HIGH SCHOOL

The rearrangement of school district boundaries in a New Jersey town greatly changed the school population in several of the schools. The X School had had a highly homogeneous pupil population drawn almost entirely from a wealthy residential section. The new arrangement brought into this school about 12 per cent of the school population from a Negro section and so changed the total so that about 41 per cent of the total population now came from middle or lower socioeconomic classes in the community. A great number of changes

were noted in the school. During the second year after the change in school population, several of the women teachers asked to be relieved of playground duty. They said there were too many fights and too much disorder for them to handle. A very spirited discussion immediately ensued. One group of teachers was certain that most of the fighting and disorder was due to quarrels between the white students and the Negro students. Evidence was also supplied that there was considerable feeling not only against Negroes but also against the Jews, Catholics, and "country clubbers." Another group of teachers suggested that a lot of the "new" children in the school just couldn't do the class work, and so in their frustration took it out in disorder and in fighting with other people. One teacher stated that he was sure that we were no worse off than we used to be. He pointed out that a Negro boy had been elected vice-president in the eighth grade. Two Negro teachers had been added to the school with the change in districting, and one of them said that certain schools were getting good results with these problems with intercultural programs in the schools.

The first meeting ended up with certain questions being asked: (1) Are there more fights and more tensions in the school than is normal? (2) Is the tension due to intergroup friction? (3) What is the truth about the native ability of these minority groups? Can they do the work or not? (4) Can we and should we stop the fights?

These questions were presented for study and for further discussion at a second faculty meeting. Those who said there had been no more fights than there had been in the past were confronted with evidence taken from the school record. For nine years before the redistricting, there had been an average of seven fights a year, always, of course, between white boys. In the two years since the redistricting the fights had increased from an average of seven to an average of twenty-four. The number of fights between white boys was the same as ever, but was three times as great between white and Negroes as between white and white.

At this point one of the colored teachers presented a sociometric chart which she had made of her class showing very clearly the relationships and feelings between the various students in her class. A great number of

---

[7] Based on notes supplied by Morris L. Cogan, who was then a teacher in the school in question and who is now an instructor at the Harvard Graduate School of Education.

teachers were immediately interested, many of whom were not familiar with the sociometric techniques. Then someone said with considerable emphasis that there should be more information on the ability of these children before we condemned them as being unable to do the work.

Discussion in this meeting ended up with formation of volunteer committees. One was to gather information on the native endowment of the various racial and religious groups now in the school. A second committee was to find out if there were any means of discovering the extent and nature of the intergroup tensions within the school. A third group volunteered to supplement the second group's findings with some background material on intergroup tensions in the country generally.

The teacher who presented the sociometric chart was asked to lead a study of this area for the faculty. This she did by means of a bulletin containing an excellent annotated bibliography. Group discussion and demonstrations followed. The use of this technique gave the faculty valid data about relationships among the student groups. Other instruments were used to determine social distance, cultural acceptance, and the like.

The supervisory leader hoped that the necessity would become apparent for including parents and other community members, and for bringing in resource experts from outside. This did not appear during the reading and study but did later.

The committees on native endowments, on local tensions, and on the national situation supplied annotated bibliographies which were used by the faculty as the basis for group discussion.

A windfall came when some parents objected to the annual student "Minstrel Show," asking that there be an end to dialect jokes, to blackface, and to the featuring of certain national characteristics (so-called). The P.T.A. group making this suggestion was touring the school and was invited to the faculty meeting. Committees added parent members.

An intergroup steering committee emerged. The annual show was built around the theme "One School and One World." The P.T.A. offered to pay for a team of resource persons. A workshop on intergroup tensions and schools was set up at a nearby teachers college. The school paper carried a series of explanatory articles. A "Round the World" dance for the whole school was held.

The general line of study then continued.

CASE 5[8]

A PLAN TO IMPROVE THE MAKING OF ASSIGNMENTS BY JUNIOR HIGH TEACHERS AS A TRANSITIONAL STEP TOWARD THE DEVELOPMENT OF SUBJECT-MATTER UNITS, FRAMINGHAM, MASSACHUSETTS

The Memorial School is judged to be a better than average junior high with a good average staff. The tendency was definitely toward traditional methods of instruction and of administration, with an emphasis on subject matter. Ample information on the pupils and their achievement was available.

A principal's bulletin invited all teachers to list three or four areas in which study for the coming year would improve the teaching-learning situation with special reference to the problems of the teachers replying. This produced a list of six major areas with twenty-four subpoints. Only three received more than two votes. The two with the highest ranking were within the area of pupil work habits and were: "Better preparation of homework," and "Better study habits." Important to note is that a school-board rule requires that seventh- and eighth-grade pupils spend one hour per evening on homework.

A second bulletin summarized the votes, supplied an excellent brief bibliography for the chief areas, and indicated that the next meeting would be devoted to selecting an area or related areas for study.

The principal, because of the votes on preparation and study habits, because of the town regulation on home study, and because he believed that many other subpoints listed by teachers could be improved by means of improved assignments, deliberately steered the discussion in this direction.

The general plan that emerged was: (1) to study statements of principles governing assignments; (2) to analyze and evaluate these principles in the light of local objectives and conditions; (3) to develop a statement of principles by the teachers; (4) to analyze a series of their own assignments in the light of the accepted principles; (5) to endeavor to put the principles increasingly into practice.

Committees were set up to carry forward the phases of the program. The principal secured a very large amount of reference ma-

[8] Based on notes suppled by Albert C. Reilley, who was principal of the Memorial Junior High School and who is now Assistant Superintendent of Schools in Framingham.

terials not merely on the principles of assignment but covering also motivation, needs, and interests; study guides; social purposes; individual differences and the adjustment of learning activities to these differences; appraisal of pupil achievement; pupil participation in assignments.

Eventually a descriptive list of "items to observe" was set up covering all phases of the assignment.

The program was carried on during the year with notation from time to time of objectives which arose and which would be taken up the next year.

CASE 6[9]

A PLAN TO IMPROVE AND UNIFY THE GUIDANCE PROGRAM IN THE WATERTOWN, NEW YORK, PUBLIC SCHOOLS

A Director of Guidance, Curriculum, and Research (a new office) was appointed in 1945, directly responsible to the superintendent of schools. Previously the supervisor of elementary schools, the supervisors of art, of music, and of attendance carried on independent programs. There was, moreover, little co-ordination between elementary, junior high schools, and senior high school. The program in elementary schools was reasonably modern and flexible with much attention to individual differences. The junior high schools were less flexible. The senior high was proud of its subject-matter emphasis and record. Many teachers in the junior and senior schools were, however, not too well satisfied with the rigid academic programs.

Wide discussion among all staff officers and teachers, plus officers of the P.T.A. associations, suggested that an over-all study (scrutiny) of the curriculum of the system should be made. Questions raised were: (1) What is to be done in making a curriculum study? (2) Who is to do it? (3) How can it be organized?

A preliminary plan emerged from discussion and study. A Central Planning Committee was set up which gathered an excellent bibliography and supplied leadership in detailed organization. Reports of curriculum programs in neighboring cities were secured, and visits made to these communities. A consultant was invited to review for the staff the general procedures and problems of curriculum study. It was then decided to (1) start with problems important to many teachers; (2) aim for goals attainable within a reasonable time; (3) involve as many teachers, pupils, and citizens as possible.

Teachers suggested seventy-three topics for attack, reorganized into twenty-six by the central committee. The most urgent were: (1) What sort of person do we expect as a result of our high-school education? (2) How can we improve the reading program? (3) How can we build in our students a desire for responsibility and success in their efforts?

A bulletin summarized events to date, indicated that committees could be set up to follow the various questions raised, and called for volunteers. More than enough volunteers responded. Committees were set up including representatives from all levels. Each committee set out to study pertinent literature, summarize and make recommendations. Preliminary summaries were first circulated to the whole staff, discussed and revised as needed.

To abbreviate: the first year saw the following achievements:

a. A better understanding between teachers from various school levels.

b. As a result of recommendations made by both the Reading Committee and the Committee on Objectives, Regents examinations, which for many years were required for graduation from high school, were made optional.

c. A revised report card in the secondary schools was based on the stated philosophy and objectives of the schools.

d. The English program has been made more flexible by introducing courses for both college entrance and noncollege pupils in the fourth year.

e. Teachers are using guidance record cards to much greater extent.

f. More guidance counselors have been added to the staff to take care of the extra counseling involved.

g. The teachers' association has developed several committees having to do with the school calendar, salary schedules, and other matters of school policy. These committees follow the procedure of study, analysis, and making recommendations.

h. Special books dealing with remedial reading are used to assist slow readers in the senior high school.*

i. Experimental reading groups have been set up in one of the junior high schools.

* Parsons and Center, "Problems in Reading and Thinking."

[9] Based on an account supplied by Robert J. Daly, then (1950) Director of Guidance, Curriculum, and Research.

j. Diagnostic reading tests are used in both junior and senior high schools to find out more about the progress of individual pupils.*

k. Teachers in elementary schools have listed specific learning activities and practices which are used to implement specific objectives.

l. Above practices for all grades will be evaluated next year. The criteria for evaluation will be set up by committees of teachers and elementary supervisors.

Eight new problems emerged as the year's study went on. Above all, the need for improving and unifying the guidance program stood out. A very broad program then emerged with extensive study of materials and examination of guidance processes elsewhere. Extensive use was made of group processes. Parents were participants. A series of summaries were made indicating desired guidance practices at all levels for both everyday classroom procedures (which are guidance whether we know it or not) up to specialized, technical analyses and recommendations for given cases.

The illustrations given are all for city-wide plans. Plans for helping individual teachers are also important. Materials on this are included in Chapter 15.

Principle 5. *Evaluate the effectiveness of the program in the light of accepted objectives, by reputable means of appraisal, to determine what improvement has been achieved.*

The plan should set forth what criteria and instruments of appraisal will be used. Some of these will be well-known instruments which are easily available to all. Others will be instruments devised by those operating the program as a part of the program itself. Evaluation is a constant and inherent part of any teaching or supervisory activity. The common means of appraisal are set forth in Chapter 9; specific appraisals of given programs are reviewed in Chapter 18.

The characteristics of an acceptable supervisory plan. The details of planning will differ widely with varying situations and groups. Certain common features should appear regardless of location or of the group doing the planning.

1. A statement, lengthy or brief as the case may be, of the situation out of which the program grew, of the survey techniques used, of the needs and problems revealed.

2. A set of objectives, clearly stated and definite enough to be achievable. Some will be continuing objectives, others new. All should be integrated with the common long-term objectives of all education.

3. An outline of the possible, and very probable, means likely to be used in attaining the objectives. Provision for flexibility and continuous readjustment should be indicated.

4. An outline of the criteria, checks, or other evaluational procedures to be used in determining the degree of success achieved by the program.

The co-ordination of plans within a system. The individual building is increasingly recognized as the effective unit for educational effort. The system as a whole, however, has certain over-all general needs. A problem in co-ordination arises.

Line-and-staff organization in small cities usually provides for co-ordination through the superintendent's office or through an assistant superintendent in charge of supervision. Co-ordination in larger cities is accomplished through a central council, or a superintendent's cabinet, or a committee set up for that purpose. The central council or cabinet may include all supervisors and principals, together with representative teachers in systems small enough so that the group will not be unwieldy. Central councils and committees in larger systems will probably be representative bodies, with all groups sending elected delegates to the meetings.

Co-ordination in a democratic organization will be accomplished through discussion in a series of local committees doing the planning which are in turn represented in a central committee. Co-operative group decisions are characteristic here. Principles and general processes were set forth in detail in Chapter 5.

Adaptation of planning and leadership to size of system, type of staff, and so forth. The foregoing discussion applies to systems

* Iowa Silent Reading Tests.

possessing requisite time, money, and staff. Obviously, adaptations must be made when time and staff are insufficient or small. Something can be done in every situation, and handicaps should not be permitted to halt supervision. Students who are principals or superintendents in very small cities often ask: "How can I do any of these things when I teach all day without even a single period for administration or supervision?" This question is all too often presented as an indirect defense for a do-nothing policy. School officers who do present it and who sincerely desire to carry on some supervision should be encouraged to begin just as the staff of a large system would begin, namely, by diagnosis of the existing conditions. Careful analysis will doubtless reveal that even in the most crowded program some supervision is possible. If hard-pressed and harassed superintendents and principals do nothing more than inspire the staff to read and discuss one good book a semester, they have accomplished something. If they set aside one hour a week for conference, if they can answer only a few questions for a teacher, if they can dismiss a class for fifteen minutes to enable someone to visit a classroom which evidences good teaching, if they can issue a one-page bulletin occasionally, they are to be highly commended.

Objections to planning. Objections are raised from time to time against planning. Certain of these are trivial and silly; others are based on honest misunderstandings and false premises; still others are legitimate and must be answered or explained.

First, it is sometimes said that planning takes too much time and work. A given system of planning could be so cumbersome, so unnecessarily detailed, so arbitrarily imposed from above that it does take too much time and energy. The criticism here is not of planning as a principle but of the persons doing the planning and of their general philosophy. Administrative and clerical details in some systems are so onerous that no time remains for planning. This is equivalent to

saying that the supervisors have to do so much other work that they cannot supervise! Criticism again rests with persons and general philosophies and not with the planning principle. An unqualified statement that planning takes too much time and energy is merely silly. Leadership in planning and participating in planning are just what the entire staff is paid to do.

A second objection states that planning is by nature undemocratic. This is such futile nonsense that it would not be discussed here except that it is raised by individuals who are quite honest in their ignorance of both planning and democracy. What is really meant, doubtless, is that certain given cases of planning have been carried on undemocratically. The truth is that the heart of modern democratic procedure in or out of school is planning together for what needs to be done. Genuine participation of all types of workers in formulating plans is an essential of democracy. Principles and techniques have been presented in Chapters 4 and 5.

An objection often stated separately (but which is actually a part of the one just stated, lack of democracy) is that a plan stifles initiative and creative effort. An arbitrary plan predetermined by one group and imposed upon another will effectively discourage initiative, responsibility, and creative contribution. The fault lies again with the theory and practice of planning held by the given administration. Democratic planning is highly effective in stimulating initiative, the assumption of responsibility, and creative contribution.

Third, it is said that each pupil, each teacher, each situation is unique, individual, different. We cannot, therefore, ever anticipate the needs of a situation or plan in advance the means of meeting the needs. Explanations are necessary here. Great emphasis has been placed latterly upon the uniqueness of persons and of situations; upon adapting to the not-elsewhere-duplicated nature of given persons and situations. This represents a valuable counterattack upon the authoritarian administration and the lock-step educational methods of the older school. Carried to extremes, it is as detrimental as the extremes of authoritarianism and lock-step procedure. Uniqueness of persons and situations is one part of the picture; commonalty is another. Planning takes account of both. Competent planning by trained personnel includes, first, diagnosis of specific situations and the organization of means fitted, not vaguely and in general, but definitely to the circumstances. Planning involves, second, attention to needs and problems which are common to many situations, recurrent and highly similar from situation to situation. Voluminous evidence is available showing both the uniqueness and the recurrent similarity of educational problems.

Planning in advance, stage by stage, which is based squarely upon locally derived facts, enlightened by general knowledge of similar situations, which is flexible and susceptible to replanning constantly, is possible and necessary.

The fourth objection is extremely important and summarizes the sensible portions of preceding objections. The statement of "definite objectives" and the organization of "specific and detailed" procedures violates, it is said, the whole nature of modern democratic procedure and of modern learning. The writer has no hesitation in discussing "definite" objectives and "specific" means. The argument turns squarely upon what is meant by those words. Definite objectives stated in unequivocal language are necessary wherever sensible persons work together. The planning of understandable procedures is similarly necessary. To proceed otherwise results solely and only in muddle, confusion, chaos.

The terms *definite* and *specifically planned* do not mean, as interpreted by some, "fixed," "unchanging," "imposed." A definite and specific plan is not operated arbitrarily as planned in the beginning. Two essential points must be recalled. First, the "definite" objectives are derived democratically by the

group from the actual situation to which they apply. Second, planning is always continuous, flexible, susceptible to change as situations develop. Planning is evolutionary, emergent, growing apace with the situation within which it is planned. Definite objectives and specified means are merely the simplest necessities of common sense; they cannot be inherently undemocratic. The emphasis throughout this chapter is not upon the *plan*, nor upon the verb *planned,* but upon *planning*.

A fifth objection states that if emphasis is placed on one aspect (or two or three) of a teaching-learning situation, the others will suffer. Supervision may, for instance, focus upon the improvement of work-type reading, whereupon arithmetic or spelling will suffer. Attention to developing social-moral traits in pupils may result in neglect in the development of tool skills. A major program of curriculum construction may cause teachers to neglect their everyday teaching, their health, and so forth.

The first answer is a simple one: there is no intention to neglect any phase of the setting for learning while giving special emphasis to another. Supervisory procedures which increasingly include all workers and which study unified situations avoid the criticism. Second, there is considerable experimental data available in the literature indicating that special attention to a special need does not detract from the total program. Good programs of special emphasis do, in fact, often increase efficiency in the total program.

SECTION 1

DISCUSSION QUESTIONS AND EXERCISES

In the discussion of the meaning of supervision, it was brought out that there are a great many agencies and instrumentalities that are concerned directly or indirectly with the study and improvement of the teaching-learning situation. The problem arises: How can the various elements be organized so as to locate and deal with educational problems effectively on a democratic, co-operative basis? How should the program be planned?

1. Relate for class analysis a situation within your experience where supervision was well planned. Outline very briefly the local conditions, processes of planning and evaluation, plus any comments of your own.

2. Relate similarly the facts concerning a situation where supervision was not planned. Give the local conditions, reasons for not planning, plus your suggestions for improvement.

ORAL EXERCISES

The two exercises following are among the most important in the book. They prepare directly for the written exercise which follows, which is itself a fundamental test of the students' understanding of the course thus far. One or two class periods may well be devoted to this if time permits.

1. Each student should formulate and bring to class two or three typical supervisory objectives. Preferably these should be derived from the actual situations in which the students are now working or have worked. One after another, these objectives should be analyzed and evaluated by the class. Scope, definiteness, clarity, and so forth, should be judged. Use the materials in the chapter as criteria.

2. A typical objective formulated by a student and evaluated by the group may be selected and written on the board. The beginnings of a program may be developed through class discussion much as an actual group in the field would formulate its program. Two or three objectives may be treated sketchily to show the diversity of possible attack. Varying suggestions for the same objective should be encouraged, since there is no one right procedure for a given problem. All that should be required is that suggestions be natural and appropriate, coherent, and practicable.

CLASS PROJECT NO. IV

PLANNING A PROGRAM OF SUPERVISORY ACTIVITY

Modern planning is co-operative and derived from given conditions and needs. Nevertheless, preliminary, tentative planning must be done in any situation. Practice in planning is legitimate and necessary.

Students who have operated under a plan in a previous position, or who are now operating a plan in a real situation, should be encouraged to bring in their plans for analysis and evaluation. The value of these discussions for students who have not yet participated in planning is great.

Ample time should be allowed for the formulation of a plan which would be sensible for a given situation. The project actually cannot be completed until just before the end of the course, perhaps just before Chapter 18 is taken up. Discussion and planning should go on constantly as Parts II and III of the text are taken up.

Each student, preferably should develop a plan but small committees may often co-operate on one plan.

Students who are not now engaged in supervisory work or who have never engaged in it will perforce construct a theoretical plan. This is quite satisfactory, and in fact, constitutes an excellent test of ability to envisage a situation and to anticipate it.

Pay particular attention to the caution on page 133, and the list on pages 132-133.

Project. Take any one supervisory objective, preferably one growing out of the situation where you work, and develop the possible and very probable means which might be employed to achieve the objective.

The plan need not be presented in complete detail but must be developed in sufficient detail to demonstrate the student's understanding of the proper adjustment of means to objectives, of the democratic techniques in deriving a plan through group participation.

SUGGESTED READINGS

The well-known standard texts and many of the yearbooks on supervision contain a chapter on planning supervisory activities. None is as detailed as the present chapter but each usually contains differing emphases on the various principles and procedures, hence should be consulted in connection with this chapter, and particularly while preparing the written exercise above.

The periodical literature very rarely contains accounts of planning for specific situations but the materials appearing are usually helpful.

The small number of references of all kinds bearing upon this topic and their easy availability make unnecessary a listed bibliography here.

COLLECTION OF PLANS

The single most valuable aid with this problem of making plans which the writer has found is to make over the years a collection of plans and logs of plans both from real situations and as produced by students in previous classes. Consulted by students and supervisors in service, they represent actuality, they introduce a variety of attacks, they illustrate the large number of techniques available, they illustrate the ingenuity of various leaders and groups in meeting their unique problems.

Section 2

SUBSIDIARY TECHNIQUES BY WHICH PROFESSIONAL PROGRAMS ARE CARRIED ON

A large collection of procedures is available for use in implementing either long-term or short-term programs. Various methods of listing these are available and the plan below may be revised if desired. The techniques listed for discussion are not discrete items but obviously overlap when they are actually used in a school system. The workshop, for instance, uses all the devices common to large group effort but also provides for individual interests. Group discussion is involved, specialists may be sought, reading and study used as needed.

Growth away from formal, imposed techniques toward co-operative, participatory procedures. A brief statement in Section 3 of Chapter 1 indicated an increasing use of community participation, co-operative methods, give-and-take discussion, committees, workshops, and conferences. Leadership is increasingly recognized as potential in any member of a group. A corresponding reduction is noted in the use of imposed, mechanical techniques. The situation in too many places, of course, does not show this growth.

Growth toward functional distribution of procedures among various supervisory officers. The techniques used in earlier days were largely the same for all types of supervisory workers. Chief procedures were the individual conference following a classroom visit, general teachers' meetings, institutes, and reading circles. The reading circle in its original form has nearly disappeared, being replaced by study groups and directed reading based on recognized local problems. Teachers' meetings and institutes, long a sore spot with teachers, have changed beyond recognition under good leadership. The old type of useless institute and teachers' meeting persists in many places because of incompetent leadership. Institutes and meetings today are work conferences based on local problems or on new departures which have appeared in the field. Visiting the classroom, with attendant conference, has been greatly minimized for the general or central office supervisors, but has assumed great significance as used by supervising principals, department heads, and helping teachers. Evidence given below supports the belief that these officers can make far more effective use of the immediate and direct individual techniques.

General supervisors are more concerned with long-range, system-wide, large-group processes such as: supplying leadership in the development of statements of policy, in programs of curriculum organization, in developing instructional materials, in stimulating and carrying on research, in making surveys of various types. General supervisors also serve an important function as consultants to school faculties within the system, as these faculties participate in system-wide campaigns in relation to local problems. The broad functions of central supervisors were briefly listed in Section 3 of Chapter 1, and are further identified incidentally in the tables and lists which follow.

The supervisory activities of the elementary principal.[10] Whole volumes have been written on the strategic importance of the

[10] Charles W. Boardman, Harl R. Douglass, and R. K. Bent, *Democratic Supervision in Secondary Schools* (Boston, Houghton, 1953). Footnotes and bibliography for Ch. 4 are exceptionally complete and valuable. Much of the material is applicable to the elementary principal as well as to the secondary principal.

SUPERVISORY ACTIVITIES WITHIN THE SCHOOL WHERE PRINCIPALS FEEL THEY DO THEIR MOST EFFECTIVE WORK

Supervisory Activity	Supervising Principals	Teaching Principals
1. By helping each teacher with her problems	63%	65%
2. By interviewing, studying, and adjusting individual pupils	18	17
3. By visiting classes to observe the teaching	4	2
4. By interviewing and planning with parents	3	6
5. By leading general discussion at teachers' meetings	4	6
6. By providing teachers with extensive instructional materials	4	6
7. By working with groups of teachers on problems of their own choosing	8	5
8. By asking individual teachers to report at teachers' meetings	1	*
9. By appointing committees of teachers to report at teachers' meetings	3	1
10. By giving tests to classes	1	1
11. By giving or arranging for demonstration lessons	1	1
12. By conducting and applying research studies	1	2
13. By asking supervisors to examine and to report on classes	*	0
14. By teaching or coaching groups of pupils	*	2
15. By giving lectures on instructional problems at teachers' meetings	*	0

* Indicates items of less than 1 per cent.

principal in supervision. The principal is, in fact, the officer best placed to provide leadership to the compact local staff with its common problems. The failure of incompetent principals to carry on supervision should not be allowed to obscure things as they should be. Many, many principals are exemplifying the highest type of supervisory leadership. The principal may use any and all supervisory procedures, but certain of these will be more valuable than others. We are here concerned briefly with his most important supervisory techniques. These have been listed (see table above) after an extensive study by the National Department of Elementary Principals.[11]

The supervisory activities of the department head. Supervision in the secondary school, regardless of the officer involved, has never achieved either the recognition or the effectiveness of supervision in the elementary school. A number of reasons could be offered if space permitted. Responsibility for supervision is lodged properly with the principal and with the department head. The principal may operate much as does the principal on the elementary level, but usually does very little. In the larger schools the principal rarely exercises this type of leadership. The department heads are theoretically the supervisory officers but again, little is done, though here and there brilliant exceptions occur.

Spears calls attention to a slight trend that might become very important, namely, the appointment of an instructional assistant to the secondary school principal. The new assistant ranks with present assistants, widely found, who are guidance officers, counselors, or "deans" of boys or of girls. Details are not yet clear, particularly in relation to the principal's leadership, or to the typical departmental organization of secondary schools. Spears believes that the new assistantship will probably increase, taking over whatever of good there is in the present department headship. The department heads may be stimulated by this development.

[11] *The Elementary School Principalship—Today and Tomorrow,* Twenty-seventh Yearbook, Department of Elementary School Principals (Washington, NEA, 1948), p. 103.

The writers have noted a slightly different trend in a few schools, namely, the appointment of an administrative assistant to the principal, setting the principal free for supervision. This not only places instructional leadership where it belongs but avoids some problems of organization and relationship. The principal devotes his efforts to the improvement of instruction, including methods, curriculum, and guidance.

Spears [12] presents a good summary, in the form of questions, of the supervisory functions of department heads:

1. *He assists teachers in making full use of materials.*
   Are teachers securing the benefits of all teaching guides?
   Are they making proper interpretation of such guides?
   Are they making use of available supplementary reference books?
   Are they making full use of bulletin boards and maps?
   Are they making full use of audio-visual materials available?
   Have they seen the possibilities of field trips?
   Has the most effective assignment of rooms, books, equipment, and supplies been made for them?

2. *He gives teachers suggestions about classroom methods.*
   Has he secured for them recently issued references on methods of teaching in that field?
   Has he encouraged experimentation in methods, when the teacher has more than one section of the same subject?
   Have teachers exchanged ideas on classroom techniques, and do they have the opportunity to visit each other's classes?
   Are such matters treated at departmental meetings?

3. *He leads the way in testing.*
   Have the tests and testing methods of the teacher been discussed with the department head?
   Have model or various types of tests been circulated among department members?
   Have the relative merits of different types of tests been measured in respect to the subject field?
   Has he encouraged maximum use of the results of the standardized achievement and mental maturity testing programs that are given in the school?
   Has he revealed the many uses of tests over and beyond the marking of pupils?
   Has he recognized the limitation of standardized tests in evaluating teaching and learning?

4. *He leads the way in adapting instruction to individual differences.*
   Has he helped to reveal the degree and types of variation among pupils?
   Has he revealed possible ways of caring for differences in abilities and interests?
   Are the teachers taking advantage of the possibility of making adjustments for pupils through the guidance service?
   Do they work at the job of helping the pupils establish desirable ways of approaching and carrying out study?

5. *He acts as a leader in professional growth.*
   Are the new teachers aware of the importance of participating in extra-curricular activities?
   Do they need help in distinguishing the ethical or professional action in school and community situations?
   Are the new teachers being shown examples of good teaching?
   Do they see their work in true relationship to the entire educational program?

A listing of available techniques.[13] Several methods of listing ways of working with teachers are found in the literature. The

[12] Harold Spears, *op. cit.,* pp. 190-192. *The Department Head and Instructional Improvement,* Association for Supervision and Curriculum Development (Washington, NEA, 1948).

[13] There is very little objective evidence on the actual value of any of the techniques widely used in the field. The evidence which does exist is scattered widely in periodical literature and in thesis studies. Illustrations of evidence on some of the procedures are included in Ch. 18, and there are indirect evidences in Ch. 15 and 16.

The techniques do, however, work very well when chosen with regard for appropriateness to the purpose being served; when chosen co-operatively; and when the program is clearly adapted to the needs of the group concerned. Personal preference for some techniques over others equally appropriate is also an important factor. The basic point has been made throughout the volume: appropriateness and adaptation to need rather than mere use of procedures which are available. Good judgment is always necessary in selecting techniques.

simple outline below proceeds from methods useful with large groups to individualized procedures.

1. Orientation meetings for new teachers.
2. Pre-term meetings for planning. (Often combined with orientation meetings.)
3. Workshops (of various kinds).
4. Large group conferences.
   Conventions; national, regional, local
   Institutes
   Teachers' meetings
   Whole faculty or staff
   Department
   Grade level
5. Small group conferences; study groups; seminars.
6. Committee work.
7. Bulletins and other documentary aids.
8. Audio-visual aids.
9. Provision of central library collection of books, resource materials, and a browsing room.
10. Extension or summer school courses.
11. Local field trips or excursions; travel.
12. Local research problems and/or experimental trial of new materials or processes.
13. Directed reading (small groups or individuals).
14. Group counseling.
15. Demonstration teaching, directed observation, or intervisitation (small groups or individuals).
16. Directed teaching.
17. Individual conference following visits or by request (usually on instructional problems).
18. Follow-up conferences in a series and based on a given problem or theme (individual or small group).
19. Individual counseling (on personal or professional problems).

General descriptive accounts of these methods will be found in the following pages. Illustrations of their actual operation are found chiefly in Chapter 15, with scattered cases in other chapters.

Orientation meetings for new teachers. In years gone by, the first staff meeting usually occurred just before school opened or on one of the first days of school. All too commonly (even yet), the meeting is a formal administrative affair for announcements and for distribution of materials which could have been better handled by mail. A speech, supposed to be inspirational, was usually included. Social activities were rarely a part of this type of introduction to the system. Ordinarily, the opening meeting was a dull affair.

Today an increasing number of school systems are providing interesting and enjoyable orientation programs, usually lasting several days or a week. Emphasis is on introduction of new teachers but the whole staff participates. Informality is characteristic of the program.

1. The general theory of education, the policies, and any special features of the local system are presented. This may be through a talk which may or may not be combined with exhibits, a film, a round-table discussion including old and new teachers.

2. Administrative and routine matters are disposed of quickly and with some discussion. Documentary aids and other instructional materials are given out and explained. (Often the materials are given out at time of employment, are read in advance with questions provided for at the orientation meeting.) The method of requisitioning and distributing supplies, keeping registers, making reports, is presented with illustrations and discussion.

3. Opportunities for questions are provided during all presentations and also in small group meetings.

4. Study groups, work conferences, which may or may not be continued during the year in workshop fashion are set up to serve any of several special needs.

5. There may be, and usually are, visits to the schools facilities and special services; to local educational resources such as libraries, museums, radio stations, and others.

6. Visits are usually made to certain key industries, to civic center establishments, and often to homes.

7. The social side of orientation is included in luncheons, dinners, parties of various types in which old and new teachers, patrons, civic leaders, become acquainted.

8. Aid is given in many places in finding places to stay, whether a room, an apartment, or a home. This is highly organized in some places.

Orientation conferences are most effective devices, provided the leadership is alert and original.

The relation of orientation to the planning of educational and supervisory programs may take any of several forms. Ordinarily, the major planning for long-term goals goes on continuously. Even short-term programs should be worked out during the spring for the coming year. New teachers are then introduced to the plans for the system very naturally by way of work conferences and small group meetings. In some places the initial planning for the system is done during the orientation week, but this is not as desirable as making this week a part of the regular planning which should be going on continuously. Planning which continues into the year may be of any type: committee meetings, reports, large group discussions, workshops, or any of the other techniques.

Pre-term meetings for planning. These may be in any of several forms, and may or may not be a part of the orientation program. It seems somewhat shortsighted to delay planning until school is about to open, though this is done in many places. As indicated above and throughout the chapter, planning should be a continuous activity. Planning meetings held as school opens can serve a number of purposes if they are a part of the major continuous planning done by the system.

The workshop. One of the most important devices for in-service education is the workshop. The term and the process have been used in other fields for a long time, coming into education in 1936. The first workshop was organized in 1936 at the University of Ohio under the direction of Ralph W. Tyler, then Chairman of the Department of Education, University of Chicago. This workshop was a part of the Eight-Year Study and grew out of the demands of teachers participating in this study. The group did not listen to lectures or reports but went to work on the actual problems confronting them as teachers within the experimental program.

Methods of group process were used and developed. Social as well as professional activities were included. Benefits included, in addition to professional growth with regard to the problems raised, better facility in working together, and in the exercise of leadership. Personal satisfactions also resulted. Increase in use of workshops since 1936 has been phenomenal.

Definition of the workshop is important. The term *workshop* has suffered from the unhappy tendency in education to seize on a new term and apply it to whatever one is doing. Leaders in the field are unanimous in presenting justifiable definitions and in condemning sharply the "band-wagon" thinking which applies the label *workshop* to conferences, panels, group discussions, even to committee meetings. Old-fashioned institutes with programs consisting solely of lectures have actually been labeled "workshops"! The older type of meetings do need revolutionary improvement, probably in the direction of work conferences or active committee investigations, but this is not the workshop. To label these otherwise legitimate procedures workshops is shoddy thinking. To label an institute lecture program as a workshop has been called by someone a *reductio ad absurdum*. To label a one-day conference a workshop is a reduction beyond absurdity.

A workshop is just what the name implies, a shop in which work is accomplished. This meaning was in use for centuries by artisans and craftsmen and has been applied in modern times to university offerings in which the objectives are original production and the development of the abilities of the participants. The famous "drama workshop" of Professor Baker, first at Harvard and later at Yale, is a case in point. The crux is productive work in contrast to listening to lectures, observing demonstrations, participating in conferences. All of these are useful in their own right, but workshop emphasis is upon the production of end results useful to the participants and desired by them. A second emphasis is upon the personal and

4 social development of participants as they work with others on common problems.

The problems considered in a workshop are usually related to typical instructional and curricular situations, though any educational problem may appear. Workshops have been centered upon evaluation, mental hygiene, school-community integration, community problems of various sorts as, for instance, community health, survey of community schools, leadership, intercultural programs.

The workshop utilizes the principles which should be used everywhere in teaching; readiness, personal and social needs as motives, co-operative and participatory process, experimental procedure, and continuous evaluation. Workshops are problem-centered and are of no use for the typical study of organized subject matter for which there already exist systematic methods.

A workshop serves an assemblage of persons working with expert assistance concurrently and co-operatively on common needs. Tyler's [14] early definition has been supported consistently by succeeding writers:

The workshop is an arrangement whereby a teacher or a school officer may work intensely on a problem which he brings from his own school and may obtain the assistance of staff members of the teacher-training institution. Typically a summer workshop runs for about six weeks and includes staff members from various fields of study, particularly from the fields of the curriculum, student personnel, evaluation, and administration. Workshop participants interested in similar problems form into small groups, and they also work individually with the guidance of various faculty members who give help on the particular difficulties that they face.

Laymen may participate fully as workshop participants or as specialists called in for consultation. Community surveys and other community problems afford natural and desirable opportunities for wide participation.

The active participation of community members in workshops is increasing. In some cases the workshop is set up as a community project.

Based on the analysis of an extensive literature, the writers present the following as identifying characteristics of a workshop:

1. *The length of the session must be adequate.* This refers both to over-all session and to the daily meetings.

A summer workshop is ordinarily six to eight weeks, with three weeks seemingly the irreducible minimum. Two-week sessions have been reported from several places as successful, but a great number of the shorter sessions are obviously not successful as workshops though they may be valuable conferences. It is extremely difficult to get problems defined, groups organized and co-ordinated effort under way rapidly enough to accomplish much in two weeks. Pressure, speed, or imposed organization will defeat not only a workshop but any type of educational effort.

The workshop in the ordinary six-to-eight-week summer session should be open all day, with varied activities and breaks. The point is made that a day-long *work* session is a serious grind for leaders and fatiguing to participants. Some authorities stand for half-day sessions. The real point is that program should be flexible: free time for browsing, for recreation, and for consulting leaders and colleagues.

The workshop operated by a school system during the school year should be open to all individual teachers, to self-formed groups, and to the committees or other groups which are carrying out an organized program sponsored by the school system. The workshop room serves as a depository for collections of resource materials of all kinds and as a center for work groups.

2. *The collection of resource materials of all kinds likely to be of value to participants should be as extensive as finances permit.*

a. Textbooks in principles of teaching, in educational psychology, in the teaching of the

[14] Ralph W. Tyler, "Trends in the Preparation of Teachers," *School Review* (April, 1943), pp. 207-212. Published by Univ. of Chicago Press.

various subjects, on the problems and principles of development for elementary and secondary school curriculums, and any others deemed necessary.

b. Curriculum documents of the dozen or more types which are available throughout the country. This collection should be as extensive as possible.

c. The largest possible exhibit of children's books in the elementary workshop or books for adolescents if it is a secondary workshop.

d. Collection of source units, proposed teaching units, logs of completed units, numerous charts, working plans of class groups, results of all kinds produced by a group while organizing and carrying on a unit.

e. Some daily lesson plans of the traditional type but improved as suggested in modern textbooks.

f. Typical traditional daily or short-term assignments, ranging all the way from fairly bad to excellent. A collection can be built up by instructors.

g. An extensive collection of tests of all kinds: intelligence, achievement, diagnostic, improved essay examinations, problem situations, battery tests, inventory tests, forms for interviewing, and the like.

h. A collection of new type report cards; descriptive marking systems; cumulative record cards; any and all types of blanks used in administering a large school; school registers for rural and small schools; daily plan book; and all types of instruments for securing background material about the learner and the learning situation.

i. An observation school or observation privileges or at best an ungraded room or two or three grade rooms should, if at all possible, be provided and operated in conjunction with the workshop.

j. A collection of films, visual aids, exhibits of materials.

k. Provision for excursions, for case studies of pupils.

l. The art and music workshops, where they are provided, should have parallel collections within their special field.

m. A shop with tools and the necessary materials for construction and craftwork should also be available.

3. *The staff should represent a wide diversity of personnel.*

4. *The full-time staff may be based on the ratio of one staff member for each 12-15 participants. Some of the specialists may be on part-time basis.*

Classroom teachers, general supervisors, or any officer may serve as leaders of small groups organized around common problems. Specialist consultants may be called in as needed. Ordinarily, specialists should be available in the areas of principles of teaching, psychology of learning, curriculum principles and practices on both elementary and secondary levels, the education of gifted or of retarded children.

Art and music consultants should be included without fail, and it is very desirable to have art and music workshops as parts of any general instructional workshop.

5. *The physical facilities should permit varied experiences.* In addition to a large general work room with separate rooms for art and music activities, there may be a small theater, or lecture room, projection facilities, a room and tools for simple construction activities, large display boards, filing cases, typewriters, and anything else that turns out to be needed. Trips to examine other facilities should be arranged.

6. *The over-all purpose must be clearly defined.*

7. *The specific problems of the participants must emerge and be defined without pressure or steering from above.* A preliminary survey is often desirable to identify problems. The survey may be made through small group discussions, through written lists of problems by students, or other problem census methods.

8. *Tentative and flexible grouping may be made around common problems.*

9. *The process of the workshop is co-operative and participatory throughout.* The principles and practices of group process should be utilized. They are the same as those which the teacher should be using in her own teaching, thus developing facility in modern teaching procedures.

10. *The personal and social growth of the individual participants should be provided for* as well as their growth in the solu-

tion of professional problems. Social events provide for the necessary "get acquainted" period, for the development of social skills, and for relaxation.

11. *The physical facilities should be adequate.* Ordinarily there should be an auditorium or other large room where all may meet in one group when desired; a theater; sufficient smaller rooms for small groups; art, music, and shop rooms; exhibit rooms as needed, library, and any other special rooms. The actual plant available may of course necessitate changes in the list.

Heaton,[15] in the first definitive treatment of the workshop, listed seven essential characteristics. They are stated from the point of view of the participant and indicate some of the details which are implied by the list of ten general characteristics proposed by the writers:

1. The participant is given an opportunity to make an intensive study of an interest which has arisen out of his experience as a teacher.

2. The participant shares in planning a program of individual and group activities designed to meet his needs and those of his fellow-workers.

3. The participant is provided with easy access to the services of various staff members, representing a variety of kinds of assistance.

4. Formal and informal association with other participants of varied backgrounds contributes to the participant's thinking on his specific problem, broadens his general professional orientation, and provides opportunity for experiences in co-operative activity.

5. An effort is made to interest the participant in the whole child, the whole school, and the whole community.

6. The participant's total experience as he studies a specific interest or problem tends to prepare him for the solution of other professional problems in the future.

7. Since workshops have been concerned not only with the professional problems of the teacher, but with his life as an individual, efforts have been made to afford opportunities for balanced living.

A description of a workshop in operation. A visitor who had never seen a workshop in operation visited the curriculum workshop at the University of Maine during the summer of 1944 and aided in preparing the following description:

The visitor entered during the morning session and found 172 Maine teachers, supervisors, superintendents, and normal school members scattered at long tables, working as individuals or in groups, large and small. Knots of people surrounded each of the ten staff members; other groups were engaged in animated discussion under their own leadership. Cases of books along the wall were being used, exhibits upon the 100-foot bulletin board were being analyzed, new exhibits were being fashioned in the art workshop. Teachers were trying out finger paints, making puppets, modeling in clay, learning at first hand the difficulties of working with the same materials which the children use. A film on the development of reading skill was being shown in the little theater directly across the corridor. Material from filing cases containing curriculum exhibits from all over the United States was being checked in and out by librarians. Groups broke up, re-formed, changed membership; individuals moved about; materials of all sorts were being examined, discussed, exchanged. Production of new materials was clearly under way in some places. The noise of conversation and movement was absorbed by the high-domed ceiling of the gymnasium which housed the workshop. The scene was one of movement, bustle, freedom; many varied activities were under way at the same time. The uninitiated visitor accustomed to adult students seated in rows listened quietly, answering questions under the direction of a teacher, or working individually in the library on identical assignments might be puzzled, amazed, even somewhat shocked—until he developed insight into what was really going on!

Evidence of values derived from participation in workshops.[16] The advantages claimed for the workshop rest largely on logical deduction from valid principles. Only recently has more direct evidence appeared. Workshop problems are real to participants.

[15] Kenneth L. Heaton and others, *Professional Education for Experienced Teachers: The Program of the Summer Workshop* (Chicago, Univ. of Chicago Press, 1940), pp. 21-41.
[16] See evidence from O'Rourke below and some other brief references in Ch. 18.

The process is geared to the readiness and background of participants, is stimulating, participatory effort, and develops self-evaluation. On this basis, the advantages may reasonably be as follows:

1. Security of the individual is preserved as he abandons old and familiar practices and develops new ones.
2. Professional knowledge, insight, and skill, especially in co-operative, democratic work, are increased for participants.
3. The personal and social growth of participants is enhanced.
4. A constructive group attack may be made upon local problems; upon new developments in the field.
5. Competent specialized assistance is easily provided.
6. Continued professional growth is stimulated.
7. The results in ideas and in materials are immediately useful in real situations.
8. Individual confidence and skill in attacking new problems is developed, together with an attitude of self-evaluation.

The most extensive study to date of the actual results of workshop participation is presented by O'Rourke.[17] Her survey of the literature is exhaustive, and is supplemented by a body of original data gathered from participants. A total of 261 administrators in 43 states who between them had participated in 195 workshops supplied information. A group of 51 elementary teachers in Maine and Massachusetts were interviewed and observed in the classroom. The interviews and observations were carefully structured so that controls existed in both securing and interpreting data. The effect of workshop participation on both administration and classroom practice was clear. Specified improvements were noted and observed in administrative practice, particularly in human relations; in teaching-learning situations within control of the teacher; in curriculum improvement; in understanding children; in school-community relations; and particularly in the extension of personal-professional activities.

Criticisms of the workshop. Two articles [18] making sharp but constructive criticisms have appeared. The plea, correctly, is for more careful thinking about workshops, particularly in definition of objectives, in clear-cut planning and organization. Participants, it is stated, must be aided as individuals as well as group members. The tendency, noted sometimes, to submerge the individuals' purposes in staff-influenced group-goals is properly condemned. Criticism of this sort recognizes the basic importance of the workshop and contributes to its improvement.

One popular and two professional articles making destructive criticism are available, but their authors were unfortunately ignorant of the nature of a workshop. Worse, the school authorities whose meetings were criticized were evidently just as ignorant. Their sessions did not meet a single criterion in the definition of a workshop. The meetings well merited the criticisms but not as workshops. The one value of these articles is to emphasize the point made earlier in this chapter, namely, the serious blunder of indiscriminately applying the label *workshop* to any and all kinds of meetings, particularly to meetings which were ill-conceived in the first place.

The workshop and its uses cannot be summarized briefly. Students and field workers are urged to examine the literature at this point. The periodical literature is far too extensive to summarize. Most of it is very valuable. The following major references are suggested:

Guide for Resources-Use Education Workshops, Committee on Southern Regional Studies and Education (Washington, American Council on Education, 1951).

[17] Mary A. O'Rourke, "The In-Service Workshop in Elementary Education: Its Effect upon Participants." Unpublished doctoral dissertation, Harvard Graduate School of Education, 1954.

[18] Paul R. Klohr, "So You're Having a Workshop," *New York State Education* (June, 1950), pp. 562-663.
Leo Shapiro, "Negative Reaction to Intercultural Workshop," *Educational Leadership* (April, 1949), p. 427.

DIEDERICH, Paul B., and VAN TIL, William, *The Workshop* (New York, Hinds, Hayden, and Eldredge, 1945).

DIX, Lester, *The Montclair Conference on Workshop Planning* (New York, Bureau for Intercultural Education, 1945).

KELLEY, Earl C., *The Workshop Way of Learning* (New York, Harper, 1951).

MACKINTOSH, Helen K., *Workshop Techniques in Elementary Education*, Education Briefs No. 10 (Washington, Office of Education, 1948).

ROTHMAN, Philip, compiler, *An Evaluation of Workshops in Economic Education*, Joint Council on Economic Education (New York, Committee for Economic Development, 1952).

"Workshops," *Peabody Journal of Education*. Division of Surveys and Field Services (Nashville, Tenn., George Peabody College for Teachers, 1951).

Large group conferences. These are of several types:

1. Conventions: national, regional, local.
2. Institutes.
3. Teachers' meetings.
   Faculty
   Department
   Grade level

Only brief reference can be made here to the many types of meetings employed in improvement programs. The teachers' convention is a complex organization serving many purposes, educational and otherwise; it supplies a medium for inspiration, cultural training, technical assistance, and the exchange of ideas. There can be little doubt of its value *where there is adequate planning and leadership.*

Another device of long standing frequently employed for improvement purposes is the teachers' institute. There are three fairly common types: (1) the special one-week and two-weeks institutes provided by teacher-training institutions and devoted to selected problems; (2) the one-day or two-days county or city institute held just prior to the opening of the school year; and (3) the one-day institute held by various school officials at different times throughout the school year.

Though the institute has now fallen into bad repute, it is, *with capable leadership,* still a valuable instrument for the improvement of educational practice. The new work-type institute, with its demonstrations, clinics, and visual aids, is proving an important source of professional stimulation and guidance. It has an interesting history and many years of usefulness to its credit.

Another improvement device long employed for various purposes is the general faculty meeting. Whether it is effective or not depends upon how it is employed in different learning and teaching situations. The tendency is toward the introduction of a greater variety of appeals such as the use of audio-visual aids, skilled technical and nontechnical lay speakers, and panel discussions. Routine announcements, so long the bane of teachers' meetings, are now ordinarily reduced to written form. Teachers' meetings have long provided the standard medium for the exchange of professional ideas. The intraschool and city departmental meetings may offer a valuable device for developing sequence and unity in the offerings in the different areas of learning or for discussing special methods and problems in the several areas of specialization in the average school system. In smaller schools, departmental meetings may not be at all feasible (since there may be too few teachers), but where there are several teachers in a given field of instruction—as in mathematics or languages—with representatives from different grade levels, much good can be accomplished. Grade meetings are useful in bringing together teachers of like interests at the same grade levels. Intergrade and divisional meetings can be used to bring together teachers of related grade levels: kindergarten, primary-grade, intermediate-grade, junior high-school, and so forth. This type of meeting is increasing.

Some suggestions for making group meetings effective. A number of practices can be employed in the conduct of group meetings to make them more effective. A few of the more important of these are briefly described below:

1. Group meetings should be called for clearly recognized purposes. Teachers' meetings and other group conferences should not be ends in themselves but antecedent to the satisfaction of some clearly recognized need. The planning of group conferences, whether for all or for some part of the teaching corps, will ordinarily not take place until the needs for such conferences have been clearly ascertained. The blunderbuss type of conference has gradually given way in recent years to conferences for specific purposes.

2. Group conferences should be carefully planned, both as to content and sequence. That the individual meetings should be carefully planned scarcely needs mentioning, considering the time consumed and their importance. Frequently, more than a single meeting is needed to accomplish the purpose of such meetings. Where more than one meeting is necessary to accomplish the purposes of the group conference, the meetings will ordinarily be arranged in some sequence.

3. A favorable attitude should be sought in the participants. Not infrequently teachers and other school officials are doubtful about the worth-whileness of group meetings. Such judgment about the value of group conferences arises out of past experiences with the conventional teachers' meeting. One of the best ways to secure a better attitude is to make these meetings of real value to the participants. To accomplish this end the purposes served will have to be those considered worth while by those who participate. The administrative personnel may sense needs not at all sensed by other participants. To accomplish its goal small group conferences may have to be used much more frequently than the faculty meeting.

4. The topic, or series of topics, to be discussed should deal with live issues with which the group as a whole is vitally concerned. A common mistake made in group meetings of various sorts lies in the choice of topics of limited interest. The topics chosen for discussion should be those of interest to at least the majority of the group assembled.

5. Consult the group concerned in advance about speakers, topics, and modes of procedure. Wider participation on the part of the school personnel in planning and administering group conferences will ordinarily insure better results.

6. Effective leadership should be supplied at all times. The best leaders are those who know their subjects and have the gift of clear exposition. Many persons of undoubted scholarship lack this gift of popular presentation and are unable to make their ideas intelligible and interesting to those concerned. Then, too, there are those who talk fluently but say nothing. In general, leadership chosen from the group will insure local emphasis and practical application. An occasional outside speaker of known ability may be employed with profit to supplement local efforts.

7. A mimeographed brief should be mailed out in advance to those who will be present. The brief may consist of an outline of what is to be done, a set of theses to be defended by various leaders chosen for the purpose, a lesson plan for demonstration teaching, or a set of standards for judging the teaching. If the audience is to make a thoughtful reaction to the subject under discussion, an outline of some sort would appear necessary.

8. Provide for wide participation both in presenting illustrative materials and in discussion. The group-discussion, the panel-discussion, or lecture-discussion types of faculty meetings are now generally preferred to the formal lecture type. In general, school people are more favorably disposed to the improvement programs when they can be brought to participate in them and share in their successes and failures.

9. Discussions should be carefully directed. Meetings must not degenerate into pointless, boring discussion or into a desultory talkfest. Neither the speaker on the platform nor a member of the audience has a right to make long digressions or raise irrelevant questions. This fault is one very commonly complained of by teachers. There should be a time limit on the meeting; the discussion should be kept moving; and a summary should be made. The skilful management of group discussion involves the ability to get participation in the discussion without too much discussion from any one person; the ability to bring to light different aspects, different shades of meaning, and conflicting views of the subject under discussion with harmony and consideration for all; the ability to state the problem clearly, to keep the various speakers on the subject, to keep the discussion moving, and to summarize from time to time as seems necessary. Many otherwise promising group conferences are spoiled by ineffective leadership.

10. Seek the reactions of the participants at all times. It is sometimes worth while to ask for specific suggestions, comments, and criti-

cisms of the work in progress. These opinions may be gathered by conference questionnaires or written reports. In the case of written reports, they may include reasons for approving or disapproving methods of conducting conferences, the ideas presented, or plans for future action. Wherever possible, specific instances of good and poor procedures should be cited, and definite suggestions for future improvements should be made.

11. Meetings should not be used for routine administrative purposes. This point serves double emphasis. Some meetings can be characterized as mere "guard mounts for the reception of general orders." Superintendents, supervisors, and principals manifest a crude disregard for teachers' rights as well as a lack of appreciation of the time value when they summon a great number of people together merely to hand them copies of regulations and lists of orders, or to discuss issues of concern only to a few of those present. The mimeograph will do many of these services much more expeditiously.

12. The meeting should end with a summary plus a look to the future; it should not merely come to an end. The problem may be restated, progress already made outlined, and important discussion for the next meeting should be stated. Many supervisors follow the practice of supplying all participants in group conferences with a written summary of the discussion. Such summaries serve as an official record of events, a recapitulation of important facts and principles, and as a guide to future discussion.

The most frequently noted shortcomings of larger group meetings are (1) the topics discussed may not be those considered by participants most important; (2) there may be inadequate provision for individual differences in recognizing the needs of participants and providing treatment; (3) the treatment accorded to topics chosen for discussion may be general, abstract, and theoretical; and (4) there may be inadequate leadership, poor planning, inexpert advice, and inadequate provision for teacher participation. When these shortcomings of group method are avoided, it may become a useful device for helping the school personnel and promoting the improvement program.

Choosing an appropriate time for group meetings. A difficult problem will probably arise in the choice of a time for group meetings. In attempts to get a satisfactory solution to this problem many different arrangements have been tried out: early morning meetings, noon luncheon meetings, after school meetings, evening meetings, and Saturday morning meetings. No time seems to be entirely satisfactory. Holding meetings in the late afternoon is a very common practice, but this is a time when school people are likely to be fatigued and not too alert. Many teachers prefer to use this time too for individualized work with pupils and in preparing for the next day's work. Similar difficulties arise from evening meetings, with the added disadvantage that some persons rather strenuously object to further work in the evening. Some schools provide for staff meetings on school time. One of the real difficulties with this arrangement is that while it is in general satisfactory to the staff, time is taken from the pupils. Probably a very much more promising development has been the attempt to make staff meetings an integral part of the day's program. Free time for meetings is secured by the careful planning of student activities, auditorium programs, and the like. The modern curriculum presupposes much group planning. Probably the best way to make such planning possible is to make it an integral part of the day's regular activities. Another possibility, if teachers agree, is Saturday morning, but many teachers object since they have customarily had this extra period for their own use. They may be reluctant to give it up. Many persons believe that much would be gained if a portion of the Saturday morning period were employed for this purpose. Whatever the merits of the various plans, the time chosen for group meetings should be acceptable to the majority of those participating and should be as convenient as possible.

Other problems in the planning of group meetings. Naturally the place will be a central one and suitable to the purposes of the meeting. Frequently a room with chairs and tables is more desirable than conventional nailed-to-the-floor seats. In general, meetings should be held as needed and not according to schedule, unless there are a number of such meetings. Then it would appear best to set a definite time and place. In many instances, supervisors, principals, and super-intendents assume that the regular weekly, biweekly, or monthly teachers' meeting is a foregone conclusion. Where there are to be a number of such meetings, the establishment of a definite time and place for them seems to ease the situation somewhat. These and other administrative problems will need to be carefully considered in providing satisfactory conditions for the use of group meetings as a means of training teachers in service.

Before leaving the discussion of teachers' meetings and other group devices for promoting improvement programs, we emphasize again that the trend in supervision is away from excessive dictation. The trend is, rather, in the direction of co-operative problem-solving where teachers, pupils, and parents all work together. There must first be a program or something to be done. Teachers' meetings, bulletins, and the many other devices here discussed will follow where there is a need for them. A few pages back a description of workshops was given. The workshop is a very valuable leadership device. The point we wish to make here is that group meetings and individual conferences are important subsidiary techniques in many phases of the improvement program. They can, of course, be misused as may any tool. Careful attention to the principles of effective leadership discussed earlier in the preceding chapter should help in the choice and use of supervisory techniques. Attendance at teachers' meetings is increasingly on a voluntary basis.

Panel discussions. Panel discussions have come into general use in recent years. Properly managed, this type of discussion may induce wide participation from all concerned. Certain criticisms and dissatisfactions have been expressed about panel discussions which can be cleared up by clear distinction between the purposes which panels serve.

Panels may be set up:

To solve problems.
To uncover problems.
To demonstrate a process.
To sample group knowledge, methods of thought, temperaments represented, types of mind within the group.

Criticisms of panels often state "we didn't get anything done," "didn't come to any conclusion," "discussion was random and unorganized." This is usually due to misunderstanding of the purpose of the given panel.

Informal, not too carefully structured, or controlled discussion is not only typical but necessary when we are sampling group knowledge and thinking. This type of discussion is completely out of place when solving a recognized and stated problem. The problem structures and impersonally controls the discussion.

Problem-solving panels have a stated problem before them; the chairman has the duty of keeping discussion on the point; statements must be documented; and there must be summaries of progress from time to time and at the end. Panels demonstrating a process, for instance, any phase of group process, will adhere faithfully to the central purpose. Exploratory panels, on the other hand, may encourage rather free discussion to see what will emerge. Participants may as often ask questions as make statements. Sources and proof can be called for later as the discussion narrows.

Exploratory discussions continued too long bring distrust and annoyance. The free and easy organization would be quite out of place in a problem-solving panel. The sequential and somewhat controlled problem-solving discussion will not be successful if the group has not yet clearly seen its problems and still needs exploratory experience.

Panel discussions have different purposes, hence different techniques and different outcomes. Panels should be set up in terms of the readiness of the group and proceed as the situation and purpose dictate.

The elements in a panel discussion are a chairman, a panel of three to ten members, an audience, and a worth-while situation of any of the types mentioned. An important factor in the success of a panel is the chairman. Discussion of effective leadership is given on pages 78-80; 113; 175-176; 190-193. A very early [19] summary on the duties of a panel chairman is still good:

1. To stimulate contributions.
2. To repeat or reformulate contributions enough to give the audience and panel time to consider for themselves the point made.
3. To supply illustrations when a panel member states a principle, or to generalize when a panel member gives specific illustrations. This also provides time and opportunity for understanding.
4. To give recognition by name, systematically but subtly, for each contribution made.
5. To emphasize aspects of contributions significant for the pattern or design which develop. The chairman may lead by asking questions and emphasizing, but should not dominate or direct the discussion to a specific and predetermined outcome.
6. To interpret the interrelations of diverse contributions both to each other and to the general pattern.
7. To summarize and to integrate from time to time, and at the close of the discussion.
8. To decide when the contributions of the panel have been sufficiently clarified to include the audience in the discussion.

The chairman should be well versed in the topic under discussion, should have an open mind, a sense of humor, resourcefulness, and should be tolerant of conflicting ideas. While stimulating the discussion he should avoid and prevent emotional tensions as far as possible. He should offer very few ideas himself, confining his contributions to emphasizing the significant contributions of others and to correlating the elements of the discussion to the main topic. In the final summary he has the opportunity to integrate the entire discussion.

It is suggested that panel members should be ready thinkers, facile speakers, interested and competent in the topic under discussion and, if possible, representative of a wide variety of viewpoints. It is important that the members of the panel understand the difference between engaging in discussion and making a succession of addresses. Five minutes should, ordinarily, be too long for any one person to speak at one time.

It is customary to follow the panel discussion by participation on the part of the audience. To get good results the meeting must be carefully planned.

The planning of school-administered forums. It has been repeatedly emphasized in this volume that teachers should participate in community-wide activities and projects in order that the community may have the assistance of such leadership as the school can supply, and that the schools and teachers may not be too greatly divorced from the people and the communities which they attempt to serve. It has also been repeatedly emphasized in this volume that teachers, pupils, parents, and administrators should all share in educational planning in order that the schools may have the assistance of all and that parents may be better informed about the schools. It was emphasized at the beginning of this chapter that teachers may learn while participating in large school and community-improvement programs. The school-community forums present another instrument for realizing many of these values. A number of suggestions on how to conduct them successfully follow.

Starting a forum involves the co-operative efforts of many persons in and out of school: civic leaders, parents, pupils, and teachers. The basic requirements for a balanced program are:

A. *Physical Features*
   1. A population large enough to meet the expense of good management.
   2. An area small enough to avoid unusual expenses for transportation of forum leaders.

[19] Lester K. Ade, *In-Service Education of Teachers,* Bulletin No. 155 (Harrisburg, Pa., State Department of Public Instruction, 1939), pp. 20-21.

3. Good meeting places of various sizes in all sections of the district.

B. *Administration*
   1. A director, part-time or full-time, depending upon the factors previously mentioned.
   2. Secretarial help, amount depending upon the same factors.

C. *Period of Operation*
   1. About 30 to 35 weeks per year.

D. *Speakers and Leaders for the Different Type of Forums*
   1. City- or county-wide forums (more accurately, "forum district-wide").
   2. Sectional forums (organized in a circuit so that a forum leader serving for a week or two may reach all districts).
   3. Neighborhood forums.

E. *Inexpensive Additions*
   1. Small study-discussion groups usually led by volunteers, meeting in homes, schools, or other convenient places.
   2. Institutes planned for vacation periods, organized and participated in by the staff.
   3. Leadership training courses, conducted by forum leaders to develop abilities in planning and leading group discussions and meetings of various kinds.
   4. General counseling services on techniques provided by the forum director and the leaders for forums, discussion groups, and public meetings under various, nonpublic auspices.

The main methods for conducting forum discussions are:

1. Informal group discussion, for groups of 10 to 25, led by one of the group.
2. Committee or conference discussion, for small groups of persons who must reach a decision on a matter of mutual concern.
3. Panel discussion, for large or small groups; the subject is presented and discussed by qualified students usually having different opinions; participation of audience follows panel discussion.
4. Lecture forum, for audiences of different sizes, based on the presentation of a qualified speaker who may or may not guide discussion; sometimes only questions are permitted or encouraged. Panels may be used to supplement the speaker.
5. Symposium, for audiences of different sizes, based on the expert presentation of different phases of the subject by three or more persons.
6. Debate, for audiences of different sizes, based upon presentation by two speakers of opposite points of view. There are many ways of organizing the time and making use of the skills of the speakers.

The choice of method will depend upon the purpose, the subject, and the situation.

The small group conference. The term *work conference* is often applied to this type of meeting, but it includes also discussion groups. The same general rules governing large group conferences apply here.

The small group conference may be employed wherever one finds teachers of like needs, interests, and problems. The advantages of the small group conference lie in its economy of time, its recognition of individual differences, and its informal proximity to the teachers themselves. It probably deserves much wider use in the improvement program than it now receives.

Educational committee work. It is common practice to turn over the responsibility for various educational projects to committees of school officials of one sort or another. These committees ordinarily have a definite goal such as making a curriculum; choosing educational aids and materials; developing criteria for evaluating various means, processes, and outcomes; conducting community surveys; making follow-up studies of graduates; finding the problems of pupils, teachers, and the like. They not only achieve their goal, but they also serve as a means for improving the school personnel in service. The emphasis here is upon the device rather than the uses to which it may be put. Accordingly, in spite of the fact that almost everyone has had committee experience, the writers have chosen to offer certain comments that we hope may be helpful.

Some suggestions for the improvement of educational committee work. To get good results, the membership must be well chosen; the problem, one of concern to the participants; and the leadership, good. The following summary may help:

1. Center the committee work around a task clearly defined and deemed of importance by the group.
2. Get volunteers or choose the membership of the committee with reference to the specific problem being attacked. Abilities and backgrounds very useful on one committee may not be so useful on another.
3. Make the committee small enough to allow a free exchange of ideas and large enough to represent varying points of view and to secure needed specialized assistance.
4. Select the leadership with special reference to qualifications for the task. (Principles of leadership were elaborated in Chapters 4 and 5. The following points are merely for re-emphasis.)
    a. Provide for the democratic processes of free discussion, trial summaries, and complete voicing of minority views.
    b. Recognize leadership within the group wherever it arises.
    c. Provide conditions which release creative activity and secure participation.
5. To facilitate operations, prepare an agenda carefully, provide necessary resource materials and good though informal organization.
6. Make the deliberations of the committee result in production of some observable type. There must be a tangible product useful in the situation, the continuing effect of which can be observed.
7. Make the form of the produced materials clear and definite enough to be easily useful to all concerned.

Bulletins, guides, and printed aids. There are many sorts of locally distributed, state, and national bulletins, guides, and printed aids available to the school personnel. They may be prepared, printed and distributed

1. By privately owned commercial agencies (such as the very large amount of materials distributed by travel agencies, chambers of commerce, life insurance companies and large industrial concerns).
2. By semipublic professional groups (such as the bulletin materials from labor unions, co-operatives, and teachers' associations; local, state, and national).
3. By educational foundations (such as the very large number of monographs reporting the results of foundation-supported projects in many areas of human development and education).
4. By various local, state, and national governmental units (such as the many excellent bulletins and special aids published by the United States Office of Education, state departments of education, and local governmental units).

They cover a large variety of topics and subject matter, professional and nonprofessional in character. They may be roughly classified as follows:

1. Source Materials
    a. Especially prepared resource units, as in curriculum.
    b. Free and purchasable leaflets, bulletins, and booklets on a miscellany of social, political, personal, professional, and economic topics.
2. Materials for Special Teaching Problems, such as helps
    a. With child development problems.
    b. With pupil diagnosis and remediation.
    c. With learning difficulties.
    d. With problems of evaluation.
    e. With teaching methods.
3. Professional Aids
    a. State, local, and national teacher association journals.
    b. Special bulletins.

In addition to the use of nonlocally prepared materials, some school systems maintain a regular bulletin service, printed or mimeographed; others issue special bulletins only as needed. The service bulletin has become an important instrument for the improvement of instructional practices.

As with all improvement devices, they must be chosen to harmonize with the particular purposes for which they are used, the personal idiosyncrasies of the users, and the conditions under which they are employed; like all aids they are subject to certain advantages and limitations. The deficiencies most commonly observed in the use of these aids arise from: (1) the apparent inability of some persons to prepare helpful materials; (2) the lack of interest on the part of some teachers in such materials; and (3) the failure of such materials to provide for the varying needs of particular learning and teaching situations. Such materials have the advantages of: (1) giving a sort of permanency to the assistance rendered (the materials may be kept for future reference and used in many instances time and time again); (2) assuring a certain completeness and accuracy of statement (one ordinarily exercises somewhat more care in written materials than in spoken materials); and (3) saving the time of the specialists (it is not possible for them always to be present when their services are needed and to do by individual conference or group conferences what a well-prepared service bulletin may do). Because of limited space, it is impossible to reproduce here samples of the many kinds of bulletins used in helping teachers and other educational workers, but these can be secured from friends and neighbors in other school systems by writing for them. Every worker should assemble such materials to use when the occasion arises.

Principles of guidance in the preparation of bulletins. The following list is not exhaustive. It represents the results of the work of a small committee on bulletins in a supervision seminar.

1. Educational bulletins should be sharply distinguished from notices, from summaries of regulations, from routine announcements, from news notes, and so forth.
2. A supervisory bulletin should be based upon and directed toward the solution of a definite need or problem which has been discovered by any of the usual means.
3. A bulletin should, preferably, deal with but one problem, issue, or item.
4. Educational bulletins have their own unique values and functions and should be used only when bulletins serve better than any other means.
5. Bulletins may be issued by individuals but should most frequently result from co-operative group study, discussion, and summary.

6. Bulletins should be dynamic, provocative of thought and action.
    (They should *not* be ordinarily mere summaries, reports of action taken, minutes of meetings, and so forth. Questions should be asked, actions suggested, reactions and comments invited, follow-up activities suggested, study guides and references included.)
7. Vocabulary, style, and tone should be lively and interesting, neither over-enthusiastic nor pessimistic, neither pollyanna-ish nor nagging in tone. The writing of interesting provocative bulletins is a specialized skill.
8. Bulletins should provide for individual and group actions in writing, or in group discussion, or in both.
9. Bulletins should provide for continuity on given problems through direct reference to the problem, to previous results, plus suggestions for future study, discussion, and activity. Devices and forms for measuring, evaluating, and recording progress may be included when appropriate.

MECHANICAL DETAILS

1. The format should be attractive. The title page may well have a drawing, a cartoon, or other decorative device. A provocative title is a distinct asset.
2. The general organization should be clear-cut and definite, not buried in long paragraphs nor in rambling, non-sequential discourse.
    a. The problem, issue, or purpose should be stated clearly and briefly at the very beginning.
    b. Explanation and background when necessary should be brief and follow immediately statement of the problem.
    c. The sequence should "march," that is, should go along with reasonable rapidity and brevity. Specific illustrative material, however, should be used freely. Drawings, cartoons, graphs, pictures should be used to supplement verbal descriptions.
    d. The conclusions or summaries should be concrete and definite, often in numbered outline form.
3. The relation of a given bulletin to a series should be made quite clear.
4. Credit for all quotations and for contributions from local teachers or other staff members, should be given without fail in footnote references.
5. Printing is ordinarily superior to stencil-reproduction.

The use of audio-visual aids. The general values and uses of these aids will be set forth in Chapters 13 and 17, dealing with materials of instruction. The same values and uses hold when these aids are used in supervision to aid teachers and laymen. Limited space prevents adequate discussion of all details. Brief summary will be made for sound motion pictures, educational exhibits, and museum materials since these are the most common ones.

The use of sound motion pictures. Films which combine visual and verbal presentation are coming into ever-wider use. Examples of all sorts of education processes, classroom procedures, new departures, whether good or poor, can be brought before teachers, parents, and others with ease. Often the difficulty and time associated with field trips or travel can be eliminated. The procedure for the use of films should be similar to that for any demonstration. The film should be selected in the first place because it makes a contribution to some problem-solving discussion or other project currently under way. Preview by the leader is essential. The showing should follow preparation of the group to see it, a guide to observation is desirable, and discussion both precedes and follows the showing. Films may be observed as often as necessary. The personal factor is eliminated by use of pictures, hence analysis may be as critical as desired. An excellent catalogue of films for use in teacher education exists and may easily be brought up to date from time to time by student search for more recent films:

Audio-Visual Materials in Teacher Education, Twenty-ninth Yearbook, Association for Student Teaching. 1950. Available from the Association, c/o Allen D. Patterson, Executive Secretary, State Teachers College, Lock Haven, Pa.

Catalogues are available from commercial distributors of educational films but all are included in the above reference. Many colleges and universities and state departments of education now maintain film libraries or depositories with materials suitable for use all the way from kindergarten instruction to graduate education for teachers. These materials should be used increasingly.

Film strips are becoming more and more easily available. Facilities for making them on the spot are obtainable. Still pictures should not be overlooked. Unposed pictures of classroom procedure are valuable supervisory aids.

Besides this use of sound film for demonstration purposes, the sound motion camera can be advantageously employed by those who can afford it as a means of making records of teaching and other improvement activities for self-observation and for critical analysis by others. Though this use of the sound motion picture is not generally feasible at the present time because of the cost of such films, it is one that promises to become general in the future as this obstacle is overcome.

The use of educational exhibits and museum materials. Educational exhibits are a regular feature of most state and national conventions. A number of school systems maintain rotating exhibits of textbooks, equipment, instructional materials, pupil productions, and the like. Valuable guidance and stimulus is supplied for new and beginning teachers and for experienced teachers as well.

Examples of pupil work are particularly stimulating to teachers who wish to try new methods but are doubtful of results. Exhibits may be of art or construction work, compositions, outcomes of projects of many types, lists of games and other amusements. The list is without limit. The varied means of achieving objectives as well as the results of individual differences are clearly shown. An alert staff will aid in gathering and displaying these materials. Needless to say, the exhibits should rotate often enough to be of interest and value. Exhibits of pupil work should be selected from regular, everyday classroom work. All levels of achievement should be represented. Exhibits of uniformly good or near-perfect work are of less use as aids to the teachers, and in addition tend to breed skepticism, with resultant lack of motivation.

Besides the exhibits, some school systems maintain regular museums of educational materials. Then there are public museums which can be frequently used by both teachers and pupils. The use of museum materials in art, natural history, geography, and the biological sciences should be encouraged and routinized so as to become a regular part of the training program for teachers and pupils alike.

Sound recording devices. Wide use may be made of sound recorders, with playback and resultant discussion. Phonographs may also be used. A commercial house distributes prepared records for use in teacher education:

Educational Recording Services, 5922 Abernathy Drive, Los Angeles 45, California.

Course work for teachers in service. Few persons who have not given the problem special consideration will realize the extent to which teacher-training institutions have reconstructed their offerings for the training of teachers and other staff members in service. Through summer-school courses, extension courses, correspondence courses, late afternoon and evening classes, special conferences, clinics, institutes, and service bureaus, many educational institutions are now offering to school personnel numerous opportunities for continued growth in service. Though this work may lack the immediate practical value of that offered by local leadership, it is invaluable both as a source of ideas and as an encouragement to further effort. A criticism frequently heard of such offerings is that they are remote, abstract, and theoretical. The very remoteness and detachment of some of these discussions are not, however, without value. There is a trend, too, toward more laboratory work and concrete experiences. The addition of problems courses and workshops has also increased the practical value of course work, which when properly organized, may supply very much needed assistance for teachers.

Some advantages and shortcomings claimed for course work. Like other means of stimulating growth among the personnel, course work possesses certain very definite advantages and disadvantages. Among the former frequently claimed for this means of helping the personnel are:

1. It provides expert assistance where expert assistance is needed. (The college and university teacher is usually one that has achieved a certain degree of expertness in his chosen field of specialization.)
2. It provides new and better library services than those ordinarily available to the field worker.
3. It provides an opportunity to meet and exchange ideas with persons from other school systems.

The most frequently voiced disadvantages of this plan are:

1. The problems and aspects of the subject presented in course work are frequently not those sensed by teachers as most pressing and significant.
2. Instructors seem frequently not to be able to bridge the gap between principles and techniques. General theory courses are sometimes not satisfactory because of their superficiality and neglect of the appropriateness aspects of techniques. The two approaches are ordinarily not well integrated.
3. Course work is frequently formal and academic.

Teachers should not hesitate to walk out on courses which remain unrelated to the facts and problems of the clientele. Courses in statistics and in tests and measurements are frequent offenders, though weakness may be found in any area. Criticism devolves upon the instructor. The weaknesses complained about in course work for teachers can be eliminated with speed and ease by instructors who know their business.

Field trips, excursions, and travel. School boards and superintendents increasingly recognize the value of directed excursions and of travel. Credits, salary increments, merit ratings, and other advantages are granted much as they are for course work. Travel is being added to the possible ways of meeting local regulations requiring some form of improvement work within given intervals, usually three to five years. The advantages are obvious. Reports are usually requested, sometimes presented to the teaching staff. Accompanying motion pictures, lantern slides, or still photographs are valuable.

An experienced supervisor recently expressed the belief that many teachers today are just not equal to handling modern youth with their varied out-of-school experiences, including summer travel with their families. A survey report on a New England town school system placed double emphasis on the suggestion that teachers be subsidized for travel expenses in any way the local authorities could afford. One teacher asked in the discussion meeting where teachers might travel, whereupon a staff member brought down the house by replying, with no hint of humor, "There are large geographic areas stretching in all directions from the boundaries of this town."

Travel seminars lasting from three weeks to several months, operated by teacher-education institutions or by commercial agencies, are increasing and becoming more effective.

Teacher participation in educational problem-solving or local research. One of the very best means of coming to some fairly substantial understanding of professional education is for teachers to study carefully and systematically the problems sensed by them in their everyday work as teachers. The problem-solving method has already been widely and successfully used by pupils, and there is no reason to believe that it cannot be successfully used by teachers in learning to teach. Many leaders have advocated research for teachers, pointing out that both the teacher and the cause of professional education would be promoted.

There are, however, three points to be kept in mind in attempting to stimulate research among teachers. In the first place,

most teachers under ordinary circumstances do not have time or facilities for carrying on such work. Certain progressive city administrations arrange this, however, by supplying substitute teachers or by reducing teaching loads.

In the second place, the teacher does not as a rule have the requisite training for doing research. This is a serious difficulty unless the supervisory staff or the bureau of research is in a position to supply expert assistance. There is a good deal of so-called "experimental" work going on in the classrooms throughout the country which is not experimental research in any sense of the word. It is merely the haphazard tryout of some procedure or other without controls and adequate means of evaluation. This sort of work bears no relation to careful scientific investigation of either the formal or informal sort here envisaged.

In the third place—and this is a vital point—there is some opposition on the part of certain administrative officers toward the teacher's undertaking systematic problem-solving. Many minor administrative officials have taken no advanced training over a period of many years and, as a result, are either largely ignorant of modern scientific procedure or they fear and distrust it. These people are often unsympathetic to experimentation by the teacher or sometimes actively oppose it. During the very week that this was being written, four cases came to the writer's attention. Two elementary-school principals flatly prohibited the participation of individual teachers in a small research study. A group of elementary-school principals refused permission to a research student (a teacher in service) to use twenty minutes of time in the various buildings examining some special individual cases. Another principal refused one of his own teachers access to the pupils' cumulative record cards so that this teacher could carry out a study of pupil progress over a period of years. In no single instance was the work of the school to be unduly interrupted; the last one did not even involve school time. Each study was to have been under the direction of a competent research agency. Certainly a principal must safeguard the work under his direction from undue interruption, but he stands in his own light in opposing a reasonable amount of carefully controlled experimentation. In many places, of course, these administrative officers are sympathetic to and vigorously stimulate research. Much good can be accomplished under such conditions.

Most of these difficulties can be overcome and have already been eliminated in the better school systems.

Activities providing participation opportunities for members of the school personnel. There is a very definite trend in recent years toward more participation on the part of the school personnel in the study of educational problems. This has been true everywhere. Some of the areas in which wider participation has been provided are those of discovering and defining educational problems, of helping with community projects, of formulating instructional plans and policies, of curriculum-making, of choosing instructional materials, and of developing educational criteria of one sort or another. These seem important enough to warrant special comment.

Participation in discovering and defining educational problems. Various committees of the school personnel have been employed in discovering and defining the problems of pupils. They have done good work and have grown as the result of their efforts in this respect. There are, however, many other educational problems with which the school personnel might render valuable service and might grow in the process of helping if given an opportunity to do so. We have in mind here participation in discovering the problems of teachers and other members of the school personnel. Some of these problems arise out of environmental factors and some out of the personal characteristics of the individual concerned. Some also arise out of staff relationships and admininstrative practices. Much real assistance can be provided the administration by wider participation on the part of the school personnel in discovering and defining such problems; and the personnel will be improved by the added experience and the added responsibility.

Participation in community projects. The school personnel is often too greatly divorced from the community. There are many community organizations and activities in which the school personnel might associate themselves, such as salvage campaigns, Red Cross, camps, gardens, clean-up campaigns, drives of one sort or another, councils, betterment associations, health programs, Boy Scouts, Girl Reserves, Y.M.C.A., Y.W.C.A., conservation activities, landscaping, recreation parks, playgrounds, art centers, adult education, forums, work projects, canning projects, nurseries, libraries, and better housing projects. School people are busy, but probably not any more so than other workers in the community. They should as a group plan to assist with community activities as much as they can and learn in doing so. If their school responsibilities are too heavy to permit participation, the duties should be lightened. It is the judgment of the writers that the schools as a matter of long-time policy cannot afford to be divorced from these community-wide activities and co-operative improvement programs.

Participation in the formulation of instructional plans and policies. One means of learning by doing which is rapidly growing in importance is that of teacher, pupil, and parent participation in the formulation of instructional plans and policies. The development is the result of growing emphasis upon democracy in school administration. The co-operative formulation of instructional plans and policies should create a better attitude on part of the school personnel toward the administration and school policies. These are outcomes that should be highly valued by all concerned. Though administrative and supervisory officials sometimes object to the time consumed by such an approach and the interference interposed upon the wishes of the administration, the time spent in advising with members of the school staff will ordinarily be found most valuable both from the point of view of the final product and the attitude of the persons concerned.

Participation in curriculum development. One of the most effective areas for participation by the entire staff is that of curriculum development, which as a constant, ongoing activity is in fact practically equivalent to the best in supervision. Dozens of state and city programs testify to the value of this form of participation. Very great progress has been made in recent years, including the development of new means by which teachers, pupils, parents, and other adult members of the community may participate more fully in this important activity. It has progressed to the point where one now seldom hears of important curriculum projects that do not make definite provision for extensive participation on the part of school personnel and members of the community. Lack of space prohibits the description of the many means employed to secure more adequate participation in curriculum-making. The committee plan is the one most generally used. Numerous illustrations of the means ordinarily employed in securing teacher participation in the important school activities can be found in the literature of education. Some illustrative materials will also be found in Chapters 5, 12, and 16.

Participation in the choice of instructional materials. Still another form of participation, good for the school personnel, is participation in the choice of instructional materials: textbooks, supplies, and equipment. Needless to say, the choice of instructional material is vital in securing effective instruction. Such textbooks, supplies, and equipment as are used must be purchased with their purpose in mind. In large city systems, the actual routine of buying, housing, and distributing materials may very well be handled through a central purchasing and distributing center; but whatever the arrangement, it should be made clear to all concerned that the choice of materials is of instructional concern to be passed upon by instructional officials ordinarily with the assistance of appropriate committees created for this purpose. A new curriculum with out-of-date textbooks or supplies would seem out of place and unnecessary in a well-organized, modern school system.

Participation in the development of the criteria by which the educational product and its antecedents may be evaluated. Reference has already been made in an earlier chapter to the use of especially developed criteria for the study and improvement of teaching. Through such criteria teachers may discover their growth needs. Criteria may also be applied to many other aspects of the program of the school, such as in defining pupil needs, in choosing learning experiences, and in determining the principles of sound personnel administration. To give the school personnel who use these criteria an opportunity to participate in their construction is to insure a better attitude toward them, a better understanding of their content, and a more intelligent use of them in the improvement of educational product. The careful review of the literature of education, scientific and otherwise, necessary for the construction and constant revision of such criteria will provide a convenient device for self-improvement and growth in service. Aside from this fact, it should also be pointed out that one of the frequent causes for misunderstandings between the superintendent and other members of the school staff is disagreement as to what constitutes effectiveness in various areas of responsibility. If agreement could be reached upon the criteria, one source of misunderstanding would be removed.

Directed reading. Of the various verbal means of learning, reading is one of the best. Presumably, by the time one has completed a college education, he should have acquired sufficient interest in his profession and sufficient facility in handling verbal symbols to continue a program of self-education through reading. The expectation does not seem unreasonable, and the failure of persons to continue programs of self-help after graduation seems quite unjustifiable. Lack of facility in the utilization of reading as a tool by which new knowledges and appreciations may be had must be laid at the door of institutions educating teachers and the failure of school officials to provide an adequate professional library. It would appear fair to say that no person who is not possessed of a strong desire to serve and who has not acquired sufficient facility in the use of verbal symbols for self-help and continued growth in service should be employed to teach. Given the proper personal qualities, one of the very best indices of an individual's probable growth in service will be found in the kinds and amounts of reading done, professional and otherwise.

The sources to which one may turn for guidance in this respect are far too numerous to discuss or even list here. First of all, there are bulletins, journals, and periodicals of various associations of subject-matter specialists such as the *Proceedings* of the American Historical Association, or the many professional journals such as the *Elementary School Journal,* the *School Review, Review of Educational Research,* and the *Journal of Educational Research.* There are many other journals containing excellent materials. Within these publications will also be found book reviews setting forth the merits and shortcomings of the many new books published each year. An excellent guide to professional reading will be found in the Enoch Pratt library list of the best books of the year, prepared in co-operation with the National Education Association, and published annually, usually in the April issue of the *Journal of the National Education Association.* Similar lists exist in other fields. All this reminds one of the teacher's professional library, the school professional library, the supervisor's professional library, and other available

sources of materials for continued growth in service.

The yearbooks of the professional education associations are excellent sources of new ideas and of stimulus. Among the prominent publications are those of the National Society for the Study of Education, the Association for Supervision and Curriculum Development, The Association for Student Teaching, The Department of Elementary School Principals, The National Association of Secondary School Principals, and the yearbooks of the associations of teachers dealing with subject areas, as for instance social studies, mathematics, science, English, and others.

The reading of books both for general background purposes and for assistance with specific teaching difficulties is a practice that might be much more generally encouraged among supervisors than it now is. The chapter bibliographies in this volume supply many leads to desirable reading.

Demonstration teaching. The efficacy of demonstration teaching was early recognized. As early as the nineteenth century, Barnard employed a successful teacher by the name of William G. Baker to travel from meeting to meeting in a covered wagon with his class of twelve children to give demonstration lessons of what was then considered good teaching. Demonstration lessons, when given by persons who have the ability to do this sort of thing, have always been considered an important means of helping teachers. They may be presented either to groups of persons or to an individual.

The purposes, uses, and values of demonstration teaching have changed greatly since the early days. The increasing use of modern methods which organize learning around continuing problems and which use larger blocks of time have greatly reduced the value of typical demonstration "lessons" in which the procedure of one period was demonstrated. Many schools, however, will be using formal methods for a long time and in these the older type of demonstration is valuable. In modern schools demonstration of a typical daily procedure is nearly impossible. Directed observation of procedure over a period of days is valuable here.

The chief purpose of traditional demonstration teaching is to show observers "how to do it"; to present sound and approved methods of procedure, devices, and techniques. To be most convincing, demonstration lessons should adhere rather closely to ordinary classroom conditions both as to subject matter, method, time allowance, and the like. A valuable type of demonstration, however, and one which is entirely legitimate to use, elaborates in detail a certain lesson type of procedure. The lesson is polished to a degree impossible under the classroom conditions. Such "model" lessons are often severely criticized by teachers, as being staged, unreal, and inapplicable to the usual conditions, but they seem nevertheless to serve a valuable purpose. There are times when these more elaborate and more polished presentations may be extremely helpful in making clear and explicit the use of certain procedures under more or less ideal conditions. The fact that such a lesson is an elaboration of the usual classroom procedure should, of course, be clear or be made clear to everyone concerned. No one, of course, expects the average teacher to pursue such procedures *in toto* in her everyday classes, but teachers can profit by careful observation of such more or less idealized presentations.

Careful preparation for the observation is necessary. That careful and detailed preparation for the demonstration should be made goes without saying. Preparation of the individual group to observe the demonstration does not always seem to be regarded as too important, but it cannot be too strongly emphasized that those who are to see the demonstration must be prepared for what they are to see, if they are to observe and react intelligently. Prior to the demonstration, the lesson or whatever else that may be under demonstration should be carefully analyzed, including aims, methods, and techniques. It

cannot be taken for granted that those for whom the demonstration is presented will without guidance see the most important points to be observed. We are constantly surrounded by all sorts of phenomena that are totally unnoticed by most people because these phenomena have never been called to their attention or forcibly impressed upon them. It is a serious error to assume that the physical presence of any person will lead to significant observations without direction. The outlines and check-lists discussed elsewhere in this volume are valuable devices for making clear to observers what they may see.

Observations should, as a rule, be made in terms of carefully formulated criteria. Since demonstrations, to be most effective, will ordinarily be followed by careful and critical discussion, some record of what happened would seem desirable. Such records may take any one of a number of forms, such as those discussed in Chapters 10-13. Sometimes it is worth while for observers to make a brief running outline of what is observed or a diary outline. One may wish to employ some one of the more objective data-gathering devices described on pages 238 to 253. Probably the most easily used device might be a check-list developed for the purpose. The things observed and the type of record made are in themselves excellent indices of the observer's maturity.

Demonstrations should be followed by group discussion. Next to the actual observation, probably the most important element is the critical discussion which should follow. First of all, it should establish what actually took place in the demonstration observed. Observers' impressions will often differ remarkably in this respect unless some fairly adequate means of recording happenings is employed. As soon as the facts seem to be fairly well established, the discussion should turn to the evaluations of what was observed. The criticisms, elaborations, and questions of the observers should be welcomed and analyzed. Recognition of crucial points in the demonstration, increased insight, and comprehension are achieved.

Directed observation of teaching. Sometimes it is helpful to direct an individual teacher or small groups of teachers to observe regular class work. Though this device is more common in the institutional training of teachers than it is in the training of teachers in service, it is, however, an extremely effective device when properly handled, and one quite generally used in some school systems. To put such a plan into operation some disposition must be made of the teacher's own pupils. In larger school systems this is frequently done by the use of the substitute teacher. In small school systems this is sometimes done by getting another teacher to assume responsibility for the class of the observing teacher for the duration of the demonstration. The critical discussion of the observation may follow at some other time, but not too much time should be permitted to elapse. What has already been said about careful planning and follow-up work with other demonstrations is important here. The needs of the teachers concerned will determine the plan of action. Sometimes it is best to begin with simple assignments of easily observable points such as routine matters, physical conditions, and housekeeping. This, of course, will depend upon the teacher. Later, attention may be directed to simple items of method and technique; and, as the teacher grows in confidence and skill, if this is her problem, to more difficult aspects of teacher-pupil relationships. Whatever is done should be done to fulfil the observing teacher's pressing needs.

Intervisitation. An excellent device for helping teachers is the visiting day, provided in some school systems. Some school officials strenuously object to this plan and criticize it severely, but if properly administered it may be a beneficial procedure. Usually visitation is at the teacher's request, but a better plan is to direct it in some measure. In Decatur, Illinois, for example, a plan was in operation for some years in which the supervisor took a group of teachers or a single teacher to observe one of the best teachers in the system. Any weak teacher in the system could be thus shown expert teaching related to any special difficulty confronting her. Sometimes the teacher observed was an expert in teacher-pupil relationships or she might have been noted for disciplinary skill or for efficiency in the routine factors of school management. Tact is necessary, of course, in administering such a plan because of the many human elements involved. When successful, such a scheme as the Decatur illustration stands as a good example of co-operative supervision. This device appears to have been used successfully in a great number of city systems.

The demonstration center. One of the very useful developments of recent years is the demonstration center. Large research foundations have been particularly helpful in establishing various sorts of demonstration centers in almost every phase of education. Today, many large cities have their own. Centers of this sort have been particularly helpful in providing opportunities for persons to see for themselves how different departures in practice work or do not work.

Individual conferences.[20] The type of conference between supervisor and teacher following a classroom visit (or other occasion followed naturally by conference) has been in need of discussion for some time. Originally "visitation and conference" constituted the bulk of supervision. Three factors have brought about changes. First, concepts and practices of supervision have changed greatly. The central office supervisors, it is now recognized, waste untold amount of time, energy, and money if they attempt to maintain extensive classroom visiting. This type of supervision, as stated earlier, is far more effective in the hands of the elementary prin-

[20] The discussion of the individual conference, particularly the many personal and professional problems on which individual help is needed, is abbreviated here. Further details and concrete illustrations are found in Ch. 15.

cipal or the secondary department head. Central supervisors render far greater service through system-wide activities, though they will always maintain contact with the classroom. Second, the change from formal schedules of visits and other imposed procedures to on-call supervision has affected the nature of conferences. Third, the rise of the democratic view of life with its emphasis upon human relations has exercised profound influence on all areas.

Change in the essential nature of the individual conference. The supervisor-teacher conference has been since time immemorial a meeting between a superior and an inferior officer in which the superior would aid or help or guide the inferior, and at worst give orders to be followed. The literature contains innumerable discussions of the conduct of conferences with such advice as:

Put the teacher at ease.
Find something good and praise it.
Mention a number of good things.
Introduce the weaknesses gently and indirectly.
Respect the opinion of the teacher.
Give the teacher a chance to save face.
Give aid or assistance—tell teacher what to do.

The whole tenor of earlier discussions indicates the superior-inferior relationship. Why does the teacher need to be put at ease? Instead of giving the teacher a chance to save face, we should ensure that he never loses face in the first place. Why not also "put the supervisor at ease"? (They sometimes need it!) Why not commend the supervisor for good things? This points up the undemocratic nature of conferences as commonly operated.

An individual conference is (or should be) a meeting between two persons equally interested in improving a situation. The views and facts of each party are necessary to complete the picture. Exchange of facts and ideas is focused on problem-solving and not on one of the persons in the conference. Aid and assistance will inevitably result, but the giving of aid will flow in both directions. The

general policy applicable here was set forth in detail in earlier chapters.

Persons thoroughly imbued with the democratic philosophy and practice do not need to be "put at ease"; they are at ease. Mutual respect and confidence render unnecessary contrived efforts to "create a favorable atmosphere." We may note incidentally that all of the suggestions given earlier and found in nearly all discussions are still usable, but as exchanges between equals and not as devices.

The professional view which is gaining in practice must be balanced here with some practical considerations. Some teachers are selfish, self-centered, and not at all dedicated to teaching. Others have acquired mental quirks which hinder adjustment to other persons. Supervisors are sometimes frustrated individuals who revel in authority, who like nothing better than imposing directions and "putting individuals in their places." Nevertheless, the democratic view and practice is slowly winning. The more recent books [21] on supervision are reflecting the change in relationships between persons working together.

Individual conferences should constantly improve the problem-solving skills of the participants and their skills in human relations.

The focus should be on facts; upon achieving an agreement and not on establishing one's personal view. As stated earlier, we do not know all the answers in education. We do, however, have the obligation to use such facts as there are. Educational workers should know the research literature and the accounts of critically analyzed experience. They must be able to cite references upholding any concept or practice.

Discussion based on facts and principles, and which drives steadily toward an agreement, however tentative, on solution of the problem is the desirable method. Discussion must not degenerate into debate in which one

[21] See in list of new books, Ch. 1, those by Briggs and Justman; Reeder; Spears; Wiles.

or the other becomes more interested in making a personal view dominant than in finding a solution. When differences of opinion reach this stage, it is better to take time out to consult references and to get more facts about the problem. No one anywhere has the right to defy facts and critically evaluated practice.

The discussion should be forward-looking. The entire movement of the conference should be forward-looking. The analysis of any situation is of value only as it improves that situation and will affect future situations. The evil effects of mistakes should not, in general, be dwelt upon. Time will be better spent upon constructive plans and suggestions.

Individual conferences are useful when properly used. Talking things over is one of the most effective methods for the interchange of facts and for "getting down to brass tacks," for getting and giving individualized assistance. A number of bad errors are, however, easily made, as following pages will show. The individual conference is one of the best and also one of the most abused methods of securing growth in service.

The sources of data for the conference. The data on which conferences may be based will be derived from many sources: (1) from observation of classroom activities; (2) from discussion about the observations, about materials read, about lectures attended; (3) from individuals who see certain of their needs and who ask for assistance; (4) from comments made by parents or pupils; (5) from tests and evaluations. The devices and instruments of analysis to be employed in the collection and interpretation of data with the problems growing out of their use will be discussed at some length in Chapters 8-13.

The individual conference answering a request for help. This type of conference differs in some significant aspects from the typical situation-centered conference. A teacher or other officer requests help. Focus is now on the point raised by the teacher which may or may not be personal. The relationships between the persons, while they should remain on a proper professional plane, are altered. One person asks for guidance from another who presumably has more information or skill than the first person. Despite the fact that one party to the conference has pointed out his own weakness or inadequacy and has asked for help, there is an unavoidable emotional reaction. The teacher has "put himself on the spot," and does not quite know what may happen. This will be true even though the officer asked to help is known to be effective and to manifest complete respect for other persons. Many of the suggested procedures which are not now so valuable for the typical conference may be of real value. Here there is good reason to "put the teacher at ease," to encourage by "commendation of the good." The remote goal is of course the same, to aid the teacher in developing his own problem-solving skills and to increase his professional knowledge.

Those who help must be genuinely interested in helping. Teachers often sense any lack of real interest in helping and resent the intrusion. To get teacher co-operation, those who would help must be genuinely interested in them and sincerely desire to help them. No aspect of leadership will test so completely the supervisor's understanding of people as much as the individual conference.

Create a friendly attitude by giving credit where credit is due. In conferring with the teacher, those who would help teachers must first of all create a friendly atmosphere. Principals, supervisors, and other administrative officials are really co-workers and helpers, as has been so frequently emphasized in this volume, and friendliness should be inherent in the situation. The conference must not be an inquisition. The kindest and most professional spirit must prevail. It must be purely impersonal and professional. The orthodox approach to the conference is to express appreciation of the strong points of the teacher's work, giving credit where credit is due. This is a satisfactory initial move, provided that which is said has a factual foundation and does not lead the teacher to believe that his work is satisfactory as it is.

Teachers should be led to analyze and evaluate their own teaching. There is serious doubt that the supervisor who always tells teacher what to do and how to do it is in the long run the most effective. The result of such a conference may be better teaching but not a stronger teacher. The teacher becomes then merely the agency by which the supervisor raises the level of instruction and not a human being in his own right. Many teachers have come to depend too much on instructions from supervisors. This is indicated by their comments about the kind of supervisory help that they desire.

A much higher type of conference is that in which the supervisor, by skillful questioning, leads the teacher to discover for himself the major elements of strength and weakness in his procedure and to devise means of improvement. The conference should lead the teacher to analyze, evaluate, and plan for the future. Self-analysis by the teacher is of more value to him as a means of growth than the acknowledgment of any number of shortcomings, once they have been pointed out to him. By merging his own personality into the common problem, the supervisor can, in a subtle way, set the teacher upon a program of self-improvement.

The supervisor may be positive without being opinionated. The supervisor and others who would help teachers may be positive without being opinionated and cautious without being colorless. They must know the characteristics of good teaching and must judge practice in terms of them. By being well read, they can be reasonably sure of the soundness of the advice they have to offer. The caution stated earlier, that debate and insistence on one's views be avoided, holds here also.

The discussion of teaching must be discriminating. General criticism should be avoided. If the principal or supervisor says, "The teaching was very good," but fails to point out the particulars in which it was good, he merely commends. If he says, "The work is poor," and fails to say in what respect, he discourages the teacher without offering constructive assistance. It is much better to say, "The method used in collecting papers was very economical," "The degree of attention was marked," "The explanation of the term *charter* was well given"; or "The amount of time consumed in getting started was a bit long," "The class exercise was largely questions and answers," "A few illustrations might have been used to good advantage." Discriminating comments leave the teacher better equipped to analyze his own teaching and to plan for progressive improvement.

The discussion of teaching must be constructive. As has already been pointed out, discussion of teaching must not be mere fault-finding. In general, it is unwise to tear down unless there are available better materials with which to build. To say to the teacher that a thing is wrong without offering a better procedure is merely to make matters worse by adding discouragement to wrong practices. Say instead, "Why not try starting the class exactly on time?" "A procedure that I have found helpful in explaining difficult terms is to use familiar examples," "An excellent substitute for 'hearing lessons' is a carefully devised informal test," and so forth.

The discussion must be of a professional nature. The most desirable end to attain in the direction of teaching is a professional attitude on the part of both teacher and supervisor. When the physician tells his patient that he has a weak heart, the patient not only expresses appreciation for the service but pays for it. It would never occur to him that he had been insulted, criticized personally, or otherwise injured. There is, similarly, on the part of the physician a feeling that he has rendered a professional service. Submission to treatment on the part of the patient represents a degree of confidence in the reliability of the physician. This, in turn, is based upon the successful outcome of similar past performances. Some patients refuse to accept and finally refuse to act upon medical advice. Some patients die. Some deaths are due to errors in diagnosis; some are chargeable to errors in treatment; and some are chargeable to constitutional causes for which the patient was not wholly responsible. But, in any case, the relationship is wholly professional.

Study of the situation should precede conference. Systematic preparation and thinking through the probable and possible phases of an analysis saves time and adds to the value of the conference. Most educational processes are far more complex than the outsider believes, hence careful study is necessary before judgments are made and solutions proposed. Snap judgments, or rather, quick judgments, must sometimes be made; but it is far better to take time for careful review of the facts, summary, and judgment. Judgments should be regarded as tentative and as changing as the situation changes. Both participants should have time to prepare and may use a number of aids, such as summaries of the facts, notation of any factors peculiar to the local circumstances, school records, and the like.

The use of summaries of professional information and principles. In earlier days it was good practice to hand a teacher an outline summarizing the desirable characteristics of a given teaching procedure: making an assignment, conducting a recitation, adjusting reading materials to individual differences, developing an approach to a unit, planning with children, or any other selected phase. The teacher was then directed to consider the lesson which had been observed and to estimate her own strong and weak points. Met in conference, the teacher and the supervisor would compare their views of the lesson. Good work was commended, weak procedures analyzed, and remedial suggestions given. Teachers often did not know clearly the characteristics of effective teaching, hence the conferences when properly conducted were a source of growth. Differ-ences of opinion were often neglected, whereas today these differences constitute a very valuable stimulus for discussion. Differences in standards, in knowledge of basic facts and principles, differences in interpretation of the same data can be bases for most profitable interchange. This, of course, depends upon the presence of the modern democratic view that each participant is important and that the common goal is the solution of the problem.

The procedure outlined has several weaknesses. First, the democratic method was usually lacking. Second, the summary outlines (check-lists or items-to-observe) were handed out to the teacher, having been made by other officers. Third, the teacher sometimes did not understand or agree to the items listed. Fourth, the check-lists often became, or at least tended to become, rating cards in a situation where rating was not the aim. This emphasized the barrier between supervisor and teacher.

The distribution of prepared lists of criteria for evaluation and as bases for discussion is not wrong, particularly with less-well-trained groups, provided the situation is well understood by all, and provision made for free questioning and evaluation by all.

Modern practice with better-trained staff groups is the development by the staff of a list of principles and practices characteristic of good teaching. Thus both the definition of good teaching and the observable characteristics are understood by and agreed to by the staff. Making such summaries is one of the best devices known for stimulating in-service study and growth. The lists give an impersonal basis for examination of classroom practice and for interpretative discussion. Focus is on the facts and principles already understood, and not on the teacher. The term *check-list* is an unfortunate one with its suggestion of checking performance by a superior officer. "Items-to-observe," "observation guides," or "self-study guides," are better terms, and if a still better term appears it should be seized upon. In any event, the basis for discussion is the locally derived outline of acceptable practice.

Organized follow-up conferences. A very effective procedure for stimulating study and growth is that of planning, by an individual teacher with the requested aid of one or more specialists, for a continuous attack upon a given problem. The problem is discovered and partially or wholly defined by the teacher. A program is then planned very tentatively with constant replanning as events develop. The procedure is akin to that outlined in Section 1 of this Chapter for groups. The activity may begin with any appropriate technique: reading for better understanding or to see what has been done with this problem; with a series of visits to other teachers; with classroom tryout of some method; or any other necessary analysis. The sequence of events is then developed as insights emerge. Any technique of any sort may be used, provided it is appropriate and can be used within the developing sequence. There may be many conferences, many readings, several tryouts, intervisitation, summarizing, and so forth.

Summary characteristics of individual conferences of any type. These have been clearly implied throughout the presentation.

1. The conference is essentially a meeting for the exchange of ideas between two persons equally interested in the given situation and in solving a problem.

2. A common system of values and of understandings concerning teaching must have been developed as system-wide policy.

3. Preparation for the conference must be made by each participant.

4. The principles of free discussion govern the interchange of views.

5. A summary of points agreed upon, together with remedial or other procedures for trial, should be made.

6. Records of conferences, particularly of conclusions, should be possessed by both participants. These may be used in continued observation and conference.

SECTION 2

REPORTS OF EXPERIENCE

Groups of students and of field workers may profit greatly if group members will report for discussion first-hand experiences with certain of the techniques listed in this section.

The following are new enough in practice so that reports may be made of practically any level of development:

Orientation meetings	Co-operative research
Pre-term meetings for planning	Individual or group counseling

The following are well developed in most areas now and reports should be made only if new and creative procedures are available:

Institutes	Bulletins
Teachers' meetings	Use of travel leaves

The workshop is new enough and found in several forms so that several reports might be made if possible.

CHAPTER SUPPLEMENT

INDIVIDUAL OR GROUP PROJECTS

1. Interview a number of teachers and report on the following:

  a. The difficulties or problems which they find most pressing.
  b. The aids or techniques which they think might be helpful.
  c. The comments they make upon improvement programs past and present with which they are or have been familiar.
  d. The means, briefly and in general, which you might choose for develop-

ment into an acceptable and effective service to these teachers.

2. Describe a typical difficulty of some magnitude which might confront an alert and growing teacher (or a new departure which a teacher might wish to try). Describe the situation sufficiently to furnish background.

Develop a series of follow-up activities (interviews, readings, co-operative planning, tryout, and so forth) through which teacher and staff members may study co-operatively the given problem.

3. A study program with an individual or group may be based upon a given body of ma-

ierial which is already systematically organized. This is wholly legitimate with adult students and when the material clearly relates to the typical ongoing activities and problems of teachers. For instance, teachers often ask for systematic study of facts about child nature, needs, and growth, about the relation of education to the social order, about newer techniques of evaluation. Scores of such questions arise in any dynamic situation.

Describe a body of more or less well organized information bearing upon any problem which might normally gain attention. Present in skeletonized form a training program which might conceivably be developed co-operatively by the group for the study of this necessary material.

4. Select and describe a specific problem which might be a legitimate basis for an effective teachers' meeting. The meeting should not be an isolated activity but a part of an ongoing program. Outline the preparation for and the development of such a meeting.

5. Select and describe a specific problem which would be a legitimate basis for a good bulletin. Outline a bulletin to meet the situation.

6. A committee may examine a number of supervisory bulletins, judge them in the light of criteria, and report results to the group.

DRAMATIZATIONS OR SOCIODRAMAS

The writers have found that brief dramatizations, or sociodramas, are effective procedures for enlarging insight and understanding.

One class group for instance undertook to dramatize a series of supervisor-teacher conferences (individual). First, a "traditional" type conference was shown: little preplanning, no rapport, negative criticism predominant, several unrelated topics covered, strict adherence to school rules, emphasis on superficial aspects of lesson, little participation by teacher, and no subsequent visits planned.

Second, a "signs of growth" type conference was shown: supervisor wished to help teacher, teacher encouraged to ask questions, working together, friendly feeling but not complete confidence in each other, supervisor willing but not fully competent on specific issue, supervisor flexible but within regulations, supported teacher in pupil control, good use of materials, other conferences arranged but at convenience of supervisor.

Third, a "new relationships" conference was demonstrated: only one fundamental point discussed, supervisor recognized strengths of teacher, asked questions which encouraged teacher to self-analysis, good rapport and mutual confidence but objective attitude on facts maintained, planned definitely what to do about problem, conferences at convenience of teacher and on follow-up basis.

The third type is susceptible to further development.

Other variations of conference procedures can be developed and portrayed by students and field workers:

Types of supervisor-teacher conference.

The opening meeting of an orientation week; or pre-planning conference.

Types of counseling.

Any others.

SUGGESTED READING

The periodical literature is literally bursting with materials dealing with the actual operation of all the techniques listed. New accounts appear practically every month.

Students and field workers should consult the magazines for material upon whatever procedure they happen to be using, preparing to use, or preparing to report upon.

Chapter 7

◆·◆·◆·◆·◆·◆·◆·◆

The General Outlines of Group Process

The democratic methods of group process free creative power. A group engaged in solving a problem which is real to them will find need for many kinds of ability, many types of skill and of insight. Contributions to the common problem may come from any and all members of the group. Leadership may actually be exercised by any member as the activity proceeds. Creative power in astonishing degree is stimulated as it is by no other method.

The democratic method of solving problems and determining policies, of reaching decisions, is one of free discussion wherein all are free to express views. Common agreement is reached through the interaction of individuals of all types and of all levels of insight within the group. Decisions are then understood and invite belief and loyalty. Respect for the individual and the good of the group are central. Security for the individual and solidarity for the group are secured.

The development and extension of insight are fundamental. One of the major aims and results of group study of any kind is the extension of insight for all concerned. Changes in attitudes and behaviors then follow. A significant fact is that remarkable changes in attitude and behavior do take place in activities where all may contribute, where all suggestions are received courteously, adopted or rejected after group consideration. The authoritarian situation, with acceptance or rejection depending upon the status leader for reasons often not understood by the group, sometimes accompanied by negative criticism, inhibits the free flow of ideas. Security is lost, antagonism de-

velops. Above all, democratic attitudes and behaviors are not achieved. Many current threats to democracy are based on our failure to prepare citizens versed in the democratic method. Authoritarian methods in the classroom will not disappear until the administration and supervision of the school system become democratic.

The social climate within a group and within the situation where the group operates is crucial. The pattern of interaction within any group is a major determinant of group morale and of group creativity. Responsibility rests upon all group members. Many roles may be played by each, many types of leadership exercised. The roles and nature of leadership will be elaborated a few pages further on. Meanwhile we are establishing general factors contributing to the necessary social climate. What are the determiners of desirable, co-operative, participatory behavior—the behavior of democracy? Some of the major factors include:

A permissive atmosphere. This is the responsibility of all members as well as the status leader.

Control imposed by the problem, by the available facts, by the considerations of coherent discourse. This is the balance for permissiveness.

An accepted universe of discourse thus promoting communication.

An accepted value system and conceptual scheme which also promotes communication and coherence of discourse.

Permissiveness can become lack of responsibility, with group activity degenerating into random discourse. The accepted problem and related facts are controls, and any member of the group may feel free to ask that discussion be on the point. Permissiveness is not absence of control, it is a pervading atmosphere which encourages any and all to contribute—to the point. Control is thus in the situation and not exercised by some persons over other persons.

Other factors are:

A common problem or goal which is an actual real problem to the group.

The goals set by the group (and changed from time to time as the study develops) must be clearly achievable, with the results useful in the real situation.

The experience of working together, reaching decisions, and carrying group thinking over into action.

Flexibility in setting up goals, in changing goals as necessity indicates; in processes and materials.

Group solidarity (eventually) which gives security through belonging and contributing, and also a feeling of being part of the larger whole, the school system.

Ease of communication both as to language and channels.

Unity with the larger goals of society in desired achievements. Obvious evidences of success and achievement resulting from the group process; in achieving goals; in seeing the benefits of the process itself.

Group roles with special responsibilities to the group. Democratic group process permits any member to play at one time or another any role which may properly appear. Group process, as has been stated, is not mere unorganized conversation or play. Responsibilities are delegated by the group in order that progress may be made. The major specialized roles are those of Leader, Recorder, Observer, and Resource person.

The characteristics of democratic leadership. The distinction between "status" and "shared" or "emergent" leadership was given in Chapter 4. The status leader does not monopolize the function; he aims instead to bring out the potentialities of group members. Leaders should work sincerely to establish conditions wherein all members wish to contribute their best to the common project.

Specific situations should then call forth the persons in the group with the knowledges and skills demanded by that situation. Mechanical controls are avoided, as is control through personal appeal or through fear. The process should discourage any desire to return to authoritarian methods. Docility and blind acceptance are not democratic virtues. The majority of persons imbued with the democratic view will usually rise to the new challenges.

A permissive climate is not easily achieved. The leader must abandon the traditional concepts of power and dominance, and place his faith in the willingness, sincerity, and ability of persons to solve problems which are real to those persons. The traditional urge to dominate is displaced by the more civilized urges to aid, encourage, and inspire. The success of others, which means their growth, is the reward of the status leader.

The leader's manner, personality, and type of leadership are among the most significant factors affecting human growth and socialization.

The leader should receive all problems (even "gripes"), all suggestions with courteous attention. Negative reaction inhibits adults, whereas recognition of the simplest sort frees and encourages them. The leader should build a free, permissive, and creative atmosphere by being consistent and honest. A friendly, informal manner eases tension and encourages expression. Occasionally time must be taken with trivial questions if group members are to be convinced that they may really bring up their problems. The leader may need to protect an individual or small group from more sophisticated group members who would ridicule simple questions and suggestions. Adequate detailed knowledge about the group and the individuals in it aids the leader in adjusting process to individual needs and interests, strengths and weaknesses, and to levels of maturity.

Certain other factors are less under control by educational workers but must be considered, and when possible improved.

The goals, ambitions, values, and beliefs about education which dominate the community.

The mores, customs, conventions of the homes and social classes within the community; the relationship between the classes and their values.

The living conditions, social acceptance, and health of the staff.

Evidence is emerging supporting superiority of democratic methods. The question often arises: Do we know that democratic methods are superior? Slowness, susceptibility to error, lack of competent leadership are mentioned. Not all those who oppose democratic methods are lazy authoritarians seeking an easy method of control in the interests of comfort and avoidance of effort. Some sincerely believe that nondemocratic methods of authority and imposition are better; some believe these methods necessary and inescapable. Their beliefs are honest, but unfortunately based on inherited beliefs from pre-democratic social thinking. The firm faith in the possibilities of human nature, the conviction that persons working on their own problems can supply answers, has not yet developed.

Evidence so far is not extensive but it is emerging, and so far is consistently on the side of democratic methods. Some experiments have been made with school students, others with adults in industry and in school work. In addition, a number of good logical analyses are available. Other experimental studies in the realm of administration and supervision will follow, it is hoped.

The classic study, "Patterns of Aggressive Behavior in Experimentally Created Social Climates," by Lewin, Lippitt, and White, should be well known to graduate students. Other references are available. Space will not be taken in an advanced text to repeat these basic studies and their findings. Students who have reached this stage without contact with these materials may achieve the background quickly—in fact should do so before proceeding further. The instructor and students should decide how much needs to be done with the following references:

Journal of Social Psychology (May, 1939), pp. 271-299. This study is also reported in some detail, with photographs, by Goodwin Watson, "What Are the Effects of a Democratic Atmosphere on Children?" *Progressive Education* (May, 1940), pp. 336-342. Another good brief account with excellent photographs appears in the *New York Times Magazine* (December 15, 1940).

BENNE, Kenneth D., and MUNTYAN, Bozidar, *Human Relations in Curriculum Change* (New York, Dryden, 1951). A mine of information. Use index and chapter headings.

BINGHAM, H. J., "The Relation of Certain Social Attitudes to School Environment," *Journal of Experimental Education* (December, 1940), pp. 187-191.

LIPPITT, Ronald, "An Experimental Study of Authoritarian and Democratic Group Atmospheres," *University of Iowa Studies in Child Welfare*, Vol. 16, No. 3, 1940.

The two great classics from the field of industry and still among the best despite early copyright dates:

ROETHLISBERGER, F. J., and others, *Management and the Worker* (Cambridge, Harvard Univ. Press, 1939). Account of a monumental piece of research carried on at the Western Electric Company, Hawthorne Works, Chicago, begun in 1927.

MAYO, Elton, *Human Problems of an Industrial Civilization* (New York, Macmillan, 1933).

CAMPBELL, Clyde M., reference on p. 74 of Ch. 4. Current references should be reported by students as found.

Unsocial behavior is a serious matter. Mental hygienists, students of personality, and students of human relations generally agree that unsocial attitudes and behavior are probably the most serious obstacle to personality development. The growth of democratic life, furthermore, is blocked. The inference is clear: anyone responsible for any group must provide opportunity for groups to work (and play) together in genuine group endeavor. The denial and bafflement of communication and cooperation resulting from outmoded administrative practices and directives is detrimental to the life of the individual and of the school. Social skills and competencies can be achieved only in social situations. Each individual, if not warped by previous treatment, desires to be an independent, respected, and self-respecting person, and to have at the same time satisfying reciprocal relationships with other personalities. Given any opportunity, human relationships will grow and improve.

The work of any group can be done only by the group, working as a group. The solution of group problems can come only from the group. Carrying out orders, acting under prescribed directives, may seem to bring smooth operation. The individuals, however, are not growing in social abilities and understandings; educational problems are not actually being solved.

A general definition of the democratic group process. Group process is the way in which individuals function in relation to one another while working on a common problem and toward a common goal. The relationships within a democratic group (as already stated) are co-operative and participatory. Modern psychology shows that not only are problems solved as well or better through group process, but that the basic attitudes and interactive behavior patterns are probably learned only in this way.

Group process, from simple discussion to elaborate sociodrama, is not mere conversation, idle gossip, nor play-acting. A group of uninformed persons pooling their ignorances will achieve nothing. The exchange of ignorant opinion, no matter how vivacious, serves no useful purpose. Six times zero is still zero. The group itself, as we shall see, is not a random collection of persons.

Group process ideally, as indicated and as will be elaborated later, is problem-centered. The problem must be of concern to the group, understandable by members, dynamic enough to beget action, and realistic enough to be solvable. Reality motivates group members to search for information, to utilize all resources within themselves and the environ-

ment. The degree to which the problem is shared determines the degree of "groupness." Above all, the problem must be one susceptible to development and solution through a "meeting of minds," and not one for which a precise, demonstrable answer is available. Group process is not adaptable to the learning of subject matter as such, but it motivates the study and use of much subject matter necessary to the problem under consideration.

Group process is not merely another "trick" in administration or supervision. It is the basic method of democracy. Participation and interaction do far more than develop good solutions to problems; they affect profoundly the individuals themselves. Each person in contributing affects not only the problem and its setting, not only other persons; each affects himself as no other experience can. He develops the personal-social-moral traits of the socialized individual.

Extension of this brief description should be obtained from:

American Association for the Study of Group Work, *Main Currents in Group Work* (New York, Association Press, 1940).

BAXTER, Bernice, and CASSIDY, Rosalind, *Group Experience: The Democratic Way* (New York, Harper, 1943), Chs. 1-3.

BENNE, Kenneth D., and BOZIDAR, Muntyan, *Human Relations in Curriculum Change* (New York, Dryden, 1951). Extensive material. Use the index.

BURTON, William H., *The Guidance of Learning Activities,* 2nd ed. (New York, Appleton-Century-Crofts, 1952). Ch. 8. A compact summary.

COYLE, Grace, *Group Work with American Youth* (New York, Harper, 1948).

DIMOCK, Hedley S., and TRECKER, Harleigh B., *The Supervision of Group Work and Recreation* (New York, Association Press, 1949).

Educational Leadership (February, 1948). Issue devoted to group dynamics.

DE HUSZAR, George B., *Practical Applications of Democracy* (New York, Harper, 1945). Chs. 1-3, 10, 11 especially, but the whole volume is one of the best single references.

The Journal of the National Education Association, September, 1948, to May, 1949, inclusive. A series of monthly articles.

KOZMAN, Hilda C., ed., *Group Process in Physical Education* (New York, Harper, 1951), Ch. 5.

OLSON, Willard C., *Child Development* (Boston, Heath, 1949). Use the index.

SLAVSON, S. F., *Creative Group Education* (New York, Association Press, 1948).

STILES, Lindley J., and DORSEY, Mattie F., *Democratic Teaching in Secondary Schools* (Philadelphia, Lippincott, 1950), Chs. 12, 13.

TRECKER, Harleigh B., *Social Group Work: Principles and Practices* (New York, Woman's Press, 1948).

WILES, Kimball, *Supervision for Better Schools* (New York, Prentice-Hall, 1950). Actually an excellent account of group process.

WILSON, Gertrude, and RYLAND, Gladys, *Social Group Work Practice, the Creative Use of Social Process* (Boston, Houghton, 1949).

Caution: group process is not always satisfactory. The account of group process given in this chapter is deliberately simplified in order to make its major characteristics stand out. The process as presented will, it is hoped, be usable and generally successful in everyday situations calling for group attack on problems. Critical analysis has been omitted, except for this cautionary paragraph, in the interests of a simple account. Critical studies are, however, becoming increasingly available and certain dangers are revealed. These studies are not concerned with misapplication and misuse of group process but with dangers appearing in situations where use of the process is legitimate. Certain individuals, for instance, simply do not respond to group dynamics even after some experience. Tensions, frustrations, antagonisms, and disintegrative conflict result. The unintentional pressure of the group situation causes some individuals to desert opinions and standards which would be of real value if maintained during discussion. Others, sensing this background pressure, resent the situation and may resort to stubborn opposition. Pressure distorts judgment even when no pressure is intended. A serious difficulty arises when individuals hold private opinions and conclusions which are quite different from their expressed opinions and conclusions. Other illustrations can be given. Some difficulties are remedied through study and practice with various group techniques; others do not respond to experience.

Two summaries are available:

CARTWRIGHT, Dorwin, and ZANDER, Alvin, *Group Dynamics* (Evanston, Ill., Rowe, 1953). A comprehensive critical summary of valid research to date of publication. Specific difficulties revealed and discussed. Some of the accounts are in the difficult language of a certain school of research and will need to be translated for the average school worker.

Human Relations: An Assessment of Experience, 1947-1953, National Training Laboratory in Group Development. (Washington, NEA, 1953). A good readable account. Pp. 67-77 refer to selected studies of a critical nature.

See also article on certain phases:

KERLINGER, Fred N., "The Authoritarianism of Group Dynamics," *Progressive Education.* (April, 1954), pp. 169-173. Excellent analysis. Good footnotes.

Dangers in the misuse of group process. Group process is not a passing fad; it is the method of democracy in action. Training in the method is inescapable in a democracy. Like any new procedure, however, it is subject to misuse and inept use as we learn to use it. Many persons have been antagonized by many examples of thoroughly shoddy thinking which is passed off as group process. Quite a number of individuals who do not know the principles and have not yet understood the skills proceed as if any random flubdub conversation is group process. Time-wasting, disorderly, ignorant-of-facts procedures in planning or in a sociodrama are accepted as group attack. This is nonsense.

The dangers which precipitate the incompetent procedures are, some of them:

1. The procedure is not problem-centered at all, but deals with the study of an area or topic, that is, of systematic subject matter. This is gross misapplication of the method.

2. The problem may be a fictitious one, not real or compelling to the group. This results in

forced and unreal discussion or no discussion at all.

3. The problem may be one susceptible to precise answer on the basis of available data. Problems for group attack must be those which are to be solved through consensus, the meeting of minds. Nothing is more time-wasting or infuriating to informed persons than to see a group wrangle (however earnestly) for an hour or more over a point that could be settled through looking in the *Encyclopedia of Educational Research,* the *World Alamanac,* or any standard reference work.

4. The problem may be too difficult for the group. The lack may be in information, in skill in group attack, or in general maturity of outlook in the field. A senseless waste of time ensues, not to mention the development of false ideas of group work. To repeat an earlier statement, the exchange of uninformed opinion will not develop valid conclusions.

5. Inept leadership, whether authoritarian or laissez faire (mistaken for permissiveness), can effectually distort or destroy group process.

6. Irresponsible demands for participation by groups which have heard that this is the method of democracy but who have no knowledge of the process and who (as yet) feel no responsibility to study the method and develop skill. These are the individuals who cite "my experience," or "my opinion" and who do not know the difference between this and evidence or reasoned conclusions.

Deliberate sabotage by subversives and other trouble-makers may be mentioned here.

The physical setting for group process. This is far more important than is thought at first. A pleasant room with comfortable furniture is essential. Chairs and tables should be arranged so that all group members can see each other. Ample blackboard space is necessary for keeping summaries or developing charts. Facilities for showing motion pictures of film strips are desirable. Recorders can be used effectively. Quiet and protection from interruptions should be secured. The simple device of serving tea or coffee with cakes is important. The chief purpose of all these arrangements is to secure as normal and pleasant a social situation as possible. Discussion can still go on without some of the desirable facilities if the group is sincerely interested, but improved physical arrangements are very helpful.

The birth and growth of a group. When first introduced, group work gets off to a slow start. A defensive attitude is often noted at first, as individuals consider what is acceptable behavior, and look around to see who's who. Some time may elapse with younger groups before group process begins to function, though more mature groups may get under way more rapidly. Even with adults there will be some uncertainty, reluctance, and even open opposition. It is well to spend some time getting acquainted.

The situation is further complicated because each individual brings with him certain values, conventions, social patterns of his own. Worse, he brings a number of verbalizations and stereotypes to which he has become conditioned by his life experience so far. The stereotypes will almost certainly be authoritarian and not democratic.

A leader or a number of interested persons cannot make, or form a group, or call it into being. All a leader or committee can do is provide the permissive conditions and atmosphere in which a democratic group and group processes can emerge. The leader, however, is not passive, nor does he follow the laissez-faire attitude. Above all, he cannot be authoritarian. He takes certain actions as we shall see later. The extent and nature of the participation of a status leader will depend upon the level of growth and insight present in the group itself.

A good analysis of the growth of a group has been given by Thelen and Dickerman in reporting the operation of the 1948 session of the National Training Laboratory on Group Development.[1] The phases of growth

[1] Report of the Second Summer Session, National Training Laboratory in Group Development (Washington, Division of Adult Education Services, NEA). Available also in *Educational Leadership* (February, 1949), pp. 309-316; and summarized in Kenneth D. Benne and Bozidar Muntyan, *Human Relations in Curriculum Change* (New York, Dryden, 1951), pp. 105-114.

set forth are not necessarily sequential, nor are they always found just as described. First, the stereotypes derived from past experience drive individuals to attempt to place themselves in those positions within the authoritarian leadership hierarchy to which they have been accustomed. Each sees others as individuals and not as group members. The leader will run things so that we "get things done," and other similar ideas dominate. Second, if the leader truly believes in democratic process and will stand fast against the effort to establish authoritarian protocol, he will precipitate a period of hostility, conflict, and frustration. Group development will "make or break" at this point. Wrangling over problems which are really carry-overs from older accustomed beliefs and procedures may destroy the group, or more accurately, cause it to be stillborn. The utmost skill is necessary so that the group may see the difference in goals, processes, and decisions between authoritarian and democratic life.

Third, if the hazards of level two are conquered, an important characteristic develops, namely, cohesiveness among members. This, however, is cohesiveness based on a beginning realization of the nature of a group but not yet on realization of the purpose of a group. A good deal is learned at this point, however, about the attitudes, processes, and positions within the group. Fourth, a group finally sees that it is the purpose and real problem-solving that is crucial. The arguing of side issues disappears as important problems capable of solution and of affecting the life of the group come to the fore. The group is then eager to go about its proper business.

Major types of group processes. All phases of democratic process, particularly the details, cannot be included in a general volume such as this. The short descriptions and supplementary readings are summarized compactly to give supervisors, it is hoped, guidance and stimulus in getting started.

Group work on a project or problem
  A problem arises and is defined.
  A plan for attack and solution emerges and is revised constantly as the project develops.
  A tentative summary or conclusion emerges.

Subsidiary group processes valuable in defining, attacking, and solving problems
  Group planning.
  Committee work.
  Sharing findings and results.
  Research for the group.

Group discussion (*useful at any stage*)
  The buzz group.

Group rôles with special responsibilities
  Leader   Observer
  Recorder   Resource person

General member rôles
  (Listed later in discussion.)

Role-playing
  Psychodrama.
  Sociodrama.

Group attack on a problem or project. The following list of procedures is based on wide trial in the field by the authors plus aid from listings by other authors. The latter sources are listed in the bibliography. Instructors and supervisors in the field may wish to develop their own listing or adaptations of this one.

1. *A problem arises.* A dynamic school system has at all times a number of continuing problems. The absence of problems, in fact, is the best evidence of incompetent leadership and of an indifferent staff. Other problems may be discovered or suggested by any staff member from beginning teacher to the superintendent, or by any member of the community.

The given problem may be one of making changes in basic policies, of reorganizing the curriculum, of in-service study of an area preliminary to tackling problems within that area. The problem may be a limited one, dealing with the development of a new type report card, some specified aspect of teaching reading or arithmetic, of the development of audio-visual materials, of learning how to use modern evaluation techniques. Problems may involve the whole community, or just the professional staff of the school system, or the staff and pupils of a small section of the system.

Our thesis is: problems are revealed by appraisal experiences which reveal inadequacies in the educational product. Appraisal may be formal or informal and done by experts or by casual observers.

Problems large or small, general or more technically professional, may be first mentioned by a pupil, by a parent or group of parents, by a teacher or other staff member, by a community organization, by the cab driver who takes the superintendent to the station one day. Problems are discovered in lacks revealed by evaluational programs, in criticism or complaints, in the desire of alert teachers to introduce new departures or to set up an experimental procedure, in the writings of frontier thinkers, in new findings of research, and in many other places.

2. *The problem is defined.* Stating a problem is not the same as defining and delimiting it. Definition and clarification is also an important learning experience for the group. All members engage in discussion and/or reading in order to define the problem so that it is susceptible to attack in the given circumstances, so that all members have a common understanding. Suggested lines of attack and resources will inevitably appear here as the problem is clarified, but systematic attention to this comes later. Sometimes a small committee may be selected to do preliminary spade work on definition which might be unduly cumbersome if done in the group. Redefinition takes place constantly as the attack on the problem develops.

3. *The problem is explored.* Applicable principles, available facts, personal and material resources are examined. Implications and consequences of all proposed procedures or probable results are particularly examined. The achievability of the problem and the desirability of the results will be studied. The method of group discussion (see later pages) is basic, but many other methods will appear.

4. *The general process* is that of problem-solving, the outline of which is well known. The information and skill immediately available within the group will be pooled. Knowledge and experience beyond that of the group is sought or set up. Consultants are invited to participate. Tentative summaries and conclusions are made and tried out. Consequent action leads, in turn to further analysis, modification, retrial, and to continuous study and growth.

A crucial "make or break" point again appears, namely, permissiveness and opportunity for all to participate. All group members have unique contributions to make, odd as that may sound in some groups. All have both right and responsibility to contribute. Creativity appears anywhere. All contributions must receive courteous attention and be accepted or rejected only after group insight into merits and defects. Authoritarian direction can destroy the democratic process of problem-solving.

5. *The machinery for co-operative process develops out of the situation, is not set up in advance.* A separate chapter (5) is devoted to this important problem. Suffice it here to point out that councils, committees, and other subsidiary groups will be set up to pursue various aspects of the problem and its solution. Channels of communication must be provided which will work both ways. Co-ordination of the efforts of many persons and committees must be provided. Responsibilities, rights, and authorities will be defined.

6. *Evaluation goes on continuously.* This deals with two areas. First, the effectiveness of the problem-solving is appraised. What have we accomplished? How nearly does this approximate a solution? Have we utilized all resources? Other items may be listed. Second, the process itself is scrutinized. How wide and how effective has participation been? How efficiently have we co-operated? What desirable changes have taken place in insights, attitudes, and patterns of behavior?

7. *Tentative summaries and conclusions are made and their consequences tested in actual situations.*

Subsidiary group processes valuable in the solution of problems. The brief summary here will be illustrated in part by later chapters, but supplementation must take place through reading and demonstration.

Group planning. The general nature of this has been clearly indicated in the foregoing outline, and was illustrated concretely in Chapter 6 on planning supervisory programs. Meanwhile, a number of points may be summarized.

The general initial technique is the group discussion indicated above in defining and exploring the problem. The staff and leader talk over what may be done, list the things which must be done, provide for division of labor, sharing findings.

Lists of subproblems, questions, and tasks are formulated. These may include formulating policies, making minor decisions and tryouts, developing bibliographies, doing so-called library research, making card indexes, blueprints, working models, designing experiments, and others.

Charts or running outlines of what to do are developed. Work is laid out by the group for long- and short-term phases of the problem. Charts may vary all the way from listings of very general questions, problems, or tasks with very general directions or guidance, to the listing of the minute questions and tasks together with specific suggestions concerning procedure. The charts supply guidance for action and also the basis for evaluation during process and at completion.

Lists are made of resources of all types, personal and material; sources of information, tools, and construction materials.

Division of labor is provided.

Provision is made for unification through sharing and through discussion looking toward integration of all efforts into the original plan.

Committee work. The work on a problem is co-operatively distributed among individuals and groups. Committees may be large or small, and organized around any phase of the problem, and may be set up at any time. Committee findings are brought to the whole group. Far more work is done, many more resources utilized than could be handled by a leader or a group working as a whole. Individual talents and interests may be utilized for the good of the whole group.

Staff members may choose their committees; may be suggested for membership by colleagues; may be chosen by a chairman; and may sometimes be assigned by the status leader. Staff members usually choose to work on areas in which they have background and skill, and to work with congenial persons. Committee memberships change as the work develops and may be changed sometimes by the group. Staff members thus learn to work with many types of persons, have opportunity to study new areas. The development of cliques in the faculty is minimized. Committees will usually have a chairman, a secretary, plus any special officers as needed. Committees should not go to work until plans have been so clearly developed that all members know what is to be done, at least as a starter.

Sharing experiences, findings, summaries, is necessary. All individuals and committees are obligated to present results to the whole group so that the common project may go forward. Regular sessions will be provided in which the staff hears or sees the contributions of its selected individuals and committees. The materials are assessed and utilized in furthering the project, or the committees may be continued to pursue their assignments further.

The status leader, and eventually the group, through its morale and solidarity, will encourage sharing whenever needed and will manage without dominating to see that contributions are aroused and keep coming. Protection will develop as a result of group sensitivity and awareness so that undue or hypercritical criticism does not arise to discourage individuals or committees.

Research for the group. This may be, as indicated, so-called library research wherein the literature is examined and summarized for the guidance of the group. It may include visits to other situations, consultation of various persons or organizations, or it may be experimental inquiry. The latter is usually done or directed by research specialists.

Group discussion is useful at all stages. A little fear and insecurity inevitably accompany first attempts at democratic discussion. Status leaders and group members long conditioned to authoritarian domination have difficulty learning the new skills of leadership and of participation. The actual details can be learned only by engaging in group discussion. Time and experience will refine understanding and skill.

Group discussion may be aimed at clarifying a goal or policy or setting these up in the first place. It may be devoted to exploring implications, resources available, at developing an orderly method of attack, at forecasting consequences of certain procedures or decisions. Consensus within the whole group rather than a majority agreement is the desired outcome. More will be said of this later.

Conclusions developed may or may not

agree with given views already in print. Even when the group arrives at a conclusion already well known in the field, the supporting arguments have been developed by the group. The decision, reasons for it, and consequences are clearly known to the individuals and hence beget loyalty. This is important, since individuals and groups must be committed to action based on their thinking. The group is also interested in the processes of arriving at conclusions whether by consensus or by majority vote.

Initiating discussion. Anyone can start a discussion, although it may be some time before group members can conquer their fears and stereotypes left over from authoritarian procedures. A real problem cannot fail to start individuals thinking and talking. A statement may be made or a question asked by an administrative officer, whereupon a teacher may suggest a modification because of the actual conditions in his building. Other teachers and principals will support or deny the original statement. The status leader may need to supply the legal or board ruling on the problem. A resource person may inject a wholly new interpretation of the problem or of the immediate phase. Vigorous give-and-take may result, with small groups sometimes becoming absorbed in their circle of discussion. The whole group will eventually receive and use the thoughts of the small groups. The status leader provides conditions for free and easy argument and is aided by emergent leaders and by increasing participation. Each alert person, probably within an hour, has exercised leadership by contribution of special knowledge, by asking a question, by making a creative suggestion. An individual may emerge as a leader for a considerable period if he becomes the center of a definite interchange. Each group member may be a leader or a participator at any time. This may go on for an hour or for a series of meetings covering a semester or year.

The difference between formal logic and thought-in-progress. Orderly, sequential procedures in thinking are highly desirable as an ideal for which to aim. The actual processes of thought in the solution of actual problems, however, follow no such orderly and smooth sequences as formal outlines of problem-solving or of logic would imply. Formal logic, in simple terms, represents a summary of correct thought after the thought has taken place. Logic is the process of proof of thinking rather than thinking itself. The summary is smooth and sequential. The actual process of thought-in-progress is something very different. The term *dynamic logic* is widely used to designate the logic of inquiry or process, as distinguished from the logic of proof or of post-procedural summary. A better term is *thought-in-progress.*

Actual problem-solving in process includes innumerable errors and corrections, digressions, discussions ending in blind alleys, the laborious trial and checking of guesses, the tedious process of validating and evaluating. Terms must be defined and redefined; schemes for classifying one's ideas must be made and often scrapped. Analysis, selection, and discrimination of ideas and processes are continuous. Many, many errors and successes appear before a difficult problem is solved. These and many others are the essence of thought-in-progress [2] but are never seen in the summaries of formal logic. The individual learns the best methods of proceeding, of avoiding errors, by discovering flaws within his own problem-solving processes. Experience with problem-solving will enable one to achieve the understandings and skills of orderly thought without having them thrust upon him through the formulas of formal logic.

Thought-in-progress has its own order and controls. The values of democratic interchange must not obscure the necessity for order, control, and reasoned conclusion.

[2] John Dewey, *Logic: The Theory of Inquiry* (New York, Holt, 1938). Advanced students may wish to examine this excellent but difficult treatment.
John Dewey, *How We Think,* rev. ed. (Boston, Heath, 1933), Ch. 5 contains a much simplified discussion suitable to beginning students.

Controls in dynamic thought reside in the problem, in known facts, in "reasonableness" of process, and finally in the democratic obligation to stay on the point and to accept responsibility for what one says. Any member of the group may demand that contributors "stay on the point," that sources of facts be given, that statements be supported by more than assertion, and that one accept all inferences fairly drawn from his statements. One may not wander aimlessly as is done in ordinary conversation, may not skip from item to item without connection, may not escape responsibility for random, inconsistent, or even contradictory statements. One may not "agree" or "disagree" with demonstrable factual materials. One cannot hide behind such expressions as "my experience shows" or even worse, "one opinion is as good as another." He must cite facts and sources. No one has a right to an opinion when contrary competent, sufficient, and valid facts are available. Anyone has the right, of course, to question the facts, to examine the methods and controls under which the facts were derived, to suggest further investigation or experiment. To hold opinions in defiance of all the facts we have is not independence, it is infantilism. Attempting to establish something through pooling of opinion when there exists in reality a basis in measurement and experimentation is absurd. This not only befuddles discussion but sets up false ideas about validity and proof. Conversely, the attempt to reduce to figures materials which can rest only on verbal description, while less frequent, equally confuses thinking.

A group cannot chat itself to truth. The enthusiastic exchange of ignorant opinion is not democratic discussion. The democratic right to participate carries the democratic obligation to stay on the point, to base one's contribution on facts or carefully critical analysis of experience, to accept responsibility.

Some groups starting group discussion try to use Roberts' Rules of Order. This is natural in view of past experience. The preceding pages should make clear that "rules of order" are a definite handicap to free democratic discussion. There must be order but the chairman and the group will be responsible for keeping it subordinate to the free discussion. Free give-and-take motivated by purpose and engaged in by sincere individuals will not require rules of order.

Difference of opinion is inevitable and desirable. When all persons participate in planning policies, in organizing plans of action, and in making decisions, will there not be endless argument, disagreement, even dissension? The preceding paragraphs do not mean that everyone must think alike, that all must agree in every detail. This would be impossible even if desirable. There will always be diversity within agreement, differences within unity. A few persons are genuinely annoyed, others are discouraged by the variety and diversity of human opinion and thought. Some say that there is no need to study carefully educational theory and practice because today's theory is replaced by tomorrow's. Some objectors are merely lazy or untrained persons; others are earnest and sincere. The latter are no less uninformed than their unprofessional colleagues, but their opposition is honest. Reference is to be had to the history of civilization and of education. Principles, philosophies, practices, even classroom devices should not change capriciously or at random. They can change continuously in a reasonably systematic, orderly, and progressive way. The successive waves of emphasis on new ideas in education are not mere passing fancies or fads. New principles and procedures are not disconnected interjections into the educational process. To say that "things are always changing in education" and that "it is no use discussing all these plans and ideas," or "just go on as we are and the old ideas will come back," is a good index of ignorance and lack of training. The alert educational worker will seek discussion of new ideas, will examine new suggestions. To refuse to engage in vigorous discussion of new curriculums, methods, policies, building plans, instructional materials is to be somewhat immature intellectually and emotionally.

Difference of opinion and exchange of ideas so annoying to some are, in fact, a wholesome sign. The situation has vitality and the individuals are growing. New research, creative contributions, will always stir discussion between conservatives and liberals. Persons of different levels of ability, training, and experience inevitably will differ. The resultant discussion and study among honest persons under a competent chairman is the road to growth. Even objectors of a somewhat temperamental type, extremists perhaps, are valuable members of the group. They not merely prevent complacency but often contribute new ideas of real worth. Unorthodox thinkers, "heretics," should not be excluded or ignored. They may be a nuisance at times, but they do serve the group well upon occasion.

Endless argument, quarreling, and quibbling dispute do go on in many groups. The cure is not a return to imposed authority but earnest effort to rise to the level of mature democracy. Group discussion will be effective in so far as (1) we have faith in individuals, (2) the group possesses sincere convictions on the value of democratic actions, and (3) the chairmen are competent leaders of discussion.

The continuous discussion of differences of opinion, of the implications of facts, will develop a core of group-accepted principles and processes. Attention to the remaining periphery of diversity is important both for securing new ideas and for guaranteeing democracy.[3]

Consensus and majority vote. The most sensitive phase in group discussion is that of decision-making. Writers are unanimous that group consensus and not majority vote is desirable. Antagonism to group process develops just at this point among persons and groups who are confronted with necessity for action immediately or very soon. Consensus cannot possibly be achieved in time. Fully understood, however, the idea of consensus will be acceptable to all. The "either-or" reaction is never fruitful. Examination of statements from students of the field should be made. Thelen [4] says:

The description of the goal should represent group consensus, not majority vote. It is the description of the goal that makes individual action meaningful because of the proper relationships in time and among the group of individual actions can be understood only in the light of the group's purposes. If all members do not feel commitment to the same goal, then there will be continuous friction in working, the capacities of some members will be only partially utilized, there will be ambiguity in the evaluation of contributions (and hence lack of security), and there will be minorities that may induce disintegrative forces. For consensus, the alternatives must be discussed or studied or practiced with until only one emerges as being clearly advantageous (i.e., with more positive vaience than the others).

The level of aspiration must be selected realistically with an eye to expectancy of the group in its particular situation.... The selection of the level of aspiration represents the action of two conflicting tendencies; to avoid the hurt of failure by keeping the level below probable achievement, and to gain the highest social approval by pushing the level above probable achievement. The level of aspiration should make probable (actual) success (possible) as distinguished ... from "success without success," " spurious success," and failure.[5] The continual clarification of goals, of group recognition of the extent to which barriers are too high or too low for the individual members, and of provision for evaluation of group and individual progress help in making group participation a success experience.

The level of aspiration must be continually revamped in response to changing perception of the changing realities in the situation. The

[3] The writer is indebted to Ralph F. Strebel for a sentence here taken from an unpublished manuscript, "Let's Try Education This Time."

[4] Herbert A. Thelen, "Engineering Research in Curriculum Building," *Journal of Educational Research* (April, 1948), pp. 579-596. (Available also in Benne and Muntyan, *op. cit.,* pp. 84-98. Excellent statement. See also footnotes there.)

[5] L. P. Bradford and Ronald Lippitt, "Employee Success in Work Groups," *Personnel Administration* (December, 1945), pp. 6-10.

higher the level of aspiration, the more change is required for success, and *therefore the more threat to the group*. As long as a group deals with the problem at the "irreal" level of academic debate and speculation, the level can be quite high with a minimum of threat; one can *discuss* possible desirability of making over the entire social order. But when the discussion becomes a consideration of desirable immediate behavior which is visualizable, the level of aspiration will have to drop considerably if the threat to the group is to remain at the same level. Much of the disappointment and complaint of group members stems from failure to understand and accept this fact.

A similar statement is made by Benne, Bradford, and Lippitt: [6]

Where persistent difference occurs, it is usually better to ask the group to find what it can agree on and where it differs and to commit itself as a group only insofar as it has reached common agreement. Where a group is not committing itself to group action but to personal action by members of the group, a variety of commitments may be invited over and above the common commitment of all members. It is healthy for members to commit themselves publicly to do something about the problem discussed, even if personal commitments differ. However, the expectation which the group is building as to successful group discussion is toward consensus as the only adequate basis for common action.

A clear statement is presented by Miel: [7]

Allow plenty of time for pooling of facts and harmonizing of conflicting values.

Before final votes are taken use straw votes to uncover minority opinion early in the process. In this step allow each voter to register as many choices as he wishes.

Seek for a consensus by allowing full discussion of the minority view before entertaining final motions.

If after adequate discussion the group is still fairly evenly divided as to the proper course of action on a given matter, consider whether or not a decision really must be made at the time. Often it is better to postpone making a decision until further study can be made by all parties.

If a decision of some sort must be made, have it understood that the decision is a trial one whose results will be carefully reviewed in order that the large minority will co-operate as wholeheartedly as possible.

The key lies in the level of aspiration. If consensus on one level cannot be achieved we may try for it on another. Emphasis upon the trial or tentative nature of a decision also makes for consensus. Delaying decisions for further study is often necessary.

Decision by majority vote will continue to be used for a long time, and will often be used where it is not necessary. Understanding of the mechanism is therefore of real importance. We quote Benne, Bradford, and Lippitt [8] again:

The group rightly aims then at consensus in action as the goal of discussion. Can it always be achieved? The answer is obviously "No." At times majority opinion is the best that can be attained. This is usually adequate in procedural matters, e.g., when and where we shall meet, whether we shall break up into smaller groups for certain phases of discussion, whether we shall invite in a certain consultant, etc.

The writers, accepting fully the aim of consensus, would venture to say that majority vote will be used often in more important matters than indicated by the paragraph quoted. Endless differences between individuals, between individuals and groups, would paralyze action if there were no mechanism for reaching decision. When all levels of insight and background are represented in policy-making and action-planning there are bound to be differences, sometimes of considerable extent. There is no other way to proceed if we are faithful to the method of democracy.

Mankind long ago evolved the concept of majority vote to meet the need for action. Majority rule can be a tyranny, however, as well as an instrument of democracy. First,

[6] K. D. Benne, L. P. Bradford, and Ronald Lippitt, "Stages in the Process of Group Thinking and Discussion," in Kenneth D. Benne and Bozidar Muntyan, *Human Relations in Curriculum Change* (New York, Dryden, 1951), pp. 68-84.

[7] Alice Miel, *Changing the Curriculum: A Social Process* (New York, Appleton-Century-Crofts, 1946), pp. 139-140.

[8] *Loc. cit.*, pp. 80-81.
See also Fred N. Kerlinger, *op. cit.*

no one should ever be *coerced* by or into following a majority decision. Second, a majority decision should be reached only after the freest discussion among all members, after all have been heard, after all objections have been elaborated, after all minorities have presented their arguments. Every participant has thus had the opportunity to help form the decision. More important, all minorities have had full opportunity to win the group to their views. Third, the majority decision is accepted as "tentative, with results to be carefully reviewed." Fourth, and most important, the decision may be re-examined upon request from any individual who presents new evidence or points out a blunder in the reasoning, or if results are not in line with expectancy. Re-examination of decisions is the safety valve.

A decision reached under these conditions represents a freely achieved agreement among a considerable number of the group. It is the best thought of the group to that moment. We must be sure that the decision actually was freely determined and is not a hasty, or superficial, or imposed conclusion. Faith in the group is a democratic principle. Are we not justified in having faith that "a large minority will co-operate as wholeheartedly as possible" under the conditions indicated? A group truly endowed with a democratic conscience should recognize an obligation to "go along" with the best group decision at the moment, to avoid "continuous friction," to see that "capacities of all members are utilized," and to control "disintegrative forces." The rights of the minority are fully protected by the democratic process itself.

The Illinois State Department of Education has developed within the curriculum program what is probably the most extensive body of material dealing with the problem of consensus and the development of agreements. A score or so of bulletins is available, most of which deal with the discussion process as well as with the specific curricular area under consideration.

Samples include:

What Do You Think About Our School's Extra-Class Activities Program? Consensus Study No. 1 (Springfield, Ill., Illinois Secondary School Curriculum Program, 1951).

What Do You Think About Parents and Teachers Working Together for Better Schools? Consensus Study No. 8 (Springfield, Ill., Illinois Curriculum Program, 1952). Other bulletins dealing with specific areas are available.

How the Illinois Secondary School Curriculum Program Basic Studies Can Help You Improve Your High School, Bulletin No. 13 (Springfield, Ill., Secondary School Curriculum Program, 1951).

HAND, Harold C., *What the People of Bloomington, Illinois, Think About Their Public Schools* (Bloomington, Ill., Board of Education, 1951).

Further discussion of methods which are valuable in bringing about changes in one's perceptions, insights, and beliefs is given in Chapter 16.

SOME SUGGESTIONS FOR PARTICIPATING IN CO-OPERATIVE THINKING THROUGH GROUP DISCUSSION

Prepared for the
Michigan Study of Secondary
School Curriculum

by

J. Cecil Parker [9]

1. Each person should do his own thinking. Don't try "to save time" by telling the group the right answer. The leader is not a group instructor, but a social engineer, trying to arrange conditions so that each will do creative thinking.

2. Group discussion is not a debating society. We do not argue for the fun of it. The issues are of great importance; wise men disagree in their views; our task is to find more truth than we bring to any group meeting. We are in a co-operative quest. Our thinking is creative rather than combative.

3. Ask yourself which ideas, experiences, and differences are basic, fundamental and most worth discussing.

4. When discussion wanders, restate the question and get a new start. Sometimes, if the

[9] Adapted from Goodwin Watson, William H. Kilpatrick, H. S. Elliott, S. A. Courtis, and others.

side-line is especially important, put it up to the group, "Shall we follow this interesting issue that has come up, or shall we return to the plan of discussion originally adopted?"

5. Make short statements; not speeches.

6. Do not pass any important matter that is not clear to you. Sometimes individuals hear unfamiliar terms and assume that everyone else must understand; hence they fear it would be humiliating to ask for explanations or illustrations. This is untrue. Have you not often been glad when someone else asked for clarification on a point on which you had been none too clear? Others may profit too, but you are in the group to learn, and you must not hesitate to ask.

7. If you find yourself talking more than other members of the group, train yourself to pass over minor points and to speak on only a few carefully chosen issues.

8. Use special care to be fair to positions represented by a minority or not represented at all in the group. If you are aware of a position not being adequately represented, present it as its adherents would like to hear it stated, then explain your disagreement.

9. Challenge contributions you cannot fully accept. Do not keep your disagreements quiet in the mistaken notion that it is better manners to pretend to agree when you do not. Make inquiry concerning the assumptions involved in the contribution.

10. The "either-or" attitude is on the whole not fruitful. Search rather for new means which enable both sets of values to be pursued without clash. Our concern in co-operative thinking is not simply to choose between two ways we now know, but if possible to find a way of integrating the values of both, thereby creating an improved solution. However, avoid smoothing over differences. Differences should be probed with questions to make them clear and sharp.

11. When there is some confusion over a diversity of opinions expressed, a minute of silence can do much to help members rise to a clearer perspective of what has been said. In suggesting this pause, the chairman should restate the precise issue under discussion. After the pause the members may be more able to co-operate in detecting the root of the disagreements. This may be in the partial nature of the experience and evidence used, or in a difference in the sense of values. Try to keep in mind some ends everyone wants.

12. Be on the lookout for different uses of the same word. Call for illustrations whenever this difference becomes confusing. Do not wrangle over a verbal definition.

13. Trust the group. There is no person in it who is not superior to the rest in at least one respect. The experience of all is richer than the experience of any. The group as a whole can see further and more truly than its best member. Remember that every member of the group is an individual just as you are.

14. For every discussion there is available a limited amount of time. Each individual should help make it possible to utilize the time more effectively. To attempt too much in too short a time fosters a habit of slipshod and superficial thinking.

15. Summarize (1) whenever a major point is finished before going on to the next; (2) whenever the discussion has been fairly long drawn out or confused; (3) shortly before the close of the period. Try to use the words of members of the group, rather than your translation.

Another set of guides, bringing out two or three points not included in the foregoing, is taken from Miel.[10]

1. Give full opportunity for every member of the group to contribute every suggestion that occurs to him.

2. Keep the gathering of suggestions as a phase of the discussion separate from the evaluation of the suggestions. (This usually ensures a more impersonal discussion of suggested solutions.)

3. Allow plenty of time for pooling of facts and harmonizing of conflicting values.

4. Before final votes are taken use straw votes to uncover minority opinion early in the process. In this step allow each voter to register as many choices as he wishes.

5. Seek for a consensus by allowing full discussion of the minority view before entertaining formal motions.

6. If after adequate discussion the group is still fairly evenly divided as to the proper course of action on a given matter, consider whether or not a decision really must be made at the time. Often it is better to postpone making the decision until further study can be made by all parties.

7. If a decision of some sort must be made, have it understood that the decision is a trial one whose results will be carefully reviewed in order that the large minority will co-operate as wholeheartedly as possible.

[10] Alice Miel, *op. cit.,* pp. 139-140.

Further information on the discussion method will be found in the following references:

AUER, J. Jeffery, and EWBANK, Henry, *Handbook for Discussion Leaders* (New York, Harper, 1947).

BENNE, Kenneth D., BRADFORD, Leland P., FENNER, Mildred, and LIPPITT, Ronald, *Role-Playing and Discussion Method* (Washington, NEA, 1950).

DENNY, George V., Jr., *A Handbook for Discussion Leaders* (Town Hall, 123 West 43rd Street, New York).

EWBANK, Henry, and AUER, J. Jeffrey, *Discussion and Debate*, 2nd ed. (New York, Appleton-Century-Crofts, 1951).

FANSLER, Thomas, *Discussion Methods for Adult Groups*. A pamphlet which with others may be obtained from the Service Bureau for Adult Education, Division of General Education, New York Univ., New York.

Group Discussion and Its Technique, Bureau of Agricultural Economics (Washington, Government Printing Office).

HALL, D. M., *The Dynamics of Group Discussion* (Danville, Ill., Interstate Printers and Publishers, 1950).

A Handbook for Discussion Leaders (Carnegie Endowment for International Peace, 405 West 117th Street, New York). Topic No. 9 contains excellent specific discussions of mechanics and arrangement of groups.

EVANS, Hubert M., "The Social Character of Problem Solving," *Progressive Education* (April, 1949), pp. 161-165.

It Pays to Talk It Over (Washington, National Institute of Social Relations).

Learning Through Group Discussion (Junior Town Meeting League, 400 South Front Street, Columbus 15, Ohio).

SLAVSON, S. R., *Creative Group Education* (New York, Association Press, 1948).

Suggestions for Discussion Group Members (Washington, Department of Agriculture).

Talking It Through, A Manual for Discussion Groups, National Department of Secondary School Principals (Washington, NEA, 1938).

UTTERBACK, William E., *Decision Through Discussion* (Department of Speech, Ohio State Univ., Columbus 10, Ohio).

The buzz group. An effective supplementary device for large group discussion is the buzz group, sometimes called the "six-six" procedure. Groups of approximately six persons consult for about six minutes for various purposes.

A large group often inhibits individuals from expressing themselves, especially in a close argument. The problem often is not sharply clarified. Differences of opinion are not easily handled in the large open discussions. The extent of agreement or disagreement is not always clearly assessed. Small groups which consult or "buzz" for from five to thirty minutes carry group thinking forward rapidly. Each group reports quickly to the reassembled groups. The small groups can be formed on a moment's notice or they can be set up a day or more ahead, depending on the nature of the problem or impasse. Often the six or so persons sitting next each other can simply draw together without dispersing the large group into separate rooms. Sometimes a longer period and dispersal is necessary. Groups may be formed at random or by choice of given aspects of the immediate problem. The "buzzing" can be completely informal, without even a chairman, or it can be carefully structured with an outline, chairman, recorder, observer, and even resource person. The teacher is often the resource person.

Buzz groups must know exactly what is to be done before going into session.

Clarify the problem, topic, or issue, either the major one or any subproblem as it arises.

List the specified agreements and disagreements within the groups.

List a series of questions to which the large group should adhere in place of random discursive discussion.

Advantages of the buzz group are:

Explanations of any topic or process can be given more effectively in small groups.

Getting acquainted more rapidly can be achieved.

Wider participation is encouraged.

(Any number of very specific points may be used as a basis for buzzing, depending upon the given problem or topic under discussion by the total group.)

Reporting to the main group can be oral, with a master list kept on the blackboard to prevent repetition and loss of time. A combined report may be prepared by the reporters from the several groups. Reports are often effectively dramatized through sociodrama, skits, or pantomimes.

Teachers can develop with children excellent understanding and use of this device, which is also a real-life procedure.

Excellent supplementary discussion will be found in:

KOZMAN, Hilda C., ed., *Group Process in Physical Education* (New York, Harper, 1951), pp. 167-169.

Characteristics of a democratic leader. Leadership under legal authority and with power concentrated is a relatively simple matter. Leadership under democratic conditions is a subtle and difficult procedure. Certain personal characteristics and principles must be achieved. Growth is necessary; the desired characteristics do not appear in mature form as a gift of God. They cannot be achieved, either, through reading "fifteen minutes a day" in some of the quack volumes on personality and how to exercise influence over others. Reading of competent volumes in the psychology and practice of leadership in important human affairs, done in conjunction with efforts to develop leadership in actual situations, is of definite assistance.

1. A leader is selected for a given special ability or fitness to lead a specified co-operative project. A leader has ordinarily demonstrated some ability or power better than the ability or power of other members of the group. This is the opposite of selection of a leader on the basis of seniority, political power, religious or social affiliations, and so forth. Any member of the group may become a leader at a given time.

2. A leader has the willingness and ability to create a truly co-operative spirit and procedure.

   a. Ability to suppress natural primitive urges to mastery, dominance, and authority.

   b. Ability to substitute the more civilized and mature urges to aid, encourage, inspire; to guide followers in defining, understanding, and attacking a problem (gets personal satisfactions thus instead of bolstering ego through dominance—which is childish).

   c. Willingness and ability to secure sympathetic insight into the mental processes, attitudes, prejudices, ideals, motives, and aims of other individuals in group.

   d. Ability to create an atmosphere of serious, critical, analysis of problems and procedures.

   e. Willingness to listen to, to understand, to try out if practicable, any well-thought-out proposal of a group member.

   f. Willingness to recognize leadership in others—to accept it as a contribution to his group project and to allow others to take over the leadership temporarily or for the duration of the project.

   g. Willingness to wait patiently for the more sure results which come from understanding the nature of learning; understanding the specific levels of the group members rather than to seek the quicker and so-called more efficient results of authority.

   h. Willingness to recognize and to accept from colleagues intelligence and contribution superior to his own; willingness to accept with consideration and attention the contributions of slower and duller individuals.

3. A leader has better than average intelligence and emotional balance.

4. A leader has confidence in self, ability, aims, but also at times a profound feeling of humility, sometimes even distrust of self. Both attitudes contribute directly to leadership.

5. A leader has confidence in human nature, its improvability, the creativity of all individuals. A leader at times is profoundly critical of human nature, recognizing its dangerous shortcomings at given moments. Each attitude spurs to leadership.

6. A leader recognizes critical points in the democratic development of policy, recognizes when issues must be brought into the open, thoroughly discussed and decisions secured. A leader recognizes, even in the midst of democratic discussion, crises when agreement, vote or even poll of opinion cannot be secured; recognizes emergencies in which it would be fatal for him to dodge responsibility for making

decisions even authoritatively. A leader in these instances, however, recognizes that he has taken responsibility and must take the consequences; particularly must he make frank statements as to what he has done and why.

An interesting specific analysis of two types of leadership was made by a classroom teacher and quoted by Koopman, Miel, and Misner.[11] The teacher was portraying characteristics derived from actual situations experienced by her.

The Autocratic Administrator	*The Democratic Administrator*
1. Thinks he can sit by himself and see all angles of a problem.	1. Realizes the potential power in thirty or fifty brains.
2. Does not know how to use the experience of others.	2. Knows how to utilize that power.
3. Cannot bear to let any of the strings of management slip from his fingers.	3. Knows how to delegate duties.
4. Is so tied to routine details that he seldom tackles his larger job.	4. Frees himself from routine details in order to turn his energy to creative leadership.

5. Is jealous of ideas. Reacts in one of several ways when someone else makes a proposal:
  a. Assumes that a suggestion implies a criticism and is offended.
  b. Kills a suggestion which does not at once strike him as excellent with a withering or sarcastic remark.
	5. Is quick to recognize and praise an idea that comes from someone else.

c. While seeming to reject it, neatly captures the idea and restates it as his own, giving no credit to the originator of the idea.	
6. Makes decisions that should have been made by the group.	6. Refers to the group all matters that concern the group.
7. Adopts a paternalistic attitude toward the group: "I know best."	7. Maintains the position of friendly, helpful adviser both on personal and professional matters.
8. Expects hero-worship, giggles of delight at his attempts at humor, and so forth.	8. Wishes to be respected as a fair and just individual as he respects others.
9. Does not admit even to himself that he is autocratic.	9. Consciously practices democratic techniques.
10. Sacrifices everything, teachers, students, progress, to the end of a smooth-running system.	10. Is more concerned with the growth of individuals involved than with freedom from annoyances.
11. Is greedy for publicity.	11. Pushes others into the foreground so that they may taste success.
12. Gives to others as few opportunities for leadership as possible. Makes committee assignments, then outlines all duties and performs many of them himself.	12. Believes that as many individuals as possible should have opportunities to take responsibility and exercise leadership.

[11] G. Robert Koopman, Alice Miel, and Paul J. Misner, *Democracy in School Administration* (New York, Appleton-Century-Crofts, 1943), pp. 15-16.

The authoritarian leader may be a benevolent despot, may be humane in highest degree, but his aims differ from those of the democratic leader. The authoritarian speaks of the logical perfection of assignment of duties through defined lines, of the smoothness and efficiency of the system, of precision in routine matters, of careful balance and check. The authoritarian leader may in some cases be cold and insensitive. This type regards the staff as instruments designed to carry out his policies, almost as extra arms and legs in some cases. He is annoyed when orders are not carried out with flawless efficiency. Breakdowns of the impersonal machinery are blamed on the "dumbness" of staff members. Annoyed, he may be heard to say, "I cannot get anyone able to carry out my policies. No one has any initiative anymore! Why don't people use their judgment?" Initiative and judgment are not compatible with a rigid authoritarian scheme. The effects upon the prized efficiency are soon apparent. "Efficiency" actually disappears. Worse than that there are many evil effects upon mental hygiene and creativity. Study and growth wither away. The staff become "yes-men."

The democratic leader sees his chief responsibility as co-ordinating the abilities, talents, enthusiasm, and contributions of his co-workers. He surrounds himself with the most competent persons his budget will allow. He places them where their specific individual contributions will be most helpful. He may be heard to say, "Go to it! Try out your idea. We will see what happens. What help do you need in your particular situation?" This leader quietly prepares situations in which the leadership of others may appear and flower and in which his subordinates will experience success. This leader welcomes creative contributions from anyone and gives the creative individual opportunity before the group and in tryout. The genius and originality which appear under these conditions is almost beyond belief. The democratic leader protects his staff from unjust criticism and attack. The democratic leader rises with his staff, not above it.

The status leader and the appointed leader have responsibility for starting discussion, keeping it going, and indicating the need for summary. Any responsibility of a status leader may be assumed at any time by a member of the group.

1. Start the discussion (if it does not start itself) by asking a question or a series of them, by making comments on the selected topic, by asking someone to express an opinion, by referring to a newspaper or magazine article, a cartoon or picture, or by any other of many devices.

2. Guide discussion by calling for comments upon any contribution, by asking for evidence for statements, by asking questions, by calling for transitional summaries: "How far have we progressed?" "What comes next?" "What points of disagreement remain?"

3. Ask questions or call upon persons to ensure that all shades of opinion are brought out.

4. Endeavor to make discussion general by refraining from answering questions from the platform; through throwing questions back to the group; by encouraging answers and contributions from all parts of the group.

5. Call ceaselessly for facts back of statements. This is a most effective means of keeping out senseless remarks and encouraging the sincere group members.

6. Summarize or call for summary, raise direct questions, call for further pointed comment at any point where the discussion bogs down; then openly move on to the next point.

7. Remain, so far as responsibilities permit, in the background, but do not neglect the duty of guidance and stimulation.

A permissive climate is not easily achieved. The leader must abandon the traditional concepts of power and dominance, and place his faith in the willingness, sincerity, and ability of persons to solve problems which are real to those persons. The traditional urge to dominate is displaced by the more civilized urges to aid, encourage and inspire. The success of others, which means their growth, is the reward of the status leader. A number of statements of the principles of leadership as applied to teacher growth have appeared in the literature of education. The statement below, which may be taken as representative of the emphasis in this field, is based upon statements by Corey,[12] Goslin,[13] and Spears:[14]

1. *Leadership should be problem-centered.* Necessity develops novel approaches; people work best when what they do seems important.
2. *The need for group action must be felt by those participating in the undertaking.* It must not be imposed from without or above.
3. *Start where the group is.* Groups are usually quite heterogeneous in many respects; they differ in readiness, capacity, and the energy that they bring to bear upon what is to be done.
4. *Slow progress is the rule.* Real learning which involves changes in practices rather than changes in verbalizations never comes quickly.
5. *Actually do something.* Guard against the enervating tendency to discourse and discourse until everyone is disgusted with chatter and anxious to do something else.
6. *As far as possible the activity should be of a co-operative sort involving wide participation from those concerned.* Get teachers, pupils, and members of the community all working together.
7. *The leadership must stimulate those concerned to the best of which they are capable.* It should release energy, not bottle it up.
8. *Leadership is constantly alert to new opportunities to do and grow.* The task must be approached with creative imagination.
9. *The group should employ the principle of alternate leadership.* Get as many different persons as possible into positions of leadership.
10. *A free exchange of ideas is basic to group action.* As far as possible those attempting to express ideas should have a high sense of fairness, objectivity, and truth.
11. *Discussions should be fashioned out of the combined thinking of those affected.* Democracy must supplant authoritarianism.

12. *Cordial interpersonal relationships are important.* Teachers who know and like one another personally are more apt to change as a consequence of group action than are teachers who interpret a professional difference in point of view as a personal attack.
13. *The group should encourage constant evaluation.* Evaluation is important in indicating both needs and progress in meeting these needs.
14. *Good records are necessary.* Good, terse, permanent records of group accomplishments should be scrupulously kept.

Space does not permit comment upon these several principles individually. They are all important, however, and worthy of wide acceptance and application. We would like to emphasize the importance of group action.

The effects upon behavior of democratic and authoritarian atmosphere and leadership. A most useful summary is presented by Rokeach, based[15] upon his analysis of three research studies on the subject. The summary, as the author points out, may be used as a general check-list by any administrator wishing to evaluate the atmosphere of his own group.

Effects of Democratic Atmosphere	Effects of Authoritarian Atmosphere
1. More "we-feeling"; more frequent use of "we," "us," "ours."	1. More "I-feeling"; more frequent use of "I," "me," "mine."
2. "Group-minded suggestions"; relatively few demands for individual attention.	2. Suggestions more designed to command individual attention from leader.

[12] Stephen M. Corey, "Co-operative Staff Work," *School Review* (June, 1944), pp. 336-345.
[13] W. E. Goslin, "When We Work Together," *Educational Leadership* (January, 1944), pp. 221-229.
[14] Harold Spears and others, *Leadership at Work,* Fifteenth Yearbook, Department of Supervisors and Directors of Instruction (Washington, NEA, 1943).
[15] Milton Rokeach, "Psychological Aspects of Authoritarian and Democratic Leadership," Ch. 4 in Clyde M. Campbell, ed., *Practical Applications of Democratic Administration* (New York, Harper, 1952), pp. 107-108.
A. Bavelas, "Morale and the Training of Leaders," in Goodwin Watson, ed., *Civilian Morale* (Boston, Houghton, 1942).
Kurt Lewin, Ronald Lippitt, and R. K. White, "Patterns of Aggressive Behavior in Experimentally Created Climates," *Journal of Social Psychology* (May, 1939), pp. 271-301.
Ronald Lippitt and R. K. White, "An Experimental Study of Leadership and Group Life," in Theodore M. Newcomb and Eugene L. Hartley, eds., *Readings in Social Psychology* (New York, Holt, 1947).

Effects of Democratic Atmosphere	*Effects of Authoritarian Atmosphere*
3. Positive identification with whole group, including leaders and non-leaders.	3. No group identification; identification with the leader rather than with the group.
4. Relatively greater group cohesion as a result of positive group identification.	4. Relatively less group cohesion. Sometimes the group may unite to rebel or defy the leader, but this sort of cohesiveness is temporary and does not necessarily incate the existence of genuine group identification.
5. Greater group productivity.	5. Less group productivity.
6. Group activity begins before leader arrives and continues during his absence.	6. Group activity decreases with absence of leader and increases with his presence.
7. Greater job satisfaction.	7. Less job satisfaction.
8. Higher morale.	8. Lower morale.
9. Few or no rumors.	9. Relatively more anxiety about the present and future, leading to the formation and spreading of rumors.
10. Relatively little aggression toward leader and other members. Generally more friendly behavior.	10. Considerable aggression toward other members.
11. When frustrated, aggression is directed toward the real source of aggression.	11. Greater tendency to displace aggression to ''scapegoats,'' strangers, newcomers. Under some circumstances, perhaps when frustration is very great,

Effects of Democratic Atmosphere	*Effects of Authoritarian Atmosphere*
	apathy and inwardly directed aggression are evident.
12. Relatively little "griping" about leader; fewer "gripe sessions."	12. Considerable "griping" about leader; more "gripe sessions."
13. Relatively little "horseplay."	13. Considerable "horseplay."
14. Relatively less de-dependence on leader.	14. Overdependence on leader. In extreme situations, there may be regression toward childlike dependence.
15. Relatively less submissiveness toward leader.	15. Considerable submission toward leader.
16. Greater liking for leader.	16. Greater dislike of leader.
17. Relatively broader time perspective; perception of present in relation to past and future.	17. Shorter time perspective; inability to perceive present in relation to past and future; piecemeal rather than whole perception of problems.
18. Greater variability and flexibility of behavior.	18. Greater rigidity of behavior.
19. Satisfaction at a reality level.	19. Satisfaction on a fantasy level.

The foregoing summary on leadership may be supplemented immediately by wide reading.

BENNE, Kenneth D., and MUNTYAN, Bozidar, *Human Relations in Curriculum Change* (New York, Dryden, 1951). This, with the Wiles volume listed below, are two of the best references available. See particularly pp. 115-132.

CAMPBELL, Clyde M., ed., *Practical Applications of Democratic Administration* (New York, Harper, 1952), Chs. 1, 2, 3, 4. Excellent material.

DE HUSZAR, George B., *Practical Applications of Democracy* (New York, Harper, 1945). Whole volume but particularly Chs. 1, 2, 3, 10, 11, 12.

Leadership at Work, Fifteenth Yearbook, 1943, Department of Supervisors and Directors of Instruction (now the ASCD) (Washington, NEA, 1943). Chs. 1 and 2, but particularly pp. 1-17 which contain the now famous fable "Joe Brown of Centerville." This should be required reading for all.

KOOPMAN, G. Robert, MIEL, Alice, and MISNER, Paul J., *Democracy in School Administration* (New York, Appleton-Century-Crofts, 1943).

WILES, Kimball, *Supervision for Better Schools* (New York, Prentice-Hall, 1950). Whole volume but particularly Chs. 2, 3, 4.

The recorder. The recorder is like a secretary, but he has the further responsibility of sorting out pertinent comments. He records the major issues and selects contributions that bear on the issues. Careful listing must be kept of those topics or problems raised but referred for later discussion. The recorder ordinarily makes his report at the close of the session, but may break in if too many issues get before the group without being disposed of systematically.

The observer. The observer, unlike the recorder, pays little attention to the content but focuses sharply on the method or process of the discussion. An outsider, or out-group observer, is usually more effective at first until the role is understood, whereupon in-group members may act as observers. Observers must preserve and demonstrate honesty and objectivity, must avoid any appearance of superiority to the group, or the report and advice will be ineffective. Groups are always a little afraid of observers at first, but skillful observers and leaders plus helpful objective analyses of group activity, will overcome this. The observer's comments and interpretations may be rejected by the group. The observer, as hinted, may confine reports to descriptions of what took place or may include interpretations. This depends upon the maturity and willingness of the group and upon the ability of the observer.

The feedback of comment from the observer aids all members to become aware of their own characteristics: aggressiveness, defense, escape, earnestness, sincerity, courtesy and tact, or too great bluntness.

The observer and the group evaluate process. The observer will be greatly aided by use of criteria or guides, not only to keep the observations pertinent and objective, but also to evaluate the group activity. Jenkins [16] has suggested three levels of evaluation: group discussion observation; end-of-meeting suggestion slip; and the flow chart.

GROUP DISCUSSION OBSERVATION

Name of Group . . . .   Date . . . . . .

A. *Direction and Orientation*
  1. How far did we get? (Was agenda covered? Times spent on details?)
  2. To what extent did we understand what we are trying to do?
  3. To what extent did we understand how we are trying to do it?
  4. To what extent were we stymied by lack of information?

B. *Motivation and Unity*
  1. Were all of us equally interested in what we are trying to do?
  2. Was interest maintained or did it lag?
  3. To what extent did the group feel united by a common purpose?
  4. To what extent were we able to subordinate individual interests to the common goal?

C. *Atmosphere*
  1. What was the general atmosphere of the group?
    a. Formal or informal?
    b. Permissive or inhibited?
    c. Co-operative or competitive?
    d. Friendly or hostile?

Observations on the contributions of individual members of the group:

A. *Contributions of members*
  1. Was participation general or lopsided?

---

[16] David H. Jenkins, "Feedback and Group Self-Evaluation," *Journal of Social Issues* (Spring, 1948), pp. 54-55, by permission of *Journal of Social Issues.*

2. Were contributions on the beam or off tangent?
3. Did contributions indicate that those who made them were listening carefully to what others in the group had to say?
4. Were contributions factual and problem-centered, or were the contributors unable to rise above their preconceived notions and emotionally held points of view?

B. *Contributions of special members of the group*
   1 How well did special members serve the group?
     a. Leader?
     b. Recorder? (may ask for clarification at times which in turn helps the group)
     c. Resource person?

END-OF-MEETING SUGGESTION SLIP [17]

What did you think of this meeting? Please be frank. Your comments can contribute a great deal to the success of our meetings.
1. How did you feel about this meeting? (check)
   No good ( ) Mediocre ( )
   All right ( ) Good ( ) Excellent ( )
2. What were the weaknesses?
3. What were the strong points?
4. What improvements would you suggest?

The third level, the flow chart, is so-called because it reveals the flow and the direction of discussion. Lines drawn from the speakers indicate the type of interaction and of digression. Lines may be from individual to individual, or toward the center to indicate remarks directed to the whole group. Lines leading outside the grouping indicate digressions, straying from the point.

The resource person. The term *resource person* is self-explanatory. Any type of group may have need for someone with special information. The leader will serve thus with many groups, though every opportunity

should be taken to use group members with special backgrounds or experiences. Outsiders are also brought in. Ordinarily, the resource person contributes when the group sees the need and requests help, but assistance may be volunteered.

The resource person in most instances meets with the group, sitting with them, contributing as needed. More formal methods of utilizing resource persons are the *panel,* the *forum,* the *symposium,* the *round table,* the *demonstration.* Older, more familiar forms are the lecture and lecture-demonstration.

General roles played by members. All members of a group play from time to time brief roles as they contribute, ask questions, or object. Several writers in the field have identified groupings of these roles which cannot be elaborated in detail here. The titles are mostly self-explanatory.

Roles which facilitate and co-ordinate group activities are:

Initiator-contributor	Elaborator
Information seeker	Co-ordinator
Opinion seeker	Orienter
Information giver	Evaluator-critic
Opinion giver	Energizer
Procedural technician	

Roles which build up group attitudes and encourage group morale include:

Encourager	Expediter
Harmonizer	Standard setter
Compromiser	Follower

Roles are apparent also which indicate that individuals are trying to satisfy their own needs, often by ill-advised methods. These roles are inimical to group-centered development, and need to be diagnosed and remedied.

Aggressor	Playboy
Blocker	Dominator
Recognition seeker	Help-seeker
Self-confessor	Special-interest pleader

[17] *Ibid.,* p. 56.

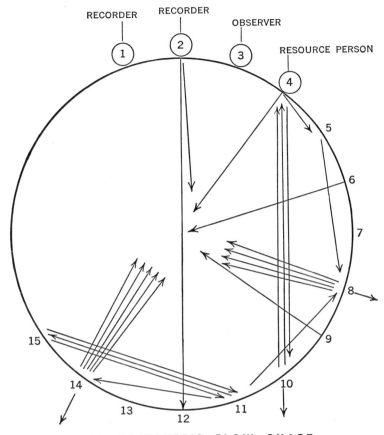

AN OBSERVER'S FLOW CHART

This represents the third quarter-hour of a one-hour discussion. The sample is given because the lines for an hour become too congested. This group had no chairman. Two recorders were necessary to catch all action. The resource person entered the discussion, twice to comment to individuals, once to the group as a whole, and was twice called upon. The resource person was not called on during the first half hour. The recorder gave one student information, evidently voluntarily and once threw in advice for the group. Two students said nothing, and only three were off the point. The majority of contributions were to the whole group, showing good interaction. Interchanges between two persons are also shown.

Supplementary material on special and general roles will be found in:

BENNE, Kenneth D., and MUNTYAN, Bozidar, *Human Relations in Curriculum Change* (New York, Dryden, 1951). Entire volume contains excellent materials. Use the index. Refers to adults dealing with the curriculum but is easily adapted to classroom use.

————, BRADFORD, Leland, FENNER, Mildred, and LIPPITT, Ronald, *Group Dynamics and Social Action* (Washington, NEA, 1950).

KOZMAN, Hilda C., ed., *Group Process in Physical Education* (New York, Harper, 1951), pp. 145-156, 191-194.

Portfolio of Teaching Techniques (Washington, Educator's Washington Despatch, 1948).

STILES, Lindley J., and DORSEY, Mattie F., *Democratic Teaching in Secondary Schools* (Philadelphia, Lippincott, 1950), pp. 381-403.

An excellent project for any group is to compile suggestions for countering the blocking or nonsupporting roles. Techniques are now found in widely scattered sources. The list can be extended through the creation by the group of new procedures. Rules of thumb or listed devices will not suffice. The leader and group members must be able to adjust and adapt to fit the particular problem as it arises.

Role-playing in psychodrama and in sociodrama. Role-playing, in simplest terms, is the unrehearsed acting out of a problem or situation confronting a group. All persons play roles in real life. Spontaneous drama and discussion are natural outlets for tension, natural methods of disseminating views and of informing one's self.

The psychodrama was developed originally as therapy, and concerns the analysis and guidance given to an individual within the group. We need not be concerned with it very much for use in everyday supervision.

The sociodrama can be used by groups at all levels. Several members of the group enact a scene in the presence of the whole group. The scene may deal with real problems of human relations within the class, or with any materials being studied which permit different interpretations. Any typical supervisory problem may provide opportunity for a sociodrama.

By virtue of role-playing, skill in the democratic process is improved. Communication is speeded. More important, however, individuals gain greater insights into their own beliefs, tensions, honest convictions, and prejudices. Greater understanding of other persons results. Real attitudes and values are revealed. The analysis of difficulties in group thinking is enhanced. Roles may be reversed for a second playing. The audience is invited to participate and make suggestions both during the scene and after.

Spontaneity is the essence; hence there should be no rehearsal. The actors should have a brief period together for planning the general setting, line of development, and views to be expressed. The discussion following the scene is thought by many to be the most valuable part of this technique. (Typical dramatization used in school for years is still valuable but for other reasons. A planned sequence, a script, and rehearsal are in order with dramatization.)

The general procedure [18] is as follows:

A. *Demonstrating a sociodrama for a new group*
   1. Select a simple, illustrative situation that will be fun and meaningful.
   2. Select a volunteer cast.
   3. Arrange the scene, using a few simple props if necessary.
   4. Inform the cast about the scene and what is to be done.
   5. Develop and enact the scene. As it progresses, the director may secretly suggest to one of the cast a problem which will encourage argument or discussion.
   6. Encourage audience participation by stopping the scene from time to time to get new ideas.
   7. Try out new ideas. The actors may be asked to try out suggested ideas of members of the audience. Members of the audience may be asked to replace members of the cast for that purpose.
   8. Reverse roles. Members of the cast may be asked to exchange roles to increase opportunity and variety of participation.
   9. Discuss the scene after it is concluded. The director asks questions regarding the subject of the scene, the problems presented, and the solutions suggested.
   10. Limit the demonstration to ten or fifteen minutes.

B. *Performing a real-life situation*
   1. Select a scene which is related more directly to the kinds of problem situations this group has encountered.
   2. Decide roles. The director may ask the audience to help in selecting the roles and indicating how they should be played.

Extensive materials on the sociodrama are available in many sources. Volumes already cited in this chapter contain discussions. Additional references are:

HAAS, Robert B., ed., *Psychodrama and Sociodrama in American Education* (New York, Beacon House, 1949).

[18] Hilda C. Kozman, ed., *Group Process in Physical Education* (New York, Harper, 1951), pp. 206-207.

Moreno, J. L., *Who Shall Survive?* (New York, Beacon House, 1934). The early classic in the field; covers many aspects of sociometry.
———, *Psychodrama*, Vol. I (New York, Beacon House, 1946). Descriptions of typical life situations, reactions of role players, instructions to players, etc.
Shoobs, Nahum E., *Psychodrama in the Schools*, Psychodrama Monographs, No. 10 (New York, Beacon House, 1944).

Note other Psychodrama Monographs, also the magazines *Sociometry, Sociatry,* and any others dealing with human relations or personnel problems whether in school or in industry.

Psychotherapy through group membership and work. Discussion of therapy through everyday activities has been increasing for some time. The literature of education includes discussions ranging from the teaching of little children to the administration of large adult groupings. Agreement is wide that teachers can aid learners of all ages to live more normal, happy, adjusted lives, and to overcome fears, frustrations, and tensions as they arise. The typical principles of good teaching everywhere contribute to this. Teachers accept individuals as they are and treat all persons with respect and with sensitivity to the inner life as expressed by the child. Individuals are accepted as unique, each with possibilities for development. Controls are properly permissive and properly firm, but always sympathetic.

The same facts and relationships hold for adults. Normal, happy, integrating individuals are those whose inner drives and basic desires are not in conflict with reality and with the necessity for purposeful, controlled behavior. Disturbed human relations, feelings of isolation and insecurity, belief in the hostility of others result in defensive behavior, aggression, withdrawal, or some substitutive reaction.

Organized therapeutic treatment by trained personnel is not our concern here. The proposal is heard, however, that all professional workers who deal with human relations acquire a core of understandings and skills. Administrative and supervisory leaders in education can have marked effect for good or ill on the lives of co-workers; the co-workers on the lives of each other.

Some may object on technical grounds, others on the ground that this is just one more added responsibility and task in an already overloaded job. It is more than that. Democracy is concerned for the individual, his growth and development. Responsibility rests in some measure upon all of us to deal with the individual's problems and their solution. The increasing complexity of society and its demands upon individuals have disturbed human relations and personal tranquillity to the point of public concern.[19]

The use of group methods provides excellent opportunity for therapy. Co-operation, free discussion, mutual aid and affection, the opportunity to make personal contributions to group effort with accompanying recognition, all give security, "belongingness," and confidence. Feelings may be expressed; obstacles resulting in tension and frustration may be openly expressed and examined. The individual gains insight and courage to attack his own personal difficulties positively. The defense mechanisms once used no longer are necessary.

Freedom to choose one's co-workers (sociometric grouping), to change committee membership or be reassigned, to choose freely one's project and study area, or a part in the group project, are all aids to tranquillity.

This topic, vital as it is, cannot be treated at great length in a general volume. Students will doubtless have further contact with it in child study, in adolescent psychology, in mental hygiene courses where given. The

[19] Lawrence K. Frank, *Society as the Patient* (New Brunswick, N. J., Rutgers Univ. Press, 1948).
Karen Horney, *Our Inner Conflicts* (New York, Norton, 1945).
———, *The Neurotic Personality of Our Times* (New York, Norton, 1937).
Kurt Lewin, *Resolving Social Conflicts* (New York, Harper, 1948).
Other similar references are available in considerable number.

periodical literature is packed with current materials. Supplementary readings are found in many references, particularly in the bibliographies in these volumes.

DIMOCK, Hedley S., and TRECKER, Harleigh B., *The Supervision of Group Work and Recreation* (New York, Association Press, 1949).

HAAS, Robert Bartlett, ed., *Psychodrama and Sociodrama in American Education* (New York, Beacon House, 1949).

HARSHFIELD, H. W., and SCHMIDT, J. P., "Playing out Our Problems in Sociodrama," *Sociatry* (December-March, 1948).

JENNINGS, Helen, *Sociometry in Group Relations* (Washington, American Council on Education, 1948).

LEWIN, Kurt, *A Dynamic Theory of Person-*

ality (New York, McGraw, 1935).

LIPPITT, Ronald A., *Training in Community Relations* (New York, Harper, 1949).

MENNINGER, William C., *Psychiatry in a Troubled World* (Macmillan, 1948).

MORENO, J. L., *Who Shall Survive? A New Approach to the Problem of Human Interrelations* (New York, Nervous and Mental Disease Publishing Co., 1934).

OVERSTREET, H. A., *The Great Enterprise* (New York, Norton, 1952).

———, *The Mature Mind* (New York, Norton, 1949).

ROGERS, Carl H., *Counseling and Psychotherapy* (Boston, Houghton, 1942).

SYMONDS, Percival M., *The Dynamics of Human Adjustment* (New York, Appleton-Century-Crofts, 1946). Use index.

CHAPTER SUPPLEMENT

DISCUSSION QUESTIONS

The class is assumed to be reasonably well informed from the readings about:

The general nature of group process, its philosophy, psychology, and purposes.

The appropriate occasions and problems on which it may be used.

The typical procedures and how structured.

The kinds of groups which may be formed: by purpose; by level of maturity and background; others.

The major roles with responsibilities; the supporting member roles; the nonsupporting roles.

The general principles governing the operation of group processes.

The methods of arriving at decisions, of keeping discussion and thinking moving along, of avoiding impasses, of carrying decisions into action.

The necessary and desirable physical arrangements.

The values and limitations, facilitating factors and obstacles, advantages and disadvantages.

The author has found that it is absolutely essential that class members do have preliminary understanding, even if limited, of the foregoing. To proceed without understanding is to invite pointless, rambling discussion, annoyance, and eventually antagonism to group process.

INTRODUCTORY PROJECTS AND EXERCISES

Two things are essential as preliminary to any analysis of this process. Students must have clear understanding of (1) the difference between an area, a topic, a question, a problem; and (2) the difference between the solution of a problem through group attack, and the study of an area or topic—the acquisition of subject-matter background through systematic teaching. Students should ask questions before proceeding if any of the above is not clear.

1. The following questions are samples of those raised by many class groups:

How is group process initiated?

Is group process worth the time it takes? Might this differ with the types of problem, level of maturity, and background of experience of the group?

What should a group do with "unreconstructed rebels," that is, individuals who flatly refuse to participate?

Does group process in school administration, supervision, and curriculum development indicate lay participation?

What are the rights and duties of minorities in group discussion, in arriving at decisions, and after decisions have been accepted?

How do we preserve the security of the individual as he moves over into new and strange processes; that is, eliminate fear of

the untried or of personal discomfiture?
Will groups (children or adults) learn best by participating in group processes; by a preview and discussion of principles and techniques; or by demonstrations?

Is a group decision *always* the best decision? Why or why not? What is meant by *best* decision?

Can group process be forced upon the group?

2. Another good method of introduction is afforded by oral reports from any students in the class who might have had previous experience with group process in any of its forms.

3. A third method of introduction is through demonstration of certain procedures:

Sociodrama	Symposium
Panel	Round table
Forum	Group discussion

For this demonstration it is essential that a real problem or the description of a real problem—a case—be available. The case report should be read by all first. Often a student or the instructor can relate in a few minutes a case of sufficient interest to form the basis of one of the processes. Note that certain of the procedures require previous study or the presence of an already informed resource person (for instance, the panel, the symposium, and the like).

Students in the audience should note and report the way in which the responsible roles were played; the number and effectiveness of member roles which appeared.

Roles may be exchanged in the case of the sociodrama and the discussion repeated.

EXERCISES

The questions accompanying the chapters in this volume are, with a very few exceptions, problematic in nature. Interpretations or applications to hypothetical situations are required. Group discussion is therefore the desired method. Real problems are often brought in as discussion proceeds, particularly by experienced teachers.

The hypothetical and real problems often lead to more elaborate treatment, thus involving other group methods from planning to sociodrama.

(The text is not designed to be handled by typical recitation methods [repetition of content] and should not be so handled. Classes lacking sufficient background may need to acquire content, but if so the situation should then be handled as systematic instruction for this purpose. Group attack on problems must then wait until sufficient background and experience in the field has been achieved.)

1. The class discussions may be used, when facility has developed, to illustrate the making of flow charts, to give practice for observers, recorders, leaders, resource persons.

2. The class may be divided, one-half acting as observers, to note and report the ways in which responsible roles were played, and the number and effectiveness of member roles which appeared. Critical analyses should be participated in by the whole group.

3. A valuable exercise for all levels of students is to list the actions which should characterize the procedures of the leaders, recorders, observers, and resource persons. Textbooks and articles give good lists in general terms, but few give the actual processes, for instance, of keeping the discussion on the point, of avoiding or overcoming an impasse, of controlling trouble makers, of moving toward a partial summary.

4. A group of experienced teachers who bring in a real problem from the field which warrants extended treatment may manage it as a group project. All the phases of group planning, discussion, committee work, sharing information and experience will enter. Use can be made as justified of the sociodrama, the panel, the forum, the symposium, the round table, the demonstration.

The instructor may be assigned the role of observer or resource person. With inexperienced groups attempting a project, the instructor may well act as leader for one or two meetings, though it is better if group members can assume leadership from the beginning. (A few advanced classes have, on occasion, taken over part of the course and managed it.)

5. Students observing experienced teachers may report upon the social climate of the classroom, giving key characteristics and reasons for desirable and undesirable climate, high or low morale. Make similar report on any aspects of group process observed. (Protect teachers at all times by refraining from the use of names.) Experienced teachers may report their own problems, difficulties, or successes, for discussion and analysis.

6. Report any periodical articles dealing with experimental studies of social climate, extending the list in this chapter.

7. The instructor will need to judge how far a general course can go into the matter of

therapy in the classroom. Other courses will, in many institutions, give further detail. Reports may be selected, if time permits, from such areas as:

The dominative or integrative behaviors of group members.

The effect of the leader's personality on group behavior.

(A similar study can be made of the effect of the teacher's personality on classroom behavior.)

The carry-over effect on group participation and behavior of outside personal problems or tensions.

(A similar study can be made of a classroom group.)

Causes of frustration and aggression; methods of alleviating the conditions; the same for fears and other insecurities.

Summary of conditions making for desirable social behavior.

Summary of some studies of personality patterns.

Studies may be made when possible of isolates among a group of adults; of rejected persons; of popular supporting persons; of the overly aggressive or overly recessive individuals. (This can always be done in terms of general principles and behaviors, but if studies can be made of actual situations without knowledge by the subjects this should be attempted.)

Projective techniques may be used if the maturity of the group permits. Sociometric studies can usually be made without difficulty. (These tests are described further in Chapter 9.)

Reports on psychiatry and psychosomatic medicine may be made if competent consultants are available to bring this to the group.

(The list could be extended indefinitely. Students and teachers will find enormous amounts of material. If interest develops in advanced discussion of psychotherapy, students may review and make quick summaries from such sources as Frank, Lewin Myrdal, Freud, Adler, Jung, Horney, and from writers on mental hygiene generally.)

8. The class should make extensive study and set up detailed lists of the characteristics of the socialized personality. The same thing may be done for behaviors characteristic of the unsocial, or antisocial individual.

READINGS

The extensive bibliography on this general subject would be unduly cumbersome if given in one list; hence it has been distributed by major topics through the chapter.

WRITTEN

Read and analyze discussions of the three levels of democracy (talk-democracy; consent-democracy; do-democracy) until you are reasonably familiar with the meaning, characteristics, and particularly with the consequences of each.

Report orally or make written summary of the appearance of each in your everyday life. Look at social gatherings, local governmental affairs, church management, club management, or any other group to which you belong or can observe. Note also assumptions concerning this which lie behind editorials, commentators' columns, speeches, sermons, and so on.

Write a brief, compact paper based on a series of classroom observations showing the prevalence of any or all of the levels of democracy listed above. Experienced teachers may write their contacts and conclusions since ordinarily they will not be in a position to observe.

Note. The situation indicated in Question 4, a real problem brought in and developed in some detail by group process, may occur with any of the areas treated in this textbook. Group process may be used at any time during the course when such a problem emerges and is of sufficient reality to the group.

Part **II**

◆·◆·◆·◆·◆·◆

THE EVALUATION OF THE EFFECTIVENESS
OF THE EDUCATIONAL PROGRAM

Chapter 8

◆·◆·◆·◆·◆·◆·◆·◆·

The Evaluation of the Total Educational Program: A Co-operative Process

Section 1

THE NATURE OF EVALUATION

EVALUATION IN EDUCATION is a continuous process of inquiry concerned with the study, appraisal, and improvement of all aspects of the educational program of a community. Ideally, this process should be carried on co-operatively by all concerned with the growth and development of children. On the basis of the information about the growth and development of youth secured by suitable evaluative procedures, judgments can be made by all concerned as to the quality of the total educational program and the effectiveness with which it meets the needs of individuals and of the community as a whole. The strengths and weaknesses of the program are revealed and plans for dealing with the problems that emerge can then be considered. Those steps can then be planned and taken that are most likely to assure more effective growth and development of the individual members of the community and the improvement of life in the community as a whole.

In recent years, widespread interest in evaluation has led to the systematic study and appraisal of educational programs in many parts of this country [1] and at all levels of the school from the nursery school through the university. Policies and plans for action based on the results of this appraisal have led to many forward-looking changes in the work of the schools and improvements in the environment that have enriched the life of the people.

The most satisfactory basis for evaluating an educational program is to study it "in terms of its philosophy of education, its individually expressed purposes and objectives, the nature of the pupils with whom it has to deal, the needs of the community which it serves, and the nature of the American democracy of which it is a part." [2]

All American schools are instrumentalities for transmitting and improving our American heritage and American ideals. However, there is no single best way of achieving this goal. Each school, therefore, should be free to determine its own educational policies and programs for achieving the ideals of American civilization.

The problem-solving approach. The approach to evaluation should be essentially that used in the study and solution of any problem:

1. Sensing a need or difficulty.
2. Defining the need or difficulty and formulating the problem clearly and definitely.
3. Setting up tentative procedures for dealing with the problem and possible solutions based on past experience and educational science.
4. Working on the problem.
   a. Recalling known information.

[1] *Citizen Co-Operation for Better Public Schools,* Forty-third Yearbook, Part I, National Society for the Study of Education (Chicago, Univ. of Chicago Press, 1954).
[2] "The Evaluation of Secondary Schools," General Report of the Co-operative Study of Secondary School Standards (Washington, 1939), p. 57.

b. Determining the need for further information.
c. Locating and selecting possible sources of information.
d. Setting up means of securing information.
e. Securing and organizing information.
f. Analyzing and interpreting the findings.
5. Drawing conclusions.
    a. Considering possible conclusions.
    b. Determining which are most logical and reasonable.
    c. Making value judgments.
    d. Arriving at a conclusion.
6. Carrying out a plan of action growing out of the conclusions drawn.
7. Considering the results of the program undertaken and making changes in it from time to time as may appear to be advisable.

Evaluation, in the true and effective sense of the term as currently applied, is a process of making value-judgments on the basis of pertinent information than can be gathered about any significant aspect of the educational program. The basic concepts that underlie this approach are that judgments about factors affecting the status and growth of learners should be made in light of the values and goals that are accepted; and that the validity of any judgment concerning the effectiveness of the educational program is sure to be increased if it is based on definite reliable information, data, and facts that define and clarify the problem or issue being faced, and on the basis of which practical judgments can be made of "what to do next."

The evaluation [3] of any given set of data may be made by reference to values and goals, to objective standards or norms that may be available, or by application of subjective criteria previously prepared by competent specialists or set up independently on the spot by any group involved with the study and solution of some problem.

In deciding what steps are to be taken to bring about an improvement in the situation, choices also must be made on the basis of the informed judgment of the group involved, that is, in the light of all available information as to the effectiveness of the proposed program or procedures in bringing about desired changes in similar situations.

Subsequently it again becomes necessary to evaluate the improvement program by making value-judgments about the changes that have taken place and the progress or growth that has been made by the learners.

The basic steps in the evaluative process. Certain basic steps are essential in the process of evaluation:

1. All major goals and values of the educational program must be determined and accepted. These reflect the ideals and wishes of the community.
2. The objectives should be based on a systematic analysis of individual and community needs. They should be clarified and formulated in terms of desirable behavior on the part of the individual and groups concerned.
3. Steps must then be taken by appropriate procedures to collect evidence of growth with respect to the established goals and values as revealed by changes in the behavior of the learners, in the work of the school, and in community life.
4. There should also be an examination of the school environment and practices which are used to achieve the goals, including the experiences of children both in and out of school.
5. The synthesis and interpretation of all of the findings concerning pupil growth and educational practices is the final step, leading to redefinition of goals and values, the setting up of new goals and objectives, and the planning of improved ways and means to attain the modified objectives and new objectives.
6. The schools should act to secure the co-operative participation of parents and all community agencies concerned with the growth and development of children and youth in evaluating the total educational program and in planning its improvement.[4]

[3] *Citizen Co-operation for Better Public Schools.* Sec. III contains excellent suggestions of principles underlying co-operative procedures in the evaluation process.

[4] "Research on Human Relations and Programs of Action," *Review of Educational Research* (October, 1953), contains a valuable summary of research dealing with many aspects of community participation in the study of the education program.

An illustrative approach to problem-solving. An excellent illustration of a basic approach that can be used in any school system to secure widespread participation of all members of the staff and also parents in the study of problems and in the formulation of educational policies is a recent city-wide study of promotion and grouping procedures in New York City. The situation that presented itself when the study began was as follows: retardation (overageness) had been reduced between 1925 and 1950 from 26.3 per cent to only 4.4 per cent in regular grades; nonpromotion had been reduced from 9 per cent to only 0.8 per cent. This is truly a remarkable change for the schools as a whole to bring about. These data do not include special classes for handicapped and retarded learners. The average level of achievement in reading and arithmetic in grades 3 and 6 in spite of this change was practically the same as the standard norms for those grades, although there was a wide variation on the scores for individual pupils.

Meanwhile many problems arose in the schools for which answers were not readily available, such as:

At what age should children be admitted to the kindergarten?

How large should classes be?

On what basis should children be grouped into classes and within classes?

What are the essentials of a readiness program?

What provisions should be made for gifted and talented children?

What additional provisions should be made for slow learners?

How adequate are our clinical services?

What special services should be provided for schools in which unusual social and economic problems exist?

Under what conditions, if any, should a child be required to repeat the work of a grade?

Should we change from the present system of annual "reorganization" to semiannual promotion?

The administrative staff decided that it would be unwise for the staff itself to attempt to formulate policies along these lines. Instead it was decided to secure the views of teachers and field workers as to what policies should be adopted. A study guide was therefore prepared in which current policies were summarized. Issues also were listed which pertained to the various policies. Questions were included as guides for discussion. The staff of each school was invited to study the policies and be prepared to make recommendations about them. The services of specialists and consultants were made available. Ideas were to be pooled by representatives of the schools in district meetings, and finally the composite judgment of the entire staff was to be determined. On this basis, policies would then be established. The problems were of genuine concern to most teachers, and observers of conference groups indicated that there was keen interest in the discussions. Parents often participated. It will be interesting to see what emerges from this significant program.[5] Judging from the progress made during the first year of the study, it seemed evident that because of the great variability among the conditions from school to school, the ultimate policy would be to leave it to the professional staff of each school to deal with its own problems, guided by whatever advice and assistance consultants could make available. The necessity of a continuing study of local problems and experimentation with ways of solving them was evident, an undertaking in which the central staff of the school system would be expected to supply leadership.

[5] *Study Guide on Policies and Practices Affecting Elementary Schools* (New York, Board of Education, Association of Assistant Superintendents, 1952). The problems listed above are not listed in the Study Guide but were assembled by an observer who was interested in the program of study and who contacted numerous schools and supervisory personnel in the course of a visit of about two months.

Section 2

EMERGING CONCEPTS THAT AFFECT EVALUATION

Evaluation in the field of education has been particularly affected by three forces: (1) the efforts to apply scientific procedures to the study and solution of educational problems, (2) the findings of research into the nature of child development and the learning process, and (3) the changing concepts of the role of the school in the social order.

1. Scientific procedures applied to educational problems. In the past few decades, many measuring devices and other less formal evaluative techniques have been devised for appraising educational outcomes and the characteristics of the learner, such as standard tests of intelligence and of achievement in academic areas. A great deal of experimental work also has been done to devise suitable procedures for evaluating less tangible educational outcomes that are not readily appraised by older types of testing procedures, such as personality and character traits, mental health, interests, attitudes, appreciations, methods of work, and social efficiency. These procedures usually involve the observation of behavior in a variety of situations and its evaluation by reference to criteria which reflect desirable educational outcomes.

In recent years, the scope of evaluation has been extended to include the appraisal of all aspects of the educational program by means of a wide variety of systematic procedures, including surveys of local educational needs, the application of lists of evaluative criteria to various elements of the total teaching-learning situation, and similar procedures for securing definite information to aid in making judgments about the merit of the educational program. Several such programs will be described in Section 3.

2. Research on child development and the learning process. As knowledge concerning child growth and development and the learning process accumulated, there was growing dissatisfaction with numerous beliefs and practices. The scrutiny of new and changing values has led to new emphases in curriculum and instruction and to the development of new bases for appraising the educational program and its outcomes. Such concepts as the following suggest factors related to child growth and development that must be considered in making judgments as to the quality of educational outcomes and the appropriateness and effectiveness of various educational procedures:

1. The fact that there is a wide range of individual differences among the members of any group of learners from almost any point of view from which the group may be viewed.

2. Learning as a growth process which makes it necessary to adjust the educational program to differences in rates of growth of learners, as contrasted with the traditional "lock-step" system.

3. The role of the school in dealing with the needs and interests of the learner.

4. The ways in which both heredity and environment condition intelligence levels and learning ability.

5. Learning as a process involving first-hand experiences by children in school and community so that what they learn may be meaningful and socially significant to them.

6. The necessity of considering available evidence as to the relative effectiveness of various kinds of school organizations, curriculums, instructional procedures and learning materials when evaluating any practice.

7. Instructional and environmental factors that contribute to mental, emotional, and social health and adjustment.

8. The need of improving human relations in school and community.

9. The importance of practicing democracy in school and community.

3. Changing conceptions of the role of the school. The changing conception of the role of the school in the social order has an important bearing on the evaluation of any phase of the educational program in any community. On the one hand, the school may serve the limited function of the school of the past as a dispenser of knowledge, skills, and abilities restricted to a formal academic curriculum. On the other hand, the school may serve as a vital force in man's efforts to achieve the goal of the "good life." An educational program has vitality and strength when it has as its goal the improvement of the living of each individual and of the larger community. In a community school, the heart of the educational program is the problems of the people. Education is seen as a power in the solution of these problems. The school must help children and youth as well as all other citizens to identify these problems and give them experience in dealing with these problems by bringing intelligence and community resources to bear on their solution. From these experiences the learners gain skills in problem-solving, an appreciation of the value of the problem-solving procedure, and the ability to work with others democratically and co-operatively in the improvement of community life. The community school is not concerned alone with the problems of the local community. Its ultimate goal is to make it possible for people to bring their values, skills, and insights to bear upon the study and solution of the broader problems present in larger areas, even in the world as a whole.

It is evident that this point of view has an important bearing not only on the evaluation of the educational product, but also on the appraisal of all aspects of the educational program. The school because of its very nature and functions is concerned with community needs and ways of meeting them. The program of the school can never be set up in isolation without regard to the values and wishes of the community.

It is evident that the school is better able to serve some needs than any other community agency. However, in any particular situation the decision as to where and how the school can make its greatest contribution must be arrived at co-operatively. The com-

munity school thus has a dual role: (1) arranging rich, vital educational experiences for children, youth, and adults; and (2) supplying leadership in directing the attention of the people to the areas of community living in which improvement is needed and assisting in planning and carrying out the necessary measures for improving conditions.

The statement [6] that follows is an excellent summary of principles underlying the emerging concept of the role of the school as an instrument for social progress:

1. The community school is organized and administered in a manner which would further the commonly accepted beliefs and goals of the society in which it operates. A community school which is located in a democracy would of necessity stress democratic ideals and processes in its organization and operation.
2. Community members and school personnel co-operatively determine the community school's role in attacking problems and thus plan its curriculum.
3. Community members and school personnel alike function in seeking community problems for study and serve co-operatively in sensitizing the community to them.
4. The community school is but one of many agencies; it independently attacks some problems, serves as a co-ordinating agency in other situations, and participates as a team member in still other circumstances.
5. The community school uses the unique expertness of all community members and agencies as each is able to contribute to the program of the school and, in turn, is utilized by them as it can contribute to their efforts, all in the common cause of community betterment.
6. The community school is most closely oriented to the neighborhood and home community; nevertheless, solutions to local problems are sought not only in relation to local goals and desires but also in the light of the goals and desires of each wider community.

Tasks to be faced. There are many aspects of educational programs about which there is widespread agreement as to practices. However, there also exist differences

[6] Adapted from pp. 59-61 in *The Community School,* Fifty-second Yearbook, Part II, National Society for the Study of Education (Chicago, Univ. of Chicago Press, 1953).

in points of view on a number of moot questions, judging from practices observed in the schools. These problems grow out of conflicts that have a long history. The decision relative to any practice should be based on the values inherent in our American culture and on available evidence that can be brought to bear on the issue. Typical operational jobs to be worked out can be stated briefly as follows:

1. *Organization of the School*
   a. Developing democratic policy, organization, and practice in administration and supervision.
   b. Grouping pupils in the light of known facts about individual differences, levels of maturity, aims of education on different levels; heterogeneous grouping where proper, homogeneous grouping where proper.
   c. Setting up modernized pupil progress and promotion policies

2. *Curriculum*
   a. Developing on appropriate levels unified curriculums, broad fields, subject curriculums, core offerings.

   b. Ensuring preparation for life and also participation in life today.
   c. Determining the general education to be required of everyone and the provision of special education to fit special needs.

3. *Instruction*
   a. Ensuring the achievement of meanings, attitudes, skills, and all desirable outcomes.
   b. Ensuring meanings without falling into verbalisms, skills without meaning; providing wide experience, mastery through use and practice, repetitive drill after insight.
   c. Ensuring attention to individuals within class groups.
   d. Developing pupil-teacher co-operation in planning classroom activities, minimizing complete teacher control.

4. *School-Community Relations*
   a. Developing widespread participation in community life, minimizing isolation of school.
   b. Participating in leadership within community, in solution of community problems, replacing indifference toward community life.

Section 3

THE SCOPE OF EVALUATION

Evaluation is concerned with:

1. The scope and quality of the goals, purposes, and functions of the total educational program and the extent to which they meet the needs of the various individuals and are in line with the desires and needs of the community as a whole.

2. The progress being made in the achievement of these goals as measured not only by the present status of the achievement, characteristics, and behavior of the learners, but primarily by the *growth* that they have made in attaining socially desirable objectives both as individuals and as members of the larger social group.

3. The appraisal of all elements of the total teaching-learning situation that contribute to effective and economical learning, with a view to their improvement, including:

1. The organization and administration of the school.
2. The school curriculum and the undirected experiences of the learners.
3. The teaching-learning process.
4. The instructional materials, equipment, and facilities.
5. Community life and school-community relations.

1. Evaluating goals and purposes. Ultimate goals and purposes of education are the expression of the wishes and ethical values of the society. They vary from one form of society to another, for example, the educational goals of a democratic society differ from those of a totalitarian dictatorship. The goals of our American schools should reflect the ideals of our form of social and political life; their influence should be evident in all aspects of our educational program, especially in the ways in which it operates.

These values are expressed in many sources, such as the Declaration of Independence, the Constitution of the United States and of the various states, and in the regulations and bylaws of official controls of the schools. Various unofficial controls also tend to operate in the establishment of values, such as the program of the school, and the relationships among teachers, pupils, and parents.[7] Local traditions, the standards set up by accrediting agencies, the attitudes of organized special-interest groups, the general views of political, religious, business, labor, patriotic groups, and civic agencies also all exert a strong influence on the educational program of any community. The schools of a democracy belong to all the people and reflect their ideals and wishes.

The more immediate and specific goals of the educational program itself should reflect the values and insights of all who are concerned more or less directly with the growth and development of the individual as well as with the improvement of the life of the community, primarily the views of the professional staff.

The establishment of meaningful goals is a most valuable guide for both learner and teacher and also for parents and social agencies. The goals should be related closely to the needs and interests of the individual at various levels of the school and also to the needs of the community in which he lives.

Educational objectives for various levels of the school and for major areas of the curriculum should be defined by listing the kinds of behavior they imply and the results expected. The school and community must enable the learner to have many satisfying experiences that will give him the opportunity to practice the desired forms of behavior. The following list of needs is adapted from an analysis that was developed by the committees that constructed *Evaluative Criteria for Secondary Schools*. It includes the

areas where the learner encounters problems that the school and community must take steps to meet co-operatively through the educational program.

1. How to live happily and effectively with other human beings as learners and as citizens in a democratic industrial society.
2. How to achieve and maintain sound mental and physical health.
3. How to live intelligently and appreciatively in the natural and scientific environment.
4. How to think logically and to state ideas clearly through the use of various media of expression.
5. How to acquire satisfactory control of the various tools of learning and efficient methods of study and work.
6. How to use leisure time well.
7. How to live esthetically.
8. How to carry on the activities of one's calling.

Problems in each of these various areas range from those that are immediate and personal to learners to issues that are broadly social in their nature.

2. Evaluating pupil growth and development. The evaluation of pupil growth and development is essentially a process of making value-judgments about their achievement and behavior as they progress through the school, and also after their formal education has been completed. The basis of these judgments should be dependable information as to the status of the learners and the progress they have made toward desirable educational goals, with due regard for the mental capacity, health, interests, and needs of the individuals. Consideration must also be given to environmental influences [8] that may affect the rate and direction of growth of the learner, such as the nature of his home life, the influence of community agencies, such as the church, recreation facilities, welfare or-

---

[7] An excellent discussion of these forces is found in M. H. Willing and others, *Schools and Our Democratic Society* (New York, Harper, 1951).

[8] See Ch. 16 for brief discussion of community influences.

ganization, political parties, and the like, and the general merit of the instructional program itself.

There are three basic methods of securing information about the status and growth of the learner:

1. Observation of his behavior and reactions.
2. Testing his knowledge, skills, abilities, attitudes, and character traits by informal procedures.
3. Measuring his characteristics and behavior by means of standardized devices and testing procedures.

The evaluation of observed behavior is largely a subjective procedure in which value-judgments are used. Tests and measures are simply more exact ways of observing behavior. By means of standard tests we can measure growth. Measurement as such does not involve value-judgments. Measurement is a process of determining the amount or relative amount of something, such as level of achievement, general intelligence, reading ability, amount of functional knowledge, readiness for new work, and ability to solve problems. Judgments as to the quality or merit of behavior as revealed by measurement are based on comparison of test results to established standards or norms, with due consideration of all factors that are significantly related to the outcomes and that may affect their rate of development.

In its early stages, the standard testing movement was largely devoted to the development of paper-and-pencil devices that afforded standardized measures of specific and relatively easily appraised academic knowledges, skills, and abilities by which the status of learners in restricted areas of subject matter could be determined. Efforts also were made to increase the quality and reliability of teacher-made examinations. Considerable emphasis was placed on the development of objective or new type tests.

The interpretation of the results of standard tests became increasingly difficult due to the evident undesirability of applying uniform standards to individuals who differed widely in intellectual ability, rate of learning, physical development, background of experience, interests, and needs. The widespread use of intelligence tests, aptitude and readiness tests, physiological tests, personality and character tests, and tests of social development emphasized the wide range of individual differences that were revealed by achievement tests.

It also became clear that many outcomes of learning that were being increasingly stressed, such as interests, attitudes, appreciations, ability to deal effectively with problems of daily life, and social sensitivity, could not be measured directly by paper-and-pencil procedures.

Research in child development also emphasized the importance of considering more fully the growth made by the individual rather than only his present status. Recognition of the fact that learning is not merely reaction to stimuli, but rather a process of interaction between the learner and the environment in which learning takes place, led to the development of methods of studying and appraising pupil behavior observable in learning situations. Methods of recording pupil behavior in problem situations were devised; behavior records were developed; inventories to secure data as to interests, activities, and problems were constructed; sets of criteria were prepared by which behavior, a performance, or some creative product could be evaluated; sociometric methods of studying interaction among the members of a group were devised. Educational literature contains hundreds of descriptions of the use that has been made of these and similar procedures for studying the behavior of children. In general, the evaluation of behavior consists largely of the analysis of information about the performance of the learner in controlled and uncontrolled situations and the making of value-judgments as to the quality of the behavior in terms of subjective criteria set up by those making the appraisal. See Chapter 9 for illustrations.

3. Evaluating elements of the total teaching-learning situation. In recent years there have been many attempts to devise ways of evaluating the educational programs of elementary and secondary schools, and also of colleges. Five of the most significant reports of these investigations are the following:

A Guide for Self-Appraisal of School Systems by Paul MORT and Francis G. CORNELL, 1937.
Elementary School Inventory, New York State Department of Education, 1941.
Handbook for Self-Appraisal and Improvement of Elementary Schools, Texas State Department of Education, 1948.
Evaluative Criteria (Manual), Co-operative Study of Secondary School Standards, 1950 edition.
Evaluating the Elementary School, by the Commission on Research and Service of the Southern Association's Co-operative Study in Elementary Education, 1951.

Brief descriptions of the methods used in these five programs will assist the reader to sense differences in the points of view from which the problem of evaluation has been approached and the trends toward more widespread community participation in the evaluation process. The detailed description of specific procedures applied to various aspects of the education program is left to the related chapters that follow.

1. *The Mort-Cornell Guide.*[9] In this guide the authors state: "This instrument is designed to serve as a basis for the appraisal of individual school systems with respect to their adaptation to current educational needs which differ from those of past generations as a result of economic and social developments or of improved understanding arising from the progress of educational science."

The guide consists of a series of checklists of what the authors regard as items that reflect forward-looking "adaptations" in (1) classroom instruction, including the curriculum and pupil activity; (2) special services for individual pupils, including provision for individual differences; (3) educational leadership, including supervision, school organization, school administration, and community-school relations; and (4) physical facilities and business management. The specific adaptations were based in part on theoretical considerations, in part on the results of surveys of practices in what were regarded as better types of school systems. In all there are 23 subsections in the guide, including a total of 182 specific adaptations.

A decision as to the presence or absence of a given adaptation in a school system is based on the analysis of documents and the results of observations and interviews by a survey staff. In the guide, each item given is followed by a question which suggests the nature of the documents, observations, and interviews that are used to secure information which forms the basis for judging whether or not the adaptation has been made. The question is followed by three or four sample statements of indications of each adaptation which serve as further guides for observation and interviews. Associated with each statement there is a place for recording a Yes-No entry to indicate the presence or absence of the adaptation. No provision is made for estimating the merit or quality of the adaptation; its existence alone is to be indicated.

A score sheet is provided for summarizing the results. The number of adaptations in each subsection is first indicated. Weightings are given for each of the 23 subsections, ranging from 5 points for each adaptation in such areas as grade and subject organization, administrative planning, and the school site, to 13 points for the subsection for adaptations in the fields of learning. The total number of points possible is 1003. Mort and Cornell report that "there is a fairly close relationship between the score obtained and the level of expenditure of the school system." They also report in the manual scores for various school systems ranging from 130 points to 730 points on the scale. This in-

[9] New York Teachers College, Bureau of Publications, Columbia Univ.

formation reveals that there is a wide range in the quality of educational programs.

The guide serves as the basis of a survey to determine the extent to which practices in a school system are in line with best practices. The check-lists also make available for any school system a list of forward-looking ways of dealing with educational needs. The guide was originally applied by visiting specialists in the appraisal of educational programs; however, there is no reason why it cannot be used by the professional staff of any school system, in co-operation with interested citizens, to determine what can be done to improve many aspects of the local educational program. The guide makes no direct reference to the formulation of the values underlying the total educational program or to the appraisal of the educational product. The appraisal and analysis of the aspects selected for improvement is "through the fourfold approach of (a) quantification, (b) controlled interview, (c) controlled observation, and (d) documentation." In the manual there are no specific suggestions that a school system might follow to bring about an improvement.

2. *The Texas Handbook for Self-Appraisal and Improvement of Elementary Schools.*[10] This handbook consists of a series of scales for appraising many important aspects of the educational program of an elementary school, including (1) provisions for meeting the needs of children, including enrollment, classification and promotion practices, provision for health and safety, welfare services, and the special needs of children; (2) the teacher and the responsibility of the community to the teacher; (3) the program of school life, including the curriculum, pupil-teacher relationships, and the care of teaching resources including the school library; (4) equipment and supplies; (5) home, school, and community relations; (6) the school campus, including site, building, service systems, classrooms, and special activity rooms; and (7) administration and supervision.

For each of these seven aspects there are several scales that are used to appraise the existing program. Each scale consists of descriptions of five levels of practices. Level 1 in each case contains "the minimum legal requirements of Texas" and, where no specifications are mentioned in the law, what are regarded by the committees that prepared the scales as "the very minimum of acceptable practices." Level 5, on the other hand, "represents features and procedures drawn from the frontier of thought and research in elementary education." In the handbook the statement is made: "Level 5 represents the ideal as reflected by the modern literature on elementary ducation." Level 5 thus "represents a goal toward which schools may strive." The intervening levels 2, 3, and 4 represent characteristics on "a graduated scale" between levels 1 and 5. The handbook indicates that "the differences between any given level and its succeeding higher level were intended to represent the more normal evolutionary stages through which a school system might move in its effort to keep abreast of the changes in education in a changing culture."

The plans for using the handbook are flexible and the importance of initiative by school administrators in planning the study of local schools is stressed. The handbook suggests that initial work should be done with the school faculty so that its members will become familiar with the content of the handbook and be able to participate effectively in "subsequent activities with school trustees and patrons." The handbook points out that it is highly desirable to give the staff of the schools, school trustees, and the general public the opportunity to discuss the characteristics of a good elementary school of today so that school improvement may proceed with community and school support.

The steps in appraising school practices with this handbook may be summarized as follows:

10 Austin, Texas State Department of Education.

1. The staff should familiarize itself with the content of all five levels pertaining to the topic being considered.

2. The staff should take a careful inventory of present practices. This inventory may be taken informally or it may be made as objective and definitive as may be feasible by individuals, teachers, committees, or the faculty as a whole.

3. To evaluate present practices, those concerned should identify the level on the scale in which the descriptive items or statements correspond most closely to present practices in the school.

4. In the column in the handbook headed "Notations on Major Needs and Next Steps for Improvement," a summary is to be made of the conclusions of those making the appraisal as to the limitations of existing practices and also their judgments as to the procedures to follow that are most likely to bring about improvement.

5. On the school summary blank, which is graphic in form, the rating for each item on the scale provided on the blank is to be recorded. There it is possible to make a school profile by connecting the various ratings with lines. This profile gives a graphic picture of practices in the school as "mirrored against" the contents of the handbook.

It will be observed that the Texas plan does not include either the formulation of goals and objectives by the group or the evaluation of the educational product and the analysis of community needs. It is largely a plan for evaluating existing practices in terms of a scale of values growing out of extended study and experimentation. As new evidence accumulates, these values may change. Hence the scales undoubtedly will require continuous study and revision by the state. The use of these scales in evaluating existing practices is a powerful stimulus to any staff to improve the educational program.

3. *The New York Elementary School Inventory.*[11] This inventory consists of a series of four check-lists to be used in the appraisal of practices in any school or school system "in guiding pupil growth." The four areas involved are identified by the following headings: (1) curricular experiences; (2) organizing and implementing the educational program; (3) school, home, and community relations; and (4) recording, evaluating, and reporting procedures. The check-lists "are based chiefly upon the digest of publications issued or sponsored by the State Education Department." They are hence the expression of the point of view sponsored by an agency of official control. The items in each check-list express desirable educational practices. The check-lists were developed by committees of school people; in their final form they are the outgrowth of several revisions after extensive preliminary trial in typical schools. A digest of official and nonofficial publications pertaining to the items in the check-lists is available for schools that wish to study the items more closely before applying them to a particular situation.

The sequence of steps to be taken in using this inventory in any school is as follows:

1. The staff should first familiarize itself with the contents and purpose of the inventory. It may be significant that the plan does not provide for the participation of children, parents, or representatives of community agencies in the evaluative process.

2. The members of the staff next express judgments as to the desirability of each practice listed, preferably as a group judgment growing out of study and discussion in faculty meetings and committee reports.

3. The staff then surveys the local situation to determine the extent to which the various desirable practices have been put into effect in the school.

4. The staff attempts to identify local conditions and considerations that have caused the rejection in whole or in part of desirable practices that are not fully operative.

5. The ultimate step is the formulation of a working philosophy upon which to base the school's program and the provision of help for the individual teacher to "find expression for her own philosophy in the work of the school."

It is evident that throughout the evaluative process contained in this inventory, group thinking by the staff of a school is emphasized. Thinking in this case is guided, even directed, by a system of values included in a semiofficial statement of practices that

[11] Albany, N. Y., State Education Department.

are regarded as desirable. There is no reason why the staff of any school, in co-operation with parents and others in the community concerned with the education of youth, should not modify the list or even work out co-operative a similar list of desirable practices which it finds more acceptable. The inventory emphasizes the point that "every school or school system should re-examine its theory and practice as a basis of planning and action." It is obvious that many undesirable practices continue because no one critically examines them; many desirable practices not now operative would be adopted if they were really examined.

4. *Evaluative Criteria for Secondary Schools.* Since 1933 a co-operative study of secondary school standards has been underway. The committee in charge of the program, with the assistance of numerous subcommittees, has prepared sets of criteria by which the staff of any secondary school can evaluate many aspects of its program. These criteria have been applied in many places and steps taken subsequent to evaluation of existing programs have led to important changes in many schools.

In 1950 the committee published a report of progress which contained a series of recommendations for evaluative procedures and also extensive revisions of the evaluative criteria previously published. The following discussion is based on this revision.

The point of view of the committee is expressed in the following statement of guiding principles:

The school exists primarily for the benefit of the boys and girls of the community which it serves. The types of people, their vocations and interests, their tendencies and prejudices, their abilities, their racial characteristics, their hopes and prospects regarding the future, their customs and habits, the similarities and differences of groups within the community, are different from those of other communities. The school should know the distinctive characteristics and needs of the people and groups of people of the school community, particularly those of the children. But every school community inevitably is interrelated with other communities and is a part of larger communities, particularly the state and nation. The school should therefore adapt its general philosophy and specific purposes to its own community and to the larger communities of which it is a part.[12]

The program of evaluation which the committee recommends begins with the securing of basic data about the pupils of the school, such as enrollments and graduations, age-grade distributions, mental ability, stability of school population, withdrawals, educational and occupational intentions, and follow-up data of graduates. The information regarding the pupils is supplemented by basic data about the community, including population, occupational and educational status of adults, financial resources, rural and tuition pupils, agencies affecting education and additional socioeconomic information.

The next step in the program requires the school to set up a summarizing statement of its purposes and responsibilities in meeting the educational needs of all youth of secondary school age. To assist the school in formulating its basic philosophy, *Evaluative Criteria* lists eight major areas of needs. Each area is clearly and extensively defined. The staff of the school is (1) to indicate the extent to which it accepts meeting each of these needs as a responsibility of the school, (2) to discuss any qualifications which it cares to make concerning a need as stated, and (3) to indicate its judgment as to the extent to which the existing program of the school meets the need, as "slightly," "moderately," or "extensively."

To assist the school then to evaluate its program of studies in the light of the data about the school population and community, the analysis of educational needs of youth, and its own expressed philosophy, the report contains an extensive series of check-lists giving criteria for analyzing and appraising (1) general principles underlying the program of the school, (2) curriculum-development procedures, (3) program of studies, in-

12 Page 20 of Manual for *Evaluative Criteria,* 1950 edition.

cluding extent and nature of offerings, (4) general outcomes of the program of studies, (5) special characteristics of the program of studies, and (6) general evaluation of the program of studies.

The criteria in the check-lists consist of provisions, conditions, and characteristics found in what are described in the report as "good secondary schools." The check-lists are intended to provide the factual bases for the evaluation of any secondary school.

Each section of the check-list first requires that an estimate be made of the extent of provision for some item; when the item is missing an estimate is to be made as to whether or not the item is needed or is not desirable or appropriate for the particular school. Finally the check list calls for an evaluation of each of the provisions or conditions on a 5-point rating scale defined as follows:

5.—*Excellent:* the provisions or conditions are extensive and are functioning excellently.

4.—*Very good:*
  a. the provisions or conditions are extensive and are functioning well, or
  b. the provisions or conditions are moderately extensive but are functioning excellently.

3.—*Good:* the provisions or conditions are moderately extensive and are functioning well.

2.—*Fair:*
  a. the provisions or conditions are moderately extensive but are functioning poorly, or
  b. the provisions or conditions are limited in extent but are functioning well.

1.—*Poor:* the provisions or conditions are limited in extent and are functioning poorly.

Similar check-lists are also included for (1) the pupil activity program, (2) library services, (3) guidance services, (4) school plant, and (5) school staff and administration.

Charts for making a statistical and graphic summary of evaluations for all areas are provided in the plan. A rating of the total program is based on the average of ratings for each category.

The committee maintains that a secondary school is best evaluated if the staff of a school, including both professional and non-professional members, first makes a self-evaluation using the *Evaluative Criteria,* and then has this self-evaluation checked by a visiting committee composed of "experienced and well-prepared professional workers in the field of education." The committee reports that in some cases schools have found it profitable to include representatives of pupils, parents, community organizations, and official boards of control as participants in, or observers of, the self-evaluation. However, no specific recommendation as to this procedure is given.

Evaluative Criteria provides an excellent basis for evaluating the programs of secondary schools. The procedures described can be modified and adapted as may seem desirable to the staff of any given school. Undoubtedly further revisions of the *Evaluative Criteria* will be made in the future.

5. *Evaluating the Elementary School.*[13] The extensive use of the *Evaluative Criteria* for secondary schools among the schools of our southern states stimulated the Southern Association of Colleges and Secondary Schools to organize in 1948 the Co-operative Study in Elementary Education. The publication, *Evaluating the Elementary School: A Guide for Co-operative Study,* which appeared in 1951, is the outgrowth of widespread experimentation by the schools of various states in the development of suitable procedures and instruments for evaluating elementary schools. The program suggested has a number of interesting features that represent new departures in evaluation.

The guide is divided into five parts: (*a*) viewpoint, that is, the formulation of values

[13] Atlanta, Ga., Commission on Research and Service, Southern Association of Secondary Schools.

and goals; (*b*) the listing of functions that elementary education is to serve; (*c*) the program of the school, including knowledge of children to be taught, scope of the program, organization for learning, and the teaching-learning process; (*d*) resources, including the school plant, facilities and materials, community resources, and personnel; and (*e*) planning next steps to improve any or all aspects of the total educational program.

The contents of each section are set up in the form of a study guide to serve as the basis of a continuous evaluation of the work of the school so as to determine how effectively the educational program meets the needs of the individual learner and group of learners, of the community as a whole, and "of an ever-changing society." In sections (*A*) and (*B*) of the guide the study activities are so arranged that the existing values underlying the total educational program and practices are systematically examined. This study ordinarily will culminate in the formulation of values and purposes of education that are acceptable to both school and community. Measures can then be taken to provide better learning experiences for children and also to improve the life of the community. Sections (*C*) and (*D*) serve as guides for studying and planning ways of improving the program of the school and the quality and use of educational resources. Each section contains subsections which include questions to be discussed by the group making an evaluation, and desirable provisions and practices—"specific examples" of which the group is expected to "cite"—that are present in the local situation. Next the guide calls for the listing of the needs and shortcomings that apparently exist in the specific area being considered. Finally, the group is called on to formulate the long-range goals and to indicate the immediate steps that should be taken to develop a more effective program in the area. There is no provision for making an actual quantitative or qualitative rating of existing practices as is done in several of

the evaluative procedures that have been described above. The guidance of thinking and study is the primary purpose.

The last section of the guide, (*E*), deals with the procedure for planning a co-ordinated program of action along all lines on a co-operative basis. Planning is regarded as a part of the entire process of evaluation. It is to be participated in by parents, pupils, and all members of the staff of the school. As the scope of planning varies, so the personnel of the group making the study will vary. Out of the total effort a comprehensive, co-ordinated, co-operative program should emerge. The professional staff of the school then faces the problem of setting up an educational program that will carry out the wishes of the community and that is most likely to achieve the accepted values.

Evaluation guides developed by city systems. Many larger city school systems are producing their own guides, similar to the state-wide or regional guides. A good illustration is *The Evaluation Handbook for Elementary Schools* issued by the St. Louis, Missouri, schools. Other similar guides may be examined.

Evaluation guides developed by institutions. The number of these may be expected to increase. A good illustration is *Elementary Evaluative Criteria*, Boston University School of Education, Boston, Mass., 1953. Copyright is held by James F. Baker, leader of the group which developed the criteria.

Trends in evaluation. A comparison of the procedures used in the earlier of the evaluation programs described above with those in the more recent plans indicates certain significant trends that should be borne in mind in planning future supervisory programs:

1. The necessity of formulating a meaningful educational philosophy as a guide for instruction is being recognized as a prerequisite for effective evaluation.

2. There is definite evidence that the view is emerging that educational programs should be evaluated primarily to determine the extent

to which they meet the needs of youth, rather than merely on the basis of such external aspects as the quality of school buildings, the organization of the curriculum, the size of classes, and salary schedules.

3. There is a clear tendency to make considerable use of democratic procedures involving the co-operation of professional and community groups in planning and carrying out programs of evaluation and improvement.

4. Criteria reflecting the results of critical thinking by "best minds" rather than directives of official agencies of control are being set up as guides for the study and improvement of many aspects of the educational program.

5. Stress is being placed on methods of self-evaluation of educational programs by individual schools and communities rather than on evaluation by visiting experts or officials.

6. Increasing emphasis is being placed on the use of evaluation programs as a means of continuous in-service education of all members of the professional staff and as a basis of effective public relations.

7. Programs of evaluation are becoming more comprehensive and are being planned on a long-range basis.

8. Programs are becoming increasingly flexible and are being adapted to varying conditions from place to place and among the schools of any single locality.

9. There is evidence that the trend is away from the earlier practice of rating a school in quantitative terms toward making a critical subjective evaluation of current practices in terms of criteria of various kinds and expressed as value-judgments.

The changing role of state and national testing programs. State testing programs have a long history. They began soon after the establishment of the graded school system. The purpose of these examinations was to ascertain how the schools and grades were conforming to "standards" set by educational authorities and to judge the efficiency of the schools. In most instances the tests were not standardized and were poorly constructed. They were limited to testing knowledge of narrow bodies of subject matter. They were compulsory for certain schools, often for only certain grades. Each year teachers spent long periods of time preparing their children for these examinations by drilling on earlier

forms of the tests, a practice that had disastrous effects on the nature of classroom instruction.

There has been a marked change in both methods and purposes of state examinations in recent years.[14] The principal change in method has been the introduction of standardized aptitude tests and achievement tests, the former to serve as an aid in interpreting scores on the latter. In some states, the achievement tests are prepared by research divisions of universities and state departments; in others, tests are used that are distributed by national and commercial agencies. The use of these tests is in most cases voluntary, and testing programs are conducted on a co-operative basis.

The purposes of testing programs have also changed from their use for rating schools and pupils to their use for various kinds of instructional purposes. Texas, for example, lists eight functions of the state testing program, including (1) selection and admission, (2) placement, (3) guidance and counseling (4) control of learning, (5) remedial teaching, (6) motivation for teachers and pupils, (7) evaluation of progress, including interpretation of the results on the basis of tests of aptitudes, interests, and emotional factors, and (8) research.

There is a definite tendency from state to state to try to assist the schools to use tests of various kinds for such purposes as discovering strengths and weaknesses in pupil achievement at various school levels; discovering their aptitudes as a basis for instruction; and for educational and vocational guidance. Their use for rating schools has practically disappeared.

There also are nation-wide testing programs largely at the secondary level. Testing services are provided by various test publishers and nonprofit testing agencies. The most notable of nonprofit national programs at the present time are the programs of the

[14] David Segel, *State Testing and Evaluation Programs,* Office of Education Circular No. 120 (Washington, Federal Security Agency, 1951).

Educational Records Bureau, 21 Audubon Avenue., New York 32, N. Y., the Co-operative Test Service of the American Council of Education, Washington, D. C., and the Educational Testing Service, Princeton, New Jersey. They include a variety of tests of achievement and scholastic aptitude. At the high-school level, these programs are practically compulsory because of the widespread use of the test results as a basis of selection and guidance by higher institutions of learning.

The influence of nation-wide examinations in academic fields depends on the nature of these tests and the use made of the results, since they affect greatly how and what pupils study and what teachers teach. This is particularly true of the college entrance board type of examination which so frequently tests knowledge of relatively sterile, lifeless bodies of subject matter that in the opinion of many educators should not be included in the general education of most pupils of high-school age. Furthermore, there is real danger that objectives and curriculum content to be tested will be determined arbitrarily by testing agencies, thereby leading to the freezing of the existing curriculum and standardization of method, both barriers to further evolution of secondary education. The relatively narrow outcomes that can be most readily measured by paper-and-pencil tests also are sure to be stressed. When teachers seek to prepare students to take poorly devised state and national examinations, cramming, regimentation, and undesirable uniformity are certain to result. This applies also to many city-wide testing programs in elementary schools. Good tests stimulate good teaching and efficient learning, but poorly constructed tests that stress outcomes that are relatively of little consequence are actually harmful in their effects on instructional practices.

Values of the co-operative appraisal of educational programs. There are many valuable outcomes of an intelligent, systematic, co-operative study and evaluation of any educational program and the planning of ways to improve the learning experiences of children and factors that affect their growth and development. The authors of *Evaluating the Elementary School* [15] list the following as "probable" outcomes that result where faculties and the community have seriously undertaken and effectively worked at the process of self-evaluation:

1. *Improved School-Community Relationships*

As the school faculty works with pupils and parents in an evaluation program, citizens begin to realize more fully what the school is trying to do for children. As citizens gain more understanding of what teachers are trying to do with available materials and resources, they work to secure the additional facilities needed for a good school program.

2. *Professional Growth of Staff Members*

As faculty members work together in the self-evaluation process, they develop unity of purpose, greater teamwork and a deeper sense of group loyalty. Out of thinking together teachers are challenged to learn more about children, about the community in which the school is located, and about the cultural values of society.

3. *Better Teaching-Learning Conditions*

Because teachers are participating in co-operative endeavor and are having a real share in planning what they shall do and how they shall do it, they tend to introduce such practices into their classrooms. Usually co-operative planning by pupils and teachers increases as the result of the evaluation.

4. *Better Utilization of Physical Facilities*

As the faculty, with pupils and parents, begins to look over the school plant and the available resources, it usually find that more effective use can be made of presently available facilities. Plans are made for more efficient sharing and for rotation of equipment.

5. *Better Utilization of Community Resources*

A deeper awareness on the part of both the school and the community of the resources each has to offer has usually grown out of the evaluative activity. As a result, children have more direct contact with community life, and patrons

[15] *Loc. cit.*, p. 7.

participate more actively in teaching young community members.

6. *Direct Benefits to Pupils*

The real measure of the effectiveness of the evaluative activity is, in a large degree, deter-mined by the extent to which pupils have better living and learning experiences at home and school. As parents, pupils, and teachers plan together, direct and observable benefits usually do and certainly should accrue to pupils at all levels.

Section 4

PRINCIPLES UNDERLYING AN EFFECTIVE PROGRAM OF EVALUATION

An analysis of the five programs of evaluation discussed in Section 3 and others that have been reported elsewhere shows that a group of fundamental principles is emerging which may serve as criteria in planning future programs for the study and improvement of the work of the school. An illuminating formulation of these principles is given in the following statement which appears in a report [16] of the evaluation program of Virginia, one of the states that has participated extensively in the development of the procedures reported in *Evaluating the Elementary School*.

Evaluation is a process that is used to ascertain to what extent values and goals are being achieved. In education it may be defined as the process of determining the effectiveness of the school program in meeting the needs of boys and girls in the school and community and in improving the quality of total community living. Evaluation of the elementary school is a continuous process of looking at and improving the purposes of the school, the program designed to accomplish these purposes, and the personnel and plant provided to further this program.

An effective program of evaluation in education has certain characteristics which obtain within the various steps of the entire process:

1. It must be *comprehensive* in scope and method. It is concerned with all aspects of the growth of the child and/or his community and the means and processes whereby he achieves that growth. It seeks many kinds of evidences through many different procedures.

2. To be consistent with the principles of a democratic society of which the educational system is such a vital part, evaluation must be *co-operative*. Teachers, administrators, pupils, and parents should be involved at different levels of participation in the formulation and definition of goals and values, and in the collection and interpretation of evidence.

3. If the school is to perform its function of contributing to better living for children, it must subject its values, goals, objectives, materials, and processes to *continuous* self-examination in terms of what these have done to contribute to the growth of the individuals involved. Evaluation is not a process which is used at the end-point of a year's work nor at any set time during the year.

4. Evaluation is allied with all that goes on in the classroom and in the school. It is not a program within itself but is an integral part of the planning and learning process in the total school program. It *emphasizes growth* and is concerned with progress made in terms of needs and objectives and not merely with determining the status of the group, the school, or program in relation to a norm or scale.

5. It is both a *long-term and immediate process*. The extent to which growth has been made in some areas may be determined within a short period of time while in others it will involve study over many years in order to determine the genuine effectiveness of the program.

6. It must be *economical*. While data should be cumulative, the process of preserving it should involve a minimum of clerical work and yet be effective. Materials and techniques of the basic processes of evaluation should be established in terms of simplicity, clarity, and economy.

[16] *Looking At Our Elementary School* (Richmond, Va., Division of Elementary Education, July, 1949), Vol. 32, No. 5, pp. 5-6.

CHAPTER SUPPLEMENT

INTRODUCTORY DISCUSSION QUESTIONS

1. Why is the evaluation of educational programs a complex undertaking?

2. What values are there in public participation in planning ways of improving educational programs? Give concrete examples.

3. Be ready to discuss a program of evaluation in which you may have participated. Tell about how the program began, reasons for it, procedures used, public participation, if any, in the program, findings, and difficulties. What suggestions have you for improving the program? An alternative would be to discuss an evaluation program with some person who has participated in it, and be ready to tell about it.

4. How would you go about securing community participation in the study and evaluation of some aspect of the educational program? Be specific. Should pupils participate in evaluation programs? If so, how?

5. Why is the problem-solving approach likely to be effective?

6. Comment on the relative merits and limitations of the five evaluation programs described in this chapter. In what ways could any one or all of them be improved? Be specific.

7. Is there any merit to the limitations of nation-wide testing programs discussed in this chapter? Do these limitations apply in any way to city-wide testing programs?

8. Give illustrations of effective school-community co-operation in studying and improving aspects of educational programs.

9. Should local plans of evaluation be used rather than plans developed by some regional or national agency or organization?

10. What are the values and limitations of self-evaluation by the faculty of some school?

11. Comment on the desirability of having a visiting group check up on the self-evaluation made by some school.

WRITTEN EXERCISES FOR INDIVIDUALS OR GROUPS

1. Individuals or groups may apply some selected section of one of the evaluation plans described in this chapter to a local school situation and prepare a report of the findings. This experience will reveal to the student the procedures used in the plan and give some notion of the usefulness of the results.

2. Individuals or small committees may interview members of staffs of nearby schools or school systems to determine policies and practices regarding public participation in evaluating and planning improvements in educational programs.

3. Secure a report of a survey of some school system and prepare a statement of the extent of public participation in the evaluations made and in the planning of improvements.

4. Make a list of specific educational problems that you believe might well be made the basis of co-operative study and planning by school and community.

5. Comment on the trends in evaluation given on pages 218 and 219. Do you think that they are in the right direction? What changes if any seem desirable?

6. Prepare a critique of one of the volumes listed in the bibliography.

7. Look up current literature dealing with school-communty co-operation in studying and improving educational programs. Write short reviews of a few of the most valuable reports.

SUGGESTED READINGS

BENNE, Kenneth D., and MUNTYAN, Bozidar, *Human Relations in Curriculum Change* (New York, Dryden Press, 1951).

CAMPBELL, Clyde M., ed., *Practical Applications of Democratic Administration* (New York, Harper, 1952).

Citizen Co-operation for Better Public Schools, Fifty-third Yearbook, Part I, National Society for the Study of Education (Chicago, Univ. of Chicago Press, 1954).

CLAPP, Elsie R., *Community Schools in Action* (New York, Viking, 1939).

DURRANCE, Charles L., and others, *School-Community Cooperation for Better Living* (Gainesville, University of Florida, College of Education, 1947).

Forces Affecting American Education, 1953 Yearbook, Association for Supervision and Curriculum Development (Washington, NEA, 1953).

FISK, Robert S., *Public Understanding of What Good Schools Can Do* (New York, Teachers College, Bureau of Publications, Columbia Univ., 1944).

HAND, Harold C., *What People Think About Their Schools* (Yonkers, World Book, 1948).

HILLMAN, Arthur, *Community Organization and Planning* (New York, Macmillan, 1950).

HUTCHINS, Robert M., *The Conflict in Education* (New York, Harper, 1953).

HYMES, James L., *Effective Home-School Relations* (New York, Prentice-Hall, 1953).

LEONARD, J. P., and EURICH, A. C., *An Evaluation of Modern Education* (New York, Appleton-Century-Crofts, 1942).

McCHAREN, William K., *Selected Community School Programs in the South* (Nashville, Tenn., George Peabody College for Teachers, 1948).

MENGE, J. Wilmer, and FAUNCE, Roland C., *Working Together for Better Schools* (New York, American Book, 1953).

MIEL, Alice, *Changing the Curriculum: A Social Process* (New York, Appleton-Century-Crofts, 1946).

MUNTYAN, Bozidar, "Community School Concepts," *Journal of Educational Research* (April, 1948), pp. 597-609.

OLSEN, E. G., *School and Community Programs* (New York, Prentice-Hall, 1949).

————, *The Modern Community School* (New York, Appleton-Century-Crofts, 1953).

OLSON, Clara M., and FLETCHER, Norman D., *Learn and Live* (New York, Alfred P. Sloan Foundation, 1946).

"Research on Human Relations and Programs of Action," *Review of Educational Research* (October, 1953). Excellent review of research on the problem discussed in this chapter.

RUGG, Harold, and BROOKS, B. Marian, *The Teacher in School and Society* (Yonkers, World Book, 1950).

SHANE, Harold G., and McSWAIN, E. J., *Evaluation and the Elementary School Curriculum* (New York, Holt, 1951). Extensive bibliography at end of book dealing with many aspects of evaluation.

SUMPTION, M. R., *How to Conduct a Citizens School Survey* (New York, Prentice-Hall, 1952).

The Community School, Fifty-second Yearbook, Part II, National Society for the Study of Education (Chicago, Univ. of Chicago Press, 1953).

What Schools Can Do—101 Patterns of Educational Practice, Metropolitan School Study Council (New York, Teachers College, Bureau of Publications, Columbia Univ., 1947).

WHITELAW, John B., *The School and Its Community* (Baltimore, Johns Hopkins Press, 1951).

WILES, Kimball, *Supervision for Better Schools* (New York, Prentice-Hall, 1950). Extensive bibliography of books and articles dealing with the human relations aspect of supervision.

YAUCH, W. A., *How Good Is Your School?* (New York, Harper, 1951). A handbook to help parents to judge the quality of local schools.

YEAGER, William A., *School-Community Relations* (New York, Dryden, 1951).

Chapter 9

◆·◆·◆·◆·◆·◆·◆·◆

The Appraisal of the Educational Product

Section 1

THE BASIS OF APPRAISING EDUCATIONAL PROGRAMS

The contributions of evaluation to supervision. It would not be difficult to defend the proposition that the quality of any educational program can most directly be measured by an appraisal of the characteristics of its product, that is, by an evaluation of the behavior of individuals and groups in social situations encountered throughout life, both in and out of school. This evaluation necessarily must be based on the values and ultimate goals that school and community establish, as described in preceding chapters. The professional staff of the school, in cooperation with other interested community agencies, faces the problem of determining the extent to which the values and goals for which the school is responsible are being achieved, as reflected by the growth and development of the children as they progress through the school and ultimately by their success in dealing with personal and community problems that arise in daily life. In the light of any strengths and weaknesses of the educational product that are indicated at various stages of development, the school and community can study the educational program and act to improve it. The technical aspects of the problem are the immediate responsibility of the professional staff which should provide the necessary leadership.

The traditional basis for appraising educational programs has been an analysis of data about the excellence of the school plant, the amount of money spent, the training of the teachers, the number of books in the library, the size of classes, and similar extraneous items. The inadequacy of such an approach is quite obvious, particularly when divorced from appraisal of the educational product. A beautiful school building, for example, may house a curriculum that is very narrow and limited; teachers may have a high level of academic training but lack skill in guiding the learning activities of the pupils; the number of books in the library may be large, but the selection may have been made on a very unintelligent basis. The reverse of these conditions may also be found. There are many apparently excellent educational programs offered in schools that are inadequately housed, where the lack of finances makes it impossible to pay satisfactory salaries, and where the educational materials are very limited. It is, of course, true that there is a general relation between the excellence of a program and the kind of provisions a community can make, but the correlation is by no means perfect.

The tendency has been for society to expect the school to assume not only its traditional function of transmitting the social heritage but also many of the educational functions for which in the past other social institutions have been responsible. Numerous instances can be given. Schools in some states are now required by law to give instruction in humaneness, patriotism, and citizenship—outcomes affected by many influences in the community. Most schools now carry on programs of character training, formerly a major function of the church and the home. Some schools now offer courses in social etiquette, sex education, safety education, driving of automobiles, fire prevention, and similar training for which the home was formerly held responsible. The system of medical examinations required in many schools and the provisions made by some schools for corrective treatment demonstrate the extent to which society expects the schools to assume responsibility for the physical development of its youth. The guidance carried on in many schools by highly trained specialists was formerly undertaken by parents and friends.

Is the school responsible for the quality of all outcomes? Current criticisms of the schools that appear from time to time in books, magazines, and newspapers in most instances reflect the concern of individuals and groups about the effectiveness of the educational programs of various communities. The criticisms in many instances deal with apparent deficiencies in the educational product in such areas as control of basic tools of learning and expression, attitudes toward institutions and persons, emotional stability, and character traits.[1]

Undoubtedly the school contributes to the development of the learner along all of these lines, and is directly responsible for helping the child to master the basic tools of learning, in so far as he is capable of doing so.

It is obvious that the school cannot rightfully be held accountable for the quality of many outcomes in these fields because in the community there are conditions affecting them over which the school has little, if any, control.[2] The school, however, is a convenient place in which to study under fairly favorable conditions the characteristics of large numbers of children. At the same time, the school must scrutinize the behavior of its product in life outside the school. Such a study supplies fundamental information that can be used by the community in the further development of the total educational program.

The effectiveness of a school's program depends on its ability to set up immediate objectives whose attainment will lead to the achievement of ultimate educational objectives. Ultimate objectives are those characteristics of the individual that are manifested in wholesome, desirable methods of adult living. In general, they may be defined as those qualities, attitudes, and abilities that are essential for efficient living in an evolving, industrial, democratic society. The immediate objectives of the school are guidance and the development of desirable forms of behavior, consistent with ultimate objectives, as the individual progresses through the school. The work of any class is largely determined by its immediate objectives. To the degree that they are valid they will lead to the attainment of the ultimate goals.[3] Under such conditions it may be assumed that any measure of the characteristics of the pupils at a given level of the school is an indirect index of the extent to which ultimate goals are likely to be achieved.

The results of a typical evaluation program. An interesting and revealing account of an effort to assess an educational program by evaluating its product is given in the reports of the *Regents' Inquiry into the Character and Cost of Public Education in the State of New York*. By a wide variety of

[1] *Forces Affecting American Education*, 1953 Yearbook, Association for Supervision and Curriculum Development (Washington, National Education Association, 1953).

[2] *Juvenile Delinquency and the Schools*, Forty-seventh Yearbook, Part I, National Society for the Study of Education (Chicago, Univ. of Chicago Press, 1948).

Mass Media and Education, Forty-third Yearbook, Part II, National Society for the Study of Education (Chicago, Univ. of Chicago Press, 1954).

[3] Eli Ginsberg and D. W. Bray, *The Uneducated* (New York, Columbia Univ. Press, 1953).

Ruth Eckert, *Outcomes of General Education* (Minneapolis, Univ. of Minnesota Press, 1943).

Paul I. Lyness, "Patterns in the Mass Communication Tastes of the Young Audience," *Journal of Education Psychology* (December, 1951), pp. 449-467.

Paul Witty, "Children's Interests in Comics, Radio, Motion Pictures, and Television," *Educational Administration and Supervision* (March, 1952), pp. 138-147.

techniques, information was gathered about the "social competence" of youth at the time they were leaving school. The results of this investigation were stated in part as follows: [4]

Numerous and varied though its positive effects have been, the educational program has not been equally successful with all types of young people. It has done more, on the whole, for boys than for girls. It has been more effective with the academically able pupils than with those whose talents have lain in other directions. It has provided better for city pupils than for boys and girls in the small towns and the country.

Moreover, the current program has not always swept clean in those areas in which its positive results are most apparent. Though it has equipped most young people with the tools of learning, it has allowed appreciable numbers of boys and girls to leave school without having learned to read and write and use arithmetic well enough to meet normal, out-of-school needs. It has been most effective, in the main, with young people whose abilities are of a bookish sort; but even among boys and girls of marked academic ability it has failed to challenge many to their best achievement.

The present educational program has notably failed to develop certain types of competence. Though it has supplied much academic information, it has neglected to equip boys and girls with pertinent knowledge about their local communities, their chances to make a living, and the educational opportunities open to them once they leave the high school. As a result, thousands of young people just out of school are equipped to take no well-informed part in civic affairs; they look at random for jobs which may never materialize; they plan for further education which they can never attain, and which would often be of little use to them even if they could get it.

Despite some success in acquainting boys and girls with their rights as citizens, neither the schools nor any other social influences have developed in these boys and girls an active social conscience. High-school pupils on the point of leaving school display, on the contrary, a disturbing inclination to evade social responsibility, and young people who have left school undertake few activities which will contribute in any way to the public good.

Nor have any large numbers of these young people attained standards of enjoyment which lead them to make particularly discriminating use of their leisure time. What boys and girls read when they are free to choose what they will read, what they like to listen to on the radio, what they see in the movies, give evidence of little discriminating preference, except the preference for something that is exciting, romantic, or "funny."

In the field of competence which is most on the minds of the boys and girls themselves—vocational ability—the present program seems to have done least of all for the young people who have been subject to it. The majority have developed no salable vocational skills; they have learned nothing about the kinds of work in which they are most likely to be successful; they do not know how to make the most of the jobs they eventually get.

In all these matters the present educational program fails large numbers of high-school pupils in New York State. It falls farthest short of developing competence on the part of the boys and girls who most need help—the young people from homes low in the social scale, whom financial need or lack of encouragement or lack of success with traditional academic work drives out of school before they have earned a high-school diploma.

On the basis of the information thus secured and of an analysis of the influences to which the students had been exposed—including the curriculum, instruction, materials of learning, conditions in the community, and the social trends in general—certain definite recommendations for bringing about an improvement were presented. The approach represents the point of view presented in this volume.

Integration of evaluation and learning. Evaluation should also be an integral part of the learning process, and it should grow out of or emerge from that process. Although for some purposes it is necessary for the teacher or other community agency to evaluate some phase of the pupil's personality, the learner should be led to see the importance of evaluating his own behavior and traits in the light of desirable educational

[4] F. T. Spaulding, *High School and Life* (New York, McGraw, 1938), pp. 118-119. A similar discussion of pupils at the end of the elementary school is included in a report, L. J. Brueckner and others, *The Changing Elementary School* (New York, Inor Press, 1939).

objectives and social standards. In many instances the pupils, with the help of the teacher, can formulate evaluative criteria of their own. The expert in evaluation should not prescribe specific means and methods of appraisal to be used in instruction but rather should assist the teacher to devise techniques of evaluation that will function as an integral part of teaching-learning procedures. Evaluation should be continuing, and new methods of appraisal should be devised as new needs arise.

Section 2

PLANNING APPRAISAL PROGRAMS

Emphasis on educational objectives. The selection of means of appraising the educational products depends on the conception one has of the nature and scope of outcomes; these may be regarded narrowly in terms of knowledges and skills, or broadly in terms of all of the accepted objectives of a field of instruction. Most of the present tests of achievement in the various subjects deal with a narrow range of outcomes; standard tests in arithmetic, for example, are limited largely to the measurement of ability to compute and to solve verbal problems. Recently, several have been devised that deal with the informational and sociological functions of arithmetic. Similar limitations exist in regard to the extent to which most of the tests of reading, spelling, English, social studies, languages, and other subjects measure the range of desired outcomes. Many were originally devised as measuring devices, and in their construction little attention was paid to the types of educational objectives with which they dealt. The use of these tests had a marked influence on teaching. Teachers, whose skill was often rated on the basis of the scores made by the pupils, consequently stressed the types of outcomes measured by the tests; and, as a result, teaching tended to become as narrow and as limited as the specific objectives dealt with in the meager range of outcomes that were to be measured.

The work of Tyler,[5] Eurich,[6] Brueckner,[7] and others has brought to our attention the desirability of using methods of evaluation that determine the extent to which all of the major desired outcomes of instruction are being achieved. This point of view has not only influenced instruction in a favorable way but has also led to important constructive developments in the use of new means of appraising educational outcomes.

As a foundation for the development of means of appraisal, Smith and Tyler set up the following list of ten major educational objectives: [8]

1. Development of effective methods of thinking.
2. Cultivation of useful work habits and study skills.
3. Inculcation of social attitudes.
4. Acquisition of a wide range of significant interests.
5. Development of increased appreciation of music, art, literature, and other esthetic experiences.
6. Development of a social sensitivity.
7. Development of better personal-social adjustment.
8. Acquisition of important information.
9. Development of physical health.
10. Development of a consistent philosophy of life.

These ten objectives are a synthesis of many similar statements that have been issued in recent years. They may be regarded as basic to all areas of instruction in the field of general education. They are more specific as well as more comprehensive than most

[5] R. W. Tyler, *Constructing Achievement Tests* (Columbus, Ohio State Univ. Press, 1934), pp. 6-7.

[6] A. E. Eurich, in *Studies in College Examinations* (Minneapolis, Univ. of Minnesota Press, 1936), pp. 51-66.

[7] L. J. Brueckner, "Intercorrelations of Arithmetic Abilities," *Journal of Experimental Education* (September, 1934), pp. 42-44.

[8] Eugene R. Smith, R. W. Tyler, and members of Evaluation Staff, *Appraising and Recording Student Progress* (New York, Harper, 1942), p. 18.

earlier formulations and include all aspects of personality. They indicate very clearly the general kinds of outcomes that should serve as goals of instruction at all levels. Statements of objectives for specific curriculum areas can be made on the basis of this general list. The "3 R's" are implicit in items 2 and 8 in the list.

Characteristics of a modern evaluation program. A modern evaluation program consists not only of a basic testing program concerned with the status of basic knowledges and fundamental skills but also with the continuous evaluation by all suitable procedures, both objective and subjective, of all aspects of the growth and development of the learner. The characteristics of a modern program of evaluation have been well stated [9] as follows:

1. *Consistent with accepted educational objectives.* Practices in evaluating do not ignore or violate one objective in overemphasizing another, but harmonize with all sound goals.

2. *Democratic in providing for participation by all concerned.* Children being evaluated have a share in determining objectives, selecting techniques of appraisal, and interpreting results.

3. *Continuous throughout the child's years in school.* Appraisal of development is cumulative throughout the child's career in school, week to week, month to month, year to year.

4. *Integral with teaching.* Evaluation is a daily, even hourly, occurrence—a continuous activity representing a vital aspect of the teaching process—rather than being limited to periodic emphases such as end-of-month or semester tests.

5. *Comprehensive in treatment of all phases of child development.* Attention is given to attitudes, habits, understandings, and appreciations; to physical welfare and social adjustment; to ideals and aspirations; to factual information and skills.

6. *Flexible in the selection and use of an appropriate variety of techniques.* Means of appraisal are not limited to paper-and-pencil tests, check-lists, and rating scales but include all appropriate means of collecting information needed. Moreover, the appropriateness is determined by the differing characteristics of individuals and groups of children.

7. *Descriptive in terms of desired behavior.* The actions of children which represent their achievement of objectives must be clearly identified. Everyone concerned must be clear as to his goals. Descriptions of behavior are simple, clear, and as complete as possible.

8. *Specific with reference to desirable teacher objectives and the appropriate abilities and interests of children.* The chief concern is with progress in the all-around development of children rather than with status in comparison with an abstract "average child" or the "passing" of artificial hurdles.

9. *Good for the children whose behavior is being appraised.* The procedures, techniques, and instruments used in the program of evaluation themselves contribute to the educative process. There is simply no justification for evaluation procedures that are unfair, negative, or destructive in their total educative effect. Above all, the child must be permitted to keep his self-respect.

The planning of an appraisal program is a co-operative venture. Any program for appraising the educational product should be carefully planned and systematized. Such programs may range in scope from one that is organized by a state department to evaluate a state system of instruction to one that may be devised by the teacher of a class to appraise the work of an individual pupil. They may deal with achievements in one or more areas of learning, with the analysis of behavior both in and out of school.

The greatest value of such a program will accrue if it is carefully integrated with a planned program for the improvement of learning. So that teachers may be aware of this point, it is desirable to secure their participation in the planning and administration of the appraisal program. They should have a part in the determination of the nature and scope of the testing program, in the selecting of the tests, in the giving and scoring of the tests, in the tabulating and scoring of the results, and in the planning of the steps to take following the analysis and evaluation of the results. Likewise, they should participate in the development and carrying out

[9] J. B. Burr, L. W. Harding, L. B. Jacobs, *Student Teaching in the Elementary School* (New York, Appleton-Century-Crofts, 1950), pp. 187-188.

of plans for gathering other kinds of information about the educational product. These general procedures should be supplemented by a cumulative and continuous appraisal of the behavior of individual pupils by the classroom teachers, since evaluation should be regarded as an essential integral part of the learning process. To this end self-appraisal by pupils is fundamental.

The following steps in the organization and use of an appraisal program should be recognized by the supervisor and by the corps of teachers:

1. Formulate clearly the purposes of the evaluation program. This should be a co-operative enterprise participated in by all concerned with the growth and development of the learner: parents, pupils, teachers, and all others whose opinions should be considered. Attention should be given first to the setting up of educational objectives to be used as the basis of instruction. Then the group should select areas of instruction or experience about which reliable information must be gathered in order to appraise the product of the schools. The need for information may be the result of shortcomings observed in the behavior of students that are regarded as of serious enough import to be investigated thoroughly. The appraisal program may also be conducted as a means of gathering general information on a variety of points for its own value rather than because of any evident faults or shortcomings, noted by the group. Strengths and weaknesses in the product not suspected can thus be brought to light.

2. Consider the types and the possible sources of information that should be secured about the pupils. The sources may be school records, reports by teachers or parents, results of tests, court records, and so forth.

3. Select means that may be used to secure the desired information. These may consist of any of the kinds of devices that are discussed in this chapter, varying from standard achievement tests to the analysis of records of social agencies. The sources and devices selected should yield accurate, reliable information.

4. Prepare adequate instructions which will explain in detail the procedures to be used in the fact-gathering program.

5. Give the necessary preliminary training to those who are to participate. Clerical workers can undertake the analysis of the available school records. When trained examiners are not available, teachers and principals must be taught how to administer the tests. The co-operation of specialists of social and civic agencies not under the direct control of the school should be secured, and the essential data in their records and reports should be analyzed. The co-operation of parents should be secured in this fact-gathering program.

6. When tests have been administered and the other essential kinds of data have been gathered, tabulate the data by classes and by schools, and then summarize the findings for all classes and evaluate the results. The strengths and weaknesses of the educational product should be determined by comparison of test scores with available standards and in terms of the growth made toward goals and objectives. Manuals that describe in detail the methods of scoring tests and tabulating and interpreting the results are available for practically all tests. The supervisor must be prepared to assist the teachers or others in the analysis and interpretation of the results.

7. Organize and present the information obtained in the form of a report, including suitable tabular and graphic exhibits. Point out the strengths and weaknesses revealed by the program of evaluation.

8. Consider with the group concerned possible reasons for unfavorable results. As has been indicated in an earlier chapter, these may be resident in the pupil himself; they may be located in the instruction and in the personality of the teacher; they may be in the curriculum; they may be in the socio-physical environment, both in and out of school, including the plant, the community, and the materials of instruction. Then set up with the group a series of investigations to establish the factors thought to be at the root of the matter.

9. When these have been determined, plan and carry out an improvement program for removing those factors that have been demonstrated to be the most probable source of the difficulty. Check from time to time to see if there is evidence that desired changes are taking place and be prepared to make any necessary adjustments.

The teacher is the key person in the evaluation program. It is obvious that the most effective evaluation of learning is the appraisal made by the learner himself of his behavior, performances, and achievements. With the guidance of the teacher, the children can learn how to appraise their work from day to day and to assume responsibility for improving it. Evaluations made by some outside agency, such as a research department or survey staff, are not nearly as effective as appraisals made on the spot by the teacher and the learner. The teacher is the key to the effective use of evaluative procedures in the classroom. Wrightstone [10] has listed the following procedures to illustrate the ways in which a teacher can study and appraise the characteristics and behavior of the learners as a basis for effective instruction.

1. She will learn as much as she can about her new class before meeting them. To this end, she will:
   a. Inspect the cumulative records and the health record cards.
   b. Inspect any special reports on individuals.
   c. Confer with the supervisor and the children's previous teachers.
2. She will observe the children as she becomes acquainted with them. She will notice:
   a. The spirit of the class; signs of friendship groupings.
   b. Individuals who are outstanding, for one reason or another.
   c. Apparent interests; apparent level of maturity.
3. To find out where her children are in relation to their academic work, she will:
   a. Consult office records to see what units and other major experiences the class has had in previous years.
   b. Give formal or informal tests to find group and individual ability in skill areas. (If recent data exist, this step may be omitted. However, there is often some loss of skill over the summer vacation.)
   c. Be alert to evidences of competence and knowledge apparent to children's informal talk, in work habits, in their sharing of teacher-pupil planning, etc.
4. To discover how her children are responding to the program being developed with them, she will:
   a. Observe carefully the processes in which the children take part: how they go about a task, how they work together, how they do research, how they discuss and share information and ideas, how they report, how well

they manage the transition from one activity to another, etc.
   b. Watch for evidences of the quality of the children's thinking.
   c. Give brief and fairly frequent tests by which the children may be kept informed of their progress in skills and in facts which they need to remember.
   d. Give special attention to children having exceptional needs, and devise ways by which they can test their own progress.
   e. Interpret the results of city-wide test programs in such a way that she can:
      (1) Adjust her instructional program to serve group and/or individual needs revealed by the results.
      (2) Consider the standing of her class in relation to the given norms with due allowance for all the factors involved—the children's background, recent community changes, individual problems, etc.
      (3) Give the scores their rightful place in the total picture of each child. Experienced teachers know that children may grow by spurts and lags, rather than steadily. Children may appear to stand still in one area while speeding ahead in another. They may seem to be regressing in all aspects at once. Much must be known about the individual to account for these changes and lack of changes. Teachers must take the whole child into consideration in evaluating any score and are not discouraged by occasional lapses.
5. To enlist the children's optimum participation in the evaluative program, the teacher will:
   a. Provide opportunities according to the children's maturity for them to carry on evaluations frequently and in relation to their plans, their goals, their activities, the tools and materials they use, and the results of group efforts.
   b. Explain to them as much as they can understand of the purpose of testing

[10] Mimeographed statement by J. W. Wrightstone, New York Board of Education, Brooklyn, New York.

and other evaluations; permit them to apply evaluation to the tests used.

c. Provide the guide opportunities for the children, within the limits of their maturity, to work with the teacher or in groups to devise simple tests for specific uses within the class.

6. To gain information that will aid her in understanding all aspects of the child's life, and in guiding him wisely, she will:

a. Confer with parents, when possible, in a manner as informal and unhurried as can be arranged and in a spirit of co-operation and common interest, when necessary or desirable.

b. Confer with others in a position to know about various aspects of the child's life such as representatives of community agencies or of child guidance services and experts in any appropriate field.

c. Observe his behavior in supervised and unsupervised situations and make such notes as will be useful in estimating his personal social growth and needs. The notes may be in the form of anecdotal records, ratings on a scale, checks on a check-list, or any other kind of notation the teacher prefers. These notes will prove helpful when the teacher is called upon to enter personality ratings on the Cumulative Record Card.

As the teacher evaluates the growth of the children in the class, she is also making an evaluation of herself as a teacher. She studies her teaching techniques in order to discover whether they are effective or whether she needs to see better ones. The way in which materials are being used and the manner in which routines are taken care of, help the teacher to evaluate her effectiveness. Some teachers keep diaries for purposes of record and in order to be able to appraise their own effectiveness. A diary may take any one of many forms and may focus on a variety of points. It may be a running account of the progress of a unit, a narrative showing how the class has learned new ways of getting along together, a report of incidents that required attention and of plans for meeting the problems revealed, or a behavior journal following the development of a particular child (often one who needs special help and understanding). A diary may be the joint product of the teacher and a child: for instance, the teacher writes suggestions and comments in the daily log book, and the child in charge of the log for the day reports his activities on the job and his reactions to the teacher's written comments.

THE CONSTRUCTION AND SELECTION OF APPRAISAL INSTRUMENTS

Steps in the development of means of appraising outcomes. The supervisor should assist teachers in selecting methods of evaluating the important outcomes, and when satisfactory methods of appraisal are lacking, in taking steps to develop them. The steps in developing such procedures may be listed as follows:

1. Formulate the objectives clearly. The desired objectives of instruction should be stated in terms that can be understood by all. Detailed analyses of the objectives in several fields are already available. In other fields they have not been formulated. The analysis given below [11] lists major aspects of social sensitivity that formed the basis of a series of tests for measuring the social sensitivity of high-school students during the Eight-Year Study.

1. *Social thinking;* e.g., the ability (*a*) to get significant meaning from social facts, (*b*) to apply social facts and generalizations to new problems, (*c*) to respond critically and discriminately to ideas and arguments.

2. *Social attitudes, beliefs, and values;* e.g., the basic personal positions, feelings, and concerns toward social phenomena, institutions, and issues.

3. *Social awareness;* that is, the range and quality of factors or elements perceived in a situation.

4. *Social interests* as revealed by liking to engage in socially significant activities.

5. *Social information;* that is, familiarity

[11] E. R. Smith, R. W. Tyler, and members of Evaluation Staff, *op. cit.,* p. 161.

with facts and generalizations relevant to significant social problems.

6. *Skill in social action,* involving familiarity with the techniques of social action as well as ability to use them.

To be most helpful, a general analysis of objectives should be further broken down so as to indicate the specific objectives for each stage of growth. Such an analysis would be of value both to the teacher and to the one who is constructing means of appraisal.

An example of the breaking down of the general objectives for a particular field of learning into those of development levels is the following statement of the aims of five stages in the development of reading ability:[12]

1. *The stage at which readiness for reading is attained.* This stage usually comprises the preschool years, the kindergarten, and often the early part of the first grade. The chief purpose of the guidance recommended is to provide the experiences and training that promote reading readiness. In addition, steps should be taken to overcome physical and emotional deficiencies that might interfere with progress.

2. *The initial stage in learning to read.* For pupils who advance normally, this stage usually occurs during the first grade. Among other attainments, pupils acquire keen interest in learning to read and a thoughtful reading attitude. They learn to engage in continuous meaningful reading, read simple interesting material with keen interest and absorption in the content, and begin to read independently.

3. *The stage of rapid progress in fundamental reading attitudes and habits.* This stage of development occurs usually during the second and third grades. It is characterized by rapid growth in reading interests and by notable progress in accuracy of comprehension, depth of interpretation, independence in word recognition, fluency in oral reading, and increased speed of silent reading. By the end of this stage of development pupils should read silently more rapidly than orally and should be able to read with reasonable ease, understanding, and pleasure both informational and literary materials such as are usually assigned early in the fourth grade. To do this efficiently, a grade score of 4.0 in silent reading should be attained.

4. *The stage at which experience is extended rapidly and increased power, efficiency, and ex-*cellence *in reading are acquired.* The fourth stage of development occurs normally during grades four, five, and six and is characterized by wide reading that extends and enriches the experiences of the reader and broadens his vision. The chief purposes of the guidance provided are to promote greater power in comprehension and interpretation, greater efficiency in rate of reading and in reading for different purposes, improvement in the quality of oral reading, the extension of the pupil's interests, the elevation of reading tastes, and greater skill in the use of books and other printed sources of information. A grade score of 7.0 in silent reading is desirable by the end of this stage of development.

5. *The stage at which reading interests, habits, and tastes are refined.* The fifth stage of development occurs as a rule during the junior high-school, senior high-school, and junior-college periods. The chief purposes of guidance in reading during these years are to promote further development and refinement of the attitudes and habits involved in various types of reading, to broaden interests and elevate tastes in reading, to develop increased efficiency in the use of books, libraries, and sources of information, and to secure a high level of efficiency in all study activities that involve reading.

In the yearbook Gray [13] lists specific objectives and aims of instruction for each of these five levels. As an illustration of the specific nature of the objectives listed, the aims for Stage III are paraphrased below:

1. Participation in a rich variety of reading experiences based on the world's greatest stories for children and on informational materials that challenge interest, including topics relating to various curricular fields.

2. Keen interest in reading wholesome books and selections for pleasure and to establish the habit of reading independently.

3. Rapid progress in the development of habits of intelligent interpretation when reading for a variety of purposes.

4. Increase in the speed with which passages are read silently within the limits of accurate comprehension. (This includes rapid increases in span and rate of recognition and a corresponding decrease in number and duration of

[12] *The Teaching of Reading,* Thirty-sixth Yearbook, Part I, National Society for the Study of Education (Bloomington, Ill., Public School Publishing Co., 1937), pp. 76-77.

[13] *Ibid.,* p. 101.

eye-fixation per line in both oral and silent reading.)

5. The development of desirable standards and habits involved in good oral reading.

6. Continuous development in accuracy and independence in word recognition.

7. Training in the skillful use of books and increased familiarity with the privileges and opportunities of libraries.

To help the teacher to visualize more clearly the significance of these aims, Gray [14] also describes the characteristics pupils should possess before they can be regarded as having completed the requirements of the period successfully. The characteristics listed for the end of Stage III are as follows:

1. They have established the habit of reading independently.

2. They interpret accurately the materials related to other curricular fields.

3. They seek reading materials that relate to activities in which they are interested.

4. They read more rapidly silently than orally.

5. They are able to read at sight materials suited to their stage of development.

6. They show increasing skill in combining contextual clues with visual and auditory elements in recognizing unfamiliar words.

7. They show increased ability to make the adjustments required when reading for different purposes.

8. They exhibit rapid progress in acquiring wholesome and diversified reading interests.

This analysis recognizes the fact that the ability to read is the result of a long process of development and that at each of the five levels there are definite objectives which should be adjusted to the growth process. The objectives are not stated by grade levels as is so frequently done in courses of study, but according to recognized stages of growth. It is known that pupils do not progress from stage to stage at the same rate in any field. The significance of this listing of objectives by successive levels of growth rather than by grades is clearly revealed by a statement in the same yearbook that gives the following essential steps which must be taken to provide adequately for these individual differences in rates of learning: [15]

1. Systematic and continuous study of the attainments and needs of pupils through the use of both informal and formal methods.

2. A flexible scheme of grouping pupils within a grade or classroom that recognizes individual differences and provides for them.

3. The provision of different kinds of guidance in reading in the same grade or classroom in harmony with the varying needs of the pupils taught. (The adoption of this procedure should result in greatly reducing the need for so-called "remedial teaching.")

4. Differentiation in the materials and methods of teaching in order to provide adequately for differences in capacity and rates of learning.

5. The provision of extended periods of work, uninterrupted by failure, whereby pupils may make satisfactory progress from one level of advancement to the next.

6. The exemption of pupils from systematic effort to improve their mastery of basic reading habits as soon as they are able to engage efficiently in all the reading activities essential in meeting the general curricular demands at their respective levels of advancement.

7. The substitution of various aspects of child growth for progress in reading as the basis of promotion from grade to grade.

Further discussion of these general principles of adapting instruction to individual differences in all areas of learning will be deferred until Chapter 14.

2. Clarify the objectives. The objectives must be further clarified by describing them in terms of student behavior which represents change in the direction of the desired objectives. In constructing or selecting a test, this question should be considered: "Does the kind of behavior required on this test relate to an important objective of the course? Do the kinds of behavior required in these tests give evidence about the status of all of the important objectives of the course?"

The following statement by Tyler will make clear what is meant by clarifying objectives by describing them in terms of pupil behavior: [16]

[14] *Ibid.*, p. 107.

[15] *Ibid.*, pp. 77-78.

[16] R. W. Tyler, in *Educational Diagnosis*, Thirty-fourth Yearbook, National Society for the Study of Education (Bloomington, Ill., Public School Publishing Co., 1935), pp. 114-115.

To define the behavior to be evaluated is essentially to determine all the kinds of behavior that are particularly significant for the purposes under consideration. The reactions of any human organism are so many and varied that it is necessary to isolate the particular reactions that are significant for a given purpose. For example, during the process of instruction in a subject, such as arithmetic, pupils are reacting in many different ways; some are talking; some are smiling; some are moving about in their seats, but these are probably not significant kinds of behavior from the standpoint of arithmetic intruction. In making an appraisal of value in the field of arithmetic it is necessary to define the kinds of behavior that are significant in arithmetic, so that we may discover whether the pupils are reacting in desirable ways. This definition would probably include behavior such as the ability to determine the total amount of an itemized grocery bill, a feeling of the importance of accurate numerical computations, the ability to determine the arithmetic processes to use in solving typical problems encountered in everyday life, and so on. Similarly, one must define social adjustments in order to evaluate the effectiveness of a child's adjustment in a social group. Many reactions are made by a child when in a social group; some of them are random and of little or no significance from the standpoint of social adjustment; others are vitally related to social adjustments. It is therefore necessary to identify the significant behavior.

An excellent example of the method used to clarify the meaning of the second major objective listed on page 227, the cultivation of useful work habits and study skills, is the analysis given below, prepared by Smith and Tyler [17] as a guide to developing means of appraising outcomes related to this objective:

1.1 *Effective Use of Study Time*
  1.11 Habit of using large blocks of free time effectively.
  1.12 Habit of budgeting his time.
  1.13 Habit of sustained application rather than working sporadically.
  1.14 Habit of meeting promptly study obligations.
  1.15 Habit of carrying work through to completion.

1.2 *Conditions for Effective Study*
  1.21 Knowledge of proper working conditions.
  1.22 Habit of providing proper working conditions for himself.
  1.23 Habit of working independently, that is, working under his own direction and initiative.

1.3. *Effective Planning of Study*
  1.31 Habit of planning in advance.
  1.32 Habit of choosing problems for investigation which have significance for him.
  1.33 Ability to define a problem.
  1.34 Habit of analyzing a problem so as to sense its implications.
  1.35 Ability to determine data needed in an investigation.

1.4 *Selection of Sources*
  1.41 Awareness of kinds of information which may be obtained from various sources.
  1.42 Awareness of the limitations of the various sources of data.
  1.43 Habit of using appropriate sources of information, including printed materials of various types, lectures, interviews, observations, and so on.

1.5 *Effective Use of Various Sources of Data*
  1.51 Use of library.
    1.511 Knowledge of important library tools.
    1.512 Ability to use the card catalogue in a library.
  1.52 Use of books.
    1.521 Ability to use the dictionary.
    1.522 Habit of using the helps (such as the index) in books.
    1.523 Ability to use maps, charts, and diagrams.
  1.53 Reading.
    1.531 Ability to read a variety of materials for a variety of purposes using a variety of reading techniques.
    1.532 Power to read with discrimination.
    1.533 Ability to read rapidly.
    1.534 Development of a more effective reading vocabulary.

[17] Smith, Tyler, and staff, *op. cit.,* pp. 31-33.

1.54 Ability to get helpful information from other persons.

    1.541 Ability to understand material presented orally.

    1.542 Facility in the techniques of discussion, particularly discussions which clarify the issues in controversial questions.

    1.543 Ability to obtain information from interviews with people.

1.55 Ability to obtain helpful information from field trips and other excursions.

1.56 Ability to obtain information from laboratory experiments.

1.57 Habit of obtaining needed information from observations.

1.6 *Determining Relevancy of Data*

1.61 Ability to determine whether the data found are relevant to the particular problem.

1.7 *Recording and Organizing Data*

1.71 Habit of taking useful notes for various purposes from observations, lectures, interviews, and reading.

1.72 Ability to outline material for various purposes.

1.73 Ability to make an effective organization so that the material may be readily recalled, as in note-taking.

1.74 Ability to make an effective organization for written presentation of a topic.

1.75 Ability to make an effective organization for oral presentation of a topic.

1.76 Ability to write effective summaries.

1.8 *Presentation of the Results of Study*

1.81 Ability to make an effective written presentation of the results of study.

    1.811 Habit of differentiating quoted material from summarized material in writing reports.

    1.812 Facility in handwriting or in typewriting.

1.82 Ability to make an effective oral presentation of the results of study.

1.9 *Habit of Evaluating Each Step in an Investigation*

1.91 Habit of considering the dependability of the data obtained from various sources.

1.92 Habit of considering the relative importance of the various ideas obtained from various sources.

1.93 Habit of refraining from generalization until data are adequate.

1.94 Habit of testing his own generalizations.

1.95 Habit of criticizing his own investigations.

3. Collect test situations. A test should consist of situations that are representative of the variety of situations in which the pupil ordinarily uses the skills, information, or other items to be appraised. If we wish, for example, to find out how well a pupil spells in the kinds of writing he does in life situations, we must note and record his behavior in such situations—a list test will not do this. To find out about a pupil's mechanical ability we must observe his behavior as he works in functional situations on tasks requiring mechanical skills—a test of information will not reveal this. The test situations used should give direct evidence concerning the behavior being evaluated. They must give the individual the opportunity to express the behavior being appraised. Extraneous factors, such as the difficulty of the reading or the complexity of the procedure, which are likely to confuse the individual, should be controlled. The test situations should be practicable from the standpoints of time, effort, and facilities required. They should sample the defined behavior under a variety of conditions so that dependable conclusions may be drawn as to the typical performance of those tested. It is ordinarily desirable to use a variety of techniques so that a more complete measurement is possible. Numerous examples are given in Section 4 of this chapter.

4. Record the behavior. A record of the pupil's behavior is necessary so that his behavior may be evaluated. Paper-and-pencil examinations furnish one kind of record. Reports of significant observations of pupil behavior, written compositions, art productions, trait-rating devices, check-lists for recording actions, photographs, motion pictures, and similar devices are other means of recording behavior. The form of record to be used depends on the nature of the behavior that is to be evaluated.

The record should describe accurately all of the significant reactions that took place which may later be of value in interpreting the results. The larger the number of significant records, the more objectively and validly the behavior can be evaluated. The availability of a cumulative record of previous behavior and other information about the individual will greatly facilitate a diagnosis. Records should not require much time and effort or many facilities if they are to be practical.

As a basis for recording and evaluating students' reactions to their reading, the Evaluation Committee [18] first assembled overt acts and verbal responses which in the judgment of the committee would in certain situations reveal the presence or absence of the seven types of behavior listed below. A few illustrations are included for each type of behavior.

1. *Satisfaction in the Thing Appreciated*
   1.1 He reads aloud to others, or simply to himself, passages which he finds unusually interesting.
   1.2 He reads straight through without stopping, or with a minimum of interruption.
   1.3 He reads for considerable periods of time.
2. *Desire for More of the Thing Appreciated*
   2.1 He asks other people to recommend reading which is more or less similar to the thing appreciated.
   2.2 He commences this reading of similar things as soon after reading the first as possible.
   2.3 He subsequently read several books, plays, or poems by the same author.

3. *Desire to Know More about the Thing Appreciated*
   3.1 He asks other people for information or sources of information about what he has read.
   3.2 He reads supplementary materials, such as biography, history, criticism, etc.
   3.3 He attends literary meetings devoted to reviews, criticisms, discussions, etc.
4. *Desire to Express One's Self Creatively*
   4.1 He produces, or at least undertakes to produce, a creative product more or less after the manner of the thing appreciated.
   4.2 He writes critical appreciations.
   4.3 He illustrates what he has read in some one of the graphic, spatial, musical, or dramatic arts.
5. *Identification of One's Self with the Thing Appreciated*
   5.1 He accepts, at least while he is reading, the persons, places, situations, events, etc., as real.
   5.2 He dramatizes, formally or informally, various passages.
   5.3 He imitates, consciously and unconsciously, the speech and actions of various characters in the story.
6. *Desire to Clarify One's Own Thinking with Regard to the Life Problems Raised by the Thing Appreciated*
   6.1 He attempts to state, either orally or in writing, his own ideas, feelings, or information concerning the life problems with which his reading deals.
   6.2 He examines other sources for more information about these problems.
   6.3 He reads other works dealing with similar problems.
7. *Desire to Evaluate the Thing Appreciated*
   7.1 He points out, both orally and in writing, the elements which in his opinion make it good literature.
   7.2 He explains how certain unacceptable elements (if any) could be improved.
   7.3 He consults published criticisms.

5. Evaluate the behavior. Instead of using a subject score, such as an educational age or a percentile rank based on the results

[18] Smith, Tyler, and staff, *op. cit.*

of a single test, to evaluate a pupil's performance, behavior should be appraised by evaluating responses in terms of each of the important objectives of instruction. The question should be raised: What is the individual's status with respect to a particular objective? The chief problem here is the establishment of standards for evaluating performance in different kinds of test situations and for various forms of reports. In some cases appraisal is relatively simple, as in the measurement of height or weight, since objective units of measurement exist. The evaluation of achievement in such fields as reading, mathematics, and science is much more difficult since the outcomes of instruction in these subjects are numerous, many-sided, and in some instances nonprecise; furthermore, objective means of describing pupil achievement relative to many of these outcomes are lacking at the present time. Pupil progress is also highly variable.

The problem of setting up norms of achievement presents many difficulties. The present general practice is to consider the average score for children of a given chronological or mental-age group or of a given grade as the norm of achievement for all children of the group. Because of the wide range of differences in the abilities and interests of the members of a group, this method of arriving at a norm is of doubtful validity. In setting up a goal the primary consideration should be the nature of the objective and the extent to which there is evidence that there is optimum growth and development from time to time in the direction of the goal. The purpose of the teacher should be to attempt to guide the pupil "from where he is to where he ought to be," as judged by the achievements of similar children and of his own potentialities, that is, his expectancy level. Experimentation is needed to determine the feasibility of setting up goals of learning for different groups of children on the basis of such variables as differences in capacity to learn, differences in experiential background, differences in men-

tal, physical, social, and emotional maturity, and differences in basic interests and purposes. The problem of setting up norms for varying configurations of these and other factors presents interesting possibilities. Individual norms are now used in clinical and remedial work when the individual's past performance is used as the norm by which to measure subsequent progress or when performances on several tests are compared to note relative strengths and weaknesses.

Evaluation is facilitated by increasing the objectivity of the record so that, in so far as is possible, the evaluation is not unduly influenced by subjective judgment and personal bias. A form of test should be used that can be easily administered and scored. Validity should not be sacrificed, however, to secure objectivity. In general, it is recognized that if the behavior is in harmony with the accepted aims of education as a whole or of a particular area of learning it is given a high rating; if it is not in harmony, it is rated low. Problems of determining scale values for different kinds of behavior present many difficulties which are being attacked in various ways. It is important that measurement be obtained in fine enough units so that exact appraisal may be possible.

In some areas standards of appraisal are not appropriate. The difficulty of evaluating outcomes in the social studies can be made clear by a consideration of "attitude" scales which have proved useful in *describing* group attitudes toward social problems and institutions. These scales cannot be used to *evaluate* attitudes because there is no agreement as to what the attitudes should be. They are therefore useful as instruments for the *description* of attitudes rather than as means of evaluation. In the same way, interest inventories may be used to describe the interests of individuals or groups and their general patterns, but we cannot say that a given individual *should have* a given set of interests or possess them to a given degree.

Character and personality traits are at

present very unreliably appraised by most of the available tests. Many efforts have been made to develop measures of such traits as honesty, good citizenship, openmindedness, leadership, and self-control. As yet they have hardly advanced beyond the exploratory stage. Behavior records are giving us more reliable data as a basis for evaluation. The school cannot proceed with any assurance in building a program for the development of these traits until they have been adequately defined and described and until reliable means for appraising them are available.

Section 4

PROCEDURES FOR EVALUATING THE EDUCATIONAL PRODUCT

Evaluation has always been a basic element in the teaching-learning process. Historically, the school first emphasized as the primary goal of education the acquisition of specific information in the various areas of learning. Such procedures as oral and written examinations were used to evaluate the learner's mastery of the subject matter. Test performance was subjectively appraised to determine how well it met standards that were likewise subjective and also not clearly defined. Research showed that they also varied from person to person and that ratings by different persons were unreliable and not comparable. Ultimately, standardized tests were developed to assure more dependable methods of appraising the information acquired.

Later the increasingly broader interpretation of the concept of educational outcomes stressed the behavioral changes desired in children. This trend created demands for improved and more broadly conceived procedures for appraising the educational product.[19] This led to the development of less formal, and at the same time more subjective, means of studying the behavior of the learner in social situations both in and out of school, such as activity records, interest inventories, and tests of behavior in problem situations.

The accumulating information about individual differences in intelligence, rates of growth, interests and needs of persons, led to the development of methods of evaluating attainments in terms of the varying ability of the different individuals and the differences in their rates of growth and development.

Instead of merely determining the present status of a pupil's attainments by comparison of scores with standards and norms of performance, increasing recognition is being given at the present time to the desirability of determining from time to time the growth that is made by the learner with respect to attainment of desirable goals, such as the mastery of the basic tools of learning, the functional use of information, and the ability to deal with the problems of daily life. Evidence of normal growth by the learner in terms of his own capacity to learn is perhaps the most valuable measure of the effectiveness of the educational program.

In current literature a distinction usually is made between objective and subjective methods of approach in gathering data about a pupil's attainments and characteristics. The two expressions *measurement* and *evaluation* identify the difference in point of view. "Measurement" is applied to the use of precise objective methods that yield quantitative data concerning aspects of individual growth which lend themselves to quantitative analysis, such as his attainments in the various areas of the curriculum, his general intelligence and aptitude for special areas of learning, and his physical characteristics, such as his height, weight, and strength. These measures can be expressed in standard units, and direct comparisons with standards and norms are possible. "Evaluation," on the other hand, refers to the appraisal of information

19 J. W. Wrightstone, "Evaluation," in W. S. Monroe, ed., *Encyclopedia of Educational Research* (New York, Macmillan, 1950).

gathered by less objective methods, such as rating scales, anecdotal records, and interviews. Their purpose is to determine the ability of the learner to use in a functional way what he is learning. These procedures yield descriptive qualitative data about the individual's behavior and his ability to use what he has learned in a wide variety of social situations, including the learning activities planned by the school. These data obviously do not lend themselves to measurement by precise, standard units, but they are very valuable as a basis for making judgments about the quality of the learner's reactions, his methods of work, and other less tangible educational outcomes. "Subjective judgment" is not a term of reproach.

Although the approach to the interpretation of the information gathered by the less precise methods of evaluation is ordinarily not quantitative, considerable progress has been made in recent years in the development of more objective standards by which these kinds of qualitative data can be appraised. Ultimately, the distinction between the techniques of measurement and evaluation will likely be unnecessary. Both terms actually imply that certain values have been accepted and that behavior and attainments are judged in terms of these values.

In selecting methods of gathering facts to be used in the appraisal of the educational product, certain points should be given careful consideration. The outcomes to be evaluated should be comprehensive enough to include the more important objectives of the area involved. The method of appraisal should be practical and not too difficult to apply. Evidence should be secured that the procedure selected is valid, that is, that it measures what it purports to measure. The fact that the technique is reliable and yields consistent, accurate information should be established. It is essential that the data derived in a given situation by two or more persons independently should be in close agreement and also be comparable with data from similar situations. In brief, whatever the method of appraisal that is used—be it essay examination, standardized test, direct observation, interview, anecdotal record, or any other of the wide variety of techniques that are available—every effort should be made to select procedures that will assure the availability of dependable accurate information.

Obviously, the nature of the outcomes to be appraised determines the nature of the means of appraisal to be employed. A test of information, for example, can well be a paper-and-pencil examination, whereas a test of ability to use the microscope ordinarily requires the use of the instrument itself in a test situation. The present lack of means of evaluating many educational outcomes is largely due to two factors: (1) the failure to relate measurement to outcomes, and (2) the difficulty of inventing suitable appraisal techniques. No one supervisory procedure would lead more quickly to the enrichment and improvement of teaching than bringing, through appropriate techniques, the broad range of educational outcomes to the attention of teachers and helping them to discover the status of their pupils in relation to those outcomes.

Procedures for evaluating the educational product. An analysis of the literature on evaluation shows that a great many different kinds of techniques are being used to appraise various characteristics of the educational product. Some of the procedures have been in use for many years, others are of recent origin. The list below includes the more important and useful techniques of appraisal that are being used at the present time. The procedures given in Group I in general are objective and yield quantitative information, whereas those in Group II are largely subjective and lead to judgments about quality of behavior.

I. *Tests and Standardized Procedures*
    1. Standardized tests and measures.
        a. Achievements tests.
        b. Mental and intelligence tests.
        c. Tests of motor skills and abilities.

d. Aptitude tests.
e. Physiological measures and medical examinations.
f. Personality and adjustment tests of several types.
g. Interest inventories and attitude scales.

2. Unstandardized, short-answer objective tests.
    a. Simple recall or free response.
    b. Completion.
    c. Alternate response.
    d. Multiple choice.
    e. Matching.

3. Improved essay type of test consisting of questions so formulated that they can be scored on a fairly objective basis.

4. Scales for analyzing and rating a performance or a product.

5. Tests involving evaluation of responses using projective methods.

6. Case studies involving use of specialized clinical devices and procedures. (These procedures will be discussed in detail in Chapter 10.)

II. *Evaluation of Behavior by Less Formal Procedures*

1. Problem-situation tests.
    a. Direct experience.
        (1) Experiment to be performed.
        (2) Actual life situation to be met.
    b. Indirect approach.
        (1) Improved essay type examinations.
        (2) Expressing judgments about described situations.
        (3) "What would you do"?

2. Behavior records concerning in-school and out-of-school activities.
    a. Controlled situations.
        (1) Use of check-lists, rating scales, score cards, codes for evaluating personality traits, behavior, attitudes, opinions, interests, and so on.
        (2) Self-rating devices, "Guess-Who."
        (3) Time studies of attention, activities.
        (4) Photographs and motion pictures.
        (5) Stenographic reports.
        (6) Dictaphone and tape recordings.

    b. Uncontrolled situations.
        (1) Log or diary; autobiographical reports.
        (2) Anecdotal records; behavior logs.
        (3) Records of libraries, police, welfare agencies, etc.
        (4) Still or motion pictures.

3. Inventories and questionnaires of work habits, interests, activities, associates, and the like.

4. Interviews, conferences, personal reports.
    a. With the individual learner himself.
    b. With others, such as parents, associates.

5. Analysis and evaluation of a creative act or product, such as poems, music, constructions, and so forth.

6. Sociometric procedures for studying group relationships.

7. Evaluation of reactions using projective and expressive techniques.
    a. Psychodrama and play technics.
    b. Free association tests.
    c. Interpretation of reactions to selected pictures and drawings.
    d. Interpretation of free oral and written expression.
    e. Interpretation of artistic and constructive products.

In this section we shall discuss the general principles underlying the selection and improvement of these techniques of appraisal. Special consideration will be given to the diagnostic use of projective and expressive techniques in Chapters 10 and 14. In Section 5 of this chapter there is a discussion of effective ways of using the other evaluative procedures.

Functions of general achievement tests. The major functions of general achievement tests in so far as planning instruction is concerned have been summarized as follows:[20]

1. To direct curriculum emphasis by:
    a. Focusing attention on as many of the important ultimate objectives of education as possible.

[20] W. W. Cook, in E. F. Lindquist, ed., *Educational Measurement* (Washington, American Council on Education, 1951), p. 36.

b. Clarification of educational objectives to teachers and pupils.

c. Determining elements of strength and weakness in the instructional program of the school.

d. Discovering inadequacies in curriculum content and organization.

2. To provide for educational guidance of pupils by:

   a. Providing a basis for predicting individual pupil achievement in each learning area.

   b. Serving as a basis for the preliminary grouping of pupils in each learning area.

   c. Discovering special aptitudes and disabilities.

   d. Determining the difficulty of material a pupil can read with profit.

   e. Determining the level of problem-solving ability in various areas.

3. To stimulate the learning activities of pupils by:

   a. Enabling pupils to think of their achievements in objective terms.

   b. Giving pupils satisfaction for the progress they make, rather than for the relative level of achievement they attain.

   c. Enabling pupils to compete with their past performance record.

   d. Measuring achievement objectively in terms of accepted educational standards, rather than by the subjective appraisal of teachers.

4. To direct and motivate administrative and supervisory efforts by:

   a. Enabling teachers to discover the areas in which they need supervisory aid.

   b. Affording the administrative and supervisory staff an over-all measure of the effectiveness of the school organization and of the prevailing administrative and supervisory policies.

Criteria to be considered in test selection. An up-to-date discussion of the criteria that should be considered in the selection of psychological tests is contained in a special report of the American Psychological Association.[21] The list of criteria given below is adapted from this report. Those who may be interested are referred to it for a detailed statement. Information of the kinds listed below usually is included in manuals of directions.

CRITERIA TO BE CONSIDERED IN EVALUATING PSYCHOLOGICAL TESTS ADAPTED FROM PROPOSAL BY APA COMMITTEE ON TEST STANDARDS

1. *Basic General Information about the Test*

   a. Function of the test.

   b. The character of the materials.

   c. Extent to which they have been validated.

   d. Interpretation of scores and ratings.

   e. Other data to be considered in interpreting test scores.

2. *Validity*

   a. Predictive validity—correlation between test scores and subsequent criterion measures.

   b. Content validity—content samples a universe of possible behaviors which are the goals of training or some other activity.

   c. Status validity—correlation between test scores and concurrent external criteria.

   d. Congruent validity—correlation of scores and other indicators of the state or attribute.

3. *Reliability*

   a. Coefficient of internal consistency among the parts of tests as measures of a generalized homogeneous trait.

   b. Coefficient of equivalence of forms.

   c. Coefficient of stability of scores if test is repeated.

4. *Administration and Scoring*

   a. Clarity of directions for administration and scoring.

   b. Relative ease of scoring procedures used.

   c. Scorer agreement.

[21] Technical Recommendations for Psychological Tests and Diagnostic Procedures; Preliminary Proposal. *The American Psychologist* (August, 1950), pp. 461-475.

The committee made no specific proposal of criteria to be considered in the selection of *educational tests*. An older but still very useful scale for rating achievement tests is the scale by Von Borgersrode and Cole given on pp. 220-223 in the second edition of this volume.

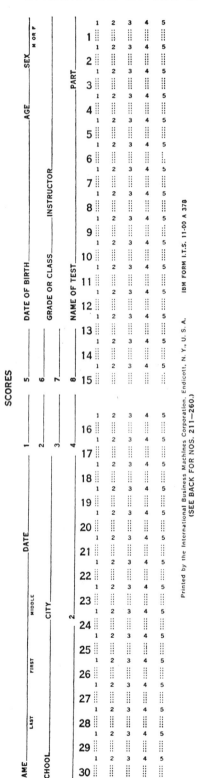

d. Objectivity—possible use of objective or machine-scoring procedures.

e. Cautions on interpreting scores when subjective processes enter into scoring.

5. *Scales and Norms*

a. Scales for interpreting scores and likelihood of accurate interpretation and emphasis by test interpreter and subject.

b. Derivation of norms or standards.

c. Populations on which norms are based defined and clearly described, as to age, sex, training, and other equally important variables.

The reader will find it an enlightening exercise to apply these standards to means of appraisal used in his school. Data needed in the case of a particular test are often given in the manual accompanying it. The general criterion should be: To what extent is this particular instrument a suitable one for the purposes I have in mind?

The Third and Fourth Mental Measurements Yearbooks,[22] edited by Oscar K. Buros, contain selected evaluations of a wide variety of tests and measures of all kinds which are of great value in making selections of appraisal devices.

In recent years the introduction of machine-scoring methods has greatly reduced the burden of scoring objective tests, including alternate response, multiple choice, and matching types. The "Test Scoring Machine" developed by The International Business Machines Corporation (IBM) is widely used in city school systems and universities and has proved highly satisfactory. Answers are recorded on special answer sheets, such as the section of a typical sheet shown on this page. The student marks his answer with a special soft lead pencil. When the answer sheet is placed in the machine, a dial electrically operated gives the total correct score. Thus an answer sheet can be scored in only a few seconds. The machine can be set to secure a summary of responses on each test

[22] Published by Gryphon Press, Highland Park, N. J. (Fourth Yearbook, 1953).

item, thereby facilitating a limited type of diagnosis. A number of test publishers supply this type of scoring service for schools using tests they distribute.

The improvement of new-type objective examinations. The use of the new-type objective examination has spread rapidly in our schools. Its use enables the teacher to sample a much larger area of subject matter than was possible by the essay-type test. Furthermore, it is possible quickly to derive a quantitative score on these new-type tests. These teacher-prepared tests should meet criteria similar to those which standards tests must meet: primarily validity, reliability, and objectivity. In recent years, local workshops and testing centers in universities have assisted teachers greatly to improve testing procedures related to the curriculums of particular schools and school systems. This work has disseminated rapidly among teachers knowledge of the principles that underlie the construction of improved objective types of informal examinations.

The following books should be consulted for information about procedures to follow and cautions to bear in mind in the construction of these types of tests as well as their values and limitations:

SMITH, E. R., and TYLER, R. W., *Appraising and Recording Pupil Progress* (New York, Harper, 1942).

REMMERS, H. H., and GAGE, N. L., *Educational Measurement and Evaluation* (New York, Harper, 1943).

GREENE, H. A., JORGENSEN, A. N., and GERBERICH, J. R., *Measurement and Evaluation in the Elementary School,* 2nd ed. (New York, Longmans, 1953).

———, *Measurement and Evaluation in the Secondary School,* rev. ed. (New York, Longmans, 1954).

WEITZMAN, Ellis, and McNAMARA, W. J., *Constructing Classroom Examinations* (Chicago, Science Research Associates, 1949).

For a detailed discussion of the advantages and disadvantages in the use of the various kinds of objective test items, such as multiple choice, alternate choice, matching,

and completion exercises, the reader is referred to the article on "Achievement Tests" by Cook in the *Encyclopedia of Educational Research* and the volume by Ross, *Measurement in Education,* Chapter 3.

Tests of motor skills. Included in this category are tests of such motor skills as handwriting, manipulation of mechanical devices, skills in sports, and motor co-ordination. Scott and French give detailed information in their book, *Evaluation in Physical Education,*[23] about a wide variety of procedures for appraising skills in sport, physical fitness, general motor ability, and knowledge. Rating scales, incidence charts, achievement progressions and illustrative tests of knowledge related to physical development are also included.

Limitations of the technique of objective measurement. The following list [24] of what are regarded as "important limitations" of the use of techniques of objective measurements was given by Traxler and his associates:

1. There are important aspects of human behavior as well as important instructional objectives which cannot be evaluated effectively by objective tests available at the present time.

2. Test results are influenced significantly by factors such as motivation, physical condition, and emotional tone, which are often inadequately controlled in the test situation.

3. One is frequently misled by operation of unrecognized factors in testing, e.g., the reading comprehension factor in arithmetic problem-solving tests, the rate-of-perception factor in closely timed tests, or the general-intelligence factor in achievement testing.

4. Tests must be employed within the limits of the accuracy and consistency with which they measure whatever they are supposed to measure. No test is perfectly reliable, and practically all tests compromise with regard to validity.

5. In the main, objective tests are used to

---

[23] Published by C. V. Mosby Co., St. Louis, Mo., 1950.

[24] Arthur E. Traxler and associates, *Introduction to Testing and the Use of Test Results in Public Schools* (New York, Harper, 1953), pp. 11-12.

describe performance in terms of comparisons with other individuals. This fact may discourage consideration of the pupil within the framework of his own individual capacities, limitations, and goals. As yet, we do not seem to have adequate statistical techniques for describing test performance in terms of individual maturation units.

6. Objective testing is criticized frequently as being atomistic—that is, as approaching an understanding of the child by searching for bits or parts of behavior which are put together to produce a "whole" personality. In at least partial support of this criticism, it must be recognized that human behavior in many situations is meaningful and understandable only in terms of the total personality in a total situation.

7. Closely related to the limitation just given is that of overemphasis on objectivity, which the device claims as its chief advantage. Individual judgment cannot be ruled out of the appraisal process. Even after "facts" are obtained by objective means, there remains the task of fitting them together. This involves judgment, intuition, and discrimination, processes which are *subjective* more often than *objective*.

8. A test score represents a sort of spot check indicating the individual's status with regard to a particular quality or capacity at a given point in his growth cycle. Since individuals vary with respect both to rate and to ceiling of growth, it is necessary to apply frequent comparable checks in order to obtain an adequate understanding of the individual. One should be very cautious in generalizing on the basis of a single test result.

The following sources give valuable information about the preparation, uses, values, and limitations of a wide variety of psychological and achievement tests:

FREEMAN, F. S., *Theory and Practice of Psychological Testing* (New York, Holt, 1950).
JOHNSON, Wendell, *Speech Problems of Children* (New York, Grune and Stratton, Inc., 1950).
JORDAN, A. M., *Measurement in Education* (New York, McGraw, 1953).
LINDQUIST, E. F., ed., *Educational Measurement* (Washington, American Council on Education, 1951).
MICHEELS, W. J., and BARNES, M. R., *Measuring Educational Achievement* (New York, McGraw, 1956).

The Measurement of Understanding, Forty-fifth Yearbook, Part 1, National Society for the Study of Education (Chicago, Univ. of Chicago Press, 1946).
REMMERS, H. H., and GAGE, N. L., *Educational Measurement and Evaluation* (New York, Harper, 1943).
ROSS, C. C., *Measurement in Today's Schools* (New York, Prentice-Hall, 1947).
TRAXLER, Arthur E., and associates, *Introduction to Testing and the Use of Test Results in Public Schools* (New York, Harper, 1953).

The use and improvement of the essay examination. Essay-type examinations have for many years been subject to severe criticism. The two major limitations discussed have been the subjectivity of scoring, resulting in the unreliability of marks, and the limited sampling of the important areas of subject matter being tested. The recognized values of essay examinations for such purposes as measuring higher mental abilities, such as the ability to organize materials or to interpret and criticize discussions, have led to widespread efforts to devise means of overcoming their limitations. Most of the resulting recommendations have to do with the selection of test content, the framing of test items, and the method of scoring the test papers. The following statement lists three steps that may be taken to improve teacher-made examinations of the essay type:[25]

1. The exact purpose of the examination must be understood by both the teacher and the pupil. The emphasis of the essay examination should be definitely on thought, reasoning, and other types of mental activity as applied to the materials of the course. The main concern is with topics which involve interest-centers or relationships and problematical issues. Questions involving judgments, synthesis, and generalizations are admittedly difficult to evaluate, but they show aspects of pupil mastery and mind-quality probably not revealed otherwise.

2. The content of the examination should be governed by its purpose. In general, a test should parallel the objectives and pupil out-

[25] H. A. Greene, A. N. Jorgensen, and J. R. Gerberich, *Measurement and Evaluation in the Elementary School* (New York, Longmans, 1942), pp. 146-148.

comes of the course. This means that there should be a proper balance of test content not only with respect to the subject matter but also with respect to the types of abilities to use and apply informations which are desired pupil outcomes. Essay-type questions have been generally open to the criticism that they are hastily and carelessly prepared. The advocates of the improved essay examination are quite positive in their insistence that the preparation and selection of suitable essay-type questions should consume at least as much time as is required to score the answers. If this is done, the value and the accuracy of the scores obtained are almost certain to be increased.

3. Definite rules should be formulated which will as far as possible control the irrelevant factors in scoring the papers. The careful use of scoring rules will bring about a definite decrease in the inaccuracy of the pupil scores.

Weitzman and McNamara [26] suggest the following plan for increasing the accuracy of scoring or rating written examinations:

1. Prepare a written key. Under each question on the key, write down the correct answer. This answer will include one or more specific parts.

2. Assign the number of score points to be given to each answer as a whole, and to each part of that answer.

3. While scoring test copies, refer often to the key. When in doubt as to whether an answer is correct, always consult the key.

4. Score all test copies on the first question. Then score them all on the second question, and so on. This procedure is more nearly accurate than scoring all the questions on one test copy consecutively.

5. On each test copy, add the score points given to all answers. This of course gives the total score. Check each addition.

6. Subtract from the total score any point deductions made for errors in spelling, punctuation, language usage, and the like—if these are to be penalized. This subtraction gives the net total score—the score usually employed in assigning grades.

With reference to penalties for spelling errors and the like, the kinds and sizes of these penalties should depend upon what the test is supposed to measure. For example, errors in spelling, capitalization, punctuation, and language usage would be penalized more heavily in an English test than in a social studies or a science test.

The evaluation of products and performances. The achievement of numerous educational objectives is expressed by means of a *product,* a direct indication of the ability of the pupil to apply information, skill, and understanding. Such products may well include specimens of handwriting, composition, and objects produced in classes in industrial arts and home economics. They may range in variety from musical compositions to tangible objects made of wood and metals. In connection with the evaluation of the product, a rating of the procedures used in effecting the product is often as important as judging the product.

Products may be evaluated either in terms of their "general merit," as, for example, specimens of handwriting, or in terms of their component features or desirable characteristics, a method in which various aspects of the product are evaluated separately. Devices of the first type are either *rating scales* or *quality scales*. The Thorndike Handwriting Scale, a device for rating the general merit of penmanship, for example, contains fifteen samples, each of which defines a quantitative value for rating general merit along a range from best to poorest. Similar scales are available for composition, art work, freehand lettering, and other kinds of products. Devices of the second type contain an analysis of the product into specific features, for each of which there are found in the best instruments descriptions of various levels of quality that aid in scoring each feature. In some instances the rating device is the product of extensive statistical investigation and analysis, whereas in others the evaluative criteria are simply derived and descriptively stated.

The evaluation of a performance or procedure is a difficult undertaking because it becomes necessary to evaluate a continuing changing process consisting of many different specific actions and aspects. One impor-

[26]Ellis Weitzman and W. J. McNamara, *Constructing Classroom Examinations* (Chicago, Science Research Associates, 1949), pp. 71-72.

tant development in this direction is the check-list developed by Tyler which is used to describe student reactions in finding an object under a microscope.[27] It consists of a list of specific activities which aids the observer to compile an objective record of the performance of an individual student on an assigned task. The analysis of the data reveals strengths and weaknesses in the steps taken by the student and affords an excellent basis of a subsequent discussion of his methods of work. Check-lists of a similar kind can be used to evaluate other kinds of performances, such as kicking a football, giving a lecture or talk, taking part in a play, or performing an experiment.

The evaluation of creative products is by all odds the most difficult of evaluation tasks. Burton lists the following reasons for the difficulty:[28]

1. Standards of taste cannot be routinized.
2. Confusion arises easily between judgments of content and judgments of form.
3. Undue analysis easily kills the creative spirit, especially with young pupils and with older ones who are beginners.
4. Individual differences may be as important here as standards.
5. Careless negative judgments have a greater detrimental effect here than in most fields.

In spite of these and other difficulties the careful evaluation of creative work must be undertaken. A helpful approach is suggested by the analysis of achievements in writing, fine or applied arts, music, research, contributions to group discussion and decisions in terms of the following characteristics and levels of "creativeness and imagination":[29]

General: Approaches whatever he does with active imagination and originality, so that he contributes something that is his own.
Specific: Makes a distinctly original and significant contribution in one or more fields.
Promising: Shows a degree of creativeness that indicates the likelihood of valuable original contributions in some field, although the contributions already made have not proved to be particularly significant.

Limited: Shows the desire to contribute his own thinking and expression to situations, but his degree of imagination and originality is not in general high enough to have much influence on his accomplishments.
Imitative: Makes little or no creative contributions, yet shows sufficient imagination to see the implications in the creation of others and to make use of their ideas or accomplishments.
Unimaginative: Has given practically no evidence of originality or creativeness of imagination or action.

Ratings in terms of these levels are admittedly subjective but they are likely to assist in the evaluation of creative products. Specialized instruments are available for several areas. Composition scales, for example, often include such criteria as originality or content, freshness of approach, originality of treatment, and facility of expression. Scales for evaluating products of work in sewing, art, cooking, and mechanical drawing have been developed in a number of places; but they have not proven very satisfactory as yet. Experimentation is still going on.

The use of problem-situation tests. The problem-situation test is an excellent means of evaluating such outcomes of learning as methods of response when faced with a difficulty, ability to apply principles in new situations, and critical thinking. A direct test involves the study of the learner's performance in some concrete situations in which he is faced with a problem to be solved. He may be asked, for example, to demonstrate his understanding of the meaning of the concept *area* by finding the area of the surface of a table or some other plane. In this case the items that may be considered in evaluating his performance include among others the following:

[27] R. W. Tyler, "A Test of Skill in Using a Microscope," *Constructing Achievement Tests,* p. 39.

[28] William H. Burton, *The Guidance of Learning Activities,* 2nd ed. (New York, Appleton-Century-Crofts, 1952), pp. 620-621.

[29] Smith, Tyler, and staff, *op. cit.,* p. 478.

1. Method of attack on the problem.
2. Skill in the use of measuring devices needed.
3. Kinds of errors made in securing needed information.
4. Correctness of computations necessary.

In another form, the problem-situation test includes paragraphs which state separate problems. The objective-test form asks, "What should be done?" The pupil is required to select from a number of solutions the one he regards as correct for each of the problems. The pupil may also be asked to write a statement of his solution as an essay examination. The test can be effectively extended by asking the pupil to indicate which of possible reasons listed support his conclusion. The results may be analyzed to show:

1. Ability of the pupil to make correct decisions and to select correct reasons.
2. The nature of the conclusions drawn or reasons selected as a basis of discovering faulty concepts and misunderstandings.
3. The types of incorrect reasons selected, such as those irrelevant to the problem or technically false, or those based on authority practice of false knowledge.
4. The number of reasons inconsistent with the conclusions drawn.

The use of behavior records as a basis of evaluation. Many aspects of learning and behavior do not lend themselves effectively to objective measurement by means of paper-and-pencil techniques. They can be more satisfactorily analyzed by observation of the pupil's behavior in controlled situations or in life activities both in and out of school. In order to discover whether or not a student knows how to locate information in the library, for example, a useful plan is to give him an assignment and then to note the procedures he uses in carrying out the task. Similar procedures of a problem-solving kind can be used in many other ways: in the laboratory, in the shop, on the athletic field, and in carrying on the activities in some class or individual project.

Less formal procedures can also be used in studying through observation of the char-

acteristics of the learner. The correctness of his speech, its precision and quality, can best be determined by noting his responses in normal group activities, during recitations, and in conferences. His abilities in art, music, science, dramatics, and athletics are probably best appraised by observing his behavior in circumstances where these abilities find normal expression rather than through paper-and-pencil tests. The performance and product can both be studied. There is always present, of course, the problem of standards for evaluating the information secured. To assist in this appraisal there are available check-lists of various kinds, rating scales, sets of criteria of fairly objective types, and other methods of increasing the dependability of the ratings given. In the absence of a standardized procedure, the teacher should not hesitate to make use of some original plan that will assist in the evaluation of performance or product.

The use of the camera, dictaphone, tape recorder, and similar mechanical devices makes it possible to preserve a permanent record of behavior or product which can be considered again and again in making an appraisal. Such records also make it easier to determine progress made from time to time by direct comparisons of performance or product. Stenographic records of conversations and discussions also are valuable for some kinds of appraisal. Other more specific clinical procedures, such as psychiatric interviews, and projective techniques, also are based to a large extent on the results of observations of behavior. These devices will be discussed fully in the chapter on methods of studying the product to determine reasons for inefficiencies and unfavorable growth.

The anecdotal behavior record and the diary. Paper-and-pencil tests, rating devices, and performance tests are inadequate means of evaluating such items as social and emotional adjustment, social interests, and level of social awareness. A more direct observational approach known as the "anecdotal behavior record" has been developed as a means of gathering facts about pupil behavior that can form the basis of evaluative judgments of his characteristics. Anecdotes are reports of what a pupil does or says in social situations both in and out of school that may be of value in making an appraisal of his behavior. The incidents that are reported may be instances of desirable behavior or of undesirable conduct. The general trend of the reports for any individual indicates the ways in which the pupil is adjusting himself and of the ways in which he is contributing to the welfare of his group. Changes in the amount and nature of the reports provide a roughly quantitative measure of the direction and extent of his development. Information of this kind gathered by teachers and other competent observers is of great value in guidance programs.

Traxler has presented the general procedure for setting up a system of anecdotal records in the following six steps:[30]

1. Enlisting the co-operation of the group.
2. Deciding how much should be expected of observers, the kinds of information to be gathered, and the consideration of possible methods to be used.
3. Preparing forms for reporting anecdotes.
4. Obtaining original records of behavior.
5. Filing reports in some central location.
6. Summarizing and interpreting the records being compiled.

To facilitate the preparation of reports of anecdotes, Jarvie and Ellingson[31] recommend such procedures as (1) providing centrally located dictaphones for use by teachers, (2) assigning secretaries to teachers at specified times to take down anecdotes and to transcribe them for the central file, (3) organizing weekly discussion groups to present instances of behavior for consideration by the staff. Periodic summaries should be made of all anecdotes reported for individuals and for the school as a whole. Those for individuals should be specific and diagnostic, whereas those for the school can be in general terms so that any important trends in their nature can be discovered. The infor-

mation thus gathered may well lead to the development of rating scales consisting of lists of descriptive categories which describe various levels of quality and desirability in such traits as responsibility-dependability, creativeness and imagination, open-mindedness, and seriousness of purpose.

The diary is a form of record for keeping a running account of activities by an individual or a class over a period of time. The data gathered by this method supply concrete evidence about behavior which is of value in making judgments similar to those made on the basis of anecdotes and incidents. Ordinarily, a diary or log is kept by some individual for personal reasons; a record of this kind, however, kept by some person as a description of the activities of others makes it possible to get a vivid picture of their behavior and reactions. The analysis of the data gathered for specific reasons and purposes set up in advance provides valuable information needed for appraisal.

The interview or questionnaire as used in evaluation. There are many facts about the characteristics of the individual, his interests, his activities,[32] and his behavior that can be effectively gathered by means of questions directed at the individual. In many cases others—parents, associates, and teachers—can also supply needed information. When this approach is used, every precaution must be taken to secure dependable reliable data. Such information as the following has been successfully secured by means of questionnaires, inventories, interviews, and personal reports:

[30] Arthur E. Traxler, *The Nature and Use of Anecdotal Records* (New York, Educational Records Bureau, 1939), p. 42.

[31] L. L. Jarvie and Mark Ellingson, *A Handbook on the Anecdotal Behavior Journal* (Chicago, Univ. of Chicago Press, 1940).

[32] W. Linwood Chase, "Subject Preference of Fifth-Grade Children," *Elementary School Journal* (December, 1949), pp. 204-211.

Frederick L. Pond, "A Simplified Method of Scoring an Inventory of Reading Experiences," *Journal of Educational Research* (April, 1942), pp. 585-597.

1. Books, magazines, newspapers, etc., read.
2. Radio programs listened to.
3. Movies, concerts, shows, meetings attended.
4. Kinds of writing and speech activities in life outside the school.
5. Participation in community and school projects and enterprises.
6. Hobbies.
7. Work experiences, money earned.
8. Things produced, as in gardens, shops, etc.
9. Home activities.
10. Problems and difficulties encountered.
11. Observed behavior reported by associates and others.
12. Group data supplied by civic, social, and welfare agencies.
13. Expressions of attitudes, interests, and opinions.

Certain principles should be borne in mind in preparing a questionnaire or inventory form. The questions should be clearly stated so that there will be no doubt about their meaning. It is often desirable to include check-questions, so that there will be a check on matters about which it is desired to secure accurate information. No hint should be given as to answers that would be regarded as acceptable, nor should there be anything that will color the responses in any way. Short, direct, specific questions are preferred. Interest, ease of answering, and willingness to answer are important factors to be considered in constructing the questionnaire and selecting persons to whom it is to be directed. Ordinarily, it is desirable to try out the form on some competent individuals and then to revise it in the light of suggestions made. The more objective the data called for and the more the information called for is within the responding individual's first-hand experience, the more dependable are the results of the investigation. Questionnaires are useful but easily misused.

An illustration of a procedure used to study pupil participation in school activities is the series of questions given below. The interpretation of the results of the question-

naire is fully explained in the reference given below.[33]

1. What kinds of things do you like to do with other students?
2. Would you like to have a club to do these things?
3. Do you belong to a club or activity group in school?
4. If YES, which clubs or activities? (Name)
   If NO, why have you not joined?
5. Do you belong to a club or group outside of school?
6. If so, which? (Name)
7. Which of the clubs or activities do you most enjoy?
   a. In school (List and say why):
   b. Outside of school (List and say why):
8. In what way has belonging to your club made a difference to you?
9. To which other clubs or activities would you most like to belong that you don't belong to now? List:
10. How does a student get to be important in student activities in this school?
11. Who do you think is the most popular student in this school? Why is this student important?
12. Do you belong to any *unorganized* crowd that gets together at school, more or less regularly?
13. Do you belong to any unorganized crowd that gets together outside of school, more or less regularly?

The use of sociometric procedures. Sociometric procedures are a valuable means for studying intergroup and interpersonal relationships and the existing social-emotional climate within a classroom. The climate in a classroom undoubtedly has some relationship to the degree of acceptance or rejection of each other by the children and of each other's needs and goals. The social-emotional atmosphere of the classroom has a direct bearing on the development of personality and on learning. In many classrooms some

[33] Hilda Taba and associates, *Diagnosing Human Relations Needs* (Washington, American Council on Education, 1951), pp. 149-150. This reference also contains numerous other devices for studying human relations, including sociometric procedures.

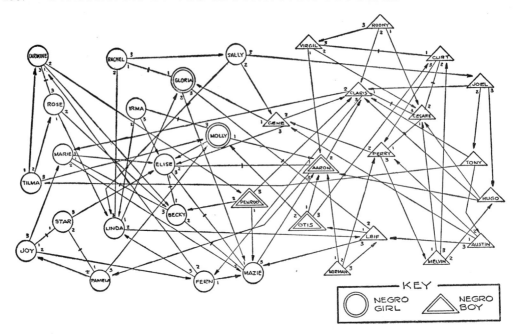

SOCIOGRAM OF A SIXTH-GRADE CLASS

From Helen H. Jennings, *Sociometry in Group Relations*, p. 78. Reproduced by permission of the publisher, American Council on Education.

children are happy and secure, whereas others are rejected by the group and hence are frustrated in their efforts to participate in the social life of the group. Information as to the intergroup relations and the emotional climate is of great value to the teacher in guiding the learning activities of a class as a whole and of individual pupils or groups of pupils.

Sociometric procedures are especially helpful in locating the leaders in a class and in finding isolated, unpopular children who have feelings of insecurity and lack of belongingness to the group. The simplest technique to use to study intergroup relations is to have the pupils answer questions such as the following to secure essential information:

1. Write the names of the three children in the class who you think are your best friends.
   a. _____ b. _____ c. _____

2. Write the names of the two children in this class with whom you play most often at school.
   a. _____ b. _____

3. What child in the class would you most like to have work with you on a committee? _____
   Why?

4. Write the names of the two children who you think contribute most to the good of the class.
   a. _____ b. _____

A sociogram such as the one shown on this page summarizes graphically the data gathered by means of a sociometric technique. It presents in visual form the social structure of a small sixth-grade class as shown by the number of times each pupil was chosen by the individual members of the class as "one of my two best friends." A teacher who has information of this kind secured by sociometric techniques can guide the learning experiences of the individuals and groups in the class much more intelligently than when such information is lacking; for example, in organizing groups and in interpreting the behavior reactions among the children in the class.

Some instruments in this category, such

as the Ohio Social Acceptance Scale—Advanced Series, provide each child with the names of his classmates and ask him to rate each on some trait according to a simple code. The Ohio Code in abbreviated form is:

1. "Very, very best friends"
2. "Good friends"
3. "Not friends but okay"
4. "Don't know them"
5. "Not okay"

By studying the result of such ratings, the teacher can discover the leaders and the isolates, the most popular and the least popular children, and the existence of cliques. On the basis of the data, the teacher can obtain a social-status rating for each child. These scores help the teacher in grouping children, in planning socializing experiences for isolates, in forming committees, and in making other arrangements for improving social relationships. This information is of such a personal nature that most teachers keep it to themselves and do not discuss it with the children directly, especially its negative aspects in so far as individuals are concerned except as a basis for guidance in certain cases.

Bogardus [34] has invented a device called "A Social Distance Scale" to determine the degree to which an individual is accepted or rejected by the group, and also to what degree he accepts or rejects the group. The volume by Cunningham [35] and associates discusses and illustrates other sociometric instruments, including (1) check sheets for opportunities in human relations, (2) check sheet for describing people, (3) "Things to Improve about Myself," (4) "Letters to the Teacher," (5) social analysis in the classroom, (6) "The Wishing Well," and (7) guides for group observation.

An excellent statement by Lee and Lee summarizes the kinds of information about children's relationships that have been secured by sociometric procedures and indicates the caution with which interpretations of data must be made: [36]

There is so much more to be learned about children's relationships that really the surface has only been scratched so far. However there are a few things we do know. We know that the children in the top eighth of the class in popularity when compared with the bottom one-eighth "proved definitely to be more extroverted, to have a higher sense of personal worth, a stronger feeling of belonging, to express more acceptable social standards, to possess superior school relations, and to be more attractive in facial appearance." Whether popularity caused these various factors or was caused by them, there is no objective evidence. Even attractive facial appearance is greatly influenced by the child's attitudes and feelings. A sullen, rebellious face is never as attractive as a happy eager one. It is most probable that popularity and these other factors all develop along together, each influencing the others.

In studying the social acceptance of children they have found that neither race, color, high social position, intelligence, nor achievement necessarily determine acceptability. There is a positive relationship between social acceptance and personal ability in intelligence and achievement, but it is not high. There is a desire on the part of most children for friendship with leaders. This was shown in the sociogram on page 98, where the isolates chose "stars" or near stars.

Pupils choose different children for different purposes. When they were asked to designate the one they had most fun with and a work mate there was little relation between these two choices. High IQ and scholastic proficiency by themselves have not proved to be sufficient qualities for acceptance as workmates.

Children recognize ability to do things and tend to enter into social relationships with the child who possesses and demonstrates such ability.

In general, the more social relationships a child has the happier he is. There is some indication that in general the brighter the child, the more social relationships he has, although other factors are more important.

[34] E. S. Bogardus, "A Social Distance Scale," *Sociology and Social Research* (January-February, 1933), pp. 265-271.
[35] Ruth Cunningham and associates, *Understanding Group Behavior of Boys and Girls* (New York, Teachers College, Bureau of Publications, Columbia Univ., 1951).
[36] J. Murray Lee and Dorris M. Lee, *The Child and His Curriculum,* 2nd ed. (New York, Appleton-Century-Crofts, 1950), pp. 102-103.

A very important fact is that the earlier the attempt is made to improve relationships the better are the chances for satisfying and lasting results. In fact, if such relationships haven't been pretty well established by the end of the sixth grade, the chances are very much less that they will be. It is also quite certain that the child will not be able to do it without specific, direct, and understanding help.

The use of projective and expressive procedures. Projective techniques enable the examiner to study the total dynamic personality of an individual or group. At present, because of their highly technical nature, the use of standard projective techniques should be undertaken only by persons who have had the specialized training necessary to use them correctly, such as psychologists and clinicians.

The projective method of studying a child involves presenting him with what may be called a stimulus situation with which he is unfamiliar, such as a word or sentence, a story, a picture, or a problem. He is asked to make an oral or written response to the situation. The examiner observes his responses and behavior closely for clues which reveal his private meanings, values, and feelings.

The two most widely used projective techniques for which standards are available are probably the Rorschach Ink Blot Test [37] and the Murray Thematic Apperception Test (TAT).[38] In the former, the child is asked to respond to each of a series of ink blots and his responses are compared to those of other people who have been categorized into personality patterns. In the Murray Thematic Apperception Test, his responses to a series of pictures are similarly evaluated. Any psychological test may be regarded as projective when the examiner is not concerned with the rating of specific answers to test items but rather with the behavioral patterns which reveal the child's personality structure. Thus in a play situation the child may unconsciously reveal his attitude toward some individual with whom he has been closely associated, such as his attitude toward a father whom he fears.

Simpler forms of projective techniques which a teacher can more easily analyze are:

1. Autobiographies, diaries, logs.
2. Free compositions about experiences, reasons for liking something.
3. Expressions of likes and dislikes.
4. Analysis of reactions to some story, person, or description of a problem.
5. Dramatic play and role playing.
6. Fantasy and other forms of free expression.

As a result of extensive study, psychologists have concluded that creative expression with such instructional materials as clay, dough, and finger paints offers excellent opportunities for evaluating personality traits. However, the process of interpreting the creative products of pupils is very difficult and intricate, and should be undertaken only by competent psychiatrists and clinicians.

The references below contain a wealth of information on sociometric and projective procedures:

ANDERSON, H. H., and ANDERSON, Gladys, *An Introduction to Projective Techniques* (New York, Prentice-Hall, 1951).

BONNEY, Merl E., and POWELL, Johnny, "Differences in Social Behavior between Sociometrically High and Sociometrically Low Children," *Journal of Educational Research* (March, 1953).

BURTON, William H., *Guidance of Learning Activities,* 2nd ed. (New York, Appleton-Century-Crofts, 1952). Chs. 8 and 10 deal with human relations.

CUNNINGHAM, Ruth, and associates, *Understanding Group Behavior of Boys and Girls* (New York, Teachers College, Bureau of Publications, Columbia Univ., 1951).

DAVIS, Allison, *Social-Class Influences upon Learning* (Cambridge, Harvard Univ. Press, 1948).

[37] Bruno Klopfer and W. M. Kelly, *The Rorschach Technique* (Yonkers, World Book, 1942).

[38] H. A. Murray, *Manual for the Thematic Apperception Test* (Cambridge, Harvard Univ. Press, 1943).
See also the articles by Symonds and associates in *Review of Educational Research* (February, 1944), pp. 81-98, and (February, 1947), pp. 78-100, for recent developments in the study and use of projective techniques.

How to Construct a Sociogram (New York, Horace Mann-Lincoln Institute of School Experimentation, Teachers College, Columbia Univ., 1947).

JENNINGS, Helen H., *Sociometry in Group Relations* (Washington, American Council on Education, 1948).

TABA, Hilda, *A Sociometric Work Guide for Teachers* (Washington, American Council on Education, 1947).

WITHALL, John, "The Development of a Technique for the Measurement of the Social-Emotional Climate in Classrooms," *Journal of Experimental Education* (March, 1949).

Section 5

USING THE VARIOUS PROCEDURES FOR APPRAISING THE EDUCATIONAL PRODUCT

Pupil attainments and behavior as a basis of appraisal. As has been indicated, the effectiveness and quality of an educational program can be appraised best by determining the extent to which accepted educational goals and objectives are being achieved. This can be accomplished by analyzing the attainments and characteristics of the learner at successive stages of development so that changes in behavior indicating growth can be discovered. These attainments and characteristics to be considered in this section can be quite conveniently grouped under four classifications:

1. Educational achievement, including the knowledge and information the pupil has acquired, his skill in the use of the tools of learning, and his ability to use in his daily life the contributions of the curriculum.

2. Character and personality traits, including items personal in nature, such as interests, attitudes, appreciations, self-control, social and emotional adjustment, and morals.

3. Societal aspects of behavior, including those types of conduct essential to effective group living in an evolving industrial democratic society, such as the ability and readiness to participate in the co-operative study and solution of problems faced by self and community, qualities of leadership, creativity in action, and social sensitivity.

4. Physical and mental development, including such items as physical growth, physical and mental health, physical defects, and athletic skills.

The principle that underlies the use of evaluations of pupil growth toward desired goals as the basis for the appraisal of educational programs is that the higher the level of achievement of educational outcomes, the better the program must be. This principle also applies to the appraisal of educational instrumentalities, such as the curriculum, instructional methods, and aids to learning. However, because of the complexity of the elements involved in any situation, it is difficult to isolate the effects of any single instrumentality. Anyone who is familiar with current literature on research methods realizes the precautions that must be taken in trying to establish experimentally the relationships among the factors involved. Consequently, in any situation in which prompt action is necessary, practical judgments [39] must be made in the light of experience and with an awareness of the available findings, if any, of educational science. Hence conclusions should not be hastily drawn and action should proceed on a tentative basis. The value of viewing the learning situation as an integrated whole rather than as a group of specific elements is self-evident.

The following pages will present selected examples of procedures and devices suitable for the evaluation of outcomes in each of these four areas and will also give references to further illustrations.

The approach to evaluation. The planning of the evaluation program can be approached from the point of view of an entire

[39] Stephen M. Corey, *Action Research to Improve School Practices* (New York, Teachers College, Bureau of Publications, Columbia Univ., 1953).

school system, of the staff of a single school, of the teachers of particular classrooms, or of an individual pupil. The leadership of a school system is concerned with the assembling of essential data about the educational product of all schools in the community so that intelligent judgments can be made by the staff about the progress that is being made from year to year in the various curriculum areas and thus to locate points of strength in the educational program and points where measures should be taken to bring about improvement. The administrative and supervisory staff of a modern school system should seek to make available to the staffs of the various schools the means for gathering necessary information about the pupils so that instruction may be more effectively adapted to their needs and abilities. In many larger cities, the selection of evaluation procedures by specialists is made in co-operation with representatives of the various schools and sometimes parent groups. Expert consultants on evaluation are available to supply technical advice as the need arises. Emphasis is placed by the central staff on long-range plans of evaluation rather than on programs to be applied immediately in a given school or classroom.

In a particular school, the staff is concerned not only with the execution of long-range programs of evaluation set up by the system as a whole but also with the development of an evaluation program that is adapted to conditions that exist locally. A long-range program should give continuous, comparable, and comprehensive information about every child's growth and development. In many elementary schools a balanced program of testing such as the following is undertaken:

1. Intelligence tests: group tests three times; individual tests as need arises.
2. Health examinations: each year and as the need arises.
3. Basic skills.
   a. Reading and arithmetic readiness.
   b. A battery of standard achievement tests in at least reading, language arts, arithmetic: three times.
   c. Study skills: one or two times.
4. Personality tests: two times.

A minimum testing program for secondary schools should incorporate tests that are necessary for educational and vocational guidance. The following testing procedures are recommended:

1. A general intelligence test—grade 9.
2. Achievement tests in the language arts and arithmetic that have diagnostic value —prior to entrance to grade 9 and at end of grade 11.
3. Vocational—interest inventory—grade 9.
4. Tests of special aptitude in mathematics, art, music, and mechanical skills—as the occasion may warrant.
5. Personality test—grade 10.
6. A test of general educational development administered at the time of leaving school.

In addition to the basic testing program outlined above, the staff of a school frequently will find it necessary to administer other tests to secure additional information needed in dealing with some problem. Informal evaluations also must be used continuously as a part of the appraisal program of any well-managed school, for instance, the collection of such evidences of growth of pupils as art products, written work, participation of children in the activities of the school, and records of conduct. (See Section 4 of this chapter.) The co-operation of professional and nonprofessional members of the staff, parents, and children in the selection of evaluative procedures is essential if the program is to succeed. The specialist in evaluation and consultants in the various curriculum areas can make many valuable contributions to the planning of such a program.

The testing program of a university high school (see pp. 255-256) illustrates the kinds of tests that are useful and the time intervals at which they are given.

UNIVERSITY OF MINNESOTA UNIVERSITY HIGH SCHOOL TESTING PROGRAM

The following is the schedule of tests which were given to the students in a recent year.

I. *Grade 7*
   - A. Achievement: Iowa Basic Skills Tests. Gates Reading Survey-Speed Test Section.
   - B. Intelligence: Otis Self-Administering Tests of Mental Ability, Intermediate Form. Stanford Binet Form L.
   - C. Personality: Science Research Associates Youth Inventory-Junior High School Form.
   - D. Interest: Kuder Preference Record-Vocational.

II. *Grade 8*

   Same as for grade 7, except intelligence testing for new students only.

III. *Grade 9*
   - A. Achievement: Iowa Tests of Educational Development. Gates Reading Survey-Speed Test Section.
   - B. Intelligence: Terman McNemar Test of Mental Ability-Form C. Stanford Binet Form L for all new students.
   - C. Personality: As in I-C above.
   - D. Interest: Strong Vocational Interest Inventory.

IV. *Grade 10*
   - A. Achievement: Iowa Tests of Educational Development.
   - B. Intelligence: Terman McNemar Test of Mental Ability Form C—for new students only.
   - C. Personality: Science Research Associates Youth Inventory-Senior High School Form.
   - D. Interest: As in III-D above.

V. *Grade 11*
   - A. Achievement: As in IV-A above.
   - B. Intelligence: Co-op English Test (college placement). English Theme (college placement). Ohio Psychological Examination (selectively). American Council on Education Psychological Exam, High School Form (college placement). Wechsler Intelligence Test, Adult Form, for new students and those not previously tested.
   - C. Interest: As in III-D above.
   - D. Personality: Minnesota Multiphasic, Rorschach Ink Blot Test, TAT (selectively administered).

VI. *Grade 12*
   - A. Achievement: As in IV-A above.
   - B. Intelligence: Wechsler Intelligence Test, Adult Form for those students not previously tested.
   - C. Personality: Science Research Associates Youth Inventory-Senior High School Form. Minnesota Multiphasic Test of Personality, Rorschach Ink Blot Test, TAT (selectively administered).

APPROXIMATE DATES FOR ADMINISTERING THE VARIOUS TESTS

First quarter

Sept. 10-11	Otis, Terman, Gates Reading Survey (grades 7-9).
Sept. 29-Oct. 2,	Iowa Test of Basic Skills and Educational Development (all grades).
Oct. 19-23,	Stanford Binet (grades 7-9).
Nov. 23-Dec. 4	Wechsler (grades 10-12).
Month of Oct.	Kuder Preference (grades 7-8).
Month of Nov.	SRA Youth Inventory (grades 7-12).

Winter quarter

Week of Jan. 11	Strong (grades 9-12). ACE. Co-op English. English Theme (grade 11).
Jan. 18-29,	Stanford Binet (grades 7-9).
Feb. 23-Mar. 5	Wechsler (grades 10-12).

Spring quarter

April 12-23	Stanford Binet (grades 7-9).
May 17-27	Wechsler (grades 10-12).

The Personnel Department does not select or administer standardized tests for classroom use in the subject-matter fields. Assistance will be given in the selection of such tests and it is highly desirable that results obtained be forwarded to the Personnel Department to be included in the folders of the individual students concerned.

The teacher in the classroom faces the problem of making effective use of the basic data that are gathered systematically through the long-range testing program so that the learning experiences of individual children will be adapted as fully as is possible to their needs and to their readiness and ability to learn. The long-range testing program is concerned with the general status of achievements and their trend over a period of years. It is necessary that standard survey tests be supplemented by diagnostic tests that are so constructed as to locate and identify in the course of classroom instruction specific deficiencies in the various curriculum areas. In cases of extreme disability, the competent teacher must be able to apply more penetrating analytical procedures, clinical in character, to determine the nature and the underlying causes of the disabilities. The teacher then must be able to take steps to make necessary adjustments of instruction to remedy the condition. These diagnostic procedures will be discussed in detail in Chapter 10. Throughout this diagnostic program, the supervisor must be prepared to assist the teacher to use the procedures that are to be applied.

Continuous evaluation by less formal methods is also an integral part of any well-managed classroom. The children should learn to evaluate their own work and their behavior in social situations both in and out of school. Many teachers have devised methods of helping children to diagnose their learning difficulties in the basic skills by means of informal diagnostic procedures that reveal desirable standards of performance, help the learner to establish goals to be

achieved, and bring out the inadequacies of his performance or product. The resulting motivation is a very valuable stimulus to learning.

Studying the educational achievements of pupils. Any technique that will yield information of a reliable, valid kind may be used to study the achievements of pupils. In general, the procedures that may be used involve some sort of test of ability or observation of behavior.

Educational tests. Educational tests available for appraising pupil achievement may be classified in various ways. One way is according to the aspect of ability they measure. *Rate* tests measure the amount of work of a uniform kind of difficulty a pupil does in a given time. *Scaled* tests consist of exercises of increasing difficulty. They measure the height or altitude to which a given general ability, such as addition, or knowledge of geographic information, has been developed. *Quality* scales in handwriting, composition, sewing, and other subjects make it possible to measure the merit of a specimen by comparing it with specimens in the quality scale. *Area* tests afford a means of surveying a wide variety of skills and specific abilities included in a field of learning. Supervisors and teachers should select tests that will measure the aspect of ability they wish to measure.

Educational tests may also be classified according to their use as *survey, diagnostic,* or *prognostic. Survey* tests aim to give a general measure of the status of achievement. They usually consist of scaled tests of some aspect of the work in each of the basic subjects of the curriculum. Tests of this kind are widely used throughout the country. Testing programs should not be limited to tests of this kind because they evaluate only a narrow range of outcomes. *Diagnostic* or *analytical* tests usually consist of a series of tests in several aspects of a single subject, such as reading, arithmetic, language, or science. From the results it is possible to determine the relative status of a class or of an individual with respect to the outcomes measured by each of the tests. A pupil may read rapidly, for example, but with poor comprehension; or he may be able to read with understanding, but not be able to locate material in reference books. The detailed discussion of diagnostic tests will be deferred until Chapter 10. *Prognostic* tests aim to predict probable success in a given field of learning such as algebra, Latin, or clerical work. Tests of readiness in arithmetic and reading are a sort of prognostic test. In all cases, the use to be made of the test results should be a guide in the selection of means of appraisal.

No attempt will be made here to supply a complete list of the different kinds of tests to be used in appraising the products of learning. Several thousand achievement tests exist and others are constantly being devised. Excellent discussions of available tests may be found in the list of references at the end of this chapter.

Test batteries may be divided into two groups. In the first group are comprehensive tests that sample the outcomes in nearly all of the elementary and secondary school curriculums, such as the following:

The Metropolitan Achievement Test (Yonkers, World Book).
The Stanford Achievement Test (Yonkers, World Book)
Modern School Achievement Test (New York, Teachers College, Bureau of Publications, Columbia Univ.)
Co-ordinated Scales of Attainment (Minneapolis, Educational Test Bureau).

In the second group are tests that concentrate on the "fundamentals," including the basic skills of reading, language, and arithmetic. Typical tests of this second kind are:

Iowa Every-Pupil Tests of Basic Skills (Boston, Houghton).
California Achievement Tests: Elementary, Intermediate and Advanced (Los Angeles, California Test Bureau).

For illustrative purposes the list of different tests included in the Iowa Every-Pupil Tests of Basic Skills is given below:

A. *Silent Reading Comprehension*
   I. Reading Comprehension.
   II. Vocabulary.
B. *Work Study Skills*
   I. Map reading.
   II. Use of basic references.
   III. Use of index.
   IV. Use of dictionary.
   V. Alphabetization.
   VI. Reading graphs, charts, and tables.
C. *Basic Language Skills*
   I. Punctuation.
   II. Capitalization.
   III. Usage.
   IV. Spelling.
   V. Sentence sense.
D. *Basic Arithmetic Skills*
   I. Vocabulary and fundamental knowledge.
   II. Fundamental operations—whole numbers, fractions, and decimals.
   III. Problems.
      Note: In the advanced form, percentage is added in Test D, Part II.

There also are numerous tests for measuring general power in single areas of the curriculum, such as arithmetic, reading, and language. Lists of tests of this kind may be found in the books for the various subjects, given in the bibliography at the end of this chapter. Typical specific-subject tests are the following:

Iowa Silent Reading Tests: Elementary and Advanced (Yonkers, World Book).
Co-operative World History Test (New York, Co-operative Test Service).
Morrison-McCall Spelling Scales.
Analytical Scales of Attainment in Arithmetic (Minneapolis, Educational Test Bureau).
Snader General Mathematics Test (Yonkers, World Book).

Other types of tests of a much more analytical nature dealing with particular subjects may be selected. The Iowa Elementary Language Tests, for example, for grades 4 to 9 contain tests in (1) word meaning, synonyms, and opposites; (2) language usage; (3) grammatical-form recognition; (4) sentence sense; (5) sentence structure; (6) capitalization and punctuation; (7) paragraph organization. Similar tests are available for other subjects of the curriculum. Results of such analytical tests afford a much more detailed analysis of the level of achievement than is supplied by general survey tests. In general, the use of such analytical tests should follow a general survey program rather than precede it. As a matter of fact many textbooks, especially in arithmetic and language, now contain well-constructed survey and diagnostic tests suitable for use by the classroom teacher. Their intelligent use by the teacher is an essential supplement to general survey testing. Diagnostic testing is an invaluable element of any good teaching program.

A wide variety of tests in high-school subjects is published by The Educational Testing Service of Princeton, New Jersey, and by the Psychological Corporation of New York. Other high-school and college tests are published by the same companies that publish tests for elementary schools.

An important development in the field of evaluation is the series of tests known as the Iowa Tests of Educational Development.[40] The series consists of a number of broadly comprehensive examinations, one for each of the major areas of the curriculum. The tests measure growth in certain general characteristics of the pupil's development with which all subjects in a general area are concerned. They are intended for use in high schools. The series includes the following tests:

1. Test of understanding basic social concepts.
2. Test of background in the natural sciences.
3. Test of correctness in writing.
4. Test of ability to do quantitative thinking.
5. Test of ability to interpret reading materials in the social studies.
6. Test of ability to interpret reading materials in the natural sciences.
7. Test of ability to interpret literary materials.
8. Test of general vocabulary.
9. Test of use of sources of information.

Cook[41] comments as follows on "the severe limitations" of the customary high-school testing program, including entrance board examinations:

1. Since tests are usually given only in those courses in which a pupil is enrolled they do not give at any one time a sufficiently comprehensive picture of the pupil's total educational development.
2. The usual high-school tests do not provide for measures of growth. A score in algebra one year and in geometry the next will not indicate how much a pupil has grown in ability to do the type of quantitative thinking required in life outside the school. Measures of growth depend upon successive measures of status in the same developmental area.
3. Subject-matter tests are usually not sufficiently concerned with the ultimate objectives of the total school program. They tend to measure what is taught rather than what should be taught and emphasize immediate objectives rather than ultimate objectives. For example, the extent to which an algebra course has contributed to the students' ability to do quantitative thinking in typical life situations is not measured.
4. Traditional tests are too much concerned with the immediate and often temporary results of instruction (factual rote learning) and do not indicate the permanent changes which have been wrought in the behavior of pupils.
5. Because of the difference in the abilities of the pupils taking different subjects the usual testing program does not provide strictly comparable measures from subject to subject and hence a differential profile of achievement is not possible.
6. There is a tendency to use test results for the purpose of teacher rating. When this is done the teacher becomes concerned with higher test averages for their own sake instead of with what the test results can reveal about the needs and abilities of individual pupils.

[40] Chicago, Science Research Associates.
[41] W. W. Cook, "Development Tests Supersede State Boards," *Minnesota Journal of Education* (March, 1950), pp. 26-27.

The major contributions of evaluation to the supervision and improvement of instruction are:

1. The classification and selection of educational objectives as guides to learning and instruction.
2. The determination of the progress made in achieving the accepted goals as measured by the growth of the learner.
3. The establishment of a basis for helping teachers to set up educational experiences adapted to the ability, needs, and interests of the learner.
4. The motivation and guidance of learning.
5. The diagnosis and treatment of learning difficulties.
6. The co-ordination of supervisory plans for improving instruction.
7. The evaluation of educational instrumentalities, including curriculum, instructional procedures, materials of instruction, facilities, and personnel.
8. The improvement of reports of pupil progress to parents.

Practical uses of evaluation. The primary purpose of evaluation in so far as the classroom is concerned is to assist the teacher to make continuing adaptations of the educational program to the needs of the children. Evaluation also supplies data needed for the grade-placement of a child in a group of children of similar intellectual ability and physical and social development. The use of standard tests of reading readiness, reading ability, work-study skills, and other areas of achievement enables the teacher to group children for instructional purposes. Evaluation by children themselves of their activities and behavior develops self-knowledge and self-direction and furthers critical thinking. The use of evaluative procedures enables the teacher to locate learning difficulties, to diagnose their nature, and to apply corrective measures. Evaluation also is essential to effective guidance because knowledge about children gathered both systematically and informally enables schools and teachers to provide experiences that are adapted to the interests and abilities of the learners. The cumulative record has been widely adopted

by our schools. The use of modern techniques of evaluation have also greatly improved the reports to parents about the achievements of their children.

Studying character and personality traits. Psychologists have devised a myriad of ways of studying character and personality traits of children. The areas with which the evaluative procedures deal can be classified as (1) personality, (2) attitudes, and (3) interests. Some of the procedures described are quite technical in nature and have little significance for the classroom teacher, since they can be used effectively only by clinicians, psychiatrists, and well-trained psychologists. However, a knowledge of the available methods of studying character and personality traits of children will enable the teacher, with the assistance of consultants, to devise less formal ways for securing information about important aspects of learning not readily appraised by paper-and-pencil tests.

The approaches to the study of personality have been classified as follows by Remmers and Gage: (1) adjustment schedules; (2) rating devices; (3) performance tests; (4) tests of knowledge and judgment; (5) observational records; (6) organized behavior descriptions; (7) external physical signs; (8) free association; (9) laboratory techniques involving apparatus; (10) psychiatric interviewing, including psychoanalysis; (11) the autobiography and life history; and (12) projective techniques. For a detailed description of these twelve procedures the reader is referred to the volume of Remmers and Gage, *Educational Measurement and Evaluation.*[42] To the above should be added sociometric procedures. For our purposes, we shall limit discussion in the following pages to a consideration of selected procedures of most immediate value to teachers. Few of these devices have passed beyond the experimental stage, but recently there have been many promising developments. There are available numerous standardized procedures

[42] New York, Harper, 1943.

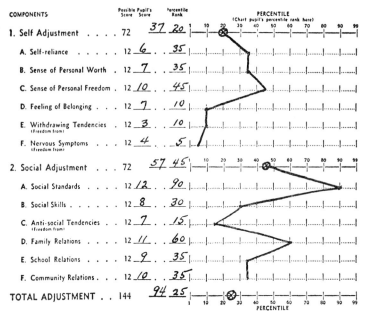

PERSONALITY PROFILE

From *California Test of Personality.* Used by permission of the California Test Bureau, Los Angeles, California.

that yield objective data which can be interpreted by reference to norms and rating methods. However, it is necessary to supplement these tests by informal evaluative procedures similar to those described in preceding sections, such as observations, interviews, analysis of available records, teacher-made tests, and the like.

Some of these devices have hardly passed beyond the experimental stage in psychological laboratories. Few have been produced of sufficient practical significance or meaningfulness to warrant extensive use in the hands of the typical classroom teacher. However, because of the obvious importance of tests and rating devices of this kind as a means of appraising these important kinds of educational outcomes, it is essential that the supervisor and teacher be familiar with the efforts being made to devise satisfactory instruments and when possible to assist in their development and application. These devices should be supplemented by less formal techniques—discussed in the preceding

section—such as observation, interviews, analyses of records of various kinds of questionnaires, and the like.

California Test of Personality provides a profile of percentile positions for total adjustment, for self- and social adjustment, and for twelve specific areas of adjustment. A typical profile is given on this page. An analysis of the ratings for the individual shows the phases in which there is lack of adjustment, particularly in terms of self. The subject rates high in social standards but rates low in freedom from antisocial tendencies.

The SRA [43] Junior Inventory by Remmers and Bauernfeind is a valuable means of determining the needs and problems of elementary-school children. It is a check-list of children's health, social, school, personal, and home problems. The SRA Youth Inventory is for high-school students. The Mooney Problem Check List [44] also affords the individual the opportunity to express his worries

[43] Chicago, Science Research Associates, 1951.
[44] Columbus, Ohio State Univ. Press, 1950.

and his needs. It is available in four forms: Junior High, High School, College, and Adult. The chief criticisms of these tests are that responses are not equally stable for all individuals and that they may be affected by a temporary mood. The person being tested can vary his answer at will, especially if his score will have practical consequences.

Attitudes tests are used to appraise attitudes toward problems—like those of a political and of a social nature—which lend themselves to differences of opinion and attitude. Scores do not correlate as highly with intelligence as do scores on tests of moral knowledge and information. The chief difficulty is that the expression of the individual's attitude or opinion on such tests may not be a true statement of his actual views. There is evidence that there are individual differences in the degree of stability and constancy of opinions. In some tests, consistency of answers or the person's tendency to take an extreme position forms the basis of scoring.

Thurstone,[45] Remmers,[46] and others have devised means of appraising the attitudes of people toward various items, such as the church, democracy, school subjects, occupations, and economic issues. Attitude scales make it possible to determine the individual's points of view and their strength or intensity and to discover conflicts or inconsistencies in them. Such scales can be administered at the beginning of a period of instruction to determine the views held and again at the end of the period to discover what changes have taken place during instruction.

How may we know for certain that an individual possesses a given [47] attitude or not? Undoubtedly, the most direct method is observation of his behavior. This method is not practical with large groups, and hence recourse has been taken to the use of verbal methods. The difficulty here is that the individual may check an attitude known to be desirable which is not consistent with his own conduct. The susceptibility to faking is being overcome by methods of checking. For example, it has been found that if two or more sets of questions or test items on the same problem are submitted at different times, with different wordings, and preferably with a concealed approach in some of the sets, a consistency in replies is found. Consistency is fair evidence that a persistent attitude or understanding is present. It has also been found that in the case of truly vigorous attitudes on some point, these will influence verbal responses more strongly than the knowledge of what the "desirable" or "correct" response is.

A scale for measuring attitude toward communism has been devised by Thurstone. The odd-numbered items in the scale are given below this paragraph. The items in the complete scale, which are here disarranged, may be thought of as being arranged in a series according to scale values. One simply checks the items in which he believes. The median or average score of the items checked is used as the index of the subject's position. One item may be judged to be the most representative point of view. Similar scales have been prepared in a wide variety of topics by Thurstone, Remmers, and their students.

ATTITUDE TOWARD COMMUNISM, SCALE NO. 6, FORM A [48]

(Prepared by L. L. Thurstone)

Put a check mark (   ) if you agree with the statement

Put a cross (   ) if you disagree with the statement

1. Both the evils and the benefits of communism are greatly exaggerated.
3. The whole world must be converted to communism.

[45] L. L. Thurstone, *University of Chicago Attitude Scales* (Chicago, Univ. of Chicago Press, 1929).

[46] H. H. Remmers and E. B. Silance, "Generalized Attitude Scales," *Journal of Social Psychology* (August, 1934), pp. 298-312.

Quinn McNemar, "Opinion-Attitude Methodology," *Psychological Bulletin* (July, 1946), pp. 289-374.

[47] David H. Russell, "What Does Research Say about Self-Evaluation?" *Journal of Educational Research* (April, 1953), pp. 561-574.

[48] By permission of Univ. of Chicago Press.

5. Communism is a much more radical change than we should undertake.
7. Give Russia another twenty years or so and you'll see that communism can be made to work.
9. Communism should be established by force if necessary.
11. I am not worrying, for I don't think there's the slightest chance that communism will be adopted here.
13. Communism is the solution to our present economic problems.
15. The ideals of communism are worth working for.
17. The whole communistic scheme is unsound.
19. We should not reject communism until it has been given a longer trial.

Measures of interests in most cases involve self-description. They probably are more valid than similar tests of emotional adjustment, since the questions are of a less personal nature. Hence the responses of the subject are more likely to be honest. When tests of interests are used to determine admission to some institution or appointment to a job, however, the subject is likely to give answers which in his opinion will make the best impression. Considerable use is made of these inventories for vocational guidance, although their value for this purpose has not been clearly demonstrated.

The best known is the Strong Vocational Interest Blank.[49] The results of this test help to determine interest patterns which are used in many places as a basis for guidance. The Kellogg-Brainard Interest Inventory[50] consists of a series of groups of items carefully selected to secure ratings of the interest of children above the sixth grade in a variety of activities common to them: construction, arts, mathematics, science, leadership, and the like. A section of this inventory follows:

Put a circle around one number after each question:

ART

How do you like		Dislike	N		Like
1. To sketch picture outlines of trees, people, houses, etc.?		1	2	3	4 5

How do you like		Dislike	N		Like
2. To draw maps or charts?		1	2	3	4 5
3. To copy cartoons or draw original pictures?		1	2	3	4 5
4. To make sketches of dresses, hats, furniture?		1	2	3	4 5
5. To model or carve figures or vases from clay?		1	2	3	4 5

Lehman's Play Quiz[51] is a device for appraising children's interests in various kinds of games. The reader is referred to the book by Fryer, *Measurement of Interests in Relation to Human Adjustment,*[52] for a detailed discussion of methods of appraising the interests of individuals.

The Kuder Preference Record,[53] suitable for grades 9 to 16, provides for the identification of nine interest patterns, including (1) mechanical, (2) computational, (3) scientific, (4) persuasive, (5) artistic, (6) literary, (7) musical, (8) social service, and (9) clerical. Another interest inventory suitable for high-school students is the Occupational Interest Inventory by Lee and Thorpe.[54] Levels of interest in three areas are identified by this test: (1) verbal, (2) manipulative, and (3) computational. The Brainard and Stewart Specific Interest Inventory,[55] suitable for ages 10 to 16, analyzes the subject's interest in particular modes of activity, such as physical work, vocal expression, and experimenting.

The Springfield Interest Finder given below is an excellent illustration of a practical device for studying the interests of children in grades 1 to 12. A detailed analysis of the

[49] Stanford University, Calif., Stanford Univ. Press, 1926-1930 (for men); 1934-1937 (for women).
[50] New York, Psychological Corporation, 1938.
[51] New York, Association Press, 1927.
[52] Dougles Fryer, *Measurement of Interests in Relation to Human Adjustment* (New York, Holt, 1931).
[53] Chicago, Science Research Associates.
[54] Los Angeles, California Test Bureau.
[55] New York, Psychological Corporation.

results of its application in an extensive study in the schools of Springfield, Missouri, is given in the reference below.[56]

SPRINGFIELD INTEREST FINDER

Name .... Boy or Girl ....
Age .... Teacher ....
Grade .... School ....
Date ....

My three wishes:
What I'd like to learn more about at school:
What I don't care to study about:
What I like best in school:
What I like best outside school (that is, away from school, when I'm not at school):
What I like least at school:
What I like least outside school (that is, away from school, when I'm not at school):
What I want to be or do when I grow up:
The most interesting thing I have done at school during the past week or so:
One of the places I especially like to go is _____:
One of the happiest days in my life:

The selected references below contain additional detailed information about character, interests, and personality tests:

For extended discussions of tests in the field of character the reader is referred to three volumes: Hartshorne and May, *Studies in Deceit* (1920); Hartshorne, May, and Maller, *Studies in Service and Self-Control* (1924); and Hartshorne, May, and Shuttleworth, *Studies in the Organization of Character* (1930), all published by The Macmillan Company, New York.

HAVIGHURST, R. J., and TABA, Hilda, *Adolescent Character and Personality* (New York, Wiley, 1949). An extension of research reported in the three volumes mentioned above.

FREEMAN, F. S., *Theory and Practice of Psychological Testing* (New York, Holt, 1950).

FRYER, Douglas, *The Measurement of Interests in Relation to Human Adjustment* (New York, Holt, 1931).

JERSILD, Arthur T., and TASCH, Ruth J., *Children's Interests and What They Suggest for Education* (New York, Teachers College, Bureau of Publications, Columbia Univ., 1949).

Review of Educational Research (February, 1953), "Educational and Psychological Testing," pp. 4-110. This is the most recent of the reviews published every three years by the American Educational Research Association. Preceding issues should be consulted by those interested.

THURSTONE, L. L. and CHAVE, E. J., *The Measurement of Attitudes* (Chicago, Univ. of Chicago Press, 1929).

Consult also the references on sociometric and projective technics on pages 251 and 252 for other valuable procedures.

A selected list[57] of tests and rating devices in the area of character, interests, and personality traits follows. Publisher's catalogs should be consulted for details as to grade or age levels at which to use them.

Bell Adjustment Inventory (Stanford Univ. Press).
Bell Personal Preference Inventory (Pacific Books, Palo Alto, Calif.).
Brainard and Stewart Specific Interest Inventory (Psychological Corporation).
Brown Personality Inventory for Children (Psychological Corporation).
California Test of Personality, Primary, Elementary and Intermediate Forms (California Test Bureau).
Detroit Adjustment Inventory by H. J. Baker (Psychological Corporation).
Haggerty-Olson-Wickman Behavior Rating Scale (World Book).
Kuder Preference Record (Science Research Associates).
Lee and Thorpe Occupational Interest Inventory (California Test Bureau).
Loofbourow and Keys Personal Index (Educational Test Bureau).
Mooney and Gordon, *Mooney Problem Check-Lists, Grades 7-9, and 10-12* (Ohio State Univ. Press).
New York Scale for Measuring School Habits (World Book).
Rogers Test of Personality Adjustment (Association Press).
SRA Youth Inventory and SRA Junior Inventory (Science Research Associates).

Tests of conduct and behavior include measures of the individual's various charac-

---

[56] Arthur T. Jersild and Ruth J. Tasch, *Children's Interests and What They Suggest for Education* (New York, Teachers College, Bureau of Publications, Columbia Univ., 1949).

[57] These tests and devices should be available for study and reference. Class reports may be made of the devices and their uses.

SAMPLE ITEM FROM HAGGERTY-OLSON-WICKMAN BEHAVIOR RATING SCALE

29. How does he react to frustrations or to unpleasant situations?

Very sub-missive Long-suf-fering	Tolerant Rarely blows up	Generally self-controlled	Impatient	Easily irri-tated Hot-headed Explosive
(3)	(2)	(1)	(4)	(5)

teristics that are undoubtedly the most significant from the social point of view. The group contains tests of honesty, persistence, co-operation, moral conduct, and the like. In many of these tests, natural life situations controlled to some extent by the examiner are used, so that the subject responds normally. Hence conduct tests are to a large extent valid. The major problem involved concerns the consistency of behavior of the individual in other situations similar to the specific test situation. Investigators have found relatively low correlations between scores on different tests of conduct.[58] This has led to the concept of specificity of character traits which presents serious problems in character education. General observation, however, shows that there is a great deal of transfer and generalization in behavior in social situations. Hence the specificity of character traits revealed by tests is at least in part dependent on the nature of the test rather than on the intrinsic nature of character itself. Correlations between scores on paper-and-pencil tests of honesty, co-operation, or moral behavior and moral knowledge are extremely low, in general about .25. There is an obvious need of developing tests of this kind that yield scores more closely related to actual conduct.

Rating scales for evaluating behavior aid in the appraisal of some of the less definite outcomes of education. Although scoring of traits by means of these scales is largely subjective and hence often unreliable, improvements in their construction have increased the reliability of the ratings.

The Haggerty-Olson-Wickman Behavior Rating Scale[59] is a typical scale. A short section of this scale, which is widely used for locating behavior problems, is given above. The teacher is asked to rate the seriousness of each of thirty-five behavior traits as they occur in a particular child. Five degrees of seriousness are provided for in the scale. Each point is described and a problem tendency score is given for each point. Ratings by the teacher undoubtedly make for more careful observing of the behavior of children as well as for more discrimination in regard to problems of conduct.

Studying the health and physical condition of children. The health and vitality of its people are great assets to a nation. Society has recognized the importance of health by assigning to the schools the task of safeguarding the health of the children. The basis of an intelligent program of general health and physical education should be an awareness of the health problems of the individual and the community as revealed by systematic examination and study.

The most important outcomes of health education are good physical condition, adequate health habits, and proper attitudes toward healthful living. The first of these outcomes can be determined by thoroughgoing physical examinations of the kind now required by law in a number of states. The data revealed by such examinations can easily

[58] Robert J. Havighurst and Hilda Taba, *Adolescent Character and Personality* (New York, Wiley, 1949).

[59] Yonkers, World Book, 1930.

be summarized, and an appraisal made of the health status of the pupils. Teachers must also learn to recognize the symptoms of common diseases and bring them to the attention of the medical authorities. The chief problems involved in the supervision of these physical examinations are their inadequacy in many instances when superficial tests are given because large numbers of children must be examined, and the difficulty of securing action by parents and teachers to correct unsatisfactory conditions. The close relation between learning and the physical condition of a pupil makes it necessary to give more thorough-going physical examinations to children experiencing learning difficulties than need be given to children who are making normal progress. A complete health record is therefore an essential element in a well-rounded pupil accounting program.

To measure the development of adequate health habits, physical efficiency and skills, and attitudes toward healthful living, numerous sorts of tests have been devised. They may be grouped as follows: (1) health knowledge and health habits, (2) physical growth and physical capacity, (3) motor abilities, (4) general achievement and athletic proficiency.

For detailed descriptions of evaluative procedures in these areas the following references may be consulted:

CLARKE, H. H., *The Application of Measurement to Health and Physical Education* (New York, Prentice-Hall, 1945).

CURETON, T. K., and others, *Physical Fitness Appraisal and Guidance* (St. Louis, C. V. Mosby, 1947).

LARSON, L. A., and YOCUM, Rachel D., *Measurement and Evaluation in Physical, Health, and Recreation Education* (St. Louis, C. V. Mosby, 1951).

McCLOY, C. H., *Tests and Measurements in Health and Physical Education*, 3rd ed. (New York, Appleton-Century-Crofts, 1954).

Studying mental-health conditions. Many writers in recent years have emphasized the importance of consideration on the part of the school of problems in the field of mental health. One reason for this movement has has been an apparent increase in the number of individuals suffering from mental illness. It is known that evidences of maladjustment appear at an early age in many cases. The sooner they are identified, the more likely it is that steps can be taken to ameliorate the condition.

The procedures for identifying mental illness vary from observations that may be made of pupil conduct by the informed teacher to clinical examination by a psychiatrist. Some symptoms can easily be identified, whereas others are deep-seated and can be recognized only by the expert. A simple classification of difficulties indicative of maladjustment that can be noted by the teacher in the classroom has been suggested by Tiegs and Katz: [60]

1. Work methods, such as lack of interest, inattention, lack of initiative, procrastination, and evasion of work.
2. Social adjustment, such as rudeness, discourtesy, annoying, bullying, fighting, tattling, selfishness.
3. Authority, such as tendency to argue, disobedience, defiance.
4. School regulations, such as tardiness, destructiveness, cheating, lying, truancy, stealing.
5. Personal adjustment, such as seclusiveness, timidity, sensitiveness, dependence, temper-tantrums.

The evaluation of these difficulties can be objectified by rating scales, records of behavior, and similar procedures described in the discussion of methods of studying personality and character traits.

Other kinds of indices of mental illness can also be recognized by the teacher. These include such nervous habits as thumb-sucking, nail-biting, tics, and speech defects. Sexual difficulties, misconduct, and delinquent behavior can also be identified. Daydreaming and feelings of inferiority are revealed by overt behavior.

[60] E. W. Tiegs and Barney Katz, *Mental Hygiene in Education* (New York, Ronald, 1941), pp. 203-204.

There are more complex forms of mental illness that the teacher should at least realize may exist. These include such complex disorders as the three types of psychoneuroses called neurasthenia, psychasthenia, and hysteria. In addition, there are also major mental disorders, such as dementia praecox, manic-depressive psychoses, paranoia, and paresis. Whenever the teacher observes unusual symptoms, such as erratic behavior, violent reactions, and abnormal conduct, the case should be brought to the attention of proper medical and psychiatric authorities. In many localities there are special agencies that are concerned with problems in the field of mental health. These include mental hygiene departments, child-guidance clinics, divisions of correction dealing with delinquents,[61] social-welfare agencies, and charitable organ-ization of all kinds. These agencies deal with many kinds of problems which are of vital concern to the school. No educational program can be effective which overlooks the data available in the files of these various agencies.

The books listed below should be consulted for further details about problems in mental health:

CATTELL, R. B., *The Description and Measurement of Personality* (Yonkers, World Book, 1946).
Mental Hygiene in the Classroom, National Committee on Mental Hygiene (New York, 1949).
OLSON, Willard C., *The Behavior Journal* (Ann Arbor, University Elementary School, 1948).
WALLIN, J. E. W., *Personality Maladjustments and Mental Hygiene* (New York, McGraw, 1949).

Section 6

ILLUSTRATIVE APPRAISAL PROGRAMS

Evaluating outcomes of an activity program. The report by Wrightstone of the evaluations made in the course of an experiment to measure the effectiveness of an activity program as compared with conventional instructional practices in the New York City elementary schools is an excellent illustration of the use of tests and other evaluative procedures in appraising a wide variety of educational outcomes. The outcomes appraised included certain basic skills, social performances, critical thinking, knowledge of current affairs, attitudes, and personality. The table below lists the aspects of learning which were evaluated in this investigation and the procedures that were used. The broad scope of the evaluation indicates the desire of the staff to consider a wide range of possible outcomes that might be directly affected by an activity program. The evaluative procedures ranged from the analysis of records of controlled observations to standard tests.[62] Direct comparisons were made between data for activity and nonactivity schools.

1. Controlled observation of social performances in classrooms
   a. Co-operative activities.
   b. Leadership activities.
   c. Self-initiated activities.
   d. Recitational activities.
2. Tests of basic skills
   a. Reading comprehension.
   b. Arithmetic computations.
   c. Spelling.
   d. Language usage.
3. Tests of critical thinking
   a. Working skills in the social studies.
   b. Drawing conclusions in the social studies.
   c. Applying generalizations in the social studies.
4. Test of knowledge of current affairs

[61] Sophia H. Robinson, *Can Delinquency Be Measured?* (New York, Columbia Univ. Press, 1936).
J. B. Maller, "Juvenile Delinquency Among the Jews in New York City," *Social Forces* (May, 1932), pp. 542-549.
[62] J. W. Wrightstone, "Evaluations of the Experiment with the Activity Program in the New York City Elementary Schools," *Journal of Educational Research* (December, 1944), pp. 252-258.

5. Tests of attitudes and personality
   a. What do you believe?
   b. Personality trait indicator.
      (1) Personal adaptability.
      (2) Social adaptability.

In addition to the evaluation of pupils, an effort was made to appraise the effects of the activity program on the school personnel by means of interviews, questionnaires about professional activities, and tests of the teachers' knowledge and interpretation of child behavior. Parents were also interviewed and they recorded their attitudes toward school practices in the type of school their children attended.

In general, the results were highly favorable for the activity schools. For details the reader is referred to the original report.

Procedures for evaluating general outcomes in a curriculum area. The analysis of procedures for evaluating certain outcomes of instruction in English given below is based in part on a discussion by Dora V. Smith [63] of recent developments in this field. Smith points out that the trend in evaluation in English and other areas is "away from concern with acquistion of mere skills and knowledge toward the measurement of more dynamic outcomes in terms of human behavior and the development of personality, and in the direction of the study of individual growth in the ability to use language effectively in functional situations." Illustrative procedures for appraising a number of important outcomes of instruction in English are given below.

Outcome	Suggested Means of Appraisal
1. Mastery of basic skills.	Standard achievement tests. Rating of quality of written composition by standard scales. Analysis of language errors in compositions, letters, and written work, and in oral expression. Appraisal of the quality of oral and written language in life situations. Rating of performance, such as a play, a talk.
2. Ways of thinking.	Tyler's test on "Interpretation of Literature" and "Critical-mindedness in the Reading of Fiction." Essay type examinations. Analysis of evaluations of books, talks. Behavior in problem situations. Anecdotal records.
3. Personal and social attitudes and beliefs.	Essays on selected topics. Observation of behavior. Interviews. Tests of attitudes. Tests of beliefs. Questionnaire. Anecdotal records. Ratings by self and others. Psychodrama.
4. Interests and appreciations.	Carroll prose-appreciation test. Check-list of books and magazines read. Ratings of the quality of books read. Records of newspaper reading. Choice of motion pictures and radio programs. Activities involving written expression in life outside the school. Participation in school club activities. Interest inventories.

[63] Dora V. Smith, "Recent Procedures in the Evaluation of Programs in English," *Journal of Educational Research* (December, 1944), pp. 262-276.

Robert M. Travers, "A Review of Procedures for the Evaluation of Outcomes of the Teaching of English," *Journal of Experimental Education* (December, 1948), pp. 325-333.

The supervisor faces the problem of assisting the teacher to select from among available techniques or to devise suitable methods of evaluating the behavior related to various objectives that have been accepted. Emphasis should be placed on the evaluation of behavior in social situations in which oral and written language functions.

A program of evalution in the social studies. Wesley and Adams [64] outlined in considerable detail elements and procedures of a broad program of appraisal in the social studies, including both measurement and evaluation techniques. It includes a wider variety of outcomes than have yet been measured. It is beyond doubt the best list of its kind available for any area of the curriculum. Some of the procedures they list are already available, some exist in only an informal way. Evaluational procedures for some of the outcomes do not yet exist and will have to be devised. The resourceful teacher will utilize those that seem to be most appropriate to the purpose of the appraisal. The outline of techniques of evaluation prepared by Wesley and Adams follows:

Entity	Techniques of Evaluation
1. Equipment.	Isolate the factors, e.g., maps, and measure by means of matched groups; record performances inspired by the use of the equipment being evaluated; pupil and teacher opinion of its value.
2. Method.	Pupil opinions of the two methods being compared; matched groups taught by different methods; teacher opinion of the value of the methods; extent of pupil interest.
3. Grading.	Relative performance of two or more successive grades; relative performance of three or four grades; diffi- culty of the material as estimated by pupils, by teachers; varying performance by pupils.
4. Organization.	Pupil preferences and reactions; pupil achievement; logic and appeal of the organization to teachers.
5. Teacher.	Self-rating scales; supervisor's ratings; pupil performance on tests; pupil conduct in the opinions of other teachers; teacher's performance on teacher examinations; popularity of the teacher among pupils, among colleagues; teacher's achievements in publication, travel, professional activity, community services, and in reading.
6. Concepts.	Ability to give examples; ability to choose correct or best definition; ability to give a definition; ability to match with an example or a definition; presence or absence of the word in the pupil's speaking and writing vocabulary; pupil-made lists of synonyms, of words by categories, and of other assigned patterns of words; measurement of the number of connotations which pupils know.
7. Locating materials.	Observations of pupils in search of materials; tests of familiar-

[64] Edgar B. Wesley and Mary Adams, *Teaching Social Studies in Elementary Schools* (Boston, Heath, 1951), pp. 440-443.

Entity	Techniques of Evaluation	Entity	Techniques of Evaluation
	ity with selected books, references, and bibliographies; time tests of skill in using index, table of contents, title page, and card catalogue and in finding words in dictionary and articles in encyclopedia; tests of discrimination in choice of sources for finding answers to given questions.		map; ability to select the right kind of map for a given purpose; knowledge of the function of colors in maps; familiarity with longitude and latitude; completion exercise in map-reading; exercises in interpreting cartoons, graphs, and tables.
8. Appraising materials.	Ability to distinguish between sources and secondary accounts, to sense degrees of reliability, to sense degrees of probability; ability to recognize authorities; lists of books read, shows attended, radio programs selected, lectures attended; tests involving attitude toward superstitions; tests for sensitivity to inconsistencies; ability to distinguish fact from opinion; the degree of difficulty in proving different kinds of statements; tests involving the recognition of the tentative nature of conclusions and generalizations in the social studies; awareness of conflicting testimony; ability to select kinds of data needed for a particular problem; ability to suspend judgment.	10. Utilizing materials.	Ability to select the proper deduction following a generalization; ability to make a logical inference, draw a proper conclusion, state a generalization; ability to make correct citations and bibliographies; ability to organize materials; ability to recognize sequences, to establish causal relationships; ability to select proper kind of graph to embody given materials; ability to put a group of headings in proper relationship.
9. Studying materials.	Ability to select leading ideas; recognition of symbols, abbreviations, and allusions; method and speed of locating a place on a	11. Interests.	Observation of choice of books from a varied assortment; observations of those portions of a newspaper which are being read after two minutes; observations of subjects of magazine articles being read after five minutes; the content of pupil conversations; choice of projects and problems; games played; questionnaires; shows attended; record of hobbies; radio programs heard.

Entity	Techniques of Evaluation
12. Co-operation.	Check-lists of instances of voluntary co-operation; check-lists with graded levels for indicating the quality of co-operation; lists of achievements which are the result of joint enterprises; the number and efficacy of typical pupil-managed organizations; check-lists of observance of courteous demeanor; tests of attitude toward co-operation.
13. Suspended judgment.	A test consisting of sets of statements followed by conclusions of which some are warranted and others unwarranted; tests to measure the change of opinions after hearing a speech, seeing a show, reading a book; tests to see if pupils will refrain from forming judgments on insufficient bases.
14. Toleration.	Tests on racial and religious toleration; a check-list of instances of favorable and unfavorable treatment of minorities, such as foreigners, Negroes, etc., in the school.

Appraisal in guidance. Wrenn and Dugan [65] outline as follows the kinds of information essential for guidance and the means by which each kind can be secured:

Areas of Information	Means of Appraisal
1. Scholastic aptitude.	Previous grades, psychological tests of ability and achievement.
2. Scholastic achievement and basic skills.	Previous grades, standardized and teacher-made achievement tests, survey and di-
	agnostic tests of basic skills, school activities, and work experience.
3. Special abilities: clerical, mathematical, artistic, and the like.	Special aptitude tests, interviews, evaluation of previous achievement or performance (work experience, hobbies, extracurricular activities).
4. Interests and plans.	Autobiographies, interest inventories or tests, stated interests, interviews, previous achievement, and both work and leisure activities.
5. Health and physical status.	Physical examination, health history, observation, attendance record and nurse follow-up, and family consultation.
6. Home and family relationships.	Observation, anecdotes, rating scales, interviews, autobiographies, themes, check-lists and adjustment inventories, reports from employers, group workers, or group leaders, and parent conferences.
7. Emotional stability and social adjustment.	
8. Attitudes.	Student questionnaires, home contacts, interviews, themes, autobiographies and other documentary information, and standardized rating scales.
9. Work experience.	Record of employer, reports of vocational counselor, interviews, and student questionnaires.

Evaluating a school's testing program. At intervals the staff of a school should evalu-

[65] C. G. Wrenn and Willis E. Dugan, *Guidance Procedures in High School* (Minneapolis, Univ. of Minnesota Press, 1950), pp. 18-19.

ate its testing program. The entire staff or a committee in charge of the testing program should consider the following points:

1. The effectiveness of the use being made of available test data by teachers.
2. The labor involved in scoring tests.
3. The care with which test scores are being transcribed on record forms and the use made of the records.
4. Areas in which additional tests would be helpful.
5. Tests that could be deleted for various reasons.
6. The use being made of the services of available specialists and consultants in evaluation.
7. The advisability of constructing local testing materials.
8. The influence of the testing program on instruction.
9. Possible changes in scheduling the testing program.
10. The degree to which the tests in use fit the local sequence in teaching basic skills.

Similar appraisals should also be made of the informal procedures of evaluation that are used by teachers and others to study educational outcomes not readily tested by paper-and-pencil tests.

Reporting pupil progress to parents. Interesting and significant developments are to be found in the nature of reports made to parents about the progress of children in our schools. Burton summarizes the characteristics of several hundred new-type report cards as follows:

1. Conspicuous changes appear in marking by subjects.
    a. Traditional unexplained single marks for subjects are steadily decreasing.
    b. Subjects are increasingly being grouped under major broad fields.
    c. Important objectives to be gained from individual subjects are listed increasingly.
    d. Definitions for marks, where retained, are increasing.
2. Social and emotional growth, special interests, attitudes, habits are increasingly included.

3. Physical growth and well-being, health knowledge and habits are increasingly included.
4. Increased opportunity for co-operation with parents is indicated.
5. Comparative or competitive marking is disappearing with considerable rapidity.
6. Individual, personalized, letter-form reports from teacher to parent are increasing slowly.
7. Conferences between parent and teacher appear both as supplements to report cards and as substitutes.
8. Special notices of failure sometimes supplement the report card.
9. New-type report cards are increasingly printed in large type, decorated, or otherwise given a pleasing appearance.
10. A very marked tendency is apparent so to organize and word all items that the report is easily and immediately understood by any pupil or parent.
11. Separate cards for various levels (kindergarten, primary, upper grades, high school) and for single subjects in high school are increasing.

It is evident that reports to parents are in many places keeping pace with changes made in other major aspects of the developing educational scene. Emphasis is being placed on growth in all phases of pupil personality rather than on the limited evaluation of achievement in subject-matter areas which was the outstanding characteristic of the report cards of the past.

Wrinkle [66] has suggested the following list of criteria to be used in evaluating marking and reporting forms and practices:

CRITERIA USED IN EVALUATING MARKING AND REPORTING FORMS AND PRACTICES

1. Have the objectives of the educational program been identified?
2. Are the objectives clearly stated?
3. Are the objectives sufficiently analyzed so that they have specific meaning?

[66] W. L. Wrinkle, *Improving Marking and Reporting Practices* (New York, Rinehart, 1947), p. 107. On pp. 10-15 there is an excellent 70-item check list for inventorying points of view on marking and reporting. A key for scoring the items is provided.

4. Are the objectives understood, accepted, and recognized as important by the students, teachers, and parents?

5. Are different objectives evaluated and reported separately?

6. Are different forms provided to serve different purposes?

7. Are different bases for evaluation utilized which are appropriate to the purposes involved?

8. Can the teacher evaluate with sufficient reliability the achievement and growth of the student with respect to the objectives which have been set up?

9. Can the reports be prepared with a reasonable expenditure of staff time and effort?

10. Do the evaluation procedures make provision for student self-evaluation?

11. Is provision made for the reporting of evidence and comments relative to the evaluations?

12. Are the forms so constructed as to facilitate recording?

13. Can the evaluations be easily translated into other symbols if the evaluations may have to be stated in terms of other systems of marking?

14. Do the forms and practices serve the various functions which they are designed to serve, that is, give information, stimulate interest in improvement, facilitate guidance, provide a basis for college-entrance recommendations, etc.?

CHAPTER SUPPLEMENT

INTRODUCTORY DISCUSSION QUESTIONS

1. What arguments can you give for or against the hypothesis that the effectiveness of the educational program of a school or community can be determined by a continuing appraisal of characteristics and behavior of its product both in school and in the affairs of daily life in the community?

2. How justified are current criticisms of the educational product appearing in printed sources and heard in public discussions? Can you cite sources and illustrations of important evidence as to strengths and limitations of the educational product?

3. Tell about the planning and organization of the evaluation program used where you may be teaching or in some school with which you may be familiar. Evaluate the program in the light of points discussed in this chapter, especially the analysis of possible procedures on pages 253-270.

4. Tell about any workshop or similar plan for improving evaluation procedures with which you may be familiar.

5. What are the advantages and disadvantages of the machine-scoring of tests? Should teachers administer and score standard tests?

6. Discuss the use of sociometric and projective procedures—their values and limitations.

7. What principles would you suggest as guides to teachers for evaluating the achievements on tests of pupils of the various levels of intelligence and social background?

8. What types of tests are found in current textbooks and workbooks for the various curriculum areas?

9. Why should evaluation be a continuing process? Who should select tests and other appraisal techniques to be used?

10. What kinds of evidence can be gathered to determine the extent to which educational purposes are being achieved? Indicate clearly the relative value of the different kinds of evidence.

11. What use can be made of the available statements of objectives in particular areas of the curriculum, such as reading or arithmetic, in appraising the educational program?

12. How adequate do you think the methods were that were used to determine the characteristics of the educational product in the New York Survey report, *The Changing Elementary School*? In some other survey?

13. Who should make the evaluation of the educational product? When?

14. What difficulties are there in interpreting results of appraisal programs?

15. How should the results of evaluation procedure be made known to pupils? to the staff? to the public?

16. What technical agencies and services are found in school systems and in the community that deal with the appraisal of the educational product? With the study and improvement of the curriculum? With the study and improvement of materials of instruction, equipment, and the socio-physical environment? With the study and improvement of factors related to instruction? With the study and improvement of factors present in the learner?

17. What are the activities that are carried on by the various agents to achieve their purposes in each of the areas listed?

WRITTEN REPORT FOR INDIVIDUALS OR SMALL GROUPS

1. Examine the report of some school survey and evaluate the methods used to appraise the educational product.

2. Select and evaluate a test of mental ability, a personality test, and a standard achievement test by applying the criteria given on page 241.

3. Make a record of significant observable actions and responses of some pupil in a classroom who presents a problem and analyze the data so as to define his strengths and weaknesses. The record could be extended by utilizing simple informal evaluative procedures, consulting available school records, observing behavior outside the classroom, and so on. A similar record for a class may be made by recording a narrower range of items of interest to the recorder.

4. Examine selected textbooks in some curriculum area, list the kinds of tests and evaluative procedures they include, and evaluate the findings.

5. Design an original appraisal device similar to the informal procedures discussed in this chapter. If possible, apply it to some learning situation and report the results. The device might be:

    a. A problem-situation test.

    b. Four (or more) valid essay questions.

    c. A best answer or multiple choice test necessitating judgment.

    Or any other preferred by the student.

6. Make a critical report upon the use of anecdotal records in your school or that you have observed. Select typical anecdotes and appraise them.

7. Apply some simple sociometric procedure in a classroom and diagram the results.

8. Describe and evaluate critically devices for appraising personality traits and moral-spiritual outcomes.

PROJECT NO. V

IMPROVING METHODS OF EVALUATING THE EDUCATIONAL PRODUCT

A valuable activity for a group of students is the careful listing of procedures to be used to evaluate some important educational outcome and the preparation of brief descriptions of the necessary appraisal devices. The writers have in some instances divided the entire class into small groups, each to set up an appraisal program for a different outcome judged by the group to be important. In one course, various means of appraising the following outcomes were selected or devised: problem-solving in social situations, co-operation, leadership, social sensitivity, mental health, respect for property, and creativity. Each item was defined in terms of behavior and then test situations were devised. The evaluation of outcomes in knowledge of subject matter, skills in the "3 R's," specific interests, health, and similar outcomes presents fewer difficulties than the appraisal of less tangible items.

The mere listing of available standard tests and of evaluational instruments will be regarded as passable but on the lowest level. The more acceptable answers will contain evidence of originality in the application of available tests; the best answers will contain new tests or evelutional procedures devised by the students. (Written report No. 5 above was a preparation for this.)

The outline below presents one grouping of areas that should be considered in making an analysis of educational objectives. Other groupings are possible. Instructors and students should feel free to make another listing if desired. There is inevitably some overlap between the divisions. Details have, of necessity, been neglected.

I. Basic types of learnings directly derivable from experience with curriculum areas
    a. Functional knowledge.
    b. Understandings; meanings, concepts; thought processes.
    c. Skills: motor, intellectual.
    d. Abilities.
    e. Methods of work and study: of attacking problems: patterns of behavior.

II. Outcomes directly related to child growth and development
This general over-all outcome is personal, mental, physical, emotional, social, and moral growth and development (not specifically related to content or what is taught).
    a. Health and adjustment—physical, mental, emotional, social and moral.
    b. Specified attitudes or tendencies to act.
    c. Specified appreciations, attitudes.
    d. Interests and purposes.
    e. Creativity in learning activities (in the arts, in language expression, in interpretation in any field).

III. Outcomes of a societal nature
  a. Problem-solving— (individual or group procedures). (Variously defined but in general as (1) ability to recognize a problem; (2) ability to formulate a problem in specific, definite terms; (3) ability to formulate a plan for solving the problem; (4) ability to secure data needed to solve the problem; (5) ability to organize and present data; (6) ability to evaluate data; (7) ability to draw conclusions, and (8) ability to apply conclusions to new life situations.)
  b. Social sensitivity. (Defined by Smith and Tyler as: (i) social thinking; (ii) social attitudes, beliefs, and values; (iii) social information relevant to social problems; (iv) social awareness; (v) readiness to participate in significant activities; and (vi) skill in social activity.)
  c. Democratic co-operation.
  d. Democratic leadership.
  e. Creativity in social situations and problems.

GENERAL PROCEDURE FOR THE PROJECT

1. Select some significant educational outcome (or group of related outcomes) to be evaluated. Specify reasons for selecting this outcome and why it is worth studying.

2. Define the outcome in a form which permits evaluation or measurement, preferably in terms of characteristics and behavior of learners.

3. Specify in outline form as shown below the means to be used in appraising the product. If standardized means are available, give titles; if informal procedures are to be used, illustrate them briefly. Construct new instruments. Use as a guide the detailed list of evaluative procedures given on pages 239-241 in the text.

Items to Be Appraised   Means of Appraisal

1.   *a.*
2.   *b.*
                           c.

4. Students in service should make efforts to apply their proposed procedures in school situations and then present findings. Comments on their significance should be included in the report. When this is impossible for students who have no direct access to classrooms or schools, brief descriptions of findings likely to result should be prepared. This exercise is a good test of the student's general knowledge of the curriculum, of typical outcomes, and of methods of appraisal.

5. An activity that grows logically out of the appraisal programs would be an analysis of probable next steps to be taken to determine possible causes of unfavorable growth and development so that finally plans can be considered for improving the situation. (This item can be omitted until later if desired.)

SUGGESTED READINGS

All major references have been included within the body of the chapter at appropriate places.

Chapter 10

The Study of the Learner: Diagnosis of Learning Difficulties

The nature of diagnosis. By means of the various procedures of evaluation described in Chapter 9 it is possible to determine not only the status of the educational product relative to a wide variety of desirable educational outcomes but also the progress that has been made over a period of time. As has been indicated, evaluation therefore should be regarded as a continuous process and should not be done according to a set schedule.

Diagnosis is the interpretation of the results of the various means of appraisal for the purpose of locating strengths and weaknesses in the educational product. The more specific the information that is secured by this evaluation, the more definitely and precisely it is possible to define the nature of a deficiency. Thus, a single test of general power in reading does not afford nearly as significant information about an individual's ability as is supplied by a more detailed series of reading tests that evaluate a group of basic reading skills. A reading profile based on the latter results may reveal at a glance a variety of both strengths and weaknesses, information of undoubted value in planning instruction.

The following has already been proposed as a generalized approach to diagnosis:

1. The setting up of educational objectives as guides to learning and instruction.
2. The appraisal of the educational product by means of a variety of evaluative procedures to locate its strengths and deficiencies, in general or in some specific area.
3. The review of previous experience and scientific investigations for ideas as to the probable factors conditioning the growth of the individual or group favorably or unfavorably.
4. A preliminary survey of the situation under investigation for evidence (symptoms) of the presence or absence of the probable factors likely to be operative.
5. The formulation of a tentative hypothesis or of hypotheses as to the factors most likely to be operative in the case under consideration.
6. The use of systematic analytical procedures to study the situation so as to establish with some assurance the presence or absence of the factors that may be suspected to be conditioning growth or achievement unfavorably.
7. The instigation of a more effective developmental program on a tentative experimental basis.
8. Re-evaluation of the behavior, growth, and achievement of the learner to establish the validity of the diagnosis and remedial program and as a basis of further guidance.

The first two points in this outline were discussed in detail in Chapters 3 and 9. In the present chapter points 3 to 6 of the outline will be considered. Points 7 and 8 will be treated fully in Chapter 14.

The purpose and scope of diagnosis. The purpose of diagnosis is to secure appropriate dependable information about the causes of poor or unsatisfactory learning, about the causes of satisfactory learning, in the individual pupil. Diagnosis will discover the abilities and disabilities of the individual learner, discover the strengths and weaknesses in his attitudes, interests, and work habits.

The scope of diagnosis includes all characteristics of the personality—physical, intellectual, emotional, social, and moral.

The data revealed by diagnosis are then used as a basis for remedial programs of instruction, or for guidance toward further development of special ability or talent.

In diagnosis we make a critical and analytical study of conditioning factors that are related, favorably or unfavorably, to a desired outcome, especially when there is evidence of unsatisfactory progress. The information thus derived helps us to understand the nature of a disability.

The causes of unsatisfactory growth and development, which are actually interrelated, will be treated separately for purposes of analysis and study. Four areas are recognized: factors inherent in the learner; in instruction; in the curriculum; and in the sociophysical environment. The first of these is treated in this chapter, the others in immediately following chapters. It is thus evident that there are many elements in a learning situation that may contribute to a deficiency. Sometimes a diagnosis based on a casual survey or on the results of a group test is adequate for ordinary purposes, but for seriously handicapped children the approach must be on an individual basis and much broader in its scope and more searching in its attack. The techniques of diagnosis are as diverse as are the deficiencies of the individuals that are to be studied and as the conditions out of which the deficiencies grow. There is thus no set formula to use in diagnosis. Available diagnostic techniques should be used in varying combinations with different individuals, the choice in each case being determined by the several elements that may require investigation.

The modern school has no desire to mold every individual into one pattern; it seeks rather to help each one to achieve the utmost of which he is capable. This utmost will vary from person to person. For this reason it is necessary to know the ability, needs, interests, and purposes of each individual as well as his special talents and aptitudes. Science has demonstrated that each individual is a unique personality. It is therefore clear that the community must plan its total educational program in such a way that it will be suited to the capacities, the interests, and the total personality of the individual.

Special consideration should be given to the discovery and development of giftedness and talent. Evidence of giftedness should be sought outside the area of general intelligence as measured by intelligence tests. There is no reason for assuming that a high IQ posits creativity, genius or near genius. No matter what his mental level, a child whose performance in any potentially valuable field is observed to be consistently remarkable might well be considered as gifted; he should be given every opportunity which his talent demands for nurture and continuous growth; constant adaptations should be made, and changes of experience that are necessary to maintain growth should be provided. These steps can be taken with assurance when continuous diagnosis and evaluation furnish reliable information as a guide for action. At the same time, his needs in other fields should not be overlooked.

Each individual has in a sense his own direction, rate, and pattern of development which differs from that of any other individual. Developmental sequences tend to be the same for all, but there are great variations in the levels attained, the amount of retrogression, and the times of attainment. Accurate prognosis of future development depends on knowledge of whether the child is progressing, standing still, or even retrogressing and the rate at which change is taking place. Furthermore, each of the integral components of the individual has its own rate and direction of growth.[1] Hence it is necessary to consider at all times the changes that are taking place in the total personality of the individual.

Nature of deficiencies. Deficiencies among learners may vary from those that are minor problems to others that are very serious in nature. (1) Some difficulties are of recent origin and can easily be corrected; (2) other deficiencies have persisted for some time and have not yielded to casual treatment; (3) still other faults are more serious and of long standing. They may pervade many areas of the learner's personality, and they have not been corrected by previous remedial measures.

Learning problems of these varying degrees obviously require different kinds of treatment. Faults of the first type usually are readily identified and respond to treatment when handled by competent teachers within regular classes. Problems of the second type require more specific attention by a person who has been given special training in the diagnosis and improvement of learning in the area involved. Such cases can be dealt with in special classes or by means of carefully adapted individualized instruction within regular class groups. Problems of the third type require the attention of a clinic where a comprehensive case study can be made by specialists to discover the subtle, less evident factors in the total situation that are interfering with satisfactory growth. Treatment here may also have to be on a clinical basis.

Kinds of deficiencies. The major types of deficiencies in the various areas of learning and their symptoms should be known in order to facilitate diagnostic study. The sources of such lists are theoretical considerations, experimental investigations, day-to-day teaching, and clinical experience in dealing with individuals. The kind of deficiencies vary from phase to phase of the total personality of the learner and for different areas of learning. Their nature also changes as the individual progresses from level to level of the school. Many deficiencies, unless corrected, become more complex and involved as the individual grows and matures.

An illustration of a formulated list of major deficiencies in a learning area is the list below for reading, prepared by Strang.[2]

1. Ineffective habits of recognition and persistent vocalization.
2. Inability to apprehend the meaning of words and sentences.
3. Inability to get the pattern of the author's thought in an entire passage.
4. Inappropriate rate of reading which may be too slow or too rapid for a given type of material and for the purpose which the reader has in mind.
5. Inadequate and incorrect interpretation, comparison, analysis, and critical evaluation of the material read.
6. The lack of ability to pronounce words correctly and to phrase properly in oral reading.
7. Ineffective applications of material read in the discovery and solution of problems.
8. Inability to get esthetic appreciation from printed sources.
9. Narrow or unsuitable reading interests, purposes, and attitudes.
10. Lack of flexibility in adapting reading methods to the reader's purpose in reading a given type of material.

Closely allied with these areas of deficiency are ineffective habits of budgeting time, planning work, and attacking a unit of study. Inefficiency in locating sources of information in books and magazines is also related to efficiency in reading. Even more important, though less frequently recognized as a deficiency, is a lack of balance in the total learning situation.

The significance of symptoms in diagnosis. There are characteristic responses and reactions of the learner that will indicate to the alert examiner the possible presence of a deficiency or defect of some kind. For ex-

[1] Willard Olson, *Child Development* (Boston, Heath, 1949).
[2] Ruth Strang, "Diagnosis and Remediation," in W. S. Gray, ed., *Reading in General Education* (Washington, American Council on Education, 1940), Ch. 9, pp. 309-310.

ample, the following classroom symptoms of visual difficulties appeared more frequently in children referred to a reading clinic than in an unselected group of children, according to a report by Knox:[3]

1. Facial contortions.
2. Holds book close to face.
3. Tense during close work.
4. Tilts head.
5. Thrusts head forward.
6. Holds body tense while looking at distant objects.
7. Assumes poor reading position.
8. Excessive head movements while reading.
9. Rubs eyes often.
10. Avoids as much close work as possible.
11. Has tendency to lose place in reading.

These and similar symptoms should suggest to the teacher the necessity of an examination of the eyes. When a visual deficiency of some kind exists, the correction of the faulty responses in reading will more likely result from a correction of the visual factor than from the use of reading exercises directed at the faulty responses.

Similar lists of symptoms should aid the observer in detecting other kinds of deficiencies, such as faulty hearing, malnutrition, glandular disturbances, incipent disease, ineffective methods of work, and the like.

There are certain kinds of mental disturbance that are of special significance, for they reflect on the adjustive process itself. The means by which the individual consciously or unconsciously meets any conflict are significant in describing his personality. The well-adjusted individual is able to face a problem and to make the adjustment necessary to avoid a conflict. When there is a feeling of frustration, aggressive action leading to conflict may be taken, or there may be some form of compensation to protect the individual from unpleasant reality, or feelings of self-pity and uncertainty may prevail. Fenton has proposed the following classification of areas of disturbance that influence the reactions and behavior of children.[4]

A TENTATIVE CLASSIFICATION OF AREAS OF DISTURBANCE IN A CHILD

1. Disturbance because of insecurity
   a. Concern over the parents' love for him; over their love for each other.
   b. Anxiety about economic problems in the home: the unemployment of parents, poverty, or material obligations of any sort; illness or death.
   c. The effects of fears: general ones, such as fear of the dark, novelty, strangers, animals, disease, or death; or specific fears, like the syphilophobia of some adolescents or the fear of specific school subjects or skills such as reading or arithmetic, or of certain instructors.
   d. Undue concern over matters of health.
2. Disturbances over social status
   a. Doubts of his own acceptance or acceptability in the group at school or in the neighborhood; feeling that he has unfortunate or unpopular personal qualities; his own conflicts over such defects (whether or not they really exist).
3. Disturbances about his own personal qualities; nonacceptance of self
   a. Feelings of inferiority because of appearance, health, size, strength, race, family occupation, or personal qualities of parents, location or appearance of home, etc.
   b. Self-doubt or distrust about ability (competence, adequacy) in schoolwork, chores, social relationships, or ability to get on in the world or to justify his family's expectations about him.
   c. Feelings of guilt over past behavior or present attitudes and feelings.
4. Disturbances over the acceptance of reality; evasion of personal and social obligations or responsibilities; disagreements with adults; lack of interest
   a. The nonacceptance of the actuality of his own life (for example, the type of home or neighborhood in which he lives).

[3] In Helen Robinson, ed., *Clinical Studies in Reading II* (Chicago, Univ. of Chicago Press, 1953), p. 100.
[4] Norman Fenton, *Mental Hygiene in School Practice* (Stanford University, Calif., Stanford Univ. Press, 1943), pp. 221-222.

b. Unwillingness to accept the authority of parents or teachers, to do what is asked of him at home or at school through lack of interest or willingness.

c. Unwillingness to co-operate with classmates, to acknowledge the rights and property of others.

d. The effects of lack of constructive interests.

e. Conflicts over choice of a life work, over relationships with the opposite sex.

a. General symptoms in ineffective learning.

Data of various kinds that can be derived from test results, observations of pupil behavior, and the analysis of available records will often indicate the existence of an unsatisfactory condition that requires investigation.

1. *Low scores on survey tests.* When the results of general survey tests show that the achievements of pupils are not up to reasonable standards or that growth has not been satisfactory, the supervisor has a valuable clue to the points at which a study should be made to determine the reasons for the unsatisfactory results. The supervisor must, of course, be certain that the survey test deals with the accepted objectives and the contents of courses being taught, and that the appraisal of the results takes into consideration the mental level of the pupils, their home environment, their maturity, the length of the school term, and similar factors that tend to condition their achievement.

2. *Low scores in one area.* Survey-test results may show that pupil achievement is satisfactory in all but one or two areas. If more detailed analytical tests have been used in the survey, the results may reveal deficiency in only one or two of the skills tested. This information will clearly indicate the points at which the attack should begin. The supervisor must recognize the fact that though the class average may be at or above the standard, there will usually be considerable numbers of pupils whose scores are unsatisfactory. This information is of great value to the teacher in adjusting the instructional program to the needs of the individuals.

3. *Failure to progress.* If observations over a period of time show that improvement or growth in ability is less than expected, the supervisor should suspect that the instruction is not adapted to the needs of the pupil and that adjustments of various kinds may be necessary.

4. *Lack of interest or attention.* If there is evidence of lack of interest in the work of the class or of inattention on the part of pupils, the supervisor should suspect that the curriculum may not be well adjusted to the interests and abilities of the pupils, that motivation is lacking, and that instructional materials may not be attractive and well arranged.

5. *Behavior difficulties.* When behavior problems arise in school among older children who are retarded and not successful in their class work, or when there is nonparticipation of pupils in various forms of group activities, the condition is a sure symptom of maladjustment which should be investigated. When records of juvenile delinquency in the community reveal an unsatisfactory situation, the school must assume the leadership in a study with a view to correcting conditions in the environment both in and out of school, that contribute to these results.[5]

6. *Statistics about overageness and nonpromotion.* The analysis of age-grade data will enable the supervisor to discover the extent to which the pupils are not making normal progress through the grades, and the number who are underage and overage. If the range in ages is very wide, the supervisor may suspect that many of the class activities do not meet the needs of either the younger or the older children. An analysis of teachers' marks and of promotion records will reveal the points at which the pupils are encountering the greatest difficulty, and the areas that are contributing to nonpromotion.

[5] This problem is fully discussed in Chs. 13 and 17.

7. *Unsatisfactory physical and psychological characteristics.* An analysis of the physical and psychological records will enable the supervisor to discover the extent to which the school is providing for children having certain defects. The presence in the classrooms of children with physical and mental defects reveals the fact that the program is not meeting its obligations to all children nor adjusting its activities to meet their needs. Overt behavior often reveals the presence of physical defects, such as faulty vision or deficiency in hearing.

b. Specific symptoms in particular fields. Symptoms of a much more specific kind than those listed above will suggest clues as to the nature of difficulty in the various areas of the curriculum. In many cases definite test techniques have been invented that enable the supervisor to determine with precision the seriousness of the condition of which the behavior is a symptom. Such detailed diagnoses in specific areas of knowledge are of basic importance, regardless of the organization of materials for learning. In an activity or experience curriculum these same difficulties are likely to arise. Difficulties will doubtless differ in type and severity under different types of learning but nevertheless need to be diagnosed and remedied. Detailed diagnostic procedures for other than subject-matter learning are indicated later in this chapter and in Chapter 9.

c. Symptoms of maladjustment. Symptoms of maladjustment are helpful in identifying various kinds of personality difficulties and forms of mental illness. Several symptoms of emotional maladjustment that can easily be identified by the careful observer are the following:[6]

1. Shyness that may become apparent in a number of ways. The adolescent may be overstudious, docile, and withdrawn. He may prefer seclusion and become irritable when parents or teachers attempt to break into his seclusion. He may daydream to the point where he confuses imaginative and realistic thinking.
2. Aggressiveness that indicates a bullying, domineering person who is emotionally uncontrolled and antagonistic and who is always against proposals made by other people.
3. Strong antisocial tendencies manifested in the overt actions of destructiveness, stealing, and lying.
4. Sexual deviations.
5. Somatic symptoms, such as headaches or vomiting, occurring in association with emotional disturbances.

The interpretation of symptoms observed in a given case should be made with care. This is advisable because of the differences in causative factors in the personality of children who present similar difficulties. Because of the uniqueness of each individual and his background of experience, it is highly improbable that the same constellation of symptoms and underlying causative factors will be present in several children. Fenton has listed the following cautions which he believes should be considered in using any schematic summary of symptoms of maladjustment.[7]

1. The meaning of a symptom for practical purposes is not absolute but is relative to the child's personality, his relations to his parents, and many other factors, including the mores and standards of the household, classroom, neighborhood, or community.
2. The terms used to designate symptoms are ordinarily vague as to the degree of seriousness involved. The same word, for example, "stealing," may mean anything from a petty and insignificant act of stealing in the home to the theft of hundreds of dollars from a store.
3. The meaning of a symptom or problem in a child can be adequately defined only by the study of its relationship to the rest of the personality of the child. A particular symptom is, to be sure, always considered in the diagnosis of the child's difficulty. But isolated symptoms are obviously not nearly so meaningful as the grouping of symptoms and problems found in the child.
4. Attention must be given to the possibility of subjective error in the descriptions of symptoms by teachers and parents because of the

[6] Milton Schwebel and Ella F. Harris, *Health Counseling* (New York, Chartwell House, 1951), pp. 180-181.
[7] Norman Fenton, *Mental Hygiene in School Practice* (Stanford University, Calif., Stanford Univ. Press, 1943), pp. 151-152.

variations among them in personal sensitivity to different types of problems in children. Some adults are excitedly overconcerned, others somewhat indifferent, in regard to identical behavior in children. The inability of the observer to record accurately what the child does or to know all the facts—which is an important aspect of the subjective error—may be a source of confusion in the description and designation of symptoms.

Section 2

WHY CHILDREN DO NOT MAKE SATISFACTORY GROWTH

Causes of deficiencies. It is very difficult to differentiate between the causes of a given deficiency and its symptoms or correlates. Competent diagnosticians speak of the "cause" of a deficiency as "the developmental sequence leading to it." In this sequence there are often certain elements that contribute more than others. For example, in one case a certain type of visual defect may contribute decisively to a reading disability, whereas in another case with the same type of defect the individual may have overcome the handicap by adjustments of various kinds. Sometimes an apparent cause of a deficiency may in fact be the result of a more remote set of circumstances. Lack of interest in reading which might lead a child to avoid reading may thus be the direct result of his inability at an earlier stage to comprehend what was read. Failure of the teacher to adapt methods and materials of instruction to the needs and abilities of different children may apparently not affect the learning of some individuals but may lead to serious maladjustments in other cases. It is thus clear that what may be a cause in one case may be merely a correlate in another with little if any significance.

For purposes of discussion the factors which often appear to operate as causes of deficiencies may be grouped as follows, although in real life they are not so clearly differentiated and rarely fall into such discrete categories:

1. Physiological factors.
2. Intellectual factors including intelligence.
3. Instructional factors.
4. Emotional and affective factors.
5. Environmental conditions.

1. Physiological factors. In this group are included such factors as health, physical development, nutrition, visual, auditory and physical defects, kinesthetic irregularities, and glandular imbalance. It is commonly recognized that ill health, retarded physical and motor development, and malnutrition interfere with optimal learning and growth. Large numbers of children suffer from various kinds of visual, auditory, and other physical defects that interfere seriously in learning such skills as reading and writing. In young children some of these sense organs are not matured enough to stand the strain on them required by the close work of the classroom. Kinesthetic irregularities, such as muscular imbalance of the eye, speech defects, lack of motor control, and mixed dominance of eyes and hands, are known to interfere with the learning of the basic skills. Gates [8] has listed as causes of spelling deficiency the following physical conditions: (1) defects of sensory mechanisms, including the visual and auditory; (2) defects of the motor mechanism, including general motor incoordination, defective writing, defective articulation, defective eye-muscle control, inappropriate eye movements, and eye-voice span in reading.

It has been clearly demonstrated that the various glands of internal secretion, such as the thyroid and pituitary glands, affect be-

[8] Arthur I. Gates, *The Psychology of Reading and Spelling,* Contributions to Education No. 129 (New York, Teachers College, Bureau of Publications, Columbia Univ., 1922).

White House Conference on Child Health and Protection (New York, Appleton-Century-Crofts, 1932).

havior. This relationship is self-evident when one considers the manner in which motivation is influenced through the avenue of the emotions. Disturbances of the glandular mechanism contribute decisively to changes in emotional tone and hence to instability of personality.

Vitamins and learning. Recent research in the field of vitamins suggests that there is some relationship between vitamin intake and efficiency of learning. Harrell,[9] for example, reports the results of an experiment which shows that in sixteen different learning experiences there was in every instance a difference in favor of a group "with increased vitamin intake." Not all of the results were statistically significant, but all differences were in the same direction. For increased mental efficiency it seems evident that the learner should be well nourished. Special attention should be given to see that there is no vitamin deficiency in the diet of the individual.

2. Intellectual factors. Thorndike[10] has pointed out that intellect has several dimensions. Intellect may be thought of as possessing *altitude* or *level,* that is, the height at which the individual can attain success with tasks arranged in increasing order of difficulty. The higher the level of difficulty at which success is attained, the higher the level of the intellect. Intellect also may be thought of as possessing *width* or *range.* The greater the variety of tasks of a given level of difficulty the individual can perform successfully, the greater range of intellect at that level. Intellect also has *area,* or *volume,* terms used to mean the total number of tasks of some specified sort at which intellect succeeds. In simple language, Thorndike means that intelligence is made up of thousands of specific abilities such as ability to compare, to discriminate, to react rapidly (or slowly), to perceive, to draw, to manage people, and so forth.

Most intelligence tests measure the altitude of the intellect. Thorndike's CAVD Tests measure a number of the specifics referred to above and thus give a measure of width and areas as well as altitude of intellect. Information about these three aspects of intellect enables one to know not only the relative power of a person's intellect but also, to a degree, what he has done with his intellect; the extent to which he has used it, and the different avenues of interest that he has explored.

In contrast to Thorndike's view that intelligence is made up of thousands of specifics, we have the *"g and s"* theory of Spearman.[11] In his view intelligence is made up of a general factor, *g,* plus any number of special factors. Spearman interprets *g* as a form of energy. It may be looked on as energy, plasticity, a favorable balance of various organic conditions, and so forth. The *s* factors are such things as musical capacity, mathematical capacity, and so on. Thorndike and Spearman differ as to the degree of relationship existing between the different items. The technical statistical research[12] is unbelievably complex and may be left for advanced students.

A more recent approach than those of Thorndike and Spearman is the basis of a series of tests devised by Thurstone for measuring the so-called "primary mental abilities." Through a complicated process of factor analysis he identified these abilities as (1) visual or spatial ability, (2) perceptual ability, (3) numerical ability, (4) logical or verbal-relations ability, (5) fluency in dealing with words, (6) memory, (7) inductive ability, (8) deductive ability,

[9] Ruth F. Harrell, *Effect of Added Thiamine on Learning,* Contributions to Education No. 877 (New York, Teachers College, Bureau of Publications, Columbia Univ., 1943).

[10] E. L. Thorndike, *The Measurement of Intelligence* (New York, Teachers College, Bureau of Publications, Columbia Univ., 1929).

[11] C. E. Spearman, *The Nature of Intelligence and the Principles of Cognition* (New York, Macmillan, 1927).

[12] L. L. Thurstone, *The Vectors of the Mind* (Chicago, Univ. of Chicago Press, 1925). Deals with multiple-factor analysis for the isolation of primary traits.

(9) ability to restrict the solution of a problem.

The SRA Primary Mental Abilities Test [13] —ages 11-17, devised by Thurstone, measures five basic learning aptitudes: verbal meaning, space, reasoning, number, and word fluency. The total score can be converted to a general ability quotient comparable to the IQ.

The range in mental levels. The wide range in the levels of intellect among individuals is commonly recognized. People vary in intelligence from the level of the idiot to the level of the genius. Success in school is in general closely related to level of intellect. Pupils at the lower levels of intelligence often encounter serious difficulty in mastering their school work. It is known, however, that in some cases pupils of a relatively high level of intelligence also experience difficulty in learning some of the essential skills.

One of the first steps in diagnosing inability to learn is to determine the individual's mental level. The most commonly used index of mental ability is the *intelligence quotient*,[14] which is the ratio of the pupil's mental and chronological ages. An intelligence quotient of less than 75 is ordinarily regarded as indicating so low a mental level that the individual possessing it should be assigned to a special class where a modified instructional program can be offered. Ordinarily cases with IQ's below 50 indicate the advisability of institutionalization.

Jordan [15] discusses four characteristics of intelligence quotients that need to be kept in mind when interpreting mental ratings based on available standards:

1. IQ's are *not inherited.* They are, as is every other aspect of mental life, the results of the interaction of inheritance and environment. Newman has shown that two identical twins who differed 13 years in education differed 24 IQ points. Each of the pair had the same *genetic constitution,* but in one case there was not enough environmental stimulation to develop this capacity. A child from a poverty-stricken family who earns an IQ of 90 has more native capacity than a child with the same IQ from an excellent environment. Children deaf from birth frequently have low IQ's simply because they have been shut off from environmental stimulation. Let us once and for all abandon the idea that the IQ is inherited like the color of our eyes or the freckles on our skin.

2. IQ's are not *constant* but vary considerably within limits. Variation of IQ's may be due to the manner in which a test is given or scored, to the fact that they are derived from tests standardized on different populations, or even to the fact that one child cheated. An IQ of 100 obtained from the correct administration of a test would vary 4 or 5 points on the second giving. There are 99 chances in 100 that an IQ of 100 would not vary more than 15 points in the administration of two forms of the same test. The variations just discussed are those arising out of the process of measurement. Radical changes in environment or emotional maladjustments may produce greater variations than those described. On the other hand, we do not expect a child with an IQ of 50 ever to be normal or one with an IQ of 130 ever to recede to 100. Intelligence quotients remain within certain definable limits from year to year, but the limits are broad.

3. An IQ is *more valuable the nearer in time* it has been computed. An IQ computed for a 3-year-old is of very little value at age 6. The testing of very small children is fraught with many difficulties, e.g., negativism. After year 6 or 7, the IQ stays more nearly the same, i.e., its variation is less. For a sixth-grade teacher to have to depend on an IQ secured in the third grade is unfortunate indeed. If it has been computed while the child was in the fifth grade it is valuable.

4. Intelligence tests, except for performance tests, measure *verbal intelligence.* This means that a poor reader in the fourth grade will be penalized by giving him a group intelligence test. Poor reading then is frequently the cause of low scores on group intelligence tests.

If these matters are kept in mind, intelligence test scores and IQ's are the most useful types

---

[13] Chicago, Science Research Associates.

[14] L. M. Terman, *The Measurement of Intelligence* (Boston, Houghton, 1916).

The term IQ is usually associated with individual tests. Various other terms are used with group tests: intelligence test score (in place of IQ), ability index, mental quotient, and others.

[15] By permission from *Measurement in Education* by A. M. Jordan. Copyright, 1953, McGraw-Hill Book Company, Inc.

of information which can be collected. They indicate the child's present learning capacity and help the teacher in knowing what procedures are best for his continuing development.

The relationship of mental factors to learning difficulties. The level of intelligence is not always directly related to achievement. Horn,[16] for example, has summarized the causes of low spelling accomplishment as follows:

1. Poor study habits.
2. Ineffectiveness of reading.
3. Slow illegible handwriting.
4. Inadequacies of instruction in written composition.
5. Faulty speech habits, particularly in pronunciation.
6. Lack of interest or presence of undesirable attitude.
7. Special disabilities in vision, auditory discrimination, and perceptual analysis.

He then points out that "positive correlations have been reported between intelligence and spelling, and children of low intelligence are very likely to be poor in spelling. On the other hand, high intelligence does not guarantee superior spelling ability."

Sometimes pupils do not learn because of special intellectual disabilities. Low scores in one area and high scores in other areas indicate the possible presence of a special deficiency. There are many different varieties of disabilities. They may be grouped under the following main heads: (1) perceptual disabilities, such as slowness of perception of diverse stimuli; (2) deficiencies in visual and auditory memory span; (3) alexia, or word blindness, resulting in inability to recognize the meaning of written or printed symbols; (4) aphasia, a defect in, or loss of, the power of expression by speech, writing, or signs; (5) agraphia, or inability to express ideas in writing; and (6) amusia, or loss of ability to produce or to apprehend melodies and musical sounds.

It is important, also, to bear in mind the fact that different kinds of intelligence are now recognized by psychologists,[17] such as abstract intelligence, the kind required for work on intellectual school tasks; social intelligence, the kind involved in social relationships; and concrete or mechanical intelligence,[18] the kind involved in working with tools, machines, and concrete objects. These kinds of intelligence exist in varying degrees in each individual, rarely to the same extent in any one person. Knowledge of the character of a pupil's intellect is of considerable value in the guidance of learning, in vocational guidance, and in the diagnosis of disability. The instructional program of pupils with below average abstract intelligence and above average mechanical intelligence should clearly not be the same as for a pupil of high abstract intelligence and low mechanical intelligence. The former should probably be guided into a course in some kind of shop work, whereas the latter appears to have the kind of ability required for more academic work. Special adjustments must be made in the work of pupils who have special kinds of mental defects that interfere with optimal growth.

Insufficient mental ability is listed here as a primary cause, but it may be in fact a secondary cause based upon a defective nervous system, glandular imbalance, or the like.

[16] Ernest Horn in W. S. Monroe, ed., *Encyclopedia of Educational Research* (New York, Macmillan, 1950), pp. 1257-1258.

[17] The expression "kinds of intelligence" must not be interpreted too literally. All the facts concerning the nature of intelligence are not yet available. At present the most careful interpretation is that intelligence, whatever it is, is a basic function of the organism. In some individuals it seems to manifest itself most effectively in dealing with abstract ideas, in others with concrete matters, and in still others with social relationships. All persons use their intelligence; that is, have some facility with all three types of material. A given person is not likely to have no facility whatever with any one of the types. "Kinds of intelligence" means different manifestations, not disparate fundamental types, of intelligence.

[18] E. L. Thorndike, "Intelligence and Its Uses," *Harper's Magazine* (January, 1920), pp. 227-235. Popular account.

George D. Stoddard, *The Meaning of Intelligence* (New York, Macmillan, 1943), Part V.

Furthermore, sharp distinction must be made between definite mental inadequacy and seeming or deceptive lack of mental ability. Lack of mental ability, so-called in many cases, actually turns out to be lack of interest in a poor curriculum and poor teaching; lack of interest or active antagonism due to unfavorable teacher personality; unfavorable home attitudes toward school; lack of energy due to malnutrition or overwork outside school; lack of interest due to continued failure, which in turn may be due to poor study habits, in turn due to poor teaching, or poor home environment not conducive to study, and so on.

Finally, it must be remembered that intelligence, defined as ability to do school work, manifests itself very differently in different situations. Previous experience, guidance, success or failure, the total educational situation all affect this. The motives and ambitions of the pupil also affect the results obtained as well as the level of mental ability.

In appraising mental endowment, it should be recognized that not only the level of intelligence must be considered but also the quality or manner in which it functions. The intelligence which an individual possesses may function normally and efficiently, or it may function inefficiently, peculiarly, unpredictably, even disastrously as in the case of a psychopathic individual or a delinquent youth. This factor of mental function correlates far more closely than mental age with our everyday social problems.[19]

Studying the mental capacities and special aptitudes of pupils. There is no question that mental capacity conditions educational progress. Many studies have demonstrated that wide variations in intelligence exist at all age levels and in all grades. Children vary greatly both in their ability to learn and in the rates at which they learn. It is therefore necessary to organize the educational program so that provision is made for these individual differences.

Intelligence tests. There are both group and individual tests. There are two types of group tests, classified as verbal and nonverbal. The verbal tests require the comprehension of verbal directions and the reading of test items expressed as words. The nonverbal tests are administered without the use of words. They utilize oral directions and pantomime to give directions, and the test items consist of pictures, diagrams, and other symbols rather than words. Nonverbal tests are primarily used with young children and other individuals whose reading ability is at a low level, or who are unable to express themselves in the English language. The names of illustrative tests of each kind that have not been discussed previously are given below. There are other excellent intelligence tests that are not listed.

1. *Group Tests*
    a. Verbal
        (1) *American Council on Education Psychological Examination for High School Students.*
        (2) *Detroit Tests of Learning Aptitude* (Public School Publishing Co.).
        (3) *Terman-McNemar Group Test of Mental Ability* (World Book).
    b. Nonverbal or mixed
        (1) *California Test of Mental Maturity* (also verbal) (California Test Bureau).
        (2) *Pintner-Patterson Scale of Performance Tests.*
2. *Individual Tests*
        (1) Arthur: *Point Scale of Performance Tests* (Commonwealth Fund).
        (2) *Kuhlman Test of Mental Development* (Educational Test Bureau).
        (3) *Terman-Merrill Revision of the Stanford-Binet Test* (World Book).
        (4) *Wechsler Intelligence Scales for Children—Verbal and Nonverbal—* (Psychological Corporation).

For a detailed discussion of the uses of intelligence tests the reader is referred to the volume by F. S. Freeman, *Theory and Practice of Psychological Testing.*

Measurement in counseling. Psychological measurement is essential in dealing with

[19] Florence Mateer, *The Unstable Child* (New York, Appleton, 1924).

individual problems of adjustment, development, and orientation that come to the counselor's attention, and also with group problems related to growth, achievement, classification of students, and educational selection for admission to higher institutions of learning. These uses [20] may be summarized as follows:

1. The objective appraisal of personality for better self-understanding and self-direction on the part of the individual himself.

2. The accurate comparison of individual performance with the performance of others for the purposes of selection, recommendation, and self-understanding.

3. Improved basis of prediction as to likelihood of success in any activity in which prospective performance can be measured and compared.

4. Evaluation of personal characteristics in relation to characteristics required for educational and occupational performance.

5. Evaluation of achievement and growth—individual and group.

6. Disclosure of capacity and potentiality as well as the diagnosis of mental disabilities, deficiencies, and aberrations.

The applications of measurement stem from the basic need for objective comparative data about individual behavior, subject as little as possible to the vagaries of subjective surmise and interpretation.

Sources of variations in performance. The most common sources of variations in performance on a test have been listed [21] as follows:

Actual differences among individuals in the general traits or general abilities being measured.

Specific abilities required in a particular test; or specific disabilities in the functions being tested.

Skill in taking tests; being "test wise," or the converse.

The "chance" acquisition of a particular piece of knowledge or information required in a test: e.g., the meaning of an unusual word, such as *ambergris;* or a bit of unusual information, such as the name of the author of a little-known work.

Effects of practice (previous test taking) or, in some instances, coaching.

Normal or expected fluctuations in performance from time to time.

Personal characteristics of the testee: motivation, health, energy level, emotional status.

Physical conditions under which the test is taken: heat, light, ventilation.

Unpredictable, or "chance" factors: noise, interference, broken pencil, misunderstanding of instructions, etc.

Fortunate guessing of answers.

Limitations of psychological tests. Mursell [22] lists seven "severe" limitations of psychological tests:

a. They cannot directly reveal a person's capacity for complex and sustained learnings.

b. Our tests cannot directly reveal capacity for disentangling concepts from complex masses of data.

c. Our tests cannot directly reveal capacity for consistent and considered choice between possible courses of action.

d. Our tests cannot directly reveal capacity for dealing sensibly and wisely with practical problems.

e. Our tests cannot reveal directly a person's capacity for controlled and effective methods of work.

f. Our tests cannot directly reveal the depth, strength, and subtlety of a person's appreciative reactions in ethical, social, or esthetic matters.

g. Above all, our tests cannot even begin directly to reveal capacity for producing original ideas and constructions—for initiative, for the original solution of problems, for creative endeavor.

Tests of special aptitude. It has been recognized that the tests of general intelligence do not give a measure of the special abilities and talents which some individuals apparently possess. This has led to the development of various kinds of tests of special aptitude for certain vocations, such as teaching, nursing, and salesmanship. Typical tests of this kind are the Stenquist Mechanical Aptitude Tests,[23] Orleans Algebra Prognosis

[20] E. F. Lindquist, ed., *Educational Measurement* (Washington, American Council on Education, 1951), p. 71.

[21] F. S. Freeman, *Theory and Practice of Psychological Testing* (New York, Holt, 1950), p. 17.

[22] Adapted from pp. 14-16 in J. L. Mursell, *Psychological Testing* (New York, Longmans, 1949).

[23] Yonkers, World Book, 1921.

Tests,[24] and the Seashore Measures of Musical Talent.[25]

The reader is referred to Hull's *Aptitude Testing,*[26] and Bingham's *Aptitudes and Aptitude Testing* [27] for a detailed discussion of methods of measuring aptitude.

There are certain limitations about the use of intelligence tests that should be borne in mind. They have been well stated by Witty as follows: [28]

During the past ten years, intelligence tests have been subjected to careful study, and experimental data now enable one to appraise them with considerable fairness and impartiality. Today we are aware of the limitations as well as the values of these tests. It is evident that many of the high hopes and claims of mental-test enthusiasts have not been fulfilled. For example, we are fully aware that a single test is not a reliable measure of the individual's mental ability. We have noted some of the hazards in predicting mental growth from test results, and the fallacies and dangers involved in certain educational practices have been cited. In addition, we are now able to see how unwarranted and false were some of our assumptions associated with race or sex differences in intelligence. Moreover, we have seen the limitations of the test scores used independently in predicting special ability or aptitude. Despite these limitations of intelligence and aptitude testing, its use still occupies a significant rôle in educational work. When test results are considered in connection with other data in arriving at an estimate of a child's nature and needs, they are of undisputed value. Treated in conjunction with developmental data covering physical, emotional, and educational growth, they help us understand children. Hazards in their use are numerous; but, notwithstanding these facts, tests may assist the teacher in arriving at a sound basis for intelligent diagnosis, intelligent counseling, and intelligent guidance of school children.

For detailed discussions of the nature-nurture controversy the reader should consult, *Intelligence: Its Nature and Nurture,* Thirty-Ninth Yearbook of the National Society for the Study of Education, Parts I and II, published by Public School Publishing Co., 1940. Another important volume in which much of the controversial data is assembled and evaluated is the volume by George Stoddard, *The Meaning of Intelligence.*[29]

3. Instructional factors.[30] Unsatisfactory growth of a pupil may be due to shortcomings in his mastery of what has been taught, to faulty methods of work and study, and to narrowness of his experiential background. If instruction has proceeded too rapidly and has not consistently checked the extent to which the pupil is mastering what is being taught, the pupil may have accumulated a number of deficiencies that interfere with successful progress. For example, in arithmetic, knowledge of the basic addition facts used in carrying is essential to successful work in multiplication. Weakness in the former will contribute directly to deficiency in the latter. Similarly failure in chemistry may be due to low reading ability, or to weakness in mathematics. Likewise, because of faulty instruction a pupil may have learned inefficient method of study and bad work habits. The following description by Atkin shows the difference in the methods of studying spelling used by children with high and with low learning indices: [31]

The outstanding characteristics of the study methods of children in spelling at the very high learning level are the presence of a very systematic and well-organized plan of study or

[24] Yonkers, World Book, 1928.
[25] New York, Silver Burdett, 1919.
[26] C. L. Hull, *Aptitude Testing* (Yonkers, World Book, 1928), 535 pp.
[27] W. C. Bingham, *Aptitudes and Aptitude Testing* (New York, Harper, 1927), 390 pp.
[28] Paul Witty, in Charles E. Skinner, ed., *Elementary Educational Psychology* (New York, Prentice-Hall, 1945), pp. 123-130, or see any standard text.
[29] Stoddard, *op. cit.*

[30] It will not be possible because of limitations of space to give more than a general statement of the nature of learning factors. The reader is referred to the classified bibliography at the end of this chapter for references in which these deficiencies are described and methods of diagnosing them in the various areas of the curriculum are presented.
[31] S. Atkin, "The Study Habits of Pupils with High and Low Learning Indices in Spelling," Unpublished Master's thesis, Univ. of Minnesota.

approach in doing their work. All of these children used a number of the following techniques in studying their spelling: visualization, vocalization, transfer, syllabication, writing down the words on paper while looking at the mimeographed form, and writing down the words on paper from memory. It is true that the children did not use the above-mentioned techniques in the same order, for variation in method was an outstanding characteristic of this group of spellers. Another marked feature of the manner in which these children did their work was the zeal with which most of them studied, and the unusual display of initiative common to both boys and girls and to those in the two grade groups.

Analysis of the study methods of children having very low learning indices reveals many noticeable weaknesses. There is a marked lack of systematic method, organization, and self-direction in the study of spelling in this group. Most of the cases show a distinct lack of concentration, lack of organized study, and lack of effective self-direction. Such devices as vocalization, syllabication, visualization, and transfer were used but seldom, and then not very effectively.

Under this heading should also be considered the influence of matters related to the curriculum, the instructional program, and the materials of instruction that condition learning. Such aspects of the curriculum as its scope, its organization, its flexibility and adaptability, and its relation to the needs and interests of the pupils should be examined. The basis for grouping the children, promotion policies, the underlying philosophy of method, techniques of discipline, the guidance program, the skill of the teacher, and the like also affect child growth. Similarly it is necessary to consider the adequacy, efficiency, difficulty, and quality of the materials of instruction as well as the general quality of the school plant and equipment. The administrative relations between members of the staff, the morale of the staff, provisions for improvement of instruction, and similar matters are more remote factors that affect the quality of instruction. These and other items related to curriculum, instruction, and materials will be considered fully in succeeding chapters.

4. Emotional and affective factors. Emotional factors (such as interests and feelings) and social factors (such as rivalry, co-operation, and place in the group) are directly related to the complex psychology of motivation. It is obvious that the responses of the individual to various kinds of stimuli are determined by a wide variety of tendencies to act. Some of these tendencies are constructive and valuable; others are unwholesome and destructive. For various reasons a pupil may have developed a dislike of some subject. He may not see its value. It may be too difficult for him. He may lack important basic foundations. It may lie outside of the range of his interests. The subject may be poorly presented by the teacher. The pupil may lack the capacity of sustained effort. The general consequences of any of these may be a bad emotional state and undesirable maladjustment.

Another pupil may not adjust satisfactorily to his classmates, his teachers, and others with whom he comes into contact. The result may either be withdrawal on his part or aggressive behavior. He may develop unsocial traits. He may commit minor misdemeanors that could ultimately lead to more serious offenses. The school must analyze and evaluate the behavior of pupils and seek to provide the type of stimulation that will initiate and sustain activity toward socially desirable goals. The sociometric procedures described in the preceding chapter are valuable in the study of these social relations.

Detjen and Detjen [32] describe a simple questionnaire to be used by the teacher to discover some of the personal and social needs of children. They are asked to identify members of the class by answering a series of questions, a portion of which is given below. Each pair of questions contains a positive trait and a corresponding negative trait. By assembling the answers the teacher

[32] E. W. Detjen and Mary Detjen, *Elementary School Guidance* (New York, McGraw, 1952), pp. 48-49.

can secure a wealth of information extremely valuable for guidance purposes.

MY CLASSMATES

What children get along best with the others in the class?

What children badly need the friendship of others?

Who are the most helpful to teachers and other pupils?

Who are the least helpful?

Which ones protect and help smaller children?

Which ones tease and pick on smaller children?

Which ones always play fairly and observe the rules of the games?

Which ones often try to take unfair advantage in games?

Which ones are especially good at active outdoor games?

Which ones would rather read, play quiet games, or watch the others play?

What children are especially good sports about doing their share of the work in a group project?

Which ones shirk and do not do their share of the job?

5. Environmental factors. There are many elements of the environment that affect the development of the individual. Some of these conditions are positive and constructive; others, wholly destructive in their influence. First of all is the general quality of the social and material environment of the school itself and the nature of the learning experiences that are provided. These will be considered more fully in Chapters 13 and 17. Then the child's behavior reflects the influence of the home, the attitudes and interests of his associates, and the experiences he has in the community. The home furthermore contributes to the child's feeling of security or insecurity. Frequent migration from one neighborhood to another, poverty, unemployment of parents, lack of food, and broken homes are truly disruptive forces that affect the personality of the individual de-

cisively. The apparent relationship between environment and delinquency brings into sharp relief the environmental forces that determine behavior. Prescott has summarized this point of view as follows:[33]

Delinquents are recruited mainly from those (a) who are victims of an intolerable hiatus between desires and the ability or opportunity to achieve these desires, (b) who are suffering unbearable repression at home and at school, (c) who find it impossible to achieve a satisfactory sense of values belonging in our society because of racial, religious, or cultural differences, or because of personal stigmata, (d) who are deprived of an adequate affectional life by broken homes or because of the personal characteristics of their parents or of themselves, (e) whose life has been overstimulated until they thirst for more and more emotion, (f) whose life has been starved emotionally until they feel that anything is better than the complete drabness they have experienced, and (g) who find in the delinquency a thrill which releases them from unbearable tensions of a wide variety of types. Homes and schools will have to concern themselves more effectively with the direction of the desires of their pupils and with experiences that influence the development of basic value concepts.

Owing to lack of contacts with social and industrial life in the community through travel, excursions, reading, and the like, a pupil may lack the background of experience necessary to make what is being learned meaningful and vital to him. The illustrations that have been given are examples of the many kinds of difficulties (which may grow out of environmental factors) that may interfere with progress and growth.

While it is evident that the causes of unfavorable development often are to be found in readily identifiable elements in the environment itself, the more fundamental questions may be raised: What in fact are the underlying reasons for the existence of these unwholesome conditions? To what extent are they beyond the control of the school? The

[33] Daniel A. Prescott, chairman, *Emotion and the Educative Process* (Washington, American Council on Education, 1938), pp. 152-153.

reasons are undoubtedly to be found partly in the social and economic aspects of community life, partly in the attitudes of the community toward education in general, and partly in the lack of educational leadership. Burton has summarized the conditions in the social order which often are the basic underlying causes of the existence of unwholesome influences that affect the growth and development of the individual unfavorably:[34]

I. *Inequitable distribution of resources,* resulting in inadequate financing of schools, poor economic status of many homes, etc.
   A. Inadequate educational situation.
      1. Poorly constructed, unattractive buildings with poor facilities; inadequate play space and other special items.
      2. Inadequate curriculum; poor or nonexistent instructional material; large overcrowded classes; inadequate pupil experiences; heavy teaching load.
      3. Poorly selected, poorly trained, poorly paid teachers.
   B. Undesirable housing, neighborhoods, inadequate recreational facilities.
   C. Low economic status of many homes.
      1. Lack of education resulting in parental antagonism toward school and in lack of co-operation; resulting in truancy and absence.
      2. Necessity to supplement family income necessitating work after school, resulting in fatigue and other contributing causes.
      3. Stress and strain within family group due to economic insecurity.
      4. Absence of books and magazines, library cards, travel experiences, and other cultural items.
      5. Malnutrition (this is found also in homes of good economic status but for different reasons).
      6. Frequent moves in search of employment resulting in changes in schools and gaps in schooling.
      7. Lack of protection from disease, failure to have adenoids removed, or other necessary care; lack of glasses or other physical aids.
      8. Lack of quiet place for study.

II. *Control of school by conservative elements* in present adult generation who received their education in the past: by *untrained, inert, and often cowardly educational leaders*
   A. Aims of education out of date: an undemocratic philosophy of education.
   B. Lack of modern scientific approach.
   C. Undemocratic administration and supervision.
   D. A curriculum poorly or not at all adapted to the needs, interests, and abilities of the pupils; to the needs of the community.
   E. Traditional teaching methods based upon an erroneous conception of the learner and of learning.
   F. Traditional grade organization, arbitrary standards of promotion, wholly theoretical grade-a-year progress.
   G. Adult standards of success set up without regard for the nature of the learner, of learning, of individual differences.
   H. Lack of an adequate program of professional improvement for the staff.
   I. Failure of the professional leaders to inform and educate the public.
   J. Inadequate local financing of school program in all its details with concomitants already listed.

III. *Low regard for education,* for teaching, and for teachers on part of substantial numbers of lay public
   A. Poor financing, equipment, and program as already listed.
   B. Poor standards for teacher selection and training, low required levels of:
      1. Professional equipment. Meager training and experience, poor methods, ignorance of modern concepts of learning, of teaching, of results, of evaluation.
      2. Physical equipment. Ordinary appearance, average or less than average good health, lack of energy.
      3. Personal equipment. Ordinary appearance, lack of poise, enthusiasm, good judgment, open-mindedness, and many other traits; lack of ambition.

[34] Adapted from William H. Burton, *The Guidance of Learning Activities,* 2nd ed. (New York, Appleton-Century-Crofts, 1952), pp. 634-635.

4. Social equipment. Lack of ability and willingness to co-operate, to adapt oneself, to be considerate, and many other items.

5. Intellectual equipment. Ordinary or less native ability, poor cultural background, narrow interests, poor general information, lack of interest in world affairs, and so on.

IV. *Inadequate understanding by parents* (on all economic levels) of principles of child care and rearing, of human motivations, control of behavior, etc.

A. Harsh, imposed, authoritarian discipline, or

B. Overprotection and coddling.

C. Failure to participate in and guide children's leisure-time activities, reading, radio listening, movie going, choice of companions, and so forth.

D. Failure to give security through the above plus inconsistent discipline, guidance, indulgence; through lack of protection from adult tensions, problems, quarrels, and so forth.

E. Failure in broken homes to protect children from the particular emotional strains involved in this situation.

F. Exposure to racial, national, religious, and political prejudices.

V. *Presence in our society of large immigrant populations*

A. Bi-lingualism in many homes.

B. Double load on pupil if required to attend native-language or religious in addition to public school.

C. Inevitable direct contact with racial, national, religious, and political prejudices.

The implications of this list of fundamental causes of less than optimum growth of individuals are far reaching and of deep social significance. The issues that are raised can in some cases be dealt with locally; whereas in the case of others, the financing of education, for example, the problems are of national concern.

Interrelations of factors. Though in certain cases some one of the five groups of factors that have been described may be the cause of the learning difficulty, in most cases several interrelated factors appear to contribute to the condition. Weakness in reading, for example, is sometimes due to combination of low mental ability, lack of experiential background, and lack of interest in reading.

The following analysis of the more immediate factors that are associated in various combinations with reading disability illustrates in a concrete way each of the five categories just discussed. The list is an adaptation of the discussion in the book by Monroe and Backus:[35]

1. *Physiological Factors*
    a. Visual defects.
    b. Auditory defects.
    c. Difficulties in motor control.
    d. Physical defects and debilitating conditions.
2. *Intellectual Factors*
    a. General level of intelligence.
    b. Verbal disabilities.
    c. Peculiarities in modes of thought.
3. *Emotional Factors*
    a. Conditions contributing to unfavorable attitude toward reading, such as emotional immaturity, timidity, predilection against reading.
    b. Conditions the result of reading disability, such as withdrawal, aggressive action, hypertension, and compensating mechanisms.
    c. Associated or conditioned responses, such as reactions associated with fear, punishment, and similar negative reactions.
4. *Instructional Factors*
    a. Deficiencies in preparation or readiness for reading.
    b. Inappropriate reading materials.
    c. Poor adjustment of methods of instruction to individual differences.
    d. Poorly motivated work.
    e. Overcrowded classes.
    f. Insufficient use by teacher of testing and diagnosis.
    g. Highly routinized and standardized instructional procedures required by supervisor which discourage flexibility and teacher initiative.

[35] Marion Monroe and Bertie Backus, *Remedial Reading* (Boston, Houghton, 1937).

h. No planned or adequate remedial program.
5. *Environmental Factors*
   a. Lack of co-operation between school and home.
   b. Emotional stress and insecurity in the home and elsewhere.
   c. Economic insecurity.
   d. Frequent migration.
   e. Illiteracy and language handicaps.
   f. Meager provision of suitable reading materials.

From the list given above of causative factors, the diagnostician can often eliminate certain factors as inoperative on the basis of preliminary information derived from observation, interview, and examination. He can then formulate a tentative judgment as to the conditions that have unfavorably affected learning to read. By means of appropriate diagnostic methods he should then attempt to establish the correctness of this hypothesis. When the causative factors have once been established, they should then be corrected or removed when possible, or necessary adjustments made. To allow for factors that cannot be corrected, such as a low level of mental ability, radical changes in the instructional program may be necessary.

The complexity of the problem of diagnosis [36] is increased when one realizes that any one primary cause may be due to a variety of related factors or causes and that it may produce different sets of symptoms in different individuals. For example, the primary cause of a deficiency may apparently be malnutrition. In one case this may be the result of poverty, in another an unbalanced diet, and in another poorly supervised eating habits. In another case lack of interest in

school work may be due to fatigue caused by a large amount of time spent in working outside of school which in turn may be due to the necessity of earning money to help support the family; in other cases lack of interest may be due to indifference of parents, to inability to master the subject matter, to a poor curriculum, to ineffective instruction, even to emotional insecurity, which again may be due to any of a score of causes. Any of these primary causes can be broken down still further into numerous details, ranging from narrowly conceived aims by the school to inadequacies of instructional materials and procedures. This complexity of causes of a learning deficiency should be recognized by the teacher and clinical worker. Hence any diagnosis should be made on a tentative basis and modified whenever there is new information indicating other possible contributory factors.

Factors on which prediction of readiness depends. There are available readiness tests in primary reading and in arithmetic at all grade levels. Readiness tests in reading [37] vary widely in the reliability of predictions based on their results. Brueckner [38] has developed a readiness test for primary arithmetic which has a predictive index of .87. Other studies by Brueckner and his associates about readiness for division and operations with fractions yielded somewhat lower predictive indices. Preliminary work [39] has also been done on readiness for spelling. Studies in other areas will doubtless develop.

In general, it can be said that readiness of any child for learning in any given field of knowledge depends on (1) the background of experiences related to the field with which he approaches the new work; (2) his physi-

[36] Sheldon Glueck and Eleanor Glueck, *Unraveling Juvenile Delinquency* (New York, Commonwealth Fund, 1950).

[37] A. I. Gates and G. L. Bond, "Reading Readiness: A Study of Factors Determining Success and Failure in Beginning Reading," *Teachers College Record* (May, 1936), pp. 679-685.

———, "A Further Evaluation of Reading Readiness Tests," *Elementary School Journal* (April, 1940), pp. 577-591.

[38] L. J. Brueckner, "The Development of Readiness Tests in Arithmetic," *Journal of Educational Research* (September, 1940), pp. 15-20.

———, "The Development and Validation of an Arithmetic Readiness Test," *Journal of Educational Research* (1947), pp. 496-502.

[39] D. H. Russell, "A Diagnostic Study of Spelling Readiness," *Journal of Educational Research* (1947), pp. 276-283.

cal development, including visual and auditory perception, and motor development; (3) his mental development, including intelligence level, maturation, concepts, and meanings; (4) language development, including speech; (5) desire to learn and evidence of interest in the new work; and (6) his emotional and social adjustment. Other factors such as the skill of the teacher and the suitability of instructional materials should be considered in making predictions. The effective use of this information about readiness enables the teacher to plan the instructional program intelligently.

The value of readiness tests as predictive devices and aids to instruction in arithmetic has been established by well-controlled experimentation. Souder [40] has also demonstrated that when teachers in grade 5 used the results of carefully constructed readiness tests that were diagnostic in nature as guides for instruction, the results were superior to those for classes for which this information was not available.

Section 3

THE TECHNIQUES OF DIAGNOSIS

Levels of diagnosis. There are different levels of diagnostic study, ranging from a casual observation by a layman that an individual seems to be hard of hearing to the clinical study of hearing by a specialist; from a general impression that a pupil has difficulty in reading to a critical analysis of the process by which he tries to get meaning from the printed page.

The classroom teacher can gain a great deal of information about the pupil's methods of work by observing him while he prepares an assignment in the library or classroom and noting his difficulties. As a check on the correctness of these impressions, the teacher can make use of the results of group tests or diagnostic tests that locate his deficiencies with greater accuracy and definiteness. In case of need of more exact knowledge to establish hypotheses about the status of the individual and the factors involved, use can be made of highly analytical clinical procedures and instruments. Discrimination should be used in the selection of diagnostic instruments, and indiscriminate testing should be avoided. The diagnosis should be only as detailed as may be necessary to reveal clearly the nature of the disability. In general, a program of diagnosis should be simple to operate and as easy to apply as is consistent with good results. The relatively few cases whose diagnosis requires the use of expensive equipment and materials should be referred to a central clinic for examination. Very few communities [41] are able to finance the installation of fully equipped clinics. For practical purposes, ingenious home-made devices can be put to considerable use. There is no hocus-pocus about educational diagnosis.

Three levels of diagnosis can be identified as follows:

1. *General:* The procedures at this level include those that are used to make a general evaluation of the characteristics of the educational product that were described in Chapter 9.

2. *Analytical:* The procedures at this level are diagnostic tests and devices that are intended to locate and identify with precision and in detail the shortcomings and deficiencies existing in some major learning area.

3. *Psychological:* The procedures used at this level determine the exact nature and also the causes of weaknesses that have been identified or located by analytical procedures. These techniques include:

　　a. Standardized individual diagnostic programs and tests.

[40] Hugh Souder, "The Construction and Validation of Certain Readiness Tests in Common Fractions," *ibid.* (October, 1943), pp. 127-134.

[41] Gertrude Boyd and O. C. Schweiring, "A Survey of Child Guidance and Remedial Reading Practices," *ibid.* (March, 1950), pp. 481-493. Reports results of a survey of 76 clinics.

b. Controlled observation of performance in test situations.
c. Analysis of written work.
d. Analysis of oral responses or accounts of procedures.
e. Analysis of some product by comparison with diagnostic devices.
f. Interview or questionnaire.
g. Projective and expressive procedures.
h. Clinical tests and laboratory procedures.
i. Analysis of information in records of various kinds.

Each method of studying a deficiency discloses certain characteristics of behavior, but each method has its limitations. Standardized and informal tests limit diagnosis to the particular situation and form of response elicited. Observation tends to limit the analysis to the elements of a situation that are most readily observable and hence diagnosis is often incomplete and overlooks vital elements. The analysis of oral and written responses is often limited by their inaccuracy and indefiniteness, and the interpretation of the information is usually subjective. In the interview there is often an unconscious bias or conflict of personalities. The development of clinical and laboratory procedures is still very limited in such areas as personality traits, but there have been rapid strides in such areas as reading and arithmetic. The practical value of these procedures has however been amply demonstrated, and the authors recommend their use with full recognition of their limitations. In the following pages these procedures will be briefly discussed. The fundamental importance of a thorough medical examination when dealing with a child having learning difficulty of a serious kind is merely indicated at this point. Special types of information helpful in diagnosing learning, that can be secured from competent medical diagnosticians and opticians, are indicated from time to time.

1. General diagnosis. The chief instruments used in general diagnosis in the various curriculum areas are standard tests of intelligence and batteries of achievement tests. The data supplied by intelligence tests are needed to interpret scores on achievement tests. Often check-lists, rating scales, records of observations and data supplied by local agencies are utilized as the basis of an overview of other aspects of behavior perhaps more important but not so readily measured by standardized procedures.

The purpose of such surveys is to secure a general picture of the status of the educational product. A comparison of the results of survey tests given from year to year reveals general trends in the growth of children in the areas tested in relation to available norms and standards. This information is of great values to administrators and supervisors in identifying strengths and weaknesses of educational programs. To be of greatest value, survey tests should be administered early in the school year so that the information can be used as the basis of instruction and supervision. The results of equivalent forms of the test toward the end of the school year provide the basis for evaluating the progress that has been made.

The procedures to follow in analyzing and interpreting the results of surveys of educational outcomes at various levels in the school system are suggested by the following headings:

1. *Superintendent and Central Staff*
   a. Analysis of city-wide results grade by grade in comparison with expected performance.
   b. Comparison with results of previous years.
   c. Consideration of the consolidated distributions of class medians for all schools at various grade levels.
   d. Overview of results for various schools.
   e. Consideration of possible causes of these variations in results among the different schools.
   f. Planning next steps for improving the educational program.
2. *Staffs of Individual Schools in Co-operation with Consultants*
   a. Comparison of results for the school as a whole with city-wide scores and

with standard scores at various grade levels.

b. General trends of progress from grade to grade as compared with results for previous years.

c. The deviation of each grade and class from expected levels of attainment in relation to the mental ability of the children, their social background, and health.

d. Consistency of levels of attainment in the various areas tested.

e. The range of test results for each area within individual classes.

f. The overlapping of test scores at consecutive grade levels.

g. Identifying strengths and weakness of the school's program on the basis of the test results.

h. Considering possible next steps.

3. *Individual Teachers in Co-operation with Principal or Consultant*

a. Overview of the results for the class as a whole, sharing the information with the pupils.

b. Analysis of results for individual pupils, preferably summarized in graphic profile form.

c. Critical comparison of educational levels achieved in relation to the mental ability of individuals.

d. Consideration of factors that might throw light on variations in achievement of individuals and deviations from levels of expectancy.

e. Consideration of discrepancies between test results for individual pupils and teacher's estimates.

f. Analysis of the test items on survey tests that have possible diagnostic value.

g. Planning a program of remedial instruction.

h. Planning the ways in which to use the data most effectively in the public relations program.

The plan outlined above will make "the people in the central office" thoroughly aware of the wide variations that are invariably discovered when the outcomes for the different schools in a single school system are compared. Under intelligent leadership, the result is likely to be that supervisory programs will be flexible and adapted to the differences in the situations revealed in the various schools. Plans can be made for strengthening good work that is being done and for dealing with points in the educational program where weaknesses appear to exist. The same flexibility of approach should be used in the planning done co-operatively by the staffs of particular schools to improve local conditions.

The steps to be taken in evaluating the information secured by other less objective methods of appraisal are similar to those outlined above for dealing with the results of tests. The evaluation will necessarily be less precise and definite than is possible with tests results because comparable standards are in most instances lacking. In all cases the analysis can be done on either an individual or a group basis. The total picture should be very revealing. On the basis of the facts thus secured, intelligent steps can be taken by the school to bring about an improvement.

2. Analytical diagnostic tests. These tests are more detailed and analytical than the survey tests discussed in Chapter 9. In analytical diagnostic tests, major abilities such as reading, or areas of the curriculum, such as the social studies, are broken into elements. The application of these tests enables the teacher to locate the specific places where weakness exists or where skills break down. On the basis of the results, it is possible to construct a profile of the individual's status which reveals his strengths and weaknesses. The Iowa Silent Reading Tests are an example of this kind of test.[42] Several other good ones are available. They measure a considerable number of reading skills, as can be seen from the list of the parts of the test given below:

IOWA SILENT READING TESTS

Comprehension
1. Paragraph meaning.
   A. Social science.
   B. Literature.
   C. Science.

[42] Yonkers, World Book.

2. Word meaning: subject-matter vocabulary.
   A. Social science.
   B. Science.
   C. Mathematics.
   D. English.
3. Sentence comprehension.

Organization

4. Sentence.
5. Paragraph.
   A. Selection of central idea.
   B. Outlining.
   C. Organization of paragraph.

Location

6. Ability to use the index.
   A. Use of the index.
   B. Selection of key words.
   C. Alphabetizing.

TOTAL COMPREHENSION SCORE

Rate

7. Silent reading rate.

These tests measure abilities in different types of subject matter, including social science, literature, and science. Four major aspects of reading are evaluated: comprehension, organization, location of materials in printed sources, and rate of reading. Tests of paragraph-, word-, and sentence-meaning are included for measuring comprehension. Under the heading of organization there are tests of sentence and paragraph organization. Three tests of paragraph organization are included, namely, selection of the central idea, outlining, and paragraph organization. There are three tests of skills in locating information: use of the index, selection of key words, and alphabetizing. These tests are illustrative of the kinds of diagnostic methods that are very helpful in locating specific strengths and weaknesses of pupils. Similar tests are now available in various subjects, including among others English, arithmetic social studies, modern languages, and science. Many of the new, up-to-date instructional materials, textbooks, and workbooks also include tests useful for diagnostic purposes. The results of these tests enable the teacher to discover points at which the class as well as individual pupils need help. In some of these instructional materials there are also given suitable corrective and remedial exercises. Analytical tests of this kind should always be used to discover specific weaknesses in fields in which the general survey tests have already indicated that a possible deficiency may exist.

Cook [43] has proposed the following criteria that a diagnostic test should meet:

1. The test should be based on experimental evidence designed to reveal the sources of learning difficulties, misunderstandings, and faulty thinking.
2. The test must be an integral part of the curriculum, emphasizing and clarifying the important objectives.
3. The test items should require responses to situations that approximate the functional as closely as possible.
4. The responses should be such as to reveal the mental processes of the learner.
5. Instructional procedures should be provided to correct the various errors or provide needed learning experiences.
6. The tests should be segmented, organized, and spaced to cover systematically a substantial sequence of learning. In fact, the testing should continue at regular intervals through the elementary-school period.
7. The tests, by affording the opportunity for a constant, systematic review of difficult elements, should reduce forgetting as well as detect faulty or inadequate learning.
8. Provision should be made for the pupil to keep a record of learning problems and to measure and record his progress systematically.

Determining the elements to include in an analytical diagnostic test. For example, the analysis given below of the skills involved in working the illustrative example at the right will reveal the possibility of a wide variety of contributory causes of disability in the total process of division:

$$\begin{array}{r} 2 \\ 27\overline{)80} \\ 54 \\ \overline{26} \end{array}$$

1. In order to find the quotient figure in this example, it is necessary first to estimate the quotient and then to correct the estimated

[43] Robert H. Beck, Walter W. Cook, and Nolan C. Kearney, *Curriculum in the Modern Elementary School* (Copyright, 1953, by Prentice-Hall, Inc., New York), pp. 188-189. Reprinted by permission of the publisher.

quotient to find the true quotient, a very diffi-cult step to learn.

2. To find the quotient 2 it is necessary to know the quotient in the division grouping $2/8$. A knowledge of all basic even and un-even division groupings obviously is basic to mastery of the process.

3. Next it is necessary to multiply 27 by 2, requiring a knowledge of the groupings and process of multiplication.

4. In working this example, addition is used in carrying after multiplying 27×2. Thus a knowledge of addition groupings and processes is also essential in division.

5. In finding the remainder, subtraction is used. Therefore a knowledge of subtraction groupings and processes is also essential to success in division.

This analysis could be extended to include various other subskills, concepts, and mean-ings underlying division.

Research by the use of diagnostic tests of each of the above skills has established the fact that some pupils who make low scores in division tests are deficient in only one of these underlying skills, for instance, subtrac-tion, whereas others reveal weaknesses in almost all of them. A systematic examination of the written work of pupils performing at a low level in division will reveal weaknesses that may be contributing to a poor perform-ance. Informal tests of each basic skill can then be applied to make certain that a defi-ciency exists. Similar procedures can be used for identifying difficulties in composition, spelling, and grammar.

To aid in the analysis of errors, extensive lists have been compiled for various subjects, such as spelling, arithmetic, composition, writing, and reading. Some of these errors are of minor consequence, whereas others are symptoms of serious weaknesses. Random, unintelligent misspellings, for example, are a much more serious symptom of disability than mere phonetic misspellings.

The values and limitations of studies that have been made of the errors and defects found in the oral and written responses of pupils have been summarized by Brueckner as follows: [44]

Detailed lists of kinds of errors pupils make in algebra, arithmetic, spelling, English, and reading are available. These lists have been supplemented by carefully arrayed descriptions of apparently faulty methods of work, ineffec-tive study habits, and undesirable behavior traits; however, these studies have a number of limitations. Some of the lists are substantially complete and of great value in diagnosis; others are so general that they are of little assistance. Many of the studies that contain detailed lists of the kinds of errors made most frequently by children contain no information as to their cruciality as symptoms of important deficiencies or as factors that may substantially lead to serious maladjustments. Very few of the studies of errors or apparently faulty methods of work contain data showing differences between the reactions of pupils whose performance is satis-factory and those whose work is unsatisfac-tory; that is, they give little evidence concerning valid methods of differentiating the peform-ances of pupils of inferior and superior ability. Some of the faults listed are found in the work of both superior and inferior pupils. Little is known concerning the prognosis of various types of difficulties and faults. Very few studies are available that deal with the persistency of error in the work of pupils, a very important factor in arriving at a valid diagnosis. Little is known concerning the extent to which vari-ous types of specific difficulties are usually eliminated as the learner matures. Little is known concerning the relation between the kinds of errors made and the performances of the learner on particular tasks that vary widely under different conditions.

Those who have made analyses of errors and methods of work have clarified many issues relative to the characteristics of learning. For some difficulties, suitable remedial exercises have been suggested; yet little exact informa-tion is available concerning the effectiveness of the various proposal remedial measures for correcting particular kinds of difficulties. That many difficulties can easily be corrected is ap-parent from the results of ordinary instruction. Teachers, individually and as a group, have ac-cumulated a mass of techniques that they apply with varying degrees of assurance and success. This same condition of uncertainty existed in the field of medicine before the techniques of modern science were applied to the study of the prevention and cure of human ills. By means of similar scientific techniques the rem-

[44] Brueckner, in *Educational Diagnosis, op. cit.*, pp. 152-153.

edies for crucial faults and learning difficulties, as well as techniques for averting their incidence, should be experimentally established in education, so that the teacher may undertake corrective work with reasonable assurance of attaining the desired results. Here are also involved materials of instruction. It is perfectly clear that at present much of our teaching is not intelligently directed toward the achievement of desired goals because we know so little concerning the effectiveness of the materials of methods of instruction that we used. The contrast between the scientifically validated techniques of the medical practitioner and the unsystematic, unscientific procedures of the educator is very striking.

Analytical diagnostic tests in specific curriculum areas. Considerable progress has been made in recent years in the improvement of the format of analytical diagnostic tests in arithmetic. The following kinds of diagnostic tests are essential tools of instruction in arithmetic that are found in modern arithmetic textbooks:

1. Inventory tests in basic skills to be administered in the fall of the year to identify areas in which there is a need for systematic diagnosis and review.
2. Diagnostic tests constructed so as to locate specific types of difficulty.
3. Readiness tests to determine how well the learners have mastered basic concepts and skills needed in new work.
4. Developmental diagnostic tests that parallel new work and are given at frequent intervals to identify promptly any weak spots in what is being learned.
5. Comprehensive diagnostic tests that include all key types of examples when instruction in a major skill, such as multiplication of fractions, has been completed.

Each of these kinds of diagnostic tests serves a specific purpose, namely, to locate or identify points where difficulty exists that should be corrected promptly. The cumulative effect of specific deficiencies in arithmetic has often proved disastrous.

The steps [45] in constructing an analytical diagnostic test in arithmetic of the developmental type listed above are as follows:

1. Make a careful analysis of the various combinations in which the basic skills involved in some process appear. For instance, the basic types of examples in addition of like fractions without carrying may be listed as follows:

a. $\frac{1}{3}$ b. $\frac{1}{4}$ c. $3\frac{1}{5}$ d. $2\frac{1}{8}$ e. 4
$+\frac{1}{3}$ $+\frac{1}{4}$ $+2\frac{2}{5}$ $+3\frac{5}{8}$ $+2\frac{1}{2}$

Each of the above examples involves a different combination of skills, as can easily be determined by inspection.
2. Arrange the different types in order of their complexity following the sequence in which they are taught in the textbook. The sequence given above illustrates the procedure.
3. Construct three examples, preferably four examples, of each type so that the pupil is given the opportunity to work several examples of each type.
4. Arrange the three or four examples of each type in rows on the test paper, rather than in disarranged order, to facilitate the location of weak spots.
5. If on the test a pupil works all of the examples in a row correctly, he clearly has no difficulty with examples of that type. If he works only one example in the row incorrectly, he should correct the error at once. When he works two or more examples incorrectly in a single row, a persistent difficulty is indicated that requires careful diagnosis by using more penetrating procedures such as are described in the next section of this chapter.

It should be pointed out that very few of the available textbooks contain diagnostic tests constructed along this line, although the results of experimental investigations are the basis for the plan outlined above. Similar procedures have been developed for reading and language skills.

Suggested analytical diagnostic tests. Useful tests for analytical diagnosis in the various major fields of the curriculum, in addition to those that have been mentioned, follow:

ARITHMETIC

Analytical Scales of Attainment in Arithmetic (Minneapolis, Educational Test Bureau, 1934). Contains tests in processes, problems, vocabulary, and quantitative relationships.

[45] L. J. Brueckner and Ella Hawkinson, "The Optimum Order of Arrangement of Items in a Diagnostic Test in Arithmetic," *Elementary School Journal* (January, 1934), pp. 351-357.

California Achievement Tests (Los Angeles, California Test Bureau). Contains tests in the four operations, and of three aspects of arithmetic reasoning.

Iowa Every-Pupil Test of Basic Skills, Test D, Basic Arithmetic Skills, three subtests (Iowa City, Bureau of Educational Research and Science, University of Iowa, distributed yearly); also by Houghton Mifflin Co., Boston, and Science Research Associates, Chicago.

READING

California Achievement Tests (Los Angeles, California Test Bureau). Contains seven subtests on reading vocabulary and reading comprehension.

Diagnostic Reading Tests and Survey Reading Test, Committee on Diagnostic Reading Tests (Chicago, Science Research Associates).

Gates Reading Survey for Grades 3 to 10 (New York, Teachers College, Bureau of Publications, Columbia Univ., 1939). Gives measures of vocabulary, level of comprehension, speed and accuracy.

Gates Primary Reading Tests (New York, Teachers College, Bureau of Publications, Columbia Univ., 1945). Gives measures of power in reading words, sentences, and paragraphs for grades 1 and 2.

Gates Silent Reading Tests (New York, Teachers College, Bureau of Publications, Columbia Univ., 1945). Give measures for speed, comprehension, and accuracy of comprehension of four basic reading skills for grades 3-6.

Iowa Every-Pupil Tests of Basic Skills, Elementary and Advanced (Boston, Houghton, 1947). Contains tests of reading and work-study skills, language, and arithmetic.

Van Wagenen-Dvorak Diagnostic Examination of Silent Reading Abilities (Minneapolis, Educational Test Bureau, 1939). Consists of a series of tests for measuring status of ten fundamental elements in reading.

ENGLISH COMPOSITION

California Achievement Tests (Los Angeles, California Test Bureau). Contains five subtests on language.

Iowa Every-Pupil Test of Basic Skills. Contains three subtests in language.

Pressey Diagnostic Tests in English Composition (Bloomington, Ill., Public School Publishing Co., 1936). Diagnostic tests in various phases of composition.

Van Wagenen English Composition Scales (Yonkers, World Book, 1923). Provide method of evaluating structure, thought, and mechanics.

SOCIAL STUDIES

Analytical Scales of Attainment in History and Geography (Minneapolis, Educational Test Bureau, 1932). Consists of two series of tests, measuring various aspects of attainment in history and geography.

Iowa Every-Pupil Test of Basic Study Skills (Iowa City, Univ. of Iowa). Consists of tests of various skills required for successful work in history and geography for elementary and high school.

STUDY HABITS

Attempts have been made to devise direct tests of study habits. Some of the most useful are listed here.

Iowa Every-Pupil Test of Basic Skills. Subtests on work study skills.

EDGAR, J. W., and MANUEL, H. T., *A Test of Study Skills* (Austin, Texas, The Steck Co., 1940).

LEWIS, E. E., *Attitudes and Skills in the Use of References: Every Pupil Test. Range: Grades 5-8, 9-12* (Columbus, Ohio Scholarship Tests, Department of Education, Ohio State Univ., 1935).

Tyler-Kimber Study Skills Test. Range: High School and College (Stanford University, Calif., Stanford Univ. Press, 1938).

WRENN, C. G., and MCKEOWN, R. B., *Study Habits Inventory. Range: Grade 12 and College* (Stanford University, Calif., Stanford Univ. Press, 1933).

A very interesting method of measuring the effectiveness of study habits in spelling has been devised by Courtis. A standard test of fifty words is dictated. Then pupils are given the list words to study for ten minutes. Following this study period, the test is repeated. The growth made during the study period is used as a measure of the efficiency of the study habits. Standards for interpreting growth in terms of a new unit of measure, isochrons, are available.[46]

[46] Helen Miller, *Creative Teaching in the Field of Spelling* (Hamtramck, Mich., Board of Education, 1928).

3. Psychological diagnosis. In cases of serious deficiency it is often necessary to make a detailed analysis of the pupil's responses and methods of work so as to make clear their characteristics as a basis for determining more definitely the exact nature of his difficulty. The analysis of the kinds of errors made, for example, in spelling, arithmetic, reading, and English, is an illustration of this kind of diagnosis. Other examples are the analyses of pupil's study habits, his attention, and his perseverance while at work on an assigned task. Diagnosis of maladjustments is another example.

Considerable progress has been made in devising analytical procedures for studying and appraising the pupil's behavior and responses. Some of the more useful of these techniques will now be described. They are in many cases not so precise as the procedures that have been discussed, but the information secured by their use is often more revealing. This is especially true if the examiner is aware of the kinds of behavior that are likely to indicate the presence of unfavorable conditions and knows how to array situations in which these responses will ordinarily be made evident.

a. Standardized individual diagnostic tests. A number of very useful standardized tests for making diagnostic studies to determine the nature of specific deficiencies of individual children in the basic tool subjects are available. Originally their use was limited to workers in clinics and remedial centers. However, in recent years because of the lack of specialists in diagnosis in most schools, many classroom teachers have taken courses in the diagnosis and treatment of learning difficulties in which both standard and informal diagnostic procedures were studied and applied. To an ever increasing degree these diagnostic techniques have been simplified and adapted to general use in classroom instruction. This is particularly true of the area of arithmetic. Up-to-date textbooks in arithmetic include inventory tests, diagnostic tests, readiness tests, and progress tests, all of which are essential tools of instruction. Their use must be supplemented in the case of pupils having unusual difficulty by informal diagnostic procedures such as those that are described in the following pages.

To enable teachers to make more effective use of informal diagnostic procedures, their preparation for teaching should include systematic study and actual experience in using such standard diagnostic tests as the following. Otherwise there must be provision for training teachers to use diagnostic tests as a part of the in-service education program.

ARITHMETIC

a. *Brueckner Diagnostic Tests in Whole Numbers, in Fractions, and in Decimals* (Educational Test Bureau).
b. *Buswell-John Diagnostic Tests for Fundamental Processes in Arithmetic* (*Whole Numbers Only*) (Public School Publishing Co.).
c. *Diagnostic Tests and Self Helps in Arithmetic,* devised by L. J. Brueckner. A series of 23 diagnostic tests of all computational skills in Arithmetic (California Test Bureau).

READING

a. *Gates Reading Diagnostic Tests* (Teachers College, Bureau of Publications, Columbia Univ.).
b. *Durrell Analysis of Reading Difficulty* (World Book).
c. *Monroe Diagnostic Reading Tests* (C. H. Stoelting Co.).

SPELLING

a. *Gates-Russell Spelling Diagnosis Tests* (Teachers College, Bureau of Publications, Columbia Univ.).

LANGUAGE

a. *Blanton-Stanchfield Speech Measurement Test* (C. H. Stoelting Co.).
b. The workbooks by Michaelson and others, *Language Drills,* published by Fowler Co. Contain numerous well-devised diagnostic these in the field of written language at each grade level from grade 3 to 8.

HANDWRITING

a. *Freeman Chart for Diagnosing Faults in Handwriting* (Houghton).
b. *The Minneapolis Self-Corrective Handwriting Charts* (St. Paul Book and Stationery Co., St. Paul, Minn.).

With both of these diagnostic instruments in handwriting the probable causes of the defect are listed, thus facilitatiing corrective work.

Essentials in education for expert clinical service. Skill in the diagnosis and treatment of deficiencies and needs in the mastery of subject matter and basic skills in various curriculum areas require, in addition to a thorough understanding of the developmental process in the area involved:

1. A mastery of techniques of administering as well as interpreting and applying the results gained by such instrument as:
    a. Achievements tests.
    b. Visual screening devices.
    c. Auditory screening devices.
    d. Individual and group intelligence tests.
    e. Systems of individual diagnosis in various areas such as reading, spelling, handwriting, speech, and arithmetic.
    f. Tests of personality and adjustment.
2. Facility in using the data gathered to determine the needs of the child, including sociological data and data from school records.
3. Skill in considering multiple hypotheses as to the causes of a child's learning difficulties and in applying available knowledge concerning needs and causes to the implementation of effective remedial procedures.
4. Skill in selecting and evaluating possible corrective procedures in light of accepted principles of remedial teaching.
5. Adaptability and versatility in adjusting instructional procedures to learning programs as treatment proceeds.
6. Sufficient knowledge of practices in such specialties as psychiatry, clinical psychology, and endocrinology to recognize symptoms requiring the services of specialists in these areas.

The prerequisites for skill in diagnosis in the area of behavior are similar to those given above.

b. Controlled observation. Because of the impossibility of appraising by ordinary tests many of the characteristics of the pupil who is having difficulty, the teacher must in many cases use the technique of controlled observation.[47] This means the observation of the activities of the pupil while he is at work on some task and the recording of his actions as a basis for later evaluation. The teacher can, for example, discover manifestations of lack of control of basic skills by observing the pupil at work. For instance, vocalization and lip movement in reading, counting in arithmetic, and incorrect use of laboratory apparatus are some of the kinds of faulty habits readily revealed by observation. McCallister[48] has assembled a list of faulty study habits used by pupils in reading and the social studies which can serve as a guide in the observation of pupils at work. Wrenn's Study Habits Inventory[49] is an excellent device for evaluating the study habits of high-school and college students. An observer can also analyze the kind of contributions and the extent of participation of pupils in class activities,[50] using as a basis of the analysis a list of the types of pupil activity that are desirable or undesirable. Blunders and failure can be noted. The reactions of various children to different kinds of incentives and to materials and methods of motivation can be recorded by means of sociometric and projective procedures. This observation can be extended to the study of behavior in the activities on the playground and in the larger community.

[47] Dorothy C. Adkins, "Principles Underlying Observational Techniques of Evaluation," *Educational and Psychological Measurements* (Spring, 1951), pp. 29-51.
[48] J. M. McCallister, *Remedial and Corrective Instruction in Reading* (New York, Appleton-Century, 1936).
[49] Stanford University, Calif., Stanford Univ. Press, 1934.
[50] E. Horn, *Distribution of the Opportunity for Participation Among the Various Pupils in Classroom Recitations*, Contributions to Education No. 67 (New York, Teachers College, Bureau of Publications, Columbia Univ., 1914).

Morrison [51] has devised the individual attention profile as a means of getting a graphic picture of the degree of attention exhibited by the pupil during a recitation or study period. To aid in the evaluation of this record, a systematic account of the pupil's behavior and conditions affecting it should parallel the profile.

The use of observation in the study of behavior is well illustrated by the elements of an outline, devised by Fenton, for the study of the individual student in terms of his needs. The outline contains seven sections with the following headings: [52]

    I. The need for a healthy body and good physique and appearance.
   II. The need for feelings of security.
 III. The need for social adjustment and recognition.
 IV. The need for feelings of competence.
  V. The need to accept the conditions and the realities of his own life.
 VI. The need to experience curiosity and pleasure and to acquire active and varied interests.
VII. The need to be considered a developing personality.

The nature of the outline of items to observe is shown by the contents of the section on the need for social adjustment and recognition given below:

III. The need for social adjustment and recognition
    A. Is the student accepted as a member of the group at home without resentment and jealousy by others there? Yes. No. Without favoritism or preferment? Yes. No. Does he feel jealousy or resentment toward anyone in the home? Yes. No. Explain:
    B. Does he feel that he belongs to his group at school? Does he feel accepted by other children? Yes. No. By the teacher? Yes. No. Explain:
    C. Does he receive recognition for legitimate achievement at home? Yes. No. In school? Yes. No. Elaborate:
    D. Does he need to seek recognition through show-off behaviors or other unwholesome attention-getting devices? Yes. No. How?
    E. Does he have some special friends in school? Yes. No. In the neighborhood? Yes. No. Does he take initiative in seeking friendships? Yes. No. Comment on the range and quality of friendships:
    F. Does he have a reasonably unselfish and generous attitude toward others? Yes. No. Is he mature enough to hold ideals of social betterment? Yes. No. Explain:
    G. Does he give evidence of prejudice or antagonisms (racial, religious, social, sex) which influence his choice of associates, or lead to the avoidance of certain classmates? Yes. No. Specify:
    H. Does he behave well and observe the ordinary social decorums in the classroom? Yes. No. Elsewhere? Yes. No. Comment:

c. Analysis of written work. A test score furnishes a helpful measure of the level of a pupil's achievement, but it gives no index as to the quality of his work nor of the kinds of difficulties he encountered or of the errors he made. It is possible to use standardized tests constructed in such a way that serious deficiencies or difficulties will be revealed.

An illustrative analysis of written spelling errors. The table below contains an analysis of the spelling errors made by a typical fifth-grade class of 35 pupils during a three-month period. The teacher [53] kept a record of misspelled words in all daily essay-type work, the regular weekly spelling test, and an achievement test. In all 5624 errors were discovered in a total of 5035 misspelled words. The table shows the types of errors identified, classified according to three major categories, namely, mechanical, phonetic, and nonphonetic.

[51] H. L. Morrison, *Practice of Teaching in the Secondary School* (Chicago, Univ. of Chicago Press, 1926), Ch. 8.

[52] Norman Fenton, *op. cit.,* pp. 173, 192-193.

[53] M. R. Wolff, "A Study of Spelling Errors with Implications Concerning Pertinent Teaching Methods," *Elementary School Journal* (April, 1952), p. 461.

DISTRIBUTION OF SPELLING ERRORS MADE BY 35 FIFTH-GRADE PUPILS

TYPE OF ERROR	MATERIAL OF ALL TYPES	
	Number	*Per Cent*
I. *Mechanical*		
1. Punctuation		
a. Capitalization	446	7.9
b. Uncrossed *t*'s	62	1.1
c. Others: hyphen, contractions, abbreviations	72	1.3
2. Letter formation		
a. Interchange of *m* and *n*	280	5.0
b. Use of *t* for *l*	28	.5
c. Interchange of *U* and *V*, *O* and *Q*, *Z* and *Y*, *I* and *S*.	14	.2
d. Loop letters *z, q, g, d, p, b, h, k, l*	59	1.0
e. Interchange *u, w, v, x, s, r*	48	.9
f. Kinaesthetic	32	.6
3. Rules		
a. Plurals and possessives	147	2.6
b. Suffixes	88	1.6
TOTAL	1276	22.7
II. *Phonetic*		
1. Vowel substitution	456	8.1
2. Vowel omission	335	6.0
3. Consonant substitution	221	3.9
4. Final *e* difficulty	189	3.4
5. Diphthongs	385	6.8
6. Doubling and non-doubling	281	5.0
7. Endings: *er, le, ly*, etc.	104	1.9
8. Entire word	69	1.2
TOTAL	2040	36.3
III. *Nonphonetic*		
1. Word not attempted, not completed, little similarity, different	557	9.9
2. Inversions	473	8.4
3. Faulty pronunciation	90	1.6
4. Homonyms	147	2.6
5. Anticipation and repetition	42	.7
6. Insertion of syllable	16	.3
7. Omission of syllable	55	1.0
8. Insertion of vowel	218	3.9
9. Insertion of consonant	101	1.8
10. Omission of consonant	449	8.0
11. Silent consonant	33	.6
12. Unaccountable consonant substitution	127	2.2
TOTAL	2308	41.0
GRAND TOTAL	5624	100.0

The recognition of the fact that mechanical errors in composition [54] are probably not as significant as other faults has led to the development of methods of analyzing compositions from the point of view of the richness of their vocabulary,[55] their freedom from faulty structure,[56] the freshness and originality of their style,[57] and their general interest to the reader. Similar techniques are available for art, home economics, and mechanical drawing.

d. Analysis of oral responses. For some purposes, the analysis of oral responses is a valuable diagnostic procedure. A record of errors in oral English is in some respects more valuable than an analysis of errors in written composition as an index of the correctness of expression in the affairs of daily life. An analysis of the kinds of errors made in oral reading often reveals the kinds of faults that interfere with success in silent reading.

The list of errors in oral reading given below is from the Gates Diagnostic Reading Test. It illustrates the use of the technique of analysis of oral responses on a test of oral reading as a basis of diagnosis of reading difficulty.

ANALYSIS OF ERRORS

Base the analysis on the first four paragraphs only.

a. Words omitted.
b. Words added.
c. Repetitions.
d. Mispronunciations.
e. Full reversals.
f. Reversal of parts.
g. Wrong order ($e + f$).
h. Wrong beginnings.
i. Wrong middles.
j. Wrong endings.
k. Several parts wrong.

CHECK-LIST OF DIFFICULTIES

Reads slowly, word by word.
Reads slowly, phrasing and emphasis poor.
Reads rapidly, phrasing and emphasis poor.
Reads rapidly, skipping or mispronouncing unfamiliar words.
Seems nervous, tense, insecure
Reads with false confidence—as if it were easy.
Reads in monotone.
Reads with artificial expression.
Voice higher pitched than conversational tone.
Voice low and indistinct.
Enunciation slurred, unclear.

CHECK-LIST OF WORD PRONUNCIATION

Usually "refuses" unfamiliar words.
Usually gives a wrong word quickly and proceeds.
Usually makes a detailed study of unfamiliar words with audible trials.
Usually stops and studies inaudibly.
Appears to depend mainly on general configuration.
Appears to depend mainly on syllabication.
Appears to depend mainly on phonograms like *tr* and letter sounds.
Appears to depend mainly on letter sounds.
Appears to depend mainly on spelling out the word.
Tries various methods of attack.
Gives up very easily.
Too quick and superficial.
Too slow and labored.
Lacks any consistent method of attack.

Having the pupils give aloud the mental steps by which the incorrect solution of an example in arithmetic was arrived at will enable the observer to discover faulty, involved procedures that cannot be found through an analysis of the written work. The results of the application of this technique by Buswell,[58] Brueckner,[59] and others

[54] Dora Smith, "Diagnosis of Difficulties in English," in *Educational Diagnosis*, Ch. 13.

[55] L. J. O'Rourke, "Rebuilding the English Usage Curriculum to Insure Greater Mastery of Essentials" (Washington, The Psychological Institute, 1934).

[56] *Van Wagenen English Composition Scales* (Yonkers, World Book, 1923).

[57] Marietta Stewart, "A Scale for Measuring the Quality of Conventional News Stories in High School Journalism," *The English Journal* (March, 1934), pp. 209-215.

[58] G. T. Buswell, *Diagnostic Studies in Arithmetic*, Supplementary Educational Monograph No. 30 (Chicago, Univ. of Chicago Press, 1926).

[59] Leo J. Brueckner, *Diagnostic and Remedial Teaching in Arithmetic* (Philadelphia, John C. Winston, 1930).

SELF-CORRECTIVE CHARTS FOR HANDWRITING*

Chart	Kind of Defect	Frequency of Oc- currence	Total by Types
1. Color	Irregular color	177	177
2. Size	Irregular size	200	319
	Too large size	62	
	Too small size	57	
3. Slant	Irregular slant	240	326
	Too much slant	61	
	Lack of slant	25	
4. Letter spacing	Irregular letter spacing	267	331
	Crowded letter spacing	62	
	Scattered letter spacing	2	
5. Beginning and ending strokes	Irregular beginning and ending strokes	270	381
	Long beginning and ending strokes	63	
	Short beginning and ending strokes	48	
6. Word spacing	Irregular word spacing	171	415
	Scattered word spacing	177	
	Crowded word spacing	67	
7. Alignment	Irregular alignment	300	374
	Writing below the line	58	
	Writing above the line	16	

* From data supplied by Ellen Nystrom, formerly supervisor of handwriting, Minneapolis, Minn.

has revealed an amazing variety of incorrect, immature roundabout procedures in working examples that lead to failure in arithmetic.

e. Analysis of product. To increase the validity of diagnosis, various kinds of objective devices may be used. A common form is to compare some product with a standard chart to determine its deficiencies or faults, for instance, in diagnosing defects in handwriting. Freeman [60] and Nystrom [61] have developed two sets of analytical diagnostic charts in handwriting. The first series contains scales for evaluating uniformity of slant, uniformity of alignment, quality of line, letter formation, and spacing. Specimens are rated according to the value assigned the sample in the scale which they most nearly resemble. The Nystrom charts have special merit because they are constructed in such a way that pupils can easily diagnose their own difficulties. Each chart consists of a series of specimens each of which exhibits a major fault that contributes to illegibility. A comparison

of the pupil's specimen with those in the chart enabled him to make the diagnosis. The list of charts, the kinds of defects they reveal, and their frequency are given above.

f. Interview and questionnaire. When the data secured by tests, observation, analysis of oral and written responses, and other methods do not yield adequate information on which to base a diagnosis, the interview must be used. For example, if a pupil is unable to write out a meaningful, systematic account of his methods of studying spelling because of his inability to analyze his mental processes clearly, an interview in which the examiner seeks by judicious questioning to bring out the essentials of his methods is the most feasible procedure.

When the examiner, having made an analysis of the pupil's written work, is uncertain

[60] F. N. Freeman, *Chart for Diagnosing Faults in Handwriting* (Boston, Houghton, 1914).
[61] Ellen Nystrom, *Self-Corrective Handwriting Charts* (Minneapolis, Farnham Press, 1927).

as to the nature of the difficulty, he should use the interview technique to verify his diagnosis. The skilful use of searching questions will usually reveal the difficulty.

In many instances it is necessary to interview the pupil's associates, his family, and other persons. The use of a formal type of interview blank makes it less likely that significant types of information or symptoms of various kinds of maladjustment will be overlooked than if a casual form of interview is employed. Because much of the information secured through an interview may be peculiar to the case, however, the examiner should always feel free to supplement the items included in a standard plan. A typical interview blank is illustrated below. It was devised by Maller and is used with the Maller tests of character and personality traits, the CASE Inventory.[62]

INTERVIEW BLANK DEVISED BY MALLER

Name .... Age ......
Height ...... Weight ...... Grade ......
Father's Occupation .... Nationality .... In what country was he born? .... How many brothers do you have? ...... How many sisters? ......
How many rooms are there in your home? .... Do you have a room for yourself? .... Do you have a radio in your home? .... A piano? .... An automobile? .... A telephone? .... About how many books are there in your home? ...... Are you a member of a club? ......
Name of club or clubs? ....
.... Which school subject do you like most? .... Which least? ....
Your favorite form of recreation? ....
...... How often do you go to the movies? .... What kind of movies do you like best? .... Give an example .... Has any moving picture ever made you want to do something good? .... What, for example? .... Name of picture? .... Has any moving picture ever made you want to do something you should *not* do? ....
What? .... Name of picture?
.... Do you

listen to the radio regularly? .... When? .... What is your favorite program? Which program don't you like at all? Why? .... Has any program ever made you want to do something good? .... What, for example? .... Name of program? .... Has any program ever made you want to do something you should *not* do? .... What, for example? .... Name of program? ....
................Do you suffer frequently from headaches? ...... Colds? .... Indigestion? ...... Other illness? ...... What occupation or vocation do you intend to follow? .... What occupation would you follow if you had your choice? .... What kind of books do you like best? ....
Do you plan to go to college?.............
Why? ....
....

A highly specialized use of the interview is the psychiatric examination. Its function is explained in the following statement:[63]

The "informational interview," as it is frequently designated for research purposes, corresponds to the questionnaire technique; it consists in asking a number of well-planned and carefully organized questions designed to elicit from an individual what he knows but what he might not be willing or able to tell under ordinary circumstances. The "educational interview" usually consists in asking a child to state his problem directly and then offering criticism and helpful suggestions. In the "psychiatric interview" situation the lead as to what should be discussed is largely left to the interviewee, but the interviewer remains much more passive than in the "educational interview" although his passivity is subject to certain technical restrictions. He tries to behave in such a way that exactly those emotions and impulses in the interviewee have a chance to come out which otherwise would be naturally suppressed (cut off from expression and action) or even repressed (cut off from conscious self-perception). In this technique it is not so much the content of the discussion as

[62] New York, Teachers College, Bureau of Publications, Columbia Univ., 1934.
[63] From W. S. Monroe, ed., *Encyclopedia of Educational Research*, p. 721. By permission of The Macmillan Company, publishers.

the emotional rapport established between interviewer and interviewee that counts.

The limitations as well as values of the psychiatric interview are presented in the following statement: [64]

The disadvantages of the psychiatric interview are obvious: no well-organized stock of material is derived from it; the collected material appears chaotic; there is no indication of the relative importance of one factor over others; and supplementary interpretation is necessary. The needed additional techniques for interpretation give rise to a whole set of new problems. Besides being a technique which is hard to learn and long in learning, it is difficult to handle, once learned. Even when the interviewer is skilled, some cases require a whole series of interviews distributed over a considerable period of time, each interview having meaning only in relation to the entire series after supplementary study.

The advantages of the psychiatric interview are equally clear: it is still the only workable way for getting at the expression of those specific factors in child behavior which would otherwise remain unexpressed and obscured; it is the only way to create the rapport between child and interviewer which is necessary to obtain desired information; the rapport developed may be useful later in the educational guidance of the child. Since the development of both positive and negative character traits includes factors which belong in this unexpressed or unconscious material, the psychiatric interview method has become an important aid in guidance, education, and particularly in reëducational therapy.

Self-appraisal by students themselves is sometimes a valuable procedure. The pupil questionnaire given below was used for self-diagnosis by pupils and as a source of information to guide teaching procedures in the public schools of Hamtramck, Michigan.[65]

This questionnaire has been made for the purpose of finding out why more students do not take part in class discussions. If we are able to find out the reasons, we may be better able to help students develop the ability to express themselves in the presence of others. The survey will be useless *if you do not answer truthfully.*

I. How often do you take part in class discussions? Check one word only.
   a. Always   *b.* Frequently
   c. Seldom   *d.* Never

II. If you seldom or never take part in class discussion, check the reason or reasons for not doing so.
1. I am not thoroughly prepared.
2. I am afraid to talk in front of large groups of people.
3. I am afraid the teacher will criticize me.
4. I am afraid the class will criticize or laugh at me.
5. I am not interested enough in the class to bother taking part.
6. I think it is foolish to take part in discussion when I can pass the course without doing so.
7. The class is so disorderly and noisy that it is useless to try to take part in a discussion.
8. I am too lazy.
Add other reasons not listed above.

III. If you take part in the discussion frequently, check the following reasons for doing so.
1. I take part in the discussion frequently so I will get a better mark.
2. I take part in discussion because I like to express my ideas.
3. I take part in class discussion because I think it helps others to hear my ideas.
4. I take part in the discussion because I believe that everyone has something worth while to contribute and that if I do my share others will do theirs.
Add any other reasons.

IV. Do you feel that small group discussions help you to understand the problems? Yes _____ No _____

V. Whom would you rather have conduct the discussion? Teacher _____ Chairman _____

g. Projective and expressive methods.

The procedures under this heading that were described in the preceding chapter perhaps should have been described in this section dealing with psychological diagnosis. Some of the techniques are especially adapted for

[64] From W. S. Monroe, ed., *Encyclopedia of Educational Research*, p. 722. By permission of The Macmillan Company, 1950, publishers.
[65] Quoted in *Learning the Ways of Democracy*, Educational Policies Commission (Washington, NEA, 1940), p. 415.

the study of the personality of individuals whereas others are intended for the study of interaction among the members of a group. The underlying procedures have perhaps already been adequately described for our purposes. Those who are interested in the study of this approach to diagnosis should consult the references given in Chapter 7. Sociometric methods are also often of value in the diagnostic study of the behavior of individuals, especially interviews with individuals about the findings.

h. Clinical tests and laboratory procedures. When a more precise analysis than can be secured by ordinary tests and diagnostic procedures is desired, the systematic, exact techniques of the laboratory or psychological clinic may be employed. Numerous easily administered laboratory tests have been devised. The Betts Telebinocular Tests, for example, are very valuable devices for measuring visual and auditory factors essential to success in reading. They include tests of visual and auditory readiness, and visual sensation and perception. Special apparatus easily manipulated by teachers is needed to give these tests. The Monroe Reading Aptitude Tests measure auditory memory, articulation, language control, and lateral dominance. These are individual tests, also easily administered. The audiometer is a dependable device for measuring hearing.

When a permanent record of a pupil's performance is wanted, the examiner can use the Kymograph, the ophthalmograph, the motion-picture camera, the dictaphone, or a combination of the voice and motion-picture methods. Such records often reveal small but important symptoms that ordinary observation does not detect. These records make possible repeated studies of the same performance and more precise analysis of characteristics of behavior than can be obtained by other methods. The valuable contributions of the laboratory study of eye movements to the improvement of reading are an excellent example of the ways in which exact clinical procedures have affected instruction.

Though at present the use of laboratory methods is largely limited to clinics and child-guidance centers in universities and laboratories, it is apparent that these services will be made increasingly available for all schools.

i. Analysis of available records. School and community records contain a wealth of information of value in making a dagnosis of causes of learning difficulty.

An analysis of the pupils' record of progress on practice tests in reading, arithmetic, spelling, and handwriting serves as a very effective basis of guidance. If the record shows improvement, in most cases further diagnosis is not necessary. If the record shows that no progress is being made or that there is even a loss in ability, steps must be taken to discover the causes of the condition. Loss in ability may be due to some fault that is undermining the basic skills, to indifference, or to lack of effort.

In some cases, a record of the way the pupil spends his time in and out of school reveals valuable information. This record may be compiled either by the pupil or by the examiner. Assuming that the report is a true one, such facts are revealed as that the pupil has no systematic study program, that he does not begin work promptly, that he wastes much time, that he spends an excessive amount of time on some subject, and other evidence of the unwise use of time available for study.

Large numbers of school systems use cumulative-record systems for recording information about pupils. The systems vary from simple record cards containing only a few items to large folders on which numerous facts are recorded and which at the same time serve as containers of informal current reports about the activities of the learner. An analysis by Segel of cumulative records used in 177 school systems showed wide variation in the items the forms included. His findings are tabulated on page 309.

The record forms in use have often been developed by state and city school systems. Several have been issued by commercial pub-

FREQUENCY OF OCCURRENCE IN PERCENTAGES OF EACH ITEM ON RECORDS STUDIED* (177 SCHOOL SYSTEMS)

Item	Elementary (113 records)	Junior High (87 records)	Senior High (136 records)
Scholarship (marks)	96	100	100
School progress	80	92	79
Attendance	86	85	77
Entrance and withdrawal	71	86	79
Home conditions and family history	70	71	69
Intelligence test results	58	77	71
Social and character ratings	73	71	63
Health	65	64	56
Space for notes	58	63	57
Achievement test results	51	56	49
Extracurricular activities	19	64	63
Vocational and educational plans	17	45	44
Residence record	38	26	21
College or vocation entered after leaving school	15	34	33
Special abilities	14	23	16
Photograph	7	23	16
Out-of-school employment	5	20	18

* David Segel, "Nature and Use of the Cumulative Record," Office of Education Bulletin No. 3 (Washington, Government Printing Office, 1938), p. 6.

lishing houses. Many of the forms reflect the practices of the traditional school, but there is clear evidence in many cases of modern developments. The type of record to be used should take into consideration both the needs and the objectives of the school and the kinds of objective evidence which support the items it includes. The Progressive Education Association investigated the types of records an ideal system of individual records should contain. The following items were recommended:[66]

1. *Personal pattern of goals.* "Since the school exists, in some measure, to help achieve the goals he (the pupil) sets for himself and to lead him to formulate even clearer, more consistent, more attainable, and more socially valuable goals, it is important to ascertain what these goals are and to record progress toward them. This requires a carefully planned conference technique in which the counselor discusses with the pupil such areas of goals as his life work, school work, school life, home and friends, sports, hobbies, the arts, reading, and other recreational activities." The pupil is to write out at intervals of perhaps a week or a month the goals in which he is interested and his success in attaining them.

2. *Records of significant experiences.* To be written out by pupil at irregular intervals.

3. *Reading records.* A record of the free reading, which is a good index of intellectual maturity; must be interpreted on basis of type and quantity of material.

4. *Records of cultural experience.* Attendance at plays, concerts, listening periods on radio, etc.

5. *Records of creative expression.* Diederich is not certain about the way in which this should be reported. He recommends that teachers experiment. He suggests that some common elements might be: names of pupil and teacher, the date, the name, title or subject of the creative product, the medium of materials, the approximate number of hours of work represented, statement by the pupil of the purpose or central idea of his product, what he learned in creating it, and how successful it was in achieving his purpose. An interpretation by the teacher should be included.

6. *Anecdotal records of pupils, and interpretation by the teacher.*

7. *Records of conferences.*

8. *Record of excuses and explanations.*

9. *Record of tests and examinations, with an interpretation by the teacher.*

[66] P. B. Diederich, "Evaluation Records," *Educational Method* (May, 1936), pp. 432-440.

10. *Health and family history.*

11. *Oral English diagnosis.* A diagnosis of the pupil's pronunciation, enunciation, quality of voice, diction, usage, force, etc., without knowledge of pupil. To be used in subsequent work.

12. *Minutes of student affair.*

13. *Personality ratings and descriptions.*

14. *Questionnaires.* These include all interest and personal questionnaires pupils are asked to fill in. Should be interpreted and filed in the pupil's folder.

15. *Records of courses and activities.*

16. *Administrative records.*

At the close of this list of recommended items Diederich added: "It is not suggested that any school attempt to install all these forms of records at once. They are only intended to present alternative possibilities among which schools may choose, and to illustrate the richness and variety of types of evidence which are available for the evaluation of even more tangible outcomes of progressive education if schools are willing to develop, collect, and interpret them."

In recent years many schools have greatly extended the information included in their pupil records in order to have a sound basis of guidance. Such items as the following indicate some of the trends:

1. Records of interests, abilities, and achievements in special areas such as art, music, hobby clubs, and athletics.
2. Records of vacation experiences, travel, and employment.
3. Educational and vocational plans at various stages of maturity.
4. Information about personality traits.
5. Case histories of pupils evidencing serious social, emotional, and educational maladjustment.
6. Anecdotal records of significant behavior.
7. Records of contributions to life of the school and participation in student and community activities.

Traxler [67] lists the essential characteristics of a good cumulative record system as follows:

1. The cumulative record should grow directly out of the objectives of the school in which it is used.

2. The cumulative record should bring together and summarize all kinds of information about the individual which are needed in counseling.

3. The form should be planned in such a way that it is intrinsically a growth record.

4. The record should consist largely of objective data and of summary statements interpreting these data.

5. Since the cumulative record is seldom, if ever, a form for original entry, a variety of forms on which original data are entered by teacher, counselor, school psychologist, and others need to be related to the main form.

6. Some cumulative records are planned to serve as file folders as well as record forms, but as far as possible the main items of information should be written on the card itself.

7. Every cumulative record should be accompanied by a carefully prepared manual of directions.

Ayer [68] points out that the cumulative record card is the center of child accounting records. He suggests that the cumulative record itself should include the following supplementary forms:

1. Health card.
2. Test record.
3. Individual inventory.
4. Guidance card.
5. Special educational sheet.
6. Personality inventory.
7. Clinic report.
8. Anecdotal record.
9. Occupational inventory.
10. Sociometric form.
11. Case study.
12. Problem check-list.

For a detailed analysis of present-day record forms, the reader is referred to the following:

AYER, F. C., *Practical Child Accounting* (Austin, Texas: The Steck Co., 1949).

Guidance in Educational Institutions, Thirty-seventh Yearbook, National Society for the Study of Education (Bloomington, Ill., Public School Publishing Co., 1938). Part I contains an excellent discussion of various kinds of records and their use in guidance.

[67] Arthur E. Traxler. "The Cumulative Record in the Guidance Program," *The School Review* (March, 1946), pp. 156-157.

[68] Fred Ayer, *Practical Child Accounting* (Austin, Texas, The Steck Co., 1949), p. 9.

Handbook of Cumulative Records, A Report of the National Committee on Cumulative Records, Bulletin 5 (Washington, Government Printing Office, 1944).

REED, G. M., and SEGEL, D., *Minimum Essentials of the Individual Inventory in Guidance,* Vocational Division Bulletin No. 202, Occupational Information and Guidance Series, No. 2 (Washington, Office of Education, 1940).

SEGEL, David, *Nature and Use of the Cumulative Record,* Office of Education Bulletin No. 2 (Washington, Government Printing Office, 1938). Contains a wealth of helpful material on the nature and use of the cumulative record.

WRINKLE, W. L., *Improving Marking and Reporting Practices* (New York, Rinehart, 1947).

Individual collections can be made.

Section 4

ILLUSTRATIVE DIAGNOSTIC TESTING PROGRAMS

Outline of a typical diagnostic testing program. Because there is such a large variety of defects and possible causes of difficulty in any curriculum area, diagnostic testing programs usually call for the gathering of a wide variety of information given in school records and from individuals with whom the learner comes into contact, especially the teacher and the parents, that will assist in the diagnosis and treatment of the difficulty. The essential data include information about the learner's educational background and school history, environmental influences to which he is exposed in the home and community, his emotional and social adjustment, records of test results and of medical examinations, and similar types of pertinent data.

The diagnostic testing program in reading devised by Gates [69] provides a three-level attack on reading problems. It includes (1) a survey test for measuring general power in reading to be administered to the class as a screening device; (2) analytical tests of a number of major reading skills at the primary and intermediate grade levels to determine the level to which each major skill has been developed; and (3) a standard reading diagnostic test to be administered to individuals having serious reading difficulties in order to determine the nature and causes of the deficiency, so that steps can be taken to plan an improvement program.

The nature of the individual Gates Diagnostic Test in Reading can be seen from the outline of its content which follows.

For illustrative purposes, the list of tests and subtests included in the Gates Reading Diagnostic Tests is given below:

Oral Reading
1. Gates Oral—Total Score
   a. Omisions, words
   b. Additions, words
   c. Repetitions
   d. Mispronunciations
   e. Full reversals
   f. Reversal of parts
   g. Wrong order (e + f)
   h. Wrong beginnings
   i. Wrong middles
   j. Wrong endings
   k. Wrong several parts

Vocabulary
1. Gates Oral Vocabulary
2.

Reversal Test
1. Total errors
2. Per cent reversals

Phrase Perception
1. Number phrases correct

Word Perception, Analysis, etc.
1. Flash presentation
2. Untimed presentation

Spelling
1. Gates Test

Visual Perception Techniques
1. Syllabication
2. Recognition of syllables
3. Recognition of phonograms
4. Blending letter sounds
5. Giving letter sounds
6. Reading capital letters
   a. Speed
   b. Errors
7. Reading small letters
   a. Speed
   b. Errors

Auditory Techniques
1. Blending letter sounds
2. Giving letters for sounds
3. Giving words— initial sounds
4. Giving words— ending sounds

[69] Arthur I. Gates, *The Improvement of Reading,* rev. ed. (New York, Macmillan, 1947).

The tests are all administered individually. Norms are available for interpreting scores on each test. The form on which to summarize test results for one child is on page 304. In addition to the above data, consideration is given to information that is available on cumulative records and that can be secured by other laboratory tests and general tests of reading ability.

Gates points out that this program emphasizes the testing and direct observation of the techniques used by the pupil in various reading and word-study situations and the relations of the pupil to other persons concerned with his difficulties. Motivation is stressed because improvement depends on the ability of the teacher to secure the co-operation of the learner, a more or less perplexed personality. Many of the instruments in Gates's inventory are designed to measure and to diagnose ability at the same time. Each one diagnoses one of the essential reading skills. The series of tests was designed primarily to lead to the application of appropriate forms of remedial instruction. Measurement, diagnosis, and remedial teaching are therefore intimately related.

The necessity of using informal diagnostic procedures. Standard procedures for diagnosing many educational outcomes are lacking at the present time. The teachers, however, should be encouraged to devise methods that may be helpful in analyzing and evaluating the extent to which desirable objectives are being achieved. Procedures similar to those that have been standardized for various fields may serve as models.

An illustrative informal diagnostic examination procedure. The general procedure to follow in selecting pupils for diagnostic study and the method of conducting a detailed examination are similar for all areas of learning. Although in serious cases it is desirable to make use of special apparatus and standardized materials, the teacher can in many instances make a fairly adequate diagnosis by using materials available in textbooks or devise simple home-made devices. The following statement of procedures to use in arithmetic diagnosis describes a general plan of attack:[70]

1. The teacher should observe the quality of the pupils' work from day to day in the classroom to note evidences of difficulty in arithmetic. The results of standard survey tests and of informal progress tests included in textbooks are especially helpful in locating pupils whose progress is not satisfactory. Minor difficulties can be diagnosed and corrected as they appear from time to time in the course of instruction.

2. An examination of the results of a well-devised survey test will indicate areas which apparently present serious difficulty to some of the children. To identify weak spots in some operation, such as subtraction of fractions, the teacher should administer an analytical diagnostic test in that operation. Some modern textbooks contain such tests. When they are not available, the teacher can quite easily prepare informal tests that will serve the purpose by following standard directions for these tests.

3. The teacher should then select for special study pupils whose work is seriously deficient in one or more of the processes. In the average class not more than 10 per cent of the pupils will require this diagnostic study. Ordinarily these pupils should be examined by the teacher at a time while the others in the class are at work on some seat assignment, so that all will be profitably occupied.

4. After the class has begun to work on the assignment, one pupil who has been selected for special study should be called to the teacher's desk, or to a table conveniently located in the room. The pupil should be told that the purpose of the teacher is to help him to determine the cause and nature of his arithmetic difficulties, and he should be encouraged to assume a co-operative attitude in the undertaking. The teacher should think of his part of the examination as being like that of a physician who is making a clinical diagnosis of the cause of the illness of an individual. The purpose of the diagnosis by the teacher should be the location of faulty methods of work, lack of knowledge on the part of the pupil, and other possible causes of inefficiency of work. At this step the teacher should not be concerned with remedying the situation by teaching correct procedures.

[70] Adapted from L. J. Brueckner and E. O. Melby, *Diagnostic and Remedial Teaching* (Boston, Houghton, 1931), pp. 212-214.

5. The teacher should next select a standardized diagnostic test in the process to be investigated, such as the Buswell-John [71] or Brueckner [72] tests, or if they are not available, should use some similar set of examples prepared for the purpose. Usually not more than one process at a time should be studied, to avoid fatigue on the part of the pupil.

6. The teacher should explain to the pupil that he will make it easier to diagnose his difficulties if he will do his work aloud, so that the teacher may observe his procedure. The teacher should illustrate the method by working one or two typical examples. Pupils readily respond to these directions and demonstrations, especially if the teacher has created the right attitude, and if the examination is conducted in a friendly, helpful spirit.

7. As the pupil works, the teacher should make notes of the types of faults that are discovered. Such a record is facilitated by the use of the record blanks that are prepared on certain of the standard diagnostic tests. These blanks contain lists of the most common types of faults revealed by extended clinical studies of the work of pupils deficient in arithmetic. It is obvious that the teacher must have a first-hand appreciation of the various kinds of errors that may be discovered and of their symptoms. Sometimes the pupil stops in the middle of an example and apparently is blocked by some difficulty. By careful questioning the teacher should make an effort to get the pupil to tell what his mental processes are during the period of apparent inactivity. While the method of securing the pupil's testimony as to his mental processes may not be a wholly reliable one, because of his inability to describe them accurately, nevertheless an observing teacher with insight can usually secure quite a vivid picture of what mental activity takes place. The length of the time required for a diagnosis will of course vary according to the extent and nature of the faults discovered in the pupil's work. The average time required for a single process is between fifteen and thirty minutes.

8. When the work of the test has been completed, the teacher should carefully analyze the notes taken during the examination and summarize the findings of the diagnosis. These may be recorded on the standardized blank, on the pages of a notebook in which records of a diagnosis are kept, or may be filed in some other convenient form for reference.

9. The necessary reteaching and remedial work should then be undertaken in the light of the findings of the diagnosis.

Checking a diagnosis. When a diagnosis has been made of the nature of a learning deficiency and its probable cause has been at least tentatively established, the diagnosis should be checked by an examination of other available data. The structural, organic, and functional aspects of the learner's physical and physiological mechanism should be examined; the history of the learner should be investigated to discover significant data concerning his growth and development, illnesses, school experiences, social life, work experiences, and emotional adjustment. The characteristics of the family and of life in the home also bear scrutiny in many cases. The diagnosis may require modification after this study. On the basis of all available information a program for improving the condition can then be undertaken.

Synthesis and analysis of diagnostic findings. After the breaking down and analysis of the student's need for assistance and development have been completed and the contributory factors have been examined, there should be a discriminatory consideration of the information assembled. A synthesis should then be made of the most significant data bearing on the case in such a way that the causal relations and clinical meanings become evident. Several alternative steps or solutions may then open up which should be considered by all concerned with the welfare of the individual, including himself. The treatment that is most likely to be effective should be selected and put into operation. Subsequently a re-evaluation should be made to discover the nature of the changes produced in terms of pupil growth and welfare so as to determine the correctness of the diagnosis and treatment and to

[71] *Buswell-John Diagnostic Tests for Fundamental Processes in Arithmetic* (Individual Test) (Bloomington, Ill., Public School Publishing Co., 1925). A test for psychological analysis of arithmetical errors.
[72] *Brueckner Diagnostic Tests in Whole Numbers, Fractions, and Decimals* (Manuals and Record Forms) (Minneapolis, Educational Test Bureau, 1929).

determine future needs. The details of improvement programs will be discussed in Chapter 14.

Sources of description of case studies. The real significance of educational diagnosis can only be grasped by the study of reports of cases in which are assembled all of the data that bear on them. Limitations of space here do not permit at this point the presentation of any detailed reports of case histories describing methods and findings of diagnostic procedures in the several fields of the curriculum. For the convenience of the reader, however, there is given at the end of this chapter a classified list of sources in which detailed procedures and findings for numerous cases are described. The reader is referred to this source of materials for help.

CHAPTER SUPPLEMENT

INTRODUCTORY DISCUSSION QUESTIONS

1. How may factors inherent in the pupil, such as the following, affect his growth and development unfavorably?

    a. Physical traits, nutrition, defect.
    b. Mental capacity, intelligence level.
    c. His control of basic knowledges, skills, and abilities.
    d. Emotional and personality traits, interests, attitudes, etc.
    e. Social and experiential background.

2. For which of these factors is the school primarily responsible? For which are other agencies at least in part responsible? Explain.

3. What is meant by general diagnosis? Analytical diagnosis? Psychological diagnosis?

4. What techniques are used for each of these three levels of diagnosis? Which are included in textbooks and workbooks?

5. To what extent are teachers qualified to do diagnostic work?

6. What are the limitations of educational diagnosis?

7. What special services are provided to aid in diagnosis?

8. How should children be grouped?

9. What are the educational implications of a policy of "100 per cent promotion"?

10. Is there any similarity between educational diagnosis and diagnosis in medicine?

11. What sciences have made important contributions to educational diagnosis? How?

12. How can one identify a pupil definitely in need of systematic diagnostic study?

13. State in your own words the steps to take in making a diagnostic study of an apparently serious learning difficulty in some area. Describe the procedures you would use.

14. What types of informal diagnostic procedures should teachers use in the course of day-to-day teaching? Give concrete illustrations of their application.

15. What are the possibilities of self-diagnosis by pupils?

16. How do curriculum and instruction contribute to learning difficulties?

ORAL REPORT

1. Report on the specific techniques of diagnosis in some area described in one of the references in the chapter bibliography. Illustrate the three levels of diagnosis discussed in this chapter.

2. What special provisions are made by schools (your school in particular) to assist in the diagnosis of various types of learning difficulty and behavior problems? What clinical services are available, local, regional, or state? How are cases referred?

3. Describe a case in which one, or more, of the causes of difficulty discussed in this chapter actually was operative.

4. What kinds of tests and clinical apparatus are needed in diagnosis?

5. Secure a report of a case study and present details as to procedures used and the various agencies contacted.

6. What provision is made in preparing prospective teachers to utilize diagnostic procedures, formal or informal?

WRITTEN REPORTS—INDIVIDUAL GROUP

1. Observe instruction in some classroom and make a note of the kinds of diagnostic procedures the teacher and pupils actually use. Evaluate them. If possible, discuss the topic with the teacher. Suggest additional procedures that the teacher or pupils might have used.

2. Make an outline of causes of difficulty in some phase of a major curriculum area; in health; in character traits; in personality.

3. Prepare a systematic description of the various means and techniques of diagnosis in

some curriculum area, described in the references.

4. Outline a plan for diagnosing unfavorable character traits; personality traits; interests; attitudes; appreciations.

5. Make an actual case study and report the results to the class. (Only advanced students with special training should undertake this assignment.)

CLASS PROJECT NO. VI

Develop a paper on diagnosis similar to Project No. V on evaluation.

Select a typical case of difficulty in learning and specify in outline form how you would proceed to diagnose the suspected difficulty. Include special services when justified.

The same general directions that were given for the evaluation project hold here. Introductory question No. 4 will supply a start on this project.

SUGGESTED READINGS

General

BRUECKNER, L. J., and MELBY, E. O., *Diagnostic and Remedial Teaching* (Boston, Houghton, 1931).

CONKLIN, Agnes M., *Failures of Highly Intelligent Pupils: A Study of Their Behavior*, Contributions to Education No. 792 (New York, Bureau of Publications, Teachers College, Columbia Univ., 1940).

Encyclopedia of Educational Research, W. S. Monroe, ed. (New York, Macmillan, 1950). Look up articles dealing with evaluation, diagnosis in teaching, and all subject areas for summaries of research on diagnosis.

FERNALD, Grace, *Remedial Techniques in Basic School Subjects* (New York, McGraw-Hill, 1943).

GREENE, H. A., JORGENSON, A. N., and GERBERICH, J. R., *Measurement and Evaluation in the Elementary School*, 2nd ed. (New York, Longmans, 1953).

HILDRETH, Gertrude, *Learning the 3 R's* (Minneapolis, Minn., Educational Publishers, 1947).

National Society for the Study of Education, Thirty-fourth Yearbook, *Educational Diagnosis* (Bloomington, Ill., Public School Publishing Co., 1935).

REMMERS, H. H., and GAGE, N. L., *Educational Measurement and Evaluation* (New York, Harper, 1943).

Mental and Physical Development and Health

BAKER, H. J., *Introduction to Exceptional Children* (New York, Macmillan, 1953).

Commission on Teacher Education, *Helping Teachers Understand Children* (Washington, American Council on Education, 1945).

FENTON, Norman, *Mental Hygiene in School Practice* (Stanford University, Calif., Stanford University Press, 1943).

HOLLINGSWORTH, Leta S., *Children Above 180 IQ* (Yonkers, World Book, 1942).

HOLY, T. C., and WALKER, G. L., *A Study of Health and Physical Education in the Columbus Public Schools* (Columbus, Ohio, Ohio State Univ., 1942).

JENSEN, Kai, "Electrical Activity of the Nervous System," *Journal of Experimental Education* (December, 1938), pp. 233-282.

STODDARD, George D., *The Meaning of Intelligence* (New York, Macmillan, 1943).

ZACHRY, C. B., and LIGHTY, Margaret, *Emotion and Conduct in Adolescence* (New York, Appleton-Century-Crofts, 1940).

Arithmetic and Mathematics

BRESLICH, E. R., *The Teaching of Mathematics in the Secondary Schools* (Chicago, Univ. of Chicago Press, 1930).

BRUECKNER, L. J., *Diagnostic and Remedial Teaching of Arithmetic* (Philadelphia, John C. Winston, 1930).

———, and GROSSNICKLE, F. E., *Making Arithmetic Meaningful* (Philadelphia, John C. Winston, 1953), Chs. 11, 12, and 13.

BUSWELL, G. T., and JOHN, Lenore, *Diagnostic Studies in Arithmetic* (Chicago, Univ. of Chicago Press, 1926).

Mathematics in General Education, A Report of the Committee on the Function of Mathematics in General Education, Progressive Education Association (New York, Appleton-Century-Crofts, 1940).

English and Related Subjects

National Society for the Study of Education, Forty-third Yearbook, *Teaching Language in the Elementary School* (Chicago, University of Chicago Press, 1944), Part II, Ch. 9.

ORTON, S. T., *Reading, Writing, and Speech Problems for Children* (New York, Norton, 1937).

RUSSELL, D., *Characteristics of Good and Poor Spellers*, Contributions to Education No. 727 (New York, Bureau of Publications, Teachers College, Columbia Univ., 1937).

SPACHE, G., "Spelling Disability Correlates," *Journal of Educational Research* (April, 1941), pp. 561-587; (October, 1941), pp. 119-138.

TRAVIS, L. E., *Speech Pathology* (New York, Appleton-Century, 1934).

Reading

BETTS, E. A., *Diagnosis of Reading Disabilities* (Meadeville, Pa., Keystone View Co., 1934).

Clinical Studies in Reading, edited by Helen Robinson. Supplementary Educational Monograph, No. 77 (Chicago, Univ. of Chicago Press, January 1953).

DURRELL, D. D., *The Diagnosis of Reading Disabilities* (Boston, Houghton, 1935).

GATES, Arthur I., *The Improvement of Reading* rev. ed. (New York, Macmillan, 1947).

HARRIS, Albert J., *How to Improve Reading Ability* (New York, Longmans, 1947).

HARRISON, M. R., *Reading Readiness,* rev. ed. (Boston, Houghton, 1939).

KIRK, S. A., *Teaching Reading to Slow Learners* (Boston, Houghton, 1940).

MONROE, Marion, *Children Who Cannot Read* (Chicago, Univ. of Chicago Press, 1932).

WITTY, P., and KOPEL, D., *Reading and the Educative Process* (Boston, Ginn, 1939).

Social Studies

Department of Superintendence, Tenth Yearbook, *Character Education* (Washington, NEA, 1932), especially Chs. 5, 6.

HARTSHORNE, H., MAY, M., MALLER, J. B., and SHUTTLEWORTH, F. R., *Studies in the Nature of Character:* I. Studies in Deceit; II. Studies in Service and Self-Control; III. Studies in the Organization of Character (New York, Macmillan, 1928-1930).

HORN, E., *Methods of Instruction in the Social Studies* (New York, Scribner's, 1937), Ch. 2.

———, "Another Chapter on Tests for the Volume of Conclusions and Recommendations," *The Social Studies* (January, 1935).

KREY, A., and KELLEY, T. L., *Tests and Measurements in the Social Sciences* (New York, Scribner's, 1934).

WILSON, H., *Education for Citizenship* (New York, McGraw-Hill, 1938).

Fine and Industrial Arts

GOODENOUGH, Florence, *The Measurement of Intelligence by Drawings* (Yonkers, World Book, 1926).

KWALWASSER, J. *Tests and Measurements in Music* (Boston, C. C. Birchard and Co., 1927).

NEWKIRK, L. V., and GREENE, H. A., *Tests and Measurements in Industrial Education* (New York, Wiley, 1935).

STANTON, Hazel M., *The Measurement of Musical Talent,* Studies in the Psychology of Music, Vol. 2 (Iowa City, Univ. of Iowa, 1935).

———, *Prognosis of Musical Achievement* (Rochester, N. Y., Univ. of Rochester, 1929).

THORNDIKE, E. L., *Prediction of Vocational Success* (New York, Commonwealth Fund, 1934).

Chapter 11

◆·◆·◆·◆·◆·◆·◆·◆·◆·◆·◆

The Study of Instruction

Section 1

FACTORS THAT AFFECT INSTRUCTION

THE METHODS OF INSTRUCTION in any curriculum area, broadly conceived, are affected by the quality of all of the instrumentalities through which the goals of education are achieved, by the effectiveness with which the instrumentalities operate. Conditions may, in fact, exist within a teaching-learning situation that prevent a teacher from doing the superior kind of teaching he may be competent and ready to perform, and force him to carry on an inferior kind of program until conditions can be improved. These factors have been discussed in various chapters and will be briefly summarized at the close of this section. We will be concerned in this chapter with those factors which are immediately and directly concerned with instruction. These are:

1. The teacher.
2. The choice and kind of methods used.
3. The competency of the teacher in using the methods chosen.

Factors inherent in the teacher. When studying instruction in the classroom, it should be borne in mind that the personality of the teacher is only one of the factors that determine the nature of the learning experiences of the children. The teacher is, however, perhaps, the single most important element in the situation and we need to know his characteristics as they affect instruction.

1. Personal qualities, such as intelligence, health, emotional stability, and attractiveness.
2. Competencies as director of learning ac-

tivities, skill in following the learning process, and skill in instruction.
3. Background, including scholarship, general culture, professional knowledge and background, interests, attitudes, and ideals.
4. Social relationships with pupils, staff, and community members.

The teacher is more than a classroom operative. He must be considered as a personality and as having responsibilty for several kinds of activity. He is a (*a*) director of learning; (*b*) friend and counselor of pupils; (*c*) director of extracurricular activities; (*d*) member of a school staff; and (*e*) member of the community. The teacher may have problems in any one or more of these categories.

Factors inherent in kind and choice of methods of teaching. In any given learning situation, the various factors discussed above appear in combinations that perhaps are almost wholly different from those appearing in other situations. The teacher is faced with the problem of planning an educational program that is most likely to be effective in this complexity of forces that affect choices of teaching methods. The effectiveness of instruction can only be judged by the growth made by the learners in the direction of desirable goals. When progress is not satisfactory, the underlying causes should be determined, one of which may be the quality of instruction. It is apparent that there is no such thing as a method of teaching that is good for all kinds of subject matter at all times and in all places. However, it may be true that there are best methods of achieving

317

a certain definite purpose in a certain kind of situation with pupils of certain types of ability and backgrounds of experience and with available instructional equipment. Methods are dynamic and instrumental, and they must be chosen in view of the ends to be achieved and in the light of conditioning circumstances. The choice of method should be made in light of existing evidence as to the effectiveness of the teaching procedures in similar situations. This point of view should be borne in mind by any supervisor or principal who is observing the work of a teacher with a view to evaluating it.

Factors inherent in the level of competency in the use of classroom methods. The previous paragraph stated that choice of method will depend upon the ends to be achieved and the conditioning circumstances in the specific situation. Ignoring the latter fact, conditioning circumstances, leads to a common error in evaluating instruction. A teacher using traditional methods is often given a low rating for competence even though in fact he is employing the traditional methods with a high degree of competence. The supervisor is committed to modern methods and is giving a warped judgment because conditioning circumstances are overlooked. The teacher should be judged first in terms of competence, and then the choice of methods may be taken up. A teacher who knows no other than traditional methods but who is operating within a situation with full scope for modern methods needs one kind of help, namely, assistance in developing competence with the modern procedures. A teacher using traditional methods because the administration insists on this, or because materials and aids are not available, or because of community pressure, needs another kind of help, namely, assistance in improving his competency in the use of these methods.

The statement of teaching competencies which follows is not only an excellent illustration of definition of the types of behavior which characterize good teaching, but can be used by supervisors in evaluating either traditional or modern methods. The list, furthermore, can serve as a guide in evaluating at the preparation-of-teachers level and in appraising the work of teachers in service. It focuses on the type of behavior that is desired rather than on general qualities of the teacher, such as personality, intelligence, and appearance. Such qualities are reflected in the behavior of teachers, but many contributory skills, attitudes, and insights may be identified that depend on the person and on the situation in which the individual teaches. The analysis below was developed by the California Council on Teacher Education.

THE CALIFORNIA STATEMENT OF TEACHING COMPETENCE[1]

The competent teacher:

1. *Provides for the learning of students*
   1.1 Uses psychological principles of learning.
       1.11 Uses effective and continuing motivation.
           1.111 Recognizes and makes use of the interests, abilities, and needs of students.
           1.112 Uses the experiences of students and draws upon life situations and the interests inherent in subject matter.
       1.12 Provides varied learning experiences.
       1.13 Uses a variety of teaching procedures, such as discussion, review, etc., effectively.
       1.14 Plans co-operatively with students.

   1.2 Uses principles of child growth and development in learning situations.
       1.21 Provides for differentiated activities and assignments to meet the needs and abilities of students.
       1.22 Knows the health (mental and physical) status of his students and adapts activities to their needs.

[1] Quoted from pp. 7-11 in *Evaluation of Student Teaching,* Twenty-eighth Yearbook, Association for Student Teaching (Lockhaven, Pa., State Teachers College, 1949).

1.3 Maintains an atmosphere in the classroom that is conducive to learning and is marked by a sense of balance between freedom and security.

  1.31 Maintains an effective working situation.

  1.32 Helps students increasingly to assume leadership and responsibility.

  1.33 Provides opportunities for students to co-operate and to exercise leadership in the activities of large and small groups.

  1.34 Provides opportunity for expression of independent critical thought with emphasis on freedom of expression and open-mindedness.

1.4 Plans effectively.

  1.41 Aids the students to define worth-while objectives for large units, daily class work, and special class activities.

  1.42 Organizes his teaching well by choosing wisely learning experiences, subject-matter content, and materials of instruction.

  1.43 Selects and uses a wide variety of materials of instruction (e.g., books, pamphlets, films, bulletin boards, flat pictures, radios, recordings, etc., . . .).

  1.44 Uses resources of the school library and the community.

1.5 Uses varied teaching procedures.

  1.51 Uses teaching procedures (such as group reporting, discussion, planning with pupils) designed to achieve desired purposes in teaching.

  1.52 Builds effectively upon the students' participation in class activities.

  1.53 Develops study skills of students.

  1.54 Stimulates creative activities of students.

  1.55 Aids the students to evaluate their own achievements.

1.6 Uses diagnostic and remedial procedures effectively.

  1.61 Is familiar with common diagnostic tests in his own and related fields.

  1.62 Constructs, administers, and interprets diagnostic tests.

  1.63 Uses other appropriate diagnostic procedures.

  1.64 Plans and uses remedial procedures.

1.7 Uses adequate procedures for evaluating the achievement of students.

  1.71 Uses informal evaluation procedures (anecdotal record, interview, questionnaire) for collecting and interpreting needed information.

  1.72 Uses standard achievement tests.

    1.721 Is familiar with the more common ones in his field.

    1.722 Selects, administers, and interprets the results of tests and uses them in planning.

  1.73 Uses teacher-made tests.

    1.731 Constructs appropriate tests skillfully.

    1.732 Interprets the results and uses them in planning.

  1.74 Keeps accurate and adequate records, e.g., case studies, cumulative records.

  1.75 Makes effective reports to students and parents concerning the progress of students in their growth.

1.8 Manages the class effectively.

  1.81 Plans satisfactory routine for handling of materials, equipment, and supplies.

  1.82 Uses own and pupils' time effectively.

  1.83 Is attentive to the physical well-being of students in such matters as heating, lighting, ventilation, and seating.

2. *Counsels and guides students wisely*

2.1 Use sound psychological principles concerning the growth and development of children in guiding individuals and groups.

  2.11 Maintains objectivity when dealing with behavior that is aggressive and abnormal.

  2.12 Is sympathetic with and sensitive to students' personal and social problems as well as their academic needs.

2.13 Makes adjustments in the curriculum and other requirements in light of pupils' needs.

2.14 Secures sufficient rapport with students so that they come voluntarily for counsel.

2.2 Maintains effective relationships with parents.

    2.21 Explains the needs, abilities, interests, and problems of the students to their parents.

    2.22 Obtains co-operation from parents in helping students with their problems.

2.3 Collects and uses significant counseling data.

    2.31 Administers aptitude and intelligence tests.

    2.32 Interprets the results of such tests.

    2.33 Uses results collected in counseling with students.

    2.34 Keeps research suitable for guidance.

2.4 Uses suitable counseling procedures.

2.5 Maintains appropriate relations with guidance specialists, recognizing their role, and the limitations of his own skill and ability.

3. *Aids students to understand and appreciate our cultural heritage*

3.1 Organizes the classroom for effective democratic living.

3.2 Directs individuals and groups to significant life applications of classroom learnings.

    3.21 Uses subject fields to develop understanding of social, economic, and political problems.

    3.22 Develops an understanding of wide significance of various fields of subject matter.

3.3 Draws on his own background of experience to elicit the cultural growth of individuals and groups.

3.4 Helps students to know and to apply in their daily lives the democratic principles which are rooted deep in our historical development.

4. *Participates effectively in the activities of the school*

4.1 Plans co-operatively the means of achieving educational objectives.

4.11 Shares effectively in curricular revision and is able to evaluate progress toward attaining educational objectives.

    4.111 Defines objectives clearly.

    4.112 Collects data efficiently and draws appropriate conclusions from them.

    4.113 Employs appropriate remedial procedures.

4.12 Shows flexibility in modifying his plans and procedures to fit with those of the entire school.

4.2 Assumes his share of the responsibility for school activities.

    4.21 Carries out effectively the administrative responsibilities delegated to him.

    4.22 Participates in planning and administering extracurricular activities.

4.3 Maintains harmonious personal relations with his colleagues.

5. *Assists in maintaining good relations between the school and the rest of the community*

5.1 Acquaints himself with available community resources and uses them in classroom activities.

5.2 Obtains the co-operation of parents in school activities.

5.3 Aids in defining and solving community problems.

    5.31 Helps in defining community problems and in developing awareness of them in students and parents.

    5.32 Draws on available and appropriate resources within the school in attacking community problems.

5.4 Takes part in community affairs and projects.

5.5 Observes professional ethics in discussing school problems, particularly with lay persons.

6. *Works on a professional level*

6.1 Gives evidence of the social importance of the profession to parents, students, and other members of the profession.

6.2 Adheres to a professional code of ethics.

6.3 Contributes to the profession by membership in professional organizations and participation in their activities.

6.4 Assumes responsibilty for his own professional growth by planning an appropriate program for professional betterment.
6.41 Continues professional study through courses, lectures, institutes, professional reading, and other activities.

6.5 Aids in supervising student teachers and in the orientation and induction of beginning teachers.

This listing serves to identify strength and weakness in the work of any teacher or group of teachers. The methods of analysis and identifying them are discussed in the following sections.

Diagnosing factors contributing to instructional problems. The supervisor is concerned not only with the discovery of instructional problems but with the diagnosis of the factors contributing to them. Just as was the case in the diagnosis of the learning difficulties of pupils, it is possible to make fairly systematic studies of factors contributing to teaching problems. Unless a diagnosis can be made, correction is likely to be exceedingly difficult. First, the supervisor should try to identify symptoms of difficulty, and then use systematic methods of diagnosis to confirm his judgment.

Symptoms of teaching problems. So far as the authors are aware, no systematic study has been made of symptoms which show that teaching difficulties probably exist. A preliminary and wholly tentative analysis of a few symptoms is presented below for the consideration of the reader. It should be extended after discussion. The symptoms become evident sometimes in the behavior of the pupils, sometimes in the behavior of the teacher, sometimes in other aspects of the teaching-learning situation.

SYMPTOMS OF TEACHING PROBLEMS

1. Disorderly conduct of pupils.
2. Low level of pupil interest.
3. Poor group relations among pupils.
4. Test results considerably below those expected of pupils.
5. Excessive truancy and unlawful absence
6. Failure of pupils to complete assignments.
7. Evidence of poor planning and preparation for lesson by teacher.
8. Evidence of lack of basic knowledge by teacher.
9. Emotional instability and physical fatigue of teacher.
10. Poor personal relationships with teacher associates and parents.
11. Limited participation by teacher in school and community affairs.
12. Evidences of "poor housekeeping."

Steps in diagnosing typical teaching difficulties. The existence of a teaching problem may be shown through observation of the teacher at work, through examination of reports by the teacher and by other persons about the work and personality of the teacher, and through an analysis of measures of pupil growth and development. Once a problem is clearly shown to exist, the sequence of steps to take in identifying factors that prevent optimum teaching performance is as follows:

1. Review previous experiences and scientific information for ideas about the possible reasons for less than optimum teaching performance. As has been indicated, the factors may be resident in elements of the total teacher-learning situation itself or inherent in the teacher.

2. Make a preliminary investigation of the situation for evidence as to the factors that are conditioning the work of the teacher unfavorably.

3. Formulate a hypothesis as to the probable factors that are operating unfavorably in the situation.

4. Make a systematic investigation, using suitable fact-finding procedures, to determine the presence or absence of the factors believed to be the causes of the condition.

5. Instigate an improvement program in cooperation with the teacher involved.

6. Reappraise the performance and per-

sonality of the teacher to determine the effectiveness of the improvement program.

7. Make any necessary adjustments in the program.

Levels of diagnosis applied to teaching. The three levels of diagnosing learning problems of pupils that were discussed in Chapter 10 can also be applied to the diagnosis of teacher problems as outlined below:

1. *General diagnosis*
    a. Studies of growth by children.
    b. Analysis of personnel records of teachers.
    c. Tests of teaching aptitude.
2. *Analytical diagnosis as applied to teacher*
    a. Health—physical, mental, emotional, social.
    b. General culture tests and social background.
    c. Tests of personality traits.
    d. Measures of scholarship and general professional knowledge.
    e. Intelligence level (in some cases).
    f. Anecdotal records.
    g. Analysis of a performance or product.
3. *Psychological diagnosis*
    a. Tests of attitudes toward children, toward teaching, toward social agencies and institutions.
    b. Observation of classroom procedures; teacher behavior in social situations; participation in community affairs; sociometric records.
    c. Analysis of oral responses for clarity, correctness of form, general quality, coherency of ideas.
    d. Analysis of written responses, in class materials or in lesson plans, letters, questionnaires, etc.
    e. Interviews about problems, needs, difficulties.
    f. Projective methods.
    g. Clinical procedures in severe cases where the help of specialists seems necessary.

The comprehensive discussion of these three levels of diagnosis given in Chapter 10 makes it unnecessary to repeat details at this point. In general, the supervisor can adapt procedures for studying children to the study of adults. There are special adaptions of diagnostic procedures applied to teachers that will be briefly discussed below.

The primary causes of teacher difficulty are in general quite similar in most respects to the primary causes of failure of the learner to grow satisfactorily, discussed in Chapter 10. They will be analyzed more fully in Chapter 15 in connection with the discussion of more immediate causes of teacher difficulty and means of remedying them.

Other factors which affect instructional practice. Many factors other than those inherent in the teacher, his choice of methods, and his competency, affect instruction. These will turn up as we investigate the three factors which are the concern of this chapter, but are not our interest at this time. Before taking up the subject matter of this chapter, we may note for the record a summary of these other factors, all of which are discussed in detail elsewhere in this volume.

1. The formulated statement, if any, of the ultimate purposes of education which serves as a guide for teaching. Obviously, these objectives may be viewed dynamically and broadly or they may be narrowly conceived; they may be meaningful to the teacher or their significance may not be comprehended.

2. The comprehensiveness of the immediate objectives of instruction in the various areas of the curriculum.

3. The organization of the curriculum, which may vary from a compartmentalized, scientific subject arrangement to a broad experience type of program.

4. The subject matter to be taught as outlined in the course of study, its difficulty, the amount of it, and its relation to the needs, purposes, and interests of the learners.

5. The organization of learning experiences, for example, departmentalized teaching, time allotment.

6. The conception of the role of the school as a force for social progress and for preparation for citizenship.

7. The accepted responsibilities of the school for improvement of community life.

8. The quality and richness of instructional materials and equipment.

9. The adequacy of facilities for carrying on the educational program.

10. The potentialities and limitations of the children with whom the teacher must deal.

11. The ways in which the children are grouped for instructional purposes, including

class size, special classes, clinical services, and so on.

12. The methods used by school administrators to measure the aspects of instruction, including pupil tests, teacher rating scales, promotion policies, and the like.

13. Community attitudes toward education and the school.

14. The quality of educational leadership.

15. Provisions for maintenance of morale and good working conditions for teachers.

The organization of the rest of this chapter is as follows:

Section 2. Methods of studying instructional practice.

Section 3. Values and limitations of analytic procedures.

Section 4. Using data-gathering devices.

Section 5. Analysis of instruction a co-operative procedure.

Section 2

METHODS OF STUDYING INSTRUCTIONAL PRACTICES

There are four basic methods of securing data about instructional practices that assist the supervisor to determine strengths and limitations of the program as a whole, in various curriculum areas at various grade levels, in particular schools, and in the work of a given teacher:

1. Analysis of measures of pupil growth, attainments, interests, and methods of work.
2. Direct observation of instructional practices.
3. Analysis of reports from individual teachers, pupils, observers, and groups.
4. Examination of personnel files.

In this section we shall describe a variety of fact-gathering procedures; in Section 3 their values and limitations. In the final section we shall illustrate the application of different kinds of procedures useful for three major purposes, including (1) describing existing instructional practices, (2) rating and evaluating teaching, and (3) diagnosing underlying causes of difficulties.

1. Analysis of measures of pupil growth. It seems obvious that one of the most effective ways of locating areas of learning in which results are inferior is the analysis of various measures of pupil growth, achievement, interests, and methods of work as well as the results of evaluative procedures such as were discussed in Chapter 9. The more analytical the measures used were, the more definitely a possible shortcoming in the instructional program can be identified. For example, if a learning test in spelling shows that the children of a certain teacher seem to have very ineffective study habits, it can be assumed that instruction at some point has not been adequate. This fact can be established, or be demonstrated to be incorrect, by a closer inspection of the total teaching-learning situation, including instructional procedures at preceding levels of the school as well as in the classroom concerned. Similar procedures can be applied in connection with needs in any curriculum area or with respect to any educational outcome.

This procedure is subject to all of the limitations inherent in evaluating educational outcomes that were discussed in Chapter 9 and in Section 1 of the present chapter. The data do give a supervisor a clue as to a point which may require systematic study of classroom practices.

2. Direct observation of instruction. The observer's approach will differ according to the status of the individual being observed and the purpose of the observer; for instance, the purpose of an observation of a student-teacher would be quite different from that underlying the observation of a new teacher on probation who is having serious difficulty, or of a master teacher. In the first case the purpose would be selection and guidance; in the second case the purpose would be diagnosis; whereas in the third case the purpose might be merely to get new ideas or to find desirable practices to be reported to other teachers. In none of these cases is the purpose of the observer served by merely getting a general impression of the work under way; it is necessary to devise and keep some kind of record of the activities of teacher and pupils. The supervisor and teacher can then analyze the data, consider their implications, and interpret the findings. Steps to bring about improvement can then be planned.

The supervisor must be familiar with the various kinds of fact-gathering techniques that can be used during observations and aware of their limitations. The supervisor must also be skillful in choosing procedures to apply in a given situation. Educational literature [2] contains a wealth of information about these analytical procedures and their use by supervisors. There is given below a list of some devices that are useful for securing a record of various aspects of classroom instruction. In some instances the record will be merely descriptive; in others there is the implication of evaluation. The choice of procedures to use in a given situation depends on the supervisor's purpose and the appropriateness of the method to conditions that prevail in the classroom at the time.

OBSERVATION OF INSTRUCTIONAL PRACTICES

1. Free observation of teacher and pupil activities.
2. Observation in controlled planned situations.
3. Checking items in a check-list of some kind, such as teaching difficulties, objectives, classroom management, etc.
4. Time studies showing distribution of time.
5. Diagramming teacher-pupil activities on a chart.
6. Taking running notes of teacher or pupil activities, blunders, etc.
7. Using inventories of desirable practices and materials.
8. Judging levels of instruction by using descriptive "levels" of instruction, as in the Texas guide.
9. Using a rating scale to evaluate a performance or a product, with supporting data.
10. Recording behavior in social situations; making anecdotal records; listing contributions to school programs; and to school-community relations; using tape recorders, motion pictures, photographs.
11. Checking for applications of principles of learning, such as provision for individual differences, etc.
12. Checking on use of community resources.

A careful scrutiny of the data gathered by these procedures will reveal problems and needs that may be made the basis of more intensive investigation. The data are invaluable in conferences with teachers.

The use of sound and sound-motion recording devices. One of the most interesting recent developments in the gathering of data is the use of sound and sound-motion recording devices.[3] Reference has already been made to the use of stenographic reports and other devices for recording the happenings of the class period. The use of sound and sound-motion recording devices is merely one more step in the direction of securing more adequate records of teacher and pupil activities in concrete learning and teaching situations.

Few persons who have not attempted to make studies of teaching have any appreciation of its complexity and elusiveness. The evaluation of teaching really involves a threefold operation: (1) the securing of adequate records of the purposes and conditions that prevail in the learning-teaching situation under consideration, (2) the collection of reliable data relative to teacher and pupil activities, and (3) the evaluation of the data collected. When sound-recording instruments and combinations of sound and motion-recording devices are employed in making

[2] Many illustrations are available in the periodical literature and in textbooks.
[3] A. S. Barr and C. D. Jayne, "The Use of Sound Recording Equipment in the Study and Improvement of Teaching," *Journal of Experimental Education* (March, 1936), pp. 279-286.

records of teaching, they do solve quite satisfactorily the problem of getting permanent and accurate records of what takes place, that is, as far as observable behavior is concerned; but they do not solve the problem of evaluation. In the older set-up the evaluator had to record, analyze, and evaluate the happenings simultaneously; and in a complex situation, with many things taking place in rapid succession, that was a difficult assignment. With the sound record or the sound picture, teachers and supervisors can analyze and evaluate the events associated with learning and teaching in a more leisurely fashion. Many schools cannot as yet afford such equipment, but when such records are made they can be examined in detail and as often as necessary by those concerned. The evaluations may be made subjectively or through the application of established criteria. If one does the evaluating purely subjectively, then the evaluations are subject to all of the limitations of this method. Unfortunately, some supervisors have thought that with such records their problems of evaluating teaching had been wholly solved. They confuse, thus, the two phases of analysis: (1) the observing and recording of facts, and (2) the evaluating of the events observed. The evaluation of teaching even with adequate records is still a very complex activity.

3. Analysis of reports. Because of the impossibility of observing practices at first hand in the large number of classrooms there are in most places, the supervisor must often solicit the co-operation of others in securing basic information about instruction. The most feasible procedure is to secure reports from others in some effective, dependable way. A report may be made by the teacher, a pupil, observers, and sometimes by citizens in the community. Those who are to prepare reports of information should be carefully instructed as to the nature of the report and when possible given preliminary practice in using the form. When the form itself is developed co-operatively by supervisors and teachers, it will be meaningful and there will

be an appreciation of the significance of the information gathered.

One series of procedures for securing information about instruction is given below. Supervisors may wish to make out similar lists to suit their needs.

SECURING REPORTS ABOUT ASPECTS OF INSTRUCTION

1. Scrutinizing informal reports, such as letters, requests, newspaper articles, etc.
2. Securing answers to specific questions about practices, materials, objectives.
3. Using check-lists of practices, objectives, etc., to secure reports of various kinds.
4. Analyzing plan books, lesson plans, etc.
5. Securing inventories of materials available.
6. Interviewing teachers about difficulties, needs, etc.
7. Analyzing objective records, such as stenographic reports, tape recordings, movies of lessons.
8. Analyzing reports of rating of teachers, levels of instruction, objectives, etc.
9. Analyzing logs of work.
10. Using sociometric procedures.
11. Helping teachers to use methods of evaluating their own procedures.
12. Group conferences for discussing problems.

The systematic analysis of well-designed reports gives the supervisor a wealth of information about current practices and reveals strengths and weaknesses in the instructional program. When a persistent weakness appears in a large number of classrooms, a sound basis for planning an improvement program is established. Individual teachers are also often helped to study their own practices by carefully constructed check-lists, inventories, and similar reporting procedures.

Teachers' needs indicated through a survey of research on instructional difficulties. A large number of studies have been made to discover and define the difficulties that teachers experience in attempting to provide desirable conditions for learning. An analysis of these leads to definitions of specific needs. A summary of 475 of these research studies covering reports from 12,372 teachers has been made by Hill as follows:[4]

1. Difficulties in providing for individual differences among pupils... 19*
2. Difficulties in teaching method.... 18
3. Difficulties of discipline, control, social development of the pupil... 17
4. Difficulties of motivation, getting children interested, getting them to work 12
5. Difficulties in the direction of study 9
6. Difficulties in organizing and administering the classroom 8
7. Difficulties in selecting appropriate subject matter 6
8. Lack of time during the school day for all the things that need to be done 6
9. Difficulties in organization of materials 6
10. Difficulties in planning and making assignments 5
11. Difficulties in grading and promotion of pupils 5
12. Inadequacy of supplies and materials 4
13. Difficulties in testing and evaluating 4
14. Personal difficulties of the teacher. 4
15. Difficulties arising from conditions of work 3
16. Difficulties involved in diagnosing and correcting particular pupil difficulties 3
17. Difficulties in teaching reading... 3
18. Difficulties in making plans for teaching 3
19. Difficulties in promoting desirable habits 2
20. Difficulties in securing study aids.. 2
21. Difficulty in securing pupil participation 2
22. Difficulty because pupils talk while others are reciting............. 2
23. Outside interruptions of class work 2
24. Miscellaneous problems mentioned in only one study .... 40†

* Number of studies in which difficulty was among the first six.
† These were mostly specific problems. Seven were difficulties in teaching this or that subject. Others were rural school problems such as "only one pupil in grade," or "too many grades in one room."

An examination of the difficulties listed above reveals that they arise chiefly out of the teacher's responsibilities as a director of learning; they do not adequately illustrate the teacher's work as a friend and counselor of youth, as a director of extracurricular activities, as a member of a school staff, and as a member of a community. The report lists merely the difficulties of performance; many of the improvement needs of teachers are likely to be found, however, in the background factors such as personality, morale, and social pressures that condition performance. The limited purpose of this summary prevents its use as a truly satisfactory illustration of all of the growth needs of teachers.

Helping a faculty to become aware of educational needs. The principal and the co-ordinator of instruction in some area can make effective use of such means as the following to help teachers not only to become aware of instructional needs of the school as a whole but also to make them sensitive to their own individual teaching strengths and problems:

1. Identification of school problems through co-operative faculty and community study and evaluation of the existing educational program.
2. Co-operative development of school policy by the whole staff on methods of dealing with some problem or need revealed by a staff appraisal of the existing program and practices.
3. Presentation of evidence concerning some emerging school or community problem, to sensitize the staff to it.
4. Making appraisal devices available for teachers to apply in studying and evaluating their own instructional practices.
5. Conferences and informal discussions with groups of teachers and individuals to consider instructional problems.
6. Lectures on current educational problems and related topics by stimulating speakers.
7. Discussions of ways of meeting the needs of individual pupils who present special learning problems.
8. Reports by individual staff members of experiences, meetings, trips, intervisitation, research, community contacts, etc.
9. Study groups and committees concerned

[4] George E. Hill, "Teachers' Instructional Difficulties: A Review of Research," *Journal of Educational Research* (April, 1944), pp. 602-615.

with the analysis of particular needs and problems of school and community and the proposal of ways of dealing with them.

10. Participation by staff in community surveys leading to knowledge about the environment and its problems.

11. Parent-teacher conferences about factors affecting pupil progress and related problems.

12. A growing, co-operatively maintained professional library.

Specific questions in particular curriculum areas. An illustration of the types of specific questions that may be resolved by the staff of any school system in a single curriculum area is the following statement prepared by Gray and Iverson:[5]

1. How well do our pupils read? Are they doing as well as might be expected in terms of their ability to learn? Are they able to meet reasonable demands made upon them in study activities? Are they growing as rapidly as they should in ability to read independently and with penetration and discrimination? If not, what are the reasons for their shortcomings?

2. Do we have a well-balanced, sequential reading program throughout the elementary and the high school? Does the program provide for the development of basic reading habits, for guidance in reading in the various curriculum areas, for the stimulation and guidance of personal reading for pleasure or information, and for meeting the special needs of the poor reader?

3. Is reading narrowly or broadly conceived? That is, do we teach reading as if it were a set of specific skills that can be applied uniformly once they are learned, or do we recognize that reading is a form of experiencing and learning that differs in important respects with the kinds of material read and the purposes for reading?

4. Do we recognize and provide effectively for individual differences with respect to the time at which instruction in reading begins, the rate of progress expected, the demands made on pupils for reading in the various curriculum fields, and the nature and variety of reading materials provided?

5. Are we giving balanced emphasis to all the important aspects of reading? Some of the important aspects are recognizing words accurately and independently; grasping the sense meaning of what is read; interpreting the ideas apprehended according to all the reader knows that throws light on their meaning; reacting critically to the facts presented and the conclusions reached; and making use of what is read in clarifying thinking, solving problems, and guiding action.

6. Have we explained our program and practices to parents so that they know what we are doing and why?

Any supervisor can, with the assistance and co-operation of members of the staff, set up a similar series of questions for any curriculum area. This would be an excellent committee project.

4. Personnel files. In most school systems, personnel files are kept in which information of various kinds is assembled. The richness and variety of information they contain will depend on the purposes for which the files are kept. In a sense, the data are a cumulative record of information that is likely to be used for such purposes as:

1. Selection of teachers.
2. Guidance in service.
3. Placement.
4. Recording ratings, problems, relationships.
5. Recording information useful in promotion and making special assignments.
6. Recording evidences of professional advancement.
7. Anecdotes about special contributions to pupils, to the school program, and to school community relations.
8. Listing test data, reports of medical examinations, etc.

These records can be examined by the supervisor to secure a wide variety of information helpful in planning supervisory programs, such as the extent to which teachers have had advanced professional study in some area, their travel and work experiences, and evidence as to felt needs on their part. A more detailed analysis may be made in the case of an individual teacher.

[5] W. S. Gray and W. J. Iverson, "What Should Be the Profession's Attitude Toward Lay Criticism of the Schools? (With Special Reference to Reading), *The Elementary School Journal* (September, 1952), pp. 39-40.

VALUES AND LIMITATIONS OF ANALYTICAL PROCEDURES

Early attempts at analysis. School systems have always faced the problem of evaluating instruction. At first teachers were rated arbitrarily by untrained, unqualified persons, such as school commissioners and members of school boards. Gradually there were developed crude score cards for rating teachers. Their use proved very dissatisfying. and unreliable. Ultimately there developed, in connection with school surveys conducted early in this century, various plans for describing in factual terms some of the characteristics of instruction, intended to give the readers of the reports of surveys a realistic picture of classroom procedures. The following statement [6] lists the typical kinds of objective data that were included in reports of school surveys:

When the members of the survey staff made their written reports on the recitations, they included some simple notes designed to indicate whether the teachers were mainly engaged in questioning pupils to find how well they remembered what they had studied in the books, or whether they were trying to help the children through observing, thinking, and discussing.

In the first place they noted whether it was the teacher or a pupil who was talking when the visitor entered. In seven rooms out of every ten it was the teacher who was doing the talking, while in the remaining three it was a pupil.

Similarly a record was made as to whether the recitation was predominantly one in which the teacher heard the pupils recite or whether she was attempting to stimulate them to think for themselves. In seven rooms out of every ten the records show that in the judgment of the visitor the teacher was mainly engaged in hearing the pupils recite what they had learned in the book.

Another record made at each recitation related to the type of questioning mainly employed by the teacher. The results showed that in eight out of each ten rooms the observer judged that the questions were predominantly of such a nature that the pupils could answer them only by stating facts or giving definite in-

formation. In two out of each ten rooms the object of the questioning was mainly to get the pupils to describe or explain.

A fourth set of records related to the answers of the pupils and showed whether these mainly consisted of single words, of phrases, or of sentences. These records show the pupils in five rooms out of every ten answered mainly in single words, while in two cases they used phrases, and in the remaining three the answers were mostly in complete sentences.

The interpretation of these data depends on the point of view of the reader and the values he accepts. The survey staff made no attempt to evaluate the information as a measure of teaching competency and left the interpretation to those who read the statement.

The development of objective analysis of teaching. Many specialists in supervision began at about that time to devise ways of making objective analyses of various aspects of classroom instruction to establish a dependable basis for rating the teacher and for studying the influence of factors that condition teaching. The development of the testing program for measuring pupil attainments was an important factor in this approach to the study of teaching.

Questions began to arise as to the reliability and validity of these analytical procedures. For example, how reliable a picture of usual practices is the information gathered in the course of a single lesson? How good an index of teaching ability is any given body of information about the work of a teacher, such as the distribution of time during a lesson or the number of questions asked by the teacher? Information about these and other problems is given in the first edition of this book and may be reviewed by those concerned with the problem. At this point we

[6] L. P. Ayres, *Public Schools of Springfield, Illinois* (New York, Russell Sage Foundation, 1914).

shall merely summarize some of the most significant conclusions:

1. Teaching is a highly variable activity. Hence specific data about the work in one lesson is not a reliable index of what will take place in succeeding lessons. This important conclusion should be borne in mind by any supervisor who by force of circumstances limits his observations of teachers to short, infrequent visits.

2. Ratings given a teacher by different supervisors after an observation of a lesson usually vary widely and also are wholly unreliable, indicating a lack of common standards and the influence of differing points of view held by the observers.[7]

3. There is very little, if any, relationship between ratings given teachers by supervisors and the numerous kinds of specific acts that the teacher performs in conducting a lesson. This is partly due to the inadequacy of almost all of our teacher-rating devices; furthermore, in most of these studies the mere fact that a certain activity took place a certain number of times was recorded, but no consideration was given to the appropriateness of the act at the time.

4. There are no specific teaching procedures that are "always" good under all circumstances. It is apparent that the effectiveness of teaching procedures depends on the objectives and purposes of the teacher, the persons involved, the principles that one holds to be true, and other special limitations of the particular situation at hand.

5. Evaluation of teaching should be in terms of principles rather than in terms of specific activities. Much of our educational literature, whether of a philosophic, scientific, or personal nature, eventually becomes a summary of generalizations, principles, and theories. Principles of one sort or other become controls over practice. For instance, it is not difficult to determine by analyzing instruction to what extent a teacher recognizes the principle that instruction must provide for individual differences among children. In this volume there are numerous illustrations of sets of principles of learning that may be regarded as fundamental in the evaluation and improvement of instruction.

Growth of pupils as a criterion of success. The mounting evidence as to the lack of merit of current teacher-rating procedures led to the adoption as a criterion of teaching ability the growth made by the learners. An extensive series of investigations has been made by Barr and his associates of the relationship between growth of pupils and the prediction of teaching success. The results appear to be promising.

McCall pointed out some years ago that the ultimate criterion of teaching success is the number, kinds, and amounts of desirable changes produced in pupils.[8] If this approach is made to the measurement of teaching ability, it should be remembered that certain important assumptions have been made. Two are noted here. (1) It is assumed that we possess adequate measures of the major changes produced in pupils. Excellent progress has been made in the development of new means of evaluating pupil growth but in no sense can the data-gathering devices now available in this field be said to be adequate. (2) It is assumed that factors other than teaching ability can be controlled, equated, or otherwise held constant as in experimental research. Teaching is only one of the several factors conditioning the changes produced in pupils. If the gains in test scores for one teacher are to be compared with those of another, those factors other than teaching ability affecting the products of learning must be controlled, equated, or otherwise held constant, as in experimental research. This latter condition is sometimes not possible in research conducted in school situations.

The use of measures of pupil growth in evaluating the efficiency of teachers is an exceedingly difficult process. Although the method is theoretically sound, more harm may be done than good unless it is applied

---

[7] The 1938 edition of this book contains a fairly exhaustive study of the validity, reliability, and objectivity of analytical procedures for studying classroom instruction that summarizes research dealing with these problems. The bibliography at the close of the present chapter contains a selected list of more recent studies in this area. The reader should consult these references for details. Class reports by individuals will help to clarify the issues.

[8] William A. McCall, *How to Measure in Education* (New York, Macmillan, 1922), pp. 150-152.

with great care. Whether or not measures of pupil growth should be used by administrative officials to evaluate the efficiency of instruction will depend upon: (1) the attitude of the teaching corps, (2) the kinds of measures that are available, and (3) the care with which data are collected and the results interpreted. As instruments of measurement become more refined, one would expect that the more efficient teachers might demand, of their own accord, that their performance be evaluated in terms of the number of desirable changes produced by them in pupils instead of the less accurate and subjective methods now generally in use.

Difficulties in applying the growth criterion. The problem involved is a very difficult one to investigate. In the first place, we lack adequate methods of measuring many important educational outcomes, a limiting factor in current studies. In the second place, the teacher is only one element in a complex situation that affects pupil growth, and it is exceedingly difficult to isolate the influence one teacher may have on what is learned from the influence of other factors, such as previous educational experiences, the quality of home and community life, and the adequacy of instructional materials. In the third place, it has proved to be very difficult to arrange comparable learning situations in which the effects produced by different teachers can be measured directly so that they will be comparable. Finally, the merit of a teacher cannot be measured merely by measuring the growth of the children in a relatively narrow range of outcomes in academic areas; it is generally agreed today that merit ratings must also consider the contributions the teacher makes to the school program and policies as well as to school-community relations. At present we lack suitable means of evaluating these important aspects of teaching. The whole problem is unbelievably complex, but the issues are quite clear. The problem of setting up experimental studies is being painstakingly investigated in various centers. The results of these studies should be examined by all supervisors.[9]

The pupil-growth index of teaching efficiency holds considerable promise not only for evaluating efficiency but for the study of the relationship of various teacher factors to pupil growth. For illustrative materials both on the use of pupil growth as an index of teaching efficiency and on the relationship of various teacher factors to teaching efficiency, the reader is referred to Barr and others, *The Measurement of Teaching Ability.*[10]

The statistical treatment of changes in pupil scores. We have indicated briefly in the immediately preceding paragraphs some of the more important assumptions underlying the use of measures of pupil growth as indices of teaching efficiency. Not only must the data be collected with great care but they must have adequate statistical treatment. It is not within the scope of this volume to discuss the intricacies of correct statistical procedure, but we would like to suggest that what is done should be done with great care. Dependable results will be had only when such is the case.

Besides the pupil-change scores discussed above, a number of derived measures of teaching efficiency have been developed. Courtis,[11] after much very careful work, developed a very complicated system of iso-

---

[9] Two Reports of the Committee on Criteria of Teacher Effectiveness of the American Educational Research Association have appeared recently, the first in "Teachers and Nonacademic Personnel," *Review of Educational Research* (June, 1952), pp. 238-270, and the second in *Journal of Educational Research* (May, 1953), pp. 641-659. The reader who is interested in the technical problems involved in this problem will find a comprehensive technical discussion of its various aspects.

[10] A. S. Barr and others, *The Measurement of Teaching Ability,* Experimental Educational Monograph (Madison, Wisc., Dembar Publications, March, 1945).

[11] S. A. Courtis, "The Prediction of Growth," *Journal of Educational Research* (March, 1933), pp. 481-492.

———, "Maturation Units for the Measuring of Growth," *School and Society* (November, 1929), pp. 683-690.

chron units. The technically informed student in this area will doubtless want to know more about his efforts to devise measures of teaching efficiency. A somewhat less complicated but equally interesting approach is the MA unit proposed by Seyfert [12] and others. Lack of space prevents discussion of these interesting developments.

Correlation studies of teaching success. Several hundred studies have sought to identify qualities essential to teaching success by calculating correlations, between measures of various qualities and aspects of teaching and measures of teaching success. Variations in the conditions under which the studies were made, and the nature of the measures of teaching success used, make the comparison and interpretation of the results of the various studies difficult. On pages 332-333 is an adaptation of a comprehensive compilation by Barr [13] and others which attempted to bring together the results of studies of correlations of measures of teaching success and aspects of teachers or teaching, including student-teaching rating, in-service ratings, college grades, pupil growth, consensus of judges, and miscellaneous items. The data are totals for all criteria combined. The headings give the degree of relationship with teaching success, broadly considered, for a long series of items. "Positive" means positive findings, "negative" means inverse relations, and "zero" means no relationship between the item and teaching success. The figures in parentheses indicate the number of studies for the item. Each item in the list is fully defined in the reference, [13] which also gives details for each aspect considered.

The summary shows that most of these studies have dealt with the more general characteristics or aspects of teaching efficiency, such as personal qualities, and knowledge of subject matter both academic and professional. Important specific competencies have not been investigated to any extent. The number of items for which there are given both positive and negative relationships, together with the many cases in which there is a zero relationship, make it apparent that the identification and definition of teaching competencies is as yet by no means satisfactory. For example: in 31 studies of the relationship of emotional stability to teaching success (item I-4) there were 33 cases in which a positive relationship was indicated while in 13 cases there was a zero relationship. There were no cases in which a negative relationship was found in this instance. Notice the variety of relationships shown for teaching aptitude (item I-1) and teaching success. The three types of relationships were found. The confused results may be due to the inadequacy of the measures used and the lack of control of conditions in the experimental design. On the whole, few negative relationships were found.

We clearly lack satisfactory means for measuring teaching competency and aptitude. Barr suggests that research "should be directed toward identifying those teacher abilities, traits, and qualities which make for a high level of efficiency for different purposes, persons, and situations"—rather than to try to identify general characteristics of teaching efficiency.

Next steps to be taken. In the practical school situation, the supervisor is faced with the problem of taking steps to analyze and deal with instructional problems as they arise. In general, his approach should be that used in studying any problem. First, he should be clear on what objectives are to be achieved, and the extent to which they are being achieved; then he should try to determine, in co-operation with his associates, by suitable analytical techniques the needs of the system as a whole, the needs in a particular area of the curriculum; and he should ultimately try to help the individual teacher to meet the

[12] Warren C. Seyfert and Balfour S. Tydal, "An Evaluation of Differences in Teaching Ability," *Journal of Educational Research* (September, 1934), pp. 10-15.

[13] A. S. Barr and others, *The Measurement and Prediction of Teaching Efficiency: A Summary of Investigations* (Madison, Wisc., Dembar Publications, 1948).

FREQUENCY OF MENTION OF CORRELATION BETWEEN ASPECTS OF TEACHERS OR TEACHING AND CERTAIN CRITERIA OF TEACHING SUCCESS

ASPECTS OF TEACHING	RELATIONSHIPS WITH CRITERIA OF EFFICIENCY		
	Positive	Negative	Zero
I. Personal qualities			
1. Teaching aptitude (6)	16	2	14
2. Resourcefulness (8)	8	0	2
3. Intelligence (40)	44	1	16
4. Emotional stability (31)	33	0	13
5. Considerateness (27)	98	0	3
6. Buoyancy (24)	42	0	1
7. Objectivity (20)	26	0	1
8. Drive (11)	19	0	0
9. Dominance	24	0	9
10. Attractiveness (24)	27	0	0
11. Refinement (8)	8	0	0
12. Co-operativeness (10)	13	0	0
13. Reliability (11)	28	0	0
14. Personality, general (19)	34	0	2
II. Competencies (abilities to do)			
A. As a director of learning			
1. Skill in identifying pupil needs (0)	0	0	0
2. Skill in setting and defining goals (2)	2	0	0
3. Skill in creating favorable mind set (motivation) (9)	12	0	0
4. Skill in choosing learning experiences (2)	2	0	0
5. Skill in following the learning process			
a. In providing for individual differences (7)	7	0	0
b. In making activities meaningful (2)	2	0	0
c. In locating and overcoming difficulties (—)	0	0	0
d. In organizing learning experiences into meaningful wholes (7)	7	0	0
e. In supervising study (4)	4	0	0
f. In directing discussion (4)	7	0	0
6. Skill in using learning aids (3)	4	0	0
7. Skill in teacher pupil relations (28)	38	0	0
8. Skill in appraising pupil growth and achievement (2)	4	0	0
9. Skill in management (6)	8	0	0
10. Skill in instruction (20)	34	0	1
B. As counselor and friend of pupils (1)	1	0	0
C. As a member of the profession (—)	0	0	0
D. As a member of a community (1)	1	0	0
III. Effects of teacher leadership (results) (8)	14	0	0
IV. Behavior controls			
A. Knowledges			
1. Knowledge of subject matter taught or of activity directed (29)	27	0	3
2. Knowledge of child behavior and development (2)	4	0	0
3. Knowledge of professional practices and techniques (27)	46	0	5

ASPECTS OF TEACHING	RELATIONSHIPS WITH CRITERIA OF EFFICIENCY		
	Positive	Negative	Zero
4. General cultural background (17)	14	0	7
5. Scholarship grade point average (27) ..	55	1	3
B. Generalized skills			
1. Skill in problem-solving (1)			
2. Work habits (6)	7	0	1
3. Skill in human relations (see II A 7) ...			
4. Skill in use of language			
a. Speech (14)	27	0	0
b. Reading (6)	7	0	3
c. English usage (2)	8	0	1
C. Interests, attitudes, ideals			
1. Interest in pupils (4)	7	0	0
2. Interest in subject or activity (1)	1	0	0
3. Interest in teaching or school work (16)	20	0	5
4. Interest in community (4)	5	0	2
5. Social attitudes (4)	11	2	6
6. Professional attitudes (6)	6	0	0
7. Efforts toward self-improvement (3) ..	2	0	1
8. Interests-general (4)	7	0	0
9. Interests in extracurricular activities (7)	8	0	0
D. Health (11)	12	0	2
E. Morale (—)	0	0	0
V. Status facts			
1. Age (7)	4	2	2
2. Height (1)	0	0	1
3. Weight (—)	0	0	0
4. Training (4)	2	1	1
5. Experience (10)	8	0	5
6. Sex (5)	0	0	5
7. Salary (4)	3	0	1
8. Recommendations (3)	2	0	1
9. Photographs (1)	1	0	0
10. Socioeconomic status (2)	2	0	1
11. Tenure (2)	2	0	0
12. Applications	1	0	1

needs of a group of pupils in the classroom. In every way possible he should assist the teacher to analyze and evaluate his own practices in the light of criteria accepted by the group.

The choice of data-gathering devices. Many different data-gathering devices will be described in the pages that follow. Ordinarily only a limited few of these devices will be used at any one time or in any one learning-teaching situation. The following three suggestions may assist in choosing appropriate data-gathering devices:

1. *The device should fit the purpose for which it is to be used.* As has already been said, one may desire (1) to secure a general picture of the situation in a number of schools, school systems, or states as in a survey, or detailed information about an exceptional case of ineffective performance as in a program of individualized assistance; (2) to study performance or to study teacher factors conditioning performance; or (3) to accomplish some temporary short-time purpose or some more remote goal of reconstruction. The choice of instruments will depend on these purposes.

2. *The devices should provide data of the desired degree of accuracy.* Sometimes the need is for very accurate data; at other times

estimates, guesses, and approximations will suffice. By and large, there are very many more instances in life in which one relies upon estimates, guesses, and approximations than there are instances demanding precise measurement. In general, the devices used to collect data about teachers should reach the standards of accuracy expected in other areas of measurement and evaluation.

3. *The device should be in keeping with the limitations placed by the immediate learning-teaching situation.* There are limitations of time, money, and energy; and there are limitations imposed by the attitudes of those concerned and by the availability of help and materials. All of these will circumscribe what one may choose to do in a particular learning-teaching situation.

Section 4

USING DATA-GATHERING DEVICES

Purposes which data-gathering devices serve. The use of the various data-gathering devices that were evaluated in the preceding sections serves three major purposes:

1. Describing instructional programs.
2. Rating the teacher at work.
3. Gathering data about the teacher's characteristics and background.

In this section we shall illustrate practical uses of data-gathering for these purposes.

1. Describing instructional programs. A supervisor who is new to a school system ordinarily will wish to secure information about the status of instruction before setting up a program of improvement. The closer the contact with actual classroom work, the more dependable the information gathered about various aspects of instruction will be and the more likely it is that the actual needs will be discovered. The steps taken in a survey of reading in the schools of Detroit suggest a good plan for a busy supervisor to follow. They were outlined by Gertrude Whipple,[14] supervisor of reading, as follows:

1. The provisions made for developing readiness for the reading activities were observed, noted in writing, and appraised to determine whether they were adequate for the purpose.
2. The reading activities underway were appraised in terms of the aims of basic reading instruction. The specific types of growth being stressed were determined, and tabulations made

of the number of times each type was stressed in order to find out the emphasis in instruction.

3. The extent to which visual aids were used, and the particular uses to which they were being put in teaching reading were analyzed.

4. The books on hand for reading in each room were inspected to estimate the number and quality; the types of books preferred by the teachers were ascertained in answer to a questionnaire prepared for that purpose and used in interviewing a large sampling of teachers.

5. Teachers' and principals' suggestions for the further development of the reading program were assembled and are now being put into effect as far as possible.

6. Detailed records were kept of superior classroom activities; these records were broadcast in the written reports prepared for the teachers and principals.

7. The provisions made for removing reading retardation were observed, noted in writing, and studied.

Throughout the survey the supervisor, who has taken part in several such surveys in large cities, endeavored to have the impartial attitude of an outside investigator. Also, in a system the size of Detroit responsibility for the reading program is shared by many officials, particularly the principal of the school who serves as the building supervisor and the central administrator who is especially responsible for giving his support to constructive measures and for implementing the program with reading material and standardized reading tests. The abilities of the pupils, another element, in

[14] In File No. 4828, December 15, 1945. Department of Language Instruction, Detroit, Mich. (mimeographed).

a survey are dependent upon their previous experience and training as well as the quality of their present guidance.

In order to avoid the disadvantage of interpreting the survey findings from a single point of view, the supervisor constantly checked her judgment against that of teachers, principals, and other school officials. Those consulted gave most helpful suggestions showing no disposition to regard the survey as narrowly inspectional.

The guide that was used by the supervisor to record the information about each lesson that was observed contained seven major items, with necessary space for writing. The items were the following:

1. Evidence of stimulation to read (e.g., pictures and exhibits on the theme of the reading; bibliographies suggesting further reading; attractive library books).

2. Preparation of the pupils for the reading activities (e.g., What steps are taken to build the background essential to good reading? To what extent are interests stimulated? What effort is made to insure purposeful reading? Are the books fitted to the pupils' reading ability? Does the teacher provide for overcoming difficulties in the reading material?).

3. Attention to individual differences (e.g., through grouping pupils for reading; providing reading material of different degrees of difficulty; setting up purposes which lead to more advanced forms of reading by accelerated pupils; providing further opportunities for reading by pupils who finish ahead of their classmates).

4. Pupil initiative (e.g., shown by voluntary comments and questions; voluntary reading; contributions based on experiences outside of school).

5. Types of growth in reading which the teacher is promoting.
   a. Comprehension (e.g., getting the meaning in the form presented by the author).
   b. Interpretation (e.g., grasping the underlying meanings and implications appraising the ideas).
   c. Meaning vocabulary.
   d. Recognition vocabulary.
   e. Reading for study purposes (e.g., skimming; note-taking; outlining; summarizing).
   f. Speed of silent reading. (It should be developed only so long as comprehension is not sacrificed.)
   g. Fluent oral reading.
6. Attention given by pupils to the activities (e.g., alert, interested discussion as opposed to passivity; close application to the reading as opposed to the frittering away of time).

7. Evidences of activity growing out of the reading (e.g., written paragraphs which the pupils have based on their reading; drawings depicting things read about; lists of books read; scrapbooks and other books prepared by the pupils to extend an interest developed through reading).

The consultant in any curriculum area can prepare a similar series of items as a basis of a survey of instruction in that area. The list should be prepared co-operatively with teachers and principals so that all will be aware of the points being considered in observing instruction.

Check-lists as guides to observation. In studying the nature and quality of instruction in one or more classrooms, check-lists may be used as a guide for recording information or for self-analysis by the teacher. Check-lists serve as reminders of various aspects of instruction that should be brought under observation, for example, the objectives of teacher and pupils, the types of instructional activities, the instructional materials used, and the organization of the class for work. Each major classification in the check-list can be further defined by appropriate items. Ideally such check-lists should be developed co-operatively by teachers and supervisors and be used by both to study and to improve instruction. General trends of practices in a school system also can be determined by the supervisor by assembling data for a sampling of classrooms.

An illustration of a typical check-list is the Pistor rating scale [15] for studying the ways in which democracy is practiced in classrooms. The check-list consists of the following twelve categories of items stated as questions:

1. Curriculum opportunities.
2. Selecting and planning classwork.
3. Personal relationships of pupils.

[15] Frederick Pistor, "A Standardized Measure of Classroom Democracy," *Journal of Educational Research* (November, 1941), pp. 183-192.

4. Relationships with community.
5. Discussion and class-conference periods.
6. Silent-reading and directed-study periods.
7. Construction and experimentation periods.
8. Appreciation and creative-work periods.
9. Drill and practice periods.
10. Recreation and game periods.
11. Routine affairs and maintenance work.
12. Organization of classroom materials.

An excerpt illustrating the questions asked is given below:

3. *Personal Relationships of Pupils*

Never Seldom Sometimes Often Always

a. Do the pupils seem to be happy and successful in their work? 1 2 3 4 5
b. Do the children know the achievements, interests, and ambitions of each other well enough to sense that they belong to a group? 1 2 3 4 5
c. Are the children developing a concern for the welfare of all others? 1 2 3 4 5
d. Do they respect each member of the class as a responsible co-worker? 1 2 3 4 5
e. Are the pupils encouraged to communicate freely so they may share their ideas, discuss their plans, and evaluate their results? 1 2 3 4 5
f. Do all of the children have opportunity to lead in some activity part of the time? 1 2 3 4 5
g. Are the pupils courteous and friendly in their relationships with others? 1 2 3 4 5
h. Do the children consider the teacher an efficient and friendly guide of the group as well as competent instructor? 1 2 3 4 5

Never Seldom Sometimes Often Always

i. Do the pupils continue to work freely when the principal or the supervisor visits the class? 1 2 3 4 5
j. Do the children continue to work efficiently when the teacher leaves the group or the classroom? 1 2 3 4 5
Total value of this section ......

A descriptive check-list to be used to secure information about instruction in arithmetic is given below. The check-list may be used by a supervisor as a means of recording observations or as a basis for reports of practices observed by others. Similar check-lists can be developed for other curriculum areas.

SURVEY OF SELECTED INSTRUCTIONAL PRACTICES IN OBSERVED LESSONS IN ARITHMETIC IN GRADES 4, 5, AND 6

(Conducted under the auspices of the National Council of Teachers of Mathematics)

School .... *City* ....

State .... *Grade* ....

Length of Period ...... *Time of Day* ......

Number of Pupils .... *Experience of Teachers*

(*in Years*) .... *Type of School* { Platoon ....
Traditional ..
Experimental
Other ......

TRAINING: Grade 9, 10, 11, 12 Normal or Teachers College 1, 2, 3, 4 University or College 1, 2, 3, 4 (Encircle highest year attended)

DIRECTIONS: This blank is to be used to record certain observed facts in *one* typical lesson in arithmetic, in a room having only one full class in it. Split classes should not be included. The observer will check the items below applying to this *one* lesson alone. Space is provided in each group of items for additional facts that may appear to be vital.

1. The apparent *major* objective of the lesson. (Check not more than two, preferably only one unless two are very evident.)

....*a.* To develop skill in computation.
....*b.* To develop skill in solving problems stressing processes rather than social applications of number.
....*c.* To develop an understanding of the *social* applications and uses of number in life.
....*d.* To develop interest in number through various types of projects, creative activities, and the like, planned by the pupils under the guidance of the teacher.
....*e.* Others, such as ....

2. Types of instructional activities occurring. (Check all those observed.)

....*a.* Development of new process by direct teaching.
....*b.* Practice on the new process.
....*c.* Review of previous work through discussion and questions.
....*d.* Formal written drill on previously acquired skills.
      (1) With standard drill materials.
      (2) With teacher prepared materials.
....*e.* Games.
....*f.* Test not including practice tests listed in *d.*
      (1) With test prepared by the teacher.
      (2) With a standardized test in arithmetic.
....*g.* Pupils give original problems illustrating topic under consideration.
....*h.* Teaching pupils how to solve problems using prepared problem-solving helps.
....*i.* Practice in solving problems dealing with social applications of number.
....*j.* Practice solving problems to illustrate some computational process.
....*k.* Discussion of historical aspects of number.
....*l.* Discussion of present-day social social applications and uses of number.
....*m.* Planning and executing class project involving practical application of number.
....*n.* Reports on assigned topics, assigned reading, etc.
....*o.* Worthwhile voluntary independent contributions made by individual pupils.
....*p.* Dramatizations of applications of number.

....*q.* Systematic diagnostic work with individuals by the teacher.
....*r.* Pupils taught how to diagnose their own difficulties.
....*s.* Pupils diagnose their own difficulties.
....*t.* Systematic remedial work adapted to individual needs.
....*u.* Oral practice exercises for speed work.
....*v.* Independent group work by some pupils.
....*w.* Completely individualized work (Winnetka plan).
....*x.* Presentation of uses of number in other subjects, as geography, health, etc.
....*y.* Construction of graphs and other types of geometric design.
....*z.* Others, such as ....

3. Instructional materials used. (Check all those used.)

   a. Books.
   .... (1) No books used.
   .... (2) Basic text in hands of the pupils.
   .... (3) Supplementary textbooks.
   .... (4) Reference books, encyclopedias, etc.
   .... (5) Pamphlets, bulletins, magazines, etc.
   .... (6) Selections found in readers, geography texts, history texts, etc.
   .... (7) Others, such as ....

   b. Practice exercises.
   .... (1) Exercises in textbook.
   .... (2) Standardized drill cards adapted for individualized progress.
   .... (3) Unstandardized materials on cards prepared by the teacher.
   .... (4) Mimeographed materials.
   .... (5) Workbooks.
   .... (6) Materials on blackboard to be copied by pupils.
   .... (7) Dictated materials to be copied by pupils.
   .... (8) Problems or examples given orally to be solved mentally.
   .... (9) Flash cards.
   .... (10) Others, such as ....

   c. Other equipment.
   .... (1) Blackboard used by teacher.
   .... (2) Blackboard used by pupils.
   .... (3) Slides, films, etc.
   .... (4) Class progress graph (in use or on wall).
   .... (5) Individual progress graph.
   .... (6) Charts, diagrams, pictures, etc., not in textbook.
   .... (7) Objects, such as cubes, measures, sticks, rulers, instruments, etc.

.... (8) Illustrative materials collected from the community.

.... (9) Bulletin board display of current applications of number.

.... (10) Prepared exhibits of materials supplied by commercial houses.

.... (11) Neatness scales to set standards.

.... (12) Others, such as . . . .

4. The organization of the room for work.

.... (a) The entire class does the same work on processes.

.... (b) The entire class does the same work on problems.

.... (c) Pupils are divided into two or more groups according to progress made.

.... (d) There are independent groups working on various group projects.

.... (e) There is completely individualized instruction on number processes.

.... (f) Others, such as . . . .

5. Basis of the class work. (Check one.)

.... (a) Teacher-directed activities limited almost wholly to the organization and content of a single textbook or of the drill exercises.

.... (b) Variety of materials is introduced by the teacher to supplement the textbook to enrich instruction and to develop interest by the pupils.

.... (c) Work is organized in large units of subject matter devised by the teacher and executed by the pupils. (Contracts, Morrison units, etc.)

.... (d) The class work is organized in the form of activities planned and executed by the pupils under the guidance of teacher. (Projects, creative activities, etc.)

Person making the observation

. . . .

Position . . . .

Applying criteria describing instructional practices. In 1934 the Committee on Educational Problems of the New York Principals' Association voted to make the activity movement a major topic of study during the current school year. In February, 1935, the Committee recommended a limited program which was started in thirteen schools; in September, 1935, the program was extended to seventy schools. In 1936-1937 an extensive program of evaluation was initiated in nine activity and in nine paired nonactivity schools. The testing was continued through 1938, 1939, and 1940. In 1938 the New York City Board of Education recommended that the superintendent of schools invite the State Education Department to make a survey of the experiment. Plans for the survey were submitted to the superintendent in November, 1940, and completed in April, 1941. An excerpt from the criteria used in this survey is reproduced below:[16]

1. *The extent of planning.* With the teacher's guidance, children plan projects, units of work, activities, and the daily schedule.

3. *Origin of activity or work observed.* Units, projects, and activities have their origin in the interests and needs of the children who with the teacher's guidance determine and objectives and desired outcomes.

7. *Exercise of initiative.* Through exercise of initiative, children develop qualities of leadership.

18. *Attention to social outcomes.* Both teacher and children are alert to discover growth in the social behavior or conduct of the individual and the group.

29. *Whole group enterprises and experiences.* Children share experiences through the use of bulletin boards, home-made movies, class or school newspapers, assembly programs and other such enterprises.

34. *Workshop-like appearance.* The room is arranged and equipped to facilitate many types of work.

37. *Pupil participation.* Children are eager to participate in the program in progress.

41. *Leader-group responsibility.* Group insists on action and progress, holding the leader responsible for the discharge of his functions.

44. *Freedom of movement.* Children move freely around the room to obtain and use materials and in the performance of tasks related to the work at hand.

46. *Pupil-pupil relations.* Children's relations with one another are informal and natural, marked by courteous, socially desirable behavior.

51. *Rapport between teacher and pupils.* There is a fine understanding and working re-

[16] J. Cayce Morrison and others, *The Activity Program: A Survey of the Curriculum Experiment with the Activity Program in the Elementary Schools of New York City* (New York City Board of Education, September, 1941), pp. 29-32.

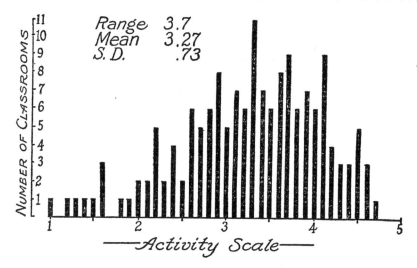

Range 3.7
Mean 3.27
S. D. .73

**THE AMOUNT OF ACTIVITY IN SELECTED CLASSROOMS
OBSERVED BY THE ADVISORY COMMITTEE**

The distribution on an activity scale ranging from 1.0 to 5.0 of 158 classrooms in
37 activity schools observed by members of the Advisory Committee. From J. Cayce
Morrison and others, *The Activity Program: A Survey of the Curriculum Experiment
with the Activity Program in the Elementary Schools of New York City* (New York
City Board of Education, September, 1941).

lation between pupils and teacher, marked by
an attitude of friendship and mutual respect.

55. *Parent participation.* Parents are given
the opportunity to participate in the work of
the school and to demonstrate a desire to be
helpful.

The scale from which this excerpt is taken
is composed of 57 items each defined on a
five-step scale. The 57 items were grouped
into nine categories as follows:

1. Pupil's participation in planning.
2. Experiencing as a basis of learning.
3. Keeping records and evaluating work
   done.
4. The pupil's relation to content of instruction.
5. Supplies and equipment.
6. Physical properties and arrangement in
   classroom.
7. Pupils' activity in classroom and school.
8. Intraschool relationships.
9. Relations of school to home and community.

On the basis of observations, each class
was given a rating on each point and finally
a composite rating. The range in the ratings
by the survey committee in 158 classrooms

in 37 schools is shown in the graph above.
The report makes a detailed comparison of
the amount of activity in activity and nonactivity schools.

Principles of learning applied to teaching.
Mursell has made a valuable and interesting
attempt to show how basic principles underlying learning may be applied in the classroom. First he examined what is known
about the psychology of learning. On the
basis of this analysis, he formulated six conditions under which good learning takes
place. For each principle he set up a hierarchy or scale of applications by which a
teacher or observer can evaluate instructional practices. The purpose of the scales is
not to set a pattern but to provide an opportunity for the teacher to apply the six principles at the highest possible levels.

The six principles as stated by Mursell [17]
and the scale of levels indicated by Roman
numerals for each principle are listed on the
following page.

[17] Adapted from J. L. Mursell, *Successful Teaching* (New York, McGraw, 1946).

1. *Context*

Meaningful learning must proceed in a context exemplifying the meanings involved.

   I. Textbook only.

   II. Textbook together with collateral or supplementary readings in general of somewhat similar type, academic in character and aiming at further exposition.

  III. Nonacademic and current materials, such as magazine articles, newspaper clippings, advertising items, brochures, poems, and so forth. May be accompanied by either or both of the foregoing or not.

  IV. Graphic materials such as pictures, movies, maps, charts, tables, graphs, "visual aids" generally, also phonograph recordings. May be accompanied by any or all of the foregoing.

   V. Demonstrations, museum trips, excursions, presentations by visiting "experts," e.g., traffic policemen, fire wardens, etc., in general, chances to observe phenomena and events more or less in natural setting. May be accompanied by any or all of the foregoing.

  VI. Personal, social, community undertakings, either in school or out. May be accompanied by any or all of the foregoing.

2. *Focus*

Meaningful and effective learning must be organized about a focus.

   I. Learner's task defined by page assignment in textbook, by exercises to be completed, etc. Simple, crude, uniform organization of learning, routine in character.

   II. Focus established by announced topic, together with page or chapter references, etc. Lends itself to more extensive and varied learning patterns, but again chiefly an information-getting memorizing process.

  III. Focus established by setting up broad concept to be comprehended or problem to be solved; may or may not have to do with current experience; makes for still more varied learning patterns, and tends to break away from routines and memorization.

  IV. Focus established as a concept to be understood, a problem to be solved, a skill to be acquired in order successfully to carry on some undertaking in progress.

3. *Socialization*

The meaningfulness and effectiveness of learning depends to an important extent upon the social setting in which it is done.

   I. Social pattern characterized chiefly by submission; function of the group is to respond to questions and directions from the teacher; imposed discipline.

   II. Social pattern characterized typically by contribution: members of the group allowed and encouraged to volunteer suggestions, raise issues, etc. Discipline still imposed, but sympathetic.

  III. Social pattern characterized chiefly by co-operation: group function is to carry through common undertaking in which all have responsible share; self-generated discipline.

4. *Individualization*

Meaningful learning must proceed in terms of the learner's own purposes, aptitudes, abilities, and experimental procedures.

   I. Uniform tasks on uniform schedule with individualization showing in differential performance.

   II. Homogeneous grouping on two or more levels on IQ, MA, EA combined in some formula: differences in level between groups, differential performance within them.

  III. Contract plans on two or more levels: allows some choice and so more flexible than the above.

  IV. Individual instruction: Dalton and Winnetka plans as typical.

   V. Large units with optional related activities and experiences.

  VI. Individual undertaking stemming from and contributing to the joint undertaking of the group of learners.

5. *Sequence*

The sequence of meaningful learnings must itself be meaningful, if authentic results are to be obtained.

   I. Sequential blocks of content: (lessons; courses). Held together chiefly by requirements, prerequisites and logical order:

Basic assumption, additive accumulation of knowledge and skill.

II. Attempts to knit learnings (lessons; courses) more closely together by introductions, previews, pretests, and the rearrangement of the order of material:
Basic assumption, apperception.

III. Sequence organized in terms of readiness.

IV. Sequence organized in terms of lines of emerging meaning.

6. *Evaluation*

The effectiveness and success of any job of learning is heightened by a valid and discriminating appraisal of all its aspects.

I. Evaluation on results only: chiefly direct results.

II. Evaluation chiefly on results, emphasizing transferability and objectives: some attention paid to process.

III. Evaluation on total learning process, including results.

Observers of classroom instruction and teachers themselves can quite easily determine by systematic analysis the level at which these principles are being applied in a given situation. A profile may be made, showing graphically the results of the analysis, thereby revealing points where improvements can be made. The application of these principles by a group of teachers and supervisors to an observed unit of teaching will assist all to sense their significance. Helping teachers to apply them to their own teaching is probably the most valuable use that can be made of these principles in improving instructional procedures.

An illustrative report on application of principles. Krause reported the results of a series of 217 intermediate-grade classroom observations in 60 schools in 10 different systems, showing the extent to which "principles of modern and progressive classroom procedure" were being practiced. The principles grew out of a systematic analysis of the writings of modern educational leaders.[18] He listed on a guide sheet items to identify each of the 25 principles shown in the table below, each of which he defined by both positive and negative explanations to stabilize the record of his observations. The table

shows the percentage of classes visited in grades 4, 5, and 6 in which each principle was observed in operation.[19] It presents an interesting description of what he saw.

Krause evaluated the data he reported as follows:

In all but five of the classrooms visited at least one of the twenty-five principles was observed in each classroom. The average number of modern and progressive principles which was practiced in each classroom was four. The range of principles found in operation in any classroom was from 0 to 21.

The reader may wonder whether or not one could expect to find many of the twenty-five principles in operation during one class period and whether or not the principles would apply more to social studies than to reading classes or more to language work than social studies, etc. When considering the observations in which thirteen or more of the principles were in practice, it was found that each of the academic fields—arithmetic, reading, social studies, language, and science—was represented. Regardless of the academic work in progress, it was possible that a majority of the principles could be employed. In seven of the 217 observations nineteen of the principles were practiced on the average.

The ages of teachers as a whole who showed more progressive evidence came within the interval of thirty-two and thirty-six years. For those observations in which thirteen or more principles were noted, the ages ranged from twenty-two to forty-five years with a mean age of thirty-three years.

One could reasonably expect to find a few modern and progressive principles employed in the average classroom. More than likely they would involve those which are easier to perform such as teacher *pleasantness, movable furniture* and *homelike rooms.* Less often one would find *enthusiastic, democratic teachers* who would be *allowing a desirable amount of freedom.* Still less frequently teachers would be *using pupil interests, encouraging clear thinking,* and *acting as guides.* Probably an average of 30 per cent of the classes would be *alert and*

[18] L. W. Krause, "A Method of Noting and Evaluating Modern and Progressive Practices in the Classroom," *The Elementary School Journal* (March, 1941), pp. 521-532.

[19] L. W. Krause, "What Principles of Modern and Progressive Education Are Practiced in Intermediate Grade Classrooms," *Journal of Educational Research* (December, 1941), pp. 251-262.

COMPARISON BY GRADES OF THE PERCENTAGE OF MODERN AND PROGRESSIVE EVIDENCE NOTED FOR EACH OF THE TWENTY-FIVE PRINCIPLES*

Principles	Per Cent for Grade 4	Per Cent for Grade 5	Per Cent for Grade 6	Average
THE TEACHER IS				
1. Pleasant	87	79	82	83
2. Enthusiastic	25	25	30	27
3. Conducting her room on democratic principles.....	17	20	20	19
4. Using pupil interests......	12	10	15	12
5. Encouraging clear thinking	17	17	10	15
6. Helping children evaluate..	3	1	1	2
7. Keeping several groups working harmoniously....	1	3	1	2
8. Guiding and suggesting...	15	13	10	13
9. Allowing freedom........	22	20	19	20
10. Giving skills practical application	1	3	1	2
11. Teaching facts for a definite need	4	3	0	2
THE CHILDREN ARE				
12. Alert and interested......	28	25	28	27
13. Showing signs of self-discipline	13	15	8	12
14. Helping to plan work....	4	4	3	4
15. Working as a social group	1	7	5	4
16. Active physically........	1	4	3	3
17. Active creatively........	10	10	10	10
18. Active intellectually	9	10	6	8
19. Using some of their own initiative	13	15	9	12
THE ENVIRONMENT				
20. Has movable furniture...	51	42	46	46
21. Includes a variety of materials	19	15	13	16
22. Shows signs of previous activities	15	10	11	12
23. Is homelike.............	44	51	47	47
24. Is reasonably quiet.......	20	17	15	17
25. Has a unit of work in progress	3	1	0	1

* Figures in all tables are to the nearest per cent.

interested, and an average of 10 per cent of the classes would *show signs of self-discipline, use their own initiative,* and *be active creatively and intellectually.* From 10 to 20 per cent of the classrooms would include *a variety of materials, show signs of previous activity,* and be *reasonably quiet.*

The writer believes that in few classes would one find *group work, evaluation activities, practical application of skills,* and *information being learned and used for a definite need.* Classes *working as a social group* would be rare, too, as well as *activities of a physical nature.*

From this survey and data the writer would conclude that the practice of modern and progressive principles are well established in from 5 to 7 per cent of the public classrooms; moderately established in 15 to 20 per cent of the classrooms; and in 70 to 80 per cent of the classrooms they are rarely practiced.

General uses of descriptive procedures.
The supervisor should utilize or modify any of the analytical procedures that are discussed in Section 3 when studying any important aspects of instruction; sometimes new analytical procedures must be devised to meet the situation. All of the aspects of instruction listed below have been studied by the various means that are given at the right. The list could be extended almost indefinitely.

SECURING DESCRIPTIVE DATA ABOUT INSTRUCTION

Aspect of Teaching	*Analytical Procedure Used*
Objectives.	Check-lists; reports; observations.
Levels of teaching.	Descriptive scales; reports.
Apparent conception of the nature of learning.	Observations; check-list; tests; interviews.
Organization of curriculum.	Analysis of daily program.
Organization of class.	Check-list of grouping procedures.
Principles of learning.	Use of check-list; reports; records.
Participation of pupil-teacher.	Time studies; diagrams of activities.
Provision for individual differences.	Check-list of possible methods; reports by teachers; observation.
Personal and group relations.	Sociometric procedures.
Materials and use of community resources.	Check-lists; observation, interview.
Apparent needs and difficulties.	Reports; interviews; observation.

2. Rating the teacher at work. Undoubtedly the most dependable way of measuring the effectiveness of the teacher is by studying the growth of the learners. In very few schools is this policy followed. Instead teachers are rated by teacher-rating scales of the traditional type. This device was employed long before many of the new-type of evaluative procedures described above were developed.

Current trends in teacher evaluation. The results of a recent survey [20] of current practices in teacher evaluation, based on replies to a six-item questionnaire by seventy of eighty persons consulted, were as follows:

Ranking		*Method*
1.	I.	No formal rating plan.
2.	II.	Rating scale or check-list.
3.	III.	Verbal reports of principal to superintendent.
4.	IV.	Written reports following classroom visitation by administrators.
5.	V.	Self-appraisal form prepared by the teacher.
6.	VI.	Group evaluation by each teacher's fellow workers.

The survey report indicates that methods V and VI were used very infrequently, while methods II and III followed method I closely in frequency. Numerous comments made by those who replied indicated that there was considerable dissatisfaction with the evaluation procedures being used and that experiments leading to improved methods of evaluation would be welcomed.

The recent widespread interest in research on criteria of teacher effectiveness grew out of such needs [21] as the following:

1. Securing dependable measures of teacher effectiveness.
2. Selecting teachers for appointment.
3. Determining whether permanent tenure should be granted.
4. Granting special considerations, such as salary increment or special assignment.
5. Determining whether a student in a teacher-education program should be granted a certificate or be recommended for a position.
6. Determining suitability for admission of a student to a teacher-education program, retention in the program, or guidance needs.

[20] Mimeographed statement on *Teacher Evaluation,* prepared by Grosse Pointe, Michigan, Administrative Group, dated December 2, 1952.

[21] These needs were discussed in "The Second Report of the Committee on Criteria of Teacher Effectiveness," prepared by a committee of the American Educational Research Association, which appeared in the *Journal of Educational Research* (May, 1953), pp. 641-658.

The problem is to identify "predictors" of teacher effectiveness on three levels; (*a*) pre-training, (*b*) in-training, and (*c*) in-service. These would include such items as personality characteristics, attitudes, interests, knowledges, skills, and teacher performance which would serve as valid measures of teacher effectiveness.

Because of their association with their administrative uses, rating scales are not generally regarded as instruments of improvement; however they can be a source of much valuable assistance in this respect when properly used. Rating scales, like all other data-gathering devices discussed in this chapter, are best employed when co-operatively developed and applied. At no time in this discussion are we thinking of the conventional, administrative, applied-from-without type of evaluation. We stress the possibilities of self-rating and diagnosis.

Types of rating scales now in use. There are six types of rating scales now in general use for evaluating the efficiency of teachers: (1) point scales; (2) graphic scales; (3) diagnostic scales; (4) quality scales; (5) man-to-man comparison scales; and (6) conduct or performance scales.[22] Because of the importance of these several instruments in studying the teacher at work, each kind will be described briefly; the reader should relate each in turn to four approaches to evaluation, namely, the mental-prerequisites approach, the qualities-of-the person approach, the performance approach, and the pupil-change approach. Professional educators are not always agreed as to where the emphasis should be placed in evaluation, whether upon the situation, the person, the performance, or the results. We believe, however, that all are important and need careful investigation. It is quite clear in the illustrative material to follow, as well as that which has preceded, that the emphasis upon these different aspects of the learning-teaching situation varies.

Elements of a point scale for evaluating student teaching. Bach[23] reported the results of an analysis of rating scales used by 126 teacher-training institutions in the United States. He found that 83 different items appeared in four or more of the scales. Bach then regrouped the traits into 48 general categories. Finally he condensed the list to 25 traits and prepared a five-point rating scale in which the traits were grouped into three main classifications, as shown in the scale below. The scale can also be used for evaluating teaching in regular classrooms.

Ratings
1 2 3 4 5

I. *Competencies*
   1. Skill in selecting learning experiences (including assignments).
   2. Skill in discovering pupil needs and formulating objectives.
   3. Skill in classroom management.
   4. Skill in directing learning (including supervised study).
   5. Skill in evaluating pupil achievement.
   6. Skill in pupil-teacher relationships (discipline).
   7. Skill in group leadership (questioning, motivation).

II. *Behavior Controls*
   A. Knowledges
      1. Subject matter (scholarship).
      2. Principles and techniques of teaching.

[22] W. C. Reavis and D. H. Cooper, *Evaluation of Teacher Merit in City School Systems,* Supplementary Educational Monograph No. 59 (Chicago, Univ. of Chicago Press, 1945). This volume contains a fairly comprehensive analysis of rating practices in this country, and also a table giving a list of items included in rating scales.

A. S. Barr and L. M. Evans, "What Qualities Are Prerequisite to Success in Teaching?" *The Nation's Schools* (September, 1930), p. 62. An analysis of qualities listed in 209 rating scales.

[23] "A Scale for Evaluating Student Teaching," *Evaluation of Student Teaching,* Twenty-eighth Yearbook Association for Student Teaching (Lock Haven, Pa., State Teachers College, 1949), pp. 128-130.

Ratings

1 2 3 4 5

3. Understanding children.
4. Principles of action (including human relationships and principles of learning.)

B. Interests, Attitudes, Ideals
   5. Professional attitude towards one's work (including objectivity, co-operation, openmindedness, attitude toward criticism).
   6. Interest in children, subject, and teaching.

C. Generalized Skills
   7. Voice expressiveness and use of English.

D. Physical Resources
   8. Health (vitality).
   9. Freedom from physical defect. (If answer is "no," enumerate and describe under general comments at end of scale.)

III. *Essential Qualities*
   1. Intelligence (including personal and professional judgment, foresight, intellectual acuity).
   2. Emotional stability poise).
   3. Reliability (including dependability, sense of responsibility, conscientiousness, promptness, and punctuality).
   4. Leadership (forcefulness).
   5. Adaptability.
   6. Attractiveness (appearance, dress).
   7. Considerateness (courtesy, tact, and sympathy).
   8. Initiative (originality, resourcefulness, creativeness).
   9. Enthusiasm, energy, drive.
   10. Sense of humor.

Sum of all scores   *Total Score*   _____
Total Score divided by 25 equals
    Average Score   _____

Low Score of Part I times Low Score of Part II times Low Score of Part III equals   Product Score   _____
    Letter Grade   _____

Statement concerning Estimate of Probable Success of Student Teacher (Include statement of physical defects, if any, and reasons for any trait rating of 2 or less.)

Date _____   Signed _____
    Critic or Supervisor

Bach summarized the results of an analysis of the rating scales and a questionnaire about rating practices as follows:

1. Although the majority of teacher-training institutions use rating scales as a means of evaluating student teaching, there is a general trend away from their exclusive use to the use of anecdotal records, diaries, interviews, and other informal techniques.

2. Over half of the rating scales received were constructed by committees usually consisting of faculty members and supervisors.

3. The scales varied in length of use from those recently constructed to others used for twenty-three years; the average length of use was approximately seven years.

4. The number of revisions under way indicates an effort on the part of these institutions to improve their present system of evaluation.

5. The frequency of expressions of dissatisfaction with their rating device and the number of revisions underway in almost one-fourth of the institutions show a dissatisfaction with present rating devices.

6. There has been little change in terminology of traits used in rating scales for the past twenty years, but the emphasis on particular traits is shifting.

7. Only one-third of the scales used descriptions or definitions of their items.

8. The majority of the scales used a five-point system of marking, with an average of twenty-two items.

Bach also suggested the following principles underlying the use of rating scales:

1. Each rating scale should be tried out experimentally to determine its validity, reliability, objectivity, and practicability.

SAMPLE OF THE ALMY-SORENSON RATING SCALE

	Score	Basis for Judgment

1. Resourcefulness—Means for meeting situations and overcoming them.

10	9	8	7	6	5	4	3	2	1	0
	Skillfully meets every difficulty.		Usually equal to every difficulty.		Successful in most situations.		Rather mechanical. Often overcome.		Unable to cope with difficulties. Easily "floored."	

Basis for Judgment: Definite General Inadequate Score: ( )

2. Enthusiasm—Lively manifestation of zeal and earnestness.

10	9	8	7	6	5	4	3	2	1	0
	Shows lively interest.		"Self starter." Usually interested.		Is moderately zealous.		Quite dead and indifferent.		Dead. Inanimate.	

Basis for Judgment: Definite General Inadequate Score: ( )

3. Leadership—Capacity or ability to instil into action.

10	9	8	7	6	5	4	3	2	1	0
	Children manifest whole-hearted response.		Very seldom does teacher fail to activate children.		Ordinarily children are responsive.		Ineffective in conducting children.		Children not responsive. Ignore teacher.	

Basis for Judgment: Definite General Inadequate Score: ( )

4. Coöperation—Collective and concurrent effort or labor.

10	9	8	7	6	5	4	3	2	1	0
	Works splendidly with others for common objective.		Works well with others.		Usually coöperative.		"Solo worker." Reluctant in common endeavor.		Completely individualistic. Neither gives nor takes.	

Basis for Judgment: Definite General Inadequate Score: ( )

5. Trustworthiness—Worthy of confidence—Can be depended upon.

10	9	8	7	6	5	4	3	2	1	0
	Always dependable. Does work 100%.		Very seldom fails to do work properly.		Generally to be trusted.		Uncertain. Spasmodic.		Unreliable. Can't accept trust or duty.	

Basis for Judgment: Definite General Inadequate Score: ( )

From *Almy-Sorenson Rating Scale for Teachers* (Bloomington, Ill., Public School Publishing Co., 1930).

2. The rating scale should be used in conjunction with a variety of other appraisal instruments; it should not be used to evaluate behaviors appraised more directly by other techniques.

3. Evidence to support the ratings should be gathered periodically throughout the total student teaching experience.

4. The supervisor or other rater should, in conference, explain and interpret the rating scale to the student or teacher who will be rated.

5. The final rating given the student or teacher should be interpreted in a conference with the student. In certain situations it will be helpful to have the student rate himself with the scale.

Three problems confront those interested in the development of point scales. First, there is the problem of the selection of traits, characteristics, and qualities representative of teaching success. The traits chosen for use in the scale must be known to characterize good teaching. Second, there is the problem of the description of each trait in such terms that the judgments about it are made objective. The description of such traits is usually highly subjective. And third, there is the problem of the weighting of each trait and the degree of control over it in such a way that the teacher's total score correlates with his observed success as a teacher. High positive correlations are not frequently attained.

Graphic scales. A graphic scale is similar to a point scale except that the degree of control exercised over each item is portrayed graphically. An excerpt from the Almy-Sorenson rating scale is reproduced opposite. The scale is composed of twenty items as follows: resourcefulness, enthusiasm, leadership, co-operation, trustworthiness, honesty, fairness, sympathy, tact, patience, courteousness, love for children, progressiveness, poise, kindness, originality, good humor, helpfulness, promptness, and foresight. The graphic aspects of such scales are interesting and worth while, but they in no manner lessen *the necessity for carefully choosing, defining, and weighing the aspects of teachers and teaching considered in such instruments of measurement.*[24]

Diagnostic scales. A diagnostic scale is a point scale organized around the different aspects of teaching in such a manner as to reveal levels of attainment with reference to the different characteristics ordinarily associated with teaching success. An excerpt from the Torgerson Diagnostic Teacher Rating Scale given below will illustrate this type of scale.[25]

1. *Assignment*
    . . . . *a.* Indefinite assignment.
    . . . . *b.* Number of pages in a textbook.
    . . . . *c.* Topical assignment from textbook.
    . . . . *d.* Problem assignment.
    . . . . *e.* Problem-project or unit assignment.

2. *Discussion Period*
    . . . . *a.* Class discussion limited to brightest pupils.
    . . . . *b.* Entire class participates in the discussion.
    . . . . *c.* Class discussion shows lack of purpose.
    . . . . *d.* Pupils take no active part in the discussion.
    . . . . *e.* Discussion period seldom provided.

3. *Pupil Diagnosis*
    . . . . *a.* Only class difficulties analyzed.
    . . . . *b.* Only obvious difficulties of class given any attention.
    . . . . *c.* Special attention given to retarded pupils only.
    . . . . *d.* Individual pupil difficulties basis for all reviews and remedial teaching.
    . . . . *e.* No attempt to analyze pupil or class difficulties.

4. *Remedial Instruction*
    . . . . *a.* Reviews and reteaching based upon individual pupil difficulties.

[24] H. C. Almy and Herbert Sorenson, "A Teacher-Rating Scale of Determined Reliability and Validity," *Educational Administration and Supervision* (March, 1939), pp. 179-186.

[25] *Torgerson Diagnostic Teacher Rating Scale* (Bloomington, Ill., Public School Publishing Co., 1930).

....*b.* No reviews or reteaching provided.

....*c.* Class reviews with additional help for dull pupils.

....*d.* Occasional class reviews.

....*e.* Carefully prepared program of class reviews.

5. *Drill Material*

....*a.* Teacher makes up drill material to supplement textbook.

....*b.* Drill material rarely ever used.

....*c.* Available standardized practice exercises always used.

....*d.* Only drill material provided in text used.

....*e.* Standardized practice exercises used at times.

The Torgerson Diagnostic Teacher Rating Scale is composed of eighteen items, as follows: assignment, discussion period, pupil diagnosis, remedial instruction, drill material, measurement of individual differences, provision for individual differences, technique of measuring results, sequence of topics, types of criticism, pupil attention, results of motivation upon pupils, pupil activity, attention to heating, lighting and seating, use of instructional materials, control over pupils, method of handling problem cases in discipline, and corrective measures. Though by no means a perfect instrument of analysis, the Torgerson scale does represent a promising development in this field.

Quality scales. A quality scale is one in which the different degrees of teaching merit, each described in terms of its characteristic aims, methods, and procedures, are arranged at equal intervals according to a system of scale values from zero merit to perfection. The method of constructing these scales is similar to that used in constructing handwriting, art, and composition scales. The scales by Brueckner,[26] Mead,[27] and the Committee on the Evaluation of Instruction of the Department of Classroom Teachers [28] are of this sort. An excerpt from one of Brueckner's scales (the compulsion type) for evaluating the teaching of geography in grades 5 and 6 is reproduced here: [29]

SAMPLE FROM BRUECKNER'S SCALE FOR THE RATING OF TEACHING SKILL

TYPE I. Compulsion

The subject matter is organized wholly in terms of logical arrangement, usually of textbook arrangement. It is presented either orally or by text, with or without some explanation by the teacher. Pupils are expected to study same and learn it by heart. The recitation consists in having the children give back what they have learned. Usually the form in which it is given must be exactly that of the text. Much dependence is placed on repetition, review, and drill. There is complete teacher domination and control, and almost perfect attention because of rigid discipline maintained by teacher by force. Results in terms of knowledge are emphasized. Respect and unquestioning obedience are demanded of children.

Teacher A　　　　　*Scale Value 16.2*

The teacher was a rigid disciplinarian. Every child was compelled to keep in perfect order, to sit rigidly in the standard position, to pay absolute attention to everything that was said, and to strive to acquire perfection in all his work.

Every child worked during his study period at his top speed, because the lessons assigned were generally sufficiently long to require it, and the compelling force back of the command made by the teacher to know these important facts served to make everyone sit up and concentrate on what he was doing. On the other hand, if the material was difficult, the lessons assigned were short, so that it was possible to learn them.

Papers were marked with care, every *i* not dotted and every *t* not crossed being noted and later corrected by the pupil. Answers to questions which were not in the exact language of the book were counted wrong, and there were no supplementary readings or discussions. Any

[26] L. J. Brueckner, "Scales for the Rating of Teaching Skill," *Educational Research Bulletin* No. 12 (Minneapolis, Univ. of Minnesota, 1927).

[27] Cyrus D. Mead, "Scaling Lesson Taught," *Journal of Educational Method* (November-December, 1926), pp. 115-119, 168-174.

[28] Guy M. Wilson, chairman, "Report of the Committee on Evaluation of Instruction of the Department of Classroom Teachers of the National Education Association," *Proceedings* of the National Education Association, 1925.

[29] Brueckner, "Scales for the Rating of Teaching Skill," *op. cit.,* p. 12-16.

child could ask any formal question he wished about anything he did not understand, but the question had to be asked during the study period, not during the recitation.

The teacher was absolutely fair and impartial, knew every pupil's weakness and success, held herself up to the standards set for the class. Deliberate misbehavior was sure to receive swift and vigorous corporal punishment; failure to learn meant additional drill.

There was much well-organized drill and review. Class questioning was vigorous and snappy and enjoyed by the entire class. When the study of France was concluded, the children could answer any question on the continuous list, which the teacher had given, without hesitation, and with no deviation from the words of the text.

Teacher E   *Scale Value 9.8*

"For the next assignment take pages 118-119, and be ready to answer questions 10 to 20, particularly emphasizing 11, 14, 16, and 18. Look up difficult words in the dictionary and refer to the large map of France in the textbook in locating places wanted in your reading."

Three or four pupils whose inattention the teacher failed to check were required to get their assignment from their neighbors. No connection was made between the previous lesson and the new assignment.

The teacher deviated occasionally from the logical order due to lack of preparation on her part, thus confusing several of the pupils, and as a result time was wasted in getting back on the track. All questions were stressed alike in spite of the fact that she had asked the pupils to pay particular attention to certain definite ones. No reference was made to the map and dictionary assignment. She stated that answers must be in the exact words of the book, but in four or five instances let inaccuracies slip by. A fair amount of drill was given over part of the work.

She asked questions of most of the pupils, but never worried if she failed to reach three or four of the same pupils each day. Seven or eight of the pupils failed to answer the questions they were asked, and only in two instances did she find out their difficulties. Instead they were marked zero, and someone else was called upon to give the answer. Two pupils were corrected, one for not standing on both feet, the other for leaning on the desk, but no attention was given to incorrect sitting posture of the other children.

At least three-fourths of the class were attentive during the whole period and these learned some answers to most of the questions in the lesson. There was a strong bond of sympathy between the bright pupils and the teacher, but little attention was paid to the lower group, and as a result these pupils came to class reluctantly.

Teacher I   *Scale Value 5.0*

The class had one more day to complete the study of France.

"Get out your books and begin where we left off." Several pupils who did not seem to know where the point was wasted most of the study period thumbing through their texts, because they were afraid to disclose this fact to the teacher and dared not ask a neighbor.

During the recitation that followed, the textbook map-question list furnished the line of least resistance for the teacher. She attempted to ask the questions in their logical order. Frequently she lost her place or asked the same question twice, because it was often necessary to stop the lesson to check disorder in the class, which occurred when she was off her guard. Then, to save time, she skipped two pivotal questions around which the subject was organized with the remark, "We haven't time to take that up now."

Not once was the map on the wall referred to by either teacher or pupils. No attempt was made to check the pupils' answers, as she scarcely waited for them to reply until another point was taken up. Hence many inaccuracies crept in.

Several pupils who failed to answer any questions were given no help, and her only comment was, "It's your own fault; you should never have been promoted to this grade anyway."

After many interruptions and outbursts of disorder the work was only partially covered.

The entire class had a "don't care" attitude, and even the bright pupils gained only a vague and inaccurate notion of far-away France.

Brueckner's scales were developed in accordance with Courtis' suggestion that more reliable rating scales might be developed if rating scales were constructed that differentiated between the teacher's method of teaching and his skill in utilizing these methods. This is an important point. As has been repeatedly pointed out in this discussion, the evaluation of teaching is a very

MICHIGAN EDUCATION ASSOCIATION

TEACHER RATING CARD—Long Form

HUMAN SCALE METHOD

Teacher................ Experience........Years. Building or Department..........

Quality Groups		1	2	3	4	5	6	7	8	9	10
Letters or Scale Words Indicating Degrees of Quality	Points Assigned to Scale Steps	Vitality	General Personality	Dynamic Personality	Growth and Progressiveness	Team Work	Attitude Toward Children	Preparation	Skill in Control and Management	Skill in Teaching (Technique)	Skill in Teaching (Results)
A or Very Superior...........	50										
B or Superior............	40										
C or Average............	30										
D or Inferior.............	20										
E or Very Inferior.........	10										

DIRECTIONS:. Use of the "human scale" is strongly urged. (See III and IV on the reverse side of this card.) After determining the degree of merit in each quality group, place a dot in each vertical column opposite the proper degree of capability as indicated by the scale words in the lefthand column. (The horizontal lines, not the space between them, indicate the steps of the scale. No dot should ever be placed in the space above the line of the scale step "Very Superior," as that line represents a perfect score.) Connect the dots by lines. If it is desired to weigh qualities double the number of points in groups 7 and 8, and quadruple the number in groups 9 and 10. Interpret the total score as follows: .180-299, E, or very inferior; 300-479, D, or inferior; 480-659, C, or average; 660-839, B, or superior; 840-900, A or very superior; 900, perfect score.

Total Numerical Rating { (1)........... General Rating { (1)......... Date { (1).........
(2)........... (2)......... (2).........
(3)........... (3)......... (3).........

Principal or
Supervisor.........

Note:—The general rating "Average" may be designated "Fair" or "Good" accordingly as it may be low average or high average.

SAMPLE SCORE CARD OF THE HUMAN SCALE METHOD

From A. S. Barr, *An Introduction to the Scientific Study of Classroom Supervision* (New York, Appleton-Century, 1931), p. 352.

complex activity. By and large, the evaluation of teaching has not been very well handled. One of the many sources of confusion has to do with the failure of many evaluators to differentiate between the method per se as distinguished from control over method. An ineffective teacher may have a good method and handle it poorly, or a poor method which she handles reasonably well. It would seem that our thinking about teaching has been considerably sharpened by a distinction of this sort.

Man-to-man comparison scales. On a man-to-man comparison scale, judgments about the degree of control exercised by the teacher over the different qualities selected for consideration are derived by comparisons between the teachers rated and named individuals previously judged by the raters to be average, inferior, superior, or what not. The human scale furnishes a fairly objective mode of rating teachers. Its chief limitation is the difficulty of administering such a scale because, despite the effort at objectivity, the personal element enters. Ratings of the teacher are arrived at through comparing the teacher rated with the rater's personal standards of teaching ability. The second limitation lies in this lack of commonly accepted standards despite the effort to indicate them in the language of the scale. The number of qualities considered in such scales is usually small. In the illustrative scale on page 350, ten qualities are considered: vitality, general personality, dynamic personality, growth and progressiveness, team work, attitude toward children, preparation, skill in control and management, skill in teaching (technique), and skill in teaching (results). The scale possesses limited diagnostic possibilities.

Conduct or performance scales. Connor, a number of years ago, after presenting an analysis of current methods of rating teachers, suggested that teaching and not teachers be rated, and that teaching should be measured in terms of results only. He suggested

seven standards of pupil performance as measures of teaching efficiency: (1) thinking, (2) emotional reaction, (3) knowledge and skill, (4) morale in dispatch of work, (5) initiative in socially significant situations, (6) ethical self-control in situations socially significant, and (7) deportment. Each standard is defined, and a number of concrete acts representative of the standard are given.

SAMPLE FROM THE CONNOR RATING SCALE

IV. MORALE IN DISPATCH OF WORK

General definition: Confidence, courage, loyalty, self-reliance, promptness, and persistence with which work is performed. *Definition of Standard:* Confident, courageous, loyal, self-reliant, prompt, and persistent spirit of pupils at work.

Standard IV. Morale

1. Attends school regularly, and arrives promptly at the opening of each session.
2. Is cheerful and agreeable when he cannot have his own way.
3. Moves to and from classes and about halls in a prompt and orderly manner.
4. Is loyal to teachers and the work they assign.
5. Is loyal to school officers and rules they make and enforce.
6. Is loyal to the school and its undertakings.
7. Obeys all ordinary requests promptly and cheerfully, and in spirit as well as letter.
8. Does not talk back or sulk when corrected.
9. Does not fret or worry over school tasks, but seeks to understand them and does his best cheerfully.
10. Does not cry, whine, or tattle over little things.
11. Is not discouraged by defeat or failure.
12. Does hard or otherwise disagreeable work without expectation of praise.
13. Works in the confidence that he and his classmates can do what other boys and girls have done and are doing, and a little more.

[30] W. L. Connor, "A New Method of Rating Teachers," *Journal of Educational Research* (May, 1920), pp. 338-358.

14. Relies upon his own efforts in preparing a lesson.
15. Undertakes with courage work he knows to be difficult.
16. Finishes assigned lessons even if he is compelled to spend more time on them than some of his brighter classmates.
17. Begins work promptly and plunges into the heart of it.
18. Faces duties and responsibilities squarely—does not "sidestep" or "pass the buck."
19. Does not hunt for and elect supposed "snap courses."
20. Is conscious of some of the important habits which go to make up a worthy character, and strives to act so that these habits will be formed.

Yet another approach to performance has been made by Barr in the Barr-Harris Teachers' Performance Record.[31] A record is first made of performance: teacher and pupil activities, purposes and conditions; then the performance is evaluated with reference to teacher and pupil purposes; accepted principles of learning and teaching; pupil growth, learning and achievement; and conditions. The recording of the facts about the learning-teaching situation is thus separated from the evaluation. An interesting and very much simpler application of the same idea will be found in the Wisconsin Adaptation of the M Blank. The evaluation is organized around eight questions: (1) Is the teacher well prepared? (2) Has the teacher the personal prerequisites essential to effective work? (3) Are the goals and objectives set by teacher and pupil satisfactory? (4) Are the observed teacher and pupil activities well chosen? (5) Does the teacher show skill in directing activities? (6) Are the learning aids adequate and effectively used? (7) Are methods of checking results satisfactory? (8) Is there evidence of desirable pupil growth and achievement? An excerpt from the scale is reproduced below.[32]

1. Is the teacher well prepared?
   ( ) In general; academically, culturally, professionally.
   ( ) For the day's work or activity observed.

Anecdotal evidence   *Comments*
. . . .
. . . .
. . . .

Evaluation: (underline one)

Outstanding; above average; average; below average; poor.

4. Are the observed teacher and pupil activities well chosen?
   ( ) *a.* Are they in keeping with stated goals, purposes, and objectives?
   ( ) *b.* Are they in keeping with limiting aspects of the learning-teaching situation?
   ( ) *c.* Are they in keeping with accepted principles of learning and teaching?

Anecdotal evidence   *Comments*
. . . .
. . . .
. . . .

Evaluation: (underline one)

Outstanding; above average; average; below average; poor.

8. Is there evidence of desirable pupil growth and development?
   ( ) *a.* In interest and application.
   ( ) *b.* In work habits.
   ( ) *c.* In pupil growth and achievement.

Anecdotal evidence   *Comments*
. . . .
. . . .
. . . .

Evaluation: (underline one)

Outstanding; above average; average; below average; poor.

In looking back over the discussion of rating scales, one can see that many different approaches have been made to the study and improvement of teaching. Each approach has its advantages and disadvantages. We believe that if the interrelatedness of the several factors in the learning-teach-

[31] A. S. Barr and A. E. Harris, "Barr-Harris Teachers' Performance Record," *Journal of Experimental Education* (1943).
[32] *Evaluative Criteria,* 1950 ed. (Washington, Co-operative Study of Secondary School Standards). The numbers are those from the original scale.

ing situation is to be understood, all of these approaches need to be made. We need to know results. But we need to know, too, the situation; the kinds of teacher and pupil activity that precede the results; and the sort of persons involved—their qualities as persons and their mental prerequisites to effective performance. Anyone who evaluates teaching should be concerned with both on-the-scene activity and background information.

A note on the validity and reliability of teacher-rating scales. The scales just referred to have been chosen for discussion principally because they illustrate ways of appraising teaching. All have been subjected to systematic study, and although some meet the statistical tests of validity and reliability better than others, they all meet these tests better than do general merit ratings. Most of these scales are accompanied by a teachers' manual that supplies, among other things, data on the methods by which each was validated. Detailed data on the statistical validity and reliability of a number of these scales are presented by Barr and others [33] in the references here cited.

Merit ratings. In a considerable number of places, efforts have been made to devise methods of rating teachers as to merit as a basis for salary adjustments, promotions, and recognition of unusual services rendered. In New York State a law requires that each teacher is to have opportunities to qualify for "promotional increments" through satisfactory teaching service, and, in addition, objective evidence of special contributions in one or more of the following ways:

1. Exceptional service to the pupils for whom the teacher is individually responsible.
2. Exceptional service to the community through nonschool activities directly related to the interest and well-being of young people.
3. Participation in nonschool activities, such as summertime work or social service projects.
4. Substantial increases in the value of service to pupils as a result of education not formally credited to a degree.

The law requires that "classroom teachers shall participate in the formulation, application and review of standards" by which their work is judged. Rating thus becomes a two-way operation. Boards of Education, with the assistance of advisory committees including teachers, adopt by-laws governing the granting of promotional increments. These bylaws indicate the weight to be given each of the areas listed above, the types of evidence to be considered for each, techniques for gathering and processing the evidence, and procedures for evaluating the evidence. The advisory group is a continuing group responsible for reviewing the effects and application of its recommendations.

Morrison [34] has listed some fundamental problems about merit rating that have arisen in New York:

1. The difficulties that arise when a new idea emerges that is not fully grasped by those whom it affects in some way.
2. The unwillingness of certain teachers to participate in the program.
3. The widespread belief that the quality of teaching cannot be evaluated.
4. The development of democratic leadership in administering the merit rating program.
5. The undue emphasis placed in the past on credit hours and degrees rather than on the scope and quality of services rendered and contributions made to pupils, school policy, and school-community relations.

As the result of an extensive study of rating teachers for merit, McCall [35] came to the following conclusion:

This research failed to find any system of measuring teacher merit which the writer is willing to recommend be adopted as a basis for paying the salaries of all teachers. This study did establish that the existing system is of little

[33] A. S. Barr and others, *op. cit.*
W. H. Lancelot and others, *The Measurement of Teaching Efficiency* (New York, Macmillan, 1937).
[34] Mimeographed statement by J. Cayce Morrison, State Education Department, Albany, N. Y.
[35] William A. McCall, *Measurement of Teacher Merit* (Raleigh, N. C., State Department of Education, 1952), No. 284.

value if salaries should be paid on merit, and the system of merit rating by official superiors which the state was considering for adoption is of no value.

If ever a group of teachers actually could agree on and set up a local set of standards for judging merit which they themselves could operate, it perhaps would be possible to carry out a merit-rating program. This would mean that the staff would have to come to a common agreement on a framework of principles and practices within which merit ratings could be given, even though precise measurements of factors might not always be possible.

A broad, inclusive view of teaching. Instead of viewing teaching as a variety of activities limited to the classroom, supervisors generally recognize today that the effectiveness of a teacher should be evaluated in terms of contributions in three major areas: (1) effects on the pupils, their growth and development; (2) effects on school operations and policies; and (3) effects on school-community relations. D. E. Beecher developed a special form, The Exceptional Teacher Service Record, on which could be compiled written evidences of unusually valuable contributions by teachers in these three areas. This evidence could be used as a basis for measuring their general merit. On the form [36] are listed "areas of service," sample types of evidence for each item, and a place for recording a file number locating similar evidence about an individual teacher. The items listed under the heading "Direct service to pupils" illustrate the plan:

1. Meeting the personal and social needs of pupils intelligently and effectively.
2. Providing effective guidance in pupils' personal problems; educational, vocational and leisure-time guidance.
3. Providing rich school experience for pupils including broad curricular content, leadership opportunities, co-operative and competitive opportunities, opportunities for creative expression.
4. Successful adaptation of materials and technics to individual differences of pupils.

5. Development and effective use of new materials.
6. Organization and effective use of a variety of material.
7. Effective use of pupil interests, experiences and hobbies in classroom procedure.
8. Effective use of community resources, lay experience, local, state and national institutions.
9. Stimulation of pupil growth in academic achievement, attitudes, habits and ideals, in keeping with abilities and aptitudes.
10. Exceptional service through work in positions of special responsibility and difficulty, such as remedial classes, retarded groups, foreign-speaking groups, classes in problem neighborhoods, physically and mentally handicapped groups.
11. Promoting desirable pupil-teacher relationships to an exceptional degree through fairness, sympathetic understanding, cheerfulness.
12. Stimulating and organizing wide participation by pupils in class and extraclass activities.
13. Assistance to pupils in activities other than regular class work.
14. Development of programs which provide for continuous evaluation of pupil growth in terms of general and specific objectives recognized by the teacher.
15. Consistent application of the concept of functional teaching.

The evaluation of the information compiled about the teacher cannot be done on an objective basis. Rather must the appraisal be based on value-judgments by those concerned with the evaluation of the record. The availability of the information is certain to assure a more dependable evaluation than would be possible under ordinary circumstances.

3. Gathering date about the teacher's characteristics and background. A means of collecting data about teachers, and one where use has grown rapidly during the last ten years, is that of tests of qualities commonly associated with teaching success. Much remains to be done, but tests have already appeared which measure in a man-

[36] Distributed by author, State Teachers College, Potsdam, N. Y.

ner many of the qualities that condition teaching success. One of the earliest tests to be published was the Knight [37] test of teaching aptitude. A revised form of this test was prepared by Bathurst, Knight, Ruch, and Telford.[38] Other tests of teaching aptitude have been developed by Coxe and Orleans,[39] by Moss, Hunt, and Wallace,[40] and by Jensen.[41] These tests are now a number of years old and of interest chiefly for historical reasons. Although they have been classified as aptitude tests, most of them require a certain amount of knowledge of professional education.

Tests of professional information. There are now available in the literature of education a rather large number of tests of professional information and achievement. The reader may find interesting and worthy of study the tests of Lewerenz and Steinmetz,[42] Van Hosen,[43] Odell and Herriott,[44] Weber,[45] Flanagan and others,[46] and Harnly.[47] The Lewerenz and Steinmetz Orientation Test is composed of seven subtests related to the commonly accepted objectives of education: (1) health, (2) education, (3) worthy home membership, (4) vocation, (5) civic educa-

tion, (6) worthy use of leisure time, and (7) ethical character. People known to be superstitious and dogmatic receive low scores; individuals who have a scientific outlook and an open mind receive high scores. Van Hosen's Comprehensive Examination in Education, designed primarily for junior and senior high-school teachers, is a subject-matter test covering the following fields: educational psychology, principles of education, educational applications, history of education, and philosophy of education. The test by Odell and Herriott is a test of principles of teaching; that by Weber a test of aims, attributes, and functions of secondary education.

One of the most pretentious undertakings in tests of professional information is the National Teachers Examinations [48] developed by the American Council on Education. This test aims to test reasoning ability, reading comprehension, skill in English, cultural background, knowledge of the child, pedagogical facts and principles, contemporary affairs, and the subjects to be taught. Another instrument of somewhat different sort is that developed by Harnly.[49] He at-

---

[37] F. B. Knight, *Qualities Related to Success in Teaching,* Contributions to Education No. 120 (New York, Teachers College, Bureau of Publications, Columbia Univ., 1922).

[38] J. E. Bathurst, F. B. Knight, and others, *Aptitude Tests for Elementary and High School Teachers* (Washington, Bureau of Public Personnel Administration, 1927).

[39] W. W. Coxe and J. S. Orleans, *Coxe-Orleans Prognosis Test of Teaching Ability* (Yonkers, World Book, 1930).

[40] F. A. Moss, T. Hunt, and F. C. Wallace, *Teaching Aptitude Test,* George Washington University Series (Washington, Center for Psychological Service, 1927).

[41] Milton B. Jensen, *Stanford Educational Aptitude Test* (Stanford University, Calif., Stanford Univ. Press, 1928).

[42] Alfred S. Lewerenz and Harry C. Steinmetz, *Orientation Test: Concerning Fundamental Aims of Education,* rev. ed. (Hollywood, Calif., California School Book Depository, 1935).

[43] Ralph Van Hosen, *Comprehensive Examination in Education, Forms A and B* (Ann Arbor, Mich., Ann Arbor Press, 1933).

[44] C. W. Odell, *Standard Achievement Tests on Principles of Teaching in Secondary Schools, Form 1* (Bloomington, Ill., Public School Publishing Co., 1925).

——— and M. E. Herriott, *Standard Achievement Test on Principles of Teaching in Secondary Schools, Form 2* (Bloomington, Ill., Public School Publishing Co., 1926).

[45] Joseph J. Weber, *Standard Achievement Test on Aims, Purposes, Objectives, Attributes, and Functions in Secondary Education, Form A* (Bloomington, Ill., Public School Publishing Co.).

[46] John C. Flanagan, "A Preliminary Study of the Validity of 1940 Edition of the National Teachers Examinations," *School and Society* (July, 1941), pp. 59-64.

Daniel Ryans, "The 1948 National Teachers Examinations," *Journal of Experimental Education* (September, 1948), pp. 1-25.

[47] Paul W. Harnly, "Attitudes of High School Seniors Toward Education," *School Review* (September, 1939), pp. 501-509.

[48] *Op. cit.*

[49] Harnly, *op. cit.*

tempted to measure a number of different aspects of teaching, including the choice of purpose, content, and method.

Tests of social behavior. Teaching is above all a very human activity, and many persons believe that the most important element in a teaching situation is the human element involved in teacher-pupil relationship.[50] One of the earliest and most generally used tests of social behavior was the George Washington University Social Intelligence Test.[51] Another test of considerable promise in this area is the test of Theory and Practice of Mental Hygiene [52] by T. L. Torgerson, B. R. Ullsvik, and L. F. Wahlstrom. This test is a measure of teacher-pupil relationships from the mental-hygiene point of view. A review of the more important developments in this field can be found in Murphy, Murphy, and Newcomb, *Experimental Social Psychology.*[53]

Tests of the attitudes of teachers. Three very interesting tests have appeared in this field. It is sometimes said that the most important thing to know about an individual is his philosophy of life. Though such a test is not available, Raup, Peterson, and Williamson [54] have produced a test of the teacher's philosophy of education. Several points of view are measured in this test: (1) the static-dynamic point of view, (2) the academic-direct-life point of view, (3) the science-philosophy point of view, (4) the individual-social point of view, (5) the hereditary-environment point of view, (6) the passive-active point of view, and (7) the

separate mind-naturalistic point of view. Another test of considerable interest in this field is the test of Social Attitudes of Secondary-School Teachers prepared under the auspices of the Yearbook Committee of the John Dewey Society for the Study of Education and Culture.[55] The test is in four parts. Part I, 106 items, aims to measure the subject's attitude toward controversial issues; Part II, an essay test, asks the examinee to describe in some detail his notion of an ideal society; Part III, one hundred items, aims to measure the examinee's attitudes toward various issues of public concern; Part IV consists of a personal data sheet. A third test of quite a different sort falling in this field is the Yeager Scale for Measuring Attitudes Toward Teachers and the Teaching Profession.[56] This test is composed of 44 items to be answered: agree, $(+)$, disagree, (0), and doubtful, $(?)$. Besides these there are available in the literature of education, psychology, and sociology numerous other tests designed to measure the attitudes of adults on various problems. An excellent discussion of these tests will be found in *Experimental Social Psychology* by Murphy, Murphy, and Newcomb.[57]

Cook and his associates have devised a test for measuring teacher-pupil relations. The test is known as the Minnesota Teacher Attitudes Inventory. In this test the teacher is asked to indicate the degree to which he agrees or disagrees with each of a lengthy series of statements about pupil behavior. On the basis of responses, a score is derived

[50] M. E. Haggerty, "Crux of the Teaching Prognosis Problem," *School and Society* (April, 1932), pp. 545-549.

[51] F. A. Moss and others, *Social Intelligence Test* (Washington, Center for Psychological Service, 1930).

[52] T. L. Torgerson and others, "Theory and Practice of Mental Hygiene." Unpublished materials, Univ. of Wisconsin, Madison, 1937.

[53] Gardner Murphy, Lois Barclay Murphy, and Theodore M. Newcomb, *Experimental Social Psychology* (New York, Harper, 1937), pp. 769-888.

[54] R. B. Raup and others, *Teachers' Views on Some Problems in General Educational Theory*

(New York, Teachers College, Bureau of Publications, Columbia Univ., 1931).

[55] W. H. Kilpatrick and others, *The Teacher and Society,* First Yearbook of the John Dewey Society (New York, Appleton-Century, 1937), pp. 180-189.

[56] Teresa C. Yeager, *Scale for Measuring Attitude Toward Teachers and the Teaching Profession,* from *An Analysis of Certain Traits of Selected High-School Seniors Interested in Teaching,* Contributions to Education No. 660 (New York, Teachers College, Bureau of Publications, Columbia Univ., 1935).

[57] *Op. cit.,* pp. 889-1046.

by using a scoring key. Cook summarized some of the earlier findings about this test as follows: [58]

It has been established that teacher-pupil relations in the classroom are highly related to the teacher's attitudes toward pupils. Teacher-pupil attitudes can be measured with high reliability. A measure of the teachers' attitudes will predict with high accuracy the type of social climate which prevails in his classroom.

In general the attitudes of teachers toward pupils tend to deteriorate with age and experience. Inferior teachers tend to be at their best during their twenties. Superior teachers appear to be at their best during their thirties. It is possible that the attitudes of superior teachers improve during the first years of experience while those of inferior teachers deteriorate. This hypothesis needs to be checked. Among superior teachers those who had taken courses in mental hygiene ranked higher than those who had not. This was not true of inferior teachers.

Primary teachers have the most wholesome attitudes toward children, intermediate grade teachers are next with senior high school teachers third, and junior high teachers low. At the high school level academic teachers rank higher than teachers of art, music, home economics, industrial arts and physical education.

At the University of Minnesota there was a significant shift of attitudes in the desirable direction during the junior year when professional courses in education were taken. During the senior year when student teaching and special methods courses were taken, attitudes remained static. During the first six months of teaching in the field there was significant deterioration. The loss after six months of teaching equaled the gain of the junior year.

When juniors in the College of Education were instructed to fake the *Attitudes Inventory* to get as high a score as possible, there was a net mean gain of 5.4 score points. This is about one fourth of the standard deviation of the Inventory scores (Standard Deviation 19.39). When the test was repeated with standard directions, the mean gain was 4.2 points. When the directions to "fake good" are given at the first administration of the Inventory and standard directions are given at the second administration, the mean score difference is only 1.8 points. The Inventory is not subject to faking to a high degree. Both high- and low-scoring teachers tend to believe that their attitudes toward children are the correct and desirable ones. A large proportion of low-scoring teachers lower their scores when instructed to "fake good."

Tests of personality factors in teaching success. One of the earliest tests of personality factors for use with teachers is the Morris Trait Index L.[59] This test is composed of six sections: (1) likes and dislikes for different activities—five responses, forty-six items; (2) choice of comments for different kinds of pupils—six responses, fourteen items; (3) characterization of typical situations as amusing, embarrassing, necessitating firm control, interesting, or necessitating correction of mistake—five responses, seventeen items; (4) selection of best response to typical situations—four responses, twelve items; (5) a five-step true-false test about various items of personal interest—five responses, forty-one items; and (6) a feelings test about school situations—six responses, seven items. There is no definite time limit. An excellent summary of the instruments available for the study of adult personality may be found in *Experimental Social Psychology* by Murphy, Murphy, and Newcomb.[60]

Tests of other qualities commonly associated with teaching success. The mental capacity of the teacher can be determined through the application of any one of a number of tests of mental ability. The American Council on Education[61] Psychological Examination prepared by Thurstone

[58] W. W. Cook, C. H. Leeds, and R. Callis, "Predicting Teacher-Pupil Relations," in *The Evaluation of Student Teaching,* Twenty-eighth Annual Yearbook, Association for Student Teaching (Lockhaven, Pa., State Teachers College, 1949), Ch. 4. The scale is published by Psychological Corporation, 522 Fifth Avenue, New York, N. Y.

[59] Elizabeth H. Morris, *Morris Trait Index L* (Bloomington, Ill., Public School Publishing Co., 1929).

[60] Murphy, Murphy, and Newcomb, *op. cit.,* pp. 769-888.

[61] Gertrude H. Hildreth, *A Bibliography of Mental Tests and Rating Scales* (New York, Psychological Corporation, 1933).

and Thurstone [62] will be found to be particularly useful in this field. The National Teachers Examination [63] has, in addition to the test of professional information, sections on reasoning, knowledge of contemporary affairs, reading comprehension, skills in expression, general culture, and mastery of subject matter that supply valuable information about the intellectual and cultural backgrounds of teaching candidates. Advanced subject-matter tests can be employed to determine the teacher's academic preparation. There are several good tests now available for measuring general cultural background.[64] Hult [65] has developed a test of professional judgment.

The most accurate measure of the teacher's health will probably be found in a thorough medical examination.

General comment on the use of tests to measure teaching efficiency. The foregoing discussion is by no means complete, but it is hoped that enough has been said to indicate the more important developments in this area. The tests cited vary greatly in practical value and statistical validity, but they all illustrate important new approaches to the analysis of teaching ability. It is not thought that these tests will be extensively used by supervisors and administrators except possibly in extreme cases of malperformance. They may, however, find rather extensive use among teachers who desire to have more information about their own abilities in various respects. Combinations of these measures have been found to yield high correlations with teaching efficiency.[66]

Questionnaires, inventories, and interviews widely used. Closely related to the tests of qualities commonly associated with teaching efficiency are the rather large number of standardized questionnaires, inventories, and interviews now available for use in collecting information about a number of aspects of teaching efficiency.

Waples [67] made extensive use of the questionnaire and interview techniques in discovering the problems and difficulties of teachers. In his *Research Methods and Teachers' Problems* he and Tyler set forth a whole scheme of informal research by which teachers' problems might be discovered and solved. The procedure outlined by them occupies a position somewhere between the teacher's offhand solution of difficulties and more accurate methods of research. The volume is one that contains useful material on both the discovery and the solution of teaching problems, and is thus recommended to those who wish to approach the study of the teacher at work from a study of the needs sensed by the teacher. The methods of making such analyses are worthy of careful consideration. Barr and others [68] report the use of a standardized interview to secure information about such important matters as (1) reasons for choosing teaching as a vocation; (2) interest in children, teaching, and the subject to be taught; (3) willingness to accept the personal, social, and financial rewards associated with teaching; (4) interest in the service and reformational possibilities of teaching; (5) concern with social problems and issues; (6) emotional balance and adjust-

[62] L. L. Thurstone and Thelma G. Thurstone, *American Council on Education Psychological Examination* (Washington, American Council on Education).

[63] David G. Ryans, "Measuring the Intellectual and Cultural Backgrounds of Teaching Candidates," *Measurement and Guidance* (New York, Co-operative Test Service, 1941), Vol. 1, No. 1.

[64] E. F. Lindquist and others, *General Culture Test* (New York, Co-operative Test Service, 1936).

[65] Esther Hult, *A Study of the Effectiveness of Instruction in the Nature and Direction of Learn-*

ing. Unpublished doctoral dissertation, Univ. of Wisconsin, 1944.

[66] A. S. Barr and others, *The Measurement of Teaching Ability,* Experimental Educational Monograph (Madison, Wisc., Dembar Publications, 1945).

[67] Douglas Waples and Ralph W. Tyler, *Research Methods and Teachers' Problems* (New York, Macmillan, 1930).

[68] A. S. Barr and others, *Wisconsin Study of Teaching Ability* (Madison, Univ. of Wisconsin Press, 1947).

ment to conflict; (7) relations with others (children, contemporaries, and adults); (8) work habits and energy patterns; (9) recreational interests and activities; (10) physical health, energy, and drive; (11) initiative, originality, and creativeness; and (12) future plans and ambitions.

Three inventories not particularly designed for use with teachers but nevertheless quite valuable for this purpose are the Personality Inventory by Robert G. Bernreuter,[69] the Social Adjustment Inventory by J. N. Washburne,[70] and the Minnesota Multiphasic Personality Inventory.[71] There are many other tests.

Studying attitudes and opinions of staff. Science Research Associates[72] has developed a valuable procedure for securing expressions of attitudes and opinions of individual staff members in strictest confidence concerning a number of different aspects of the school system as a whole, such as working conditions, confidence in the administration, quality of curriculum materials, and adequacy of communication. The individual reads a statement, for example, "The inservice-education program is adequate," and then checks one of three choices as to his opinion about it: agree, no opinion, and disagree. Analysis of the findings of the inventory gives a measure of morale within the system, insights into the relationships among teachers and supervisors, areas in which the system is weak or strong, and basic information useful in the formulation of policies.

A summary statement on measures of teaching efficiency: The evaluation of teachers and teaching should be viewed broadly. From what has been said in this chapter, it can be easily seen that the evalu-

ation of teaching is a very complex activity. The efficiency of teachers depends upon many different qualities, abilities, understandings, and auxiliary competencies. Through the use of such devices as have been described valuable data may be collected about many of the important aspects of teaching. These various measures of teachers and teaching reduce themselves to five general types:

1. Means that attempt to evaluate the contributions of the teacher to the learning-teaching situation through the study of the teacher's performance.

2. Means that attempt to evaluate the teacher's contribution to the learning-teaching situation by tests of qualities of the teacher commonly associated with teaching success.

3. Means that attempt to evaluate the teacher's contribution to the learning-teaching situation through measures of the mental prerequisites to teaching efficiency.

4. Means that attempt to evaluate teaching efficiency through measures of pupil change.

5. Means of appraising contributions to school and community.

Means of the first sort ordinarily take the form of check-lists, rating scales, and various kinds of more or less standardized criteria. Measures of the second sort ordinarily take the form of observations, reports, tests, and rating scales. Measures of the third sort are the many tests of intelligence, academic training, professional information, and the other qualities commonly associated with teaching. In the fourth group fall the many measures of pupil growth and achievement. In the fifth group are included methods of evaluating teacher contributions to life in the school and community. Each of these sets of measures serves its own particular purpose and is subject to its own peculiar limitations. All in all, teaching is a very

[69] Robert G. Bernreuter, *The Personality Inventory* (Stanford University, Calif., Stanford Univ. Press, 1931-1938).

[70] J. N. Washburne, *The Social Adjustment Inventory* (Syracuse, N. Y., Syracuse Univ., 1932-1940).

[71] S. R. Hathaway and J. C. McKinley, *Minnesota Multiphasic Personality Inventory* (New

York, Psychological Corporation). First published in 1943.

A. R. Gilliland and Russell W. Colgin, "Norms, Reliability and Forms of the MMPI," *Journal of Consulting Psychology* (October, 1951), pp. 435-448.

[72] *SRA Educator Opinion Inventory* (Chicago, Science Research Associates, 1953).

complex activity, and the haphazard, un-scientific, and superficial study of teaching that characterizes much of our supervision today should not be tolerated. While our means of studying teachers and teaching are still crude and most inadequate, the work in this field has progressed to a point where general impressions and the hit-and-miss methods of studying the teacher at work can no longer be justified. Just as we have developed improved methods of studying pupils and their habits of work, so we must develop improved methods of studying and assisting teachers.

Section 5

GETTING THE CO-OPERATION OF ALL CONCERNED

Who shall study the teacher at work? There will be many persons "inspecting" the teacher's work: parents, members of the board of education, the principal, state and local supervisors, the superintendent of schools, other teachers, pupils, and, we hope, the teacher himself. Very few teachers are naïve enough to believe that their work is not appraised. All who will come in contact with the teacher's work will form opinions about it. It has always been so and will probably continue to be so as long as there are teachers. Instead of being disturbed by this fact, as some persons appear to be, those of us in teaching should be happy that the concern is so general. The concern arises in part out of two important facts: (1) parents are interested in the welfare of their children; (2) the public is concerned with having good schools. In a democratic society it is only natural that many persons are going to be concerned with teaching efficiency.

Our hope is that judgments made about teachers and teaching will be good judgments. No teacher can rightfully object to having his teaching subjected to scrutiny; his only hope is that the judgments reached about his over-all efficiency and the factors contributing to his success and failure may be sound judgments. It is not an easy matter to arrive at sound judgments about so complex an activity. The objection is not to evaluation but to unthoughtful evaluation. It is hoped when pupils, supervisors, administrators, parents, members of the board of education, and other citizens of the community attempt to evaluate teaching and its contributing factors that their judgments will be fair, sound, and worthy of the profession. The purpose of all that has been said thus far in this chapter was meant to improve the judgments of ordinary people: teachers, pupils, parents, superintendents, supervisors, board members, and all others who will have opinions about the teacher's efficiency. Although much of what has been said will appear to some to be far too technical to be comprehensible to the layman, we have attempted to lay the foundation for better work and fairer judgments in this field. The problem of evaluating teaching efficiency and of determining the teacher factors that contribute to pupil growth and achievement is much more complicated than would appear to the uninitiated.

Parents and pupils can help. It has been frequently urged in this volume that supervision be looked upon as a co-operative activity. Parents and pupils are a part of the larger partnership working for good schools. Better progress will be made when help is solicited from all concerned. Too many teachers approach the problem from a negative point of view. Instead of seeking the assistance of all concerned, they actually resent attempts to help as intrusions and as reflections upon their competency. The whole movement to engage the assistance of pupils and parents in the improvement of teaching is a part of the trend toward greater democracy in education.

Pupil appraisal of teaching. In keeping with the trends toward wider participation in the improvement program, many teachers are now seeking the full co-operation and assistance of pupils both in evaluating and improving the teaching process. Being as closely associated with the teaching-learning situation as they are, pupils will have many very excellent ideas about how the process can be improved. Many persons have in recent years urged greater participation both in planning [73] and in evaluating the efficiency [74] of what is done. Although they do not approach the problem from quite this point of view, many persons [75] have recently urged pupil participation in teacher evaluation and have proposed means by which this might be done; parents might assist too.

Teacher self-evaluation. The most alert person of all to good and poor teaching should be the teacher himself.[76] Many of the instruments discussed in this chapter, used primarily by supervisors, are equally useful to teachers who would like to know more about their own effectiveness. In evaluating one's own efficiency, it is frequently necessary to seek assistance in recording the happenings of some particular segment of teaching, but the evaluation of the data can be made by the teacher himself. If the teacher does not feel free to call upon the principal or some supervisor to help with the collection of data, he might then use some older pupil or a parent. For those who can afford it, there are now good recording devices that can be used for this purpose. Teachers are already trained to evaluate carefully pupil growth and achievement. Now we suggest

that they study their own performance in relation to this growth and plan improvement where help is most needed.

Some time, money, and energy problems. It will be readily apparent to most persons that to do all that one ought to do in the study and improvement of teaching would take considerable time, money, and energy. When one adds to this the fact that teachers, pupils, and administrators are all already overloaded with important things to do, the more systematic study of teaching may seem impracticable. If helping teachers to analyze and improve their work is an item with a low priority rating, it is not going to get the attention that it deserves. Some extra time, money, and energy may be had, however, by refocusing the efforts of all concerned upon the chief purpose of the school, namely, the facilitation of pupil growth and development. There are many persons who seem to have their minds on extraneous matters or some detail not too important in the learning-teaching situation. It may help, also, to engage the assistance of pupils and parents. Some relief may arise, too, from better comprehension of what is to be done and the resulting economies. Much that has been suggested can be done, but only under thoroughly competent leadership.

The study of teaching: a co-operative undertaking pursued in a democratic framework. It has already been emphasized in an earlier chapter of this volume that supervision should be democratic.[77] If the

[73] Harry H. Giles, *Teacher-Pupil Planning* (New York, Harper, 1941).

[74] Roy C. Bryan, *Pupil Rating of Secondary School Teachers,* Contributions to Education No. 708 (New York, Teachers College, Bureau of Publications, Columbia Univ., 1937).

———, "Eighty-Six Teachers Try Evaluating Student Reactions to Themselves," *Educational Administration and Supervision* (October, 1941), pp. 513-526.

———, "Reliability, Validity, and Needfulness of Written Student Reactions to Teachers," *ibid.* (December, 1941), pp. 655-665.

[75] Robert B. Boyce and Roy C. Bryan, "To What Extent Do Pupils' Opinions of Teachers Change in Later Years?" *Journal of Educational Research* (May, 1944), pp. 698-705.

[76] Maurice E. Troyer, "Self-Evaluation in Teacher Education," *ibid.* (March, 1942), pp. 528-543.

[77] A. S. Barr and W. H. Burton, *The Supervision of Instruction* (New York, Appleton-Century, 1926), pp. 83-85.

A. S. Barr, *An Introduction to the Scientific Study of Classroom Supervision* (New York, D. Appleton-Century, 1931), pp. 17-20.

A publication of the Department of Supervisors and Directors of Instruction also gives emphasis to this point. S. A. Courtis and others, "Teachers and Co-operation," bulletin issued by a committee in charge of the Yearbook on Co-operation, Department of Supervisors and Directors of Instruction (Washington, NEA, 1937). This early yearbook is still a good reference.

principles of democracy are put into operation, we believe that the practice of supervision will be changed in many respects. In the first place, we believe that more people will be involved. There is much isolationism in teaching today and inability to use the assistance of others; too many teachers are trying to do single-handedly what could be done better if several people worked together. Secondly, the inspectorial, teacher-centered type of supervision will be abandoned for the co-operative group type of activity. Attention in the new type supervision is shifted from the teacher to the task to be performed. Teachers, pupils, community agencies, parents, supervisors, and administrators will all work together harmoniously for the achievement of the purposes of education. Finally, teachers will take the initiative in seeking and securing wider participation on the part of all concerned. Parents still have a profound interest in and fundamental responsibility for the education of the young. Teachers will capitalize upon this interest. The pupil is always closely associated with the educative process. Accordingly, they will understand better what they are trying to do and why: they will make better progress when they are provided with opportunities to plan what they do and evaluate the effectiveness of their effort. Supervisors will help when they can. Valid data can be collected in a democratic setting if all concerned are willing to set their minds to the task of doing so.

Chapter summary. The purpose of this chapter has been to describe the means by which one may discover the improvement needs of teachers. In choosing what to study it has been frequently pointed out that teaching must be viewed comprehensively. It must be viewed broadly to include, first, not merely those activities performed by the teacher in the classroom, as a director of learning, but a wide range of school and community activities all of which are thought to condition pupil growth in its wider ramifications; to include, second, not merely "method" in its conventional, restricted sense, or even behavior in its broader sense, but the background determiners of these as well; and to include, finally, many relational factors involving the manner in which the elements in each learning-teaching situation fit together to produce the total effect observed both in teaching effectiveness and pupil growth. In this latter respect the teacher and his effectiveness must be studied in close relation to the school, the community, the pupil, the curriculum, the materials of instruction, and all other factors that affect pupil growth. Much has been said in this chapter about data-gathering devices and their trustworthiness. Many persons will evaluate teaching and offer judgments on what makes for effectiveness in the teaching act. Most of those who offer such judgments will be poorly equipped both by training and temperament for this responsibility. It is hoped that what has been said will help to better judgments. Few have the judicial temperament and the sense of evidence that one would like for a complex task of this sort. Evaluation, like improvement, is a co-operative enterprise involving group action and individual initiative.

CHAPTER SUPPLEMENT

INTRODUCTORY DISCUSSION QUESTIONS

1. Give illustrations of ways in which the factors other than the teacher that are inherent in the situation, discussed on pages 317 and 322, affect the quality of instruction.

2. Give illustrations showing how factors inherent in the teacher as a person have affected instruction. How can these factors be identified and diagnosed?

3. Evaluate the California analysis of teaching competence.

4. Analyze the list of observational devices on page 324 for studying instructional practices; analyze also the use of the various kinds of reports listed on page 325.

5. Why is it difficult to use measures of pupil growth to evaluate teaching efficiency? For what outcomes are dependable appraisal devices lacking?

6. What traits of teachers or aspects of teaching are dependable criteria of teaching success? Which are not?

7. Why are the activities of teaching so variable? How does variability of teacher performance affect supervisory visitation?

8. How might a consultant new to a school system go about securing dependable information about current instructional practices and problems as a basis for developing a program for improving the situation? Be specific about procedures to use. Could he observe? Could he secure reports? What other procedures could he use? Why is such a preliminary survey desirable?

9. Comment on the procedure used by Krause, described on pages 341-342. Evaluate the list of "principles" he gives.

10. Illustrate the methods of securing descriptive data about instruction listed on page 343.

QUESTIONS DESIGNED TO CARRY ANALYSIS FURTHER TOWARD ACTUAL PROBLEMS IN THE FIELD

1. What are some of the basic principles related to purposes, learning, and socio-economic trends to be considered in evaluating instructional procedures?

2. What are some of the causes of ineffective instruction? Can they be readily isolated? What techniques of diagnosis are useful?

3. What kinds of general information about the qualification, preparation, and experience of the staff should be available?

4. How can a dependable analysis of general instructional problems and practices be made?

5. What techniques can be used to determine a teacher's needs and difficulties? What are symptoms of poor morale? What are the causes?

6. What has been discovered about the validity and reliability of quantitative analyses of specific aspects of teaching procedures?

7. What are the values and limitations of the techniques for rating teachers?
   a. Point scales.
   b. Graphic scales.
   c. Diagnostic scales.
   d. Quality scales.
   e. Man-to-man comparison scales.
   f. Conduct or performance scales.

8. What evidence is there that teaching ability can be measured?

9. Outline a plan for making an analytical study of instruction, or of the work of a teacher, in some area of education.

10. Have the class as a group (or committee, if class is too large) observe teaching in several rooms and make a record of the objective evidences of teaching efficiency, observable teacher and pupil activities, materials and conditions for work. Then proceed to: (1) critically analyze the records made and repeat the observations until the members of the class distinguish between inference and evidence; (2) prepare a list of evidences collected about the teacher that would seem to indicate that he is a good, a mediocre, a poor teacher; (3) enumerate the criteria employed in making the judgments called for in (2) above; (4) indicate briefly how one might proceed to reduce differences in judgments among the observers.

11. What are the values and weaknesses of current plans of teacher rating? Should teachers be rated?

12. How can teaching merit be determined?

13. Illustrate concretely the three levels of diagnosis of teachers' needs described on pages 322-323.

14. The great variation in observational judgments in teaching may be greatly reduced by (1) setting up reputable criteria of judgment, (2) giving training in the application of these criteria to actual situations, and (3) considering the appropriateness of teacher and pupil activities for the specific situation under scrutiny.

Outline a procedure by which the three factors might be achieved.

15. It is sometimes interesting to compare the professional preparation, teaching practices, and pupil changes secured by two or more teachers of supposedly different levels of efficiency. Make the data as complete as possible; arrange the data for the several teachers in parallel columns for comparative purposes. What likenesses and differences do you note?

16. The purpose of this chapter is to lay the basis for more accurate study of teaching ability. In many instances the analysis herein contemplated may be of the case study sort. Through the use of techniques suggested in this chapter, prepare a careful case study of the work of some teacher who is willing to serve as a subject for this purpose. On the basis of the data collected, prepare a list of the teacher's strong points and his weaknesses. If time permits, test the validity of your diagnosis by

showing that the correction of the observed weaknesses improves the teacher's efficiency.

17. The chapter and several of the exercises emphasize the importance of criteria under which to evaluate the teacher's procedures. From a careful examination of scientific investigations in this field and from summaries thereof prepare a set of criteria which would be useful in your own work. Indicate the sources and data supporting each of the criteria. Any form may be used.

18. The method of activity analysis, especially when based upon a few visits, does not seem highly reliable. Such analyses are, however, very valuable in practical supervision. Show how this is true.

19. Report for class analysis any experience you have had in participating in a local survey of growth needs. (Students without experience may make critical analysis of methods used in a printed survey report.)

20. One authority states that weaknesses common in the teaching body are: (1) too much dependence on those in authority; (2) lack of information and conviction on the current economic, political, and social problems; (3) remoteness from the stream of community life. What evils result from these items? Outline at some length the general lines of attack upon these items.

21. List three or more serious weaknesses, other than those in Question 20, found generally among educational workers. Similarly, list half a dozen specific difficulties or problems limited to given situations. Outline at some length the general methods of attack upon the weaknesses noted.

WRITTEN REPORTS FOR INDIVIDUALS OR GROUPS

1. Prepare a list of current instructional problems for some curriculum area similar to the list for reading on page 327. How can these problems be identified in classrooms?

2. Evaluate and extend the list of symptoms of teaching problems given on page 321.

3. Devise a plan of securing reports from teachers as to their instructional difficulties and points on which they desire assistance.

4. How can one study pupil-teacher relations?

5. How can one study teacher-community relations?

6. Describe in some detail the steps to be taken to diagnose some actual teaching problem, as described on page 321. Show when and how to use the three levels of diagnosis.

7. Secure and make a critical evaluation of teacher rating devices and procedures used in local schools. What use is made of professional tests?

8. Evaluate the kinds of information about teachers contained in local personnel files.

9. Evaluate local plans for selecting new teachers. Suggest improvements.

10. Prepare a report on the nature and uses of the National Teachers Examination.

11. Examine the first edition (1938) of *Supervision* by the authors and report the evidence given as to the validity, reliability, and objectivity of analytical studies of teacher activities as a basis of evaluation.

12. A group may devise a plan for surveying instructional practices in some field similar to Whipple's program for studying various aspects of reading instruction.

13. A group may apply Mursell's principles, given on pages 339 to 341, to some lesson observed. How closely do the numbers of the group agree? Comment on possibilities of self-evaluation by applying these principles to your own teaching procedures.

14. A group or you yourself may apply Krause's principles to some lesson or a series of lessons.

15. A group may observe a lesson and rate the work of the teacher by applying selected rating scales discussed in this chapter.

SUGGESTED REFERENCES

ALEXANDER, Theron, Jr., "The Prediction of Teacher-Pupil Interaction with a Projective Test," *Journal of Clinical Psychology* (July, 1950), pp. 273-276.

ALILUNAS, Leo J., "Needed Research in Teacher Mental Hygiene," *Journal of Educational Research* (May, 1945), pp. 653-665.

ANDERSON, H. H., and BREWER, H. M., "Studies of Teachers' Classroom Personalities, I. Dominative and Socially Integrative Behavior of Kindergarten Teachers," *Applied Psychological Monograph*, No. 6 (1945), p. 157.

———, "Studies of Teachers' Classroom Personalities, II. Effects of Teachers' Dominative and Integrative Contacts on Children's Classroom Behavior," *Applied Psychological Monograph*, No. 8 (1946), p. 128.

———, and REED, Mary Frances, "Studies of Teachers' Classroom Personalities, III. Follow-Up Studies of the Effects of Dominative and Integrative Contacts on Children's Behavior," *Applied Psychological Monograph*, No. 11 (1946), p. 156.

BARKER, M. Elizabeth, *Personality Adjustments of Teachers Related to Efficiency in Teaching* (New York, Teachers College, Bureau of Publications, Columbia Univ., 1946), pp. 10-97.

———, "Summary of the Relation of Personality Adjustments of Teachers to Their Efficiency in Teaching," *Journal of Educational Research* (May, 1948), pp. 664-675.

BARR, A. S., "Wisconsin Studies of Teaching Ability," *Journal of Educational Research* (May, 1948), pp. 170-171.

———, and others, "The Prediction of Teaching Efficiency," special issue of *Journal of Experimental Education* (September, 1946).

———, "The Measurement and Prediction of Teaching Efficiency: A Summary of Investigations," complete issue of *Journal of Experimental Education* (June, 1948).

Better Than Rating, Association for Supervision and Curriculum Development (Washington, NEA, 1950).

BOARDMAN, Charles, DOUGLASS, Harl, and BENT, R. K., *Democratic Supervision in Secondary Schools* (Boston, Houghton, 1953), Chs. 6-13.

BROOKOVER, W. B., "Person-Person Interaction Between Teachers and Pupils and Teaching Effectiveness," *Journal of Educational Research* (December, 1940), pp. 272-287.

BRYAN, Roy C., "Reliability, Validity, and Needfulness of Written Student Reactions to Teachers," *Educational Administration and Supervision* (December, 1941), pp. 655-665.

BUSH, R. N., "A Study of Student-Teacher Relationships," *Journal of Educational Research* (May, 1942), pp. 645-656.

BYERS, L. M., and MATHER, Irving A., "Adjustment of Men and Women Student Teachers," *School and Society* (May 20, 1950), pp. 311-314.

COOK, W. W., and LEEDS, Carroll H., "The Construction and Differential Value of a Scale for Determining Teacher-Pupil Attitudes," *Journal of Experimental Education* (December, 1947), pp. 149-159.

COREY, S. M., "Evaluating Technical Teaching Competence," *Elementary School Journal* (April, 1941), pp. 577-586.

FLANAGAN, John C., "A Preliminary Study of the 1940 Edition of the National Teacher Examinations," *School and Society* (July 26, 1941), pp. 59-64.

GRIEDER, Calvin, and NEWBURN, H. K., "Temperament in Prospective Teachers," *Journal of Educational Research* (May, 1942), pp. 683-693.

HULSE, M. L., "Student Rating of Teachers in Service as a Teacher-Training Device," *Educational Administration and Supervision* (January, 1940), pp. 1-12.

LEEDS, Carroll H., "A Scale for Measuring Teacher-Pupil Attitude and Teacher-Pupil Rapport," *Psychological Monographs*, Vol. 4, No. 26 (1950).

NANCE, R. D., "Masculinity-Femininity in Prospective Teachers," *Journal of Educational Research* (May, 1949), pp. 658-666.

RATHS, Louis, *The Ohio Teaching Records Anecdotal Observation Form*, rev. ed. (Columbus, Ohio State Univ. Press, 1941).

Rating Employee and Supervisory Performance, ed. by Dooher and Marquis (New York, Management Association, 1950).

RYANS, David G., "A Study of Criterion Data: A Factor Analysis of Teacher Behaviors in the Elementary School," *Educational and Psychological Measurement* (Autumn, 1952), pp. 333-344.

———, "The Use of the National Teacher Examination in Colleges and Universities," *Journal of Educational Research* (May, 1949), pp. 678-689.

———, "The Criteria of Teacher Effectiveness," *ibid.*, pp. 690-699.

———, and WANDT, Edwin, "Investigations of Personal and Social Characteristics of Teachers," *Journal of Teacher Education* (September, 1952), pp. 228-231.

SEAGOE, May V., "Prognostic Tests and Teaching Success," *Journal of Educational Research* (May, 1945), pp. 685-690.

SYMONDS, Percival M., "Personality of the Teacher," *Journal of Educational Research* (May, 1947), pp. 652-661.

———, "Education and Psychotherapy," *Journal of Educational Psychology* (January, 1949), pp. 1-32.

———, "Reflections on Observations of Teachers," *Journal of Educational Research* (May, 1950), pp. 688-696.

TIEDEMAN, S. C., "A Study of Pupil-Teacher Relationships," *Journal of Educational Research* (May, 1942), pp. 657-664.

TROYER, M. E., "Self-Evaluation in Teacher Education," *Journal of Educational Research* (March, 1942), pp. 528-543.

TROYER, M. E., and PACE, C. R., *Evaluation in Teacher Education* (Washington, American Council on Education, 1944).

WITTY, Paul, "An Analysis of the Personality Traits of the Effective Teacher," *Journal of Educational Research* (May, 1947), pp. 662-671.

Chapter 12

◆•◆•◆•◆•◆•◆•◆•◆•◆•

Studying the Curriculum in Operation

Curriculums and their accompanying documentary materials must be constantly evaluated and improved.[1] The materials and methods of education have been subject to criticism and improvement from earliest times. The remote general reason for this is the recognition of lag between education and life, and of lag[2] between educational processes and research findings concerning those processes. An immediate, and we hope temporary, reason for some criticisms is the insecurity and uncertainty resulting from the current period of world crisis and social revolution. A gap probably will exist always between curriculums and processes of the school and the life of society and of the individual, but the gap should be narrowed as far as possible.

First, then, we need constantly to study and improve curriculums in order to keep them in line with the needs of a changing society, and with the needs of the individual living within that society. A general overview of the processes of social change was presented in Chapter 2.

Second, we need to evaluate all proposals to expand the functions of the school as a social instrument. Desirable changes in educational aims necessitate changes in the curriculum. This is particularly true in the area of teaching loyalty to the democratic way of life; in the area of self-realization for the individual; in life-adjustment programs, and others.

Third, we need constantly to revise the curriculum to bring it in line with emerging research findings on the nature of the learner, of the learning process, of the teaching process.

Fourth, we may note that the American

---

[1] A general volume cannot give extensive detail on studying and improving the curriculum. Students and field workers are assumed to have had course work and experience with field projects before studying this volume. For those without this background, extensive work must be provided both in curriculum theory and in analysis of printed accounts of curriculum-development programs. Field experience with a real project would be ideal but would ordinarily be too time consuming for this course. Advanced students and experienced field workers may also profit from study of the constantly appearing new materials in the field. We have tried to supply useful references within the body of the chapter.

For instance, the historical background may be extended through:

Harold L. Rugg, *American Life and the School Curriculum* (Boston, Ginn, 1936), Chs. 1 and 2, and if possible 3-8; 12-25.

J. Minor Gwynn, *Curriculum Principles and Social Trends*, rev. ed. (New York, Macmillan, 1950), Chs. 2-5, 15, 18, 19, 20.

L. Thomas Hopkins, *Interaction* (Boston, Heath, 1944), Chs. 1, 2, 3, 5.

J. Abner Peddiwell (Harold Benjamin), *The Saber-Tooth Curriculum* (New York, McGraw, 1939). A witty and devastating satire on the gap between the curriculum and life.

Early chapters in B. Othanel Smith, W. O. Stanley, and J. H. Shores, *Fundamentals of Curriculum Development* (Yonkers, World Book, 1950), contain good historical and philosophic background with the bulk of the book devoted to principles and procedures for improving curriculums.

The first chapter in H. L. Caswell and associates, *Curriculum Improvement in Public School Systems* (New York, Teachers College, Bureau of Publications, Columbia Univ., 1950), contains a good historical summary. The bulk of the book describes admirably a number of actual programs.

[2] Materials on the lag are summarized very briefly in Appendix A. This should be read before taking up this chapter, plus some browsing in the references in footnote 1.

way is and has been from the beginning that of experimentalism. Our country was founded thus, and its continued development on a new continent was guided by a tentative, experimental philosophy. Our core of reasonably stable values was produced in part by our experimental view and procedure, plus contemplation. To borrow a much overworked word, we may say without levity that it is "un-American" to wish to retain the status quo in the curriculum, to insist on the curriculum under which our fathers were trained. It is downright (and here we are being facetious) subversive to demand a "return to the '3 R's!'" (We never deserted them.) Experimentalism has helped us throughout our national life to meet new conditions in our political, economic, and social life. So also with the materials and processes of education.

The criticisms and dissatisfactions with school curricula currently expressed stem, even if the relationship is not always clearly seen, from the factors listed above. We hear on the one hand that we should educate for international understandings and one world, and on the other that we should educate for national loyalties and oppose international views. Education for family life, for moral and spiritual values, and for safe driving of automobiles in many cases represent the range of demands. Those who demand a "return to the '3 R's'" think they are opposing change in the curriculum, but their stand represents also a dissatisfaction and a demand for change. A later chapter will present methods of studying and utilizing dissatisfactions.

Dissatisfaction with the educational product is the chief reason for scrutiny of local courses and curriculums. The commonest immediate cause for investigation of a local curriculum is some deficiency, real or imagined, in the growth and achievement of the learner. The weakness may be revealed by test results, by observational and anecdotal records, by questionnaire or interview results, by complaints or questions from par-

ents, lay groups, teachers, pupils. Comments in the public press may call community attention to the problem. The suggestion that some new departure, either of material or methods, be added to the program is an indirect criticism of existing procedures and results.

Evaluation of curriculums and of printed materials a difficult task. Extensive programs of curriculum improvement and of the production of documentary materials have been developed during the last quarter of a century. At first there was little or no critical evaluation of either procedure or results. Publication of new "courses" was in many instances regarded as sufficient proof of the value of local effort and product. Many new courses were in fact great improvements over the old; many were no better; some were poorer than those replaced. The introduction of an "activity curriculum" was regarded as self-evident proof of curriculum improvement. The substitution of "units" for "subjects" was accepted uncritically. All this is natural. Valid and reliable data about the ultimate value of documentary aids and curriculums are difficult to secure. The complexity of the situation makes difficult the application of the limited, precise methods of scientific investigation. First, the time interval between use and result is long. Second, it is very difficult to secure an extensive, reliable description of life behavior of the learners. Third, it is even more difficult to assess the value of the various factors which contribute to a given behavior pattern. Social pressures; economic status; type and influence of home and neighborhood; health; conflict among the aims of pupil, school, and society; the policy and decisions of the educational leadership—these and many others modify the results achieved by learners. Excellent teachers may develop a good curriculum from poor materials; less able instructors, a poor curriculum from a good material. The materials and the teacher are but two factors among many. The inherent variability of human nature is another complicating factor. Fourth, the naïve, so-called "practical" attitude of many field workers has contributed to the neglect of proof.

Evaluation is, nevertheless, an inescapable part of any program for producing materials or improving curriculums. We cannot wait for the final results in life. We must determine as best we can as we go along how well the course or curriculum seems to be functioning. The problem must be attacked courageously, despite the handicaps. A very few experimental comparisons between curriculums have been made and deserve careful study. Judgment guided by criteria has been exercised on both courses of study and curriculums. This may be the only applicable method for some aspects. Data-gathering instruments are being evolved and used.

The criteria will change from time to time. There will be differences of opinion regarding both criteria and the results of application. Let no one be discouraged. That is the way life is. All we can do is use the best criteria and the best judges we have and then say, "To the best of our knowledge and belief this is better (or worse) than that." Constant, earnest effort to make honest judgments in the light of principles and facts is the way to reduce differences of opinion. Greatly divergent differences of opinion, let it be mentioned incidentally, are not nearly so frequent as the uninformed rank and file believe. Contrary to the naïve statements of many teachers, there are not many flatly contradictory aims, definitions, and so forth, among competent thinkers. Differences of opinion on means, on details, on interpretation of new techniques or discoveries are wholesome.

Students in seminars, as part of their training, will often examine printed materials and curriculums in operation. Field workers may often examine a collection of courses of study in their search for information or stimulus. Logs, diaries, units of work written by teachers, and other written curriculum records will be scrutinized. Daily programs, policies for grouping and promoting pupils,

methods of reporting progress, instructional techniques, the type and amount of instructional aids are all factors to be scrutinized in evaluating specific courses and specific curriculums.

Evaluation and improvement of documents and of curriculums in real situations is a simultaneous and interactive process. Arbitrary distinction between evaluation of documents and of curriculums will be made henceforth in this chapter only to facilitate discussion.

Materials and curriculums will be judged to be good or poor in the degree to which they contribute to the effectiveness of learning; to growth and achievement by the learner.

Preliminary definitions. General definitions will be necessary before we turn to methods of observation and analysis. The terms *curriculum* and *course of study* are still confused by many persons, despite the great amount of activity concerning them during the past quarter century. The concept connoted by the term *course of study* has in addition changed so greatly in modern times as to necessitate careful statement of what is meant. The definitions given here represent common agreement and usage today within developing trends. A few differences of opinion may be expected.

The definition for *curriculum* has shown steady change over the years, always away from narrow, static, content-centered concepts to broad, dynamic, experience or action-centered concepts. Curriculum originally meant the subject matter to be covered. Curriculum and course of study were here equivalent. Curriculum often meant program of studies. The desired learnings, whether stated as aims or as outcomes, were sometimes used to define the curriculum. More recent definitions emphasized the experiences which learners have under the guidance of the school. Differences in definition up to this point turn on the relative emphasis put upon aims or objectives, content, the teaching-learning processes. Until recently, programs of curriculum improvement turned upon the study and refinement of aims, content, and teaching-learning processes. These are clearly important parts of the program but not the most important parts.

The curriculum results from the interaction of many factors in addition to aims, content, and processes. Among the other interactive factors are persons; power structures among persons; material facilities; the aim and the political, economic, and social structure of the surrounding society; the aims and philosophies of the community and of those operating the educational system, together with their decisions concerning methods and materials, teacher selection, salaries, physical plant. Still other factors affecting the curriculum are the types of learners, their abilities, needs, and attitudes, past experiences, social class and cultural backgrounds. A course of study containing statements of aim, content, and preferred organizations for teaching is but one of the factors.

We borrow from Benne and Muntyan [3] and reword slightly what we believe to be a significant definition of the curriculum:

The curriculum is the series of experiences which learners enact and undergo in the process of their deliberate induction into the culture, and which the school as a social system influences significantly.

These authors stress also that it is the interaction of all the factors listed earlier that determine what experiences learners will have and, consequently, what they will learn.

This definition focuses attention on the factors: persons, school as a social system,[4] interaction, and doing by the learners. These are the elements of the curriculum which are susceptible to improvement. Improvement in statements of aim, in selection and arrangement of content, in organizations for teaching will improve educational practice only if the persons who operate the social structure of the school accept the new aims. Otherwise the personnel continues to operate with old aims still in their minds, and with old values still retained. New content, new arrangements of scope and sequence, will be disregarded if the persons have not changed their views. Unit organizations, provisions for individual differences, stress on real experiences for the learners, no matter how vividly expressed in the documents, will not affect practice unless the persons accept the new and identify themselves with the new.

To be successful, a program of curriculum improvement must bring about many important changes within persons as well as within the elements of the setting for learning. Changes within persons will be in their values, insights, beliefs, attitudes and appreciations, and skills. More of this in a later chapter. We are for the moment concerned only with setting up definitions preliminary to studying the existing curriculum.

A curriculum can be developed only in individual schools and classrooms. Teachers and pupils actually make the curriculum in all schools, aided directly and indirectly by parents, organized lay groups, administrators, supervisors, and various specialists in subject matter, in the psychology of childhood, in the diagnosis of learning difficulties, and other factors.

The view expressed in the preceding paragraph and similar statements by curriculum writers are often quoted out of context. Uninformed and unfair criticisms of modern practice result. The immediate curriculum is developed always within the general societal aims and values. This has been clearly indicated several times in this chapter and in Chapter 3.

The term *documents made available to the teacher* has come into general use to designate courses of study, source units, guides to child development, curriculum

[3] Kenneth D. Benne and Bozidar Muntyan, *Human Relations in Curriculum Change* (New York, Dryden, 1951), p. 5. The whole volume is very valuable, but reading may be delayed until we take up the improvement of curriculums.

[4] W. W. Charters, Jr., "The School as a Social System," *Review of Educational Research* (February, 1952), Ch. 5.

records of various types, bulletins on innumerable individual topics and problems. The new term is primary, with "course of study" used as a subordinate item. The change is not merely one of terminology but represents an important change in educational thought. The concept of the course of study as it has been used for many decades might well pass out of our thinking.

The typical *course of study* as we have known it for decades consists usually of a subject-matter outline. Early courses often stopped with this; later ones have increasingly included some suggested learning activities, teaching procedures, diagnostic devices, and evaluational techniques. The subject matter was regarded as essential. Everyone from parents to pupils believed that the subject matter must be "mastered," that is, memorized. The heading within the printed course often was the "prescribed" subject matter. Early courses went further, prescribing the day-by-day amounts of subject matter to be covered, specifying the number of minutes per day to be devoted to the segments, and listing the specific fact questions to be used. This concept of the course of study was deserted long ago by many. The development of new kinds of courses is increasing rapidly, even though the older type is still widely used. One large city issued a new course of the older strait-jacket type but it is almost unique among current publications.

The traditional type of course was based upon the educational philosophy which regarded the aim of education as the preparation of the child for adult life through use of adult selected and arranged subject matter. Courses of study of this type have actually hindered education as we have come to understand it in modern times. The materials selected and assigned by adults to given school levels were often not easily comprehensible to the children at those levels. Connections between the interest and abilities of the pupils could be made only with difficulty or not at all. The natural re-

sult has been memorizing and verbalism, the opposites of functional learning.[5]

A pertinent commentary by Biddick summarizes this.[6]

Often such a course (even when the teacher has been permitted the greatest possible freedom in its use) has tempted him to unduly influence pupils to "choose" study subjects that do not truly relate to their interests and needs. Then there was always the fear of being criticized for having failed to "cover" the course of study, or of jeopardizing the security of pupils in their later work. In the study of a problem of importance teachers were often tempted to get outside of "their fields," but were called back by the fear of "trespassing" on the subject areas of others. In short, they were thwarted in their desire to be of real service to their pupils.

In many schools the net result of this has been that teaching guides—materials designed to aid the teacher in deciding what and how to teach—have ceased to be of much help. The burden which this has placed upon the teacher has been tremendous. Further, it has left many teachers with a very serious sense of insecurity —of having nothing to fall back upon or to work from. Many teachers and principals have asked for some new type of guide that would not check them in their desire to meet the real needs of pupils—indeed something that would help to set them on their way.

New forms of printed or stencil-reproduced materials to aid teachers are appearing widely and in ever increasing quantity. The concept that the school can best prepare for adult life through guiding the pupil as he lives and grows is becoming dominant. The understandings, attitudes and appreciations, abilities and skills which the pupil needs *now* in the solution of his *current* problems, turn out to be similar to those which he will need *later* in solving *adult* problems. Understandings, attitudes, and abilities needed in adult

[5] For expanded treatment of these ideas see William H. Burton, *The Guidance of Learning Activities,* 2nd ed. (New York, Appleton-Century-Crofts, 1952), Chs. 1-5, 10, 11-13. L. Thomas Hopkins, *Interaction* (Boston, Heath, 1941). Use the index.

[6] Mildred L. Biddick, *The Preparation and Use of Source Units* (New York, Progressive Education Association, no date, probably 1940), pp. 2-3.

life begin their growth in the nursery and are developed through continuing experiences until the learner emerges into adult life. The narrow outline of "prescribed" subject matter is replaced by a wealth of suggested materials and experiences. *Modern guides for teachers,* far from minimizing subject matter, suggest far more of it better adapted to use by pupils and classes of varying levels of ability and of interest.

Modern courses of study materials, paradoxically, are not called courses of study. The one-bulletin type of guide is giving way to many publications of various types. The various bulletins may be on the teaching of various subjects, on the organization of experience units with subject lines disregarded, on the characteristics of the children who are doing the learning. Bulletins and source units may describe and illustrate great numbers of varied learning experiences, of teaching procedures, of ways of using many different types and amounts of subject matter; may contain sources of instructional aids, and of evaluational techniques. Extensive bibliographies may be presented. Still other documents give definite suggestions for the construction of units, of evaluational techniques, or other items of similar nature.

The purpose of modern documents developed by and for teachers is to stimulate the teacher to evolve his own organizations and procedures, that is, to develop a curriculum suited to his particular group of learners within a given community setting. Even yet, however, the textbook dominates classroom procedure. A teacher trained to study children and who understands the nature of learning experiences will be able to choose, to eliminate, to adapt materials and experiences to the needs of the learners. This activity will in turn contribute to the development of better documentary materials.

The chief forms in which new documents for teachers appear are so far:

1. Courses of study as we have known them but greatly improved as to content, organization, and aim.

2. Source units, sometimes called course of study units, resource materials.
3. Guides to child development.
4. Curriculum records of various types such as logs of units developed, diary accounts, illustrative teaching units, and the like.

These major types, which are usually organized into a sequence from kindergarten through high school, are supplemented by numerous supplementary documents, sometimes called course-of-study bulletins but which might better be known as documentary aids to teachers. Illustrative titles include:

The Aim and Philosophy (or Viewpoint) of Our Schools.
New Concepts of Elementary Education.
A Design for Curriculum Development.
The Growth and Development of Children.
Characteristics of Children at Developing Maturity Levels.
The Community as a Setting for Learning (or as a Source for Problems and Materials of Learning).
Audio-Visual Aids Available in Our Schools.
The Junior Primary. Other titles are Getting Ready for School; —And So to School; Curriculum Guides for Five- and Six-Year Old Learners.
Creative Art for Little Children.
The Technique of Group Discussion.
Assisting Teachers to Make the Transition from Traditional to Modern Methods.
Planning a Daily Program under Modern Principles.
Schedule-Making in the Secondary Schools.
The Special Problems of the One-Room Rural Schools.
Public Relations as an Aid to Improving the Curriculum.

The chief type of document replacing the typical course of study. The most widely developed of the new materials is the *source* or *resource unit.* The following criteria may be used.

A source unit is [7]

1. Organized around a problem or need in some area of living or, in less advanced situations, around a subject-matter area. It is not

---

[7] For details of some of these organizations see Biddick, *op. cit.,* p. 5; Hopkins, *op cit.* Use index for several references.

prepared for a given class, often not for a given grade. It provides a wide range of materials and experiences useful in meeting the wide range of interests and abilities within any one grade or several adjacent grades.

2. Filled with far more subject matter and many more activities than one class could ever use. It is not a prescribed outline of limited subject matter, or rigid day-by-day procedure, but rather a provocative source of suggestions for the teacher. It is a source of many diverse teaching units developed by teacher and pupils.

3. Developed by a local group and adapted to the situation which produced it. The local group may be the faculty of one school, or of a group of schools. A series of source units in continuity is produced by a city, county, or state, with wide participation of many local units.

4. Not built to a specific pattern, though several similar general organizations are in use.

The curriculum *guides to child development* are similar but usually cover more than one source unit does. Descriptions of children at different levels of maturity, discussions of the nature of growth, suggestions for adjusting the school to the child are found. This information is sometimes found in the source unit as well. The guides usually present also a sequence of possible learning experiences over two or three grades, or for several teaching units within a grade, or for several learning groups not separated rigidly into grade levels.

The *curriculum records* of various types are written accounts of the actual sequences as they developed with a given group of learners. These, together with *illustrative*

teaching units, are increasingly popular as aids to the teacher.

The better school systems are moving steadily toward supplying not a "course of study" but a wealth of continuing documentary materials based upon the observed or expressed needs of the group. Sincere efforts made to improve the older type courses of study will nearly always lead to the adoption of the new procedures.

The *improvement of a curriculum* and of a *course* are not one and the same thing. Improvement of the curriculum necessitates bringing about changes in many persons and factors operating within the setting for learning. This is accomplished through a long-time study of the major factors entering into the instructional program. Improving the curriculum is not achieved through rewriting the course of study.

Improvement of course materials, documentary aids to teachers, is actually improvement in writing and editing materials which have been derived from instructional activities. The course materials have all too commonly been thought of as the basis for the curriculum. The course is produced first and the curriculum based upon it. The opposite is the sound procedure: develop a curriculum and then produce a course, or, rather, extensive materials for the teacher. Even more accurately, the improvement of curriculums and of courses is an interactive and reciprocal process. The guiding principle is: Determine needs of teacher and learners and prepare related guides to aid them.

Section 1

GENERAL METHODS FOR EVALUATING THE CURRICULUM

The study of a specific curriculum may be approached in either of two ways. Evaluations may be based upon:

1. Observations of a given curriculum in operation.
2. Applying criteria in the analysis and evaluation of the documents made available for teachers such as courses of study, source units,

guides to child development, curriculum records of various types, bulletins on innumerable individual topics and problems.

The two methods are interrelated and are usually carried on together in a given situation. The details of method will be discussed separately, Section 1 being given to procedures for studying the curriculum in operation, and Section 2 containing methods for the analysis of documents.

The analysis of a curriculum in operation is difficult because the curriculum is a moving, shifting, dynamic process. It cannot be handled, it cannot be stopped for analysis at leisure. It must be observed as it moves by. Data must be gathered from this stream of experiences, and judgments based thereon. The log or diary account of classroom events is a valuable aid to judgment even though it is static and of necessity incomplete. Experimental comparisons between curriculums can be made provided that in interpreting results, the influence of many variables and outside factors is recognized. Seeing the events happen, interpreting them in the light of known facts in educational science, and of the implications of democratic philosophy, is the general method.

Evaluation of a curriculum is effected by:

1. Analysis of the educational product as shown by tests, behavior records, interviews, questionnaires, follow-ups.

2. Analysis of learning products obtained from different curriculums experimentally compared.

3. Analysis of the degree to which the curriculum has been affected favorably or unfavorably by certain extraneous factors (legal requirements, fixed examinations, public pressures, research, tradition, social changes, professional leadership, and others).

4. Analysis of the general activities of teachers and of the use made of resources within the setting for learning.

5. Noting the effects of the curriculum program upon the professional activities of teachers, and upon the community.

6. Analysis of the methods used, if any, to develop a program of curriculum improvement.

Evaluation is continuous and participation should be complete. Study of the curriculum should be going on continuously as a regular part of the school operation. Study and improvement of curriculums should be in fact the chief in-service growth activity within a school system. Everyone has a role to play, both in scrutiny of the current program and in production of new materials and provision of better experiences. Administrators and supervisors, principals, teachers, pupils, laymen, and outside specialists and consultants should all participate.

Evaluation through analysis of the education products. Test results, usually casual and fragmentary, it will be recalled, are often an initiating factor in an evaluation program. A comprehensive testing program may also be one of the first and most direct evaluational procedures used. Growth of the learner in personal-social-moral traits (understandings, attitudes, appreciations, values, abilities) and achievement of fact and skill learning typically associated with school subjects will be extensively surveyed. Numerous and varied achievement tests, observational and anecdotal records of behavior, projection techniques, and creative productions are used to secure a wide sampling of results. The results revealed by these measures are products of several factors. Interpretations must therefore take into account the general level of ability among the learners, the socio-economic status of the community, the influence of home and neighborhood, and other factors. Many of these are susceptible of reasonably precise description. A testing program, when properly supplemented and interpreted, is a legitimate and revealing method of evaluating a curriculum.

Sometimes the use of tests may grow out of a preliminary scrutiny of a course of study. We believe on inspection that there are weaknesses. Tests are then used to corroborate or to alter our impressions.

The use of tests, behavior records for controlled and uncontrolled situations, and subjective methods was treated at length in Chapter 9 and need not be summarized here.

The curriculum is examined finally to see wherein it may be responsible for desirable results, for poor outcomes, or for downright deficiencies in the product.

Evaluation through examination of promotional policy. Closely related to the foregoing are studies of age-grade-progress within a school. Promotional policy and practice may be an aid to learning or it may be a hindrance. It may or may not be in accord with the educational policy of the school, hence may be working for or against the curriculum as it stands. In general, a continuous progress policy on elementary levels will provide for better learning than will a rigid graded system. Arbitrary failure imposed on pupils by conditions beyond their control should be replaced by experiences which show young children how to meet and solve problems through their own efforts.

The introduction of a continuous progress [8] policy into a curriculum geared to a graded system, without distinction between types of learnings, makes for incredible muddle. Continuous progress is impossible in an unreconstructed and undiscriminated curriculum. Distinction must be made between skill learnings and what may be called the personal-social-moral learnings. Learners differ widely in the rate at which they acquire skills. Within reasonable limits, learners should have the opportunity to make continuous progress at their own rates. Learners differ also in the ways and rates at which they achieve understandings, attitudes, appreciations, and the like. Furthermore, there is no necessity that all achieve the same level of insight; in fact, they cannot. Skill learnings may be handled individually; the other types are developed in group activity. The modern unit method provides ideal conditions for the working together of learners who differ in many ways. The learning of skills is motivated by good unit work but the ideal method for handling this is unknown.

When the learner reaches the level of exploratory courses and specialized subjects leading to eventual vocational or professional training, the situation changes fundamentally. The standard of success or failure lies clearly outside the pupil. The standard is now the achievement of certain knowledges, attitudes, and skills which are demonstrably necessary for success in given vocations or professions. Levels may now be set within the preparatory subjects which the mature pupil must attain or fail. This change in policy of promotion affects the curriculum, particularly in its scope and sequence. Further discussion will be found in Chapter 14.

Much muddled thinking about the curriculum results from applying a standard and policy of promotion, which is wholly sensible in special education, to general education where it is senseless.

Evaluation through studies of drop-outs, through follow-up inquiries, and through opinion polls. Many studies can be made both in relation to the types of study indicated above, and as direct evaluations in themselves. A sampling is indicated below.

Studies of *holding power,* sometimes called studies of *drop-outs,* will reveal several specific shortcomings in the academic curriculum, in the vocational offerings, in extracurricular opportunities, in methods of instruction, and other phases of the school life. This type of appraisal may initiate a program of curriculum change, as we indicate in Chapter 16. Meanwhile it is an excellent evaluational device. A reduction in number of drop-outs may reveal that the program and curriculum improvement is proving effective.

BOYER, Phillip A., DESING, Minerva F., and LAIRD, Mary A., "Conditions Affecting the Guidance Program," *Review of Educational Research* (April, 1951), pp. 89-90. Reports studies from Denver, Detroit, Louisville, and Syracuse, and from West Virginia.

DILLON, Harold J., *Early School Leavers* (New York, National Child Labor Committee, 1949).

HAND, Harold, FINLAY, Filbert C., and DOLIO, Ardwin J., "Illinois Inventory of Pupil Opinion," in Harold Hand, *What People Think of Their Schools* (Yonkers, World Book, 1948), pp. 171-194.

[8] An excellent definition and brief explanation of continuous progress is found in Willard S. Elsbree and Harold J. McNally, *Elementary School Administration and Supervision* (New York, American Book, 1951), Ch. 10. See also bibliography of the same chapter. Good periodical literature is also available.

How to Conduct a Holding Power Study, Bulletin No. 3, Illinois Secondary School Curriculum Program (Springfield, Ill., State Superintendent of Public Instruction, 1949). This is an outline in complete detail of the procedures.

Summaries on both the instrument for study and on results can be obtained in mimeographed form from a number of school systems.

Studies of *holding power*, or *drop-outs*, should be combined with *follow-up* investigations both of those who dropped out of school and those who were graduated. Results must be interpreted with due regard for the human errors in memory, the halo effect of memory, and for the students' present status after several years out of school.

The many "youth studies" made during and immediately after the depression years contain much information similar to that derived from studies of holding power and from follow-ups. Similar analyses may be made on a small scale.

The Illinois Secondary Curriculum Program made a number of other studies which have direct bearing upon evaluating the program and with indirect implications relating to the community.

How to Conduct the Hidden Tuition Costs Study, Bulletin No. 4.
How to Conduct the Study of the Guidance Services of the School, Bulletin No. 5.
How to Conduct the Participation in Extra-Class Activities Study, Bulletin No. 5.

The use of data revealed by these studies is obvious, both for evaluating the curriculum and for initiating further improvement.

The use of *opinion polls* or surveys of opinion has been increasing in various phases of public life. The names Gallup and Roper are familiar to most citizens in this connection. A good bibliography exists which outlines the construction and use of "opinion-aires," together with their shortcomings and errors in interpretations.

CANTRIL, Hadley, *Gauging Public Opinion* (Princeton, Princeton Univ. Press, 1944).

GALLUP, George, *A Guide to Public Opinion Polls* (Princeton, Princeton Univ. Press, 1948).
LARRABEE, Harold A., *Reliable Knowledge* (Boston, Houghton, 1945), pp. 427-432. Excellent brief analysis.
PARTEN, M. P., *Surveys, Polls, and Samples: Practical Procedures* (New York, Harper, 1950).
POWELL, N. J., *Anatomy of Public Opinion* (New York, Prentice-Hall, 1951).
University of Denver, National Opinion Research Center. Various publications.
University of Iowa, *Iowa Conference on Attitude and Opinion Research* (Boston, Holt, 1949).
University of Michigan, Survey Research Center, *Measuring Public Attitudes*. Paper, 1951.

Opinion polls about the curriculum are made by asking parents, other laymen, school administrators or supervisors, teachers, and pupils to state their beliefs. Statements of opinion are not entirely reliable nor are they wholly valid evaluations of anything, but when carefully gathered from earnest individuals they do supply some guidance, especially when checked against other analyses. Many states, cities, and survey centers have constructed their own. The Michigan State Department,[9] for instance, had a four-page questionnaire developed by a committee of laymen and educational workers to deal with current criticisms of the schools. Four sample questions are given from this document, *How Would You Answer This?*

1. In your opinion, are today's youngsters who have finished grammar school as well educated as those you knew when you were a child?
2. How about those who graduate from high school nowadays—do you believe they are as well educated as high school youngsters were when you were of that age?
3. Some people have the feeling that *too many* new ideas, experiments and changes are made in the schools of today. Do you agree?
4. How do you feel about today's teachers? Do you consider them well-trained and up-to-date?

[9] Lee M. Thurston, *How Would You Answer This?* (Lansing, Mich., State Department of Public Instruction, 1951).

The Center for Field Studies at the Harvard Graduate School of Education developed an instrument similar to that of the Michigan Department. Still others are available, as listed later. Samples from the Harvard questionnaire are:

7. Some pupils have difficulty in learning to read. Would you favor a special program to improve the reading of these children?
    1. I do not feel that such a program should be provided.
    2. I am undecided.
    3. I feel such a program should be provided.
    4. I strongly feel that such a program should be provided.

12. What is your opinion as to the value of school activities such as sports, music, and plays?
    1. I feel they are very valuable.
    2. I feel they are valuable.
    3. I feel that their value is limited.
    4. I feel that they have no value.

21. Do you believe that reading, writing, and arithmetic should occupy all of the elementary school day?
    1. Decidedly, yes.
    2. Probably.
    3. I don't know.
    4. Probably not.
    5. Decidedly, no.

The word *think* or *believe* would be an improvement over the word *feel* in these questionnaires. Other minor improvements can be made.

Probably the most easily obtainable source of such instruments, together with discussion of their construction and use, is:

HAND, Harold, *What People Think of Their Schools* (Yonkers, World Book, 1948). In addition to excellent discussion of the values, limitations, shortcomings, construction and uses of opinion polls, this booklet contains illustrative inventories of parent opinion, teacher opinion, and pupil opinion on upper-elementary level and secondary level.

Other instruments [10] of this type which have been used in other places are:

What Do We Know about Our Schools? Questions raised by some 200 people as they themselves have become involved in studying their schools. Published by the National Citizens Commission for the Public Schools, 2 West 45th Street, New York 19, N. Y., 1951. 15¢ each.

15 Ways To Find Out. A list of 15 questions proposed by Wilbur A. Yauch in his article, "How Good Are Your Schools?" *American Magazine* (September, 1951).

Just a Second. A questionnaire which purports to find out, "How would you do it if you had the job of planning the very best schooling for your boys and girls?" Published by the National School Service Institute, Chicago, Ill. 2¢ each.

How Good Are Your Schools? Presents six qualities as the basis for evaluating your schools, and describes three levels—Grade C, Grade B, and Grade A—of desirability for each of the six. Prepared by William G. Carr of the NEA and distributed by the National Citizens Commission for the Public Schools, 2 West 45th Street, New York 19, New York. 10¢ each.

Schools Are What We Make Them, A Handbook for Citizens. Presents a check-list to help you judge how much you know about your schools. Offers suggestions as to the kinds of things you should know and where to get some of the answers. Prepared by the NEA Research Division and published by Bell and Howell Co., 7100 McCormick Road, Chicago 45, Illinois. Single copy free.

Characteristics of a Good School. Presents in question form standards for evaluating a school, its facilities, its staff, and its program. Pamphlet No. 7 of School Board Reference Library. Prepared for and distributed by the Illinois Association of School Boards, First National Bank Building, Springfield, Illinois. 35¢ each.

How Good Is Your School? A "test" of 63 questions prepared by *Life* magazine as a practical way to measure the education children are getting. *Life* (October 6, 1950).

These instruments aid school administrators to gauge the general climate of opinion with which schools have to deal.

Another general instrument of value is in the booklet,[11] "How Can We Help Get Better Schools," published by the National Citizens Committee for the Public Schools.

---

[10] *American School Curriculum,* Thirty-first Yearbook, American Association of School Administrators (Washington, NEA, 1953), p. 350.
[11] 2 West 45th St., New York 19, N. Y.

The experimental evaluation of curriculums. Careful comparative evaluations between curriculums in terms of learning products achieved are rare. One of the first, if not the first, was Collings' extensive experiment published under the title, *An Experiment with the Project Curriculum.*[12] A modern experience type of curriculum was developed and used for four years with one group of children. A traditional subject curriculum was taught by traditional methods to a matched control group. Typical subject-matter mastery tests were given to both groups at the conclusion of the period. This was an early study and some criticism arose about controls and type of evaluation. The experiment and its results are, nevertheless, significant and have had marked effect upon teaching and curriculum-making. Results were significantly in favor of the new curriculum.

A more extensive study was made by Oberholtzer[13] in Houston, Texas, in which an "integrated" or modern type of curriculum was compared with a traditional one. Entire curriculums were compared, but controlled comparisons were made in fourth and fifth grades with 73 teachers and 1662 pupils. The method was that of comparison between matched experimental and control groups. Evaluations were based on typical tests of achievement, on the expressed reactions of teachers, pupils, parents, and principals. The modern curriculum secured equal or better achievement in typical fundamentals; provided more enrichment; more time for problem-solving; and more participation in other activities. The thinking, interest, and enthusiasm of pupils and teacher were favorably affected.

One of the most extensive studies of curriculum is the so-called Eight-Year Study in which more than 3000 students were followed through four years of high school and four of college. A number of colleges agreed to accept, from thirty selected secondary schools, graduates recommended as fit for college work but who had not covered the standard "college entrance" subjects or requirements. The thirty schools, freed from these requirements, were encouraged to develop curriculums fitted to student needs. Variation was great, as would be expected. The traditional curriculum persisted in many, while other schools developed curriculums which differed fundamentally from the standard college preparatory sequence. Comparisons were made of college records for over 3000 students, divided between the experimental and the formal schools. The general technique was that of comparison between matched groups and between matched pairs of students. Items evaluated were: subject-matter achievement indicated by marks; study habits; participation in college activities; clarity of objectives and ability to plan own program; intellectual hobbies; creative and esthetic experiences; and others. Students passing through the modernized curriculums were definitely superior in many points, slightly superior or equal in others, and inferior in two items. The accounts of this significant experiment are contained in five volumes which should certainly be known to all school leaders.[14]

An experiment similar to the Eight-Year Study was carried on for six years in New York City with the elementary schools. A total of 75,000 pupils in 69 elementary buildings was involved. Approximately one-half the schools continued to use the standard formal subject curriculum, while one-

[12] Ellsworth Collings, *An Experiment with the Project Curriculum* (New York, Macmillan, 1923).

[13] Edison E. Oberholtzer, *An Integrated Curriculum in Practice,* Contributions to Education No. 694 (New York, Teachers College, Bureau of Publications, Columbia Univ., 1937).

[14] The general title for the five volumes is *An Adventure in American Education.* The separate volumes published between 1942 and 1945 are: I. *The Story of the Eight-Year Study;* II. *Exploring the Curriculum;* III. *Appraising and Recording Student Progress;* IV. *Did They Succeed in College?;* V. *Thirty Schools Tell Their Story* (New York, Harper, 1942-1945).

Considerable periodical literature is also available, some of it highly critical of the study.

half were given a modern experience curriculum in so far as materials and levels of teacher training permitted. A number of technical articles based on this study have appeared, but most are difficult reading.[15] An excellent simple account appears in *Progressive Education* for April, 1944.[16] The final account in lively readable form is contained in the volume *The Activity Curriculum,* issued by the State Department of Education, Albany, New York. The State Department was invited to make the evaluational survey of the experiment, hence published the final report.

Evidences of the superiority of the modern curriculum were found in increased professional spirit, better supervision, increasing understanding and co-operation from the lay public, better materials, better buildings, a continuing interest in curriculum improvement, not to mention distinctly superior achievement by pupils.

An excellent summary of individual studies, all of which bear upon experimental comparisons between curriculums, will be found in *An Evaluation of Modern Education,*[17] by J. Paul Leonard and Alvin C. Eurich.

Another early study,[18] somewhat similar to the two preceding experiments, showed interesting variations in procedure. One group of children who had come through first and second grade with "traditional" methods was given a "progressive" program in grades 3 and 4. Another group was continued under "traditional" methods for all four grades. Comparisons were then made in grades 5 and 6. The experimental group generally showed superiority over the control or "traditional" group, in all academic achievement testing. Both groups were also observed for the appearance of some thirty-eight "trait-actions," such as co-operation, exercising initiative, displaying resourcefulness, and others. Observations for these traits were distributed over different types of classroom work, such as problem-solving, drill, creative work, planning, directed study, and before-school periods. Tests at the beginning of the experiment in grade 5 showed the experimental group to be superior in all thirty-eight traits but with significant differences in only fourteen.

At the conclusion of grade 6 the experimental group was significantly superior in thirty-four of the traits. All details are not reported, hence the findings are not conclusive, but they are clearly suggestive and stimulating.

Wrightstone[19] made extensive investigations of the curriculums and classroom practices of elementary and high schools, under his designation of "newer-type" and "conventional" programs. We need not go into details. The general results were as in the studies already quoted. The same criticisms were made as of other early studies, that is, that all details were not controlled, all data are not adequately described. Nevertheless, these studies as a group give us provocative evidence of differences between curriculums, and they have stimulated other more sharply controlled studies.

Still another variation in type of investigation is found in the study by Knight and Mickelson[20] in which the subject-centered

[15] *Review of Educational Research* (June, 1942), p. 282, gives references to ten or more articles on the New York City Experiment.

[16] John J. Loftus, "Learning Comes to Life: New York City's New Program of Elementary Education," *Progressive Education* (April, 1944), pp. 186-189. Note references there to New York City bulletins.

[17] J. Paul Leonard and Alvin C. Eurich, eds., *An Evaluation of Modern Education* (New York, Appleton-Century-Crofts, 1942).

[18] F. A. Pistor, "Evaluating Newer School Practices by the Observational Method," in Sixteenth Yearbook, Department of Elementary School Principals (Washington, NEA, 1937), pp. 377-389.

[19] J. W. Wrightstone, *Appraisal of Newer Elementary School Practices* (New York, Bureau of Publications, Teachers College, Columbia Univ., 1938).

———, *Appraisal of Experimental High School Practices (ibid.,* 1936).

[20] S. S. Knight and J. M. Mickelson, "Problems vs. Subjects," *The Clearing House* (September, 1949), pp. 3-7.

and the problem-centered methods of instruction were compared. This does not give us comparative data between types of curriculum organization but compares two methods of organizing and teaching within the subject curriculum. Four subject areas were used: English literature, English composition, life science, and social studies. Details aside, the results favored the problem-centered type of organization and teaching.

Evaluation of the curriculum in the light of certain favorable and unfavorable extraneous circumstances. Adequate and valid judgments cannot be made merely by looking at the results achieved. We must also take note of certain powerful factors which influence, sometimes coerce, curriculum makers. The factors working within complex social situations are never wholly positive nor wholly negative. An item may be positive in one era and place, negative elsewhere. The long-time weight of most factors can be seen however to be chiefly positive or chiefly negative.[21] The next few pages will list these factors and comment upon their influence.

Factors which maintain the status quo and generally retard progress. Through insistence upon certain entrance requirements, *colleges and higher schools* have seriously retarded wholesome improvements in the curriculums of the lower schools. We may note here that several factors to be discussed overlap and interlock in many ways. The *college entrance* requirements are in turn partially the product of the older *faculty psychology,* with its emphasis upon *mental discipline* through formal exercises. The earlier social usefulness of the required subjects has been almost completely lost to sight. *Prestige* and *social approval* develop, which in turn support the entrenched curriculum against the demands for needed improvement. Eventually a *tradition* develops which makes the task of improvement more difficult than ever.

Let it be noted in passing that far too many secondary administrators and teachers use the "college entrance examinations" as an excuse for certain procedures in cur-riculum requirements and in methods of instruction that are not easy to justify. Individuals hiding behind this smoke screen are, many of them, refusing to consider the facts and to change methods of teaching in the light of the facts. Others may be naïvely ignorant of the great improvements made in recent years in the college entrance examinations. All the examinations have been brought more into accord with modern knowledge about learning and teaching, with one of the best illustrations to be found in the subject area of English. The requirements are, in general, two: comment in an informed manner on any piece of literature worth reading and commenting upon; write an acceptable piece of English composition on a subject of your own choosing. The requirements in some high schools, defended to the death by the faculty are, in the light of the true requirements, simply incredible.

Examinations—college entrance, eighth-grade, "regents," and the like—generally retard curriculum improvement. The use of standard tests alone as final measures may seriously restrict both curriculum and teaching procedures. Modern evaluation programs, directed at far more than fact and skill outcomes, should enhance curriculum improvement.

Textbooks in earlier times were a serious handicap; but in *modern times,* textbooks under the influence of modern psychology have been increasingly useful in curriculum improvement.

Boards of education in earlier times determined the course and hence the curriculum and were a strong influence against improvement. The surrender of many powers by the board has reduced their influence over the curriculum.

Tradition, despite the glamor often attached to the word, has been in general the

[21] The summary here is sharply abbreviated because of lack of space. Points are adapted from two or three important research studies which are noted in the bibliography, particularly those by Lawson, Miel, and Saylor.

most effective blockade to improvement of courses and curriculums. Several factors listed above often combine to form a tradition or to give added power to an established tradition.

Factors which exert positive or negative influence at different times and places. As a method of curriculum control, *legislation* is largely a nuisance. Power to select texts or content may be placed legally with certain boards or commissions. Certain subjects or parts of subjects may be forced into the curriculum by law: notably subject matter on the evil effects of alcohol and narcotics, formal citizenship training and rituals, certain desirable materials on health and physical education. Reading of the Bible is rigidly prohibited by law in some states; just as rigidly required in others. Responsive to momentary public pressures, legislation is unsystematic and capricious. History shows that legislative effort to determine curriculum content is unnecessary, and in many cases quite ineffective.

War as an influence is closely allied with legislation, since the one often results in the other. War usually expands curriculums temporarily to meet immediate demands. Wartime expansion in aviation, advanced mathematics, nursing, production and conservation of food are illustrations. Additions due to war often remain as permanent additions, for instance material in civics, citizenship, physical education, health, and so forth.

Public opinion has practically never initiated any important improvements of fundamental importance but it has often brought about minor changes, desirable and undesirable. Public opinion usually retards badly needed improvements but supports them vigorously once professional school leaders accomplish the reforms.

Factors which have in general significantly promoted the improvement of curriculums. The *superintendent,* especially in larger systems, seems to be the single most important agent in promoting curriculum improvement. Programs are initiated, in-

spired, financed, and protected by the superintendent or his professional staff. The climate necessary for growth is provided by this leadership. *State departments* of education are beginning to exercise leadership in the same manner.

Superintendents, at first, often had to overcome inertia and opposition within the staff. Certain individual superintendents, particularly in given regions are often the chief obstacles to all growth and improvement. The superintendency, however, is one of the powerful influences for progress. The *professional staff* shares in this, and in larger systems exercises much of the leadership. *Educational research,* which at first supported the status quo, has increasingly become a factor influencing growth. Research workers in early days were not always aware of unstated objectives and assumptions, hence tended to study existing procedures. Currently research workers aid in moving ahead from the status quo. A secondary achievement has been to aid in breaking down opposition which was due to ignorance of the facts.

Social change within our national life, political, social, or economic, is a factor difficult to assess but unquestionably of great importance. Prior to 1900 schools paid little attention to the emerging social order and its problems. The turn of the century saw growing sensitivity to the relationship between school and society. Explicit attention to this relationship and systematic attack has added to and expanded the curriculum considerably but seldom eliminated any materials.

Leaders, "frontier thinkers," have had considerable influence, since their writing usually reports and analyzes the social changes taking place. Attempts to predict future developments have had their influence.

Changing theories about learning have had both positive and negative influence, usually positive in modern times. The older faculty psychology, for instance, with emphasis upon mental discipline through formal exercises was (and still is) a serious obstacle to improvement. The modern psychology with its organismic concept of the learner and its dynamic interpretation of mind and of learning is beginning to exert a powerful influence for good.

The *practice of other school systems* has had great influence upon curriculum programs, at first operating to retard growth through emphasis upon frequency of practice, but latterly to accelerate growth through stimulation to critical comparison and analysis.

Teachers committees and associations, in the beginning of the modern curriculum movement, were vigorously opposed to any and all changes. This was due in part to honest but thoroughly mistaken beliefs about the value of certain subjects, to honest ignorance about the learner and his methods of learning. Teacher opposition to curriculum improvement is to this day still based upon ignorance of the facts. Opposition was also due to inertia, to unwillingness to give up cherished routines and vested interests. Teacher committees, as the curriculum movement got under way, came to participate and co-operate under direction but usually failed completely to see the implications. This was partly due to autocratic leadership. Teacher committees in modern times, particularly under democratic administrations, are increasingly becoming one of the most powerful factors not only in contributing to but in initiating desirable curriculum-improvement programs.

Agents and influences working from *within* the system seem to have far greater influence than those working from without.

Evaluation of the curriculum through analysis of the general activities of teachers and of the use made of resources within the setting for learning. The general technique is that of observing classroom procedure in the light of a summary of desirable and undesirable techniques so far as we know these. The typical instrument is a "list of items to observe" which is merely a memory aid and guide to observation. *Checklists are not rating scales.* The lists should be developed co-operatively by the educational workers using it. The items within the list thus become a commonly agreed upon summary of significant items and a basis for common discussion of observed classroom events. The amount of detail may vary greatly: one list containing a small number of major items; another going into precise detail about some or all phases of classroom procedure.

Literally scores of such instruments are available in the literature and in bulletins issued by school systems. The construction of such a list is an excellent in-service project. These lists and other instruments will be illustrated freely in the immediately following pages. Each of them, used here for curriculum analysis, is also a typical instrument for evaluation and appraisal of outcomes of learning. Cross reference should constantly be made to similar instruments in Chapters 8 and 9.

The type of data derived through use of these instruments affords considerable insight into some of the factors which affect the curriculum. The printed materials, notably the "course of study," exert large control over the teachers' classroom procedures. Administrative and supervisory officers who insist that teachers "follow the course" further enhance the control of materials over the teacher. A teacher who must "cover the text," must teach designated facts, must develop designated levels of skill, shows this influence unmistakably in his classroom procedures. The curriculum may be dominated by printed materials and by decisions of superior officers rather than guided by the needs of learners and of the community, and by adjustment to ability levels.

The type of documents developing in current times paradoxically controls the teacher by giving him freedom. The teacher using modern printed materials does not "cover" them, does not follow a prescribed sequence. He selects, adapts, and invents, stimulated by the wealth of materials and experiences given him. This is reflected in classroom procedure.

The Mort-Cornell Guide for Self-Appraisal of School Systems. This is an exten- sive general list covering much ground. Several items not found in other lists appear. The form of the questions used is also of interest. The following sample illustrates the instrument:[22]

1. CLASSROOM INSTRUCTION

A. THE CURRICULUM

1. *Flexibility of Curriculum.* The curriculum is sufficiently flexible to provide for individual pupil interests and abilities and to permit teachers to exercise their judgment and initiative in the choice and arrangement of activities, subject-matter and method.

Totals: YES . . . . . .   NO . . . . . .

a. *Teaching periods.* On the elementary level, part of the teacher's daily schedule should be organized in terms of long periods for broad subject matter fields as well as short periods for teaching specific skills or minor divisions of subject matter. The teacher should be free to modify her teaching periods as need arises.   YES* . . . .   NO* . . . .

Q. May I see your daily schedule? How closely do you follow it? Why?

Interview: Principal, Teachers.
Observe: Teacher's daily schedule.
Evidence . . . .
. . . .
. . . .

1. Most periods are at least 45 minutes in length.   Yes . . . . .   No . . . . .
2. The type of work within the longer periods may vary from day to day.   Yes . . . . .   No . . . . .
3. Teachers have been told that they are not expected to follow a schedule rigidly.   Yes . . . . .   No . . . . .

b. *Supplementary materials.* A variety of reference books and materials should be available for each subject or project whether in classrooms or in special rooms.   YES . . . . .   NO . . . . .

Q. What supplementary and reference materials are available for use by your class? Where are they kept and where used?

Interview: Teacher, Principal.
Observe: Books in room,
         Pamphlets, Supplies.
Evidence . . . .
. . . .
. . . .
. . . .
. . . .
. . . .
. . . .
. . . .
. . . .

1. There are encyclopedias for children in the elementary classrooms.   Yes . . . . .   No . . . . .
2. There are several sets of social studies books in the upper grade rooms or a large variety of single copies.   Yes . . . . .   No . . . . .
3. Crayons, water colors, and large sheets of paper are available in elementary classrooms.   Yes . . . . .   No . . . . .
4. A set of reference books pertinent to the subject being studied is available in high-school classrooms.   Yes . . . . .   No . . . . .

* YES-NO (in capitals) to be determined from weight of evidence as revealed by answers to the accompanying sub-items.

[22] Paul R. Mort and Francis G. Cornell, *A Guide for Self-Appraisal of School Systems* (New York, Teachers College, Bureau of Publications, Columbia Univ.. 1937).

5. Teachers are collecting and filing pamphlets, magazines and other materials useful in teaching their respective subjects.   Yes..... No.....

c. *Pupil freedom.* Elementary pupils should be reasonably free to move about the room to consult dictionary and similar reference materials.   YES..... NO.....

Q. What rules do you have concerning pupil's moving about the room, whispering, etc.?

Interview: Teacher, Principal, Children.
Observe: Activity in the room.
Evidence ....
....
....
....
....
....

1. Pupils move about the room quietly and freely in consulting reference books.   Yes..... No.....
2. Pupils work together in groups.   Yes..... No.....
3. Not all pupils are doing the same type of work all the time.   Yes..... No.....

Pistor's analysis of democracy in the classroom. This instrument developed to study democracy in the classroom actually covers a wide range of curricular activities. The list contains 120 questions evenly distributed under 12 headings. One division is reproduced here as an illustration.[23]

1. *Curriculum Opportunities*

	Never	Seldom	Sometimes	Often	Always
a. Do the children and the teacher have freedom to select and to plan their work, being restricted only by very broad outlines of curriculum scope and sequence?	1	2	3	4	5
b. Are the pupils studying topics which are relatively important to them here and now, especially problems of their own class living?	1	2	3	4	5
c. Does the class program of living consist of a wide variety of experiences to challenge and interest pupils of various levels and types of intelligence?	1	2	3	4	5

	Never	Seldom	Sometimes	Often	Always
d. Do the pupils have good habits of work induced by real tasks and the satisfaction of doing them?	1	2	3	4	5
e. Does the work of the teacher center about the study and development of desirable pupil attitudes and habits rather than merely the teaching of lessons?	1	2	3	4	5
f. Is drill work in the tool subjects individualized to the extent that no two pupils in the room must practice the same things during a given period?	1	2	3	4	5
g. Are there many experiences with unstructured materials (clay, paints, cloth, wood, etc.) for pupils to pattern in accordance with their individual values and modes of organiza-					

[23] Frederick Pistor, "Practicing Democracy in the Classroom," Experimental Edition, No. 3 (New York, Hunter College), mimeographed material.

	Never	Seldom	Sometimes	Often	Always
tion, thus giving opportunities for teacher study of personality patterns?	1	2	3	4	5
h. Do the children organize and work in many flexible, temporary, and natural groups as the program develops, thus affording many opportunities for teacher study and guidance of pupils?	1	2	3	4	5
i. Is the situation such that the pupils demand and develop greater proficiency in the use of the skills as they need them?	1	2	3	4	5
j. Do the pupils have part of the day to work alone on their individual problems or at their individual interests?	1	2	3	4	5

Total Value of
This Section

The Metropolitan School Study Council Guides. Another instrument uses questions differing in form from the preceding lists. A booklet, widely known as "the blue book," contains 57 pages of questions, 37 of which bear upon the course of study and the curriculum. Two divisions are reproduced here as illustrations.[24]

HOW ARE THE SCHOOLS TEACHING CHILDREN THE TOOLS OF LEARNING —READING, SPEECH, WRITING, NUMBERS AND OTHER SKILLS?

A. *What is included in the reading program?*

1. The reading program includes:

a. Practice in following written directions.	*	1	2	3
b. Practice designed to increase speed and comprehension in reading for thought.	*	1	2	3
c. The organization of each pupil's reading in terms of his interests and problems.	*	1	2	3
d. Experience in locating and reading material related to specific problems.	*	1	2	3
e. Opportunity for a wide variety of recreational reading encouraged by teachers.	*	1	2	3
f. Creation of many silent-reading situations on a variety of topics adapted to each individual.	*	1	2	3
g. Informal discussion of books read for pleasure.	*	1	2	3
h. Provision for reading experience related to activities outside of school, e.g., sports, camping, and gardening.	*	1	2	3
i. Oral reading in audience situations.	*	1	2	3
j. Critical reading.	*	1	2	3
k. Self-appraisal and improvement.	*	1	2	3
2. Training in the use of encyclopedias, dictionaries, and other reference books is made a part of the reading program.	*	1	2	3
3. Pupils learn to use tables of contents, indexes, glossaries and footnotes.	*	1	2	3
4. Silent-reading instruction is an integral part of all learning and is not taught as a skill for its own sake.	*	1	2	3
5. Silent reading is stressed more than oral reading in all grades.	*	1	2	3
6. Remedial instruction is provided for children who are retarded in reading skills.	*	1	2	3

[24] Paul R. Mort, Arvid J. Burke, and Robert S. Fish, *A Guide for the Analysis and Description of Public School Services* (New York, Metropolitan School Study Council, 1944), Part I, pp. 1-2.

7. A trained librarian assists in teaching pupils how to use the library.   * 1 2 3

8. There is a wide variety of reading materials including books, children's newspapers, and periodicals.   * 1 2 3

9. There is a reading clinic available in the school for pupils beyond the primary grades.   * 1 2 3

10. Classes frequently work in the library to gain firsthand experience in the use of the libraries and library resources.   * 1 2 3

B. *How is reading taught in the elementary schools?*

1. The teacher is familiar with scientific findings on reading instruction such as are published in the yearbooks of the National Society for the Study of Education.   * 1 2 3

2. A number of pre-primers are used in teaching beginning reading.   * 1 2 3

3. Many objects in primary grades have printed labels attached to them.   * 1 2 3

4. Picture dictionaries are found in primary grades; children's dictionaries are found in upper grades.   * 1 2 3

5. The diagnostic and remedial aspects of the reading program include:
   a. Measurement of speed in silent reading.   * 1 2 3
   b. Measurement of comprehension in silent reading.   * 1 2 3
   c. Vocabulary tests.   * 1 2 3
   d. Diagnosis of eye movements in silent reading.   * 1 2 3
   e. Determination of reading readiness:
   First grade   * 1 2 3
   Other grades   * 1 2 3
   f. Checking for visual and auditory defects.   * 1 2 3

6. Pupils are motivated to read:
   a. Through the provision of a wide variety of materials at every grade level.   * 1 2 3
   b. Through the provision of materials graded to the reading ability of each pupil   * 1 2 3

7. Children advance to more difficult reading material only after wide experience at the previous levels of attainment.   * 1 2 3

8. Material read for appreciation is not minutely analyzed.   * 1 2 3

9. Children are taught reading in groups or individually according to their rate of progress.   * 1 2 3

10. No pupils are lip reading while working at their seats.   * 1 2 3

11. Except in audience situations all reading is done silently.   * 1 2 3

12. Pupils measure their own progress in learning to read.   * 1 2 3

The Evaluative Criteria. A widely used instrument is the set of criteria prepared by the Co-operative Study of Secondary School Standards. The next three check-lists are samples from this collection of criteria.

I. GENERAL PRINCIPLES [25]

CHECK-LIST

The program of studies

( )   1. Is based upon an analysis of the educational needs of youth.

( )   2. Provides a wide variety of experiences to meet both the common and and individual educational needs of youth.

( )   3. Is planned to help meet both present and probable future needs of pupils.

( )   4. Provides opportunities for pupils as well as staff members to participate in the planning and development of curricular activities.

[25] *Evaluative Criteria,* 1950 ed. (Washington, Co-operative Study of Secondary-School Standards), p. 49. The blank numbers at various points are to allow for the addition of items relating to the local situation.

( ) 5. Provides for relating subject-matter fields to life problems of pupils.

( ) 6. Emphasizes critical and thoughtful approaches to present-day problems.

( ) 7. Provides opportunities for experiences especially adapted to the superior or advanced pupils.

( ) 8. Provides opportunities for experiences especially adapted to slow-learning pupils.

( ) 9. Provides organized sequences of courses carrying on through several grades.

( ) 10. Provides for co-ordination of educational experiences within each grade.

( ) 11. Places emphasis upon broad concepts taught for transfer value.

( ) 12. Is flexible in time allotments to meet individual pupil requirements (e.g., variation in number of periods for elective subjects, periods allotted to special-help and remedial work, or time devoted to pupil-initiated course work).

( ) 13. Provides for the evaluation of pupil achievement in the program in terms of each individual's aptitudes and abilities.

( ) 14. Recognizes the contributions made by the pupil activity program.

( ) 15. Encourages enlargement and enrichment of pupil's scope of interests.

( ) 16.

( ) 17.

Evaluations:

( ) a. How effectively are these general principles practiced in meeting the needs of youth of the community?

Comments:

B. Nature of Offerings [26]

CHECK-LIST

The program of studies provides

( ) 1. Opportunities for pupils to study themselves—their aptitudes, abilities, and interests.

( ) 2. Opportunities for the development of skills in reading, writing, speaking, and listening.

( ) 3. Opportunities for development of skill in foreign languages (reading, speaking, writing).

( ) 4. Opportunities for the development of mathematical skills and understandings necessary for daily living.

( ) 5. Experiences to meet the physical development needs of boys.

( ) 6. Experiences to meet the physical development needs of girls.

( ) 7. Experiences to meet the physical health needs of all pupils.

( ) 8. Experiences to meet the mental health needs of all pupils.

( ) 9. Preparation for homemaking and family living for girls.

( ) 10. Preparation for homemaking and family living for boys.

( ) 11. Experiences for pupils to become intelligent consumers of goods and services.

( ) 12. Experiences emphasizing preparation for, and participation in, citizenship activities.

( ) 13. Experiences which emphasize rights and responsibilities of citizens in a democracy.

( ) 14. Experiences planned to develop sound moral and ethical standards.

( ) 15. Experiences designed to meet aesthetic needs.

( ) 16. Experiences designed to meet leisure needs.

( ) 17. Vocational preparation related to the opportunities for beginning workers in the local community or surrounding area.

( ) 18. Work experiences co-ordinated with school experiences.

( ) 19. Preparation for education beyond the secondary school in a variety of areas.

( ) 20. Planned activities for appraising and evaluating the content and outcomes of the educational program.

( ) 21.

( ) 22.

Evaluations:

( ) a. How adequate is the nature of offerings in terms of the particular needs of individual pupils?

( ) b. How adequate is the nature of offerings in terms of the common needs of all pupils?

( ) c. How adequate is the nature of offerings to meet the needs of the community served?

Comments:

[26] Ibid., p. 52.

I. Organization [27]

CHECK-LIST

( )   1. The core program is required of all pupils.
(Indicate grades: _____.)

( )   2. Core classes meet a sufficient number of periods per week.
(The number of periods per week is _____.)

( )   3. Core class periods are of sufficient length.
(The length of period is _____ minutes.)

( )   4. A representative committee of both teachers and pupils assists in the over-all planning of the core program.

( )   5. Planning provides for co-ordination of instructional activities of the core program with different grade levels.

( )   6. Planning provides for co-ordination of instructional activities of core program with other areas of instruction on same grade level.

( )   7. The program is reorganized as necessary to meet new or changing needs of pupils.

( )   8. In-service training for staff members contributes to the improvement of the core program.

( )   9. Organization provides for pupils to participate in learning experiences outside the boundaries of the school building (e.g., field trips, community projects).

( ) 10.

( ) 11.

Evaluations:

( )   a. How extensive is the core program of this school?

( )   b. Do time allotments for the core program meet instructional needs satisfactorily?

( )   c. To what extent do the enrollments in the core program show that the needs of all the pupils for such experiences are being met? (Give enrollment data for the core program indicating name of course, normal grade level, and number of pupils in each grade enrolled for the current term.)

Comments:

The Texas Handbook for Self-Appraisal and Improvement of Elementary Schools.[28]

This is an instrument for elementary schools and is similar to the Evaluative Criteria prepared for secondary schools. Samples from the Texas Handbook appear on pages 388-391.

The Southern Association of Colleges and Secondary Schools Guide.[29] This instrument for evaluating the elementary school grew out of a co-operative study sponsored by the association, and is often referred to as "The Southwide Study." This publication has two features deserving special commendation. First, the use of "situation" for diagnosis; and second, the insistence on citation of evidence wherever questions are answered.

Under the general heading, Guiding Principles Concerning Values, the following is one of the illustrative incidents:

Situation E

While a sixth-grade group was studying South America, the discussion touched upon the meat packing industry. A pupil suggested that the class visit a local plant, and general approval followed. Much preparation took place: arrangements with the packing plant, plans for transportation, safety rules to observe, courteous things to do, reading about meat plants, and setting up things to look for and to learn. Parents were asked to become members of the group and to furnish transportation. The plant personnel had ample time to plan for the visit. A guide was provided who knew interesting facts and who also understood children.

After returning to the school a lively discussion followed which included sharing of facts, the evaluation of how well they had carried out their plans, and the determination of what they wanted to do next.

Some values contained in the situation. In this situation a cluster of values is evident— co-operative planning and working, studying facts which are related to daily living, developing an appreciation of the community and of work, bringing parents into school activities, and developing economic competence. The workers at the plant learned many things which

[27] *Ibid.,* p. 57.
[28] Austin, Texas, State Department of Education, 1948, rev., ed.
[29] *Evaluating the Elementary School: A Guide for Co-operative Study* (Atlanta (316 Peachtree St., N.E.), The Southern Association, 1951).

LEVEL I	LEVEL II	LEVEL III

C. WORKING WITH THE COMMUNITY ON SCHOOL-CENTERED PROJECTS

1. School administrators and teachers rarely if ever discuss school policies with laymen.	School administrators and teachers discuss school policies with laymen in answer to laymen's questions.	School policies are discussed irregularly and informally between school personnel and their personal friends.
2. Co-operation between school personnel and laymen concerning curriculum content is extremely limited.	Suggestions about curriculum needs are accepted by school people, but without any attempt to activate the suggestions.	Curriculum content may be discussed informally with laymen selected by the school personnel.
3. All school building planning is done by professional personnel only.	Suggestions about building plans are accepted from laymen, but without any attempt to apply the suggestions.	School officials may discuss building plans with a few lay citizens.
4. The community does not financially support experimentation beyond the bare essentials of the local school program.	No means are used to enlist financial support for experimental features of the school program.	Financial support for experimental features of the school program is dependent upon spasmodic fund-raising programs in the school and community.
5. School co-operation with other public agencies (libraries, health unit, etc.) is rarely ever initiated by school personnel because of fear of unnecessary entanglements.	Use of such public agencies as the library, health unit, etc., is left up to individual teachers, no administrative plan being made for such use.	Services of such public agencies as the public library and city-county health unit are spasmodic and infrequent, dependent largely upon special campaigns and drives.
6. Parents who offer their personal services to the school, such as assisting in field trips, etc., are rarely if ever, utilized.	Parents never are invited to give such personal services as help on field trips, office and library work, etc. to the school, but their aid may be accepted when offered.	Parents occasionally give such personal services as assisting in field trips, office and library work, temporary teaching to relieve the teacher for professional business, etc.

FOR SELF-APPRAISAL

LEVEL IV	LEVEL V	Notation on Major Needs and Next Steps for Improvement
Lay citizens are given a general invitation to make suggestions about school policies, but no procedure is set up to assure that these suggestions get official consideration.	A continuing advisory committee composed of both professional and lay members studies present and future needs of the school and helps to develop long-range plans.	
Laymen are invited to make suggestions about curriculum content and materials, but no procedure is set up to assure use of these suggestions.	Procedures are provided whereby laymen may suggest and help consider curriculum objectives and content in co-operation with professional personnel.	
Community citizens are invited to make suggestions about building plans, but no procedure is set up to assure consideration of these plans.	A definite plan provides for lay citizens to make suggestions when new school buildings are being planned. Community meetings, to which all citizens are invited, are held to discuss plans.	
Limited financial support for experimental features of the school program is provided by the parent-teacher association.	Educational experimentation in the schools is encouraged by sound financial support from lay organizations (parents' clubs, civic groups, etc.), and from private and semi-private foundations, but with final control in the hands of the legally-responsible public school officials.	
Services of such public agencies as the public library and city-county health unit are sought and encouraged by school officials, maximum use being limited only by lack of clearly-defined procedures.	Public agencies in the community aid the school in carrying out the educational program. Co-operation and interaction are continuous and in conformity with well-planned policies and procedures.	
Parents are invited to share in the work of the school, through voluntary personal services as assisting in field trips, etc., but few offer to help.	Parents and other qualified citizens frequently give the school such personal services as assisting in field trips, office and library work, temporary teaching to relieve the teachers for professional business, etc.	

LEVEL I	LEVEL II	LEVEL III

D. WORKING WITH THE COMMUNITY OR OTHER COMMUNITY PROJECTS

1. School people assume little or no leadership in the solution of community problems.	School personnel, as individuals, occasionally work with temporary committees in the solution of community problems, but have no plan for concentrated community action.	The school is represented on some type of continuing community council which constructively contributes to the solution of community problems in health, safety, recreation, etc.
2. School people give no recognition to community problems in intercultural relations.	School leaders recognize their responsibility for the improvement of intercultural relations, but have no continuing plan for attacking these problems.	School people occasionally discuss the problems of intercultural relations with interested lay citizens and groups.
3. Teachers and administrators do not admit the school's responsibility for meeting other than school problems of children as they may lead to maladjustment and delinquency.	Teachers and administrators admit the school's relation to problems which may lead to maladjustment and delinquency, but have no plans to cope with them.	Sporadic and disconnected projects are undertaken to meet children's out-of-school problems, but these projects lack a consistent philosophy and method.
4. The school's responsibility for community health is considered to consist in required courses in physiology and hygiene.	The school's responsibility for community health is considered to include health services for school children.	Occasional projects in community health are undertaken under school leadership, but without much continuity.
5. Either no adult-interest community projects (March-of-Dimes, Junior Red Cross, etc.,), are engaged in, or the school participates in every such project suggested by local community leaders.	The school participates in some adult-interest projects. Such participation usually is on a class competition basis, with special rewards to individuals or classes making the largest contributions.	The principal or superintendent selects some of the activities suggested by community leaders, purpose of the selection only being to avoid conflicts in scheduling. In money-raising projects there may be a limit on the size of individual contributions to lessen the financial aspects.

LEVEL IV	LEVEL V	Notation on Major Needs and Next Steps for Improvement
Level III plus: Community problems occasionally are discussed in classes, but there is no special effort to direct class thinking to these problems.	The school is represented on some type of continuing community council which constructively contributes to the solution of community problems in health, safety, recreation, etc. There is evidence of definite effort by many classes to consider local problems in such areas, and to arrive at some possible solutions for these problems.	
School personnel take an active part in intercultural relations projects initiated by lay groups, with children participating in some such activities.	Problems related to intercultural relations are recognized by the school, and there is evidence of a definite program for the improvement of relations between different racial and cultural groups. Such evidence may take the form of special units, inter-school visiting by pupils, observance of special holidays of minority groups, etc.	
School personnel give ready and active assistance to local agencies engaged in meeting children's out-of-school problems, there being some occasional carry-over of these activities into the school program.	Professional workers on the school staff are engaged with lay people in planning and executing a definite program to meet such school needs and out-of-school needs of children as might result in maladjustment and delinquency. There is evidence that this program has affected instruction, as in specific instances of guidance through teaching about home and family relationships.	
School leaders co-operate in community health projects initiated by local agencies. Local health problems occasionally are considered in classes.	The school and school staff are active participants with lay people in a continuing program for community health, with the instructional program showing evidence of constructive consideration of problems in this area.	
A faculty committee selects the adult-interest projects primarily for their public relations value, with some effort being made to use the instructional opportunities. Decision as to the participation rests with each local faculty, and is reached after careful study of each project.	Adult-interest projects participated in by the school are selected by a committee of faculty, students, and parents, on the basis of the possible contribution that the projects can make to the school's instructional program, and participation is under student leadership, with no element of competition between classes or individuals.	

were happening in the school as the children were learning about meat packing.

a. What other values can you identify?

b. Could more values have been secured by modifying the approach?

The following set of questions illustrates another type of inquiry in the Southwide Study. Ample space is allowed between questions but this is omitted here.

I. *Community-wide Planning by Pupils.*

Children and youth should have opportunities to participate in some of their own community-wide planning groups.

Cite evidence that pupils from upper grades who have been selected by their classmates have opportunities to think with children and youth from other schools about:

The city-wide recreation program.

Community beautification projects.

Provisions and regulations concerning safety.

The elimination of unhealthful conditions in the community.

Ways of improving city government.

Ways of co-operating with the community council which has representatives from all groups.

Ways of developing loyalty to all schools in the community rather than unwholesome allegiance to one.

Ways of developing co-operative projects among schools.

a. What other opportunities should elementary school children have to participate in community-wide planning? Cite examples of present practices.

b. What progress has already been made in developing community wide planning by pupils?

c. What problems exist in improving the amount and quality of community-wide planning done by pupils?

d. What plans have been made to extend *this year* the opportunities children have to participate in community-wide planning groups?

e. What are your *long-range* plans for extending the opportunities children have to think with other pupils about school and community improvement?

The foregoing pages should be related to the principles of evaluation set forth in Chapter 8.

Studies of pupil difficulties, "shortages," errors. The early application of scientific methods to curriculum problems produced a large number of limited but nevertheless very influential studies. Lists of common mistakes in language skills or grammar,[30] of spelling "demons," of shortages in necessary knowledge in computational skills, appeared frequently in the ten years following 1909. Greater knowledge of individual differences modified the validity of fixed uniform lists of errors or shortages, but the general idea is still sound. Research interest turned to other things, and studies of the type here mentioned died out. A revival would be valuable because children and adults do have needs within typical subject-matter areas which must be isolated. Often real needs must be revealed and this may be done by studies of shortcomings. The order of presenting material in some areas of the curriculum is aided by such studies.

The place of these studies in determination of grade placement and sequence will be shown in later pages of this chapter. Early books on the curriculum carried digests of these studies. The two most important sources are:

The Scientific Method in Education, Thirty-seventh Yearbook, Part II, National Society for the Study of Education (Bloomington, Ill., Public School Publishing Co., 1938).

Child Development and the Curriculum, Thirty-eighth Yearbook, Part I, National Society for the Study of Education (Bloomington, Ill., Public School Publishing Co., 1939).

The use of logs, diary accounts, stenographic reports, and other curriculum records. Each of these instruments produces valuable data about the curriculum, on the basis of which judgments of worth may be made.

---

[30] An illustration is found in W. W. Charters and Edith Miller, "A Course of Study in Grammar Based on the Grammatical Errors of Children in Kansas City, Mo.," University of Missouri *Educational Series No. 9,* Vol. 16, No. 2.

**RESULTS OF IMPROVEMENT IN EDUCATIONAL PROGRAM DUE TO
CURRICULUM WORK IN ALL CITIES STUDIED***

PHASES OR FACTORS OF EDUCATIONAL PROGRAM	DEGREE OF IMPROVEMENT MADE							
	Strong		Some		Little		Total	
	No.	Per cent	No.	Per cent	No.	Per cent	No.	Per cent
Richer and better subject content	61	65.9	18	19.4	1	1.1	80	86.4
Teacher growth and morale ...	62	67.0	17	18.3	0	0.0	79	85.3
Improved classroom methods ..	57	61.6	19	20.5	2	2.2	78	84.2
Pupil growth and interest	49	52.9	25	27.0	2	2.2	76	82.1
Stimulation of professional staff.	63	68.0	11	11.9	1	1.1	75	81.0
More and better books and supplies	43	46.4	22	23.8	6	6.5	71	76.7
New emphasis on research and experimentation	34	36.7	24	25.9	8	8.6	66	71.3
Board recognition of continuous program	22	23.7	28	30.2	12	13.0	62	67.0
Community recognition of worth of program	9	9.7	38	41.0	14	15.1	61	65.9
Total	400		202		46		648	

* C. C. Trillingham, *The Organization and Administration of Curriculum Programs*, Education Monographs, No. 4 (Los Angeles, Calif., University of Southern California, 1934), pp. 135-136, Table XLVII.

This table should be read as follows: Richer and better content is an outcome of the curriculum program in sixty-one cities, which is 65.9 per cent of the ninety-three cities which have curriculum programs.

Evaluation through noting effects of curriculum programs upon the professional activities of teachers. Programs of curriculum improvement [31] may be evaluated by noting the effects upon the staff which participates.

Trillingham secured from 648 superintendents opinions as to improvements in their situations as a result of a program of curriculum revision. The summary appears above.

A similar study based upon the Virginia curriculum program was made by Leonard who points out that while the method has its limitations, nevertheless the evidence derived is important.[31a]

I. *Teaching Practice*

Percentage of teachers actually using course 85

Percentage of teachers developing units of work 55

Percentage of teachers adding to course of study 49

Percentage of teachers using textbook only 6

Percentage of teachers disinterested and unwilling to change teaching.. 9

II. *Supervised Growth*

Percentage of teachers changing point of view 80

Percentage of teachers whose point of view changed by experimentation with course 32

Percentage of teachers whose point of view changed by discussions and reading 42

Percentage of teachers who have studied special subject matter this year (not professional) 67

Percentage of teachers making case

[31] The important item in this chapter is the determination of status with improvement procedures presented in Ch. 16. It is inevitable, however, that some indication of improvement processes get mentioned here.

[31a] J. Paul Leonard, "Is the Virginia Curriculum Working?" *Harvard Educational Review* (January, 1937), pp. 66-71.

studies, developing interest charts, making grade adjustments, changing pupil reports, and visiting homes .... 32 to 76

III. *Physical Equipment*

45 per cent of all the radios in the schools reporting were purchased last year, as were 26 per cent of the phonographs, and 23 per cent of the phonograph records. The Library Division of the State Department of Education reports an exceedingly large increase in the purchase of library books with and without state aid.

Parker reports briefly on a number of evaluation studies for which final data were not available at the time of report. The summary following is chiefly valuable in indicating methods of determining status and improvement in staff activities. The chief source used by Parker [32] was the California Co-operative Study of In-Service Education. A number of schools found that sociometric techniques could be applied to the formation of faculty committees with resultant improvement in kinds of participation, in increased member participation, in emergent leadership, and in the level of interaction.

A large metropolitan high school set out to increase democratic participation by everyone in the school program. The general procedure was to survey status and thus discover areas where improvements might be made. The analysis made preliminary to initiating an improvement program dealt with the following factors:

Define the objectives of the total program as it exists at present.

Determine the extent to which pupils participate in organizing the school program.

Study the extent to which the pupils participate in extracurricular activities.

Determine the bases on which grades or marks are assigned.

Survey the uses made of cumulative records and test results by teachers, counselors, students, and others.

Analyze referrals of discipline problems.

Survey student opinion on teachers and subjects liked and disliked.

Survey student attitudes toward various social, economic, and political issues.

Have the students evaluate school practices.

Survey teacher attitudes on (*a*) fundamental issues in education, (*b*) pupil behavior, and (*c*) ways of working together.

Describe opportunities available to students for making choices and for participating in determination of school policies, organization and control.

A program of instructional improvement was then to be developed around problems identified by students and teachers; gradual extension of pupil participation and responsibility in organization and control of the school; and systematic study of democratic ideals in the classroom.

The brief account indicates not only the varied activities which the staff will take up in carrying on this curriculum change, but indicates also some of the changes that are likely to follow the program.

A number of other similar studies under way are reported in Parker's chapter and will repay study.

School-community study of the curriculum. Certain results which appear in the life of the community constitute another type of evaluational evidence. These results are more frequent and more extensive when the community-wide approach to curriculum improvement is used. The first thing, again, is to determine status through a study of the community and its resources, the present use of the community as the unit in curriculum programs, the extent of lay participation and other factors. Methods for doing this are included in Chapters 13, 16, and 17. We are here concerned with scrutiny of the curriculum to see to what extent it meets community needs. The results of programs to improve the curriculum can then be studied by comparing status as determined earlier with the new situation.

[32] J. Cecil Parker, "Evaluating Improvement Programs," Chapter 5 in *Action for Curriculum Improvement,* 1951 Yearbook, Association for Supervision and Curriculum Development (Washington, NEA, 1951).

The general problem at this point is what are the schools doing about certain problems, illustrated in this list:

1. The extension of needed services within the community such as:

Health service and information

Recreation facilities

Night schools for youth

Adult education

Nurseries

Co-operative agricultural and other projects

(Many others could be noted)

2. The development of a community co-ordinating council which may then attack such problems as:

Juvenile delinquency   Parent education

(Many of those listed in (1) above)

3. The development co-operatively of an adequate system of cumulative school records understood by the community and answering questions from the community.

4. The extension of participation by the lay public in various ways, from determining policy, curriculum objectives, from study of local needs and resources, from service on fact-finding, committees and advisory boards, to aiding with school lunches, assisting in nurseries, developing room mothers clubs or other sponsoring groups.

5. Other areas for school-community co-operation are indicated in Chapters 13, 16, and 17. Extracts from the Texas Evaluative Criteria in the present chapter list many methods by which community members and organization may participate in curriculum study.

Factual records are necessary before either a valid study of the community (and curriculum), or an evaluation of the results of an improvement program, can be made.

The socioeconomic make-up of the population.

The racial, cultural, and religious affiliations.

The political groupings.

The health status of the community; hospitals, clinics, other agencies of medical care.

The statistics on juvenile delinquency, crime records, church and Sunday school membership, boy scout work,

charitable organizations, cultural organizations.

The educational levels.

The residential areas, from excellent to slum.

Voting records and election returns types of issues raised by local government and voters.

The facilities for ensuring pure water, milk, and food generally.

Certain of these facts are usually available only on a national basis, hence local schools and communities are seriously handicapped until they develop their own records. The community records when available will reveal status, that is, they are part of the study of the curriculum in operation. Cumulative records when developed in school and community will indicate some of the results of a program of curriculum improvement. The effects of co-operative school-community study will be illustrated in Chapters 16 and 18.

Illustrations of community study and appraisal of schools may be found in Chapters 6 through 14 in Hollis Caswell, *Curriculum Improvement in Public School Systems*.[33] Eight specific city and state programs are outlined from which readers may extract the materials on study and evaluation. A brief, simple account of community evaluation is found in *The Public Administration of American Schools*,[34] Chapter 18. The table on page 396 is from that volume, and shows how various levels of data tie in the school offerings with conditions in the community. Other agencies beside the school are, of course, partly responsible for both desirable and undesirable results.

The foregoing procedures supply, in addition to spot evaluation, many starting points for programs of curriculum improvement. This becomes clear in Chapter 16.

[33] New York, Teachers College, Bureau of Publications, Columbia Univ., 1950.

[34] Yonkers, World Book, 1952.

AREA TO BE EVALUATED	CONTINUUM				
	FROM MATERIALS	TO METHOD		TO SCHOOL RESULTS	TO LIFE RESULTS
Fundamental Subjects	Course of study, text-books, teacher qualifications, time allotment.	Observe teaching.	Achievement tests.	Student pub-lications.	Public library circulation. Sample of let-ters written in life situations, etc.
Health Services	Course of study, staff qualifications, etc.	Staff organi-zation. Plan of pro-cedure. Pupil records.	Standardized tests. Physical fit-ness perform-ance tests.	Compliance with notices following dental and physical exam-inations.	Draft rejec-tions. Employee ab-sence because of illness. Infant mortal-ity. Incidence of epidemics.
Citizenship	Course of study, text-books, teacher qualifications, time allotment.	Bulletin boards. Field trips. Supple-mentary materials used.	Achievement tests. Sociograms.	Activity organ-ization, student participation in school control, local social-welfare activity by students.	Delinquency rate. Percentage of voters voting. Peer group structure.
Aesthetics	Program offer-ings in expres-sive arts and in appreciation. Library facili-ties.	Classes and activity organization. Library man-agement.	Pupil produc-tion, hobby clubs, fine arts clubs.	Local patron-age of school exhibits, concerts, programs.	What movies, radio pro-grams, books, newsstand materials pupils and adults "con-sume."

Van Miller and Willard B. Spalding, *The Public Administration of American Schools* (Yonkers, World Book, 1952), p. 460.

Section 2

GENERAL METHODS FOR EVALUATING THE DOCUMENTS WHICH AFFECT THE CURRICULUM

The evaluation of printed materials fur-nished to the teacher necessitates judgment on at least five characteristics:

1. The effect of teachers' guides upon the learning outcomes stressed.
2. The effect of the guides upon the teach-ers' classroom techniques and manage-ment.
3. The extent to which the materials have been favorably or unfavorably affected by designated extraneous factors.
4. The internal structure (selection and ar-rangement) of the printed materials themselves.

5. The methods used in developing and writ-ing the materials.

The first three were adequately discussed incidental to the evaluation of the curricu-lum. The latter two will be examined here.

The documents affecting the curriculum are of two general types. The first consists of either the typical course of study, cast in more or less formal mold, or the more recently developed teachers' guides and source units. Older type courses were usually in one vol-ume, often a very small one.

The second type of material includes those various and miscellaneous bulletins upon any and all problems confronting teachers. The new guides are practically never in one volume but in a continuing series of bulletins. New materials are added at any time in response to needs. Many items not included at all in older courses are now discussed in bulletins for teachers. Literally hundreds of new type bulletins are available, published by state, county, city and even small-town systems. Special materials for different levels of ability appear. Many materials, including source units, are published also by government agencies, state and national, by commercial interests, notably banks, air lines, railroads, manufacturers of food and soft drinks, agencies interested in health, and others.

Major elements within courses of study or teachers' guides. Certain major topics will appear in both older type courses of study and in the new teachers' guides, whatever their form. The older courses are often confined to the outline of prescribed subject matter to the neglect of other vital points. Certain courses, in fact, present large amounts of subject matter without the slightest reference to the purposes to be served by the material. Newer courses increasingly include all or most of the items listed below. The teachers' guides or source units which are organized into a sequence of volumes often repeat in each volume some of the elements, for instance, a statement of aim and general philosophy. Better practice is to prepare a separate volume often called a curriculum "handbook" which contains a complete statement of all elements which apply generally to all guides or units.

The common structural elements are:

1. A statement of philosophy, or viewpoint, or educational belief.

2. A statement of general educational aim.

3. A listing in more or less detail of the specific objectives for subjects, units, or areas of experience.

4. An outline of subject matter and related materials, together with lists of suggested learn-ing activities, the two indicating the scope and sequence of the course.

    a. An explanation of the methods used in determining the scope of the course.

    b. An explanation of the methods used to select and organize the content into categories.

    c. An explanation of the methods used to determine sequence or gradation of materials and experiences.

5. A list of provisions for individual differences; administrative adjustments, differences in amount of material, in types of learning experience. (This is sometimes a part of the preceding point, though often presented separately.)

6. Suggestions for the organization of teaching sequences: segments of subject matter logically arranged for use in assign-study-recite-test procedures; subject-matter units; proposed functional or experience units.

7. A discussion of measurement and evaluation with illustrative tests and techniques.

8. A list of texts, supplementary books, pamphlets, songs, pictures, audio-visual aids, construction materials, bibliographies.

We may examine teachers' guides to determine if these necessary items are (*a*) present, and (*b*) adequate and sound. We ask such questions as these: Are objectives stated? Stated in acceptable form? Derived from life? Do the objectives and materials serve the needs of learner and of the community? Does the material contain introduction to the "great society" beyond immediate contacts? How is the content selected? Arranged for general reference? Arranged for use in teaching situations? What techniques for evaluation of outcomes are suggested? Are there adequate teaching aids, bibliographies, sources? Is the material and organization in accord with scientific knowledge about the learner; about the community? Likely to foster democratic principles and processes? Who constructed the guides? How were the writers and editors selected? What aims and principles directed the production of materials? What use was made of experts; of experimental tryout? What was the interaction between curriculum development and production of documents?

A detailed check-list will be found on pages 413-415.

Evaluation of the major elements found in teachers' guides. Dissatisfaction with learning outcomes, as has been stated, is the usual cause for scrutiny of the elements in the setting for learning. The search for causes of ineffective learning leads to, among other things, an examination of the documentary guides and other printed materials furnished teachers. The following pages contain an extremely brief summary of general methods and criteria [35] under which to examine these guides.

The philosophy, or viewpoint, or creed, and general aim. The philosophy and aim should be stated explicitly in early pages or in a separate bulletin. An astonishing number of traditional courses omit this entirely. Analysis of the course must be made in these cases in an effort to determine philosophy and aim by inference.

The philosophy will vary from democratic to authoritarian with many variations in between. Authoritarian course writers often include naïve verbalisms upholding democracy that are flatly contradicted by the actualities within the course. The general aim will naturally be stated in broad terms but need not be vague, indefinite, or platitudinous. The aim should be in accord with the values, ideals, and aspirations of society. It should not be a remote abstraction. Methods of deriving philosophy and aim again vary from democratic co-operative discussion, to consent by the group to materials developed by an individual or small group, to authoritarian imposition.

A course or guide is good in the degree to which:

1. The philosophy and general aim are in accord with the democratic philosophy and take into account relevant scientific knowledge.
2. The philosophy and general aim are stated in meaningful language.
3. The philosophy and general aim were derived through discussion by the whole group.

The specific objectives. Objectives [36] should be stated for subject areas, for grade levels, for parts of subjects or grades, for units or projects. Modern new type guides will state objectives by growth levels and will indicate that these are directional progress goals. The following questions may be asked:

1. Are the objectives stated in the form of textbook pages to be covered, wider segments of subject matter to be covered, amounts of facts or levels of skill to be acquired?
2. Are the objectives stated in the form of pupil growth in desirable understandings, attitudes, appreciations, abilities, skills, functional information?
3. Are the objectives prescriptive by grade or other arbitrary levels, or are they directional-progress goals?
4. Were the objectives determined by individual or small groups judgment, or derived from the study of the learners and from actual instructional practice with all persons participating?

A course is good to the extent that the specific objectives are stated in terms of pupil growth and achievement, are designated as directional-progress goals, and are co-operatively derived.

We may then evaluate the objectives them-

---

[35] *Special note.* The presentation of criteria for evaluating the major factors individually is sharply curtailed. *First,* general criteria only are presented. Illustrations of detailed criteria for some items may be found in the literature, or better, can be developed as needed by students and field workers. *Second,* no pretense is made of presenting the background for the criteria. The background is enormous and could not be included if desired. Familiarity with this background is, moreover, a legitimate assumption when dealing with advanced students. Wide reading in the area of course writing

and curriculum improvement has doubtless accompanied previous courses and field work including workshop procedure. The purpose of the present discussion is to furnish quick summary of the general initial attack to be made on the evaluation of courses and guides.

[36] Extensive reading materials are available on derivation and statement of objectives. An abbreviated summary will be found in Burton, *The Guidance of Learning Activities,* Ch. 4, pp. 417-423. Extended discussion is found in Briggs and Justman, Ch. 11.

selves by determining the degree to which they are:

1. *Dynamic,* indicative of action and likely to promote attack by normal learners.
2. *Socially desirable,* that is, recognizable progress goals leading toward outcomes accepted by society.'
3. *Achievable* at the indicated maturity levels; in the light of available resources.
4. *Developmental,* that is, leading to constantly higher levels of growth and achievement.
5. *Varied* enough to care for different levels of ability, and different aspects of the individual learner.
6. *Limited* enough in number and scope to permit definite organization for their accomplishment without diffusion of effort.
7. *Susceptible to evaluation.* Can evidence of pupil growth be derived?
8. *Worded clearly, definitely,* and *consistent* in form.

The selection and organization of content. Makers of teachers' guides are confronted with four questions:

1. What is to be the scope, or area, or coverage of the course?
2. How is content to be selected to fill the scope or area?
3. How is the content to be arranged? Under what categories may it be placed?
4. How is the content to be arranged in a sequence? (This is often referred to as gradation.)

Strength and weakness in courses of study may often be traced directly to the methods used in answering these questions.

Scope. The general method of determining scope in traditional courses was adult judgment on "what will be needed in life." Judgments were subjective and often arbitrary; made by individuals or by small selected groups. Judgments derived from discussion within larger groups are a more recent development. This method of determining scope usually results in determining content and sequence through naïve acceptance of text or courses already in existence.

Arbitrary judgments began to give way to those with some semblance of logic. A general aim was set up and broken down into a hierarchy of subaims. The material adjudged necessary to achieve these aims became the scope of the course.

Search was made for children's interests related to the formal culture materials possessed by society. A series of "centers of interest" was then set up which determined the coverage of the course.

The necessity for relating education ever more closely to the life of the individual and of his society led eventually to various forms of social analysis.[37] The basis for the scope of a course was found to be in the necessities of life as revealed by analysis, not by arbitrary judgment. This is a distinct advance.

The writers of modern guides are less and less interested in delimiting a course in terms of scope. They prefer to present as great and as rich a selection of materials as possible, fitted to the needs of children at different levels (either grade or growth).[38] Teachers may then organize many different curriculums with many different groups of learners.

The very poorest courses are those using the first method listed below. Traditional courses may be judged to be better as the procedures used rank numerically higher in the list. Scope is determined by:

1. Adoption of existing texts.
2. Setting up subject matter wider than one or a few texts would indicate.   -
3. Setting up a general aim with analysis into a hierarchy of subaims.
4. Setting up centers of interest based on children's interests in given areas of culture materials.
5. Analyzing social life to determine the needs of members of society; these needs then become the scope.
   a. Theoretical logical analyses, as for instance by Spencer, by Lynd, by other anthropologists, sociologists, educators.

[37] See Appendix A and references therein for brief quotations from the essays by Spencer, by Lynd, and the productions of various committees dealing with social analysis and with scrutiny of individual problems and needs.
[38] Many good examples of this are found in recently published courses.

b. Factual surveys of community or regional needs.

6. Analysis of the personal life of individuals (theoretically or by actual investigation) to determine needs and problems which then become the scope.

A combination of 5 and 6 often appears in the better traditional courses.

Modern guides are likely to use the two latter methods, but in many cases are moving toward an organization which does not delimit scope.

An enlightening exhibit is derived from comments by the writer's students as they have analyzed many scores of courses.[39]

The distance from (an Eastern state) to (a Rocky Mountain state) is approximately 2500 miles. The distance between them in understanding methods of determining scope for their courses of study is infinitely greater.

Scope and its determination are not mentioned anywhere in the course. No pattern at all observable.

(Statement from a course). Few educators have sufficient mastery of the scope or body of human achievement to enable them to choose unerringly only the best and most adaptable bodies of subject matter; to record these in definite and durable forms for use in teaching. We therefore accept the subject materials which have been tried for many years in various places. [A modern group using the premise above would arrive at the opposite conclusion that large bodies of diverse materials might be provided, scope to be determined in the curriculum, not the course.]

The method used to determine scope in the ...... course of study was to examine the content and organization of many courses and to select from them those areas which would contribute most to the life of the pupil. [This is the old "paste-pot and shears" method. The "best" is selected and becomes the scope and content of the local course. The fact is overlooked that no material can be "best" as it stands. It must be best for a given set of circumstances, hence must be derived within that situation.]

The scope for the course in Latin in ..... High Schools is determined by changes in the Latin requirements for the college entrance examinations.

The scope of the course in ..... was determined clearly through logical analysis of subject areas. The problems and needs of the individual within current society were completely ignored.

Scope was determined in the ...... course in homemaking education through the experiences of the teachers in working with pupils and adults and in the homes of the community. Problems common to individuals and to families were selected.

Scope was determined in the ...... courses produced in the ...... workshop through listing the pupils' problems as given directly by the young people.

Scope of the ninth-grade mathematics course was determined by investigating to what extent traditional content in a first-year algebra course would contribute to meeting the needs of adolescents in the basic aspects of living and in developing those characteristics of personality which are desirable. Effort was made to organize the year's work around problem situations which might arise in some of the basic aspects of living. [A pretty difficult search, is the comment by the student.]

Scope was determined by basic life activities carried on by all people without reference to particular time or place.

The scope of the ...... course in arithmetic was determined by our belief that experiences are vital to real learning and that meaning and use are initial steps in the learning process. Scope was outlined by a series of experience units on the first- and second-grade level, functional problem situations on the third-, fourth-, fifth-, and sixth-grade levels.

The courses of study in ...... are organized more and more around the problems of our people, young and old. Fifteen critical factors have been selected. We believe there is no one best choice of material for each grade level. We are quite willing to include within the scope whatever proves useful in practice with the children.

The method of determining scope was to accept subject-matter outlines or units which were based upon pupil interests.

The scope for the ...... social studies course was determined by two years' study and experimental teaching on the part of members of the committee. [The bulletin, however, fails to describe the nature of the experimentation carried on.]

---

[39] Names of schools and courses are omitted since some of the comments are sharply condemnatory. Many good practices were found. Exercises at the close of this chapter will direct students and field workers to similar analyses.

The selection of content. Who does this? By what principles and by what methods? What differences are there in this between traditional and modern courses? Wherein does the content or its method of selection eventually interfere with or enhance learning and growth?

The general basis for selecting content [40] in traditional courses is, as with scope, adult judgment guided by varying amounts of evidence. The general bases for selecting content for modern course bulletins are, on the one hand, analyses of the needs of individuals and studies of maturation levels; and, on the other hand, studies of the aims and needs of the social group.

The more direct techniques for determining content are, as would be expected, closely related to methods for determining scope. Content may be selected through:

1. Adoption of texts, or acceptance of courses prepared elsewhere, or patching together pieces borrowed from several courses.
2. Determining through logic the materials theoretically necessary to fulfil an accepted general aim with its hierarchy of subaims.
3. Determining through logic the materials theoretically necessary to meet the needs revealed by studies of children's interests in formal culture materials.

Content is selected for modern guides through:

4. Determining through judgment the materials best suited to meeting needs revealed through theoretical and factual analyses of social and community needs.
5. Determining through judgment the materials best suited to meeting personal needs and problems revealed through analysis of the life of the individual.
6. Supplementing judgments by the assistance of subject specialists, specialists in child growth and development; by experimental tryout.

The traditional methods 2 and 3 are made less theoretical by tryout of the materials in the classroom. The modern course maker usually employs 4, 5, and 6 simultaneously.

The first method was long ago ridiculed as "paste-pot and shears" procedure but still persists. The erroneous assumption is made that "best" materials can be selected from other courses or found in texts. The best materials for any given situation must be developed in and for that situation.

The strictly traditional methods are used by conservatives who do not recognize the dynamic nature of life and of education, by honest but uninformed leaders, or by lazy and inert persons. Materials in existence are accepted uncritically. They are reshuffled and rearranged. No question is raised as to whether any of this should be taught at all, though much of it has been useless for a long time. New material is introduced into such courses with difficulty. The interference with learning and with education is obvious.

Courses are judged to be good to the extent that content is selected in terms of the data of social analyses, and with the aim of meeting the needs of the learners at the time and of society ultimately.

The subject-matter outline and untrained teachers. The outline of material to be covered was the chief feature of traditional courses. The modern course has eliminated this entirely, substituting an extensive listing of many varied materials from which a teacher may choose. *The real danger in the subject-matter outline is that it is accepted as prescribed, is "covered" by the teacher, is memorized by the pupil.* Nothing could be worse in ordinary circumstances.

A question may be raised, however, concerning the use of such an outline with teachers who are hopelessly undertrained, who are working in remote rural regions where supervisory aid is practically nonexistent, and where facilities are unbelievably meager. A subject-matter outline may be far better here than a modern course which calls for much training insight, and ingenuity. The

[40] Detailed discussion of the various subprocesses in selecting content are widely available. See modern texts on curriculum construction.

The periodical literature will supply many specific accounts.

subject-matter outline, if used in such cases, must be supplemented copiously by state department bulletins fitted to the teachers' needs and abilities. Methods of using even the meager resources of remote communities may be pointed out; simple illustrations of the uses of modern materials may be attempted.

Arrangement of content into categories or divisions. Traditional and formal courses on the elementary level are usually organized into *subjects.* Correlation may or may not be suggested. The subjects are in turn organized under the principles of formal logic. This type of organization is of value to mature learners but not to children. Immature learners are in fact handicapped by this form of organization.

Major *themes, topics,* or *generalizations* may be used as categories. Subject matter is still the basis of organization, but the theme or topic is usually broader than the segments of a formally organized subject field. Themes or topics or generalizations usually run through the entire course, thus making for better articulation between elementary and secondary schools. Correlation and even more functional organizations are facilitated whether suggested in the course or not.

Elements of organization similar to the preceding are *subject-matter units.* These may appear in either elementary or secondary courses. They are usually, though not always, broader than themes or topics. Functional use of subject matter may be extensive.

Categories still broader are known as *broad fields.* These are usually the physical sciences, the biological sciences, the language arts, the fine arts, and so forth.

The methods of social analysis brought attempts to organize the curriculum according to lists of cultural-anthropological needs. The best known terminology for these *social needs* is that introduced by Spencer and modernized into the "Seven Cardinal Principles." Terms were Maintenance of Health, Earning a Living, Being a Member of a Home, Participating in Social and Political

Activities, Exercising Religious Impulses, and so forth. Courses are not easily arranged under these headings.

A later departure of similar nature is the use of *social functions* as categories. These are socioeconomic in emphasis and include Production and Conservation of Life, Property, and Natural Resources; Production of Goods and Services; Consumption of Goods and Services; Recreation; and others.

A scheme of organization often found in the secondary core course of the modern type is that of *personal problems.* How May I Adjust to the School? (find my way about, utilize advantages, secure guidance, plan program, etc.); How May I Make Friends and Get Along with Others? How May I Determine My Capacities and Limitations (and Improve My Personality)? How May I Prepare for Marriage and Home Responsibilities? How May I Protect Myself against Propaganda?

The modern secondary curriculum increasingly contains two definite and related divisions. First, there is a *core* program; and second, a selection of *subjects* or of *broad fields* in specialized areas. Traditional secondary courses are usually confined to subject divisions, with some having broad field organization. Significant trends toward modernization are to be noted within the traditional courses: functional organization within subjects, introduction of new subjects, correlation, fusion, broad fields, and finally the introduction of a core.

The core is defined in several ways, though the aim and underlying characteristics are very similar in each case. Alberty [41] and his seminar students have critically analyzed the

[41] Harold Alberty and others, *How to Develop a Core Program in the High School* (Columbus, College of Education, Ohio State Univ., 1949). Mimeographed book containing excellent account of analysis of this area by a seminar. Bibliographies.

——, *The Core Curriculum in the High School: A Digest of Books and Articles, 1938-1948.* First-class annotated bibliography up to 1948. (Same source as preceding.)

——, *Utilizing Subject Fields in High School*

various interpretations and they recognize six.

The core may consist of:

1. A number of logically organized subjects or fields of knowledge, each one of which is taught independently.

2. A number of logically organized subjects or fields of knowledge, some or all of which are correlated.

3. Broad problems, units of work, or unifying themes which are chosen because they afford the means of teaching effectively the basic content of certain subjects or fields . . . which retain their identity, but the content is selected and taught with special reference to the unit, or theme.

4. A number of subjects or fields of knowledge which are unified or fused. Usually one subject or field serves as a unifying center.

5. Broad preplanned problem areas which are selected in terms of the psychobiological and societal needs, problems, and interests of students, and are made the basis for developing the teacher-student planned learning activities.

6. Broad teacher-student planned units of work, or activities, in terms of the expressed wishes or desires of the group. No basic curriculum structure is set up.

The six types are obviously not mutually exclusive. In practice illustrations will be found which combine features from two or more types.

Two distinctive characteristics for the core are listed by Smith, Stanley, and Shores: [42]

1. The core places deliberate emphasis upon the sociomoral values of the society, upon the universals which give unity and stability to that society.

2. The core curriculum uses broad social problems or themes of social living as the basis for structure.

The same authors list four characteristics which are essential to the core but not restricted to the core:

1. The core areas are required of all students.

2. The activities and experiences within the core are co-operatively planned by teacher and pupils.

3. Provisions are made for special needs and interests as need arises.

4. Skills are taught as needed.

A further characteristic, implicit in all the foregoing, needs to be made explicit. The core includes an extension upward of the so-called fundamentals, the "3 R's." The great change in the secondary pupil population necessitates further instruction in this area. The increasing complexity of civilization requires an extension beyond elementary levels of the fundamental skills, particularly in reading and language expression. Also clearly implied is that the core places emphasis upon the development of social skills, understandings, and attitudes.

The effective operation of a core curriculum requires: [43]

1. Teachers specially trained for this type of teaching. There should be included: broad general education; special study of the social foundations of education; child and adolescent psychology; structure and dynamics of social groups; guidance; and problem-solving methods of teaching.

Core-Program Development. Excellent practical discussion. (Same source.)

———, *Preparing Core Teachers for the Secondary Schools.* Almost the only discussion in print. Brief bibliography. (Same source.)

[42] B. Othanel Smith, William O. Stanley, and J. H. Shores, *Fundamentals of Curriculum Development* (Yonkers, World Book, 1950). Statements adapted from pp. 468-474, 474-478.

[43] Smith, Stanley, and Shores, *op. cit.,* pp. 478-490. See also Ch. 21 for good discussion of problems, practices, and criticisms.

The materials by Alberty and by Smith, Stanley, and Shores are probably the most valuable available. Alberty's presentation referred to above is also found in Ch. 7 of Sec. II of the Fifty-second Yearbook, National Society for the Study of Education (Chicago, Univ. of Chicago Press, 1953).

See also:

Any standard textbook on curriculum problems and development.

Roland Faunce and Nelson Bossing, *Developing the Core Curriculum* (New York, Prentice-Hall, 1951).

Dorothy Mudd, *A Core Program Grows* (Bel Air, Md., Board of Education for Harford County, 1949).

Grace S. Wright, *Core Curriculum in Public High Schools: An Inquiry into Practices, 1949,* Office of Education Bulletin No. 5 (Washington, Government Printing Office, 1950).

Rosalind Zapf, "A Core Class in Action," a film strip available from Wayne University, Detroit, Mich., 1948.

2. Buildings, grounds, classrooms, and workshops must be large and flexible enough to permit wide variety of group activities.

3. Equipment and materials must be adequate for extensive group projects.

4. Several general-purpose or activity rooms should be available.

5. Transportation facilities for excursions and community wide study projects should be easily available.

6. Time blocks should be large and flexible.

7. Grouping of children should be flexible by age or by grade.

8. Administrative policy must be flexible enough to encourage the wide variety of activities and schedule changes.

9. Public relations concerning the core must be continuous and effective.

The core curriculum may be studied, then, by looking for the general characteristics noted by the specialists. A check-list may be developed out of the points given here and any others deemed necessary.

Space forbids detailed explanation of other new aspects of the curriculum which should be examined. Class reports may be used to get this further material before the group. Areas or general theories to be considered are: life-adjustment programs; provisions for gifted children, for very slow learners; intergroup relations; treatment of controversial issues. In addition, curriculums should be scrutinized to note provisions for mental health, for counterattacks upon juvenile delinquency. Schools are or should be trying to play a part in meeting these and other new needs emerging within our current social order or any deficiency to which the curriculum might be contributory. Many of these needs did not exist in the less complex society of yesteryear. Too often they are not recognized by the school, even though some of the problems are pressing and momentous.

The modern elementary guide is unified by substituting units for subjects. Units cannot be organized in detail actually in advance of use, but can be planned. The course units are therefore more properly *possible,* or *suggested,* units. A wealth of materials and learning experiences is included. Re-

prints of units that have been used will aid in developing "know how," but they should not be followed in detail as models.

Supplementary comment upon scope and content of curriculums-in-operation. Scope in the curriculum, unlike that of the course, cannot be determined in advance or written down. Scope of the curriculum is determined finally by the scope of the learners' experiences in satisfying his needs or solving his problems, in satisfying social needs within the controls of the given setting for learning.

Content for modern curriculums is selected through co-operative discussion of learners and teacher while planning and carrying on learning experiences. Content in traditional curriculums is selected usually from the written course with varying degrees of supplementation by individual teachers. The logically organized materials of the cultural heritage may often appear in modern curriculums and must appear on the level of special education. Subject matter beyond the maturity and experiential background of the learner may sometimes be demanded. This is quite natural in modern curriculums. The teacher may then seek for pictorial, graphic, or other aids to comprehension, may prepare original material herself within the comprehension of the learners, or exercise guidance toward simpler materials if available.

The determination of sequence, or the gradation of subject matter and experiences. The eternal questions appear: Is subject matter already in existence accepted or is new material developed in terms of needs? Is the material related to school levels only in terms of logical sequence within the material, or is the growth of the learner primary, with placement determined by the needs and maturities of growing learners?

The committee which prepared the yearbook on *Child Development and the Curriculum* [44] presented relationship between

[44] *Child Development and the Curriculum,* Thirty-eighth Yearbook, Part I, National Society for the Study of Education (Bloomington, Ill.,

course materials and the learner within accepted subject-matter divisions. The defense was that this was made necessary by certain stated practical considerations. The committee then stated its firm belief in an integrated or organic use of materials in the actual classroom (that is, in the curriculum). The chapters as a rule do present a wide range of materials covering several school levels instead of rigid allocation. The critique in the final chapter sharply challenged this procedure. The growth process of individual children was upheld as the primary fact, despite fragmentary data, with placement of subject matter subsidiary to the needs of growth in given instances. It is possible that two approaches may be complementary. The logic of the subject matter, particularly the increasing complexity of concepts or skills as they broaden, the eventual levels of competence, do need recognition. The readinesses, interests, and abilities of learners are also inescapable factors in arranging materials for use.

The course writer who accepts subject matter as primary asks:

1. What materials should be allocated (in arithmetic, spelling, social studies) to a given grade level?
2. When should reading start? When should oral reading be subordinated to silent? Should phonics be included in the first grade, the second grade, or not included at all?
3. When should formal arithmetic begin: immediately in the first grade or delayed to second, third, or sixth grades?
4. What spelling words should be allocated to what grades?
5. Where should formal grammar be placed?
6. Should algebra be taught before geometry or could this be reversed to advantage?

7. At what level should sex instruction be introduced? Courses in the family and its organization? In courtship? In personality analysis?
8. Can materials from algebra, geometry, and trigonometry be placed together to precede organized mathematics courses?
9. Can "general language" courses be successfully organized to precede systematic study of a language?

The guide writer who sees merit in both subject-matter organization and the nature of the learner as determinants [45] may ask:

1. Does a preliminary program enhance reading readiness or not?
2. What functional number experiences may come in kindergarten, second grade, etc.?
3. What use should be made of spelling lists in connection with words which pupils need and ask for in pursuing their own problems and interests?

The guide writer who accepts growth needs as primary may ask:

1. Can materials ever be allocated definitely to a given school level?
2. What will happen to arithmetic materials if offered to pupils well in advance of readiness or ability? (Odd as this sounds, it is an important question.)
3. What materials are necessary at any time or place which will contribute to the growth and achievement of a given learner or group?
4. What are the health needs of children at various stages of development?

Sequence or placement of materials was easily determined in the older traditional courses. The assumptions were that (1) a logical sequence was the learner's sequence, (2) all learning proceeds from simple to complex, and (3) there is such a thing as a "third-grade child," or a "seventh-grade

---

Public School Publishing Co., 1939). Whole volume excellent. For general arguments see Sec. II, prefatory note by Washburne, and the critique in Ch. 22 by Melby.

[45] In addition to the Thirty-eighth Yearbook mentioned above, other volumes supply excellent discussions of sequence or gradation and of time allotments. The following are but a few of those available.

Caswell and Campbell, op. cit., Ch. 11, contains extensive analysis of research.

Norton and Norton, op. cit., Chs. 4-16, contain many references to research studies.

The Implications of Research for the Classroom Teacher, Yearbook, American Educational Research Association, jointly with the Department of Classroom Teachers (Washington, NEA, 1939). References on gradation scattered through Chs. 8-14 with critical comment.

Current studies can be found in appropriate issues of the *Review of Educational Research* and in *The Education Index.*

child," and so forth. Critical analysis and later research revealed that these assumptions are not absolutes.

Traditional courses may be judged to be better as they move up through the methods of determining sequence:

1. The acceptance of a text determines sequence of materials. (The author of the text may or may not have used a reputable method of determining sequence within the book. Some seem to have used no method.)
2. The frequency of practice in existing courses is accepted.
3. The judgment of specialists on certain items is accepted.
    a. Logical sequence.
    b. Nearness in time and space.
    c. Increasing complexity of a concept, a skill, or other outcome.
4. The judgment of specialists and of classroom workers determines the theoretical relation of materials to levels of maturation, and to degrees of integration of experience within the learner.

Sequence in the modern guides is based on sounder principles and facts which are emerging out of research on certain items:

1. The characteristics of pupil maturation and growth.
2. The readiness of the learner:
    a. Physiological.
    b. Mental.
    c. Experiential.
3. The interests and needs of learners.
4. The presence of difficulties in learning.
5. The effect of failure upon learning.
6. The effect of knowledge of success upon learning.

Facts are far, far from adequate but many factors now modify our early bases for judgment, such as:

1. Wide variability in the capacities and interests of any group of pupils on any level appears.
2. Learning does not always proceed from simple to complex.
3. The initial attack upon a given problem, subject or area of experience may be more difficult than much that follows. Difficulty steadily decreases in some areas.
4. Intensity of interests may greatly affect the learner's effectiveness in surmounting difficulties.

5. Considerable variability of interests and abilities develops within any one learner.
6. The basic type of curriculum affects the learner's reaction, hence affects placement of materials.

Fixed allocation and absolute determination of sequence is not possible nor desirable. Many traditional courses do allocate certain material rather definitely in defiance of such facts as we have bearing on this. Modern guides tend to supply large bodies of material which are usable over several levels. Large place is left for teacher and pupil selection from these materials, guided by certain controls both within the nature of materials and within the nature of growth.

Courses may be judged good in the degree to which they meet certain criteria:

1. Broad general guides are set up within which learning groups may determine their own sequence.
2. A very wide variety of materials and experiences is suggested organized into large units, or areas of experience, or in broad fields, or within subjects, from which selection may be made.
3. Adequate assistance from supervisory leadership and other specialists is clearly provided to be utilized by learning groups as they develop curriculums.

Illustrations of gradation of materials. One or two cases may be of help here. The materials are from the formal skill subjects. Illustrations of placement for extensive content materials cannot be reproduced in brief space. Gradation, for instance, in social studies, health, music, is not based on the same principles used in mathematics and science. Many discussions are available in periodicals, yearbooks, and in teacher guides themselves.

Horn, in attacking gradation of words in spelling, illustrates the use of both criteria: the worth of the subject matter, and the ability and interest of the learner. He states first four fundamental considerations in the original choice of words: [46]

[46] *Encyclopedia of Educational Research* (New York, Macmillan, 1941), pp. 1247-1264. By permission of The Macmillan Company, publishers.

1. The relative importance of given words as measured by their permanent value.

2. The difficulty of the words for learning.

3. The logical relationships between words; grouping of words around a common problem and the progressive building of derived words from base forms.

4. The use of words in the pupil's own present writing.

Four questions arise as the actual placement is approached.

1. At what point is use by children frequent enough to justify introduction into the course?

2. What is the relative weight that should be given to frequency of use by children and frequency of use by adults in determining placement?

3. How deal with such words as *mumps, recess, measles,* which are frequently used by pupils but which are not among the first 5000 words in adult usage?

4. How deal with such words as *favorable, fundamental, gratitude,* which are frequently used by adults but rarely by children, even in the seventh and eighth grades?

The answers developed by Horn are:

1. In each of the first six grades, choose the basic word list from among words most important in the writing of adults and most important in the writing of children at that grade level.

2. Words frequently used by children but of marginal value to adults may be placed in supplementary lists or left to incidental teaching.

3. Words of great importance to adults but infrequently used by children may come toward the end of the period of systematic instruction.

4. The amount of review of words within a grade and in subsequent grades should be determined by the degree and persistence of their difficulty.

An ungraded course in arithmetic has recently been issued by the New York State Education Department. Material is arranged in its own sequence but with no reference to arbitrary school levels. It is available for pupils and teachers as they need it. A chart of possible grade placement is given in a pocket at the end of the book. No data on difficulty are given, however. This bulletin is the first to utilize the "directional-progress goal" concept popularized by Hopkins. A similar bulletin has been developed in Minnesota. This revolutionary development will be followed, it is hoped, by many other examples. A course in reading published by the Ohio Department of Education makes little mention of either selection or gradation of subject matter, but is rather a monograph on the teaching of reading. The teacher, it is realized, can find far more subject matter than he can use. The San Diego County *Trends in Elementary Education: A Teachers' Guide* is an extensive, illustrated book outlining trends in elementary education with cross reference to specific teaching problems in the social studies, the language arts, and arithmetic. This is one of the most imaginative and creative teacher guides to appear.

The San Francisco Teaching Guide for Mathematics, and the Cincinnati Tryout Course in Science, Kindergarten—Grade Eight, are but two of the several recent courses which show how learning material progressively develops within the given field.

Time allotment. Older courses usually gave definite time tables showing how many minutes per day should be devoted to the various subjects. Methods used to determine this were usually past practice as shown by frequency, the judgment of specialists, research upon attention span. Definite time allotments of this type often interfere with learning and with the development of a good curriculum. A more modern practice is to prescribe time allotments by the week or month, to be distributed as teacher judgment directs. A still more modern tendency is to shift attention from time allotment to pupil growth and achievement. The aim is to promote the growth of each pupil at his rate and in terms of his capacity. Rigid time allotments are not compatible with this. The modern teachers' guide facilitates this aim.

The next illustration, from arithmetic, was developed by Brueckner and his students.[47]

[47] L. J. Brueckner and F. E. Grossnickle, *Making Arithmetic Meaningful* (Philadelphia, John C. Winston, 1953), pp. 66-67.

RECOMMENDED GRADATION OF ARITHMETIC PROCESSES

MENTAL AGE *	WHOLE NUMBERS	FRACTIONS	DECIMALS	PER CENT
6-7	1. Counting. 2. Identifying numbers to 200. 3. Writing numbers to 100. 4. Serial idea. 5. Using numbers in activities of all kinds.	1. Contacts in activity units and in simple measurements.	1. Tens as basis of number system.	
7-8	1. Reading and writing numbers to 1000. 2. Concept development. 3. Addition and subtraction facts to 6.	1. Recognizing fractional parts.	1. Place value. 2. Zero as a place holder.	
8-9	1. Addition and subtraction facts and simple processes. 2. Multiplication and division facts through threes. 3. Multiplication by one-place numbers. 4. Related even division by one-place numbers.	1. Extending uses of fractions in measurement. 2. Finding part of a number.	1. Reading money values. 2. Addition and subtraction of dollars and cents. 3. Multiplication and division of cents only.	
9-10	1. Completion of all multiplication and division facts. 2. Uneven division facts. 3. All steps with one-place multipliers and divisors.	1. Extending use and meaning of fractions. 2. Easy steps in addition and subtraction of like fractions by concrete and visual means. 3. Finding a part of a number.	1. Computing with dollars and cents in all processes.	
10-11	1. Two-place multipliers. 2. Two-place divisors— apparent quotient need not be corrected. 3. Zeros in quotients.	1. Addition and subtraction of like fractions; also the halves, fourths, eighths family.	1. Addition and subtraction through hundredths.	

* Arithmetic age can be substituted in the first column.

MENTAL AGE *	WHOLE NUMBERS	FRACTIONS	DECIMALS	PER CENT
11-12	1. Three- and four-place multipliers. 2. Two-place divisors, apparent quotient must be corrected.	1. Addition and subtraction of related fractions; as ⅓ and ⅙; also of easy unrelated types, ½ and ⅓. 2. Multiplication. 3. Division of whole numbers and mixed numbers by fractions.	1. Addition and subtraction extended to thousandths. 2. Multiplication and division of decimals by whole numbers.	
12-13	1. Three-place divisors.	1. Addition and subtraction of types: ¾ + ⅚; 4⅝ — 3⅚. 2. All other types of division examples.	1. Multiplication and division of whole numbers and decimals by decimals. 2. Changing fractions to decimals, and vice versa.	1. Cases I and II in percentage using whole per cents.
13-14	1. Extending uses of whole numbers.	1. Extending uses of fractions.	1. Extending uses of decimals.	1. Case III of percentage. 2. Fractional per cents.

Provisions for individual differences. Traditional courses often contained no reference to differences among learners. All were to learn what was provided at the same rate, or were to fail. Research on the type and number of individual differences brought about a number of mechanical adjustments based on the subject-matter-mastery concept. Courses may be judged poor which do not go beyond the following:

1. Minimum essentials for all, plus two or more levels of achievement beyond the minimum requirements; differentiated assignments.
2. Various systems of grouping to accommodate different levels of ability and rates of learning; two- or three-track systems.
3. Suggestion on the secondary level that the number of subjects carried by individuals be varied.

Slightly better are:

1. Provision for individual progress in some types of learning, similar to the Winnetka or Dalton plans.
2. Voluntary projects in or out of class.

Modern course writers turn away from juggling subject matter to provisions for individual differences in terms of the learner himself. Guidance comes from the research, mentioned earlier, on maturation, readiness, interests, difficulty, failure and success. Courses may be judged good in the degree that they meet these criteria:

1. Units are suggested with explanation of their natural provision for wide differences in readiness, for many levels of ability, for differences in interests, differences in rate and types of growth.
2. Exploratory and tryout experiences are copiously provided for increasing levels of maturity.
3. An advisory service and suggestions are clearly indicated for aiding pupils to determine their own interests and capacities.
4. A diagnostic and remedial procedure is embodied within the course.
5. The study of special cases by specialists is indicated and the sources of readily available help indicated.
6. Administrative techniques of various types are indicated.

Several of these can be extended in considerable detail. (See, for example, Chapter 14, on "the Improvement of the Achievements, Interests, and Work Habits of the Pupil.")

The suggested organizations for teaching purposes. The general procedures usually presented are (1) the typical assign-study-recite-test sequence, and (2) some form of the unit.[48] Criteria for judging each of these are widely available in the literature on principles of teaching, and sometimes in texts on the curriculum. Space will not be taken here to reproduce these lists. See further discussion in Chapter 15.

The suggested learning activities. Learning activities included in modern courses and curriculums are numerous and varied, in sharp contrast to the limited and formal experiences within traditional courses and curriculums. Listening, reading, reciting, answering questions, writing papers, and using references constitute the bulk of learning experiences in formal situations. Good traditional teachers do, of course, introduce into their curriculums increasingly more varied experiences borrowed from modern organizations. The total number of possible types of learning activities available runs well over seventy. Diederich, for instance, presents approximately 177 possible activities organized in eight groups.[49] Other lists are available. Readers unfamiliar with these lists should examine them.

Courses are examined to see what type of learning activities is implied or directly suggested, how many, and in what variety. Learning activities observed in curriculums-in-operation may be scrutinized to see if they are:

1. Recognized by children as usable in achieving their purposes.
2. Recognized by the teacher as leading to socially desirable ends.
3. Appropriate to the maturity of the group; challenging, achievable, leading to new learnings; providing for application of old learnings.
4. Adaptable enough to provide for bal-

anced development of the learner; many types of individual and group activity.
5. Possible within the resources of school and community.
6. Flexible enough to provide for individual differences within the group.

The suggested techniques for evaluation of outcomes. Many traditional courses either neglect this item, or give merely a list of typical formal standard tests, plus a few suggestions for improving the traditional essay examination. Modern guides give extensive lists of modern evaluational instruments, together with many suggestions for application and interpretation. Modern guides also encourage the development by the teacher of his own evaluational techniques suited to his outcomes. The instruments themselves have been adequately presented in Chapter 9.

The bibliographies, lists of sources of material, audio-visual aids. Courses increasingly include extensive lists. Criteria are presented in Chapters 13 and 17.

Evaluation of the methods used in producing documents and guides for teachers. A professor of history in a well-known university was heard to say, "I will write the state course of study in history for high schools during the last two weeks of my summer vacation." The illustration is admittedly extreme, but course writing by individuals and small isolated committees still appears. The course is seen as an outline of prescribed materials, or as a list of courses to be covered, sometimes even as a series of assignments in one book or a few references.

Modern programs of course construction, in striking contrast, include the co-operative efforts of many persons and continue over

[48] Explicit criteria for both assign-study-recite and for various forms of the unit will be found in Burton, *Guidance of Learning Activities,* 2nd ed., 1952, Chs. 11, 12, 13, 14. See also standard texts in principles of teaching and on curriculum problems.

[49] Paul B. Diederich, "A Master List of Types of Pupil Activities," *Educational Research Bulletin* (Columbus, College of Education, Ohio State Univ., September 16, 1936). Burton, *op. cit.,* see pp. 437-443 for quick summary.

the years. Desirable methods of course development, of editing and writing materials, have been hinted at throughout preceding pages. A summary will suffice here. Courses of study are good to the degree in which they meet the following criteria for methods of construction which may be used as a scale for scrutinizing local practices.

1. The course should grow out of the aims and needs of the learners and of the community in which they live, with due regard for the nature of the great society beyond the local community.

2. The course content should be derived from the instructional activities within the system from casual or experimental tryout, from the continuous in-service study by the staff.

3. The instructional activities from which the course grows will themselves be the product of co-operative group effort by a personnel as wide as the community itself, and as wide as the scholarship which is relevant to the problem. Professional leaders of all types, specialists in various fields, teachers, pupils, parents, interested lay groups, community organizations and agencies will participate.

4. The course materials should be edited and written by individuals and committees specially selected because of their abilities in these specialized tasks. Preferably these individuals will be found within the total group which developed the instructional program from which materials are drawn.

5. The organization for course production should be developed on the spot by the personnel concerned, and to fit needs as they arise.

Courses do not always set forth explicitly the methods used. Examination and inference will be necessary.

The foregoing discussion is limited to the listing of criteria which contain indications of methods to be used. Extended discussion of the actual procedures in producing courses and guides appears in Chapter 16.

Section 3

ANALYTIC OUTLINES FOR SUMMARIZING THE CHARACTERISTICS OF DOCUMENTARY GUIDES FOR TEACHERS

The detailed analysis in preceding pages is a study and training device. A final report on a course or guide will usually summarize in abbreviated form the findings derived from extended analysis of details.

Astonishing contrasts appear as we examine courses the country over. Some exhibits would cause black despair were it not for the existence of truly inspiring exhibits from elsewhere. The writer has on file course bulletins in history, geography, and literature, printed in 1911 and used in a small Massachusetts community. Drill materials originally printed in 1880 are currently used in another community. Modern texts and alert teachers have circumvented these incompetent materials in many cases but not everywhere. Side by side with these is a state bulletin from Maine, "Teaching Art in the Modern Way." Developed by a committee of teachers out of their own problems, containing excellent illustrations of children's work and dealing with specific problems in a definite way, the bulletin of a few mimeographed pages has influenced teachers out of all proportion to its size. Deft references to basic principles accompany the specific discussions. Bulletins in some systems have been unchanged for decades; in others, a continuing series of dynamic materials is constantly emerging. Improvement in some communities will not take place, barring miracles, within a foreseeable time; in others, continuous programs of vigorous, unselfish effort are under way.

Illustrative summary outlines for guiding evaluational reports of documentary guides. Scores of these are in use and easily found in the literature. No one of them covers all items or satisfies all individuals. Desirable procedure in a given situation is to develop an outline co-operatively. Two illustrations of summary outlines are given on pages 412-415.

ANALYSIS OF SELECTED STATE COURSES OF STUDY*

	Arith-metic	History	Geography	Health	Art	Spelling
Date of publication	1924	1933	1931-32 1935	1936	1927	1929
Aims and objectives						
General philosophical	No	Yes	Yes	Yes	Yes	No
Specific analytical sub-subject . .	Yes, by grade	Yes, by grade	Yes	Yes	Yes	Yes
Attitudes, interests, personality.	No	No	No	Yes	No	No
Method of procedure						
Outline of subject-matter	Yes, by grade	Yes, by grade	Yes, by grade	Yes, general	Yes	Yes
Helps on method	Yes	Yes	General	General	Yes	Yes, at beginning of course
Scientific evidence cited	No	No	None	Many references	No	Yes
Suggested activities						
Teacher	Some	Yes	Yes	Yes	Yes	Yes
Pupil	None	Yes	Yes	Yes	Yes	Yes
Interrelating subjects	Yes	No	Yes	No	Yes	No
Flexibility	None	None	None	Yes	Incidentally	Method does
List of books and supplies						
Textbooks	None	None	None	Yes	Yes	None
Supplies and equipment	14 kinds	No list; general	Quite specific	Yes	Yes	None
Teachers' references	Yes	Yes	Yes	Yes	Yes	Yes
Tests	Four	Nine	None	Yes	None	None
Type lessons, not bits of lessons						
By subject	None	None	None	Yes	None	None
Stressing relationships	None	None	None	None	Rarely	None
Time allotment	Yes	No	For some types	No	No	Yes
Work divided into definite periods						
Definitely divided by years	Yes	Yes	Yes	No	Yes	Yes
Not definitely divided	No	No	No	Yes	No	No
Basis of development			On Committee	On Committee
Specialist in department	No	No	No	Yes	On Committee	On Committee
Committee	Yes	Yes	Yes	No	Yes	Yes
Extensive teacher participation	No	No	No	Yes	No	Not indicated
Reviewing committees	No	Yes	Yes	No; read by a number of persons	Yes	Yes
Bibliographies of supplementary books						
Teachers' informational references	None	Yes	Yes	Yes	Yes	Yes
Pupil references	None	Yes	Yes	Yes	Yes	No
Professional references	Yes	Yes	Yes	Yes	Yes	Yes

* L. J. Brueckner, *The Changing Elementary School* (New York, Inor Press, 1940), pp. 110-111.

Summaries may be in paragraphs of running discourse. The statement following is from a seminar report on a history course used in a Massachusetts city.

This is a traditional course, not related in any way to the life experiences of the pupils, to their interests and abilities, individual or social growth, to their community, to current conditions. While it is remotely possible that a creative teacher could use it constructively, the form and content do not encourage the idea that this would occur, and certainly no aid, either in viewpoint, objectives, or suggested procedures, is included. It is wholly fact centered and takes no account of the pupil as a person.

Scope is determined by the subject-matter outline which is adult conceived and prescriptive. The subject matter is divided into topical units with no apparent functional basis, and consists of historical facts arranged in an arbitrary sequence under such clichés as: George Washington, Our First President; Abraham Lincoln, The Savior of Our Country; Theodore Roosevelt, A Strenuous American. There is no evidence in the printed outline to indicate how the teacher is to achieve the listed aims and purposes of the course.

An excerpt from a report dealing with a course in art used by a Delaware city presents a contrast:

This course represents probably the very best in modern development. The aim is clearly one of general education and not the specialized development of talent within the field of art. Fixed scope and content have been avoided, replaced by a wealth of material from which teachers can draw inspiration and definite assistance for many different problems. Objectives, materials, and suggestions for teaching are at the beginning based squarely upon the abilities and natural interests of children. The principles of readiness and maturity are everywhere apparent. Art principles and techniques will develop out of the learner's own activities. Diversity of interest and ability are amply provided for. Extensive use of art illustrations found within the community is indicated.

Still other reports contrast course writing by individuals or small specialized committees with development by extensive staff participation.

An analytic method of listing items and findings which present certain characteristics of courses of study was developed by Brueckner for use in the New York survey of state school systems (see p. 412). Still other lists are available in the literature, one of the best known being that by Stratemeyer and Bruner.[50]

Students in the writer's seminar groups developed a list of questions calling for the citation of definite evidence. The weakness of mere identification, or of "yes" and "no" answers, is thus avoided. Evidence is derived by inspection and analysis, and judgments are based thereon.

QUESTION LIST FOR ANALYSIS OF TEACHERS' GUIDES

(Burton and many student groups)

A. *Evaluation of statement of aim, philosophy, or viewpoint. Cite evidence that:*

1. The general viewpoint and aim are in accord with democratic values and principles.

2. The general viewpoint and aim are in accord with known facts concerning

   a. The nature of the learner, his interests, needs, typical activities, maturation levels.

   b. The nature of the learning process.

   c. The structure and needs of the community for which it is developed and with due regard for the larger community of nation and world.

   d. The nature of the Great Society as dynamic and emergent, working toward ever higher values, controlling and regulating as well as emancipatory and creative in its institutions.

3. The philosophy and aim are stated in meaningful language.

4. The philosophy and general aim were derived through discussion by the whole group.

---

[50] Florence B. Stratemeyer and Herbert B. Bruner, *Rating Elementary Courses of Study* (New York, Teachers College, Bureau of Publications, Columbia Univ., 1926). Certain refinements in the original standards will be found in H. B. Bruner, "Some Requirements of the Elementary School Curriculum," *Teachers College Record* (January, 1938), pp. 273-286.

See also the Mort-Cornell and the Mort-Burke-Fish references earlier in this chapter, the Evaluative Criteria, the Southwide Study, the Texas Elementary Evaluation Guide, and others.

B. *Evaluation of statements of objectives by areas and by levels. Cite evidence that:*

1. The objectives are stated as textbook pages to be covered, wider segments of subject matter to be covered, amounts of fact or levels of skill to be attained.

2. The objectives are stated in the form of pupil growth in desirable understandings, attitudes, appreciations, abilities, skills, functional information.

3. The objectives are prescriptive by grade or other arbitrary level or are in the form of directional progress goals or developmental tasks.

4. The objectives were determined by individual or small group judgment, or were derived from study of the learners and from actual instructional practice with all persons participating.

5. The objectives are (*a*) dynamic, (*b*) socially desirable, (*c*) achievable by the indicated maturity levels, (*d*) developmental, (*e*) varied enough to care for individual differences, but (*f*) limited enough in number and scope to permit organization, (*g*) susceptible to evaluation, (*h*) worded clearly and consistent in form.

C. *Evaluation of the organization of course materials. Cite evidence that:*

1. The method of derivation and development was community-wide and fully participatory; consultants were used whenever necessary.

    a. A community survey was made revealing community needs, strengths and resources, types and channels of opinion and influence, supporting and restraining influences, groups, and individuals.

    b. A procedure for continuing study was included.

    c. Provision was made for co-ordination with out-of-school institutions and processes which also provide education.

    d. The program and machinery for continuing study and for co-ordination of all community agencies is emergent, and in its constant revision taking account of (1) the constantly appearing fund of new facts about the learner and learning; and (2) the evolutionary nature of our social, political, and economic institutions and processes.

2. The scope was

    a. Determined by existing texts.

    b. Determined by subject-matter materials wider than a few texts.

    c. Determined by setting up a general aim with analysis into a hierarchy of subaims.

    d. Determined by setting up centers of interest based on children's interests in given areas of cultural materials.

    e. Determined by analyzing social life to determine needs of members of society.

    f. Determined by analysis of the personal life of the individual (inferentially or by actual investigations) to determine needs and problems.

    g. Delimited or left without limits so that curriculum scope could be determined in actual operation.

3. The content was

    a. Determined by (1) existing texts or acceptance of courses prepared elsewhere, (2) logical analysis based on a hierarchy of pre-determined aims, (3) logical analysis based on statements of children's interests, individual problems, or social needs.

    b. Narrow and prescribed; or supplied in wide variety so that content could be selected for given situations.

    c. Derived in part from actual experience in guiding learners which will reveal materials necessary in meeting pupils' needs and for introducing them to the society in which they live.

4. The sequence was

    a. Based on research facts concerning the characteristics of pupil maturation and development with special emphasis upon (1) readiness, (2) interests and needs, (3) difficulties in learning, (4) effect of failure in learning, (5) effect of level of aspiration, (6) effect of knowledge of success in learning.

    b. Organized around broad, general guides within which learning groups may determine their own sequence.

    c. Prescribed in given order; or inclusive of a wide variety of materials and experiences organized into large units on all levels from which selection may be made.

5. The suggested learning experiences

    a. Are organized into units which are

based upon both socially desirable outcomes and pupil purposes, recognizable by learners as usable in achieving their purposes, recognized by the teacher as socially valid.

b. Are appropriate to the maturity of the group; challenging and achievable, leading to new learnings, providing for application of previous learnings.

c. Are organized to provide for continuous, integrative, interaction with other persons, with the social physical environment; for participation in the life of the community.

d. Are possible within the resources of the community.

e. Are as wide as the life of the learner permits, as wide as the society will permit.

f. Are varied enough to provide for the balanced development of the whole child. (Are visual, verbal, oral, listening, writing, drawing, motor, mental, esthetic, creative experiences provided?)

g. Possesses breadth as shown by avoidance of the so-called "minimum essentials" concept, by provision of creative work, of problem-solving experiences, of meanings and appreciations beyond the commonplace (by types of experience in (e) above).

h. Are varied enough to provide effectively for individual differences; for flexibility in operation toward this end through wealth of materials, flexibility in scheduling, provision for variation in pupil contribution.

6. The suggested outcomes to be achieved by learners.

a. Are stated in terms of patterns of pupil behavior, or controls of behavior: meanings, attitudes, appreciations, work-study skills, ways of attacking problems, methods of personal-social adaptation. (Or are stated in terms of incomplete sentences, vague and meaningless generalities.)

b. Are flexible and adaptable to individual differences in rate and level of achievement; or are rigid, final, and attached to grade levels.

7. The scope, content, sequence, and suggested outcomes are in line with the philosophy and general aim.

D. *Evaluation of teaching suggestions given. Cite evidence that:*

1. The teachers' guide is to be a guide, not a dominating agency.

2. The general procedure is to be flexible with constant adaptation to pupil needs and the necessary social demands.

3. The organization for teaching-learning situations is either a modernized version of assign-study-recite, or the unit. Illustrations are included.

4. The evaluational procedures are continuous and a part of the teaching process. Lists or samples are given of objective tests, improved essay questions, behavior or anecdotal records, observation techniques, case study outlines, of techniques of co-operative evaluation.

5. Ample lists are given for

a. Sources of materials.

b. Sources of books, pictures, magazines.

Section 4

THE EVALUATION OF THE EXTRACURRICULAR PROGRAM

Educational activities supplementary to the "regular" course or curriculum have appeared since earliest times. They became prominent in the United States during the period of the academy and have increased steadily in number and value. The formal school and its administrators first ignored and then opposed the so-called extracurricular activities. The modern school with its greater understanding of the nature of the learner, of the learning activities, and of the integration of experience recognized that the so-called "extracurricular" activities were in fact excellent experiences. The extra activities have been moving over steadily into the curriculum. The extra activities are in fact based upon a principle basic to modern education; pupil participation in selecting, planning, and carrying on learning activities. Educational values have always suffered when an extracurricular activity became so important financially or politically that adults took it away from the learners, for instance, interscholastic athletics.

Extended treatment is not possible here. An extensive literature is available. While examining programs of co-curricular activities on either elementary or secondary level we may ask:

1. Is an extensive program of student participation in the government of the school indicated?
   a. Student councils and policy-forming committees.
   b. Participation in management of school functions: registration, commencement, dances and other parties, assembly programs, special drives and campaigns.
   c. Participation in minor routines of traffic control, classroom management, record-keeping.
2. Is a home-room program outlined with educational as well as administrative objectives?
3. Is there a wide variety of club activities indicated?
   a. Literary and debating.
   b. Vocational and avocational (hobbies).
   c. Dramatic, musical, artistic.
4. Is there an adequate list of school publications?
   a. Newspaper.
   b. Yearbook.
   c. Student Handbook.
   d. Literary magazine.
   e. Humorous magazine.
5. Is there provision for activities giving training in the management of money?
   a. School banks and thrift programs.
   b. Handling money for school activities.
6. Is a varied program of school excursions and trips included?
7. Is there an extensive program of intramural sports and games, with reasonable interscholastic contacts?

The following listing is not exhaustive but is helpful in initiating an analysis of co-curricular activities in either elementary or secondary schools.

CO-CURRICULAR ACTIVITIES

City. . . . . School. . . . .

Directions: Please check below all clubs in your school; add others not listed.

I. MUSIC
.. Boys' Glee Club
.. Girls' Glee Club
.. Mixed Chorus
.. Band
.. Orchestra
.. Harmonica Club
.. String Ensemble
.. Brass Ensemble
.. German Band
.. "Hill-Billy" Group
.. Soloists' Club
.. Rhythm Band
.. Folk Dancing
.. Tap Dancing

II. SERVICE
.. Student Council
.. Safety Patrols
.. Hall Captains
.. Lunchroom Committee
.. Milk Committee
.. School Bankers
.. Playground Supervisors
.. Jr. Red Cross Council
.. Visual Aids Operators
.. Messengers
.. Hosts-Hostesses
.. Bulletin Board Committee

III. ATHLETIC
.. Football
.. Basketball
.. Baseball
.. Volleyball
.. Tennis
.. Track
.. Tumbling
.. Stunts
.. Boxing
.. First Aid

IV. LITERARY
.. Dramatics
.. Creative Writing
.. Choral Speech
.. School Paper
.. Annual

V. SCIENCE
.. Nature
.. Bird
.. Star
.. Animal
.. Weather
.. Electricity
.. Chemistry
.. Radio
.. Camera
.. Collections

VI. HANDICRAFTS
.. Art Crafts
.. Poster
.. Soap Carving
.. Clay Modeling

.. Wood
    Crafts
.. Airplane
.. Metal
    Crafts
.. Puppetry
.. Sewing
.. Embroidery
.. Cooking
.. Scrapbook

VII. SOCIAL RELA-
    TIONS

  .. Personality
  .. Social Con-
      tacts
  .. Etiquette
  .. Travel
  .. Stamp

VIII. COMMUNITY

  .. Boy Scouts
  .. Cub Scouts
  .. Girl Scouts
  .. Brownies
  .. Girl Re-
     serves
  .. Campfire
    Girls

.. Four-H
.. Blue Birds

IX. OTHERS

.. . .
.. . .
.. . .

CHAPTER SUPPLEMENT

DISCUSSION QUESTIONS FOR GENERAL INTRODUCTION

1. How do you suppose school work came to be organized in the form of "subjects"?

2. How were the particular subjects now in use selected?

3. How do you suppose the content for the various subjects was selected in the first place?

The foregoing three questions deserve special comment. Student thinking will be greatly aided through avoidance of an odd error which constantly appears here. Do not answer by saying that subjects were selected or organized as they are because of "tradition." This common answer would be genuinely comic if it did not reveal (1) serious ignorance of simple historical facts, and (2) serious superficiality of thinking. To be selected because of "tradition" the subjects must have originated and established themselves before they became "traditional"! The questions ask students to tell or to infer how the subjects arose in the first place.

4. How did Latin and cooking come to be offered in the same school?

5. What other organizations for materials have you encountered besides subjects? Upon what are they based?

6. Why are some subjects required, others elective?

7. Why do we not give everywhere courses in child rearing, care of children's diseases, city management, beautifying the home, and so forth?

8. The public pays for educating some individuals in some trades and professions. Why not others? Should the public pay for all types of training or not; plumbers, surgeons, carpenters, lawyers, teachers, engineers, telephone operators? This is a fundamental and far-reaching question.

9. If Spencer were to analyze secondary education found in typical medium-sized towns in the United States today, could he make the same criticisms he made in England nearly a century ago? Wholly, partially, not at all? Be specific.

10. What is the explanation and the significance of the similarity between Spencer's list of aims and the list prepared by the Commission on the Reorganization of Secondary Education? Of the differences?

11. Of all types of curricular material, which has received the most attention in the past? Which should receive increasing attention?

12. What part does formal discipline play in selection of subject matter? Actually? Supposedly?

DISCUSSION QUESTIONS DEALING WITH CRITERIA AND GENERAL PROCEDURES

1. What criteria should be considered in evaluating the *curriculum* of an elementary school? What are the major issues in this area?

2. What procedures can be used to secure information about the *curriculum* in actual practice in the classroom?

3. How can courses of study and other kinds of teachers' guides be appraised?

4. What are the advantages and disadvantages of state courses of study; of state instructional guides? Are you in favor of state examinations?

5. How can the co-curricular program be analyzed and appraised?

6. How can the supervisory program related to the curriculum and its development be analyzed and appraised?

7. Outline in some detail a plan that you might use in making a study and evaluation of the curriculum as a whole or in some area of learning in some school or school system.

INDIVIDUAL AND GROUP REPORTS

1. Report for class analysis the methods used in studying *courses* and *curriculums* in operation in your own school system. Note

placement of local practices in terms of levels (pp. 700-701) and periods (pp. 593-594).

2. What is being done locally to provide enrichment of experiences for gifted and talented children?

3. Describe and evaluate the *curriculum* of some school other than your own, applying principles discussed in this chapter.

4. Describe and evaluate quickly four *courses* (may be distributed among class members) *of study* in some curriculum area. Include major aspects of such documents and evaluate in terms of this chapter. (This prepares for the Class Project below.)

5. Report any extensive investigation of a given *curriculum* in operation carried in current periodicals, in city or state bulletins. Individuals or small committees may bring this to the whole group.

6. Evaluate the extracurricular program in some school using the outline of activities on page 416 as a guide. The class may compare programs reported and determine the point of view which underlies each.

7. Describe and evaluate a *curriculum study program* in some locality nearby, preferably in your own system.

8. What is the status of research in curriculum making in any selected curriculum area? Can you locate any studies? What are "minimum essentials"?

9. Individual committees or small committees may volunteer to make organized general comparisons between modern courses and good ones published between 1890 and 1910. (This often proves to be a most enlightening exercise.)

10. Course-of-study units may be evaluated here if the group desires, but this can be done to advantage in connection with Chapter 14.

CLASS PROJECT NO. VII

THE CRITICAL EVALUATION OF A COURSE OF STUDY DOCUMENT

Exercise No. 4 above prepares for this more extensive and detailed analysis.

Make a detailed analysis of a course of study, either from your own schools or from the library collection. The course may be of any type, traditional or modern, subject or unified, elementary or secondary.

a. Critically evaluate the statement of aim, philosophy and viewpoint.

b. Critically evaluate the statements of specific objectives on any and all levels.

c. Critically evaluate the organization of the course (scope and sequence—often called

selection and gradation of subject matter).

d. Judge whether the content actually is in line with the general aim and specific objectives stated or with some other implicit aim.

e. Critically evaluate the outcomes listed in the course of study. (Sometimes these are listed separately and in addition to the specific objectives, sometimes assumed to be the specific objectives in the degree achieved.)

f. Critically evaluate the suggested learning experiences.

g. Critically evaluate the suggestions given concerning general teaching methods, or organization for teaching, devices, methods of testing or evaluating, diagnosing, and so forth. (Students may use any set of criteria which appeals and need not be confined to the set in this chapter.)

A Special Exercise

The selection of content and learning experiences within any subject field or area of experience will present problems of special interest. The selection of materials and experiences useful in developing social insight are, however, the concern of educational leaders generally. All curriculum workers and teachers should therefore make brief answer to the following questions: [51]

1. What problems and materials will most illuminate the present social situation for the student?

2. What points of contrast between the present and the past will bring the student to a realizing sense of the perennial character of social problems?

3. What knowledge will throw into relief the bases of present and past social standards?

4. What social situations will bring to light the incongruity of man's behavior as he carries over standards from the past and crowds them in with those of the present?

5. In what ways has intelligence operated in this field to develop new instrumentalities and institutions?

6. What new responsibilities have these instrumentalities and institutions brought to the individual?

7. What materials will best show the play

[51] H. G. Hullfish, "Educational Confusion," *Educational Research Bulletin,* March 2, 1932 (Ohio State University), pp. 118-119.

of human intelligence in the creation of new standards?

8. What interests of the student will illustrate these same conflicts of standards and place on him the burden of critically establishing a unified outlook?

9. What class procedures will lead the student to a reconstruction of his present view as he thus sees knowledge at work leading man both to deepened insight and to social maladjustment?

SUGGESTED READINGS

A number of basic references have been included in the body of the text and will not be repeated here. Authors were:

American Association of School Administrators
Association for Supervision and Curriculum Development
Benne and Muntyan
Caswell and associates
Faunce and Bossing
Gwynn
Rugg
Smith, Stanley and Shores

The following references are of equal importance:

ALBERTY, Harold, *Reorganizing the High-School Curriculum,* rev. ed. (New York, Macmillan, 1953). Probably the best summary available. The bibliographies contain reference to other valuable texts.

BECK, R. B., COOK, W. W., and KEARNEY, N. C., *Curriculum in the Modern Elementary School* (New York, Prentice-Hall, 1953). First chapter gives much historical background quickly. Excellent general summary. See bibliographies.

BOBBITT, Franklin, *The Curriculum* (Boston, Houghton, 1918). Practically the first book to present modern theory. Interesting philosophic treatment. Valuable despite date.

DEBOER, John L., and others, *The Subject Fields in General Education* (New York, Appleton-Century-Crofts, 1941). Excellent analysis of the general subjects in the light of modern concepts of learning.

DOUGLASS, Harl, ed., *Education for Life Adjustment* (New York, Ronald, 1950).

FEATHERSTONE, William B., *A Functional Curriculum for Youth* (New York, American Book, 1950).

FLAUM, Laurence S., *The Activity High School* (New York, Harper, 1953). A bold statement applying the activity concept to the secondary school. Should be read. Excellent bibliography.

The Foundations and Techniques of Curriculum-Making, Twenty-sixth Yearbook, National Society for the Study of Education (Bloomington, Ill., Public School Publishing Co., 1926). Excellent extensive discussion of methods and achievements to 1926. Valuable historical reference for discussion of trends and methods of procedure.

JERSILD, Arthur T., *Child Development and the Curriculum* (New York, Teachers College, Bureau of Publications, Columbia Univ., 1946).

KRUG, Edward A., *Curriculum Planning* (New York, Harper, 1950).

LAWSON, Douglas, *Curriculum Development in City School Systems* (Chicago, Univ. of Chicago Press, 1940). An excellent critical analysis of factors affecting courses and curriculums in ten large cities. Valuable collection of factual materials. (This study could well be repeated based on current programs.)

MIEL, Alice, *Changing the Curriculum: A Social Process* (New York, Appleton-Century-Crofts, 1946). A better reference for Ch. 16 but excellent general reading here. Probably first statement concerning social process as basic to curriculum change.

SAYLOR, Galen, *Factors Associated with Participation in Co-operative Programs of Curriculum Development* (New York, Teachers College, Bureau of Publications, Columbia Univ., 1941). One of the best summaries available on the topic. This study, like that of Lawson above, might well be repeated.

STILES, Dan, *High Schools for Tomorrow* (New York, Harper, 1946). First class semi-popular discussion. Very provocative. Anticipates Flaum somewhat.

GENERAL SOURCES OF ORIGINAL MATERIALS APPEARING CURRENTLY

The *periodical literature* constantly contains accounts of new courses, of critical evaluation. These should be reported by individuals or small committees.

The journal *Educational Leadership,* with which the *Curriculum Journal* was merged, is the chief periodical source in this field.

The *bulletins* of city, county, and state departments of education, while usually dealing with programs of curriculum development in progress, often contain analytic materials also.

REFERENCES ON THE CO-CURRICULAR
PROGRAM

JOHNSTON, E. G., and FAUNCE, R. C., *Student Activities in Secondary Schools* (New York, Ronald, 1952).

JONES, Anna M., *Leisure Time Activities, a Handbook of Creative Activities for Teachers and Group Leaders* (New York, Harper, 1946).

McKOWN, Harry C., *Activities in the Elementary School* (New York, McGraw, 1938).

———, *Extracurricular Activities,* 3rd ed. (New York, Macmillan, 1952).

OTTO, Henry J., and HAMRIN, S. A., *Co-Curricular Activities in the Elementary Schools* (New York, Appleton-Century-Crofts, 1937).

TERRY, Paul W., *Supervising Extracurricular Activities* (New York, McGraw, 1930).

Wichita, Kansas, Board of Education, Report of group studying extracurricular activities, 1949. (Look for similar reports from other school systems.)

See also texts on guidance, principles of secondary education and secondary school administration, as well as voluminous periodical literature.

Chapter 13

◆·◆·◆·◆·◆·◆·◆·◆·◆

The Study of Materials of Instruction and the Socio-Physical Environment

IN THIS CHAPTER we shall deal with three major topics: (1) methods of studying and evaluating materials of instruction, (2) the study of the socio-physical environment of the school itself, and (3) methods of studying the community.

The growth and development of the pupil in the modern school are affected not only by the nature of the curriculum and the quality of instruction but also by the environment that the school and community provide. The modern pupil is literally surrounded by a profusion of aids to his learning, such as concrete materials of all kinds, books, visual aids, audio-aids, exhibits, and hundreds of others. Learning takes place in an environment that is more or less comfortable and stimulating. The facilities and equipment provided determine the richness and variety of his experiences. At the same time, he encounters personalities that affect his own personality in many different ways. In addition to these factors that affect his growth, it should be remembered that he is exposed to a wide variety of influences in life outside the school that in many cases are wholesome and constructive but that too often are known to be destructive and damaging. The school is faced with the problem of determining the extent to which these many elements of the learning situation may be leading to unfavorable child development. Often the study of these conditions can be most effectively conducted if there is a co-operative attack by all agencies in the community that are concerned with raising the level of living for all members of the group. Success has attended such efforts in many places.

The basic importance of the environment for learning is attested by the fact that the Association for Supervision and Curriculum devoted the 1954 Yearbook to this topic under the title, *Creating a Good Environment for Learning*. This volume is replete with both concrete illustrations and statements of basic principles. Its contents should be examined in relation to this chapter and also to Chapter 17.

It is an unfortunate fact that wide variations exist in the level of educational facilities among the schools of this country. These differences are due in part to differences in the wealth of the communities, differences in their willingness to support well-rounded educational programs, and, unfortunately, often to educational leadership which does not have a clear vision of what is desirable. In many localities where there are severe financial limitations, we find excellent programs conducted by a staff that by exercising ingenuity is able to make the most of what is available. The problem of equalizing educational opportunity is being given careful consideration in this country. Its seriousness is revealed by the fact that the per pupil cost [1] for the school year, 1950-51, by states ranged from $82 to $300.

---

[1] *Advanced Estimates of Public and Elementary and Secondary Schools for the Year 1950-51,* Bulletin of the Research Division (Washington, NEA, 1950).

421

The influence of the socio-physical environment on child development is clearly revealed by Ludden in a study of delinquents in a large city in New York. In this investigation, data were assembled for two groups of pupils in grades 7 to 9; one of them consisting of pupils who had come into direct contact with the court; the other of pupils who had not had such contact. An analysis of the data showed significant differences between the groups on the following list of characteristics: [2]

Factor	*Critical Ratio*
1. Living in a delinquency area..	9.10
2. Chronological overageness—any amount	8.88
3. Living in a low rent area—average under $20 a month...	8.40
4. Living in a broken home.....	7.50
5. Different homes lived in, if more than one	6.76
6. Poor school attendance—over five absences	6.43
7. Terms repeated in school—over one	6.40
8. School failures—more than one subject	6.19
9. Terms with failing marks—two or more	5.61
10. Intelligence below 90 on Otis test	4 to 6
11. Low employment status of father	4.72
12. Times tardy at school—any number	4.65
13. Illegal absences from school—over five	4.32
14. Intermediate position in sibling group	2.10

It can be seen that in the list of items that often accompany delinquency, there are six that are related to the home and eight that are related to the school environment. Five of the six related to the home, namely, delinquency area, low-rent area, broken home, mobility of the home, and low economic status of the father, are closely associated with economic conditions. They should be matters of concern to the entire community. Poor school adjustment of delinquents is indicated by most of the factors related to the school. Correction of the conditions over which the school has direct control would undoubtedly do much to eliminate the factors that contribute directly to delinquency. Close co-operation between the school and community agencies is necessary if social and economic conditions in the community are to be improved. They are the result of trends in modern life that are matters of profound concern to all who are seeking to make living for all people richer and more wholesome. Their correction may require many far-reaching social, economic, and political reforms.

Section 1

METHODS OF STUDYING AND EVALUATING MATERIALS OF INSTRUCTION

Kind of instructional aids. To carry on the activities of the modern school a great variety of instructional aids are necessary. The use of some of them requires special apparatus. The value of community resources as a means of vitalizing instruction and making it meaningful is generally recognized. As a basis of preliminary analysis, the following list of kinds of instructional aids is presented:

I. *General Instructional Supplies*
   A. Printed or written materials.
     1. Books, periodicals, bulletins, pamphlets.
     2. Charts, diagrams, graphs, tables.
     3. Cartoons, clippings.
     4. Maps and globes (relief, product and industry, population, rainfall, etc.).
     5. Posters.
     6. Practice exercises, workbooks, tests of various kinds.

[2] Wallace Ludden, "Anticipating Cases of Juvenile Delinquency," *School and Society* (February 12, 1944), pp. 123-126.
See also, W. C. Kvaraceus, *Juvenile Delinquency and the School* (Yonkers, World Book, 1945).

B. Visual aids.
  1. Pictures (photographs of persons, places, processes, reproductions of works of art).
  2. Motion pictures with and without sound.
  3. Lantern slides, still films, film strips.
  4. Stereographs.
  5. Television.
C. Audio aids.
  1. Radio presentations and transcriptions.
  2. Phonograph records.
  3. Plays and dramatizations.
  4. Tape recordings.
D. Concrete materials.
  1. Exhibits (specimens of fauna and flora, models of machinery or places, industrial and natural products, business forms).
  2. Museum collections.
  3. Measuring instruments.
  4. Gardens, animals, toys.
  5. Laboratory apparatus.
  6. Manipulation materials.
  7. Materials for self-expression.
II. *Apparatus Required*
  A. Motion picture projectors and screens; sound projectors; television.
  B. Phonographs and radio sets.
  C. Blackboards and bulletin boards.
  D. Sand tables, aquaria, green house.
  E. Construction materials, tools, work benches.
  F. Health education apparatus, equipment, supplies, games.
  G. Musical instruments, science equipment.
  H. Museum rooms and exhibit cases.
III. *Contacts with Community Resources*
  A. Trips, excursions, tours, journeys.
  B. Direct participation in community affairs—social, economical, political, industrial, recreational.
  C. Community surveys, clean-up campaigns, etc.
  D. Church, theater, recreation, welfare agencies, press, industry, government.

Determining the adequacy of various kinds of instructional materials. In appraising the instructional materials that are available and the use that is made of them, teachers and supervisors must bear in mind the purposes which different kinds of materials serve. An overview of the functions of various aids to learning is given in the analysis below. The grouping of materials according to the three functions that are listed enables the teacher and supervisor to analyze the materials that are actually being used. This grouping of materials also brings to attention possible steps to take to increase the variety of learning materials that could be used in a particular situation to serve the various purposes.

1. *Materials for Developing Individual Capacities*
  Textbooks, workbooks, diagnostic tests.
  Practice materials for mastering skills.
  Manipulative materials for developing meanings.
  Visual aids to give insight.
  Materials for slow and fast learners.
  Special equipment needed for corrective work.
  Tools and construction materials.
  Enrichment materials.
  Materials to explore and foster special interests.
2. *Materials for Use in Group Situations*
  Models, specimens, pets, plants, foods.
  Resource persons.
  Written requests for materials.
  Materials gathered from community.
  Measuring devices.
  Exhibits, trips, excursions.
  Clippings, newspapers, pamphlets, pictures, cartoons.
  Films, slides, television, radio, recordings.
  Reference books and supplementary materials.
  Maps, charts, graphs, diagrams, tables.
  Service projects in the school.
3. *Materials for Developing Creative and Integrative Aspects of Learning*
  Art objects, paintings, records.
  Materials for preparing murals, artistic materials.
  Musical instruments, supplies, etc.
  Materials used in dramatic and expressive activity.
  Materials used to explore, stimulate, and develop speical talents and aptitudes.
  Materials for enriching all important areas of the school's program.
  Museums, art galleries, theatre.
  Library, book corner, bulletin boards.

Beautifying school, classroom, community.

Participation in community projects.

A check-list for determining the adequacy of the instructional materials available in a specific curriculum area is illustrated in the following analysis of the kinds of learning aids needed for arithmetic: [3]

1. *Concrete and Manipulative Materials*
   Objects to use to help children to discover number groupings and facts.
   Devices to teach meanings of number, such as the abacus.
   Place value charts to teach meaning of number system.
   Materials used in demonstrating meanings of operations.
   Cutouts to show fractional values and relations.
   Instruments of measurement, such as rulers, scales, clocks, coins.
   Construction materials, field work, projects.
   Mechanical computing devices.
2. *Visual Aids*
   Illustrations that visualize the meanings of operations.
   Pictures, photographs, drawings to extend meanings.
   Beautiful designs and patterns.
   Motion pictures, strip films, television.
   Bulletin board exhibit.
3. *Symbolic or Abstract Materials*
   Textbooks, workbooks, practice materials.
   Diagnostic tests, progress tests, remedial exercises.
   Simplified instructional materials for slow learners.
   Charts, tables, graphs, diagrams.
   Reference books, pamphlets, bulletins.
   Business forms, blanks, bills, checks, receipts.
   Clippings, cartoons, maps.
   Games.
4. *Community Resources, Field Trips, Excursions*
   Stores, banks, other places of business, markets, governmental buildings.
   Health facilities, developmental centers, libraries, weather bureau.
   Museums, exhibits.
   Sport centers, transportation centers.
   Farms; local construction projects.

Similar check-lists of essential instructional materials for other curriculum areas can be prepared for the guidance of teachers and supervisors.

Studying the quality of instructional equipment. Whenever studies of equipment have been made, wide variations in the quality of supplies have been found. The differences from place to place are due to such factors as lack of funds, a narrow view of the possibilities and requirements of a subject, the limited viewpoint of the supervisory and teaching staff, and the indifference or lack of initiative of the teaching staff. The problem is further complicated if the pupils are required to purchase their own textbooks and other supplies, since this almost always results in a severe limitation of materials.

Several plans have been devised for studying the quality of instructional materials. For example, after a study of the reading materials used in a number of school systems, Zirbes [4] prepared a series of four levels for rating the adequacy of available reading materials. Her approach is most suggestive; the content of her scales could be brought up to date by any interested group. Baldwin [5] devised a somewhat different plan for determining the quality and adequacy of equipment in the social studies. He first made a careful study of the kinds of materials used in many school systems in social studies classrooms. He then checked the equipment to see how well it served generally accepted objectives of the subject. He also had the materials rated as to their value. On the basis of his analysis, he then drew up lists

---

[3] Based on suggestions given in *The Teaching of Arithmetic,* Fiftieth Yearbook, Part II, National Society for the Study of Education (Chicago, Univ. of Chicago Press, 1951), and L. J. Brueckner and F. E. Grossnickle, *Making Arithmetic Meaningful* (Philadelphia, John C. Winston, 1953).

[4] Laura Zirbes, *Comparative Studies of Current Practices in Reading with Techniques for the Improvement of Teaching,* Contributions to Education No. 316 (New York, Teachers College, Bureau of Publications, Columbia Univ., 1928).

[5] J. W. Baldwin, *Social Studies Laboratory,* Contributions to Education No. 371 (*ibid.,* 1929).

of the kinds of equipment that are necessary for efficient teaching of the social studies, with assigned ranks as to their importance. By checking the equipment available in any school against the Baldwin list, it is relatively simple to determine deficiencies. Baldwin's procedure is most suggestive but the contents of his check-list require revision to bring them up to date. The reader who is interested in the details should consult the references below.

Trends in the selection and adoption of textbooks. At the state level,[6] there has been a marked change in recent years in policies underlying the adoption of textbooks. There was a time in certain states when a single textbook was adopted for all schools as the basic textbook in a given curriculum area. Its use was required by law, and local schools had no choice among books. Later a plan was developed of adopting multiple lists of textbooks from which the schools were permitted to make a selection. The use of books not on the official list was illegal. In some states, schools were later given the right by law to purchase any desired book that was available on the open market. There have been abuses of all procedures of centralized adoptions and, in general, educational authorities do not approve of them. In theory, each school system should be free to select, with the help of competent specialists and teachers, the instructional materials that it desires and for which funds are available. In this way the needs of the schools can be met in making a choice of books.

The selection of textbooks in school systems was in the past often made by the superintendent's staff and specialists in the curriculum areas involved. The adoption often was made on the basis of personal factors, too infrequently on the basis of the systematic application of sets of criteria by those concerned. The criteria sometimes were wholly subjective; in other cases criteria were set up that required an objective analysis of the contents of the textbook so that dependable comparisons between competing textbooks were possible. In some places this analysis was made by research bureaus which prepared reports of the findings for those who were concerned with the actual adoption. In other cases it was made by committees of principals or teachers, under the guidance of supervisors or consultants. The data provided a basis for judgments as to merit, so that adoptions were no longer based on mere general impressions, such as the attractiveness of the pictures, the size of type, the use of color, and similar extraneous factors, but rather on a systematic analysis and evaluation of the contents of the various textbooks.

In recent years, in line with the principle of using democratic methods in dealing with problems of the schools, school administrators have invited teachers to participate in choosing textbooks. Sometimes this action has been limited to the participation of teacher committees, in some cases secretly appointed. In other instances the choice has has been made by majority vote of all teachers. The latter procedure is of very doubtful value unless the teachers have access to objective data about the textbooks; otherwise choices are made on general impressions as to the attractiveness of the books and various personal considerations.

The selection of textbooks is too important an undertaking to be done by haphazard methods such as are describd above. It should be done by committees under the guidance of supervisors and in consultation with specialists on the evaluation of instructional materials, so that there is a likelihood that adoptions will be made on the basis of a careful study of the merits of the books, rather than on the basis of personal and impressionistic considerations and uninformed judgment. Under competent leadership, various available sets of criteria and score cards should be examined and evaluated. The staff can modify any of them in line with the

---

[6] Victor R. Durrance, "Public Textbook Selection in Forty-eight States," *Phi Delta Kappan* (January, 1952), pp. 262-266.

thinking of the group as may be desirable, or set up co-operatively a new set of criteria. The experience the group has in applying well-conceived criteria under competent leadership will lead to a deeper appreciation on their part of the problems of textbook authors and publishers and to the recognition of the actual merits of the books that are finally adopted.

State uniformity of textbooks. Until recent years, about one-fourth of the states had the policy of state adoption of single textbooks to be used uniformly in public schools. Because of pressure by both professional groups and private agencies, the trend has shifted in the direction of multiple listings in an effort to remove some of the arguments against state uniformity. The following arguments for and against state uniformity of textbooks have been reported by Burnett: [7]

For State Uniformity
1. Uniform texts make possible a uniform course of study.
2. Local adoptions increase the possibilities of graft.
3. State adoption provides expertness of selection.
4. Mobility of population makes uniform texts desirable.
5. Uniformity brings lower prices for textbooks.

Against State Uniformity
1. Scope of adoption makes state competence impossible.
2. State adoptions have political implications; sizes of contracts increase threat of graft.
3. Ill-advised action has state-wide effect.
4. State adoptions show disrespect for teaching profession; stifle local initiative.
5. No state is a homogeneous unit.
6. State adoptions do not result in better choices of books.
7. State adoptions involve long periods of time during which new and better books cannot be adopted.

Arguments for and against free textbooks. In most places textbooks are either supplied free of cost or are rented to pupils, particu-larly in elementary schools. The issue of free textbooks for years was a subject of controversy. A summary of typical arguments in favor of free textbooks and against free textbooks as reported by Keesecker [8] follows:

In Favor of Free Textbooks
1. The textbook is an essential part of the American public-school system, and free textbooks make educational facilities more nearly equal and complete.
2. Distribution of free textbooks at the opening of the school term promotes dispatch and efficiency in inaugurating and proceeding with school work.
3. Free textbook systems promote uniformity of textbooks and efficiency of instruction.
4. Free textbooks promote economy when changes in textbooks are made and relieve many parents from buying textbooks which can be used for only one year.
5. Free textbook systems generally provide for the distribution of textbooks to children at the school and thus relieve parents and children from the frequent task of purchasing various books from local dealers.
6. Children are required to attend school, therefore they should be provided the tools with which to work. Free textbooks also tend to promote better school attendance.
7. Free textbooks enable children of poor parents to attend schools as well equipped with school facilities as children of well-to-do. When textbooks are free only to indigent children it is difficult to avoid unpleasant distinction, as such children are made to appear as charity pupils.

Against Free Textbooks
1. Under the free-textbook system many pupils receive used and unattractive

[7] Doctoral dissertation at Stanford Univ., 1948. Lewis W. Burnett, "Textbook Provisions in the Several States," *Journal of Educational Research* (January, 1950), pp. 357-366.

[8] Reprinted in a note on p. 261 of *Phi Delta Kappan*, Vol. 33 (January, 1952).
See also Ward W. Keesecker, "Free Textbook Trends Across the Nation," *School Life* (December, 1949), pp. 44-45.

books due to the fact that books which have been used one year are passed on to other pupils in succeeding years until they are worn out or a new adoption is made.

2. Free textbooks which are used by different students are often said to be unsanitary.
3. Publicly owned textbooks are used with less care than individually owned books.
4. Free-textbook systems impose unpleasant administrative and custodial duties upon teachers and interfere with instruction.
5. Free textbooks discourage home libraries and individual pride that comes from ownership.
6. The expense of free textbooks increases school taxes.

Criteria to be considered in rating textbooks. Score cards that are used in rating textbooks range from short lists of items to elaborate scales in which the various items are given weightings in terms of their significance. The rating a book receives is based on a composite of these weighted results.

The specific contents of score cards vary according to the fields of subject matter involved. In less valuable types of score cards, the items are stated in such a way that the ratings are merely expressions of subjective judgments of the rater based on general impressions. In other instances, the items are stated in such a way that it is necessary to assemble objective information about the contents of the books being rated, so that direct quantitative comparisons are possible between selected characteristics of different books as a basis for judging their merits; for instance, the vocabulary load, the kinds and usefulness of illustrations, the number of arithmetic problems or examples, the readability of the contents, and so on.

The list below contains a general classification of the items that should be considered in examining and rating single textbooks or a series of textbooks:

1. The degree to which the textbook (or series) emphasizes the educational objectives of the curriculum area involved that have been set up by the schools.
2. The value, authenticity, and freedom from bias of the contents.
3. The appeal of the contents to the interests of students.
4. Suitability to the maturity and reading level of the majority of students who will use the textbook.
5. The organization of the contents.
6. The scientific basis of the methods of teaching utilized in the development.
7. Aids to learning and teaching included in the contents.
8. Provisions for individual differences.
9. The physical make-up of the book.
10. The attractiveness of the format and the use made of illustrations.
11. The total instructional program of which the textbook is an integral part, including essential supplementary materials.
12. The experience and reputation of the authors.

An old but still valuable list of items found in rating scales is included in an article by Gertrude Whipple, "Procedures Used in Selecting Textbooks," which appeared in *The Elementary School Journal,* Vol. 36 (June, 1936), pp. 760-775.

Selected rating scales for evaluating textbooks. Many rating scales have been devised for evaluating textbooks, some of which contain excellent lists of criteria that led themselves to objective analysis. The following sources may be consulted by those interested in devising scales for rating textbooks.

BRUECKNER, L. J., and GROSSNICKLE, F. E., *Making Arithmetic Meaningful* (Philadelphia, John C. Winston, 1953). Ch. 14 contains a scale for rating arithmetic textbooks.

DAVIS, H. J., "Criteria for Selecting Science Books," *School Science and Mathematics* (April, 1942), pp. 360-364.

GREGORY, W. M., "Scoring Plan for Elementary Geography Texts," *Education* (December, 1934), pp. 307-313.

KOPEL, David, and O'CONNOR, J. F., "Criteria for Evaluating Reading Textbooks," *Journal of Experimental Education* (September, 1943-June, 1944), pp. 26-33.

———, "Procedures for Evaluating Textbooks in Reading," *Journal of Experimental Edu-*

cation (September, 1943-June, 1944), pp. 34-36.

MELBO, I. R., and WATERMAN, I. R., "Evaluation of Textbook Materials in Handwriting," *Elementary School Journal* (November, 1935), pp. 204-210.

NEWLUN, Chester, "The Selection of Basal Readers," *Elementary School Journal* (December, 1931), pp. 285-293.

SMITH, Dora V., chairman, "Evaluation of Composition Textbooks," Report of National Council Committee, *English Journal* (April, 1932), pp. 280-294.

SPRACHE, George, "Selection of Spelling Textbooks," *Elementary English Review* (February, 1940), pp. 51-59.

WATERMAN, I. R., *The Evaluation of Arithmetic Textbooks*, Bulletin No. 19 (Sacramento, Calif., State Department of Education, 1932).

————, and MELBO, I. R., "Evaluation of Spelling Textbooks," *Elementary School Journal* (September, 1935), pp. 44-52.

The State Textbook Commission of California [9] has devised a number of excellent scales for rating textbooks, illustrated below.

[9] Ivan R. Waterman, "When You Choose a Textbook," *Phi Delta Kappan* (January, 1952), pp. 267-271.

SCORE CARD FOR EVALUATING BASIC TEXTBOOKS IN READING FOR GRADES FOUR AND FIVE

Criteria	Weightings
1. *Nature of the Material*	100

The material shall include a wide variety of
- a. Stories of today's science, adventures, heroes, and inventions.
- b. Stories of the past, its heroes and enduring literature.
- c. Stories that seek to develop high ideals, good character, and appreciation of other peoples.
- d. Stories designed to develop an appreciation and love for American ideals and institutions.
- e. Good poems—old and new.

2. *Quality of the Material*	100

- a. It shall be interestingly and well written. It shall be devoid of careless errors and crude English.
- b. It shall be characterized by simplicity, beauty, and imaginativeness.

3. *Function of the Material*	200

Provision must be made for the adequate development of the following reading abilities:
- a. Analytical reading.
  - (1) Getting central thought or general idea.
  - (2) Evaluating, comparing, inferring, drawing conclusions.
  - (3) Summarizing, organizing, outlining.
  - (4) Following directions.
  - (5) Reading for specific information.
  - (6) Reading for comprehension.
  - (7) Interpreting attitudes, various expressions, and humor.
- b. Location of materials.
  - (1) Skimming for particular information or details.
  - (2) Using titles, chapter or section headings, paragraph headings.
  - (3) Using table of contents, indexes, glossaries, bibliographies, appendices.
  - (4) Using encyclopedias.
  - (5) Using dictionaries.
  - (6) Using graphs, diagrams, charts, maps, and tables.

Criteria	Weightings

    c. Vocabulary growth.
        (1) Word meanings.
        (2) Word recognition study.
    d. Oral reading.
        (1) Suitable selections for oral reading.
        (2) Appropriate selections for dramatization.

4. *Organization of the Material*   100
The material must be arranged and organized on the basis of a definite and acceptable plan.

5. *Appropriateness of Material to Children's Capabilities*   150
    a. The concepts treated must be within the understanding of children for whom the material is intended and must be designed to extend and enrich their experience. Emphasis must be directed toward the development of efficient silent reading for information and enjoyment.
    b. The vocabulary, sentence structure, and paragraph organization must be in accord with the ability of the children of the various age groups.

6. *Amount of Material*   75
The book, or combination of books, must contain an adequate amount of material.

7. *Illustrations*   50
There should be accurate up-to-date illustrations, with much use of color, that
    a. Illustrate the story.
    b. Develop concepts and vocabulary.

8. *Format*   75
The format and other mechanical features must conform to acceptable standards for
    a. General appearance.
    b. Face and size of type.
    c. Margins and arrangement of material on page.
    d. Cover design.

9. *Instructional Aids*   150
    a. There should be intrinsic teaching aids, such as
        (1) A paged list of new words developed in the reader.
        (2) An accessible and usable glossary which presents phonetic spelling and defines accurately various meanings of words.
        (3) A well-organized table of contents with page references to authors and story titles.
        (4) A functional pronunciation key.
        (5) References to other books for children to read and interesting comments upon such books.
        (6) Provisions for checking children's achievement.
    b. There should be a teacher's manual which
        (1) Offers a wide variety of suggestions for teaching.
        (2) Gives short, usable synopses of stories to aid in planning the teaching objectives.
        (3) Suggests ways of checking growth in the various abilities and provides some exercises for that purpose.
        (4) Provides a systematic plan for developing word recognition and word meanings.
            TOTAL   1000

The following table gives the criteria and distinction of weights for scoring on the California arithmetic score card.

Criteria	Scoring
Problem Material	125
Processes Presented	125
Practice Material	150
Measurement of Achievement	150
Provision for Individual Differences . .	50
Grade Placement and Sequence	75
Informational Arithmetic	50
Vocabulary and Sentence Structure . . .	50
Balance	100
Teacher Aids	75
Physical Features	50
TOTAL POINTS	1000

Evaluating teaching aids found in textbooks. A procedure that should be useful in evaluating the contents of textbooks is implied in an analysis reported by Lawrence [10] of the extent to which 170 biology teachers stated that they used fourteen kinds of teaching aids contained in all biology textbooks used in the State of Connecticut. These aids were defined as follows by Lawrence:

1. *References.* Any listing of books, newspapers, magazines, and other sources of information pertaining to the area of study under discussion.

2. *Projects.* Individual or group activities—many types: includes collections of samples, community surveys, chart making, and the like.

3. *Problems.* Major questions of large scope —usually involve group planning on a long-term basis.

4. *Reports.* Individual or committee oral reports to the class. May include summary of an experiment, project, or book.

5. *Tests.* May be of several types—essay, multiple-choice, completion, true-false, others.

6. *Demonstrations.* Teacher or student presentation of experiments or other materials to the class.

7. *Vocabularies.* Lists of scientific terms.

8. *Field trips.* Any excursion, visit, or "outside the classroom" work of an educational nature.

9. *Experiments.* Individual or group work on the testing of scientific laws or observations —includes laboratory work.

10. *Principles.* Lists of basic truths, scientific laws, or rules of action—includes applications or scientific methods and attitudes.

11. *Visual-aid sources.* Lists of sources for securing charts, models, films, film strips, microprojection equipment, and the like.

12. *Outlines or summaries.* Important conclusions to be drawn from the area of study.

13. *Review questions.* Usually found at the end of the chapter. Designed to test the student's understanding of the area under study. Under this heading are found "written exercises."

14. *Guide questions.* Usually found at the beginning of the chapter. Designed to control the area of study and to stimulate thought.

The table on page 431 shows the extent to which teachers indicated in interviews that they used these different kinds of aids.

There are wide differences in the value of these aids as measured by the extent to which they appeared in textbooks (X) and by the extent of their use. For instance, references were given in almost all textbooks, but they were seldom if ever used. Teachers indicated that they preferred current newspaper and magazine articles. Field trips, visual aids, sources and problems in textbooks were seldom used, since teachers preferred to use their own materials and local sources. On the other hand, such aids in textbooks as vocabulary lists, review questions, and outlines or summaries were used extensively.

Other aspects of textbooks subject to analysis. Similar objective analyses can be made for other characteristics of textbooks, such as:

1. The amount of material devoted to major topics.
2. The percentage of material in readers devoted to such types as true stories, biography, drama, poetry, and the like.
3. Provision for practice exercises on various leading skills.
4. Number of illustrations of various kinds.
5. The kinds of tests and diagnostic procedures provided.
6. Distribution of practice on arithmetic processes.
7. The variety of social applications of problems.

[10] F. S. Lawrence, "Teaching Aids in Biology Texts," *Phi Delta Kappan* (January, 1952), pp. 288-289.

SUMMARY OF THE EXTENT OF USE OF TEACHING AIDS

Teaching Aids	Scoring Key for Interview [a]						
	X	A	B	C	D	E	Tot.[b]
1. References	3	57	60	42	3	5	167
2. Projects	5	55	62	38	8	2	165
3. Problems	8	63	61	23	8	7	162
4. Reports	41	36	46	29	14	4	129
5. Tests	97	26	12	13	9	13	73
6. Demonstrations	70	21	34	36	8	1	100
7. Vocabularies	23	18	16	31	30	52	147
8. Field trips	26	116	23	5	0	0	144
9. Experiments	36	42	43	41	6	2	134
10. Principles	100	26	13	19	6	6	70
11. Visual-aid sources	83	66	11	5	3	2	87
12. Outlines or summaries	38	37	27	36	14	18	132
13. Review questions	3	30	31	48	29	29	167
14. Guide questions	77	38	11	25	13	6	93

[a] The teachers were asked during the interview to respond by letters. The code letters, and meaning, were as follows:
X—if the item does not occur in the textbook
A—if the item occurs, but is never used
B—if the item occurs, but is rarely used
C—if the item occurs and is frequently used
D—if the item occurs and is almost always used
E—if the item occurs and is always used
[b] This column indicates the number of teachers using textbooks which contained the item.

8. Provision for individual differences.
9. The gradation of spelling words in terms of difficulty and frequency of usage.
10. The reading difficulty and readability of the contents.
11. The relation of contents to objectives and contents of local courses of study.

Difficulty of materials. Dependable methods for studying the difficulty of materials included in textbooks are available. The two basic methods used are the comparison of the contents of book with materials of standardized difficulty, and the actual testing of pupils on materials selected on a sampling basis from the books to be evaluated.

Lorge [11] listed the following characteristics that have been shown experimentally to be useful in measuring the readability of materials:

1. *Some measure of vocabulary (always used)*
   a. Number of running words.
   b. Percentage of different words.
   c. Percentage of different infrequent, uncommon, or hard words.
   d. Percentage of polysyllabic words.
   e. Some weighted measure of vocabulary difficulty.
   f. Vocabulary diversity (related to *b*).
   g. Number of abstract words.
   h. Number of affixed morphemes (prefixes, inflectional endings, etc.)
2. *Some measure of sentence structure or style (usually used)*
   a. Percentage of prepositional phrases.
   b. Percentage of indeterminate clauses.
   c. Number of simple sentences.
   d. Average of sentence length.
3. *Some measure of human interest (much less frequently used)*
   a. Number of personal pronouns.
   b. Number of words expressing human interest.
   c. Percentage of colorful words.
   d. Number of words representing fundamental life-experiences.
   e. Number of words usually learned early in life (related to *b*).

There has been considerable criticism of the use of word lists in evaluating the vocabulary load of textbooks and other reading materials, particularly by teachers of English

[11] Irving Lorge, "Predicting Readability," *Teachers College Record* (March, 1944), pp. 404-419.

and by semanticists. The position is taken that pupil interest and need often require the use of materials in which the vocabulary is considerably beyond the limits of these word lists, for example, in an experience program in reading in the primary grades. It is also contended that since words have different meanings, particularly in different contexts, the uncritical use of a list of words in evaluating a textbook is a basically unsound procedure.[12]

There is undoubtedly some merit in these contentions. It should, however, be pointed out that studies of textbooks have shown that there is a great unevenness in the vocabulary load, especially in the primary grades. The burden is often so great that slow pupils have considerable difficulty in reading. The teacher who knows the vocabulary loads of books and their reading difficulty is able to make effective adaptations of materials to the level of ability of the pupils. Word lists should in any case not be regarded as fixed and final. Teachers should recognize the fact that words in lists may have many different meanings and present them accordingly in a variety of settings. To assume that a word has only one meaning is definitely misleading. Everyday conversation with children reveals the difficulty here.

Washburne has published a formula which enables the supervisor to determine the level of reading ability required to read a particular book. Washburne's description of the application of this formula to a particular book follows: [13]

It is not necessary here to explain in detail how we finally determined the best combination of elements for the making of the formula. Suffice it to say that after many trials and much study we found a combination which gave us a high correlation (.86) with grades all the way from the first to the ninth, which corrected the skewing of the Winnetka Graded Book List, and which was simpler than the earlier formula and predicted with satisfactory accuracy the degree of reading ability needed by children to read a given book with pleasure. The probable error of estimate was 0.8 of a grade—as close as could be desired or warranted.

The three elements that go into this new formula are simple:

1. In a thousand words, from a systematic sampling of the book, how many different words are there?
2. Of this same thousand words, how many are not among the 1,500 commonest in the English language?
3. Out of seventy-five sentences, sampled systematically, how many are neither complex nor compound?

These are combined in a regression formula as follows:

Number of different words in 1,000 multiplied by .00255,

Plus number of different uncommon words in 1,000 multiplied by .0458,

Plus, a constant: 1.294,

Minus the number of simple sentences in 75 multiplied by .0307,

Yields the grade of reading ability for satisfying reading of the book.

Perhaps this formula will be a little more intelligible if it is applied to a book:

Tom Sawyer, for example:

Number of different words in 1,000	$-373 \times .00255 =$	0.951
Plus: Number of different uncommon words in 1,000	$-117 \times .0458 =$	5.359
Plus: Constant		1.294
		7.604
Minus: Number of simple sentences in 75	$-18 \times .0307 =$	.553
		7.051

Tom Sawyer can be easily read, therefore, by a child with a reading ability of grade 7.1. Practically, this figure means that the book is suitable, as far as difficulty is concerned, for children of seventh-grade ability or higher.

Spache [14] gives the following regression equation for those who wish to use his for-

[12] Irving Lorge, "Word Lists as Backgrounds for Communication," *Teachers College Record,* Vol. 45 (April, 1944), pp. 543-53.

E. W. Dolch, "Tested Word Knowledge vs. Frequency Counts," *Journal of Educational Research* (February, 1951), pp. 457-470.

[13] C. W. Washburne and Mabel M. Vogel, "Grade Placement of Children's Books," *Elementary School Journal* (January, 1938), pp. 355-364.

[14] G. D. Spache, "A New Readability Formula for Primary Grade Reading Materials," *Elementary School Journal* (March, 1953), pp. 410-413.

mula for measuring the readabilty of primary reading materials: Grade level of textbook = .141 × average sentence length per 100 words + .086 × words outside the Dale "Easy Word List" of 769 words + constant .839.

The sum of the items represents the reading difficulty of the book. Thus if the sum is a figure such as 2.267, the reading difficulty of the book is grade 2.3, that is, 2.267 rounded off to the nearest tenth.

Aspects of the content of textbooks that influence their difficulty. The problem of preparing readable, usable textbooks is ever present for authors and publishers, because pupils in apparently increasing numbers are encountering serious difficulty in reading assigned materials with adequate comprehension. It was ·at one time believed that theme, nature of subject matter, and unity were the most significant aspects of content influencing its readability. Consideration was also given to various aspects of style of expression, presentation, and organization.

In more recent years, three different groups of variables have been widely used in estimating and predicting readability of textbooks and other printed materials. In the following statement Gray [15] defines these three groups and indicates the types of additional factors that should be investigated in order to secure more dependable estimates of readability:

Three groups of variables have been used widely in predicting readability of passages and books. They are (a) vocabulary, including number of different words, percentage of different, infrequent, uncommon or hard words, percentage of polysyllabic words, vocabulary diversity, number of abstract words, or number of affixed phonemes (prefixes, inflectional endings, etc.); (b) sentence structure, including such items as average sentence length and complexity; and (c) some measure of human interest, such as number of personal pronouns, words expressing human interest, colorful words, and words representing fundamental life experiences.

Whereas all these factors are of great importance, research in the field of readability should be carefully studied in the future. We need to know far more clearly than at present the extent to which such factors as the following influence the readability of textbooks: kind of themes; nature of content; patterns of organization; abstractness of treatment; use of verbal and pictorial illustrations; compactness of ideas. This list could be greatly extended. Since the influence of many of these factors will vary among individuals of different background, it is important to determine which of the factors are most constant in influencing difficulty and which are most variable.

The immediate object of the research here proposed is not another formula for determining readability. That might follow in the course of time. The basic aim sought is a clearer understanding of the various factors that make for difficulty in understanding the content of textbooks.

Interest appeal of pictures. Whipple [16] made a study of the interest appeal of illustrations in six fourth-grade textbooks. Altogether 150 children were given the opportunity to select three illustrations, by examining in pairs six prepared booklets of illustrations cut out of the books, thus suggesting that the stories accompanying them would be the most interesting to read. This plan was designed to measure the *potential* interest in the accompanying text, defined as "narrative interest value." The original report should be consulted for details as to factors that are related to interest appeal of pictures.

Whipple states that the narrative interest value of different books may be estimated by ranking the books, using all or a sampling of the illustrations, with respect to the following specific standards:

1. The proportion of the illustrations that have a definite center of interest which draws the eye to a particular point. Such a center is usually large and impressive, easy to interpret, and not subordinated by too many details.
2. The proportion of the illustrations that

[15] A short statement by W. S. Gray in a symposium on "Needed Research on Textbooks" in *Phi Delta Kappan* (January, 1952), p. 298.

[16] Gertrude Whipple, "Appraisal of the Interest Appeal of Illustrations," *The Elementary School Journal* (January, 1953), p. 269.

depict action. The more interesting the moment of action, the more appealing the illustration. The action ranks high if it tells a story in a sequence of pictures.

3. The extent to which color is used in the illustrations. An illustration in several colors has greater merit than a black-and-white picture. The artificial use of a single color other than black is less appealing to children than the realistic use of three or four colors.

4. The average size of the illustrations. The larger the area devoted to the illustration, the higher the interest value, other characteristics being equal.

5. The number of illustrations included in the book. The larger the total number of illustrations in the book, the higher the interest value. This statement holds up to an undefined point of saturation. Too many illustrations would reduce the amount of reading matter and make the textbook a mere picture-book.

6. The extent to which the illustrations deal with eventful topics as opposed to still-life topics. An illustration which presents a theme having marked human interest, displaying the supernatural, or relating to exciting adventures has greater merit than an illustration on an uneventful topic.

Special aids for the teacher in making scientific appraisal of books. The supervisor should be familiar with objective scientific techniques that can be utilized in evaluating instructional materials and be able to assist teachers to apply at least the simpler procedures in the study of equipment prior to its selection and purchase. The selected references below are grouped by categories that can be investigated as may be desired. They should be consulted for details as to procedures of analysis. Reports of selected studies may be made in courses.

BASIC VOCABULARY CONTENT

BUCKINGHAM, B. R., and DOLCH, E. W., *A Combined Word List* (Boston, Ginn, 1936).

DALE, Edgar, "Dale List of 3000 Familiar Words," *Educational Research Bulletin*, Vol. 27 (1948), pp. 45-54. Columbus, Bureau of Educational Research, Ohio State Univ.

FITZGERALD, James A., "Spelling Words Diffi-
cult for Children in Grades II-VI," *Elementary School Journal* (December, 1952), pp. 211-228. (Summary of research.)

GATES, A. I., *A Reading Vocabulary for the Primary Grades* (New York, Teachers College, Bureau of Publications, Columbia Univ., 1926).

HORN, Ernest, *A Basic Writing Vocabulary*, University of Iowa Monographs in Education, First Series, No. 4 (Iowa City, Univ. of Iowa, 1936).

KRANTZ, L. L., *The Author's Word List* (Minneapolis, Curriculum Research Co., 1945).

RINSLAND, H. D., *A Basic Writing Vocabulary of Elementary School Children* (New York, Macmillan, 1945).

THORNDIKE, E. L., *The Teacher's Word Book* (New York, Teachers College, Bureau of Publications, Columbia Univ., 1921).

————, and LORGE, Irving, *The Teacher's Word Book of 30,000 Words* (New York, Teachers College, Bureau of Publications, Columbia Univ., 1944).

VOCABULARY LOAD

GENTRY, Lillian, "Study of the Vocabulary Load of Sixty-Six Pre-Primers," *Journal of Educational Research* (March, 1950), pp. 525-532.

HOCKETT, J. A., and NEELEY, Deta, "A Comparison of the Vocabularies of Thirty-three Primers," *Elementary School Journal* (November, 1936), pp. 190-202.

LEWERENZ, A. S., "A Vocabulary Grade Placement Formula," *Journal of Experimental Education* (March, 1935).

PATTY, W. W., and PAINTER, W. L., "A Technique for Measuring the Vocabulary Burden of Textbooks," *Journal of Educational Research* (September, 1931), pp. 127-134.

SERRA, Mary C., "The Concept Burden of Instructional Materials," *Elementary School Journal* (May, 1953), pp. 508-512.

THORNDIKE, E. L., "The Vocabulary of Books for Children in Grades 3 to 8," *Teachers College Record* (December, 1938-February, 1939), pp. 196-205, 316-323, 416-428.

Note: Most publishers of primary-reading textbooks will be glad to supply lists of the vocabulary used, indicating the amount of practice on the various words, the number of new words per page, and similar kinds of statistical information.

FORMAT, SIZE OF TYPE, COLOR OF PRINT

BAMBERGER, Florence, *The Effect of the Physical Make-up of a Book upon Children's Selection* (Baltimore, Johns Hopkins Univ., 1922).

BUCKINGHAM, B. R., in *The Textbook in Education,* Thirtieth Yearbook, National Society for the Study of Education (Bloomington, Ill., Public School Publishing Co., 1931).

PATERSON, D. G., and TINKER, M. A., "Black Type Versus White Type," *Journal of Applied Psychology* (June, 1931), pp. 241-247.

PATERSON, D. G., and TINKER, M. A., "Studies of the Typographical Factors Influencing Speed of Reading: XI. Role of Set in Typographical Studies; XII. Printing Surface; XIII. Methodological Considerations," *Journal of Applied Psychology* (December, 1935), pp. 647-651; (February, 1936), pp. 128-131, 132-145.

RUDISILL, Mabel, "Children's Preferences for Color versus Other Qualities of Instruction," *Elementary School Journal* (April, 1952), pp. 444-451.

TINKER, M. A., "Hygienic Lighting Intensities," *Journal of Industrial Hygiene* (November, 1935), pp. 258-262.

———— and PATERSON, D., "Differences Among Newspaper Body Types in Readability," *Journalism Quarterly* (June, 1943). (Reprint.)

PICTURES AND ILLUSTRATIONS

Dow, Sterling, "Illustrations in Textbooks," *Journal of General Education* (January, 1951).

FRENCH, John E., "Children's Preferences for Pictures of Varied Complexity of Pictorial Pattern," *Elementary School Journal* (October, 1952), pp. 90-95.

GROSSNICKLE, F. E., "Illustrations in Arithmetic Textbook," *Elementary School Journal* (October, 1946), pp. 84-92.

MALTER, M. S., "Studies of the Effectiveness of Graphic Materials," *Journal of Educational Research* (December, 1952), pp. 263-274.

MELBO, I. R., and WATERMAN, I. R., "Pictures in Geography Textbooks," *Elementary School Journal* (January, 1936), pp. 363-376.

MELLINGER, Bonnie E., *Children's Interests in Pictures,* Contributions to Education No. 516 (New York, Teachers College, Bureau of Publications, Columbia Univ., 1952).

READ, John G., "Picture Indices for Basic Readers," *Elementary School Journal* (February, 1950), pp. 339-340.

STERNER, Alice P., *Radio, Motion Picture, and Reading Interests,* Contributions to Education No. 932 (New York, Teachers College, Bureau of Publications, Columbia Univ., 1947).

WHIPPLE, Gertrude, "Appraisal of the Interest Appeal of Illustrations" *Elementary School Journal* (January, 1953), pp. 262-269.

INTERESTS

BRUNER, H. B., "Determining Basic Reading Materials Through a Study of Children's Interest and Adult Judgments," *Teachers College Record* (January, 1929), pp. 285-309.

GATES, A. I., *Interest and Ability in Reading* (New York, Macmillan, 1930).

JORDAN, A. M., *Children's Interests in Reading,* Contributions to Education No. 107 (New York, Teachers College, Bureau of Publications, Columbia Univ., 1921).

MANUCK, Inez L., and SWENSON, Esther J., "A Study of Children's Recreational Reading," *Elementary School Journal* (November, 1949), pp. 144-150.

MCCAULEY, Lucile, "Children's Interests in Poetry," *English Review* (November, 1948), pp. 426-441.

POLLOCK, C. A., "Children's Interests as a Basis of What to Teach in General Science," *Educational Research Bulletin* (January 9, 1924).

SCANLAN, W. J., "One Hundred Most Popular Books of Children's Fiction Selected by Children," *English Review* (February, 1948), pp. 83-97.

WASHBURNE, C. W., "A Grade Placement Curriculum Investigation: A Study of Children's Interests," *Journal of Educational Research* (April, 1926), pp. 284-292.

————, and VOGEL, Mabel M., *What Children Like to Read* (Chicago, Rand McNally, 1929).

WASHBURNE, C. W., "A Grade Placement Curriculum Investigation: A Study of Children's Interests," *Journal of Educational Research* (April, 1946), pp. 284-292.

ZELLER, Dale, *The Relation and Importance of Factors of Interest in Reading Materials in Junior High School Pupils,* Contributions to Education No. 841 (New York, Teachers College, Bureau of Publications, Columbia Univ., 1941).

DIFFICULTY AND GRADATION
OF CONTENT

AYER, Adelaide, *Difficulties in Elementary School History,* Contributions to Education No. 212 (New York, Teachers College, Bureau of Publications, Columbia Univ., 1926).

BRUECKNER, L. J., and GROSSNICKLE, F. E., *Making Arithmetic Meaningful* (Philadelphia, John C. Winston, 1953). Ch. 3 contains data on the difficulty of various processes in arithmetic.

BRUECKNER, L. J., and IRVING, J. A., "A Technique for Comparing the Difficulty of Problems in Arithmetic Textbooks," *Elementary School Journal* (December, 1932), pp. 283-285.

BRUECKNER, L. J., and LAUMANN, G. S., "The Measurement of Accuracy of Judgments of the Difficulty of Arithmetic Problems," *Educational Method* (March, 1933), pp. 338-345.

Child Development and the Curriculum, Thirty-eighth Yearbook, National Society for the Study of Education (Bloomington, Ill., Public School Publishing Co., 1939). Part I contains an authoritative discussion of research in all areas of the curriculum on the gradation of subject matter. Ch. 16 contains a detailed summary of the recommendations of the Committee of Seven.

MATTHEWS, C. O., *The Grade Placement of Curriculum Materials in the Social Studies,* Contributions to Education No. 241 (New York, Teachers College, Bureau of Publications, Columbia Univ., 1926).

WASHBURNE, C. W., "Mental Age and the Arithmetic Curriculum," *Journal of Educational Research* (March, 1931), pp. 3-24. For a discussion sharply critical of the work of the Committee of Seven, see W. A. Brownell, "A Critique of the Committee of Seven's Investigation of the Grade Placement of Arithmetic Topics," *Elementary School Journal* (March, 1938), pp. 495-508.

WISE, "The Spelling Difficulty of 1102 Words Found in Twenty Spellers," *Elementary School Journal* (December, 1935), pp. 281-289.

READABILITY

DALE, Edgar, and CHALL, Jeanne S., "A Formula for Predicting Readability," *Educational Research Bulletin* 21 (January 11, 1948, pp. 11-20; February 17, 1948, pp. 37-54).

FARR, James W., JENKINS, J. J., and PATERSON, D. G., "Simplification of Flesch Reading Ease Formula," *Journal of Applied Psychology* (October, 1951), pp. 333-337.

FLESCH, Rudolf, *Marks of Readable Style* (New York, Teachers College, Bureau of Publications, Columbia Univ., 1943).

GRAY, W. S., and LEARY, Bernice, *What Makes a Book Readable?* (Chicago, Univ. of Chicago, Univ. of Chicago Press, 1934).

LORGE, Irving, "Readability Formulae: Evaluation," *Elementary English* (February, 1949), pp. 81-95.

MALLINSON, G. G., STURM, H. E., and PATTON, R. E., "The Reading Difficulty of Textbooks in Elementary Science," *Elementary School Journal* (April, 1950).

MILLER, Leo R., "Reading Grade Placement of the First 23 Books Awarded the John Newberry Prize," *Elementary School Journal* (March, 1946), pp. 394-399.

RUSSELL, David H., and FEA, Harry L., "The Validity of Six Readability Formulas as Measures of Juvenile Fiction," *Elementary School Journal* (November, 1951), pp. 136-144.

SPACHE, George, "A New Readability Formula for Primary-Grade Reading Materials," *Elementary School Journal* (March, 1953), pp. 410-413.

VOGEL, Mabel, and WASHBURNE, C. W., "An Objective Method of Determining Grade Placement of Children's Reading Materials," *Elementary School Journal* (January, 1928), pp. 373-381.

Other means of appraisal of textbooks. Several other means of studying the merits of books and workbooks may be suggested. They may be tried out in the classroom to observe how the children react to them and how easily they can be administered by the teacher. Book reviews and appraisals by experts can be consulted. Various types of statistical procedure can be applied to the contents to study the overlapping of several books. The amount and distribution of practice can be found by simply counting the examples or words on each page and finding the total. In all cases the supervisor will find it helpful to make some sort of quantitative study of instructional materials so that the conclusions will be based on facts rather than on general impressions.

The evaluation of workbooks. For years there have been available commercially prepared drill materials in the form of practice exercises in arithmetic, reading, language, and the social studies; reading charts; and many others. In recent years there have been published large numbers of workbooks which contain a wide variety of instructional aids and practice exercises. Many workbooks are designed to accompany a given textbook; others supply materials in some field without reference to any particular textbook. The better workbooks are so well organized and prepared that they are practically self-instructive, and their use enables the teacher to adapt the work to the needs, rate of learning, and interests of individual pupils. Less desirable workbooks merely include a mass of supplementary miscellaneous drill material which is so organized and arranged that it is practically impossible to adapt instruction to individual differences. Furthermore, there is real danger that the use of these inferior kinds of workbooks will lead to isolated and meaningless drill that is assigned indiscriminately as a form of busy work. In so far as is possible, practice based on materials in workbooks should grow out of needs derived from meaningful experience or be readily integrated with such experiences.

The criteria to be considered in evaluating workbooks should be formulated in terms of the functions they serve. These vary from subject to subject. Criteria for evaluating a workbook in primary reading, for example, are not likely to be the same as those for appraising an arithmetic workbook for the intermediate grades.

Andreen [17] reported the results of observations of the use of workbooks in a large number of classrooms in several school systems. In many classes, the workbook represents merely a "series of convenient tasks and exercises, the doing of which is to be rigorously directed by the teacher." In other classes, teachers regard the workbook "as a service tool to be used by the student in ways dictated by his individual needs and desires."

"A majority of teachers" depend upon these workbooks to the extent that "their own personality is almost entirely removed from the teaching-learning situation." He adds the significant comment, "Teachers who assign the teaching function to a printed page within a workbook are not giving the optimum of learning service to their pupils." Further studies of this problem are much needed.

The effective use of well-constructed workbooks by teachers who understand their functions as well as their possible limitations is an important factor in the guidance of the learning activity. The elimination of workbooks that are nothing more than compilations of routine drill exercises, that are to be assigned as "busy work," should be a supervisory goal. The selection of any workbook should be done on the basis of criteria that stress the contribution such materials should make to the guidance and improvement of learning. A good workbook in the hands of a skillful teacher is a valuable instructional aid.

The following criteria for evaluating any workbook are derived from a study of workbooks in various curriculum areas by the authors:

1. The contents contribute to the achievement of desirable objectives, general or special.
2. The functions of the workbook are stated clearly. They should be evaluated in terms of the functions that the group wishes the selected workbook to serve.
3. The organization of materials is such that their specific purposes are clear to teacher and learner.
4. The directions to pupils are stated in simple direct language.
5. The contents of the workbook effectively supplement a basal instruction program and provide numerous and varied experiences and practice of the skills and abilities being developed.

[17] Earl P. Andreen, "A Study of Workbooks in Arithmetic," *Journal of Educational Research* (October, 1938), pp. 108-123. Contains list of criteria.
H. A. Schneider, *The Place of Workbooks in the Teaching of Arithmetic,* Supplementary Educational Monograph No. 66 (Chicago, Univ. of Chicago Press, 1948), pp. 54-67.

6. The activities are challenging and are likely to be interesting to the learners.

7. Special activities for more able learners are included.

8. Diagnostic tests and devices facilitating self-diagnosis are included, together with extensive and flexible provisions for corrective and remedial work to follow diagnosis.

9. Informal means of determining progress are included.

10. The workbook is attractively illustrated, well made, and there is ample space for pupil work.

The supervisor, with the assistance of groups of teachers, can adapt these criteria more specifically to the evaluation of workbooks in any particular curriculum area.

Illustrative statement of criteria [18] *for workbooks in a specific curriculum area.* An illustrative statement of the functions that are served by a typical sixth-grade reading workbook suggests the kinds of contributions that any well-planned workbook can make to the improvement of learning:

1. Extending reading experiences in new content that is enriching and closely related to the reader which it supplements.

2. Giving further experience with the vocabulary in new and varied content so that the words can be more readily recognized.

3. Developing the comprehension abilities that the child must master in order to continue to gain in reading power and efficiency.

4. Reviewing and refining abilities introduced earlier, presented so that the child may not lose any of the competencies which have been taught previously.

5. Building readiness for abilities to be developed later, so that the child's growth can be smooth and free from undue hazards.

6. Giving added experience with and direct instruction in a variety of word-recognition techniques so that the child can become an independent reader of material of increasing difficulty.

7. Giving specific instruction in and experience with the various basic study skills so that the child can use his growing reading power in study-type reading situations.

8. Expanding meaning vocabulary and encouraging the habit and desire to study words and their varied meanings, and by developing an understanding of the meaning values of structural elements.

9. Encouraging the development of a differentiated attack necessary for reading various types of content for a variety of purposes.

10. Developing independent study habits so that the child may learn to rely on his own resources and will become increasingly independent of the teacher.

11. Making the processes of reading meaningful to the child through isolating them for specific attention in contextual and real reading situations.

12. Developing habits of accuracy and self-checking so that the child may become aware of the need for understanding the printed page fully and so that he can study his own progress.

13. Enabling the teacher to make continuous diagnoses of learning difficulties of each child so that a minor difficulty need not develop into a major problem.

14. Providing the opportunity for additional practice on a specific skill or ability which needs re-enforcing for a given child in order to prevent the need for remedial work later.

Obviously, criteria for evaluating the contents of workbooks will vary from field to field and in accordance with the functions they are to serve. A most fruitful experience for a group of teachers is to set up criteria, under the leadership of the supervisor, to be applied in selecting workbooks. The items should lend themselves if possible to objective analysis so that the data secured will be helpful in comparing contents of workbooks and evaluating their merits.

Selection and use of "nonlisted" instructional materials. Many valuable instructional materials do not appear on official lists. They are offered to the schools by many outside organizations, institutions, and special-interest groups. These offerings fall into the categories of printed materials, visual aids, auditory aids, and concrete materials. For the most part they are inexpensive, some are free, some are rentals, some are gifts.

Most school heads encourage the use of such materials because they enrich learning experiences. However, because of their vast variety, few of them can be "officially listed"

[18] Adapted from pp. 57-59 in Teacher's Guide for *Stories to Remember* (Chicago, Lyons and Carnahan, 1952).

for use in the schools. They also vary greatly in quality and appropriateness. Recently the Board of Education of New York City approved the following group of general principles [19] for selection of "nonlisted" instructional materials as guides for teachers, principals, and supervisors:

Commercially-Sponsored Materials

1. The material should make a significant contribution toward educational goals.
2. The advertising content of the materials should be minimal, unobjectionable, and unobtrusive.
3. The advertising matter should be in good taste. It should be fair, accurate, and free from excessive promotional or competitive presentation.
4. Wherever possible, the materials used should be those provided by the industry as a whole rather than by individuals or companies.
5. In commercial and technical subjects, in which identification of machines, apparatus or other illustrative materials by reference to trade or firm names is necessary or unavoidable, materials containing such illustrative matter may be used.
6. Appropriate materials carrying advertising may be used in consumer education for the purpose of analysis and evaluation of advertising methods used. In this case the purposes for which these materials are used should be made quite clear.

Materials Offered by Special-Interest Groups and Materials on Controversial Issues

1. Materials, so far as possible, should be accurate and objective in their presentation of issues and trends, reflecting competent scholarship.
2. Where differences in quantity or effectiveness of available materials representing opposing points of view exist, the teacher should try to create a balance of materials.
3. Materials used should promote American democratic ideals and moral values. They should, therefore, be free from objectionable propaganda, overemphasis, or misleading bias. To the same end, appropriate materials may be used, under careful teacher supervision, for the purpose of developing skill in propaganda analysis.

4. The material should make a significant contribution toward educational goals.

Materials Issued Serially

1. The material should make a significant contribution toward educational goals.
2. Periodical material used in classroom instruction should be free from excessive or objectionable advertising matter.
3. Decision to use periodically issued materials should not imply advance acceptance of every issue. Each succeeding issue should be appraised before distribution and use.

Materials Sold in School Book Fairs or Bazaars

1. The material should make a significant contribution toward educational goals.
2. The choice of materials to be purchased by or for pupils through parents' associations or through the schools must be governed by the principles applying to the selection of all other materials. This is the responsibility of the head of the school.

Criteria such as those given above are of undoubted value in studying the kinds of supplementary materials used in any school. Their application is likely to prevent the use of undesirable types of learning aids.

Using concrete experiences as materials of instruction. Because of the extreme bookishness and verbalism of much of classroom instruction, schools are making increased use of a wide variety of concrete experiences to make learning less formal and more meaningful. There are many sources of such experiences: objects, models, museum exhibits, excursions, field trips, constructive activities, and direct participation in community enterprises. Their use not only clarifies ideas but also stimulates pupil interest, encourages pupil activity, and breaks down the barriers between life and the school.

The criteria for evaluating any concrete experience are (1) its usefulness in achieving the purposes of instruction, (2) its con-

[19] Board of Education, New York, *Curriculum and Materials*, Vol. 7, No. 1 (September, 1952), p. 3.

tribution to the meaning and understanding of some important concept, or of a social or an industrial process, (3) the extent to which it stimulates critical thought, and (4) its authenticity and genuineness.

In a discussion of constructive activities, Horn [20] shows that some of those used widely in our schools today have little if any authenticity, whereas others are true to life and involve the participation of pupils in real lifelike community enterprises. His analysis classifies activities into five groups according to the degree of reality that is achieved and thus provides an excellent basis for appraising the merits of such activities in any classroom. He defines these five levels as follows: [21]

1. Lowest of all are the constructions that are largely fanciful and almost wholly erroneous. An Indian peace pipe is represented by a large bowl with enough stems so that all members of the council can smoke at once; and a drawing of a single person climbing a steep hill to reach a lone hut at the top depicts the capture of Vicksburg.

2. A little higher in the scale are various types of construction that are illustrative, in a limited sense, but that are so far removed from the realities they purport to represent as to distort rather than clarify the student's ideas. Most paper construction belongs to this class. Trees, animals, garden vegetables, bridges, boats, trains, castles, and whole cities are made with scissors and paste. In the same category are most representations of scenes and episodes in sand, clay, and similar materials. Although such constructions are generally ludicrous in their inadequacy, many show a degree of effort and ingenuity that deserves a better outlet.

3. Other types of models are on a much higher intellectual level than those described above. Modeling natural features and regions in relief with sand, clay, paper pulp, or other plastic materials is no longer used so extensively as it formerly was, but the practice is not uncommon even today. Such models usually involve much more careful study than in the case of most of the historical and geographical scenes described above, yet they suffer from the same limitations that are always found in the attempt to reproduce extensive and complicated features in miniature. The objection to such small models is that unless they are made to scale, they distort the physical features, and if they are made to scale, they fail to bring out the significance of these features. It is in the understanding of more simple objects, however, that models have proved most useful.

4. Closely akin to the construction and use of working models are those constructive activities that help the student to understand the processes by which fundamental material needs are satisfied. The methods of obtaining food, clothing, and shelter are most frequently illustrated, but considerable attention is given also to related problems, such as those involved in transportation, communication, recreation, the improvement of health, the keeping of records, and the making of tools and utensils. Primitive processes and those of the period of relative self-sufficiency are most often duplicated. The chief steps in the transformation of raw materials into usable products are illustrated.

5. The direct participation in the solution of community problems, while not adequately described by the term *constructive activity,* has, nevertheless, much in common with the type described in the preceding section. Many advantages inhere in these out-of-school activities. They display social problems in all of their complicated human relationships. Because they demand the solution of practical difficulties, they strengthen moral and intellectual fiber to a degree not easily matched in the protected circumstances of the school. They give a sense of the responsibility and dignity of induction into citizenship that is not equaled by any other type of project, and certainly not by types of instruction that consist only in make-believe or even in reading and talking about community problems. They are preeminent in the development of the various concomitants usually claimed for activities in the school.

The discussion of methods of improving the use of concrete experience will be fully considered in Chapter 17. At this point we are merely concerned with the basis on which the teacher and supervisor can evaluate the use being made of this kind of activity in

[20] Ernest Horn, *Methods of Instruction in the Social Studies* (New York, Scribner, 1937).
[21] Adapted from *Methods of Instruction in the Social Studies* by Ernest Horn by permission of Charles Scribner's Sons, pp. 420-429. The illustrations given are taken from actual classroom activities.

the classroom. This series of levels can be used as the basis of discussions of ways of improving the use of concrete experiences.

Audio-visual aids in instruction. To bring about desired changes in the behavior of children, the modern school uses a wide variety of visual aids: still pictures of all kinds, sound and silent motion pictures, school journeys of various kinds, museum materials models and exhibits, charts, maps, and graphic representations. In addition to these aids, commonly recognized as visual, there is a wide variety of concrete materials which are also visual in nature that are used to give meanings and manipulative experience.

In general, the experimental studies of the uses of these aids, particularly those dealing with the motion picture and excursion, show that they have genuine value in teaching. Significant gains in learning have resulted from their use, especially in such areas as the assimilation and retention of information, the development of interests and attitudes, and the acquisition of skills and occupational techniques. There is an excellent summary of these studies in the *Encyclopedia of Educational Research,* under the heading, "Visual Education," to which the reader is referred for further details and a bibliography. These studies have shown that the effectiveness of the use of these aids depends on a variety of factors such as the following:

1. The purpose for which they are used.
2. The age and background of the children or group using them.
3. The type of materials studied.
4. The skill and method of presentation.
5. The authenticity of the materials.
6. The influence of the teacher.

Methods of studying the use made of visual aids. Visual aids should be used for educational purposes to develop meanings, to broaden experience, and to arouse genuine interest in the activity at hand. They should be true to life, artistic, and correct to scale so that the pupils will be likely to establish correct concepts and will be stimulated to desirable kinds of responses and behavior.

If projection equipment is used, special attention should be given to such matters as good lighting, clarity of projection, comfortable seating, and ventilation. The visual aids selected by the teacher and pupils for the unit of work should be correlated with other kinds of sensory appeals, especially those of hearing and kinesthetic sense, so as to form a balanced multi-sensory experience.

In studying the use made of visual aids, attention should be given to such matters as the extent of use being made of these aids, their quality and adequacy, the use being made of community resources in instruction, the difficulties teachers and pupils encounter in the use of these aids, especially the technical equipment needed, the training teachers have had in the use of visual aids, the extent of film damage, the training and use of student operators to assist the teachers, the storage facilities available, and the kinds of visual aids accessible in the community.

The procedures to use to gather these different kinds of information are similar to those used to secure facts about any other aspect of instruction: observation of the classroom use of the materials, interviews with teachers and administrative officers, questionnaires, reports, analysis of records of the use of materials, requests for assistance, and the like.

The relation of motion pictures and child development. In the average motion picture theater, about one-third of the audience is of adolescent age or younger. Three per cent are less than seven years of age. The great majority of children attend movies either once or twice a week. As would be expected, attendance varies greatly with the day of the week. Sometimes the theater is a clean, cool place; often it is hot, stuffy, and poorly ventilated.

The movies children see at the theater are determined in part by what they like but mostly by what is available. The great majority of films are adult in theme, such as crime, sex, and love. Even though the material is adult, it is presented in a form intelligible to immature minds; hence, it may be dangerous. The choices of children are not necessarily the same as those of adults.

Research has shown that children remember as much of a picture as do adults. Of action they best remember sports, crimes, acts of violence, and scenes with a highly emotional appeal. Sad as well as humorous details are also well remembered. Restlessness during night sleep is increased from 15 to 25 per cent after attendance at a movie; consequently, fatigue and irritability are often present the next day.

Frequent attendance at movies has some unfavorable effect on school work, but not decisively so. The delinquent child sees more movies than does the normal child. This may be a protest against the barrenness and drabness of his daily life. It is quite likely that pictures depicting violence and crime produce a most unwholesome effect on children of poor background and on those who tend to be oversuggestible.

Movies and television have to some extent replaced reading. In so far as they have reduced the amount of reading of excellent children's literature, they may be regarded as a detriment. On the other hand, a glance at the average audience will convince the observer that it contains many individuals who are not the type that ever finds enjoyment in reading good books. For them the new media bring enrichment of experience and understanding of human motives, and often an uplift of spirit; the social values of this elevation cannot be overestimated. The school faces the problems of gradually raising the standards of the children and of making suitable use of motion pictures in the instructional program, because they are an instrument of tremendous potential value. At the same time producers and exhibitors must take steps to raise the general tone and quality of the films to a higher level.

Value of films. In the *Encyclopedia of Educational Research,* 1950 edition, the evidence concerning the value of films is summarized under the following nine headings:

1. Learning factual information.
2. Retention of material learned.
3. Habits and skills.
4. Development of relationships.
5. Description and explanation.
6. "Thinking" and "education."
7. Imagination.
8. Development of interest.
9. Responses to elements of films.

Because of lack of space it will not be possible to comment on these items in detail. Suffice it to say that with few exceptions, research studies point to the positive value of films as an aid to learning. Those interested should consult the summary in the *Encyclopedia* for details and consult the bibliography there attached.

Criteria for the selection of motion pictures. Many sets of standards for evaluating instructional films have been proposed. A survey of these suggests the following criteria:

1. The film should be chosen because it contributes directly to some need of the pupils that arises in the course of the ongoing activity.
2. The film should be appropriate to the school level at which it is to be used.
3. The social values inherent in the film should be carefully weighed.
4. The film should appeal to socially approved native interests and to wholesome emotional responses.
5. Careful consideration should be given to the mechanics of the film, including such factors as the quality of photography, vocabulary, continuity, duration, captions, and clarity.
6. The cost and accessibility should also be considered.
7. The material should be accurate and up-to-date.

Standards for the selection of film projection equipment include the following: simplicity, safety, portability, adaptability, durability, economy of operation, and quality of sound produced.

The radio in education. In nine out of ten homes, adults and children spend several hours a day listening to radio broadcasts of varying degrees of excellence. The extent of use of the radio in classrooms as a means of instruction has not been determined for the country as a whole by systematic investigation. There is evidence that its use is increasing in recent years due to the provision of better types of programs by interested agencies. The Texas School of the Air is a striking example of an excellent state program. Many cities have local programs operated by the schools. The same is true for television programs which are being rapidly developed in a number of centers.

In many schools the use of audio aids is very unsatisfactory, a situation due to a variety of causes, among them lack of appreciation of the value of these aids, the failure of available programs to integrate with the curriculum, difficulties of scheduling, and lack of training by the staff in the use of the radio.

Criteria for appraising radio broadcasts. There is a wide variation in the value and quality of radio broadcasts for instructional purposes. Many of them are for entertainment only. While there is reason why the school should include such programs in its activities, by far the more valuable type of program is one that is intended more definitely for instructional purposes. Tyler has proposed the following three major criteria for evaluating the merits and adequacy of a broadcast: [22]

1. *Educational Value*
   a. Is the information authentic?
   b. Are the generalizations the children are likely to make from the program sound?
   c. Are various points of view on controversial matters presented?
   d. Are the implied concepts accurate?
   e. Are the emotional reactions of the listeners likely to be wholesome?
2. *Clarity and Comprehensibility of Content*
   a. Can the program be easily followed and understood?
   b. Is the program "good radio"?
   c. Does the material presented lend itself to sound treatment?
3. *Interest and Appeal*
   a. Is the material suitable for the level of maturity of the audience?

   b. Is the material "talked down" to too low a level?
   c. Does the subject matter deal with content within the range of experience and interest of the children?

Such additional factors should be considered as the availability for teachers of helps in conducting the program, its relation to the content of the curriculum, its timeliness, and the source of the program.

Methods used to appraise audio aids. Audio aids may be evaluated by means of one or more of the following procedures:

1. Observations may be made of the ability of the pupil to use the aid.
2. Evidence may be secured of the extent to which they contribute to meanings and understandings.
3. A study may be made of pupil interest in the aid and attitude toward it.
4. The extent of use made of the aid by teachers and pupils is an important consideration.
5. The reactions of pupils of different mental levels can be checked during lessons.
6. The authenticity of the information should be checked.
7. Tests and examinations may be given after their use to discover how much has been learned.
8. Aids may be rated by means of checklists and rating scales.
9. The appropriateness to the age and background of the pupils can be analyzed.
10. Special attention should be paid to the durability, construction, hygiene, and general attractiveness of the materials.
11. Experimental studies of the value of these materials are the most desirable basis of making an eveluation of these aids.

Pupil participation in evaluation of these materials is desirable. They can readily give their reactions as to the value of different kinds of aids. Often they prepare materials of this kind as a part of the regular class work. Standards for appraising materials

[22] Adapted from the article by I. Keith Tyler, "The Educational Evaluation of Radio Programs," in *Radio and the Classroom* (Washington, NEA, 1941).

produced by pupils should be developed cooperatively by teacher and pupils. In many schools, the pupils are also taught how to operate the apparatus required.

Certain administrative features should also be considered when appraising the use made of these aids. Special attention should be given to the protection and preservation of these aids. Special attention should be given to the protection and preservation of the materials. It should be noted whether or not they are conveniently located and readily available when needed. The system of requisitioning, obtaining, and returning them should be examined to see if it operates efficiently.

Evaluating audio-visual materials. Dale [23] has suggested a series of questions that may be used in evaluating audio-visual materials:

1. Do teaching materials make those who use them more critical-minded?
2. Do the audio-visual materials give us a true picture of the ideas which they present?
3. Does the material contribute meaningful content to the topic under study?
4. Is the material appropriate for the age, intelligence, and experience of the learners?
5. Is the material used worth the time, expense, and effort involved?
6. Is the physical quality of the audio-visual materials satisfactory?
7. Is there a Teachers' Guide available to provide help in effective use of audio-visual materials?

Teacher competence in the use of audio-visual materials. The instructional value of audio-visual aids is generally recognized. However, there is a wide variation in the extent to which they are used in classrooms and the skill with which they are employed by teachers. This was shown by a recent study of teacher competence in the use of a variety of visual aids in the schools of Wisconsin. White [24] prepared a series of six competency levels in the use of six kinds of audio-visual materials. The following description of the competency levels for 16 mm. motion pictures illustrates the procedure used in defining competency.

COMPETENCY LEVELS—16 MM MOTION PICTURES

LEVEL VI. *Selection:* On basis of previous knowledge or by careful searching; knowledge of several good sources; final selection based on accepted evaluation principles.
Utilization: Always previews or has intimate knowledge from previous viewing; does vocabulary work if at all necessary; careful preparation of students; re-shows if need exists; used as an integral part of the learning situation; follow-up work explored.
Evaluation: Written evaluations for future use; evaluation on accepted principles; methods of utilization evaluated.
Operation: Operates with no fear; gets very good projection results; is able to teach others to operate; realizes the need to make operation as unnoticed as possible.

LEVEL V. *Selection:* Found by search of materials already in that school but including BAVI (Wisconsin) catalog; limited knowledge of sources.
Utilization: Usually previews or has seen films before; gives only a brief introduction; some discussion afterward; little or no follow-up.
Evaluation: Informal evaluation of both film content and method of presentation.
Operation: Operates but not confidently; prefers to have someone else do it.

LEVEL IV. *Selection:* Films ordered by others; uses films obtained for other teaching purposes, very limited knowledge of sources.
Utilization: Seldom or never previews; little or no introduction of film; limited student preparation; uses films for other than basic teaching purposes.
Evaluation: Concern ends with showing of film; no evaluation of film or utilization procedures.

[23] Adapted from Edgar Dale, *Audio-Visual Methods in Teaching* (New York, Dryden, 1946), pp. 500-506. (See also 1954 edition.)
[24] F. A. White, "Teacher Competence in the Use of Audio-Visual Materials," *Audio-Visual Communication Review* (Spring, 1953), pp. 91-98.

PER CENT OF THE 106 TEACHERS PERFORMING ON THE VARIOUS LEVELS

Level	16 mm Films	Chalk-board	Film Strips	Magnetic Recorder	Opaque Projector	Radio
VI	6.6%	9.4%	3.8%	7.5%	0.0%	0.9%
V	50.9*	67.0*	17.0	18.9	3.9	9.4
IV	26.5	23.6	17.0	14.1	1.8	26.5
III	0.9	0.0	4.7	10.4*	35.8	5.6
II	2.8	0.0	6.6	8.5	25.4*	5.6
I	12.3	0.0	50.9*	40.6	33.1	51.8*

* Indicates median level.

Operation: No knowledge of operation or has forgotten and not relearned; does not operate the projector.

LEVEL III. Equipment not available to the teacher.

LEVEL II. Availability of equipment not explored by the teacher.

LEVEL I. Equipment available but not used by the teacher.

White then interviewed 106 teachers and their supervisors and arrived at a rating for the teachers' competency in the use of each of the media listed in the table above.

The conclusions drawn by White follow:

1. As a group these teachers (only two of whom had had an audio-visual course) did not use all of the audio-visual methods and materials at their disposal.

2. Those teachers who did use the six audio-visual methods did not perform at the highest levels of usage.

3. These teachers were cognizant of their own deficiencies in the area of audio-visual methods but only to that point where their knowledge of the methods would allow them to realize and recognize their deficiencies.

4. The inservice training programs now found in schools such as those in which these teachers taught cannot be depended upon to provide competency in the area of audio-visual methods.

5. The attitude of these teachers and their supervisors toward the subject of audio-visual methods and toward the interviewer in this study was a very pleasant and encouraging one. It leads to the strong belief that all concerned are eager to have teachers better prepared to use audio-visual methods than were members of this group.

6. The supervisors believe that beginning teachers should be fully prepared to use audio-visual methods when those teachers leave college. The supervisors want the teachers they select for their schools: (*a*) to be acquainted with the materials that apply to the teacher's own fields, (*b*) to be competent in the mechanical aspects of the materials, (*c*) to understand and appreciate the pedagogical values of audio-visual methods of producing a more effective learning situation, (*d*) to know how to use them so as to achieve most effectively their inherent values, and (*e*) to know how to evaluate the methods and the results they produce.

Budgeting expenditures for textbooks and library books. The amount of money spent for textbooks and library books varies widely from place to place. In a recent study of practices in New York the range in amounts spent and books available given in the table on page 446 was revealed. The data are for a selected group of secondary schools typical of the state as a whole.

The variations shown in the table are very striking. The highest amount spent per pupil was $4.43; the lowest amount spent was nothing at all. The range in number of books available ranged from 22 books per pupil to 2 books, a ratio of 11 to 1. The number of books added to the library varied from 0.9 to no books. An additional check showed that the percentage of books recommended by *The Standard Catalog for High School Libraries* actually available that year varied from 54 per cent in a suburban school

VARIATIONS IN PROVISIONS OF BOOKS IN SELECTED NEW YORK SCHOOLS*

Level	Amount Spent for Textbooks per Pupil	Average Number of Books per Pupil in Library	Books Added That Year per Pupil
Highest	$4.43	22—	0.9
Median	0.58	4—	0.2
Lowest	0	2—	0

* Data are adapted from a table in Dora V. Smith, *Evaluating Instruction in Secondary School English,* English Monograph No. 11 of the National Council of English (Chicago, 1941), p. 130.

to only 9 per cent in a small central rural school. The problem of purchasing books is complicated for the larger schools by the numbers of pupils involved. Provision for an adequate range of books for limited numbers of pupils taxes the resources of smaller communities. Hence the need for state and federal aid.

Locating needs for instructional materials. There are many ways in which the supervisor can locate needs for instructional materials. The analysis of the requirements of the course of study will indicate some of the kinds of materials needed for effective instruction. Results of tests will show the fields in which there are weaknesses that may be due to lack of the proper kind of instructional equipment. In many schools, teachers make out formal written requests for materials they need to carry on units of work. An analysis of these requests is a very helpful means of locating needs. The study of inventories will reveal limitations of supplies. Library records will indicate the kind and extent of free reading done by the pupils. Any deficiency here may be due to the fact that there is an inadequate supply of interesting books and other reading materials. An analysis of books, magazines, and periodicals supplied to children by private and rental libraries may prove to be very revealing.

A survey by the supervisor of the extent to which the teachers have drawn upon the resources of the community to vitalize their teaching through excursions, visits, and first-

hand contacts may show the need of bringing these possibilities to the attention of the teachers.

The most direct method of locating needs is by observation of the work in the schools and by interviews with principals and teachers. One procedure that has been very helpful is the use of check-lists to record the kinds of materials observed in use during lessons. Such a plan is more significant than securing from teachers lists of supplies on hand, since the fact that they are on hand does not assure either that they are being used or that they are being used effectively.

The results of one application of this procedure are shown by the data in the table on page 447. They are based on reports of observations of lessons by principals of the kinds of materials used by a selected group of teachers from all parts of the country during typical arithmetic lessons. The table shows the wide variety of materials that can be used. It also shows the relatively small number of teachers who were using such means of vitalizing instruction as supplementary pamphlets, progress graphs, objects, bulletin boards, exhibits, and illustrative materials collected from the community. The textbook, mimeographed materials, and exercises copied from the blackboard constituted the major sources of the work of the class. Similar data for any curriculum area based on reports of observations in one school or in one school system would furnish the supervisor with ample information as to the use of various kinds of ma-

NUMBER OF TIMES EACH TYPE OF INSTRUCTIONAL
MATERIALS WAS OBSERVED IN 505
ARITHMETIC LESSONS*

| Instructional Material | Grade | | | All | % of 505 Classes |
	4 No.	5 No.	6 No.		
A. Books					
1. No books used	48	62	71	181	36
2. Basic text in hands of the pupils	71	86	100	257	51
3. Supplementary textbooks	18	13	11	42	8
4. Reference books, encyclopedias, etc.	0	0	4	4	1
5. Pamphlets, bulletins, magazines, etc.	1	4	10	15	3
6. Selections found in readers, geography texts, history texts, etc.	0	4	9	13	2
7. Others, such as _____	7	14	9	30	6
B. Practice Exercises					
1. Exercises in textbook	53	70	75	198	39
2. Standardized drill cards adapted for individualized progress	16	13	14	43	8
3. Unstandardized materials on cards prepared by teacher	20	28	11	59	12
4. Mimeographed materials	20	38	26	84	17
5. Workbooks	22	15	22	59	12
6. Materials on blackboard to be copied by pupils	54	74	68	196	37
7. Dictated materials to be copied by pupils	17	32	28	77	15
8. Problems or examples given orally to be solved mentally	26	44	33	103	21
9. Flash cards	18	11	12	41	8
10. Others, such as _____	6	9	8	23	5
C. Other Equipment					
1. Blackboard used by teacher	107	138	137	382	76
2. Blackboard used by pupils	96	131	133	360	72
3. Slides, films, etc.	0	0	1	1	1
4. Class progress graph (in use or on wall)	29	27	40	96	19
5. Individual progress graph	26	31	47	104	21
6. Charts, diagrams, pictures, etc., not in textbook	22	20	24	66	13
7. Objects, such as cubes, measures, sticks, rulers, instruments, etc.	16	15	22	53	11
8. Illustrative materials collected from the community	4	4	10	18	4
9. Bulletin-board display of current applications of numbers	2	6	7	15	3
10. Prepared exhibits of material supplied by commercial houses	0	0	2	2	1
11. Neatness scales to set standards	6	4	1	11	2
12. Others, such as _____	3	5	7	15	3
Number of classes	153	170	182	505	

* The Teaching of Arithmetic, Tenth Yearbook, National Council of Teachers of Mathematics (New York, Teachers College, Bureau of Publications, Columbia Univ., 1935), p. 46.

terial in classrooms. Since the supervisor cannot conveniently visit all classes, he should secure the help of principals in gathering the desired information. Reports by teachers are a valuable stimulating device.

Evaluating uses of materials. The availability of good materials does not insure their effective use. An excellent plan for evaluating the use of textbooks by teachers is based on an analysis of their uses in representative schools in New York State, which appeared in the bulletin, Informal Teaching Series, Circular 3, "The Use of Textbooks." Three levels of use are described: the formal, less formal, and the informal. The descriptions suggest steps that may lead toward better practice. The plan is presented in the chart that follows.

PLAN FOR EVALUATING USE OF TEXTBOOKS*

Formal	Less Formal	Informal
1. *Who determines the choice of textbooks?*		
Teachers and supervisory officers immediately responsible have little or no choice in the selection.	Chosen by principal and supervisors.	Chosen co-operatively by securing judgment of every one concerned including teachers.
2. *What is the administrative provision for the use of textbooks?*		
Kept as a set for the exclusive use of one class.	Texts lent to class for the period of time needed.	Exchanged freely among various classes.
3. *How are textbooks used in making assignments?*		
Curriculum determined by textbooks.	More than one textbook used. Teacher supplies other materials.	Texts and other books used as references. Pupils seek and use other materials.
4. *What provision is made for differences in pupil ability to use texts?*		
All pupils in same class use same set of books simultaneously.	Teachers choose different books which pupils may use.	Various books of different degrees of difficulty used at same time depending upon ability and interests of pupils.
5. *How do teachers use textbooks in oral work?*		
In classes such as oral reading or social studies, pupils are required to follow silently in their own books.	One group takes turns reading pages of story to other group.	Class becomes audience for new story which one pupil has chosen and prepared in advance.
6. *What is done if the book is too difficult for some pupils?*		
Teacher reads difficult portions to pupils who cannot understand text.	Pupils having difficulty are required to reread with special emphasis upon vocabulary.	If texts are too difficult easier books which pupil can understand and enjoy are made available.
7. *What provision is made for individual differences?*		
Entire class is assigned same number of pages.	Amount of work varied for different sections of class.	A common theme or topic is followed but materials and references are varied according to individual abilities and interests.

Formal	Less Formal	Informal
8. To what extent are pupils required to master the contents of books?		
Pupils must know what author says and agree with ideas of teacher.	Pupils allowed to question author's or teacher's statements.	Pupils are taught to reserve judgment, seek evidence and exchange ideas before forming opinions.
9. What is the goal to be attained in the use of textbooks?		
Mastery of subject matter is the goal.	Mastery of the tools of learning is the goal.	Desirable attitudes, appreciations, abilities, habits and skills are the goals.
10. How are pupils tested after the completion of their work?		
Class is given written examination on content of text and is required to attain a fixed standard.	Pupils may not be examined but teachers mark on daily recitations.	Success is measured by the satisfactory completion of tasks chosen or assigned on the basis of the individual pupil's age, progress, and ability to achieve.

* Published by the State Education Department, Albany, N. Y.

Accessibility of instructional materials. The accessibility of materials is an important factor determining their use. The supervisor should determine whether materials are stored in convenient places or whether they are placed in central depositories that are difficult to reach. Often the regulations governing the loaning and use of materials loaned by libraries, museums, visual-instruction departments, and other agencies are so complicated and rigid that teachers hesitate to ask for these supplies. There may be no good system of collection or delivery of loaned materials; hence there may be long delays in securing desired supplies. If there is a supply of materials in the school, it may not be arranged in good order or catalogued so that desired items can easily be located. The financial arrangements for purchasing new supplies may be unnecessarily involved so that there is a long interval of time between the time the order is placed and the receipt of the materials. These and similar problems should be carefully investigated by the supervisor. Not the least important question is the accessibility of pupil records and reports, professional books for teachers, and supplies of tests and similar materials. This can be improved very easily in most schools.

The following set of criteria will be helpful in studying the variety of procedures that may be used by schools in handling materials and supplies. The criteria deal with the characteristics of the materials, their selection and storage, and the responsibilities of the teachers and pupils for their care. The three types of conditions described are outgrowths of different philosophies of teaching and supervision.

VARIETY OF PROCEDURES IN HANDLING MATERIALS AND SUPPLIES*

Formal	Less Formal	Informal
1. Who selects the materials and supplies?		
Central authority makes selection and determines distribution.	Uniform supply list made by principals, special teachers, and classroom teachers working together.	Selected by those using them, teachers and children, in the light of the varied activities to be carried on. Provision made by administrative officers for examination, experimentation and evaluation of new materials.
2. What are the desirable characteristics of materials and supplies?		
Standardized. Uniform for all children in each group. Small enough to be used at desks. Planned to supplement the teaching of skills. Limited to a few types. Use to be dictated by teacher.	Planned to supplement the teaching of skills but used as individuals need them. Limited to a few types. Printed directions for their use a common accompaniment.	Variety in type. Adapted to variety of uses. Lend themselves to uses made of them outside of the school. Suggestive of other needed materials. Suggestive of many and varied uses to suit individual's and group's growing demands. Use is determined by the individual's or group's purposes. The use of such conducive to child health. Tending to large rather than small activities. Suitably esthetic.
3. What is adequate storage space?		
Small cupboards, narrow shelves. Uniform spaces. Placed for teacher's use.	A few wide shelves. Many bookshelves. One or more cupboards available to children.	Well-lighted space conveniently arranged. Easily accessible to the work at hand. Adjustable to changing demands. Much storage space to care for large and small materials. Conveniently placed for children's uses.
4. What is the teacher's responsibility in respect to materials and supplies?		
Central office sends from supply list items needed to complete course of study. Teacher selects, distributes and carries responsibility for care and economical use of these supplies.	Co-operates in making up yearly supply list. Appoints certain children to make available to the rest of the group the daily supply.	Contributes to the general list of sources and supplies. Searches new sources for needed materials. Contributes material of her own. Constructs needed materials. Experiments with possibilities of materials. Makes available to children sources for and means of securing needed materials. Makes children responsible for care and use of materials.

Formal	Less Formal	Informal
*5. What are the children's responsibilities with respect to materials and supplies?*		
Use materials given them as directed. Distribute and collect materials when appointed to do so.	Most capable children have opportunities for the selection, distribution, and care of material. All children made responsible for care and use of certain materials assigned to them.	Contribute materials from their own supplies at home. Construct needed materials at school and at home. Seek available sources of material. Secure needed material from available sources in a proper fashion. Children develop a growing responsibility for the care and economical use of their own materials used by all the group.

* "Materials and Supplies in Unit Teaching," Circular No. 2, Informal Teaching Series (Albany, N. Y., State Education Department, 1933).

Section 2

THE STUDY OF THE SOCIO-PHYSICAL ENVIRONMENT OF THE SCHOOL

What are the requirements for school buildings that make the maximum contribution to productive school living? The American Association of School Administrators has provided a rigid test:

Curriculum adequacy—Do they provide the space and facilities for the educational program that your community needs for its children, youth, and adults?

Safety and well-being—Do they not only protect against danger but also provide a positive influence for improving the health and physical welfare of the pupils?

Interfunctional co-ordination—Are they so planned that the activity in each part of a building may be co-ordinated harmoniously with related activities and may be carried on effectively without disturbing other activities?

Efficiency and utility—Are they so planned that the handling of materials and the comings and goings of pupils, school staff, and the public are accomplished with a minimum of interference and a maximum of ease and satisfaction to all concerned?

Beauty—Are they pleasing in appearance, with simplicity, usefulness, and balance as ideals, rather than ornamentation or symmetry?

Adaptability—Are they so planned that they can be enlarged or rearranged internally to meet new educational demands with a minimum of additional cost?

Economy—Are they so planned that in original outlay and in future operation the utmost in educational utility can be secured for every dollar spent? [25]

A recent report [26] of the federal survey shows that many school buildings fail to meet these and similar standards.

The fundamental requirement for a wholesome social environment in the school is the presence of rich, well-integrated personalities. Personalities that exercise a destructive influence upon teachers, pupils, and others should be removed from the school system. Questions related to the problems of personalities will be discussed fully in the chapters dealing with teacher development. Here we shall be concerned with means of studying the physical aspects of

[25] *American School Buildings,* Twenty-seventh Yearbook, American Association of School Administrators (Washington, NEA, 1949), p. 8.

[26] *First Progress Report, School Facilities Survey,* Office of Education (Washington, Federal Security Agency, 1952).

the school and classroom that affect learning. In the next section we shall consider elements of the community as a whole that affect learning.

Studying the school plant. The intimate relation between the school plant and the quality of the educational program, as well as its outcomes, is not generally recognized or understood. It seems clear that the program of the school may be seriously restricted and impeded by an inadequate plant. The school building should not be planned and equipped merely as a place in which formal instruction is to be the dominant activity; it should be planned as a functioning part of the total educational program of the community; it should be flexible enough to meet effectively the new demands that society is constantly making for the enrichment and broadening of learning opportunities and for the extension of the functions of the school to meet changing conditions. The development of the entire school plant should be regarded as an integral part of a community planning program.

A number of check-lists have been devised that may be used to appraise the construction of the school building, the arrangement of the facilities, provisions for special services, and the adequacy of the equipment. In rating any school building, the rater should take into consideration such factors as the following:

1. The underlying philosophy of education.
2. The expressed purposes, functions, and objectives of the school, since these differ widely.
3. The needs and nature of the student body it serves.
4. The nature and needs of the community.

A particularly valuable approach to the evaluation of the school plant was developed by the Co-operative Study of Secondary School Standards.[27] The assumption was made that evaluation alone is not enough; it was recognized that if evaluation stimu-lates the faculty or the citizens of a community to take steps to bring about an improvement, the results of the application of a rating scale are likely to be of greater value than if the scale is merely applied in a routine way. Thus the application of the scale can serve two purposes: evaluation and stimulation. The need of a flexible scheme of rating was also recognized because of the wide variety of purpose, size, and function of the secondary schools in this country. The scale finally devised as a result of the activities of a large number of individuals consists of "promising conditions or characteristics found in good secondary schools." It was pointed out in the report that not all of the items are necessary, or even desirable, in every school.

There are given below the major items and the subheads included in this rating scale, and the number of items (shown in parentheses) included for each of these subheads.

RATING OF SCHOOL PLANT

1. Site
   a. Location (13).
   b. Physical characteristics (14).
2. The building or buildings (29)
3. Building services
   a. Illumination (12).
   b. Temperature and ventilation (12).
   c. Water and sanitation (17).
   d. Miscellaneous building services (10).
4. Classrooms (16)
5. Special rooms and services
   a. Auditoriums (19).
   b. Lunchrooms, dining rooms, and kitchen (25).
   c. Office and staff rooms (10).
   d. Clinics, infirmary, or hospitalization facilities (12).
   e. Sleeping and study quarters (18).
6. School buses (5)
7. Special characteristics of school plant (5)
8. General evaluation of the school plant (2)

[27] See action on "School Plant," in *Evaluative Criteria for Secondary Schools*, 1950 ed. (Washington, Co-operative Study of Secondary School Standards).

The extent of provision for each item is indicated by five symbols as follows:

√√ Provision or condition is made extensively.
√   Provision or condition is made to some extent.
X   Provision or condition is very limited.
M   Provision or condition is missing but needed.
N   Provision or condition is not desirable but does not apply.

Evaluations, representing the best judgments of those making the study of a building, are expressed for each item by means of this rating scale:

5 Excellent
4 Very good
3 Good
2 Fair
1 Poor

Other useful rating scales are listed below. In the manuals that accompany the score cards listed below, the standards for appraising each item are described. An examination of the details of the rating will make clear the shortcomings of a building. The chief limitations of these and similar scales is that they are at best only expressions of expert opinion, since the validity of most of the standards employed has not been established.

Useful rating scales developed since 1920 are the following:

Butterworth School Building Score Card for One-Teacher School Buildings (Yonkers, World Book, 1921).
ENGELHARDT, N. L., *Elementary School Building Score Card and Survey Manual* (New York, Teachers College, Bureau of Publications, Columbia Univ., 1936).
EVENDEN, E. S., STRAYER, G. D., and ENGELHARDT, N. L., *Scorecard for Physical Plant of Normal Schools and Teachers Colleges* (New York, Teachers College, Bureau of Publications, Columbia Univ., 1924).
HOLY, T. C., and ARNOLD, W. E., *Score Card for the Evaluation of Junior and Senior High School Buildings* (Columbus, Ohio State Univ., 1936).

STRAYER, G. D., and ENGELHARDT, N. L., *Score Card to Be Used in the Selection of School Building Sites* (New York, Teachers College, Bureau of Publications, Columbia Univ., 1929).
———, *Standards for Elementary School Buildings* (New York, Teachers College, Bureau of Publications, Columbia Univ., 1933).

The following references contain the most recent available information about up-to-date features of modern school buildings:

American School Buildings, Twenty-seventh Yearbook, American Association of School Administrators (Washington, National Education Association, 1949).
CYR, F. W., and LINN, H. H., *Planning Rural Community School Buildings* (New York, Teachers College, Bureau of Publications, Columbia Univ., 1949).
Designing Elementary Classrooms, U. S. Department of Health, Education and Welfare, Special Publication No. 1 (Washington, Government Printing Office, 1953).
ENGELHARDT, N. L., ENGELHARDT, N. L., Jr., and LEGGETT, S. F., *Planning Secondary Schools* (New York, Reinhold Publishing Co., 1949).
———, *Planning Elementary School Buildings* (New York, F. W. Dodge Corp., 1953).
Guide for Planning School Plants, 1949 ed., National Council on School House Construction (Nashville, Tenn., George Peabody College for Teachers, 1949).
Organizing the Elementary School for Living and Learning (Washington, National Education Association, 1947).
PERKINS, L. B., and COCKING, W. D., *Schools* (New York, Reinhold Publishing Co., 1949).
REID, Kenneth (compiler), *School Planning* (New York, F. W. Dodge Corp., 1951).
WAECHTER, H. H., and WAECHTER, Elisabeth, *Schools for the Very Young* (New York, F. W. Dodge Corp., 1951).

Studying single aspects of the school environment. The rating of school buildings by use of score cards has definite limitations, primarily because ratings are in fact summations of subjective judgments rather than actual measurements. Furthermore, buildings differ so greatly in size, structure, and arrangement that in many cases score cards simply do not apply. Nor, as has been shown above, are experts agreed as to items to be considered.

The present trend is in the direction of studying single aspects of the school environment by use of criteria that suggest the desirable features that should be present rather than trying to arrive at a composite rating. An illustration of this approach is found in the following chart,[28] which can be used to survey school-health environmental conditions.

SURVEY OF SCHOOL-HEALTH ENVIRONMENTAL CONDITIONS

Environmental Factors	*Desirable Conditions*
A. *School site* 1. Location and surroundings. 2. Landscaping.	Accessibility, attractive surroundings, no dumps or undermining influences. Attractive as any home.
B. *Buildings* 1. Type of structure, number of floors. 2. State of repair. 3. Provision for fire protection. 4. Heating. 5. Ventilation. 6. Acoustical treatment.	Elementary schools one floor if possible, elevator for others to provide for physically handicapped. All necessary repairs made for economy, safety and attractiveness. Fireproof buildings if possible. Exits, fire escapes, alarm systems, extinguishers. Modern heating with proper humidity—thermometer control. If possible, no-draft windows, circulating air (washed). Of ceiling and walls.

C. *Classrooms*
1. Number and size of seats.
2. Temperature
3. Humidity
4. Special rooms
5. Illumination
 	
  a. Window shades.
  b. Wall color.
6. Desks and seats.
7. Blackboards.
8. Floors.
	Sufficient number, and size to fit child (adequate space between seats as an aid in control of contagion).
	68 to 70 degrees Fahrenheit—thermometer control.
	Controlled through heating and ventilating system.
	Health service, teacher rest rooms, shops, etc.
	Adequate brightness and brightness ratio; double-switch control to permit illumination for desks removed from windows when daylight illuminates only the outside rows.
	Upper and lower shade diffusing light.
	Dull finish and light color.
	Dull finish and adjustable.
	Dull finish, placed in good light; dustless chalk, eraser cleaners.
	Cleaned and washed, vacuum system if possible, composition flooring if possible.

D. *Service system* 1. Drinking fountains. 2. Toilet facilities. 3. Hand-washing facilities.	On each floor, side spout if possible; sufficient number. Adequate heat, ventilation, light; cleaned daily with a disinfectant; at least one toilet for every twenty children; open-front type; self-flush. On each floor; several basins with liquid soap, paper towels, hot water.

[28] *The Expanding Role of Education,* Twenty-sixth Yearbook, American Association of School Administrators (Washington, NEA, 1949).

Environmental Factors	Desirable Conditions
E. *Operation of school plant*	
1. Cleaning.	Floors cleaned daily, vacuum method preferred; windows washed when needed.
2. Dusting.	Oil dusting daily.
3. Storage of materials.	Fireproof compartment.
4. Personnel qualifications.	Well-trained custodian, engineer, helpers (physical examinations—pre-employment, periodic).
5. Lunchrooms.	Hot lunches in clean, comfortable, well-ventilated rooms at minimum costs; lunchrooms with sound-deadening wall and ceiling treatment.
6. Play facilities.	Space and equipment in building other than gym for play in inclement weather.
F. *Teaching personnel*	Complete physical examination on entrance; at least once in three years thereafter.
G. *Adjustment to children's health needs*	
1. Seating.	Adjustment to each specific health need, e.g., pupils with
2. Rest periods.	vision and hearing problems should be near the front
3. Special placement.	of the room; rest periods should be provided for those with heart trouble or any debilitating disease.

Checking items that affect classroom comfort. There can be little doubt that the classroom environment has a definite influence both on child health and on the comfort with which the pupil participates in learning activities. The school should take steps to check environmental influences that may affect adversely the child's normal growth and development. Eyestrain, improper seating, inadequate lighting, crowding, and extreme fluctuations of the temperature of the classroom obviously affect the comfort with which the child works.

The following list includes the important items related to comfort that should be noted in studying the conditions under which learning proceeds:

FACTORS INVOLVED IN CLASSROOM COMFORT

1. *Conditions Causing Eyestrain and Hearing Difficulty.*
   a. Evidence of eyestrain and hearing difficulty.
   b. Location of pupils with visual and auditory deficiencies.
   c. Noise and disturbing conditions.
2. *Seating Provisions That Affect Posture.*
   a. Proper desk height.
   b. Proper seat height.
   c. Placement and slant of work surface.
   d. Spacing.
   e. Arrangement.
   f. Surface for work.
3. *Illumination.*
   a. Adjustment to location of pupil in classroom.
   b. Adjustment to characteristics of pupil.
   c. Adjustment to task undertaken.
   d. Intensity of light on working surfaces.
   e. Supplementation of natural light by artificial light.
   f. Adequacy of light for rooms used for different purposes.
4. *Glare and Excessive Light.*
   a. Direct from sun or artificial sources.
   b. Reflected glare from surface, globe, etc.
5. *Shades.*
   a. Quality.
   b. Adjustability.
6. *Luminaries.*
   a. Type: direct, semi-direct, indirect.
   b. Location, spacing and arrangement.
   c. Intensity of lighting in various parts of the room.
   d. Distance from working surface.

7. *Windows.*
   a. Cleanliness.
   b. Ratio to wall space (norm 20-25 per cent).
   c. Location: side; rear.
   d. Continuity.
8. *Interior Decoration.*
   a. Quality of paint.
   b. Color scheme.
   c. Reflection factor.
9. *Blackboards.*
   a. Composition.
   b. Surface.
   c. Area.
   d. Placement and height.
10. *Arrangement of Furniture.*
11. *Condition of Air.*
    a. Humidity.
    b. Temperature.
    c. Movement of air.
    d. Ventilation.
    e. Smells; dust; smoke.
12. *Presentation and Display of Instructional Materials.*
    a. Placement.
    b. Angle of vision.
    c. Clarity and size of print.
    d. Interferences with vision.

In most instances, there are no generally accepted standards by which to evaluate the items in the list. Certain standards of illumination are recommended for different kinds of rooms which can serve as a guide. Thus 15 foot-candles are regarded as the desirable level of illumination for classrooms, offices, shops, laboratories, and gymnasiums; 25 foot-candles are recommended for rooms where sewing and other fine detail work is done; in auditoriums, locker rooms, and corridors a level of 5 foot-candles is sufficient. In general, the chief point to be borne in mind is that everything possible should be done to eliminate conditions that cause fatigue, strain, and discomfort. The most complete and systematic source of authentic information available about most of the factors in the list is the monograph by M. E. Broom, C. E. Thompson, and H. Gordon, *Improving the Classroom Environment,* published in 1943 by the El Paso Public Schools, Texas. The volume can be secured at a small cost.

Determining the extent to which school facilities serve the community. The term *community school* is currently used to define a school that has two distinct emphases: namely, (1) service to the entire community, not only to children of school age, and (2) the discovery, development, and use of the resources of the community as part of the educational facilities for carrying on the program of the school. The community school seeks increasingly to democratize life in the school and outside its walls. It co-operates actively with other social agencies and groups in improving community life. The community school is concerned not only with local matters but also with problems of the larger community: state, the region, the nation, and the world. The school serves also as a service center for youth and adult groups. It has been easier to develop schools of this kind in rural areas than in urban centers because of the greater complexity of social organization in city life. Important developments, however, are also taking place in this direction in large centers of population.

The adequacy of the provisions for carrying on a well-rounded community school program can perhaps be best judged by comparing these provisions with those that are regarded by experts as essential. The following list can serve as a basis of analysis. It is compiled from the volume by Engelhardt and Engelhardt, *Planning the Community School,* in which separate chapters are devoted to the discussion of the details for each of the major items in the list.[29]

PROVISIONS FOR PROGRAMS OF COMMUNITY SCHOOLS

1. A community school auditorium, equipped for radio and motion picture programs.
2. Indoor game spaces.

[29] Adapted from chapter headings in N. L. Engelhardt and N. L. Engelhardt, Jr., *Planning the Community School* (New York, American Book, 1940).

3. Social recreation spaces.
4. Cafeterias.
5. Housing provisions for orchestra, choral society, and similar community musical groups.
6. Workshops for arts and crafts with ample exhibit space.
7. Home living laboratories, including home demonstration, practice home, suite of laboratories.
8. Community school library.
9. Facilities for co-ordination, co-operation, and guidance, including psychiatric and health service, medical and dental clinics, vocational and educational guidance.
10. Small group discussion, planning, and study rooms, including forum rooms.
11. Facilities for vocational growth and adjustment, including retraining and rehabilitation.
12. Community school grounds, recreation areas, gardens, farm plots.

Either these facilities can be placed in separate buildings intended primarily for the use of adults, or adaptations can be made of existing facilities in schools; in the latter case, the same resources can be used by all individuals living in the community. Few places have gone as far as the implications of the recommendations by Engelhardt and Engelhardt would extend the program. In larger communities, the establishment of schools designed for adults is likely to be the common practice, whereas in smaller localities the development is likely to be in the direction of a single integrated plant for the entire community. Whatever the trend may be, the possibilities are almost limitless. The extension of the program of the school and its enterprises not only helps to vitalize its activities but it also helps to improve the quality of living in the community.

Section 3

METHODS OF STUDYING THE COMMUNITY

Importance of considering environmental conditions outside the school. It is becoming increasingly evident that the school must consider the effects on children of environmental factors outside the school. A striking example of these effects is reported by Burt [30] who compared 197 delinquent boys and girls with 400 nondelinquents of the same age, the same social class, living on the same streets, and attending the same school. The table on page 458 summarizes the comparative data for the two groups for hereditary, environmental, physical, and psychological conditions. There is a very striking difference in the results for these classes of children. The frequency ratios are largest for psychological and environmental conditions. In the latter group are included influences both within and without the home. Though these differences are closely related to problems of delinquency, they also have a bearing on other aspects of personality and learning. In some respects the school must seek to counteract the unwholesome effects of undesirable community contacts. It is clear that the supervisor must therefore take into consideration the home and community environment in planning the program of developmental and remedial teaching. Many detrimental factors may be overcome.

Surveying the community. The intelligent planning of an educational program depends on the availability of information about local conditions and needs. The importance of this fact has led to the undertaking of surveys of existing social, political, industrial, economic, and moral conditions in many communities. On the basis of the information thus secured, the supervisory staff has been able to make effective adaptations of the total instructional program to meet local needs. Continuing surveys are made in some communities.

[30] Cyril Burt, *The Young Delinquent* (New York, Appleton-Century, 1925), p. 21.

RELATION BETWEEN JUVENILE DELINQUENCY AND FOUR SETS OF CONDITIONS

Conditions	Percentage of Cases		Fre-quency Ratio	Coefficient of Association
	Delin-quent	Non-delinquent		
1	2	3	4 *	5
I. Hereditary Conditions:				
A. Physical	36.9	22.7	1.63	.17
B. Intellectual	25.4	7.7	3.30	.34
C. Temperamental (with patho-logical symptoms)	24.4	10.7	2.28	.24
D. Temperamental (with moral symptoms)	54.3	17.5	3.10	.41
Average	....	....	2.58	.29
II. Environmental Conditions:				
A. Within the home:				
1. Poverty	52.8	38.2	1.38	.15
2. Defective family relation-ships	57.9	25.7	2.25	.33
3. Defective discipline	60.9	11.5	5.30	.55
4. Vicious home	25.9	6.2	4.18	.39
B. Outside the home	45.2	20.2	2.24	.29
Average	....	....	3.07	.34
III. Physical Conditions:				
A. Developmental	21.3	5.5	3.87	.37
B. Pathological	69.0	54.7	1.26	.15
Average	....	....	2.56	.26
IV. Psychological Conditions:				
A. Intellectual	68.5	27.5 †	2.47	.41
B. Emotional:				
1. Inborn:				
a. Specific instincts	59.4	12.0	4.95	.53
b. General emotionality	48.2	11.7	4.12	.46
2. Acquired:				
a. Interests	45.7	13.2	3.46	.40
b. Complexes	64.5	20.5	3.15	.45
Average	....	....	3.63	.45

* Figures in Column 4 are obtained by dividing the figures in Column 2 by the figures in Column 3. The frequency of each item among the nondelinquents is taken throughout to be unity.
† Cases of supernormal ability not included.

The community-survey approach has also been utilized by many individual schools [31] and teachers to study the local environment to locate illustrative materials and conditions that can be used to relate the work of the pupils more closely to their experiences in

[31] E. G. Olsen, *School and Community,* 2nd ed. (New York, Prentice-Hall, 1954).

———, *School and Community Programs* (New York, Prentice-Hall, 1949). Companion book to preceding reference.

———, *The Modern Community School* (New York, Appleton-Century-Crofts, for the Association for Supervision and Curriculum Development, 1953). Excellent cases.

S. E. T. Lund, *The School Centered Community* (New York, Anti-Defamation League of B'nai B'rith, 1949).

William A. Yeager, *School-Community Relations* (New York, Dryden, 1951).

Citizen Co-operation for Better Public Schools, Fifty-third Yearbook, National Society for the Study of Education (Chicago, Univ. of Chicago Press, 1954).

life outside the schools, and to make the instruction more vital and meaningful. Programs of excursions to local institutions and places of interest can also be effectively planned as the basis of such a survey.

The steps in a community survey are as follows:

1. The awareness of some problem or need, social, economic, political, religious, educational.

2. A fact-finding study of the situation and an analysis of community agencies already operative and their functions.

3. The development as a basis of discussion of a proposed program of appropriate action and co-ordination to fit the local situation.

4. The adoption and institution of the proposed program as approved by the community.

Measuring the "goodness" of life in a community. Thorndike has provided a series of selected items by which American cities can evaluate the "general goodness of life for good people." His little book, "Your City" [32] contains the necessary information for a complete and critical understanding of his technique. The "Ten-Item City Yard-Stick" below reveals the approach any city can use to measure its "general goodness." These items were selected from an index consisting of 37 selected items as applied to 310 cities. Thorndike indicates that data for these ten items can be obtained for "almost any city in a few hours and will tell fairly well how the city stands in its general goodness."

TEN-ITEM CITY YARD-STICK

Item 1. Get from the health officer of your city the infant death rate, that is, number of deaths per year of infants 1 to 365 days old per 1000 live births. Subtract this number from 120, and multiply the result by 2.

Item 2. Get from the city-treasurer the year's expenditures for the operation and maintenance of parts, playgrounds and other means of recreation, that is, the figure he would report to the census authorities as "Government-cost payments for operation and maintenance of the department of recreation." Divide this amount by the estimate population of the city, and take

ten times the quotient expressed as dollars. For example, if the amount is $46,350,000 and the population is 60,000, the quotient is $0.7721, and ten times it is 7.7 (or 8 to the nearest whole number).

Item 3. Get from the city-treasurer the estimated value of all the city's property in the form of schools, libraries, museums, parks and other recreational facilities. Divide this amount by the estimated population of the city; then multiply the result expressed in dollars by 1.25.

Item 4. Get from the city-treasurer the total value of all public property (exclusive of streets and sewers), both that (such as schools, fire engines, and jails) used for municipal services, and that (such as water-works, docks and power plants) used for public-service enterprises. Get also the net public debt, subtract the latter from the former, then divide by the population. Enter a credit of 1 for every $3 per capita excess of property over debt. In case your city owes more than its public property is worth, enter the appropriate negative number.

Item 5. Get from the city-treasurer or from the superintendent of schools the expenditures for the operation and maintenance of schools. This does not include capital outlays or payments of interest on school debts. Divide this amount by the population. Multiply the number of dollars in the quotient by 2. That is, enter a credit of 1 for every 50 cents per capita spent for teachers' salaries, books, and supplies, heat, light and care of the schools, or any educational item.

Item 6. Get from the superintendent of schools the number of persons who graduated from senior high school during the year, and divide this number by the city's population. Multiply the quotient by 14141. This is equivalent to giving a credit of 10 for every 7 graduates per 10,000 population.

Item 7. Get from the person in charge of the public library the circulation of books as he would report it to the American Library Association. Divide this number by the city's population. Multiply the result by 5.

Item 8. Get from the superintendent of schools the number of pupils in school who were aged 16 years 0 months to 17 years 11 months at the date when the school enrollment was taken. Find what per cent this number is of the estimated number of persons 16 years 0 months to 17 years 11 months living in the

[32] From *Your City*, copyright, 1939, by E. L. Thorndike. Reprinted by permission of Harcourt, Brace and Company, Inc.

city at that date and give a credit of 1 for each per cent.

Item 9. Get from the superintendent of the telephone company the number of subscribers, or estimate the number by counting the names on 30 pages taken at random from the phone book. Multiply the number of phones by 3,000, and divide the product by the city's population. That is, give a credit of 1 for every three phones per thousand population.

Item 10. Get from the electric light company the number of homes that are supplied with electricity. Multiply by 200 and divide by the city's population. That is, give a credit of 2 for each domestic installation of electricity per hundred population.

Sum the ten entries to obtain your city's total score. . . .

The Ten-Item Yard-Stick scores in 1930 for the cities over 30,000 run from about 300 to about 1000. The average was about 575; about 10 per cent were below 400 and about 10 per cent were above 750.

Some study of cities from 10,000 to 29,000 in population indicates that the following adjectives are appropriate for their scores in the 10-item City Yard-stick:

200-350.   Far below the American standard.
351-500.   Inferior.
501-650.   Ordinary.
651-800.   Superior.
801-950.   In the class of Evanston, Glendale, Newton, Oakland, Springfield, Mass., Grand Rapids, and the like.
951 or more.   Among the world's highest 1 per cent.

The relation of educational leadership to the quality of the educational program in a given school is well illustrated by the following statement: [33]

Schools *A* and *Z* are located in depressed areas of St. Louis. If Jimmy's parents happen to reside in the community served by School *A*, he probably will attend this school which is served by a dynamic principal who feels strongly that the home, the school, and other community agencies should work together to contribute to Jimmy's maximum development. The influence of this attitude is apparent in the school program.

Although the school does not possess the support of a financially able parents' association and lacks many of the facilities present in more recent buildings, these deficiencies are overcome, at least in part, by utilizing community agencies to the maximum. The school, for example, has no library, but Jimmy and his classmates will walk five blocks on a regular schedule to be helped by the teachers and the public librarians in the use of these facilities. The playground area is almost negligible, but the class will make use of a near-by play area provided by the Board of Education. Though the school has no room for school gardens, arrangements have been made for the use of three vacant lots close by. These lots have been cleared by the pupils and, when not under cultivation by the garden enthusiasts, will be utilized for marbles, rope jumping, hopscotch, and other games during free periods.

Among the activities which should interest Jimmy will be many club activities, a student council with representation from all grades, interschool and intraschool baseball competition and marble tournaments, and a great many trips to places of educational interest—all that School *A*'s quota from the Board will allow, and as many extra trips as the Central Office can furnish. These will be supplemented by walking trips to points of local interest. Boy Scouts, Girl Scouts, and Brownies will meet in the building. There will be a milk station providing nourishment for all who can pay and 125 free bottles per week for those who cannot. From the meager funds of the parents' association copies of *Young America* and the *Story Parade* will be furnished, supplemented by magazines contributed from other sources.

Nor will the activities be limited to Jimmy and other elementary school pupils. A formerly utilized room has been adapted to house a WPA nursery unit, which Jimmy's small brother will be able to attend. WPA adult education classes will be held several times a week. Enlisting the services of WPA orchestras, the school will sponsor dances for its former pupils and older pupils at intervals during the year. Girl graduates will be forming a homemaking club which will meet in the building.

The most recent evidence of co-operation with community agencies is that the school has been made an agency for Wyman Camp, a camp for underprivileged youngsters, located outside the city. This arrangement will enable fifty children from School *A*, with some of their mothers, to spend two weeks each summer at this outdoor camp.

[33] Adapted from G. W. Ebey, *Adaptability Among the Elementary Schools of an American City* (New York, Teachers College, Bureau of Publications, Columbia Univ., 1940), p. 18 ff.

If, however, Jimmy's parents happen to reside in the community served by School *Z,* his formal educational environment will be everything that the word *formal* implies. The atmosphere will be one of rigid regimentation, of straight lines and folded hands. There will be no trips and excursions because, as one teacher explained, "The principal doesn't believe in them." There will be no clubs because, according to the principal, the school doesn't believe in "extracurricular stuff." There will be no milk station and no youth organizations meeting in the school because these activities are "not the job of the school." In spite of the fact that the school has one of the few elementary school auditoriums in the city, there will be no school orchestra and no dramatization of classroom work. Jimmy will not be encouraged to use the public library because, in the opinion of the principal, "it is filled with fables and fiction." If Jimmy breaks a citizen's window and the citizen complains to the principal, the case will be referred to the police, for they are responsible for the protection of property. The principal will not be able to understand "why the children are bad on the outside when they are perfect ladies and gentlemen in school."

Essential elements of a survey of community resources. A useful check-list of community resources and suggested sources of information concerning them is given below.[34] The teacher's purpose should not be to guide the pupils in a study of all aspects of the community, but to find and select for study those aspects of life in the community whose consideration is most likely to have educational outcomes of value. The list also suggests the broad aspects of community with which the teacher should be familiar and which can be used to vitalize and enrich learning experience and to make them realistic and meaningful.

RESOURCES AND SOURCES OF COMMUNITY STUDY

RESOURCES	SOURCES
I. *Geography*	I. *Geography*
Soil.	Teachers.
Configuration.	Local experts.
Drainage.	County agents.
Erosion.	4-H club leaders.
Need of reforestation.	Grange officers.

RESOURCES	SOURCES
Elevation.	Agricultural surveys.
Latitude, longitude.	Geodetic survey maps.
Length of growing season.	Relief maps.
Temperature, extremes, average.	Weather reports.
Natural resources.	Crop reports.
Timber.	
Minerals.	
Water power.	

II. *Population*	II. *Population*
Ratio males to females.	Census reports.
Number by age groups.	Industrial reports.
Rate of increase.	Church records.
Average family size.	Court records.
Births.	Patriotic societies.
Deaths.	Telephone installations.
Marriages.	Water, gas, and electric installations.
Divorces.	
Density of population.	Election returns.
Internal migration.	School records concerning parents.
Percentage of voters.	Interviews.
Nationalities represented.	
Percentage and numbers.	
Attitude toward foreign groups.	

III. *History.*	III. *History*
Origin of community homes.	Local histories.
Date of settlement.	Historical societies.
Place of settlement.	Old residents.
Reason for settlement.	Newspaper files.
Identity of early settlers.	Old maps.
Recent immigrants.	Records of churches, clubs, and societies.
Early leaders.	Town records.
Reasons for community growth.	Diaries.
Outstanding events.	School records.
Outstanding industries.	Business records.

[34] E. B. Wesley and Mary A. Adams, *Teaching Social Studies in Elementary Schools* (Boston, Heath, 1952), pp. 387-391.

RESOURCES	SOURCES	RESOURCES	SOURCES
IV. *Farms*	IV. *Farms*	IX. *Occupations*	IX. *Occupations*
Number.	Census reports	Professions.	Interviews.
Average size.	Agricultural	Number in each.	Salaries.
Crops.	yearbooks.	Services.	Income taxes paid.
Livestock.	Local crop reporter.	Farmers.	Payrolls.
Poultry.	County agent.	Laborers.	Relief records.
Fruit.	Outstanding		
Farm mortgages.	farmers.	X. *Standard of Living*	X. *Standard of Living*
Tenancy.	Assessor's lists.	Housing.	Interviews.
Farm labor.	Questionnaires.	Types and condi-	Observation.
Kinds of	Visits.	tions.	Tax rolls.
machinery.	Interviews.	Slums.	Building permits.
Roads.		Relief rolls.	Housing projects.
Conveniences—		Business buildings.	Building activity.
electricity, gas,		Bathrooms.	Sales records.
telephones, mail.		Electricity.	Telephone book.
		Refrigerators.	
V. *Industries*	V. *Industries*	Sweepers.	
Number and types.	Interviews.	Telephones.	
Location.	Business records.	Radios.	
Number of	Observation.	Automobiles.	
employees.			
Conditions of work.		XI. *Health*	XI. *Health*
Wages.		Birth rate.	Vital statistics
Standard of living.		Death rate.	reports.
Unemployment.		Prevalent diseases.	Health records.
Distribution of		Number of doctors.	Hospital records.
products.		Hospitals.	School health
		Health regulations.	records.
VI. *Commerce*	VI. *Commerce*	Water supply.	Accident records.
Stores.	Interviews.	Garbage disposal.	School lunches.
Chain and local.	Visits.	Sewage disposal.	
Mail order business.	Freight records.	Accidents.	
Co-operatives.	Bank statements.	Malnutrition.	
Peddlers.	Advertisements.		
		XII. *Government*	XII. *Government*
VII. *Transportation*	VII. *Transportation*	*Services*	*Services*
Railroads.	Specimen counts of	Police.	State laws.
Kinds of trains.	passengers.	Fire department.	Local ordinances.
Bus lines.	Observations.	Health department.	Safety patrols.
Truck lines.	Interviews.	Public library.	Council proceed-
Water transport.	Number of tickets	Traffic control.	ings.
Airport.	sold.		Election returns.
Automobiles.	Classified directory.		State guide books.
Roads.	Advertisements.		Visits.
Volume of traffic.	Automobile license		Interviews.
Principal freight.	bureau.		
	Railroad and bus		
	folders.	XIII. *Recreation*	XIII. *Recreation*
	Maps.	Parks, playgrounds.	Visits.
		Hunting, fishing.	Participation.
VIII. *Communication*	VIII. *Communication*	Sports.	License records.
Newspapers.	Newspapers.	Picture shows.	Advertisements.
Telephones.	Interviews.	Poolrooms.	Broadcasting
Telegraph.	Visits.	Recreational clubs.	announcements.
Radios.	Telephone book.	Radio programs.	
Mail.			

RESOURCES	SOURCES
XIV. *Education*	XIV. *Education*
Schools.	School records.
Attendance.	Certificates.
Curriculum.	Library files.
Costs.	Circulation records.
Libraries.	Nurse's reports.
Books available.	School staff.
Adult education.	Members of com-
Lectures.	munity.
Lyceums.	
XV. *Churches*	XV. *Churches*
Number.	Membership lists.
Denominations.	Conference records.
Membership.	Marriage records.
Attendance.	Sunday School lists.
Activities.	Baptismal records.
Ministers.	Interviews.
Influence.	Observation.
XVI. *Social Ideas*	XVI. *Social Ideas*
Traditions.	Old residents.
Rivalries.	Newspapers.
Local leaders.	Social workers.
Crime.	Ministers.
Attitude toward	Teachers.
Sunday amuse-	Town officials.
ments.	Observation.
Drinking.	
Smoking.	
Dancing.	
Divorce.	

The type of information desired will determine the technique to be used.[35] The survey can most profitably be undertaken as a co-operative community enterprise in which the staff, the pupils, and other interested members of the community participate. The pattern of community life reflects the concern of all of its members for their common and mutual welfare.

Techniques for studying the community. There are many methods of studying special aspects of life in the community. Some of these procedures, such as the social survey, are highly technical and require the services of an expert. The most useful techniques that the teacher and interested individuals can employ to gather information concerning the community include some of the following:

1. *The group interview*—a method of studying a situation in which the interviewer seeks to draw information or expressions of attitude from an assembled group of interested people rather than through conversations with individual persons.

2. *The personal interview*—a method of specialized directed conversation in which the interviewer guides the responses of the interviewee in a particular premeditated direction.

3. *The questionnaire*—consisting of a series of questions prepared to be submitted to a number of individuals to obtain mass data of a rather elementary type about some condition or situation.

4. *Participant observation*—a method requiring the observer to take up residence among a group and to share its experiences. The method involves excursions, visits, field work, active participation in work and play activities, and similar procedures.

5. *The ecological method*—that is, the study of "space relationships" of the conditions of community life, usually involving the preparation of a social base map, showing the location of various elements of the environment, such as areas of crime and poverty, recreation facilities, poor housing, and so forth.

6. *The use of documentary sources*—the census, newspapers, school records, records of social agencies, reports of research by other agencies, books, museums, diaries, and so forth.

7. *Rating of elements of the community*—various devices which can be used to get data about the social and economic status of the homes of the pupils. One such plan, the Sims Score Card for Socio-Economic Status,[36] requires the pupil to supply various kinds of information about his home that gives a very reliable index of its social status. In this way it is possible to secure information for a large number of homes in a relatively short time. Chapin's Social Status Scale [37] requires the actual visit to the home by some competent social worker. This procedure is time-consuming but nevertheless essential in dealing with problem cases. A portion of Chapin's scale is reproduced below.

[35] An excellent example of plan for a community survey is given in E. A. Wesley, *Teaching the Social Studies* (Boston, Heath, 1937), pp. 436-440.

[36] Bloomington, Ill., Public School Publishing Co., 1927.

[37] Minneapolis, Univ. of Minnesota, 1936. See also Alice M. Leahy, *Minnesota Home Statue Index* (Minneapolis, Univ. of Minnesota Press, 1936).

A PORTION OF THE CHAPIN SCORE CARD FOR MEASURING SOCIO-ECONOMIC STATUS

PART I. MATERIAL EQUIPMENT AND CULTURAL EXPRESSION OF THE LIVING ROOM OF THE HOME

1. Floor, softwood (6) .... ____
   hardwood (10) .... ____
2. Large rug (8) .... ____
3. Windows with drapes each window (2) .... ____
4. Fireplace with 3 or more utensils (8) .... ____
5. Artificial light, electric (8) .... ____
   kerosene (−2) .... ____
6. Library table (8) .... ____
7. Armchairs (8 each) .... ____
8. Piano bench (4) .... ____
9. Desk: personal-social (8) .... ____
10. Bookcases with books (8 each) ... ____
11. Sewing machine (−2) .... ____
12. Couch pillows (2 each) .... ____
13. Alarm clocks (−2) .... ____
14. Periodicals (8 each) .... ____
15. Newspapers (8 each) .... ____
16. Telephone (8) .... ____
17. Radio (8) .... ____
    Score on Part I .... ____

PART II. CONDITION OF ARTICLES IN LIVING ROOM

To provide some objective rating of qualitative attributes of the living room, such as "esthetic atmosphere" or "general impression" the following additional items may be noted. The visitor should check the words that seem to describe the situation. Some of the weights are of minus sign, and so operate as penalties to reduce the total score of the home.

18. Cleanliness of room and furnishings
    a. Spotted or stained (−4) ...... ____
    b. Dusty (−2) .... ____
    c. Spotless and dustless (+2) .... ____
19. Orderliness of room and furnishings
    a. Articles strewn about in disorder (−2) .... ____
    b. Articles in place or in usable order (+2) .... ____
20. Condition of repair of articles and furnishings
    a. Broken, scratched, frayed, ripped, or torn (−4) .... ____
    b. Articles or furnishings patched up (−2) .... ____
    c. Articles or furnishings in good repair and well kept (+2) .... ____

21. Record your general impression of good taste
    a. Bizarre, clashing, inharmonious, or offensive (−4) .... ____
    b. Drab, monotonous, neutral, inoffensive (−2) .... ____
    c. Attractive in a positive way, harmonious, quiet and restful (+2) ____
       Score on Part II .... ____
       Total Score,* Part I and II .... ____

* With penalties deducted.

The value of the community survey procedure. A well-organized and carefully conducted community survey leads to the gathering of a body of information through the use of systematic procedures about some significant aspect of life in the community. The consideration of these data establishes a basis for intelligent planning of the steps that are necessary to improve conditions. These facts are also of undoubted value in the selection of curriculum content and serve as a means of vitalizing the work in the classroom.

Participation by the pupils in a community survey properly adjusted to their level of maturity is a valuable educative experience. Not only do the pupils have worth-while practice in the use of systematic procedures for gathering the necessary data and organizing it for purposes of analysis and evaluation; they also participate in the co-operative group planning and action required to conduct a survey. They gain an insight into the social process and see at first hand some of its weaknesses. According to Olsen, the survey technique: [38]

1. Fosters comprehensive understanding of community structure and processes in every-

[38] From *School and Community,* by E. G. Olsen. Copyright, 1945, by Prentice-Hall, Inc. Reprinted by permission of the publishers. (See also 1954 edition.)
See also E. G. Olsen, *The Modern Community School* (New York, Appleton-Century-Crofts, 1953).
Citizen Co-operation for Better Public Schools, Fifty-third Yearbook, National Society for the Study of Education (Chicago, Univ. of Chicago Press, 1954).
The Community School, Fifty-second Yearbook (*ibid.,* 1953).

day operation, interaction, and complexity.

2. Stimulates depth of insight into vital community problems and trends as these have been influenced by past conditions, present developments, and future prospects.

3. Discloses problems which should be met, not because teacher or textbook loftily says so, but because the evidence itself inescapably reveals the need.

4. Suggests possibilities of student participation in the on-going processes of the community. Such constructive participation, co-operatively carried on, provides fine personal satisfactions, as well as essential training in democratic citizenship.

5. Develops awareness of human interdependence and of the practical necessity for general civic co-operation in carrying on successful individual and group living.

6. Promotes superior citizenship by providing extended experience in the making of critical judgments concerning existing conditions. Students learn, through personal actions, to base conclusions and recommendations upon factual data carefully assembled, objectively interpreted, and meticulously verified.

CHAPTER SUPPLEMENT

INTRODUCTORY DISCUSSION QUESTIONS

1. Summarize quickly from experience or general reading a few points showing:

   a. How living in slum areas affects the development of pupils as learners and as persons.

   b. How the extent of financial support affects the richness and adequacy of instructional equipment and supplies.

   c. How to provide materials adapted to individual differences among pupils.

   d. The use of community resources to make learning realistic and meaningful.

   e. Factors to be considered in selecting sites for school buildings.

   f. The school as a community center.

ORAL REPORTS FOR INDIVIDUALS OR SMALL COMMITTEES

1. List several of the most important material and social elements in your community that you think affect pupil learning definitely for better or for worse.

2. Outline briefly and make critical analysis of the methods used in your system for the selection of instructional materials.

3. Do the same for methods used to supply materials adapted to the range of ability found in all class groups.

4. Describe briefly any project in which you or a group attempted to make systematic use of community resources. (If inexperienced with this, select any typical school survey and critically evaluate what was suggested.)

5. Describe briefly and critically evaluate any project in which you may have participated aimed at conducting a survey of community resources. (If inexperienced, find the account of such a survey in the library and proceed as above.)

6. Describe and evaluate the use made of motion pictures, television, and the radio in some school. What sources or catalogues of these aids are supplied to the teachers?

7. What are the various kinds of instructional supplies and equipment that should be provided in a modern school?

8. By what standards can the quality and adequacy of these materials be appraised?

9. How can that use and adaptation to the needs of children in the school be evaluated?

10. What kinds of tests, clinical apparatus, and special aids should be available?

11. How can the methods of selecting supplies and their availability be studied?

12. What factors related to the comfort of the pupils should be considered in studying the socio-physical environment?

13. How can the adequacy of the equipment and plant for meeting the needs of a modern educational program be studied?

14. How can the use of community resources be studied?

15. What techniques can be used to make a survey of the elements in the social environment outside of school that may affect child growth and development unfavorably?

16. Outline in some detail a plan that could be used to make a systematic study of some aspect or phase of material, supplies, equipment, and socio-physical environment.

WRITTEN REPORTS FOR INDIVIDUALS OR SMALL COMMITTEES

1. Develop a blank for gathering information about materials in reading (or language arts, or social studies, etc.) similar to that for

arithmetic on page 447. If possible, apply the blank in some school situation.

2. Apply to some school or individual classroom the criteria for use of materials outlined on pages 448-449. Would you suggest any changes in these criteria?

3. Consult the original study of Zirbes and prepare improved levels of reading materials for lower or upper grade levels.

4. Make a study of the adequacy of available materials in some school in any field; arithmetic, social studies, language, geography, etc. Try to suggest at least three levels of materials for the field chosen. (Schools using a unified, in contrast to a subject organization, will still be using materials recognizable by the above classifications.) Point out limitations and suggest improvements.

5. Select a score card for rating texts (several are available in the library) and apply it to two or more texts. Evaluate the score card as well as reporting findings on the texts.

6. Prepare a score card for texts in a field where instruments are lacking.

7. Make a detailed and highly critical analysis of a set of workbooks. (This is an important exercise in view of the wide use of extremely poor materials.)

8. Make a list of the kinds of objective information you could secure about the content of a textbook in arithmetic, reading, language, history, etc., that could be used in evaluating it.

9. Determine the level of reading difficulty for some book through application of one of the formulas referred to in the text or found in the library.

10. Make an inventory of the visual aids, mechanical equipment and other instructional materials available in some room or building.

11. Check your school library against the American Library Association's starred list of titles for children. Several other lists issued by school systems and publishers are also available. (A recent survey of this type revealed differences between schools, some of which had 6 per cent of the books and others 60 per cent.)

12. Make a critical analysis of radio, television, and motion-picture programs offered in your community. What can be done by the school to improve the quality of programs given commercially? What is now being done by interested groups of producers and of school workers to improve the quality and to increase the number of educational films available?

13. Describe and suggest improvements (if necessary) in the methods used by your system in housing and distributing instructional materials.

14. Apply a score card to any nearby school building, or some aspect of the plant.

15. Describe a plan whereby your school staff might initiate and carry on a community survey. (Make a miniature survey if possible.)

16. Describe a plan whereby your school staff might co-operate in the selection and evaluation of instructional materials. Evaluate current procedures.

BIBLIOGRAPHY

Consult selected bibliographies given throughout the chapter for details.

Part III

THE IMPROVEMENT OF THE EDUCATIONAL PROGRAM

Chapter 14

◆·◆·◆·◆·◆·◆·◆·◆·◆

The Improvement of the Achievements, Interests, and Work Habits of the Pupil

Section 1

THE GUIDANCE FUNCTION OF THE SCHOOL

Education as guidance. Instruction may be regarded as being both developmental and corrective. On the basis of dependable, systematized information about the individual learner—his needs, abilities, interests, traits, and capacities, and his experiential background—the school through an efficient program of guidance attempts to help him to set up goals that are meaningful and significant to him. The school arranges a variety of functional learning experiences that, if effective, will lead to the well-rounded growth and development of all wholesome aspects of his personality. The chief problem involved is to provide fully and efficiently for individual differences among learners. The continuous study of the pupil by the teacher by carefully selected means of evaluation and also self-appraisal by the individual himself are both important elements of a well-conceived guidance program. Whenever there is any realistic evidence that growth and development are not proceeding satisfactorily, it becomes necessary to identify the nature and causes of the deficiency or shortcoming by appropriate diagnostic procedures, so that the necessary corrective and remedial measures can be taken as soon as possible. Thus evaluation, guidance, and diagnosis are intimately intertwined parts of a continuing unitary process of guiding learning.

The guidance function of the school re-

quires the creation, with that part of the environment under its control, of conditions most likely to be conducive to wholesome growth; and in that part of the environment not under school control, the securing of the co-operation of the pupils and all other members of the social group in creating an environment that stimulates and sustains the growth of all. The school should help the individual to set up standards of attainment and behavior by which he can at all times and in all places evaluate his conduct. Dewey points out that "the planning must be flexible to permit free play for individuality of experience yet firm enough to give direction to continuous development of power." [1]

The fundamentals of an effective educational program. The relation of mental hygiene to instruction and learning has only recently been recognized. The integrated attack on mental-hygiene problems by school and community has barely been begun.

The phenomena of human personality are undoubtedly the most complex and elusive of all of the factors with which the school has to deal. The solutions of the problems involve procedures that are subtle and devious and that undoubtedly vary from individual to individual. They pervade all

[1] John Dewey, *Experience and Education* (New York, Macmillan, 1938), p. 65.

important aspects of the life of the school and community that affect the nature, direction, and quality of individual growth and development. The changes of a political, social, and economic kind that must take place if the principles of social justice are to prevail in the life of the community are too comprehensive and complicated to be presented in this volume, but the need for certain basic changes is fully recognized by the authors. In so far as the school itself is concerned, the steps to be taken to insure the provision of an effective educational program can be stated concisely as follows:

1. The school should provide a curriculum consisting of varied educative experiences adapted to the age, ability, needs, and interests of the individual with the aim of helping him to live a satisfying productive life; experiences also with the aim of aiding him to develop that core of values and beliefs and skills which all must have in common.
2. There should be a broad, rounded instructional program conducted by competent well-adjusted individuals, and organized and administered according to modern principles of education.
3. There should be an attractive physical plant and a wholesome environment containing concrete instructional materials, aids, and equipment that will stimulate learning of a socially desirable type.
4. There should be a well-conceived guidance program with an adequate testing and record system which assists pupils maladjusted in varying degrees, educationally, physically, socially, and emotionally, to adapt themselves to normal school and community life.

In this chapter we shall consider briefly certain broad underlying principles related to these steps. The means of improving instruction, curriculum, and materials will be discussed fully in succeeding chapters. In this chapter we shall discuss the direct steps the school can take to improve the growth and development of all pupils, primarily those whose progress is not satisfactory.

The curriculum of the modern school.
The curriculum may be regarded as the succession of educative experiences for which the school is responsible. The school is also interested in the nature and quality of life outside the school and with the steps that can be taken by the social group to improve living conditions so as to make life happy and satisfying for all. This is inevitable because the school wishes to do all in its power to insure the optimum growth of all members of the social group.

In planning the curriculum, the school must take into account the stage of growth of each individual in so far as his physical and mental development, his interests, purposes, and experiential background are concerned. The objectives of education should encompass all aspects of the personality of the learner, including his physical, mental, social, and emotional development and his educational achievements. To insure well-rounded growth, the school should provide a comprehensive balanced program of experiences, including both in-school and out-of-school activities. The school should recognize the need of helping the individual and the community to develop an active wholesome program of recreation and a plan for using leisure time worthily.

The curriculum should provide for the direct participation of youth in the management and control of their activities in school and elsewhere, so that they will learn through use the ways of democracy. They should consider their own problems and also problems and issues of persistent long-time social concern so that they may understand social life and develop a desire to participate constructively and co-operatively in the solution of the problems of life.

The curriculum should allow for a large amount of creative activity. All experience may be made creative. The solution of problems provides a most valuable opportunity for creative action. This is also true of construction activities, appreciative experiences, sports, and even of those procedures concerned with the acquisition of basic skills and techniques of work and study. Special provision should be made for opportunities for the learner to explore and cultivate his interests and aptitudes through a wide variety of co-curricular activities. In up-to-date schools these experiences have become an integral part of the life of the school and are no longer regarded as "extracurricular." It is recognized that there is need of guidance in creative expression, especially for those who display special skills and interests.

Provision should also be made for work experience and work interests. There should b opportunity for the exploration of vocational aptitudes at all times, especially as the student approaches maturity. To develop desirable attitudes toward work, the learner should be led to see that work experience should be evaluated in terms of what it produces, its social value, and its appeal to the worker. Society faces the problem of providing work opportunities for all members of the social group, an exceedingly complex task involving major economic adjustments. Probably the most valuable contribution the school can make is to carry on a continuous study of the local situation and to inform the community as to the situation and the trends to be expected in the future. A co-operative community, even state or national, attack on the problem is fundamental. The school should make certain that it has as effective a program of vocational guidance, training, and placement as is possible, extending beyond the limits of the high school and including all members of the community who desire assistance and training.

The necessity of providing for the acquisition of special skills and abilities by which all intellectual activity is carried on, including language and the use of quantitative procedures, must be recognized. The need of a control over these techniques is constantly revealed to the learner by the experiences he has in life, and this awareness of their social significance is a valuable means of motivating the efforts required to master them. In traditional schools, there are usually set aside special periods for "drill,"

thus isolating the practice from the situations in which the need for the skill arises. In many cases little if any effort is made to lead the learner to see the social value of the techniques and the contribution they make to the more efficient management of the affairs of life. Drill thus often becomes routinized repetition of material that has little meaning to the learner. In the more modern school, every effort is being made to integrate as closely as possible the use and practice of these skills and abilities, emphasis being placed on their ultimate improvement and mastery by use in meaningful situations. The need of direct intensive practice to develop skill and precision in essential skills can best be provided for on an individualized basis and through the use of instructional materials that make possible a self-directed attack by the learner, independently of the teacher in many cases. This plan requires the careful continuous study of the needs and progress of the individual and the use of appropriate instructional procedures when difficulties arise as learning proceeds.

Range of individual differences far greater than commonly thought. The results of standard tests and informal evaluation procedures are basic data that must be considered in evaluating prevailing school organizations and instructional practices, and the assumptions underlying them. The single most significant fact that has been revealed by measurement is the wide range of differences in intelligence and achievement among the members of any group, and the apparent increase in this variability grade by grade and age by age. In summarizing the results of a carefully devised study of variability of intelligence by Terman and Merrill, Cook[2] stated that in a typical school

(1) The first-grade teacher will find that 2 per cent of the pupils have mental ages of less than

[2] In E. Lindquist, ed., *Educational Measurement* (Washington, American Council on Education, 1951).

four years and that 2 per cent will have mental ages of more than eight years; (2) the sixth-grade teacher will find that 2 per cent of the pupils have mental ages of less than eight years and that 2 per cent will have mental ages of more than sixteen years; (3) the high school teacher will find a range of from eight to ten years in mental age at each grade level; and (4) these conditions will be found to exist whether the school enforces strict policies of promotion and failure or promotes entirely on the basis of chronological age.

Cook also summarized similar data from a number of studies on variability in achievement. Here again he found a wide range of differences:

The range in achievement (2nd to 98th percentile) at the first-grade level is between three and four years; at the fourth-grade level, between five and six years; and at the sixth-grade level, between seven and eight years, in the areas of reading comprehension, vocabulary, the mechanics of English composition, literary knowledge, science, geography, and history. In arithmetic reasoning and computation the range is somewhat less, between six and seven years at the sixth-grade level. These conditions are found to prevail whether the study is based on a large standardization sample representing many schools or on the median variability of single classroom groups.[3]

There also is a great overlapping in the test results for consecutive grade levels, a fact that should be borne in mind in establishing policies for gradation, grouping, and promotion. The teacher of any group faces the problem of adapting instruction so as to provide for this wide range in ability and achievement of the pupils. Unfortunately, the implications of these and similar data about variability in intelligence and achievements of pupils in our schools for the organization of instructional programs have commonly been ignored.

In addition to data about intelligence and achievement which can be expressed in precise quantitative terms, the teacher in planning learning experiences must bear in mind the equally important information about other aspects of pupil behavior that cannot be expressed objectively in precise

units. It is obvious that variability among learners in problem-solving, ability interests, attitudes, adjustment, and ability to work co-operatively with others is probably relatively at least as great as the variability in intelligence and achievement described by Cook. Furthermore, there sometimes is little relationship between the level of achievement as measured by tests and social behavior. The significance of these data will be more fully discussed in the following pages.

Adapting instruction to individual differences. The problem of aiding individuals to develop and improve is complicated by the very great range of individual differences. The expression "individualization of instruction" appears frequently in discussions of educational procedures. To some, individualization means that the individual works alone on some task, not as a member of a group. This point of view is a gross misconception. There is no inherent contradiction between the child working as a member of a group and at the same time carrying on activities adapted to his individual needs, interests, and abilities. The teacher who wishes to adjust the learning activity to differences among individuals so conducts the work of the pupils that each can make his own contribution to a group interest. If the class is allowed to participate in the selection and planning of the activities to be undertaken, it is more likely that strictly individual capacities and talents will be developed than if an uninformed teacher, unaware of the differences among individuals in a class, makes arbitrary uniform assignments of subject matter to be learned by all the pupils. Effective guidance of the learning activity depends on knowledge by the teacher of the characteristics and background of each pupil. To overcome learning difficulties that arise in even the most well-conducted instruction, the teacher must know how to utilize diagnostic procedures to locate specific weaknesses, to establish the

[3] *Ibid.,* p. 11.

causes of the difficulty, and then to undertake the kinds of corrective and remedial measures likely to bring about an improvement. Clearly the "lock-step system" that characterized the schools of the past is outmoded.

Because of the need of providing for the individual differences among the pupils of a grade or class, the instructional program should be highly flexible. The contents of the curriculum should be adapted to the ability and level of development of the group of pupils in the class. The program for groups of superior children should be enriched. Special adjustments should be made to explore the talents of gifted children. Activities should be organized to promote the discovery of aptitudes, interests, and appreciations of individuals. A systematic program of educational and vocational guidance is an important element in differentiated instruction.

The list below gives a helpful analysis of the wide variety of instructional procedures that are used in our schools to adapt instruction to individual differences and to provide valuable experiences in group learning activities:

1. The use of experience units which provide for a wide variety of activities on different levels of difficulty.
   a. Problem-solving, research, and experimentation.
   b. Construction activities, resulting in intellectual or material products.
   c. Appreciation experiences enjoyed by the individual.
   d. Creative activities resulting in original thinking, acting, and producing.
   e. Excursions, field trips, and participation in community enterprises.
   f. Opportunities for learning through use and direct experience.
2. Grouping of pupils according to their needs, interests, and level of development.
   a. Classification into groups of similar social maturity and intellectual status.
   b. Promotion at irregular intervals.
   c. Program planned in terms of future needs of individual.

   d. Exploratory courses.
   e. Classes for gifted children.
   f. Special provisions for talented children to insure stimulating experiences.
   g. Rich program of co-curricular activities.
   h. Adapting program of work to level of pupil ability.
3. Differentiation of work in classes by such means as:
   a. Readiness programs adjusted to needs of individuals and groups.
   b. Differentiated curriculum.
   c. Differentiated assignments.
   d. Differentiated standards to be achieved.
   e. Differences in scope of course requirements.
   f. Differences in time allowed for completing work.
   g. Supplementary assignments.
   h. Special assignments for more able pupils or those with special interests.
   i. Use of books and materials of several levels of difficulty.
   j. Use of workbooks.
   k. Enrichment activities.
4. Laboratory methods, such as:
   a. Individualized instructional materials to develop basic skills, such as those used in the Winnetka plan.
   b. Dalton plan of assignments of different levels of difficulty and comprehensiveness.
   c. Morrison plan of guide sheets and differentiated assignments.
   d. Individual progress plans in laboratory and shop courses.
   e. Diagnosis of difficulties that arise in the course of learning.
   f. Remedial and corrective measures to eliminate causes of difficulty.
   g. Provision of a wide variety of materials for developing meanings.
   h. Use of appropriate community resources to vitalize and enrich learning experiences.
5. Special provisions for maladjusted and slow-learning pupils.
   a. Adjustment and coaching teachers.
   b. Opportunity classes.
   c. Ungraded classes.
   d. Hospital classes for serious problem cases.
   e. Special classes for students who have failed some required courses.

6. Guidance services which assist in orienting the student and in planning a program of work adjusted to his needs, interests, and potentialities.
   a. School psychologists and personality consultants.
   b. Visiting teachers and social workers.
   c. Counselors and vocational-guidance experts.
   d. Home-room teachers and advisory periods.
   e. Medical and psychiatric services.
   f. Clinicians to study behavior problems and cases of serious retardation.
   g. Recreation integrators.

Selected references of special value in studying the problem of providing for individual differences are the following:

BERTHOLD, Charles A., *Administrative Concern for Individual Differences* (New York, Teachers College, Bureau of Publications, Columbia Univ., 1951).
COOK, W. W., "Individual Differences and Curriculum Practice," *Journal of Educational Psychology* (March, 1948), pp. 141-148.
TRAXLER, Arthur E., "Current Organization and Procedures in Remedial Teaching," *Journal of Experimental Education* (March, 1952), pp. 305-312.
WOLFF, Sister M. Roberta, "A Study of Spelling Errors with Implications Concerning Pertinent Teaching Methods," *Elementary School Journal* (April, 1952), pp. 458-466.

The necessary adjustments to individual differences must not obscure the point that there must be also experiences which develop the likenesses as well. The individual, while different, is also like many other individuals in a number of important ways. The "commonalties" must be developed as well as the differences.

The staff should use the above list of procedures as the basis of an inventory of current practices. The inventory may grow out of observations of practices in classrooms by the supervisor or perhaps a self-inventory by the teacher. Instructional specialists should be available to assist in planning methods of improving the organization of instruction so that school and teachers can more effectively adapt instruc-

tion to individual differences. Study groups of interested teachers can be formed to examine various aspects of the problem as a part of the program of in-service education. The outgrowth of this study should be systematic experimentation by the staff with methods of differentiated instruction that are judged to be most useful.

Special provisions for the highly endowed. There is widespread interest in the education of the gifted, talented, highly endowed at all levels of the school. A considerable literature in this field is appearing in which various aspects of the problem are being discussed and practices evaluated. The most commonly used plans are included in the list of methods of providing for individual differences on pages 473 and 474. There are many other interesting innovations that should be at least mentioned at this point. The nature of some of them is indicated by the brief descriptions that follow:

1. Outstanding students participate in the management and operation of school enterprises.
2. They establish and operate organizations for dealing with their problems, such as credit unions, insurance companies.
3. They participate in a wide variety of community enterprises, such as surveys of housing, cleanup campaigns, etc.
4. Groups meet regularly with a special teacher to receive special training in the use of research procedures and library materials in the solution of problems.
5. Groups study major topics, such as the American Heritage, for an extended period of time in lieu of the regular class work.
6. Special classes are set up to help the school and the learners to uncover talents and special abilities.
7. They serve as guides for visitors, office assistants, etc.
8. They participate in discussions, forums, debates, etc.
9. They conduct exhibits of hobbies and creative products.

In general, there are three basic administrative plans of providing for more capable learners: (1) acceleration, (2) grouping, and (3) enrichment.

Acceleration is synonymous with more rapid progress, made possible by special promotions. This plan is questionable, since from the standpoint of personal and social adjustment it could be a dubious practice to group immature youngsters with much older students.

Grouping of the more capable children into special classes emphasizes competition rather than co-operative group participation in activities with individuals of all levels of ability, a normal social situation. Partial grouping for special kinds of experiences has considerable value.

Enrichment seems to be a by far better approach to the problem than either acceleration or grouping. The skillful teacher easily can enrich the work in the various curriculum areas by planning for the more capable learners special activities that will broaden and deepen their insights and lead them to explore areas beyond the normal course content. Nonacademic experiences can be added to their programs to enable them to develop leisure-time and quasivocational skills. The more capable learners should also be given special opportunity to develop qualities of leadership in studentbody activities of many different kinds.

Where modern unit teaching is used, there is certain to be excellent provision for individual differences, for slow or for gifted children. (See Section 3.) Emphasis is being placed on the necessity of getting some of the very bright students through the secondary school at an earlier age because of the long period of preparation required for some of the professions. The selected references below contain basic information on educating the gifted:

CARROLL, Herbert A., *Genius in the Making* (New York, McGraw, 1940).

The Education of the Gifted, Educational Policies Commission (Washington, NEA, 1950).

Education of Exceptional Children, Forty-ninth Yearbook, Part II, National Society for the Study of Education (Chicago, Univ. of Chicago Press, 1950), Ch. 14.

HILDRETH, Gertrude, *Education of Gifted Children* (New York, Harper, 1952).

HOLLINGSWORTH, Leta S., *Children Above 180 I.Q.* (Yonkers, World Book, 1942).

TERMAN, L. M., and ODEN, M. H., *The Gifted Child Grows Up* (Stanford University, Calif., Stanford Univ. Press, 1947).

WARNER, W. L., HAVIGHURST, R. J., and LOEB, M. B., *Who Shall Be Educated?* (New York, Harper, 1944).

WITTY, Paul, ed., *The Gifted Child* (Boston, Heath, 1951).

———, "Educational Provisions for Gifted Children," *School and Society* (September 20, 1952), pp. 177-181.

———, and BLOOM, S. W., "Education of the Gifted," *School and Society* (October 17, 1953), pp. 113-119.

Special adjustments for slow-learning pupils. Instructional adjustments can be made also for slow-learning children and for children with various handicaps. Hildreth (see p. 476) suggests that the same philosophy of education which demands provision for the gifted demands also that the needs of slow learners be met. The use of units as instructional organization, with their provision for various contributions on various levels, serves both types of learner. The dullard should not be regarded as a nuisance, and above all, not be made to feel that he is one. He is a citizen. As an individual he is entitled to the respect accorded all individuals.

A simple environment with fewer changes and interruptions than is common is desirable. First-hand, concrete experience is essential, with generalizations and abstractions introduced more slowly. Real-life experience with the environment provides ideal instructional materials. Guidance must be sympathetic and rather continuous. Every opportunity for success should be provided. There is as yet little valid evidence about methods of instruction, but we do know that "bringing them up to normal" is an idle dream—and detrimental as well. Confining the program to drill on skills is equally undesirable. The slow learner is entitled to deal with meanings, to attempt creative work on his level. A program of opportunity for slow learners to experience widely and to achieve on their own level is far better than (sometimes overpressured) remedial programs later.

The bulk of the literature on this topic is in the periodicals, and is extensive. Two general references contain good summaries and also extensive bibliographies:

HILDRETH, Gertrude, *Child Growth Through Education* (New York, Ronald, 1948), Ch. 22.

The Education of Exceptional Children, Forty-ninth Yearbook, Part II, National Society for the Study of Education (Chicago, Univ. of Chicago Press, 1950). Whole volume.

Effective materials of instruction. The importance of an attractive, stimulating environment as a factor in learning is commonly recognized. Learning cannot proceed easily and successfully unless the materials of instruction are attractive, interesting, and well organized, and unless their difficulty is adjusted to the ability of the children. Because of wide variations in the mental capacity of the pupils, it is usually desirable to have books of different levels of difficulty at hand. There should also be a wide variety of reference books and instructional materials. Standards for evaluating and selecting materials are fully discussed in Chapters 13 and 17.

There are also numerous reading, spelling, language, and arithmetic workbooks which a wide-awake teacher can use to adapt instruction to individual differences.

It should be emphasized that much wider use than at present should be made of the available types of instructional materials which make it possible to adapt instruction in the basic tool subjects to the differences in the rates at which children learn.

Necessary diagnostic and remedial materials. To enable the teacher to adjust instruction to the needs of the pupils, cumulative records of work in former grades, such as have been described in Chapter 10, should be accessible. To aid in the discovery of faults, diagnostic tests should be available. The necessary remedial materials should also be provided. When they are lacking, the teacher must devise them. Because of their value as incentives, methods of showing the pupils their progress from time to time, such as graphs of tests results, progress charts, and similar devices should be used regularly.

Guidance and counseling. In many secondary schools and higher institutions of learning there is provided a systematic program of guidance and counseling. Guidance from the beginning was concerned chiefly with vocational choices of students. It was later extended to include educational guidance, that is, the selection of courses suitable to the interests and future careers of the individual. More recently, the concept of guidance has been broadened to include what is now usually called "counseling," which is concerned with advice on all aspects of learning, including personality development, in both elementary and secondary schools as well as at the college level. Wrenn has defined counseling as follows: [4]

Counseling is a personal dynamic relationship between people who approach a mutually defined problem with mutual consideration for each other to the end that the younger, less mature, or more troubled of the two is aided to a self-determined resolution of his problem.

From this point of view, guidance is a function that pervades all aspects of the educational program, including curriculum, instruction, extracurricular activities, administration, and community relations. Guidance leads to the focusing of attention on the learner, his needs and problems, rather than on the courses he is taking. It affects the administration of the school in such matters as flexibility of scheduling, attitude toward extracurricular activities, regulations about attendance, discipline, and school-community relationships. The pur-

[4] *Guidance in Educational Institutions,* Thirty-seventh Yearbook, Part I, National Society for the Study of Education (Bloomington, Ill., Public School Publishing Co., 1938), p. 121.

pose of guidance is the optimum development of each individual in the light of his potentialities.

The basis of effective guidance and counseling is information about all essential aspects of the learner's personality that may help in the solution of any problem that may arise. The types of information include many of those that are useful in educational diagnosis, namely, data about his school history, his aptitudes and abilities, his home background and the community environment in which he lives, his goals, purposes, and interests, his social and emotional maturity and adjustment, his health, and his economic and financial background.

The techniques used to secure information about the individual's vocational preferences and aptitudes are similar to those used in studying his educational achievements and in making educational diagnoses, except that they are focused primarily on matters related to choice of occupation. These procedures include first of all various kinds of tests, such as intelligence tests, achievement tests, personality tests, tests of vocational aptitude and skills, and guidance tests and inventories.

Numerous less formal objective methods are also used to secure essential information, similar to the techniques of diagnosis described in Chapter 10, including the analysis of records of social, civic, and protective agencies of the community. The most useful devices are rating scales, inventories of information, interviews, observations of behavior in arranged situations, reference to diaries, anecdotal records, questionnaires, and case histories. The advantages of a well-kept system of cumulative records and personnel folders as a source of information for guidance purposes are obvious.

For details in the area of guidance, the interested reader is referred to the following selected references:

DARLEY, J. G., *Testing and Counseling in the High School Guidance Program* (Chicago, Science Research Associates, 1950).

DETJEN, E. W., and DETJEN, Mary F., *Elementary School Guidance* (New York, McGraw, 1952).

DUNSMOOR, C. C., and MILLER, L. M., *Principles and Methods of Guidance for Teachers* (Scranton, Pa., International Textbook Co., 1949).

FROELICH, C. P., *Guidance Services in Smaller Schools* (New York, McGraw, 1950).

————, and DARLEY, J. G., *Studying Students* (Chicago, Science Research Associates, 1952).

Pupil Personnel Services in Elementary and Secondary Schools, Office of Education (Washington, Federal Security Agency, 1951), Circular 325.

STRANG, Ruth, *Counseling Technics in College and Secondary School* (New York, Harper, 1949).

TRAXLER, Arthur E., *Techniques of Guidance* (New York, Harper, 1945).

WILLEY, Roy D., *Guidance in Elementary Education* (New York, Harper, 1952).

Counselors in elementary schools. The use of special counselors in elementary schools is a promising new development, especially in larger school systems. Usually their function is to co-ordinate activities in schools dealing with personnel work with all pupils, mental hygiene, measurement and evaluation, social work, clinical services, and adjustment problems. Bailard [5] has outlined the responsibilities of elementary school counselors as follows:

LEGITIMATE SERVICES OF AN ELEMENTARY-SCHOOL COUNSELOR

The counselor is directly responsible to the principal in her building. Her services will be subject to his approval. The counselor's time should be used in promoting the services indicated below if a well-balanced guidance program is to be developed.

General Services

An elementary school counselor should be responsible for:
1. A testing program.
   a. Make provision for ordering and administering tests—survey, intelligence, special building achievement, individual, and other.

[5] Virginia Bailard, in *Handbook for Counselors* (Long Beach, Calif., Public Schools), pp. 70-71.

b. Interpret results.

c. Make provision for the scoring of group tests. This may be done by junior clerk or classroom teacher, or by counselor when necessary.

2. Gathering, organizing and keeping significant pupil data (permanent record, pupil analysis blank, etc.).
3. Recording and filing of all pupil data.
4. Routine procedures for transferring pupils.
5. Aiding principal in registering pupils.
6. Assisting principal with the organization of pupils into socially satisfactory groups.
7. Aiding principal in the selection of pupils who need individual work.

Services Concerning the Child With a Problem

1. Helping teachers to understand, accept and deal more effectively with the individual child who presents special problems in behavior and learning, or who is clearly emotionally and socially maladjusted.
2. Gathering data about the child through observation, testing, interviews, etc.
3. Utilizing and co-ordinating the services of school personnel workers who contribute to the welfare of the child.
4. Aiding principal in conferring with parents in an effort to arrive at a satisfactory plan of action which would be most beneficial to their child.
5. Co-operating with local agencies when they are concerned with an individual child with a problem.
6. Working with the child directly when that seems advisable.

Services Concerned With Teachers

1. Helping teachers to accept and understand all children.
2. Helping teachers individually and in groups, through demonstrations and conferences, to develop acceptable techniques of collecting, interpeting and using behavioral data.
3. Assisting principal in guiding teachers in making constructive and wise reports to parents.
4. Organizing pupil-study conferences and interesting teachers in participating in them.
5. Helping teachers use group work as an adjustive process for making pupils feel that they "belong."

6. Assisting principal in planning programs for faculty meetings which would make for greater understanding of the guidance point of view.
7. Being genuinely concerned about the mental health of the teacher, giving her as much help and support as possible.

Mental-hygiene aspects of instruction. In recent years increased attention has been given to the mental-hygiene aspects of learning and to the need of considering the development of the emotional aspect of personality. The school should make every effort to identify children whose emotional responses do not fall within the general range of accepted behavior. Experiences should be provided in the school that will stimulate the development of patterns of emotional reactions that are recognized as mature in terms of the growth level of the individual and are acceptable to the cultural patterns of the community. Creative esthetic expression and purposeful activities should be encouraged as a means of maintaining a high level of morale, of relieving tensions, and of sensitizing learners to the beautiful. Children should be given the opportunity to develop genuine, effective loyalties through participation in a wide variety of group experiences and through re-evaluation of their loyalties in the light of experience. The evidence is very clear that teachers who persistently force children to undertake purposeless, difficult distasteful tasks that have little if any significance for them are deliberately taking the risk of creating frustrated, neurotic, rebellious children and adults.

The selected references below—there are many others—consider problems of mental hygiene in the learning process:

CUNNINGHAM, Ruth, and others, *Understanding Group Behavior of Boys and Girls* (New York, Teachers College, Bureau of Publications, Columbia Univ., 1951).

DOLLARD, John, and others, *Frustration and Aggression* (New Haven, Yale Univ. Press, 1940).

FENTON, Norman, *Mental Hygiene in School Practice* (Stanford University, Calif., Stanford Univ. Press, 1943).

HAVIGHURST, R. J., and TABA, Hilda, *Adolescent Character and Personality* (New York, Wiley, 1949).

LEWIN, Kurt, LIPPITT, Ronald, and WHITE, R. K., "Patterns of Aggressive Behavior in Experimentally Created Social Climates," *Journal of Social Psychology* (May, 1939), pp. 271-299.

LOWENFELD, Viktor, *Creative and Mental Growth: A Textbook in Art Education* (New York, Macmillan, 1947).

MURPHY, Gardner, MURPHY, L. R., and NEWCOMB, T. M., *Experimental Social Psychology* (New York, Harper, 1937).

PRESCOTT, Daniel, *Emotion and the Educative Process* (Washington, American Council on Education, 1938).

WALLIN, J. E. W., *Personality Maladjustment and Mental Hygiene* (New York, McGraw, 1949).

Consult also reader's guides for current materials.

A schedule for evaluating a mental-hygiene program. The basis for studying and improving the mental-hygiene program of a school is suggested in the following schedule prepared by Fenton.[6] The evaluation should be undertaken as a group enterprise in which all persons concerned with the problem have the opportunity to participate. The ratings, while subjective and qualitative, are likely to reveal to the staff where the weaknesses in the program lie and to suggest the points at which improvements can be made. In a sense, the items in the schedule constitute a series of suggested standards.

SCHEDULE FOR THE EVALUATION OF THE MENTAL-HYGIENE PROGRAM OF AN ELEMENTARY SCHOOL

KEY FOR RATING: A—Excellent; B—Good; C—Fair; D—Poor; E—Very inadequate

1. Does the organization and conduct of the school contribute to the wholesome personality adjustment of teachers and pupils?
   a. To what degree are special efforts made to understand the needs of individual pupils through the employment of counselors and other guidance specialists who use: (1) tests of academic aptitude, (2) measurement of educational achievement, (3) study of social history, (4) personal interviews, (5) physical examinations?
   b. How much is done by way of remedial instruction in (1) reading, (2) arithmetic, (3) speech, (4) study skills, (5) other fields?
   c. Does the health program stress preventive as well as therapeutic aspects of pupil well-being?
   d. To what degree are happy, spontaneous, and constructive recreational experiences provided for all pupils?
   e. To what extent was the system of evaluation (1) developed through faculty participation, (2) understood by the faculty, and (3) understood and accepted by the pupils?
   f. In the promotion of pupils, to what extent is their physical, emotional, and social status considered as well as their academic achievement?
   g. Does the special education program make adequate provision for (1) the superior, (2) the retarded, (3) the physically handicapped, and (4) the socially maladjusted?
   h. As for records: (1) How adequate are pupil records? (2) How freely are these records available for the use of teachers?
   i. How well is the school equipped (1) to give individual guidance? (2) to employ the guidance conference to give teachers a better understanding of the pupils?
2. Do the conditions under which the teachers work contribute to their occupational adjustment and mental health?
   a. How pleasant, clean, and cheerful are the physical surroundings?
   b. To what extent do the community mores permit the teachers a reasonable amount of personal freedom?
   c. How adequate are the salaries of teachers with regard to personal security and independence?
   d. To what extent do teachers feel that their job tenure is secure?
   e. Is there adequate provision for sick leave?
   f. Do the teachers have health insurance?

[6] Norman Fenton, *Mental Hygiene in School Practice* (Stanford University, Calif., Stanford Univ. Press, 1943), pp. 9-11.

g. To what extent does the teachers' lounge (1) provide reasonable quiet and privacy, (2) contain furniture and cooking equipment for teacher comfort?

h. How adequate is the plan of teacher rating?

i. How fairly is the distribution of extra duties handled?

j. Can the teacher feel secure in adapting her methods to her own background and ability?

3. Does the community accept its responsibilities for the mental hygiene of teachers?

a. How well are the teachers welcomed into the community life?

b. How far does the teaching profession enjoy prestige comparable to that of other professions?

c. Are the demands upon teachers' time and effort, in addition to professional duties, reasonable?

d. How well are the teachers' efforts at self-improvement appreciated and rewarded?

e. How much does the administration encourage teachers' recreational enjoyment?

f. Does the teacher have a sense of belonging and of contributing to the community?

4. Does the mental hygiene of the school reflect itself in the mental hygiene of the parents?

a. To what extent do parents in general have a sympathetic knowledge and understanding of what is going on at school?

b. Do parents understand and accept the system of pupil evaluation?

c. Are parent-study classes planned (1) to interest the parents in the work of the school? (2) to instruct them in child psychology?

d. How advanced are the plans to have parents spend time at school observing the program?

e. How much does the Parent-Teacher Association enter into the life of the school?

f. How extensive are the opportunities other than the Parent-Teacher Association offered for parental participation in school life?

g. To what degree are teachers friendly and hospitable in their relationships with parents?

5. Is the scope of treatment in mental hygiene broader than the school itself?

a. To what extent does the school refer behavior problems to guidance specialists in the community?

b. How far does the school co-operate with the family-welfare agencies in the community?

c. How much is the school involved in the various after-school recreational and other welfare programs of the children?

d. To what degree does the school co-operate with youth organizations such as the Scouts?

The use of the schedule should make it clear that mental hygiene is not something new and unfamiliar but a vital and significant force that operates in any well-conducted school. This factor is receiving ever increasing attention.

Records essential for effective guidance. The purpose of school records should be to aid the staff to understand individuals so that effective guidance can be given. A well-devised set of records requires the setting up of educational objectives and provides for the gathering of information which enables the staff to determine the extent to which they are being achieved. Records should contain as complete and reliable information as possible on the basis of which reports of pupil progress and development can be made to the home, so that school and home can deal co-operatively and consistently with the individual. The records should at all times be available to the staff. Records should give evidence regarding a pupil's readiness for succeeding educational experiences. Transferable records assure continuity of guidance. The following statement from the volume by Smith and Tyler sets up a series of criteria to be used as the basis of evaluating any system of records: [7]

1. Any form devised should be based on the objectives of teachers and schools so that by its use a continuing study of a pupil will throw light on his successive stages of development

[7] Eugene R. Smith, Ralph Tyler and the Evaluation Staff, *Appraising and Recording Student Progress* (New York, Harper, 1942), pp. 467-468.

in powers or characteristics believed to be important.

2. The forms dealing with personal characteristics should be descriptive rather than of the nature of a scale. Therefore "marks" of any kind, or placement, as on a straight line representing a scale from highest to lowest, should not be used.

3. Every effort should be made to reach agreement about the meaning of trait names used, and to make their significance in terms of the behavior of a pupil understood by those reading the record.

4. Wherever possible a characterization of a person should be by description of typical behavior rather than by a word or phrase that could have widely different meanings to different people.

5. The forms should be flexible enough to allow choice of headings under which studies of pupils can be made, thus allowing a school, department, or teacher to use the objectives considered important in the particular situation, or for the particular pupil.

6. Characteristics studied should be such that teachers will be likely to have opportunities to observe behavior that gives evidence about them. It is not expected, however, that all teachers will have evidence about all characteristics.

7. Forms should be so devised and related that any school will be likely to be able to use them without an overwhelming addition to the work of the teachers or secretaries.

8. Characteristics studied should be regarded not as independent entities but rather as facets of behavior shown by a living human being in his relations with his environment.

The significance of individual and trait differences. Any program of instruction must take into consideration the important facts about individual and trait differences that have been revealed by the studies set forth in earlier chapters of this volume. There exists in any realm of activity a wide range in the endowments of individuals. The distribution of aptitude approximates the normal curve of distribution. This is true of achievement in reading, athletic skill, general intelligence, and artistic talent, as well as all other native and acquired traits. Individuals cannot readily be classified into specific types, however, since the various levels merge gradually and are not sharply differentiated.

The evidence is clear that the degree to which the individual possesses different traits also varies.[8] The wider the range of acquired traits appraised the greater appears to be the range of talent. Graphs of the results of diagnostic tests in reading usually are not symmetrical in form. Their unevenness shows that in many cases the various skills have not all been developed to the same level. The profile given on page 482 is an illustration of the unevenness of the development of various traits in arithmetic for a fifth-grade pupil. The chart shows unusual strength on some points and serious weakness on others. Charts for other students differ markedly from this one, indicating the necessity of recognizing individual differences in planning remedial instruction. Brown[9] has demonstrated the fact that "dull boys and bright boys show an equal amount of unevenness in all abilities" and that the "same type of class organization and treatment" is required for both groups.

The data in the chart also show the importance of evaluating the wide range of skills and abilities of the various areas of learning by comprehensive testing programs so that any deficiency can be located. If the student whose profile appears on page 482 had been given only the test in signs and symbols he would have rated high in arithmetic. His weakness in number concepts would not have been detected until much later, if at all.

Children do not all profit equally from the same experience because of the differences in their mental levels, in their readiness for the task, in the effectiveness of their study habits, in their background of experiences, and in the effort they put forth. They do not respond to the given incentive in the same way. Children also differ in the rates at which

[8] C. L. Hull, *Aptitude Testing* (Yonkers, World Book, 1928), pp. 21-50.

[9] A. W. Brown, *Unevenness of the Abilities of Dull and of Bright Children,* Contributions to Education No. 220 (New York, Teachers College, Bureau of Publications, Columbia Univ., 1926), p. 109.

SAMPLE PROFILE—CALIFORNIA ARITHMETIC TEST

A Test Given in October to a Low 5 Pupil. Age, 124 months. Mental Age, 132 months.

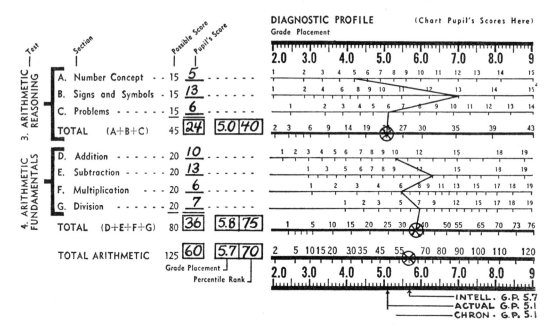

they are maturing physically, mentally, and emotionally. They differ in the rates at which they learn the basic skills involved in spelling, writing, reading, and computing. These differences are caused in part by differences which appear to be fixed by heredity in original inborn nature and in part to differences in environmental influences to which they have been exposed. These factors also decisively condition behavior.

The individual should be continuously evaluated in terms of his own potentialities, developmental progress, and experiential background. Because the educative process continuously modifies the total picture, including the needs, interests, attitudes, and potentialities of the individual, evaluation must be continuous. The need is for a flexible educational program conducted by a staff which proceeds on a tentative experimental basis to adapt instruction to the wide range of individual differences.

At the same time consideration must be given to the problem of developing the common attitudes, interests, and knowledges re-

garded as basic in life in a democratic society. Hutchins [10] has stated the issue sharply:

Since education in the West is built largely on the doctrine of individual differences, so that the study of the individual child and his individual interests is supposed to be the principal preoccupation of his teachers from his earliest days, and premature and excessive specialization is a common characteristic of both the American college and the British public school, it will be argued that a program of liberal education ignores the most important thing about men, and that is that they are different. I do not ignore it; I deny it. I do not deny the fact of individual differences; I deny that it is the most important fact about men or the one on which an educational system should be erected.

Men are different. They are also the same. And at least in the present state of civilization the respects in which they are the same are more important than those in which they are different. . . . Now, if ever, we need an education that is designed to bring out our common humanity rather to indulge our individuality.

[10] Robert M. Hutchins, *The Conflict in Education in a Democratic Society* (New York, Harper, 1953), pp. 88-90.

An illustration of variability in achievement. Some of the problems of effective guidance arise out of the wide variations in the ability of pupils in the same group. The table on page 484 gives the scores on the Stanford Achievement Test of six pupils of approximately the same educational age and in five cases of about the same chronological age.

Their educational ages do not vary more than two months; however, there is a wide variation in their subject ages. The range is from fourteen months in arithmetic reasoning to seventy-nine months in language usage. An examination of the scores for each pupil shows that the nature of their profiles varies also. Pupil *D* has a consistently average rating. Pupil *C* has an extremely variable rating, the range being from 10-6 in literature to 16-5 in language usage. It is obvious that these pupils present greatly different problems to the teacher. They are typical individuals and do not represent unusual cases. Effective adaptation of instruction to these differences presents serious difficulties. Obviously they are not a homogeneous group. The problem becomes exceedingly complex with large groups.

Variability among schools. Not only is there wide variability among the achievements of pupils, but there is also almost as great variability in the average achievements among the schools of a city or state. The table below illustrates not only the variability in achievement among a large group of eighth-grade junior high school pupils but also the wide range in school average scores in a single city, in this case New York. The data are for achievement in reading.

It can be seen from the table that the variation in individual scores was from below 4.9 grade level to above grade 12 level. The median 7.6 was practically the same as the 1940 norm for the test used; the range for the middle 50 per cent was from 5.9 to 9.8. It is obvious that the schools of the city face a serious problem, especially in so far as they are to deal with the large number of students with very low reading ability.

The setting up of a reading program for the city as a whole is complicated greatly by the wide range in average scores for individual schools. School averages range from the grade 5.0-5.9 level to the grade 10.0-10.9 level, indicating that the problem of organizing a reading program for retarded readers is critical in some areas but of little significance in others. The range in school average scores is almost as great as the range in individual scores.

It is evident that a supervisory group responsible for instruction in reading should not try to set up a uniform program to be carried out by all schools; it should be their purpose to assist the staff of individual schools to set up reading programs that are adapted to the local situation and to the needs of the pupils and staff of each school. This conclusion applies not only to reading but to all areas of the curriculum. The supervisory program should be flexible and adapted to the need of particular schools, even of individual teachers. These principles were discussed in Chapter 6.

VARIABILITY IN READING GRADE FOR EIGHTH-GRADE PUPILS IN NEW YORK JUNIOR HIGH SCHOOLS IN STANFORD READING TEST 1, 1940 NORMS

Reading Grade	Individual Scores	School Average Scores
12-	2298	
11.0-11.9	2134	
10.0-10.9	2507	1
9.0- 9.9	2727	14
8.0- 8.9	3654	22
7.0- 7.9	4358	26
6.0- 6.9	3989	21
5.0- 5.9	4381	4
4.9 and below	3300	
Total	29,348	88
Median	7.6	
Q_1	5.9	6.8
Q_3	9.8	8.6
Q_3-Q_1	3.9	1.8

(Data adapted from Tables I and II in May Lazar, ed., *The Retarded Reader in the Junior High School* (New York, Bureau of Educational Research, Board of Education, Publication No. 31, September, 1952).

SCORES ON STANFORD ACHIEVEMENT TEST

For six pupils with educational ages which do not vary more than two months. Expressed in specific subject ages

Pupil	Boy or Girl	Age		Tests												
		Years	M'ths	1 Par. Mean.	2 Word Mean.	Total Reading	3 Spell.	4 Lang. Usage	5 Lit.	6 Hist. and Civ.	7 Geog.	8 Phys. and Hyg.	9 Arith. Reas.	10 Arith. Comp.	Total Arithmetic	Educational Age
A	B	14	2	12.8	13-9	13-3	12-	12-7	9-10	12-11	11-8	12-8	12-3	11-0	11-7	12
B	B	13	3	10-10	11-5	11-2	11-8	13-3	11-6	11-9	10-10	12-11	12-3	12-7	12-6	11-10
C	B	14	4	11-10	13-9	12-8	14-10	16-5	10-6	12-7	12-2	15	13-5	12-7	12-11	11-11
D	G	13	10	12-2	12-6	12-3	12-7	12-3	10-6	12-10	11-11	11-5	12-3	11-3	11-8	11-11
E	B	14	7	10-10	12-	11-5	12-6	12-8	11-6	11-8	11-1	11-1	12-3	13-3	12-8	11-10
F	B	15	11	10-9	10-9	10-9	11-9	9-10	11-6	13-1	12-7	12-6	13-5	13-7	13-7	11-10
Range in months			32	23	36	42	26	79	20	15	21 ·	47	14	31	24	2

Section 2

EDUCATIONAL POLICY AND PUPIL PROGRESS

The administrative organization of the pupil population for instruction. Certain principles of a more or less administrative character are basic to all good instruction and must be taken into account in organizing the educational program.[11]

The grouping of pupils. The first essential to good teaching is a carefully considered plan for grouping the pupils. The pupils in a grade or some educational level may be divided into classes on various bases, such as age, achievement, or ability, and the classes then further subdivided into groups, according to their needs, their interests, and special aptitudes, depending on the nature of the work. These groups should be changed whenever conditions may warrant it. The primary consideration should be the needs and abilities of the individual children, as established by available records of achievement, interests, and intelligence. Special classes for mentally defective and seriously subnormal children who are unable to profit from the regular class work should be provided. Suitable provisions should also be made by health services for children who are physically handicapped or otherwise not up to par because of bad teeth, poor vision, and the like. Clinical facilities and specialists in remedial instruction to aid in the diagnosis and treatment of severe learning difficulties should also be available. In small places, the superintendent or some teacher with special training can often give teachers the needed help. Details about clinical services will be discussed in Section 4.

Readiness for learning. In the lower grades it is especially important that the readiness of young children for the study of such areas as reading and arithmetic be determined before instruction is begun. There is good reason for believing that considerable difficulty can be averted by adapting methods and materials of instruction to the mental, physical, educational, and social maturity of the children, when the time comes that there is some value to the activity.

Burton points out that "readiness is the pedagogical counterpart, so to speak, of maturation, but includes social and intellectual maturity as well." He points out that this important principle is often and easily misinterpreted. He says: [12]

We are led to think of "readiness" as a definite locus or condition. This leads to three subsidiary errors: (*a*) neglect of the growth and development of any power, skill, or understanding; (*b*) waiting for a given condition of readiness to appear of itself; (*c*) assuming without investigation that readiness must be present.

In regard to (*a*) we know that growth is a steady, ongoing process. The designation of any given point in the developmental sequence as readiness for the given learning must be largely arbitrary. The (*b*) type of error may cause teachers to overlook the value of stimulation, opportunity, and tryout, thus unduly delaying a given learning. The (*c*) error may result in too early stimulation and forcing because readiness is deemed to have been attained. This results in frustration and in formal attempts to bring on or induce readiness. . . .

Regardless of differences of interpretation, a very important point is involved, namely, when to introduce certain learning experiences. The problem is one of balance or pacing. The only way we can tell whether a state of readiness has been achieved is to give learners the opportunity to learn and then to watch what happens. The concept of a series of readinesses is probably safer than the concept of a fixed locus for readiness. Guided by the learner's reactions we can adjust to readiness or—if it is preferred —to growth.

[11] *The Grouping of Pupils,* Thirty-fifth Yearbook, Part I, National Society for the Study of Education (Bloomington, Ill., Public School Publishing Co., 1936), is devoted to the discussion of the problem of grouping. It emphasizes the importance of considering social grouping as well as grouping on an intellectual or achievement basis.

[12] William H. Burton, *The Guidance of Learning Activities,* 2nd ed. (New York, Appleton-Century-Crofts, 1952), pp. 192-193.

The following selected references discuss problems of readiness:

BRUECKNER, L. J., "The Development and Validation of an Arithmetic Readiness Test," *Journal of Educational Research* (March, 1947), pp. 495-592.

HARRISON, Lucille, *Reading Readiness* (Boston, Houghton, 1939).

HILDRETH, Gertrude, *Readiness for School Beginners* (Yonkers, World Book, 1950) (general).

SOUDER, H. C., "The Construction and Evaluation of Certain Readiness Tests in Common Fractions," *Journal of Educational Research* (October, 1943), pp. 127-134.

Earlier bases of grouping. For many years, various administrative plans were used to group children. Some schemes, such as the Batavia system and the Santa Barbara Plan, were designed to assist the slow pupil so that he could complete the work of a grade in the same length of time as the normal pupils. Other plans, such as the Cambridge Plan, the St. Louis Plan, double- and multiple-track plans, such as the Portland Plan, permitted the more able pupils to advance at a faster rate than the slow. Few of these plans are used at the present time.

More recently, because of the availability of objective test procedures, attention was given to new forms of organization which enabled each pupil to progress at his own rate. For example, the plan still in use in Winnetka provided for completely individualized instruction in skill phases of the curriculum.

Pupils were grouped on the basis of their mental ability alone; new plans were devised for adapting the curriculum to these ability groups, such as the Detroit XYZ Plan; new kinds of individualized instructional materials were constructed.

In order to secure more homogeneous grouping of pupils, many schools have used plans of ability grouping, that is, dividing children into classes according to their mental ability. Research has revealed the fact, however, that homogeneous grouping on this basis is actually not achieved. Even under the most careful and scientific groupings, there are found large differences in pupil achievement among the different curriculum areas, even within a single area, which must be provided for in teaching.

In many quarters the social desirability and the educational effectiveness of ability grouping have been seriously questioned. The studies of ability grouping also show that in so far as achievement of pupils is concerned, homogeneous grouping is not only actually not feasible but it is neither advantageous or disadvantageous because of variability among the various traits of learners. It is also necessary to take into consideration the social maturity and physical development of the pupils. Whatever the form of grouping that is used, the proper adaptation of experiences, methods of teaching and materials of instruction is essential.

A summary of research findings is given just below which, despite early date, is still useful to those still attempting to deal with homogeneous grouping without further analysis. The real crux is the statement just above about social maturity, and we might add intellectual maturity.[13] Grouping is necessary at all levels. In *general* education we form groups and then regroup within classes in any number of ways, especially when we use units or adapt instruction to pupil needs following testing and diagnosis. In *special* education, when we begin specialization and take up organized subject areas, for example, algebra, we group on the basis of aptitude and set standards which pupils must meet. The standards in *general* education can only be levels of growth which pupils can make in terms of their individual organismic patterns. Heterogeneous grouping is essential in *general* education, homogeneous in *special* education.

The feasibility of homogeneous grouping. As a result of an experimental study of various methods of grouping children and related promotion policies, Cook drew up

[13] For a more detailed discussion, see *ibid.,* pp. 22-24, 622-623.

the following series of statements about factors limiting attempts to use homogeneous groups for instructional purposes: [14]

1. When the various abilities required for school are measured in age units, we find a range of from six to ten years at the sixth-grade level, with greater differences above that level and lesser differences below.

2. When we attempt to reduce the ranges of abilities by retarding slow-learning-pupils and accelerating fast-learning pupils, we increase the proportion of slow-learning pupils in each grade, we lower average grade achievement, we do not decrease the range of abilities in instructional groups, and by placing fast learners who are relatively young in the same group as slow learners who are overage we create serious social as well as educational problems.

3. When we attempt to reduce the ranges of abilities through homogeneous grouping on the basis of intelligence or general achievement test scores we find that the variability of the instructional groups with reference to specific achievement scores is reduced only by approximately 20 per cent.

4. When pupils in the lower 5 to 10 per cent of classes are failed because of low achievement they do not necessarily become better adjusted educationally or socially in the retarded position. The available evidence indicates that on the average they achieve as much, if not more, by being given regular promotion. The all-important factor seems to be not whether they are promoted or failed but whether their needs are met, wherever they are placed.

5. The variability of instructional groups with reference to limited goals set largely in terms of material to be memorized may be reduced by a driving type of teaching procedure. Such limited goals tend to cultivate the memory rather than the higher mental processes; they are usually too advanced for the slow-learning pupils and too simple for the fast-learning pupils. When unlimited goals are set in terms of understandings, skills, and abilities that each pupil can achieve in situations challenging him to do his best, the variability of the group tends to increase after a period of instruction. The better the teaching the greater the increase in variability.

6. Probably the best bases for grouping children are chronological age, physical development, and social development. The idea that grade levels indicate rather definite stages of achievement should be abandoned, for in reality they represent very broad, overlapping bands of achievement.

Flexibility of grouping within classes. Grouping within classes should be flexible and adapted to the existing situation. Sometimes the teacher will take the whole class as a unit in developing a skill needed by all or in working on some activity; at other times the teacher will form several broad groupings according to achievement levels to help in arranging specific activities of different levels of complexity; sometimes a group will be formed on the basis of level of ability in some area to be helped to increase power in that area; sometimes pupils of several levels of ability will be grouped for remedial instruction in some area; sometimes the teacher will wish to work with an individual child who needs special help in some area; sometimes a group with a common interest will be formed to work together on some problem but the pupils may work on materials of different levels of difficulty. When groupings of this kind are made, it is possible to adjust the work of the class to individual differences in ability, needs, and interests. The wide variety of pupil activities inherent in the modern instructional unit enables the teacher to effectively adapt instruction to these differences.

How good instruction affects variability in achievement. It is commonly believed that instructional groups are made more homogeneous through effective teaching. This belief is used as the justification of such educational practices as the setting up of courses of study giving specific outlines of what is to be taught, the selection of textbooks that include the required subject matter, and the specification of dates by which sections of the content are to be completed. These practices are all in violation of what is known about individual differences in rates of learning.

[14] W. W. Cook, *Grouping and Promotion in the Elementary School* (Minneapolis, Univ. of Minnesota Press, 1941), pp. 57-58.

Are individuals more alike or less alike with respect to a specific skill or to what is known about a given subject after a period of instruction? After reviewing experimental studies bearing on this issue, Cook [15] arrived at the following conclusions:

The research indications are somewhat contradictory, and many technical problems are involved in their interpretation. But for our purposes the following generalization seems warranted: if the responses to be learned are sufficiently simple and the goals that have been set so limited that a high proportion of the group can master them during the period of learning, the variability of the group becomes less; if the task is complex and the goals unlimited, so that the abilities of the most apt members of the group are taxed during the period of learning, the variability of the group increases.

These experiments indicate that learning involving problem-solving relationships and the operation of the higher mental processes are relatively permanent and that unrelated facts and mere information are relatively temporary. Unless learning involves differentiation and integration of old and new responses into a problem-solving type of mental process or into an organized behavior pattern, it has little permanence or value. *How was it learned?* is the important question.

The permanent results of the educational process are measured by such tests as: (1) vocabulary, (2) reading comprehension in the natural sciences, social sciences, and literature, (3) problem-solving in mathematics and the sciences, (4) ability to use the library and basic reference materials, and (5) ability to write and speak effectively. It is with reference to such objectives that great heterogeneity in achievement exists, and the more effective the instruction, the greater the heterogeneity.

It would seem then that the emphasis which some schools place on striving for homogeneity in classes, getting students over the passing mark, and providing for individual needs with a view to bringing all pupils up to a standard, encourages teachers to set limited goals for instruction which result in temporary factual learning involving mainly the lower mental processes. When the ultimate goals of education, involving the higher mental processes and permanent learnings, are striven for and each student is stimulated to capacity effort, the variability of instructional groups increases.

Promotion policies and pupil growth. Promotion policies vary widely in the schools of this country. In many school systems the percentages of nonpromotion in elementary schools have been reduced to a very low level compared with what they were one or two decades ago.[16] However, it is also unfortunately true that in some school systems an alarmingly high percentage of children are required to repeat the work of a grade; sometimes the practices vary widely from school to school in the same system. Through careful guidance and systematically differentiated curriculum programs, many secondary schools have also greatly reduced the extent of nonpromotion, particularly in the areas of general education. On the other hand, in many secondary schools the rate of elimination of pupils is high largely because of excessive nonpromotion in academic and special subjects.

The arguments that have been most frequently advanced for nonpromotion are the following:

1. Repeating the work of a given grade will assure mastery of the subject matter taught at that grade level.
2. Nonpromotion will result in the formation of a group of pupils at the next grade level that is more homogeneous in ability and level of attainment, and hence problems of instruction will be reduced in so far as adapting the work to individual differences is concerned.
3. The threat of nonpromotion will cause the pupil to make a greater effort to learn and thus assure a higher level of attainment.

The fallacy of these assumptions has been established by a number of important experimental studies. After an analysis of the results of these investigations, Saunders drew the following conclusions which summarize very effectively modern views on the un-

15 In E. F. Lindquist, ed., *Educational Measurement* (Washington, American Council on Education, 1951), pp. 21-23.
16 H. Caswell and A. Foshay, *Education in the Elementary School* (New York, American Book, 1951), pp. 354-378. Presents recent data on the problem.

desirability of a policy of nonpromotion of the traditional kind: [17]

1. Nonpromotion of pupils in order to assure mastery of subject matter is not a justifiable procedure. Many children who are not promoted learn less than they would have learned had they been advanced to the next grade.

2. Nonpromotion does not result in homogeneity of achievement within a grade.

3. Nonpromotion cannot be justified in terms of discipline administered to the child or to his parents.

4. Nonpromotion usually intensifies emotional instability of children.

5. Nonpromotion because of inadequate mentality, insufficient attendance, imperfect health, or lack of emotional stability is not based on valid causes or reasons.

6. Nonpromotion is an admission of inefficient teaching, inappropriate administrative practices, and inadequate educational planning.

7. Nonpromotion has no place in a school in which children are properly motivated and work to the level of their individual capacities.

Relation of promotion to general and special education. By general education we mean the content of educational experiences that all good citizens should have. The rate at which knowledge and skills are acquired will vary from individual to individual, and it is not feasible to set standards that all should achieve at a certain age level. Nor is it to be expected that all pupils will learn the same thing in the course of a given learning experience. In general education, the rate of progress is largely determined by factors that are inherent in the individual, and the teacher has the problem of providing learning experiences adapted to his aptitudes, interests, and rate of growth.

By special education we mean the content of educational experiences that are intended to prepare the learner for a particular vocation or educational career for which, for example, certain aptitudes and manipulative dexterity are essential, as in the case of engineering or typewriting. In this instance, standards of achievement are based not on factors inherent in the individual but on demands made by society. If a pupil's work

shows little aptitude for a given line of endeavor, such as typewriting, and that he lacks the manual dexterity and language skills necessary to success, his prospects of success in this field are at a low level and he should be helped to make a choice more nearly in line with his potentialities and capacities. The same would be true for curriculum areas such as technical courses in mathematics, required for entrance into professional training, for instance, algebra. In large high schools where the number of pupils makes a three-level series of courses possible, under competent guidance pupils are enrolled in courses in algebra, general mathematics, or high-school arithmetic in accordance with what is known about their aptitudes and their future destiny. This plan has reduced nonpromotion in ninth-year mathematics in many schools almost to the vanishing point.

Variations in promotion policies. An examination of promotion polices in our schools shows that in the main three general practices prevail. They may be identified as:

1. Grade or subject-standard plan.
2. Continuous promotion plan.
3. Uninterrupted continuity plan.

By the grade or subject standards plan is meant the setting up of definite standards to be achieved by a pupil in various curriculum areas at a given grade level or in a given course if he is to be promoted. This is the traditional policy which led to the large number of nonpromotions that were characteristic of most schools early in the present century. The use of the results of state examinations or standard test norms as a basis for uniform standards of promotion that were applied indiscriminately to all pupils, regardless of their levels of ability or the quality of the educational program through which they had passed, were particularly disastrous. Unfor-

[17] C. W. Saunders, *Promotion or Failure for the Elementary School Pupil* (New York, Teachers College, Bureau of Publications, Columbia Univ., 1941), p. 44.

tunately, there is ample evidence that this policy still prevails in both general and special education in many schools at the present time. It is utterly out of place in the field of general education.

By the continuous promotion plan is meant the policy of advancing all pupils at regular intervals to the next higher level regardless of the status of their performance or achievement. Such a plan is obviously not suited to the requirements of special education outlined above. In general education the plan has both values and limitations. It is not to be expected that all learners will learn the same things, and what they learn will vary with their capacities, needs, and interests, and with their rates of growth. For instance, the children in a class may all participate in the activities involved in the study of a realistic problem in the social studies or science, but it is not possible to set up uniform standards of achievement to be met by all of the learners. In the mastery of basic knowledge, skills, and methods of work the situation is quite different. In each of these areas it is possible to measure the status of the learners' progress at any given time. However, the information thus secured would serve more appropriately as a basis for diagnosis and subsequent guidance, rather than as standards on which to make a promotion to the next higher level. Where the continuous-promotion policy is applied arbitrarily in the area of special education, on the basis of directives from those in authority, ridiculous situations sometimes develop. For example, the promotion of all pupils, regardless of their achievements in a course in algebra in a small school where it is not possible to offer a series of differentiated mathematics courses, makes the grades or credits received practically meaningless for guidance purposes as indications of what has been learned. On the other hand, it is difficult to conceive of conditions under which a school would be justified in failing a pupil in such fields of general education as health, music, and community life problems.

The uninterrupted-continuity plan as applied to general education means that the teacher is concerned not with promotion as such, but rather with guiding the learning experiences of each learner in such a way that there is evidence of continuous growth and progress on his part in line with what can be expected in terms of his capacity, needs, interests, and future destiny. The teacher is expected to make systematic use of diagnostic tests to make the learner conscious of his strengths and weaknesses in basic knowledge skills and methods of work, and then to provide the necessary learning materials and instruction to correct deficiencies and to assure continuing growth along these lines. Standards of attainment are thus individual in nature and learning is evaluated in terms of the progress made by the learner toward the achievable goals that he and the teacher have established co-operatively. The application of this policy to the area of special education has serious limitations. For example, if the progress made by a learner in mastering the skills of a trade is so slow that the length of time required to achieve ultimate standards would be excessive, steps should be taken to bring about a change in his plans so that he will shift to a field that is more in line with his aptitudes. Similarly, if a pupil reveals little aptitude for such fields as Latin or geometry, it is questionable whether he should be allowed to continue the work in courses in which he is making little if any progress, since the final outcome will likely be failure with all of its unfortunate personal and social consequences.

The staff of a school should carefully consider the issues discussed above in evaluating its promotion policies. The first of them, the grade or subject standard plan, prevails in many high schools and colleges but is rapidly being discarded in most elementary schools as being inapplicable. In a considerable number of elementary schools and in some secondary schools, the continuous-promotion plan is being adopted without a recognition of its implications. The uninterrupted-continuity plan has many values in line with modern educational theory, but experimentation is necessary to study its application in the schools.

Reducing the amount of retardation. Caswell [18] has pointed out that the evidence as to the value of nonpromotion as an educational policy is almost wholly unfavorable but that the practice still exists to what many regard as an alarming extent. In some schools an attempt has been made to eliminate the practice by executive order directing that nonpromotion be reduced to a minimum. Such a procedure obviously does not solve the problem. Unless necessary adjustments are made, the pupil is in the predicament of being continually faced with work which is more and more beyond his ability. A much more effective plan for solving the problem is for the entire staff to undertake a cooperative study of the issues involved and then to map a program to achieve the desired end. The goal should be the working out of a plan for providing adequate educational opportunities for all of the pupils, a plan adapted to their needs and maturity and adjusted to their level of ability. If this is done, the teachers and others concerned will become familiar with all phases of the problem of nonpromotion and with the difficulties of solving it; and they will understand the reasons for the steps that are proposed or taken as the result of group action. A list of possible procedures is given below.

The measures to be taken to reduce the amount of nonpromotion in our schools necessitate many adjustments of educational practices. Special consideration should be given to methods of adapting instruction to individual differences which will be great whatever the plan of promotion adopted. These include such items as:

1. More effective readiness programs to prepare the pupils for new work.
2. The utilization of instructional procedures which provide adequately for differences in the rates at which pupils learn.

3. The adaptation of the difficulty of instructional materials to differences in the ability of the pupils so that all may be successful.
4. Effective guidance procedures which enable the teacher to study the growth of the student and to make any necessary adjustments.
5. A well-graded curriculum in which adequate provision is made for the wide range of interests and ability of the pupils, including a well-rounded program of co-curricular activities.
6. Effective grouping in terms of development.

Cook has made a valuable series of suggestions as to the steps the elementary school can take to meet the great variability within instructional groups, whatever the basis of grouping or the policy of promotion may be. His recommendations may be summarized as follows: [19]

1. The administration should make available to every teacher in the school instructional materials with a range of difficulty adapted to the range of ability that she finds in her classroom. The interest appeal of the material should also be broad enough to reach all pupils. This means an adequate and well-selected school library, for the selection of books is more important than the number of books available.

In addition to a wealth of books there must be in the classroom magazines, newspapers, art materials, tools, work benches, simple science laboratory materials, pictures, and visual aids of all types. The administration must recognize that asking teachers to eliminate non-promotion and to provide for the individual differences in their classes, at the same time providing only textbooks of the traditional type as instructional materials, is perhaps the lowest form of administrative incompetence.

2. The administration should reduce the teaching load to approximately thirty pupils a teacher. There is no evidence to support this recommendation except the opinion of teachers who are skilled in the art of adapting group procedures to the needs of individual pupils.

3. Educational achievement should be thought of not in terms of the grade in which a pupil happens to be placed but in terms of the individual pupil's progress and level of achievement in specific areas.

4. The pupils should have a large share of

[18] H. L. Caswell and A. W. Foshay, *op. cit.,* Ch. 13.

[19] Cook, *op. cit.,* pp. 58-62.

responsibility not only in setting the immediate goals toward which they strive but in criticizing their own work in terms of these goals. This procedure insures that the pupil's attention will always be focused on the next steps in their progress.

5. The grade levels at which certain knowledges, skills, and abilities should be taught cannot be determined with any degree of specificity. The important thing is to teach those items that are needed, at the time they are needed, in the reading, writing, speaking, computing, and manipulating activities in which children engage. When sixth-grade pupils write letters to a sick classmate the errors made by some pupils will be typical of second-grade pupils, while others will be typical of ninth-grade pupils. The teacher must be prepared to lead each pupil through the next steps in his development, regardless of the level.

6. Since life outside the school recognizes and rewards a great variety of aptitudes and combinations of aptitudes, the school should do likewise. The broadening of the elementary school curriculum to include various forms of practical arts, fine arts, a school paper, extended educational field trips, participation in community affairs, stimulation of hobbies, participation in school government, the safety patrol, radio programs, and community health programs is evidence of the acceptance of this principle. The elementary school should be a proving ground in which the individual discovers his peculiar strengths and weaknesses. If every child is to find himself, the offering of the school must be as broad as the culture of which it is a part.

7. Although correlations between desirable traits are always positive for large groups, an individual tends to vary greatly in specific traits. In order to know a pupil's strengths and weaknesses it is necessary to measure him in many traits and to construct and study his profile.

A large number of specific traits enter into a child's achievement in any one area. The peculiar combination or pattern of an individual's traits is much more important than strengths and weaknesses in specific traits. Since the pattern of traits of an individual is unique, the school should be a testing ground upon which the individual with his pattern of traits is brought to grips with complex tasks set by the culture in order to determine what the individual can do.

8. Grouping within the class by the teacher upon a wide range of bases is one of the most essential procedures in meeting pupil's needs.

In the primary division from three to five groups within each grade is common, with the pupils grouped differently in each subject-matter or skill area. Because the range of individual differences increases in the upper grade one might assume that more sub-groups are required on these levels. This, however, is not necessary because the books and materials used in the upper grades are more flexible and can be adjusted to a wider band of abilities than can be done with primary-grade materials.

Nonpromotion at upper grade levels. The adoption of a program of uninterrupted continuity at the level of the elementary school has important implications at the level of the junior high school. There are those in our secondary schools who maintain that no pupil should be admitted to the junior high school until he demonstrates the mental ability and the degree of control of the basic intellectual tools of reading, language, and arithmetic required to pursue successfully the program of studies provided at that level. They maintain that pupils who are not adequately prepared should be retained in the elementary school until they achieve the stated skills and can be certified as ready and able to do the work offered in the junior high school.

Such a policy on the part of the junior high schools cannot be too severely condemned. If adopted, it would result in the piling up of large numbers of children at the sixth-grade level, many of whom would undoubtedly become serious problem cases, especially if they were not promoted for any considerable length of time as so often happens now at the sixth-grade level in states with state examination systems. A much sounder policy for the junior high school to adopt would be the one now operating in many places, namely, the admission of all pupils from elementary schools at about the age of 12 years and the adaptation of the program of the junior high school to the abilities, needs, and interests of these pupils. As a matter of fact, why need we any longer regard the elementary and junior high schools as different kinds of institutions, each with peculiar functions to perform? Why should we not, rather, consider them as phases of a continuous-development program in which what is best for each individual is the primary consideration? Incidentally, this program of uninterrupted continuity at the lower levels has many implications for the senior high school.

Section 3

THE GUIDANCE OF LEARNING EXPERIENCES

Foundations of modern instructional procedures. Instruction is the efficient sympathetic management of the educative experiences of children, a continuous "planning" activity. The primary purpose of the school is to assist boys and girls to improve their daily living. In a democracy, instruction recognizes the worth of creative human individuality and seeks to develop in each pupil the disposition, ability, and power to consider and explore the problems that are faced by himself and the social group, and the factors that give rise to them. In many cases these problems should be those about which the pupils can do something to effect their solution in a co-operative democratic way, so as to produce conditions that promote and sustain creative experience for all. Pupils thus come to expect further change by intelligent action and get ideas as to the direction of expected change. They become habituated to the use of scientific methodology in dealing with problems. They discover for themselves the social values for which mankind has for many generations been struggling. The modern school, furthermore, seeks to help the students to understand and learn the ways of democracy by exemplifying in its program and practices the way of life which our nation is striving to achieve.

Learning is an active social process. Dewey's educational philosophy has presented the view that education should be regarded as an active social process. This view has had a powerful influence on instruction in this country because of the emphasis that it places on learning through "activities" and first-hand experiences in life-like social situations. The salient points in his philosophy have been summarized as follows: [20]

> Knowledge originates in "active situations," or problems; that education is pre-eminently a social process, and that school life and social life must be unified, the school becoming "co-operative society"; that this facing of problems, considering the means, making choices, making mistakes, achieving successes, and going on to other and more difficult problems under the drive of social inspiration rather than that of mere authority is the true path to character; and that education, thus actively considered, is in harmony with democratic philosophy—is in fact the normal education of the free man in a society that he and his fellows create and recreate. Historically considered, it is the resultant of many tendencies of centuries past, to which brief allusion has been made, but it is more than that. It is a careful, critical synthesis of these, in the light of a more advanced knowledge of psychology and sociology, with a profound appreciation of the demands that democracy makes of education, and that must be satisfied if government by the people is to be more than a phrase.

The educational program must provide a rich, wholesome, stimulating environment which continuously presents the child with new and interesting possibilities that keep him moving forward with zest and initiative and give him the opportunity to practice those skills, abilities, and behavior patterns which it is desired to develop. The personalities with which the learner comes into direct contact should be well balanced, poised, and cultured because of the great influence they have on the development of the

[20] Thomas Woody, in *The Activity Movement,* Thirty-third Yearbook, Part II, National Society for the Study of Education (Bloomington, Ill., Public School Publishing Co., 1934), p. 39.

personality of the pupil. Positive, encouraging, helpful suggestions are much more effective in eliciting desirable conduct and result in more enduring satisfying behavior than discouraging, negative, unfavorable contacts.

Principles that should guide instructional processes. The curriculum should be so organized that it is adapted as fully as is possible to the needs, interests, and talents of each individual. Learning experiences should be rich and varied and should be so organized that they are flexible and adapt themselves both to social change and to the growth of the individual; they should be so arranged that the learner will understand his experiences while he is in the process of having them. The following[21] statement summarizes an effective expression of this point of view:

1. Teachers should, as a first step in instruction, have clearly formulated in their minds the educational objectives they are to attain through the instructional process. This means that if a teacher undertakes to develop a unit of study on the Soviet Union, for example, he should know what the children ought to derive from the experience.

2. Educational objectives should be translated into behavior patterns—patterns of knowing, understanding, appreciating, desiring, adjusting, doing, and thinking that become functional aspects of the child's daily living.

3. Educational objectives become patterns of response of the type just enumerated as children have the guided experiences designed to achieve these objectives.

4. The primary task of the teacher is to manipulate the classroom environment so that children will have educative experiences. This manipulation takes the form of selecting and organizing experiences which are educative and of guiding the directing children in these experiences.

5. New behavior patterns, both desirable and undesirable, are established in terms of the goals which children themselves attempt to reach through their activity.

6. Goals for learning activity are established in terms of children's motives—their wants, needs, interests, or drives.

7. A first step in the actual instructional process is to formulate, with the children as

participants, the goals to be attained as they work and learn.

8. Content and activity are means to ends, these ends being new behavior patterns. Content and activity are not ends in themselves.

9. Learning takes place or fails to take place in terms of the individual child. While instruction is usually a group procedure, learning is always an individual process.

10. The teacher as an individual personality is an important element in the learning environment. The way in which his personality interacts with the personalities of the children being taught helps to determine the kind of behavior which emerges from the learning situation.

11. Interpersonal interactions among pupils are important elements in the learning environment. These personal interactions are in part responsible for the kinds of social, emotional, and intellectual behavior which emerge in the learning situation.

12. Evaluation is an integral part of the instructional process. Teachers and pupils should be continuously considering together the contribution of different experiences to goals sought. The ongoing experiences should be restructured in light of the evaluations being made.

The unit as an organizational plan is presented briefly in Chapter 15. Extended discussion will be found in Chapters 12, 13, and 14 of Burton, *The Guidance of Learning Activities.*[22]

Contrasting principles underlying traditional and modern practice. An excellent summary prepared by Wrightstone[23] states the older principles of instruction and reveals their implications:

1. The classroom is a restricted form of social life, and children's experiences are limited therein to academic lessons.

2. The quickest and most thorough method of learning lessons is to allot a certain portion

[21] G. L. Anderson and others, "The School As a Learning Laboratory," in *Learning and Instruction,* Forty-ninth Yearbook, Part I, National Society for the Study of Education (Chicago, Univ. of Chicago Press, 1950), pp. 337-338.

[22] *Op. cit.*

[23] J. Wayne Wrightstone, *Appraisal of Newer Practices in Selected Public Schools* (New York, Teachers College, Bureau of Publications, Columbia Univ., 1935), p. 9.

Also in Burton, *op. cit.,* p. 324.

of the school day to instruction in separate subjects, such as reading, phonics, word drill, language, arithmetic, history, geography, health, and stories.

3. Children's interests which do not conform to the set curriculum should be disregarded.

4. The real objectives of classroom instruction consist to a major degree in the acquisition of the content matter of each subject.

5. Teaching the conventional subjects is the wisest method of achieving social progress.

The same author has summarized the implications of modern principles as follows:

1. The classroom is a form of democratic social life and the children reconstruct their experience therein.

2. These experiences grow from the children's social activities, and various parts of the newer type of curriculum are integrated around a central problem suggested by the children's social activities.

3. The organization of the curriculum for integration of pupil personality is paramount to traditional and formal organization of subject matter.

4. A dynamic organismal-environmental concept of learning is preferable to a mechanistic stimulus-response concept.

5. A pupil's interests are viewed as signs and symptoms of growing powers and abilities.

6. Interests and powers are developed by activities, and not alone by passive assimilation of knowledge.

7. A mastery of principles and practices of intelligent living is more important than memory of specific facts.

8. Each pupil personality is inherently social in origin and character.

9. The true unit of educative experience is a realistic study of a problem and a co-operative creative solution.

10. Education is the foundation upon which social progress and refinement are based, and consequently education must concern itself with vital problems in the world of both child and adult.

First-hand pupil experiences in co-operative action. The skills and attitudes necessary for working together are learned by doing, as are all other educational achievements. A large number of activities through which children have direct experience with

co-operative group action can be given under the guidance of the school. The ability to work together democratically and co-operatively in dealing with problems that arise is an objective widely recognized in our schools. The list of activities given below affords an excellent basis for a consideration by supervisors and teachers of effective ways of achieving this important objective.

DIRECT PARTICIPATION IN GROUP CO-OPERATIVE ACTION

1. Group co-operative action for the common good.
   a. Safety patrols.
   b. Junior Red Cross organization.
   c. Construction of needed equipment.
   d. Participation in drives, cleanup campaigns, and similar group activities.
   e. Beautification of the classroom and of the school building.
2. Participation in planning, executing, and evaluating units, assignments, and group experiences in the classroom.
   a. Consideration of ways of meeting needs and of solving problems and conflicts that arise from time to time.
   b. Planning excursions and trips.
   c. Committee work on group assignments.
   d. Preparation of exhibits, displays.
   e. Dramatizations of episodes; pageants.
   f. Committee work related to management of home room routines.
3. Participation in out-of-class school activities.
   a. Participation in student council.
   b. Student control of conduct in halls, on playground, etc.
   c. Student services to the school.
      (1) Care of building and grounds.
      (2) Care of equipment, such as radio and motion pictures.
      (3) Assistance in library, cafeteria, and store.
      (4) Care of bulletin boards, attendance, etc.
      (5) Service clubs.
      (6) School gardens.
   d. Operation of school paper.
   e. Sale of stamps, school supplies, etc.
4. Participation in recreational and social-group activities.
   a. Organized community groups, such as Boy Scouts, Girl Scouts.

b. Musical organizations.
c. School clubs of various kinds.
d. Athletic programs.
e. Camps and playground group activities.
f. Field trips and excursions.
5. Participation in community activities.
   a. Community surveys.
   b. Production of foods needed.
   c. Conservation of resources.
   d. Beautification of community.
   e. Red Cross.
   f. Campaigns for funds for various purposes.
   g. School elections at the time of local elections.

Instruction in fundamental skills and abilities. It is not possible to specify the grade levels at which certain knowledge, skills, and abilities are to be taught or the degree of mastery to be required at each grade level. This is true because of the large differences in the rates at which children will learn them. Instruction in these skills and abilities must be so organized that the teacher is able to lead each child through successive stages in his development regardless of the level he has achieved at any given time.

These fundamental skills should be learned in their natural setting. At regular intervals, as a part of the learning activity itself, the teacher should administer inventory tests to measure the progress made. Grouping pupils within a class on the basis of similarity of their status and needs in specific learning areas is one of the most valuable procedures available for adapting instruction to the needs of individuals. The teacher must be prepared to make extensive use of instructional materials so organized as to make it possible for children to progress at different rates. The diagnosis and correction of learning deficiencies is an essential element of such a program. The purpose of diagnosis should be to keep both teacher and learner conscious of individual needs and learning problems. Instruction must be flexibly organized so that the teacher can adapt the learning activities to the needs, interest, ability, and level of development of the learners.

Guidance of specific learning activities. Numerous statements of rules for effective study and work are available in the literature of education. The basic principles underlying the general rules on study have been summarized by Barr as follows: [24]

1. Distributed practice is more effective than concentrated practice.
2. Learning by wholes is more effective than learning by parts.
3. Reactions accompanied by satisfying effects are more quickly learned than those accompanied by dissatisfaction and annoyance.
4. Pupil interest is closely related to pupil ability: interest in an activity cannot be secured unless the child can successfully function in that activity.
5. Meaningless material is sooner forgotten than meaningful material.
6. Reactions acquired in one situation tend to transfer to other situations; everything else being equal, that method of instruction is best which secures a maximum amount of spread.
7. Demonstration and active participation are often superior to verbal descriptions in learning.
8. Functionally taught subject matter is longest retained and easiest applied. The absence of any one of the above conditions may constitute an adequate cause of poor work.

These and other factors are fully discussed in current treatises on the psychology of learning and on how to study,[25] and will not be reviewed here.

[24] A. S. Barr, *Introduction to the Scientific Study of Supervision* (New York, Appleton-Century, 1931), p. 166.
[25] See, for example, Charles Bird, *Effective Study Habits* (New York, Appleton-Century, 1931); W. F. Book, *Learning How to Study and Work Efficiently* (Boston, Ginn, 1926); A. L. Hall-Quest, *Supervised Study* (New York, Macmillan, 1916); Guy M. Whipple, *How to Study Efficiently* (Bloomington, Ill., Public School Publishing Co., 1927); John Dewey, *How We Think*, rev. ed. (Boston, Heath, 1933); W. S. Hunter, "Experimental Studies of Learning" in Carl Murchison, *The Foundations of Experimental Psychology* (Worcester, Clark Univ. Press, 1920), pp. 564-627.

Horn [26] recently summarized the research about methods of study in learning to spell a word. His statement is an excellent illustration of the application of the principles of learning listed above:

1. The student's efforts should be focused upon words or parts of words which a pretest has shown him to be unable to spell.
2. The mode of sensory presentation should be predominantly visual. The visual presentation of words in syllabicated form is apparently not in itself advantageous, and for certain types of words, such as *awhile* and *therefore,* it may be a disadvantage. It is possible, however, that, if systematically accompanied by careful pronunciation, with a focus on the syllables where errors have been made on pretests, the combined effect may be beneficial. The correct pronunciation of the word by syllables has been found to be important. In the actual process of learning, auditory and kinesthetic appeals are also commonly utilized.
3. The emphasis during learning should be upon visual imagery, but auditory imagery, which accompanies pronunciation, and kinesthetic imagery, which attends both the pronunciation, and the writing of the word, increase the effectiveness of learning. The use of imagery is obviously related to the practice of recall.
4. Aggressive efforts to recall should be interspersed with sensory impression. Investigations in all fields of learning have shown the beneficial influence of recall. In the application of spelling in written language, moreover, it is the ability to recall the word that is required. It has been found difficult to get pupils to utilize recall, in spelling as in other subjects, but it is not impossible. The amount and character of the emphasis upon recall will vary with individual pupils.
5. Distributed learning seems to be better than mass learning, but the student's efforts in any learning period should aim to attain temporary mastery. The general plan of reviews should afford a minimum distribution, but this plan should be supplemented, particularly in the case of students of low ability, by additional distributed learning periods.
6. Both in the original learning period and during each review words should be overlearned, i.e., they should be learned beyond the point of one successful recall. The term "overlearning" is somewhat inept, since overlearning contributes to mastery and in the long run saves time. The amount of overlearning that is efficacious in spelling has not been accurately determined, but the desirable amount may be expected to vary with individual students.

Similar analyses of research on learning in other curriculum areas are available. Teachers who attempt to apply these principles that are the outgrowth of experimental investigations can proceed with considerable assurance that their instructional procedures have a sound, defensible basis.

Horn has prepared a statement of principles the application of which by both teacher and the learner will, he believes, make the best provisions for the retention of ideas and the development of experience in the social studies. These are the outgrowth of a critical review of the existing experimental evidence in the field of memory. The principles, detailed in Horn's *Methods of Instruction in the Social Studies,* follow: [27]

1. Both teacher and students should know the chief characteristics of forgetting and the best ways of providing for the retention and development of experience.
2. There should be a clear understanding on the part of both teachers and pupils of what is to be learned, whether facts, concepts, principles, attitudes, ways of working, or knowledge of sources.
3. The amount and quality of what is retained are heavily conditioned by what is done in the period of original learning.
   a. The instructional materials should be organized in terms of one or more significant purposes.
   b. Students should be encouraged in an aggressive, active, and purposeful attitude toward the problems under attack. Of special importance is the determination to learn and remember.
   c. It is imperative that all important ideas be clear, accurate, and well organized. Otherwise, efforts to provide for future use will be largely a waste of time.

[26] Ernest Horn in W. S. Monroe, ed., *Encyclopedia of Educational Research* (New York, Macmillan, 1951), p. 1258.
[27] The list of principles, comments, and subprinciples with amplifying discussion appears in Ernest Horn, *Methods of Instruction in the Social Studies* (New York, Scribner, 1937), pp. 497-509.

d. The impression, whether through reading, hearing, or observation, should be interspersed with attempted recalls, in order to show shortcomings and necessary corrections in the result of the impression.

e. Overlearning appears to be economical in the long run, even in the early stages of learning. Much more thorough work must be done in the original learning period than at present before the point of overlearning is even approached.

f. The contribution of interest is fundamental.

4. There must be definite provisions for review. No matter how well any material is understood or learned in the original learning period, it tends to be gradually forgotten unless definite provision is made for maintenance and growth.

5. There must be a material reduction in the amount to be learned. This insistent emphasis upon the reduction of the amount to be learned does not imply a curtailment of details or a diminution of the rigor of the search for truth. What is needed is more rigorous thought, operating on more details, but devoted to the study of a smaller number of basically important matters.

In each of the above cases the emphasis is on principles of learning. Pupils must be taught how to adapt these general principles to their own particular needs. Because of differences among individuals, no attempt should be made to impose a single pattern of work and study on all learners. Through careful guidance however, pupils should be led to select from among techniques of known merit those that are most effective for themselves. For analyses of principles of methods of teaching and study in other major curriculum areas the reader should consult the *Reviews of Educational Research* listed in the bibliography at the end of the chapter.

Section 4

THE BASIS OF CORRECTIVE AND REMEDIAL INSTRUCTION

Types of cases needing remedial treatment are revealed by tests. The analysis by the teacher of the results of a testing program invariably reveals wide variations in the levels of performances of individual children on the various tests. On an achievement-test battery some pupils will score very high on all parts of the battery. They can be excused from further routine work in the areas involved, their experiences can be enriched, and steps taken to develop special abilities, talents, and interests. Another group will perform at a level that is as high as can be expected in view of their aptitude. For them, no other teaching than regular instruction is required. In a third group the performance of the pupils will be uneven, indicating the need of special help on certain phases of learning, but not on others. In a fourth group there will be children whose ratings are somewhat below their level of expectancy but whose difficulties can in most cases be corrected by working with them in groups. Finally, there will be others whose performance indicates that serious deficiencies exist in one or more areas which require individual attention.

It is obvious that the "lock-step system," in which children were taught as though they were all alike and could learn the same things at the same rate, is completely outmoded. The supervisor should make every effort to assist teachers to devise means and procedures such as have been described for adapting instruction to the individual and trait differences that exist in their classes. The authors wish to emphasize again the point that deficiencies exist not only in subject-matter areas, but also in the entire range of less tangible outcomes whose appraisal was discussed in Chapter 9.

Difficulty of correcting unsatisfactory conditions. It has been repeatedly demonstrated that training and practice ordinarily produce marked changes in specific traits. For instance, teaching procedures that stress rate of reading will under normal conditions produce a marked increase in the pupil's rate of reading.[28] Similarly, emphasis on problem-solving in arithmetic will yield excellent results.[29] If a pupil does not readily respond to instruction, the teacher must attempt to locate the source of the difficulty and apply appropriate remedial and corrective measures.

There are marked differences in the ease with which desirable changes can be brought about. Some deficiencies, such as mental defects, due to heredity, disease or birth injury, cannot be corrected by any known techniques. Other faults such as stuttering are often very difficult to correct, although in most cases careful treatment will produce marked changes.[30] Hygienic measures can in most cases greatly alleviate physiological weaknesses, such as faulty vision, malnutrition, and glandular disturbances. Many of the minor difficulties that arise at various stages in the learning of the various school subjects, for example, lip movements in reading or counting in arithmetic, disappear with the passing of time and growth in control of the basic skills. Other faults such as failure to learn basic skills in arithmetic or the vocabulary of a foreign language are cumulative and become more serious the farther the student progresses. The redirection of character traits, interests, attitudes, and the like is often extremely difficult to accomplish because of the inability of the school to control the influences in the community that condition them. The correction of these faults is usually an individual problem and should be approached from this point of view.

The mental-hygiene factor in remedial instruction. Burnham has made the following statement on the place of mental hygiene in the instructional program: [31]

1. The primary aim of mental hygiene is the preservation and development of a wholesome personality and the prevention of personality disorders.
2. Hygiene requires respect for the personality of each pupil as a unique and independent individual—an object for observation and study, but never for snap judgments.
3. Hygiene requires regard for the whole personality as an integrated unit, the whole child as shown in his interests and behavior, in home, playground, and the like, as well as in the school.
4. For the preservation and the development of a wholesome integrated personality, hygiene requires a task of his own for each pupil and the maximum of freedom in the choice and doing of the task.
5. Hygiene requires the adjustment of the task to the personality and stage of development of each pupil, so that each may receive the stimulus of success.
6. Hygienic activity is attentive activity, for attention is integration. In many schools with methods now used, the teachers' usual complaint of inattention suggests that much of the work is not hygienic.
7. Hygiene requires the avoidance of conditions disintegrating and confusing in the instruction and training, especially harsh criticism, sarcasm, blame, and anything that reflects upon the personality of the pupil, such as words and actions that call attention to a personal defect of inferiority.
8. Hygiene emphasizes the health value of the objective or scientific attitude, or, in educational terms, the learning attitude in its highest form; thus emphasizing truth rather than opinion, learning rather than teaching, and the value of training in the scientific attitude in all school activity.

Basic considerations [32] underlying a remedial program. In planning a remedial program for dealing with a deficiency in some basic area of learning, the following questions require careful deliberation:

1. Is the condition in fact a disability requiring the attention of a specialist? The nature and severity of the disability should be established by suitable diagnostic procedures.

[28] Arthur I. Gates, *The Improvement of Reading,* rev. ed. (New York, Macmillan, 1934).
[29] Worth J. Osburn and L. J. Drennan, "Problem Solving in Arithmetic," *Educational Research Bulletin* (March 4, 1931), pp. 123-128.
[30] Lee E. Travis, *Speech Pathology* (New York, Appleton-Century, 1934).
[31] W. H. Burnham, *The Wholesome Personality* (New York, Appleton-Century, 1932), pp. 476-477.
[32] These questions are based on suggestions by Guy Bond, Univ. of Minnesota.

2. Who should deal with the disability? The regular teacher, a social worker, a clinical diagnostician, a psychologist, a physician.

3. What kind of instructional program is most likely to correct the deficiency?

4. How can this program be managed most satisfactorily? Scheduling, materials, location, grouping, using available services.

5. What changes in conditions present in the learner are necessary? Correction of visual defects, malnutrition, low level of interest in reading, etc.

6. What changes in the environment are necessary? Home, school, classroom, community, instruction, materials, group relations.

Organizing remedial instruction. Observations of practices in all parts of the country reveals a wide variety of plans for organizing remedial instruction. The staff of any school system should adopt a plan that most nearly meets the needs of the local situation or those that exist in a particular school. The following brief descriptions of the essentials of plans that have proved helpful may be of assistance in formulating a program:

1. The regular teacher is responsible for both diagnosis and corrective measures, which can be applied on a group basis, even in the case of individuals whose problem is not too complex.

2. A specialist is available to assist teachers in planning ways of diagnosing and treating a learning deficiency.

3. Learners seriously retarded in some area such as reading are referred to a remedial reading teacher in the same building for one or more hours a week for special help. They also attend the regular classes.

4. Children from several schools are sent to a remedial teacher in some conveniently located center for a part of each day for special help.

5. Children may be referred directly to a central clinic or a branch for special help when severe disability exists.

6. Children with extremely serious and complicated learning difficulties along academic, physiological, social, and emotional lines may be sent to a special school for clinical treatment.

The selection of corrective and remedial procedures. Many reports are available of corrective and remedial procedures that have proved effective in particular cases. The specific measures applied varied from case to case in terms of the needs of the individual. Very rarely did a single approach serve to bring about improvement; in most cases a group of adjustments and methods had to be used, including medical care, the use of psychiatric and psychological procedures, modification of the curriculum, the use of special types of instructional procedures, instructional materials, adapted to the needs of the case, and various adjustments in the social and physical environment.

An analysis of the methods that appeared to bring about improvement in a large number of cases of different kinds is the basis of the list of corrective and remedial procedures given below. The wide variety of means used to deal with learning problems is quite striking. They point out the necessity of a comprehensive, manysided approach to remedial instruction. The contents of the list should be referred to by the teacher and supervisor for suggestions as to measures to be applied in a particular case. The study of the list can well be undertaken in courses, workshops, and study groups as a part of the inservice education program. Case studies would make the work very concrete and vital. Adaptations to particular areas of skills in the curriculum can also be made by interested groups.

PROCEDURES IN CORRECTING LEARNING DIFFICULTIES

1. *Medical Care*
   a. Correction of physiological defects of vision, hearing, etc.
   b. Elimination of factors causing fatigue.
   c. Change in nutrition and diet.
   d. Glandular therapy.
   e. Elimination of focal infections of teeth, tonsils, etc.
   f. Cure of disease, such as syphilis, encephalitis, etc.
   g. Recreation.
   h. Relaxation and rest.
   i. Corrective gymnastics.
2. *Psychological-Psychiatric Procedures*
   a. Making the learner aware of the

status of his difficulty and its significance.

b. Developing confidence in therapist and awareness of progress.

c. Using rewards, approval, and constructive incentives.

d. Using penalties, punishment, and disapproval.

e. Using competition, with self and others.

f. Developing interest in what is being learned or done.

g. Changing undesirable attitudes toward associates, school, community.

h. Providing release from emotional conflicts.

i. Insuring appreciation and sympathy of associates through planned group contacts.

j. Using suggestion, advice, persuasion, direction, reasoning.

k. Requiring shift of hand used in activity, as in writing, because of dominance.

l. Providing practice using faulty procedure though knowing correct one.

m. Substitution of interests, stimuli, or goals for present ones.

n. Kinesthetic sensation as in tracing correct forms of letters.

o. Play therapy.

p. Psychodrama.

q. Nondirective therapy.

3. *Modification of the Curriculum*

a. Adaptation of content of instruction to developmental level of the learner.

b. Careful analysis of steps of difficulty in learning.

c. Use of rich social experiences to broaden the learner's background of meanings.

d. Adjustment of work to ability, interests, and needs of pupils.

e. Use of content of social value.

f. Means of exploring new interests and special aptitudes.

g. Use of concrete materials from the locality.

h. Opportunity for effective functioning within the limitations of the individual.

i. Special hospital classes for severe disability cases.

4. *Methods of Instruction*

a. Self-diagnosis by learner to locate and clarify his shortcomings.

b. Securing co-operation of learner in the application of corrective procedures.

c. Clear explanation of corrective treatment to be applied.

d. Setting goals possible of achievement by individual learner.

e. Direct attack on specific shortcomings and difficulties.

f. Adjustment of instruction to level of progress of the individual.

g. Such reteaching as may be necessary when difficulties arise.

h. Teaching of effective methods of procedure and perception.

i. Use of manipulative and visual aids to make work meaningful.

j. Teaching of effective study habits.

k. Correction of faulty mental processes and steps in procedure.

l. Correction of faulty handling of materials and tools of work.

m. Demonstration of accepted procedures.

n. Provision of good models for study and imitation.

o. Teaching of "crutches" and aids to learning.

p. Provision of practice on desired trait or ability.

q. Distribution of practice so as to avoid boredom and fatigue.

r. Awareness of learner of success and rate of progress.

s. Adaptation of instruction to interests, needs, and ability of learner.

5. *Materials of Instruction*

a. Proper level of difficulty and adapted to specific needs.

b. Interest and appeal to the learner.

c. Variety of types of exercises and experiences adjusted to development of the desired particular traits, skills, and abilities.

d. Abundance of materials suited to purposes of learners.

e. Adequate provisions for study and practice.

f. Scientific specifications used in constructing reading materials.

g. Provision for individual differences in rates of progress.

h. Facilitation of self-diagnosis of difficulties by learner.

i. Provision for treatment of specific deficiencies.

j. Progress graphs to show results of efforts to improve.

    k. Provision for maintenance of skills and abilities.
    l. Rich variety of supplementary aids to learning.
    m. Hygienic conditions in classroom.
6. *Environment*
    a. Removal of learner from unwholesome environment.
    b. Correction of unfavorable conditions in the physical environment.
    c. Securing co-operation of associates.
    d. Psychotherapeutic treatment of parents, teachers, etc.
    e. Securing co-operation of various social agencies.
    f. Provision of recreation facilities.
    g. Improvement of home life.
    h. Improvement of recreational and leisure-time activities.

Principles of remedial and corrective instruction. Under ideal conditions, the number of pupils who do not make satisfactory progress will be reduced to a minimum. But under existing conditions there will be found in almost every class numbers of pupils who are encountering learning difficulties of varying degrees of seriousness. Numerous studies have been made to discover ways of eliminating these faults. These methods are fully described in the references at the end of this chapter and in the bibliography in Chapter 14. They will not be reviewed in any detail at this point.

The following eight general principles may be regarded as basic in a program of remedial and corrective instruction if improvement is to result:

1. *Consider the growth of the individual.* The primary consideration in planning an instructional program should be the growth of the individual. Instead of thinking of means of improving particular skills or the work in some subject, the teacher should focus attention on the problem of facilitating the well-rounded growth of the learner and discovering the reasons why particular learners are not making satisfactory progress. The latter approach is more likely to establish a comprehensive basis of developmental and remedial teaching than the former. There is then some assurance that all aspects of the learner's personality, including his physical conditions, his intellectual level, his scholastic achievements, his attitudes and interests, and his general behavior will be considered. If attention is focused on the improvement of some narrow skill, many important aspects of personality such as those listed previously are likely to be overlooked.

2. *Use instructional procedures likely to achieve desired goals.* Instruction must be guided by clearly formulated educational objectives. Means must be devised for determining the extent to which these outcomes are being achieved. The teaching methods that are used should, in so far as is possible, be selected from among those that have been validated by scientific study, so that the teacher may operate with some assurance of success.

3. *Consider the relative value of the outcomes.* In planning the instructional program, due weight must be given to the relative value of educational objectives. If test results show that a sixth-grade pupil is low in division of decimals, the teacher must consider whether or not time should be spent on the practice needed to secure mastery, or whether the time could be spent more usefully on some other kind of work. Obviously, an excessive amount of time spent on intensive drill on skills and knowledge will lead to the neglect of other important outcomes, such as attitudes, interests, and appreciations, and will usurp time allotted to other areas such as art, music, literature and the like.

4. *Integrate developmental and corrective instruction.* It must be recognized that even though there may be well-organized, efficient instruction, some pupils will have learning difficulties for various reasons, many of them beyond the control of the teacher. One or more of the various factors described in the preceding chapters will be operating to produce this condition. It is the teacher's problem to make a systematic study of the

work of the pupil to determine the factors that are interfering with desirable progress and to take steps to bring about improvement. Remedial instruction should be regarded as an important element in any well-rounded program of instruction. Except in unusual cases, the remedial program should be in charge of the classroom teacher rather than conducted by some teacher of a remedial class who does not have the opportunity the regular teacher has to make the necessary adjustments of instruction in all phases of class work to the needs of the individual child. The responsibility for the treatment of any pupil should be delegated to one person.

5. *Attack specific points directly.* The more definitely the root of the specific difficulty can be determined, the more effectively can the remedial program be planned. A child may be having difficulty in reading because of a deficiency of the eye, for example, muscular imbalance or astigmatism. Any remedial program that fails to take this visual defect into consideration is likely to be futile. Pupils who are having difficulty in long division may have a deficiency in subtraction which is needed in this process. Practice in long division is likely to be a waste of time until this basic weakness has been corrected. There is ample evidence that well-directed practice aimed at specific difficulties will in most cases yield large returns. In general the rule applies that the best way to overcome a specific weakness or fault is to attack that point directly. The findings of educational science and related sciences such as neurology, psychiatry, sociology, and psychology, are making it increasingly possible for the teacher to apply remedial measures that will produce the desired changes.

6. *Correct physical, emotional, and environmental factors interfering with learning.* It is essential that steps be taken from the beginning to correct physical handicaps and environmental factors that may contribute to maladjustment. Visual and auditory de-

fects, malnutrition, and so forth must be remedied as soon as possible. If the learner has a faulty attitude toward the school, a subject, or his associates, positive steps must be taken to substitute good attitudes for bad ones. It may be necessary to make curricular readjustments of various kinds. It may be advisable to change the instructors. Unsatisfactory conditions in the home must be changed. If it appears that the unwholesome influences of the neighborhood in which he lives are affecting him unfavorably, it may be necessary to remove him from the immediate locality. It is obvious that in the correction of all of these there must be close co-operation between the school and all social agencies concerned with the care and development of children. The community council is of great help here.

The effects of environmental influences on the behavior of individuals are strikingly revealed by the results of a survey [33] of the rates of delinquency in nine mile-zone areas in Chicago. The nearer the zone was to the Loop District, the greater was the amount of delinquency. Over a period of a generation the delinquency rate had remained constant in certain interstitial areas, although there had been a marked shift in the national character of the population in them. As these groups moved out into new suburban areas, their delinquency rates dropped to figures appropriate to the new environment. It thus is clear that fruitful steps to reduce delinquency are either to remove the individual from an unwholesome environment or to change the local conditions that contribute to the deficiency. The achievement of such a result is possible only when all agencies in the community in any way concerned with the care and development of the individual co-operate in the steps taken to bring about an improvement.

It is being increasingly recognized by sociologists, psychiatrists, and others concerned with various aspects of the care and develop-

[33] Clifford R. Shaw and others, *Delinquency Areas* (Chicago, Univ. of Chicago Press, 1929).

ment of the individual that the prevention of crime and juvenile delinquency must be regarded as a community enterprise in which the schools must exercise leadership. The Gluecks [34] published a book on preventive programs which gave samples of school programs, co-ordinated community programs, police programs, intra- and extra-mural guidance programs, boys' clubs, and recreation programs. From this mass of concrete illustrative detail, the writers set forth a number of principles that should underlie preventive work. Some of the more important of these principles may be summarized as follows:

1. Crime prevention should take into account the evidence that most criminals show definite antisocial tendencies of attitude and behavior early in childhood.
2. In most instances, children should be kept away from typical contacts with police stations, courts, and correctional institutions until more scientific and sympathetic efforts have failed.
3. An experimental attitude should govern the establishment and conduct of crime-prevention programs.
4. It cannot be definitely concluded as yet that any one type of crime-preventive activity is necessarily superior to or should be exclusive of any other.
5. Existing community agencies and institutions should be used to their fullest capacity.
6. A crime-prevention program should recognize that children must have ample outlets for their energies.
7. Trained personnel should be liberally employed in crime-preventive activity.

Although much good can be accomplished by whatever qualified agency in a community assumes the leadership in crime prevention, the public schools can play an especially significant role.

The Gluecks suggest that the schools should

1. Recognize physical and mental handicaps.
2. Determine dissatisfaction with school curriculums.
3. Unearth other reasons for maladjustment to the requirements of society.
4. Discover means of making school work more attractive.
5. Establish special classes or schools for children possessing special abilities or disabilities.
6. Counteract tendency to an undiscriminating mass treatment of children.[35]

In a number of communities there have been established child-guidance clinics that are primarily concerned with the study and treatment of behavior disorders. A well-trained staff makes an intensive study of all aspects of the personality of the individual, his associates, and home background, with a view to locating the factors that contribute to the maladjustment. After a careful consideration of the case, a tentative method of meeting these needs is set up. The treatment facilities used in improving the situation include the facilities of the clinic itself, the machinery of the law when necessary, the home, the school, professional case-working agency not connected with the school, organized recreational programs, and, if necessary, placement outside the home. Diagnosis continues throughout the treatment, and the treatment is modified whenever it seems advisable to do so.

Strang has summarized the most important steps that can be taken to improve conditions leading to unfavorable personality development as follows: [36]

1. Change the attitude of personnel workers, teachers, parents, other members of the family, and other children toward the child.

[34] Sheldon Glueck and Eleanor Glueck, eds., *Preventing Crime: A Symposium* (New York, McGraw, 1936). Also see their *Juvenile Delinquents Grown Up* and *Criminal Careers in Retrospect* (New York, Commonwealth Fund, 1940 and 1943).
[35] A more recent book by the Gluecks contains a vast amount of information on causes of delinquency and discusses possible means of prevention. See *Unraveling Juvenile Delinquency* (New York, Harper, 1951).
[36] Ruth Strang "Guidance in Personality Development," in *Guidance in Educational Institutions,* Part I, Ch. 7, pp. 197-229.

2. Change or rearrange other elements in his environment.

3. Help him to acquire certain skills and social routines that will enable him successfully to take his part in a group.

4. Help him to acquire insight into a situation and to discover for himself better ways of meeting difficulties, or by helping him to gain information on the basis of which to make intelligent choices.

5. Provide play and other forms of outlet that enable him to work through and solve his conflicts for himself.

6. Use special techniques, for example, psychoanalysis.

7. Self-guidance through goals accepted or set up by the individual.

7. *Proceed on a tentative basis and modify procedures when it appears advisable.* Because we cannot be certain in most cases what the cause of a deficiency is, remedial instruction must proceed on a tentative basis. When the teacher has isolated what appears to be the root of the difficulty, remedial measures should be applied. The correctness of the diagnosis will be shown by a resulting improvement. It may, for example, appear that the reason for difficulty in a course in history is a reading deficiency. If a remedial reading program results in improvement in history, the diagnosis probably was correct and the remedial program was the proper one. Because of the difficulty of making such a clear-cut diagnosis in many cases, owing to the effects of several factors not readily isolated, the teacher must be prepared to alter the remedial program at any time. If little improvement takes place, a new attack must be made on the problem. This varied procedure, adapted as wisely as possible to the apparent needs of the learner, must be continued until the solution to the problem is found.

8. *Secure the interest and co-operation of the learner.* In all cases the teacher must make every effort to secure the whole-hearted, intelligent co-operation of the learner. The learner must be led through self-diagnosis to an insight into the nature of his difficulty. If the teacher can give him

a real appreciation of the significance of his difficulty and can make clear to him the steps that are most likely to lead to improvement, a willing attack on the problem is in most cases insured. Children of superior mental ability can analyze their difficulties more easily than inferior pupils can. The former do not need as definite guidance as the latter. Intelligent pupils can usually correct difficulties when they are pointed out to them. The teacher must assign the child of inferior mental ability well-graded tasks that he can master. The goals to be achieved should be adjusted to his capacity for growth. From the very beginning of the remedial program, the teacher should try to make clear to each pupil the improvement he is making, even though it may be taking place in very small increments. It is important that at all times the teacher use instructional materials and methods which fully recognize differences in the rates at which pupils learn.

The use of apparatus in diagnosis and treatment. In recent years there has been a rapid development in the use of various kinds of apparatus for diagnostic and remedial purposes, especially in the field of reading. They are highly technical in nature and special training in their use is necessary. They are mentioned here briefly to bring them to the attention of the reader. Some of the most important are the following:

Betts Telebinocular Tests, distributed by the American Optical Company, Southbridge, Mass., measure a number of important visual traits.
Ophthalmolograph, distributed by the American Optical Company, is an instrument which produces a photographic record of eye movements.
Metronoscope, distributed by the American Optical Company, is a device for improving eye movements.
Harvard Reading Films, distributed by Harvard University for a small charge, are designed for improving eye movements.

The following references discuss the values of these and similar devices in the instructional program:

ANDERSON, Irving H., and MORSE, William C., "The Place of Instrumentation in the Reading Program: I. Evaluation of the Ophthalmograph," *Journal of Experimental Education* (March, 1946), pp. 256-263.

TRAXLER, Arthur E., "The Value of Controlled Reading: Summary of Opinion and Research," *Journal of Experimental Education* (June, 1943), pp. 280-292.

Sources of help on developmental and remedial programs. It will not be possible, because of limitations of space, to discuss in any detail the many remedial and developmental exercises that have been devised. In some cases there can be applied very specific corrective measures which will bring about a big improvement.

There are many books which contain detailed descriptions of developmental and remedial programs in the various areas of the curriculum. Excellent general discussions are included in most of the books on measurement mentioned in the bibliography in Chapter 9. Several books discuss diagnostic and remedial procedures in considerable detail. The following are among those most useful:

Educational Diagnosis, Thirty-fourth Yearbook, National Society for the Study of Education (Bloomington, Ill., Public School Publishing Co., 1935). All areas of curriculum.

BRUECKNER, L. J., *Diagnostic and Remedial Teaching of Arithmetic* (Philadelphia, John C. Winston, 1930).

———, and GROSSNICKLE, F. E., *Making Arithmetic Meaningful* (Philadelphia, John C. Winston, 1953).

———, *How to Make Arithmetic Meaningful* (Philadelphia, John C. Winston, 1947).

BRUECKNER, L. J., and MELBY, E. O., *Diagnostic and Remedial Teaching* (Boston, Houghton, 1931). All areas of curriculum.

Encyclopedia of Educational Research, 1950 edition (New York, Macmillan, 1950). See articles under subject titles for reviews of research on diagnosis and treatment of learning difficulties.

FERNALD, Grace, *Remedial Techniques in Basic School Subjects* (New York, McGraw, 1943).

GATES, Arthur I., *The Improvement of Reading,* rev. ed. (New York, Macmillan, 1947).

HARRIS, Albert, *How to Improve Reading Ability* (New York, Longmans, 1947).

Manual of Gates-Russel Diagnostic Test in Spelling.

McCULLOUGH, Constance, STRANG, Ruth, and TRAXLER, Arthur E., *Problems in the Improvement of Reading* (New York, McGraw, 1946).

HOW TO DEAL WITH PROBLEMS OF MALADJUSTMENT

Education of Exceptional Children, Forty-ninth Yearbook, Part II, National Society for the Study of Education (Chicago, Univ. of Chicago Press, 1950).

FENTON, Norman, *Mental Hygiene in School Practice* (Stanford University, Calif., Stanford Univ. Press., 1943).

Fostering Mental Health in Our Schools, 1950 Yearbook, Association for Supervision and Curriculum Development (Washington, NEA, 1950).

GLUECK, Sheldon, and GLUECK, Eleanor, *Unraveling Juvenile Delinquency* (New York, Commonwealth Fund, 1950).

PRESCOTT, Daniel A., *Emotion and the Educative Process,* Report of the Committee on the Relation of Emotion to the Educative Process (Washington, American Council on Education, 1938).

ZACHRY, C. B., and LIGHTY, M., *Emotion and Conduct in Adolescence* (New York, Appleton-Century-Crofts, 1940).

The complex nature of remedial programs illustrated. In a recent study, Glueck and Glueck set out to determine if there were characteristic differences between two groups of boy, one consisting of 500 delinquent boys, the other of 500 bona-fide nondelinquent boys. The age range was from 11 to 17 years. The groups were matched by age, ethnic derivation, general intelligence, and residence in underprivileged urban neighborhoods. Systematic studies were made of the traits and characteristics of the individuals, their family life, their school background and their employment of leisure time. A summary of the basic findings and a discussion of specific targets of delinquency prevention are included in a small volume, *Delinquency in the Making.* A full account of the study will be found in a major report.[37]

The enormous complexity of the problem of juvenile delinquency and of the factors underlying it is made clear by the data in the report. The Gluecks make a number of specific recommendations of possible steps that may be taken to prevent juvenile delinquency. As they see it, the school and the community as a whole have important roles to play. Their basic recommendations are indicated by the following abridged quotations from their report. The original should be consulted for full details:

a. The Delinquent Himself. What can be done, specifically, about the constitution, traits, and characteristics that distinguish delinquents as a group from nondelinquents?

The greater incidence of mesomorphic constitutional physique among delinquents, and the "growth spurt" of these boys at thirteen to fourteen years, provide targets for specific action. The excess of mesomorphy among delinquents as a class ought to suggest to all persons and agencies intimately concerned with the guidance of youth—parents, teachers, community recreational agencies, and others—that special allowance must be made in all major channels of self-expression for the greater energy output of certain boys, if their drives are not to take antisocial expression. The days of "winning the West," of the whaling ship, and of other fields of action for energetic, adventure-hungry youth are no more. To supply legitimate substitutes is a challenge to the ingenuity of schools, recreational authorities, and vocational guides. There is obviously a need for greater variety in curriculum patterns, in leisure-time programs and in vocational opportunities, and a more specific fitting of types of boys into areas of activity.

The greater inclination of the delinquents to the practical, concrete forms of mental activity and their disinclination to abstract, verbalistic intellectual processes furnish specific targets for designers of school curricula. In regard to such qualitative intellectual traits as incapacity for objective interests, unrealistic thinking, lack of "common sense," and unsystematic approach to mental problems, those who plan curricula need to consult with experts in clinical psychiatry and psychology, because such traits are especially entangled with emotional tendencies.

In weighing the characteristics of delinquents as derived from the Rorschach Test and psychiatric interview, school and clinic have the greatest opportunity for action directed toward specific goals. These are so clearly of a nature to interfere with a satisfactory taming of primitive impulses and to facilitate uncontrolled, unthinking antisocial self-expression, that they furnish specific targets for preventive activities on the part of family clinics and school agencies. Among them, it will be recalled, are assertiveness, defiance of or ambivalence to authority; excessive feelings of hostility, suspiciousness, destructiveness; unconventionality in ideas and behavior oral-receptive and sadistic-destructive trends; marked emotional impulsiveness, and defective self-control; sensuality and acquisitiveness; deficiency in conscientiousness and self-criticism; preponderance of extroversive trends and/or the tendency to resolve emotional conflicts by an impulsive "acting out."

Such traits tell their own story as to why it is that so frequently the efforts of juvenile courts and other agencies dealing with delinquents, devoted and intelligent as these often are, can accomplish so little in changing a course of habitual antisocial conduct. The deep-seated nature of the temperamental and character traits found to differentiate persistent delinquents from nondelinquents, and the extremely early age at which delinquents first manifest marked difficulties in adjustment as expressed in misbehavior, should make us realize how absolutely essential it is for schools, particularly, to be equipped to discover *potential* delinquents before the trends of maladaptive behavior become too fixed. For the schools are in a strategic position to note such marked deviations and difficulties of adaptation at the age of around six when the child first enters grade school. *Character prophylaxis*—the testing of children early and periodically to detect malformations of emotional development at a stage when the twig can still be bent—is as necessary as are early and periodic medical examinations. A crying need of the times in this field is a *preventive medicine of personality and character.*

b. Family Life. Many crucial differences were found between the parents of the delinquents and those of the other boys—the greater intellectual and emotional abnormalities of the delinquents' grandparents (and other distant relatives) and parents, the higher incidence of

---

[37] Sheldon Glueck and Eleanor Glueck, *Unraveling Juvenile Delinquency* (New York, Harper, 1951).

alcoholism and criminalism in the families in which the parents of the delinquent boys had themselves been reared; their more extensive physical, intellectual, and emotional handicaps, as well as drunkenness and criminalism; their greater dependence on various social welfare agencies. All this suggests that the community must somehow break the vicious circle of character-damaging influences on children exerted by parents who are themselves the distorted personality products of adverse parental influences. This can be done only through intensive instruction of each generation of prospective parents in the elements of mental hygiene and the requisites of happy and healthy family life. It calls for a tremendous multiplication of psychiatric, social, religious, educational and other community resources for improving the basic equipment of present and prospective parents in the assumption of a wholesome parental role. For there cannot be the slightest doubt, in the light of the facts marshaled in the preceding pages, that it is futile to treat the child, delinquent or otherwise, apart from the family that contributes much to make him what he is. Without concentration on the family, particularly the parents, we may set up boys' clubs, recreational centers, clinics, and the like, and we may inveigh against the movies, comics, and crime-suggesting toys; but we shall still be trying to sweep back the tide of childhood maladjustment and delinquency with pitifully inadequate brooms.

Under modern conditions of city life, especially in the underprivileged areas, what used to be a problem that tended to take care of itself in rural and semirural America, when families were large, cultural ideas and ideals more uniform, and life simpler, has become difficult and perplexing. It is obvious that little progress can be made in the prevention of juvenile delinquency until family life is strengthened through a large-scale, pervasive, continuous program designed to bring to bear all the resources of mental hygiene, social work, education, and religious and ethical teaching upon this central issue.

The differentiative traits of the parents of our boys lead to the conclusion that all the community's agencies for the guidance of young people in the proper selection of mates and in preparation for marriage—agencies specializing in marital problems, church groups, family welfare organizations—need to enlarge and enrich their techniques.

The evidences of disruption in the family life of delinquents are specific targets at which to aim. To cite but one illustration—if agencies interested in the recreational movement, boys' clubs, and other methods for constructive use of leisure were to formulate their plans and activities around a working principle of encouraging recreations that would engage the interest of the family as a unit, this one principle alone might serve to counteract the tendency to family disintegration. Beginning with the cementing influence of family-group recreation, the path might be opened to improvement in other constituents of the unhealthy family pattern.

It will be recalled that certain other unwholesome parent-child relationships, apart from those already noted, were found strikingly to differentiate the family atmosphere of delinquents and nondelinquents. Far more of their homes were broken; far more of the mothers of the delinquents allowed their children to shift for themselves during leisure hours; far fewer of their fathers evinced sympathy and affection for their boys; and while there was much more warmth on the part of the mothers generally, fewer of the delinquents' mothers had a healthily affectionate relationship to the boys. Far fewer of the delinquents were, in turn, warmly attached to their fathers and mothers; a far lower percentage of the delinquent boys accepted their fathers as desirable models for emulation; to a greater extent the former believed that neither of the parents was genuinely concerned for their welfare; and the disciplinary practices of the parents of the delinquents were far less adequate.

Here is a dynamic area of intrafamily crosscurrents that in large measure accounts for the persistent maladjustment of the boys who became delinquent. Again we have a situation which, though highly involved and complex, might be attacked by concentrating on a series of specific constituents of the entire emotion-laden area. If, for example, there were community agencies to instruct parents systematically in regard to the emotional significance of various disciplinary practices and to demonstrate to them how behavior situations usually improve when discipline is fair and firm and unaccompanied by anger, they might learn to adopt such practices with socializing effect on their children. Again, if parents were systematically taught simple elements of the dynamics of parent-child relationships; of the struggle the young child must go through in adjusting his instinctual drives and their emotional accompaniments in relation to mother, father, and brothers and sisters; of the role of the father as the first "ego-ideal," and, in general, of the great part played by early parent-child experiences in the crystallization of the child's basic personality and character traits which will be carried into adulthood and become more difficult to modify with the passage of time, some headway might be made in rendering intrafamily life more hygienic and happy.

The problem is enormous in scope. It calls for the widespread co-operative endeavor of child-guidance clinics, school teachers, family welfare agencies, church and other communal resources. In most communities it will be found that there are not enough facilities, such as clinics, and that the effort of public and private agencies is not planfully articulated so as to give the most economical results.

c. The School. A great deal of time, and at a very impressionable age, is spent by children in schools. Our findings have shown that much more goes on in the intraschool situation than the mere commerce in ideas about "readin', writin', and 'rithmetic," and that what does transpire is of an essentially emotional nature. On the part of the teacher, she cannot altogether get rid of her own emotional problems through the channel of drilling students in the curriculum. On the part of the little pupils, they do not, when they enter the classroom, leave behind their emotional freight, their worries about parental anger, neglect, drunkenness, criminalism.

We have seen that delinquent boys largely possess certain temperamental and personality traits and special abilities and disabilities which distinguish them from the general run of nondelinquents. We have also seen that because of the poor parent-child relationships predominating in delinquents' families the boys have difficulty in finding an emotionally sympathetic adult as a symbol for emulation around whom ideals and standards of behavior can be woven to form the core of character. Such facts—and there are other relevant ones—suggest that fundamental changes in school curricula and teacher training must be made.

Forcing certain types of children into the traditional mold results in increasing tension, frustration, revolt, and delinquency. Much greater flexibility in school curricula is called for; a rich variety of satisfying school experiences must be devised which will enlist the interests of different types of children.

The marked differences between the delinquent boys and their nondelinquent counterparts again afford specific targets at which to direct preventive action in this area: Among the delinquents as a group there was more school retardation, poorer scholastic achievement, greater dislike of school, less academic ambition, greater preference for adventurous activities. But these traits are not essentially chargeable to a difference in general intelligence, for the two groups were similar in average IQ. Their true roots are apparent from the other differentiative traits and behavior manifestations in which the delinquents were different from the other lads: They did not adjust themselves as well to their schoolmates; almost all the delinquents, compared to but 86 of the other lads, indulged in all forms of misconduct in school, ranging from defiance, stubbornness, lying, and persistent inattention to truancy, stealing, and sexual misconduct. It will be recalled, further, that while such misbehavior occurred at eight or less among a third of the delinquents (their average age at first school misbehavior having been 9.5 years), it occurred as early as this among less than a tenth of the few nondelinquents who had misbehaved in school (their average age at first misconduct in school having been 12.5 years).

These facts suggest not only that a boy's school misconduct as a harbinger (and sometimes an accompanier) of misconduct in the general community is not only of emotional origin, but that the emotional difficulties are deep-rooted, reaching into the most tender years. When, to the early age of first school misconduct is added the early age of first antilegal behavior (almost half the delinquents were only eight at the time), it becomes clearer than ever that the evidences of persistent delinquency arise essentially before puberty and that the elementary school therefore stands in the front line of attack on the problem.

In an enlightened educational system the school could function as the litmus paper of personality and character maladaption, reflecting early in the child's growth the acid test of his success or failure in his first attempts to cope with the problems of life posed by a restrictive society and code of behavior. In such a system, the best psychiatric, psychologic, medical, social, and other facilities would then be focused on the specific traits shown to be most largely related to personality distortion and maladapted behavior at a critical point in the child's development when character and habit are still sufficiently plastic for effective therapeutic intervention.

d. Leisure Time. In their life on the city streets, as well as in the other respects noted, we have seen that the delinquent boys are worse off than the nondelinquents: Their families moved about more frequently, interfering with whatever stabilizing influences there are in attachment and loyalty to a definite community. To a greater extent than the nondelinquent lads, the delinquents worked in street trades where they were subject to the hazards of unsupervised employment at an impressionable age. Their recreational as well as work preferences were for risky and adventurous energy outlets, reflected not only in excessive truck hopping, keeping late hours, bunking out, running away from home, destroying property, and the like, but also in seeking out play places at a considerable distance from their homes, and other enticing locales of risk and adventure such as railroad yards and waterfronts. These tendencies are also shown in the greater extent to which delinquents had serious street accidents and even (vicariously) in their much more frequent movie attendance. Most of the delinquents became gang members, and many preferred companions older than themselves. There is also strong evidence that the delinquents disliked the confinement of playgrounds, supervised recreations, or attendance at clubs or other centers which they rarely joined of their own desire. Finally, they were more neglectful of church attendance than the nondelinquents.

Here we have a series of behavior manifestations that unquestionably suggest that settlement houses, school community centers, church centers, boys' clubs, and other agencies must take into account the preferences of these adventure-thirsty boys who dislike intensive supervision and tend to turn to delinquency as a congenial way of life. Such agencies should experiment with various means of attracting and guiding youngsters of this type into at least socially harmless, if not positively constructive, channels. In a busy, exciting, urban community of individualists "on the make," these boys drift among the general population unattached by loyalties except to those of similar energy drive and consuming interest. There is obviously a crying social need for coping with this problem through well-planned community action, based upon careful surveys of local conditions, liabilities, facilities, and needs. A number of communities have made promising beginnings in this direction.

The contributions of specialists and clinical services. The function of specialists and clinical services is to assist the teacher to help the individual who is experiencing serious learning difficulty to adjust through diagnostic study and therapeutic treatment for which most classroom teachers are untrained or haven't the time, and for which special equipment and apparatus are required. There are various kinds of educational specialists in schools that are concerned with diagnosis, including (1) those concerned with physical and mental health, for example, school physicians, pediatricians, psychiatrists, dentists, optometrists; (2) those concerned with social aspects of the teaching-learning situation, for example, attendance officers, recreation leaders, visiting teachers, and social workers; (3) technical clinical personnel, such as testing specialists, school psychologists, psychometrists, psychiatric social workers, academic clinicians, and audiometer technicians; and (4) those concerned primarily with treatment and therapy of deficiencies of various kinds, for example, speech correctionists, remedial reading teachers, teachers of exceptional and handicapped children, teachers of corrective gymnastics, and home room teachers.

The services rendered by these specialists vary widely. They may be classified as:

1. Directing testing programs in such areas as intelligence, achievement, aptitude, readiness, personality, and health.
2. Diagnosis in such areas as mental health, emotional stability, social adjustment, academic work, physical traits, and vocational aptitude.
3. Treatment and therapy of mental, emotional, social, and physical aspects of personality, and of serious disabilities in academic areas.
4. Advisory and consultative services for administrators and supervisors for dealing with educational problems of the school and community, also for parents, teachers, and pupils, and for such community agencies as the courts, welfare agencies, placement services, and employment services.
5. Educational activities, such as conducting workshops for the in-service education of teachers and staff, assisting in teacher selection, parent education, experimentation with educational programs and materials, and the school public relations program.

The services rendered by the various special services also vary according to the size of the school system, the needs of particular schools, the resources available, and the readiness of the teachers and others to make use of their contributions. In small school systems one individual, for example, a school psychologist, may be required to perform the functions of several different specialists. In this case, private sources must be consulted when the need arises. In large systems there is often a multiplicity of specialists and clinical services difficult to integrate and co-ordinate so that their contributions may be fully effective.

Clinics operate at various levels. For example, there are clinical services that operate at the state level and in various regions in a state as traveling clinics, in school systems as a whole, in particular schools, in remedial centers, in hospitals, and in universities and colleges. Sometimes consultants are available on call, sometimes according to a schedule. Sometimes specialists are employed on a part-time basis.

The names given to special and clinical services vary widely from titles that suggest limited functions, such as psychological clinic, child guidance center, and reading clinic, to other more inclusive titles that indicate an integration of a number of related services, such as Bureau of Child Services, Division of Guidance Services, and Department of Educational Counsel. The value of an integrated approach in dealing with educational problems is very evident when one observes the procedures in staff meetings in which various clinical specialists bring to bear their several contributions on how to deal with the case at hand. Under such conditions there is little danger that the case will not be approached from all points of view, and there is every assurance that treatments will be as comprehensive as facilities and staff permit.

The support of clinical services presents many problems. In some states there is state aid for at least a part of the program; in many localities support comes only from local public taxation; in some places clinical services are maintained by groups of parents and other interested persons; in other places private clinics are operative that are supported by fees paid by those who utilize their services. In a number of instances, clinics have been established by educational foundations for demonstration purposes, for example, in the so-called 3-School Project in New York City. In this case three schools have been selected in which serious educational and social problems exist and steps have been taken to bring to bear on these needs the services of broadly conceived psychological and educational clinics, local social agencies, welfare groups, recreational staffs, and similar agencies which have contributions to make to a comprehensive improvement program. The outcomes of this approach, in terms of changes in behavior of youth and improvements of community life, are to be studied over a period of years to determine its effectiveness, with a view to extending it to other areas of the city.

Those concerned with the improvement of the work of these clinics and special services face many problems. There is a lack of adequately trained personnel; the training of specialists is often very narrow and not fitted to the actual situations that exist in the schools; diagnosis is frequently limited to the study of only one or two phases of personality, for instance, emotional maladjustment, and overlooks related aspects of the situation; there often is a long delay in making reports of findings to the referring agencies, and suggestions as to treatments are often very limited or so general as to be of little value; there is a need for research on the improvement of diagnostic procedures and the validation of remedial measures; schools often are not prepared to "follow through" the recommendations of clinics; in many places facilities assigned to clinics are inferior and woefully inadequate; in certain cities there is a lack of support for special services due to failure of the responsible authorities to appreciate the great value of their services.

Undoubtedly, the most valuable contributions of specialists and clinics are made when they work co-operatively, directly, and at close range in school situations with the immediate problems faced by the staff and the pupils. Specialists should make every effort to make their contributions of immediate and practical value to the schools and community and to assist teachers to carry out improvement programs intelligently and skillfully. Where there is only a small staff to serve several schools, for instance, one consisting of a school psychologist, a psychiatric social worker, an academic clinician, and a competent pediatrician, their time should be so divided that not only will all schools secure the minimum essential services but there will be time for giving special attention to situations in which the need is greatest. Smaller systems frequently share the services of specialists. Often the services of consultants from nearby colleges and universities can be secured on a part-time basis. Many classroom teachers are taking special work in diagnostic procedures and are prepared to make their services available when the need arises.

Standards for appraising programs for the physically handicapped. Crayton made an exhaustive study of the provisions for the care of various kinds of handicapped children in the states and cities of this country. Wide variations in practices were found. The different plans were appraised by a commission which then proposed policies for the state of Kentucky for dealing with this problem. Very suggestive standards for evaluating state and local programs were drawn up. The following standards for the care of crippled, cardiac, and tubercular children illustrate the criteria that were adopted for evaluating the provisions for the various kinds of handicapped children. They may be applied in the appraisal of the provisions for these children in any community. Crayton's report contains similar standards for appraising programs for each of the other kinds of handicapped children. Crayton's complete series of standards was used to evaluate provisions for handicapped children in the schools of New York state. The results are reported in Brueckner's *The Changing Elementary School.*

STANDARDS FOR EVALUATING PROVISIONS FOR CRIPPLED, CARDIAC, AND TUBERCULAR CHILDREN [38]

1. There should be some practical and efficient program for locating and diagnosing the needs of the crippled, the cardiac, and the tubercular. This would perhaps include:
    a. A law requiring that birth records indicate the existence and type of congenital defect.
    b. A law requiring that the school census note the existence of obvious defects.
    c. School clinics.
    d. Traveling clinics.
    e. County surveys.
    f. Tubercular tests and roëntgenological examinations for all children exposed to open tuberculosis and for other suspicious cases.
2. Provisions should be made for the hospitalization of those cases which require it. In general, two types of hospital facilities have demonstrated their worth.
    a. A centralized orthopedic hospital supported by the state and administered either by the state or by the state medical school. (This plan seems better adapted than any other for reaching cases in isolated rural communities.)
    b. Orthopedic facilities of local general or children's hospitals checked and approved by the state for the care of the state's patient. (This plan is better in that it makes use of existing facilities and makes it unnecessary for many children to go far from home for treatment.)

[38] From Sherman C. Crayton, "A Proposed Program for the Care and Education of Kentucky's Handicapped Children, Based upon Current Practice and Philosophy within the State and Current Throughout the United States," *Bulletin of the Bureau of School Service,* Vol. 7, No. 1 (Lexington, Univ. of Kentucky, September, 1934). Quoted in Leo J. Brueckner and others, *The Changing Elementary School* (New York, Inor Publishing Co., 1939), pp. 231 ff.

3. Provisions should be made for the care of children under treatment and those convalescing from operations. Under varying circumstances four different types of care are feasible.

    a. Convalescent homes, sometimes in connection with hospitals which handle orthopedic cases (approved as a means of caring for children for long periods at less cost than in the orthopedic hospital).

    b. Nurses to visit children convalescing in their homes to supervise diet and care, and to adjust braces (usually feasible only in or near cities and in cases where home conditions are favorable).

    c. Clinics to which children are taken at regular intervals.

    d. Tuberculosis sanatoriums.

4. The state should bear the responsibility of directing and financing, at least in part, the education of the crippled. Various types of arrangements must be made, the choice depending upon the situation and the physical condition of the child.

    a. Private instruction in the home (sometimes very unsatisfactory, but certainly better than none, although it deprives the child of youthful companionship and outside contacts).

    b. Bedside or class instruction in hospitals and in convalescent homes.

    c. Special schools and special classes in public schools (usually practicable only in cities of 14,000 and over).

    d. State aid to assist children who wish to board in a city near a special class or school.

    e. Provisions for free transportation to special day schools and classes for children who require it.

The procedure to follow in applying these standards is simply to consider the items listed as they apply locally or to the state and to check those that are adequately provided for or are not provided for. The standards for the other types of handicapped children may be applied in the same way.[39]

CHAPTER SUPPLEMENT

QUESTIONS TO INTRODUCE GENERAL DISCUSSION

1. How significant a factor in learning and instruction do you regard mental hygiene to be?

2. Is there any basis of grouping pupils that you regard as satisfactory? Explain.

3. Give examples of how some teacher provided effectively for individual differences; for gifted children.

4. How desirable are hospital classes for pupils not able to progress satisfactorily? What clinical services should be available?

5. What can be done to *prevent* the incidence of learning difficulty?

6. What policy of promotion of pupils is operative in your schools? Would you subscribe to a policy of uninterrupted continuity and complete elimination of nonpromotion at all levels of the school? At any level? What bearing does nonpromotion have on child development?

REPORTS

1. Describe some case in your experience in which systematic steps taken to correct some learning or personality weakness apparently were successful.

2. How can school medical examinations be improved so as to provide data needed for diagnosis?

3. What kinds of remedial materials are available, for example, in reading?

4. What guidance provisions are there in your school? How adequate are they?

5. What clinical facilities are there available in your locality?

6. What provisions are made by local schools for handicapped children?

7. Criticize the basis of grouping pupils used in your school.

8. What are the general elements of an educational program that are likely to lead to favorable growth and development of normal pupils and the achievement of the purposes of education?

    a. The curriculum.

    b. Instruction as such, and teacher traits.

    c. The materials, equipment, plant, community life.

[39] G. L. Hilleboe, *Finding and Teaching Atypical Children,* Contributions to Education No. 423 (New York, Teachers College, Bureau of Publications, Columbia Univ., 1930).

A. A. Strauss and Laura E. Lehtinen, *Psychotherapy and Education of the Brain-Injured Child* (New York, Grune and Stratton, 1947).

d. The grouping and promotion of pupils.

e. Special services for slow learning and handicapped children as well as gifted and talented.

9. What adjustments are possible for pupils having the following deficiencies?

a. A pupil with a very low level of reading ability in grade 4.

b. A specific deficiency in arithmetic, such as inability to subtract numbers when borrowing is necessary.

c. Inferior legibility of writing.

d. A boy showing a tendency to delinquent behavior.

e. A stutterer with emotional difficulties.

f. A child suffering from malnutrition.

g. A girl with a lack of interest in music.

h. A group reads books of inferior quality only.

10. Why is guidance becoming such an important aspect of teaching?

WRITTEN REPORTS FOR INDIVIDUALS OR SMALL GROUPS

1. Select a specific pupil weakness in some curriculum area and indicate in detail how you would proceed to correct it. Preferably take some difficulty in the case of a particular pupil identified by diagnostic procedures. Plan a remedial program applying to him. Review Chapter 10.

2. Make a list of remedial materials you think should be available for the classroom teacher. The materials may be for some grade level or for some single area of learning. Examine textbooks and workbooks in this connection.

3. Compare remedial measures proposed by authors in references in the bibliography for a particular weakness. To what extent do they agree?

4. Make a study of the work of some teacher and note the kinds of remedial measures she uses. These may include steps taken at any stage of learning to eliminate learning difficulty.

5. What evidence is there that corrective and remedial work produces results?

SUGGESTED READINGS

Adapting the Secondary-School Program to the Needs of Youth, Fifty-second Yearbook, Part I, National Society for the Study of Education (Chicago, Univ. of Chicago Press, 1953).

AIKIN, Wilford M., *The Story of the Eight-Year Study* (New York, Harper, 1942).

ALBERTY, Harold, *Reorganizing the High School Curriculum* (New York, Macmillan, 1947).

BECK, R. H., COOK, W. W., and KEARNEY, N. C., *Curriculum in the Modern Elementary School* (New York, Prentice-Hall, 1953).

BLAIR, G. M., *Diagnostic and Remedial Teaching in Secondary Schools* (New York, Macmillan, 1946).

BOND, Guy L., and HANDLAN, Bertha, *Adapting Instruction in Reading to Individual Differences* (Minneapolis, Univ. of Minnesota Press, 1948).

BOSSING, N. L., *Principles of Secondary Education* (New York, Prentice-Hall, 1949).

BRUECKNER, L. J., *Adapting Instruction in Arithmetic to Individual Differences* (Minneapolis, Univ. of Minnesota Press, 1947).

———, and GROSSNICKLE, F. E., *Making Arithmetic Meaningful* (Philadelphia, John C. Winston, 1953).

BRUECKNER, L. J., and others, *The Changing Elementary School* (New York, Inor Publishing Co., 1939).

BURTON, William H., *The Guidance of Learning Activities,* 2nd ed. (New York, Appleton-Century-Crofts, 1952).

CASWELL, H. L., and FOSHAY, A. W., *Education in the Elementary School* (New York, American Book, 1950).

COOK, W. W., *Grouping and Promotion in the Elementary School* (Minneapolis, Univ. of Minnesota Press, 1941).

DALE, Edgar, *Audio-Visual Methods in Teaching* (New York, Dryden, 1946).

DAVIS, R. A., and BALLARD, C. R., "The Effectiveness of Various Types of Classroom Incentives," *Educational Method* (December, 1932), pp. 134-136.

Education for All American Children, report by Educational Policies Commission (Washington, NEA, 1948).

Education for All American Youth, Educational Policies Commission (Washington, NEA, 1944).

Education in Rural Communities, Fifty-first Yearbook, Part II, National Society for the Study of Education (Chicago, Univ. of Chicago Press, 1951).

FAUNCE, R. C., and BOSSING, N. L., *Developing the Core Curriculum* (New York, Prentice-Hall, 1951).

FENTON, Norman, *Mental Hygiene in School Practice* (Stanford University, Calif., Stanford Univ. Press, 1943).

FERNALD, Grace M., *On Certain Language Disabilities: Their Nature and Treatment,* Mental Measurement Monographs, Serial No. 11 (Baltimore, Williams and Wilkins, 1936).

———, *Remedial Techniques in Basic School Subjects* (New York, McGraw, 1943).

FLAUM, Laurence S., *The Activity High School* (New York, Harper, 1953).

FOX, Lorene K., *The Rural Community and Its School* (New York, Kings Avon Press, 1948).

GATES, Arthur I., "The Necessary Mental Age for Beginning Reading," *Elementary School Journal* (March, 1937), pp. 497-508.

GILES, H. H., *Teacher Pupil Planning* (New York, Harper, 1941).

Group Planning in Education, 1945 Yearbook, Department of Supervision and Curriculum Development (Washington, NEA, 1945).

HARRIS, A. J., *How to Increase Reading Ability,* rev. ed. (New York, Longmans, 1947).

HAVIGHURST, Robert, *Developmental Tasks and Education* (Chicago, Univ. of Chicago Press, 1948).

HILGARD, E. R., *Theories of Learning* (New York, Appleton-Century-Crofts, 1948).

HOPKINS, L. T., *Interaction* (Boston, Heath, 1941).

JERSILD, Arthur T., and TASCH, Ruth J., *Children's Interests* (New York, Teachers College, Bureau of Publications, Columbia Univ., 1949).

KEARNEY, Nolan C., *Elementary School Objectives* (New York, Russell Sage Foundation, 1953).

KRUG, E., and ANDERSON, G. L., *Adapting Instruction in the Social Studies to Individual Differences,* Fifteenth Yearbook, National Council of the Social Studies (Washington, NEA, 1944).

Learning and Instruction, Forty-ninth Yearbook, Part I, National Society for the Study of Education (Chicago, Univ. of Chicago Press, 1950).

Learning the Ways of Democracy, report of the Educational Policies Commission (Washington, NEA, 1940).

LEE, J. M., and LEE, D. M., *The Child and His Curriculum,* 2nd ed. (New York, Appleton-Century-Crofts, 1950).

LOWENFELD, Viktor, *Creative and Mental Growth: A Textbook in Art Education* (New York, Macmillan, 1947).

Meeting Special Needs of the Individual Child, Nineteenth Yearbook, Department of Elementary-School Principals (Washington, NEA, 1940).

MEIER, Arnold, CLEARY, F. D., and DAVIS, Alice M., *A Curriculum for Citizenship* (Detroit, Wayne Univ. Press, 1952).

MONROE, Marion, *Children Who Cannot Read* (Chicago, Univ. of Chicago Press, 1932).

MORT, P. R., and VINCENT, W. S., *Modern Educational Practice: A Handbook for Teachers* (New York, McGraw, 1950).

OTTO, Henry J., *Principles of Elementary Education* (New York, Rinehart, 1949).

ROBINSON, Helen, *Why Pupils Fail in Reading* (Chicago, Univ. of Chicago Press, 1946).

ROGERS, C. L., *The Clinical Treatment of Problem Children* (Boston, Houghton, 1939).

SIMPSON, Ray H., *Improving Teaching-Learning Processes* (New York, Longmans, 1953).

SMITH, B. Othanel, "The Normative Unit," *Teachers College Record* (January, 1945), pp. 219-228.

———, STANLEY, W. O., and SHORES, J. H., *Fundamentals of Curriculum Development* (Yonkers, World Book, 1950). Ch. 23 contains excellent discussion of process units.

SPAULDING, F. T., *High School and Life* (New York, McGraw, 1938).

STILES, Lindley J., and DORSEY, Mattie F., *Democratic Teaching in Secondary Schools* (Philadelphia, Lippincott, 1950).

THUT, I. N., and GERBERICH, J. R., *Foundations of Secondary School Method* (New York, McGraw-Hill Book Co., 1949).

WILLEY, R. L., *Guidance in Elementary Education* (New York, Harper, 1952).

WINSLOW, C. E. A., *The School Health Program* (New York, McGraw, 1939).

WRIGHTSTONE, J. Wayne, "Research Action Programs for Research Bureaus," *Journal of Educational Research* (April, 1949), pp. 623-629.

See also the bibliography at the end of Chapter 16. In most of the books listed the reader will find suggestions of ways of improving learning in the various curriculum areas.

Consult files of the periodical, *Review of Educational Research,* for extensive reviews of current research on guidance, child growth and development, mental hygiene, education of exceptional children, curriculum, and other topics related to the theme of this chapter.

Chapter 15

◆·◆·◆·◆·◆·◆·◆·◆·◆

The Improvement of Instruction

Section 1

IMPROVEMENT OF INSTRUCTION VIEWED AS A GROWTH PROCESS

Distinction made between training teachers and facilitating teacher growth. The expression "training of teachers in service" is no longer in good repute; at least, its standing is not so clear as it was some time back. The expression as used by many is undoubtedly very closely associated with the teacher-centered concept of supervision which we hope now may be supplanted by a goal-centered, co-operative type of group activity in which teachers, pupils, supervisors, administrators, and all others concerned work and grow together. The supervisors and administrators as well as the teachers are the learners. It is readily clear that pupils are learners, but not so readily clear that teachers, supervisors, and administrators are learners. All work together, however, for the achievement of the purposes of education and learn in the process of doing so.

The phrase "training in service" connotes teacher-centered and imposed supervision. The teacher is *given* devices, techniques, skills, and *trained* in their use. The teacher is *corrected* in his detailed techniques through *handing out* ready-made procedures. The modern concept holds that teachers (and all educational workers) should have *opportunities for growth* through the *co-operative analysis* of problems and through *choosing* from among several techniques or *devising* new ones based on the situation confronting the teacher. Teachers (and

educational workers) are not ordinarily to be *given* limited specifics but are to *develop* judgment in choosing or devising techniques which fit the situation. The teacher is to be aided in studying the significant factors in the situation, in evaluating the strength and weakness of his present procedures, and in the choosing or devising of techniques. There will arise, within the total range of supervisory situations, many instances in which the giving out of specific procedures may be the only possible action, but we "take over" only with very definite reservations and when the situation clearly indicates the necessity of extreme action.

Growth must be considered in relation to the total situation. There are two quite different approaches that we would like to refer to briefly in getting under way this discussion of helping teachers grow in teaching effectiveness. In one approach, teacher growth is considered apart from pupil growth; in the other, the growth needs of teachers are considered in relation to the larger improvement program of which they are a part. We wish here to consider the program for facilitating the teacher's growth as a part of the larger ongoing activity of helping pupils grow. Examples of these larger programs are given subsequently in this chapter. The difference between the approaches does not turn upon the amount of help given individual teachers, but rather upon the approach, frame of reference, or point of departure, and upon the manner in which assistance is given. The help given teachers will not be in either case accidental, but careful and systematic. In the approach chosen here, the program for helping teachers grow in teaching effectiveness will take its point of departure from the teachers' felt needs,—needs that arise in promoting pupil growth. The program will return continuously to pupil growth for validation. All educational workers, as well as the citizens of the community, participate in aiding the teacher to meet pupil needs and are in turn stimulated to growth.

Some supervisors fail to create favorable attitudes toward newer methods of teaching. The motivational methods of supervisors are not always effective. The supervisor, out of his experience, many contacts, and professional reading, comes to see the necessity for educational change. Seeing the importance of change, he comes to advocate modified procedures in learning and teaching and in other aspects of the school system for which he is responsible without giving teachers an opportunity to see the need as he sees it. Teachers are frequently without the supervisor's background of experience and contacts. Teachers are, however, faced with the responsibility of putting educational theory into practice. Under these conditions, they are naturally much more conservative and doubtful about change than are persons less well acquainted with the demands of the immediate situation. Then there are many inertias. One of the very best illustrations of the influence of inertia can be seen in the great gap between theory and practice in the classes taught by some college professors of education. A relatively small number practice in their own teaching the things that they preach. Supervisors seem to forget these very important facts in their work with teachers; and instead of planning improvement programs co-operatively, they frequently leave the problem to chance sales talks and verbal devices. If the supervisor is a good salesman and presents his ideas

well, he may secure the outward co-operation of the majority of his teaching staff, at least temporarily, until the new idea runs into difficulty. As already has been said, there is always a wide gap between theory and practice, and what is easily advanced in theory may be most difficult to put into practice. These difficulties will be discovered in attempting to put the new program into operation; and as difficulties arise, the teachers will have questions to ask, first, as to detail, and later, as to the general feasibility of the program as a whole. Such inquiries will stimulate other less convinced teachers to raise questions until sooner or later the supervisor finds himself committed to an educational program without the support of his teachers. This is a thing that occurs, as we all know, all too frequently in American education. The failure of supervisors to catch the psychology of this situation gives rise to much of the conflict and ill-will that exists between teachers and supervisors.

Discussed in terms of the basic approaches to learning—such as verbal activities, observational activities, and direct contact activities—the thing that has happened in this case is somewhat as stated below. The supervisor has relied upon verbal communication as a means of securing the necessary new attitudes. Though the verbal method is not without value, as witnessed daily by salesmen and saleswomen of all sorts, it has, however, certain limitations in education, particularly when the ideas presented appear later to come into conflict with the experiences that one gathers from direct contact with the thing itself, or where teachers may observe others to react negatively. The supervisor forgets that although it is true that the presentation to him may have been a verbal one and yet sufficient, the social situation provided by college classes and conventions may be very different from that provided in the local school system. The general attitude of college classes and educational gatherings is ordinarily positive.

The audience is selected and made up of persons already favorable to new ideas and not infrequently already committed to the idea presented. The prestige of the speaker is an important factor. Not to conform under such conditions is to incur the ill-will of the group of which the observer is a member. Back home the situation is different. Instead of relying upon social pressure to force recalcitrant individuals into line, the supervisor may be confronted with a community and teaching corps that are temporarily or even permanently hostile to the ideas presented. There is frequently no very strong positive social pressure persuading teachers to newer modes of behavior. Under these conditions the verbal method of creating new attitudes is frequently not successful, and some more convincing procedure may need to be applied. Co-operative group attack, let it be repeated, will be more effective.

To turn from the negative to the positive, it may be helpful to recall that we are generally more convinced about things that we have experienced directly through contact than by verbal presentation. This suggests that exposure to new ideas should be so managed that individual teachers or small groups of teachers may first try the new ideas out for themselves, without too much negative social pressure, and see that they work; and see that more progress will be made through the use of the newer ways. New attitudes may be developed; but to create favorable attitudes in negative climates, it would appear best to rely less upon verbal appeals and to rely more upon group planning and reactions from experience with concrete learning and teaching situations where teachers can experience directly the new values and feel surer about them. Supervisors should create situations where teachers can see for themselves that proposed changes are of value to the teachers in their own efforts to teach more effectively. The fact that new interests are grown from old interests and that we value those things that work for us is just as true of teachers as of pupils and points the way to a more effective type of leadership than that frequently supplied. The psychology of this situation is deserving of more attention than it gets.

Teacher growth is a learning process. Six principles of learning that are particularly important in facilitating teacher growth are the following:

1. The learning experience must grow out of a felt need.
2. Interest is an important factor in learning.
3. Satisfaction and success must attend the learning activity.
4. Teachers differ in interests, needs, and capacities, and provision must be made for these differences in the improvement program. People also differ in the rates at which they learn and in the ways in which they respond to different experiences.
5. Learning is most effective when the learner's attention is directed to the significant elements of a learning situation and he reacts to them and evaluates them.
6. Knowledge of progress is an important condition for effective learning.

Here we emphasize the importance of the principles of economical learning in facilitating teacher growth; in the materials to follow we shall discuss some principles of leadership. What one may wisely do in any particular situation will depend upon (1) the need or purpose; (2) the sorts of persons involved; (3) the principles of learning, teaching, and leadership that we hold to be true; and finally (4) the limiting aspects of the immediate situation. Principles, then, are one of the important general guides as to what to do and how to proceed in facilitating teacher growth.[1]

[1] *Better Than Rating,* Association for Supervision and Curriculum Development (Washington, NEA, 1951).

Section 2

THE FOUNDATIONS OF IMPROVEMENT PROGRAMS

Foundations of modern methods of teaching. The California statement of teaching competence given on pages 318 to 321 obviously envisages a high level of teaching which emphasizes the participation of children in rich, vital learning experiences under the guidance of well-qualified teachers. Limitations of space make it impossible to discuss details of method at this time. However, we shall attempt to characterize briefly the kinds of instructional procedures that are identified with modernized units, an up-to-date approach to teaching that is in line with modern educational theory. This description will serve as a frame of reference to be borne in mind throughout the discussion of ways of improving teaching that follows.

Foundations of method. Modern educational theory stresses the point that instruction should be so organized that the pupils not only learn subject matter and skills of genuine social value and significance, but also acquire patterns of thought and effective habits of thinking. So-called "subject-matter units" aim chiefly at substantive outcomes, derived from the subject matter through assimilative experiences. Smith[2] has suggested that the name "process unit" be used to designate any instructional unit that stresses patterns and habits of thought. Typical goals of process units are the discovery of generalizations, explanations, and principles, the formulation of policies and plans of action, and the development of the ability to evaluate critically statements, actions, plans, or various kinds of proposals.

There is no reason why apparent differences between subject-matter units and process units should be emphasized except for purposes of definition. Ideally, the goals of all effective teaching units will be a combination of subject-matter mastery and development of effective thought processes.

These goals are most likely to be achieved through purposeful, realistic learning activities suited to the needs, interests, and maturity of the learners. In a good learning situation there is a rich and varied series of experiences unified around a vigorous purpose and carried on in interaction with a rich, varied, and provocative environment. To comprehend and accept a principle through the study of printed materials is not at all the same as to achieve that principle through the study of actual problems and by undergoing actual realistic experiences in the course of which the principle emerges.

The emphasis to be placed on the components of units for a given group of pupils will be determined by their level of maturity, their experiential background, and their level of aspiration, as well as by their purposes, needs, and interests. Burton[3] points out that this means:

The education of *little children,* of *beginners* on almost any level, and of all classes *in the area of general education* will proceed best via units wherein the purposes, problems, interests, and "felt needs" of the learners largely determine the amount and complexity of subject matter to be included and the degree of attention to be given to the study or thought processes; wherein direct experience predominates over the vicarious.

The education of students who have *adequate reading ability,* who have achieved sufficient maturity to be able to *learn through verbal abstractions,* and who are entering upon *areas of specialization* which involve a look to the future will proceed best via units wherein ultimate social goals and more remote personal goals,

[2] B. O. Smith, W. O. Stanley, and J. H. Shores, *Fundamentals of Curriculum Development* (Yonkers, World Book, 1950), Ch. 23.

I. N. Thut and J. R. Gerberich, *Foundations of Secondary School Method* (New York, McGraw, 1949).

[3] William H. Burton, *The Guidance of Learning Activities,* 2nd ed. (New York, Appleton-Century-Crofts, 1952), p. 394.

with due regard for the necessity for challenge now, will largely determine the amount and complexity of subject matter and the degree of attention to the study of processes of learning and of thought; wherein greater use will be made of vicarious experiences.

Unit teaching differs sharply from the traditional assign-study-recite-test process that is widely characteristic today of instruction in American schools at all levels. This traditional teaching procedure is the outgrowth of the days when pupil mastery of bodies of subject matter set up to be learned was the primary objective of the schools. Sections of textbooks are assigned from day to day for study by pupils by strongly memoriter methods for subsequent re-citation or "giving back" in answer to questions asked by the teacher. Repetitive drill is emphasized in teaching skills. Supervised study is used as a basis for guiding learning activities. Finally, tests are administered to determine how well the subject matter and basic skills have been learned.

Burton [4] has summarized the "evils" inherent in this traditional kind of teaching as follows:

1. The underlying psychology is unacceptable. The atomistic-mechanistic concept of learning, adding fact upon fact (or skill, or concept) does not add up to useful learning outcomes.
2. The outcomes—fragmentary isolated facts, learning in non-functional situations—are not usable in real life. Some pupils do learn by this method and carry over the learning for use in life, but the mediocre and dull do not. It is uneconomical learning at best.
3. The functional learning outcomes—understandings, attitudes, appreciations, skills, and special abilities—are for most pupils actually precluded by the recitation procedure. The initiative, judgment, creativity, and personal development of the individual are stifled for the most part. The premium is upon rote memory and not upon developing power to cope with meaningful problems.
4. The teacher dominates. A number of scientific studies now available show the value of pupil participation.
5. The teacher is at best a hearer of lessons; at worst, a policeman or dispenser of punishment. To do better than this requires ingenuity, much hard work, and thorough insight into the processes of learning.
6. The impression made on pupils is undesirable. An attitude of antagonism, distrust, and suspicion is engendered. This is the direct opposite of the desired attitude and ability to do co-operative work.
7. The individualistic, competitive recitation is antagonistic to the democratic, co-operative philosophy of life and of education. The recitation situation is not lifelike.
8. The nervous tension created inevitably results in bad mental hygiene.
9. Individual differences among learners are often neglected, sometimes arbitrarily disregarded.
10. Time is wasted in large quantities.

The chart on pages 522 and 523 summarizes the characteristics of the assign-study-recite procedure in general terms and the contrasting emphases within units suitable for pupils of different levels of maturity and purpose.[5]

Factors involved in changing points of view. There are few reports available which show how the points of view of teachers changed in the course of an improvement program and the factors that brought about the change. It is very difficult to change attitudes along some lines. An excellent example of the extent to which points of view can be changed is the discussion of the outcomes of a year's study by the staff of the Norris School in Tennessee of ways in which to evaluate more effectively the school's entire program.[6] The purpose of the study was to clarify the objectives of the whole school and to assist teachers to develop instruments and procedures for determining how well the objectives were being achieved.

[4] *Op. cit.,* pp. 375-76.
[5] *Ibid.,* pp. 402-403.
[6] Maurice E. Troyer and C. Robert Pace, *Evaluation in Teacher Education* (Washington, American Council on Education, 1944), pp. 280-281.
See also Ch. 16 for another aspect of the problem of changing one's viewpoint; the reduction of forces operating to retard change.

The activities of the study under the guidance of a steering committee were of many different kinds, including staff meetings, discussions, conferences, committee work, construction of evaluative devices, their application in classrooms, case studies, workshops, study groups, reading books, observations, and informal undertakings of many kinds. The staff had the help of a full-time consultant who was a specialist in evaluation.

The report of the study indicates that at the beginning of the study the points of view of the staff toward evaluation were as follows:

Analysis of appraisal procedures used by teachers at the beginning of the study and ideas expressed in the early meetings of the committees on objectives showed that teachers believed that certain types of specified behavior should be achieved by all pupils, that such behavior should be appraised with test instruments that could be easily administered to large groups of pupils, that progress of pupils should be judged on the basis of standard behavior (test norms), and that evidence of progress toward all of the schoolwide goals should be collected for each pupil.

As a result of the year's study, there was a marked change in the points of view of most members of the staff. The report goes on to comment as follows on the factors that were believed to have contributed to the modification of these views:

The teachers concluded that their earlier approach to evaluation was impracticable. Whereas, at the rate they were going, it would be at the earliest the following winter or spring before measuring instruments of any significant degree of validity or reliablity could be completed for use, they desired to secure evidence of changed pupil behavior during the fall months. Many of them concluded that the most practical way of doing this was to observe boys' and girls' actions in the classroom, in the halls, on the playground. This approach, the teachers agreed, could be used with varying degrees of intelligence and validity by most teachers, and it would not require additional time on their part in their already crowded school day.

A second relevant factor in the transition involved the teachers' experience in trying to define their objectives. As the teachers got well into this job, they found themselves confronted with doing something which contradicted previously held values. In specifying behavior which was to exemplify attainment of a school objective, they were, in effect, saying that it was a good thing for all boys and girls in the school to acquire these specific behavior characteristics. Several teachers had to reject this procedure because they believed that to try to have all pupils exhibit *certain specific* behavior characteristics ignored individual configurations of behavior and individual needs, and assumed that a certain kind of behavior was an end in itself, irrespective of its significance in the life of an individual child.

Another factor that influenced the decision of several teachers to lessen emphasis on pencil and paper and other indirect means of measurement was their intense interest in pupils as individuals. Rarely did such teachers discuss "what my class is doing" or "what my pupils need." Their references were to individual cases. This interest seemed to make the teachers more sensitive to the individuality of pupils and the necessity to deal with individual drives and motivations.

A fourth factor was the growing belief of some teachers that evaluation should be as much a pupil concern as it was a teacher concern. In a classroom where evaluation deals primarily with teacher concerns the problem (of evaluation) is simple: the teacher wants to know how her pupils are getting along with respect to some objective, and she wants to know now. The problem is solved by giving the class a test. Some teachers began to ask such questions as: What is happening to the pupils? Do they consider the behavior measured by the test important in their lives? Are they anxious to take the test and to study the results in relation to their life goals and drives? (Not to be determined simply by asking all those who want to take a test to raise their hands.) What would happen if taking the test was to be made optional? To what extent are *their* criteria of achievement compatible with those of the teacher? (Not that incompatibility is to be considered undesirable. When it exists, however, it has implications concerning *how* the teacher secures evaluative evidence.)

The teachers who began to ask such questions as these have been trying to insure a maximum of pupil participation in evaluation. When the classes of these teachers have a discussion

COMPARISON OF FORMAL ASSIGNMENT PROCEDURE AND UNITS ON TWO LEVELS

Assignments as typically used. (The extreme type of formal assignment is the basis here. Many assignments are far superior to those indicated here, but the formal type is still dominant. Improved assignments will be characterized by closer approach to the characteristics of units.)	Units for little children and beginners, and for all levels within the area of general education; units which are dominated by the immediate purpose of the learner.	Units for more mature students and within areas of specialization; units which are dominated by more remote personal purposes and by social goals.
1. Begin in the intention of adults to teach approved subject matter to students.	Begin in the intention of the learner to achieve some immediate purpose; to satisfy some felt need.	Begin in intention of learner to achieve more remote personal and social purposes, the values of which he sees now. Can begin with acceptance of purpose from teacher. Learner accepts aid in either case from teacher in clarifying and stating purpose.
2. Are for the purpose of having students "cover" the material and acquire the logically arranged material as the learning outcome. (Good assignments increasingly aim to derive useful learnings from the subject matter.)	Are for the *immediate* purpose of satisfying a need of the learner, with the *ultimate* purpose of developing desirable meanings and facts, attitudes, skills, and patterns of thought.	For the purpose of deriving systematic knowledge in the form of principles or facts, attitudes, and patterns of thought, not as ends but as aids in the satisfaction of more remote goals.
3. Are organized logically around a core within the subject matter. (It must be noted that many assignments and the subject matter used have no organization of any sort.)	Are organized psychologically around the purpose of the learner.	Increasingly organized around systematic materials with more attention to developing patterns of thought, but always with due regard for the purposes of the learners. (Again the materials and patterns are not isolated nor ends in themselves.)
4. Are prepared in advance, by the teacher, or by a course of study committee familiar with the materials and their logic. (Good assignments are increasingly using pupil participation.)	Are organized as they develop by a group facing a new situation for the first time, and not familiar with the materials and patterns of thought necessary to meet the situation.	Can be preplanned to considerable degree by teacher and accepted by pupil, but always with pupil goals in mind and with as much pupil participation as the given situation permits.
5. Are usually organized (when organized at all) logically in terms of the materials, usually from simple to complex, often chronologically.	Are usually organized functionally and in disregard of subject lines; from simple to complex but often from complex to simple.	Are organized far more in terms of the systems within materials and patterns of thought, but always with regard to maturing student purposes.
6. Are controlled by the teacher, by adult committee, by course of study.	Are controlled by a co-operating group of learners which includes the teacher as an active participant; uses course of study as needed.	Controlled by the social purposes of the school and by systems of thought within the subject matter, but always with regard to pupil purpose and with pupil participation as warranted.
7. Are usually centered in the past, in the "accumulated, not the accumulating" culture; little reference to present or future; reference to future usually theoretical.	Are usually centered in present and future; use accumulated materials from past freely in solving present problems.	Usually concerned with future needs which are, however, recognized now by learner, and with social needs; uses current materials and accumulated materials (subject matter), the future value of which is sensible to the learner now.

Assignments as typically used. (The extreme type of formal assignment is the basis here. Many assignments are far superior to those indicated here, but the formal type is still dominant. Improved assignments will be characterized by closer approach to the characteristics of units.)	*Units for little children and beginners, and for all levels within the area of general education; units which are dominated by the immediate purpose of the learner.*	*Units for more mature students and within areas of specialization; units which are dominated by more remote personal purposes and by social goals.*
8. Rely on formal methods, assignments, distinct lesson types, and printed materials as chief sources; learning experiences few and formal.	Utilize co-operatively planned procedures suited to the situation, uses sources in great variety; learning experiences numerous and varied.	Utilizes and increases facility in the use of meanings and patterns of thought which were derived earlier in the co-operative experiences; printed materials and more sophisticated patterns of thought prominent, supplemented by many references and aids.
9. Give all pupils the same contact with the same materials; some provision for individual differences.	Gives contact with many materials and patterns of thought; individual differences cared for variously and almost automatically.	Gives contact with many materials and patterns of thought, but with more conscious attention to their intrinsic value; individual differences cared for systematically.
10. Have fixed outcomes known in advance, required uniformly for all learners.	Do not have fixed outcomes known in advance and required uniformly of all learners.	Same in all units.
11. At conclusion, evaluate through the use of formal tests of subject-matter acquisition, usually of fact or skill.	Evaluate many complex outcomes continuously, with constant use of many instruments, formal and informal.	Same in all units.
12. Close with a backward look, so-called "review," and are done with when finished.	Leads to new interests, problems, and purposes.	Same in all units.

to appraise some project, or decide to write up something as a class paper, or respond to a questionnaire, or take a test, the decision usually is one which most members of the class have arrived at themselves without pressure from the teacher.

The next factor was the desire of teachers to know what aspects of the child's experience account for his changes in behavior. Some teachers were not concerned with changes apart from those elements in the environment that account for them.

They considered knowledge of the processes through which an insecure child develops greater security to be as important as the fact that a change in the child's security status did occur. Many testing instruments (interest indices, etc.) would reveal only likes or dislikes and would not relate them to classroom procedures which produced them.

A sixth factor which helps to account for the shift from indirect to direct methods of getting evaluative evidence is that some of the teachers

indicated a growing dislike for picturing the growth of pupils in terms of statistical numbers and percentages. Such a procedure "loses the flavor," as one teacher stated, which comes from studying boys and girls in flesh and blood as they participate in school activities.

An overview of this program reveals some significant points that should be borne in mind in planning any improvement program in which the problem of modifying attitudes, points of view, and beliefs of members of the group may arise:

1. The study covered a period of a whole school year. It was not a short-time undertaking. It takes time to change ways of thinking. People do not all learn at the same rate.

2. The enterprise grew out of problems that were real and vital to the participants as professional workers. There was genuine interest in the enterprise. There was a desire on the

part of the participants to study their present practices with a view to their improvement.

3. The planning was continuous and highly flexible. It was developed co-operatively. Plans were modified from time to time as the judgment of the entire group or of the steering committee believed advisable.

4. The services of a consulting specialist were available to assist the steering committee and teachers in carrying out the technical aspects of the enterprise.

5. A wide variety of activities was carried on in the course of the study, including group and individual participation in study, listening, and observing activities and also direct concrete experience in constructing and applying evaluative procedures. Because a given experience affects different people in different ways, it is highly desirable to provide a wide variety of experiences designed to affect individuals who differ widely in their reactions from one situation to another. It is probably impossible to predict how a particular individual or a given group will react to a particular stimulus in a particular situation. People learn in different ways.

6. The "give-and-take" of group discussion by interested and informed individuals is a potent factor in the modification of points of view.

7. As ideas become clarified and their implications become meaningful, changes in present practices are likely to take place.

The reader should add to the above other notions that may occur to him about changing the attitudes and points of view of individuals and groups.

Factors that make it difficult to change attitudes. Some of the factors that make it difficult to change educational practices are the mores of the community, tradition, prejudices, and the attitudes of influential but conservative and reactionary individuals and agencies in the school and community, including the members of the staff of the school. Fear, insecurity, low morale, lack of insight, inferior educational leadership, and sheer unwillingness to try new procedures are some of the important factors that cause teachers to resist change. The reader should extend this list by reviewing his own attitudes and experiences.

A summary of statements [7] about difficulties encountered in preparing elementary school teachers to adopt and utilize practices in line with sixteen modern curriculum trends illustrates the difficulties that could be encountered with experienced teachers in service:

Rigidity and crystallization of practice; indifference and inertia of public schools in which student teaching must be done. Students cannot practice what they have been taught. Cannot secure enough competent supervising teachers.

Academic colleagues have traditional concept of education and resist curriculum changes.

Students have become so accustomed to traditional practices in their own school experiences that it is difficult to change them.

Teaching loads too heavy, classes too large in public schools.

Students fear newer practices will be disapproved.

Training period too short. Two-year curriculum.

No selection, or inadequate selection of candidates for teaching.

Supervising teachers have little training for guiding student teachers.

Lack of adequate materials in public schools.

Too few opportunities to observe better practices in public schools.

Lack of co-operation between personnel in professional courses and in laboratory experiences.

Insufficient supervision available for student teachers.

Restrictive influence of achievement testing, programs which measure textbook coverage rather than child growth. [8]

The staff of a school system should analyze the local situation to discover the extent to which the above elements and additional items may make it difficult for teachers to adopt newer methods, and then consider steps that may be taken to remove or remedy the restrictive conditions.

[7] *Curriculum Trends and Teacher Education*, Thirty-second Yearbook, Association for Student Teaching (Ann Arbor, Mich., Edwards Bros., 1953).

[8] *Ibid.*, pp. 36-37.

THE MOST SERIOUS OBSTACLES ENCOUNTERED IN PROGRAMS OF IN-SERVICE EDUCATION

Obstacle	Number of Schools Listing the Obstacle as a Very Serious One	Per Cent of Schools
Lack of time, heavy teaching loads, heavy extracurricular loads, no suitable time of day	112	45.5
Unprofessional attitudes of teachers	99	40.2
Lack of money for providing professional books and magazines and suitable library facilities for staff	34	13.8
Lack of planning	21	8.5
Conflicts in personality between teachers and between teachers and administrators	14	5.7
Weariness of teachers, teacher ill-health	12	4.9
General unrest in the school and community	11	4.5
Authoritarian administration	10	4.1
Teacher turnover	9	3.7
Lack of supervision	8	3.2
Life certificates	8	3.2
Petty arguments	7	2.8
Reading of bulletins by the principal	6	2.4

ANALYSIS OF THE OBSTACLE "UNPROFESSIONAL ATTITUDES OF TEACHERS"

Types of "Poor Teacher Attitudes"	Number of Schools Listing This to Be Very Serious Obstacle	Per Cent of Schools Listing "Poor Attitude"
Older teachers who have little interest in any kind of in-service education	25	25.2
Indifference, inertia, complacency of teachers	22	22.2
Vested interests of departments	11	11.1
Lazy teachers who shun work	9	9.1
Degree-itis, teachers think Master's degree makes study unnecessary	8	8.1
Opposition to change of any kind	7	7.1
Teachers "pass the buck" to administrators	6	6.1
Tenure makes teachers indifferent	5	5.1
Suspiciousness	4	4.1

Obstacles to improvement programs. Weber [9] has compiled a list of the most serious obstacles occurring in programs of in-service education. The list is given above together with an analysis of one obstacle, unprofessional attitudes of teachers. The list is self-explanatory.

Adequate background necessary for good judgment in determining needs. In the co-operative frame of reference here

[9] C. A. Weber, "Obstacles to Be Overcome in a Program of Educating Teachers in Service." *Educational Administration and Supervision* (December, 1942).

envisaged, pupils, teachers, and supervisors are all making judgments about what to do. Presumably, teachers have more skill and insight than do pupils—supervisors, more skill and insight than do teachers; but as we all know, this is not always the case. Besides the teachers, pupils, and supervisors, there are others not so intimately associated with the situation as they who will be making judgments too, as, for example, parents, board members, and other adult members of the community. The latter, however, are ordinarily not too much concerned with the more technical aspects of professional education. In any case, the judgments made by these various persons are not always good, and the question here is how can these judgments be improved. There are many things that one might do. First of all, those who reach judgments about what to do in specific situations might be helped by understanding the framework within which judgments are made. What one does in a particular learning and teaching situation will depend partly upon one's purpose; partly upon the persons involved (teachers, pupils, parents, supervisors, and so forth), and their understanding, skills, capacities, and attitudes; partly upon one's system of values, standards of achievement, and other generalizations that one holds to be true; and finally upon one's ability to perceive and infer the implications of unique features of the immediate situation.

Secondly, we believe that judgments about what to do should improve with experience, particularly when the results of each decision are carefully noted and there is a deep desire to improve. One may learn by doing if one is willing to modify means, methods, and materials to get better results.

Finally, we believe that judgments about what to do in specific situations may be improved by providing appropriate background training. Making good judgments presumes certain fundamental abilities, knowledges, skills, attitudes, and ideals. To promote the making of sound judgments, then, one will need to make certain that there is understanding of the framework within which judgments are made, that there is provision for practice in making judgments under supervision, and provision for background training in basic abilities. We are here emphasizing the basic importance of these behind-the-scene determiners of human behavior.

There are very many behind-the-scene determiners of human action with which teachers and supervisors will have to concern themselves. Some will be summed up in the qualities of the person, such as considerateness, honesty, and objectivity; and others will be summed up in the knowledges, skills, attitudes, interests, and ideals which constitute the prerequisites to good teaching. Some will be native and not acquired. Some will be given in teacher-training institutions; and some, acquired on the job in developmental programs such as those here under discussion. One of the real problems of professional education is that of getting relevant background essential to good teaching, or that of handling this background in such a manner that its relevancy will be seen by the individuals concerned. There must be background, but the background must be pertinent and applicable.

PLANNING IMPROVEMENT PROGRAMS

The steps in an improvement program. The sequence of steps in a program for improving the general level of instruction in a school or school system has been indicated in preceding chapters. They may be outlined as follows:

1. Formulate co-operatively the objectives in the area involved.

2. Use suitable evaluative procedures to determine the strengths and weaknesses of the educational product.

3. If, in the judgment of the group, the diagnostic procedures used to identify causes that were discussed in Chapter 10 indicate that on the whole ineffective instruction seems to be a decisive contributory factor, steps should be taken to develop co-operatively plans for improving the methods used by teachers. The program for the staff as a whole should be so designed that probable causes are attacked directly. The program should be flexible and adapted to the needs of groups of teachers. It should provide for a wide variety of experiences thus recognizing differences in the needs of the various teachers and of other members of the staff. Similar procedures would be used in improving the curriculum, the selection and use of instructional materials, and aspects of life in the community.

4. The effects of this generalized approach to the improvement of teaching can be measured after a time by the extent and quality of the modifications of instructional practices that are used by teachers in the classroom and elsewhere.

The sequence of steps outlined above as the general approach for improving the instructional practices of large groups of teachers must be modified when helping a particular teacher who is encountering unusual or serious difficulties. In this case, the approach to the improvement program must be more analytical and special kinds of experiences must be planned that are adapted to the particular needs of the individual teacher. It may even be necessary to secure the assistance of specialists of various kinds, if they are available, in determining the nature and causes of the unsatisfactory situation and the steps to be taken that are most likely to bring about an improvement. The sequence of steps in dealing with the problems and needs of an individual teacher may be outlined as follows:

Steps 1 and 2—same as those given above.
3. Use diagnostic procedures such as those described in Chapter 10 to determine the degree to which instruction is contributing to unfavorable growth of children. Self-evaluation by the teacher should be encouraged at this point.

4. Review past experience and experimental studies quickly for possible factors that may be operative in the present situation, including those present in the teacher as a person and those present in the instructional procedures. For the present we may assume that the curriculum, instructional materials, school plant, and community are not the immediate causes of the teacher's problems.

5. Examine the situation with the teacher to determine which of these factors are most likely involved in the present difficulty.

6. Set up a hypothesis indicating which factor or factors are most likely to be the source of the problem. Usually a complexity of factors is involved.

7. Check this hypothesis if possible by securing in co-operation with the teacher any available information that will verify it; or alter conditions related to the factor or factors identified, and observe the effects of these changes. The changes may involve altering the characteristics of the teacher as a person, trying new instructional procedures, and/or changing the social and material environment. Of course, in many instances curriculum and materials of instruction also will often be involved, but at this point we are concerned with remedying instructional problems. The procedures for bringing about necessary modifications in teaching and in the teacher are discussed in the following sections.

8. Continue the procedure in Step 7 until the problem is solved.

An analysis of teaching problems. The basis for the improvement of teaching should be a clear analysis of what a teacher's problems or the problems of groups of teachers actually are. If the problems can be formulated by the teachers themselves, a big step forward has been taken in dealing with them. A list of teachers' problems [10] such as that in the table on page 528 should be of value to all supervisors, since it represents an analysis of 2227 teaching problems reported by 1075 public school teachers of Colorado for all levels of the school. The list reveals the areas into which fall the teaching problems that were sensed by the Colorado teachers. In the original report

[10] Robert A. Davis, "The Teaching Problems of 1075 Public School Teachers," *Journal of Experimental Education* (September, 1940), pp. 41-60.

FREQUENCY OF TEACHING PROBLEMS REPORTED

TYPE OF PROBLEM	EDUCATIONAL LEVEL				
	Elementary school Per cent of total	Junior high school Per cent of total	Senior high school Per cent of total	All levels combined Frequency	All levels combined Per cent of total
Motivation	17.2	30.9	32.6	565	25.4
Testing and evaluating	16.1	14.5	16.9	359	16.1
Diagnosing and correcting difficulties	17.0	7.3	8.4	267	12.0
Modes of presentation	10.9	12.4	10.0	242	10.9
Individual differences	15.3	6.6	6.1	230	10.3
How to study	2.7	5.6	4.2	85	3.8
Transfer of training	2.4	3.7	4.6	77	3.5
Relationships with administration	3.6	2.6	3.2	73	3.3
Lack of materials and equipment	2.5	2.1	3.7	64	2.9
Curricular and extracurricular activities	3.2	2.3	1.8	56	2.5
Thoroughness and mastery	3.3	2.1	1.5	54	2.4
Discipline	1.0	4.9	2.7	53	2.4
Pupil participation in class	1.3	2.8	2.3	43	1.9
Guidance	0.8	1.2	1.5	25	1.1
Racial differences	2.0	0.7	0.0	23	1.0
Parent-teacher relationships	0.6	0.2	0.5	11	0.5
TOTALS	997	427	803	2227	

by Davis, each problem is defined by a series of illustrative sub-items which the reader should consult for details. Similar analyses of the problems of local teachers can be made by the supervisory staff of any school system.

At all levels, problems of motivation were those most frequently reported. Problems in motivation, according to the report, include the need of different methods of motivation for different pupils, the "get by" attitude of many, lack of interest in ideals, irresponsibility, and similar problems. Problems in testing and evaluation, and in diagnosing and correcting difficulties, bulked up large at all levels. Problems related to individual differences were more numerous for elementary teachers than for those at other levels. Problems in modes of presentation of content were of major importance in all schools, especially in high schools. Under these five headings there are included almost three-fourths (74.7 per cent) of all problems listed. The other kinds of problems

were not mentioned frequently, but they may have been of great significance in the situations in which they arose.

Problems in motivation, modes of presentation and individual differences are closely associated with both curriculum and instruction. In the present chapter we are primarily concerned with problems related to the latter, instruction.

Illustration of co-operative attack on a problem. A constructive procedure for helping teachers to identify and clarify instructional problems is illustrated by a plan used by an instructional consultant in assisting a group of teachers and their principal who felt that arithmetic operations were not being made meaningful to the pupils. They felt the need of expert assistance on the problem. The issue was discussed with the consultant and arrangements were made for a series of observations of classroom instruction which would enable him to evaluate instructional procedures and materials of learning. It should be said that the consultant was an expert in the diagnostic analysis of instruction. Subsequently he discussed with the staff what he had observed and pointed out certain inadequacies in both teaching and materials. Then, through discussion and study under the leadership of the consultant, a group of underlying principles was developed; methods of applying them were demonstrated; necessary materials were secured; and direct assistance on classroom procedures was given to individual teachers when the need arose. This approach to the problem obviously was constructive and helpful; it illustrates a plan that can be adapted to the study of any instructional problem.

Personal problems faced by teachers. Teachers face many problems of a personal nature which interfere with their efficiency. Symonds,[11] for example, made an analysis of problems of 98 teachers enrolled in a course in mental hygiene. The problems were discussed in confidential compositions to be read by the instructor alone, and undoubtedly represented the free responses of the teachers. Symonds reports that to his "surprise, personal problems quite overshadowed all others." In his article he lists 47 kinds of problems which were discussed by one or more of the teachers. The 14 kinds of problems given by ten or more teachers were the following:

1. Family relationships 48
2. Love life 37
3. Feelings of inadequacy and inferiority 36
4. Health 26
5. Difficulties with teaching 23
6. Financial problems 22
7. Difficulties in making social contacts . 21
8. Difficulties with superior officers.... 18
9. Problems related to position 12
10. Aggressive tendencies 12
11. Difficulty with colleagues 11
12. Deaths 11
13. Miscellaneous personal problems.... 11
14. Problems related to graduate and summer study 10

Problems of a professional nature, such as types 5, 8, 9, 11, and 14, represented a small fraction of the total number listed. Personal problems were much more frequently discussed. Many of them are typical problems encountered by any normal individual, whereas others are closely related to mental health, especially types 3, 7, 10, and 11. Problems growing out of difficulties with superiors were mentioned by about one-fifth of the group, a point worth noting for supervisors and principals.

The solution of most personal problems such as are listed above probably depends on the whole on private arrangements; problems of a strictly professional nature may be alleviated by the help of educational specialists of various kinds; problems in mental hygiene when severe must undoubtedly be dealt with by medical and psychiatric services of the community, both public and private. Many school systems provide special counseling services to assist teachers in dealing with their problems in human relations.

The reader who is interested in mental-health problems of teachers will find many articles dealing with this topic in current literature. The references given below are typical and their contents illustrate varied approaches to the problem.

ALILUNAS, Leo J., "Needed Research in Teacher Mental Hygiene," *Journal of Educational Research* (May, 1945), pp. 653-665. Extensive bibliography.

DOWNIE, N. M., and BELL, C. R., "The Minnesota Teacher Attitude Inventory as an Aid in the Selection of Teachers," *Journal of Educational Research* (1953), pp. 699-704.

Encyclopedia of Educational Research, 1950 Edition (New York, Macmillan, 1950). See article on Mental Hygiene, pp. 732-744.

MASON, Frances, "A Survey of 700 Maladjusted School Teachers," *Mental Hygiene* (July, 1931), pp. 576-599.

RANKIN, P. T., and DORSEY, J. M., "The Detroit School Mental Health Project," *Mental Hygiene* (April, 1953), pp. 228-248.

Review of Educational Research, Special issues on Teacher Personnel: June, 1940; June,

[11] P. M. Symonds, "Problems Faced by Teachers," *Journal of Educational Research* (September, 1941), pp. 1-15.

1943; June, 1946; June, 1949; June, 1952. Reviews of research; extensive bibliography.

SYMONDS, P. M., and HAGGERTY, H. R., "The Therapeutic Value for Teachers of the Course in Mental Hygiene," *Journal of Educational Psychology* (November, 1942), pp. 561-583.

————, "Suggestions for the Adjustment of Teachers," *Teachers College Record* (March, 1943), pp. 417-432.

————, "Needs of Teachers as Shown in Autobiographies," *Journal of Educational Research* (May, 1943), pp. 662-677.

————, "How Teachers Solve Personal Problems," *Journal of Educational Research* (May, 1945), pp. 641-652.

WICKMANN, E. K., *Children's Behavior and Teachers' Attitudes* (New York, Commonwealth Fund, 1928).

The mental hygiene of the teacher. We cannot in this volume present an extended treatment of the mental hygiene of the teacher, which belongs elsewhere. A brief note does seem necessary, since it is obvious that many unfortunate influences on children and learning flow from frustrated, maladjusted teacher personalities. Maladjusted teachers clearly produce maladjustment in children.

A number of studies [12] of teachers attending summer schools showed them to be a little less well adjusted than other women students. Studies of teachers in service revealed serious maladjustment in many cases. The study [13] of New York City teachers made some years ago showed, in the opinion of the examiner, that 1500 of the 37,000 teachers were mental cases, some of them severe. Psychiatric examination would have benefited about 4500 more. The examiner in this case, however, believed the percentage of psychotics among teachers to be no higher than in the general population. Even then, approximately 40,000 children would be exposed to a psychotic teacher each year. The same study cited the figures from a New Jersey investigation showing that a child had a 7 to 1 chance to have at least two emotionally maladjusted teachers somewhere during elementary and secondary schools.

These studies, and those [14] made in fields other than teaching, all stress the necessity for normal, balanced living, for attention to health, and particularly for recreation. One study [15] showed that former teachers confined in an institution for mental cases had none of them ever had a hobby or avocational interest. Fair and honest administration and supervision, alleviation of too heavy loads, pensions, congenial associates, and community approval all make for emotional normality.

Personality traits of teachers. In the analysis of teaching problems given above there is no direct reference to personality traits of teachers. Many efforts have been made to list desirable traits of teachers. The listings vary somewhat in length and content, but are so general that it seems as though they list the kinds of characteristics that one would wish any friend to possess whether a teacher or not.

An interesting and revealing approach to the study of teacher personality traits has been reported by Witty. He secured letters

[12] Leigh Peck, "A Study of the Adjustment Difficulties of a Group of Women Teachers," *Journal of Educational Psychology* (September, 1936), pp. 401-416.

[13] Leo J. Alilunas, "Needed Research in Teacher Mental Hygiene," *Journal of Educational Research* (May, 1945), pp. 653-665.

[14] Dorothy Baruch, "Let the Teachers Have Their Vices," *Educational Method* (February, 1942), pp. 230-235.

John A. Bronson, "Problem Teachers," *Educational Administration and Supervision* (March, 1943), pp. 177-182.

Fit to Teach, Ninth Yearbook, Department of Classroom Teachers (Washington, National Education Association, 1938).

Paul C. Palmantier, "Why Teachers Go Crazy," *Journal of Education* (December, 1947), pp. 290-291.

J. B. Stroud, "The School Administrator and Problems of Teacher Adjustment," *Elementary School Journal* (April, 1945), pp. 451-454.

[15] Frances Mason, "A Study of 700 Maladjusted School Teachers," *Mental Hygiene* (July, 1931), pp. 576 ff.

Many others are available.

from about 14,000 pupils in grades 2 to 12, as part of a "Quiz Kid" program, in which they were asked to describe the characteristics of "the teacher who has helped me most." The list below contains the twelve "positive" traits mentioned most frequently in the letters:

1. Co-operative, democratic attitude.
2. Kindliness and consideration for the individual.
3. Patience.
4. Wide variety of interests.
5. Personal appearance and pleasing manner.
6. Fairness and impartiality.
7. Sense of humor.
8. Good disposition and consistent behavior.
9. Interest in pupils' problems.
10. Flexibility in ways of teaching.
11. Use of recognition and praise.
12. Unusual proficiency in teaching a particular subject.

The emphasis on aspects of mental hygiene is the outstanding feature of the list. Boys and girls are grateful to the school and its staff in proportion to the degree to which it offers security, individual success, shared experience, and opportunities for personal and social adjustments; all factors that promote good learning.

Witty [16] also listed the twelve most frequently mentioned "negative traits," as follows:

1. Bad-tempered and intolerant.
2. Unfair and inclined to have favorites.
3. Disinclined to help pupils.
4. Unreasonable in demands.
5. Tendency to be gloomy and unfriendly.
6. Sarcastic and inclined to use ridicule.
7. Unattractive appearance.
8. Impatient and inflexible.
9. Tendency to talk excessively.
10. Inclined to talk down to pupils.
11. Overbearing and conceited.
12. Lacking sense of humor.

The possible improvement of such unfavorable personality traits as these is discussed in Section 5. They clearly reflect poor mental hygiene. In teacher-education institutions, the kinds of personality traits that are generally regarded as desirable should be defined and brought to the attention of the students and efforts made to develop them. At the same time, steps should be taken to change traits that are not acceptable to pupils and associates in social and professional groups.

Section 4

GENERAL MEASURES FOR IMPROVING TEACHING

Developmental measures for improving teaching. As far as the authors know, there have as yet been few systematic analyses of specific steps actually taken by school systems and individual supervisors to bring about a change for the better in the work of individual teachers. Nor has the actual effectiveness of specific means for improving particular instructional weaknesses been established by experimental method, a method that would be exceedingly difficult to apply in the complex situation in which learning takes place. However, the fact that instructional problems exist is universally recognized. Supervisors and teachers everywhere face the problem of discovering instructional needs, determining their causes, and deciding on ways of improving the situation.

It seems quite clear that steps leading to the improvement of instructional practices must be along at least three general lines:

1. The strengthening of educational leadership.
2. The improvement of factors inherent in the teacher as a person.
3. The improvement of instructional competencies.

[16] P. A. Witty, "Evaluation of Studies of the Characteristics of the Effective Teacher," in *Improving Educational Research*. Official Report of American Educational Research Association, 1948, pp. 198-204.

1. The strengthening of educational leadership. The basic principles underlying democratic leadership are discussed in Chapters 5 and 7. Where there is effective educational leadership, such conditions as the following prevail which make good instruction possible.

a. There is a formulated educational philosophy, accepted by school and community, which serves as a guide for all members of the staff.
b. Systematic efforts are made co-operatively by all concerned to evaluate all aspects of the educational program, including especially pupil growth and achievement, so that school and community have dependable information on the basis of which to plan a more effective educational program.
c. There is a planned, continuing study and evaluation of the curriculum so that its content and organization are adapted to children's needs and to the needs of the larger community.
d. There are available competent consultants and instructional specialists who assist the staffs of particular schools to provide a flexible program of effective learning experiences for the pupils and to help teachers to solve instructional problems.
e. A rich variety of learning materials is available so that the classroom can function as a learning laboratory, and the educational facilities are such as to make possible a well-rounded program of learning experiences.
f. School-community relations are cordial and intelligent, and the community accepts its obligations to maintain an up-to-date modern educational program.
g. Steps are taken from time to time by the administration in co-operation with the staff to maintain conditions which promote a high level of morale among the members of the staff.

In connection with the above comments, the reader should review the discussion in Section 1 in Chapter 11 of factors that affect the choice of methods of teaching. All of the items listed above have been quite fully discussed in preceding chapters, except con-

ditions that affect teacher morale. We shall explore this item in some detail shortly.

Provisions that are likely to increase the effectiveness of in-service educational programs are the following: [17]

1. Special provisions of the salary schedule.
2. Sabbatical leave allowances.
3. Expense allowances for educational travel.
4. Allowances for visiting schools.
5. Funds for substitute service to relieve teachers for conferences, visiting, special assignments, etc.
6. In-service institutes and allowance of time for attendance and funds for consulting service.
7. Bonuses for advanced professional study.
8. Subsidizing of services provided by teachers' colleges for departments of education in faculty advisory service.
9. Compensation for preschool and postschool conferences by the faculty.
10. Summer workshop costs, both those arranged locally and those in which teams of teachers work as a unit in university summer schools.
11. Expense allowances for attendance at state and national educational conferences.
12. Funds for publication of bulletins, study guides, outlines, and curriculum brochures used in the improvement of instruction.
13. Provision of time for special in-service activities.
14. Provision for comprehensive professional library service, including curriculum laboratory, current periodicals, collections of past educational references, and assistance in gathering data from other sources on special problems.

2. The improvement of factors inherent in the teacher as a person. In Chapter 11 a wide variety of methods of studying aspects of the teacher as a person were discussed, including the personality of the teacher and professional competency. The causes of poor teaching may be found in such aspects

[17] Clyde M. Campbell, ed., *Practical Applications of Democratic Administration* (New York, Harper, 1952).

of the teacher's total personality as the following, although the establishment of the exact cause in a given situation might be difficult because of other contributory factors in the environment which will be discussed shortly:

a. The teacher's health, physical development, strength, and handicaps.
b. The teacher's level of intelligence and scholarship.
c. The teacher's emotional and social adjustment.
d. The teacher's cultural background, interests, and appreciations.
e. The teacher's social relationships in school and community.
f. The teacher's attitudes toward children, social institutions, and education as a career.
g. Morale.
h. Personality traits.

The teacher-training institution bears a heavy responsibility in the selection of its students and their certification for teaching positions.

The selection process should be so carefully conducted that individuals with serious physical, mental, scholastic, emotional, and social handicaps will be identified at an early stage in their training, so that steps can be taken to protect children and society from serious unfortunate consequences that might result if they became teachers. In many institutions, when limitations of cultural background, interests, and appreciations are discovered, the educational program for the individual is adjusted accordingly. The teacher-training institution must also scrutinize the social relationships, attitudes, morals, and personality traits of its students, so that here also steps can be taken to bring about desirable changes, in so far as this seems feasible, desirable, and practical. The important point is that prior to graduation and certification much can be done by teacher-training institutions to reduce the number of unqualified persons who enter the profession and subsequently present serious problems for those in super-

visory positions. It of course is true that many personality difficulties and instructional problems arise in the actual school situation that did not appear in the training institution. This suggests the desirability of a careful follow-up program of graduates by teacher-training institutions to discover the needs and problems. In the light of these findings, the institution can study its program and make adjustments that may meet the needs. In any case, a school system cannot expect that all of its new and inexperienced teachers will come to it as finished products who will have all of the knowledge, skills, attitudes, and personality traits that good teachers have.

There is a considerable literature on the improvement of personality traits which we shall also examine briefly. This problem should be of concern to all members of the supervisory staff, particularly principals and counselors with whom teachers come into close daily contact. Their guidance is essential in the improvement of personality traits.

The Detroit School mental-health project. A report by Rankin and Dorsey [18] describes in detail the nature of a five-year mental-health project in Detroit. Problems in mental health in this rapidly growing industrial center with its complex social and economic environments led to the appointment of a committee on mental health which, in cooperation with Wayne University and the University of Michigan, developed the mental-health project discussed in the reference below.

The nature of the activities carried on in the project was varied and in some cases quite novel. The program was subsidized by funds from private sources. The main activities are listed below in summary form:

1. A basic course in mental hygiene for teachers in which 2856 persons enrolled during the five-year period. The course was for 16

[18] P. T. Rankin and J. M. Dorsey, "The Detroit School Mental Health Project," *Mental Hygiene* (April, 1953), pp. 228-248.

USUAL PRACTICES IN SELECTING TEACHERS

Practice	Number	Per Cent
Hold personal interviews with applicants	1609	100
Collect information and opinion from persons named as references	1402	87
Have applicants fill out a formal application blank	1382	86
Require applicants to submit transcripts of college preparation	1031	64
Require proof of legal certification for position sought	853	53
Verify experience records reported by applicants	789	49
Observe classroom work of applicant	624	39
Establish lists of eligible candidates	485	30
Require applicants to submit to a physical examination	460	28
Given by the school physician or other physician approved by board	118	7
Given by any licensed physician	319	20
Status of examiner not specified	23	1
Require applicants to take written examinations	51	3
a. Other practice: includes the following practices—require chest X-ray; require blood test; require birth certificate; have applicants write informal letter of application; careful examination of materials from placement bureaus; personal visit to placement bureau; visit home of applicant; require oral examinations; and check with persons *not* given as references.		
Number of cities reporting	1615	...

weeks with 2½ hour meetings consisting of ½ hour of viewing films and listening to radio transcriptions, a 1 hour lecture, and finally 1 hour devoted to group discussions of the lecture and related problems under specialists in child growth and human relations. A consultant in psychiatry was also available at intervals.

2. An advanced course in mental hygiene was also offered in which 558 persons enrolled.

3. There were 27 two-day institutes for special groups and for teachers who did not enroll in the regular courses, so as to contact as many individuals as possible.

4. Books, bulletins, and periodicals were made available in rich variety for study purposes.

5. A series of radio programs was offered at the time of regular teachers' meetings.

6. A special study was made of the implications of group dynamics of mental health, especially psychodrama and role-playing by members of courses.

7. Trips and excursions were made by groups to mental-health centers.

8. One-act mental-health plays were performed to demonstrate problems and ways of dealing with them.

9. In one school the psychiatrist visited classes during one afternoon a week usually on invitation of teachers and after school met with teachers interested and discussed what he had seen and the implications for teachers.

All in all, according to the report, the results of this well-conceived program were far reaching and valuable, and instruction has been modified in many ways. Helpful contributions also were made to the mental health of teachers.

Improvement of practices in selecting new teachers. Because of the numerous problems that often arise subsequent to the appointment of new teachers, school systems are trying to eliminate at the time of making a choice those candidates who, it appears, are likely not to succeed. The screening process involves such practices as listed in the table above, which are reported in February, 1952, for 1615 cities in the United States.[19]

It is obvious that a member of the staff apparently well qualified from all points of

[19] *Teaching Personnel Practices, 1950-51: Appointment and Termination of Service,* Research Bulletin 30, No. 1 (Washington, NEA, 1952).

view at the time of appointment may subsequently, for a wide variety of causes, have teaching or personal difficulties that require prompt attention if the situation is to be corrected.

The Detroit plan for evaluating candidates for teacher contracts illustrates the steps being taken by school systems to insure the appointment of persons who are well qualified from all points of view:

COMMITTEE EVALUATION OF CANDIDATES FOR TEACHER CONTRACT STATUS

Detroit Public Schools
January, 1952

Independent Evaluation. In recent years, group judgment through carefully chosen committees has become a basic feature of the selection process for Detroit Public School teachers. It is important that each committee member exercise independent judgment based on factual evidence. The degree to which this is done determines the success achieved in the selection of good teachers for Detroit Public Schools.

Procedure. Each candidate who appears before a committee has met all technical requirements as to degree, teaching certificate, and adequacy of training in his teaching field. Previous to the committee interview, each candidate has been screened by the Personnel Department, interviewed personally by the supervisor in his teaching field, and tested with a comprehensive battery of tests at the Psychological Clinic. In each case the committee is given a summary of the candidate's credentials —his scholastic preparation, experience, recommendations, achievement on the battery of tests, and other factual evidence gained through personal interviews reported separately by the supervisor and a psychologist at the Clinic.

Majority Vote. Following the committee interview with the candidate, each member casts a secret, signed, independent vote rating the candidate as a prospect for a contract position in the Detroit Public Schools. In general, to be approved for the eligibility list, a candidate must receive a majority vote of the committee of "average" or higher rating on the scale. A ballot marked "doubtful" or "undesirable" constitutes a negative vote in regard to a candidate. The names of recommended candidates are presented to the Superintendent for his review

and approval, including borderline cases with split votes, for placement upon the eligibility list or exclusion.

Basic Considerations. In conducting the committee interview, we recommend the following in the interest of objective evaluation and in personal consideration of each candidate as an individual:

1. Each candidate is to be treated with full respect for his personality, social point of view, employee affiliations, political affiliations, religious faith, race, and sex.
2. No committee member will raise questions or make remarks tantamount to a "sales talk" for or against a given candidate.
3. All questions will be pointed toward a better understanding of the candidate as an employee able to fill a teaching vacancy in his teaching field.
4. Any committee member is at liberty to direct questions to the candidate in the spirit of the foregoing statements.
5. Each committee member is expected to draw his own conclusions and cast his independent secret vote after the candidate has been interviewed and all credentials have been considered. Each vote is a final vote—not subject to change.

3. The improvement of instructional competencies. The California statement on teaching competence which appears in Chapter 11 affords an excellent basis for studying the work of teachers in service with a view to determining specific instructional incompetencies and difficulties. The wide variety of possible needs of teachers is revealed by the scope of the outline. In fact, the essentials of the professional program in institutions preparing teachers for all levels of the school are revealed by the California analysis, in so far as it is complete.

Since it obviously is not possible for any teacher-training institution to prepare its graduates to deal competently, intelligently, and skillfully with all of the technical aspects of the work of the teacher included in the analysis, it necessarily becomes the responsibility of those in charge of school systems to provide additional training when the need arises. This is the primary function of the members of the supervisory staff. The problem is especially pressing at the present time when so many new teachers are required because of the rising tide of school enrollments.

Many procedures are used to improve the general level of teaching in a school system. The actual merit of few of them has really been experimentally established. The particular purpose the supervisor has in mind and the number of persons involved will determine the choice of the improvement procedures to use in a particular situation. As has been indicated in the discussion of planning in Chapter 6, the possible procedures can be classified from various points of view: (*a*) the degree to which they provide for individual differences, as in individual and group techniques, (*b*) the degree of participation provided, whether active or passive, and (*c*) the individual's approach to learning, as (1) learning by doing, (2) observational learning, and (3) verbal learning.

In the classification of improvement procedures given in Chapter 6 the three bases are combined. In selecting an improvement device, the supervisor should bear in mind the size of the participating group, the approach to be taken to learning by the members of the group and the expected degree of participation by individuals.

A typical in-service education program. The supervisory staff of Long Beach, California, over a period of years has developed an in-service education program that is adapted to the needs of teachers new to the system, inexperienced teachers, and mature teachers no longer on a probation status.[20] The essential components of the program for 1948, which is one of the best the authors have found, were the following:

1. Preschool conferences at the beginning of the school year, primarily for new teachers.
2. Observations of prepared lessons, films, etc. and discussions.
3. Intervisitation.

4. Meetings to discuss problems, methods, materials, etc.
5. Conferences with faculty, groups, individuals.
6. Workshops of many different types.
7. Excursions.
8. Curriculum-development program.
9. Committees on general and special problems.
10. Extension classes for staff.
11. Summer school courses.
12. Institute sessions.
13. Participation in public relations.
14. Study groups.
15. Bulletins, courses of study, documentary aids.

The following extracts from the Long Beach statement illustrate the nature and purpose of the activities included under eight of the headings given in the list:

1. *Observations and discussions*

Scheduled throughout the year are group observations of commendable classroom work. These observations are always followed by an informal group discussion in which, under the guidance of an able leader, the basic practices observed are highlighted and the possibility of their application in other situations is considered. These guided observations of outstanding classroom work prove to be the most fruitful type of in-service education.

Teachers attending these observations are released from their classrooms for the necessary time by having a substitute teacher provided; by the principal or vice-principal's teaching for them; or by having some other teacher in the building take charge of two classes.

A problem of great importance in carrying forward this work is that of insuring a common understanding among those who are to assume major responsibility for the series of observations in a chosen field. To accomplish this, the practice has been established of preceding each series of grade observations with a pre-observation for the teachers and leaders who are to serve in the subsequent meetings of the series. They observe together and consider what teachers might well carry away from a similar type of work. By following this practice, not only

[20] Mimeographed statement prepared by elementary supervisors of Long Beach, September, 1948.
This discussion further illustrates the presentation in Sec. 1 of Ch. 6.

has the main purpose of unity in thinking been achieved, but the entire level of the subsequent observations has been raised.

Some of the most valuable outcomes of the observations and discussions are as follows:

a. Inspiration and incentive to new effort on the part of the strong teachers in the system.

b. Recognition of teachers who, though not strong in many fields, do have specialized abilities.

c. Solution of common problems and establishment of new standards toward which to strive.

d. Clarification of the thinking of supervisors, principals, vice-principals, and teachers regarding desirable classroom procedures and materials of instruction.

e. Extension of the understanding and use of curriculum publications which have been made available.

f. Co-ordination of the efforts of all who are concerned with developing a better educational program.

2. *Intervisitation*

Teachers needing help not available through the scheduled group observations are frequently sent individually or in a small group to see some associate who does that work well.

Superior teachers in the system are not overlooked. They are allowed time to visit one another or to see especially strong work in neighboring cities.

3. *Meetings*

Some discussion meetings apart from observations are held. Among the purposes of these are the following:

a. To increase the efficiency of teachers of special reading groups.

b. To consider various aspects of the primary reading program, such as:
(1) Quiet-time activities for junior first, first, second, and third grades.
(2) Chart development.
(3) Introduction of new stories in books.
(4) Use of the basal and supplementary book lists.
(5) Ways to help children to become independent readers.

c. To discuss social studies units. Meetings for this purpose are usually scheduled at the end of the first semester. A teacher for each unit listed in the Scope and Sequence is chosen to share her room environment and to discuss how the unit

was initiated and developed with the children in her group.

d. To introduce new guides or courses of study, or to explain policies.

e. To select, review, or to become acquainted with new audio-visual aids, phonograph records, and other concrete instructional materials.

f. To learn techniques; e.g., how to paint, work with clay, use rhythm band instruments.

g. To learn folk dances.

h. To discuss control and guidance.

i. To discuss techniques for conducting parent conferences.

4. *Conferences*

In a city as large as Long Beach, and with three supervisors for primary and intermediate education, it is necessary that each type of conference be as far-reaching as possible.

A principal requests the supervisor to visit his building. The reason may be one of many; e.g.,

a. To survey the teaching in some particular field such as arithmetic, language arts, social studies. In this case, a conference with the whole group of teachers is scheduled so that all may discuss common problems and/or share the fine work being done.

b. To survey a field in one particular grade. In this case, a conference similar to the one described is held with the teachers of that grade.

c. To help a few teachers with common problems and one or two with individual problems. In this case, it is better to schedule a group conference for the few teachers with the common problems and individual conferences for the others.

d. To have a faculty meeting with all of the teachers to discuss without visitation some phase of the program that can be handled in this way.

e. To discuss with the entire staff an area of instruction common to all classes and to return at an interval of 3 to 6 weeks to visit the classrooms for a "follow-up."

f. To confer with the principal in making short- or long-term plans for his building.

5. *Workshops*

Workshops are another source of help for teachers. Usually they are held in a centrally located elementary school and cover many aspects of the school program.

Workshops are planned each year in Long Beach after the principals and teachers indicate the needs for that year. As a result, this year special supervisors worked in conjunction with the supervisors of primary and intermediate education.

    a. Industrial Arts and Quiet-Time Activities for Reading.

    b. Audio-Visual.

    c. Music.

    d. Other fields.

As requested by the teachers, a few workshops in art and physical education are conducted by the respective supervisors.

The possible contributions of workshops are only beginning to be realized. As workshops grow in popularity, because of their value, doubtless others will be added.

6. *Excursions*

Another important medium for helping teachers is the excursion. Trips are arranged under an able guide to: the harbor, the dairy, the creamery, Southwest Museum, the wholesale market, the airport, the Press-Telegram, telephone office, the bakery, the Post Office, and other places that contribute to the enrichment of the teacher's background.

7. *Curriculum development*

Some of the richest opportunities for the teacher growth are offered in the field of curriculum development.

Division committees made up of principals, teachers, and supervisors analyze the needs of the various grade divisions of the school system and bring before a general committee recommendations for curriculum projects to be undertaken during the year.

When agreement has been reached as to the work to be undertaken, committees of classroom teachers are organized to proceed with the work under the counsel of the supervisor of that field.

As soon as plans and ideas take sufficient form that recording seems desirable, one or two members of the committee are released from classroom work to give exclusive attention to the preparation of the manuscript for the curriculum guide. Frequently, the work is accomplished in summer workshops, those participating being remunerated on the basis of the regular salary.

From time to time as the writing goes on, conferences are held to review what has been recorded and exchange ideas regarding possible improvements.

If the content of the new publication has not been tried out in a sufficient number of classrooms to prove its worth, it is printed in tentative form only. The final publication follows a thorough "tryout" in several classrooms with resulting revision based upon the recommendations of those using it.

8. *Committee*

Teachers frequently gain from participation on committees as they share ideas and think through problems.

From time to time, teachers and administrators are asked to serve on committees for reasons other than curriculum development. The purposes may be:

    a. To review and evaluate the books on the basal and supplementary book lists.

    b. To make recommendations for special play equipment, visual aids, instructional supplies, and the like.

    c. To compile summer reading lists for children.

    d. To evaluate a tentative guide and to make recommendations for improvement.

    e. To share and evaluate materials used for quiet-time activities during reading periods.

    f. To share the sequences developing in a specific social-studies unit.

    g. To review the books on the kindergarten list.

An examination of the above discussion shows that some of the procedures are group devices, others individual devices; some of them involve "doing" by the members of the group, whereas in others the participation is largely passive. Some are verbal in nature, others are observational. In some cases, for instance, workshops, all of these different kinds of characteristics can be identified.

Descriptions of many similar city-wide supervisory programs have been published. Individual reports about them and discussions of their merit as well as of local programs would be an excellent activity for classes in supervision.

A large number of supervisory procedures that have been found to be useful in promoting the general improvement of the work of groups of teachers are:

Discussion of an instructional problem.

Study of some topic; securing necessary information.

Library shelf of reference materials on problems.

Observation of films, dramatizations, lessons.

Television programs.

Lectures, institutes.

Panels, forums, debates.

Role-playing; psychodrama.

Reports of visitations, travel, meetings.

Workshops—a wide variety of possibilities.

Self-diagnosis of needs by teachers.

Evaluation of aspects of the educational program.

Excursions, field trips, field work.

Exhibits, demonstrations.

Community surveys.

Preparing instructional materials.

Experimental studies.

Committee assignments—school; system; special.

Working with community groups; parents.

This list of group procedures can be extended almost indefinitely by supervisors and students as a class or study-group project. A choice can be expressed of methods judged to be suitable for dealing with some particular problem of concern to the group.

Evaluating improvement devices. It is highly desirable that supervisors and teachers from time to time evaluate the improvement experiences in which they engage. The evaluation can be based on general impressions as to the reactions of participants, but such a procedure sometimes leads to an incorrect appraisal. On the other hand, systematic evaluative procedures can be devised which yield a wealth of information as to the reactions and suggestions for improvement. These data can be examined subsequently and changes that seem desirable can be made. Systematic procedures for evaluating the effectiveness of supervision and supervisory practices will be discussed in Chapter 18.

Teachers' estimates of the effectiveness of improvement techniques. The best-planned study of teachers' judgments of the effectiveness of supervisory techniques is still that made by Weber [21] in 1942. An investigation by Boardman in 1949, confined to the high-school level, corroborates the general findings by Weber. The techniques mentioned as most promising by the teachers of twenty or more schools are given below:

1. Organizing teachers into committees to study problems.
2. Organized study of special topics in general staff meetings.
3. Providing a professional library and browsing-room for teachers.
4. Having teachers (not administrators) give reviews of articles in current educational magazines.
5. Giving special financial awards for participation in programs of in-service education.
6. Co-operatively engaging in a systematic evaluation of the school, using the criteria of the Co-operative Study of Secondary-School Standards.
7. Carrying out a well-planned attack upon the problems of curriculum development.
8. Holding forums where parents, pupils, teachers, and board members participate.
9. Attending summer workshops.
10. Visiting teachers in one's own school or in other schools.
11. Holding small group meetings to study revisions of the course of study in a department.

The techniques listed as most promising by the teachers of at least ten schools, but fewer than twenty were as follows:

1. Panel discussion by teachers.
2. Experimentation with new classroom procedures.
3. Making surveys of pupil problems.

[21] C. A. Weber, "Promising Techniques for Educating Teachers in Service," *Educational Administration and Supervision* (December, 1942), pp. 691-695.

Charles W. Boardman, *What Are Good Techniques in Achieving Democratic Administration in High School?* Bulletin of the National Association of Secondary School Principals (April, 1949), pp. 206-215.

See also Fred C. Ayer and Dorothy R. Peckham, *Check List for Planning and Appraising Supervision* (Austin, Texas, The Steck Co., 1948). Contains 291 practices organized under ten principles.

**POINTS OF GREATEST DISAGREEMENT BETWEEN
SUPERVISORS AND TEACHERS IN RANKINGS
OF CERTAIN SUPERVISORY ACTIVITIES
IN ORDER OF RELATIVE IMPORTANCE**

Activity	Supervisors' Rankings *	Teachers' Rankings
1. Plan, conduct, or follow up the results of demonstration teaching	61	3
2. Read educational literature	2	24
3. Attend professional meetings outside the school system	3	30
4. Make case studies of problem pupils or have such studies made	40	4
5. Hold membership or office in professional organizations	5	42
6. Visit other school systems and study educational practices	36	5
7. Provide means whereby teachers may rate systematically their own traits and activities	65	10
8. Direct and co-ordinate the work of all supervisors in the school	69	11
9. Help to fill vacancies in teaching positions	46	8
10. Co-operate with normal schools, colleges, or universities to improve quality of, or to increase the number of summer-school, extension, or correspondence courses available to teachers	63	13

* The rankings of the supervisors are taken from Fred Engelhardt, William H. Zeigel, Jr., and Roy O. Billett, *Administration and Supervision*, pp. 155-157. See also National Survey of Secondary Education Monograph No. 11, which is the United States Office of Education Bulletin No. 17, 1932 (Washington, Government Printing Office, 1933).

4. Attending professional meetings.
5. Having teachers prepare and issue handbooks for new teachers.
6. Planning an orientation program for new teachers.
7. Holding informal meetings of the staff.
8. Home visitation.
9. Field trips for teachers.
10. Making surveys of graduates.
11. Participating in the eight-year study.
12. Participation in interschool studies of curriculum development.
13. Encouraging teachers to write magazine articles by offering cash awards.
14. Attending guidance conferences.
15. Individual conferences.

The following techniques were listed as most promising by fewer than five schools:

1. Visitation of classes by the principal.
2. Talks by the principal.
3. Reading of papers by teachers.
4. Using rating scales.
5. Requiring special readings.
6. Demonstration teaching.
7. Issuance of bulletins by the principal.
8. Requiring summer-school attendance.

Teachers and supervisors do not always agree. Peterson and Messenger [22] found that teachers and supervisors do not always agree upon the effectiveness of different techniques as shown in the table above.

The teachers in 1945 thought that demonstration teaching was an effective device; supervisors in 1932 thought not; the same was true of case studies and visits to other school systems. Supervisors placed a high value on membership in professional organizations, and attendance at professional meetings outside the school system; teachers did not. The teachers' emphasis of twenty or thirty years ago upon the immediate and individual techniques continues today, so far as we can tell from informal studies and seminar reports. The giving of individual assistance has, as noted, been largely taken

[22] O. E. Peterson and Helen R. Messenger, "Why Not a Planned Attack on That Forty-Year Lag?" *Elementary School Journal* (February, 1945), pp. 317-323. Published by The University of Chicago Press.

POINTS OF GREATEST AGREEMENT BETWEEN SUPERVISORS AND TEACHERS IN RANKINGS OF CERTAIN SUPERVISORY ACTIVITIES IN ORDER OF RELATIVE IMPORTANCE

Activity	Supervisors' Rankings *	Teachers' Rankings
1. Visit classroom teachers	1	1
2. Write professional articles for publication	58	58
3. Maintain a system encouraging teachers to offer suggestions for the improvement of the educational program of the school	15	14
4. Encourage teachers to address professional groups outside their own school system	57	58
5. Survey the school plant and equipment	47	48
6. Develop and maintain, or help to develop and maintain cumulative records of pupils	27	25
7. Recommend teachers for bonus or salary increases	67	65
8. Plan and follow up the intervisitation of teachers	50	48
9. Plan, conduct, and follow up the results of individual conferences	4	2
10. Study the interests, abilities, talents, experience and training of staff supervised	10	7

* The rankings of the supervisors are taken from Engelhardt, Zeigel and Billett, *op. cit.*, pp. 155-157. See also National Survey of Secondary Education Monograph No. 11, which is the United States Office of Education Bulletin No. 17, 1932 (Washington, Government Printing Office, 1933).

over by the principal, or should be so taken over.

Teachers and supervisors in these early studies agreed upon several items. Analysis reveals several significant things. First, the preferences in the early studies differ considerably from those in Weber's study, which probably reflects the modern view that had developed by the time Weber gathered his data. Second, teachers and supervisors agree, in the early study, on the value of classroom visits and individual conferences, but supervisors in the later study recognize that these processes are of less value to them and of greater value to the principal. An odd finding in Weber's study was the low rating by teachers for "visitation of classes by the principal." This probably indicates an important point, namely, that studies of this type are greatly affected by the experiences of the persons responding. The effectiveness of any technique actually depends upon its appropriateness for the purpose at the time and on the skill with which the procedure is used. Techniques are not good and bad in general, but good or bad for different purposes, persons, and conditions. Distinctions between use by various type of supervisors can, however, be made.

Group counseling. Group processes used to attack common problems are valuable not only for the professional skills and insights, for solutions to problems, but also are excellent opportunities for counseling and therapy. Co-operation, free discussion, mutual aid and affection, the opportunity to make personal contribution to group effort with accompanying recognition, all give security, "belongingness," and confidence. Feelings may be expressed, obstacles resulting in tensions and frustration may be openly attacked and examined. The individual gains insight and courage to attack his own personal difficulties positively. The defense mechanisms once used are no longer necessary. The leader exploits all the opportunities inherent in group work to help individuals achieve better personal and social adjustment. The leader contrives opportunities for contribution, success, and recognition for those who need it; contrives experiences designed to give pause to the overly aggressive, egocentric individuals. The timid and hypersensitive group members are gently brought into discussion. The danger of dependence on the counselor in individual work is less likely to appear in group counseling.

Two good references on group counseling are:

HERRICK, Virgil E., and COREY, Stephen M., "Group Counseling with Teachers," *Educational Administration and Supervision* (September, 1944), pp. 321-330.

ROGERS, Carl R., *Client Centered Therapy* (Boston, Houghton, 1951).

The use of sociometric methods is as valuable with adults as with children. Freedom to choose one's companions for work or committee deliberation, to change membership or be reassigned, to choose one's free reading material, one's project, or part in the group project, are all aids to tranquillity, and hence to effective work.

All the methods of securing information about individuals which are used with children are applicable to adults, from cumulative records to projective techniques. Many of these are indicated in Chapters 9-10.

Section 5

IMPROVING PERSONALITY TRAITS

The improvement of personality. The personal factor is of basic importance to all activities in which individuals or groups work together. This is true even when an individual or group has power over other individuals or groups. Democratic leadership exercised among equals is impossible without certain characteristics of personality. The prime importance of this for administration and supervision has already been indicated in Chapters 4 and 5. A partial list of the characteristics of a good leader was given there. The importance of desirable personal characteristics in the teacher is obvious to all observers. Growth in desirable personality characteristics is, then, important for all staff members.

The development of a desirable personality is possible and not unduly difficult if seriously attempted. Popular interest in this is manifested by the great number of books, pamphlets, newspaper columns, and magazine articles dealing with personality and its

improvement. A great deal of the popular material is shoddy quackery, resulting in superficial changes or surface manifestations only. The underlying structure of personality is not affected. Valid facts and principles are available, however, together with reputable methods of improvement. Important growth in desirable personality can be achieved.

An adequate discussion of personality and its improvement cannot be presented in a general volume such as this. Effort is made here to present a reputable outline in extremely skeletonized form. Students are urged to read extensively in the excellent literature available. It is to be noted also that personality is interpreted in somewhat different ways by various scholars in the field. The account here is admittedly but one of several, though effort was made to present a consistent theory and practice.

Various bases of interpretation.[23] A simple framework for thinking will be of

[23] A list of primary sources would cover several pages. Many treatments on this level are too difficult for the average reader. Fortunately, there now exist several excellent general volumes which summarize the research and present interpretations. Prominent among these are:

John E. Anderson, *The Psychology of Development and Personal Adjustment* (New York, Holt, 1949). Good interpretation and summary. Easily

read. Useful to anyone wishing background and summary of principles. Good bibliography.

Gordon W. Allport, *Personality: A Psychological Interpretation* (New York, Holt, 1937). Despite early date is probably still the best single book, particularly for field workers interested in applications. The next reference extends, strengthens, and corrects several points in the 1937 volume.

Gordon W. Allport, *The Nature of Personality:*

great assistance to students attempting to interpret and evaluate various divergent pronouncements on personality.

An individual is first of all a mechanism. In the eyes of some, that is all he is. But he is also a biological organism, his organismal structure being superimposed on the mechanistic base. Finally, as both common sense and controlled observation indicate, he is a purposive agent, capable of will and choice. At least he changes his opinion and, within limits, acts as if from choice in such a way as to defy prediction on mechanistic and organismal assumptions. The individual is predictable, but he is also creative and original. Integration, or systematic internal organization, is the most important aspect of personality on any level. Dynamic organization is necessary in order that the individual may make adjustments both routine and creative to his environment.

Briefly, this means, first, that a man possesses a body, particularly a neuromuscular system, capable of response, and a certain few reflexes. He easily acquires a large number of conditioned reflexes or habits. Breakdown of any part of the mechanism affects the activity of the whole. All of these are aspects of the personality, mechanistic in nature. Warning should be sounded here that the student be not misled by the brevity of this and following paragraphs into thinking that this simple statement disposes of the problem. Undue simplification is dangerous, but simple statements of this extremely complex process are all that can be given in this volume.

Selected Papers (Cambridge, Mass., Addison-Wesley Press, 1950). Contains a series of essays from 1935 to 1947. Excellent material for both advanced student and the field workers.

Charles M. Harsh and H. G. Schrickel, *Personality: Development and Assessment* (New York, Ronald, 1950). An easily read summary, similar to Anderson reference above.

Ross Stagner, *Psychology of Personality* (New York, McGraw, 1948). Similar to Anderson and to Harsh and Schrickel but with more immediate references to research background and primary sources. Extensive bibliography. An excellent all round treatment.

Second, it means that man possesses the organs and functions of a living organism. He must carry on the processes leading to survival and reproduction. The fundamental drives of anger, fear, love, and sex operate and are vital components of his personality. The functioning of his endocrine glands is so important that a whole literature has sprung up around their relation to personality. Disease and injury affect the personality through effect upon the organism. The innumerable acquired loves, hates, and fears are also factors.

But third, man is not merely a mechanism at the mercy of stimulus and response, or an organism controlled by heredity and environment. He can—and this is most important—choose, examine, and manipulate causes, deliberately using them to achieve his purposes. When man makes conscious analysis and choice among the factors of his environment he might make use of a mechanistic response to an environmental stimulus not as an end in itself but as a means toward some chosen consequence. Man is a seeking, choosing, creative being. He is self-conscious and aware of himself. Normally he has an organized system of concepts, values, attitudes, and motives. Any account of personality must take into consideration the incalculable factors of inherent variability, and of will and choice operating in purposive behavior, and the further effect of this behavior on the personality. In seeking his adjustments, the individual engages in equal and reciprocating intercourse with other individuals and with the world. He affects other

Percival Symonds, *The Dynamics of Personality Adjustment* (New York, Appleton-Century-Crofts, 1946). Good common-sense discussion, easily read by all levels of students.

Kimball Young, *Personality and Problems of Adjustment,* 2nd ed. (New York, Appleton-Century-Crofts, 1952). A well-known book with good basic summary together with reference to improvement of personality.

(Each of these references contains material dealing with adjustment or improvement of personality. Comment on this together with additional specialized references will be given a few pages further on.)

individuals and the environment and these in turn affect him. Instead of being wholly bound by his environment, he changes and produces environment with far-reaching effects on his personality. He is a social-moral being.

Personality is affected by an individual's inherited mechanism and functions; by his organismic nature; by his creative, purposive ability; and by the effects of environment upon all of these.

Those enamored of the mechanistic view lean toward the method of trait analysis, the listing of many traits, and the treatment of them statistically as if they were discrete parts of an operating mechanism. This type of thinking consciously or unconsciously operates in many discussions of the rating of teachers.

Those regarding organismal nature as dominant interpret personality in terms of "instincts," racial drives, urges, appetites, and so on. Here we find emphasis on the sublimation of sex and anger, bringing them to heel in the service of the organism. The Freudians go to the extreme of catharsis through free expression, whereas others argue for intelligent and rational repression or suppression. The development of various desirable "drives" is important. As indicated above, glandular action and disease are scrutinized in their relation to personality. Traits are described in terms of behavior reactions and, adequately delimited, are open and susceptible to statistical treatment and practical discussion.

The third group stresses the uniqueness of the individual, growth and development of a system of ideals and standards, attitudes, the growth of judgment and reflective thought, and the effect of environment. The variable and creative aspects are regarded as important.

Despite extremely clever arguments for interpreting personality on one or another of these levels, it seems intelligent, in the absence of complete, final data, to examine all three levels in interpreting this factor so

important in our lives. Let us summarize briefly.

1. The individual is a mechanism. As such he is a space-time-energy pattern susceptible to scientific analysis. As in all mechanisms, the parts are simultaneous and function in one direction. The principle of explanation is simple mechanical cause and effect.

2. The individual is a biologic organism. As in all organisms, the functions of the parts are determined by the life function of the whole. The function of one part may be taken over by another. These parts function in two directions. The principle of explanation is heredity and environment.

3. The individual is a purposive agent, a social-moral being. He is engaged in reciprocal response with other individuals and with the outside world in seeking adjustment. The principle of validation is intelligent purposing.

With this all too brief, and perhaps rather abstract, framework for guidance, let us examine various statements as to total personality and separate traits.

The personality is an organic whole, not a collection of "traits." The general principles of modern biology and psychology, not to mention the broad trends in philosophy, stress the importance of the living whole in contrast to a summation of parts. A personality is not the sum of a large number of discrete elements; it is a functioning whole.[24]

Confusion between whole and part widespread in common discussion. Common, everyday use of terms in this field shows either serious misunderstanding of meanings or great carelessness. First, the word *personality* is widely used in everyday conversation and in some more serious discussions when actually but *one aspect or characteristic* of the total personality is meant. The single "trait" is often a striking but relatively unimportant aspect of a total personality. A girl utterly lacking in seven-tenths of the

[24] Discussion is confined to the normal personality, no reference being made in this brief summary to disturbances or derangements within a personality or the more serious schizophrenia, i.e., split personality.

elements of mature personality is often said to have a "fine personality" when what is meant is that she is merely pretty, or vivacious, or active in social affairs. In the business world *personality* is used to refer to extreme social polish, tact, great ability to manage men; to salesmanship; to undue aggressiveness or impertinence, and so forth. Certain savants possessing most elements included in mature, balanced personality of the highest type are sometimes referred to as having poor personalities when what is meant is that they lack affability, do not talk the vacuous nonsense of the day, refuse to be interested in trivial concerns which "made a good newspaper story." The obvious stupidity of much everyday discusion of "personality" should have long since indicated that there was incoherence or irrelevance somewhere, but the average citizen is not ordinarily interested in exactness of terminology.

Second, a tendency opposite to that just described is encouraged by methods of activity or job analysis which give a picture of personality as made up of scores, even hundreds of "traits." It is quite common to see lists of these desirable and undesirable traits compiled by writers advising young people and upon rating cards for teachers or commercial employees. When it is considered that the terms used are subjective and largely undefined, the chaos is even greater. If such trait summaries were in fact reliable, no one could begin to understand personality, a complexity of myriad aspects. It is doubtful, however, if analysis applied to mechanisms can be applied in like manner, if at all, to organisms. The natures of the two are different. As will be shown briefly later, analysis suitable to personality research is more arduous than the mere listing of characteristics. Rating-card lists as they stand are reckless arrays, indiscriminate conglomerations of symptoms, fundamental attitudes, sheer notions, commonplace designations, including many noncomparable items. Such an approach would give us a "rag-bag" theory of personality. Present trends indicate that the fundamental aspects of personality are very few. These rating-card trait lists, when compiled with discrimination and when used by competent observers, do have a value as will be shown later. Published without explanation, minus strict definition of terms, and used without understanding, they engender much fallacious thinking.

Illustrating a more reputable view of whole and part. The chief error illustrated in the foregoing paragraphs is the belief that arbitrarily defined traits—ranging from *sincerity, initiative, resourcefulness,* and *judgment,* through *tact, enthusiasm, cooperation,* to *neatness, docility,* and *thrift*—are entities, basic elements of the personality. Some of them are, and some are not. To be a trait, an item should be established on rational grounds or should be statistically demonstrable as an independent variable and should be persistent. Most items in trait lists are mere symptoms, indications, clues to the presence or absence of underlying understandings and conduct attitudes which are, in fact, the genuine elements of personality. A simpler way to say the same thing is to point out that *initiative, resourcefulness, honesty,* as commonly used, are but colloquial names used to designate and describe certain types of observed reaction. These actions, dubbed honest or dishonest, resourceful or imitative, as the case may be, are indications of the functioning or failure to function of fundamental ideas, values, native intelligence, of training and discipline, etc. One or two simple illustrations, even though very briefly outlined, may make this clearer.

A man returns a purse containing a considerable sum which he has found in the street. Everyone then speaks of him as being *honest,* as if honesty were a characteristic like blue eyes, short stature, or quick reaction time. What is really meant is that the action may be classified as honest. Instead of saying that the behavior may be classified as honest or that the man acted in an honest manner, we make a natural mistake encouraged by careless language and say that it is the individual who is honest. This, of course, is not serious if understood, and it serves common intercourse satisfactorily. But when it leads to the attribution of "honesty" as a positive something in the individual's make-up, thoroughly muddled thinking ensues. There is no such thing as "honesty," except as the name used to describe actions. The true personality elements here are probably (1) systems of ideas concerning the nature of property, (2) sufficient intelligence to distinguish between *meum* and *tuum,* and (3) an attitude of desiring to act in accord with the right. The latter factor in some cases might not be conscious or analytic but the result of training. These items, not "honesty," are the elements of personality in the individual. At the risk of being repetitious, we may say the individual is not honest in the sense that he possesses some trait characteristic, or mysterious personal attribute, known as honesty. There is no such thing. He is honest, that is, acts honestly, because he has acquired certain understandings (ideas) and values, which are the fabric alike of personality and of civilization, and has the intelligence to operate these ideas and values. When these are present and functioning, we call the resultant behavior *honest.* When absent or not functioning, we call the behavior *dishonest.* A further absurdity in thinking of honesty as a positive attitude or power is seen in the fact that the actions of an individual may be classified as honest in certain fields and cases, though quite dishonest in others. This is usually, though not always, a question of judgment or discrimination (intelligence) for the better types of individual, and of values and training for the less mature. The more generalized one's concepts and habitual modes of reaction are, the more nearly his actions come to being always honest, and vice versa.

Similarly, individuals who steal, lie, and cheat, do not do so because possessed of a characteristic known as *dishonesty, immorality, untruthfulness.* Depending upon cases, they do so because, (1) they do not have the intelligence to see consequences of the act, or (2) knowing the consequences, they do not have the intelligence to see they cannot escape those consequences. Put positively, this last means they think they "can get away with it," which is usually an error in judgment! Still others (3) knowing they *can* and *will* get away with it, do not possess the attitudes, values (standards), and discipline that enable them to resist temptation. Some still more primitive mentalities do not understand the nature of property, the values of truth, the value of confidence engendered through playing fair. Individuals who steal and cheat do so because they are not strong enough to solve their problems otherwise, or because their personalities are underdeveloped either through native inability or lack of training.

If the basic elements in personality can be in fact thus reduced to understandings, appreciations, attitudes, and patterns of behavior which are somewhat, even if not absolutely, consistent, the relationship to the curriculum becomes clear. *It is quite possible to develop personality, or character, or "honesty" by providing for the experiences leading to the desired understandings, ideals, and patterns.*

An illustration of a positive characteristic shows the same susceptibility of reduction to other and basic elements. Resourcefulness, like honesty, is often referred to as if it were a fundamental attribute of the individual. There is no such thing as *resourcefulness,* though certain acts may be called *resourceful* and may be regarded as indicating the presence of fundamental personality elements. In this case these would include (1) native reaction-time, (2) trained alertness of attention, (3) wide training in the field which supplies information and systems of ideas, (4) long experience with occasions demanding resourceful behavior, etc. As with honesty, individuals may be marvelously resourceful in one field and hopelessly naïve in another.

The effect of environment on personality cannot be overlooked. The material and social factors which surround an individual exert an important influence upon personality and behavior.[25] A teacher is placed in congenial surroundings, given work to his liking, treated with respect by superior officers, given credit for suggestions and opportunity to use his own judgment. Under these circumstances the teacher eagerly furthers the purposes of the organization of which he is a member, carries out the policies, performs experiments, makes suggestions, and voluntarily assumes responsibility. He is rated highly by superiors on *co-operation.* We may assume for the moment that the error is not made of regarding this as an attribute but properly as a name for actions performed, the true personality elements being intelligence and certain concepts and attitudes. For the moment we are on the trail of another aspect of the problem, namely, the influence of conditions. Let us now assume a change, involving a new chief who is arbitrary and arrogant, who enforces petty regulations, who steals suggestions from co-workers. The competent teacher of mature personality will try to co-operate until stopped by rebuffs, increased load, and threatened loss of respect. He settles back to routine work, dropping voluntary projects, doing what is to be done but without spirit. The new chief rates him very low on *co-operation!* Obviously the crucial thing here is the working conditions, both spiritual and material, supplying a further clue to the interpretations of personality. The operation of fundamental personality attributes, as revealed by actions, is vitally affected by the situation in which they are exercised. A study of factors conditioning personality is as important as a study of the attributes themselves, and is discussed briefly under morale.

A definition of personality. Two errors in definition, it is clear, are to be avoided.

First, we must avoid the trivial and fragmentary definition common to everyday conversation and used widely by businessmen, salesmen, popular lecturers, and "the man in the street." Personality is not to be defined in terms of one (or several) striking, obvious, or unusual characteristic. Second, we should avoid definitions which refer to a "collection" or "sum total" of traits or characteristics. Several definitions of this type are widely used. Personality is not a collection or sum total of anything; it is an integration or systematic organization of something. The best definition in the sense of most enlightening and useful is that advanced by Allport in 1937,[26] and further supported by his collection of essays published in 1950: "Personality is the dynamic organization within the individual of those psychophysical systems that determine his unique adjustments to his environment." Many later volumes, significantly, use this definition.

A dynamic organization implies, first, change and growth, together with motive toward action, plus self-regulation. Second, there is avoidance of the useless listing of discrete traits or characteristics. Third, the development and improvement of personality based on principles can be predicted by trained workers. The principles bringing about the development and integration of understandings, attitudes, and patterns of behavior are known, even if not yet completely.

The principle of integration. Different schools may vary greatly in stating the components of personality, but most of them agree on integration as an indispensable characteristic.

[25] The relation of the total culture to personality is generally obvious to all sincere observers. Excellent discussions of this are found in the writings of social psychologists, as for instance, Bogardus, Linton, Kimball Young, and many others. Social anthropologists studying social communities in the United States also supply much valuable information.

[26] *Op. cit.*

On the mechanistic level, integration means co-ordination in operation resulting in successful performance. Certainly, part of any personality is an orderly, efficient, bodily mechanism.

On the organic level, we have what was probably the original use of the term *integration:* the proper functioning of those processes by which organisms maintain themselves and survive. The terms *self-preservation, survival, reproduction,* are commonplace. *Health, strength, vigor* are indices of integration here.

Integration in an intelligent, purposing agent means sanity or wholeness of mind. That is, the various characteristics, urges, powers, and abilities are fused together so that fundamental unity is achieved. This makes possible the co-ordination of ideas and impulses, the control of strong urges and appetites, the ultimate resolution of conflicts through intelligent choice, absorption and coherence in pursuit of a chosen and worthy purpose.

An integrated personality is one which can participate in the life of the group in a responsible and consistent manner. The maturing person has developed and is further developing a core of values, beliefs, attitudes, motives, and purposes, together with understandings of his society and its problems. This core guides his choices and contributions.

Obviously, there are differing degrees of integration; uneven development of the constituent factors. Minor conflicts and inconsistencies do appear which are clues to the necessity for growth. Severe conflicts give us abnormal personalities of various known types, but this is not our concern here. A fundamental tendency toward integration is observable and this is confirmed by research studies.

The development and modification of personality. One school of thought regards personality as nonmodifiable or modifiable only with great difficulty, and then only within limits. A fair percentage of school leaders join with the average citizen in making this blunder. Everyday observation, on the other hand, should convince alert observers that personality is in fact modifiable, in some cases readily and with ease. Research is quite clear on this: personality can be modified, many of the principles and practices are known. The testimony of many general writers and research workers is clear on these points.

A large number of studies [27] are available dealing with the diagnosis and improvement of personality factors. Many references could be included here but the research aspects are not our concern. The materials are, furthermore, easily available both in summaries and in primary sources.

The improvement of personality may be made the object of conscious attack. Methods and results will vary with individuals, with groups, with levels of maturity, and with the specified aspects of personality. The general principles are those of diagnosis and planning for processes of improvement; of learning; and of integration.

The principles and processes of diagnosis were summarized fully in Chapter 10 and will not be repeated here.

Caution must be exercised when we speak of learning. Broadly speaking, the processes of learning include anything and everything which one does; the products include all achievements by the learner. Learning used thus coincides with the use in education generally, and particularly in texts on teaching. Learning as used by traditional systematic psychologists is far narrower. The efforts of systematic psychologists to develop internally coherent "learning theory," legitimate as that is, do not aid us much in classroom learning and teaching. The educational worker accepts from the various systems

---

[27] See, for instance, earlier references to Anderson, Allport, Stagner, Symonds, and others. A summary which is excellent for the research student but not so valuable for the field worker is found in Raymond B. Cattell, *Personality: A Systematic Theoretical and Factual Study* (New York, McGraw, 1950).

principles [28] which are consistent and which are useful in his area. This must not, however, be uncritical eclecticism. We know for instance that learners do better when:

1. The learning situation is dominated by a purpose and goal set up by the learner.
2. The goal grows out of the life of the learner and serves purposes within that life.
3. The experiences through which learning takes place, and the outcomes, are unified around the purpose.
4. The learning process consists chiefly of doing, experiencing, undergoing, the actual thing to be learned, although many other varied activities accompany and contribute to the central process.
5. The learner is aided by others whether through counseling, assistance, stimulation to analysis, to readings, or other procedures.
6. The situation invites wholehearted identification and participation from the learner when his whole organism is involved.
7. The learner is ready for the experiences specified.
8. The learner is aided by an environment which is encouraging to expression and participation; by human relationships which are sympathetic and supporting; by experiences wherein chances of success are high.

Integration is, as we know, the desired over-all outcome of learning carried on under the guidance of the principles summarized above.

The texts on personality such as have been referred to throughout the earlier pages of this section deal with the growth and development of personality [29] as it takes place naturally from earliest infancy to adulthood. The deliberate modification and improvement of personality is treated only incidentally in some, and not at all in others, of these references. A good deal can be inferred from some of the volumes.

The desired modifications of personality may range from the elimination of a trivial but annoying mannerism to the development of a profound and justified self-confidence. Some may need experiences designed to build good human relations, that is, understandings, attitudes, and skills used in working with other persons. Others may need to overcome shyness and develop self-confidence through participation in group activities, through exercising leadership even if only for a moment in making a suggestion. Still others only need to be given opportunity to exercise their valuable skills in group projects. A few may need redirection. Feelings of inferiority may be overcome through acceptance of contributions to group effort, through individual success. Fears, anxieties, worries may be simple or profound, and may need sympathetic treatment. The confidence and social sensitivity of the mature personalities in the group serve as steadying

[28] Principles of learning of this type will be found in detail in such volumes as:

William H. Burton, *The Guidance of Learning Activities,* 2nd ed. (New York, Appleton-Century-Crofts, 1952), Chs. 1-10.

James L. Mursell, *Developmental Teaching* (New York, McGraw, 1949), Chs. 1-4.

Lindley J. Stiles and Mattie F. Dorsey, *Democratic Teaching in Secondary Schools* (Philadelphia, Lippincott, 1950), Chs. 8-16.

Other references are also available.

[29] Books dealing with the improvement of personality are extremely rare, except for the superficial volumes which attempt to develop what are actually symptoms rather than basic personality elements. The basic references given earlier do contain much indirect guidance. The respectable books on counseling, on individual and group therapy also contain material of use to teachers and supervisors. Several of the books on mental hygiene and on psychoanalysis present material usable to advanced students. We do not in this volume pretend to go into the more remote details of personality improvement or modification. One volume which is of interest here is:

Fred McKinney, *Psychology of Personal Adjustment* (New York, Wiley, 1949). Particularly Chs. 7, 8, 10, 14, 15, 16.

Currently there is interest in books written for laymen in the field of personality. One of the best which will supply background for school workers is:

Rollo May, *Man's Search for Himself* (New York, Norton, 1953).

Interest is also great currently in psychiatry and in the correction of personality maladjustments. The following reference is but one of many reliable volumes available:

Phillip Polatin and Ellen C. Philtine, *The Well-Adjusted Personality: Preventive Psychiatry for Everyday Use* (New York, Lippincott, 1952).

factors and quite unconsciously serve as guides and goals. The breaking of undesirable habits and the development of desirable ones follow the general known principles of habit formation.

The following general principles are based upon analysis of many case studies and upon the reasoned conclusions of general theorists. They may guide the individual working upon his own personality development, and also the group leader endeavoring to give guidance to individuals or groups and to work out co-operatively the environments conducive to desirable personality growth.

SUGGESTIONS FOR THE IMPROVEMENT OF PERSONALITY

1. Define personality, particularly the characteristic you wish to eliminate or develop.
2. List as adequately as possible the specific objective manifestations of the given characteristic, or of its absence.
3. Perform honest analyses in terms of these definitions of behavior indexes.
4. Attempt to apprehend the reasons (understandings, ideals, and attitudes) for the value of such conduct, and then rather consciously attempt to grow into the desired attitude and behavior. Seek experiences toward this end.
5. Seek advice from friends and from those who are indifferent. Observe and imitate good models.
6. Study physical conditions and immediate environment for possible hindrances or modifications, making such changes as are possible.
7. Secure an understanding of, and consciously adopt what is known as, the "objective attitude" in the whole matter. Secure understanding of and attempt to avoid rationalization, wishful thinking, and other forms of magic.
8. Believe in the worth of one's self and of one's task in the world, noting also that a variety of interests should go with devotion to one major purpose.
9. Understand that genuine effort and persistence are necessary. No hocus-pocus nor mumbling of incantations will achieve the difficult change in one's personality.

The basic characteristics of desirable personality. More and more one is forced to the conclusion that the essentials are not numerous, as would be implied by most interpretations of trait lists. As indicated in the foregoing pages, the few essentials include a good bodily mechanism and adequate native intelligence. With the full implications made explicit, personality could be epitomized in the ancient statement, "A sound mind in a sound body." There is a meager list of inherited automatic responses, a few racial drives, a few emotional reactions. By far the largest part of complex human personality is made up of acquired beliefs and attitudes about the world and man, acquired values, and tendencies to act in accord with those values.

Remembering that characteristics of personality will cover all levels, remembering particularly that the uniqueness of individual personality is paramount, remembering finally that "personality" should be individual and not generic in its reference, we may venture a tentative summary. The general major items here indicated can each be broken down into lists of understandings, ideals, and attitudes. These, in turn, are susceptible of treatment in the course of study. Experiences designed to develop them may be provided in the curriculum.

1. First and foremost may be listed bodily *health*, or physical well-being. Not only do ordinary everyday activities necessitate this, but enthusiasm, good spirits, morale, or optimistic outlook, enabling continuous performance of one's duties, all depend upon a good physical basis.

This means, first, that the individual is possessed of knowledge about care of the body, habits exemplifying this knowledge, and a desire to employ these habits. This could be amplified interminably into details of personal hygiene of the nervous system, the respiratory, digestive, and excretory systems. It means, second, avoidance of disease and injury, or when these are inescapable, intelligent effort to avoid permanent untoward consequences. It means, third, absence of such physical defect or deformity as would seriously interfere not only with physical functioning but with emotional and intellectual attitudes and efficiency.

2. Second may be noted desirability of adequate *native intelligence*. There should be balanced mental development, including habits and skills of attention, good judgment, memory, imagination, clear perception; ability to analyze,

organize, and present the results of critical thought.

3. Third, *emotional balance* and tranquillity are important. That is, it is important that one have what is commonly called a disposition which is cheerful and optimistic. This involves control, training, sublimation of racial drives into any number of acquired drives. Specifically it means control of anger, jealousy, etc., the development of a sense of humor, and perspective.

4. *Integration* of the whole physical and mental individual has been stressed continuously. It is interesting to note that *health* comes from a Saxon word meaning "whole." The desirable personality is whole, balanced, integrated. This is characterized by euphoria on the physical, and by a sense of reality on the mental side. Professor Burnham phrases it thus: [30]

"The wholesome personality is characterized by a sense of reality, of validity, and of security. This is comparable to the euphoria that accompanies a condition of complete physical health. An individual who lacks this sense of personal health has a sense of unreality, of insecurity, and apprehension that may at times be alarming."

These fundamentals may be supplemented by a number of functional attitudes and abilities which enable the personality to function, and which themselves are aspects of the personality.

A. The following fragmentary list is illustrative of desirable intellectual characteristics:
1. Respect for another's point of view; the ability and willingness to weigh and understand the present position, status and motives of "the other fellow," anyone with whom one must deal.
2. Knowledge that any worth-while attainment in the world necessitates serious training, arduous effort, and persistence; disbelief in "getting by."
3. An adequate knowledge of the immediate and remote goals of life, and particularly of one's work in life.
4. Ability and willingness to become absorbed in one's task.
5. The objective attitude, willingness, and ability to face the facts; refusal to waste time arguing with the inevitable.
6. Belief in an orderly world, entailing consequences from causes, and responsibility in agents.

7. A sensitive curiosity concerning the nature of things.
8. The habit of delayed response, involving the suspension of judgment, weighing of further data, etc.
9. Belief in the evolutionary, experimental nature of the world and of life.

B. The following list of "conduct attitudes" proposed by H. C. Morrison,[31] even if incomplete and tentative, is illustrative of the desirable values and ideals to be included in the personality. The values which should be found are those which clearly further the right or the good in the long run. There is of course vigorous, almost violent, controversy over what is good or right, much of it honest, but much of it selfish sophistry. Among careful thinkers of wisdom and insight there is considerable agreement concerning ideas of duty and responsibility which are manifestations of values. As stated, Morrison's list is an admirable illustration of attitudes based on recognition of certain values. As attributes of personality, those attitudes constitute functioning conduct controls.

1. The acceptance of deferred satisfaction.
2. A sense of the consequences of one's own actions.
3. Altruism.
4. A sense of fair play.
5. A sense of property rights.
6. Spirituality in the sex relationship.
7. Right acceptance of criticism.
8. Acceptance of the value of co-operation.
9. Fidelity to promises.
10. Obedience to constituted authority.
11. Sustained application, capacity for hard work, effort.
12. A sense of duty.
13. Willingness and ability to assume leadership.
14. Fortitude.
15. Punctuality.

On the higher levels, these involve conviction plus a tendency to act in accord therewith. On the lower levels, reactions may be habitual rather than reasoned responses. Professor Morrison's penetrating and highly

[30] Burnham, *op. cit.*, p. 674. See also Gardner Murphy, Lois B. Murphy, and T. M. Newcomb, *Experimental Social Psychology: An Interpretation of Research upon the Socialization of the Individual*, rev. ed. (New York, Harper, 1937).

[31] H. C. Morrison, *The Practice of Teaching in the Secondary School*, rev. ed. (Chicago, Univ. of Chicago Press, 1937), Ch. 20.

stimulating discussion may well be made the subject of a class report. There is overlap with the preceding list of understandings.

The symptomatic characteristics of desirable personality. We may now return to the lists of "traits" which are actually symptoms of basic characteristics. Studies of these supply valuable guidance for practical everyday discussions. An early study of desirable personality in teachers [32] was based upon the opinions of 3725 high-school seniors. An abbreviated sample from a much longer list reveals several important facts.

The lists are significant. The "traits" listed are symptomatic of the desirable attitudes, abilities, and understandings listed earlier. The first item in "Reasons for Liking Teacher 'A' Best" deals with teaching technique but the great majority of the others are characteristics of the personality which is effective with learners. The comments are specific with generalities emerging only toward the end of the longer list from which the sample is taken. The least specific characteristic, "cultured and refined" (a typical verbalism), was last of all with but twenty mentions. Mastery of subject matter, which is essential but badly overrated by specialists, ranks sixteenth in both lists.

Hart's general findings have been corroborated many times by later studies. [33] The best current discussion of discipline selects one of the traits mentioned by Witty [34] for special comment:

A sense of humor is obviously the most essential characteristic of skillful handlers of discipline problems. One personality trait most injurious to successful discipline is false dignity. We know of no other single personality trait which would cause so much confusion, uproar and mismanagement as this one.

We may stress also "consistent behavior." Few things confuse children more, or produce undesirable behavior more quickly than inconsistent treatment from adults. Consistent fairness and fulfillment of promises from adults give the child a sense of security. This in turn begets confidence and effort. Baxter's earlier detailed studies of teacher-pupil relationships gave conclusive evidence that the behavior of teachers has great effect upon the pupil's sense of security, freedom from tension, courtesy, resourcefulness, and seeking of social recognition. Repeated some years later, the analyses corroborated the early findings.

One study reversed the usual form of question and asked, "From what did you suffer most in school?" The answers are revealing and should be taken to heart by teachers. "Sarcasm, excessive demands, contempt, and corporal punishment." Sarcasm can result only from genuine stupidity or from a frustrated personality. Excessive demands result in much unnecessary failure by pupils, with accompanying antagonism and bad behavior.

Many other studies [35] dealing with elementary and secondary teaching are avail-

[32] Frank W. Hart, *Teachers and Teaching* (New York, Macmillan, 1934), pp. 131-132, 250-251.

[33] Paul Witty, "An Analysis of the Personality Traits of the Effective Teacher," *Journal of Educational Research* (May, 1947), pp. 662-671.

[34] George V. Sheviakov and Fritz Redl, *Discipline for Today's Children and Youth,* Department of Supervision and Curriculum Development (Washington, NEA, 1944), p. 59.

[35] Bernice Baxter, *Teacher-Pupil Relationships* (New York, Macmillan, 1941).

William U. Snyder, "Recent Investigations in Mental Hygiene in the Schools," *Educational Research Bulletin* (November, 1945), pp. 222-224.

Willi Schohaus, *The Dark Places in Education,* trans. by Mary Chadwick (New York, Holt, 1932).

Wilbur B. Brookover, "Person-Person Interaction Between Teachers and Pupils and Teaching Effectiveness," *Journal of Educational Research* (December, 1940), pp. 272-287.

Robert N. Bush, "A Study of Student-Teacher Relationships," *Journal of Educational Research* (May, 1942), pp. 645-656.

R. H. Ojeman and F. R. Wilkinson, "The Effect on Pupil Growth of an Increase in Teacher Understanding of Pupil Behavior," *Journal of Experimental Education* (December, 1939), p. 143.

Weston A. Bousfield, "Student's Rating on Qualities Considered Desirable in College Professors," *School and Society* (Feb. 24, 1940), pp. 253-256.

Reasons for Liking "Teacher A" Best, Arranged in Order of Frequency of Mention, as Reported by 3725 High School Seniors	*Frequency of Mention*
Is helpful with schoolwork, explains lessons and assignments clearly and thoroughly, and uses examples in teaching	1950
Cheerful, happy, good-natured, jolly, has a sense of humor, and can take a joke	1429
Human, friendly, companionable, "one of us"	1024
Interested in and understands pupils	937
Makes work interesting, creates a desire to work, makes classwork a pleasure	805
Strict, has control of class, commands respect	753
Impartial, shows no favoritism, has no "pets"	695
Not cross, crabby, grouchy, nagging, or sarcastic	613
"We learned the subject"	538
A pleasing personality	504
Patient, kindly, sympathetic	485
Fair in marking and grading, fair in giving examinations and tests	475
Fair and square in dealing with pupils, has good discipline	366
Requires that work be done properly and promptly, makes you work	364
Considerate of pupils' feelings in the presence of the class, courteous, makes you feel at ease	362
Knows the subject and knows how to put it over	357
Respects pupils' opinions, invites discussion in class	267

Reasons for Liking "Teacher Z" Least, Arranged in Order of Frequency of Mention, as Reported by 3725 High School Seniors	*Frequency of Mention*
Too cross, crabby, grouchy, never smiles, nagging, sarcastic, loses temper, "flies off the handle"	1708
Not helpful with schoolwork, does not explain lessons and assignments, not clear, work not planned	1025
Partial, has "pets" or favored students, and "picks on certain pupils"	859
Superior, aloof, haughty, "snooty," overbearing, does not know you out of class	775
Mean, unreasonable, "hard-boiled," intolerant, ill-mannered, too strict, makes life miserable	652
Unfair in marking and grading, unfair in tests and examinations	614
Inconsiderate of pupils' feelings, bawls out pupils in the presence of classmates; pupils are afraid and ill at ease and dread class	551
Not interested in pupils and does not understand them	442
Unreasonable assignments and homework	350
Too loose in discipline, no control of class; does not command respect	313
Does not stick to the subject, brings in too many irrelevant personal matters, talks too much	301
"We did not learn what we were supposed to"	275
Dull, stupid, and uninteresting	275
Too old-fashioned, too old to be teaching	224
Not "fair and square" in dealing with pupils	203
Knows the subject but "can't put it over"	193
Does not hold to standards, is careless and slipshod in her work	190

able. Studies are also available on the college level which show that the more mature students still rank first the professor's interest in his students and their problems, and his willingness to give attention to them.

The general attitude of the teacher. An older study by a psychiatrist supplies excellent guidance in this problem. Anderson,[36] after listing such general traits as insight, sense of reality, adaptability, interest, integration, social adjustment, sense of responsibility, resourcefulness, and good work habits, makes an enlightening comment upon the teacher's total attitude:

The mental attitude . . . of an individual probably constitutes the most important element in the atmosphere of the classroom. The disgruntled, sour, sarcastic, sharp and bitter teacher has a general attitude of mind that is most dangerous to the shy, timid, over-sensitive child. The suspicious, doubting, supercilious teacher does untold damage to the pupil whose daily life is filled with one long series of threats against his own security. The over-anxious, demonstrative, worried teacher has built up an attitude of mind that commonly develops in the classroom regression tendencies in pupils, is responsible for baby ways of behaving, and halts the maturing process so essential to the mental health and growth of children. And so it is, in their effect on the personalities of each and every pupil in the classroom, those influences emanating from the teacher's attitude of mind are fraught with the greatest possibilities for good or evil.

The studies by Lewin and his associates, quoted earlier in Chapters 1 and 7, testify to the positive side of this same problem. Learners preferred the democratic teacher to the autocratic or laissez-faire leaders. *Mere preference* is not the point. Learners *accomplished more* with the help of co-operative, democratic teachers, both in subject-matter learning and in the development of personal-social-moral traits. The superiority of settings for learning under the guidance of democratic personalities was overwhelming.

Tiedeman[37] discovered the significant fact that dislike for and antagonism toward the autocratic, domineering type of teacher personality increases with the age of the pupils, at least through junior high school. Added experience and maturity evidently increased insight into the evils of poor personality, and increased respect for the co-operative teacher.

An extensive series of recent studies[38] supplies even more specific evidence. Differences between dominating and socially integrative teachers were studied in second-grade rooms. Four degrees of domination were listed, ranging from domination in conflict to domination while working together with no conflict. Integration was described on two levels: (1) teacher and pupils not working together, but the class feeling secure in consulting the teacher, and (2) full co-operative participation by the teacher. The most extreme differences were found, as would be expected, between the teacher who dominated in conflict and the completely integrative teacher. All previous resu.ts were conclusively corroborated. Children's reactions, attitudes, and personalities were most favorably affected by the integrative teacher. The dominating teacher stimulated increased resistance from the children with detrimental results on mental hygiene and behavior. The study revealed also that the bad behavior learned under the dominative teacher did not persist when the children encountered a new

[36] V. V. Anderson, *Psychiatry in Education* (New York, Harper, 1932), p. 300.

[37] Stuart C. Tiedeman, "A Study of Pupil-Teacher Relationships," *Journal of Educational Research* (May, 1942), pp. 657-664.

[38] Harold H. Anderson and Joseph E. Brewer, *Studies of Teachers' Classroom Personalities II,* "Effects of Teachers' Dominative and Integrative Contacts on Children's Classroom Behavior," Applied Psychology Monograph No. 8, American

Psychological Association (Stanford University, Calif., Stanford Univ. Press, June, 1946).

Harold H. Anderson, Joseph E. Brewer, and Mary F. Reed, *Studies in Teachers' Classroom Personalities III,* "Follow-up Studies of the Dominative and Integrative Contacts in Child Behavior," Applied Psychology Monograph No. 11, American Psychological Association (Stanford University, Calif., Stanford Univ. Press, December, 1946).

teacher in the third grade. This is another practical illustration of the effect of the immediate social situation on human beings. The domineering teacher continued to be domineering with her new second grade; the integrative teacher also proceeded as before. The dominating teacher persisted in techniques that clearly contributed to conflict and turmoil in her room, and which repressed initiative and spontaneity. Very significant was the finding that the integrative teacher materially reduced the resistance of the few children who were in conflict with her; the dominating teacher did not.

Section 6

MORALE AS A FACTOR IN TEACHER GROWTH

Morale is a natural outgrowth of all the factors which contribute to the development of an adequate, successful, and satisfying setting for one's work. Morale is not an end in itself which can be achieved by special methods. To aim at morale as a special and separate matter is likely to result either in a false and insincere spirit which evaporates under pressure, or in contempt for leadership, contempt which is in itself a form of low morale. Morale is a natural accompaniment of growth and in turn an excellent stimulus to growth; it supplies an emotional atmosphere conducive to growth.

An extensive literature on morale now exists, particularly with reference to industry, business, and the army. Literature on morale relating to education is growing steadily. Morale has been defined in various ways. The following is a composite, attempting to include salient points:

Morale is the esprit-de-corps or *elan* of a group. It is the inner confidence on the part of the individuals and a mutual faith among individuals which makes possible concerted group action. It is a unity of understanding, sympathy, and purpose within the group.

Psychological evidences of the presence or absence of morale. A very good statement is found in Small's [39] study of executive ability. Under good conditions, all levels of workers will clearly manifest the following attitudes:

1. He is enthusiastic and self-confident. He respects his own judgment and is willing both to make decisions and to accept full responsibility for any course of action which they involve.

2. He likes and respects those in authority over him and his fellow-workers and is confident that they like and respect him. He is jealous of their good opinion and is careful to be worthy of it.

3. He enjoys his work and takes just pride in its quality and in his ability to accomplish results. He believes that those in authority appreciate this ability, and he will go to endless pains with difficult problems in order to accomplish results which will justify their esteem and confidence.

4. As he is sure of the high regard in which he is held by his employers, he is confident of the retention of his position and the security of his future. He is free from worry, cheerful, optimistic, and contented. He is able to enjoy his leisure because he leaves his business problems at his office.

Before making application to educational work, we must again note that the statements above are drawn from business organizations. Authority is stressed, and there is apparent some propaganda designed to keep employees happy as employees. In education we must substitute the term *leadership* for *authority* and stress more the co-operative relationship than that of employer and employee. Intelligently interpreted, however, the four items supply valuable guidance.

Obviously, the attitudes of persons of poor morale are the opposite of those stated. Small's statements are reproduced below because they are more than mere reversals of

[39] Sumner G. Small, "How to Develop Executive Ability Through Personality," *Industrial Management* (February, 1921), pp. 115-116.

the positive points. The details supply much additional guidance.

1. They lack enthusiasm and self-confidence. They avoid decisions or responsibility, always attempting to pass the decision and responsibility to those over them, even preferring to accept their snap judgment, and to proceed on a course they know to be wrong rather than to act on their own initiative. They feel they will obtain little credit for correct action, but know they will be highly censured for mistakes, and even fear the loss of their positions.

2. They dislike and do not respect their superiors or fellow-workers, with the exception of a few in a clique formed defensively for mutual protection. They feel that the blame for all mistakes is shifted to their shoulders by their superiors or fellow-workers for the purpose of advancing their cause and discrediting them in the eyes of the management.

3. They dislike their work and take little pride in it, for it is seldom commended. They think the managers fail to appreciate their ability, they dislike to tackle anything which may result in criticism and the further jeopardy of their positions, and they concentrate their energies in avoiding or concealing those matters which have been the subject of past censure.

4. They are sure they lack standing with the management and are constantly in danger of losing their positions. They are worried, depressed, pessimistic, and unhappy. Their leisure is clouded by worry about the uncertainty of their future.

With the change of some words and interpretations, these points are of value in considering the morale of school workers.

The bases of morale. The various studies all show that good human relations is the most significant factor among several. Any given individual, however, may be motivated or otherwise affected by any one of the various factors. The general psychological factors making for good human relations are

now a commonplace, due to the many studies in all fields:

a. Participation in policy-making, defining goals and problems, planning and carrying out plans.
b. Recognition by fellow-workers, acceptance by them of one's contributions.
c. Stimulating leadership which encourages emergent leadership, co-operative effort, and participation by all.
d. Consistent policies under which to work, consistent treatment from status leaders.
e. Achievement, production of useful results.
f. Satisfaction from, and security in one's work which comes from fair treatment, participation, achievement, and recognition.
g. General administration which is democratic, sympathetic, and stimulating.

Coffman's [40] study showed the area of human relations to be of highest importance among teachers as other studies have shown it to be among other groups of workers. Hedlund and Brown [41] showed that living and working conditions were highly important and that several factors were more important than salary. The same thing is shown by practically all studies in business or industry, contrary to popular opinion. Financial status is, of course, important especially when an individual or family is constantly on the edge of financial difficulty. Schultz [42] showed that subjects taught, size of community, amount of experience were not too important; that salaries were related to morale; but that working conditions, supplies, and equipment were of more importance. The most dissatisfied teachers were the most sharply critical of conditions, supplies, and equipment. Administration was identified by those of both high and low morale as a focal point. An older study by Cralle and Burton [43] made a detailed analysis

[40] W. E. Coffman, "Teacher Morale and Curriculum Development: A Statistical Analysis of Response to a Reaction Inventory," *Journal of Experimental Education* (June, 1951), pp. 305-332.

[41] P. A. Hedlund and F. S. Brown, "Conditions That Lower Teachers' Morale," *Nation's Schools* (September, 1951), pp. 40-42.

[42] R. E. Schultz, "Keeping Up Teacher Morale,"

Nation's Schools (October, 1952), pp. 53-56.

[43] Robert E. Cralle and William H. Burton, "An Examination of Factors Stimulating or Depressing Teacher Morale," *California Journal of Elementary Education* (August, 1938), pp. 7-14.

Articles are available also of a general discussional nature.

S. Dowdell, "Building Morale from the Super-

of administration and morale, listing a large number of specific items which are merged with items in the general summaries.

Teacher morale and student achievement. A high level of morale is desirable for many reasons; but we may ask especially if teacher morale is in any way related to student achievement. Anderson [44] investigated this problem in twenty secondary schools in Iowa. Student achievement was determined by the Iowa Tests of Educational Development. The morale level among the teachers was determined by a scale made up of factors believed to affect morale. Teachers responded to multiple-choice answers in this scale and were also interviewed. Statistical analysis revealed significant differences in achievement between schools in which there were also differences in teacher morale. Groups ranking high in pupil achievement were those with teachers ranking high on the morale scale; groups with low pupil achievement were those with teachers who ranked significantly lower on the morale scale. The implications are important. First, the maintenance of morale in teaching staffs does have an effect on student achievement. Second, teacher-training institutions should endeavor to attract and retain candidates with enthusiasm for teaching. This study by Lester Anderson, combined with those by Harold Anderson [45] and his associates, shows clearly that we cannot ignore the attitudes of persons toward teaching. The attitudes do affect student achievement. More research is needed along these lines but preliminary indications are that morale of the teachers is clearly related to achievement by the learners.

Factors favorable to the development of morale. A number of summaries are available, out of which the following composite has been made:

I. *Leadership by the Administration in Developing Good Community Relationships*
   A. Securing community recognition and respect for the school and its workers.
   B. Providing, in so far as an administration can, opportunities for adequate and desirable social life.
   C. Aiding in the securing of adequate and comfortable living conditions.
   D. Minimizing, in so far as an administration can, unnecessary and unwarranted restrictions upon and interferences with private lives.
II. *Leadership by the Administration and in the Effective Operation of the Schools*
   A. Maintaining a consistent policy and practice of orienting all new staff members socially and professionally.
   B. Inviting and providing for continuous participation in policy- and plan-making, recognizing contributions and suggestions.
   C. Maintaining a consistent and rational policy of administration and supervision, thus making for confidence and security.
   D. Maintaining a good physical plant, adequate supplies and equipment; adjusting teacher loads; preventing undue time pressures.
   E. Maintaining a sound employment policy.
      1. Selection, appointment, and promotion on the basis of objective techniques and merit.

visor's Point of View," *School Executive* (July, 1951), pp. 43-44.

M. R. Ahrens, "Helping Teachers with Their Tensions," *Childhood Education* (January, 1952), pp. 211-215.

C. W. Campbell, "Security and Freedom Requisite for Morale," *School Executive* (July, 1951), p. 41.

J. F. Huey, "Teachers' View of Professional Morale," *California Journal of Elementary Education* (August, 1951), pp. 14-26.

J. Connor, "Satisfactions That Help Keep a Teacher on the Job," *Childhood Education* (May, 1952), pp. 396-398.

A. E. Diettert and C. C. Diettert, "What Can the Principal Do for Staff Morale?" *American Teacher* (February, 1953), pp. 10-11.

See also several appropriate chapters in the many texts on Industrial Management, on Human Relations (in each of several fields), and on Group Dynamics.

[44] Lester W. Anderson, "Teacher Morale and Student Achievement," *Journal of Educational Research* (May, 1953), pp. 693-698. An article based on Anderson's unpublished doctoral dissertation, "A Study of Teacher Morale," Univ. of Iowa, 1950.

[45] Harold H. Anderson, and others, *op. cit.*

2. Assignments and transfers made with due regard to the difficulties and necessities of preparing for and adjusting to a new situation.
3. An adequate salary schedule based on a plan, reasonably automatic in operation, and with an open top.
4. Reasonable security of tenure and avoidance of annual elections and contracts.
5. Elimination of causes of rapid or too great turnover in so far as possible.
6. A retirement, pension, or annuity plan.
7. A fair policy of sick leave, reasonable ease of security, sabbaticals for travel or study.

Oddly enough, none of the studies or discussions mentions health as a separate and distinct factor in morale; however, it is unquestionably indicated by a dozen or so of the items which are listed. Hence, we may emphasize health as a prime requisite for morale.

Factors inimical to the development of morale. Again we may present a composite based on several summaries.

I. *Factors in Community Life*
  A. Lack of community respect and cooperation; public lack of regard for teachers and the teaching profession; anti-intellectualism.
  B. Attempts to secure extra community service for teachers by pressure toward Sunday school teaching; requiring presence in town over weekends; requiring local residence.
  C. Prohibitions on freedom of speech and action placed on public employees; demands for oath taking, pledges, and other verbalisms designed to control employees.
  D. Lack of opportunity for desirable social life.
  E. Presence of unnecessary restraints, prohibitions, and interferences with private lives; prohibitions against dancing, card-playing, smoking. Proscription of marriage. Prohibition of certain outside interests which do

not interfere with school work. Rules against receiving gifts or accepting social invitations.

II. *Factors in Unintelligent Administration and Supervision*
  A. Failure to orient new staff members socially or professionally.
  B. Failure to invite participation in policy- and plan-making; failure to recognize contributions or good teaching.
  C. Failure to maintain consistently a sound, defensible policy of administration and supervision.
  D. Failure to maintain a sound employment situation.
    1. Selection, appointment, promotion on capricious, personal, or political bases, undeserved appointments and promotions, political interference with technical requirements.
    2. Last-minute assignments and transfers.
    3. Maladjustment of salaries.
    4. Too short contractual periods; insecurity of tenure.
    5. Rapid turnover of both administrative-supervisory staff and teaching group.
    6. Absence of retirement or pension plan.
    7. Restriction or absence of sick leave, of sabbaticals for travel or study.
  E. Failure to supply good working conditions; properly constructed buildings; properly equipped rooms; laboratories and playgrounds; proper sanitary facilities; adequate and comfortable retiring rooms for relaxation, etc.
  F. Failure to supply ambitious, enthusiastic, technically adequate professional leadership.

Supervision and the maintenance of morale. Supervision has a very special place, if not the crucial place, in developing morale. We may recall at this point all that was said in Chapter 4 about the principles and techniques of democracy which are at the heart of this problem. In conclusion, we present a set of suggestions for the supervisor in morale work.

Supervisors will contribute to morale:

1. Through manifesting faith and confidence in all their co-workers.
2. Through expertness in professional leadership displayed.
3. Through a willing and unselfish expenditure of time and energy in meeting problems and in rendering service.
4. Through maintaining a policy of co-operative attack and solution in all problems and tasks.
5. Through giving full public credit for all contributions.
6. Through judging contributions, suggestions, and results achieved in terms of the persons concerned and the conditions involved, instead of by some arbitrary standard; through objective data and standards, however fragmentary, instead of by personal or capricious standards.
7. Through leadership and administration which is kindly, sympathetic, and co-operative, and at the same time objective and impartial.
8. Through providing every opportunity and facility for the exercise of freedom, initiative, and experimental attack upon problems and tasks.

If morale is absent or seems to be disintegrating, the workers concerned should immediately (1) locate and define the fault, (2) make a diagnostic analysis of conditions creating the weakness, (3) formulate co-operatively definite measures for correction of the conditions, and (4) apply these measures, that is, do something about it. All too often morale work is confined to vague, sentimental appeals and evangelical exhortations. Action is a far better builder of morale.

Section 7

MEETING THE NEEDS OF INDIVIDUAL TEACHERS

Principles underlying the improvement of the work of individual teachers experiencing difficulties. In their courses the authors have often discussed with their students possible principles that should underlie the supervisory program as it bears on the problem of improving the personal traits and performance of individual teachers. The following series of principles, which is the outgrowth of the thinking of many persons, is proposed for further discussion. It is also based on rather systematic studies of improvement programs in all parts of the country; however, the list may be modified or extended by any group after careful examination that chooses to do so. Note that there is some similarity between these principles as applied to teachers and those given in Chapter 10 for dealing with learning difficulties of children. Improving teaching should be regarded as a learning process.

1. *Consider all aspects of the teacher's personality in planning an improvement program.* It is almost self-evident that the improvement program must take into consideration not only growth needs with respect to instructional procedures, but also such factors as the teacher's health, attitudes, interests, emotional adjustment, personal problems, social characteristics, and community relationships. In this connection, counseling and guidance services provided in many cities play an important role. In smaller places their functions must be performed by supervisors, principals, and friends. In many school systems special assistance is given to new teachers and others on probation by "helping" teachers and special consultants.

2. *Secure the co-operation of the person or group concerned in the establishment of needs, and in the planning of the improvement program.* Self-evaluation and self-study under friendly guidance are undoubtedly two of the most helpful ways of determining needs and instructional problems. When the individual has a clear realization of a need, his sincere co-operation in an improvement program is usually assured. Feelings of security are likely to emerge in a constructive friendly atmosphere, a condition under which

most people are ready to engage in a variety of new and vital experiences likely to bring about improvement.

3. *Adapt the improvement program to the specific needs of individuals and groups having common problems.* While there is great value in extensive participation by teachers in the study of major educational problems and community needs, there nevertheless are vital problems that some teachers face which must be dealt with on an individual or group basis. Teachers vary widely in professional background, interests, and education; other individual differences similar to those found among pupils exist among teachers; there are also many differences in the conditions under which they teach, as was pointed out in Section 1 of Chapter 6. All of these factors should be borne in mind in planning an improvement program.

4. *Integrate the improvement program as far as is possible in the in-service education of teachers.* The general in-service education should be planned in such a way that it meets the needs of as many teachers as possible. Part of the in-service education should consist of larger group activities in which problems of general significance to the schools and the community are discussed and studied by the entire staff; provision should also be made for smaller study groups and workshops concerned with specific problems and needs of smaller numbers of teachers; provision should also be made for special kinds of learning experiences that are intended to help individual teachers to improve their personal characteristics and to master more effective instructional procedures, such as conferences with consultants, guidance in reading and study, demonstrations to observe, intervisitation, guided practice in acquiring underlying skills, and similar direct learning activities.

5. *Attack specific needs, faults, and shortcomings directly.* For instance, if there is evidence of the need of medical care, rest, or recreation, this should be promptly arranged for, probably on a personal basis. If specific lacks exist, such as weakness in diagnosing pupil difficulties in some curriculum area such as reading, spelling, or arithmetic, steps can be taken at once to deal with the problem. When specific personality problems exist frank discussions of their significance and ways of dealing with them with competent counsellors and specialists in many cases will lead to an improvement. In general, it is best to begin a developmental program by attacking some condition in which it is most likely that a change for the better can be brought about rather than some large complex vaguely defined area of difficulty. These needs vary from person to person and should be approached on an individual basis.

6. *Correct environmental factors that contribute to teaching problems.* This can be done in most instances by removing or altering the factors or elements that are causing difficulty, in some instances by transferring the teacher to some position where conditions may be more favorable. Conditions that reduce the level of teacher morale should be corrected. When school and community relations are unsatisfactory insofar as an individual is concerned, the situation should be canvassed to determine possible steps to take to bring about a change. Items such as quality of the school plant, adequacy of instructional materials, and availability of community resources also should be carefully examined with a view to their possible improvement where they are deficient.

7. *Familiarize the teacher with instructional methods and materials of demonstrated validity and value.* This goal may be achieved in part by making available professional literature, by faculty discussions, by study groups, by demonstrations, by films,[46] by lectures, and other suitable ways. When the teacher feels assured that suggested changes of methods and in the use

[46] *Audio-Visual Aids in Teacher Education,* Twenty-ninth Yearbook, Association for Student Teaching (Lock Haven, Pa., State Teachers College, 1950).

of materials will probably lead to an improvement, it is likely that there will be greater readiness to adopt them and master them than if the teacher is merely required to use specific technics and routine procedures prescribed by a supervisor, for which no dependable basis has been established.

8. *Provide guided experience and practice to develop skill and proficiency in instructional procedures of demonstrated value which the teacher desires to master.* Normally teacher-training institutions provide at least a minimum of direct experience in teaching; however, many new problems arise "on the job" for which there has been inadequate preparation. The teacher in the classroom is constantly learning more about how to teach, sometimes by trial and error, sometimes by fumbling and success. This wasteful uneconomical learning process can be to a considerable extent cut short by effective guidance through in-service education activities, such as workshops, courses for teachers, laboratory work, internships, demonstrations, and directed practice. Programs of this kind for new teachers are found in many cities; there is sometimes a need for similar experiences for mature skillful teachers who wish to keep abreast of modern educational developments in methods and materials.

9. *Help the individual from time to time to measure his progress so that he may be aware of the degree to which his efforts are proving successful.* Learning is a developmental process, and the rate of growth will vary among individuals. Awareness of success is a powerful force for improvement. Judicious encouragement and commendation by the principal, supervisor, and fellow teachers encourages the individual to even greater effort. The satisfaction growing out of an awareness of progress is a reward for the efforts that have led to this improvement.

10. *Proceed with the improvement program on a tentative basis and adjust or modify it if this seems advisable or necessary.* Because there are in most instances several different approaches to a problem, those selected may not prove to be very effective. In that case, changes should be made from time to time that may be judged by all concerned to be more helpful until a measure of success has been achieved.

Procedures useful in helping individual teachers. Individual teachers often present problems that must be dealt with on an individual basis because of their specific nature.[47] In some cases the condition proves quite amenable to treatment; for instance, in dealing with dietary needs and simple personal problems; in others the condition is rather difficult to correct, for instance, a bad attitude toward children, or a speech or personality defect; in others it is almost impossible to remedy the condition, for instance, the presence of mental disease and emotional instability.

In some of the above cases the supervisor, a consultant, or an educational specialist can give direct help to the teacher to overcome the problem; in other cases the services of specialists are required, such as social workers, psychiatrists, and endocrinologists. In some cases the school system is able to provide the necessary services with members of its own staff; in other cases the services must be supplied by other agencies. In some cases treatment should be sought by the individual on a personal basis; in others the school system through its counseling and guidance divisions can assist in the corrective program. In many places groups of teachers have arranged privately co-operative plans for dealing with health and personal problems. Participatory programs in which the system as a whole and the teachers share the cost of recreation and entertainment exist in any number of places.

The outline below contains a list of illustrative procedures that have been found helpful in improving the work of individual teachers whose problems required assistance

47 Lewis M. Brammer, "Counseling for Teachers: The Supervisor's Opportunity and Responsibility," *Educational Administration and Supervision* (May, 1953), pp. 259-268.

beyond that which would be included in the broader in-service education of teachers. Most of the activities involve the active co-operative participation of the individual. To be effective, participation in the experiences should be active rather than passive as it is in the case of large group activities. The slogan should be "Learn by Doing!" The list is wholly tentative and preliminary in form. It is for discussion purposes only. The list should be studied by those interested in the improvement of instruction in general and also in particular cases. The list is incomplete and can be expanded in the light of a critical examination of practices that have been found useful in particular cases with which members of a study group or class may be familiar.

ILLUSTRATIVE DEVELOPMENTAL PROCEDURES USEFUL IN HELPING INDIVIDUAL TEACHERS SOLVE THEIR PROBLEMS

1. *Medical Care*
   a. Correction of physical and physiological deficiencies.
   b. Changes in nutrition and diet.
   c. Glandular therapy.
   d. Psychiatric treatment.
   e. Rest and relaxation.
2. *Psychological-Psychiatric Measures*
   a. Personality development (as outlined on pages 550 to 554).
   b. Considering implications of conduct or actions.
   c. Establishing feeling of security.
   d. Changing attitudes by deliberate choice of individual.
   e. Expanding interests and appreciations.
   f. Establishing confidence in therapist and treatment.
   g. Play therapy and psychodrama.
   h. Releasing tensions.
   i. Improving morale (see pages 557 to 558).
3. *Participation in the Co-operative Study and Solution of Problems of School and Community*
   a. Individual points out problems of children, school, or community.
   b. Assignment of responsibility.
   c. Assumption of specific duties.

d. Working with individuals and groups interested in similar problems.
e. Preparing reports and defending recommendations.
f. Carrying out decisions of group.
4. *Improving Methods of Teaching*
   a. Study and reading: courses; independent.
   b. Observation and evaluation of work of good teacher.
   c. Visitation of other schools, teachers, systems.
   d. Workshop participation.
   e. Conferences, discussions about principles of learning and their application.
   f. Guided practice under competent leadership.
   g. Experimentation with new procedures.
5. *Improving the Selection and Use of Instructional Materials*
   a. Participation in selection of materials.
   b. Demonstrations, exhibits, displays, museums.
   c. Workshops and laboratory exercises.
   d. Excursions, field trips.
   e. Travel.
   f. Work experience.
   g. Films, film strips, television.
   h. Intervisitation.
   i. Guided experience in using new materials.
6. *Changing Environmental Conditions*
   a. Transfer to a different position or school.
   b. Beautifying the school, classroom, community.
   c. Travel, camping.
   d. Developing recreational program.
   e. Community surveys.
   f. Participation in program for improving living conditions in the community.
   g. Participation in youth groups and community activities.

Principles of value in "dealing with reluctant or antagonistic teachers." As a general rule, teachers welcome suggestions as to methods of improving instructional procedures and use them when they are once understood. Even "reluctant and antagonistic teachers" are entitled to the opportunity to study and grow. A statement giving the following group of selected principles of value in dealing with this type of individual appeared in a Maine Curriculum Bulletin: [48]

SELECTED GENERAL PRINCIPLES OF VALUE IN DEALING WITH RELUCTANT OR ANTAGONISTIC TEACHERS

1. Teachers who have fixed views along certain lines do not change these views suddenly. The converting of these teachers to better methods of instruction will require much time and patience. The departure from their stereotyped methods must be gradual.
    a. Set up a long range plan for teacher improvement.
    b. Make use of any desirable methods which the teacher is at present employing. Ways of improving these methods will be worked out so as to bring to the classroom a greater variety of real experiences which can be used under these circumstances.
2. Teachers will accept more readily those things of which they can see the worth and the purpose. If these teachers are to be converted to better methods of instruction, they must be able to see definite improvement in the results obtained with the pupil.
    a. Invite the teacher to serve on a committee to investigate the worth of new methods of instruction.
    b. Cite results of comprehensive studies on the evaluation of modern methods of instruction.
    c. Arrange for the teacher to observe classes taught by modern methods and see how the pupils react in actual situations where these methods are used.
    d. Make use of demonstration lessons.
    e. Invite the teacher to take part in panel discussions on desirable methods of instruction.
3. Teachers are most likely to accept views contrary to those now held if they participate in the investigating and planning of better methods of instruction.
    a. Take advantage of any chance remarks that the teacher might make relative to difficulties encountered in daily work to suggest places to find help.
    b. Provide for the teacher to visit other teachers to see how they do things. Attempt to apply with the teacher those things observed which are applicable to her situation.
    c. Go over difficulties with the teacher and formulate a plan with her on points on which to work and places in which to find information on these points.
    d. Invite the teacher to work on committees which are concerned with investigating and planning new methods of instruction.
    e. Encourage and commend any new ideas which the teacher may have developed from her investigations.
    f. Encourage the teacher to plan a simple unit and teach it. Attempt to arrive at some conclusions with the teacher as to the values derived from such methods. Attempt to find solutions to difficulties encountered in teaching unit.
4. Individuals may often be won over through participation in situations where no factor insults the intelligence of the participant.
    a. The teacher may be invited to participate in a series of meetings, on a committee, on a panel, to investigate a problem arising within the system and obvious to all. The problem selected, however, should be one on which the evidence for better procedures is overwhelming and conclusive. The reading, discussion, and contributions of the rest of the group will likely have a very wholesome effect.
    b. The teacher may be invited, because of her long experience, to summarize for the faculty a recent article, experimental study, monograph, or book. The material should be so selected that the modern procedure is overwhelmingly supported by evidence which is simple, direct, and easily understood.

This statement was then supplemented by a list of approaches involving [49] "pressures of a distinctly professional sort" that were believed "to be legitimate in extreme cases" when exercised "with full recognition of the democratic process":

[48] *A Forward Step,* Curriculum Bulletin No. 7 (Augusta, Me., State Department of Education, 1948), pp. 104-105.
[49] *Ibid.,* p. 113.

1. Present detailed analysis of test results or other evaluational data; press courteously for rational explanations of unexpected results, inconsistencies, deviations. Group discussions of unidentified figures are helpful as a device.

2. Ask teachers to outline methods of teaching in reasonable detail and to justify procedures on objective grounds, either with research data or through agreement with known principles of teaching. The same thing can be done for materials, learning activities, programming, methods of evaluation, discipline, etc.

3. Ask for a list of the chief learning activities engaged in by children; ask the teacher to compare these with lists of possible activities and to justify her procedures.

4. Ask the teacher to outline any procedures she herself has used to improve her work within six months; any new departure she has attempted; any new devices, books, or materials; any effort to solve case of nonlearning, of discipline, of maladjustment of any kind; books studied, articles read, courses taken, etc.

5. Analyze community comments, questions, complaints; pupil comments. Carry through in friendly objective fashion to reasons, explanations, and needed improvements.

6. Request that the reluctant teachers attack all problems with a professional attitude, relying upon accepted authority to support their stand, not the limited experience of one individual.

Adjustment counseling for individual teachers.[50] The emphasis so far has been upon the professional improvement of the individual. Teachers, like all persons, have many problems of an emotional or personal-social nature. Emotional adjustment is as important for effective work as is professional skill. All individuals need security, a sense of worth, recognition from associates, membership in a group engaged in worthwhile work. Certain supervisors have objected to the addition of counseling to their already heavy load. Difficult cases do, of course, call for the technical services of the trained counselor, but much can be done for everyday cases. Supervisors can undoubtedly aid teachers to overcome fears, frustrations, and tensions as they arise, to move toward happy, adjusted lives. Disturbed human relations, feelings of isolation and insecurity,

belief in the hostility of others usually results in defensive behavior, aggression, withdrawal, or some substitutive reaction. Supervisors or other leaders can through everyday activities have marked effects for good or ill on the lives of other persons. Organized therapeutic treatment by trained practitioners is not our concern here.

The typical method is through interviewing, though often it is a matter of listening by the counselor before any interchange can take place. Emotionally disturbed individuals or anxious persons need to express their feelings, to "talk it out." Sympathetic help can then be given to enable the disturbed individual to map out a tentative solution and then to work toward it. The very working out of a solution gives feelings of security, confidence, and resourcefulness, so necessary to the uncertain individual. The counselor must never give directives or tell what must be done. The very process of bringing problems, feelings, and value judgments into the open is a part of the therapy.

The summary below may be of assistance.

1. The counselor accepts and treats persons as individuals with unique potentialities for development, who are capable eventually and progressively of solving their own difficulties.

2. The counselor accepts each individual as he is, alert or dull, dedicated or not to teaching, bright or stupid, co-operative or resistive, energetic or lazy, orderly and workmanlike or disorderly and slovenly.

3. The counselor will treat individuals with patience, sympathy, respect, and with sensitivity to the inner life and feelings as expressed.

4. The counselor will endeavor to be prop-

[50] F. J. Roethlisberger and W. J. Dickson, *Management and the Worker* (Cambridge, Harvard Univ. Press, 1941).

Virgil E. Herrick and Stephen M. Corey, "Adjustment Counseling with Teachers," *Educational Administration and Supervision* (February, 1944), pp. 87-96; also "Group Counseling with Teachers," *op. cit.*

Carl R. Rogers, *Client Centered Therapy* (Boston, Houghton, 1951).

H. A. Curtis, "Improving Consultant Services," *Educational Administration and Supervision* (May, 1953), pp. 279-292.

erly permissive and properly firm, and always kindly, warm and outgoing.

5. The counselor will not exert authority, will not argue with the interviewee, and above all will not give moral admonition.

6. The counselor will not ask questions except as necessary:

a. To put the interviewee at ease with the counselor, to relieve any fear which would affect relations between the two.

b. To redirect the discussion to some area which has been neglected or omitted.

c. To bring out any implicit meanings or values if this can be done safely.

d. To indicate appreciation for an accurate report of intimate thoughts and feelings.

e. To keep the interviewee talking.

Principles underlying improvement programs. Gray and Iverson [51] list a series of widely accepted principles that underlie good procedure in the study and improvement of teaching in any field. Their statement is an excellent summary of the general point of view emphasized by the authors of this volume:

1. The improvement of teaching should be conceived as a co-operative enterprise. Similarly, responsibility for results should be shared by the entire administrative and teaching staff.

2. The specific duties and responsibilities of each type of staff member should be clearly defined and fully understood. Such definitions should indicate the area in which initiative and creative effort will be most effective.

3. Constructive work should begin at the level of current practice and should lead gradually to improved types of teaching. The ultimate goal in the case of reading is a program of adequate breadth and excellence, based on the needs of contemporary life, the major purposes of schooling, and the results of scientific studies.

4. All who aid in the improvement of teaching should co-operate actively in critical appraisals of current practice and in intensive studies of the recommendations of experts in specific fields and of the results of related scientific investigations.

5. Desirable changes and readjustments should be defined clearly and illustrated concretely in order that they may be attacked intelligently. Only those changes should be undertaken, however, which may be introduced in a given school system with wisdom and prudence under existing conditions.

6. Constructive steps should be recommended as rapidly as they can be introduced without placing undue burden on the staff or without distracting attention from other legitimate phases of the school's program.

7. As teachers endeavor to make significant changes, continuous help and guidance should be provided for those teachers who need it. Stimulating and constructive help is especially needed when difficulties are first encountered or during periods of discouragement.

8. Continuous study should be made of the progress achieved and of the difficulties encountered in effecting desirable reforms. The program adopted should be extended or modified as rapidly as the need for such changes is established.

9. Teachers should be stimulated at all times to take interest in raising instruction to successively higher levels in harmony with forward-looking trends and the results of research. An inquiring attitude concerning such trends and results should also be cultivated.

10. The more capable teachers of a staff should be encouraged to assume leadership in the study of specific problems, in the selection or development of new materials of instruction, and in providing other types of service that may be needed.

11. Recognition that stimulates and inspires should be given to members of the staff for valuable service rendered or for unusual progress in improving teaching.

CHAPTER SUPPLEMENT

INTRODUCTORY DISCUSSION QUESTIONS

1. Describe and evaluate a program of inservice education for teachers with which you are familiar.

2. What can be done to help inexperienced teachers and others new to a school system? Evaluate current plans and practices.

3. What is your belief about placing new teachers on probation? about tenure?

4. How can a teacher be helped to identify

[51] W. S. Gray and W. J. Iverson, "What Should Be the Profession's Attitude Toward Lay Criticism of the Schools? (With Special Reference to Reading)," *Elementary School Journal* (September, 1952), pp. 40-41.

a possible instructional fault or personal difficulty? What help can be given in planning and carrying out an improvement program? Why are teachers sometimes not aware of their limitations?

5. What services can schools and teachers organizations provide to assist teachers to solve personal problems? professional problems?

6. What kinds of experiences are most helpful in improving instruction by teachers as a group? by individual teachers? Describe several particularly helpful experiences.

7. Describe conditions and policies with which you are familiar that contribute to a high level of teacher morale; a low level.

8. Discuss procedures that have been used by some individual to improve some personality trait.

9. What are causes of teacher inertia? What can be done to stimulate teachers of experience and also master teachers to consider the results of the scientific study of educational problems and to modify their practices accordingly?

WRITTEN REPORTS FOR INDIVIDUALS OR GROUPS

1. Suppose that you are a teacher and wish to increase your effectiveness. What do you consider your chief assets? Liabilities? Choose one respect in which you would like to improve and indicate how you think you might be helped to get good results. What difficulties do you anticipate? How do you expect to meet these difficulties? To what principles of learning do you expect to give major attention? How do you expect to determine whether you have learned?

2. Suppose that you are responsible for helping a beginning teacher in the first week of teaching. What difficulties do you anticipate? How would you meet these difficulties? To what principles of learning would you give major attention? How would you expect to determine whether the teacher had been helped?

3. Suppose that you are responsible for helping a mature teacher who has developed a personality problem. What difficulties would you anticipate? How would you meet these difficulties? To what principles of learning would you give major attention? How would you determine whether the teacher had been helped?

4. Select some specific performance difficulty that you have observed or that has been reported to you by one of your teachers. How would you proceed? What background information would you desire? To what principles of learning would you give major attention? What

improvement measures are possible? How would you determine whether you had helped?

5. Suppose that you wished to make a co-operative attack upon some situation in need of improvement, such as group morale. How would you solicit the assistance of others? How would the group determine the respects in which the situation needs improvement? How would the group choose the means and methods by which the situation may be improved? How would the leader reconcile differences of opinion about what to do? How would the group evaluate the effectiveness of its efforts?

6. Individuals or small committees may present to the class summaries of research studies made on the typical difficulties of inexperienced and experienced teachers. (This is important in connection with Exercises 2 and 3 given above.)

7. The chapter indicates clearly that staff members often need to know far more than they do concerning some given area or topic, as for instance, child nature and needs, the nature of the social order, the nature of interaction between individual and social group, and many others.

Suppose that a genuine need or problem has been discovered. Describe a body of more or less well organized material bearing upon the problem which exists or may be assumed. Present in skeletonized form a program designed to initiate a co-operative study of this material. Two or three groups of students may report original programs for class analysis. A committee might work on an extensive illustration.

8. (Read the entire question carefully before beginning an answer.)

   A. Miss Cadwallader, a very traditional teacher of the fifth grade in the John Alden school, says she *knows* her methods work. Her methods, she explains, depend upon tolerating no foolishness in her class. She makes her pupils learn whether they like it or not. She knows what is best for them. After all, isn't she an adult and trained as a teacher? When asked for evidence to prove that her methods work, she replies tartly: "I get results. That's how I know my methods work."

    a. Describe very briefly four results Miss Cadwallader *thinks* she is getting.

    b. Suppose, in support of one or more of her "results," she cites scores on standardized tests convincingly above the fifth grade norm. How would you account for this?

c. What *undesirable* learnings, unbeknown to Miss Cadwallader, are very likely being acquired by her pupils? Why?

d. What *desired* learnings are her pupils probably failing to achieve?

B. Miss Montgomery, a fifth-grade teacher who thinks she is following "progressive methods," also says she knows her methods work. She does not plan her program in detail and allows the children to engage in long, unguided discussions. She is not much concerned with subject matter, but talks a good deal about "initiative," "responsibility," and "felt needs." She encourages the children to plan lessons, to make decisions, but does not herself participate. She does not wish to "dominate" the children. Asked for evidence, she replies, "Oh, you can just see the children grow."

a, b, c, d. Answer the same questions as above for this teacher.

C. The above four items for A and B should be answered in a sentence or two each. The important part of the question, on which you may express yourself at greater length, now follows.

Oddly enough, each of these teachers needs the same *general* help and guidance from the principal, supplemented by other advice *specific* to each case.

a. Outline the *general* lines you would follow in aiding these teachers to improve. What questions might you raise? To what bodies of materials might you refer them?

b. Give briefly two suggestions of any type which you would make to each teacher dealing with her *specific* difficulties.

SUGGESTED READINGS

ANTELL, Henry, "Inventory of Teacher Interests as a Guide Toward Their Improvement in Service," *Educational Administration and Supervision* (January, 1945), pp. 37-44.

BEALE, Howard K., *A History of Freedom of Teaching in American Schools*, report of the Commission on the Social Studies in the Schools, American Historical Association (New York, Scribner, 1941), p. 343.

BOARDMAN, Charles, DOUGLASS, Harl, and BENT, R. K., *Democratic Supervision in Secondary Schools* (Boston, Houghton, 1953), Chs. 19 and 20.

BRIGGS, Thomas H., and others, *The Emotionalized Attitudes* (New York, Teachers College, Bureau of Publications, Columbia Univ., 1940), p. 107.

BURTON, William H., "The Teacher's Morale as an Important Factor in Teaching Success," *California Journal of Elementary Education* (May, 1938), pp. 218-226.

CRALLE, Robert E., and BURTON, William H., "An Examination of Factors Stimulating or Depressing Teacher Morale," *California Journal of Elementary Education* (August, 1938), pp. 7-14. Companion to article by Burton published in same magazine in May, 1938.

DALDY, Dorothy M., "A Study of Adaptability in a Group of Teachers," *British Journal of Educational Psychology* (February, 1937), pp. 1-22.

DAVIS, Robert A., "The Teaching Problems of 1075 Public School Teachers," *Journal of Experimental Education* (September, 1940), pp. 41-60.

DURANT, Henry, "Morale and Its Measurement," *American Journal of Sociology* (November, 1941), pp. 406-414.

Evaluating the Elementary School, A Guide for Co-operative Study, Southern Association Co-operative Study in Elementary Education (Atlanta, Ga., Commission on Research and Service, 1951).

EMANS, Lester M., "In-Service Education of Teachers Through Co-operative Curriculum Study," *Journal of Educational Research* (May, 1948), pp. 695-702.

HARTMAN, G. W., "Social Attitudes and Information of Elementary School Teachers," *Journal of Educational Sociology* (April, 1938), pp. 506-510.

HEATON, K. L., "Co-operative Approach to Improvement of Teachers in Service," *National Association of Secondary-School Principals* (January, 1941), pp. 5-9.

Helping Teachers Understand Children (Washington, American Council on Education, 1945).

HILL, George E., "Mental Hygiene of the Teachers," *Educational Administration and Supervision* (October, 1937), pp. 501-512.

KELLEY, Earl C., *The Workshop Way of Learning* (New York, Harper, 1951).

KOOPMAN, George R., MIEL, Alice, and MISNER, Paul J., *Democracy in School Administration* (New York, Appleton-Century-Crofts, 1943).

Leadership at Work, Fifteenth Yearbook, Department of Supervisors and Directors of Instruction (Washington, NEA, 1943).

LEWIN, Kurt, in Gertrude W. Lewin, ed., *Resolving Social Conflicts* (New York, Harper, 1948).

LINGREN, Vernon C., "Criteria for the Evaluation of In-Service Activities in Teacher Education," *Journal of Educational Research* (September, 1948), pp. 62-68.

PATTERSON, Walter G., "Personnel Policies as the Basis for Teacher Morale," *American School Board Journal* (October, 1943), pp. 26-27.

PRALL, C. E., and C. L. CUSHMAN, *Teacher Education in Service* (Washington, American Council on Education, 1944).

Principles and Procedures of Teacher Selection, American Association of Examiners and Administrators of Educational Personnel (Xenia, Ohio, Central State College Press, 1951).

SHARP, George, *Curriculum Development as Re-education of the Teacher* (New York, Teachers College, Bureau of Publications, Columbia Univ., 1951).

SILVERMAN, E. L., "Administrative Practices Which Help to Build Morale," *National Elementary Principal* (February, 1943), pp. 125-127.

TABA, Hilda, *Leadership Training in Intergroup Education: Evaluation of Workshops* (Washington, American Council on Education, 1953).

Teachers for Democracy, Fourth Yearbook, John Dewey Society (New York, Appleton-Century, 1940).

TROYER, Maurice, and PACE, C. R., *Evaluation in Teacher Education* (Washington, American Council on Education, 1944).

WICKMAN, E. K., *Children's Behavior and Teachers' Attitudes* (New York, Commonwealth Fund, 1928).

YAUCH, Wilbur A., *Improving Human Relations in School Administration* (New York, Harper, 1949).

◆·◆·◆·◆·◆·◆·◆·◆·◆

The Improvement of Curriculums

A "CURRICULUM" DEVELOPS in answer to the needs of a group of learners and to the demands of a given society. A curriculum is made by a teacher and his pupils as they work together, but actually the whole community participates, as we shall see. Teacher and pupils receive continuous assistance directly and indirectly from many persons and from many sources. The superintendent, principal, supervisors, subject-matter specialists, school psychologists, lay groups and social agencies, and advisory commissions all contribute, usually through the teachers' guides and through the curriculum-improvement program which developed the guides. Many contributions are made on the spot. The development [1] of a specific curriculum is, then, a co-operative community activity in which many persons participate. The curriculum is a process, not a fixed existence.

The *documents made available to the teacher,* course of study, or teachers' guide, or series of source units, or other specialized bulletins, do have existence and play a

vital part in the development of curriculums.

The amount of help or guidance a given teacher may receive from several sources will vary with amount of training, professional skill, and professional attitudes possessed. Teachers of less training and with mediocre professional insights, attitudes, and skills will of necessity receive far more guidance, even direction, than alert, dynamic teachers. One aim of in-service programs of growth through curriculum improvement is to raise the levels of teacher initiative and responsibility.

Types of curriculum programs. Three types of improvement program are recognized by Saylor: [2]

1. Programs designed solely for the preparation of courses of study.
2. Programs planned in terms of course-of-study preparation, but organized so as to promote acceptance of the completed course by teachers through participation of representative teachers in its preparation.
3. Programs planned on a broad basis for the improvement of instruction, with course-of-study preparation only one, though an important, aspect of the program.

---

[1] We must note again, as with Ch. 12, that it is impossible to include extended detailed discussion of curriculum development. The aim here is to supply students and field workers with a compact outline together with the primary sources.

B. Othanel Smith, W. O. Stanley, *Fundamentals of Curriculum Development* (Yonkers, World Book, 1950), Chs. 25, 26, 27, 28.

H. L. Caswell and associates, *Curriculum Improvement in Public School Systems* (New York, Teachers College, Bureau of Publications, Columbia Univ., 1950), Chs. 1, 2, 3, 4, 5.

Edward A. Krug, *Curriculum Planning* (New York, Harpers, 1950), whole volume.

Alice Miel, *Changing the Curriculum* (New York, Appleton-Century-Crofts, 1946), whole volume.

Action for Curriculum Research, 1951 Yearbook, Association for Supervision and Curriculum Development (Washington, NEA, 1951), whole volume.

Kenneth D. Benne and Bozidar Muntyan, *Human Relations in Curriculum Change* (New York, Dryden, 1951), whole volume.

Ronald C. Doll and associates, *Organizing for Curriculum Improvement* (New York, Teachers College, Bureau of Research, Columbia Univ., 1953), whole volume.

[2] J. Galen Saylor, *Factors Associated with Participation in Co-operative Programs of Curriculum Development* (New York, Teachers College, Bureau of Publications, Columbia Univ., 1941), p. 2.

The three types illustrate the development of thought from the traditional preparation of formal, static courses to processes used in the modern development of dynamic curriculums.

A *program of curriculum improvement* is far broader than the development of a given curriculum or the writing of a course or series of guides. An improvement program includes study of all the major elements which affect the individual teacher's curriculum and which enter into production of documents. A reputable curriculum program necessitates far-flung study by all staff members and by groups, based upon defined local needs. The political, economic, and social structure and aim of the surrounding society, its hopes and aspirations, its tensions and shortcomings, need to be understood. Public opinion toward education must be known. Programs of advice or information for the public may be part of a curriculum program. The aim and philosophy of current educational practice need to be studied and understood. The nature of learners, their growth and development, their characteristics at various levels of growth, all need to be examined and used. The abilities, needs, purposes, and individual differences among learners must be studied. The origin and nature of subject matter, the development of present curriculums, all need to be scrutinized. The nature of the educative process and the effect upon it by persons and material facilities must be analyzed. The nature of modern outcomes of learning and the many new techniques of evaluation need special study.

A program of curriculum improvement will go further than developing curriculums in given classrooms, further than writing course-of-study aids. *A program of curriculum improvement to be successful must bring about many important changes within persons and within the elements constituting the setting for learning.* Changes within persons will be in their attitudes and understandings, in appreciations and skills. Participants in a curriculum program will develop knowledge and conviction concerning the aim and philosophy of education in a democracy. They will develop facile knowledge of the nature of experience as the essence of the educative process. They will have a wider grasp of subject matter and better understanding of its uses. They will learn better how to evaluate the complex and subtle outcomes of modern education.

A program of curriculum improvement is a, if not the, major concern of supervisory leadership. A staff engaged in such a program is demonstrating professional aims and attitudes, engaging in professional activities of the highest type. A curriculum-improvement program is the vehicle for most of the general supervisory program.

We may note in connection with the types of programs that there are also several typical ways of organizing and operating. The program, particularly the preparation of documents, may be carried on

a. By one man.
b. By a secret, or at least nondemocratically selected, committee.
c. By a dominated committee.
d. By a democratically selected and organized committee, with the center of gravity in the local units but with regard for central co-ordination of those aspects which are system wide.

Differentiations are also to be made in terms of state and local leadership, when and if state participation is involved.

Educational workers, in order to participate effectively in curriculum development, will either possess or will develop in the course of the activity:

1. A critically appraised philosophy of education.
2. A clear conception of the process of reorganizing and integrating experience.
3. A detailed knowledge of the growth and development of children.
    a. Characteristics of growth levels.
    b. Individual and social-class differences.
    c. Readiness for given educational materials and experiences.

4. Skill in discovering and developing pupil needs; community and social needs.
5. Skill in organizing learning experiences for the development of various types of learning outcomes: behavior patterns, meanings, attitudes, appreciations, generalized abilities, skills, functional knowledge, and other substantive outcomes.

Section 1

THE PRINCIPLES GOVERNING A CURRICULUM-DEVELOPMENT PROGRAM

The discussion to follow draws heavily upon other summaries in earlier chapters and hence is abbreviated and cross-referenced to avoid repetition.

Action in the area of the curriculum results, as does action in any field, from disturbance of an equilibrium. Tensions which need to be reduced arise from dissatisfactions and criticisms, from new needs which arise and demand reorganization of an existing curriculum and the development of new materials.

The specific factors to which satisfaction or dissatisfaction are attached may range from the immediate "results" of instruction in the common branches, or the type of category used within the curriculum, or any phase of classroom instruction, or the personnel in teaching or administration, to more remote factors such as the philosophy and policy of the professional staff, or the degree to which the school is thought to serve the general "life needs" of the population, or the extent to which the school and its processes are abreast of developments in the world and in research in education.

The actual state of affairs in any given community may range from almost complete complacency to extreme dissatisfaction. First, many persons and groups will assert that change in the curriculum is nonsense, a fad, activity for its own sake. The old curriculum has served all our needs, so why change? These individuals need to be introduced to the world in which they live—or rather to the world in which almost everyone else lives. Second, there are those to whom almost everything is "out-of-date." Teaching is ineffective, the children do not learn to read and write, adolescents are not "prepared for life." These individuals too, need introduction to the facts in and out of school. Third, and more typical, will be those situations in which are heard temperate, sensible criticisms of some aspects of the school and its work, together with equally sensible recognition of satisfactory processes, materials, and results.

The justified criticisms and dissatisfactions present in the community should be seized upon and channeled by the professional leadership toward a program of study, experimentation, and continuous improvement of the curriculum. A climate of unjustified complacency needs to be disturbed so that curriculums and methods which can be shown to be outmoded and ineffective within the value system of the surrounding society may be progressively modified. The process of disturbing an unjustified complacency is actually a problem of modifying the perceptions of the individuals concerned, that is, of modifying their insights into actual conditions, their ideas held about the current situation. Many techniques are available for shocking complacency and modifying perception, as we shall see.

The security of all, administrators, supervisors, teachers, laymen, and the children, must be preserved during the difficult and disturbing process of abandoning old, familiar materials and processes, and substituting for them new materials and processes. Maintenance of security is one of the crucial aspects of curriculum change, and one of the greatest challenges to leadership. The leadership must assume that change toward progressive improvement is the order of the day and must provide for it. This prevents crystallization, and tends to prevent periods of violent disturbance from time to time. The latter is a greater threat to security and effective education than is orderly change based on appraisal and study. The following list of nine principles is not laid down as the law but may be reworded or modified to suit specific situations.

Principle 1. *A curriculum-development program emerges out of an accurate picture of what the curriculum is now doing.*

Principle 2. *The program may be and is initiated by seizing upon an existing criticism or dissatisfaction, or by bringing shortcomings up for discussion, or by introducing a new departure in education.*

The program will originate, ideally, in some current appraisal, or criticism, or dissatisfaction, some suggestion concerning a new departure, some individual experimental work under way. Any item of appraisal or evaluation may be capitalized by the group under leadership.

The direct procedures for initiating a program:

a. Make an appraisal of the products of instruction, both subject-matter achievement, and personal and social growth.

b. Initiate a community survey to determine needs, facilities, possibilities, or to determine the validity of certain community criticisms of education.

c. Actively seek the comments, critical and otherwise, of the community through opinion polls of parents, other laymen, and the learners.

d. Seize upon any current discussion of a new departure in education, or important research finding.

The techniques through which these procedures are carried on have been outlined in several preceding chapters, notably Chapter 12 on studying the curriculum, and Chapter 9 on the appraisal of the educational product.

The foregoing procedures are likely to produce real problems which immediately arouse the thinking and acting of the staff and community groups. Motivation in other instances will be indirect, growing out of deliberate stage-setting by the leadership or small committee. A program indirectly motivated will be accepted to the extent that it brings out issues or projects which meet the needs of the group and the actualities of the situation. A number of techniques are available which may or may not uncover real problems. Many of the early state and city programs began with the study of an area or topic which led to problems. Procedures of this study type include:

a. Engage in faculty study of any major area: the social and/or psychological foundations of education; relation of the individual to the social order; the organismic concept of the learner and his growth; the socio-economic make-up of communities and of the local school population; the extent of participation in student activities of various groupings of students; the present status of graduates of three, four, five, or more years ago. Any of a dozen areas will serve, depending on local conditions.

Study the social scene itself with eventual relation to the adequacy of the curriculum. The strength and success of our social order, the tensions and maladjustments, appearing trends, all have vital significance for the program of education.

b. Engage in faculty-layman study of any of these areas, preferably sections thereof.

c. Encourage individual teachers to make detailed case studies of individual children, dull, average, gifted, handicapped, with problems. Relate findings to offerings of curriculum to meet the several needs. Case reports for faculty information.

d. Examine a collection of courses of study with special reference to their methods of meeting any of the problems indicated in the preceding study areas.

e. Examine the local curriculum to note how it meets or fails to meet the several major areas mentioned in the accepted statement of the general aim of education.

f. Equip a local workshop for use by teachers on any of their problems; encourage attendance at summer curriculum workshops; at curriculum conferences held within the area.

g. Encourage attendance at summer school or extension courses in curriculum development or related areas: ask nearby teacher education institutions to organize courses for the staff (either at the college or locally).

h. Encourage attendance at state, regional, national conferences both general programs and those devoted to special interests, social studies, English, etc. Take an active part in making the programs at conventions worthwhile to the audience.

i. Study the literature on principles of teaching generally, or with special reference to the teaching of a given area; study the characteristics of learners at various levels.

Out of any of these general and indirect procedures a focus may arise in the form of a problem real and provocative to the local staff. The staff can identify itself with a real problem and become genuinely involved. The focus or problem which arises may be as limited as improving materials and methods for teaching spelling in the intermediate grades; or as wide as a survey of existing curriculums by areas, or subjects, or levels.

Principle 3. *A community diagnosis must be made in order to show accurately the existing constellation of convictions, opinions, attitudes; the channels of influence and power, the key persons and organizations.*

The many forces affecting community thinking on school problems must be identified, listed, and weighed. The channels of influence within the community and the pivotal persons affecting public opinion must be similarly identified and taken into account. The same type of analysis must be made for the school community.

Whatever the focus or problem which emerges as a likely basis for a curriculum project, the state of affairs concerning it must be accurately known. This is the crucial phase which will make or break any curriculum program. The procedure outlined below may appear lengthy and involved, but it cannot be omitted. It can be simplified greatly for small or limited projects.

Changes in the curriculum, or any other phase of education, are basically changes in people. We look first, then, not toward changes in course outlines and other documentary aids, in methods or materials, but to values, convictions, and opinions concerning these things held by the professional staff, the community members, and the school population.

The summary to follow is sharply abbreviated and must be supplemented through reading and tryout. An outline is presented here in order to give some form to the somewhat complicated discussion.

1. The first phase, whether existing dissatisfactions have been seized upon, or have been brought to consciousness through deliberate disturbance of complacency, is to make an "equilibrium diagram" or other description of the forces at work in a given situation.

2. The second phase is to analyze the forces (illustrated below) and to select lines of action.

3. The third thing to do is to study and plan a course of action toward reducing tensions and dissatisfactions. Positive forces may be augmented, negative ones reduced in power, or changed in direction.

4. The fourth phase is the production of actual changes in any of the forces or influences in the situation, with eventual change in educational materials and processes.

An illustration of an equilibrium diagram[3] **or force field.** The following paragraphs are adapted from the presentation by Jenkins, which is the clearest found by the writers. Jenkins'[4] illustration shows how certain forces in the group might affect an effort to improve the "teacher-pupil planning" method of classroom procedure. The procedure is equally applicable to community diagnosis preceding curriculum improvement. The arrows in the diagram pointing downward represent restraining forces which work against the desired improvement in method. Upward pointing arrows represent favoring forces. Length of

[3] Kurt Lewin, "Frontiers of Group Dynamics: Concept, Method and Reality in Social Science, Social Equilibria and Social Change," *Human Relations* (June, 1947), pp. 5-41. Contains the original statement concerning equilibrium diagrams.

[4] David Jenkins, "Social Engineering in Educational Change: An Outline of Method," *Progressive Education* (May, 1949), pp. 193-197. Other articles in this same issue are also valuable.

arrow represents relative force at the point represented—the longer the arrow the stronger the force.

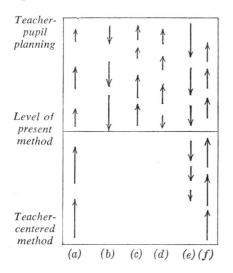

Force (*a*) might be a generally progressive theory of education held by the teachers which would have a favoring effect through all levels of method. Greater pressure from this force would come at the lower level of equilibrium, that is, where method is more teacher-centered. But the teacher might not possess the skills necessary for carrying on participatory planning, hence this becomes force (*b*), a strong restraining force against going beyond present levels. The teachers probably believe sincerely that more pupil participation will increase their own satisfaction and efficiency, hence force (*c*) represents this and should stimulate efforts to go beyond present levels. Force (*d*) is important as an illustration of change in direction. The administration, let us say, is hesitant to make changes because of obvious difficulties, but once a change has been decided upon, will carry through faithfully. The hesitancy which would act to restrain and keep practice where it is, becomes a favorable force. Forces (*e*) and (*f*) represent differences of opinion among parents. Some believe that the newfangled methods are detrimental or at least wasteful; others believe them to be valuable and useful. A campaign of education and public relations might conceivably convince more parents of the value of democratic, participatory methods. Force (*e*) would then be reduced, and (*f*) augmented. Both operate at all levels within the field.

Categories of forces present in practically all communities. The influences operating within any community may be classified in any of several ways. The one given here may be modified to suit local levels of insight.

1. Restraining forces that can be changed or eliminated only with the greatest effort, or those that cannot be changed economically.
2. Restraining forces which can be reduced or eliminated with least effort.
3. Restraining forces which can be changed in direction.
4. Positive forces which can be increased.

Forces may be modified. A staff and community leaders may proceed in several ways. The positive or driving forces may be *strengthened,* the restraining forces may be *reduced, eliminated,* or *changed* in direction. Many principles and techniques have been developed (see later) with which curriculum workers may work for change in attitudes or beliefs that must precede any change in the curriculum. Attention must be given to preserve security of the persons in the situation.

Restraining forces that can be changed or eliminated only with greatest effort, or those that cannot be changed economically. Some writers distinguish "crucial" forces, those that must be changed or there can be no change in the curriculum. The writers believe: (*a*) that all forces are crucial in the sense that change of some sort must be brought about or curriculum change will be retarded; and (*b*) that all forces can be changed, given time, energy, leadership, and "propitiousness of time." We recognize, however, certain other factors: (*a*) limitations in principles, techniques, and abilities of leaders for given situations; (*b*) certain forces that are so powerful that efforts to change them may not be worth while in terms of physical or emotional expenditure. Effort may well be expended more profitably on other forces in the situation. There is, as we say, "no use banging one's head against a stone wall." The success of a curriculum worker may, in fact, be evaluated not only by the shrewdness with which he appraises these community forces, but also by the realism with which he matches the "equipment" available against the obstacles, and by his ability to seize the "psychological moment" (propitiousness of time).

Illustrations of forces in this class might include:

a. Resistance of a wealthy New England suburban town to any modification of the college preparatory curriculum.
b. Resistance of a predominantly Catholic community toward "sex education."
c. Resistance of a southern, rural, Protestant community toward employing Catholic teachers.
d. Resistance of certain economically powerful persons and groups toward "consumer education," consumer research, toward critical, even though friendly, analysis of the strengths and maladjustments of our economic system.
e. Resistance of certain groups toward that type of "social study curriculum" which brings learners into contact with the actualities of local politics, state and national policies; pressure groups, propaganda, and the like.

Restraining forces which can be reduced or eliminated with least effort. The reduction of restraining forces is, in general, better procedure than the augmenting of positive driving forces, especially in early stages. Increasing a driving force without reducing the opposing forces may make for more conflict and insecurity. Illustrations of forces which might be reduced with little difficulty are:

Belief that the modern program has no place for teaching skills.
Belief that the "3 R's" are not adequately taught.
Belief that the values of democratic citizenships are neglected.

The huge volume of fact bearing upon the first two usually convinces all but the truly bigoted. An illustration is found in the relatively quick reduction of these two in popular thinking during the recent rash of attacks on the schools. Critics opened their attacks in ignorance of valid data which could be understood by anyone. The cry of "communism in the schools" is dying harder because of the emotional involvement and because the criticism can be used to make political capital. It is dying, however, under the slow, tedious process of getting the facts and then presenting them to the public.

Low morale in a staff can be reduced by identifying sharply the actual causes for the poor spirit and then attacking them directly. A series of successes here engenders confidence for attacking more difficult items.

Lack of skill in dealing with pupil participation, for instance, can be remedied through development of these skills through a program of in-service education which includes study and discussion of principles, development of techniques, tryout with assistance. Again a series of successes develops confidence not only for this factor but for the approach to others.

Further general suggestions would include:

1. Proceed slowly at first, thus ensuring security as small changes take place to build security.
2. Recognize that several factors are being dealt with at once. (The foregoing paragraphs have dealt with one element at a time for the sake of clarity but several will be included in a real situation.)
3. Select for a point at which to begin those forces which can probably be affected most easily, quickly and with little threat to security.
4. Select those forces which, when modified, are most likely to produce desired changes.
5. Proceed at all times by means of fully participatory group action.

Restraining forces which can be changed in direction. Jenkins believes this to be one of the most effective initial attacks. Teachers, for instance, would probably entirely agree that children and youth must be educated for democratic citizenship and patriotism, but disagree widely as to the classroom methods suitable for this goal. Some of the opinions held would be strong forces operating against developing pupil participation. A study program might convince all or many that co-operative planning in the classroom is in fact an effective technique in democratic education. The teachers already possess a positive motive in the general *goal* of citizenship. A restraining opinion about *method* is now replaced by a positive belief.

Changing direction can also be seen when the cry arises that the current curriculum meets the needs of the students adequately. An investigation by means of a study of drop-outs and a follow-up on graduates over a period of years usually changes public opinion. Parents are often startled at the keen analyses made by their own children on this problem.

Teachers in a small Massachusetts system became alert to the possibilities of creative education through reading, summer school, and observation. The superintendent was violently opposed, condemning all creative education as "chaos." (Forces operating upon him were, among others, doubtless: (1) ignorance of the nature of creative expression among children; (2) insecurity due to the ignorance; (3) insecurity because he had no idea of what to do.) The teachers, however, converted the community and thus developed a strong driving force, replacing indifference and some antagonism. The superintendent acquiesced but eventually was removed because he could not free himself from the forces controlling his thinking. In another Massachusetts community, the Harvard Center for Field Studies, called upon to make a survey, found the community members and the local newspaper to be strong forces against change in the curriculum or teaching. Slow patient gathering of data, plus more and more *involvement of local people* in the process converted laymen and newspaper from opposition to strong support of the new program.

Illustrative influences which may be given changed direction:

Factions within the community which want better education, but are fighting with one another to see who will control the change.

Persons or groups within the community who want better education, but who, misled by recent irresponsible newspaper and magazine publicity, identify any change with the "evils of progressive education."

Persons in the community who are basically friendly toward better education but who have had unfortunate experiences with previous personnel.

Critical, negativistic teachers who have never been encouraged to think through their own criticism to discover the real reasons, and thence on to constructive change.

Positive forces which can be increased. This is not too difficult. The general method with the professional staff is through co-operative, democratically operated programs of in-service study, observation, and tryout. The general method with community personnel is through involvement in the professional programs, through furnishing facts, through demonstrated successes. More will be said about techniques of involvement in a few pages.

The number of available favorable forces is far larger than is generally recognized. The list here is merely illustrative:

Teachers who are frustrated under present system and believe there must be something better.

Persons in the community who believe that the local schools are not doing the best job possible.

Progressive members of the school board.

Teachers who are experimenting with different methods in their classrooms.

Born skeptics who can pose penetrating questions.

Specific persons on the staff who may have experience and skill with group process.

Teachers' genuine desire to prepare good citizens (despite presently inadequate educational practices).

Illustrations of forces present in practically all school situations. An adequate list would cover several pages. Field workers will discover the range and large number of forces through experience in diagnosing community situations. Students should supplement the lists here with others. (See at end of chapter, "Individual and Group Reports," Nos. 18-22.)

The opinions, beliefs, values, and feelings possessed by persons individually and in organized groups are likely to range from one extreme to another on any question, in school or out. The brief list below deals with education, is illustrative only, and does not belabor the nevertheless important fact that nearly every point has an opposite statement. This is important in view of the fact that we can reverse many forces.

Positive forces likely to be found operating within a faculty:

Confidence that one's principal will back up his teachers; will not play favorites; will accept suggestions and abide by group decisions; will take responsibility when he should and not "pass the buck" to subordinates.

Confidence that the central administration will work for the good of education and of the staff; will protect from unjustified criticism; will not evade questions raised.

High morale due to the foregoing and also to acceptance by the community, good working conditions, confidence in each other.

Desire to teach well, to make work interesting and meaningful to learners, to contribute to educating loyal citizens, to achieve results in basic skills.

Belief that there is opportunity for advancement and recognition.

Conviction that modern methods are more effective than traditional.

Knowledge that supervisory assistance will be forthcoming and that supervisors will assume joint responsibility for any tryouts.

The reverse of those listed become negative forces. Others may be noted:

Low morale (for any of various reasons).

Lack of confidence in the administration (either for its leadership or its honesty).

Fear of new because of lack of knowledge or lack of necessary skills.

Fear that "essential subject matter" will be left out: or that the "fundamentals" will not be well taught.

Consciousness of criticism from parents (on results; on treatment of children; on ability or preparation; religion; personal life).

Feeling that teachers are not socially accepted by the community.

Belief that one's suggestions or efforts will not be received or appreciated.

Forces positive and negative likely to be operating among laymen:

Belief that the present curriculum prepares quite well for life (or equally strong belief that it does not).

Beliefs about "essential subject matter" and the "3 R's" as above.

Conviction that modern methods have been adequately proven to be superior (or the opposite).

Belief that a guidance program is urgently needed (or that this is a frill and that the home should give the necessary guidance).

Strong beliefs for (or against) sex education.

Objection to "experimentation on our children." (Often balanced by desire for the very best new things for our children.)

Firm conviction that "too much tax money goes to the schools." (Often balanced by strong beliefs about outmoded "firetrap" or unsanitary buildings.)

Belief that teachers are the servants of the community and need not participate in policy-making, nor raise questions.

Forces operating among the learners will include similar beliefs about the adequacy of the curriculum, treatment by teachers, adequate help with study problems or personal problems (or lack of this help), adequacy of extracurricular opportunities. Various attitudes and beliefs for or against certain socioeconomic classes, nationalities, or races will appear.

The forces here listed are stronger for or against desirable educational change when held by organized groups. Generally speaking, favorable and augmenting forces will be expressed by such organizations as the League of Women Voters, the Association of University Women, and similar associations of women in business or the professions. The taxpayers' associations are practically always against the improvement of education because of costs. The Chamber of Commerce locally and nationally, the various associations of industrialists and business men, may be favorable or unfavorable in different localities. An excellent opportunity for educational leadership is presented in connection with these groups. The national headquarters of the American Legion has gone on record as against unjustified criticism and attack on the schools and as generally favorable to improvement. Local posts often exert strong influence against the schools, as does the official magazine at times. The so-called "patriotic" groups, while strongly for what they believe to be education for patriotism and national loyalty, are more often negative influences on education. The Parent Teachers organization nationally is a strong positive force and can be made so locally. A large number of "front" groups, or "hate" groups, are strong forces against improvement in education, in fact against public education itself. The press in some places is one of the strongest forces for improvement, in others the single strongest force against the schools. Labor unions, the National Citizens Commission for the Public Schools, and the Anti-Defamation League are very strong positive forces.[5]

Extraneous factors working for or against curriculum improvement. The factors summarized on pages 379-381 in Chapter 12 must also be accounted for in a given situation. Recall the discussion there of legislation, college entrance examinations, research, frontier thinkers, teachers' associations, and others.

Device for sorting out forces and their bearings. The chart[6] on page 579 is one method and may suggest others to readers. The illustration is not intended to be final or exhaustive.

Channels of school-community influence and persons controlling the channels. Despite the dynamic word *force,* the various forces do not operate themselves. Community influences[7] of all sorts are channeled through individuals and small groups. Asked off-hand to identify the influential persons in a community, the average citizen is likely to name the "big-shots," those who enjoy prestige because of family background, wealth, or a status position. These "prestige bearers" do have influence, as witness the use of big names as honorary chairmen and as sponsors for community projects. Studies show, however, that frequently these individuals are not those who influence others most effectively. Very often those with greatest influence in a community, particularly in a neighborhood, may be found in everyday positions. The effectiveness of these individuals rests on the confidence of their neighbors and is based on past performance in aiding others with problems, in diagnosing and advising upon community issues. The sum of several neighborhood leaders of this type adds up to substantial community influence.

Lewin suggested the term *gatekeeper* for those individuals who exert real influence in channeling community thought and ac-

[5] For details on this phase, see *Forces Affecting American Education,* 1953 Yearbook, Association for Supervision and Curriculum Development (Washington, NEA, 1953).

[6] The writers wish to express their appreciation for the assistance rendered by members of Burton's seminar on curriculum problems at the Harvard Graduate School of Education. The chief contributors to the general discussion here and who will be referred to specifically from time to time included:

Joseph W. Cole, faculty member, State Teachers College, Geneseo, N. Y.

Joseph J. Young, Jr., Executive Secretary, Rhode Island Institute of Instruction (State Teachers Association).

Donald W. Oliver, Teaching Fellow. Formerly teacher in the Helen Baldwin School, Canterbury, Conn.

Joseph Carroll, Teaching Fellow. Formerly teacher in the Cascade, Mont., High School. Now assistant business manager, Newton, Mass., public schools.

[7] Kurt Lewin, "Forces Behind Food Habits and Methods of Change," *Bulletin of the National Resources Council,* Vol. 108 (1943), pp. 35-65.

ANALYSIS OF FORCES*

Force	Operates as		Operates on				Nature of Force		
	Augmenting Forces	Restraining Forces	Students	Teachers	Lay Public	Administration	Direction Can Be Changed	Can Be Increased	Can Be Reduced
1. Morale	x	x	x	x	x	x	x	x	
a. Economic recognition	x			x		x		x	
Economic neglect		x		x		x			x
b. Job security	x			x		x		x	
Job insecurity		x		x		x			x
c. Good physical work cond.	x		x	x		x	x	x	
Poor physical work cond.		x	x	x		x	x		x
d. Good psychological cond.	x		x	x		x	x	x	
Poor psychological cond.		x	x	x		x	x		x
e. Recognition (effort-perf.)	x		x	x	x	x	x	x	
Lack of recognition		x	x	x	x	x	x		x
2. Fear and insecurity from									
a. Lack of skill		x		x		x			x
b. Concern over nature of change		x	x	x	x	x	x		x
c. Regard over ability to adjust to change		x	x	x	x	x			x
d. Regard over loss of something valued		x	x	x	x	x	x		x
e. Concern over cost change		x				x	x		x
f. Fear of economic loss		x		x		x	x		x
g. Fear of loss of prestige		x		x		x	x		x
3. Forces inherent in a group									
a. Cohesiveness	x	x	x	x	x	x	x	x	x
b. Commonness of purpose	x	x	x	x	x	x	x	x	x
c. Adherence to group stand	x	x	x	x	x	x	x	x	x
d. Acceptance by group	x		x	x	x	x		x	x
4. Concern over welfare of child	x	x		x	x	x		x	x
5. Desire for self-improvement	x			x		x		x	
6. Curiosity	x		x	x	x	x		x	
7. Lack of money, facilities, etc.		x	x	x	x	x	x		x

* Suggested by Joseph Cole.

tion. Several kinds of gatekeepers may be distinguished. First, we may call "status" gatekeepers those who exert influence because of their position in the community: the leading banker, a priest or minister, a political boss, a prominent physician or lawyer, a member of the first families. Second are the officers of organized groups in the community, and in fact the groups themselves; labor unions, religious bodies, associations of business men or of men in the professions. Third are the "natural" gatekeepers, those individuals close to the problems, questions, fears, and hopes of their neighbors. A gatekeeper here may be a housewife, a small shop-keeper, a barber, a well-beloved local physician, or other member of the "plain people." The writer remembers a western pioneer town in which the single most influential person was the owner of the local barber shop. This friendly, optimistic, extroverted individual was possessed of unusual shrewdness in social or political affairs and was consulted by everyone who knew him. Another community had as most influential a crippled ancient who had crossed the plains in an ox-cart and who manifested sharp insight into human affairs. Very few things were ever undertaken in the two communities without consultation with these two. Another waterfront community had as leader the owner of the combination respectable hotel, gambling place, tough saloon, and bawdy house. The "good" people never succeeded in overcoming his influence, partly because they could not organize. The latter fact has a message for all community leaders including school men; influences and channels of influence must be known, taken into account, and if not organized at least given a voice.

The school community has as status gate-keepers, superintendents and other administrative officers, and the school board. A principal and the department head operate swinging gates, channeling information and sentiment both ways; from administration to teaching staff and from staff to administration. Officers of teachers' associations, unions, or other professional organizations are in this category. The leaders of those informal groupings or cliques which exist in all faculties (in fact in all groupings) are important natural gatekeepers. Individuals of insight and sympathy and a known willingness to listen to other persons and to give sincere advice are also very important natural gatekeepers.

Anyone who wishes to work with a school staff or a total community cannot operate without knowledge of the channels of influence and the gatekeepers, as well as of the forces listed earlier. These basic factors cannot be discovered by guesswork, by using conventional beliefs about prestige and influence. No fool-proof methods for locating channels and gatekeepers have been devised and only a few actual investigations have been made. The best method to date is the well-known sociometric technique already being used in classrooms for the forming of better work groups. One study [8] to locate gatekeepers devised a fifteen-point questionnaire with a number of subquestions. Illustrative samples are:

1. Have you given advice to anybody at all recently:
    (1) On what kinds of things?
    (2) Can you give some other instances?
4. When people you know have some personal trouble, to whom are they most likely to turn for advice?
    a. Why do you think they would go to him (or her)?
    b. Are there any others to whom they might turn with such problems?
12. Who would you say are the important people in town? (Ask for each name given the indicated follow-up questions. Be sure to ask, "Any others?" until the respondent has mentioned at least five persons. If he finds it diffi-

[8] Frank A. Stewart, "A Sociometric Study of Influence in Southtown," *Sociometry,* J. L. Moreno, ed. (February, 1947), pp. 11-13.

———, "A Study of Influence in Southtown," *Sociometry* (August, 1947), pp. 273-286. The two articles are actually one account. The questionnaire is reproduced in full. Interesting results are given showing the actual influence of "prestige bearers" and persons whose positions might indicate influence. Further studies are needed, especially looking toward the discovery of the more local and subtle channels and the less well-known "natural gatekeepers." (The questionnaire used here is also reproduced in full in Smith, Stanley, and Shores, *op. cit.,* pp. 685-687.)

Robert Bartels and Frank A. Stewart, "How Briarcliff Manor Took Inventory," *The American City* (September, 1948), pp. 104-105.

R. K. Merton, "Patterns of Influence: A Study of Interpersonal Influence and Communications Behavior in a Local Community," in Paul F. Lazarsfield and Frank N. Stanton, eds., *Communications Research* (New York, Bureau of Applied Social Research, Columbia Univ., 1948-1949), pp. 180-219.

Other good materials will be found in the general literature dealing with sociometry and leadership; in texts on social psychology; on industrial management.

See also references in Ch. 7.

cult to name more than one or two persons, probe by asking, "Are there any others like Mr. *A,* or Mr. *B?"*)

    a. In what ways is Mr. *A* important? (If this question proves too vague for the particular respondent, ask, "What makes you think of Mr. *A* as important?")

    b. Now that you stop to think about it, how do you suppose Mr. *A* came to be important?

    c. Who else is important in town?

Sociometric methods are not perfect but they are susceptible to improvement and even as they are, they are far superior to guesswork or the use of conventional standards concerning social interaction.

Curriculum programs (or any social project of whatever nature) will make or break at this point. A school leader or staff, or any leader in any social process, simply cannot succeed in any undertaking without explicit attention to community forces, channels of influence, and the gatekeepers who direct the influences. An extensive, detailed equilibrium diagram need not be made in simple situations, but a definite listing and weighing of the factors noted must be made if only in simple running discourse. The general process of problem-solving outlined in these pages is applicable also to any problem which involves changing human behavior. The preceding account, abbreviated as it is, is still long enough, relative to the rest of this chapter, almost to constitute a digression. This testifies to the basic importance of the process for curriculum improvement.

We all know superintendents who will make no move to improve anything because, say they, school leaders who get new buildings, or who inaugurate programs of curriculum improvement, or who attempt to upgrade teaching, always end up by getting dismissed. This is not an accurate diagnosis. Leaders who lose out over new programs do so not because of the new program, but because they failed to assess the community situation, failed to involve community members, and thus carry them along with the program.

We hear school and community leaders with a do-nothing policy criticized for laziness, apathy, inertia, or even cynicism toward improvement. These words have no meaning outside the vague muddled world of casual conversation, and their very use prevents the desired improvement. There is no such thing in the world as "laziness" or "apathy." The words are loose, blanket terms referring inaccurately to a type of behavior. Persons act in such manner as to be designated as lazy or apathetic for definite given reasons. Indifference or apathy are due to discoverable fears and insecurities. A superintendent does not know how to initiate a curriculum program, does not possess the social skills necessary, is afraid to try. A community may be perfectly satisfied with its schools, quite unaware of actual shortcomings, unaware of new developments. What is needed is the type of careful analysis and assessment of forces and influences at work in persons and groups, outlined in these pages. To attribute failure to do anything to apathy or cynicism gets us nowhere. Bringing the causes for the so-called apathy out into the open, assessing them, and planning a systematic program for their reduction or elimination is the first step in getting anything done on a social project.

The whole problem reported here is too important to drop with this abbreviated outline. Field workers and students are urged to do further reading, to analyze given situations whenever possible. A few illustrative references:

BAVELAS, Alex, "Some Problems of Organizational Change," *Journal of Social Issues* (Summer, 1948), pp. 48-52.

BERI, Susan, and others, "Techniques for the Diagnosis and Measurement of Intergroup Attitudes and Behavior," *Psychological Bulletin* (May, 1948), pp. 248-271.

BRADFORD, Leland P., "Involving Parents in School Problems," *Progressive Education* (May, 1949), pp. 214-219.

GOODSON, Max R., "Social Engineering in a School System," *Progressive Education* (May, 1949), pp. 197-201.

JAQUES, Elliot, "Interpretative Group Discussion as a Method of Facilitating Social Change," *Human Relations* (August, 1948), pp. 533-549.

JENKINS, David H., "Social Engineering in Educational Change: An Outline of Method," *Progressive Education* (May, 1949), pp. 193-197.

JENNINGS, Helen H., "Sociometry in Group Relations" (Washington, American Council on Education, 1948), pp. 1-85.

KNICKERBOCKER, Irving, "Leadership: A Conception and Some Implications," *Journal of Social Issues* (Summer, 1948), pp. 26-28.

LEWIN, Kurt, "Group Decision and Social Change," in Theodore M. Newcomb and Eugene L. Hartley, *Readings in Social Psychology* (New York, Holt, 1947), pp. 340-344.

——, "Frontiers in Group Dynamics: Concepts, Methods and Reality in Social Science; Social Equilibria and Social Change," *Human Relations* (June, 1947), pp. 5-41.

——, and GRABBE, Paul, "Conduct, Knowledge and Acceptance of New Values," *Journal of Social Issues* (August, 1945), pp. 56-64.

MIEL, Alice, *Changing the Curriculum* (New York, Appleton-Century-Crofts, 1946), pp. 40-47.

McGREGOR, Douglas, "The Staff Function in Human Relations," *Journal of Social Issues* (Summer, 1948), pp. 10-13.

THELEN, Herbert A., "Resistance to Change of Teaching Methods," *Progressive Education* (May, 1949), pp. 208-214.

——, "Engineering Research in Curriculum Building," *Journal of Educational Research* (April, 1948).

——, and DICKERMAN, Walter, "Stereotypes and the Growth of Groups," *Educational Leadership* (February, 1949).

A number of references on social structure with particular reference to locus of power in community attitudes and beliefs is given below.

BIERSTEDT, Robert, "An Analysis of Social Power," *American Sociological Review* (December, 1950), pp. 730-738.

COOK, Lloyd A., and COOK, E. F., *A Sociological Approach to Education* (New York, McGraw, 1950).

COUNTS, George S., *School and Society in Chicago* (New York, Harcourt, 1928).

FOA, Uriel G., "Verbal Attitude and Actual Behavior: A Tentative Method of Measuring Social Pressure," *Sociometry* (February, 1948), pp. 85-87.

GOLDHAMER, Herbert, and SHILS, E. A., "Types of Power and Status," *American Journal of Sociology* (September, 1939), pp. 171-182.

HANKS, L. M., ed., "Social Research in Political Decision," *Journal of Social Issues* (Fall, 1947), entire edition.

HUNTER, Floyd, *Community Power Structure* (Chapel Hill, Univ. of North Carolina Press, 1953).

KEY, V. O., Jr., *Politics, Parties and Pressure Groups,* 3rd ed. (New York, Crowell, 1953).

LASSWELL, Harold D., and KAPLAN, Abraham, *Power and Society* (New Haven, Yale Univ. Press, 1950).

LUNDBERG, George A., and LAWSING, Margaret, "The Sociography of Some Community Relations," *American Sociological Review* (June, 1937).

LUNDBERG, George A., and STEELE, Mary, "Social Attraction Patterns in a Village," *Sociometry* (January, 1938), pp. 375-419.

TANNENBAUM, Frank, "The Balance of Power in Society," *Political Science Quarterly* (December, 1946), pp. 481-505.

WILLIAMS, R. H., Jr., *American Society: A Sociological Interpretation* (New York, Knopf, 1951).

Precise data on community pressures and influences are meager but emerging.
A series of studies [9] currently under way sponsored by the Harvard Graduate School of Education and the Harvard Laboratory of Social Relations has produced some enlightening preliminary data. Full accounts should be available in print within a year of this date.

[9] The studies, several of them, are known as the *School Executive Studies* are under the direction of Dr. Neal Gross, with the assistance of men in sociology and psychology. Financing is by the Rockefeller Foundation, the Kellogg Foundation, and from other funds. The summary here is from the specific study entitled *The Pressures and Dilemmas of the Superintendent.*

A popular account of Dr. Gross' study will be found in: Henry F. Pringle and Katharine Pringle, "Pity the Poor School Superintendent," *Saturday Evening Post,* Sept. 4, 1954, pp. 32-33; 42-44.

Findings were derived from interviews with 48 per cent (105) of the superintendents in Massachusetts and with 500 school-board members. The purpose in this study was to develop information about the relations between superintendent and school board. A number of startling facts emerged. Superintendents were sure that certain attitudes were present in the community which inquiry showed to be absent. The opposite was also found. Certain administrators were convinced that community influence was strongly against the introduction of, for instance, sex education, whereas there was actually a very favorable attitude. The same was true concerning "controversial discussions" in the classroom. Community leaders often misjudged community sentiment. (The two specific illustrations were taken from another source but illustrate similar situations in the Harvard studies.) One of the striking findings of the Harvard studies was that flatly contradictory pressures often play upon the superintendent.

Fifty-nine per cent of the superintendents reported strong pressure to "return to" or to put more emphasis upon the "three R's" whereas 64 per cent were under the directly opposite pressure, namely, to expand the limited curriculum with new courses and subjects.

Thirty-nine per cent received protests against new services by the school, e.g., guidance, health programs, hot lunches, whereas 63 per cent received demands that such services be introduced.

Forty per cent faced demands from the community for less emphasis on athletics, 58 per cent were under pressure to more emphasis.

Forty-six per cent were confronted with demands that school contracts be awarded to certain firms. The same percentage was under demand for appointment of teachers for reasons other than competence. The same situation existed regarding dismissals.

Many other similar facts are contained in the study.

Pressures differ by groups. Politicians and businessmen are more likely to exert influence on tax issues, bond proposals, and contracts. The press, the service clubs, and some school-board members are likely to demand more interschool athletics. Superintendents reported community pressures from the following sources:

Parents (92 per cent reported such pressures)
School board members (75 per cent)
Teachers (65 per cent)
Taxpayers' groups (49 per cent)
Finance committee or city council (48 per cent)
Local politicians (46 per cent)
Business or commercial organizations (45 per cent)
Economically influential individuals (44 per cent)
Personal friends (37 per cent)
"Old line" families (31 per cent)
Local newspaper (36 per cent)
Church or religious groups (28 per cent)
Veterans organizations (27 per cent)
Labor unions (27 per cent)
Chamber of Commerce (23 per cent)
Service clubs (21 per cent)
Fraternal organization (13 per cent)

Certain questions concerning the "dilemmas" of the superintendent are posed in the following passage. Later published materials will contain positive suggestions for meeting the situations.

How do you balance professional standards against the unprofessional standards and practices of some school-board members?

What do you do when you discover that undercover religious and nationality conflicts are at the heart of many of your school problems?

What do you do when one or more school board members insist on misrepresenting you or your ideas and policies, who make unfounded charges against you? Do you attempt to remove the unfavorable ideas developed in the community or do you "stay out of local politics"?

What do you do with strong cross pressures within the community, e.g., strong groups insisting on a winning football team and another insisting on the de-emphasis of athletics?

A number of helpful recommendations are available which are too long to reproduce here but many of which bear on the discussion of the preceding part of this chapter.

Understanding must be developed between the school administration and community opinion. Public opinion should be developed against the use of the schools for local patronage, and strongly for truly educational goals and procedures. Techniques should be developed for frank discussion between superintendents and community leaders, groups, "gatekeepers."

Principle 4. *A participatory process should be used providing for the widest possible involvement of the professional staff and the community members.*

The desired changes must be made not merely in materials and methods of instruction, but in the beliefs, values, attitudes, and practices of the persons concerned. A successful process must therefore provide for (*a*) growth of the personnel, and (*b*) observable results within the instructional materials and methods. These in turn produce a third characteristic of good process; (*c*) a desirable type of security within the staff, the pupils, and the community. The process must also provide for (*d*) continuity of effort.

A few persons are irritated at discussions of process. They focus on the goal and drive toward it, regardless of methods used. A number of evils result, not the least of which is that the chosen goal may not be reached at all. Others regard process as a collection of clever techniques, "tricks of the trade," a list of "how to's." This gives rise to distrust and suspicion of process; it becomes merely manipulation and an end in itself. Process should never be regarded as a set of techniques, should never be permitted to become an end; it must be designed for solving stated problems within a given setting. We may disregard those who regard attention to process and its control as futile. The result is laissez faire and drift. Progress is not possible without attention to and effort to direct a desirable process.

The process which has proved most effective is that of participatory group approach and study, group decision and tryout, and continuing study. The process will provide for maximum interchange of ideas, will allow sufficient time for development and assimilation of concepts, sufficient time for development of a consensus or near-consensus. One aim will be a synthesis of all pertinent materials, including conflicting theories and beliefs. There will be division of labor to expedite the process, together with careful record-keeping of discussion and decision, of the results of tryout. The principles and mechanisms for operating participatory programs, together with warnings and cautions about the process were set forth in Chapter 7. The emergence and use of the actual mechanisms—study groups, workshops, conferences, and others—are outlined in Chapter 6.

Principle 5. *A functional organization and machinery must be developed.*

An organization of some sort is necessary to carry forward any complex undertaking. An error of the past has been to assume that the *form* of the organization was the important thing, instead of *functional relation* of the organization to the problems and needs under consideration. A functional organization will be semipermanent and changeable, will provide for uninhibited flow of ideas in both directions. The machinery develops as needed. An organization handed down from above violates the first principle of administration, namely, that organizations should develop functionally.

The specific characteristics or details of a desirable organization for a curriculum-development program cannot be suggested in advance. The number, size, and kind of committees cannot be stated in advance nor interrelationships indicated. Any and all kinds of study groups, production committees, experimental groups, editing committees may appear. A succession of leaders may arise to serve different purposes. Consultants and specialists will be called on as needed.

The situation here is similar to that of developing a functional organization for administering a school system. The functional organization, as indicated in Chapter 5, may appear to be very similar outwardly to the formal. So it is with organization for curriculum improvement. The differences, however, are more fundamental than the likenesses. The functional organization grows up from the problems and is fashioned to meet needs. The formal organization grows down from the central authority and is fashioned to meet abstract logical principles. The differences in general structure, in number and names of committees, in provisions for intercommunication may be slight; but they are the key to the basic principle: organizations must grow out of needs, that is, be functional.

Some general characteristics of a desirable organization. The following summary emphasizes points presented many times in preceding pages. The curriculum organization devised in any given situation:

1. Should grow out of the problems found there.
2. Should be close enough to the actual problems and be flexible enough to ensure freeflowing interpersonal exchanges, to ensure the utilization of the contributions of many types of persons within typical heterogeneous groups including pupils and lay groups.
3. Should provide for the necessary co-ordination between groups and units within the system as the program develops from its simple beginnings.
4. Should provide for continuity of effort.
5. Should be subservient to its purpose and not become the important feature of the situation.
6. Should develop all committees functionally as needed to serve temporarily or with membership rotated.
7. Should develop all standing committees to deal with major persistent factors. (Membership may rotate under a stagger system.)
8. Should develop a general policy under which the group operates. (Subcommittees are thus given power to act under policy.)
9. Should keep records, publish summaries, and eventually produce materials of use in improving instruction.

A democratic, functional organization for a curriculum program is desirable, first, because it is the most efficient method in the long run. Second, it provides full opportunity for individuals and minority groups who often have important contributions to make. Third, it is likely to encourage and to utilize social invention. Fourth, it ensures, as far as anything can ensure, group solidarity, growth for individuals and groups, and accomplishment, all of which give that security necessary to mental hygiene. Accomplishment of desirable results is more likely to ensue.

The chart on page 586 shows the organization developed in Weston, Massachusetts, for a community-wide survey and improvement campaign. Eventually every adult in this small, closely-knit community was involved in the program.

The keynote of both process and administration for curriculum-development programs is participation. Principles 4 and 5 above have stressed the fundamental importance of wide participation by school personnel and laymen. In addition, evidence exists in several studies which supplies factual backing for the principles. Banning's [10] study of junior-high-school teachers in a Massachusetts community revealed that the single most important factor in winning over teachers to a curriculum program was the opportunity for real participation. Attitudes of these teachers favorable to curriculum change correlated significantly on this point above all others; the teacher's feeling that he was a real participant and that his individual contributions really counted in policy-making and in implementing that policy. Scrutiny of several of the early state programs which were successful shows wide participation to be a characteristic.

The general challenge here in curriculum programs is to provide, in so far as humanly possible, the factors which facilitate co-operation, and to prevent or alleviate the effects of weakness in these factors. How can par-

[10] Evelyn Banning, "Teacher Attitudes Toward Curriculum Change: A Study of the Junior High School Teachers in [a Massachusetts community]." Unpublished doctoral dissertation, Harvard Graduate School of Education, 1953.

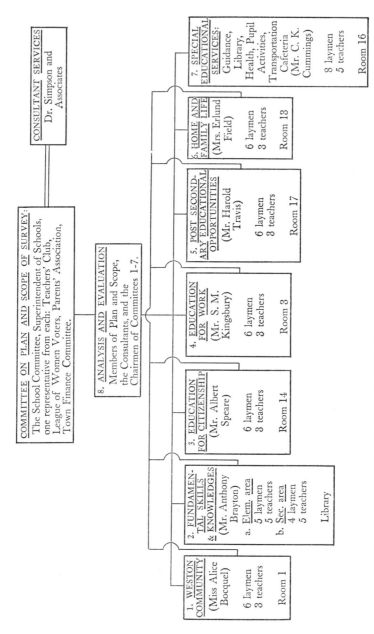

CONSULTANT SERVICES
Dr. Simpson and Associates

COMMITTEE ON PLAN AND SCOPE OF SURVEY:
The School Committee, Superintendent of Schools,
one representative from each: Teachers' Club,
League of Women Voters, Parents' Association,
Town Finance Committee.

8. ANALYSIS AND EVALUATION
Members of Plan and Scope,
the Consultants, and the
Chairmen of Committees 1-7.

1. WESTON COMMUNITY
(Miss Alice Bocquel)
6 laymen
3 teachers
Room 1

2. FUNDAMEN-TAL SKILLS & KNOWLEDGES
(Mr. Anthony Brayton)
a. Elem. area
5 laymen
5 teachers
b. Sec. area
4 laymen
5 teachers
Library

3. EDUCATION FOR CITIZENSHIP
(Mr. Albert Speare)
6 laymen
3 teachers
Room 14

4. EDUCATION FOR WORK
(Mr. S. M. Kingsbury)
6 laymen
3 teachers
Room 3

5. POST SECOND-ARY EDUCATIONAL OPPORTUNITIES
(Mr. Harold Travis)
6 laymen
3 teachers
Room 17

6. HOME AND FAMILY LIFE
(Mrs. Erlund Field)
6 laymen
3 teachers
Room 13

7. SPECIAL EDUCATIONAL SERVICES: Guidance,
Library, Health, Pupil
Activities,
Transportation
Cafeteria
(Mr. C. K. Cummings)
8 laymen
5 teachers
Room 16

ORGANIZATION OF THE PARTICIPATORY SCHOOL SURVEY, WESTON,
MASSACHUSETTS, 1944-1945

ticipation be stimulated? What are the obstacles? An excellent study of these factors in the Virginia state program was made by Saylor. His general conclusions have been corroborated by other fragmentary studies of various programs. He lists the chief facilitating factors as:

1. Dynamic, competent leadership.
2. Economic ability sufficient to finance a good program.

Saylor believes that leadership is the critical factor, going so far as to say:[11]

In fact, a dynamic superintendent of schools can, if he so desires, probably overcome almost any handicap to participation by his school system in a state co-operative curriculum program of the stimulative type organized in Virginia.

The two factors are interlocked. Good leadership is undeniably attracted by better rewards and by better support of the program. High economic ability is, however, no guarantee of competent leadership. Many wealthy systems employ mediocre leaders and teachers. Good leadership is sometimes found in systems of low economic ability, exercised usually by young men and women on their way to better positions.

The economic factor does clearly affect items which facilitate co-operation:

    a. Provision of competent and sufficient supervision.
    b. Provision of better salaries and conditions for teachers.
    c. Provision of more generous supplies of books, instructional aids, and other material factors.

Saylor notes a negative factor which becomes of great importance in rural states, or rural areas within states:

3. Physical and cultural isolation.

Isolation as a factor presents one of the most direct challenges in any program. Urban situations and nonisolated rural areas are likely to possess good economic ability, first-class leadership, reasonably well-trained and -paid teachers, ability and willingness to carry on a competent program. Co-operation is not too difficult to secure if the leadership is good. Isolated communities, on the other hand, are handicapped not merely by distance and transportation difficulties which make supervision, intervisitation, and various cultural contacts difficult. Isolated communities develop a feeling of segregation and neglect. They become sensitive about backwardness, feel hopeless about improvement, and develop unconcern, if not antagonism, toward developments in more favored areas.

Saylor believes that the Virginia program did not always succeed in securing active participation in the more remote rural and isolated areas, low in economic ability and lacking leadership. The program was one of the earliest state programs and doubtless progress has been made subsequently.

The developing program in Maine has the problem of isolation in serious proportions. Distances are great and Maine contains a large area of "unorganized territory." The challenge is being met squarely by the state department. Maine has the only state officer "in charge of unorganized territory" in the United States. The general consultant has visited a number of the most isolated one-room schools to observe conditions, to get the teachers' problems at first hand, thus to participate in developing aid for these teachers. State supervisors and district superintendents make earnest effort to bring supervision to these isolated schools. The 1945 workshop included a rural section. Teachers in this group attacked their own problems with vigor and produced excellent materials which became a state bulletin for distribution among rural teachers.

[11] Galen Saylor, *Factors Associated with Participation in Co-operative Programs of Curriculum Development* (New York, Teachers College, Bureau of Publications, Columbia Univ., 1941), whole volume, but Chs. 3 and 8 particularly, p. 234. Saylor presents excellent detailed data for all the points developed. Space prohibits extended reference. Students and field workers should read the original study.

Types of participation which should be provided. First, of course, there should be free participation by the professional staff; administrative and supervisory officers, curriculum co-ordinators, teachers. Second, participation in several ways should be provided for the children and adolescents in the schools. Third, there should be consultants of various types, general and special, and small specialized committess. Fourth, the participation of lay groups will be greatly extended over that provided by early programs. The details of the first two forms of participation have been made amply clear throughout this and other volumes. Lay participation needs a further brief note.

Lay groups serve best as sources of public opinion about the strength and weakness of current programs, of opinion on the soundness of proposed improvements. Lay groups render excellent service in helping to develop general policy through discussions with professional leaders. They serve also as sounding boards before which to present explanations or denials of criticism, explanations and research backgrounds for new developments. Convinced of the soundness of technical explanations made by the professional staff, the lay participants then become centers for dissemination of information about and support for the new program. Proposed improvements, no matter how sound, will fail if public misunderstanding arises; are far more likely to succeed if there has been public discussion and review. Lay participation is not to "sell" a program after its development, but actually to aid in the development of the new program. Denfinite provision for study by lay members must be made, not of technical details but of general principles and trends.

Inert professional leadership in a few local communities has given rise to initiation and direction by an exasperated public of an improvement program with the professional staff subordinated or ignored. The results are usually disastrous. Lay groups should not be asked to make decisions on technical problems, but rather to demand clear, non-technical explanations, convincing to the public.[12]

Field workers and students should investigate further the roles of the various participants. (See Reports at chapter end.)

How participation is achieved: techniques of involvement. Participation in affairs which interest one, or which affect one significantly, is easy and natural. Ordinarily, little effort is actually necessary to secure participation, though this fact is often overlooked. Deliberate effort and planning may be necessary in cases where necessity and effects are not immediately apparent. What, then, are some of the techniques of involvement?

Presentation and study of results of an appraisal program. Unless this is a humdrum statistical report, interest in and difference of opinion will lead to involvement.

Surveys. The same is true of general surveys of needs, facilities, financial situation, or any factor; opinion polls of various groups; a series of structured interviews; recordings of discussions, panel presentations; or other group presentations. Partial

[12] Arkansas Congress of Parents and Teachers, *Arkansas Co-operative Program to Improve Instruction: Study Program,* Bulletin No. 1 (Little Rock, Ark., State Department of Education, 1933). An old but good reference. Consists of a bulletin produced by a workshop.

New York State Department of Education, *Problems Confronting Boards of Education: A Manual for Community Participation in Educational Planning* (Albany, N. Y. State Department of Education, 1944). Another older but good reference.

Caswell and associates. Nine good illustrations in various programs. Use the index.

Educational Leadership (February, 1952). Issue devoted to lay participation.

J. H. Hull, "Some Principles of Lay Advisory Committee Organization," *American School Board Journal* (September, 1949), pp. 30-31.

D. H. Ross and others, *The Agencies and Processes of Change in Schools* (New York, Metropolitan School Council, 1951).

Helen F. Storen, *Laymen Help Plan the Curriculum,* Association for Supervision and Curriculum Development (Washington, NEA, 1946). An excellent pamphlet.

See also texts on Public Relations; on the Community School; on Group Dynamics.

participation is often achieved in the making of the survey itself.

Projective techniques. The views, the experience, the open or hidden beliefs and attitudes will be revealed. Unrecognized assumptions and attitudes will often lead to discussion, study, or overt project.

Sociometric techniques. The application is similar to that in the classroom, presented in Chapter 7. Relations between persons and groups, some of which are blocking co-operation and some of which would be aids to participation, are brought out.

Prestige of leaders or of certain groups will often encourage participation by other individuals and groups.

Group processes, particularly free discussion, sociodrama, and role-playing are not only processes of participations but are invitations to participation. This is particularly true when well done and obviously honest in intent.

Workshops, study groups, conferences are both processes of, and invitations to, participation.

Opportunity to explore new ideas, to try out new procedures is often effective.

Complacency shock, as the result of presentation of unanswerable facts, or of new results of research, or of success by similar groups in similar situations, may be used in some situations.

Catharsis, through expressing one's dissatisfactions, "gripes," one's honest criticisms, or requests for new ideas, for supervisory leadership, is actually a projective technique but is often mentioned separately. Expression usually changes the attitude and circumstances making for far more favorable attitudes toward involvement and possible change.

Psychotherapy is mentioned by nearly all writers but obviously requires specially prepared leaders and occurs, probably, in special situations.

Basic to the whole problem is the development of sincere conviction that one may participate freely, that contributions will be respected and will be used wherever possible, that reprisals will not follow criticism or disagreement.

Specific illustrations for some of the techniques are given:

1. Participation on committees to make choice of textbooks in any curriculum area; to develop a new report card; or other project.
2. Gathering facts regarding topics that may be controversial in local schools.
    a. Review of the literature to discover research findings.
    b. Engaging in action-research or experimentation to gather new facts.
3. Helping to develop a survey program to determine community needs, knowledge, or beliefs with respect to the school program.
    a. Developing a questionnaire.
    b. Visiting homes to interview parents; visiting schools to see exhibits, to ask questions, to inform selves.
    c. Analyzing data from whatever source.
    d. Preparing a report of findings for presentation to professional-lay groups.
4. By participation in a sociodrama to demonstrate a particular problem in your school system. (A disagreement over the marking system or the mark given a particular pupil, or the marks given by a given instructor; over social-studies content; over athletic policy, or any of a score of others.) Roles to be played and when possible reversed for a second playing include parent, principal, teacher, board member, student, supervisor, coach, and others.

Principles on which techniques of involvement may be based.[13] The following list is neither fixed nor exhaustive. Field workers and students may wish to make changes or to develop lists of their own.

1. *The principle of identification.* Individuals tend to view as their own products toward which they have contributed. The ideas are thus internalized and the individual tends not to go contrary to these ideas. Probably the most important principle.

DE HUSZAR, G. B., *Practical Applications of Democracy* (New York, Harper, 1945), pp. 12-13, 16-17. Uses the word *participation* instead of *involvement.*

[13] The valuable assistance of Joseph J. Young, Jr., is gratefully acknowledged in the preparation of this list.

2. *The principle of changing the group standard.* The group is frequently the anchorage of the attitudes of the individual. Changes will be greater and more lasting if a group anchorage is provided for the new attitudes.

FESTINGER, Leon, SCHACTER, Stanley, and BACK, Kurt, *Social Pressures in Informal Groups* (New York, Harper, 1950), p. 5.

3. *The principle of prestige.* Certain individuals tend to identify their attitude with those of "status" persons in community or group.

LURIE, W. A., "The Measurement of Prestige and Prestige-Susceptibility," *Journal of Social Psychology* (May, 1938), pp. 209-225.

4. *The principle of guarantee of success.* Success must be reasonably in view. The satisfaction resulting induces persons to participate and to change views. Unpleasant results inhibit desired changes.

Many available references in psychology and in education.

5. *The principle of dissatisfaction.* Discontent and dissatisfaction always exist and can be utilized for participation and eventual change of attitude.

Many available references.

6. *The principle of tension reduction.* Disequilibrium and frustration always produce tensions which are in turn productive of efforts toward equilibrium. The tensions may be isolated and utilized.

Many available references.

7. *The principle of reduction of resistance.* This was discussed in presenting the techniques. Tension may produce aggressiveness which can be minimized by reduction of the resisting forces.

Many available references.

8. *The principle of contact.* Hostile attitudes toward persons and ideas may often be reduced through intimate contact. The nature of the contact, needless to say, is crucial. Some contacts can easily increase hostility.

WILLIAMS, R. N., *The Reduction of Intergroup Tensions* (New York, Social Science Research Council, 1951).

Others are available in quantity.

9. *The principle of complacency shock* (the word *trauma* is often used here). Attitudes may change quickly and deeply if incontrovertible evidence confronts complacency. Limited use probably.

MURCHISON, Carl L., ed., *A Handbook of Social Psychology* (Worcester, Clark Univ. Press, 1935). The article by Allport on attitudes. Available also in Allport's own writings. Allport suggests still other terms which might be principles and which are probably already implied by others in the list here: *integration, differentiation, adoption.* The *Encyclopedia of Educational Research,* p. 78, discusses these briefly.

10. *The principle of inducements.* This is obvious and well known. Inducements may be material rewards, personal nonmaterial opportunities or satisfactions, desirable working conditions, opportunity for enlarged participation, for working with chosen companions.

BARNARD, Chester, *The Functions of the Executive* (Cambridge, Harvard Univ. Press, 1948), p. 142.

11. *The principle of the gatekeeper.* This was explained in some detail in earlier pages. Many references are available.

12. *The principle of knowledge* (information and education). We all know that attitudes and feelings are not ordinarily changed by facts alone. Facts are powerful aids, however, under certain circumstances.

WILLIAMS, R. M., Jr., *The Reduction of Intergroup Tensions* (New York, Social Science Research Council, 1951).

Others available.

13. *The principle of finding acceptable words or symbols.* We all know that certain words are "fighting words" for given individuals or groups. Other words may, in the course of events, acquire distasteful connotations. The very words *curriculum program* have become anathema in given school systems because of unfortunate experiences. Simple substitution often changes attitude and general atmosphere.

SAENGER, Gerhart, *The Social Psychology of Prejudice* (New York, Harper, 1953).
KRUG, Edward A., *Curriculum Planning* (New York, Harper, 1950).
CASWELL, H. L., and associates, *Curriculum Improvement in Public School Systems* (New York, Teachers College, Bureau of Publications, Columbia Univ., 1950). Many illustrations.

The preservation of security during change. We come now to the most crucial aspect of practically any human undertaking.

Opposition to change, to obvious improvements and advantages, stems very often from plain fear. Individuals are reluctant to admit this, often in fact are not aware of their real motivations. Everyone fears, however, departure from known things, from practiced routines. Can we successfully operate in the new situation? Will we fail? Will our failure be apparent to others? There are, of course, other causes of reluctance to consider the new, of active opposition to it, but fear and even frustration resulting from real or fancied loss of security is basic in many cases.

Everyone operates, whatever his occupation in life, within a structure of relationships with other persons, within a set of expectancies of certain behavior from others. One's self-respect is involved in playing one's role. Change disturbs the relationships and upsets the expectancies. Distrust, fear, and insecurity are quite normal reactions to change. One basic aspect of social engineering anywhere is concern for adjustment to new relationships and expectancies, to the playing of new roles, thus aiding in preserving security during the difficult transitional period. The approval of co-workers, the support of others, and knowing one's own role plus skill in playing it are basic to adjusted personality.

The over-all general strategy is (1) to develop insight into the situation, and (2) to develop appropriate skills for the new roles. This is likely to bring (1) confidence that one can cope with the new, which in turn is likely to bring (2) success in new undertakings. The circle is completed. A series of small changes and successes is better than attempting a major problem first with increased possibility of difficulty and failure. The need for security, being normal, must be respected and not, as sometimes happens, sneered at by leaders. The following suggestions may be of value:

1. Begin with problems real to the individuals concerned. Avoid general problems which are "in the air," perhaps nationally.

2. Select problems for initial approach which will likely yield successes.

3. Impersonalize discussions as much as possible (discuss ideas, not people).

4. Use simple, direct language; avoid "fighting words," or words for which a local distaste has been developed.

5. Develop a strong group feeling, but with full respect for individuals within the group.

   a. Through co-operative selection of goals and problems.

   b. Through provision for free participation by all.

   c. Through group control of the process; minimizing of status leadership; acceptance by the group, however, that there must be direction and control by themselves.

   d. Through acceptance by status leader of responsibility with group for decisions and results.

6. Provide support in the form of recognition of contribution, praise for results.

7. Provide reassurance of job security.

8. Avoid direct attack on special interests of individuals or groups, i.e., do not create hostility by derogatory references to materials or beliefs approved by others. (Often these things must eventually be approached. Time, the development of intragroup confidence, and indirect approaches will help.)

9. Recognize and build upon differences in interests, special abilities within the group.

10. Avoid reference in early stages to eventual major changes; make haste slowly.

11. Avoid lengthy and philosophical discussion regarding aims, objectives; avoid getting entangled in bickering over general values or issues. These vital matters of philosophic principle and value should have been cared for elsewhere before an actual problem comes up. Efforts to solve real problems will, of course, provide for refinement of values and principles.

12. Provide an atmosphere of freedom and spontaneity.

   a. Voluntary meetings; informal meetings; social phase included.

   b. Opportunities to express grievance, to "gripe," to question, as well as to contribute.

   c. Avoidance of pressure, but make sure group stays on point.

   d. Preservation of self-decision principle (feeling that "I will have a voice" in decisions).

   e. (See Chapter 7 for details of group process.)

13. Provide adequate resources, money, material, time, consultant services. Much effort, in many places, will need to be for some time on a voluntary basis.

Principle 6. *The program should be based upon a geographic and administrative unit small enough to permit face-to-face contact, with provisions for necessary co-ordinations among small units.*

A city- or state-wide attack upon improvement of instruction is likely to become a course-writing program because of sheer size. Participation by personnel is of necessity limited to representatives, thus curtailing opportunities for growth by the whole group. Courses are written with varying degrees of participation and presented to the total group for approval and acceptance. Extensive tryouts are sometimes used to reduce the gap between the materials and the total group.

The individual school is increasingly used as the unit in modern programs. Small districts may be used in small towns or in semi-urban areas. The Maine program began with the individual classrooms and is developing appropriate co-ordinations.

The advantages of the individual school as unit are, first, that the school staff and local community have in most instances come to know each other. The resources of the community are known. The patrons have some understanding of the aims and methods of the school. Second, the ideal situation for curriculum development exists and is under some control, a known group of learners within a given setting. Third, face-to-face contacts between persons engaged in a common task are usually far more satisfactory than exchanges over a distance. Fourth, participation by all is more easily arranged. The principal, the teachers, the pupils, the parents, and others interested may each have responsible and important parts in the program. Fifth, the large group of indifferent members of a social group can more easily be interested and drawn in by their own

neighbors and the problems can be brought home sharply.

The heterogeneity of attack through small local units stimulates originality and individuality in meeting problems. The chances for social invention, for the development of new departures, for genuinely creative contributions are multiplied. The advantages of this "broken front" attack must not be lost, however, through pure scattering of effort, or through attention to diverse fragments. Balance must be secured by co-ordinations of various types. Certain needs are common to many units. Agreements on certain specified instructional policies and practices are necessary for the development of rounded programs.

Co-ordination within the school itself may be secured, first, by constituting the faculty a committee of the whole. In larger schools a representative committee or council may be used. Needs common to several areas within the school, and the common agreements referred to above, may be worked out through these agencies. The student council is also a co-ordinating device of this type. Co-ordinations between schools will thus be, second, an extension of an already familiar technique. In large cities, third, there will be more numerous committees and a central council. These will include committees and conferences for interschool effort as well as for wider co-ordination. An excellent method of securing co-ordination is, fourth, to have all members of the central staff participate directly in activities on the local firing line. First-hand contacts of this type will greatly aid common agreements, understandings between groups, and closer co-ordination of activities between the center and the periphery. The interchange among units of any advances made anywhere within the system not only accelerates the program but is another method of co-ordination. Discussion will be curtailed at this point because of comments in Chapter 5 and in preceding pages about mechanisms for co-ordination.

Principle 7. *A balance must be maintained between gradualism and rapidity.*

Social change is a long, slow, tedious process. Human beings simply do not change ideas easily and quickly, especially ideas dealing with any aspect of organized social life. Ideas dealing with mechanics, machinery, material things will change far more rapidly but we can make no such assumption about changes in more subtle affairs. Time and study plus demonstration continue over a period of time. A curriculum-development program must, therefore, be a gradual process. At the same time, however, it must be kept ever in mind that "civilization is a race between education and disaster." We must not be misled by those who mouth the old cliché "you must not go too fast." We cannot sit around and wait for progress to take place. The deliberate control of social change is necessary. Proceed at a pace consistent with the development of social thinking—but do something to accelerate social thinking! Recent developments in the physical sciences make imperative an acceleration of the process of social change.

Principle 8. *The necessary financial aid, material facilities, specialists, and adjustments on the loads of local participants must be arranged.*

This principle is self-explanatory. Its importance was indicated in preceding discussions of the various factors facilitating participation.

Principle 9. *A program must justify itself through continuous evaluational processes and summaries thereof.*

The techniques which are applicable here were illustrated in Chapters 9 and 10. Other illustrations are available in the literature.

Principle 10. *Curriculum-development programs should be continuous rather than spasmodic.*

Principle 11. *Curriculum programs, while comprehensive in scope and in attention to all factors in the situation, should make progress on a "broken front" rather than uniformly.*

Section 2

THE GENERAL CHARACTERISTICS OF ILLUSTRATIVE, LONG-TIME CURRICULUM PROGRAMS

The general history of curriculum development in the United States has been outlined in a number of volumes. The following abbreviated summary of high points is adapted from the excellent account by Caswell and associates.[14] The first period, roughly up to the turn of the century, developed no sensible curriculum theory or practice. Courses were added as needed, resulting in a crowded collection of unrelated fragments. The second period was marked by effort to introduce order by development of sequences of courses. National committees and text writers dominated the process. Emphasis was on course-of-study writing. Considerable lack of organization and consistency for the over-all curriculum persisted. Chief influences were from outside the curriculum.

The development of larger central administrative and supervisory staffs brought the curriculum problem down from the national level to that of the individual or local system. Emphasis was still upon the production of course outlines by which the administration directed the teachers. Courses were to be followed closely. A few suggestions were, in a few places, secured from the teachers and used in revision. The basic characteristic was still separate subjects with no reference to the total curriculum.

A third period began at the close of

[14] *Op. cit.,* Ch. 3. See other historical references also.

World War I, when attention began to turn to comprehensive programs dealing with the total offering of the school. The new programs stressed (*a*) the development of statements of general objectives (sometimes very extensive) as a basis for the curriculum, (*b*) correlation between the subjects, and (*c*) a basis for organization, a scope and sequence. The over-all goal was a highly desirable one: to develop a curriculum related to life and to the nature of the learner. Emphasis was still on the production of course outlines. Chief procedures were the use of production committees, development of course outlines by these committees, and then installation of the new materials throughout the system. Supervisors found that teachers did not use the new materials effectively, even though representative teachers had participated in their development. Improvement, however, was in the air.

Two influences brought a change. First, the difference between the course and the actual experiences of the learners was realized. Good course materials did not always affect the experiences of the children. Second, the concept of learning by experiencing became more widely accepted. To provide more effective experiences for learners became the teacher's chief function.

A fourth period emerged, then, in the thirties. Attention shifted in part to instruction. The curriculum was actually made by teachers, hence the necessity for participation by all and not merely by representative committees. The final impetus occurred when it was realized that change in the beliefs, attitudes, and values of the persons involved was basic to change in the curriculum materials. The curriculum programs were now truly comprehensive both in materials and personnel, and in general basic theory. Production was no longer confined to course outlines, but shifted to development of a very wide variety of bulletins and guides (listed in Chapter 12). Courses were no longer prescriptive outlines to be followed but were actually guides, containing a wealth of materials and suggestions for teaching from which teachers and learners could choose. This period saw also the change from a uniform movement throughout the curriculum and the school, to the concept of the "broken front." Advances are made where and when facilities and readiness of personnel warranted. Various types of consultants were increasingly invited to participate. Wide and continued study by professional staff and lay participants accompanied all phases of the program. This brings us up to date with the principles of administration and of process generally set forth in this volume and particularly with those in the preceding section of this chapter.

State-wide curriculum programs emerged. More than half the states now have programs of curriculum improvement as a regular part of their educational activities. Wide influence is exercised on local programs through leadership from the state department, as indicated in Chapter 5. State programs are, in fact, almost equivalent to local programs in rural, village, and county schools. The larger independent city districts may be included or may develop their own programs. The leadership in state programs must, in fact, be careful not to overinfluence local situations with their own particular needs and resources. The first of the extensive programs was the Virginia project which began in 1931-1932 and which influenced many later programs. Succeeding programs over the years developed many improvements.

A representative program of the study type. The Mississippi [15] program which began in 1934 illustrates well the programs of that period. Note the reference to areas for study, the offer of assistance from the state department, the involvement of institutions of learning and teacher preparation.

[15] *Mississippi Program for the Improvement of Instruction: Study Program,* Bulletin No. 1 (Jackson, Miss., State Department of Education, 1934), pp. 8-9.

The first year will be spent on study, analysis, and discussion of our present program and of our educational needs. Attention will also be given to possible methods of improvement. Study and discussion groups will be organized throughout the state. Every effort will be made to assure such groups a profitable period of study. Materials are presented in this bulletin which suggest general areas and procedures for study. Members of the State Department and of the higher institutions of learning will provide counsel and guidance. The central state committees will be at work during this time preparing materials for guidance of the second year's work.

During the second year, the teachers of the State will be encouraged to make exploration into new materials and new procedures. These materials will be appraised and organized by state committees.

The work of exploration and expansion will be continued during the third year and, at the same time, materials previously collected will be put into the hands of selected teachers to be tried in practical classroom situations.

A further extension of the use of new materials by all teachers will be encouraged in the fourth year. Provisions will be made for the continuous revision of the instructional materials.

During the fifth year, materials which have been selected from the work of the preceding years as being of special value to all teachers in the State, will be made available on a state-wide basis and teachers will be aided in their use.

Other state programs which began in this period or later and which developed ever more extensive and more democratic activities include those in Kansas, Oklahoma, Michigan, Louisiana, Georgia, North Carolina, Tennessee, and Michigan. Later programs include Maine, Illinois, Delaware, Florida, Alabama, Connecticut, Minnesota, Missouri, Pennsylvania, and others.

A program with heterogeneous approach. The Maine program represents the other extreme from that of study areas used as opening maneuver. The state commissioner called a preliminary conference for informal exploration of possibilities in 1943. Participants were state department supervisors, normal school and state university faculty

members, representative superintendents, and a special consultant. Laymen and teachers were to have been included but short notice prevented this. Laymen have been consulted and have participated, while teachers soon came to play probably the most important part. Conferences, interviews, field reports, and correspondence developed the following principles and procedures:

1. The proposed curriculum program will make its primary attack upon improving the work of classroom teachers in doing whatever they are now doing.
2. Leadership will be vested in local superintendents and their teachers. Assistance will be on a service basis, in answer to direct questions from the field, and given by the state department, the state normals and university, and the general consultant. Special consultants will be called in as needed.
3. A common understanding of aim and philosophy, of viewpoint, recognition of the necessity for a survey of needs, will emerge out of the efforts to improve instruction. The scope and sequence will emerge similarly.
4. The machinery of committees, councils, channels; the additional personnel will be developed as demanded by ongoing activities.
5. Written courses-of-study bulletins will grow out of the curriculum program rather than vice versa.

Activities were suggested as follows:

1. A series of regional conferences based upon questions submitted in advance by teachers and superintendents.
2. Local study groups to deal with the immediate problems and questions of the teachers concerned.
3. A series of bulletins in answer to pressing needs as demonstrated by questions submitted and by the regional conferences.
4. A workshop for teachers sponsored by the state department and staffed by the normal schools and the university.

A program illustrating multiple approach, democratic processes, emphasis on quality of life as well as on education, and provision for continuous curriculum improvement. The Florida program began naturally with the improvement of instruction and materials in schools and expanded to include education of all citizens and emphasis upon the interrelation between education and the life of the people. General features include:

1. *Citizens Committee*—a group of prominent citizens from many walks of life appointed by the Governor at the suggestion of the State Superintendent of Public Instruction to study the school needs of the state and make appropriate recommendations to the state legislature. An interracial committee of professional educators served as technical advisors to the Citizens Committee.

2. *Minimum Foundation Program*—the state-wide educational plan for improving education in the state; a direct culmination of the recommendations of the Citizens Committee to the legislature. It includes such things as provision for a tenth month (with pay) for school program planning, 180 actual teaching days for every school in the state, kindergartens, junior colleges, twelfth-month programs for schools, a state-wide system of curriculum workshops, etc.

3. *Preschool period*—a block of time carved from the tenth month and used for planning the curriculum for the current school year; usually two or three weeks.

4. *Post-session, or post-school period*—a block of time provided at the termination of the teaching year, ostensibly for evaluating the effectiveness of the year's program.

5. *State Board of Education*—the top policy-making body in education and is comprised of the Governor, the Secretary of State, the Treasurer, the Attorney General, and the State Superintendent of Public Instruction.

6. *Courses-of-Study Committee*—a committee of nine members recommended by the State Superintendent and appointed by the Board of Education. Its chief duty is to examine carefully courses of study in current use with a view to utilizing "the best ideas obtained in revising from time to time courses of study for the Florida schools."

From a list of some seventeen statements about its operational principles in relation to local schools, the following ones which deal especially with curriculum engineering were drawn:

1. Analyze what must be done to improve the quality of living and learning in schools and communities.

2. Contain within itself the possibility of in-fluencing living and learning in all schools throughout the state.

3. Place emphasis upon local initiative.

4. Reflect co-operative planning at the state and local levels.

5. Work primarily with leadership, both lay and professional.

6. Develop educational leadership throughout the state.

7. Direct efforts wtih respect to individual schools through the school principal.

8. Plan major emphasis upon finding the principals and teachers who are willing and able to carry out worthwhile undertakings to improve schools and communities.

9. Take into account the availability and need for appropriate materials and resources.

10. Plan work in such a way that each staff member understands his individual role in the activities of the department.

11. Provide a method of perodic evaluation of what is done.

12. Inform the schools concerning educational activities throughout the state.

13. Provide findings of research and indicate sources of research to the schools.

14. Provide continuous study of state staff services in the light of discovered needs.

The Continuing Education Council is made up of representatives of eighteen groups in Florida,[16] including teachers' associations, women's clubs, veterans, labor unions, chamber of commerce, school board association, prominent industrialists, and officers of institutions preparing teachers.

Space prohibits further details of state programs but field workers and students are urged to consult the bulletins or other accounts of programs in New York, Illinios, Michigan, Wisconsin, and Minnesota.

County programs in Alameda and San Diego, California, may be studied to advantage. Montgomery and Harford counties in Maryland have had extensive programs for some time. Others may be found in the literature.

[16] The writer is indebted to several graduate students from Florida, to correspondence with Sam H. Moorer and conversations with Dora S. Skipper, both of the state department. Detailed accounts of the Florida plan and of the Michigan plan are found in Caswell and associates, *op. cit.*, Chs. 13 and 14.

Regional curriculum programs may develop in the future. The Southern Association of Colleges and Secondary Schools, inaugurated in 1948-1949, has a regional program which is representative of a new development. Each state in the region set up a committee to define problems, plan programs of action, suggest areas for regional co-operation, to try out proposals and to evaluate what goes on. Each state financed its own local program and the association was aided by the General Education Board. The general procedures are similar to those in state programs. The following suggestions for inaugurating regional projects are given by Drummond: [17]

Enlist the support of an established, functioning organization which already has prestige and influence throughout the area served.

Enlist the support of the state departments of education, the professional associations, and the teacher-education institutions.

Develop committees which cut across levels of the school system and represent those particularly interested in the improvement of elementary schools, including parents.

Provide for co-ordination among the various states through a central committee, but avoid the growth of a large central office.

Secure, if possible, some financial assistance to support the program until it is well established. The program should soon enlist sufficient support to be self-sustaining.

Work at the regional level on the problems identified by the representatives of the various states. State the objectives clearly.

Focus attention on securing wide participation in solving regional problems.

Encourage state groups to work on other problems of concern in addition to those identified for co-operative regional action.

Develop some specific plans for rotating leadership responsibilities.

City programs. The number of curriculum programs under way in cities and small towns is so large that it is futile to attempt a listing. In general, the city programs illustrate the same principles and practices found in the state programs. Local workshops and curriculum laboratories are prominent. Lay participation is increasing in amount, especially in individual school units. Prominent among city programs are those in New York, Philadelphia, Denver, Long Beach (Cal.), San Diego, Santa Barbara, Minneapolis, Kingsport (Tenn.), Glencoe, Battle Creek, Des Moines, Wayne (Mich.), Portland (Ore.), and scores of others. Bulletins and other materials are available. Many of these are discussed in the periodical literature.

The story of the development of a curriculum for the Wells High School in Chicago from the opening of the school in 1935 is a unique story in American education. The volume *Developing a High School Curriculum* [18] is excellent reading for all curriculum workers. The detailed accounts of participation by staff and community are simple and enlightening.

Two older volumes by Spears [19] are also of great value: *The Emerging High School Curriculum,* which is an account of some thirteen experimental programs, and *Experiences in Building a Curriculum,* which relates the development of the program in Evansville, Indiana.

A good collection of fragments illustrating many new departures in curriculum development in many places is included in *Toward a New Curriculum,* [20] the 1944 Yearbook of the National Department of Supervision and Curriculum Development.

[17] Harold D. Drummond, "Southern States Work Co-operatively to Improve Elementary Education," *The National Elementary Principal* (October, 1952), p. 30.

[18] Paul R. Pierce, *Developing a High School Curriculum* (New York, American Book, 1942).

[19] Harold Spears, *The Emerging High School Curriculum* (New York, American Book, 1940); *Experiences in Building a Curriculum* (New York, Macmillan, 1937).

[20] *Toward a New Curriculum,* 1944 Yearbook, Association for Supervision and Curriculum Development (Washington, National Education Association, 1944).

The Community School, Fifty-second Yearbook, Part II, National Society for the Study of Education (Chicago, Univ. of Chicago Press, 1953).

See also the several books by E. G. Olsen on community-school relationships, noted in earlier chapters.

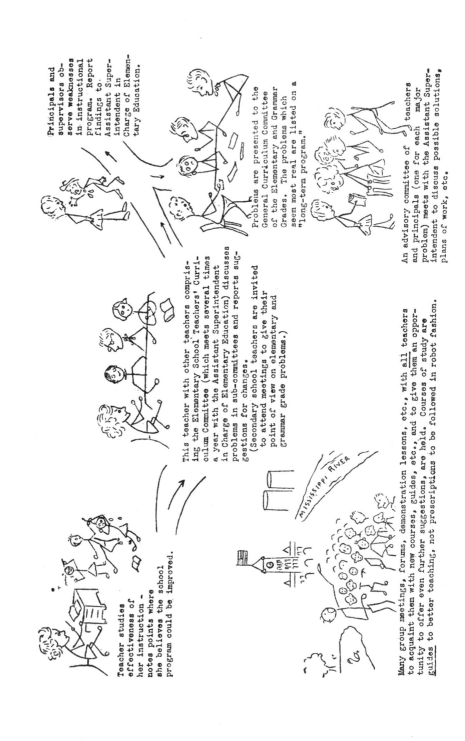

Teacher studies effectiveness of her instruction - notes points where she believes the school program could be improved.

This teacher with other teachers comprising the Elementary School Teachers' Curriculum Committee (which meets several times a year with the Assistant Superintendent in Charge of Elementary Education) discusses problems in sub-committees and reports suggestions for changes.
(Secondary school teachers are invited to attend meetings to give their point of view on elementary and grammar grade problems.)

Principals and supervisors observe weaknesses in instructional program. Report findings to Assistant Superintendent in Charge of Elementary Education.

Problems are presented to the General Curriculum Committee of the Elementary and Grammar Grades. The problems which seem most real are listed on a "long-term program."

An advisory committee of teachers and principals (one for each major problem) meets with the Assistant Superintendent to discuss possible solutions, plans of work, etc.

Many group meetings, forums, demonstration lessons, etc., with all teachers to acquaint them with new courses, guides, etc., and to give them an opportunity to offer even further suggestions, are held. Courses of study are _guides_ to better teaching, not prescriptions to be followed in robot fashion.

MISSISSIPPI RIVER

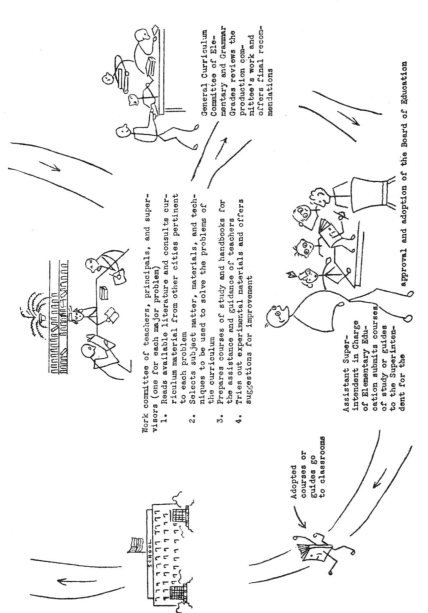

Work committees of teachers, principals, and supervisors (one for each major problem)

1. Reads available literature and consults curriculum material from other cities pertinent to each problem

2. Selects subject matter, materials, and techniques to be used to solve the problems of the curriculum

3. Prepares courses of study and handbooks for the assistance and guidance of teachers

4. Tries out experimental materials and offers suggestions for improvement

General Curriculum Committee of Elementary and Grammar Grades reviews the production committee's work and offers final recommendations

Assistant Superintendent in Charge of Elementary Education submits courses of study or guides to the Superintendent for the approval and adoption of the Board of Education

Adopted courses or guides go to classrooms

HOW MAJOR INSTRUCTIONAL OR CURRICULUM PROBLEMS ARE HANDLED

From "A Brief Presentation of the Plan for Curriculum Construction and Improvement" (Minneapolis, Department of Elementary Education, Minneapolis Public Schools, March, 1942). This chart has also been used in the Washington, D. C., program.

Still other valuable sources of material on curriculum programs are the bound volumes of the *Curriculum Journal,* and those of *Educational Leadership* with which the *Curriculum Journal* merged. The volume by Lawson listed in the bibliography is a mine of information. The Third Yearbook of the John Dewey Society (1939) and the Tenth Yearbook (1937) of the Department of Supervisors and Directors of Instruction contain valuable accounts of many early programs.

The best recent collection of accounts of actual programs is the volume by Caswell and associates,[21] *Curriculum Improvement in Public School Systems.* The Thirty-first Yearbook of the American Association of School Administrators, *American School Curriculum,*[22] contains some brief accounts which are useful. The general tenor of this volume is naïve and the curriculum theory quite out of date but the specific illustrations are sound. A volume which does not discuss any specific programs but which proposes a definitely new type of secondary program is Flaum's *The Activity High School.*[23] Although on general theory it is revolutionary, it should be very valuable to curriculum workers in local projects.

Illustrations of process charts from Minneapolis, A Curriculum Council from Kalamazoo,[24] a plan for faculty organization[25] from Lincoln, Nebraska, and a co-ordination chart from San Diego County will be found on pages 598-603.

A high-school staff set out to improve the provision for individual differences in their classrooms. An opinionaire supplied data showing the perceptions of the teachers on this problem at the beginning of the operation. The opinionaire was offered again at the end of the study. Group discussions were held; interviews between individual teachers and the supervisor-co-ordinator got down to details. Tape recordings were made of discussions which, with the interviews, showed: the problems most important to the teachers; kinds of assistance requested; whether the

aid was given or not; what teachers did to help themselves; descriptions of the actual changes being made in the classroom; and finally the changes in perception of difficulties in the area. Bibliographies were furnished, librarians and other specialists were brought in, class logs, and other sources of data were used. Teachers wrote a summary at the end outlining practices now used in class which were not used before; practices still used but in lesser degree than formerly; practices no longer used.

The effects upon the community of curriculum programs, briefly summarized. The following categories may be noted:

1. The typical improvements and extensions within the course or curriculum more numerous and more far-reaching when the community approach is used.
2. Numerous extensions of needed services within the community stimulated by the curriculum program:

Health service and information	Nurseries
Recreation facilities	Co-operative agricultural and other
Night school for youth	projects
Adult education	(Others may be noted)

3. The development of a community council with its accompanying attack upon problems of juvenile delinquency, recreational facilities, parent education, and so forth.
4. Extensive participation by the lay public in planning and carrying on the work of the schools. This may range from serving the school lunches, managing nursery schools and the like, to extensive study of the local needs, resources, and fact finding by committees and advisory commissions.
5. The more effective gearing of the curriculum to the needs and resources of the community within which the curriculum develops. (Material is included also looking toward the understanding of the ever wider community.)

[21] *Op. cit.,* 1950.
[22] *Op. cit.,* 1953.
[23] Laurence S. Flaum, *The Activity High School* (New York, Harper, 1953).
[24] Helen F. Storen, "The Role of Laymen in Curriculum Planning," *Educational Leadership* (February, 1952), p. 278.
[25] Gilbert S. Willey, "Organizing for Curriculum Improvement," *Educational Leadership* (October, 1949), p. 44.

DIAGRAM OF THE ORGANIZATION OF THE CURRICULUM COUNCIL AND ITS COMMITTEES*

KALAMAZOO PUBLIC SCHOOLS, CURRICULUM DEPARTMENT

The major purpose of the Curriculum Council is to understand and improve our education program.

Curricular Committees

I. Public Relations Committee

II. All-School Reading Committee

III. General Education Committee

IV. Special Education Committee

V. All-School Social Studies Committee

VI. Junior High School Curriculum Committee

VII. Citizenship Education Committee

VIII. Mathematics Committee

IX. Social Travel Committee

X. Science Committee

XI. Primary Unit Committee

XII. Intercultural Workshop

XIII. Unified Studies Committee

XIV. All-School Audio-Visual Education Committee

XV. Child Growth and Development Committee

XVI. Professional Growth Committee

XVII. Central High School Curriculum Evaluation Committee

XVIII. Industrial Arts Committee

XIX. Home Economics Committee

XX. Art Committee

XXI. Music Committee

XXII. Physical Education and Health Committee

Curriculum Council	
1 representative elected by each school or a combination of small schools	15
1 representative elected by the specialized subject matter areas of music, art, physical education, industrial arts, and home economics (a few representatives represent both these areas and schools)	5
1 representative elected by the senior high school subject matter departments (social studies, language arts, science, mathematics and business education)	5
4 administrative staff members	4
1 representative elected by the supervisors	1
1 representative elected by the principals	1
20 representatives of the P.T.A.	20
1 representative elected by special education	1
2 student representatives elected by the senior high school government	2
1 representative elected by the Kalamazoo Federation of Labor	1
1 representative elected by the Junior Chamber of Commerce	1
1 representative elected by the Social Agencies	1
2 recent high school graduates (1 vocational worker, 1 college student)	2
1 representative elected by the Department of Research and Guidance	1
1 representative elected by the Parent Education Council	1
22 chairmen of curriculum committees	22
4 representatives of the A.A.U.W.	4
	87

* From Helen F. Storen, "The Role of Laymen in Curriculum Planning," *Educational Leadership* (February, 1952), p. 278.

6. Great increase in community understanding of the nature of education; of the learning process; of the relation of education to the community; of the necessity of active experiencing and participation by all; of the meaning of democratic interaction.

7. Increased knowledge of the nature of the organized educational system as exemplified in the local school; of the place of the school in civilized society.

8. Increased understanding and acceptance of the dynamic point of view that curriculums and methods of teaching will always be under constant improvement.

9. Increased financial support for better buildings, materials, and salaries; increased moral support for innovations, for increased standards of teacher training, and so forth.

10. Greatly increased co-operation between teachers and parents.

11. Increased recognition of the teacher as a citizen of the community.

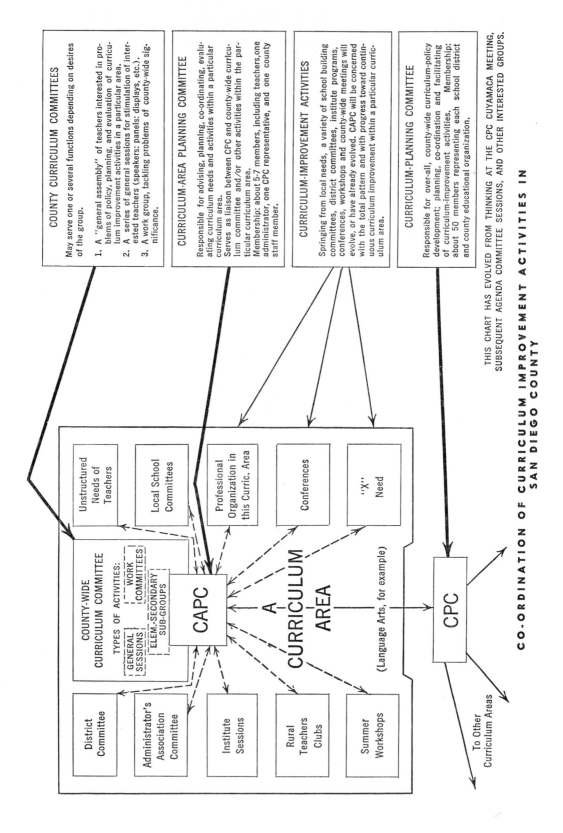

COUNTY CURRICULUM COMMITTEES

May serve one or several functions depending on desires of the group.

1. A "general assembly" of teachers interested in problems of policy, planning, and evaluation of curriculum improvement activities in a particular area.
2. A series of general sessions for stimulation of interested teachers (speakers: panels: displays, etc.).
3. A work group, tackling problems of county-wide significance.

CURRICULUM-AREA PLANNING COMMITTEE

Responsible for advising, planning, co-ordinating, evaluating curriculum needs and activities within a particular curriculum area.

Serves as liaison between CPC and county-wide curriculum committee and/or other activities within the particular curriculum area.

Membership: about 5-7 members, including teachers, one administrator, one CPC representative, and one county staff member.

CURRICULUM-IMPROVEMENT ACTIVITIES

Springing from local needs, a variety of school building committees, district committees, institute programs, conferences, workshops and county-wide meetings will evolve, or have already evolved. CAPC will be concerned with the total pattern and with progress toward continuous curriculum improvement within a particular curriculum area.

CURRICULUM-PLANNING COMMITTEE

Responsible for over-all, county-wide curriculum-policy development; planning, co-ordination and facilitating of curriculum-improvement activities. Membership: about 50 members representing each school district and county educational organization.

Unstructured Needs of Teachers

Local School Committees

Professional Organization in this Curric. Area

Conferences

"X" Need

COUNTY-WIDE CURRICULUM COMMITTEE
TYPES OF ACTIVITIES:
GENERAL SESSIONS
WORK COMMITTEES
ELEM.-SECONDARY SUB-GROUPS

CAPC

District Committee

Administrator's Association Committee

Institute Sessions

Rural Teachers Clubs

Summer Workshops

A CURRICULUM AREA

(Language Arts, for example)

CPC

To Other Curriculum Areas

THIS CHART HAS EVOLVED FROM THINKING AT THE CPC CUYAMACA MEETING, SUBSEQUENT AGENDA COMMITTEE SESSIONS, AND OTHER INTERESTED GROUPS.

CO-ORDINATION OF CURRICULUM IMPROVEMENT ACTIVITIES IN SAN DIEGO COUNTY

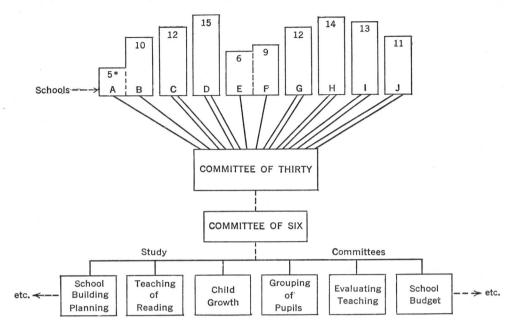

* Indicates number of teachers in buildings

SUGGESTED PLAN FOR FACULTY ORGANIZATION IN LINCOLN, NEBRASKA

From Gilbert S. Willey, "Organizing for Curriculum Improvement," *Educational Leadership* (October, 1949), p. 44.

Data as to the desirable effects on the community can be secured only if adequate cumulative community records exist upon which to base the program. Facts will evaluate the curriculum, that is, indicate how well needs are being met, and will form the basis for continuous improvement of the curriculum. This in turn will be reflected in the life of the community.

Section 3

OBSTACLES TO CURRICULUM IMPROVEMENT

The negative content of this section should not unduly discourage anyone. Obstacles and blocks to curriculum development are deliberately listed in order that they may be overcome. Severe criticisms of leadership, of personnel generally, of picayune efforts, of lay interference, must be read as a contrast to the excellent, stimulating leadership found in many places, and well-trained staffs engaged in difficult comprehensive programs, and the many excellent examples of lay participation and support.

The foregoing sections have prepared us to consider the constellation of forces and influences at work within a staff and within the community. Certain of these forces are sure to be antagonistic. The following very general listing of typical obstacles may be rearranged to suit the purposes of any group.

1. Educational workers in many places and on many levels are not convinced and committed to curriculum improvement.
2. Authoritarian administration in general prevails, and specifically in directing curriculum programs.

Co-operative group methods, known to be more effective, are not utilized either through ignorance or fear of them. This means that:

  a. Antagonisms springing from vested interests, or from limited views of the educational process, are not brought out for free discussion and attempts at consensus.
  b. The staff and laymen do not get together. The staff looks askance at "lay interference"; laymen criticize the staff for technical jargen; laymen persist in outmoded concepts of education.
  c. Roles of participants, including outside consultants, are not clearly defined, if at all.

3. Leadership, even where it transcends authoritarianism, has often confined efforts to tinkering, to shifting courses, with no real program.

4. Educational research results are often unknown, often defiantly ignored.

This means that many subjects are retained in the curriculum for their mythical transfer value. Others are retained because they are supposed to prepare for college. Methods of teaching take no account of the extensive research on motivation, especially in regard to levels of aspiration, to praise, rewards, and punishments. Comparative studies of social climate in the classroom are unknown to many. The effects of such simple things as lighting, humidity, and furniture on learning are constantly ignored. Sociometric techniques, so very helpful to leaders of any group, are not used.

5. Antagonistic or skeptical attitude toward change itself generally, and in education specifically.

6. Certain working conditions: load, salary, pension, acceptance in community, tenure, turn-over.

Weber,[26] in an excellent early study, believed the greatest single block to be working conditions: lack of time, heavy load, extracurricular duties, clerical work. Weber investigated separately a group of 99 schools reporting unprofessional attitudes on the part of teachers as a serious block. He found that there was a positive correlation of .42 between unprofessional attitudes and authoritarian, inspectorial, and prescriptive supervision by the principal. A negative correlation of $-.26$ was found between unprofessional attitude and democratic leadership in the school. Weber then made the interesting comment that unprofessional attitudes held by teachers were more dependent upon the type of teaching techniques used by the teachers than upon age or training. This hypothesis and other findings by Weber were corroborated by Banning's study[27] of junior-high-school teachers in a Massachusetts community ten years later.

1. Favorable attitudes were correlated positively with the feeling that one was a real participant; that one's individual contribution to policy-making and to implementation would be considered; that one had the support and approval of the administration.

2. Favorable attitudes were correlated positively with the more desirable methods of handling disturbances in the classroom. Teachers who habitually gave reprimands, dismissals from class, or sent the offender to the principal were unfavorable to change. Those who handled such incidents in such manner as to stimulate the growth and self-discipline of the pupil were favorable to change.

This is a revealing point, with many far-flung implications. Teachers who know how to teach and to handle children enjoy better relations with their pupils, are more poised and secure, and are also quite favorable to change or study. The converse is true. An indirect point which may have a bearing here is that teachers with liberal arts training or college training generally were more dissatisfied with conditions but less inclined to do anything about it. Teachers-college graduates were less inclined to criticize conditions or the state of the program but were

[26] C. A. Weber, "Obstacles to Be Overcome in a Program of Educating Teachers in Service," *Educational Administration and Supervision* (November, 1942), pp. 609-614.

[27] Evelyn Banning, *op. cit.*

more favorable toward curriculum study and change.

3. Favorable attitudes were correlated positively with the role of the teacher in the community. Acceptance and respect from the community, as we might expect, accompanied attitudes favorable to study and change.

A valuable monograph dealing with the problem of re-educating teachers toward curriculum improvement, or for that matter, toward improvement of any aspect of the program is:

SHARP, George, *Curriculum Development as Re-education of the Teacher* (New York, Teachers College, Bureau of Publications, Columbia Univ., 1951).

The single most valuable reference here is:

ALBERTY, Harold, and others, *Removing the Blocks to Curriculum Improvement in the Secondary School* (Columbus, Department of Education, Ohio State Univ., 1951, mimeo.). Bibliography.

Our general book on supervision does not allow space for details of solutions.[28] Many methods of overcoming obstacles have been given or implied in preceding pages. Reference should be made to Alberty's detailed summary.

Alberty's monograph clearly defines each obstacle and then follows with an equally clear summary the proposed remedies. Curriculum workers will find this one of their most valuable handbook aids. The following outline of major types of obstacle, with illustrative items under each was adapted from Alberty's summary by one of his doctoral candidates.[29]

I. *Influence of Colleges and Accrediting Agencies*

1. Traditional policies and programs of colleges tend to retard curriculum reform in the secondary schools.

    a. Imposition of rigid college admission requirements dictates the development of a college preparatory curriculum.

    b. Liberal arts colleges have not clearly stated the purposes of general education, making it difficult for secondary schools to agree on the best kind of preparation for those who expect to go to college.

2. Teacher education in general fails to develop teachers and administrators who are prepared for initiating and participating in curriculum development in the secondary schools.

    a. Lack of a co-ordinated effort between liberal arts colleges and teacher training colleges, absence of unified underlying principles, and emphasis on unrelated and too specialized subjects lead to a fragmentation of teacher education programs.

    b. Poor understanding of actual conditions in the secondary schools by teacher education institutions produces teachers who are not qualified to effect curriculum changes.

3. Accrediting agencies tend to perpetuate the status quo rather than to encourage curriculum experimentation in the secondary schools.

    a. Standards of evaluation based on how well high schools meet college preparatory requirements, and inspectorial accreditation procedures block curriculum improvement.

II. *Federal, State, Local Legal and Technical Blocks to Curriculum Improvement*

4. Federal support of vocational education tends to widen the gap between vocational and general education and impairs the unity of action needed for curriculum improvement.

    a. The creation of a dichotomy of purposes results in conflicting practices that impede curriculum reconstruction.

5. State-wide testing and curriculum programs often result in "freezing" the curriculum.

    a. Emphasis placed on test results and on academic achievements tends to perpetuate subject-centered programs.

[28] See also Kenneth Benne and Bozidar Muntyan, *op. cit.,* for general theory bearing on human relations and curriculum change.

[29] Daniel S. Noda, "A Study of Successful Practices Used to Remove the Major Blocks to Curriculum Implementation in the Secondary School." Unpublished doctoral dissertation, Ohio State Univ., 1952.

   b. State courses of study promote conformity to prescribed curriculum practices.

   c. Supervision from the state level is still mandatory and fails to release creative leadership.

6. State laws tend to restrict the curriculum through dictating curriculum content and prohibiting teaching in certain valuable subject areas.

   a. State statutes limit the scope of curriculum content by specifying what should be taught with matters concerning government, patriotism, and religion.

   b. Loyalty laws cause teacher retrenchment in dealing with curriculum programs that stress examination of social issues.

7. Local boards of education often exert a restraining influence on curriculum improvement by their stated policies and their insistence upon maintaining the status quo.

   a. Tendency of boards of education to assume the functions of administration hinders effective leadership.

   b. Resistance to consolidation and redistricting in marginal areas retards curriculum development.

III. *Community Blocks to Curriculum Improvement*

8. Indifference or hostility on the part of the general public toward the school results in lack of support of the school program.

   a. Prevalence of negative criticisms of the schools results in inadequate financial support while public complacency means withdrawal of active participation and co-operation which are so indispensable to curriculum improvement.

9. Certain traditional conceptions of education held by the public tend to restrict curriculum improvement by restraining efforts at change.

   a. Constant demands to keep schools as they are—"What's good enough for me is good enough for my children" —and a laissez-faire attitude toward the schools do not stimulate experimentation and research.

   b. Vested interests exert pressures to keep things as they are in the schools while certain patrons insist that the schools gear their programs to meet college requirements.

10. Homogeneity in a community frequently has a restraining effect on curriculum improvement.

   a. The development of the school program in terms of narrow occupational interests or strong denominational beliefs fixes curricular practices.

   b. Imitation of curriculum programs of wealthy college preparatory schools by smaller schools results in undesirable homogeneity.

11. Heterogeneity may, on the other hand, have a restraining influence on curriculum improvement.

   a. Profound differences of opinion on matters pertaining to religion, politics, race, and basic socioeconomic issues preclude unity of school aims, and the status quo is maintained to sustain harmony among the various groups in the community.

12. Community organizations sometimes exert pressures which adversely affect the content, organization, and purposes of the curriculum.

   a. Undue time and effort given to community-sponsored contests, competitive sports, and well-meant drives, campaigns, etc., leave the schools little time for curriculum improvement; and fragmentation ensues.

   b. Special-interest groups attempt to promote their point of view by providing free literature while others exploit the schools by using them merely as a market place.

13. Many schools do not have sufficient financial support to provide an adequate educational program.

   a. Limited financial support and unwise spending mean an unqualified staff, insufficient supplies and equipment, and poor teacher morale.

IV. *Blocks Within the School*

14. The lack of a co-operatively developed functional school philosophy leads to inconsistency and confusion of purposes and practices.

   a. Philosophy conceived and developed by the administration alone ends in teacher hostility, smugness, and a static curriculum.

15. The failure of teachers to keep pace with new developments in educational research causes a serious lag between practice and theory.

a. Prescribed curricular practices, loss of security, and the sanctity of the textbooks are detrimental to teacher growth.

16. Undesirable relationships among administrators, supervisors, teachers, and students impede effective curriculum planning.

   a. Dictatorial and "hands off" leadership fails to release teacher creativity and resourcefulness.

   b. Division between supervision and administration causes unhealthy staff and human relations.

c. Compartmentalized teaching produces teachers who feel responsible for their own fields of specialization rather than for the educative process as a whole.

d. Evaluation processes that leave out teachers and students result in an unrealistic appraisal of the school curriculum.

e. Teaching methods that do not allow room for student planning and participation ignore the needs and interests of students.

Section 4

THE PERSONNEL AND PROCEDURES INVOLVED IN PRODUCTION OF DOCUMENTS FURNISHED TO TEACHERS

The writing of a *course of study* or *teachers' guide,* or of *source units,* is a specialized task requiring certain specialized skills, sufficient time, facilities, and money. Committees or groups are given responsibility for developing a bulletin or series of bulletins known as the course or guide. The work is that of selecting, organizing, editing, and unifying materials from many sources and from tryouts into such form that the teacher may use it easily in the synthesis which is the specific curriculum.

The modern course, as has been indicated, should grow out of a curriculum-improvement program, or develop simultaneously with it.

Teachers will participate in this work by serving on various councils and committees, but they cannot participate en masse as they do in curriculum-making. The far-flung efforts of all teachers to improve their own curriculums is one of the most important sources from which the course writers draw their materials. The work of many committees organized in the curriculum-improvement program will be utilized and in some instances the committees continued. The contributions of many types of specialists in subject matter, in the psychology of learning, in the growth and development of children and youth, in behavior problems, in community problems, will be utilized by course

writers. The specialists and consultants will be both lay and professional.

Differences in structure from traditional to modern courses affect the methods of production. The nature and make-up of the published courses reflects the educational philosophy of those producing the courses. Methods of production are affected, therefore, by the type of course desired. The differences between older and more recent courses, made clear in a previous chapter, cause certain differences in production.

Organization for writing formal courses. The earlier programs of course production generally developed extensive machinery. The actual writing was usually done by a central Committee on Editing (or Unifying, or Reviewing), working closely with a series of Production Committees. The latter were organized around subjects, or areas of experience, depending on the type of course desired.

A number of other committees set up anew or carried over from the curriculum program included one on Philosophy (or Viewpoint, or Principles), one on Aim, one on Definitions, one on Scope and Sequence, and one on Evaluations. Other specialized groups appeared in some programs. Earlier programs set these committees up and produced a Viewpoint, Aims, Scope, and Sequence in executive session and by "taking thought." The results were handed out as the framework of the course. Later programs saw these committees serving to utilize, to review, to edit, and to write in acceptable form the results derived from the long, detailed, specific studies and activities of the curriculum-improvement program.

Questions have been raised concerning separate committee organization. Are separate committees in keeping with principles of integration and of democratic co-operation? Can an organization of separate committees see the project whole? Would it not be better for all who work upon the project to see it whole and to participate in all steps and procedures? This may necessitate course production by a central committee of the whole which may delegate certain specialized tasks to subcommittees of its own members, who will report to the total group.

Organization for writing modern guides. Principles set forth in several places earlier hold here. Organization will be loose and flexible, with easy reorganization possible. Machinery will grow out of the curriculum program instead of the reverse. Production committees will appear early, emerging out of local study groups, conferences, workshops, and from individual experimentation. These committees will not at first be controlled by a central organization and frame of reference but will produce these things as needed. Statements of philosophy and aim, definitions and the like will be produced by the original groups as needed.

Production committees for elementary materials may be of two types, depending on the local theory of education. The more formal situations will have committees on reading, writing, arithmetic, social studies, spelling; the less formal will have committees developing source units of many types cutting across subject lines, constructing bulletins on characteristics of learners at different levels, on diagnostic and remedial procedures, guidance, and the like. The subject-matter committees will, of course, give

attention to these latter areas; the makers of source units will consult subject-matter specialists.

Production committees on the secondary level will usually include two types: one on core curriculum materials where this curriculum exists, and another on subject areas. The latter are sometimes organized horizontally by school levels, sometimes vertically from kindergarten through twelfth grade.

The "installation" of courses of study. Early programs which produced courses through central organization, or with a minimum of participation, had the problem of "installing" courses, that is, securing use throughout the system. The typical procedure was to distribute the courses to everyone, together with a bulletin governing use of the course. Courses were usually prescriptive, to be "followed," were to be used immediately, and in so far as possible, similarly by all teachers with all groups of persons. Provision for variation in use was made in many courses.

Current knowledge about education and about learning denies the validity of these procedures. Courses should not be prescriptive, but provide for many options in use suitable to the diverse conditions within any system. Use cannot be immediate but will be based on further group study and individual experimentation, aided by supervisory assistance. Courses are not to be "followed," but used as guides and aids to teacher ingenuity in adapting to given situations. The modern curriculum program avoids the problem of installation as formally interpreted. The nature of a curriculum program, made clear in this and other chapters, explains this. Materials for teacher use emerge out of the efforts to improve instruction which are going on in all sorts of small units, individual classrooms, or schools. Materials are produced in answer to needs, both individual and social, immediate and remote. General needs emerge and with them representative councils or committees to produce materials of general application. The great volume of materials, from bulletins on limited specific problems to series of extensive resource units or volumes, will be available for use by any interested teacher or faculty. Leadership is the key to use. Valuable materials will be widely used. With leadership absent, materials will not get wide use, even under requirement from the central office. To summarize: installation under regulation is not likely to be effective in any real sense; the problem of installation disappears in a modern program where participation and good leadership are widespread.

Guidance for conservative systems with less well-trained staff. The programs of curriculum development and production of documents described in this chapter and in Chapter 12 represent advanced practices in the hands of well-trained personnel, prepared for modern procedures. The question is asked about approaches in less favorable situations. Illustrations were requested by students as this volume was being prepared. Space simply prohibits lengthy illustrations of less advanced practices. Aid to systems which are feeling their way is nevertheless important.

First, we may say that modifications of the most advanced practices may be attempted by any system. Second, the initiation of programs in more conservative systems will likely be by the leadership rather than by derivation from on-going activities by any staff member. Third, corollary to the second, participation will be far less widespread. Fourth, in-service programs are likely to be imposed rather than arising in response to demand. The study program will be more limited and progress slower than in advanced situations. Emphasis at first is likely to be on formal courses and study of books, moving slowly toward workshops, committee work, and experimental tryout. Fifth, printed materials will likely be prepared by small representative groups with programs of installation prominent. Sixth, the production of documents will likely be more prominent than the development of curriculums. Progress can be made toward better procedures.

Accounts of conservative programs are less frequent in the periodical literature. Bulletins for such situations can be secured and studied. Exercise No. 4 at the close of the chapter enables student groups to summarize materials here.

CHAPTER SUPPLEMENT

INTRODUCTORY QUESTIONS FOR USE WITH GROUPS WHICH NEED TO DEVELOP BACKGROUND

(Need not be used with advanced students)

1. The first four questions on policy and general procedure in Appendix B will be found stimulating and valuable. Others in the list may be used as needed.

2. A series of critical summaries may be made of the literature on the strengths and weaknesses of: the subject curriculum; the activities or experience curriculum; the broad-fields curriculum; broad-fields organizations; the core (various interpretations). The relation of expertness of teaching to the stimulation of integrative learning experiences, regardless of curriculum organization, should be considered.

INDIVIDUAL AND GROUP REPORTS

1. Critically evaluate the general methods used in your own system to *initiate* a curriculum-improvement program; to *develop* and carry on the program; to *evaluate* program and outcomes; to *produce* materials. Include comment upon the administrative machinery used.

2. Report for class analysis your own personal experience in participating in the program.

3. Students without this first-hand experience may report critically upon any city or state program as set forth in bulletins or in the periodical literature.

4. An individual or small committee may summarize the characteristics of extremely limited or of very conservative curriculum programs as found in the bulletins of given

systems, in the literature, or in one's personal experience.

5. Present specific suggestions for the improvement of some curriculum-study program now under way. This may be the one in your own system or in another.

6. Enumerate specific desirable changes which might be made in the curriculum or in course-of-study documents in a given school. Outline the means which might be used to bring about the improvements.

7. Compare, point by point, several course-of-study documents of earlier days (get some very old ones, if possible, as well as more recent ones) with current documents. State guides, local bulletins, collections of bulletins from various systems, periodical literature may be consulted.

8. List principles and practices useful in converting conservative teachers to more modern curriculum practices.

9. Make a list of beliefs and practices held by elementary and secondary teachers which would have to change if these teachers sincerely accepted the newer curriculum views. If possible, interview several teachers; otherwise answer from past observation and belief. (It is assumed, of course, that a good curriculum program would be operating to stimulate teacher growth toward desirable changes.) This is a far-reaching question and an organized answer is important.

10. In the early decades of the present century, numerous investigations were made to select curriculum content on the basis of "social utility," for instance, in spelling, arithmetic, and language; on the basis of "shortages" or mistakes made.

    a. Reports on selected research studies of this period may be made.

    b. How useful were and are the results of these studies?

    c. List a few studies of this type which might be made profitably today.

11. How, in general, can state curriculum programs be improved?

What kinds of services can the state best provide to assist local communities in their study and development of the curriculum?

What kinds of teachers' guides or other curriculum documents should the state provide, if any? The federal office or other national agency?

12. What sources of aid in the selection and planning of units of work should be made available to teachers?

13. In what sense is the teacher in the classroom a curriculum maker? What is the "emergent" curriculum?

14. Should the school have a co-curricular program?

15. What can the school do to raise the general level of the leisure time activities of the pupils in life outside the school?

16. In what ways can the elementary school more closely relate its program to the needs of the community?

17. Outline in some detail the steps that can be taken by a small school system to study and improve its curriculum.

18. Make, if circumstances permit, a brief analysis of the beliefs, attitudes, values held by a given group regarding education in general and preferably toward a given issue or practice. The beliefs, attitudes, etc., will be the sources of requests or pressures exerted by these individuals. (The class itself might be used; the faculty of a nearby co-operating elementary or secondary school, a parent-teacher group, or any other might be used.) Reduce your findings to a simple diagram or listing.

19. Outline very briefly how a leader or a group might go about changing, eliminating, or increasing a stated factor as revealed in your analysis. (If an analysis cannot be made take the pattern of influences revealed in some printed study.)

20. Relate any personal experience (or observation) in a situation where a local gatekeeper was prominently involved. Characterize the gatekeeper and his operations.

21. Describe the techniques of involvement used to secure wide participation in a situation within which you yourself were a participant. (Or an observed situation.)

22. Describe the steps taken to maintain security and to avoid emotional upsets in a given situation in which you participated or observed.

QUESTIONS ON MIEL, "CHANGING THE CURRICULUM"

This volume should be read in connection with this chapter.

1. The treatment of the curriculum problem differs significantly from all treatments prior to its date of publication (1946). Since then the chief point of difference has been picked up by some other texts.

    a. What was the one most significant difference between Miel and earlier texts?

    b. Mention three or four other important differences.

2. Note without discussion a number of principles of curriculum change derivable from Miel which are applicable to other areas within education.

3. Note without discussion a number of principles directly applicable to the problem of curriculum, differentiating

a. Those already presented in our chapter without notable change in language or emphasis

b. Those included here but which are treated by Miel with change in language and emphasis

c. Those which are found in Miel only.

4. Where, according to Miel, are the most important changes to be made within a program of curriculum improvement? Present a brief argument agreeing or disagreeing with her point here.

5. To what one major phase of curriculum reorganization does Miel's material chiefly apply? (All phases are affected, but one major point of emphasis is discernible.)

6. Organize a brief statement giving the practical implications of the two points, one in Question 4 and one in Question 5. This is a far-reaching question, and three or four items should be listed.

7. What are some of the major factors stressed by Miel as stimulating to the production of social changes? What can we do about this?

8. List and describe a number of "social inventions" in such way as to demonstrate your understanding of the term. Use illustrations, preferably from fields well outside education and curriculum organization.

(A certain amount of overlap between certain of the questions is deliberate. Students discovering this will not be confused if they recognize that a major point has been approached from more than one angle.)

Read Peddiwell's *Saber Tooth Curriculum*, particularly pages 28-44, but whole volume if time permits.

Are there any questions or comments stemming from this reading?

Are there any questions or comments based on the various Appendices at close of this volume (*Supervision*)?

Chapter 17

◆·◆·◆·◆·◆·◆·◆·◆·◆·◆

The Improvement of the Use of Materials of Instruction and the Socio-Physical Environment

IN THIS CHAPTER we shall discuss four major topics:

1. Improving the use of materials.
2. Improving the socio-physical environment of the school.
3. Improving the use of community resources to vitalize instruction.
4. Improving the quality of living in the community.

The relation of materials to educational objectives. Many problems are presented to supervisors and teachers by the rapidly accelerating rate at which instructional materials are developing and the growing belief in the necessity of closely relating the work of the school to life outside the school. Choices of materials must be made, and rigorous selection for use is required. The selection must be made in terms of factors which condition effective and fruitful learning. The emphasis that is being placed by current educational thought on preparing children for life in a democratic society demands a different conception of the functions of instructional materials from that held when the primary objective of the school was the transmission of the social heritage and the development of basic intellectual skills.

This broadening conception of the purpose of education is emphasized in the emerging concept of the community school whose characteristics and functions are well expressed in the following statement:

(1.) The school is closely identified with the social, economic, political, and ethical life of the community and with the personal life of the citizens; and the curriculum is designed to meet realistically the needs of the community and its individual members; (2) the school utilizes all types of community resources, including the services of the community agencies and the capabilities of individual citizens as well as material resources, in its educational program; (3) the school, in its turn, serves an entire community through participation in projects for community betterment, provision of leaders and leadership training, full utilization of the school plant by the community; it also acts as an integrating force in community life; (4) it relates the people of the community to the outside world by helping them avail themselves of the services of state, regional, and national community-serving agencies and by interpreting the relationship of the local community to conditions, issues, and problems of the larger society; and (5) it is democratic in its administrative and instructional policies and practices in its community relationships.[1]

This conception stresses the necessity of seeking to develop in pupils the growth of creative capacity, the ability to adjust to the demands of the situation, power in self-direction, and the enjoyment of experiences

[1] Edgar Grim, "School and Community Development," in Clyde M. Campbell, ed., *Practical Applications of Democratic Administration* (New York, Harper, 1952), p. 116.

Another excellent supplementary volume here is the 1954 Yearbook of the Association for Supervision and Curriculum Development, referred to in Ch. 13.

by the help of what can be drawn from the accumulated wisdom of the human race. Such a program requires an environment of concrete, problem-solving, laboratory materials, an environment which stimulates investigation and other forms of self-expressive activity. These materials may be located in the school, or they may be found in the social life outside the school. A sure way to make the learning activities directed by the school vital and meaningful is to draw on the community and its activities for illustrative materials, or to contact these agencies directly through a series of excursions and visitation.

Effective instruction also requires the provision of scientifically organized materials which will insure the mastery of the essential tools of learning with a minimum of difficulty. It also requires a wide variety of materials which are adapted to the differences in interests and aptitude of the children. Instructional materials must be selected because they will contribute effectively to the achievement of worthy objectives and purposes.

Section 1

IMPROVING THE USE OF MATERIALS OF INSTRUCTION

Improving the selection of materials. The selection of instructional materials should take place as the result of co-operative action by all who are affected by them, in some cases including even the pupils and members of the community who are competent to express judgments. The selection should be made on the basis of criteria accepted by the group. These standards of selection may most suitably be set up by a specialist in the field, by the supervisor, or by the group responsible for the selection of the materials. If teachers under the leadership of the supervisor set up the criteria, and if all issues involved are given adequate consideration, the professional stimulation is considerable. The selection of materials should be made, in so far as this is feasible, in a scientific manner, that is, on the basis of facts derived from systematic analysis of the items, experimental trial in the classroom, and the recommendation of experts. A typical statement of principles and procedures for such groups is the one developed by the school staff in Pasadena [2] that follows:

To make certain that outstanding instructional materials will be selected, the system-wide Learning Materials Committee has established specific criteria and procedures. These represent a composite of many years of thinking and experience. Since a considerable number of these policies have been in effect for several years, they have been tested in actual practice. New provisions have been added only after very penetrating and thorough consideration. As a result, therefore, of a great deal of careful deliberation, the Committee has succeeded in establishing the following principles:

1. There is a consistency at all levels. Learning materials are carefully selected and adopted for the kindergarten through the fourteenth grade, for regular day school and for extended day.

2. Like functions are treated alike. Procedures for the selection and adoption of the same kinds of materials are alike whether they are for the elementary school, junior high school, or junior college. For example, library resources are acquired in the same way regardless of whether they are for the elementary library, the junior high and the junior college libraries, or the audio-visual service.

3. There is a sufficient flexibility of procedures in order to provide for the peculiar needs of each level without, on the other hand, sacrificing the basic protection to students, teachers, the school system, and the community. To achieve this, the following safeguards have been included:

[2] *Procedures in the Selection and Adoption of Learning Materials in the Pasadena City Schools*, prepared by the Learning Materials Committee (Pasadena, Calif.: Division of Instructional Service, May, 1952), pp. i-iv. This report includes numerous check-lists for selecting various kinds of instructional equipment.

a. Schools must request the adoption of any learning material which will be used in quantity.

b. At least three qualified individuals must read and submit a documentary analysis and judgment on any material requested for adoption.

c. The Board of Education takes final action on all adoption requests and any purchase orders resulting therefrom.

4. Initial analysis and review of materials is done at the teaching level. In short, teachers who will be teaching with the learning materials participate actively in the selection and adoption process.

5 Every person responsible for co-ordinating the selection and adoption of particular learning materials has the guidance of an advisory council. For example, a junior-high-school librarian can turn for assistance to his building library advisory board; the supervisor for a subject field can call upon the services of the system-wide Learning Materials Committee; the Supervisor of Audio-Visual Service can confer with his advisory board. Any subcommittee may, in the final analysis, turn for assistance to the system-wide Learning Materials Committee. This Committee stands ready to act on problems relating to the selection, adoption, and utilization of instructional aids.

6. Requested materials are evaluated in terms of criteria approved by the Learning Materials Committee. (Criteria forms and adoption request forms are appended to the report.)

7. Membership on committees dealing with the selection of learning materials shall be determined by the following means:

a. One to four teachers shall be nominated by the principal of each building. The Pasadena Elementary School Principals' Association shall nominate principals; the Junior High School Principals' Group shall do likewise. From the master list of nominees, the Superintendent of Schools shall select the principal and teacher delegates to these committees, basing such appointments on the following factors:

(1) The membership on the several elementary school learning materials committees shall be so distributed that every school shall be represented on at least one committee dealing with learning materials.

Each junior high school shall be represented on every committee working on learning materials for the junior high schools; each junior college shall be represented on similar committees for the junior college level.

(2) Each elementary school committee shall consist of an equitable distribution of members from small and large schools and from the different geographical locations.

(3) Each elementary school committee shall consist of one teacher from each grade level (kindergarten through sixth grade) and two principals.

8. Every teacher and staff member of the Pasadena City Schools has the responsibility for making sure that outstanding instructional aids are chosen.

This process for the selection and adoption of learning materials represents the best judgment of a great many trained professional persons. In order that it operate efficiently, it necessitates the co-operation and continuous evaluation of everyone.

Levels of learning materials. Direct, firsthand experience with concrete materials undoubtedly is the most effective means of helping young children and beginners in any field to learn. As pupils become more mature, they are increasingly more able to learn through vicarious experiences involving materials of greater "remoteness from reality" until finally they are able to utilize highly abstract symbols and thought processes. The following scheme illustrates a series of levels of remoteness from reality, beginning with direct experience and proceeding by stages until the point is reached when highly abstract symbolic representations are used in learning.

1. *Direct experience through*
    a. Actual participation in enterprises and activities.
    b. Manipulation of objects and concrete learning materials.
    c. Construction of models.
    d. Undergoing treatments, exposures, contacts.

e. Dramatizing actual episodes and events using realistic settings and costumes.

2. *Vicarious experience through*
    a. Direct observation.
        (1) Seeing events take place and processes used.
        (2) Seeing pantomimes and dramatizations.
        (3) Seeing exhibits, museum materials.
    b. Viewing pictorial representations.
        (1) Motion pictures portraying events and processes.
        (2) Seeing photographs of places, events, persons, objects.
        (3) Television.
    c. Analysis of graphic and semiconcrete representations.
        (1) Maps, charts, diagrams, blueprints, and other ways of representing places, facts, and relationships.
    d. Verbal means.
        (1) Reading narratives, explanations, and descriptions.
        (2) Listening to narratives, explanations, and descriptions.
    e. Interpretation of highly abstract symbolic representations.
        (1) Technical symbols and terminology, indices, formulae, coefficients, tabular materials, graphs.

Suggestion for use of materials immediately at hand. Some of the ways in which easily available materials can be used or arrayed to stimulate children to activity are stated by Burton [3] as follows:

A. *Approaches may be derived from the natural ongoing activities of the learners in and out of school; from events in or characteristics of the immediate environment*
    1. Seize upon any pupil discussion, argument, comment, or question out of which a unit may be developed readily. These opportunities may appear in and out of class, in formal or informal groups. The range of opportunity here is as wide as the life of the group.
    2. Utilize any materials brought from home: curios, souvenirs, utensils, clothes, *objets d'art* from foreign countries or from other regions within our own country; pets; toys; flowers, seeds, fungi, minerals, and other material from the natural environment; apparatus from mechanical areas.

B. *Approaches may be developed through the arrangement of the environment*
    1. Arrange an attractive exhibit or display on the bulletin board, the wall, a table, or exhibit shelf.
        a. Pictures, posters, picture postcards, of historic or geographic places and events, of costumes, of customs, of festivals, of living conditions, of industrial or agricultural processes. These may be ancient or modern, or show contrasts between the two.
        b. Book covers, extracts from reviews, illustrations.
        c. Books opened to interesting pictures or exciting passages.
        d. Apparatus from science, from medicine, from industrial or agricultural processes; household appliances. These, too, may be ancient or modern.
    2. Arrange a "beauty spot." This is a form of exhibit or display, but is listed separately because it usually has an esthetic instead of a utilitarian emphasis.
        a. Artistic flower arrangement.
        b. Artistic productions of any type: graphic art, ceramic products, textiles, and so forth, from foreign countries or other regions of our own country.
    3. Capitalize upon any important event which occurs. Deliberately ask questions or otherwise initiate a conversation upon:
        a. Any important current event reported in the papers or occurring locally.
        b. The presence of foreign visitors.
        c. A motion picture showing locally.
        d. A vacation or other trip taken by teacher or pupil.
        e. Any other interesting or remarkable experience undergone by any member of the group.
    4. Make an excursion or visit to a famous place or person; to a factory,

[3] William H. Burton, *The Guidance of Learning Activities,* 2nd ed. (New York, Appleton-Century-Crofts, 1952), pp. 423-424.

a farm, or some other place of special interest.

5. Read an extract from a book, a magazine article, a poem.

6. Show motion pictures, lantern slides, stereoscopes; play records.

7. Refer to experiences in a previous unit.

8. Undertake a local project suggested by school, or by some local organization, such as beautifying the school grounds, conducting a clean-up campaign, or holding a garden contest.

The use of current materials in problem-solving. The foundation of the democratic process is problem-solving. American education has the obligation of providing learning experiences in which the pupils face significant problems of their own and of the community as whole. These problems inevitably overlap. The nature of the activities and materials of instruction in a classroom serves as a means of identifying the acceptance of this responsibility. A classroom in which current problems are being studied utilizes whatever sources of information there are that will lead the pupils to understand them. The learner must learn to use these sources wisely and effectively; he must learn how to locate and appraise the sources consulted.

An excellent analysis [4] of the kinds of current materials that are useful in observing and studying problems at first hand follows:

1. Current materials are all sources of adult information on current problems and affairs. They consist of classroom papers, daily newspapers, magazines, booklets, yearbooks, almanacs, recent books, and practically all other types of printed matter which is of recent origin and which deals with matters of concern to students.

2. Of major importance are magazines and newspapers. The Council believes that students should learn to utilize the current news weeklies, the available newspapers, government publications, and fugitive pamphlets and booklets. These materials are not suitable for every grade; consequently, school newspapers and magazines should also be used. Their use, however, should

also lead, especially in the upper grades, to the utilization of adult materials.

3. Current materials include posters, pictures, leaflets, advertisements, folders, time tables, travel guides, price lists, catalogues, and other more or less fugitive matter which nevertheless provides ideas, facts, and images useful to students.

4. Current materials include community resources from which students can derive information and understanding. Museums, art institutes, historical markers, monuments, parks, playgrounds, churches, railway and bus stations, airports, factories, stores, banks, courtrooms, city halls, hospitals, and farmers' markets are examples of the wealth of opportunities which almost every community provides.

5. Current materials include cities, areas, states, and distant countries. If occasion enables a student to visit a national park, a state capitol, an interesting area, a foreign country, he can utilize his opportunity greatly to enrich his information and understanding.

6. Current materials include the available human resources. Professional speakers, businessmen, parents, factory workers—whoever can meet with the students, at school or in their place of activity—and give them help in learning.

7. Current materials include the resources that are peculiar to a particular community. One town produces artichokes in greater quantities than any other center. For the local school this industry is a peculiarly valuable resource.

8. Current materials include films and radio and television programs which are pertinent to student problems.

9. Current materials include forums, lectures, debates, and even conversational opportunities that provide help in understanding today's problems.

The close relation between learning and the meaningfulness of learning materials is well expressed in the following statement by Ryans: [5]

---

[4] Reprinted from *Better Learning Through Current Materials,* edited by Lucien Kinney and Katharine Dresden with the permission of the editors and of the publishers. Stanford University Press. Copyright, 1952, by the Board of Trustees of Leland Stanford Junior University.

[5] David G. Ryans in *The Psychology of Learning,* Forty-first Yearbook, Part II, National Society for the Study of Education (Bloomington, Ill., Public School Publishing Co., 1942), pp. 308-309.

The meaningfulness of learning materials is dependent upon:

1. A broad background of related experience, of facts and principles about the situation, course, or subject-field with respect to which learning is sought;

2. The awareness of the relationships existing between the old and the new, between past experience and present experience. New learning should be related to situations in which the learner already possesses information and interest. This may be accomplished either directly or indirectly;

3. The organization of the material to be learned. The logical relationships of the situations must be used to advantage; and

4. The awareness of relationship between the learning situation and the possible future applications of the learning. The purposefulness of learning is always directly related to its meaning.

Trend in textbook construction. The textbook is perhaps the most important educational tool in this country. It is used almost universally, and, in fact, in many classrooms serves as the course of study. Some years ago Judd [6] and Whipple [7] discussed problems of textbook construction and suggested possible steps to improve their content and organization. An examination of modern textbooks in reading and arithmetic reveals the following trends, many of which indicate the desire of authors to keep textbooks abreast of best practices in our schools.

1. *Reading*
   a. Attractive titles for individual books.
   b. No grade designation of the books.
   c. Some designation of the level of difficulty of books.
   d. Readiness program for young children included.
   e. Primary books of three levels of difficulty.
   f. Organization of content in major units.
   g. Control of vocabulary.
   h. Consideration of reading skills needed in reading in various content fields.
   i. Supplementary workbooks geared to the textbooks.
   j. Informal testing procedures.
   k. Readers for various curriculum areas.
   l. Complete helpful guides for teachers.

2. *Arithmetic*
   a. Contents arranged in light of known facts about their learning difficulty.
   b. No grade designation for the books to identify them.
   c. Attractive titles for the books for the different grades.
   d. Contents provide for two- or three-level program.
   e. Readiness program for young children.
   f. Emphasis on meanings and relationships.
   g. Use of manipulative and visual aids to supplement textbook.
   h. Use of functional rather than decorative pictures and illustrations.
   i. Comprehensive diagnostic testing program.
   j. Stress on social uses of arithmetic in daily life.
   k. Consideration of interests of the learners.
   l. Activities for enriching the work for fast learners.
   m. Workbooks specifically intended for slow learners.
   n. Rich, detailed guides for teachers.
   o. Application of research findings about methods.

Similar trends may be noted in textbooks for other curriculum areas. Textbook construction is a difficult, highly technical undertaking. The skill of the authors is shown by the evidence that they are keeping pace with educational progress and recognize the implications of the results of research about the learning process in the construction of instructional materials, for example, providing for individual differences.

Proposed standards for selecting textbooks. Recently the American Textbook Publishers Institute sponsored a statement of twelve standards to which, in the judgment of publishers, procedures used by school systems in selecting textbooks should

[6] C. H. Judd, "The Significance for Textbook Making of the Newer Concepts in Education," *Elementary School Journal* (April, 1936), pp. 575-582.
[7] G. M. Whipple, "Needed Investigations in the Field of the Textbook," *ibid.* (April, 1935), pp. 575-582.

conform in order to insure a wise choice. The policies which were all fully defined and justified in the statement are as follows:

1. The committee should not be secret.
2. The committee should be small.
3. The committee's task should be kept within reasonable bounds.
4. The committee should be given adequate free time.
5. A time schedule should be part of every procedure.
6. Publishers should be notified of pending adoptions.
7. Provision should be made for interviews.
8. Hearings may be desirable.
9. Outside consultation should be prudent.
10. Committees should be encouraged to study all aspects of the publisher's program.
11. Development of a course of study and the selection of textbooks should go hand in hand. It is an unwise and wasteful procedure to attempt to develop a course of study without regard to instructional materials available. One sure way to have a course of study which will *actually* function in the classroom is to (*a*) define the broad objectives of the program, (*b*) prepare a tentative draft of the course of study, (*c*) select the teaching materials that come closest to meeting the broad objectives in the tentative draft, (*d*) after textbooks are selected, revise the tentative draft in terms of the materials adopted.
12. Individual judgment should be emphasized. There are, of course, a few quantitative measures for what is good in teaching materials: vocabulary counts can be made, illustrations counted, sentence and paragraph length tabulated, number of exercises determined, and so forth. But if undue weight is placed on such quantitative factors there is grave danger that not enough attention will be given to what is probably the most important single factor for evaluating instructional materials—*the skill with which the author develops ideas.*

To determine this, the committee member must spend time actually thinking through with the author the exposition and development of certain ideas. She must ask, do these materials meet the learning problems which children encounter? Is the content worth while and valid? Are generalizations supported by details? Taking these into account, and also considering vocabulary, length of sentence and paragraph, quality and teaching value of illustrations, are these textbooks *good learning materials* for the subject and grade for which they are intended?

An intelligent answer to these questions requires careful thought and judgment. Quantitative measures may contribute to the selection but they should not determine it. Subjective judgments are essential.

Such questions as the following have been raised which may serve as a basis of discussion by any interested group:

1. Who is to appoint the committee on selection?
2. What types of positions should be represented on the committee?
3. By what criteria are the textbooks to be evaluated?
4. What role can teachers and experts play in the formulation of criteria?
5. What kinds of objective data about competing textbooks can be assembled that will aid in making judgments about their merits?
6. How can teachers be informed about the evaluations of various textbooks?
7. What voice should the corps of teachers have in the final selection and recommendation of textbooks for adoption?

An illustrative plan of textbook selection. The following statement presents the policies and procedures of selecting textbooks [8] officially adopted by the schools of Cincinnati, Ohio, in 1952:

The selection of textbooks in the Cincinnati Public Schools is part of a comprehensive program of curriculum development. A first consideration in the selection process is the degree to which the books fulfill, in terms of content and organization, the requirements of carefully developed courses of study in the various areas of learning. The courses of study are written by teachers, principals, and supervisors, at times with the assistance of outstanding consultants; are continuously evaluated under exacting classroom conditions; and are periodically revised when warranted changes are indicated. The development of courses of study, locally, allows for the selection of content that is in harmony with the particular needs and abilities of pupils and the special demands of the community. Textbooks are selected, therefore, to assist teachers in the achievement of instructional objectives set forth in soundly constructed courses of study.

[8] Mimeographed statement supplied by the Cincinnati Board of Education.

The following procedure is used in the selection of all textbooks:

1. A committee of representative teachers and principals is appointed by the Assistant Superintendent in charge of instruction and approved by the Superintendent of Schools with the specific charge of examining textbooks in a particular field and recommending the adoption of one or more of them.

2. Notification of the appointment of the committee, a description of the course for which the text is needed, and a list of committee members is sent to all educational publishers with the advice that they submit for consideration any books falling within the description.

3. The books are evaluated by the committee members individually and the committee meets as frequently as necessary to consider together the books submitted.

4. Selection is made by secret ballots which are tabulated at a full meeting of the committee. The book receiving the largest vote is recommended.

5. The recommendation of the committee is made in writing to the Superintendent of Schools who, when he has received and accepted it, transmits it to the Board of Education with his recommendation for approval.

Improving the use of workbooks and remedial materials. In Chapter 13 criteria for the selection of workbooks were discussed, and their value for purposes of instruction was pointed out. Numerous investigations have shown that when well-organized, functional practice materials are used correctly, the gains that result in terms of such outcomes as growth in ability, grasp of subject matter, skill in the use of the tools of learning, interest in the subject, and breadth of understanding are definitely greater than when traditional procedures are followed.

It is unfortunately true that workbooks and similar prepared practice materials are often misused. Some teachers apparently believe that adjustment of instruction and materials to individual differences is not desirable. All pupils are assigned the same practice exercises in workbooks despite the fact that their weaknesses and the causes of the weaknesses may differ. To have all pupils, irrespective of their difficulties, perform the same exercises is a "shot-gun" approach. The effective use of workbooks and remedial practice materials requires the study by the teacher of the individual pupil to establish his needs and the direction instruction should take to eliminate the individual pupil's particular weakness or weaknesses. Pupils having similar deficiencies can, of course, be taught as a group.

Some teachers apparently regard a workbook as a panacea. They never deviate from the order of the workbook and never go beyond it. Unfortunately, a workbook does not include exercises that will remove the causes of difficulty; for example, a pupil who is not able to work out independently the new words that appear in practice exercises in reading should not be given a reading assignment in a workbook until necessary help has been given in phonetic analysis. Similarly, if he has a visual defect, this should be corrected before intensive practice is done. Workbooks also are often not very interesting to the pupils. The teacher must therefore take steps to develop a desire on the part of the pupil to do the practice exercises in the workbook. The successful use of workbooks and prepared practice exercises requires that the teacher supplement the text with a variety of experiences, materials, exercises, and methods adapted to the needs of the individual.

Some teachers apparently believe that assigning a large amount of drill is a guarantee that effective learning will take place. The fact is that unguided drill actually strengthens inefficient habits and skills, because the pupil repeats the same errors and faulty procedures again and again with no improvement in performance. For example, it is practically certain that a pupil who uses an incorrect roundabout procedure in working examples in subtraction will not hit upon the correct method of work independently. Unless his fault is discovered by careful diagnosis by the teacher and the correct procedure is taught before practice is assigned, the drill work will be useless and may actually be harmful.

The kind of motivation used is also an important consideration in the use of workbooks. Some workbooks provide a means of keeping a graphic record of performance to show the progress made. But because of the unstandardized and variable nature of the materials and tests on which the scores are sometimes based, they are not directly comparable and hence the ratings derived from them are not dependable or reliable. Even when such extrinsic methods of motivation as progress graphs are used, the teacher should stress the value and importance as well as the necessity of the remedial measures and the practice that the pupil is expected to do. Because of their intrinsic nature, the satisfaction and enjoyment to be derived from improved skill are much more valuable sources of motivation than progress graphs. If the children can see the need for the use of practice exercises in workbooks, if it emerges in the ongoing activity of the class, it is obvious that the practice will more likely be purposeful and meaningful than if it is assigned arbitrarily without any plan for showing the children why the practice has been assigned or is necessary.

Workbooks and remedial materials are likely to be most helpful if they meet the following standards:

1. They should be organized in such a way that the purpose of the material is evident to the pupil.
2. The activities involved should be related to socially desirable objectives and should be vital and meaningful to the children.
3. These materials should make definite and effective provision for differences in the needs, ability, and rate of learning of the pupils.
4. They should include reliable devices by means of which the teacher and the pupil can locate strengths and weaknesses in particular areas. The more specific the diagnosis, the more likely it is that underlying causes of deficiency can be identified.
5. They should provide a wide variety of developmental and remedial materials of dem-

onstrated value which may be used in the light of the diagnostic analysis. The keying of instructional materials and remedial practice to diagnostic tests facilitates a self-directed attack by the pupil on his particular difficulties and assist the teacher to adapt the work to the needs of each individual.

Principles underlying the preparation of individualized instructional materials. It is undoubtedly true that no two pupils are actually ready for a particular phase of work at the same time, especially in the learning of techniques and skills. It is therefore necessary to provide materials which enable each child to work independently of the others in the class. In Winnetka this is still accomplished by the following plan: [9]

1. Instructional materials in the form of workbooks or textbooks are written in such clear, simple, concrete terms that they are practically self-instructive. This makes it possible for each pupil to proceed at his own rate with a minimum of help from the teacher. The teacher is always ready to give assistance on difficult points.
2. Each child works on the unit for which he is ready and when that is completed passes on to the next unit, regardless of the progress made by other members of the group. A definite effort is made to limit the scope of the work to what is called the common essentials, including the skills, knowledges, and concepts necessary to maintain social relationships. The emphasis is placed on sytematic learning in accordance with the child's development.
3. Maximum effort is stimulated through short periods of intensive work. Long periods of practice are avoided.
4. The pupils score their work on practice lessons that are carefully checked by diagnostic tests administered by the teacher when a unit of work has been completed. Any further instruction apparently needed is given at once by the teacher.
5. When the pupil at any time during the year has completed the requirements for some area for a given grade he may proceed to the work of the next grade at once without changing rooms.

[9] Adapted from the discussion in C. W. Washburne, *Adjusting the School to the Child* (Yonkers, World Book, 1932).

6. If the pupil has not completed the work of a given grade in June, he begins in September at the point where he left off.

7. The individualized work is continuously supplemented by a series of creative socialized activities in which the children are given ample opportunity to utilize the facts and processes they are learning, to consider carefully the relationships involved, and to make generalizations. In this way the work is extended beyond the level of concrete experience.

Adjusting difficulty of materials to pupil ability. In a discussion of factors related to the difficulty of reading materials, Leary points out the necessity of considering a variety of elements before recommending a book to a particular student because of the desirability of adapting the work to the ability and interest of the individual. The list of items to be considered, according to Leary, is as follows: [10]

1. Observe the format, noting whether the material is attractive in size and appearance, approachable, legible, etc.

2. Consider the type of subject matter and the literary form, deciding whether they are appropriate for the student's purpose, interest, and ability.

3. Evaluate the content of the book for the quality of ideas presented.

4. Judge the degree of compactness of the ideas and facts presented, estimating whether they are too compressed for the students to interpret readily.

5. Observe the author's choice of words.

6. Examine the author's arrangement of words in sentences.

7. Predict the difficulty of the book by sampling the book, analyzing the passages for significant elements, and applying a formula of prediction.

8. Synthesize the facts pertaining to the difficulty of the book under consideration and relate them to what is known about the reader in order to determine whether the book is suited to his interests, abilities, and purposes.

[The application of this series of steps can be done by the teacher either in a systematic way, or informally by a fairly detailed analysis of the book by inspection. When it is planned to make use of a basic body of materials for instructional purposes, it is a good plan to establish with considerable accuracy the relative difficulty of each item included as a basis of effective direction of the learning activities of each item included as a basis of effective direction of the learning activities of pupils. This is essential if adequate provision is to be made for individual differences.]

The specific procedures that may be used to determine the difficulty of various kinds of materials have been discussed in Chapter 13, and will not be reviewed at this point. Standards for the allotment of materials to classes should recognize the need for materials of varying levels of difficulty so that proper adjustments to the variations in the abilities of the pupils can be made.

Improving library facilities. The educational value of printed matter is widely recognized. In most communities, special provisions have been made to ensure the accessibility of wholesome reading materials through efficient library service. It is necessary to supply strong incentives toward the "better" publications that are written sincerely, present truth without bias, depict life by emotionalizing the truths of human experience, and distinguish the heroic from the normal. The library seeks to condition youth against the "worse" publications which are more numerous and more easily available than the "better." The most widely read publications are those that are most accessible. Even when good books are available and more accessible than the "worse," the better will be neglected unless the right incentives are applied. Readers must be led to prefer them by sympathetic guidance, usually on an individual basis.

The school library represents the most direct step that has been taken to improve and broaden reading interests. The school library can serve many purposes. It should be a place to which children can go for study, relaxation, and enjoyment. It can also serve as a place for group activities, pupil-teacher conferences, and reference reading.

[10] Bernice Leary in W. S. Gray, ed., *Reading in General Education,* A Report of the Committee on Reading in General Education (Washington, American Council on Education, 1940), pp. 301-302.

The pupils should be given much freedom in the use of the library as a source of inspiration, a stimulation of creative activities, and a place for exhibiting the products of their activities. When the library is supplemented by reading alcoves or corners in all classrooms, it is possible to integrate the services of the library with the ongoing learning activity. Here can be made available for the pupils the materials needed in the activity that is under way.

The following types of materials should be available in the well-equipped school library:

1. Supplementary books with authentic material related to curriculum areas.
2. Different kinds of reference books, dictionaries, encyclopedias.
3. Well-selected literary materials for enrichment purposes and for recreational reading.
4. One or more newspapers, local or national.
5. Selected magazines for children and for older pupils.
6. Sets of reading materials organized by subject or topic arranged for class use.
7. Books loaned by city, county, regional, or state library, if available.
8. Pamphlets, bulletins, dealing with vocations and occupations.
9. Pictorial aids, such as pictures, films, slides, maps, etc.
10. Bulletin board for posting clippings, reviews, advertisements, etc., to simulate interest in reading.
11. A small space for museum exhibits and for exhibits of pupils' productions.

Improving the accessibility of materials. Teachers and pupils should grow in their ability to find or devise materials that are needed in the course of their activities. When great varieties of materials are available, some of the value that comes from locating needed supplies or using ingenuity in devising materials is lost. Some of the equipment needed for instruction, such as textbooks, maps, and reference books, is of a more or less permanent nature, whereas other supplies such as clippings, pictures, and periodicals are soon out of date and need not be preserved.

The establishment of a materials bureau offers many advantages, since it provides centralized facilities for storing and filing materials to be preserved. It may take the form of a central bureau for all schools in a system, under the direction of some competent person. Any teacher may requisition materials from this bureau or visit the bureau to select the materials desired from among those available. In many schools, materials bureaus for the single school have been established, sometimes as part of the school library and under the charge of the school librarian, sometimes in a special room set aside for the collection. The resources of this bureau are available to all teachers and pupils. Sometimes materials bureaus are developed for single classrooms where adequate storage and filing space is available. This is especially necessary for classrooms designed for social science, science, and industrial arts. The pupils should be taught to assist in collecting and preserving necessary materials and in keeping them up to date. They can also participate in the activities involved in mounting, filing, cataloging, indexing, and lending the materials. In the course of time such a bureau can assemble an excellent variety of instructional aids.

The sources of materials in the community should also be explored systematically. References to libraries, museums, art galleries, collections of various kinds, exhibits, and other sources should be compiled by the staff, and the lists should be made available with notes as to what each source can provide. Names of places of historic interest, the names of firms, stores, business houses, farms, and so on, willing to give pupils access to them for purposes of study or other kinds of contacts should also be compiled for the information of all.

To make teachers familiar with sources of new materials, several steps can be taken. The supervisor or a committee of teachers interested in the problem of supplies can make a systematic scrutiny of publishers' catalogs and advertising matter. Exhibits of materials at professional meetings should be examined to locate new kinds of instructional materials. Reports of new types of supplies and equipment often included in books, articles, and new courses of study should also be analyzed. Observations at experimental centers and elsewhere are another valuable source of information. Special steps should be taken to bring to the attention of the staff some new use that is being made of some older type of material. This may be done by means of special bulletins or orally at staff meetings. In general, the supervisor should enlist the help of the entire staff and pupils to locate or devise the necessary kinds of instructional aids and take steps to keep them informed as to the best sources.

Materials to be secured free or at small cost. At the present time, an increasing amount of instructional materials of various kinds is being made available for the schools. This material is most useful in supplementing the textbook. The following list shows the kinds of materials that can be secured free or at very small cost by any school:

1. *Printed materials*
   Annotated bibliographies.
   Catalogs, bulletins, pamphlets, folders.
   Papers, magazines, children's newspapers.
   Time tables, schedules.
   Publications of local and regional public and private agencies.
   Programs—radio, music, theater, museum.
   Clippings, advertising matter.
   Reviews of books, plays, movies.
2. *Visual and illustrative materials*
   Posters, cartoons, sketches, diagrams.
   Pictures, paintings, prints, photographs, postcards.
   Graphs of different kinds, time lines.
   Tapestries, wall hangings, ceramics.
   Road maps, pictorial maps.
   Exhibits, made available by business firms.

Collections of stamps, coins, minerals, mountings, etc.
   Models—local museums; businesses.
   Properties and costumes.
   Films, slides, recordings.
3. *Community resources*
   Containers.
   Measures and measuring devices.
   Specimens of fruit, food, etc.
   Materials brought from homes for illustrative purposes.
   Materials for simple experiments in science.

The value of visual aids. Because it is not feasible for the student to have first-hand contacts with many aspects of life past and present, extensive use must be made of visual aids to give meanings. The motion picture more or less faithfully reproduces scenes, settings, processes, and actions representing the history, literature, and life of all parts of the world. The sound film has greatly increased the potentialities of the motion picture as a means of instruction. Pictures, film strips, graphs, models, posters, maps, clippings, and exhibits are other kinds of visual aids used in our schools. Horn has summarized as follows the claims and experimental evidence of the value of these aids: [11]

1. Motion pictures, like other pictures, but to a superior degree, contribute materially to the accuracy, the richness, and the significance of students' concepts. This is particularly true of descriptive aspects. Places, people, events, and processes are made to seem more real.
2. As a consequence, thinking is made more effective, empty verbalism reduced, vocabulary increased, and language made more meaningful.
3. Learning is made more active: the imagination is stimulated; students write more, talk more, carry on more "projects," and ask more questions.
4. Interest is more easily aroused and maintained.
5. Voluntary reading is encouraged rather than discouraged.

[11] Ernest Horn, *Methods of Instruction in the Social Studies* (New York, Scribner, 1937), pp. 373-374.

6. A marked contribution is made to retention.
7. Children who are lacking in imagination, low in intelligence, or below the average, are helped especially.
8. The total desirable results, both direct and indirect, exceed those attained by any other media that were used in teaching the topics chosen for these various experiments. It is important to know, however, that the best results were obtained when the films were used in conjunction with other recognized methods of instruction.

Locating educational films. In a number of states and larger institutions of learning such as state universities there are visual-education departments that supply films free or at a small cost. The use of these resources should be encouraged and their latest catalogs of films should be on file in some convenient place. There are also similar bureaus in many of the larger cities. The production of films by school systems has been handicapped because of the cost of producing them and the lack of any kind of organized effort by educational organizations to develop the field. There have been several noncommercial organizations interested in the production of educational films but their output has been small. Many of the films produced by the motion picture industry for general distribution are excellent for school use, but often the rental is high and they are out of date before they become available. Usually they are too long for class use and are not intended for instructional purposes.[12] The great value of films as an aid to instruction, revealed by their use in the war training program, should greatly stimulate their production for wider use in the schools. If better films, more closely integrated into the school's program, were available, and if the cost of the necessary equipment were reduced, there would undoubtedly be a big increase in the use of the film in teaching.

Teachers will find their own state university and state departments of education the best sources of information about audio-visual aids. Local and state courses of study and teachers' guides also contain many suggestions.

The following selected sources contain a wealth of information about audio-visual and other kinds of aids of all types and for various curriculum areas. They may be consulted for detailed information:

Audio Visual Aids for Instruction, Forty-eighth Yearbook, Part I, National Society for the Study of Education (Chicago, Univ. of Chicago Press, 1949).
Audio Visual Materials and Methods in the Social Studies, Yearbook, National Council of Teachers of the Social Studies (Washington, the Council, 1947).
BRUECKNER, L. J., and GROSSNICKLE, F. E., *Making Arithmetic Meaningful* (Philadelphia, John C. Winston, 1953).
DALE, Edgar, *Audio-Visual Aids in Teaching* (New York, Dryden, 1946).
McKOWN, H. C., and ROBERTS, A. B., *Audio Visual Aids to Instruction,* rev. ed. (New York, McGraw, 1954).
Multi-Sensory Aids in the Teaching of Mathematics, Yearbook, National Council of Teachers of Mathematics (New York, Teachers College, Bureau of Publications, Columbia Univ., 1945).
OLSEN, E. G., *The School and the Community,* 2nd ed. (New York, Prentice-Hall, 1954).
The Teaching of Arithmetic, Fiftieth Yearbook, Part II, National Society for the Study of Education (Chicago, Univ. of Chicago Press, 1951), Ch. 9.
WITTICH, W. A., and SCHULLER, C. F., *Audio-Visual Materials: Their Nature and Use* (New York, Harper, 1953).

Numerous distributors of films, film strips, slides, and other visual aids publish catalogs giving detailed information about their materials. Among the leading distributors are the following firms:

Coronet Films, Coronet Building, Chicago.
Encyclopaedia Britannica Films, Wilmette, Illinois.

[12] W. W. Charters, *Motion Pictures and Youth* (New York, Macmillan, 1935). Summarizes twelve studies of the influence of motion pictures on children.

Knowledge Builders, 625 Madison Avenue, New York.

United World Films, 1445 Park Avenue, New York.

World Book Co., Yonkers, New York.

Young America Films, 18 E. 41st St., New York.

Certain organizations publish periodically lists and reviews of current visual aids. The following are typical:

Educational Film Guide (annual). New York, H. W. Wilson Co., 950 University Avenue; also *Film Strip Guide,* published annually.

Educational Film Library Association, Suite 1000, 1600 Broadway, New York.

Federal Radio Education Committee Bulletin, Federal Security Agency, Office of Education, Washington (monthly, free).

School Films, 6047 Hollywood Blvd., Los Angeles, California.

Sources of Teaching Material, Teaching Aids Laboratory, Bureau of Educational Research, Ohio State University, Columbus; also *The News Letter.*

The value of audio aids. There are several important kinds of audio aids to instruction, including the radio and the phonograph. Not only do these aids affect instruction but they are widely utilized in life outside the school as a means of recreation and enlightenment. The potential uses of the radio and phonograph in classroom instruction have barely been touched in this country. The conscious use of the radio as a social force by Hitler is ample testimony of the power of this instrument. The schools are face to face with the need of adopting some policy as to the extent to which steps should be taken to guide the learners' choices of program and their methods of listening. The use of the radio as an instrument of classroom instruction raises many administrative and teaching problems. The effectiveness of the radio compared with other kinds of instructional aids must be determined and its peculiar contributions established. The apparent advantages of the radio as a means of instruction have been summarized by Cantril and Allport as follows: [13]

1. Radio can reach incomparably larger audiences.
2. Figuring per capita cost, its services are probably cheaper than any other medium of instruction.
3. The varied content possible in its programs promotes interest and attention.
4. Its varied methods do the same thing.
5. Dramatization and showmanship make education pleasurable.
6. In many regions, it can supplement poor local teachers with good radio teachers.
7. It probably has a favorable effect upon the exercise of visual imagination.
8. It can make important events and personages more real to the people.
9. It can bring good music into every locality.
10. The pupil becomes less provincial in his outlook; the excellence of talks and music heard may fire his ambition and arouse talents that might otherwise lie dormant.

The following plan for reporting on the utilization of radio programs is of very significant value to the classroom teacher since it lists procedures and items which the teacher can use to judge the quality of the use made of any radio program. The checklist was prepared by a group on evaluating school broadcasts. [14]

UTILIZATION REPORT

1. Did you have an opportunity to prepare your students for listening to this program before the time of the broadcast?
   _____Yes. _____No.
   If you did, when was this done?
   _____*a.* Immediately before the broadcast began.
   _____*b.* At an earlier time on the day of the broadcast.
   _____*c.* At some time before the day of the broadcast.
   If you did, underline the number which most nearly approximates the number

[13] H. G. Cantril and Gordon Allport, *Psychology of Radio* (New York, Harper, 1935), p. 252.

[14] Reported by W. B. Levenson and E. Stasheff in *Teaching Through Radio and Television* (New York, Rinehart, 1952), pp. 294-296.

of minutes spent in advance-preparation activities:

Less than 5   5 to 10   10 to 15   15 to 20   20 to 30   30 to 40   45 or more.

2. Check any of the following types of activity that were employed in preparing your class for listening to this broadcast:

_____a. The teacher consulted the printed manual about this broadcast.

_____b. The teacher explained to the students what the broadcast was to be about.

_____c. Questions about which the broadcast was expected to provide information were listed.

_____d. Key words, names of people, places, or dates were listed on the blackboard.

_____e. Students discussed the subject of the broadcast.

_____f. Materials such as books, pictures, maps, clippings, etc., related to the topic of the broadcast were consulted.

_____g. Students maintained a few moments of silence.

3. Check any of the following things you did to facilitate listening:

_____a. Made sure window shades were properly adjusted before program began.

_____b. Carefully checked heat and ventilation of the room.

_____c. Allowed students to move to places where they could hear better (if radio set is located in the room).

_____d. Tuned in the station, beforehand, to check reception.

_____e. Turned on the program promptly at the beginning, and shut it off promptly at the end of the broadcast (if centralized radio is used).

_____f. Checked with the office to make sure the broadcast would be turned on as scheduled.

4. Check any of the following things which you did during the broadcast:

_____a. Checked reception in all parts of the room.

_____b. Permitted freedom of pupil activity so long as it did not interfere with group listening.

_____c. Kept a few notes on the broadcast for use in later discussions.

_____d. Wrote, on the blackboard, names, dates, new words, and the like, that were mentioned in the broadcast.

_____e. Pointed to locations on a map, or to words listed on the blackboard.

_____f. Listened attentively with the students.

5. Were you able to allow time for a period of follow-up activities after the students had listened to the broadcast? _____Yes. _____No.

If so, when did these follow-up activities take place?

_____a. Immediately after the broadcast was concluded.

_____b. At a time during the day of the broadcast.

_____c. At some time after the day of the broadcast.

If so, underline the number which most nearly approximates the number of minutes spent in follow-up activities:

Less than 5   5 to 10   10 to 15   15 to 20   20 to 30   30 to 40   45 or more.

6. Check any of the following types of follow-up activities that were employed in connection with this broadcast:

_____a. Students had a brief period of relaxation.

_____b. Students took part in a free discussion of the broadcast.

_____c. Students discussed points in the broadcast they considered important.

_____d. Students discussed the broadcast in terms of previously listed questions.

_____e. Students listed important points which the broadcast had failed to mention.

_____f. Parts of the broadcast were explained by the teacher.

_____g. Questions raised, but not answered, in the broadcast were pointed out for further consideration.

_____h. Sources where additional information about the topic of the broadcast might be found were suggested.

_____ *i.* Students drew pictures or wrote about things suggested to them by the broadcast.

7. Write, in the space below, any observations which indicated that the broadcast (including preparation and follow-up) was a valuable educative experience for the students of your class.

Tape recordings are valuable in the study and improvement of speech difficulties, since they enable both student and instructor to note changes that take place. They are also useful in recording oral discussions, oral compositions, and other uses of speech in the classroom. In some school systems, recordings are used to reproduce panel discussions, lectures, and similar activities for groups that were unable to attend the original presentations.

Improving the use of the radio and audio aids. As a result of the survey of audio aids in Ohio, reported in Chapter 13, a series of nine recommendations for the improvement of the use of audio aids in the classroom was made by the staff. The complete list of recommendations is given below because of its general usefulness as a basis of studying and improvement in this direction in any school system: [15]

1. That every effort be made by school systems, by parent groups, and by other educational and civic organizations to provide schools with radios.
2. That special efforts be made to stimulate the use of radio in rural schools and especially in one-room rural schools.
3. That schools with central radio sound systems (and other radio equipment) examine carefully the actual and potential uses made of that equipment.
4. That schools with record-playing equipment make more effective use of that equipment by purchasing records usable and valuable in different curricular areas.
5. That school administrators who believe in the educational potentialities of radio not only make public their approval of radio education but also design and put into action a program of radio production, utilization, and in-service education of teachers.
6. That teachers colleges, state and county departments of education, and the administra-

tive units of city school systems develop more effective programs for the pre-service and in-service training of teachers in the use of radio in the classroom.
7. That broadcasters, particularly the network broadcasters, design their school programs for elementary-school listeners.
8. That teachers and administrators interested in the educational values of radio listening at home become familiar with the rich variety of programs on the air.
9. That teachers and administrators re-examine their curriculums to see whether radio should or should not be emphasized in different courses and in different grades.

The use of the phonograph. The use of the phonograph should be greatly extended in our schools. It can be used when there is no radio available. When records are at hand they can be used at any time they may be needed—an advantage they have over the radio. The records can be repeated as often as is desired. The results of what is undoubtedly the most comprehensive investigation to date of the use of the phonograph in the classroom are given in a report of an experiment in the rural schools of New York. Miss Bathurst summarizes the suggestions and recommendations about the use and production of records growing out of this study as follows: [16]

1. When properly made for the purpose, the phonograph record is a useful aid to learning in the rural elementary school.
2. To be a useful learning aid, the record's content must not only be carefully selected but keyed to the curriculum and to the experience and ability of the children with whom it is to be used. This requires competent curriculum research.
3. The effectiveness of the phonograph record is dependent not only upon its content, but also upon the skill of the script writer, the skill of the actors or persons making the recording and the quality of production in its manufacture.

[15] "Radio in the Schools of Ohio," *Educational Research Bulletin* (May 13, 1943), pp. 115-148.
[16] Effie G. Bathurst, *Phonograph Records as an Aid to Learning in Rural Elementary Schools* (Albany, N. Y., State Education Department, 1943), pp. 148-149.

4. The chief test of the value of the phonograph record as an aid to learning is the extent to which it stimulates children to pursue other useful learning activities such as group discussion, observation of their surroundings, and the use of reference works to find the answers to their own questions.

5. A secondary test of the record's value is observed in the children's responses—their exclamations of approval, the character of their discussion, and the number of times they ask to have the record replayed.

6. In many areas such as bird study, regional studies, and study of environment, the phonograph record is a more effective aid when supplemented by visual aids, such as lantern slides or mounted pictures.

7. The phonograph record should be planned as a supplement to and not as a substitute for other teaching aids such as the radio, the sound film, and the printed page.

8. The phonograph record should be designed to aid the teacher where sound is especially important, as in the recording of songs of birds and the record on choral speaking. The elementary school has need of many series of records of this type.

9. Since the teacher in rural schools has limited supervisory assistance, the phonograph record can provide some of the help that would be given by a master teacher in specialized areas. This is illustrated by Allen's records, "Do You Know the Birds?" Using these records the children are in the presence of master teachers of elementary-school science, children's literature, and creative writing.

10. The phonograph record may enrich children's opportunity for learning through bringing the artist into the classroom, as in Dorothy Lathrop's, "How I Make My Books."

11. Production of phonograph records as an aid to learning requires skill in the techniques which have proved effective in producing radio programs; but the record has three values not inherent in the radio program: it can be adjusted to the time schedule of the classroom; it is available for replaying or review; and it can be used in schools which are not equipped for using electrical transcriptions of radio programs.

Television. In recent years there has been a rapid development in the educational role of television. The number of homes in which television sets are found has grown by leaps and bounds. A recent study in Cincinnati showed that sixth- and seventh-grade children averaged about thirty hours a week in televiewing. About half of them reported that no restrictions were placed by parents on programs they were allowed to watch, a fact that has serious implications for the schools.

A recent review by Finn [17] of research on television and education led to the following generalizations:

A. *The television audience*
   1. While television, early in its introductory phases, represented a luxury to be afforded by groups that had the economic means to purchase sets, this situation no longer holds true.
   2. As with the introduction of other mechanical devices into American life, an immediate tendency is set up to spread the advantages of television throughout all levels of society. Television is fast becoming a general necessity.
   3. All groups of Americans can be reached in equal amount through television broadcasts if set owning is the criterion of availability.

B. *The effects of television on leisure time and other social activities*
   1. Television in the home definitely has an effect on all the other leisure-time activities carried on by the family.
   2. Most investigators agree that radio listening, motion picture attendance, reading, and "going out" are decreased when a family owns a television set.
   3. The evidence with respect to the so-called novelty effect is not clear. There is some reason to believe that the initial effect of television on leisure-time activities may be modified, but not erased, as the set remains in the home over a period of time. However, the duration of the novelty effect is longer than most investigators had suspected.

C. *Effect of television on children and education*
   1. Where television is available, children of all ages view it extensively,

[17] James D. Finn, "Television and Education: A Review of Research," *Audio-Visual Communication Review* (Spring, 1953), pp. 106-126.

with the average running over 2 hours per day on school days and more than that on weekends. Averaging the results of all the studies, it would seem that children spend in the neighborhood of 20-25 hours per week watching television.

2. The preoccupation with television causes a decline in almost all other kinds of leisure-time activities. While it cuts down on the use of other media, it also cuts into participating activities such as playtime. The net result is that children's exposure to the mass media is increasing.

3. There as yet is no demonstrable effect of television on school achievement. The evidence in this regard is conflicting.

4. Television has had an effect on the family life of children. It has influenced their eating, sleeping and social habits generally in an undesirable direction from a psychological point of view.

5. If Lewis' data is confirmed by other investigators, there would be some reason to believe that a leveling-off factor will begin to operate after four years of set ownership and that television will be integrated more comfortably into family life. Further controlled research is definitely needed here.

D. *The content of television programs*
1. The amount of time devoted to programs which, even broadly interpreted, are educational in nature is very little when compared to the total programming in a saturated television area.

2. The bulk of programs which are available are in classifications which, while they may be entertaining, are not useful to the general public in helping them solve the tremendous problems which confront the nation nor do these program classifications illustrate many possibilities of expanding and enriching the cultural experience of the viewers.

3. The entertainment programs designed for children contain a tremendous amount of crime and violence to the exclusion of other possible dramatic, exciting, or comic material which might have a more wholesome effect.

E. *Effectiveness of television as a means of instruction*
1. Television is an effective medium of instruction.

2. Instruction by television is remembered by those who experience it.

3. All studies report that learners like to receive instruction by television.

4. Although more study is needed to establish specific technics that are most effective for television instruction, it seems to be established that direct instruction, supplemented by printed bulletins, is one effective way to use television. Dramatic and other complicated technics would seem to need further investigation.

5. Television as used for in-school broadcasting is also an excellent public relations medium.

Many teachers have had no training whatsoever in the use of television programs. In many school systems, supervisors are organizing workshops and conferences to provide the necessary experiences for the teachers. Important commissions are studying the role [18] of television in education and formulating principles underlying its uses.

The elements of in-service education in audio-visual aids. McKown and Roberts [19] have suggested the following outline of an in-service program for teachers in audio-visual aids:

1. *Objectives*
    a. To help the teacher to recognize and appreciate the place and possibilities of audio-visual aids in general.
    b. To familiarize the teachers with the literature in the field, both descriptive and evaluative.
    c. To teach the basic principles to be observed when using audio-visual materials.

[18] Section III of *Mass Media and Education,* Part II of the Fifty-third Yearbook of the National Society for the Study of Education, contains an excellent discussion of the topic, "What the Schools and the Public Can Do about the Mass Media" (Chicago, Univ. of Chicago Press, 1954).

[19] By permission from *Audio-Visual Aids to Instruction,* by H. C. McKown and A. B. Roberts, pp. 546-547. Copyright, 1949, McGraw-Hill Book Company, Inc.

d. To acquaint the faculty with the various types of audio-visual aid, their instructional possibilities, and the advantages and limitations of each.

e. To demonstrate the different types of equipment and to provide instruction in operating them.

f. To familiarize the group with the techniques and procedures to be observed when utilizing these tools in the classroom.

g. To acquaint the staff with the audio-visual center and its services.

h. To show the procedures to be followed in requesting materials or service from the center.

i. To acquaint the faculty with the various sources from which these materials may be obtained.

2. *Skills to be acquired:* The audio-visual course should be based upon actual laboratory activities that will assist the staff in acquiring the necessary skills. The following will illustrate:

a. Operating all types of still-picture projector—opaque, 2″ x 2″, standard slide, filmstrip, and micro.

b. Operating motion-picture projectors, both silent and sound.

c. Learning to place the projector and screen in order that all observers will be seated in the correct viewing angle.

d. Operating recording and playback machines—disc, metal tape, or wire.

e. Recognizing and compensating for ear defects when using auditory aids.

f. Making handmade slides.

g. Making microslides.

h. Using camera in making slides, either black and white or color.

i. Using guides to locate a specific aid required.

j. Acquiring techniques and procedures for the best utilization of these materials in the classroom.

Local systems are preparing manuals for teachers on the effective use of radio and television programs in connection with courses of study. The following outline of a detailed guide has been proposed: [20]

1. Introductory Information

Advance listing of all programs, dates, etc.

The purpose and plan of the radio program.

Suggested seating arrangement.

Suggestions for distributing materials.

Reception in the classroom—the teacher's function.

Hints for teaching with radio.

General follow-up techniques.

Suggestions for using visual aids.

2. The Individual Program

Objectives of the program, possible outcomes.

Before the Broadcast

Materials needed—the teacher's responsibility.

If pupil worksheet is used, copy is attached.

During the Broadcast

Activity by the teacher.

Type of student participation.

After the Broadcast

The teacher's responsibility: immediately after the program; between radio programs.

Pupil's responsibility: individual progress chart.

Scope and summary of the program.

Suggested references: for teacher, for pupil.

Optional tasks for superior pupils.

Related vocabulary to be emphasized.

Test questions; key for grading.

Means of promoting uses of instructional materials. The supervisor can use various simple and direct means of making teachers keenly aware of the educational values of concrete materials and stimulating them to use new kinds of instructional materials.

Exhibits. The supervisor can arrange exhibits of supplies in some centrally located place. Traveling museums, art exhibits, and libraries are also very helpful in bringing materials to the attention of teachers. Exhibits during Book Week are used in many systems. Publishers' exhibits at teachers' conventions and elsewhere are other means of making teachers aware of the existence of new kinds of materials.

[20] W. B. Levenson and E. Stasheff, *op. cit.,* p. 493.

Materials bureaus. The supervisor can make available for teachers on their requisition collections of various kinds of materials such as slides, books, pictures, and the like which the ordinary teacher cannot collect unaided. The pooling of the resources of several schools will greatly increase the amount and variety of materials available for all of them.

Surveys of the community. The supervisor can assist teachers greatly by making a systematic survey of the places in the community which are suitable for excursions and for illustrative purposes, in connection with the study of social institutions and occupations. The attention of teachers can be called to places of historical interest and natural beauty. Arrangements can be made with such local interests as industries, banks, the post office, and so on for their first-hand observation by pupils. A direct study of the current health, social, and economic needs of the community through teacher excursion and study groups will be a rich source of suggestions of problems that are likely to be of vital concern to large numbers of pupils.

Intervisitation. If teachers are given the opportunity to study the kinds of materials in use in other schools and classes in terms of their value to children, they ordinarily have been led to introduce new kinds of equipment into their own classrooms. Reports of observations by representative teachers have also been found to be very fruitful.

Demonstrations. In many school systems, the supervisors or some teachers demonstrate for groups of teachers the use of new kinds of materials being introduced into the schools. The wise supervisor will be on the lookout for interesting and suggestive work being done by individual teachers which should be brought to the attention of all teachers through demonstrations.

Study groups. It is often helpful to organize study groups of teachers who wish to increase their skill in the use of new kinds of materials. Such groups can also make a systematic appraisal of the available supplies and equipment with a view to the elimination of unsatisfactory materials and the recommendation of the purchase of additional supplies.

Experimental studies. The supervisor should encourage the teachers to make experimental studies of the values of new kinds of materials. Such investigations need be nothing more than a systematic recording of the reactions of pupils to the various items. It has been repeatedly shown, however, that there is awakened a real interest on the part of teachers in the study of the value of materials when they have participated in a well-planned investigation of an experimental kind.

Section 2

IMPROVING THE SOCIO-PHYSICAL ENVIRONMENT OF THE SCHOOL

Improving school buildings. It seems quite obvious that school buildings should be planned in terms of the kind of instructional program that is to be carried on in them. In the traditional school, the primary consideration was the provision of facilities for teaching the subject matter of a variety of special curriculum areas, sometimes defined as the "scientific subject" curriculum. In the modern school, consideration is given not only to the teaching of the subject matter of broad curriculum areas but also to the development of personality traits, interests, attitudes, appreciations, mental and physical health, and methods of democratic living. The modern school building should be planned so as to provide the facilities that are needed to carry on a wide variety of learning experiences, such as are listed below, which contribute to the achievement of this increasingly broad range of educational objectives.[21]

TYPICAL ACTIVITIES IN MODERN EDUCATION FOR WHICH FACILITIES AND EQUIPMENT MUST BE PROVIDED

1. Mastering basic learning skills, including reading, writing, speech, and arithmetic.
2. Studying community life (social studies).
3. Recreating community enterprises in the classroom.
4. Carrying out experiments in science.
5. Caring for animals and fish.
6. Making models and simple constructions.
7. Growing plants.
8. Cooking and sewing.
9. Playing house (primary grades).
10. Using records and transcriptions.
11. Viewing films, pictures, television.
12. Using art as a medium of expression.
13. Developing hobbies and use of interest materials.
14. Participating in musical activities.
15. Making exhibits, displays, collections.
16. Dancing and rhythms.
17. Puppetry, marionettes.
18. Dramatics.
19. Participating in sports, games, recreations.
20. Securing information from printed and other sources.
21. Participating in group and committee work.

The kinds of facilities that should be provided to carry on the rich program of experiences of the modern elementary school are listed below. The list is based on an analysis by the authors of provisions found in modern schools they have visited and of up-to-date books on the planning of school buildings. At the present time, the tendency is to reduce the size of school buildings so that there can be more intimate contacts of the staff with individual children than is possible in the very large schools found today in many cities. It is highly desirable that supervisors and teachers participate in planning school buildings because of their sensitivity to the needs of children.

DESIRABLE FACILITIES FOR MODERN ELEMENTARY SCHOOLS [22]

1. Self-contained classroom units for groups of 25 children each.
   a. Classrooms set up as learning laboratories.
   b. Flexible structure—readily enlarged.
   c. Built in facilities for books, supplies, and children's products.
   d. Corners for reading, social studies, and arithmetic.
   e. Special rooms for exceptional children.
   f. Provision for very young children— ages 2-4.
2. Facilities for activities beyond classrooms.
   a. Library—a center for films, records, books, museum materials, exhibits.
   b. Outdoor play area.
   c. School garden and greenhouse.
   d. Indoor play area or gymnasium with corrective facilities.
   e. Auditorium for school and community use.
   f. Science laboratory.
   g. Arts and crafts workshop.
   h. Kitchen unit, primarily for cooking.
   i. Space for animals, birds, pets.
3. Special rooms.
   a. Cafeteria and lunch room.
   b. Health suite and rest provisions.
   c. Teachers' rest lounge and recreational facilities for men and women.
   d. Conference rooms for school and community groups, school psychologists, etc.
   e. Principal's office.
4. General facilities.
   a. Materials bureau.
   b. Toilets and washrooms.
   c. Storage space for supplies, equipment, etc.

[21] The authors have drawn freely for ideas in preparing this analysis on various books, especially from N. L. Engelhardt and others, *Planning Elementary School Buildings* (New York, Reinhold Corp., 1949).

[22] A class report on the procedures used in the following volume will be of interest to many: Frank M. Long, *Desirable Physical Facilities for an Activity Program,* Contributions to Education No. 593 (New York, Teachers College, Bureau of Publications, Columbia Univ., 1933).

Criteria for planning school buildings.

The traditional secondary-school building was planned in terms of a curriculum which prepared solely for college entrance. Few other needs were considered. Many new emphases have emerged in the program of secondary education which are being considered today in planning high-school buildings. An excellent analysis [23] of some of the more significant of these basic criteria follows:

A. Education is not merely a preparation for future life work but it is a process of eventful, constructive, and happy living. Society depends upon education for the integration of its membership in a successful, co-operative and democratic organization.

B. School and community must be thought of as working harmoniously in the conservation of the resources of childhood and adulthood.

C. The secondary school should plan its facilities to provide for all needs of all children who could reasonably profit from any program of education.

D. The secondary school plant should not be planned merely to meet the needs of traditional age groups but should provide for possible expansion of these groups.

E. The school's function includes teaching of the techniques of civilization, the development of physical well-being, the instruction of all individuals in the idealogy of their society, the introduction of students into cultural areas, and the socialization and guidance of the individual toward effective membership in his society.

F. The school plant must be closely interwoven with a comprehensive program of city planning.

G. The school plant should be in harmony with its surroundings, both natural and man-made.

H. The secondary school building should reflect the achievements, the aims, and the highest ideals of the community.

I. The school building should not be institutionalized, but the plant should be thought of as a community in itself where direct contact is given with the problems of living.

J. Good planning is evident in the secondary school plant by the degree to which its space provisions meet the particular needs of the community and are free from stereotypes.

K. The education service rendered in a school plant is constantly changing, thus requiring a high degree of adaptability in construction.

L. With increasing emphasis upon the problems of the air age, high schools must be planned to provide adequate training for work in a three-dimensional world.

M. The pupil-teacher relationship has also witnessed considerable modification. The teacher today is the companion and fellow-worker rather than the teacher-dictator.

Eliminating sources of accidents.

There are many sources of accidents that should be checked in site planning and building design and construction. The following list [24] includes the principal sources of accidents which should be subjected to careful scrutiny in connection with safety.

SITES
1. *Proximity of traffic hazards*
   a. Major arteries.
   b. Railroad tracks.
   c. Streets which invite speeding such as those receiving high-speed traffic from rural areas.
   d. Roadways without sidewalks.
   e. Curved and blind highways.
   f. Multiple, irregular, blind, and grade intersections.
   g. Steep hills.
   h. Interference of school loading and parking facilities with student pedestrian traffic.
   i. Roadways separating school property.
   j. Playground areas unprotected from streets.
2. *Recreational areas and landscaping*
   a. Roadways through playground areas.
   b. Improper fencing allowing children to run into streets or off school property to recover balls.
   c. Lack of proper surface treatment of school grounds.
   d. Holes, ledges, rocks, ruts, tree stumps, and ditches which might cause children to fall.

[23] N. L. Engelhardt and others, *op. cit.*, pp. 25-26.
[24] N. L. Engelhardt and others, *op. cit.*, pp. 31-32.

e. High or abrupt cliffs left unprotected.

f. Football goal posts left unpadded.

g. Wire fences either too low or too light for good visibility.

h. Unprotected construction in progress.

i. Poorly constructed bleachers.

j. Improper layout of play areas which cause interference of players.

k. Interference of pedestrian traffic with players.

BUILDINGS

1. *Gross structures*

   a. Lack of proper building codes.

   b. Use of inferior materials and labor in construction.

   c. Poor design.

   d. Lack of fire-resistive materials in roof, walls, flooring, and flues.

2. *Interior arrangement*

   a. Unprotected vertical openings, such as stairways, ventilating ducts.

   b. Inadequate distribution of exits and stairways.

   c. Inadequate size of corridors, exits and stairways.

   d. High risers and slippery, narrow treads on stairs.

   e. Obstructions in corridors.

   f. Doors which open inward or against the direction of traffic.

   g. Inclusion of attic.

   h. Improper maintenance.

   i. Storage under stairs.

   j. Improper protection of danger spots including heating units, fuel rooms, custodian's supply rooms, industrial shops, cafeterias, kitchens, and chemical laboratories.

   k. Lack of automatic control devices and fire warning signals.

   l. Insufficient or inadequate distribution of fire-fighting equipment.

   m. Improper natural and artificial lighting.

   n. Slippery floors in shower rooms and swimming pools.

   o. Wells between double stair runs.

   p. Turns and blind curves in corridors.

   q. Steps into rooms of corridors.

3. *Facilities and equipment*

   a. Improperly padded apparatus in gymnasiums and exercise rooms.

   b. Sharp corners, rough edges on equipment.

c. Inadequate waste receptacles.

d. Improper arrangement in segregating hazards in shops and laboratories.

e. Unprotected shop equipment, including lack of guards on lathes, grinders, and machine saws.

f. Drinking fountains, fire extinguishers, and other apparatus protruding from walls in corridors.

g. Radiators protruding into rooms and corridors.

h. Low unprotected windows.

i. Lack of panic bolts on outside exits.

j. Railings on stairs which are too high or too low.

k. Use of anything but a wire glass adjacent to fire escapes.

l. Unprotected motion picture projectors.

m. Lack of proper fire doors and curtains at critical points.

n. Unprotected power panels in shops and laboratories.

o. Easily operable gas fixtures.

The value of checking building equipment has been quite fully discussed in Chapter 13 and will not be reviewed at this point. Suffice it to say that if buildings are constructed according to up-to-date specifications [25] that are now available, there will be little cause for complaint about the adequacy and merit of school buildings.

It is extremely difficult to set up standards on such points as ventilation, lighting, and similar points about buildings because there is a lack of agreement among authorities about these. There are even differences among experts in interpreting the results of experiments. Tinker comments on the difficulty of setting up standards for illumination as follows: [26]

Since so many factors (distribution of light, condition of the eye, etc.) are involved in determining hygienic illumination, it is hazardous to set up standards of light intensity for read-

[25] Alice Barrows, *Functional Planning of Elementary School Buildings,* Bulletin No. 19 (Washington, Office of Education, 1936).

[26] M. A. Tinker, "Facts Concerning Hygienic Illumination Intensities," *School and Society* (January 22, 1938), pp. 120-121.

ing. It is possible, however, to suggest tentative specifications that provide for a margin of safety for efficient and comfortable seeing: Never read in light of less than 5 foot-candles unless there happens to be a very bad arrangement of direct lighting. In such a situation a slight reduction in the brightness will be less fatiguing to the eye; with the fair distribution of light that is found in most homes use 5 to 10 foot-candles; with good distribution of light, use 10 to 15 foot-candles. If no glare is present, higher intensities may be employed with safety but without any practical advantage. A recent international commission on illumination recommended 8 foot-candles as a minimum in classrooms.

In certain situations higher intensities are essential for hygienic vision. Both the defective eye (refractive error) and the eye changing with age (presbyopia) are benefited by relatively bright illumination. Light intensities should be increased somewhat when poorly legible print is being read or when very fine details are being discriminated.

Trends in classroom construction. Another valuable publication in this field is the report compiled by Jean Betzner, entitled "School Housing Needs of Young Children," published in 1939 by the Association for Childhood Education, Washington, D.C. This forty-page bulletin contains photographs of modern classrooms and classroom equipment, a discussion of the materials and standards, and a selected bibliography on the subject.

A still more recent publication is Portfolio A, *Elementary School Classrooms,* compiled by N. L. Engelhardt and School Planning Associates, and published by the Bureau of Publications, Teachers College, Columbia University, in 1941. It contains a collection of classroom plans from all parts of the country and represents many different educational philosophies. The details of the plans were carefully analyzed and the findings discussed. Eighty plates are presented with sixteen pages of discussion, check-lists, index, and an excellent bibliography. This material contains a wealth of valuable information to be used by groups in planning classrooms adapted to instructional needs.

A way in which a supervisor can assist any school to evaluate and plan ways of improving any aspect of the school environment is suggested in the plan for improving the attractiveness of the school environment given below. It is contained in the section dealing with that problem in the guide *Evaluating the Elementary School,*[27] which was discussed in Chapter 12. First, the school, in co-operation with local interested citizens, is expected to study its own present program, then to indicate its strengths and weaknesses and to suggest ways of improving the environment, and finally to consider immediate and long-term plans for improvement. On the original form there is space provided for writing the necessary information.

1. *Providing an attractive school environment.* The school needs to teach appreciation of beauty and desire to contribute to beautiful surroundings.

In the space below each of the following suggestions cite specific illustrations which indicate the ways you are teaching esthetic values through the school environment by:

Giving children opportunities to help landscape the school grounds.

Planning with children how to achieve orderliness and cleanliness of buildings and grounds.

Planning with children and giving them opportunities to redecorate their own classrooms.

Giving the school council responsibility for keeping attractive exhibits of creative work in halls.

Hanging at eye-level many pictures which appeal to children and changing the pictures frequently.

Planning with children and parents to make the cafeteria as homelike as possible.

Giving children opportunities to accept responsibility for attractive bulletin board displays.

a. What else should be done to provide an attractive school environment? Use bibliographical references for suggestions.

[27] *Evaluating the Elementary School:* A Guide for Co-operative Study (Atlanta, Ga., 316 Peachtree St., N.E., The Southern Association, 1951), pp. 121-125.

Cite examples to illustrate what you are doing.

b. List the strengths and the weaknesses of the school environment as it exists with reference to attractiveness. As the basis for your analysis use the preceding suggestions and these which you identified in "a". Be sure that experiences are selected in terms of the child's maturity.
   Strengths
   Weaknesses

c. What do you plan to do *this year* to improve the attractiveness of the school environment?

d. What are your *long-range* plans for improvement?

Section 3

IMPROVING THE USE OF COMMUNITY RESOURCES TO VITALIZE INSTRUCTION

Vital learning experiences in the community. There has been steady progress in this country toward the use of the community to add greater vitality and reality to school experiences. Concreteness is secured by bringing the pupils into contact with geographical and physical features of the community life. By observing the activities of members of the social group, the learners are brought into contact with many social and economic relationships and may gain a better understanding of aspects of life in a modern society. They become familiar with the opinions, attitudes, prejudices, and purposes of people.

The supervisor should help the teachers to examine the community to locate sources of concrete instructional situations and illustrations. The school should also secure the co-operation of interested groups of laymen in the study of local questions such as public health, recreation, guidance, relief, religious education, delinquency, and the like. These should then be related to the curriculum and their possible usefulness recognized. To lead to the easy use of these experiences, necessary administrative adjustments must be made by the principal and supervisor.

Two kinds of community contacts have been recognized. In one kind, the contacts come into the classroom, as when exhibits are brought into the school or when some businessman addresses the students on topics related to his occupation and its community relations. In the other kind of experience, the pupils leave the school and see the agency or activity in its natural setting; for example, they may visit a creamery, interview some governmental agent, or visit a factory to gather information about working conditions.

The activities in which the pupils and teachers may engage may be of various sorts. The three types most commonly employed are:

1. Observation—field trips, films, exhibits.
2. Actual participation in the study of community problems.
3. Contributory activities.

Field trips for teachers. The excursion is one of the most valuable means to acquaint teachers with community resources. A typical program of community excursions is reported in the reference below.[28] The committee in charge of the program had the following purposes in mind:

1. To acquaint teachers with certain features of their environment in Springfield which would serve to deepen and make more realistic their understanding of what is actually involved in group living in the modern world.
2. To reveal new and vital resource materials that teachers could use in their classes.
3. To increase teacher understanding of the problems faced by boys and girls outside the realm of school.
4. To bring elementary and secondary teach-

[28] Paul Mitchum, Alice Pittman, and Harry P. Study, "Excursions to Acquaint Teachers with Community Resources," *The National Elementary Principal* (July, 1952), pp. 358-362.

ers together in a joint project that would increase the number of common understandings.

5. To convince teachers that a school is
only part of a community, not all of it.

6. To reveal agencies other than schools
that are providing educative experiences for
boys and girls.

7. To encourage teacher respect for other
social agencies that compete with schools for
the public money.

8. To further sell to the community its
teachers and its schools by showing the
teachers' genuine interest in community affairs.

A questionnaire was submitted to the
teachers to determine what trips to plan.
It contained the following headings: (*a*)
distributive industries, (*b*) manufacturing
industries, (*c*) transportation facilities, (*d*)
utilities, (*e*) communication facilities, (*f*)
service organizations, (*g*) government agencies and services, and (*h*) miscellaneous.
On the basis of the returns, a master schedule was drawn up. A booklet for each trip
was prepared, containing pertinent data
about places being visited, "stimulating
questions" to suggest the kinds of items to
notice, "understandings that might be contributed to by a study of this place," and
finally a page of "modern problems suggested by a study of this place."

The following statements indicate the
nature of teacher participation in the program and the observed results of the trips:

THE TRIPS

Beginning with the second Wednesday of
vacation, the scheduled trips began. At some
of the more popular places, more than one
visit was made to accommodate the number
wanting to go. Usually the number allowed to
go on any one trip was kept to a maximum of
ten to fifteen persons.

A typical Wednesday boasted one excursion
to the Youth Center and another to a wholesale grocery establishment in the morning and
a study of the gas and electric plant in the
afternoon. At the gas and electric plant, a lesson
in community interdependence was learned
from the arrangement which Springfield and
surrounding towns have to supply one another
with electricity if and when any local source
of supply fails.

For two summer months teachers were all
over the city, following workmen around,
snooping here and there, asking hundreds of
questions, and frequently gazing in wide-eyed
amazement at what they saw. Those in charge
of the agencies visited provided workmen-
guides to explain the "why and wherefore."
These guides showed considerable pride in their
companies as well as in their knowledge of
what "makes the wheels go 'round." Teachers
took pages of notes on the booklets with which
they were provided but of course could not
adequately record all their impressions. The
response to these trips was so enthusiastic that
plans were made for additional trips to be
taken during the coming school year.

THE RESULTS

In the fall a special committee set to work
compiling the data provided by the summer
visits. In several cases follow-up discussions
were arranged. Thus, the director of the Medical Center was asked to explain the underlying
philosophy of the United States penal institutions.

The most important result, however, was
that teachers began to utilize more fully the
resources of the community, selecting more dynamic problems for classroom study and taking
pupils out into the community to learn through
actual firsthand contacts and from original
data. Topics were chosen for study which involved significant social understandings. These
ranged from questions of food, communication, and transportation to those of conserving
natural resources and living in a machine age.
The use of firsthand community resources
helped the children to become more keenly
aware of the interrelationships among various
social forces and institutions. Thus, in studying the conservation of natural resources they
discovered that the government was an important factor. Likewise, in their study of how
clothing is produced and provided they developed the concept of a region and of the
dependence of local activities on the resources
of that region. Trips into the community were
used specifically to build important social concepts and to create an increasing awareness of
the functioning of a community as an interrelated unit.

Destinations of school trips. The following list [29] will suggest some of the places

[29] H. C. McKown and A. B. Roberts, *op. cit.,*
pp. 261-263.

to which school classes may profitably take trips:

Agriculture: farms,—grain, stock, fruit, tobacco, cotton, dairy, school, experimental, irrigated, dry; processing plants, packing, ginning, stemming, milling, pickling, canning, condensing, stockyards, elevators, warehouses and storage plants.

Art: galleries, exhibits, architecture; churches, homes, and furnishings—rugs, wallpapers, pictures and statues; cemetery; public works; landscapes and seascapes.

Clothing: factories, stores; cleaning, dyeing, and pressing, laundry.

Clubs: fraternal, professional, and social; YMCA, YWCA, YMHA, commercial, country.

Communication: telephone and telegraph—offices, exchanges, plants, radio broadcasting station and studio.

Community groups: religious, social, racial, national, artistic, occupational.

Courts: justice of the peace, magistrates, city, traffic, police, juvenile, county, circuit, supreme.

Educational: schools—public, private, parochial, night, adult, open air, military, nursery, higher institutions—colleges, university, technical school, business; museum, gallery, library, theatre, various exhibits.

Engineering: bridge, highway, dam, viaduct; aqueduct; canal; garbage disposal plant; buildings, drainage and sewer systems; flood and erosion control; hydro-electric plant, dam, pumping station, power house; improvements.

Expositions: fairs and exhibits of all kinds.

Factories: automobile, building supply, machinery, clothing, glass, ceramic, soap, tools, weapons, implements, furniture.

Federal: post-office, court, lock, dam, mint, power plant, flood and erosion control devices, experiment stations, nature preserves, improvement projects.

Financial: bank, clearing house, broker's office, stock exchange.

Food and drink plant: bottling, ice cream, breakfast food, dairy products, ice, canning, packing, pickling, baking.

Health: center, clinic, sanitarium, hospital, first aid station, safety-first provision in streets, homes, offices, factories, fire and disease prevention.

Historical: buildings, homes, settings, sites, shrines, memorials, markers, monuments, battlefields, cemeteries and burial plots; old forts; expositions; exhibits—documents, weapons, utensils, clothing and costumes, relics, old village, pioneer home, and furnishings.

Homes: slum, middle class and exclusive districts; buildings—exterior; furnishings, equipment, appliances, grounds.

Hotels: flophouse, middle class and exclusive, apartment and resort; restaurant.

Literary: library, exhibit, bookstore, publishing house, authors' homes and haunts, graves, shrines, story settings and inspiration spots, dramatic events and activities; newspapers and magazine offices.

Meetings: board of education, city council, court, legislature, political rally, conferences, forum, debate, lecture, address, symposium, program.

Military: fort, reservation, armory, post, airfield, school.

Mines and quarries: coal, zinc, lead, stone, gravel, granite, processing plants.

Municipal: departments, offices, plants; services—police, jail, safety, health, utilities, garbage disposal.

Music: concerts, opera, studio program, composers' homes and graves, exhibits, publishing and recording companies, manuscript rooms, school conservatory, instrument manufacturing plants, stores.

Nature: water and land forms—river, pond, lake waterfall, island, hills, mountains, valleys, cave, geological formations; woods and fields; nature and forest preserves; bird and game sanctuaries; public and private parks, arboretums, planetarium, floral and vegetable gardens, greenhouses; botanical and zoological gardens, scenic spots, phenomena and curiosities.

Naval: station, ships, air station, docks, yard, school.

Oil: wells, refining and processing plants, station, pipe lines, tanker filling station.

Penal institutions: workhouse, detention home, industrial school, jail, farm, penitentiary.

Professional: offices of physician, dentist, lawyer, minister, banker, publisher, weather forecaster, insurance salesman, real estate agent.

Public works: buildings, aqueduct, viaduct, bridges, streets, tunnel, waterworks, flood-control, and other protective devices.

Recreational: swimming pools, beaches, playgrounds, parks, courts, courses, camps, stadium, gymnasium, skating rinks.

Religious: cathedral, churches, synagogues, missions, schools.

Shops: machine, plumbing, blacksmith, printing, barber, beauty.

State: institutions, buildings, preserves, sanctuaries, services, organization.

Stores: wholesale and retail; department, general, jewelry, grocery, street market, book, meat market, bakery, fuel, second hand, five and ten, chain.

Transportation: railway, surface, elevated and subway lines; bus lines; trucking corporations; terminals; offices, equipment; repair shops, freight and express services; automobiles and trailers, parking stations, camps, highways; water—ships and boats, ferry, docks, canal, dam, locks, ford, bridge; air—airport, hangars, planes, offices, shops, air events, races and shows, museum.

Utilities: municipal and private; water, heat, power, light, gas.

Welfare: settlement house, community center, agencies and institutions.

The following statement [30] presents an excellent series of excursion possibilities for children in the elementary grades of a large city. It can be adapted to the possibilities of any community.

1. How do people on various social and economic levels live?
   a. The richer residential sections of the city; i.e., Park Avenue, Fifth Avenue, Riverside Drive, and Central Park West.
   b. The poor residential sections of the town; i.e., Lower East Side.
   c. The wealthy hotels; i.e., Waldorf-Astoria.
   d. The breadlines.
2. How can housing for the poor be improved?
   a. The Lavanbury Houses.
   b. Co-operative houses.
3. What are the racial and religious groupings of the community?
   a. Little Italy, Little Russia, Harlem, Chinatown, and Yorkville.
   b. Temple Emmanuel, and East Side Synagogue, the Cathedral of St. John the Divine, St. Patrick's Cathedral, and Riverside Church.
4. How does the city get its power? A large power plant.
5. How do people make a living?
   a. The garment center.
   b. Wall Street.
   c. A metal manufacturing firm.
6. How and where do people get their life necessities?
   a. A dairy farm.
   b. A bottling plant.
   c. A bakery.
   d. A clothing factory.
   e. A department store.
   f. A freight depot.
   g. A trucking corporation.
7. How do people travel to places?
   a. Subway and surface cars.
   b. A ferry.
   c. Bridges.
   d. Automobile assembly plant.
8. How do people communicate?
   a. A telephone exchange.
   b. The central post office.
   c. A central telegraph office.
   d. A radio station.
9. How are people informed quickly and accurately about events?
   a. The city room of a large newspaper.
   b. The processes of printing and distributing.
10. How do people govern themselves?
   a. A political rally.
   b. A meeting of a legislative body.
11. How are people protected?
   a. The police department.
   b. A magistrate's court.
   c. A fire station.
   d. The street-cleaning department.
12. How do people enrich their lives?
   a. A recreational center.
   b. A public library.
   c. The theater section.
   d. A museum.
   e. A radio broadcasting studio.
13. How does a particular community exchange products with the outside world?
   a. A railroad depot.
   b. A steamship dock.
   c. An airport.
14. How do people work towards another social order?
   a. A meeting of a party aiming at social reconstruction.
   b. Symposia, debates, and discussions.

[30] W. A. Weaver, "Excursions in a Metropolitan Center," in *Aids to Elementary School Teaching,* Thirteenth Yearbook, Department of Elementary-School Principals (Washington, NEA, 1934), pp. 292-293.

The management of field trips and excursions. Dale[31] has prepared a detailed check-list to assist teachers in using excursions as an instructional procedure to the best advantage. The list suggests the items that a supervisor should bring to the teacher's attention when the necessary plans and arrangements are being made:

A CHECK-LIST FOR TEACHERS

I. *Preparation*
  A. Teacher Preparation:
    1. Arrange through administrative department for consent to make trip, including parental consent where necessary.
    2. Make preliminary survey, with listing of situations and points of interest, etc.
    3. Estimate length of time involved; also round-trip schedule.
    4. Decide if entire class or select group should go.
    5. Make arrangements with school authorities and with authorities at place of destination.
    6. Plan transportation route, in detail, and arrange financing.
  B. Pupil Preparation:
    1. Arouse pupil interest in the projected field trip (by class talk, photographs, bulletin board, etc.).
    2. Discuss in class the problems that the trip can help solve.
    3. Make clear to pupils the purpose or purposes of the trip.
    4. Develop background by consulting reference materials.
    5. Work out for pupils the points to observe during the trip.
    6. Set up with them standards for safety and behavior.
    7. Give to pupils any materials that they can use during trip.
II. *Actual Observation*
  A. Guide is to be given clear idea of the purpose of the trip (set of questions prepared jointly by teacher and pupils).
  B. Pupils observe and hear the guide's explanations.
  C. Question period, in which individual questions from pupils are presented

and answered by guide and/or teacher and pupils.
  D. Period for note-taking and sketching by pupils.
III. *Follow-through*
  A. Group Discussion in Classroom:
    1. Critical evaluation of the place visited.
    2. Supplementing and correcting incomplete or hazy understanding.
    3. Introduction of new problems.
  B. Creative Projects:
    1. Drawings, poems, stories, construction, bulletin board displays, diaries, etc., based on the trip.
    2. Writing a letter of thanks to the guide, etc.
  C. Tests to Determine:
    1. Information gained, 2. Attitudes formed, 3. Generalizations made.
  D. Reports from Pupils:
    1. General reports—the all-over subject.
    2. Special features, reported by pupils to which these had been previously assigned.
IV. *Evaluating—Before and After*
  A. Before—
    1. Is this destination the best choice for this particular teaching purpose?
    2. What plans need be made by teacher and pupils?
    3. Is there reading material on this particular pupil level?
    4. Is the time involved likely to prove worth the undertaking?
    5. What relationship can this trip have with other pupil experiences?
    6. What emotional effects is the trip likely to have on the pupils?
  B. After—
    1. Did the trip serve the purpose?
    2. Were attitudes affected in the expected manner?
    3. Did the trip stimulate the pupils into new activities?
    4. Did it develop in them a spirit of inquiry and curiosity?
    5. Has the trip had any final effect on pupil conduct and behavior?

[31] Edgar Dale, *Audio-Visual Methods in Teaching* (New York, Dryden, 1946), pp. 155-156.

Evaluating uses of community resources.
An illustrative procedure for assisting a
school to evaluate its use of community resources and to plan for improvement is
found in the guide for study given below
in *Evaluating the Elementary School*.[32] In
the original form, space is provided for
writing information.

COMMUNITY RESOURCES

Teachers should use human, institutional, and
material resources of the community and the
total school district in the instructional program
whenever the resources can make an effective
contribution. A survey of available resources
should be made, and an up-to-date catalog of
community resources should be furnished to
teachers.

Cite examples which indicate how the school
is effectively using the following community
resources:

Public library.
The high school.
Churches and church organizations.
Civic government, including fire and police
    departments.
Service clubs (such as Rotary, Kiwanis).
Other clubs.
Parks.
Recreational centers.
Welfare agencies.
Individual community members.
Public buildings (courthouse, auditoriums).
Newspapers.
Radio and television.
Community council.
Scouts.
Extension services.
Health department.
Industries.
Businesses.
The P.T.A.
Audio-visual aids owned by nonschool
    groups.
Theaters.
Gardens, rock formations, and rivers.

a. What other community resources should
   be used by the school in the instructional
   program? Cite examples of present use
   of each additional resource which is mentioned.
b. What progress has already been made in
   using effectively the resources of the community in the instructional program?
c. What problems must be solved in order

to use community resources effectively in
the instructional program?

d. What plans have you made for more effectively using community resources in
   the school program *this year?*
e. What are your *long-term* plans for discovering and more effectively using the
   good learning resources which exist in
   the community?

An excellent project for a supervisor and
a group of teachers, in co-operation with
the pupils, is the preparation of a list or
catalog of available community resources
based on some such pattern as that provided
by the McKown-Roberts list given above.
The project itself actually serves as an integral part of any curriculum-making program. A community-resource file should be
prepared in the form of alphabetized cards
listing possible excursion points of interest
and giving essential information about each
place, the times most suitable for visitation,
the persons to contact, and suggestions
about planning the trip. It is astounding
what information about available exhibits,
materials, and places of interest the pupils
will gather if given the opportunity to do so.

**Pupil participation in improving condi-
tions in the community.** In the participatory
type of contact, the pupils take some sort
of active part in a community enterprise.
They actually engage in some activity which
adds to their understanding of community
affairs and increases the wideness and effectiveness of their participation in the affairs of the community in which they live.
An excellent example of the kinds of participatory contacts pupils may make is the
following outline of possible activities developed as a joint enterprise of the Civic
Pride Association of Greater Detroit and the
schools of that city. The activities were to
be those in which the children of the city
would and could actually participate.[33]

[32] Pp. 249-255 in *Evaluating the Elementary
School.*
[33] Reported in *The Social Studies Curriculum,*
Fourteenth Yearbook, Department of Superintendence (Washington, NEA, 1936), from a type-
written statement by Anna Willard Winkler, teacher
of social studies in Hamtramck, Mich., pp. 263-265.

POSSIBLE ACTIVITIES OF CIVIC PRIDE JUNIORS

A. *Healthful City*
  1. Things which child could do himself
     a. Killing rats.
     b. Killing all insects.
     c. Keeping animals clean.
     d. Prohibiting spitting on sidewalks.
     e. Reporting all contagious diseases to board of health.
     f. Having board of health inspect homes that are not fit to live in.
     g. Reporting to board of health any violations of health regulations.
     h. Insisting on children coming to school clean.
     i. Removing unnecessary clothing in school.
     j. Bathing regularly.
     k. Keeping windows open while sleeping.
     l. Trying to get children not to play with rubbish left in alleys.
  2. Things on which child would need adult help
     a. Providing smoke screens on all factories, large buildings, trains, etc.
     b. Disinfecting garbage cans.
     c. Prohibiting farm animals in city.
     d. Keeping ice in summer.
     e. Keeping screen doors and windows in summer.
     f. Reporting violations of pure food laws.
     g. Doing away with dead animals.
     h. Putting garbage in tin can containers and keep covered.
     i. Having public rest rooms.
     j. Having teachers and parents teach correct health habits.
     k. Establishing a municipal hospital.
     l. Getting toxin-antitoxin treatments.
     m. Getting vaccination.
B. *Clean City*
  1. Things which child could do himself
     a. Keeping alleys, streets, and sidewalks clean.
     b. Keeping garages and porches clean.
     c. Keeping yards clean.
     d. Sweeping sidewalks.
     e. Getting rid of glass and tin cans.
     f. Cleaning cages for pets.
     g. Cleaning all vacant lots.
     h. Trying to get children to clean their feet before entering a building.
     i. Raking up and burning dead leaves.
     j. Putting empty cans and bottles in receptacles.
     k. Keeping billboards clean (billboard license ordinance).
     l. Collecting loose papers.
  2. Things on which child would need adult help
     a. Providing smoke screens on all factories, large buildings, trains, etc.
     b. Disinfecting garbage cans.
     c. Prohibiting farm animals in city.
     d. Putting rubbish in separate containers from garbage.
     e. Having no dumps.
     f. Making storekeepers assume responsibility for keeping the pavement in front of their stores clean as well as alleys in back.
     g. Keeping ashes in ash cans.
     h. Burning piles of rubbish.
     i. Sprinkling all streets daily.
     j. Paving alleys.
     k. Appointing committees to see that school buildings are kept clean.
     l. Cleaning homes thoroughly at least once a week: windows, floors, woodwork, basements, and attics.

There then follow similar series of activities grouped under the headings, "Orderly City," "City of Security," "City of Leisure-Time Activity," "Other Possible Activities."

Contributory activities.[34] In the contributory type of contact, the pupils make

[34] For further detailed discussion of contributory activities see:

William H. Burton, *The Guidance of Learning Activities,* 2nd ed. (New York, Appleton-Century-Crofts, 1952), pp. 527-529.

Stuart Chase, "Bring Our Youngsters into the Community," *Reader's Digest* (January, 1942), pp. 5-8.

Morris R. Mitchell and others, "Youth Has a Part to Play," *Progressive Education* (February, 1942), pp. 88-109. Available also as a separate pamphlet.

a definite contribution or addition to their environment. This involves originality and creativeness on their part. A class, for example, may make a survey of health conditions in a community, prepare plans for improving the situation, submit them to local health authorities, and then help to arouse the interest of the community in the enterprise. Some of the activities suggested in the list on page 642 may be regarded as possible examples of the contributory type of activity. This type of activity is increasing rapidly in schools.

Criteria such as the following should be considered in selecting community problems for study and investigation:

1. The problem should be one that is within the realm of the interest of the pupils, of definite concern to them, and on a maturity level in keeping with their abilities.

2. The activity should permit the pupils to assume the responsibilities of citizenship and should be of such a nature that the pupils can complete it with a minimum of adult dominance.

3. Special consideration should be given to the study of problems which the community itself asks to be investigated, perhaps after they have been brought to the attention of the citizens by the school. This approach insures wide-spread interest and their willing participation in fact-gathering activities and an understanding of the basis of any solutions that may be proposed or adopted.

4. The activities of the pupils should lead to actions and conclusions that will be of service to the community.

5. The study of the problem should lead to the discovery of a body of information on the basis of which the pupils will be able to formulate sound and significant generalizations.

The list of contributory activities below is selected from numerous descriptions of experiences given in the volume by Alice Miel and associates, *Co-operative Procedures in Learning*.[35] It illustrates the kinds of contributory activities in which the pupils in any school can engage:

Planning to contribute to a science exhibit.
Making a safer playground.
A problem in ethics.
Planning to sell tickets for a school operetta.
Beautifying a barren hillside.
Making plans for a cathedral window.
Surveying first-aid supplies.
Beautifying the community.
Thanksgiving donations.
Improving the reputation of a community.
Sending a parcel overseas.
Setting up a lost-and-found center.
Taking charge of a Junior Red Cross Drive.

Section 4

IMPROVING THE QUALITY OF LIVING IN THE COMMUNITY

The relations of the school and the community. The educational program of a community consists of the total range of influences in the environment to which the individuals are exposed. The school is obviously the special agency set up by society to guide and direct the learning experiences of the children of the community; however, it is almost everywhere recognized at the present time that there are many other agencies in every community that affect either directly or indirectly the nature of the experiences that condition the growth of the children. Sometimes these influences affect growth favorably but in some instances their effects are definitely harmful. The home obviously is a major factor in determining the kinds of experience to which children are exposed in life outside the school and homes vary widely in their quality. Then there are numerous social influences that must be reckoned with: the radio, television, the motion picture, the press, the church, rec-

[35] New York, Teachers College, Bureau of Publications, Columbia Univ., 1952.

reational center, the neighborhood contacts, charitable agencies, youth organizations of all kinds.

There are also many governmental agencies that contribute to child development: health departments, police and juvenile courts, city planning commissions, public libraries, welfare and relief agencies, and others. In many localities these agencies proceed altogether independently of each other, duplicating efforts in an uneconomical, inefficient manner and doing little in an integrated way to improve the total environment to which youth is exposed. In other places there have been developed systematic plans for bringing about a co-ordinated attack by all agencies dealing with any aspect of the care and development of the individual.[36] Steps are being taken to bring about the elimination of unwholesome conditions in the community through what is most commonly called the "co-ordinating council" procedure. In these councils the schools usually take an active part, often assuming the leadership of the community in its endeavors to improve the conditions—social, economic, political, industrial—under which the youth of the locality grow up. It should be recognized that this co-operative movement has developed much more widely in some parts of the nation than in others—for example, in California.[37] The development of this program should be pushed throughout the entire country. Wherever the school takes an active part in the endeavors of the social group to improve its total general level of living, we can feel fairly safe in assuming that the influences which condition child development are being raised to a higher plane. When the school neglects this problem, the school is not playing its proper role. This becomes clearer with each new investigation.

In a number of places in this country, the community school has made valuable contributions to the improvement of life in the community. Certain principles are emerging from these experiments and demonstrations that can well serve as guides for all schools: [38]

1. Since education is a continuous process, it cannot be confined within fixed administrative divisions; but for education to be most effective, there must be co-ordination of all educational services in a community.

2. When educational activities are based upon the needs and interests of those for whom they are planned, community problems assume primary importance in the school's curriculum, and the school utilizes the community resources in the solution of community problems.

3. The democratic method in education is a practicable method to use in an educational program based on community problems and interests.

4. An educational program designed for all age levels of a community is characterized by flexibility—space and equipment serve multiple purposes; the materials of instruction are adaptable and methods pliable; requirements for attendance and credit are adjustable.

5. The teacher in a community school is a member of the community.

6. A community school makes its physical plant and environment a community center and demonstration of desirable operation and maintenance of property.

Community use of the school plant. The program of the school must recognize the need of those living in the community, especially the children and youth, for wholesome recreation and play. For this reason, it should arrange activities that permit participation in worth-while leisure-time pursuits. These may be in the nature of group and club activities: discussion groups, sports activities, musical and dramatic programs, the use of the library, and the like. There are many schools that conduct successful

[36] *Citizen Co-operation for Better Public Schools,* Fifty-third Yearbook, Part I, National Society for the Study of Education (Chicago, Univ. of Chicago Press, 1954). An up-to-date discussion.

[37] Kenneth S. Beam, "Co-ordinating Councils in California," Bulletin No. 11 (Sacramento, Calif., State Department of Education, September 1, 1938).

[38] *Curriculum Reconstruction,* Forty-fourth Yearbook, Part I, National Society for the Study of Education (Chicago, Univ. of Chicago Press, 1945), pp. 216-222. Quoted by permission of the Society.

recreation centers in the schoolhouse. Most schools are not well adapted to community programs of this kind but through careful study and clever planning, needed adjustments can be made. The school can also serve as a community center, concerning itself with broader aspects of the welfare of the entire family and community for twelve months in the year, such as health, planning production programs, improvement of living conditions in the community, and the elimination of community influences that contribute to juvenile delinquency. Where these programs have functioned most successfully, there has been a fine type of co-operation between the school and community agencies. Seldom do they succeed where the school sets up a program without securing the interested participation of the people of the community in planning the activities.

In some states, legislation is needed to make such programs possible and to provide the funds that are needed. It appears that adequate legislation on this subject should: [39]

1. Authorize local school boards to establish and maintain social centers in connection with the public schools, specifying some of the principal activities to be maintained.

2. Authorize school boards to set aside a certain amount of funds for the maintenance of such functions; and to extend to the people the right to increase the amount by an election held for that purpose.

3. Provide for the employment of competent directors and personnel to supervise social-center activities.

4. Authorize school boards to grant the use of school property to voluntary community organizations to maintain and operate social, recreational, or civic activities, and prescribe under what conditions school properties may be used for such purposes.

5. Provide a method whereby, in case school boards do not establish social centers, the question may be submitted to the electors of the district by petition therefor.

6. Grant school boards considerable discretionary power concerning the type and character of community activities for which school property may be used.

The community workshop approach. The Michigan Community Health Project represents another interesting and very valuable method of bringing about an integrated attack on local problems by communities. The purpose of this project was to bring to four selected communities the most promising current ideas as to ways of bettering living conditions, especially in the field of health, happiness, and well-being of children. Community workshops were established where leaders of the community together with members of the staffs of the schools studied local conditions. Specialists were brought to these workshops to lead the discussions and to supply expert advice. It was believed by those who planned the project that those who were directly concerned with the problems could best work out the answers. Some of the assumptions underlying the project were the following: [40]

a. Rural areas have a variety of resources, human and physical, which, with appropriate stimulation and assistance, can be developed into effective forces for human betterment.

b. The strength and permanence of a program depend largely on the development of local resources rather than the implantation of extraneous and frequently temporary services or facilities.

c. Steady and more lasting progress can be made if all of the component elements in a community are moving forward at the same time and are co-ordinating their efforts toward a common goal.

d. The most lasting contribution of assistance from an outside agency is the education of the people in the area.

e. The program develops from, with, and for the people of the area.

The school and the co-ordinating council. A co-ordinating council consists of individuals and representatives of local groups that organize for the purpose of

[39] *Youth Education Today,* Sixteenth Yearbook, American Association of School Administrators (Washington, NEA, 1938), p. 168.

[40] Henry J. Otto and others, *Community Workshops for Teachers in the Michigan Community Health Project* (Ann Arbor, Univ. of Michigan Press, 1942), p. 1.

working co-operatively to improve the general and social welfare within the community. In the pre-World War II period most co-ordinating councils were organized for the purpose of ameliorating poverty and preventing juvenile delinquency. The problems that grew out of World War II, such as local defense, need of providing recreation for war workers and members of the armed forces, housing problems, racial relations, caring for children of women in war industry, and conservation of resources required the joint action of numerous agencies in all communities of the country. The key to the success of these activities was the co-ordination of the work of all of the agencies concerned. In hundreds of localities community councils of different kinds were established. These councils were largely advisory in nature. Their purpose was to clarify problems and needs and to stimulate existing agencies to more intelligent and co-operative efforts in meeting these problems and needs.

The membership of these councils varied from community to community. They usually included representatives of various governmental services such as the schools, the courts, health departments, and recreation departments. They also included representatives of private social agencies and youth organizations, of civic organizations such as service clubs, parent-teacher organizations, and veterans organizations, and of religious federations. Often this list was supplemented by representatives of industrial groups, trade unions, and professional bodies such as the Bar Association and Medical Association.

The role of the school is of particular importance in the work of the co-ordinating council because it is the only permanent agency which is supported by all of the people and which serves all of the children and youth. The special obligations of the school in connection with the activities of the community council may be listed as follows: [41]

1. To provide leadership and to act with others in making and keeping the council a potent educational force in the community.

2. To maintain the democratic values of group discussion, group planning, group decision, and the scientific values of objective thinking about controversial issues.

3. To guide the council in the use of evaluative procedures so that results may be reliably appraised and purposes adjusted to changing needs.

4. To aid in sensitizing the council's membership to youth needs, youth interests, and youth problems.

5. To endeavor to widen the base of council membership so that young people are included in the deliberations and are encouraged to participate actively in both planning and executing policies.

The steps that should be taken in starting a co-ordinating council in any community are as follows:

1. A study should be made to discover pressing problems and needs of the community.

2. The limitations of the community and its resources should next be scrutinized to discover people interested in some crucial problem as well as agencies that should be concerned about it.

3. A meeting should be called of a few key people to face the facts about the situation that will clarify the problem and reveal its significance.

4. Steps should then be taken to develop a small co-operative program to deal with an issue that is of greatest concern to the group.

5. The program of activities should be extended slowly and gradually until the group has had considerable experience in working together.

6. A conference should then be called of representatives of all community agencies concerned with the general welfare of the citizens of the community. Preliminary steps can then be taken to explore the possibility of establishing a council.

7. A permanent organization should then be developed. This should be kept flexible so

[41] From *School and Community*, by E. G. Olsen. Copyright, 1945, by Prentice-Hall, Inc. Reprinted by permission of the publishers.
See also E. G. Olsen, *The Modern Community School* (New York, Appleton-Century-Crofts, 1953).

that additions can easily be made as the occasion arises.

8. Steps should be taken to inform the community about the findings of the council. Meetings should be held at which the situation is discussed and the facts are presented.

9. Under the leadership of the council a constructive program of social action should then be initiated.

10. It is desirable that the results of any action by the council be constantly evaluated so that the community may be made aware of the success of the program undertaken. When necessary, adjustments should be made in the activities engaged in.

An analysis of the reports of the work of co-ordinating councils shows that many improvements have resulted from their activities. The excellent bulletin, "A Guide to Community Co-ordination," gives the following list of some of the changes that have taken place as a result of the activities of co-operative group organizations: [42]

The following list gives some conception of the improvement councils have made in their communities through co-operative planning:

1. *Recreation facilities.* Practically all councils report more activity in this field than in any other. They report the lighting of playgrounds; securing of new playgrounds, new facilities, equipment, club houses, swimming pools, community centers; extending present programs, securing directors, promoting back-yard playgrounds, improving life-guard service, and securing the use and control of streets for play.

2. *Improving public service.* Councils frequently discover ways by which public service can be extended to areas not yet reached or new forms of service introduced. This applies to every type of public service, particularly health, sanitation, fire protection, probation, police, libraries, and public schools.

3. *Health and safety programs.* Clinics for children and mothers have been promoted, medical treatment provided for individual cases, health education stimulated, and hot lunches provided. Councils also have secured crossing guards and have improved traffic conditions.

4. *Organizations for boys and girls.* Councils assist in the extension of boys' and girls' organizations through a variety of activities: leadership training and promotion; securing leaders for individual groups; assisting in organizing new Boys Clubs, Boy Scout troops, Cub Packs,

Girl Scouts, Camp Fire Girls, Y.M.C.A. and Y.W.C.A. groups, toy loan centers, and vacation church schools. The councils are particularly interested in extending these organizations to areas and to groups not hitherto served.

5. *Employment for youth.* The councils recognize this as one of the major problems facing practically all communities. They have assisted by increasing the school facilities for vocational training, counseling, and placement service. A number of councils have provided special employment bureaus for youth.

6. *New youth groups organized.* Councils have endeavored to meet social and educational needs of youth by assisting in the organization and supervision of community dances, social outings, drama classes, youth forums; courses on the preparation for marriage, homemaking and parenthood; young married people's clubs, music clubs; clubs to promote athletics, gardening, study of radio, bicycle and automobile safety.

7. *Educational opportunities for adults.* Councils have realized the need of assisting adults as well as youth and have played a prominent part in encouraging Americanization classes, public forums, adult education courses, citizen education centers, consumer education classes, parent education classes, mothers' clubs, mothers' educational centers, nursery schools and leadership training. In rural districts councils have assisted in providing recreational counseling for school teachers, teacher-training in service, and county school trustees' institutes.

8. *Improving community conditions.* Councils have found it necessary in many communities to use their influence in preventing the sale of liquor to minors, the circulation of salacious literature, the use of gambling machines, the showing of undesirable motion pictures, and unwholesome conditions in dance halls and skating rinks. They have also played an active part in improving housing conditions.

9. *New organizations and agencies formed.* When a council discovers that a new organization is needed, it takes steps to create it and then leaves it to function quite independently of the parent council. Councils have thus launched community choruses, community theaters, motion picture estimate service, farm produce markets, and cold storage facilities. Several councils have successfully organized community chests and social service exchanges. Junior councils are now putting in their appearance in a number of cities. The chart on page 648 illus-

[42] "A Guide to Community Co-ordination" (Co-ordinating Councils, Inc., 1941).

Objectives:
1. Better relationships within the family.
2. The growth and development of individuals within the family.
3. Better relationships between the family and the community.
4. Improvement and extension of community services affecting the family.

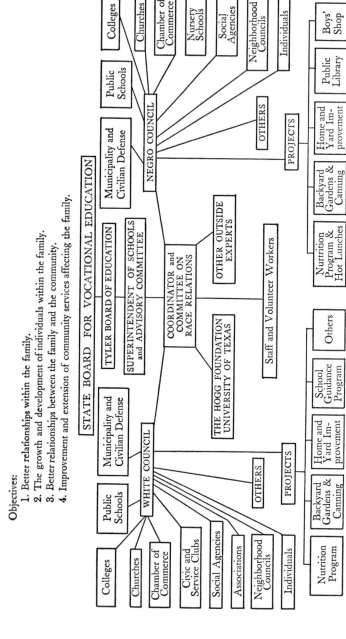

A CO-OPERATIVELY PLANNED PROGRAM FOR COMMUNITY WELL-BEING, TYLER, TEXAS

STATE BOARD FOR VOCATIONAL EDUCATION

TYLER BOARD OF EDUCATION

SUPERINTENDENT OF SCHOOLS and ADVISORY COMMITTEE

COORDINATOR and COMMITTEE ON RACE RELATIONS

THE HOGG FOUNDATION UNIVERSITY OF TEXAS

OTHER OUTSIDE EXPERTS

Staff and Volunteer Workers

WHITE COUNCIL
Colleges
Churches
Chamber of Commerce
Civic and Service Clubs
Social Agencies
Associations
Neighborhood Councils
Individuals
Public Schools
Municipality and Civilian Defense
OTHERS
PROJECTS
Nutrition Program
Backyard Gardens & Canning
Home and Yard Improvement
School Guidance Program
Others

NEGRO COUNCIL
Municipality and Civilian Defense
Public Schools
Colleges
Churches
Chamber of Commerce
Nursery Schools
Social Agencies
Neighborhood Councils
Individuals
OTHERS
PROJECTS
Nutrition Program & Hot Lunches
Backyard Gardens & Canning
Home and Yard Improvement
Public Library
Boys' Shop

From Lillian Peek, "Team Work on the Home Front: The Story of a Program of Education in Which the Entire Community Works Together to Provide for the Health and Well-Being of All" (Austin, Texas, The Hogg Foundation, University of Texas, 1943), p. 36. A printed pamphlet Good discussion of place of co-ordinator. List of achievements.

trates how one community organized for the improvement of community life.

The chart on organismic supervision on page 14 visualizes the wide variety of impacts of educational, social, and governmental agencies on the individual learner, and a possible plan for integrating their influences in a constructive way through the establishment of a community council on education consisting of representatives of all major agencies. The primary concern of this council should be the improvement of all aspects of community life that affect the growth and development of all members of the community.

Co-ordinating councils have not in all cases functioned effectively and in some cases have been discontinued. As a result of twelve years of contact with the movement in cities in Michigan, McClusky [43] listed the following conditions which appear to favor the successful operation of community councils:

1. The community council needs *clear-cut goals* which are understood by council members and the organizations they represent. Overemphasis on machinery of organization (constitution and by-laws) and neglect of objectives is usually the first and often final step toward the suspension of council programs.

2. A council thrives on a *broad and inclusive membership base.* Young people, both sides of the tracks, farmers, townspeople, over-all workers, white collar workers, etc., should be represented.

3. Special measures should be taken to assure *continuity of leadership.* The method of alternate or deputy leaders has been successfully used by many councils to prepare persons to take over important tasks when the original leaders have given up their responsibilities.

4. The *quality of leadership* is a crucial factor in council success. The leader who works well with others appears to be more effective than one who dominates his colleagues. This is especially true of councils with wide differences in membership.

5. The *communication of information to council members* and the organizations they represent is an important feature of successful operation. The most effective method of communication appears to be a face-to-face exchange of ideas by the persons directly involved.

6. Successful councils have made excellent use of *working sub-committees* to secure facts, diagnose community needs, and formulate plans, as well as to operate projects. These small committees may call on the services of anyone in the community, regardless of membership on the council. These committees are often the proving ground for new leaders.

7. Councils are sustained by *evidence of achievement.* Interest appears to grow when the program of the council occasionally leads to some tangible outcome which the community can see.

8. Successful councils are aware of and make *use of the resources* in and outside their communities in planning programs, in training leaders and in solving problems requiring technical and specialized knowledge.

CHAPTER SUPPLEMENT

DISCUSSION QUESTIONS FOR GENERAL INTRODUCTION

1. What bearing upon selection of materials of instruction has the current stress being placed on the fact that we are living in changing, emerging, democratic society had?

2. Make a brief illustrative list of instructional aids and materials found in modern schools and which were not used in schools fifty years ago, twenty-five years ago.

3. What differences are there in the kinds of materials that should be available for pupils on various levels of ability?

4. What are some forward-looking trends in school buildings, and their construction; and their relation to modern curriculum and methods of instruction?

ORAL REPORTS FOR INDIVIDUALS OR SMALL GROUPS

1. Examine two textbooks in some curriculum area published thirty years apart (longer interval if desired) and summarize the differences and improvements.

[43] Howard Y. McClusky, "Twelve Years of Community Councils in Michigan," *School of Education Bulletin*, Ann Arbor, Mich., Univ. of Michigan, Vol. 20 (May, 1949), pp. 113-115.

2. Describe and critically evaluate the procedures used in some school system for selecting and improving the instructional materials available. Do the same for accessibility of materials. How can this be improved?

3. Describe in some detail for the benefit of the class any experience you had in participating in teacher or community workshops, in organizing, and operating a workshop. Evaluate the activities and suggest further developments.

4. Make a detailed report of the literature on community workshops. (This could be a written report if class interest is indicated.)

5. Describe and critically evaluate the type of excursions made by classes in some school system. Note particularly preparation necessary, dangers, and so forth. Note differences in purpose and nature between growth levels.

6. Describe and critically evaluate the uses made by the community of the school plant. Summarize any literature on recent developments.

7. How can teachers be aided to provide more effectively for the comfort of the children?

8. What facilities are needed by the Community School?

9. What have community councils done to improve living conditions in various communities?

10. Discuss evidences of community interest in improving aspects of community life.

WRITTEN REPORTS FOR INDIVIDUALS AND SMALL GROUPS

1. Summarize for the class or for your school system the recent developments in classroom construction necessitated by the changing educational program.

2. Develop a plan whereby teachers can assist in developing ways of making more effective use of instructional materials and community resources.

3. Develop a plan whereby you would cooperatively set up a workshop in your system to study instructional materials (either a summer workshop, or the use of local workshop as needed during the regular year).

4. Experienced teachers may report upon any program of observational and participatory experiences carried on in their systems. Isolated excursions or random projects need not be reported. (This report could be given orally if class interest is indicated.)

5. Describe and critically evaluate contributory learning experiences in your schools. (If no plan exists in your system indicate some of the opportunities which might be used.)

6. Experienced teachers in committee may prepare a list of field trips for teachers based on their own community. (This exercise cannot be completed successfully on the basis of memory or "general knowledge." The committee will need to visit, to consult local authorities, use guidebooks and available historical references.)

7. Teachers in committee may prepare a list of places of interest and value in their own communities which might be used for pupil excursions. State whether the specific excursions are to be used within the generalized core curriculum or within a special subject on the elementary or secondary level, within the unified elementary program.

8. Select a deficiency in some specific aspect or element related to the topic of this chapter and outline in some detail the steps that might be taken to bring about an improvement.

9. Prepare a list of sources of free and inexpensive materials. Indicate what is available.

10. Outline a plan based on your community which might bring about the establishment locally of a community council to study local conditions with a view to improving them.

SUGGESTED READINGS

American School Buildings, Twenty-seventh Yearbook, American Association of School Administrators (Washington, NEA, 1949).

ATEYO, H. C., *The Excursion as a Teaching Technique,* Contributions to Education No. 761 (New York, Teachers College, Bureau of Publications, Columbia Univ., 1939).

Audio-Visual Materials and Methods in the Social Studies, Eighteenth Yearbook, National Council on the Social Studies (Washington, the Council, 1947), Chapter 10—illustrations.

Better Learning through Current Materials, edited by Lucien Kinney and Katharine Dresden (Stanford University, Calif., Stanford Univ. Press, 1952).

BLACKWELL, G. W., *Toward Community Understanding* (Washington, American Council on Education, 1943).

BUTSCH, R. L. C., "A Comparative Study of the Effects of Different Kinds of School-Building Ventilation on the Health of Pupils," *Elementary School Journal,* Vol. 30 (September, 1929), pp. 16-26; (October, 1929), pp. 123-131; (November, 1929), pp. 208-217.

CLAPP, Elsie R., *The Use of Resources in Education* (New York, Harper, 1952).

Creating a Good Environment for Learning, Association for Supervision and Curriculum Development (Washington, NEA, 1954).

GLUECK, Sheldon, and GLUECK, Eleanor, *Unraveling Juvenile Delinquency* (New York, 1951).

HANNA, P. R., and others, *Youth Serves the Community* (New York, Appleton-Century-Crofts, 1937).

Juvenile Delinquency and the Schools, Forty-seventh Yearbook, Part I, National Society for the Study of Education (Chicago, Univ. of Chicago Press, 1948).

KOOPMAN, Margaret O., *Utilizing the Local Environment* (New York, Hinds, 1946).

LONG, Frank M., *Desirable Physical Facilities for an Activity Program,* Contributions to Education No. 593 (New York, Teachers College, Bureau of Publications, Columbia Univ., 1933).

MCCHAREN, W. K., *Improving the Quality of Living: A Study of Community Schools in the South* (Nashville, Tenn., George Peabody College for Teachers, 1947).

NORTON, T. L., *Education for Work* (New York, McGraw, 1938).

OLSEN, E. G., ed., *The Modern Community School* (New York, Appleton-Century-Crofts, 1953).

OLSEN, E. G., *The School and the Community* (New York, Prentice-Hall, 1945).

Organizing a Community Council, Michigan Council on Adult Education (Lansing, Mich., State Department of Public Instruction, 1944).

PANUSHKA, Warren, *This Is Your Town, A Field Trip Handbook,* Curriculum Bulletin No. 43 (St. Paul, Minn., Board of Education, 1951).

The Community Is Your Classroom (Lansing, Mich., State Department of Education, 1951).

The Planning and Construction of School Buildings, Thirty-third Yearbook, Part I, National Society for the Study of Education (Bloomington, Ill., Public School Publishing Co., 1934).

The Teaching of Contemporary Affairs, Twenty-first Yearbook, National Council for the Social Studies (Washington, The Council, 1951).

WHITEHEAD, W. A., and others, *A Guide for Planning Elementary School Buildings* (Columbus, Bureau of Educational Research, Ohio State University, 1947).

WINSLOW, C. E. A., *The School Health Program* (New York, McGraw, 1938).

WITTICH, W. A., and SCHULLER, C. F., *Audio-Visual Materials: Their Nature and Use* (New York, Harper, 1953).

Part IV

♦··♦··♦··♦··♦··♦·

THE EVALUATION OF PROGRAMS OF SUPERVISION

Chapter 18

◆·◆·◆·◆·◆·◆·◆·◆

The Appraisal and Improvement of Supervisory Personnel and Programs

The desirability of appraising supervision. Just as teachers and pupils have profited both directly and indirectly from the introduction of more accurate methods of measurement into the realm of teacher and pupil growth, there is every reason to believe that supervisors and administrators too would profit by the introduction of similar means of evaluation into their own work as school leaders. Every person with leadership responsibility should be expected to furnish tangible evidence of the effectiveness of the improvement programs that he proposes and puts into operation. Desirable as having this information is, few administrative officials today have much notion, aside from general impression, of the effectiveness of the leadership which they provide. They sometimes create a considerable amount of commotion, as a bad boy might who pitches brickbats over a wall into a group of people whom he cannot see; but just how valuable this commotion is, is yet to be determined, especially in particular cases of so-called leadership. Of course, such officials do have a general impression of the effectiveness of their work; but this evidence, as we all know, is frequently very unreliable. The problem is to make these ordinary evaluations more valid, reliable, and objective.

It has been repeatedly pointed out in this volume and elsewhere that only by knowing as accurately as possible the results of instruction can the processes of education be improved. The same situation pertains to improvement programs. There are many different ways of improving pupil growth. Teachers, supervisors, and administrative officials will naturally all want to use the most effective means, methods, and materials that they can command. To improve their selection of improvement programs, they must have some mode of evaluating the results of these programs. The point has been repeatedly made in this volume of the fact that the ultimate measure of the effectiveness of any means, method, or device will be found in whether it effectively promotes teacher and pupil growth. And so it is with methods of leadership.

Supervisors and administrative officials seem, in general, to have been more interested in the development of programs of activities than in their evaluation. As a consequence, we find ourselves in the position of having reported in the literature of education many kinds of improvement programs and activities recommended by various members of the school personnel, on the basis of their own personal experience, but without scientific validation. It is true that from general observation it would seem that many of these programs are effective; but a closer study of them may show, as it has in other fields, that in fact they are often not particularly effective. Unfortunately, such activities set other activities in motion, which in turn inspire still others, and so on; until not only are isolated instances of ineffectiveness allowed to creep into the means and methods of leadership, but also whole systems of doing things that could not be tolerated under more careful evaluation. Educational leadership today is decidedly hampered in many respects by traditional practices that would undoubtedly be eliminated with the introduction of more effective means and methods of evaluation. If the methods of educational leadership are to be constantly improved, steps must be taken to develop more accurate instruments for the continuous evaluation of their effectiveness.

The necessity for developing methods of evaluating leadership through supervision grows out of such problems as:

1. The need for justifying the establishment and maintenance of various services having supervisory functions.

2. The need for evaluating the services rendered by members of the supervisory staff.

3. Planning for the continued improvement of supervisory personnel, procedures, and services.

4. The recruitment, training, and selection of principals and supervisors which cannot proceed effectively unless the desirable qualities, skills, and abilities such individuals should possess are determined and can be evaluated.

The basis of evaluation. The effectiveness of supervision may be evaluated by measuring or describing in specific terms the changes and improvements that take place over a period of time in the total educational program, or in any phase or element of it, as an apparent result of the leadership provided by those who are responsible for the improvement of learning and instruction. The areas in which these changes can be identified are the same as those that must be considered in evaluation of the effectiveness of the total educational program, namely, (1) growth and development of the learner toward accepted educational goals and objectives, (2) improvement of the curriculum, (3) improvement of instructional practices as well as in general teacher personal development, (4) improvement in the quality and use of

instructional materials and aids to learning, and (5) improvements in school-community relations.

The effectiveness of supervision may be determined either through the application of criteria designed to judge the value of the activities performed by supervisors, or through the measurement of the immediate and more remote outcomes of the supervisory program. The effectiveness of both teachers and supervisors can also be indirectly estimated through the measurement of qualities commonly associated with success in teaching or supervision: intelligence, social judgment, health, knowledge of subject taught, skill in expression, and the like, and changes in these. Measurement thus gives one information about the status of some constituent of something under consideration; evaluation carries the process at least one step further and involves the comparison of the status of the object and its constituents with some expected value, outcome, or standard. Much valuable information can be had about the quality of the educational leadership in any given areas of responsibility by examining the character of the program of activities provided by it. To appraise the educational program, it is necessary to secure judgments and opinions about it. These opinions may be based upon reports secured from the personnel and other interested individuals through interviews, inventories, and questionnaires; they may be based upon observations of the program in action, as for example, in the observation of community forums, educational workshops, and faculty meetings; or upon a study of documentary evidences of one sort or another, such as those found in the records, the learning aids supplied pupils, or printed courses of study; or upon estimates, guesses, and general impressions; or upon the systematic application of criteria designed for this purpose. We are here interested in the more systematic attempts at evaluating the educational program.

As has been indicated, the effectiveness of supervision cannot be satisfactorily judged by the existing status of conditions in any of these areas at any given time unless comparisons with conditions at some preceding or subsequent time are possible. It is obvious that the effectiveness of the activities of a supervisory staff, or of any supervisor or consultant can best be determined by an evaluation of available evidence as to the fruits of their endeavors as measured by changes that take place in any of the above five areas in which they have been actively at work. The supervisor faces the problem of gathering valid and reliable evidence by which he will be able to evaluate his effectiveness. Supervisory programs should be planned with this problem in mind. Just as we determine the effectiveness of the educational program or of a given teacher by appraising the characteristics and behavior of the product, so we should evaluate the effectiveness of the supervisory program by measuring its outcomes in some way.

Difficulty of evaluating specific supervisory practices. The usefulness of any particular supervisory practice or procedure can be measured in a similar way, although its actual value is difficult to determine since the complex situation in which it is embedded contains many associated factors whose effects are difficult to control or to measure. Initially, the approach to the evaluation of specific practices may often have to be the case method, in which the effects of a specific procedure in a single clearly defined situation can be studied and evaluated. Data for a number of cases accumulated in this way can lead to the formulation of generalizations about the practice that may be applied in working with others. In general, it is probably true that the choice of supervisory procedure will depend on the purpose of the supervisor, needs and nature of the person or persons involved, and the conditions under which

any action to improve the situation will have to take place.

An important point to bear in mind is that the evaluation must be made in the light of the basic philosophy underlying it, and the skill with which those who supervise carry on their duties. The approach may range from autocratic to democratic; skill may range from a low level to a high level. These concepts are clearly indicated by the chart showing four levels of supervision, given on pages 86-87. Later in this chapter we shall return to this matter.

Methods of evaluating supervision and educational leadership. Since 1920 there has been considerable research on the value of supervision. In most cases, the earlier investigations dealt with an appraisal of the results of the activities of an individual supervisor as measured by the growth made by pupils in specific knowledge and information as measured by tests. In more recent years, the tendency has been to evaluate supervision as a function operative in comprehensive improvement programs dealing with all aspects of the educational situation, including the learner, curriculum, instruction, and school-community relations. In the following pages we shall review some of the more significant research dealing with the evaluation of supervision and suggest additional approaches to the problem of evaluation under the following headings:

METHODS OF EVALUATING EDUCATIONAL LEADERSHIP

1. Statistical data showing changes in pupil progress.
2. Measures of changes in pupil mastery of what is learned.
3. Determining changes in factors conditioning pupil growth and achievement.
   a. Curriculum.
   b. Instruction and teaching efficiency.
   c. Changes in materials of instruction.
   d. Socio-physical environment, including school-community relations.
4. Appraisal and improvement of supervisory personnel.

PERCENTAGE OF PUPILS OVER AGE*

Grade	1921	1950	Change
1	9.1	1.9	− 7.2
2	18.1	3.6	−14.5
3	28.0	3.9	−24.1
4	34.8	6.6	−28.2
5	43.5	6.3	−37.2
6	46.2	7.7	−38.5
7	54.0	9.1	−44.9
8	40.2	14.4	−25.8
9	35.7	11.2	−24.5
10	33.6	9.1	−24.5
11	52.4	8.7	−43.7
12	60.9	7.3	−53.6
Total	34.9	7.4	−27.5

* Adapted from data in Austin School Survey, Part II—The Instructional Program, by Bureau of Field Studies and Surveys, College of Education, Univ. of Minnesota, 1952.

Section 1

STATISTICAL DATA ABOUT PUPIL PROGRESS AND ELIMINATION

Studies of pupil progress. In almost all school surveys of the early part of the present century, it was customary to present age-grade tables showing the rates of progress of the children through the schools and also tables showing the rates of promotion at various grade levels. A comparison of data about retardation for a given school system for two different years separated by a fairly long interval of time, such as is shown in the table above, affords a measure of important changes in educational practices to which leadership undoubtedly has made vital contributions. It is, of course, assumed that normal progress of pupils is a desirable policy for a school system to adopt.

The table shows that in 1921, 34.9 per cent of all pupils in grades 1 to 12 of the schools of Austin, Minnesota, were over age, whereas in 1950 only 7.4 per cent were over age, a reduction of 27.5 per cent. In 1950 only 52 pupils or 1 per cent of the total school population of 4298 were more than one year over age. In 1921 only 51.2 per cent of the Austin pupils made normal progress, whereas in 1950 the corresponding

figure was 86.2 per cent. Since retardation is due to nonpromotion, the above data reveal a marked change in the policy of requiring pupils to repeat the work of a grade in the direction of a policy of continuous regular progress.

Similar data can readily be secured for any community. New York reported recently that overageness in elementary schools had been reduced from 26.3 per cent in 1925 to 4.4 per cent in 1950, and nonpromotion from 9 per cent to 0.8 per cent. Changes of this kind entail modifications of the organization of classes, teaching procedures, instructional materials, and curriculum policies, all of which can be evaluated by criteria discussed in preceding chapters. Supervisory programs in these cases had to be adjusted to the modern policy of regular school progress.

Studies of the holding power of the school. A valuable measure of the effectiveness of educational leadership is the increase in the holding power of the schools over a period of years. A marked increase in the holding power of secondary schools has recently been revealed by several important investigations. However, the rate of elimination varies considerably from school to school, indicating the desirability of a careful study of the problem, a task that presents a real challenge to educational leadership. Where an improvement in holding power can be shown over a period of years, it is possible to make a judgment as to the effectiveness of the leadership provided in adjusting the educational program to the needs and abilities of youth.

The method of conducting a study of holding power is given in the Illinois bulletin on that subject by Harold Hand, and referred to in Chapter 12.

Section 2

MEASURES OF CHANGES IN PUPIL MASTERY OF WHAT IS LEARNED

During the years 1920-1935, a considerable number of studies were made to demonstrate the value of supervision by measuring by standard tests the changes in pupil mastery of what was learned in supervised and unsupervised classes over a period of time, usually about a year. A considerable group of these studies is reviewed in the Eighth Yearbook of the Department of Superintendence, *The Superintendent Surveys Supervision*. The outcomes appraised were largely limited to the types of knowledges, skills, and abilities in the "three R's" that were most readily measured by the available standard tests. The less tangible outcomes, such as interests, appreciations, study skills, personality traits, and social behavior were not evaluated in these studies. The reader should consult the yearbook for details as to the supervisory procedures that were used. There is little evidence of the use of co-operative methods in these supervisory programs such as are stressed in modern literature on supervision. The skill with which supervisors conducted their activities cannot reliably be inferred from the descriptions of the various programs, although the wide variations in growth of learners suggests that there were large differences in the effectiveness of the supervision.

In the yearbook [1] the results of these researches were summarized as follows:

The studies of growth in pupil achievement that are reported show uniformly that the growth is greater in supervised schools than in unsupervised schools. In each case, supervision is defined as personal supervision carried on by an expert. It is assumed in all cases that the supervisor carried on his work with an adequate degree of skill. The limitations of tests as means of measuring the outcomes of instruction should be considered in interpreting and evaluating these studies.

In the Austin survey [2] referred to above, there is more recent interesting information about differences in pupil intelligence level and performances on the same standard tests of reading and spelling that were administered in two schools of Austin in 1921 and 1950. Cook summarized the results as follows:

The median IQ of pupils in grades 3-6 in the Lincoln and Shaw schools in 1921 was approximately 94; in 1951 it is approximately 110, a difference of 16 IQ points. This difference is due largely to the fact that 46 per cent of the pupils in these schools were retarded in 1921, and only 6 per cent were retarded in 1951. The results of hoarding slow learning pupils in the elementary grades is clearly evident in these comparisons.

Pupils in grades 3-6 in the Lincoln and Shaw schools score from one-half to one full year higher in reading ability in 1951 than they did in 1921 on the *Haggerty Reading Examination*.

[1] *The Superintendent Surveys Supervision*, 8th Yearbook, Department of Superintendence (Washington, NEA, 1930), p. 139.

[2] *Austin School Survey, Part II—The Instructional Program*. Bureau of Field Studies and Surveys, College of Education, Univ. of Minnesota, 1952, p. 19.

The *Buckingham Extension of the Ayres Spelling Scale* shows the Austin schools to be below standard in spelling ability both in 1921 and 1951. In the Shaw school there is very little difference between the scores of 1921 and 1951. In the Lincoln school spelling ability is higher in 1951 than in 1921. In the seventh and eighth grades of Central school there has been deterioration in spelling ability since 1921. The validity of the norms on this spelling scale is questioned.

The difference between the results for reading and spelling indicate where the leadership has been effective and also that improvements in instruction appear to be necessary in certain areas.

In general, it may be said that marked growth in pupil performance results when attention of the staff is focused on some specific area of instruction but that there is little change in the level of learning in other fields. Special attention should be given to the evaluation of supervisory procedures by measuring the outcomes of co-operative improvement programs dealing with outcomes of a less tangible nature but possibly of greater importance, such as mental and emotional health, appreciations, attitudes, problem solving ability, social sensitivity, creativity, and ability of learners to participate effectively in co-operative democratic action. Evaluation procedures such as those described in Chapter 9 can be used for this purpose.

It should be clear that the supervisor is only one element in a complexity of factors that operate to produce a change. It is questionable whether it is possible to secure any kind of definite quantitative measure of the value of the contribution of the supervisor to the results of an improvement program. The fact that evidence can be produced that growth has or has not taken place will be one helpful index of the effectiveness of the leadership provided.

Conditions that limit the use and validity of statistical studies where controls are lacking. In general, statistical measures of the products of learning constitute fairly reliable

measures of the effectiveness of the educational leadership in particular school situations when the measurements are extended over a considerable period of time and when the factors conditioning the products measured are within the control of those to be evaluated. There are many factors to be considered if the evaluations are to be valid; some of these factors are resident in the teacher, some in the pupils, some in the curriculum, some in the materials of instruction, and some in the socio-physical conditions for learning. A detailed discussion of these has already been presented in earlier chapters of this volume. Looking over a list of these factors, one can readily see that the amount of control exercised by various school officials—principals, supervisors of special subjects, superintendents, and the like—varies from individual to individual, from position to position, and from one school system to another. The superintendent of schools possesses a larger amount of control over the factors conditioning the products of instruction than does the principal or the supervisor of special fields of learning, and consequently, statistical measurements of the products of learning constitute a better index of the effectiveness of the superintendent's supervision than they do of either principals or supervisors of special fields of learning. The superintendent of schools employs the teachers; establishes an organization; develops educational policies; constructs with appropriate assistance a curriculum; directs and supervises the instruction; provides textbooks, supplies, and equipment; and in a measure controls the physical environment. He thus possesses a large amount of control over the factors conditioning the products of learning, and because of this control, his effectiveness can be very rightly evaluated over a period of years through the use of well-chosen measures of the products of learning. To the degree that principals and supervisors of special subjects have less control over these factors, the measures of the products of learning are less valid indices of their effectiveness except, of course, as these factors may be controlled in controlled investigations.

Comparing pupil achievements in different fields of learning, schools, and school systems. In the absence of complete control over the factors conditioning pupil growth and achievement, it is sometimes possible, nevertheless, to secure some ideas of the effectiveness of one's work by comparing the achievement of the pupils of one's own field of learning, school, or school system with that of the pupils having similar advantages in other situations. In making such a comparison, it is recommended that data be collected relating to the factors conditioning the products of instruction as well as with respect to the products themselves, as follows: *the pupils:* their chronological age, mental capacity, maturity, age-grade progress, achievement, interest and effort, methods of study, and the like; *the teacher:* his age, training, experience, interest, effort, success as a teacher, and the like; *the curriculum and objectives:* the nature of the curriculum, its selection, gradation, and organization, the teacher's purpose, and the like; *the materials of instruction:* books, supplies, and equipment; *the socio-physical environment for learning:* the heating, lighting, ventilation, and freedom from disturbance. Though not without very definite limitations, objective data of this sort may, when the comparisons can be made between comparable groups, constitute a valuable indication of the effectiveness of particular supervisors and supervisory programs.

Charts showing pupil progress can be employed to indicate general instructional trends for those areas of learning, schools, or school systems for which such information is desired. The measures should be selected in such a manner as to make it possible to appraise not only the more formal aspects of learning but the less tangible products, such as changes in character, attitudes, ideals, and so on. In comparing the achievement of pupils from different areas of learning, schools, and school systems, the groups should be as nearly comparable as possible. There are many problems of a statistical character that those who attempt such studies will need to keep in mind in the treatment of test scores for this purpose. For a treatment of these more technical aspects, the reader is referred to any one of a large number of texts on the subject of statistics.[3]

Controlled studies of the general worth of supervision. Besides the uncontrolled studies of the efficiency of supervisors and supervision discussed in the preceding section, there are many controlled investigations of both the general worth of supervision and the effectiveness of particular supervisory programs reported in the literature of education. Many of the early studies in the field of supervision were of the general worth of special leadership of one sort or another.

One of the first studies of this sort to be conducted in this field was conducted by Courtis [4] and Barnes in the Detroit public schools. The purpose of this study was to compare the achievement of pupils in geography in supervised and unsupervised schools. The experiment was carefully controlled in its procedure, and the results were interpreted with due regard for contributing factors. On September 19, 1918, geography tests were given to approximately twenty-five thousand pupils in grades 4, 5, and 6 in the Detroit public schools. On the basis of these tests, the schools were divided into four equal groups: (I) an unsupervised group, (II) an inspected group, (III) a

[3] Henry E. Garrett, *Statistics in Psychology and Education,* 2nd ed. (New York, Longmans, 1941).

B. J. Underwood, C. P. Duncan, J. A. Taylor, and J. W. Cotton, *Elementary Statistics* (New York, Appleton-Century-Crofts, 1954).

J. E. Wert, C. O. Neidt, and J. S. Ahmann, *Statistical Methods in Educational and Psychological Research* (New York, Appleton-Century-Crofts, 1954).

[4] S. A. Courtis, "Measuring the Effects of Supervision in Geography," *School and Society* (July 19, 1919), pp. 61-70.

group supervised by schools, and (IV) a group supervised by classes. Schools in group I were not visited by the supervisors; schools in group II were visited, but on the old inspectional basis; for schools of group III, the supervisor received information of the general standing of the school and did his best to make both teacher and principal understand what was expected; in group IV, the supervisor used such detailed information as could be furnished by the Department of Research and centered his attention upon teachers whose classes were below the general level of attainment in geography. The work was continued for six weeks. The groups were then retested. The original scores were retabulated in order to maintain the original equality of the groups which had been distributed by changes in pupil population. Comparisons were then made, and various interpretations of the results presented. In comparing the relation of actual gain made by pupils to the possible gain, the author concludes that:[5]

In the unsupervised group, the teachers succeeded in making 49.5 per cent of the desired gain. Supervision by inspection raised the figure to 54 per cent, supervision by schools to 68 per cent, and by classes to 69.5 per cent. That is, visit of the supervisor under the conditions of Group IV resulted in an increase of achievement of 40 per cent.

Another comparison was made in terms of point scores:[6]

The children in the unsupervised group were able to locate correctly twenty-eight states on the map in the initial test and forty-three states in the final test, a gain of fifteen states in the median scores of the group.

In the group supervised by schools the gain was nineteen states. That is, as measured by the change in median scores of the group, adequate supervision increased the effects of teaching 30 per cent. In terms of the per cent the actual gain was of the desired gain, the results are Group I, 70 per cent, Group III, 83 per cent.

A further idea of the changes induced by supervision can be gained by inspecting the changes in distribution:[7]

In Group I the distributions for the initial and final tests overlap to the extent of 71 per cent. That is, in the final test the net result is that 29 per cent of the children have higher scores than they did in the beginning. For Group III the figures become 46 per cent. Put in different words, the statement would be, out of every hundred children in schools without supervision, twenty-nine were changed by the teaching. The effect of supervision was to raise this number to forty-six, a gain of seventeen children. Surely an agency which affects the work of teachers to such an extent, that without change in the teachers, the time, the equipment, or the size of the class, more than half again as many children are benefited by the teaching, is an important agency.

A study of the value of supervision in penmanship. An investigation in handwriting quite similar to the one in geography reported above was carried out by Miss Lena Shaw, supervisor of penmanship in the Detroit public schools. A total of 30,529 pupils was used, distributed through grades 3 to 8. A test was given at the beginning of the semester and the schools were divided into four equal groups, as in the geography study just reported. The same procedure was followed, one group being unvisited, the second inspected only, the third supervised by schools, and the fourth supervised by classes. The work was carried on for a whole semester. When the final test was given, the original scores were retabulated, and the conclusions were drawn, the supervised groups showed greater improvement than the unsupervised groups. The tables presenting the results by half grades are too long to reproduce here, but totals for the four groups appear in the table on page 663.

The conclusions drawn were: [8]

1. Supervision does pay since the schools which were not visited made only 30.1 per cent of possible gain, while Groups II, III, and IV made 36.2, 40.7, and 37.2 per cent respectively.

2. The best form of supervision is that in which the emphasis is placed where it is most needed.

[5] *Ibid.*, p. 68.
[6] *Ibid.*, p. 68.
[7] *Ibid.*, p. 69.
[8] Lena Shaw. Unpublished materials.

COMPARISON OF GROSS SCORES ON INITIAL AND FINAL
TESTS IN HANDWRITING OF FOUR GROUPS OF
PUPILS, ONE GROUP UNSUPERVISED AND
THREE GROUPS EACH SUPERVISED
DIFFERENTLY*

Gross Scores	Group I	Group II	Group III	Group IV
Retabulation	6,935	6,943	6,969	6,931
Final Score	8,460	8,778	9,020	8,819
Gain	1,525	1,835	2,051	1,888
Per cent of possible gain	30.1	36.2	40.7	37.2

* Lena Shaw, unpublished materials.

Though the second conclusion is not wholly justified by the evidence presented, both this study and the one preceding, seemed, however, to indicate that supervision was a worth-while activity from the point of view of the Detroit taxpayer.

A state program for the improvement of instruction in reading.[9] During the school year of 1935-1936, the regional supervisors of the State Department of Public Instruction of Iowa visited each school and made careful observations concerning the nature of the classroom instruction. As a result of these observations and of conferences, it was decided that a concentrated drive on the functional development of work-type reading skills with content subjects was needed. The program was carried on throughout the state, and consisted of (1) a county-wide meeting of teachers at which time the nature of the remedial program was carefully explained and the initial materials distributed; (2) a half-day demonstration in each school illustrating the use of the remedial materials; and (3) a follow-up questionnaire: one to the teacher and one to the county superintendent of schools. The schools in which the evaluation was carried out were located in three northwest and three northeast Iowa counties. The results of the testing program in three counties are given in the table on page 664.

The program was extended in 1937-1938. The testing program showed gains in this year varying from 157 per cent to 222 per cent of the normal gain. The author describes the by-products of this program as follows:

While the main objective of the work was to improve the teaching of reading in the schools, some other important developments also took place in connection with the in-service training of teachers. Changes were necessary in the organization in many schools in order that provision might be made for more supervised study. These changes resulted in decreasing the number of periods devoted to a given subject during the week, with a corresponding increase in the length of periods. Because of the longer periods, more time was used for directing study and less time was devoted to hearing lessons.

The emphasis on provision for individual differences resulted in efforts, in connection both with the academic and with the activities phase of the program, to incorporate materials that would take care of a wide variety of interests and abilities. In the academic work this object was accomplished by developing study exercises of varying degrees of difficulty and by providing supplementary reference materials representing wide ranges of reading ability and interests in the various content subjects. In the case of the latter the object was accomplished through the provision of activities of types that would appeal to many varied interests and abilities, some of which were intellectual, and some of which were more or less mechanical, in nature.

Forty-six superintendents, in a voluntary response to a questionnaire attached to the remedial circular, indicated that their teachers had

[9] H. K. Bennett, "A State Program for the Improvement of Instruction in Reading," *Elementary School Journal* (June, 1939), pp. 735-746.

RESULTS IN GRADES 4-8 ON COMPREHENSION TESTS (1-5)
OF IOWA SILENT READING TESTS GIVEN IN TOWN, CITY,
AND CONSOLIDATED SCHOOLS IN NINETEEN
IOWA COUNTIES IN 1937-38

	Grade IV 2489 pupils	Grade V 2865 pupils	Grade VI 2916 pupils	Grade VII 2751 pupils	Grade VIII 2575 pupils
Test norm:					
Pretest	34.0	57.0	78.0	102.0	124.0
Final test	48.0	69.0	93.0	115.0	136.0
Median score:					
Pretest	36.2	58.0	84.2	106.3	125.8
Final test	60.5	84.6	109.5	126.7	146.6
Gain	24.3	26.6	25.3	20.4	20.8
Percentage of normal gain	174	222	169	157	173
Percentage that final-test score is of test norm	126	123	118	110	108
Gains in reading age (in years and months) ..	1-5	1-3	1-3	0-11	1-0
Gain in reading grade ..	1.0	1.2	1.1	0.9	1.1

responded enthusiastically to the program, that the majority had succeeded in developing time schedules to provide for an increased amount of directed study, and that their teachers had succeeded in individualizing their instruction in the content subjects as a result of the program.

Moore's study of supervision in English.[10] A valuable study of the value of several specific supervisory procedures applied to the improvement of English was reported by Sister Mary Kathleen Moore. Moore's experimental evaluation of supervision dealt with the assumption that "with well-defined attainable goals as an integral part of supervision, there will be evidenced pupil growth." The 1328 pupils in thirty-eight classes in twelve elementary schools were divided into four equated groups: (*a*) one group, the control group, had no supervision, (*b*) a second group had a conference type of supervision, (*c*) a third group had a conference type of supervision with the addition of a set of goals being presented to the teachers without discussion, and (*d*) a fourth group, the chief experimental group,

received a goal-centered conference type of supervision. The effectiveness of the goal-centered conference supervisory technique was determined by the amount of pupil growth as measured by achievement tests. The "goal conference group" was the only one of the experimental groups whose pupils made significant gains over the control group. The experiment led to the conclusion that "supervision can be effective both in stimulating consciousness toward goals and in giving expert advice as to the decreasing of liabilities and increasing of assets in future performance."

Evaluation of the Georgia Program for Training Supervisors. Between 1947 and 1949, an effort was made to evaluate the Georgia program[11] for training supervisors. The effectiveness of the program was meas-

[10] Sister Mary Kathleen Moore, *An Experimental Study in Supervision* (Baltimore, Johns Hopkins University, 1948). Doctor's thesis.
[11] Jane Franseth, *Learning to Supervise Schools: An Appraisal of the Georgia Program,* Office of Education Circular No. 289 (Washington, Government Printing Office, 1952).

ured in the usual way by comparing some of the achievements of children in grades 5, 6, and 7 in supervised schools and in unsupervised schools. Growth in democratic citizenship was measured by the School Practices Questionnaire, preferred by McCall, Herring and Loftus; growth in development of reading comprehension, constructive study skills, language, and arithmetic was measured by the Iowa Every Pupil Tests of Basic Skills.

In the final report, a comparison was made between results for classes supervised by persons with and without internship experience and unsupervised classes. In general, the results in growth in democratic citizenship and in the various learning areas listed above were superior for the supervised classes. It was also shown that the results were higher for classes supervised by persons with internship experience, than by persons without this training.

Section 3

DETERMINING CHANGES IN FACTORS AFFECTING LEARNING

Supervision affects factors conditioning learning. Throughout this volume it has been maintained that there are many factors that affect the level and quality of educational outcomes, including the curriculum, instruction, and the socio-physical environment both in and out of school, as well as factors inherent in the learner himself. In the chapters that deal with these topics, many methods of evaluating the existing status of these factors have been presented. It was pointed out that under the leadership of the supervisory staff a co-operative study should be made to determine the factors that most probably are contributing to any unfavorable growth and development of the learner. It was indicated that a plan should then be developed co-operatively for improving conditions with respect to the factors judged to be interfering with optimum growth and development of the learners. It was shown that subsequently the outcomes should be reappraised in terms of pupil growth to measure the effectiveness of the total improvement program.

The quality of educational leadership will be revealed not only by the evidence as to the growth of the learners toward desirable goals but also by evidence of forward-looking changes that have taken place in the factors dealt with in the improvement program, such as changes in the curriculum and course of study, improvement in instruc-

tional procedures, more effective use of instructional materials and equipment, and better school and community relations. Of primary importance is the evidence of growth of all aspects of the personalities involved in the program and the maintenance of morale and good relationships among the members of the staff.

By applying selected evaluative procedures to curriculum, instruction, and the socio-physical aspects of the teaching learning situation prior to the improvement program, it is possible to make fairly dependable judgments as to their strengths and limitations. Later on, subsequent to the improvement program, it should be equally possible to analyze data gathered in the course of the program and subsequently in order to arrive at judgments as to the effectiveness of the procedures used and to evaluate the changes that have taken place in the factors dealt with.

At present there are no known procedures for measuring the actual improvement of the curriculum, although it is entirely possible to list the changes made and to evaluate them in terms of accepted criteria, such as those discussed in Chapters 12 and 16. Similarly it should be possible to describe, analyze, and then evaluate changes in the activities and personality traits of the teacher which appear as a result of the improvement program.

Objectives in Work Reading	Number of Lessons Reported		Per Cent of Lessons Reported	
	First survey	Second survey	First survey	Second survey
1	2	3	4	5
I. In which silent reading predominates:				
A. Ability to locate material quickly requires:				
1. Knowledge of and ability to use an index	30	54	4.84	8.64
2. Ability to use a table of contents	11	27	1.77	4.32
3. Ability to use the dictionary	20	11	3.23	1.76
4. Ability to use a library file	1	2	.16	.32
5. Ability to use reference material	10	24	1.61	3.84
6. Ability to use maps, tables, graphs	4	17	.65	2.72
7. Ability to skim	102	67	16.45	10.72
Total	178	202	28.71	32.32
B. Ability to comprehend quickly what is read requires:				
8. The establishment of rhythmic and rapid eye-movement	22	2	3.55	.32
9. The elimination of lip reading and vocalization	17	3	2.74	.48
10. Acquiring a vocabulary of accurate meanings..	122	48	19.68	7.68
11. The habit of vigorous reading	40	2	6.45	.32
Total	201	55	32.42	8.80
C. Ability to select and evaluate material needed:				
12. Judging the validity of information	2	6	.32	.96
13. Choosing ideas from different sources which explain or supplement one another	2	9	.32	....
14. Discovering different ideas in different sources	....	....	....	1.44
15. Deciding whether a given question is answered	9	37	1.45	5.92
16. Ability to sort essential and non-essential statements	4	11	.65	1.76
17. Telling what questions are answered by material	14	22	2.26	3.52
18. Finding the solution of a problem	21	44	3.39	7.04
Total	52	129	8.39	20.64
D. Ability to organize what is read:				
19. Practice in picking out central ideas	31	26	5.00	4.16
20. Practice in selecting main topics	54	69	8.71	11.04
21. Practice in outlining	48	99	7.74	15.84
22. Practice in summarizing	11	12	1.78	1.92
Total	144	206	23.23	32.96
E. Ability to remember what is read:				
23. Practice in selecting things to remember (see ability to organize)	10	11	1.61	1.76
24. An understanding of the best way to memorize	....	....	....	....
25. An understanding of the necessity for over-learning	....	....	....	....
26. Practice in remembering ...,..............	6	4	.97	.64
Total	16	15	2.58	2.40
F. A knowledge of the best sources of materials:				
27. Practice in selecting the proper reference books to gain an answer	1	2	.16	.32
Total	1	2	.16	.32

* L. J. Brueckner and Prudence Cutright, "A Technique for Measuring the Efficiency of Supervision," *Journal of Educational Research* (December, 1927), pp. 323-331.

Objectives in Work Reading	Number of Lessons Reported		Per Cent of Lessons Reported	
	First survey	Second survey	First survey	Second survey
1	2	3	4	5
II. Oral reading:				
A. *A knowledge of what makes oral reading effective:*				
28. Pupils formulate a statement of the things which make oral reading effective	2	3	.32	.48
29. Pupils discuss why the oral reading of certain directions or announcements was not effective.	1	....	.16	....
30. Pupils practice to make their oral reading more effective	8	4	1.29	.64
Total	11	7	1.77	1.12
B. *Ability to select material which is pertinent to a given oral reading situation:*				
31. Selecting and reading to the group material to prove a point under discussion	2	1	.32	.16
Total	2	1	.32	.16
C. *Skimming in preparation for oral reading:*				
32. Children discuss and illustrate the difference between reading unfamiliar and familiar material	1	....	.16	....
Total	1	....	.16	....
D. *An understanding of the purpose to be served by the reading:*				
33. Practice in reading material to serve different purposes	....	2	....	.32
Total	....	2	....	.32
E. *Ability to recognize and pronounce all the words in a selection:*				
34. Phonics	1	2	.16	.32
35. Word analysis	1	....	.16	....
36. Drill on list of words commonly mispronounced	3	1	.49	.16
37. Using the dictionary to secure the correct pronunciation of a word	2	....	.32	....
Total	7	3	1.13	.48
F. *Ability to use the voice in a pleasing, effective way:*				
38. The habit of noting the effect of a pleasing voice upon an audience	....	1	....	.16
Total	....	1	....	.16
G. *Ability to interpret the thought of a selection accurately:*				
39. Practice in reading selections to give different interpretations	2	....	.32	....
Total	2	....	.32	....
H. *Proper attitude toward an audience:*				
40. Practice in reading announcements	2	....	.32	....
41. Practice in reading directions for making things	....	....	....	....
42. Practice in reading informational material which the rest of the group wants to know ...	3	2	.49	.32
Total	5	2	.81	.32
Grand Total	620	625	100.0	100.0

Methods involving the study of changes in teaching procedures. A means by which the effectiveness of supervision may be evaluated is through the measurement of the changes brought about in the teaching. The improvement program functions eventually through the instrumentality of the teacher. Strange as it may seem, there are available in the literature of education few studies in which the activities of teachers are recorded before and after supervision. One of the best illustrations of this type of appraisal is a study carried on by Brueckner and Cutright [12] in the Minneapolis public schools to ascertain the changes in the techniques of teaching of reading brought about as a result of a supervisory program in reading. After certain preliminary steps, each teacher was asked to prepare lessons which he thought demonstrated his most effective types of work reading. A careful record was made of the materials and types of activities carried on in these lessons through the use of blanks especially prepared for this purpose. Thus a record was obtained of the actual practices of each teacher prior to the supervisory program.

The first survey was followed by a series of special bulletins on different phases of the teaching of reading on which the teachers wished help. A series of demonstration lessons for each grade was given on the types of reading not stressed according to the results of the first survey. The city was divided into districts, and all teachers were expected to attend these meetings. There were model lessons in training pupils to select and evaluate what they read and to organize what had been read. These lessons were taught by teachers who volunteered their services. Many local meetings were held by principals. A number of reading specialists, such as Anderson and Buswell, were brought to the city by the teachers' organizations to discuss different aspects of the problem, and the schools supplied themselves with the best available literature on the subject. There were numerous special demonstration lessons by teachers in individual buildings. Special talks were given by members of the research department, and the attention of all the teachers within the system was focused on this problem during the period of special study.

After this period of training, a resurvey was made in which the scheme was repeated. Teachers again taught lessons which they thought illustrated their most effective types of work reading on which the principals, in turn, made their reports. The results of this investigation are shown in the table on pages 666-667. On the first survey, 620 lessons were reported, and on the second survey, 625. The table contains a distribution of the lessons with each of the reading objectives reported on both surveys. The second column gives the number of lessons with specific objectives reported on the first survey; the third column contains the same data for the resurvey; and the last two columns show the percentages of the total number of lessons in each survey. The totals and percentages are also given for each major ability.

Analysis of the table on pages 666-667 shows that there were some interesting shifts in the teaching of reading in the interim between the surveys. For example, in the first survey there were 178 lessons whose objective was one of those listed under the heading, the "ability to locate material quickly (IA)." In the resurvey there were 202 lessons which had one of these objectives. These totals were respectively 28.71 and 32.32 per cent of the lessons reported. Though the total number of lessons with this objective remained almost the same, an analysis of the distributions for the specific abilities listed under this heading showed a considerable shift. For example, the percentage of lessons on the "ability to skim" decreased from 16.45 to 10.72; lessons on

[12] L. J. Brueckner and Prudence Cutright, "A Technique for Measuring the Efficiency of Supervision," *Journal of Educational Research* (December, 1927), pp. 323-331.

the "ability to use an index" increased from 4.84 per cent to 8.64 per cent. Other variations also can be noted. There was a decrease in the number of lessons having as their objective the "ability to comprehend quickly what is read." On the first survey, 32.42 per cent of the lessons reported have this objective; on the resurvey, only 8.8 per cent. This shift can be explained by an analysis of the data for the next two headings. The number of lessons whose objectives were to develop the "ability to select and evaluate material" increased from 8.39 to 20.64 per cent; and the lessons to develop the "ability to organize what is read," from 23.23 to 32.96 per cent of the total. This shift shows clearly the effect of the special demonstration lessons which were given during the training period. Most of the lessons during the period of demonstration were illustrations of these special objectives, because of the relative small use of them reported in the first survey. This change in emphasis may be considered a direct measure of the effectiveness of the supervisory program.

The remainder of the table shows that there had been practically no other change. The distribution of lessons on the objectives of oral reading was about the same on both surveys. This also can be explained, for the demonstration lessons in the training period did not touch oral reading.

The information which was collected does not give any evaluation of the improvement in the techniques of teaching reading. It merely shows the changes in objectives for the lessons the teachers taught after a period of training.

This technique also does not evaluate the efficiency of the teaching itself. It merely gives a picture of what, in the judgment of the principal, were the major objectives of the lessons observed. It does not show, for example, whether the teaching was skilfully done, whether the material that was used to achieve the objective was well selected, or whether the pupils increased in ability under the training given. Means can be developed which will make this information available, but it cannot be secured with the technique here employed.

The survey did not measure other desirable outcomes adequately. For instance, no measurement was given of the increased knowledge which the teachers had acquired of available reading materials. The reports showed that principals were almost unanimously of the opinion that the teaching of reading had greatly improved during the period of special study.

Surveys such as this can be devised for almost any subject and aspect of teaching. It is one of the evidences that the superior may offer as to his effectiveness as a supervisor.

Other possible methods of measuring or describing changes in instructional procedures as a basis of evaluating a supervisory program are the following:

1. Improvement of teaching as measured by ordinary rating scales of established validity.

2. Measuring the growth in the level of instruction by scales similar to those included in the Texas Program, including self-rating.

3. Improvement as measured by principles applied to teaching, such as Mursell's.

4. Growth in the ability of the teacher to utilize certain instructional procedures which had previously caused difficulty.

5. Growth in the ability of the teacher to make effective use of certain instructional materials and equipment.

6. Measured changes in general teaching method and skill based on ratings by Brueckner Scales for Rating Teacher Method and Skill.

7. Changes in social and emotional adjustment of teachers as measured by standard procedures.

Observable changes in individual teachers. Evidence of desirable changes in practices, attitudes, beliefs, and points of view observed in day-to-day contacts with individual teachers, such as described in the following reports, are very satisfying to those who work closely with teachers, even though the changes cannot be objectively measured.

SHIFTING THE EMPHASIS FROM FORMAL GRAMMAR TO FUNCTIONAL LANGUAGE

When a teacher was distressed at the children's incorrect speech habits, the supervisor might have used her comments as an indictment of formal grammar and launched into a dissertation on its ineffectiveness. Instead, he suggested that common mistakes be listed and used as a basis for planning with the children. The teacher found that needs differed considerably from the formal organization in the grammar book. Under friendly guidance, there was improvement in pupil interest and language ability.

Eventually the teacher, who had considered formal grammar drill imperative, was convinced that her previous approach had serious limitations. Through her own experiences, she had seen the results of functional language teaching and was influenced to modify her former methods. It is interesting to note that this type of supervision enables the teacher to retain her security yet improve her methods in response to self-inspired needs and experiences.

TEACHERS ARE WON OVER BY ATTENTION TO THEIR INTERESTS

Knowing that one teacher was especially interested in her pupils' health, the supervisor planned to introduce modern teaching on that plane. The teacher herself prepared the way by explaining that the children were always tired and restless during the latter part of the day. Why, she wanted to know, were active, vigorous children invariably listless and tired every day?

The supervisor asked how many opportunities they had for informal activity, and found that recess periods provided the only chance for the children to jump and run. So he showed the teacher a block-type program, well balanced and allowing for marked changes in activities, and explained that authorities believe these changes make school work less fatiguing to a small child.

Since she sensed his interest and felt no criticism of her methods, the teacher gave the program her attention. Through the use of materials he suggested, including pictures, books, and radio plays, and aids received from the school nurse, this teacher was soon putting into use some of the best known functional methods of health education.[13]

Methods of evaluating specific supervisory procedures. The improvement of supervisory procedures can be brought about by evaluating experiences that teachers have had by means of questionnaires, check-lists, criteria, and similar means of securing their reactions and judgments. An illustration is the following device [14] for rating a workshop for teachers which yielded valuable information to the leaders concerning the evaluation of the workshop by the participants. Similar plans for evaluating teachers' meetings, demonstration lessons, committee work, lectures, and intervisitation can be devised.

Directions

Cross out the appropriate number following each question to indicate your attitude.

> 5—very well satisfied, or very much, or to a great extent.
> 4—well satisfied, or much, or to a considerable extent.
> 3—fairly well satisfied, or some, or to some extent.
> 2—somewhat dissatisfied, or little, or to a small extent.
> 1—frankly dissatisfied, or very little, or to a very small extent.

1. How well satisfied are you with the progress on your individual problem?
   1   2   3   4   5
   > I feel this way because:
   > [Space for remarks]
   > I have these suggestions:
   > [Space for remarks]

2. How well satisfied are you with the help you got from your adviser?

3. How well satisfied are you with the morning interest group of which you are a member?

4. How well satisfied are you with the afternoon interest group of which you are a member?

5. How well satisfied are you with your contacts with staff members besides your major adviser?

[13] *A Forward Step*, Curriculum Bulletin No. 7 (Augusta, Me., State Department of Education, 1948), pp. 20-21.

[14] Maurice Troyer and C. R. Pace, *Evaluation in Teacher Education* (Washington, American Council on Education, 1944), pp. 338-340.

6. To what extent have you become profitably acquainted with other work-shoppers?

7. How well satisfied are you with the amount and helpfulness of your readings?

8. Of how much value has your work in a committee been to you?

9. To what extent have the general meetings been helpful?

10. To what extent has the workshop contributed to your understanding of democratic procedures?

11. To what extent do you believe that workshop procedures have been democratic?

12. To what extent has the planned social activity of the workshop been satisfactory?

13. To what extent have the unplanned social activities of the workshop been satisfactory?

14. How well satisfied are you with the length of time allotted to the workshop?

15. How well satisfied are you with the fact that you came to this workshop rather than to some other type of summer school?

An evaluation of the workshop program [15] for in-service teacher education directed by the Ohio State Department of Education, 1944-1947, was reported by Henderson. Approximately 1600 teachers, 115 principals, and 26 county, village, and city superintendents of schools participated in the program. The school systems involved enrolled approximately 35,000 children. More than 186 different consultants served in the workshops.

The evaluation instruments used were: (*a*) criteria postulated as adequate for the evaluation of democratic in-service teacher education, (*b*) two equated forms of an instrument, referred to as an "Inventory of Attitudes Toward Teaching," devised to determine attitudes of teachers prior to and at the close of the workshop experience, (*c*) a questionnaire to principals, (*d*) a letter of inquiry to consultants, (*e*) a questionnaire sent to a sample of teachers who had participated, and (*f*) a letter of inquiry for the director of elementary education in each

state department of education to determine practices and needs in in-service education on a state level.

The evaluation led to the following significant conclusion:

The superintendent of schools in the school situations in which the workshops evaluated were held was the key figure in initiating them. It was concluded further, that in view of the fact that teachers shared little in the planning, execution, or evaluation of a project for their own improvement, a number of basic weaknesses were inherent in the workshop program.

Evidence was presented, it will be recalled, in Chapter 6 from O'Rourke's study. In this study there was shown to be more participation by the teachers in the workshop planning and development.

Determining changes in socio-physical aspects of learning situations. Various methods of appraising the quality, adequacy and use of instructional materials and of analyzing elements of the socio-physical environment at the start of a supervisory program were described in Chapter 13. The effectiveness of the improvement program can subsequently be determined by a re-examination of the quality, adequacy, and use of these materials and of aspects of the socio-physical environment. The greater the degree to which these items conform to accepted criteria and available standards, the more successful the improvement program will have been.

The success of a program to improve school-community relations can be measured by observed changes in the attitudes of the citizens of the community and the evidence of progress and changes in aspects of community life that condition the growth and development of all its members. The statement that follows reveals in an interesting direct way some of the kinds of changes that take place when school and community cooperate in planning and carrying out an

[15] "Organization, Administration, and Supervision of Education," *NEA Review of Educational Research* (October, 1949), p. 338.

improvement program. Other details are given in Chapter 17.

The outcomes and values of community school service programs were summarized recently [16] by fifty local leaders in Michigan as follows:

1. A community can and will help itself to improve its democratic way of life in all phases of development through proper motivation, leadership, and organization.

2. Communities possess natural leadership that ofttimes remains latent for want of opportunities for action. Only through organized effort will a community make the most of its leadership potentialities for its welfare.

3. The effectiveness of leaders can be greatly increased by training programs specifically designed for the purpose.

4. A voluntary co-operative organization of all the agencies in a community should serve as a co-ordinating and advisory council for action committees working in the various areas of community life.

5. The school should play a major role and should provide some of the resources for any program or plan for community development. The school and the community are inseparable factors in democratic planning and living. The school should be the common meeting ground for everyone regardless of age, social position, religion, or income.

6. The school curriculum should be reorganized to utilize all the community resources to the best advantage. It must meet the needs of all the pupils in preparing for citizenship and for making a living.

7. Problem-study committees, responsible to the co-ordinating council, serve to discover community needs and assist in supporting action programs.

8. Problem-study committee membership should range from ten to twenty-five to assure adequate representation of all interests.

9. Action committees appointed as subcommittees should have a maximum of five members to assure progress in community development.

10. Membership on the action or problem-study committees should be purely voluntary. Efforts should be made to educate the members of the community to the opportunities that are available for making it a better place to live in.

11. The school administrator in a community should become a professional community worker who can serve the school and co-operate with the community in solving its problems for better living. The school staff and student body should be cognizant of how they, too, can share in the efforts for community betterment.

12. Participation in community endeavors is affected by the boundary of the natural community and the neighborhoods. Neighborhoods in the outer area of a large community tend to display a twofold loyalty—to the larger community and to the local neighborhood.

The value of parent participation in the educational program. An excellent illustration of the value of parent participation in the educational program was recently reported by Connor.[17] The study involved 2000 elementary school children and their parents in seven elementary schools in San Diego. An experimental and a control group with matched pairs of pupils were used. In the experimental schools, provision was made for parents to spend two hours a week at school. The parents spent one hour observing classroom procedures and one hour for discussions and planning with the teacher and their children. The control group had no planned parental co-operation. On the basis of achievement tests given at the beginning of the 20-week experimental period and again at the close, it was found that the experimental group had made significantly greater gains in the achievement of regular subject matter. The experimental group consistently exceeded achievements of matched partners in the control schools in other areas such a friendship status, attention, work habits and class participation. Another observation made from this study was that a great majority of the parents showed a willingness to co-operate.

[16] Clyde M. Campbell, ed., *Practical Applications of Democratic Administration* (New York, Harper, 1952), p. 133.

[17] Jay D. Connor, "Parent Participation Pays Dividends," *California Journal of Elementary Education* (February, 1951), pp. 136-146.

Section 4

APPRAISAL AND IMPROVEMENT OF SUPERVISORY PERSONNEL

Subjective evaluations of supervisory programs. There are many reports of subjective evaluations of supervision in general and also of specific supervisory procedures.

Method and skill. In a study of supervisory programs in twenty-four selected secondary schools, Harman[18] asked members of the teaching staff to indicate the general type of approach to supervision in each school with the results shown below:

STATEMENT OF TYPES	PERCENTAGE OF SCHOOLS DESIGNATING TYPE	
	Under 500	*500-1000*
A. Supervision is planned and conducted by the principal or other supervisory officers with little or no aim of securing the co-operation of teachers and others in planning, carrying out, or evaluating the program	....	....
B. Supervision is planned by the principal or other supervisory officers but teachers and others co-operate in carrying out and evaluating the program	13.3	11.1
C. Supervision represents the co-operative effort of principals, teachers, and others in identifying problems, planning supervisory activities on the basis of them, and carrying out these programs for the improvement of teaching and learning ...	86.6	88.8
Number of schools	15	9

Type C was clearly the prevailing approach in both large and small schools. Harman also asked teachers to express judgment as to the skill with which the types of supervision were carried out, using the code: 5—very high; 4—high; 3—average; 2—little; 1—very little; N—not used.

The results of this evaluation for all schools combined are shown in this listing:

Type of supervision	Size of School	Percentage of Schools Giving Median Evaluations of			
		2	*3*	*4*	*5*
B	Under 500	0	0	100	0
	500-1000	0	0	100	0
C	Under 500	0	30.8	61.5	7.7
	500-1000	0	12.5	50.0	37.5

In general, it is evident that according to the judgment of the teachers in these schools a highly democratic approach to supervision was being used with a high degree of skill by those responsible for this function. There is a need of defining more clearly what are the indices of different degrees of skill for each type of supervision. Suggestions are included in the chart on pages 86-87.

Evaluation of specific supervisory procedures. In the same 24 schools, Harman[19] asked the individual teachers to list the three most effective supervisory procedures used in their school as well as the three least effective supervisory procedures used. The results for each procedure, based on the percentages of the total number of times all items were mentioned, are given in the tables on page 674.

[18] Allen C. Harman, *Supervision in Selected Secondary Schools,* Doctoral dissertation (Philadelphia, Univ. of Pennsylvania Press, 1947), p. 107.

[19] *Ibid,* pp. 102, 104, 108.

MOST EFFECTIVE SUPERVISORY PROCEDURES AS REPORTED BY TEACHERS

PROCEDURE	PERCENTAGE OF TIMES MENTIONED	
	Schools under 500	Schools 500-1000
Studying Pupils	21.6	18.2
Conferences with Individual Teachers	17.7	12.1
Teachers' Meetings	13.8	3.0
Pupil-Testing Programs	7.9	9.1
Planning Supervisory Programs	7.9	6.1
Classroom Visitation	5.9	3.0
Teacher Conferences, by Subject-Matter Groups	5.9	12.1
Attending Teachers' Institutes, Conventions, and Conferences	3.9	....
Teacher Committees for the Study of Special Problems	3.9	15.2
Selecting Books and Other Materials	3.9	....
Teacher Conferences by Grade Groups	1.9	6.1
Developing Courses of Study	1.9	3.0
Supervisory Bulletins	1.9	3.0
Developing School's Philosophy and Objectives	1.9	3.0
Developing Pupil-Learning Activities	....	6.1

LEAST EFFECTIVE SUPERVISORY PROCEDURES AS REPORTED BY TEACHERS

PROCEDURE	PERCENTAGE OF TIMES MENTIONED	
	Schools under 500	Schools 500-1000
Developing Pupil-Learning Activities	12.5	13.4
Helping Teachers Plan Graduate Study	10.8	3.3
Classroom Visitation	9.0	16.7
Supervisory Bulletins	9.0	....
Teacher Inter-Visitation	7.1	13.4
Conferences with Individual Teachers	7.1	6.6
Demonstration Teaching	5.3	3.3
Teacher Self-Rating	5.3	3.3
Teacher Rating by Others	5.3	6.6
Developing School's Philosophy and Objectives	5.3	6.6
Teacher Committees for the Study of Special Problems	5.3	3.3
Teacher Conferences by Grade Groups	3.6	....
Teacher Conferences by Subject-Matter Groups	3.6	3.3
Attending Teachers' Institutes, Conventions and Conferences	3.6	13.4
Studying Pupils	1.8	....
Planning Supervisory Programs	1.8	....
Teachers' Meetings	1.8	6.6
Developing Courses of Study	1.8	....

Suggested standards for evaluating supervision in secondary schools. The statement that follows lists a variety of supervisory practices that may well serve as criteria by which to evaluate the supervisory program in any secondary school. It is a synthesis of improvement programs in a group of five secondary schools selected for study by Harman [20] because of what was regarded as the general excellence of the supervision practices:

The purposes of supervision expressed by supervisory leaders indicate that attention is focused upon pupil growth. Toward this end

[20] *Ibid.*, pp. 144-147.

staff members, pupils, and parents co-operate in identifying and striving for the solution of problems aimed at the improvement of teaching and learning. Furthermore, the following comments are illustrative of supervisory practices outlined in the selected schools.

Generally a project designed to improve instruction is adopted as a theme for a school year, or longer, and a supervisory program involving various procedures is developed accordingly. By means of suggesting problems and participating in subsequent activities, teachers co-operate with their supervisory leaders in planning the enterprise.

Classroom visitation is conducted for the purpose of evaluating the work of pupils and aiding teachers in solving problems related to their teaching programs. In some of the selected schools it is the practice of the principal to visit each teacher for an entire period at least two times per year and frequently, in addition, for a shorter duration. Also, the work of new teachers is observed more closely than that of individuals who have had previous experience in the school. Likewise, the number and character of visits depend upon the apparent need of pupils and teachers.

Conferences with individual teachers are informal in nature and instructors feel free to raise questions and offer suggestions. Topics considered at these meetings pertain to teaching objectives, materials of instruction, techniques, evaluation of pupils' work, student problems, and phases of the school's activities program.

Conferences of subject-matter groups are planned co-operatively by teachers of the various departments and supervisory leaders. Included among their programs are the development of courses of study in the light of the school's philosophy, evaluation of pupil progress, and the recommendation of textbooks, supplementary references, and other materials of instruction.

Grade groups, comprising subject and home-room teachers of a given grade, or home-room teachers only, are held periodically. Pupil-activities programs, individual student problems, and the selection of courses are illustrative of topics considered. Each teacher feels free to bring questions to these meetings and to participate in the discussion.

Committees for the study of special problems are appointed by school principals as needs arise. In addition to teacher representation, pupils and parents occasionally are named to membership on the committees or their opinions are sought in the study of questions. Reports are submitted at faculty meetings and recommendations are adopted.

In a majority of schools, faculty meetings, comprising all members of the staff, are held monthly, after school hours. Teachers co-operate in planning programs, generally in broad outline for the extent of a school year and in a more detailed manner for a semester. Reports are presented by individual teachers and committees of the staff, occasionally including parent and pupil representatives. In addition, guest speakers are scheduled and, at times, consultants serve as advisers in the development of projects designed to improve teaching and learning.

Teachers are encouraged to attend institutes, conferences, and conventions, outside the school district, dealing with problems in specific subject fields or programs of a general character.

In numerous instances supervisory bulletins are issued. They take the form of brief daily statements containing topics of current concern in the improvement of teaching and learning, lists of readily available professional books and magazines, digests of educational articles, course-of-study guides, and annual handbooks. These various types of bulletins are developed by leaders, such as the principal, the librarian, the guidance counselor, and committees of teachers.

Individuals are guided, also, in planning graduate study in the light of their needs and interests. Opportunities are pointed out for professional advancement as a result of additional study and chances are offered for the development of projects within the district. Planning generally takes place at conferences with individual teachers and may cover a study program projected several years in length.

Occasionally supervisory leaders and superior teachers present demonstration lessons, as a means of showing new teachers in particular, individually or in groups, specific techniques in presenting subject matter and in stimulating pupil response. Co-operative planning between leaders and teachers takes place prior to the demonstration, and a conference follows the lesson. This includes a review of the teaching plans, elements to be observed during the demonstration, and an evaluation of the results of the project.

The practice of teachers visiting classes within their own schools and in other districts is encouraged whenever there is an opportunity for an instructor to profit from observation of specific activities in other situations. Emphasis is placed upon setting up clearly defined purposes before visits take place, selecting schools where outstanding practices of the desired type are in operation, and reporting features of the visits to supervisory leaders and interested teachers, upon return to the schools where individuals are employed.

Teacher self-rating projects, reported by principals, are confined largely to those carried on as a phase of a school's program of evaluation. Occasionally, after using the "M" blanks of the Evaluative Criteria for their own appraisal, individual teachers and supervisory leaders review their ratings at conferences and, as a result of the discussions, they plan co-operatively measures for the improvement of teaching and learning.

When teacher ratings are assigned by others, the responsibility rests with the superintendent of the school and may be delegated to his principal. Frequent conferences are held during the year with teachers whose work is in question and, in all cases, it was reported that they are informed of their unsatisfactory status before an evaluation is reported in writing at the end of a year.

The statements of supervisory leaders and teachers revealed that principals, counselors, and other staff members, individually and by groups, devote special attention to the study of students' physical, mental, emotional, and social characteristics. In like manner, attention is focused on consideration of their habits, interests and activities. These data form the basis for curriculum development and pupil guidance.

Illustrations of pupil-learning activities in the several schools indicated that emphasis is given frequently to remedial and developmental activities in reading, programs for the improvement of mathematics, and projects aimed at the development of pupil leadership.

In numerous schools the principal delegates the guidance counselor or a classroom teacher to assume leadership in planning, conducting, and interpreting the results of testing programs. Features among the standardized examinations administered for the purpose of achieving objectives, co-operatively set up, are those pertaining to mental ability, achievement, aptitude, and measures of a diagnostic and prognostic character.

School philosophies and objectives are developed jointly by faculty groups. It is a common practice for a committee, appointed by the principal, to draft a preliminary statement, submit it to the faculty, and revise it in response to recommendations adopted by the staff members after round-table discussions.

Subject-matter groups assume a chief role in writing courses of study and making revisions according to pupil needs. Committees of teachers co-operate with principals, and in some instances expert consultants from areas outside the local school district, in developing projects extending over a period of a year or longer.

Finally, as an added means of team work in improving teaching and learning, departmental groups in some schools study sample copies of text books, supplementary references, and other teaching materials. Their recommendations, submitted to the principal, are frequently forwarded to the school's superintendent and purchases are made accordingly.

Evaluation by appraisal of documents reporting the procedures of supervisory officers. School records and documents of various types supply evidence of the effectiveness of leadership. As a matter of fact, one of the essential conditions for an effective program of evaluation will be found in the records kept by school systems.[21] To develop a program of self-survey one must therefore develop a comprehensive system of records. Much effort has already been expended upon developing records of the pupils, teachers, and school finance. Almost every school system has on file a variety of materials relating to the program of studies, the curriculum, textbooks, supplies, and the library. When properly studied, these all may yield valuable data on the character of the educational program and improvement activities. Chapters 12 to 16 contain a number of suggestions on the collection and use of such data. Almost all phases of the program may be so studied.

Judd's proposal for more informative school reports. The proposal for a set of standards for judging principal's reports, first made in 1934, is repeated because it is a stimulating departure from traditional procedures. Judd first points out that the usual methods of reporting are stereotyped and deal with factual trivialities. This com-

21 Reavis, *op. cit.,* pp. 134-137.

placent routine repetition year after year of meaningless statistics of attendance, costs, supplies, about the same old curriculum, the same old methods of administering pupils, the same old methods of selecting teachers, the number and dates of faculty meetings, the number of visits and conferences, bulletins, and so on, is one of the most disastrous results of the worthy efforts of standardization. The older standards based on formal statistics were necessary and valuable in an earlier day. The result now is stagnation, since most schools judge themselves as good in comparison with a set of minimum essentials derived from the average and designed to secure at least this minimum for the poorest situations.

Judd then proposes four sample standards which he thinks would result in the collection of evidences of an enlightened social theory, of dynamic attack, and of effective achievements. Evidence of vitality and not of stagnation in the school program would appear. His four samples are: [22]

From the principal of each secondary school applying for approval is required a report indicating some particular in which experimental modification has been undertaken during the past year in the curriculum, class organization, methods of dealing with the public or the pupils, or in some other phase of school work. This report shall include a clear description of the plan of the experiment undertaken and an evaluation of the results obtained by the experiment.

Report six cases in which pupils showing signs of maladjustment in their courses or in their general social relations were fully readjusted through special attention given them by the school staff. Describe the way in which these cases were discovered, the way in which they were treated, and present the evidence that the treatment was successful.

The principal of the school shall cause to be transmitted to the inspector one or more statements from committees of the faculty with regard to plans which they have matured during the year for the cultivation in the pupils of the school habits of reading or independent effort wholly outside the assignments of any course. Lists of books read or of constructive activities undertaken or of excursions organized and car-

ried to successful completion should be submitted as a part of each statement.

The principal shall give an account of the kinds of population which surrounds the school, the kinds of positions to which graduates of the school go, the available resources of the community for the support of schools. Against the background of the foregoing statements, the principal shall give a description of the curriculum administered by the school, describing the reasons for each course included.

Great improvements have been made in reports by principals and superintendents, some illustrations being in fact very informative. Good understanding of the realities of education is demonstrated. The full force of Judd's vital and enlightened proposal has not yet been widely demonstrated. Perhaps it is too far in advance of current thinking. Perhaps it would require too great effort to understand the nature of education and to do something about it. In any event, the writers commend it to the attention of supervisors as one of the most valuable and provocative suggestions for growth yet to appear in this field.

Methods of appraising the personnel. We have discussed in the preceding sections of this chapter a number of approaches to the evaluation of educational leadership. Leadership in school education is a very complex activity and its evaluation equally complex. One final approach to evaluation, especially to evaluation of the self-survey type, is the appraisal that can be made of the personnel, similar to those contained in recent supervisory rating scales and question lists. These evaluations may relate to the qualities of the person essential to effective leadership; principles of behavior governing effective human engineering; areas of responsibility; and the mental prerequisites to the successful discharge of these responsibilities. The work in this area has not progressed to the same point that it has in the areas of teacher and pupil evaluation, but important beginnings have been made (1) in developing rating

[22] C. H. Judd, "New Standards for Secondary Schools," *Journal of National Education Association* (May, 1934), pp. 141-142.

devices, and (2) in developing evaluative criteria of one sort or another. Following the pattern set by teacher-rating, much of the early effort in this area was expended in the development of rating devices.

A check-list of the characteristics of "good" elementary-school principals. A principals' workshop in San Francisco in 1949 developed a comprehensive list [23] of what were judged by the participants to be the characteristics of a good school administrator. Most of the groups of items are closely identified with the supervisory function of the principal. The list itself is of value not only for self-appraisal by the principal but also in planning the training of prospective principals and for setting up in-service education for principals already active. Because of the valuable and practical nature of its contents, the complete check-list is given below:

CHECK-LIST OF CHARACTER-ISTICS OF A GOOD SCHOOL ADMINISTRATOR

1. *Curriculum*
   The good administrator:
   1.1 Knows and accepts the existing educational philosophy of the system in which he works.
   1.2 Knows source materials which help in curriculum development.
   1.3 Adjusts the curriculum to environment and pupil needs.
   1.4 Utilizes community resources in implementing the curriculum.
   1.5 Fosters an experimental approach to teaching and curriculum among teachers.
   1.6 Is responsible for the curriculum improvement through activities of the entire school system; for example, through workshops, work of the science group, social-studies group, etc.
2. *Personnel*
   The good administrator:
   2.1 Knows, accepts, and respects the individual characteristics, educational background, and personal background of each teacher.
   2.2 Capitalizes upon individual strengths, interests, and talents of each teacher

in making assignments to classroom and other specific duties.
   2.3 Recognizes teacher weaknesses and, in so far as possible, aids the teacher in overcoming them.
   2.4 Recognizes good work and lets the teacher know about it.
   2.5 Practices the democratic process:
      2.51 Co-operative planning.
      2.52 Uses it in both individual and group relationships.
      2.53 Creates a permissive atmosphere in which teachers feel free to express problems of concern to them.
      2.54 Sees the implications of specific teacher problems in relation to curriculum, to principles of child development, to the organization of the school and its rules and regulations.
   2.6 Uses a variety of techniques to bring teachers to work with a problem or program.
   2.7 Evaluates his own behavior in particular situations, is objective in seeing good and bad points, and uses results of evaluation as a basis for future actions, behavior, and growth.
   2.8 Develops sensitivity to the way other people feel.
   2.9 Fosters and stimulates professional growth in each teacher.
3. *Public Relations*
   The good administrator:
   3.1 Uses the parent-teachers' association or similar groups for aid and help with pupil health and welfare.
   3.2 Uses the parent-teachers' association or similar groups to develop an understanding of school objectives.
   3.3 Uses the parent-teachers' association or similar groups to discover and explore needs as a basis for curriculum construction.
   3.4 Exercises leadership in promoting parent participation in common problems.
   3.5 Knows thoroughly the socioeconomic level of each family and of the neighborhood.
   3.6 Encourages parent visits; makes arrangement for such visits.

[23] James B. Enochs, "Elementary School Administrators Evaluate Themselves," *Elementary School Journal* (September, 1950), pp. 15-21.

3.7 Develops a regular, systematic method of reporting to parents upon developments within the particular school.

3.8 Increasingly uses student participation in putting across publicity about the school and its problems.

3.9 Studies techniques in training teachers to handle public relations more adequately.

3.10 Is alert to news-worthy stories on the site.

3.11 Uses parent resources to put over publicity for the school.

4. *Pupil-Teacher Relationship*
The good administrator:

4.1 Makes available to the teacher a knowledge of individual pupils and the group.

4.2 Encourages teachers to maintain professional relationship in so far as personal, confidential information about students is concerned.

4.3 Maintains records which furnish needed information, organizes reference system in which information is available, and encourages teachers to make continuing reports.

4.4 Makes time available (when voluntary effort calls for it) to visit homes; encourages home visiting.

4.5 Encourages teachers in developing respect for children as human beings.

4.6 Helps teachers to distinguish between cause and effect in problem situations and to recognize certain behaviors as symptoms of underlying causes.

4.7 Assists the teachers in solution of problems of individual children; sees implications of a problem for the total group situation.

4.8 Encourages teachers to use teacher-pupil planning as a real example of democracy in which individual pupils develop characteristics of leadership and followership.

4.9 By example, sets the tone of the school for recognizing every child as an individual.

5. *Noncertificated Personnel* (*Custodians and Clerks*)
The good administrator:

5.1 Uses the democratic process in situations in which it is applicable.

5.11 Makes the personnel feel wanted, needed.

5.12 Uses them in planning for their services.

5.2 Recognizes them as an essential part of the school.

5.3 Knows the duties to be performed by each member.

5.4 Clarifies duties in such a way that mutual understanding of duties is developed.

5.5 Checks with the central office supervisor as to duties to be performed and how they are to be performed.

5.6 Sets up definite channels through which requests for services are cleared.

5.7 Notifies personnel of special request far enough ahead of time.

5.8 Respects time-allotment schedule (work-schedule hours).

6. *Co-ordination with Central Office*
The good administrator:

6.1 Understands and tries to accept the policies, situations, and conditions under which the central office works.

6.2 Establishes rapport between the site and the central office.

6.3 Knows the uses of the proper channels for clearing, correcting, and eliminating complaints, misunderstandings, etc.

6.4 Capitalizes on the unique services available from the central office to supplement, implement, and enrich his own supervisory and other administrative duties.

6.5 Recognizes and acts upon his responsibility and opportunity to aid the central office in developing policies and plans.

7. *Guidance: Pupil Adjustment and Placement* (*Classification*)
The good administrator:

7.1 Knows the uses of various agencies outside the school to promote, develop, and protect child health and welfare (juvenile court, social-welfare agencies, etc.)

7.2 Sees the total child in relationship to his adjustment.

7.3 In so far as possible, exhausts all sources of information about each child; uses many sources rather than just one or two.

7.4 Maintains a sensitivity to the changing needs of each child.

7.5 Sees guidance as a need for every child and not just for the maladjusted child or the various deviates.

7.6 Keeps such flexibility in the school program and organization that the changing needs of the child can be taken care of.

7.7 Is sensitive to the interest patterns and abilities peculiar to each child; uses these interest patterns and abilities to aid in pupil adjustment and in furthering the learning process.

7.8 Assists teachers in collecting evidence that will help to solve adjustment problems.

8. *Articulation with Secondary and Other Schools*

The good administrator:

8.1 Has an objective professional, attitude toward co-workers.

8.2 Respects honest differences of opinion and judgment.

8.3 Maintains an objective, open mind about his own work and the work of others.

8.4 Knows the program of other schools and sees the relationship between elementary and secondary programs.

8.5 Acquaints teachers with other programs and relationships.

8.6 Arranges for visits and contacts among teachers, administrators, and supervisors within the school system.

9. *Supplies and Equipment*

The good administrator:

9.1 Knows what supplies and equipment are available.

9.2 Acquaints teachers with what is available and with ways in which it may be used.

9.3 Allots supplies and equipment upon an equitable basis.

9.4 In so far as possible, furnishes teachers with what they need:

9.41 To do their work as they see it.

9.42 To broaden their conception of what can be done.

9.5 Encourages teachers to learn of new materials which could be added to the present supply, in order to develop an on-going, expanding program.

9.6 Is responsible for submitting requests to the central office for additional supplies and equipment.

10. *Organization of Program*

The good administrator:

10.1 Organizes the school in such a way that its purpose and functions are actually accomplished; that is, so that "growth of the children" in learning and otherwise takes place.

10.2 Gets the co-operative judgment and support of the staff preparatory to planning for the school organization, so that personnel and plant are used effectively and efficiently.

10.3 Keeps flexibility in the organization.

10.4 Assumes responsibility for making decisions in terms of the over-all situation.

10.5 In so far as possible, maintains an organization that promotes mental health and emotional stability of the pupils and the teachers.

Standards of local school systems in selecting elementary-school principals. The 1948 Yearbook [24] of the Department of Elementary School Principals contains the results of a survey of practices in 689 localities in the selection of principals.

The list below contains the personal qualities needed by principals that were mentioned by more than twenty superintendents. The list suggests the basis of a rating scale to be used to evaluate the qualities of candidates.

Quality	Frequency of Mention
Ability to get along with people ...	150
Personality	135
Leadership	112
Organizing and executive ability ...	51
Tact and diplomacy	37
Good judgment and common sense.	35
Professional attitude	34
Interest in, liking for, and understanding of children	34
Ability to teach	33
Character	33
Appearance	32
Poise and emotional stability	28
Social adjustment	27
Health, energy, and vigor	27
Ability to supervise and help teachers grow	21
Interest in community affairs	21

[24] *The Elementary School Principalship—Today and Tomorrow,* 27th Yearbook, Department of Elementary School Principals (Washington, NEA, 1948), p. 138.

Among the items listed by fewer than twenty superintendents are: desire to improve, ability in public relations, willingness to work, culture, scholarship, intelligence, loyalty, sense of humor, sympathy, voice, democratic attitude, progressiveness, initiative, enthusiasm.

Characteristics of successful and of unsuccessful principals, according to superintendents, are as follows: [25]

CHARACTERISTICS OF SUCCESSFUL ELEMENTARY-SCHOOL PRINCIPALS

Characteristic	Frequency of Mention
1. Effective educational and community leadership	95
2. Ability to work co-operatively with teachers to improve teaching and the school program	94
3. Ability to get along with others	87
4. Ability to organize and carry out a good school program	53
5. Professional attitude and spirit	40
6. Genuine liking for and understanding of children	38
7. Desire and capacity to improve	19
8. Personality	17
9. Ability to build a good public relations program	16
10. Clear understanding of elementary education and the principal's part in it	14
11. Willingness to assume responsibility	12
12. Good judgment and common sense	11
13. Democratic attitude	11
14. Ability to solve problems calmly and according to sound educational principles	11

CHARACTERISTICS OF UNSUCCESSFUL ELEMENTARY-SCHOOL PRINCIPALS

Characteristic	Frequency of Mention
1. Allowing petty administrative details to occupy too much time	73
2. Lack of background in elementary education	70
3. Poor supervisory skill	60
4. Failure to assume responsibility	31
5. Lack of leadership qualities	29
6. Lack of initiative	29
7. Failure to grow professionally	29
8. Limited professional and cultural vision	24
9. Inability to establish harmonious working relationships with classroom teachers	18
10. Unprogressive and inflexible attitude	16
11. Inability to build good public relations	13
12. Dictatorial attitude	12
13. Failure to keep in touch with children	11

Many of these traits can be improved and/or developed by systematic study and experience. A small but good literature on this is available.

In only 63 cases [26] was there any evidence that systematic procedures for rating and selecting appointees were utilized. This is, unhappily, quite typical of general practice. The variety of examinations used, and the abilities appraised by examinations, interviews, and selective procedures of local school systems were as follows:

Type of Examination	Thirty Systematic Plans	Thirty-three Partly Systematized Plans
General examination on education	16	..
Intelligence test	8	1
Emotional maturity and stability test	8	2
Physical examination	20	28
National Teachers Examination	1	3

[25] *Ibid.*, p. 167.   [26] *Ibid.*, p. 142.

Abilities Appraised [27]	Thirty Systematic Plans	Thirty-three Partly Systematized Plans
General knowledge of public education	25	15
Information and understanding of elementary education ..	25	16
Information and understanding of the principalship	23	15
Knowledge and understanding of children	25	16
Understanding of teaching methods and devices	25	16
Understanding of public relations	22	14
Others *	4	1

* Others include such items as culture, philosophy, capacity for work, appearance, and ability to get along with others.

Two typical plans for selecting elementary principals which embody examinations, committee ratings, interviews and other desirable practices are given below: [28]

LOS ANGELES

A person wishing to become an elementary-school principal must have a bachelor's degree from a recognized college and five years of teaching experience, three of which must have been in the Los Angeles day schools. He need not have experience in an elementary school. At the time of taking the examination he must be an employee of the Los Angeles public schools. There is no age limit if the person is not old enough to retire, and no preference is given on account of sex. The candidate must have, at the time of taking the examination or within a specified time thereafter, a state credential authorizing him to serve as an elementary-school principal. He must satisfy the Health Service Section of the Los Angeles schools that he is physically and mentally fit.

The first part of the examination consists of an objective test on the principles and professional developments in the field of elementary education, especially educational administration and supervision, and the application of that knowledge to specific problems of school administration.

A committee set up from year to year, composed of four district assistant superintendents in charge of elementary schools, evaluates the professional growth and experience of the applicant. His efficiency as a director of learning activities, as a supervisor of personnel, as a leader in community relations, and as a director of management activities (the organization of office routines and the use of the school plant), are appraised to determine his fitness for the elementary-school principalship.

A committee set up from year to year, consisting of an assistant superintendent, elementary education division, and four elementary-school principals, when the written test and evaluation of personal growth and experience have been completed, calls for an oral interview with those candidates who have made high scores in these parts of the evaluation. The number to be called is determined by the superintendent, assistant superintendent of the elementary division, and assistant superintendent of the personnel division. It is expected that about half of those called will be placed on the eligible list. The number to be called for interview and the number to be placed on the eligible list are announced in the bulletin prior to the examination. The oral interview is for the purpose of evaluating the applicant's personal qualifications, including voice, speech and appearance, manner and bearing, alertness and comprehension, ability to present ideas, ability to get along with others, maturity of judgment, and general fitness for the position.

The candidates are arranged on the eligible list in order according to scores on the examination. Eligibility for appointment lasts two years unless a person's name is removed for cause.

MINNEAPOLIS

Applicants submit their credentials for the position of assistant principal since they ordinarily serve in that position before being appointed principals. In case of need, principals are appointed without such experience. Principals and assistant principals may be appointed from among qualified applicants employed outside the Minneapolis school system.

At present a candidate may be appointed with only a bachelor's degree, but he must acquire the master's degree with at least a minor in education by January 1, 1949. He must have had teaching or supervisory experience, including elementary-school experience, preferably in the Minneapolis public schools. The amount is

[27] *Ibid.,* p. 143.
[28] *Ibid.,* pp. 279-281.

not specified. There is no specified age limit but candidates should have the prospect of a considerable number of years of active service before retirement. There is no preference on account of sex.

A personnel committee, consisting of two elementary-school principals and four elementary-school teachers, elected by principals and teachers respectively, and a representative of the central office staff, is formed to make recommendations regarding candidates for elementary-school principalships. The committee is given a period of training and planning before beginning its work.

The personnel committee determines procedure for placing candidates on the eligible list. Ordinarily it interviews candidates and reviews papers giving pertinent information about their qualifications, taking into account such factors as experience, evidence of professional growth and training, indications of organizing abilities, and estimates of effectiveness in human relations. Eligibility lasts two years. In case of a vacancy the assistant superintendent consults the principal of the school, if available, and, upon the basis of this conference and his own judgment, recommends to the superintendent the individual on the eligible list who seems best qualified for the position in question. If there is no principal whom he could consult, the assistant superintendent would make the recommendation according to his own best judgment.

The following statement contains the recommendations of the editorial committee of the yearbook as to steps that should be taken to improve procedures for preparing and selecting elementary principals: [29]

1. That every school system should have a written statement of the basic personal and professional standards to be required of all persons appointed to the principalship. These standards should be formulated by the superintendent and his staff in co-operation with local principals' organizations.

2. That these standards should require at least two years of successful elementary-school experience, part of which includes direct classroom responsibilities.

3. That the professional preparation should not be less than the master's degree including special preparation in educational philosophy, administration and supervision of elementary schools, child psychology and development, curriculum, and instructional methods.

4. That in selecting new principals discriminations should not be made on the basis of sex, residence, or other irrelevant factors. However, it is to be hoped that future local standards for the principalship will be so clearly stated and so courageously applied that the proportion of the young people who undertake the principalship as a life career will be greatly increased.

5. That there should be, in addition to physical examinations, a series of tests of emotional stability, intelligence, professional knowledge, and cultural interests. The minimum points on these tests, below which no appointments will be made, should be set in co-operation with the local principals' association.

6. That likely candidates for the principalship should be interviewed by committees of principals as well as by the superintendent and his staff. These committees should have authority to indicate those candidates who, on the basis of the evidence, are qualified for listing in the records from which the superintendent makes his appointments.

In-service education of principals and supervisors. Many school systems provide systematic in-service education for principals. The most commonly used devices are given on page 684.[30]

CHAPTER SUPPLEMENT

DISCUSSION QUESTIONS

One of the very best ways to study supervision is to study it in operation. It is possible in many communities to secure the co-operation of principals, teachers, superintendents, special supervisors, and other members of the school community in planning and evaluating particular programs of supervision. To make such evaluations practicable, they should extend over a period of at least one school year and preferably over two or three years. In order to evaluate the effectiveness of the supervisory program, the various instruments employed in the collection of data will need to be applied at both the beginning and the end of the school year. The means by which such evaluations may be made have been set forth in this chapter.

[29] *Ibid.,* pp. 148-149. The yearbook itself should be consulted for information on all aspects of the functions of the elementary-school principal.
[30] *Ibid.,* p. 169.

DEVICES FOR IN-SERVICE EDUCATION OF PRINCIPALS— 657 PLACES

Device	Total Number	Per Cent
1. Superintendent holds group conferences with principals	591	90.0
2. Superintendent holds conferences with individual principals ..	570	86.8
3. Superintendent appoints committees to work on curriculum and instructional problems	508	77.3
4. Superintendent allows principals to attend professional conventions and conferences and pays their way so as to insure their attendance	459	69.9
5. Superintendent assigns individual principals to work on research problems	271	41.2
6. Superintendent appoints committees to work on professional standards and personnel policies applying to the principalship.	263	40.0
7. Superintendent co-operates in study program of the principals' club or association	142	21.6
8. Superintendent allows principals to attend conferences without loss of pay, but does not pay their way	36	5.5
9. Others *	47	7.2
Total number of replies to the questions	657	....

* Including workshops, committees on administrative policies, visits to other local school systems, employment of technical advisors, and encouragement toward participation in community and professional activities.

1. New studies of the value of supervision appear from time to time in the literature. Prepare a critical analysis of one of these recent investigations, indicating its adequacy as to method and results.

2. What are the strengths and limitations of the experimental studies of the value of supervision discussed in Section 2? Suggest ways in which the research could have been improved. Outline other possible methods of making experimental studies of the value of supervision.

3. Leadership is sometimes evaluated in terms of the qualities of the person providing the leadership. What qualities do you consider most essential to effective leadership? How can they be evaluated?

4. When asked if and why supervisors should be rated, teachers sometimes reply: "Yes, because teachers are rated." Tell why this answer is or is not correct. Try to secure a rating scale for supervisors and evaluate it. Better still, use the data in Section 4 to develop a useful rating scale.

5. Make a summary list of the chief weaknesses and the chief values of the teacher's evaluation of supervision.

6. The writers have emphasized in this chapter the importance of the self-survey. How may this become an instrument for the improvement of the leadership and continued growth in service? Apply Harman's criteria to some secondary school program of supervision and suggest how the program could be strengthened.

7. Show clearly how scrutiny of a supervisor's plan or of a superintendent's annual report may afford excellent symptomatic evidence as to the worth or lack of worth of the leadership provided.

8. Read rapidly through Chapter 13 in *The Supervision of Instruction* by Barr and Burton. Make a brief report indicating the nature and amount of progress which has been made since that chapter was written.

9. What is the unique feature of the proposals by Judd for appraising the effectiveness of leadership?

10. Why is it difficult to determine the extent of the changes in curriculum and instruction that are the direct result of supervision? Can they be described? Can they be measured?

11. Report for class analysis any local study of educational leadership in which you may have participated.

12. Evaluate local practices regarding the selection and rating of supervisory personnel and the program of in-service education for improving the effectiveness of supervision. Suggest improvements.

SUGGESTED READINGS

ANTELL, H., "Teachers Appraise Supervision," *Journal of Educational Research* (April, 1945), pp. 606-611.

ARMSTRONG, W. E., "What Teachers Prefer in Supervision," *Educational Method* (February, 1936), pp. 270-272.

BAMBERGER, F. E., "Effect of Supervision on the Quality of English Instruction," American Educational Research Association Official Report, 1940, pp. 164-168.

COREY, Stephen M., *Action Research to Improve School Practices* (New York, Teachers College, Bureau of Publications, Columbia Univ., 1953).

DURRANCE, Charles L., and others, *School-Community Cooperation for Better Living* (Gainesville, Fla., Univ. of Florida, College of Education, 1947).

Evaluative Criteria, 1950 Edition, manual prepared by Co-operative Study of Secondary School Standards, Washington.

FISK, Robert S., *Public Understanding of What Good Schools Can Do* (New York, Teachers College, Bureau of Publications, Columbia Univ., 1944).

Forces Affecting American Education, 1953 Yearbook, Association of Supervision and Curriculum Development (Washington, NEA, 1953).

GILLENTINE, Flora M., *A Controlled Experiment on Fifth-Grade Reading,* Contributions to Education No. 78 (Nashville, Tenn., George Peabody College for Teachers, 1930).

GINSBERG, Eli, and BRAY, Douglas W., *The Uneducated* (New York, Columbia Univ. Press, 1953).

GLUECK, Sheldon, and GLUECK, Eleanor, *Unraveling Juvenile Delinquency* (New York, Commonwealth Fund, 1950).

GREENFIELD, B. L., "A Study of the Effectiveness of a Program of Elementary School Supervision," *Journal of Educational Research* (October, 1933), pp. 123-126.

HYMES, James L., *Effective Home-School Relations* (New York, Prentice-Hall, 1953).

KELLEY, Earl C., *The Workshop Way of Learning* (New York, Harper, 1951).

KEYWORTH, M. R., "A Program of Appraisal under Functional Supervision in Hamtramck, Michigan," *Educational Administration and Supervision* (April, 1929), pp. 290-300.

KINHART, H. A., *The Effect of Supervision on High School English,* Johns Hopkins University Studies in Education No. 30 (Baltimore, Md., Johns Hopkins Press, 1941).

LINGREN, Vernon C., "Criteria for the Evaluation of In-Service Activities in Teacher Education," *Journal of Educational Research* (September, 1948), pp. 62-68.

McCHAREN, William K., *Selected Community School Programs in the South* (Nashville, Tenn., George Peabody College for Teachers, 1948).

MENGE, J. Wilmer, and FAUNCE, Roland C., *Working Together for Better Schools* (New York, American Book, 1953).

NEELY, Delta P., "The Effects of Planned Supervision on Teaching as Shown by Objective Analysis of Classroom Activities," *Educational Administration and Supervision* (May, 1938), pp. 341-354.

OGLE, F. A., "Does Supervision Pay?" *School Executive* (February, 1937), pp. 234-236.

OLSEN, E. G., *The Modern Community School* (New York, Appleton-Century-Crofts, 1953).

OVERN, A. V., "A Survey of Instruction and Supervision, East Grand Forks, Minnesota," *Departmental Bulletin,* Vol. 15 (Grand Forks, N. D., University of North Dakota, October, 1931).

PITTMAN, M. S., *The Value of School Supervision* (Baltimore, Warwick & York, 1921).

PREWIT, Irene, and MANUEL, H. T., "Differences in the Handwriting of Supervised and Unsupervised Pupils," *School and Society* (March 1, 1930).

SHAW, Lena A., "An Evaluation of Four Types of Supervisor Procedures in Handwriting," in the Eighth Yearbook, Department of Superintendents (Washington, NEA, 1930), pp. 106-107.

Southern Association Co-operative Study in Elementary Education, "Evaluating the Elementary School, A Guide for Cooperative Study," Commission on Research and Service, 1951.

The Community School, Fifty-second Yearbook, Part II, National Society for the Study of Education (Chicago, Univ. of Chicago Press, 1953).

TOWNER, Earl M., "The Formal Rating of Elementary-School Principals," *Elementary School Journal* (June, 1935), pp. 735-746.

WHITELAW, J. B., "Criteria for Evaluating the Effectiveness of Supervision," *Educational Administration and Supervision* (January, 1941), pp. 29-38.

WOODY, Clifford, and others, *The Evaluation of Supervision,* Fourth Yearbook, Department of Supervisors and Directors of Instruction (Washington, NEA, 1931).

APPENDICES

Appendix A

◆·◆·◆·◆·◆·◆·◆·◆·◆··◀

A Brief Summary of Background Materials Concerning the Current Curriculum Movement

Section 1

ABBREVIATED OUTLINE OF HISTORIC CRITICISMS OF COURSES OF STUDY AND CURRICULUMS

A SERIOUS OBSTACLE to educational progress is the tendency among certain teachers, educational leaders, and public figures to decry and to oppose current efforts to improve curriculums. "Curriculum reorganization is a passing fad." "The curriculum of the past has stood the test of time; why meddle with it?" "Men now successful in business or in scholarly fields were prepared by the standard curriculum of the past." (The only one they could get!) The "good old days" were better than the present with its uncertainty, its experimentation, its critical discussions. Persons taking this stand are clearly manifesting an ignorance of simple historical facts, an ignorance so naïve as to be almost infantile. Criticism of and change in curriculums and methods of teaching have been continuous from the beginnings of recorded history. The succession of criticisms and changes illustrates a fact of basic importance: the continuity of effort to bring curriculums into line with changing social needs, into line with ever greater knowledge of the educative process. Opposition to change in education borders close upon dangerous stupidity.

Criticism began early. Curriculums which existed many centuries before the Christian era were evidently unsatisfactory to some citizens. Clay tablets representing some of the most ancient civilizations contain statements from exasperated parents and taxpayers similar in tone to statements made during the intervening 5000-6000 years. A few almost duplicate word-for-word criticisms appearing in the current press.

Confucius, writing in the fifth century B.C., made a statement which would be accepted today by many persons.

> The teachers of today just go on repeating things in rigmarole fashion, annoy the students with constant questions, and repeat the same things over and over again. They do not try to find out what the students' natural inclinations are, so that students are forced to pretend to like their studies; nor do they try to bring out the best in their talents. What they give to the students is wrong in the first place and what they expect of the student is just as wrong. As a result, the students hide their favorite readings and hate their teachers, are exasperated at the difficulty of their studies and do not know what good it does them. Although they go through the regular course of instruction, they are quick to leave when they are through. This is the reason for the failure of education today.

Approximately one thousand years later, St. Augustine indicates that all is not well within the school:

> At enim vela pendent liminibus grammaticarium scholarum, sed non illa magis honorem secreti quam tegimentum erroris significant.

689

(True it is, that there are curtains at the entrance to grammar schools; but they signify not so much the cloth of a state of privacy, as serve for a blind to the follies committed behind them.)

About seven hundred years later and still three hundred years before America was discovered, Peter of Blois (circa 1200) holds forth in very modern tone:

Quid enim prodest illis expendere dies suos in his quae nec domi, nec militiae, nec in foro, nec in claustro, nec in curia, nec in ecclesia, nec alcui prosint alicubi, nisi dumtaxat in scholis?

(For what does it profit them to spend their days in these things which neither at home, nor in the army, nor in business, nor in the cloister, nor in political affairs, nor in the church, nor anywhere else are any good to anyone—except only in the schools.)

Another five centuries pass and Rousseau's *Emile* (1762) appears, containing vigorous criticism and proposals for reform. Herbert Spencer's famous essay, "What Knowledge Is the Most Worth," published in 1859, was a devastating attack upon the British secondary schools, pointing out that nothing whatever could be found in those schools which prepared the young Englishman to understand and to participate in the life of the great empire he was to inherit. The ancient world, its history and classic literature, dominated the curriculum to the exclusion of the new industrial and scientific world. The everyday activities of parents, homemakers, and breadwinners received no attention whatever. If our civilization were to decay and its records be studied later by archaeologists, said Spencer, it would have to be assumed that our whole curriculum was for celibates! More than half a century after Spencer's strictures, the survey of a city in the United States revealed that about nine times as much attention was given to Roman life, customs, and citizenship as to the same topics concerning the United States.

Under a title strangely reminiscent of Spencer's essay in 1859, there appeared in 1939 a significant volume by Robert S. Lynd,[1] an eminent sociologist. The book, *Knowledge for What?*, presents a compelling case for the place of social science in our culture and in education, just as Spencer had pleaded the earlier case for the physical and biological sciences. The Educational Policies Commission of the National Education Association brought out in 1944 an able booklet entitled "Education for All American Youth." The attack was positive in that a new program was proposed in some detail. Criticism of the old is indirect but clearly repeats for schools of the United States what Spencer had said of British schools eighty-eight years before: the bulk of the curriculum is of little value to the majority of pupils.

An interesting illustration of progress in the United States. In three quotations we have a significant illustration of the recency of success in studying the curriculum in operation and in improving it.

In 1923 Charters said:[2]

The school curriculum is the latest great social agency to feel the effect of the theory of evolution. Biology for sixty years has recognized the fact that living structure is modified to serve the functions of plants and animals. Sociology, economics, and history accept the fact that the forms of institutions are determined by the attempts of man to make his environment minister to his needs. . . .

While all these revolutionary changes have been under way, the theory of the formation of the curriculum has been slow to react to them. The curriculum builder has felt . . . that the specialists who organize the subjects . . . have developed the best curriculums. . . .

One would expect that those profound changes in the aims of education which follow revolutions in world thought would be reflected in equally fundamental changes in the curriculum of the school, but in practice the

---

[1] Robert S. Lynd, *Knowledge for What?* (Princeton, Princeton Univ. Press, 1939). See particularly pp. 236-237. Entire volume should be known to educational leaders.

[2] W. W. Charters, *Curriculum Construction* (New York, Macmillan, 1923), pp. vii, 3-4. Quoted by special permission of the publishers.

changes have always been tardy and have seldom been complete.

... In the present period, when the world thought has been turning to a consideration of social facts and ideals, the theory of the aims of education has been modified but the changes in the curriculum in actual operation are still quite inconsiderable.

Four years later, in 1927, Rugg in vivid, dynamic language points the issue even more sharply: [3]

Not once in a century and a half of national history has the curriculum of the school caught up with the dynamic content of American life. Whether of colonial reading or reckoning school, Latin grammar school, academy, or modern junior high school, the curriculum has lagged behind our current civilization. Although the gap between the two has been markedly cut down in the last three quarters of a century, nevertheless the American school has been essentially academic. Today, much of the gap persists.

Not only has there been a huge gap between the curriculum and American life; a similar one has persisted to the present day between the growing child and the curriculum. There are, indeed, three critical factors in the education process: the child, contemporary American society, and, standing between them, the school curriculum.

No, in more than a hundred years of systematization of the national educational scheme, the materials of instruction have not only been largely aloof from, indeed, foreign to, the institutions and culture of the American people; they have failed equally to provide for maximal child growth. If the curriculum of our schools is to serve its true function, however, it must be reconstructed on a twofold basis. Adequate provision must be made for creative personal development, and tolerant understanding of American life must be erected as the great guiding goal of education. Its reconstruction, therefore, must concentrate upon two foci —child growth and the dynamic content of American civilization. ...

In a hundred years, however, the public school has lagged far behind. It has never caught up with the momentum of industry, business, community life, or politics. Only rarely has it succeeded in dealing with contemporary issues and conditions; never has it anticipated social needs ... the halo of the past has oriented those who have made the content of our school curriculum. ...

Let us consider first, therefore, in this attempt to understand curriculum-making, the startling contrast between life and education on the North American continent from Washington to Coolidge. Because of the hiatus between the two, it is of crucial importance that we study its course. Indeed, no task confronting the curriculum-maker is of greater importance than that of bridging the current gulf between them. He who would undertake the task, however, must have a clear understanding of the development of the curriculum during the past century and of the method of its construction, as well as an appreciation of the ever increasing momentum of American life during this period. To these historical considerations we shall now address ourselves.

Rugg's emphasis upon the historical background of curriculum construction is sound. It is impossible to study intelligently the curriculum in operation without knowing the genealogy of that curriculum.[4] Meanwhile we may note that Rugg continues the account above in a thrilling, vividly written chapter which contrasts the vigorous drama of American life with the quietly conservative curriculum.

A great nation of fabulous wealth and power springs up; an agricultural civilization changes to an industrial one; political and social relationships change profoundly— the whole face of life changes! New problems and relationships of complex and terrifying import appear. And what of the curriculum—the agency which is to prepare

---

[3] Harold Rugg, "The School Curriculum and the Drama of American Life," in *Curriculum Making: Past and Present,* Twenty-sixth Yearbook, Part I, National Society for the Study of Education (Bloomington, Ill., Public School Publishing Co., 1927), Ch. I, extracts from pp. 3-16. Quoted by permission of the Society.

[4] Abbreviated summary outlines of this background will be found in William H. Burton, *In-troduction to Education* (New York, Appleton-Century, 1934), Chs. 9, 10, 15-17. Also in the first edition of the volume here revised, Appendix, pp. 965-969.

A more extended summary of historical background will be found in the Twenty-sixth Yearbook, *op. cit.,* and especially in Harold O. Rugg, *American Life and the School Curriculum* (Boston, Ginn, 1936).

for life? What part did the school play either in shaping the new civilization, interpreting it, or even understanding and preparing for it?

> ... the lazy giant—the public school—sleeps peacefully on, unaware of shaping issues! [5]

About all that can be said is that the "grandeur that was Greece and the glory that was Rome" persisted calm and undisturbed in the curriculum. To be sure there were fragmentary, limited, local efforts to adjust to new demands. Local opposition was, however, very strong. Some of these were reasonably successful, but no movement of scope and power emerged.

Ten years pass, and in 1937 there appears this paragraph: [6]

> In recent years, the school curriculum has been a focal point of criticism, conflict, and activity. Out of this welter is emerging a new and modern curriculum which differs in many fundamental respects from the placidly accepted curriculum of a few years ago. . . .
>
> The modern curriculum is an outgrowth and expression of the principles of democracy and is intended to aid in the achievement of democratic ideals. As the concept of democracy is expanded and altered in the presence of shifting social and technological conditions, so should the school curriculum which serves it be modified and revised in order that its functional values may be maintained at a maximum. The experimental philosophy underlying the modern curriculum further explains its experimental nature and its continuous state of change. The psychology of the modern curriculum is distinguished by its emphasis on pupil purposes, maturation levels, integrating experiences, and the personality effects of all aspects of school life.

The prophecy by Rugg that democratic American life and the nature of the learner would become basic considerations is borne out by Mackenzie's report. Curriculums, furthermore, are being basically reconstructed or developed instead of being merely rearranged.

Certain modern critics lag behind curriculum development. The new functional curriculum which is emerging and which is in operation in many places has brought about an odd situation in regard to public and professional criticism. Criticism, historically, was directed in the main at outmoded, static, and incompetent courses or curriculums. Valuable criticisms of this type are still heard but a new type of criticism is also emerging. Criticisms are today directed sometimes at the most sound, modern, useful, functional type of course and curriculum. The curriculum in many places, perhaps for the first time in history, is now definitely in advance of public understanding. The reasons for this, the dangers, and the corrections of the situation are important to all who exercise educational leadership. Let us examine a brief summary.

Current criticisms of modern education, its curriculum and procedures, appear in numerous articles and books. Argument has raged in both lay and professional periodicals and in the daily press. The controversy has now reached the stage in which adequate summaries of scattered materials are appearing. Extensive summaries [7] are readily available to all interested students and field workers. Because of this and in the interests of space conservation, the discussion below

---

[5] Twenty-sixth Yearbook, *op. cit.*, p. 12. Quoted by permission of the Society.

[6] Gordon N. Mackenzie, "Supervision Confronts a Changing Curriculum," *California Journal of Elementary Education* (February, 1937), pp. 136-143.

[7] *Adventure in American Education,* the story of the Eight-Year Study in five volumes: *The Story of the Eight-Year Plan; Exploring the Curriculum; Appraising and Recording Student Progress; Did They Succeed in College?; Thirty Schools Tell Their Story* (New York, Harper, from 1942-1945).

J. Paul Leonard and Alvin C. Eurich, *An Evaluation of Modern Education* (New York, Appleton-Century-Crofts, 1942). A well-written, easily read volume summarizing 154 investigations. Note the excellent bibliography. Probably the best single volume available.

William H. Burton, *The Guidance of Learning Activities,* 2nd ed. (New York, Appleton-Century-Crofts, 1952). Brief, easily read summaries. See Chs. 3 and 4, particularly pp. 81-89 and 112-120; Chs. 7 and 8, particularly pp. 234-239. Note bibliographies.

is sharply curtailed. The points outlined are stated without the usual limiting or qualifying particulars which would develop in detailed discussion. There is no intention to be dogmatic but merely to summarize in brief space the major points derived from a voluminous literature.

The principal criticisms widely voiced may be reduced to a few sentences. The modern school:

1. Does not teach the "3 R's"; does not give adequate grounding in the "fundamentals."
2. Is soft (there is no discipline; the child does as he pleases); lets "Willie express himself" but does not make him obey.
3. Lacks standards.
4. Is not producing leaders.

These criticisms of the modern school, did the critics but know it, are more applicable to the traditional school! The typical traditional curriculum to which many wish to "return," lags far, far behind our scientific knowledge about the learner and his learning processes, far behind our knowledge about adapting the curriculum to social needs. The curriculum for which many plead is actually formal, static, and badly out of step with modern knowledge. The modern curriculum, in contrast, is far from being "easy" or "soft," or neglectful of the fundamentals. It is clearly in line with huge bodies of valid facts derived from basic scientific research in biology, physiology, pediatrics, anthropology, psychiatry, sociology, not to mention psychology and education itself.

Criticism concerning the "3 R's" is so common and so widespread that before considering the factual answer below, it might be well to ponder the following counter-statement: *Many schools, far from neglecting the "3 R's," have been so preoccupied with them that they have neglected the vitally important outcomes of citizenship, social competence, and the ability to be secure in a changing, dynamic civilization.*

The four criticisms listed above may be accompanied by four suggestions made by the critics.

1. Let us "return to the '3 R's,'" return to the "fundamentals."
2. Let us "get tough" in disciplining youth; make children do as they are told; hold them to difficult distasteful tasks and "make them like it."
3. Let us return to the reputable standards of yesteryear, to the stiff, uniform, academic standards of mastery of specified subject matter; let us have "no nonsense"; let us have done with this "activity" or "experience" curriculum.
4. Let us return to stiff, ruthless competition between pupils so that leaders will emerge as the weaker ones fail.

Before taking up the more fundamental aspects, four quick summary answers may be made:

1. The school has never at any time, anywhere, deserted the "3 R's," the fundamentals. They are taught in every school in the land.
2. The modern definition of discipline and the scientific knowledge about discipline are flatly contradictory to popular belief. The development of self-discipline is quite different from the maintenance of order through repressive "discipline." Development of self-discipline is an inescapable necessity in a democracy, and it cannot be developed without opportunity, to exercise choice and to make mistakes. A very different school régime results which disturbs uninformed persons.
3. The traditional school never at any time, anywhere met its own "stiff" standards. The unreality of these standards played a part in the elimination of 50 per cent of all pupils early in the grades. The fact learnings constituting the standards were soon forgotten. *The very recurrence of the criticisms indicates failure to meet these standards.*
Worse than that, the traditional school completely neglected far more important types of learning, namely developments of behavior controls in the form of understandings, attitudes, appreciations, and so forth. It completely neglected creative education.
4. The modern definition of leadership, the type of leadership in the modern world, and the scientific knowledge about its development are flatly contradictory to popular beliefs. The modern school develops better and more rounded leaders than the old.

The causes for these erroneous criticisms are, some of them, simple; others are more complex and important. The simple reasons for the blunders in judgment are in general:

1. The critics do not know the facts, particularly concerning pupil achievement in the "3 R's," the development of more important learning outcomes, the development of leadership, the development of creative expression.

2. Critics fall into certain extremely simple logical errors:

   a. The highly selected group of pupils of the earlier period and their achievement is compared with the extremely heterogeneous group of the present, "all the children of all the people" and their achievement.
   b. A bright adult from a selected group is compared with an average or dull child now in school.
   c. Freak cases, extreme illustrations, gossip, cartoons are accepted as evidence.
   d. Individual cases are used: "I knew a boy," "I tried that and it won't work."

3. Nostalgic longing for the return of conditions which never existed in the first place is common among forty-year-old adolescents. The "good old days" were better, women were fairer, winters were hardier, flowers bloomed better—but it wasn't so!

The more serious reasons for criticism of modern curriculums are highly important and deserve attention from all educational workers. The errors of the lay critic rest in part surely upon the failure of professional leaders to explain modern educational science and to keep school patrons abreast of developments.

1. The lay public and less well-trained teachers are upset by the uncertainty and insecurity which inevitably accompanies periods of great social change.

The world is unquestionably in such a period. A new civilization is emerging, with its inevitable dislocation of settled beliefs and ways of doing things. Criticism is directed at all new beliefs and practices in government, in the industrial world, and in the social order generally. The curriculum of the school receives its share. The real cause is not weakness in the curriculum but the basic fear of uncertainty and insecurity. Teachers and the lay public all *know* the "3 R's," they *know* the multiplication table. They are sure of these, they feel safe and secure. When, however, they tackle problem-solving, teaching to think, free group discussion, the use of varied activities within a class group, they are frightened. There is no such stability to group discussion as there is to the multiplication tables or the capitals of the states! The management of group discussion and of varied activities is far different from listening to rote repetition of the tables! Certain persons are upset and plead for a return to simpler days.[8]

2. The lay public and many teachers do not believe that certain learning activities and outcomes which are primary in modern curriculums, really belong to youth and to childhood.

   a. The development of judgment, the power to chose and decide.
   b. The exercise of initiative and responsibility.
   c. The ability to plan and to develop purposeful activity.
   d. The power of self-discipline.

The public knows that a baby cannot learn to walk without practicing. No one can learn to skate or dance without practice. But when it comes to exercising judgment and learning to exercise judgment, then "children are too young." "Mother knows best" and will make all decisions for the child. Children must be taught to "do as they are told," to obey. Then all of a sudden when he grows up and becomes an adult the child is expected to exercise judgment and to be self-controlled.

All the learnings which are so important in the modern curriculum are matters of

[8] The writer is indebted for certain points and apt phrases to Dr. E. H. Reeder of the Univ. of Illinois and to Dr. Ruth Cunningham, executive secretary of the Association for Supervision and Curriculum Development. Unpublished addresses, March 24, 1945, before the Harvard Teachers Association annual convention. Similar material is now available in several later sources.

growth. Development should begin in the nursery. The "fundamentals," the "3 R's" themselves are obviously developmental, increasing in efficiency with continued practice and use. Judgment, self-control, the acceptance of responsibility can be learned in no other way than through opportunity and practice from the beginning. The public is honestly convinced that these are adult level techniques and are no part of the curriculum for childhood; the curriculum should stick to giving facts. These views are flatly contradicted by all known facts.

3. The lay public and many less well-trained teachers are completely mistaken in their belief about the nature of mind and of learning.

The following statement is admittedly oversimplified but ample extension is easily available. The average citizen's beliefs about mind and learning are usually naïve and inarticulate but can be described in part as follows:

 a. The mind is something like a cold storage plant, like a clothes closet, or other storehouse, reservoir, or depository.
 b. Parents and teachers fill this storehouse with facts; we place them there and let them stay there.
 c. The facts and ideas stored there, if they were well taught in the first place, will remain good and usable indefinitely; they can be called up for use anytime and will function as "good as new."
 d. The mind is a limited space, therefore we had better stick to fundamentals and not clutter up this limited area with other things.

These ideas again, no matter how sincerely held, are all flatly contradicted by voluminous evidence. The persistence of (c) even with trained thinkers is a mystery, since everyday experience contradicts it continuously. The mind and learning are dynamic, not static. *The things learned must be used to retain their vigor.*

A few criticisms are malicious. Educational leaders should face the fact that certain criticisms, worded as those above,

emanate from powerful persons with vested interests. There is clearly the attempt, constant through history, to curtail the enlightenment of the average citizen. These appear chiefly in the daily press and in the publications of various "associations" dedicated to saving the schools. These criticisms must be met by courageous counterattack prepared by associations of professional educators.

The responsibility of educational leaders concerning these criticisms. The basic reason for the prevalence of misunderstanding and of nonsensical criticisms of improved curriculums and methods of teaching, is the failure of educational leaders to provide for adequate community participation in developing educational programs. The value of community participation has been made amply clear in preceding chapters. The facts about education and learning have not been presented properly or adequately to the public. Presentation of factual background is even more important when participation is lacking. Earlier in the current era of improvement some leaders failed to present any evidences concerning the effectiveness of new developments. Today the situation is reversed, many critics failing to present any evidence at all. Today there is no excuse for failure by anyone to present data. The methods of deriving data concerning current programs are well known. A huge volume of validated background material is now available, some of it derived directly from ongoing programs, and some of it, as indicated earlier, from half a dozen related scientific fields.

Criticisms of new developments are likely to clear up as leaders take the public completely into their confidence and explain in simple, nontechnical terms the discoveries of modern science regarding education. This does not mean that we employ that barbarous term and concept, "selling" the schools to the public. It means to employ that basic necessity in democratic society, wide participation by the public in the actual development of the program. A public relations program as a part of the total project is legitimate.

Participation will not only remove uncertainty by substituting understanding but will familiarize the public with the psychology and process of change. The inevitability of change in a dynamic society, the principles and techniques useful in overcoming inertia, in stimulating social invention, in changing beliefs, customs, and habits, become familiar. Fear of the unknown and uncertain is thus reduced.

An excellent type of competent, informed, and dynamic leadership is required. Failing a reasonable degree of adequate leadership, the efforts of the inert, the uninformed, or the malicious will succeed in part.

Continuous criticism a sign of health. A minority of school officers and public leaders who are reactionaries of the "congenital" or "glandular" type, look upon the historic series of criticisms with smug satisfaction. "Improvement of the curriculum is just another passing fad." "Radicals and dissatisfied persons alone wish to tamper with the time-honored subject matter." "We, however, know the eternal verities." "We stick to what we are doing." "The curriculum does not ever change greatly." Another group of uncritical individuals is sometimes discouraged by the criticisms. "We do not make much progress, do we?" "We are just where we were."

The more informed attacks, on the contrary, are excellent signs of progress. Reactionaries and superficial observers alike overlook the fact that it is a different curriculum which each time is under criticism. Criticism, both negative and positive, careful analyses of curriculums in the light of life needs, and constructive effort toward improvement constitute an unending series of rotating activities. Each curriculum severely criticized was an improvement over the one just before, and so on through the centuries. The continuous, critical analysis of curriculums by competent scholars, instead of affording conservatives an opportu-

nity to stand pat, to "remain true to the fundamentals," does, in fact, supply the best evidence showing why it is impossible to stand pat.

Historical changes in curriculum procedures summarized. The basic changes which have taken place in curriculum principles and leadership have been presented in considerable detail in several places. The following is an extremely abbreviated summary:

1. *Change in Aim and Purpose*
   a. The aim is no longer to train some for leadership, many as followers, and all in the formal routines of democracy; it is toward both leadership and service for all as ability and occasion permit, toward a broad, functional belief and practice of democracy instead of a limited, formal, concept.
   b. The aim is no longer mastery of an abstract, verbal, and intellectual curriculum but is growth and development of the individual.

2. *Change in Orientation*
   The almost exclusive interest in the past is giving way to a concern for the present and the future. (The wisdom of the past, the cultural heritage, will be utilized far more effectively within a living situation than when imposed without a reason apparent to the learner.)

3. *Change in Content*
   a. From classical and traditional subject matter to functional materials and experiences dealing with current problems.
   b. From material to be accepted to material which stimulates independent thought and judgment.
   c. From emphasis upon study habits to emphasis upon work habits.

4. *Change in Organization*
   a. Elementary level: typical subject organizations are giving way to projects, centers of interest, subject-matter units, and to functional or experience units.
   b. Secondary level: a functional core is appearing which extends general education upward. The special subjects are being reorganized in the light of present-day needs. New subjects and areas of experience are being added.

5. *Change in Standards*
   The measurement of mastery of adult selected subject-matter skills at given intervals is giving way to continuous evaluation of pupil growth in desirable knowledges, skills, understandings, attitudes, behavior patterns, and so forth.
6. *Change in Methods of Development*
   a. From exclusive leadership by pro-fessors, subject specialists, administrative officers, toward co-operative leadership of these and many other persons, teachers, all school officers, child psychologists, laymen, and various specialists.
   b. From arm-chair, scissors, and paste to co-operative development and experimentation.

Section 2

A BRIEF SUMMARY OF REASONS SHOWING THE NECESSITY FOR CONTINUOUS CURRICULUM REORGANIZATION

A sketchy outline of major causes is all that is possible here. Students or field workers unaware of the necessary background are urged to avail themselves of the ample literature. To engage in educational leadership without reasonable knowledge in this area is to be intellectually reckless.

The gap between life and the curriculum must be narrowed. The one fundamental reason for curriculum revision stands out starkly. Curriculums must be under constant revision in order to keep pace with the constantly changing needs of the individual and of society. Education is one of the basic institutions and social forces through which society and civilization are perpetuated, and through which the individual may realize his own unique possibilities. Education is to introduce succeeding generations into the culture surrounding them, prepare them to live within it, and, more important, prepare them to participate in improving that culture. Society is not fixed and eternal; it is dynamic and emergent. Inventions, social and mechanical, new alignments of wealth and power, change the structure of society. Old needs and activities disappear; new ones emerge. The "fundamentals" of an education for participation in a simple, isolated, pioneer, agrarian society, are futile as preparation for participation in a complex, interdependent, urbanized, industrial, civilization. The "3 R's" are an important but small part of the truly necessary "fundamental" curriculum.

Curriculums have always lagged behind the needs of society, behind scientific knowledge about how to meet those needs. The lag does not matter much during settled, sterile periods, but becomes of very great importance in times of crisis in civilization. Survival of a civilization could conceivably be involved. Revision of the curriculum could easily become the critical factor in the "race between education and disaster."

The curriculum for the selected few must be expanded to meet the needs of "all the children of all the people." One of the aims of the American dream is that of bringing education to "all the children of all the people." Progressive tightening of the compulsory attendance laws succeeded in bringing practically all the children of all the people into the elementary school during the first quarter of this century. The events from 1929 to 1935 brought approximately 70 per cent of the possible secondary population into the schools. Large groups of persons appeared in school who had hitherto not desired or who had been denied an education. In addition there came the lame, the halt, and the blind, the tubercular, the delinquent, the mentally deficient. For the first time in the history of civilization a school system was called upon to educate *all*, not merely the able and willing.

The traditional school was organized largely for those (1) wishing to attend, (2) possessing interest and ability, and (3) probably going on in school and backed in their desire by the homes. Into this school organized for a small number of select students came hordes who (1) did not want to attend, (2) had little interest in or ability for the curriculum as then organized, (3) were not going on and who were not backed by the home. What happened? The school was entirely ignorant of the needs, desires, or abilities of the new horde, and besides had nothing to offer them if it had known their needs. The traditional formal curriculum suited to bright pupils preparing for higher institutions was set before the new groups. They could take it or leave it. For a long period they left it. School was an unhappy place, with early elimination for large numbers.

The relationship of this to bad citizenship, to delinquency, and to many lesser ills in social life was eventually recognized. The schools of the United States accepted this great challenge—and have been engaged ever since in remaking curriculums to serve new groups and new needs; to improve the offerings for older groups.

Educational research stimulated reorganization. A large literature is devoted to research and its contributions, hence but a few sentences will be used here. A half century of research and child study has developed a truly huge body of material about children and adolescents, about their growth and development, about their learning activities, about their social and emotional development, and about individual differences among them. The personal-social-moral development of the individual is as important, perhaps more important, than the narrowly intellectual development. Growth in understanding of a dynamic, interdependent society is an important part of the education of all individuals. Large numbers of new "subjects," and later "areas of experience" have been added, of necessity, to the curriculum.

The retention of traditional subjects and subject organization is not historically nor functionally sound on all levels. Inquiry into the typical subject organization of current courses and curriculums throws additional light upon the problem. What is the origin of "subjects"? How did the subject form originate? How was content for given subjects selected? Why the particular subjects now constituting the curriculum? How did Latin and home economics come to be offered in the same school? Why are some subjects elective, others required?

Subjects were organized by bright, mature, adult scholars who abstracted the necessary materials from real life. Human knowledge originated in the necessary activities connected with daily life. Early man while securing food, clothing, and shelter, evolved skills and discovered facts. Primitive minds did not separate knowledge or skill from the occasion in which it was used. Brilliant intellects later made the separation. Number could be separated from the things numbered. Numbers could be manipulated quite apart from the real things from which they had been derived. Arithmetic was organized by minds capable of abstract intellectual endeavor. Geometry, grammar, even such living things as literature and history eventually were widely separated from their origins. This is an interesting psycho-historical phenomenon.

The logic of subject organization is that of the material itself, not the dynamic logic of the immature mind learning new materials. The separate subjects, products of expert abstract thinking, of high-grade adult intellect, were then given to little children of immature intellect and with necessarily limited life experience! The typical subject curriculum in the elementary school is a patent absurdity! Revision movements have gone a long way toward a lifelike, unified curriculum. The particular subjects now in use in the secondary school were once directly useful in the real life of those who studied those subjects. Latin secured its place in the curriculum originally for the very same reason that consumer education, biology for life, propaganda analysis, the study of comparative economic systems, and courses on the family, now ask inclusion: usefulness in the real life of the times. He who clamors for the retention of the sacred elements of the present curriculum or who demands that Latin or geometry be *required* of all pupils is not merely ignorant of history, he is ignorant of the origin and nature of geometry as such. (Let it be noted here that the foregoing is not an argument for the total exclusion of Latin, geometry, or other older subjects. The argument is for realignment of the curriculum with the life needs of various groups of persons.) No list of subjects can possibly contain the elements of general education once and for all. No list of subjects has ever persisted indefinitely— despite the efforts of many intrenched routinists! The great developments in the secondary curriculum in the last fifteen years are in part due to greater knowledge of the simple structure of the curriculum divisions.

Studying the course of study and the curriculum in action are not passing fads. They are permanent and fundamental activities of the educational scene in the United States. The general movement is rapidly becoming more effective, the results more successful.

Obstacles and difficulties are present. The glamor and prestige of time-honored (and shopworn) curriculums persists. The tendency of human activities and institutions to crystallize operates in education as elsewhere. Inertia, comfort in easy routines, the security of tenure, all operate to aggravate what has been called the professional disease of teachers, the reluctance to study one's own business. The nature and administration of education develops an attitude of almost complete indifference to responsibility for results on the part of many. The distance between the classroom and proof of its effects upon the learner is a serious difficulty. Improvement in these areas will come through improvement in teacher training and selection, improvement of inservice training with its development of cooperative activities, and eventually through elevation of professional attitudes and standards. The modern movement toward continuous evaluation of results as a part of the ongoing instructional program will reduce the gap between teaching and its results.

The pace within the curriculum movement does, however, accelerate almost as we watch it. Inertia is no longer respectable and receives less tolerance. The obstructionist is treated with more decision if he persists after opportunity to study and participate. Experimentation, study groups, regional conferences, workshops are increasingly used. City, state, and national programs are emerging.

Section 3

BRIEF SUMMARY OF IMPORTANT[9] DEVELOPMENTS IN THE UNITED STATES

The history of efforts to change the curriculum in the United States. The early history of the curriculum from Colonial times until approximately 1895 is the story of the evolution of the traditional, typical subject curriculum. The curriculum became a se-

[9] *Note:* Texts in education are constantly criticized as containing unlimited, unnecessary, tedious repetition. Authors are doubtless led into this repetition by a natural desire for adequacy and coherence.

To treat adequately the historical background of curriculum development would necessitate two, if not three, chapters. This would be out of place in a supervision volume, but more important, the mate-rial (a) should already be known to competent supervisors and advanced students, and (b) is easily available in accessible references. Hence the authors have adopted the device of including here an extremely skeletonized outline. Any supervisor or student who is not reasonably familiar with the material available in the literature is urged to do some rapid reading before going further with the supervisory problem and the curriculum.

quence of graded units through which, theoretically, children passed one unit per year. The pupils were roughly in chronological groups and the curriculum supposedly adjusted to their maturity levels. Actually the curriculum was formal, logical, and adapted neither to the children nor to life.

Early demands for reform. Even before this traditional curriculum was perfected it was under criticism. As early as 1870 effort was made to break the lock-step in the grades. In 1874-1875 attacks were made on the lack of articulation between school divisions. From 1888 critical analysis and suggestions for improvement were continuous, increasing steadily in number and vigor. The Committee of Ten, formed to consider some of the criticisms, turned in a reactionary report in 1893 which retarded progress. Otherwise most of the analyses were forward-looking.

The writings and addresses of W. T. Harris, Francis W. Parker, President Eliot, President Harper, and John Dewey argued for shortening and enriching the elementary curriculum, eliminating much drill material, introducing stimulating materials earlier, adapting to the nature of the learner and to the needs of life.

The increasing effect of the compulsory attendance laws made the problem very acute, since the traditional curriculum was even less fitted to the many types of children now being brought into school for the first time.

The application of scientific methods to measuring outcomes and to the analysis of learning difficulties gave objective evidence of some of the glaring defects of the traditional curriculum.

The indictment of the traditional curriculum. Out of all this emerged a country-wide indictment of the 8-4-4 graded school with its lock-step sequence of logically arranged subject matter. It was said that too much time was consumed in educating people, life needs were not met, individual dif-

ferences were neglected, gifted children were retarded, articulation and transition from division to division were faulty. It was held that the elementary curriculum could be shortened two years and at the same time enriched; that the secondary curriculum could begin two years earlier, provide better for differences in ability and interest, be shortened, enriched, and organized into one coherent unit. The necessity for lifelike learning situations was continuously stressed.

Efforts at improvement. 1. *Administrative tinkering.* The first efforts at improvement were naturally by school administrators. This resulted in much tinkering with classification, gradation, irregular promotion periods, differentiated courses, two- and three-track systems, individualized instruction, and the like. This was a period of reshuffling and rearranging, but not of reorganizing the curriculum.

2. *Reorganization by subject-matter committees.* Numerous committees of subject-matter specialists, later including psychologists and educational authorities, attempted to write new curriculums. A very large number of committee reports on various subjects and school divisions are available. The committee technique has contributed in various ways both good and bad. The best known of these committees are the Committee of Ten (1893), the Committee of Fifteen on Elementary Education (1895), the Committees on Economy of Time which made four reports at various times, the Commission on the Reorganization of Secondary Education (1920). Other committees in more recent times are the Committee on Mathematical Requirements, the Classical Investigation, the Modern Language Study, and various others devoted to history and the social studies. Some of these committees were organized by the National Education Association or by its subsidiary departments. Others were either organized or financed by the various foundations in this country.

In classes where students are not reasonably familiar with these committees, reports on the strong and weak points of this technique, class reports should be made.

3. *The application of scientific methods to curriculum construction.* Considerable impetus was given the whole problem through the use of so-called scientific methods of attacking curriculum problems. This technique is illustrated and critically evaluated in Chapter 12 of this volume. Again the results were both good and bad. Much valuable and reliable guidance was secured, but there was an unfortunate tendency toward a narrow and limited view of the curriculum. Hence there evolved a counter-emphasis upon the philosophic consideration of values, aims, and desired outcomes.

4. *Modern co-operative curriculum construction.* The foregoing concepts and procedures dominated the field until approximately 1930, and particularly during the 1920's. The aim was to produce a course of study deemed by experts to be sound scientifically and philosophically, and then to set about the task of seeing that teachers used it effectively in developing their individual curriculums. Flexibility appeared; but, in the main, prescription of minimum essentials was dominant.

A new type of activity appeared about 1930. The organismic psychology changed our basic conceptions about the learner and his processes. Three principles of great import began to operate: continuity of growth; experience as the method of learning; and integration as continuing aim.

The principle of growth emphasized the flexible, experimental, emergent nature of the individual and of society; the continuity of the stream of experience. This made for continuous curriculum revision. Experience as the method of learning threw the many varied learning activities operating in real experience into sharp contrast with the limited formal activities of memorizing, drilling, doing tasks under assignment, and so forth. Integration emphasized the wholeness and unity of individuals and of society and made prominent the reciprocal interaction between the learner and the learning situation. The demand for maximum lifelikeness in learning situations was intensified. The inevitability of expanding the learning situation into the surrounding community became apparent.

The emerging and expanding understandings led directly to two concepts of great importance. First, the terms *course of study* and *curriculum* could not be used interchangeably. Curriculum revision is not the same thing as rewriting the course of study. Second, the individual classroom, the individual teacher, and the individual community school were recognized as the starting points. The co-operative concept and practice increasingly came to dominate. Curriculum improvement starts with effort to improve what is going on in individual classrooms and schools. All types of educational workers, teachers, subject-matter specialists, psychologists, supervisors, administrators, laymen, and others work together under democratic leadership. The technique employed is that of participatory group endeavor.

Appendix B

◆•◆•◆•◆•◆•◆•◆•◆•◆••

Curriculum Issues and Questions for Discussion

INSTRUCTORS AND STUDENTS often wish to engage in general, introductory discussion of curriculum problems. Excellent background material can be developed while we are leading up to a definite analysis of a given situation.

QUESTIONS SUGGESTED FOR IN- TRODUCTORY DISCUSSIONS OF CURRICULUM DEVELOPMENT

1. Why is the traditional curriculum, used with seeming success for years, now under such criticism, analysis, and change?
   a. How did the gap between curriculum and life develop?
   b. How did the gap between curriculum and learner develop?
   c. What are the chief general techniques for reducing these gaps?
   d. What is meant by the term, "evolutionary, emergent social order" and what has that to do with the curriculum?
2. Is the curriculum to be regarded as an instrument of social progress?
   a. What are the techniques for discovering social trends?
   b. What are the techniques for discussing controversial problems?
   c. What are the techniques in general designed to enlighten learners concerning propaganda, pressure groups, and so forth?
3. Are the general and specific aims of education, the content of the curriculum, to be determined with some definiteness in advance of actual teaching-learning situations?
   a. Should the curriculum be based upon the objectives, standards, needs and purposes which are the fabric of or-

ganized society, or upon the objectives, standards, needs and purposes which are the fabric of the individual's life?
   b. Should the emphasis be primarily upon maintaining group solidarity and security, or upon creative self-realization?
   c. Should the emphasis be upon general or special education—that is, upon general culture or vocational efficiency?
4. Is all, none, or a given part of the curriculum to be required of all learners, regardless of origin, present status, and very probable destiny?
   a. What shall be the nature of the required core, if any?
   b. What proportion—roughly—should be common and required, and what elective? What will be the effect, if any, of local conditions on your answer here?
   c. What shall be the bases of such differentiations as are provided—IQ, special ability or interest, probable destiny, and so forth?
   d. Should all members of society have free access to education without limitation other than capacity to grow? (Stated negatively—should education be limited for dull children, for poor children, for children of working classes, and so forth?)
   e. Should preparation for the next higher school be considered, ever, never, sometimes?
   f. What is the place of the so-called extracurriculum material?
5. How shall the curriculum be organized —scope and sequence determined?
   a. What are the strengths and weaknesses of organizing by subjects; through correlation; through fusion;

by units, themes, centers of interest, social functions, and so forth?
  b. What is meant by integration?
  c. How have time allotments been determined in the past? How will this problem be affected by some of the newer types of organization?
6. How shall the curriculum content be selected?
  a. What is meant by subject matter? Is subject matter still necessary?
  b. What is meant by activities? Will they take the place of subject matter?
  c. What are the criteria under which to select subject matter and activities for the curriculum?
  d. What are the techniques for securing the subject matter and activities?
  e. What techniques have played a large part in the past and still interfere with modern techniques?
7. What is the nature of experience?
  a. What is the difference between direct and vicarious experience?
  b. What curriculum problems are involved in the matter of direct vs. vicarious experience?
8. What is the nature of the true and desired outcome or outcomes of learning experiences?
  a. How should the outcomes be stated, both as objectives and as actual outcomes? Is there any difference in this item between the elementary and the secondary schools?
  b. How should pupil achievement, progress, growth, be marked, recorded, or reported?
  c. Should the curriculum (course of study) contain or suggest tests and techniques for determining progress, evaluating achievement, diagnosing learning difficulties, and so forth?
9. What should be the general procedure in reconstructing (or constructing anew) the curriculum?
  a. What general principles should guide, and general techniques be used?
  b. What part should be played by teacher committees, administrators and supervisors, a curriculum consultant, subject-matter experts, psychologists, and others? The public?
  c. What should be the place of experimental try-out, of reëxamining, and so forth?

  d. What length of time may safely be set aside within which to complete a curriculum revision in a given situation?
10. What are the criteria for evaluating a curriculum?
11. What is the relation of the teacher-training institutions to these problems of curriculum construction?

Basic issues in the curriculum as distinguished from practical tasks. The list is not arranged in any significant order.

1. To aid in a change in social regard for the various curriculums, that is, a change in prestige values attached to various offerings. This is a long-time problem of change in social values, beliefs, and values.

2. To face up to problems raised by the class structure of our society.

(We have so far asserted our traditional democratic faith in a relatively classless society or one with very easy mobility upward, but we have operated in large high schools, curriculums obviously based on class origins and probable destinies; in small high schools, curriculums designed to serve but one class and that a small one.)

Should we continue to operate as we do; asserting one thing and doing another? Or should we openly develop an educational system which accepts class divisions? Or should we bring the problem into the open and try seriously to develop curriculums which provide necessary common experience for all with defensible differentiation? This leads squarely into Problems Nos. 3 and 4, and indirectly to 5 and 6.

3. To develop common experiences within the so-called "cosmopolitan" secondary school. All pupils regardless of types and levels of ability, of social class distinctions, of probable destinies should have common experiences for reasons that are obvious.

To develop materials and experiences through which the non-visual-verbal learners may have adequate contact with the aesthetic, literary, and historical materials and traditions of their culture.

To develop materials and experiences through which the typical visual-verbal learner may have adequate contact with reality, that is, with things, tools, and processes.

4. To develop democratic methods of providing differentiation (eventually) within the common educational structure for those who

are going into the professions, the skilled technologies, the semi-skilled, and unskilled occupations. (Conant and many others.)

5. To reorganize the typical secondary school-college sequence in the light of the two foregoing points. New terminal points are being suggested; saving of time is being demanded; new alignments of offerings.

6. To clarify the place of trade or skilled vocational training in the public schools.

7. To provide for active participation in real-life affairs, to break away from informational and observational preparation for life experiences.

To develop in conjunction with the public, the. employing class, and the labor unions the necessary work experiences.

8. To what extent shall the curriculum indicate acceptance by the learners of intraschool and extraschool régimes; how far indicate discontent and protest, even defiance of such of the régimes as interfere with that degree of self-expression compatible with Judaic-Graeco-Christian and democratic ideals concerning the individual; with that degree of self-expression necessary for mental hygiene.

9. To develop materials and bring about popular acceptance for
   a. The development of international outlook and world-mindedness, together with patriotism toward our national group.
   b. The study of man and his institutions.
   c. The study of personality, its nature and development.
   d. The principles and skills of thinking.
   e. The development of moral and spiritual values.
   f. The comparative study of religion (on proper maturity levels).

10. To determine the relative merits of a curriculum which permits wide and free experimentation with materials and methods, and one which is rather closely organized to be followed as closely as good judgment indicates.

11. To modify and restate outcomes, adding to principles, facts, and skills the more recently emphasized understandings, insights, appreciations, attitudes, other personal-social-moral traits.

12. To reorganize the educational situation to utilize the educational functions of agencies outside the school; to recognize and use what the pupil actually learns outside the school.

13. To determine the relative merits of reasonably rapid revision through experimental and tentative evaluations, and a policy of slower evolutionary adjustment.

14. To what extent and on what levels may the curriculum be formulated by the learners, to what extent and on what levels formulated for them? That is, how to achieve a functioning balance between the felt needs, purposes and standards of the learner, and the objectives, standards, and necessities implicit in society and in the institutional nature of the school as agent of society.

15. To what extent may the curriculum be determined locally, to what extent by the state?

16. To develop a continuous articulated curriculum from beginning through various institutions on college level.

17. To develop teacher training in line with the emergent curriculum.

18. Should the curriculum (the school) be an instrument for social reconstruction?

19. Shall the curriculum recognize the problems involved in propaganda and pressure groups and attempt to handle them; or shall it remain aloof and attempt merely to exclude propaganda and sidestep pressure efforts; or shall it indulge in "safe" discussions of these items?

20. What stand shall the curriculum take on "indoctrination" in general? (First, what definition shall be accepted for indoctrination?) What shall be the attitude in specific reference to "indoctrination" of the principles, institutions, and aspirations of democracy?

21. How far shall the curriculum modify the traditional symbols of achievement (marks, diplomas) in favor of more truthful and realistic recognitions of actual conduct controls manifested by pupils?

A different line of attack is indicated in the following questions developed by Alice Miel.[1]

1. Is a given constellation of habits in a school making for a desirable economy of effort and providing a useful basis of continuity or does it represent a crystallization that is deterring constructive action?

2. Is curriculum change proceeding rapidly enough to prevent further crystallization and to guarantee sufficient accomplishment yet not too rapidly to threaten the security of teachers, parents, and children?

[1] Alice Miel, *Changing the Curriculum: A Social Process* (New York, Appleton-Century-Crofts, 1946), pp. 193-194.

3. How much difference in educational philosophy and teaching procedures can be tolerated from school to school and teacher to teacher? How can those differences be minimized most safely and effectively?

4. How can common goals and values be arrived at most quickly and genuinely?

5. Shall teachers, parents, and children be encouraged to express their current discontents, whether petty or not, or will this merely heighten an existing tendency to find fault with everything?

6. How will initial interest in curriculum change best be secured in a given school-community situation?

7. What internal organization is most satisfactory for a given situation?

8. Will the method of demonstration of the effectiveness of new ways by the school faculty to the community be most effective under given circumstances or is it better to secure community understanding and co-operation from the start in a particular instance?

9. When should an expert from the outside be brought into the picture and how should his services be utilized on a given occasion?

10. Under what circumstances should bulletins and written announcements replace group meetings?

11. Under what circumstances may a certain individual be given opportunities to practice techniques, such as those of leading a discussion, at the possible expense of group accomplishment?

12. To what extent should educational leaders bow before the unquestioned power of groups and individuals in the community?

13. How shall the matter of authority be managed in a community where teachers, the board of education, and the school patrons apparently expect the administration and supervisors to operate on an authoritarian basis?

14. How shall time be found for co-operative curriculum development without lengthening the teacher's working day unduly?

15. How can the status leader exert strong leadership without making others unhealthily dependent?

Another set of questions useful in initiating the survey of a community as part of a curriculum program follows:

1. What characteristics do the boys and girls for whom this program is being designed possess as individuals which influence what they should be taught and how they should be taught?

2. What is the nature of the community in which these pupils are living? How does it influence (a) what they will learn without the school's aid; (b) what they need to learn in school; (c) what their attitude toward school is?

3. To judge from this background, what are the specific behavior patterns which it should be the school's job to help pupils to develop? What skills, habits, dispositions, appreciations are to be fostered?

4. What is the nature of the vocational and avocational pursuits in which these young people are likely to engage in when they leave school and for which they ought to be prepared by the school?

5. What learning experiences are available and can be used most effectively to reach these ends? What books might be read, what activities might be undertaken, what things should be seen in order to achieve the purposes the school has set for itself?

INDEX